Classic Essays on Legal Advocacy

Edited by George Rossman
Associate Justice of the Supreme Court of Oregon

Preface by Bryan A. Garner
President of LawProse, Inc.

A garland of treatises on advocacy and the better use of the English language selected by the Scribes, an organization composed of lawyers who have done superior legal writing.

THE LAWBOOK EXCHANGE, LTD.
Clark, New Jersey

ISBN-13: 978-1-58477-997-1 (hardcover)
ISBN-13: 978-1-58477-998-8 (paperback)

Lawbook Exchange edition 2010.
Published by special agreement with Scribes, The American Society of Legal Writers.

THE LAWBOOK EXCHANGE, LTD.
33 Terminal Avenue
Clark, New Jersey 07066-1321

Please see our website for a selection of our other publications and fine facsimile reprints of classic works of legal history:
www.lawbookexchange.com

Library of Congress Cataloging-in-Publication Data

Advocacy and the King's English.
Classic essays in legal advocacy / edited by George Rossman ; with a new preface by Bryan A. Garner.
p. cm.
Originally published: Advocacy and the King's English. Indianapolis : Bobbs-Merrill, c1960.
Includes bibliographical references.
ISBN-13: 978-1-58477-997-1 (hardcover : alk. paper)
ISBN-10: 1-58477-997-7 (hardcover : alk. paper)
ISBN-13: 978-1-58477-998-8 (pbk. : alk. paper)
ISBN-10: 1-58477-998-5 (pbk. : alk. paper)
1. Trial practice. 2. Legal composition. I. Rossman, George, 1885- II. Title.
KF8915.R67 2010
347.73'52--dc22

2009040398

Printed in the United States of America on acid-free paper

PREFACE

The book you're holding, originally published as *Advocacy and the King's English*, is without doubt the finest anthology of articles on advocacy ever published. In 1960 Justice George Rossman of Oregon, as a board member of the Scribes organization, did a stunningly good job of pulling together all the leading articles — some of them undoubtedly difficult to obtain — and arranging them sensibly. Hence in one book it is possible to find all the best 20th-century thinking on a vast array of points relating to lawyerly persuasion.

Yet the book has remained obscure. The minutes of the 1961 Scribes board meeting records that the book sold only 290 copies within the first year of its publication — not enough to generate a penny in royalties from the publisher, Bobbs-Merrill. One wonders why that might be. My own guess is that the title proved off-putting: the *King's* English? What king? Elizabeth II had already been the monarch in Great Britain for several years, and in any event Americans hadn't aspired to speak the King's English (much less the Queen's English) for nearly 200 years. It's a quirky, off-putting title that must have appealed only to lawyers who were ardent Anglophiles. And it's misleading: only a handful of the 65 essays here collected have much to do with the subject of good English. Hence the decision to republish the book nearly 50 years later under a new title: *Classic Essays on Legal Advocacy*. It's certainly more descriptive.

Over the years, I've combed this text for ideas and choice quotations in my own works on advocacy. I've cited the book copiously in *The Winning Brief*, *The Winning Oral Argument*, *The Elements of Legal Style*, and the Scalia-Garner collaboration *Making Your Case: The Art of Persuading Judges*. In no other anthology is it possible to find so many gems packed so densely.

My own favorite essays in the book are those by Birkett (pp. 1 and 919), Jackson (pp. 21 and 189), Davis (p. 212) Prettyman (p.

259), Morison (p. 288), Carter (p. 296), Clay (p. 330), Lummus (p. 348), Wiener (p. 354), Steinheimer (p. 392), Rutledge (p. 429), Appleman (p. 440), Medina (p. 537), Prosser (p. 737), Blair (p. 788), Dore (p. 810), Cardozo (p. 840), Frank (p. 858), and Stryker (p. 966). I defy any advocate, however accomplished, to read any of those essays — you should read them all — and not be struck by their practical insights and their enduring value.

For those with a more academic bent, the two classic pieces by Chafee (p. 619) and Williams (p. 646) are well worth rereading periodically, as they reinforce the perennially vital principles of general semantics.

Under the auspices of Scribes — known more formally as the American Society of Legal Writers — Justice Rossman showed ingenuity and wisdom in compiling this underappreciated collection. Now half a century later, the Lawbook Exchange is to be commended for making this gold mine of advice more widely accessible. Let all right-thinking advocates, especially those who aspire to be truly knowledgeable about their craft, master its pages and tout it to others.

Bryan A. Garner
Dallas, Texas
August 2009

Advice to an Advocate

Be brief, be pointed; let your matter stand
Lucid, in order, solid, and at hand;
Spend not your words on trifles, but condense;
Strike with mass of thoughts, not drops of sense;
Press to the close with vigor, once begun,
And leave (hard the task!) leave off when done;
Who draws a labored length of reasoning out,
Puts straw in lines for winds to whirl about;
Who draws a tedious tale of learning o'er,
Counts but the sands on ocean's boundless shore;
Victory, if gained, is gained by battles fought,
Not by the numbers, but the forces brought.
What boots success in skirmish or in fray,
If rout or ruin, following, close the day?
What worth a hundred posts, maintained with skill,
If, these all held, the foe is victor still?
He who would win his cause, with power must frame
Points of support, and look with steady aim;
Attack the weak, defend the strong with art,
Strike but few blows, but strike them to the heart;
All scattered fires but end in smoke and noise,—
The scorn of men, the idle play of boys.
Keep, then, this first great precept, ever near:
Short be your speech, your matter strong and clear;
Earnest your manner, warm and rich your style,
Severe in taste, yet full of grace the while;
So you may reach the loftiest heights of fame,
And leave, when life is past, a deathless name.

—Joseph Story, Justice
United States Supreme Court
1811-1845

FOREWORD

The charm of a well selected word or of a choice literary passage is irresistible. Its appeal never fades. Such phrases can accomplish results beyond the power of argumentation. They stir the imagination, lodge themselves in the conscience, yield inspiration and open new horizons for us. Time leaves their fascination untouched. They are men's only product that can achieve immortality.

Lincoln's Gettysburg Address and his letter to Mrs. Bixby are as welcome reading today as they were when first we encountered them. The phrase, "I have nothing to offer but blood, toil, tears and sweat," which quickened Britain to new heights of national spirit when uttered in the dark days of World War II was over three hundred years old then, but it had not lost its power. The beautiful style in which Blackstone wrote his commentaries lent those law books an appeal that induced every gentleman of that day to believe that his drawing room was incomplete if it lacked a copy of the commentaries.

A well rounded phrase occurring in a judicial opinion can offset a lawyer's most skillfully contrived argument, as was demonstrated in the opinion of a western court which, in rejecting an argument that 5 cents overcharge of a tax was unimportant, replied:

> "Far be it from this court to say that a sum of money, coined by the government of the United States, and which is sufficient to furnish bread to the hungry, cheering drink to the thirsty, and to the miser the means of contributing to charity, shall be treated as unsubstantial."

And think how effectively a vain witness who insisted upon referring to himself by the use of the plural pronoun "we" was reduced to proper size when the judge quoted to him the words of Roscoe Conkling:

> "There are only three persons who are permitted to refer to themselves as 'we,' an emperor, an editor and the man with a tape worm."

The right expression is the most effective weapon which the lawyer can draw from his great arsenal, the English language. When well chosen, like the Battle Hymn of the Republic, it marches on forever. Words are in truth the liaison that unites people into a social order.

Possibly it is beyond the reach of most of us to write and speak beautifully, but it should be the purpose of all members of the legal profession to express themselves with clarity, conciseness and cogency. Ours, more than any other profession, deals with words. It is of course true that the lawyer gives his client advice, drafts legal documents and argues cases to courts and juries. But his sole means of imparting to client, judge and jury the thoughts of his mind is through the medium of words. The sculptor and the painter, in expressing the image which is in their minds, have at their command a choice of various materials with which to express themselves. The sculptor can select marble, bronze, granite, ivory and, as in the case of the great work in the Black Hills, he can choose a mountain. The painter can produce his work upon canvas, wood or parchment and has at his command the full spectrum of color. But the lawyer has only words as the medium by which he can make known what is in his mind. To the extent that he masters the English language he serves better his client and the cause of justice. If he wishes to achieve for himself the status of amicus curiae when he appears before an appellate court he can do so by eschewing crowds of words and acquiring the art of making one word do the work of two.

Speech is the gift of all, but clarity, cogency and beauty of expression are the acquisition only of those who strive for them. Bacon, who wrote his essays in a chaste English which never fails to fascinate, did not acquire his unexcelled command of English without effort. He was "a scribbler" all of his life, and those who knew him noticed that he scribbled a memorandum of any choice expression that came to his attention. Thus, he constantly sought good English and made a memorandum of it whenever he found it.

Words are the common domain of all of us. Unlike land and wealth they are as available to the poor and lowly as to the rich and mighty. But how effectively they distinguish the learned from all others! Good English is not only the mark of the capable lawyer but also of the gentleman.

SCRIBES is an organization of the members of our profession who love good English. Its members seek to improve their power of persuasion as employed in a brief, in a courtroom or at a conference table. SCRIBES has gathered from legal literature the best of the articles that the members of our profession have written on the use of good English, and is publishing this volume in the hope of encouraging the profession to write better. All of us spend a good part of our lives in reading and writing. What a boon it would be to the profession if those who write would use better diction and avoid the hum-drum style in which much of our legal literature is cast. Indeed, it is true, as said in the Old Testament, "A word fitly spoken is like apples of gold in pictures of silver."

GEORGE ROSSMAN
Supreme Court of Oregon
Salem, Oregon

Contents

Appellate Briefs and Oral Argument

I Inspirational and Introduction

II Form

III Contents

Inspirational

Advocacy

By Right Hon. Sir
Norman Birkett, LL.D.

I AM DEEPLY CONSCIOUS of the honour it is to stand where so many eminent men have stood before me in days past, to deliver the Presidential Address to the Holdsworth Club in this great University in this famous city. The subject is not strictly one of my own choosing, and that gives me freedom to say that I cannot claim to speak with any kind of authority, or that I possess any special or peculiar knowledge of the art of advocacy.

But it is perhaps right that I should also say, with that touch of sober melancholy the occasion calls forth, that it was in the courts of law of this city some forty years ago that I first put on the wig and gown, and humbly submitted that my client was the embodiment of every virtue. There were giants in those days. McCardie had just gone to the Bench, but Hugo Young, Disturnal, Hurst, Maddocks, Joy, Vachell and Cave, to name but a few, were in the full tide of their splendid careers.

No address on advocacy by me could give me any satisfaction if I did not pay tribute to the men whose methods I was privileged to observe in daily practice, whose example was a perpetual fount of inspiration, and whose kindness to me can never be forgotten. The city of Birmingham nourished and nurtured these men, and for seven years allowed me to learn their great language and catch their clear accents.

Since that time I have seen, I suppose, almost every type of advocate in almost every type of Court. I have seen the great occasions, naturally rare, when as Lord Campbell said of the first speech of Thomas Erskine "every eye was fixed on the great advocate, every syllable he uttered was quickly caught up, breathing was almost suspended, and such was the silence, that if a

The Presidential Address of the Rt. Hon. Sir Norman Birkett, LL.D., a Lord Justice of Appeal, President of the Holdsworth Club of the Faculty of Law in the University of Birmingham 1953-54, delivered before the Annual Dinner of the Club on 7th May, 1954.

flake of snow had fallen, it would have been heard to fall." But at all times and in all Courts, I have remembered the men that I first saw in action in this city practising the art of advocacy, and to them, and to the city itself, I bring to-day this grateful acknowledgment of my debt.

Truth, it is said, hath a quiet breast: but truth can sometimes be disturbing. And the disturbing truth must be faced at once that it is extremely doubtful whether anything can now be said on the subject of advocacy that has not already been said with complete authority some eighteen centuries ago, when Quintilian spoke with such discernment and insight. Many writers in all succeeding ages have embroidered and embellished the theme; but the essential things have long since been said. My modest purpose, therefore, is merely to set down some of the thoughts I have entertained on the subject of advocacy during the forty years I have followed the profession of the law. I do not aspire to teach or to instruct or to exhort: I am content to express the pleasure to be derived from the exercise of the art, to discuss some of its elements, and to assert, in the face of all detractors, that the career of the advocate is a high and honourable calling, essential to the good government of any civilised state, and one to which men and women might well devote their greatest gifts and powers.

How then shall we define the art of advocacy about which so many words have been spoken? It is not easy to give a short answer that will be entirely satisfactory, for advocacy is composed of so many diverse elements; but in its essence, advocacy may still be called the art of persuasion if that term is used in its widest sense. It is not confined wholly to persuasive speech, though persuasive speech is infinitely important, and may with truth be said to dominate everything else. Quintilian quotes with approval the saying of the Greek grammarian that forensic oratory has one main task— "to persuade the judge and lead his mind to the conclusions desired by the speaker." But whilst I am referring to persuasive speech, may I go a little out of my way to touch upon a wider theme than advocacy in the courts of law? The uses of persuasive speech are too often considered as belonging exclusively to counsel and solicitors. The truth is that wherever men seek to win others to their own opinion, the art of advocacy is being displayed, and men everywhere would do well to remember the immense power that lies in persuasive speech, and would do well also to make the necessary effort to acquire it.

We are living in what is sometimes called the Welfare State, and it is plain that one of the features of that state is that the duty of public speaking is now cast upon a larger number of people than ever before. It would be unreasonable to expect the same excessive care to be given to the art of persuasive speech as was bestowed upon it when the world was very much different. Men have ceased to "smooth the locks, to adjust the tresses, and to vary the braids of their comely creations" as did the Greeks and the Romans. But the Chairman of the Board of Directors, the Leader of the Trade Union, the parliamentarian, the preacher, equally with the advocate in the law courts, would do well to remember that the rewards of persuasive speech are not only exceeding great, but that they are not to be won without much labour. The notion that attractive and persuasive speech comes unbidden to the lips as a gift from Heaven's treasury dies hard, and the speech that delights you with its ease and spontaneity is not uncommonly the result of prolonged labour in the silent watches of the night. Men can be stirred and moved, thrilled and delighted, calmed and assured, stimulated to high endeavour or encouraged to follow the path of duty by the simple and skilful use of the English tongue. The primary rules are not many and they are easily mastered. They are to seek simplicity, to avoid verbiage, to use familiar words of plain meaning and to be natural. It is lucidity that makes speech enjoyable to the hearer; it is grace of speech that makes the spoken word memorable; and grace and lucidity come only from the observance of the primary rules and willingness to take pains. Lincoln's ten sentences spoken at Gettysburg will live so long as the language endures, and the speeches of John Bright, many of them made in this city, to use the phrase of Lord Morley, "will live to be a lamp for many a generation of Englishmen in times to come."

They stand as great examples of the unrivalled efficacy of simple speech, from which all lesser mortals in courts of law or wherever men are called upon to address their fellows, may find guidance and inspiration.

Advocacy in the courts of law requires a highly-skilled technique of its own. Persuasive speech is perhaps the most important single element, but there are other elements of very great importance too.

Mr. Justice Hilbery in *Duty and Art in Advocacy* says:

> "There are of course other duties than making speeches which an advocate in a Court is called upon to perform as incidental to the presentation of a cause. Never do you hear an account of the adroit and impeccable examination-in-chief. Yet nothing is more important and nothing better displays the craftsmanship of the master. The establishment of the facts depends upon the witnesses relating them. They will only relate them if questions are put which give them the opportunity to say what is required."

The learned judge then goes on to discuss many other essential features of the technique of advocacy in the law courts with the knowledge gained from busy practical experience.

But in some professions the art of persuasive speech is perhaps even more important than in the profession of the law, where so much depends upon technical dexterity in the 'procedure of the law courts'; and I could not refrain from emphasising the vast importance of the subject for all those who are called upon to instruct or guide or teach their fellows.

But it is of the advocate in the courts of law that I have undertaken to speak, and I must therefore say a word or two about the serious misconception in the public mind concerning him. Respect for the law is widespread, but the lawyer himself is not a very popular figure. The strongest condemnation has always been, and is, reserved for the lawyer who is also an advocate. Curiously enough (or do I live behind an iron curtain in this matter?), judges appear to be exempt from the universal disparagement. It would seem that when an advocate is made a judge he ceases to be a lawyer, a belief that is widely held in circles other than those of the general public. But the advocate is said to be a man utterly devoid of moral scruple, who will willingly espouse any cause whether he believes in it or not, and will defend the right or the wrong without hesitation, so long as he is paid. It is most unfortunate that one of the greatest of the English stylists and satirists gave currency to this view in *Gulliver's Travels.* There it was that Swift permitted himself to say that lawyers were "a society of men bred up from their youth in the art of proving by words multiplied for the purpose that white is black and black is white according as they are paid." Swift was in fact a disappointed litigant, and was venting his spleen in that capacity; but the power of his writing was such that his words are likely to endure. It is scarcely necessary for me to say that the disfavour in which the advocate is sometimes held arises almost wholly from the grave misconception of the advocate's true function. He does not profess to present his own point of view or his own beliefs to the Court. He is there as the mouthpiece of the client to say for him what he would wish to say for himself, were he able to do so with knowledge and understanding. When Thomas Erskine, perhaps the greatest advocate this country has ever produced, defended Tom Paine for a seditious libel contained in the *Rights of Man,* he was subjected to severe criticism and much abuse for undertaking the defence, and in the course of his address to the jury he took the opportunity to vindicate himself, and the vocation of the advocate in general, in language that is still remembered and quoted. He said:

> "If the advocate refuses to defend from what he may think of the charge or the defence, he assumes the character of the judge; nay, he assumes it before the hour of judgment, and in proportion to his rank and reputation, puts the heavy influence of a perhaps mistaken opinion into the scale against the accused, in whose favour the benevolent principles of the English law makes all allowance and which command the very judge to be his counsel."

Boswell records Dr. Johnson as saying pretty much the same thing in his conversation with Sir William Forbes, who had suggested that a lawyer should never undertake a cause which he was satisfied was not a just one.

> "Sir," said Dr. Johnson, "a lawyer has no business with the justice or the injustice of the cause which he undertakes, unless the client asks his opinion, and then he is bound to give it honestly. The justice or the injustice of the cause is to be

decided by the Judge. Consider, Sir, what is the purpose of the courts of justice. It is that every man shall have his cause fairly tried by men appointed to try causes. A lawyer . . . is not to usurp the functions of the jury or judge, and determine what shall be the effect of evidence, what shall be the result of legal argument . . . A lawyer is to do for his client all that his client might fairly do for himself, if he could."

It must be conceded, of course, that the art of advocacy is therefore beset with perils of a very special kind, and for that reason the first quality beyond all others in the advocate, whatever his particular type of advocacy may be, is that he must be a man of character. The Court must be able to rely on the advocate's word; his word must indeed be his bond; and when he asserts to the Court those matters which are within his personal knowledge, the Court must know for a surety that those things are as represented. The advocate has a duty to his client, a duty to the Court, and a duty to the State; but he has above all a duty to himself that he shall be, as far as lies in his power, a man of integrity. No profession calls for higher standards of honour and uprightness, and no profession, perhaps, offers greater temptations to foresake them; but whatever gifts an advocate may possess, be they never so dazzling, without the supreme qualification of an inner integrity he will fall short of the highest. "I, for one," said Quintilian, "restrict the name of orator and the art itself to those who are good." Lord Rosebery, himself a great master of the spoken and the written word, said of the oratory of Chatham—

"Assiduous study of words, constant exercise in choice language, so that it was habitual to him even in conversation, and could not be other than elegant in pre-meditated speech—this combined with poetical imagination, passion, a mordant wit and great dramatic skill, would probably seem to be the secrets of Chatham's oratorical supremacy . . . And yet it is safe to predict that a clever fellow who had mastered all this would produce but a pale reflection of the original. *It is not merely the thing that is said, but the man who says it that counts, the character which breathes through the sentences."*

The fact that the advocate is paid for his services ought not to blind the public to the true nature of the advocate's task; and indeed in a society where the administration of justice is recognised to be perhaps the most important thing affecting its welfare, it is essential that there should always be men of honour and uprightness who make the profession of the law their livelihood, trained to defend and to plead for the citizen, and zealously to guard his rights, his liberties, and, if need be, his life.

To those therefore who propose to make advocacy their vocation I would say from my experience that the golden rule to be observed is that the advocate must believe in himself, he must believe in the honourable character of the work he is to do, and he must bring to his task all the qualities with which his own personality has been endowed. For advocates are not all made to the same pattern. Some have been endowed with ten talents, some with five, and some with one only. Some are born under Jove or Saturn or Mercury, or under some planet the name of which is still unknown. Some, it would appear, may be even born under two planets. Marshall Hall, for example, was certainly mercurial, and at times he was exceedingly jovial, and at times he could be saturnine. But he was always himself, and brought the brilliant many-sidedness of his rich personality to the task he so much loved. On his good days he could dominate the Court and everybody in it, judge, jury and spectators alike, by the mere splendour of his presence and the compelling power of his forensic oratory. Patrick Hastings, on the other hand, was made in quite another mould. There was nothing flamboyant about him. He was exceedingly scornful of some forms of forensic oratory and never attempted any flights himself. He regarded the oratorical flourish much as Bishop South, with his love of plain speech, regarded the rather high-flown imagery of Jeremy Taylor, and sometimes expressed himself with the same bluntness as the Bishop did in his sermons. The strength of Hastings lay in quite another direction. He was, I think, the greatest cross-examiner I ever heard. He could destroy a witness with quite shattering power with his direct, incisive and penetrating questions, that came from him with the precision and speed of a machine gun. Remorselessly and relentlessly he broke down all defences, and when the triumph was complete he would make the briefest possible speech and sit down. The truth of all this is that in the sphere of advocacy there is room for almost every kind of human personality. There is no fixed and unalterable road to success in the art, and the wise advocate will not attempt to be the slavish imitator of somebody else, but he will be content to be himself and to develop his own powers by practice, by observation, and by industry.

If any further word is needed to emphasise the importance of the advocate relying upon his own personality, it may perhaps best be said by considering for a moment one or two of the advocates who by common consent are regarded as being supreme artists, and who have left behind them imperishable names. When Erskine made his first speech in Westminster Hall before Lord Mansfield in defence of Captain Thomas Baillie, he had had no training, and no experience, and had only just been called to the Bar. Yet Lord Campbell called that speech the finest in all the annals of advocacy; and Crabb Robinson, who heard him conduct a simple probate case at the Norfolk Assizes, confided to the Diary which he kept for fifty years that there were no words to describe the effect he created, and the emotions of that day could never be effaced from the memory.

When the unknown John Somers, the junior counsel for the Seven Bishops, rose to speak last in that memorable trial in Westminster Hall, he spoke for five minutes only; yet Macaulay says that when he sat down his fame as an advocate and a constitutional lawyer was established. It is perfectly plain that neither Erskine or Somers had anything to learn from lectures or treatises upon the art of advocacy. They stepped into the forensic arena fully equipped. They were like the poets: they were born and not made. They were no doubt highly-gifted creatures, but they were *themselves*. And it is a sobering thought that nothing can now be gained by attempting to capture their secret. In Lord Rosebery's phrase "it is the man who says it that counts, the character which breathes through the sentences."

The speeches of Erskine can be read in three massive volumes, but they give no clue to the magic and the mystery. For the great utterances, when recalled, are without the fire and the glow of the advocate's presence; the dramatic setting has vanished; and the magical moments have irrevocably gone. It is clear that the thing said can hardly be separated from the moment of its saying, and great advocacy reaches its height only at the very moment of its performance. It is designed and intended for one particular occasion. Then and then only are to be seen the many elements which in combination make advocacy what it is. The advocate himself with his own distinctive personality, his quick mind and understanding heart, his readiness, his resource, his courage; the particular occasion with all its dramatic possibilities; the particular theme, whether noble and lofty or tragic and pitiful; the form and the beauty of the words the advocate employs; the fire and glow and vehemence; the gestures, the voice, the expression—all these things are for the moment, and once gone, are gone beyond all recall. That is why the modern reader of past forensic oratory falls to wondering how those resounding triumphs were ever achieved. It is not merely that the oratory suited to one age is quite unsuited to another; it is that the one vital element of true advocacy is missing. That experienced Chancery lawyer and man of letters, Augustine Birrell, once penetratingly observed:

> "Not to see and hear these men is not to know them, and criticism without personal knowledge is in their case, mutilation. Those who did see and hear them listen in despair to the half-hearted praise and clumsy disparagement of critical strangers, and are apt to exclaim, as did the younger Pitt, when some extraneous person was expressing wonder at the enormous reputation of Fox, 'Ah! but you have never been under the wand of the magician'."

And Hazlitt, too, in one of the essays embroiders the same theme.

> "The thunder and lightning mixture of the orator turns out a mere dark-coloured suit in the person of the pure writer. We wonder at the change, and think there must be some mistake by which what appeared so fine now appears to be so worthless. The deception took place before; now it is removed. 'Bottom thou art translated' might be placed as a motto under most collections of speeches that I have had the good fortune to meet with, whether originally addressed to the people, the Senate or the Bar . . . What we read is the same; what we see and hear is different—the self-same words but not to the self-same tune. The orator's vehemence and gesture, the loudness of the voice, the speaking eye, the conscious attitude, the inexplicable dumb show and noise—all those brave sublunary

things that made his raptures clear—are no longer there, and without these he is nothing."

Those of you who are familiar with the written word of Emerson, but who never saw or heard him in the flesh, will perhaps be a little astonished at the tribute of so famous a man as James Russell Lowell:

> "Those who heard him while their nerves trembled under the breath of divine air, will never cease to feel and say:
>
> Was never eye did see that face
> Was never ear did hear that tongue,
> Was never mind did mind his grace
> That ever thought the travail long;
> But eyes and ears and every thought
> Were with his sweet perfections caught."

But perhaps I now ought to leave the great natural advocates who are a law unto themselves, and turn my attention for a moment or two to the art of advocacy as it applies to the vast majority of those who practise it. But it is already clear that advocacy is made up of many elements. There is first of all, I repeat, the importance of the advocate himself. He should count himself exceedingly fortunate if he has been endowed with a good voice. But he must use it. He must speak so that he can be heard, and he must articulate clearly. He must try to acquire tone and modulation, so that his every sentence is pleasant to the ear. To the advocate, the spoken word is the breath of his life, and it is quite astonishing to me that so little thought is given to it. I would like to see it made a part of the training of the young advocate that he should be taught how to speak, and how to produce his voice to the best advantage. Go into any of the courts of law to-day, and you will see the distressing spectacle of men addressing judges or juries who quite obviously know nothing of voice-production, and who perpetually keep on taking sips of water from a tumbler to the complete distraction of those who listen to them.

An advocate like the late Sir Patrick Hastings would speak for a whole day and never once take his eyes away from the Bench or the jury box, and never once break the invisible and all-important link by stopping to call the usher to bring water to his aid.

Unfortunately, too, there are some qualities most desirable in the advocate about which he can do nothing. A commanding presence is a great asset, but if Nature has been careless about this, the advocate must do the best he can by making up for it in other directions. When Marshall Hall or Edward Carson came into Court everybody was conscious of their presence. There was a subtle change in the atmosphere, a tightening of the tension, an air of expectation, due in some measure to the extraordinary power of reputation, but mainly due to their physical presence. But on the other hand, an advocate like the late Mr. C. F. Vachell who practised in the Courts at Birmingham, so far from possessing a commanding presence possessed the most curious and gnome-like features and a comparatively insignificant body, yet he could enthral and enchain a jury by his wit and the power of his personality.

It is well if the advocate is possessed of a quick mind, alert to seize the unexpected opportunity, to adapt himself to the sudden changes which occur in the conduct of a case, and to be ready to deal with any interventions from the Bench, whether they be disconcerting or helpful. But more important than the quick mind is the understanding heart, the insight into human nature, the natural sympathy with all sorts and conditions of men, the intuitive recognition of what the particular situation demands.

It would be easy to enumerate many more qualities and attributes that it is desirable for the advocate to possess. He should be courageous, and ready at all times to maintain the independence of the Bar; he should be resolute, able to make up his mind and take decisions and to stand by them; he should be courteous and good-mannered; he should be able at all times to control his temper; he should be severe when severity is demanded, and he should be gentle when gentleness brings its own rich rewards. In a word, the advocate should bring all the qualities of his own personality to the great task of persuasion and employ them as the circumstances dictate.

But whether the advocate possesses all or any of these qualities, there are certain desirable things which it is in the power of all advocates to do. I will not presume to speak of the elementary things which have been written and spoken about for generations, but I will mention one or two of them lest it should be thought that I had overlooked them. In the conduct of any case, whether it be in the Magistrate's court or in the House of Lords, the advocate must have made himself master of all the facts; he must have a thorough understanding of the principles and rules of law which are applicable to the case and the ability to apply them on the instant; he must gauge with accuracy the atmosphere of the Court in which he pleads and adapt himself accordingly; he must be able to reason from the facts and the law to achieve the end he desires, and he must above all have mastered the art of expressing himself clearly and persuasively in acceptable English. I do not propose to speak here of the technical matters relating to the examination-in-chief, the cross-examination, the re-examination and the like. Volumes have been written about these things and examples of them may be seen every day in the Courts; and further examples are to be found in the *State Trials* and the *Notable British Trials*.

They are, of course, supremely important, and the advocate by long practice must perfect himself in their use. A successful examination-in-chief is not too easy to achieve, and the ideal to pursue is perhaps that described by Sir Frank Lockwood as a spontaneous conversation between counsel and the witness. A great cross-examination is sometimes quite a terrible thing to behold, and is undoubtedly a most effective instrument for the ascertainment of truth. But the most effective cross-examiner will fail before the witness of truth, and the most earnest re-examination will be of no avail before the witness of stupidity. And whilst I do not speak further of these things, I confess that I have my own likes and dislikes, peculiar no doubt to myself, and so long as I keep them to myself in Court they do nobody any harm. I like to see the advocate who stands erect whilst he addresses the Court, keeping his eye fixed on the judge or on the jury, and compelling attention by his very manner. I like to see him so in control of himself that he does not need to turn aside to look at papers, but conducts his case with clearness and decision because he has got all the material he requires safely into his head. I like to see him respectful to the Bench, but not subservient, asserting the dignity and position of the advocate, as Erskine did before Mr. Justice Buller at the Shropshire Assizes in the case of the Dean of St. Asaph, with quiet courtesy, but with unflinching courage. When Erskine persistently demanded that the judge should record the verdict of the jury as they delivered it, they having said that the

Defendant was guilty of Publishing *only*, Mr. Justice Buller said to the jury: "You say he is guilty of publishing the pamphlet, and that the meaning of the innuendoes is as stated in the Indictment.

A Juror: Certainly.

Erskine: Is the word *only* to stand part of your verdict?

A Juror: Certainly.

Erskine: Then I insist that it shall be recorded.

Mr. Justice Buller: Then the verdict must be misunderstood; let me understand the jury.

Erskine: The jury do understand their verdict.

Mr. Justice Buller: Sir, I will not be interrupted.

Erskine: I stand here as an advocate for a brother citizen, and I desire that the word 'only' may be recorded.

Mr. Justice Buller: Sit down, Sir; remember your duty or I shall be obliged to proceed in another manner.

Erskine: Your Lordship may proceed in what manner you think fit; I know my duty as well as your Lordship knows yours. I shall not alter my conduct." And Erskine stood firm and resolute, for the point was of tremendous importance. But above all I like to see the advocate who has mastered two vastly important things —the art of presentation, and the command of language.

On these two matters I should like to spend just a few moments.

It is sometimes said that the whole art of advocacy consists of presentation. The late Lord Simon had many shining gifts, but everybody agrees that his strength lay in his power of presentation. Sometimes he had to present to the Court cases of great magnitude with the most complicated facts, but he had the great gift of lucidity. What might have become in the hands of a less skilful advocate a mere dry recitation of facts supported by strings of authorities, became in his hands a fascinating and enthralling narrative told with matchless skill. The facts were marshalled and arrayed, the important ones were emphasised and the less important lightly touched upon, and his mastery of the particular branch of law made the complicated matter sound clear and simple, and impressively convincing. Voice, gesture, knowledge, language, emotion—all go into the art of presentation; but it is not too much to say that all these things fall short of their full effect if the presentation of the case be not, beyond all other things, orderly. Mr. Justice Maule is affectionately remembered by generations of lawyers for the wisdom that lay concealed behind his humour. His famous judgment on the prisoner convicted of Bigamy before him was largely instrumental in securing a reform of the Divorce Laws in 1857; his rebuke to that plague of the law courts, the witness who cannot be heard, is still remembered—"Witness, for the Love of God, and your expenses, speak up"; but perhaps his most famous observation was on this very matter of presentation. Provoked by the confused blundering way in which the advocate was presenting a bewildering array of facts to the jury, he said:

> "Mr. Smith, but do you not think that by introducing a little order into your narrative, you might possibly render yourself a trifle more intelligible? It may be my fault that I cannot follow you—I know that my brain is getting old and dilapidated; but I should like to stipulate for some sort of order. There are plenty of them. There is the chronological, the botanical, the metaphysical, the geographical, even the alphabetical order would be better than no order at all."

I can now speak of course with knowledge of both Bar and Bench, and I cannot emphasise enough the great value of orderly presentation. If the case is one before a jury, they hear a statement so clear and understandable that they are never likely to forget it, however long the case lasts. Shaken the jury may be by the cross-examination, or the speeches from the other side, but that first, clear, orderly, lucid, incisive statement is beyond all price. If the case is one before the judge alone, he listens with the greater attention if the narrative is smooth and orderly, and he is grateful to the advocate for his co-operation in ascertaining the truth.

I never realised until I went to the Bench how much the judge relies on counsel for the orderly presentation of the case, for from the opening of the case until its close, the judge is thinking of the governing facts and the principles of law which will be the foundation of the decision which he must make and the judgment he must deliver.

When counsel gives an oratorical display, the judge may say to himself, "Well, you know this is the kind of thing I liked to do once," but he is really much more interested in a clear and orderly exposition. Let the advocate therefore write it down so that it shall never be forgotten, that orderly presentation is above all things to be desired.

The other important part of the advocate's equipment is what I have called command of language. This is a topic of supreme interest to me, and I must be careful not to over-emphasise it. You will observe that I have said very little of what is called the technique of advocacy, and I have abstained of set purpose. The mastery of the facts of the case, the knowledge of the relevant principles of law, the various methods by which the facts are elicited and placed before the Court, the special qualities needed for examination-in-chief, cross-examination and re-examination, the selection and formulation of the arguments, the widely-differing styles of advocacy required for particular tribunals, whether they be judge alone, or judge and jury, or the appellate court, the construction and arrangement of the opening and closing speeches—these and many other vastly important matters may be found in the books on advocacy, and it is essential that they should be diligently studied "and got by heart" as we say. But this over-riding quality—the command of language—which enriches and adorns almost every other quality of the advocate is not usually given the foremost place in the books which it deserves. The late Lord Macmillan said in this city over twenty years ago:

> "I believe that no advocate can be a great pleader who has not a sense of literary form, and whose mind is not stored with the treasures of our great literary inheritance upon which he may draw at will. The fortune of an argument depends much more than is commonly realised on the literary dress in which it is presented. A point made in attractive language sticks in the judicial memory."

One of the very greatest of the American Chief Justices—John Marshall—was of the opinion that no lawyer is justly entitled to the honourable and conventional title of "learned," if his learning is confined to the Statutes and the Law Reports and the text-books on law. Marshall was a great man of law, and the value of his opinion derives from that qualification; but he was also a very considerable man of letters. It was from the wider field that he drew his strength and his inspiration, and that quality of judgment that together make him a great figure not merely in the United States of America, but wherever lawyers are gathered together. For many years now I have been quoting the wise and discerning words which Sir Walter Scott put into the mouth of Counsellor Pleydell in *Guy Mannering:*

> "A lawyer without history or literature is a mechanic—a mere working mason; if he possesses some knowledge of these he may venture to call himself an architect."

These were not the words of a great imaginative writer merely, for Scott was a devoted and practical lawyer also, Clerk of Session of the Scottish Supreme Court, and these words represented, we may be sure, the garnered fruit of his own long experience. Do not let me be misunderstood. It cannot be too plainly stated that knowledge of the law and continuous application to the complete mastery of its principles is vital to any success of any kind in advocacy. Some branches of the law are naturally more difficult than others. The law of Rating, Patent Law, the law of Copyright and Trademarks, the law of Defamation, the extraordinary intricacies of the Rent Acts, the law relating to Income Tax—these and a score of other branches of the law require patient and unceasing industry to master their many complexities. And I must acknowledge in all honesty that there are men who could scarcely be called advocates in any usual or proper use of the term, who are yet such complete masters of their particular branch of the law, that they triumph over every disability by the sheer power of their learning and their authority. Halting and hesitant they may be, and lacking almost all the graces, it would seem, but they have yet the power to make the Court strain to catch every syllable of what is so imperfectly said. But such men are great rarities, and are not to be copied. For the general run of mankind it is desirable to pay the closest attention to the form as well as to the substance.

If the argument of the advocate is presented in clear and choice language, and language which seems to come naturally and easily from the speaker, and if in addition the advocate can make use of what appears to be quite natural gesture, the very argument itself seems the more persuasive. For many of his purposes, of course, the advocate must necessarily use technical words—the "hereinbefores," the "aforesaids," the "Whereases" and the like—in order to try and achieve complete precision.

But in the main task of advocacy, the exposition, the narrative, the summing-up, the persuasion, the advocate may use, and as I think ought to use, the full range of our wonderfully flexible English speech. For there is no speech to equal it in its amazing richness of expression, being as it is described in the Preface to the *Oxford Book of English Prose*

> "as malleable and pliant as Attic, dignified as Latin, masculine, yet free from Teutonic gutteral, capable of being as precise as French, dulcet as Italian, sonorous as Spanish"

and the advocate may captain all these excellencies to his service. The advocate must therefore be a student of words; he must know something at least of their history; their sound, their meaning, their associations, and, above all, the use that has been made of them by the great masters of the tongue. It is well if he knows his Bible in the Authorised Version, and has drunk in the glories of the Book of Common Prayer. It is well, too, if he knows something of the great triumvirate—Chaucer, Dryden and Shakespeare—who did so much to mould and fashion the language, and of men like Swift and Sterne and Defoe and the great stylists.

For I am one of those who believe that in the ordinary everyday affairs of life, even in casual conversation, the use of natural and graceful English is an accomplishment greatly to be desired. And how much more is it to be desired when the whole purpose of the advocate is to gain the ends he seeks by the impression he creates upon the particular tribunal before which he appears.

It follows from all this that I would have the advocate to be a diligent student of law, but I would have him also to be a diligent student of letters. The virtue of books is somehow communicated to the reader. To live in books with the great and wise spirits of all time is somehow to feel their virtue and mysteriously to share it; and all these things to the advocate in the exercise of his art are beyond rubies. The vocabulary is enriched and enlarged; and stored in the mind for use as the particular occasion demands, are the words the advocate will one day employ, with an effect that he cannot now imagine, at some great moment of his life's work.

When Ben Jonson wrote of the speaking of Bacon it was this quality of choice language that captured his imagination; for he said "that no man durst turn aside lest any single word be lost." When Clarendon in *The Great Rebellion* wrote of the speaking of Coventry, the Lord Keeper of Charles I, it was again "the strange power of making himself believed" by his command of the appropriate word that drew Clarendon's great tribute.

And if to orderly presentation of the material which the advocate has assimilated and mastered, there is added the adornment of memorable speech, whether it be plain and unadorned, or enriched by a thousand graces, the great end of all persuasion is the more likely to be gained and kept.

John Buchan had at one time desired to make a legal anthology of speeches and judgments which made good literature as well as good law, and he said of it:

> "It would put most professional stylists to shame. The greatest judges have usually been men of a wide and general culture. Such men as Hardwicke, Mansfield, Wensleydale, Selborne and Bowen are of this company, though there have been exceptions such as Sir Edward Coke, but they go to prove the rule."

Coke's fame rests upon what is perhaps a stronger foundation, his noble resistance to the encroachments of kingly power in the domain of law, and his outstanding contribution to the independence of the judiciary. So let me end these scattered sayings by observing that advocacy in its essence, and particularly great advocacy, is merely the particular expression of the man who produces it. He must respond to the spirit of his age, for his work touches human life at almost every point. The politics of the age cannot be without their effect upon him. Parliament, the supreme lawmaker, pours out its enactments, and those enactments cover the whole field of human activity. The advocate, as well as the judge, interprets the law, and the plea I venture respectfully to make here tonight is that the advocate when devoting his life to the law, indeed it would not be a misuse of words to say when consecrating his life to the law, should enlarge the sweep of his vision beyond the boundaries of the purely legal world, so that nothing that is human, or indeed nothing that affects humanity, should be to him common or unclean or unknown. Thus will the advocate fulfil the great words of Bacon:

> "I hold every man to be a debtor to his profession, from the which as men of course do seek to receive countenance and profit, so ought they of duty to endeavour themselves by way of amends to be a help and an ornament thereunto."

Adapted from a publication by The Holdsworth Club of the University of Birmingham (1954).

The Advocate: Guardian of Our Traditional Liberties

BY ROBERT H. JACKSON

THE FUTURE OF ANY American law school is bound up with that of the American legal profession. The profession here has been more fortunate than in a large part of the world where the independence of both lawyer and judge has been destroyed and they have been reduced to the status of civil servants doing the will of the government. While that prospect does not confront us, there is no certainty that a slow drift is not in the same direction. An increasing proportion of the Bar is in service of the Government. The judges more and more are called on to affirm and enforce executive or administrative orders without inquiry as to their factual foundation or justice and are increasingly refused access to sources of evidence. The prestige, independence and competence of the legal profession collectively is of concern to each teaching lawyer, as well as to each practicing lawyer and judge.

The lawyer performs the ultimate function of serving the welfare of society through assuming a variety of immediate duties, often in conflicting rôles. He counsels and represents individual interests against the power of the state, as well as in controversies between individuals. Also, the lawyer is the chief instrument by which society applies its laws and sanctions to the individual. Our system also throws upon the legal profession a certain guardianship of our traditional liberties and our legal institutions. Explosive political and social issues must often be adjudged by applying constitutional or statutory provisions through the cumbersome mechanism of the lawsuit. Unfortunately, both the public and legislators too often understand that to relieve them from responsibility.

The difficulty of the legal profession in performing these social functions to the satisfaction of society is substantially increased because the educational world has put our specialty so much outside of cultural life that law is no necessary part of an American liberal education. It is rarely studied except as the working tool of one practical profession. Perhaps we will get the measure of this educational lapse if we are reminded that Blackstone's *Commentaries* were written, not for professional education, but for general education of young Oxford gentlemen for citizenship, because, as the author said, "A competent knowledge of the laws of that society in which we live, is the proper accomplishment of every gentleman and scholar; an highly useful, I had almost said essential, part of a liberal and polite education."

We are keenly aware that the rules which govern the layman's life have become increasingly numerous, detailed and complex. The lawyer must apply them through the adversary system of litigation, the ethics of which presupposes in the advocate a partisanship which people do not understand. They censure the lawyer for living up to his code on behalf of an unpopular client almost as severely as for departure from high standards of honesty and fidelity. Moreover, even the educated layman does not have enough knowledge of legal method to understand how lawyers can honestly find so many uncertainties and conflicts in the law. I am convinced that most laymen without some instruction in the nature and method of the law tend to think of it as a complete and closed body of writing in which the judge or lawyer should find precise and final answers to his problem, if only he knew enough to open the right book at the right page. This leads to a suspicion that unnecessary controversies are promoted by lawyers often to serve the interests of private clients and that judges disagree about them only because one side or the other lacks competence or learning. It is too much to expect that the public or the individual client will understand with so much legislation and litigation why, with all that has been settled, so much still is in doubt.

What is this law to which we devote our lives? I suppose a score of plausible answers could be made. Whatever more it may be, is it not, as between pedagogue and student, chiefly a mode of thought, to be practiced under criticism of the tutor until it is acquired as a habit? Whatever help the student may find in recorded experiences and reflections of earlier judges, he will also find that the answer to the lawyer's concrete problem has rarely been written out; it must be thought out. And, if not before, the young lawyer will realize the sharp disparity between legal thinking and lay thinking when he begins to interview clients. He will have to sift out from what the layman thinks it worthwhile to recite much that, in the lawyer's discipline, is immaterial or irrelevant or not reliable because it is hearsay or secondary evidence. He will have to probe and search for information that, in his thinking, bears more importantly upon the questions involved but which to the lay mind seemed of no consequence. And throughout his professional life, or for that matter his public life, if he really is first of all a lawyer, he will find that his habit or way of thinking differs from that of laymen by demanding higher standards of certitude and stricter tests of relevancy. Impatient reformers will think him obstructive and technical. But if every legislature in the land should abolish what are stigmatized as "technical rules of evidence," the lawyer will stubbornly recognize the inherent superiority of direct evidence over hearsay, of "best evidence" over secondary evidence, of expert conclusions over nonexpert opinion, of the relevant over the irrelevant. These relative values can never be repealed or abolished. The lawyer's thinking should, and if he is a genuine lawyer it will be, characterized by closer adherence to the issue and higher standards of accuracy than any calling except, perhaps, the exact sciences.

Considerations of an autobiographical nature would make it immodest for me to suggest what a law school should teach and how best to teach it. I am a vestigial remnant of the system which permitted one to come to the Bar by way of apprenticeship in a law office. Except for one term at law school, I availed myself of that method of preparation which already was causing uneasiness —to which feeling I must have added, for the system was almost immediately abolished. You may be comforted to realize that I am the last relic of that method likely to find a niche on the Supreme Court.

But perhaps I can qualify to express the opinion that the greatest need and opportunity for improvement in legal preparation will be found where the practicing legal profession is most vulnerable on the score of performance. This, I believe, is in the work of the trial courtroom. It seems to me that, while the scholarship of the Bar has been improving, the art of advocacy has been declining.

I think the Bar itself has underrated the importance of trial work. It has been avoided as less remunerative, more exacting, and less suitable for senior dignitaries than the work of the office. It is sometimes forgotten that the ultimate test of the work a lawyer does in his office is whether it will stand up on its day in court. The rights of clients, like the liberties of our people, are only those which some lawyer can make good in a courtroom. Character of the lawyer in the public mind is likely to be fixed by what it sees of the profession in trials. So I concern myself today with the lawyer as an advocate, an officer of the court, a judge, perhaps, but always a public character, for better or for worse, constituting that class from whom, as Woodrow Wilson said, we used to draw our statesmen.

Every thoughtful observer must be depressed by the tendency of many of our criminal trials to degenerate into partisan wrangling and competitions in prejudicial, obstructive and contemptuous tactics. It will not do to put all the blame for this on either defense lawyers or prosecutors or judges, or even on the legal profession collectively. It behooves us to consider the causes of the mob atmosphere which sometimes surrounds and discredits a criminal trial.

The trial judge has largely lost the control of the influences that can be brought to bear upon the jury. Our procedural law regarded such control as necessary to fair trial. Its techniques were designed to keep unreliable testimony such as hearsay and irrelevant or prejudicial matters from influencing jury deliberations, by having the judge exclude them from evidence. In that way it was sought to confine the attention of the courtroom to the issues and to evidence meeting judicial tests of admissibility and subject to contradiction and cross-examination in open court. The newspaper made this insulation of the jury from outside influences more difficult, but still possible. Today, however, the radio, television, newsreels, and many editions of papers, penetrate nearly every juror's home and bring many influential communications before them, including matter which the judge rules to be inadmissible and keeps the lawyers from presenting in court. For example, long and bitter experience convinced courts that lay jurors tend to attach an importance to the mere fact of confession, regardless of its circumstances, which those familiar with such events know it does not merit. But what is gained for fair trial, when the trial judge rules a confession out of the courtroom as obtained by coercion, if the jurors hear repeatedly on the radio that the defendant has confessed and perhaps read the excluded statement in their newspaper? If made in court, even wrongly, such statements could at least be answered; but when put before the jury out of court, that defense is impossible. If given in court erroneously, a conviction would be set aside on appeal. But appellate courts cannot protect a defendant against false or prejudicial evidence introduced by publicity. Whether "planted" by prosecutors or police or just published as journalistic enterprise, such publicity for prohibited matter is a serious menace to the right of an accused to a fair trial. Examples could be multiplied indefinitely, and it is not always the defendant who is the victim. Innuendoes or worse about witnesses or parties, on whichever side, have the same effect of denying a fair trial and taking control of the proceedings out of the hands of the judge.

Then there are litigants who feel that newspapers and radio commentators marshal the weight of public opinion against them. In behalf of such, there has been a tendency of late to organize picket lines, to make visual demonstrations of sympathy and to inform the juror leaving or entering the courts by placards how the crowd feels about the prosecution or particular witnesses, or rulings of the judge. That such efforts to influence, if not to intimidate, present a menace to the fairness of the trial process and to its repute, needs no demonstration. In all fairness, however, the picket line, by its very crudeness and self-evident impropriety, is likely to offend the juror and may therefore constitute less actual danger to the administration of justice than subtler and more respectable forms of communication which convey influences to the mind of the juror without offending him.

All of these methods of by-passing the judge with communication to the jurors are defended upon the same ground—that they are exercises of freedom of speech and of press. Supreme Court decisions are cited in support of each. It is true that the Court has broadly assimilated picketing to free speech.[1] It has also sharply limited the power of trial judges to punish newspaper efforts to pressure court decisions, upon the grounds that such efforts are immunized as part of our constitutional freedoms.[2]

1 Thornhill v. Alabama, 310 US 88, 84 LEd 1093, 60 SupCt 736.
2 Craig v. Harney, 331 US 367, 91 LEd 1546, 67 SupCt 1249.

Without discussing the merits of the arguments for or against such holdings, it seems obvious that if before or during a trial the right to publicize inadmissible evidence is inseparable from our freedoms, then the trend of trials to turn on evidence and influences beyond control of the judge may be expected to continue. The custom of prejudging guilt or innocence and of injecting evidence and opinions upon the trial by publicity can easily proceed to such a point that verdicts in highly publicized American cases will no more really represent the jurors' dispassionate personal judgment on the legal evidence than do those of "People's Courts" we so criticize abroad. The plain fact is that courts and the legal profession cannot make good the constitutional assurance of fair trial except with the coöperation of the agencies that make and convey public opinion. If they do not respect the judicial process sufficiently to forego scooping it, pressuring it, or circumventing it, fair trial in this country is headed in the direction we so deplore when we see examples of farcical trials abroad.

But we must not allow these external influences to be invoked to exonerate our own profession for the threatened disintegration of the criminal trial process. There is often ground to suspect that the forces that pressure the courtroom from the outside have had aid and comfort from the inside. And disorderly, obstructive, contemptuous or defiant demonstration within the courtroom can only be charged to lawyers. The problem would be less difficult if it were due only to a purpose to discredit courts and judicial proceedings. But the more subtle danger is from the growing attitude that judicial control of the proceeding is a sort of tyranny, that a courtroom ought to be a cockpit without rules, the trial a free-for-all, into which the participants are free to throw anything they please. Many of these seem to have been influenced by the philosophy (which they often quote) expressed in a recent dissent in the Supreme Court that "Freedom of speech in the courtroom deserves the same protection" as freedom of press and speech outside of court.[3]

The analogy is so inconsistent with any kind of orderly legal procedure that it could hardly have been intended by the authors to be taken literally. If a trial, civil or criminal, is to have any semblance of order and its result is to be accepted as a sound judgment on evidence, it must be a controlled and disciplined pro-

[3] Fisher v. Pace, 336 US 155, 93 LEd 569, 69 SupCt 425.

ceeding from beginning to end. Neither lawyers, parties nor witnesses can have freedom to speak irrelevantly, intemperately or out of their proper turn. None have freedom to speak of things which are excluded because prejudicial or immaterial.

The adversary system which we employ in litigation in America is peculiarly susceptible to abuse. It relies on self-interest to bring out both sides of the case. This presupposes and stimulates partisanship in the lawyers. Even the best trial lawyers, if unrestrained by an alert and able judge, sometimes yield to the temptation to overstep.

This combat theory of litigation, particularly in criminal cases, has been carried in this country to lengths practiced in no other. Continental Europe does not employ the adversary so much as the inquisitorial system; the judge largely conducts the trial as an active inquirer for truth on behalf of society, not merely a receptive and passive moderator between adversaries. In England, and some other common-law countries where the courtroom lawyer constitutes a separate profession, the barrister accepts employment only from the solicitor, who briefs him on the facts, and his methods must commend him to those who judge by professional standards. But in the United States, neither the structure of his profession nor the system he employs provides restraining influences upon the lawyer's partisanship or his tactics. The responsibility for fair and orderly trial must be carried by the trial judge or hope of attaining it be abandoned.

I am convinced that the position in our profession which requires the most versatility of mind and firmness of character is the worthily occupied trial bench. I do not belittle the very necessary and important rôle of the appellate court, but I think it has been exalted at the expense of the rôle of the trial judge.

The trial judge sits alone and does most of his work with the public looking on. He cannot lean on advice of associates or help from a law clerk. He works in an atmosphere of strife, with counsel, litigants and often witnesses and spectators bitter, biased, and partisan; and, if the presiding judge fails of his part, they become demonstrative and disorderly.

This lone trial judge must make a multitude of quick and important decisions as the case progresses. He must rule immediately and firmly on questions upon which appellate judges may deliberate for months and then divide. He is frequently attended by poorly prepared counsel, and even diligent counsel may be unprepared on questions that are not anticipated. In training lawyers the law schools are also training these future judges, for we do not think it compatible with democracy that the judiciary, as in some Continental countries, be a separate profession specially trained for the task of judging. Either to preside over a courtroom or helpfully and successfully to conduct cases at its bar is, perhaps, less a science than an art. Some of the best trial judges I have known were not distinguished for learning so much as for wisdom and common sense and a personality that enabled them unostentatiously to dominate the courtroom and be master of its proceedings. I do not know that it would be possible to teach that kind of art, but it seems to me that the unsolved problem of legal education is how to equip the law student for work at the bar of the court and for assumption, the politicians willing, of the work of the trial bench. The two are similar in many requirements.

It may be that the law school emphasizes preparation for appellate work at the expense of preparation for the trial court. I sometimes sit in moot court, through which our schools are trying to teach advocacy. I find young men carefully trained, their research exhaustive, their arguments penetrating. But they usually argue some great issue for which they are not likely to be employed during the first twenty years of practice. Then, too, they are adapting themselves to an appellate court, which no case of theirs is likely to reach for some years. But more unrealistically, they have been given the complete facts of an hypothetical case. The difficulty with this is that they are started at the wrong end of the process. Most lawsuits are ended as soon as there is a final settlement of the facts. The success or failure of young lawyers will be determined by the way they investigate and prepare and present cases to the triers of fact. A surprising number of cases every term are thrown out of our Court because counsel in the trial courts have not made adequate records, have not preserved crucial questions or have not asked appropriate instructions or findings. The place to win an appeal, as well as a verdict, is in the trial court.

When I observe these moot courts, I cannot help contrasting the law school's preoccupation with appeals with the emphasis which the old apprenticeship method of legal preparation placed on trial work. Of course, I do not advocate a return to the apprenticeship system, for conditions in our large offices have made that impossible and always it left much to be desired. It was casual and uneven. Too much depended upon the choice of the office, and that usually was determined by some accident of relationship or acquaintance. If one were fortunate, he would serve his clerkship under a good lawyer who took a personal interest in him as something of a protégé.

Even at its best, apprenticeship left almost everything to the initiative of the individual and could rarely produce the well-rounded acquaintance with the general body of the law that is the aim of the modern law curriculum. If one acquired much of the general philosophy of the law, it was the result of voluntary and self-guided inquisitiveness, or what Einstein has called "a passion for comprehension."

However, the apprenticeship system offered some of the advantages associated with preparation at the British Inns of Court. A young lawyer of promise was soon admitted to the fellowship of lawyers. He worked with them, negotiated with them, went to court with them, ate with them, and—nostalgic admission—drank with them. Waiting about the courthouse for a case to be reached or a jury to report, he listened to their tall tales about cases they had won, laughed with them at slips in cross-examination that had cost lawyers their verdicts or oversights in proof that led to nonsuits. He came to know and respect qualities that made leaders at the bar and to recognize and imitate their skills. Moreover, he learned how eager leaders of the profession always were to know and to help a young man who they thought would carry on the traditions of the profession in which their own lives were absorbed.

The apprentice system was at its best in the smaller communities where one could appear in justice court without being admitted to the Bar and where every law office was a sort of private legal aid society. Each lawyer had poor relatives, poor friends, poor political followers, who sought his advice in their small troubles. The common sense and aptitude of the law student were tried out after a time as a counselor for such nonpaying clients. He began to learn how to deal with clients, witnesses and adversaries and how to investigate facts and law. If he showed promise, ultimately he was allowed to try the losing side of a justice court lawsuit. It was probably over a small bill for goods sold and delivered, or deceit in the sale of a horse, the latter a prolific and entertaining source of premotor age litigation. If he had a flair for trial work, he was enlisted to assist in preparing his tutor's cases for higher trial courts, to sit in at the trial, and perhaps to help on an appeal—provided the client was still indignant, and solvent. Thus he accumulated experience in the matters on which he would first be put to test in his profession. He discovered that advice may be erudite without being wise. He learned to size up a case, to know how many stories which sound credible *ex parte* go to pieces under cross-examination. He learned the feel of a lawsuit and a wholesome skepticism about his own client's statements. He learned to prove the signature on a promissory note, to prove books of account, to interrogate a witness without leading—too much, to ask a hypothetical question, to cross-examine and, most of all, when to let a hostile witness alone. He learned how to organize and present materials, not to satisfy professors, but to convince farmers and carpenters and laborers and miscellaneous humanity in the jury box. He learned to speak, not merely so he could be understood by persons of education, but so he could not be misunderstood by those without it. Such matters lie at the very root of successful litigation. They are experiences which our young men leave the law school without knowing and which of course are very difficult to teach except in actual practice.

If the weakness of the apprentice system was to produce advocates without scholarship, the weakness of the law school system is to turn out scholars with no skill at advocacy.

I pointed out that the old system of apprenticeship taught one to practice law by assigning the student to actual work in what I characterize as the private legal aid business of the office. Perhaps the law schools, too, could combine this important public service with practical experience for senior students. In any thickly populated area a large number of people need and are qualified to receive free legal aid. In most such places, legal aid societies are struggling for support, and one of their burdens is to obtain services of lawyers. I see no reason why, in cooperation with bar associations, local courts and legal aid societies, each law school should not maintain a legal clinic, as each medical school now tries to maintain a medical clinic. Law students must learn to deal with live problems instead of hypothetical cases, just as young doctors find that experience on cadavers does not teach skill with living flesh and blood. The student, of course, may not engage in law practice before admission. But he might conduct interviews with the indigent client and his witnesses, and possibly his adversaries, and prepare a brief of the facts and of the law. While he was performing a useful service, he would be learning something about the sources of evidence, how to get and weigh it, how fallible it all is, and how partial clients are in relating their own troubles. The case at that stage would be taken up by an instructor, perhaps, or a volunteer lawyer qualified to practice law. Within the faculty, the best counsel would be available in any specialty involved. If the case went to court, it could interest the services of lawyers too busy to take on the whole preparation of legal aid cases. The student could observe and perhaps assist the actual trial of an actual case, in preparation of which he had had a part. Of course, such plans require close supervision and support of the Bar and judges, and depend on the good sense of administering personnel and to some extent on local conditions.

But it seems to me that in such a way the law schools might recapture some of the values lost with abandonment of the apprenticeship system. It might prove a forward step, both in legal aid and in legal instruction. The difficulty with leaving trial experience to be acquired during clerkship after admission is that law offices which employ clerks are now rarely set up to render the systematic, supervised study of trial methods which law schools could offer.

Lord Radcliffe recently described the law as "that strange calling which is neither so masterful as a craft, nor so precise as a science, nor so imaginative as an art, and yet which mixes the elements of all three and which we are disposed to rank among the great professions." That profession can be worthily maintained only by placing standards of quality above those of quantity, and a balanced, exact and exhaustive scholarship above the impressionism of popular opinion. Such standards have values; they also have a price. While works of quality win respect within the profession, they may not earn wide recognition, for the law is a calling too occult to be appraised and appreciated by the uninitiated, and general popularity is apt to be the badge of low professional standards.

The Stanford Law School, like the Supreme Court, is now housed in new and elegant quarters. The silent eloquence of the edifice, however, pays tribute to the profession of architecture rather than to the law. But it fixes a high standard for the intellectual and spiritual life with which we must animate them.

As we gather in the imposing presence of this new home, it indicates no lack of appreciation to remind ourselves that, to a law school as to a court, men matter more than buildings. May the buildings we dedicate be peopled with consecrated men to whom the law is the first and last interest in life, to which they are single-minded in devotion, and to which they bring intellectual boldness, integrity and courage. This will make a living institution which will be both cradle and monument to our profession.

Adapted from Vol. 36, American Bar Association Journal (1950).

Introduction

Effective Presentation of the Law

By Claud B. Flora

Effective presentation of the law involves three things: First, a thorough knowledge of the fundamental principles of the law and, in addition, reasonable efficiency in applying those principles to particular facts; second, a thorough knowledge of law books and the ability to use them to the best advantage; third, the ability to present the law, after finding it, in the most effective way.

The first may be acquired through a course of studies in a regular law school. For a discussion of the second see the writer's articles which appeared in numbers 1, 2, 5 and 8, volume I of the Kansas City Law Review. The third will be the subject of this article.

The law is presented through written briefs, oral arguments, or both. Any memorandum of authorities prepared in connection with a case or legal proposition is called a brief. There are three types of briefs: Legal briefs, trial briefs and appeal briefs.

Legal briefs—A legal brief may be prepared either in connection with or entirely independent of a law suit. Thus, legal briefs may be offered at the close of or during the trial of equity cases or jury waived law cases, or in support of demurrers, preliminary motions or any other procedural matter arising in any case. The courts frequently call for such briefs if none are offered. Briefs of this type are usually prepared as a part of the general trial brief which I will discuss later.

Briefs are also frequently prepared in support of legal propositions not in litigation but which arise in connection with the transfer of property or in the course of other business dealings. The purpose of this type of brief is to keep the parties out of litigation, or at least to protect the interests of the client by pointing out the proper and legal course to pursue.

Any type of legal brief should be about in the following form: First, a concise statement of the material facts involved; second, a concise statement of the legal issues in the order of their natural sequence; third, each legal issue should then be taken up and treated in the order stated; fourth, the final paragraph should contain a general summary of the conclusions reached in such language that if the conclusions be correct, it must necessarily follow that the brief-writer should prevail.

There are also three steps in the treatment of a legal issue: First, enunciation of the principle involved; second, argument and citation of authorities in support of the principle; third, application of the principle. The second and third will necessarily be more or less interwoven.

In enunciating the principle, great care should be taken to state the principle correctly. If you misstate the principle, the remainder of your argument is wasted. However, since the courts are usually well informed as to abstract principles, the most important of the three steps, by far, is the application of the principle. A very common expression among judges after hearing an argument is, "Your statement of the principle is undoubtedly correct but I believe it does not apply to your case." So that the vital step in the treatment of a legal issue is to convince the court that the established principle applies to your case.

Any brief should be as short as possible. You should be logical, forceful, and to the point. Flowery arguments and far-fetched theories do not attract or hold the attention of the courts and tend to weaken your position.

If a particular question involved in the brief is well settled and the law in the particular jurisdiction clearly establishes your position, care should be taken to avoid citing and discussing too many cases. A few decisions exactly in point, especially if they are late cases, will be more effective than a great number of decisions, some of which may not clearly apply to the case involved. Too many cases may tend to confuse the courts. They are apt to pass over our brief lightly and possibly not read it at all if it is too long and rambling. However, before depending upon a few decisions, be sure they are controlling decisions and that they clearly apply to the case involved.

On the other hand, the question involved may be one concerning which there are two lines of decisions apparently directly opposed and the latest decision may not be exactly in point or the language of the opinion may not be strong enough, standing alone, to support your position.

In that situation it is usually more effective to take up and discuss all such cases both for and against in the order they were decided, pointing out as far as possible why the cases opposed do not apply and why the favorable cases do apply. A discussion of the reasons for the rules with a view of convincing the court that the rule sought to be applied is based on the sounder reasoning, is also usually desirable. If the latest case appears to be unfavorable you would have to show why that case does not apply. If it is favorable you should, after reviewing the former cases, show why it does apply and then call the court's attention to the fact that it is the latest and controlling decision and, therefore, determinative of the question involved, regardless of the former decisions.

Again, there might be involved a rule of law which has undergone considerable growth and change over a period of years. Your adversary might cite in his brief some early cases in support of the rule as it existed in the early stages of its development but which by reason of the changes in the rule, have now become obsolete. By explaining to the court the history of the rule and then presenting the late cases in support of the modern doctrine, you can readily convince the court that the cases offered by your adversary are no longer the law even if they have never been expressly over-ruled.

In selecting the authorities care should be taken to use the controlling decisions as to the particular question involved. Leading cases and cases which have been cited and followed extensively both in the local and foreign jurisdictions are entitled to more than ordinary weight since the history of such cases establishes their soundness. Well considered cases are almost sure to be valuable since they consider and review all of the prior outstanding cases involving the question under consideration. Avoid the use of decisions which have been criticized and above all be careful not to use cases which have been over-ruled.

Before selecting a case be sure that the rule announced in such case is actually followed by the court in rendering its decision and not merely stated as dictum. While dictum may be offered sometimes by way of persuasive authority as an indication of what the court would have decided had the issue been before it, it is not binding. Only that part of the opinion which is necessarily involved in the court's actual decision is binding and controlling.

Never attempt to mislead the court by quoting favorable extracts from a decision which is otherwise against you. Avoid the quoting of abstract principles alone. When quoting from a decision, always quote enough of the language to show the application of the principle. Otherwise, the court will likely assume that the case is not in point.

Trial Briefs—The trial brief serves the lawyer as a guide in the trial of a case. It should consist of the following parts: First, a list of the issues involved and an abstract of the pleadings which establish the issues; second, a list of the grounds for which the jurors may be challenged for cause, also a list of facts and circumstances concerning which you desire to question the jury panel touching their qualifications and prejudices; third, a statement of the essential facts which must be proved in proper sequence with references to the witnesses or documents by which each fact may be proved; fourth, an abstract of the testimony arranged according to the witnesses and documents which are to be examined and introduced; (3 and 4 should be checked with each other carefully to see that nothing is omitted); fifth, a statement of the essential facts which the adversary must prove in order to establish his case. A lawyer should be as familiar with his adversary's side of the case as his own. Proof of one side of a case will not always disprove the other. This is especially true from plaintiff's standpoint. In some instances the defendant may be proving certain facts, establish a good defense without disproving any of the essential facts which go to make up plaintiff's prima facie case. It is just as important for plaintiff to prevent the proof of such facts as it is to prove his own facts; sixth, a brief of the law of the case, showing the theory of the recovery or defense, also briefs in support of or against the admissibility of important evidence, the admissibility of which is in doubt, and briefs covering any other procedural question which might arise during the trial of the case; seventh, any statutes which are involved should be set out together with a resume of the authorities construing them; (6 and 7 may be combined); eighth, instructions.

The instructions to the jury should be carefully prepared in advance as they embody the law of the case and limit the jury's deliberations to the material fact issues. In other words, an instruction, other than withdrawal instructions and instructions as to the form of the verdict, etc., requires the jury to render its verdict for the party offering the instruction if the jury finds and believes certain facts, set out in the instruction, to be true. It then becomes important to offer the strongest possible proof of these material facts and in the argument to the jury a lawyer should concentrate on these fact issues. By preparing the instructions in advance, the case can be built around the instructions and the evidence may be presented in the most effective way.

Occasionally it will be found necessary to revise the instructions due to unexpected developments in the trial or due to mistakes or oversights in the drawing of the instructions. That possibility, however, would not justify a lawyer in waiting until the evidence is all in before giving any thought to the instructions. Ordinarily he would not have sufficient time at that point for the necessary thought and deliberation required in the preparation of proper instructions.

Each instruction should be written on a separate sheet and prepared in triplicate, the original for the court, the duplicate for your adversary and the triplicate for the trial brief. The triplicate copy should contain the citations of the authorities in support of the instruction.

It is better, when possible, to use instructions which have been approved by the supreme court or appellate courts in other cases but care should be taken to see that the particular instruction fits your case.

Most lawsuits are won through a careful preparation of the cases for trial and the preparation of the trial brief, in addition to serving you as a guide in the trial, is in effect a most thorough preparation of the case for trial.

Appeal Briefs—The purpose of the brief on appeal is to inform the appellate court briefly as to the controversy, the facts out of which it arose, the decision of the lower court, the grounds upon which a review is asked and the reasons why the decision of the trial court should be reversed or affirmed.

Generally, what has already been stated in the discussion of the legal brief applies to an appeal brief. However, the status and rules of the appellate courts usually prescribe substantially the form and contents of the brief and when it shall be filed. The brief is only a small part of the record on appeal. The statutes and rules of court prescribe the entire procedure for appeal.

The rules of the supreme court and of the three courts of appeal of Missouri contain similar but not identical provisions relating to the brief. Since the requirements are not identical, no attempt will be made here to set out the particular requirements of the various courts. However, the rules of the particular court to which an appeal is taken should be followed to the letter. Court rules are legislative enactments and, so far as they are enforced, they have the same force and effect as statutes, except that in case of conflict the statutes will prevail. Although the enforcement of court rules is discretionary on the part of the court, rules governing appeal, while reasonably enforced, are usually strictly enforced. Many appeals, therefore, are dismissed due to the failure of the appellant to observe and follow the requirements set out in the rules of the particular court.

Oral Arguments—Oral arguments may be classified as: Jury arguments and court arguments.

Jury Arguments—If the case is properly prepared for trial and the instructions properly drawn, as I stated in my discussion of the instructions, the argument to the jury is ordinarily confined to the fact issues presented by the instructions. The testimony relating to these fact issues should be reviewed in a careful and effective manner and logical argument in support of favorable inferences to be drawn from the physical facts and circumstantial evidence, should be made. Care should be taken not to patronize or insult the intelligence of the jurors and logic and lucidity of reasoning should be relied upon rather than verbosity and vehemence. Abusing the adversary, his attorney or unfavorable witnesses, should be avoided. Such tactics usually will prejudice the jury in their favor while if their conduct is really reprehensible, the jury or some member of the jury, at least, is apt to detect it without your help.

Court Arguments—Oral arguments before the court on questions of law call for a proper and effective discussion of the principles involved and the orderly presentation of the authorities. Where a great many authorities are necessarily involved, especially where you have no authorities directly in point, it is helpful to prepare a written brief which you may follow in the presentation of your oral argument. It is more effective, however, even where you are making your argument from a written brief, to have the reports containing the authorities referred to at hand and any quotations you desire to make from the cases should be read from the reports rather than from the brief.

The brief should be used merely as a guide to enable you to present your proposition in the most effective manner. If you simply read the brief, you may have difficulty in holding the attention of the court and much of the force of your oral argument is lost. The very purpose of the oral argument is to emphasize and to call the attention of the court directly to the vital points necessary to the establishment of your theories.

In a great many instances it is more effective to make a very short argument and with a few exceptions, for example, where the courts are divided on the proposition you are trying to establish, you should avoid citing and discussing too many cases.

One clear-cut case exactly in point, especially if it is a late case, is sometimes more effective than a great number of cases. However, before relying on the one case, be sure it is exactly in point and that it is the controlling decision as to the question involved. If it is, you would need only to inform the court as to the issue involved, quote the material language of the opinion, hand the book up to the court and stop. If the case thus offered is exactly in point and is the controlling decision on the point at issue, your adversary's argument will be futile, whereas, if in the first place, you had discussed and quoted from a great number of cases, many of which were not precisely in point, the court might overlook the controlling decision, especially if your adversary is clever.

Of course, where you have a mooted question or a rule of law which has undergone growth and change, it would ordinarily be better to follow in your oral argument the same plan I outlined to you for briefing such questions. In fact, in such cases it would be advisable to brief the question so that you may use the brief as a guide in presenting your oral argument.

In discussing a legal issue the same three steps which I mentioned in connection with the brief should be followed and bear in mind that the most important step of the three, by far, is to convince the court that the established principle applies to your case.

In presenting the oral argument it is, also, very important to be familiar with the cases favorable to your adversary, so that you may be prepared to meet his argument.

While you should never attempt to curry the personal favor of the court, you should maintain at all times a courteous and respectful demeanor toward both the court and opposing counsel.

Adapted from Vol. 4, Kansas City Law Review (1936).

Trial Brief

The Trial Brief

By Charles W. Joiner

For the experienced trial lawyer the material here set down will not be new or startling. He may disagree with some of the recommendations made. Particularly, he may believe that some of the steps advocated entail too much paper work and are over elaborate. Long experience has taught him short cuts which the inexperienced lawyer cannot risk.

An attempt is here made to point out and discuss the methods which, when pursued by the beginner or the lawyer who handles litigation only occasionally, should give him the greatest assurance of winning his cases. Whether he must work too hard in the process is his problem and does not arouse the sympathy of the writer. If he is unwilling to do the work preliminary to trial in a thorough and exhaustive manner, he should send the client elsewhere. (Hubert Hickam, *A Civil Action From Pleadings to Opening of Trial* (The American Law Institute, Philadelphia, Pa. 1953) 1.)

The term "trial brief" is a term of many meanings. In this discussion its meaning is limited to the papers that go to make up the trial lawyer's preparation of a case for trial. That which is given to the judge, though properly called a trial brief, is not here under discussion. The trial lawyer's trial manual, trial file, trial brief, or all of the papers which go to make up his preparation for trial is our subject.

Two matters are inherent in a discussion of such a trial brief. One is preparation for trial—what a lawyer must do in getting ready to carry his client's case to the judge and jury. The other is the means of organizing that preparation in order to present the case effectively to the judge and jury.

Initial qualification is in order. It is obvious that the suggestions in this paper will not be appropriate for all lawyers in all cases. Cases are different, both as to their content and as to the amount involved. Lawyers are different in the way they work, in their ability to remember. These facts are important in indicating the amount of preparation and the way in which that preparation should be organized. The suggestions contained herein have resulted from inquiry of ten of this country's good trial lawyers as to how they prepare for trial and their methods of organizing their cases for trial. The lawyers are: Eustace Cullinan of San Francisco, Herbert W. Clark of San Francisco, Hubert Hickam of Indianapolis, Harry Sabath Bodin of New York City, Loyd Paul Stryker of New York City, Francis X. Busch of Chicago, Joseph Burns of New York City, Max Badgley of Jackson, Michigan, Lester Dodd of Detroit, Clifford Mitts of Grand Rapids, Michigan, and Joseph Planck of Lansing, Michigan. To these suggestions I have added my own experiences and have attempted to draw the best from the composite and suggest it as a sound method of preparing and organizing the material for trial in a trial brief.

Throughout the comments of these trial lawyers ran statements which are best summarized in the words of Herbert Clark, "It is true that a lawyer who overtries a case invites disaster. Some may doubt that a case cannot be overprepared, but the reviewer believes that *it is impossible to overprepare for trial.*" However, there was this word of caution, "I do hope, however, that somewhere you will at least caution the lawyers of overelaborate trial briefs and an overzealous effort to blueprint the entire case in advance of trial." Therefore, with these suggestions in mind, I have concluded that there are two objectives and purposes of a trial brief. They are:

1. The trial brief must give you preparation without giving the appearance of a lawyer who overtries his case. This will require a document or file full of information arranged in a way that any bit of that information can be found at any time, but also arranged in such a way so as not to antagonize the judge or jury. The arrangement must be such as will prevent a lawyer from forgetting any ideas but will not stifle new thoughts as they come up.

2. The trial brief must simplify preparation and prevent duplication of work.

Content of Trial Brief

The following matters are suggested for inclusion in the trial brief. Following each is the number of lawyers suggesting its inclusion.

1. A statement of issues or an analysis of the pleadings and pretrial orders. (10)
2. A diagram and outline of proof. (7)
3. Notes for jury examination. (3)
4. Notes for opening statement. (6)
5. A list of witnesses both favorable and unfavorable. (5)
6. A resume of the expected testimony of each witness or the statements of each witness. (10)
7. Notes about each witness to assist the lawyer in handling the witness. (6)
8. Notes for cross-examination. (10)
9. Notes pertaining to trial motions or objections to testimony. (3)
10. Notes for final argument. (2)
11. Suggested requested instructions. (5)
12. Briefs of law. (9)
13. An exhibit file. (9)
14. An index and cross-index. (10)

Form of Trial Brief

The convenient form for the trial brief varied. A loose-leaf notebook, 8½ by 11 inches in size, well tabbed for ease in finding the parts of the brief was the most popular. The loose-leaf feature has the advantage of allowing insertions and deletions from the trial brief without difficulty. In the smaller case some lawyers used the ordinary legal pad. The use of 5 by 8 cards, well tabbed and indexed, was also suggested. The ordinary file folder with organized sub-file folders for the pleadings, the statements, the exhibits, the medical briefs, the law briefs, etc., was also used by some.

These suggestions have several things in common. They all provide a central storage place for the material collected in the investigation—a place that will make that material available and yet subject to change as the lawyer's preparation progresses or as his mind changes as to the proper method of presentation. This is particularly true of the loose-leaf notebook, for the material can be kept in a reasonably permanent form and yet is very accessible for change.

If a loose-leaf notebook is used for the trial brief, the use of the common Acco-type fastener to hold the material together during the preparation phase is suggested. Thus, the brief will lie flat and be housed easily in the ordinary case file. These fasteners will keep the portions of the trial brief together, will prevent loss of papers, and will allow the easy insertion of new matter. Just prior to trial, the brief can be transferred to an ordinary ring-type notebook for use during the trial itself. I know from personal experience that the ring-type notebook is a handy device to use in a courtroom; and so far as I have been able to tell, there is no adverse reaction to it on the part of the jury.

Method of Preparation of Trial Brief

Two suggestions stand out:

1. Begin the preparation of a trial brief early.
2. Memorandize everything that you do in preparation to eliminate the need for doing it again.

An early beginning of a trial brief will allow it naturally to grow with your preparation for trial. You will not be caught short on preparation if the case is unexpectedly called for trial. I urge the gradual building of a trial brief, mainly as a method of economy of preparation. For example, before you prepare an answer, you may have to look up a few cases. These cases are likely to have some bearing upon whether or not you will ultimately be entitled to a directed verdict. A memorandum of these cases will avoid the necessity of looking them up again when preparing for the motion for directed verdict. There is very little that is done early in the preparation for trial that has no bearing upon the later aspects of the trial. Care should be taken to preserve it in the trial brief. A well worked out scheme of preservation of evidence and law will save many hours of labor.

Use of Trial Brief

Statement of Issues or Analysis of Pleadings and Pre-Trial Orders

Every careful lawyer, prior to trial, makes an analysis of the pleadings. This analysis should be made early and be included in the trial brief. Obviously, an analysis of the complaint must be made before an answer is filed. Once an answer is filed in light of a clear analysis of the complaint, it is a simple task to dictate an analysis of the pleadings and issues in the case for inclusion in the trial brief. It can be used to refresh your recollection of the issues prior to trial. It will also prevent your forgetting some obscure but important point in the case. The reduction of your analysis of the issues to writing will force a more clear-cut presentation and will enable you to give more assistance to the court in developing your theory. Having such an analysis in your trial brief will give it fingertip use.

Two methods of tabulating such analysis are suggested. Write out the issues, one following the other, that are raised by the pleadings and pre-trial orders; or set up in parallel columns the plaintiff's complaint, the defendant's answer and subsequent pleadings and pre-trial orders. An accurate statement of contentions will be at your fingertips.

Diagram of Proof

Most lawyers include a diagram or outline of proof in their trial brief. In one sense the diagram of proof could be considered to be the most important part of the trial brief, although it may have very little value at the trial itself. Its major purpose is to put all of the proof in legally logical order.

The diagram of proof begins with the issues arrived at from your analysis of the pleadings, pre-trial orders, and substantive law. Each issue should constitute a section of the diagram. How each issue is handled in the pleadings and pre-trial conference, whether there still are matters to be proved on that issue, and a list of all of the facts that are available to prove it must next be set forth. Following each fact you should set forth a list of the names of the witnesses and exhibits available to prove such fact. Thus, the diagram will break down the facts from a witness-by-witness outline to an outline in terms of the law.

For example, one of the issues in your case is, "Was the defendant operating his motor vehicle on the left or wrong side of the road at the time of the crash?" Opposite this you would place, "denied in the pleadings" if such were the facts. The following then might be a sample of the rest of a simple diagram of proof on this particular issue:

FACT

Saw D car just before crash swerve to east across center line

Saw D car ¼ mile from the accident swerving across center line

All debris on east side of center line
Both cars stopped on east ditch.

The preparation of such a diagram forces one to analyze his case in light of the law applicable to the case. If prepared in a thoughtful manner, the strengths and weaknesses of the case become readily apparent. Such preparation may lead to further investigation of the facts and the law in order to strengthen the case; or it may indicate an early settlement on as favorable terms as possible. If a diagram is not made, either mentally or on paper, it is improbable that a full and accurate analysis of the case will have been made; and, therefore, it is likely that the case will not have been fully evaluated for purposes of settlement. It is true that such evaluation may be done orally or in your mind, but the drill of writing down these matters will prove to be valuable, and if done properly, will be rewarding not only to your client, but to yourself.

Such a diagram has at least two other purposes. It can serve as a checklist during the trial to keep from forgetting anything important. Of course, it is not binding. It may be rejected at the trial, but at least it has brought up matters that at one time were thought to be important. Lastly, it may serve as a reasonably decent outline for the opening statement.

Notes for Jury Examination

Any lawyer who has tried many cases before a jury will have definite ideas about juror types who can handle best the problems to be presented. However, there are often facts in a case which indicate the wisdom of selecting or rejecting certain types of jurors. These should be recorded to refresh your mind at the time of the jury examination. Of course, such notes made in advance should not be binding. They should be reminders only.

Only three of the lawyers suggested including jury notes in their trial briefs. This is perhaps due to the fact that many of them practiced in jurisdictions in which little opportunity was given to the lawyers for jury interrogation, the examination being conducted by the judge. However, the lawyer must think in advance of the types of desirable or undesirable jurors and the particular facts which, if disclosed, should indicate the use of a challenge.

Opening Statement

I agree with Loyd Paul Stryker when he said, "I consider the opening statement one of the most important aspects of the trial of a case. I have many times reduced my thoughts to writing, not with a view of mechanically reproducing them on my opening, but to have them clarified so that the opening itself will be lucid."

I have always required some notes in talking to a jury or in making any careful expository statement and inclusion of opening statement notes as a part of a trial brief is recommended. A good statement made from notes is better than a poor one made without notes. Clarity is important in an opening statement. Clarity requires organization, analysis, and thought. Put this organization, analysis, and thought on paper as a part of your trial brief.

Resume of Testimony

This is perhaps the most important part of the trial brief. In this there was almost unanimous agreement. The resume of testimony, including the statements of witnesses, the facts about witnesses, and the notes for cross-examination, has a five-fold purpose:

1. It will be the organization of your case. Decisions have to be made as to which of several witnesses to call, the order of witnesses, the order of the story of each witness. At least for the plaintiff, it is helpful to make these decisions in the quiet of one's office. The resume of testimony will help to keep us from forgetting what these decisions were. Of course, such decisions are always subject to revision at the time of trial.

2. It will organize the testimony of each witness. A witness's story can be ineffective if not presented in an interesting and understandable way. Much thought and some paper work will be required to prevent the lawyer from forgetting the effective method of handling a particular witness.

3. It will help the lawyer to remember important details during the trial. Some of us are not blessed with fabulous memories. Some of us must use notes when making a public statement as a reminder of substance and organization. The trial of a law suit, being more complicated and longer, may require notes as a memory aid both as to substance and organization. Not knowing what one will forget suggests the use of very extensive notes in the resume of testimony.

4. It serves as the basis for the conduct of the examination of a witness. The use of notes tends to avoid the danger of forgetting important details. Experience indicates that the unobtrusive use of notes is not a barrier between counsel and the witness or the jury, nor does it arouse prejudice against your case. An organized resume of the testimony of each witness is a helpful reminder of questions to ask and subject to cover.

5. It will relieve the trial lawyer or his assistant of some of the burden of note-taking during the trial. If the resume is accurately prepared from careful and accurate statements of the witness and if the trial advocate follows the resume during the witness interrogation, it should be a fairly accurate statement of the testimony of that witness. Insofar as it does not differ from the testimony, it will relieve the trial advocate or his assistant from the necessity of taking additional notes. The note-taking process not only can slow up the trial, but will act as a barrier between the lawyer and the witness and will sometimes actually cause the lawyer to miss something important during the testimony of a witness.

There are a number of ways of preparing the resume of testimony. Writing out questions and answers or writing out the narrative statement of the testimony are two that are suggested. The thought phrase is an effective device with which to make up a resume. Prior to trial one should go through the testimony of each witness, organize it as he hopes it will be presented, and extract from this testimony each of the many thoughts that will be expressed by the witness. These thought phrases are then written down in the order of effective presentation—wide margins, double or triple spaced. This paper is a reasonably accurate resume of the expected testimony of the witness. Single thoughts are put in single phrases. They are not joined by "ands" or "ors" or "buts." The purpose is to make this paper useful in examining the witness. A glance at the thought phrase prompts the question to bring out that thought to put to the witness. Such a resume serves at once for organization purposes, as a memory aid, and as built-in notes. Of course, as is always true, changes may be made at the trial in its substance or its organization, depending upon the course that the trial takes.

The resume should be so spaced that a glance will be a reminder of a question. The use of large type is suggested. This will allow the resume to be left on the table and not held up high, close to the eyes, so as to become a barrier between you and the witness. It should be so spaced that any new material may be inserted at any time. The margins should be cross-referenced to any legal briefs, exhibits, or matters that might arise during the trial.

At the beginning of each resume of testimony, a paragraph should be included containing all pertinent information about the witness—impressions about his capacity as a witness, as to how he should be handled on the witness stand, and what should be avoided. This paragraph helps prevent blundering upon something which should have been remembered from prior contact with the witness.

Although cross-examination cannot be planned as can direct examination, certain advance thought is necessary. We know many things about adverse witnesses. These should be written down as reminders during the trial. For example, there are witnesses who will be impeached in certain ways if they testify unfavorably. Unless there is some record of these, they may be forgotten or overlooked. Let the resume and witness notes be a repository of all preparation helpful in the examination and cross-examination of witnesses.

CAUTION: This part of the brief must be used intelligently. It cannot be followed woodenly. The lawyer must feel perfectly free to change his plan of attack if circumstances at the trial indicate that it should be done. Many lawyers will prefer not to use notes during the trial. Certainly if this can be done without the risk of forgetting some important detail, it is advisable. However, if the lawyer has any tendency to forget or if he feels the slightest need of a crutch, there is nothing harmful about the use of notes in conducting an examination of a witness or arguing before a jury. Notes can be a barrier between you and the witness or the jury, but if used intelligently, they will not be. If this part of the trial brief is in large type with the large margins, if it is kept from between you and the jury, and if your eyes are kept on the witness or the jury, you will be helped, not hindered. Your presentation will be clearer and more convincing.

Objections and Trial Motions

Sometimes you can anticipate motions and objections that are sufficiently complicated to require exact wording in order to raise the question properly. There is no reason why you should not have a section in your trial brief pertaining to these matters.

Notes to Final Argument

Though a number of the lawyers suggested notes for final argument as being a proper part of the trial brief, I have difficulty in justifying putting very much time and effort on a final argument prior to the inception of the trial. It is possible, of course, that advance thought about final argument will help in deciding how to try the case. Certainly it would be proper to make notes in the preparation of a final argument so that you will not forget them. But, you cannot go very far in the preparation of a final argument in advance of the trial record itself.

Instructions

A lawyer always owes his client the obligation of helping the court frame instructions for the jury. Proper instructions require careful study of the issues and applicable law. The judge, often, is introduced to the case for the first time at the inception of the trial and does not have the opportunity to make such a study. The lawyer on the other hand has been working with the case for some time and should have a good grasp of the applicable legal doctrines. He cannot wait until the last minute to prepare requested instructions, and if he did, he would probably be duplicating work which had been done before. Therefore, a section of the trial brief should be set aside to be a repository for all possible requested instructions. Not only should each requested instruction be written out in full with appropriate citations to the case or statute on which it is based, but each request should be placed on a separate piece of paper. Sufficient copies of the requested instructions should be prepared in advance as required by the procedural rules of the court. Preparation of requests does not commit you to use them. On the other hand, unless the work on requested instructions has been done prior to the trial it is probable that matters will be submitted to the jury without the appropriate aid of counsel.

Briefs of the Law

All lawyers agree that law briefs should be included in a trial brief. Law briefs have two purposes:

1. To be certain that the trial lawyer is prepared on the legal points involved in the case; and

2. To prevent the duplication of work.

The form of the briefs of law is important. Some forms will be of more use to the trial lawyer than others. The suggestion is ventured that instead of making one brief of law including all of the points involved in the case, the trial lawyer make separate briefs on each of the points. This will involve no more work; in fact, it might be less, for the work could be spread over a period of time and sandwiched in between other tasks. Several copies of each brief should always be made. The purpose of these two suggestions becomes clear when we consider how such briefs are used.

In many cases it will be desirable to file with the trial judge a trial brief of law and fact; this should be specially prepared for the purpose. It should not be confused either with the trial brief, the subject of this article, or with the briefs of law here discussed. Such a trial brief would have the purpose of explaining to the judge the issues, facts, and law that he should know to try the case.

The law briefs are briefs on legal points that may arise during the case on which authority may be needed in order to justify a position which may be taken. They may be briefs on evidence points or on expected motions. They may be briefs on instructions or any number of other matters that are likely to arise during the trial. Briefs on separate pieces of paper can be used separately. A copy can be handed to the judge at the time of a motion. This will be of material assistance to the judge in deciding the question. It will also reflect favorably on the lawyer and client. Several copies of each brief will make it possible to borrow copies from one case to another. As similar points arise in other cases, time of law brief preparation can be saved by borrowing from other files. The saving of time and work will be considerable.

Exhibit File

Nothing is more discouraging to a judge, a jury, and opposing counsel, than to have a lawyer constantly fumbling through his files or the papers on his table for an exhibit. This type of bungling approach does a disservice to the client and the profession. There is no reason why exhibits should not be organized and analyzed in advance of trial and appropriately indexed. Ability to find the correct exhibit at the appropriate time without wasting the time of the court or the jury should be encouraged. Exhibits, cross-referenced to the resume of testimony, will cut down on lost motion. The section of the trial brief dealing with exhibits will have to be flexible, for exhibits are different from case to case. Somewhere, however, in your trial brief you must have a section on an exhibit file organized, analyzed, and indexed for use at the trial.

Conclusion

As stated at the outset, it is recognized that this trial brief will be too elaborate for some types of litigation. However, a general adherence to this form and method of preparation will not increase but decrease the cost of litigation for your client. You will likely be able to try cases more rapidly. You may be better prepared, and your preparation will be at your fingertips. You may be able to settle more advantageously and to win more cases, for your advance analysis will have been more clear-cut. You may have less duplication of work in the preparation and trial. I conclude by saying that although I have compiled and believe this short statement about a trial brief, I am mainly a reporter of what other fine trial lawyers have told me as to their method of preparation and their use of trial briefs.

Adapted from Vol. 1, The Practical Lawyer (1955).

Trial

Common Sense in Advocacy: Some General Observations on Trial of a Suit

By John A. Wilson

"Advocacy" is a rather highfalutin word, more in use in Britain than here, and it tends to suggest the performances of those scintillating geniuses who were wont to destroy the opposing party utterly with one, and at the very outside two, devastating questions.

Very little in my own more prosaic experience would furnish any basis for a discourse along those lines. So for my purposes, I shall hopefully try to bring advocacy down to earth by common sense. And it is my thought to interpret advocacy broadly enough to cover certain aspects of preparation before trial as well as various aspects of actual trial.

However, lest I seem somewhat to belittle or apologize for mere common sense let me remind you of some rather notable things that have been said about it. An old Persian proverb, for example, estimates that: "One pound of learning requires ten pounds of common sense to apply it."

Also, someone, with undoubted insight, has said of common sense: "Common sense is, of all kinds, the most uncommon. It implies good judgment, sound discretion and true and practical wisdom applied to common life."

And the perspicacious Henry Ward Beecher praised common sense even more strongly when he said: "If a man can have only one kind of sense, let him have common sense. If he has that and uncommon sense too, he is not far from genius."

Much has been written and said about the qualifications of the ideal trial lawyer. I doubt, however, if anyone has ever possessed all of them in high degree. Foremost among the generally recognized qualifications might be listed as fundamental: a keen insight into human nature; a good memory; facility with language; capacity for quick and sound decision; and a sense of proportion.

To this obviously incomplete list, I should certainly add a somewhat unglamourous quality, not often sufficiently recognized—just plain physical and emotional stamina. This is the quality which enables the trial lawyer to "take it," day after day, when the trial is long and the going rough—enables him—in the pungent language of fistiana—to "roll with the punches," without "taking a nose dive," and without "sniffing the resin."

Sometimes it is said in rather picturesque language that a good trial lawyer should also possess unusual sensitivity—as it were, "intellectual and emotional antennae." There is much truth in this, and indeed, it should be most gratifying to every aspiring trial lawyer to know that the crustacea and the insecta need not have sole monopoly of these antennae—these useful "implements of decision." But a well-equipped trial lawyer must also have the courage of his convictions, a capacity for bold and forthright action when seasoned judgment calls for it. Hypercaution, timidity of approach and vacillation rarely convince anyone. As a current musical hit puts it: "You've got to have heart."

Preparation for trial, both on the facts and on the law, should begin promptly. Don't delay until the trial is almost at hand. A false start, based on an inadequate grasp of the facts and law, may require radical changes in pleadings or in bills of particulars. Such changes may then be effectively used by your adversary to discredit your case at the trial.

If your client is to be examined before trial, an early comprehension of all the facts is essential; it is also essential if you are to conduct a timely and really effective examination of the opposing party. Prompt preparation, furthermore, may disclose significant weaknesses in your case and may possibly indicate the advantages of a speedy settlement, before mounting litigation expenses make any settlement more difficult or impossible.

The most important aspect of preparation is to get the facts—all of them. As an eminent trial lawyer, former United States Attorney, Emory R. Buckner, used to say, in substance, to the young men about him:

> "Have a passion for the facts. But remember this also. There is no democracy of facts. They were not all created equal. There are master facts and there are subordinate facts. So give to every fact its proper weight and influence, its just due."

Judge Chase of the United States Court of Appeals in *Conghlin v. The Commissioner*, expressed a similar thought in this way:

> "... as is so often true of legal problems [he said], the correct result depends upon how to give the facts the right order of importance."

Further—and here is a rather cheering thought—if you get all the facts you will find that many seemingly close questions of law will evaporate and disappear. Thus, thorough preparation on the facts may pay off well with a bonus on the law.

In dealing with your client and with your witnesses, you will need to be an apt student of human nature—always a practical psychologist, and sometimes a bit of psychiatrist, as well. Be sensibly skeptical about the stories they tell you. This does not mean, at all, that you must assume that your client or his witnesses are fabricating facts. It does mean that you should always remember that personal interest tends to bias one's point of view. So be sympathetic but objective, and I need scarcely say be diplomatic too.

Do not assume, as some clients do, that everyone who sues them is necessarily a highjacker or an unscrupulous scoundrel. Sometimes, indeed, there seems to be an inordinate predisposition on the part of some defendants to approach their cases with only one separate and very distinct defense in mind—one which may be labelled somewhat facetiously: "They can't do that to us." But unfortunately *they* sometimes can, and *they* sometimes do.

Give careful thought to the arrangement and order of witnesses. Your case must be planned, produced and presented much like a play with proper regard for dramatic values. Therefore, avoid tediousness, produce as much variety as possible, sustain suspense and by proper planning provide, in advance, for periodic climaxes at the trial.

Try, if possible, to end each trial session and each day on a high and confident note like a good aria. If you are able to do that, then, in a trial as in an aria, some unavoidably faltering notes along the way may not count quite so heavily against you.

Many lawyers before they have really thoroughly investigated the facts unwisely display to their clients a premature and undue optimism about the successful outcome of the case. This is unwarranted. Adequate suspension of judgment is necessary.

Point out the weakness as well as the strength of your client's case. This should certainly tend to insure his more effective co-operation. If he has become optimistic, without warrant, however, you may find it difficult to convince him that he should accept a really good settlement. He may be unreasonable and obstinate, and may finally refuse such settlement—to his subsequent regret—and to yours.

The mechanics of trial should be carefully planned—and smoothly executed. Lost or misplaced papers, insufficient copies of important documents, disorganized files and similar mechanical disorders can and should be avoided. They slow up the pace of trial and destroy that timing and precision so essential to effective presentation.

And worse still! They upset the composure, poise and confidence of the trial lawyer. His resources of mind and emotion which should be held in readiness for unpredictable emergencies are, in fact, devoted to matters of mechanics. These could, with a little imagination and industry, have been taken care of before trial.

Often an otherwise good examination is spoiled completely because the examiner has had to waste time in a feverish hunt for papers. Confusion of counsel is the inevitable corollary of confusion of papers.

So achieve as near perfection as possible in these mechanical matters. For you will need all your wits and all your art and artistry to handle the unexpected situations which will surely arise. Prepare well and you may find that you will enjoy the trial because there is no undue strain.

Recently educators have been anxiously asking in the language of a best seller: "Why Johnny Can't Read." A somewhat related and similarly provocative inquiry might be, why can't more trial lawyers read well to a court and jury? The reading of far too many of us is inaudible, hurried, unexpressive and monotonous. Often we expend much skill and many hours getting an important exhibit into evidence, and then squander its probative value by the simple device of reading it badly.

I recall a friendly court reporter in the Southern District of New York, commenting to me, pointedly, upon this matter of ineffective reading, many years ago:

"Did you hear Assistant X read that beautifully fraudulent gold mining prospectus?" he asked, one morning during a mail fraud prosecution. "Terrible," he said rather disgustedly, "you could scarcely hear him; he raced through it; it sounded duller than a trust indenture. Don't ever do that."

If your case is of sufficient importance and expense is not a deterrent, secure four copies or photostats of each important document on which you propose to cross examine a witness. This will greatly simplify and improve your presentation. For you will then be able to hand the judge a copy, the witness a copy, your adversary a copy and you may examine from a copy which you hold in your own hand. In this way you may sometimes prevent a most awkward and embarrassing situation. Let me illustrate.

We have all observed, I am sure, trial counsel attempting to cross-examine a witness upon the contents of a document of which he has only one copy. He desires to call the attention of the witness to numerous passages in the document. Advancing confidently to the witness stand he leans nonchalantly over the witness, as he sits in his chair, to indicate those passages, asking a series of questions in a low confidential tone.

At this point, his troublesome adversary loudly announces that he not only has no copy of the document but that he cannot hear the questions. The court then admonishes examining counsel to speak up. But when examining counsel begins to question the witness in a strong loud voice, his adversary, a rather pestiferous fellow, I am afraid, next asserts that he is shouting at the witness and clearly endeavoring to intimidate him. He requests the court to direct the examiner to stand back from the witness.

Whereupon the court suggests that examining counsel take his position at the end of the jury box. The poor fellow does so, and again, feebly, and with obviously drooping spirits, attempts to recommence his questioning upon the exhibit.

Now, however, the witness gets into the act and says he simply cannot remember a thing the document contains unless he can look at it. So all the dejected examiner can possibly do is what, unfortunately he has had to do many times before, "crave the indulgence of the court" and pass on to other subject matter.

This and many similar awkward situations arising out of lack of imaginative preparation in mechanical matters, a little foresight could easily prevent.

Your opening to a court or jury is of special importance for this is your first opportunity to give them a favorable impression of your case and of you. Like all first impressions it will be rather hard to eradicate. So plan your opening carefully.

Counsel should outline the issues and the evidence very briefly when his case is short and uncomplicated. The court and jury are deprived of the acute satisfaction of suspense and of discovery for themselves if counsel details the evidence overmuch. Christmas gifts are always more appreciated if they are not opened before Christmas Day and if the recipient opens the package himself.

If in the opening statement too much of the evidence is disclosed by counsel, then when it comes from the witnesses it may seem dull and routine—inevitable, like a moving picture seen for the second time.

However, in a case which is long and involved, the issues and a full outline of the evidence should be stated—sufficiently to enable the court and jury to understand and appreciate your proof—but not so fully as to destroy the vital elements of discovery and dramatic surprise.

Do not overstate your case. State only those facts which you are sure you can prove. Promise no more. Understatement is, in itself, a powerful factor in the psychology of persuasion.

Moderation in every aspect of the trial is essential. Remember that, as I have said, the lawyer who prepares and tries a case is in a sense producing a play—a play which may need to be revised in part every night after court—and in which he must always subordinate a natural desire to feature himself in the star role. The need to restrain an inordinate impulse to star holds true not only of the opening statement, but of the examination of witnesses on direct and, to some extent, also, on cross.

By the Great Apostle we are adjured, in Holy Writ, to let our "moderation be known unto all men." However, if you and I cannot achieve that ideal at least we can be sure to let our moderation be known to every judge and jury before whom we try a case—and to the appellate tribunals as well.

Don't claim too much; don't exaggerate; be fair and reasonable; don't treat every issue as though it were framed in black and white; and recognize that truth often shades off into tones of gray. Exorbitant claims and denunciations, as some of the speeches during the recent political campaign well illustrated, have a singularly unpersuasive power.

Now what about making objections at a trial? For practical psychological reasons experienced trial lawyers keep technical objections to a minimum even though the objections are technically correct. Numerous objections tend inevitably to suggest apprehensiveness of a full disclosure of the facts. When counsel objects again and again on the ground that testimony is incompetent, irrelevant and immaterial, the jury, and perhaps the court too, may soon conclude that his real objection is that proof is available to his adversary so competent, so relevant and so material as to jeopardize the objectant's case.

If your adversary's proof is irrelevant and so immaterial why bother to object? It will actually help your case if your opponent insists on following the paths of futility. So—in the words of a song, popular a few years ago: Make it your trial policy in this matter of objections as in other matters, "to accentuate the positive, eliminate the negative, latch on to the affirmative, and don't mess with Mr. In-Between."

However, if a question is really improper and prejudicial, make an objection. But make your objection specific and short. I well recall the advice which a genial and helpful federal judge of the Southern District gave me after the trial of my first case, a narcotics prosecution. Calling me to the bench he said:

> "You tried your case very well, but let me make a suggestion about objections. Don't make purely technical objections. In fact, don't make many of any kind.
>
> But, if a question is really improper and harmful, don't hesitate to object. However, when you feel an objection coming on first take a look at the judge. Since he is supposed to know evidence too, you may well see that sustaining light come into his eye.
>
> Then your objection will probably be upheld and you will be thought a brilliant young lawyer."

Cross-examination is always potentially dangerous—a mine field full of booby traps. But quick and dependable insights and decisions become more possible if we have absorbed and assimilated all the facts and have exercised, in advance, an aggressive imagination as to the probable answers of the witness and the probable course his testimony will take.

If you perceive no real or apparent points of vulnerability in the testimony of a witness, do not magnify the importance of his testimony by attempting an extensive and vigorous cross-examination. He'll really be good the second time around—and the jury will, if anything, be more impressed. Rather—be casual! Invite him courteously to step down. It is an art to know what to ignore and how to ignore it. You do not need to score a knock-out in every round.

The best cross-examination is frequently wholly unspectacular. The witnesses are not "destroyed" as some professional writers on advocacy like to put it. The type of examination I have in mind consists of building up the facts of the examiner's own case on the examination of his adversary's witnesses.

This method of cross-examination has a steadily corrosive effect upon the case of the opposition; the opposition's case may be so progressively impaired as never really to stand up, impressively, at all. Moreover, the impact of one's own case is heightened if it can be established in large part out of the mouths of opposition witnesses.

Speaking of cross-examination and of the common admonition "never, never, never to ask a question when you do not know what the answer will be," Judge Schientag said:

> "It is really safe to use the words "always" and "never" in dealing with that unpredictable and strangely elusive phenomenon—human nature. It is helpful to know the general principles or rules, but as with salmon fishing so too with cross examination, it may sometimes be advisable, even necessary, to throw the rules overboard in order to land your fish."

With this piscatorial analogy of Mr. Justice Schientag I thoroughly agree. To shift from the piscatorial to the athletic, however: Who has not seen a football team, about to go down to defeat, turn defeat into victory because in the very last minutes of play an audacious quarterback had the quick good judgment and nerve to throw a long forward pass?

So it is with the seasoned cross-examiner. Whether or not to chance the question is determined, in part, by the sensitivity of what Emory R. Buckner once called the lawyer's "intellectual and emotional antennae." But make no mistake about it! What often passes for a flash of genius or for mere good luck is more often the result of that insight, gained from a thorough knowledge of the facts and law, which enables the examiner, dependably, to forecast the probable answers of the witness.

Direct examination is the much underrated and neglected twin brother of cross-examination. Some too readily assume that anyone can conduct a direct examination well, and too little thought is given to it. Yet I venture to say that more cases are won by good direct examination, coupled with effective summation, than by the more pyrotechnical displays of cross-examination.

Pedestrian though it may seem, the best direct examination follows a simple formula and elicits "the when," "the where," and "the what" of proof, in orderly time sequence. Direct examination, however, need not be colorless and drab. To be sure, the trial lawyer will need to restrain that impulse to star which is the father of so many leading questions. And he must be content to be the modest instrument for focusing attention and interest upon his witnesses. After all, basically, direct examination should be "the witness' show."

Nevertheless, the examiner must radiate the same interest and confidence in the testimony of his witnesses that he hopes the witnesses are creating in the minds of the judge and jury. This, more often than not, perhaps, will be a sufficient challenge to his artistic impulses.

Do not be deceived! Good direct examination is an art whose chief attributes are the quiet attributes of order, modulation and restraint—but it is an art, nevertheless, and by no means an easy one.

The summation is your opportunity to draw the evidence together and to interpret it so that the court and jury may see it "steadily and see it whole." When the evidence on both sides of your case is pretty much in balance, the summation will frequently prove to be decisive of defeat or victory.

The nature, complexity and difficulty of your case must determine the length of your summation. Do not, as some do, make a fetish of brevity on the one hand or on the other let your enthusiasm lead you into undue length of presentation. Within the time for summation allowed by the court take only such time as you really need to make your arguments persuasively—always keeping an observant eye upon the court and jury to see that they remain alert and interested.

Don't tell the court or jury, in effect, what they must think or do—as though you were omniscient. Rather take the attitude of counselling with them in their analysis and in their search for sound conclusions. Again, moderation is the watchword.

Before trial, if possible, prepare an outline of summation. It will be helpful and will save time when you are hard-pressed at the trial. But your outline will certainly need revision in the light of the actual evidence.

Never read your summation. Speech as nearly spontaneous as possible tends to produce an impression of earnestness and sincerity, and to equate communication by counsel with reception by the court and jury. It is essential to that electric circular response between speaker and audience, so necessary to sustained and intelligent interest.

The objective of summation is to persuade the judge and jury, ordinary men and women, to action in favor of your client. What you think and *feel* about your case must be conveyed to them in the form of the clearest and most direct human appeal.

And do not be overconcerned with the literary excellence of your summation. The absence of such excellence will be more than compensated by a heightened impression of sincerity. The zigs and zags, the hesitancies and even the occasional crudities of spontaneous speech should tend only to make it more persuasive.

There are those who believe that there is no longer any place for rhetorical values in the more traditional sense. They go all out for the conversational method, the homespun and homey style of address. The high value of this should certainly not be underrated. But many trial lawyers of the relatively more recent vintages are so fearful of emotional and rhetorical values that they invariably sum up with dull pedestrian restraint.

I would not defend empty flowery language, and certainly not bombast or flamboyancy. They are never appropriate. But the language of imagery, expressive of emotion, instinct with dramatic power, still has its place and should be appropriately employed. It is, at present, in my view, too much neglected. The rhetorical pendulum has swung too far.

There is no easy formula for the ideal summation. Neither use language of unusual rhetorical quality for its own sake nor talk down to the jury in a patent effort to reach the level of their imagined common-placeness. Talking down to a jury is as unwise as the bombastic oratory which is "full of sound and fury, signifying nothing." Be natural. Proceed with a sense of proportion.

Harris in his *Hints on Advocacy* illustrates what I have been saying. He points out that the oratorical flights of Burke or of Sheridan would be ludicrous in an ordinary accident case. And, he goes on to add, with a delightful touch of humor:

> "The empire is not at stake in every trial; and a British pickpocket may be defended, at least up to conviction, without a severe onslaught on the British Constitution."

No one is more conscious than I, that I have been giving rather freely, much advice, on a very old and most difficult subject. And, therefore, let me conclude on a note of caution and admonition both to myself as well as to you: As a noted woman advocate, Portia, in *The Merchant of Venice,* put it:

> "If to do were as easy as to know what were good to do, chapels had been churches and poor men's cottages princes' palaces."

Adapted from Vol. 43, American Bar Association Journal (1957).

How to Try a Case in the Trial Court from the Judge's Point of View

BY NEWELL JENNINGS

IT SEEMS THAT THE LAWYERS are interested in finding out, if possible, what effect their antics and practices have on the presiding judge. The importance of this is obvious when it is realized that the judge's ultimate decision is based largely on the impressions received by him during the course of the trial. This paper is therefore in no sense a complete treatise on the trial of a case but is rather, as the title indicates, a summary of the effect of common practices on the judge.

One further limitation should be observed and that is that the judge in question is myself. While I am not conscious of any particular abnormalities and have considered that I was an average trial judge, I am of course referring to my own reactions and to those of no one else. Not being a member of the trial bench at present I hope to be able to handle the question somewhat objectively and my fifteen years' experience in trial work should qualify me to some extent. As I have said before under similar circumstances, if the following observations seem trite and self-evident, the answer is that they are based on actual experience in court.

When a judge takes his seat after the Sheriff has opened court and picks up the file in the case ready for trial, he has a certain background of legal knowledge but the thing about which he is totally ignorant at that time is the factual situation in the case to be tried. Anything that the lawyers can do to outline this situation to the judge at an early stage in the trial will be most helpful.

Lawyers have usually lived with their case for a period of time and are prone to assume that the judge can acquire the same familiarity by some mystic process without their assistance. This of course is not true. Where the facts are at all complicated the case often advances for hours, if not for days, before the judge has full appreciation of the factual situation. It follows that the outstanding thing that a trial lawyer can do for the judge is to develop his facts early, clearly and as simply as possible.

The mental process which the judge goes through is well illustrated by the charge which I used to almost always give juries. It ran something like this:

> "You are here to decide the questions of fact raised by the issues which I have described to you. I recommend that you start with such facts as you find to be admitted either on the pleadings or during the trial. You will discover that these facts will make a fairly complete picture of the situation. Then take up the disputed facts, find out where the truth lies and sketch them in. To this completed factual picture you should then apply the rules of law which I have given you and bring in your verdict accordingly."

Nature of a Trial

Before coming to the concrete questions which will form the basis of the discussion, I should like to refer to one more general consideration. If we are to come to any conclusion about the trial of a lawsuit, we should have some idea of its character and purpose. The purpose of a lawsuit has always been to ascertain the truth and justice of a given situation. From the earliest times it has been a contest and far too often the contest which should be the means to the end sought has become the principal feature.

Many lawsuits degenerate into fights between the lawyers in which the interests of their clients are almost, if not quite, lost sight of. The reason for this is probably historical. The most primitive principle in the settlement of disputes which still has some force is that might makes right. The effort through the centuries has been to get away from this theory and to settle disputes according to accepted legal principles. In accordance with this effort the evolution of the lawsuit has been from a contest to an inquiry. The increasing use of discovery and pre-trial procedure are practical illustrations of this tendency.

There appears to be no sound reason why a lawsuit should necessarily mean a fight any more than the scientific search to isolate the germ of the common cold. This is mentioned because the judge always enjoys an inquiry more than he does a contest, especially when personalities are unjustifiably dragged into the picture. A lawsuit being an adversary proceeding, some features of a contest always will be and probably should be retained but the objects to be attained will be clearer and will be reached with much less loss of time and much less confusion if the inquiry method is pursued.

Preparation of Case

Remembering then that the gist of the matter is simplicity in the presentation of questions of fact, the preparation of the case becomes even more important than the trial. It must be clear that cases are won by adequate preparation more often than by presentation in court. In order to clearly plead and present his facts an attorney must make careful examination of the story of the plaintiff and his supporting witnesses and exhibits.

No time spent in this task is wasted. The attorney should not rely on his memory for the statements of the witness but they should be reduced to writing. A good method where the witness has sufficient intelligence is to get the witness to write out a statement in his own handwriting, or still better, write a letter to his attorney after he has left the office and understands what is required of him.

In talking with witnesses it is also always well to warn them that they will be questioned as to whether they have talked with anyone about the case. They should of course be informed that that is expected and involves no criticism of any kind.

After the facts are clear the first thing to ascertain is whether or not the plaintiff has a cause of action. This of course involves some investigation of legal principles and again no work done along this line at this time will be wasted. The complaint should then be drafted with care and attention to precedent.

Pleadings

The importance of the correct drafting of the complaint can hardly be overemphasized. If correctly drawn, it is not vulnerable to either plea in abatement, motion or demurrer and the case will reach the judge in its simplest form, to wit: complaint, answer and reply, if any.

When a judge picks up a file and finds that it is six inches thick consisting of amendments, pleas, motions and demurrers, he immediately feels that some carpenter has been at work and that the prognosis for a satisfactory trial is poor. The object of the permitted dilatory motions and pleas is of course to narrow and clarify the issues but they are not necessary if the original groundwork has been correctly performed.

There are of course exceptions to all rules and that statement should be made now once for all but speaking generally, dilatory pleas are of little value. If a plaintiff has a poor complaint, that is his hard luck and it may be and usually is of more advantage to the defendant to let him struggle with it at the trial than to fix it up for him by a series of dilatory motions.

The most important exception to this rule is of course where the suit can be definitely disposed of on demurrer. A demurrer which merely gives the plaintiff a better complaint is of no more use than a dilatory plea but one which knocks out the lawsuit saves time for everyone and is a very simple and highly desirable method of determining the issues at an early stage.

Claim for Damages

When the proper time arrives consideration must be given to the claim for the jury. Jury trials are slow and expensive compared to court trials and a much smaller percentage of cases is being claimed for the jury than was formerly the practice. Some lawyers claim everything to the jury and some claim nothing to the jury. Both are wrong.

There is of course a class of cases which cannot be claimed for the jury. There is another large class which should not be claimed. These include cases where the facts are too complicated to get before the jury, cases involving statements of account, and cases where the liability is reasonably clear. When a jury of twelve approaches the question of damages the result is necessarily a compromise and the effect is usually to give a smaller verdict than would be obtained if the matter were left to a judge. There will of course always remain a certain number of cases of sympathetic appeal and cases in which natural justice would perhaps be served by a plaintiff's verdict which could not be justified as a cold legal proposition.

In criminal cases the chances of acquittal are usually greater in cases tried to the court than cases tried to the jury. It happens often that the background of a case makes it almost impossible to secure an acquittal from a jury where a judge is better able to confine his attention to the precise issue involved.

The handling of exhibits has improved enormously in recent years. It is possible that too much time can be spent in indexing and arranging exhibits but that is unlikely. If exhibits are carefully arranged in order and a list of them prepared indicating when they are to be introduced, that is probably the minimum of preparation which should be made in this regard.

Memoranda of Law

While this paper is primarily concerned with the trial of questions of fact, full preparation naturally presupposes examination of the pertinent legal issues. These should be fairly evident by the time the case is placed on the trial list and fall roughly into three categories. Legal questions as to the admissibility of evidence and of requests to charge are discussed below. There remain the underlying legal issues. Everyone, including the judge, is presumed to know the law but in view of the variety and complexity of the questions now arising that is sometimes a violent presumption.

It is not unusual to try two or three court cases in a day and it is not too much to expect the attorney to prepare himself to assist the court with the leading cases on the subject. If a brief digest is prepared, not only of those cases on which the attorney expects to rely, but also of those which will probably be cited by opposing counsel, it will prove most useful. The discovery of the appropriate rule is generally less difficult than its application to the facts of the situation. So here we are, back with the facts again. Very often I have had occasion to say in a memorandum that a brief contained a lot of good law but that it did not apply to the facts of the case.

As I have reason to know, an almost infinite amount of time can be spent in research on a difficult legal question. As I also know, a busy lawyer has considerably less than infinity at his disposal for that purpose. This does not excuse him from making a reasonable search and being reasonably prepared to meet the legal questions which arise upon the trial.

Opening of Trial

A trial starts with some sort of introductory statement. The method in most common use is the reading of the pleadings. This has certain advantages because if they are actually read to the jury, the judge can say that "the pleadings were read to you at the opening of the case and will be in your jury room for reference should you find that necessary." As a simple presentation of the issues of fact no method could probably be worse. A carefully prepared statement defining the issues is of much greater value to both judge and jury. I personally much prefer this method.

The presentation of evidence will be discussed under exhibits, direct testimony and cross-examination. The question as to how much time should be spent reading exhibits during a trial is one which should be answered by common sense. My personal experience was that lawyers, in a praiseworthy effort to save time, did not read enough of the important exhibits during the progress of the trial. This resulted in extensive lacunae in the orderly presentation of the case which handicap the trier in reaching a tentative conclusion when the arguments are completed.

Most cases are tentatively decided at that time. Of course when the decision depends on a vital question of law or when the facts are so complicated that not even a tentative solution can be reached at the close of the case, this decision must be deferred. If the lawyers will bear in mind, however, that if they can put the judge into a state of mind where he is tentatively ready to decide the case in their favor when the arguments are completed, they are half way around the bases. Conversely, the lawyer who is in the reverse position has had two strikes called on him already.

It will be observed that in the foregoing discussion I have used the word tentative several times and that fact should be emphasized. This first impression which a judge gets at the close of a case is important, as I have said, but is a long distance from the final decision. This usually involves careful study and checking of the appropriate authorities.

Questioning of Witnesses

The effectiveness of the direct testimony is almost entirely dependent on preparation. The lawyer should know what questions to ask and the witness should know in a general way what is expected of him and should also understand that back-fence conversations are not ordinarily admissible. The witness on direct examination is ordinarily asked leading questions without objection up to the time when the important issue of the case is reached.

He is then asked some such question as this: "Please tell the court and jury what you observed from this time on" and then tells his story. It should be unnecessary to interrupt a witness on direct examination and this should never be done simply to get the same facts before the court in the precise way desired by the lawyer. Of course if a witness persists in attempting to give inadmissible testimony, it is necessary to admonish and instruct him in order that the case may proceed.

It should hardly be necessary to say that futile objections sprinkled practically continuously through a witness's testimony have a very bad effect on the judge and serve no useful purpose whatever. Care in asking the question should make objections unnecessary and unnecessary objections should never be made. It does happen occasionally that a vital question can be excluded and under those circumstances an objection should always be made and an exception taken.

Where a lawyer anticipates such an objection any preparation which he can make to meet it from a legal standpoint is highly desirable. The trial judge seldom has warning and always appreciates any assistance the attorneys can give him in solving the problem from a legal standpoint.

An illustration of the value of this occurred during one of my first terms. A six-year-old witness was offered. Not having happened to meet that situation in my practice, I was about to exclude the testimony when the lawyer offered me a Supreme Court report open on the table in front of him stating that the admissibility of such testimony lay in the discretion of the court after examination of the proferred witness.

Our rule requiring that an exception be taken to make a ruling reviewable on appeal does not exist in all jurisdictions and has been severely criticized. If the examination is conducted according to the principles here laid down, there would be no need for the rule. As long as the asking of improper questions and the making of unnecessary objections is as prevalent as I found it in my own experience, the trial judge is entitled to this protection. When, as too often happens, every other question is objected to, the phrase "overruled" is apt to become too automatic.

While I have heard it said that an exception should be taken to every adverse ruling on evidence, the stupidest lawyer can appreciate that cumbering the record with dozens of useless exceptions is poor practice. When an exception is taken, the attention of the judge is called to his ruling and an opportunity is afforded for reconsideration.

Cross-Examination

The story with reference to cross-examination may be summed up by saying that there is far too much poor cross-examination and not merely enough good cross-examination. A test to prove this hypothesis can be easily made. Take an ordinary Supreme Court record containing the evidence and read the direct testimony of each witness. Then read the cross-examination and see how much is added to the picture. This does not mean cross-examination should be abandoned.

The object of cross-examination is to break down the direct examination. It follows that if the direct examination has been harmless, no cross-examination is required and none should be indulged in. The reason for so much poor cross-examination lies partly in the most common method pursued during the examination of witnesses. This method is to write down the witness's testimony as completely as possible.

When the direct testimony is completed the cross-examiner then turns to his notes, asks the same questions and gets the same answers, with no gain to anyone and serious loss of time. Of course, it usually happens that some inconsistency is developed between the direct and cross-examination and the matter is then pursued ad nauseam with little practical result. Such examinations are boring and annoying to the trial judge. Where two attorneys are associated in the trial, the one who is not to cross-examine can spend his time profitably in making notes. These are valuable in the preparation of an argument or of the appeal. The method followed by the most successful cross-examiners as I have observed them is to listen carefully to the direct and make an occasional note if necessary.

The attention of the lawyer under those circumstances is not in making a complete transcript but in thinking about the testimony of the witness. If this method is pursued, he is then able to evaluate this testimony, determine whether cross-examination is called for and, if it is, to attack the witness along some line which is likely to yield pay dirt.

As already stated, if there is no harm in the direct there is no call for cross-examination. It sometimes happens that an attorney is confronted by a dangerous witness. He may make up his mind for some reason or other that it would be much better policy to leave the witness alone. Two courses are possible under these circumstances. The attorney can say "No questions" or he can conduct what is known as a pro forma cross-examination. This should not be attempted unless the attorney is a skillful cross-examiner as the results may be unfortunate. It fools nobody in any event and the dismissal of the witness is usually the preferable course to pursue.

Speaking now of the various attacks made by cross-examination from the standpoint of their effect on the trial judge, the most common as well as the most persuasive attack is usually to show any kind of bias. The deliberate perjurer on the witness stand is the rare exception. The differences in testimony result rather from differences in recollection, intelligence and opportunities of observation. Where the differences are of this character any bias, prejudice or interest is particularly liable to color the witness's testimony and if these facts can be brought home by the cross-examination it will yield large dividends.

The judge is always interested in the opportunities of observation which the witness has enjoyed. It sometimes develops that the admitted line of sight makes any observation made by the witness of a certain event entirely unreliable. A cross-examination which won a case and which was entirely devoted to the development of the witness's opportunities of observation will be found in *Seabridge v. Poli.*[1] The cross-examination of the plaintiff by the late Edmund Zacher was a masterpiece.

Another common method of attack in cross-examination is to lay the foundation for contradictory oral or written statements. Such a showing is as proper as it is common but in my experience the importance of its effect on the judge's mind is not as great as is usually supposed. This is because the judge is fully conscious, possibly from personal experience, of the frailties and inaccuracies of memory. It follows that often more time is spent in developing the case along this line than the results justify. The most usual procedure is to use the transcript where the witness has previously

1 98 Conn. 297.

testified under oath, either in a former trial, in a lower court or before the coroner.

A portion of his former testimony is read to him and he is asked if he so testified. The differences in the two versions are then pointed out. This is a very severe test and only a person with an exceptional memory will perform satisfactorily. Judges know this and it is for that reason that I say that the importance of this testimony is usually overrated. The same is true to a somewhat less extent where a witness is confronted with statements made to an investigator. The statements are often taken under circumstances which do not make for care and accuracy and more often than not are repudiated by the witness. They are invaluable in the preparation of a case but their use in the trial has not often been as valuable as a probative factor as would seem probable.

As before stated, all of this testimony is proper and probably has some value. My only criticism of it is that its importance is usually overrated. There is one form of this contradiction which is almost decisive.

If a witness can be pinned down to a perfectly definite, specific statement fixed in point of time and can be confronted with a letter or a statement written by himself which contradicts it, the attorney has something which can hardly be explained away. The opportunities for proof of this character are not very numerous but when available may alone decide the question of fact involved.

"With Whom Did You Discuss the Case?"

The "usual question" is still employed and, strange to say, still pays dividends. The average witness who is asked on cross-examination if he has discussed the case with anyone is usually embarrassed and tries to squirm out of it. The effect on the judge again is not as important as is usually supposed because the judge has been an attorney and knows how such things come about, but it is a proper question and is sometimes used effectively. As previously stated, each witness should be prepared for this question and told to state the facts.

Testing Credibility of Witnesses

In view of the latitude given in cross-examination to test the credibility of the witness the rule that the cross-examination must be germane to the direct is of little practical importance. It does have the effect of preventing the proof of the cross-examiner's affirmative allegations by means of the cross-examination. The general attack on credibility cannot be described by a, b or c because it necessarily must vary with the personality of each witness.

Formal impeachment is rare but devastating. By formal impeachment is meant the production of a considerable number of witnesses who will swear that the witness in question is not worthy of credit. Impeachment by proof of conviction of crime involving the moral turpitude is more common and I should say quite effective. A thief is a man who steals and a man who steals is dishonest. If he has been proved dishonest in one respect it follows that his testimony, unless pretty well corroborated, has little probative value.

Perhaps enough has been said to justify the original statement that there is too much poor and not enough good cross-examination. A judge has to learn patience if he is going to try cases and get through the boring, useless and time-wasting cross-examination as best he can. But the effect on him is at least negative and may be highly detrimental to the cause of the cross-examiner. This is particularly true when questions are pressed beyond reason after the judge has given clear intimation that he thinks they are inadmissible. Unless the attorney is very sure of his ground he would do well to consider whether by pressing an inadmissible question he may secure a favorable ruling which will eventually result in the loss of a perfectly good judgment.

Requests to Charge

The question is often asked what the trial judge wants in the way of requests to charge. One thing that he does not want is an attempt to prepare a full charge to the jury for his assistance. The opportunity for examining requests to charge is usually very scant and when, as occasionally happens, thirty or forty long paragraphs are submitted to him, he just cannot do them justice if he would and the practical result is that he is apt to throw them in the wastebasket and take a chance. Almost all disputes are settled before they actually come to trial and they usually come to trial because there is some particular point of fact or law on which the lawyers cannot come to an agreement. Where the question is one of fact a request to charge is not in order. Where, however, it is a question of law a request to charge should always be filed for the assistance of the judge and the protection of the party. Illustrations of questions of this type would be: Is the plaintiff entitled to a charge on the last clear chance? Is the plaintiff guilty of contributory negligence as a matter of law? Are assumption of risk or nuisance in the case? While a judge is supposed to cover all the fundamental legal issues in the case without a request to charge, there is always the danger where the legal issue is of this type that the Supreme Court will say that in the absence of a request to charge no charge was necessary. To summarize, requests to charge are not required on the ordinary rules of negligence, questions of burden of proof or definitions of a contract but should be filed when special legal issues are or may be important to the decision of the case.

Argument of Counsel

The question of argument is largely an individual problem with both the judge and the attorney. Of course in jury cases argument is part of the tradition and is always indulged in. Where the trial is to the court and the question is purely one of fact or credibility, my personal reaction is that argument is not particularly valuable in the ordinary case, although there are exceptions to this as to all rules. Where legal issues are involved I always used to want to hear the claims of the attorneys orally even if briefs were to be filed. As was stated earlier in discussing the reading of exhibits, a tentative conclusion is usually reached at the termination of the case and anything that the attorney can do to make that tentative determination favorable to his contentions should be done. Competent argument on legal issues is one of the things that is helpful to accomplish this result.

When specific cases are considered, the application of these principles should effectively answer many of the questions as to the effect on the trial judge of procedures adopted. Perhaps the best concrete illustration of the underlying principle of simplicity and clarity in the presentation of questions of fact occurs in criminal cases. With the exception of the issue of conspiracy, criminal cases almost invariably present clear and simple issues. When a criminal case is long drawn out it is usually because it is being poorly tried. As has been frequently stated, there are exceptions to all rules and an exception to this rule would be a charge of embezzlement involving a long series of accounts, expert testimony by certified public accountants and multiplication of exhibits. The question is "Did the accused do a certain act at a certain time and has the state proved that fact beyond a reasonable doubt?" In trying such a case only the most elementary principles are usually involved. Any testimony is relevant which helps the trier decide the issue and any relevant testimony is admissible unless excluded by some rule of law. With these as a guide such cases should be brought to a speedy conclusion. Where criminal cases are tried to the court the big question in my mind always was the fundamental one "Has the state proved its case beyond a reasonable doubt?" In my experience attorneys in criminal trials both to the court and jury are wont to pass this over as a matter of course and routine whereas it is apt to be the vital turning point of the case. Hammering on this issue will pay bigger dividends than cross-examining the state's engineer for half or three quarters of an hour inquiring about every possible measurement on the map not covered in the direct testimony.

One class of cases of not very frequent occurrence seems to violate all of the accepted rules and is mentioned for that reason. Will contests on the question of mental capacity seem to be in a class by themselves. In such cases every act of the testator from the date of his birth to the date of his death is relevant and courts and juries are at the mercy of the attorneys as to the extent of their inquiry into the life of the testator. Generally little mercy is shown and the cases are apt to continue for anywhere from three to ten weeks. The sad thing about it is that in view of the results obtained this seems to be the correct technique. It is undoubtedly true that a case presented in a day might receive scant attention from the trier, whereas the identical issue spread over a couple of months may finally impress the trier by the mere quantity of evidence submitted.

Trial of Negligence Cases

The trial of negligence cases has become pretty well standardized. The only comment I care to make is that too many negligence cases are tried which result in defendant's verdicts. Any injured plaintiff is entitled to have his claim considered but that does not mean that the case has to be tried. An attorney hired to defend the case has little option because any party is entitled to have the best defense made which circumstances permit provided an adjustment cannot be reached.

No attorney, however, is obliged to try a case for a plaintiff unless he thinks the chances of success are at least fair. Speaking from the standpoint of a trier, an attorney who gets the reputation of trying everything and failing to secure a verdict or a judgment in nine cases out of ten, in time tends to lose the "ear of the court."

After losing six or seven cases in a row the energy with which he presses his client's claims on the attention of the court is discounted to a considerable extent. In making this statement I am not unaware of the economic pressure under which lawyers are unfortunately laboring today. As I said, this consideration does not militate against taking a case but does seem to me a valid argument against trying too many cases where the chances are ten to one against a successful result.

Gathering up the result of this inquiry into the trial of a case from the judge's point of view, I have evolved the following definitions: A well-tried case is one well-prepared on fact and law in which improper questions are not asked and therefore not objected to, so that the facts are developed clearly and logically to form as simple issues as the case permits. The groundwork is thus laid for a brief, forceful and convincing argument.

This article was adapted from 3 Schweitzer, Trial Guide 1425, Baker, Voorhis & Co., Inc., New York (1945), which was adapted from the Connecticut Bar Journal, Vol. 14, No. 2.

How to Try a Case in the Trial Court from a Lawyer's Point of View

BY DAVID GOLDSTEIN

I FEEL THAT THE MOST IMPORTANT attribute which a successful trial lawyer must possess is that of experience. Experience is the greatest teacher of how a case should be tried, since in every trial an advocate learns something new. No two cases are the same, and the experience acquired through the trial of every case adds to the ability of a trial lawyer.

A young man who has just graduated from law school may feel that he is qualified for trial work through his knowledge of evidence and the theory of law which he has obtained in his courses at law school, but I am afraid that after he attempts to prepare and try a case in court for the first time, he soon realizes that there is something more to the trial of a case than mere knowledge of theory as to substantive law and rules of evidence. The application of rules of evidence during the course of a trial is only gained through the experience of trying cases.

Industry is a primary requisite of all lawyers. Lawyers may say, "Well, this lawyer got a break in the trial of that case." Such remarks overlook the fact that what appears to be a "break" is frequently only the fruit of diligent preparation. In the trial of a case, it is often necessary to spend many hours in preparation. If one is not industrious and conscientious in his preparation, he is wanting in one of the most important attributes of a successful trial lawyer.

Another essential quality is common sense. Every case is tried upon the basis of common sense and most cases are decided upon that basis. A prime requisite, moreover, is the ability to think and act quickly in an emergency. During the course of a trial the situation may change with kaleidoscopic celerity, and unless the trier's mind is geared up to cope with the exigencies of the situation, he may find that the bottom has suddenly fallen out of his case.

A very eminent and distinguished lawyer once said that the successful trial of cases depends to a great extent upon common sense, upon common honesty, coupled with uncommon industry. Unless an attorney possesses these qualities to a large degree, he should not attempt to act as trial counsel.

Before a case reaches the court for trial, there is a great deal of preliminary preparation that an attorney must make. This preliminary preparation is of the utmost importance to the successful presentation of the cause.

When a client first comes into an attorney's office and tells his story, the facts should be carefully reduced to writing and all documentary evidence should be procured and analyzed. The client should be examined and re-examined so that all pertinent information is elicited from him and so that the weaknesses of the case, which clients are prone to conceal, may be brought to the attorney's attention.

Unless these weaknesses are brought forth before the trial, they may come out at the trial in an unfavorable light. On the other hand, if the attorney learns of the weaknesses of his case before trial, he may be able to minimize them by bringing them out himself.

It is very important that signed written statements should be procured from all witnesses who are to testify to any of the facts of the case. After the statements have been procured, the witness should be warned not to sign additional statements for opposing counsel or any investigator employed by such counsel. There is always the possibility that an overzealous investigator acting for the opposing party may modify or change a statement given to him by a witness when the investigator reduces the same to writing.

In preparing for trial, counsel may obtain valuable assistance by examining the record of another case of similar nature, if such a record is obtainable. Where a case cited in the reports is factually similar to the case about to be tried, a perusal of the record in such a case will furnish an outline of what proof is necessary and facilitate the presentation to a court or to a jury.

Since there are more automobile negligence cases tried in our courts at the present time than any other kind of a case, I shall briefly touch upon the manner in which such a case should be tried. As stated heretofore, it is very essential that a thorough and exhaustive examination be made of the client. Immediately after the client is examined, photographs and a map should be made of the locus in quo and of the automobiles involved in the collision, because a change of conditions either of the locus in quo or automobiles will destroy their admissibility and effectiveness.

Photostatic copies of the motor vehicle reports of the operators of the colliding automobiles should be procured at once from the Motor Vehicle Department, or if a bus is involved, a report from the Public Utilities Commission. The information in such accident reports will be very helpful in locating witnesses who may be in a position to throw some light on the facts and circumstances surrounding the accident. It would also give counsel the benefit of the driver's version of how the collision occurred.

Just as soon as these reports are procured, an investigator should be dispatched to interview and procure signed statements from all witnesses. A search should also be made by such investigator of the vicinity surrounding the locus in quo where the collision occurred. If a thorough search is made to locate witnesses whose names are not reported in the statements on file with the Motor Vehicle Department or Public Utilities Commission, it is quite possible that additional witnesses may be found whose testimony will prove valuable in the trial of the case.

All available physical facts should be determined and evidence thereof should be preserved very carefully, since they are sometimes more important in the proof of the case than oral testimony offered by witnesses.

In a criminal case tried recently, the accused pleaded self-defense. In order to establish this defense, it was necessary for him to produce evidence that the four revolver shots fired by the deceased were shot before the accused's shotgun was discharged. An investigator succeeded in finding two men who slept in the upper story of a two-family house near the scene of the crime. These men stated that the four revolver shots were fired in rapid succession and were followed by a loud noise from the shotgun. This case serves to illustrate the importance of searching in the vicinity for additional witnesses after available witnesses have been examined.

In a contract action, it is imperative that all of the documentary evidence be minutely examined, since liability or non-liability may depend almost entirely upon the documentary evidence. The same course, moreover, should be followed as in the preparation of the ordinary case.

When the preliminary preparation of a case is finished, the pleadings must be drafted. Before they are drafted, the applicable law should be carefully examined. The time to look up the law is immediately after the determination of the facts in the case. It is imperative in setting forth a cause of action that simplicity and clarity be utilized. All available forms should be examined including the Practice Act, other form books, and Supreme Court Records.

There is no need to be original in the drafting and formulating of a complaint or any other pleadings. If a Supreme Court case is found directly in point, before the pleadings are drafted the record in this case should be examined thoroughly, not only as to the manner in which the complaint was drafted, but also as to the pleadings which follow.

The attorney then ought also to read the entire record so that he will be conversant with what proof was offered to establish the material and essential allegations of the complaint; or, if he is defending an action, what proof was offered in defense of the allegations contained in the complaint. It would, of course, be wise to select a case where competent attorneys represented the client, and also one where the proof was sufficient to establish the cause of action.

It is the duty of counsel to avail himself of all preliminary motions and of the taking of all depositions which may prove helpful to a successful trial of his client's cause. As long as laws are on statute books, there is no reason why they should not be utilized by diligent counsel; and very often statutes of this character are overlooked where their use might result in the winning of the case.

The next topic that I am about to take up is indeed a very important one, and that is whether a case should be tried to the court or to the jury. It is a recognized and known axiom that a weak case should go to the jury and a strong case to the court. From a practical standpoint, it is the general rule that an attorney will claim a case for a jury where the natural sympathy of such a trier ought to be with his client. For instance, a case is usually claimed to the jury where one of the parties is at a great disadvantage because of illiteracy, ignorance, age, or on account of sex.

On the other hand, if you are acting for a large corporation against an individual, you should never claim such a case to the jury. A complicated contract action which will necessitate the presentation of numerous documentary exhibits should not be claimed to the jury but should be left to the court to decide.

Just prior to the time when the case is to be reached for trial, the attorney should go over his entire case with a view to securing the best possible presentation. This pre-trial preparation requires a re-examination of the law in order to facilitate the argument of questions of law that may arise during the course of the trial, such as motions for a non-suit or for a directed verdict.

At this time, moreover, all witnesses should be re-interviewed so that they may be prepared to tell their stories in the most forceful and effective fashion. It is well to admonish them to be courteous and polite even though they may be harassed or annoyed by cross-examination.

Their recollection should be refreshed by the statements procured from them during the preliminary preparation of the case. Counsel should advise his witnesses to answer all questions truthfully, including the question as to whether or not he has talked to the lawyer or other witnesses relative to the facts in the case.

All exhibits and documentary evidence should be arranged in chronological order so that they may be offered in sequence. A court or jury will usually react unfavorably to an attorney who fumbles around his papers, looking for an exhibit or for a paper which he intends to introduce into evidence. The facts in each case should be marshalled for proper, orderly presentation in court.

A trial brief is always necessary in a very important case, particularly when there are numerous debatable questions relative to the admissibility of evidence. Of course, in the ordinary negligence case, a trial brief is not necessary except if counsel has had little experience in the presentation of cases of this character. A trial brief should contain the statements of all witnesses in the order in which the witnesses are to be presented during the trial. It should also contain the law of the case and authorities substantiating objections to, or the admissibility of, evidence. It is very important, also, to have all documentary evidence listed in the order it is to be used. An outline of counsel's argument to the court or jury, moreover, is of great assistance.

Selection of Jury

The next topic to be considered is the selection of a jury. After a panel has been selected for jury service, it is wise to ascertain from individuals who are acquainted with the jurors, their background, their past history, verdicts returned by the juries upon which they served in the past, and all other information which may throw some light upon the reactions of the prospective juror.

As a general rule, a panel may be interrogated collectively after a short statement of the case is made. Some of the usual questions propounded to a panel in the ordinary negligence case are:

1. Are you acquainted with any of the parties to this action?
2. The plaintiff is represented by John Mack of Bridgeport, and the defendant is represented by James Marshall, also of Bridgeport. Mr. Mack is connected with the law firm of Mack, Stillman & Stimson of the City of Bridgeport, and the members and associates of that firm are the following . . . Counsel for the defendant James Marshall is connected with the law firm of Marshall, Hays & Kaye. Have any of you ladies and gentlemen transacted any business with trial counsel in this case or any members of their respective firms? Or have you had any social, professional, or political dealings with any of counsel or the members of their firms? Are any of you ladies and gentlemen plaintiffs or defendants because of personal injuries sustained by you, or because of alleged negligence on your part which caused personal injuries to another party?

If counsel is representing a large firm, it is wise to ask this additional question:

Have you any prejudice against the defendant because it happens to be a large corporation? Would you decide this case fairly and impartially even though the plaintiff in this action is an individual and the defendant is a large and affluent or wealthy corporation?

If the defendant is a non-resident of this state, this question might also be asked:

Have you any prejudice against the plaintiff or the defendant because the plaintiff or defendant happens to be a non-resident of this state? What we are seeking in this case is a fair and impartial trial on the evidence; and, if you know of any reason why you could not sit and decide this case fairly and impartially on the evidence and the law given to you by his Honor, that fact should be made known to the court so that you may be excused.

Questions of this character should be propounded to ascertain whether any of the prospective jurors would be swayed by prejudice or sympathy in favor of one of the parties, thereby disregarding the evidence and the law in the case.

In every important case, and in some particular matters, the best course to pursue is to poll the jury. For instance, if the case is one where one of the operators of a motor vehicle has been drinking intoxicating liquor but this drinking had nothing to do with causing the collision itself, the jurors should be asked separately whether they would be prejudiced against the plaintiff if it appeared in the evidence that he had been drinking even though the drinking had no bearing on the collision. In polling a jury, one must be very careful not to antagonize the prospective juror. When questions are propounded which tend to embarrass a prospective juror, if subsequently he is accepted, he will not forget the manner in which he was treated during the voir dire.

It is very harmful to one's cause to ridicule a prospective juror because of his lack of education. Not only is the treatment resented by the talesman who is being examined, but also by many of his friends who may be on the panel. The questions should be propounded in a very pleasing manner so that the juror will be impressed with counsel's fairness and courtesy before he is accepted. If a juror is excused, a record should be made that he was excused in this action because, if he is ever in the future selected by the same attorney, he will remember that that attorney was un willing to accept him in the previous case.

Where a client has sustained serious injuries, the jury should be asked whether, if they find that the evidence warrants a substantial verdict, would they have any reluctance to return such a verdict because of the amount involved. An attorney should also inquire whether a juror will follow the law, especially if he is defending a case where on a strictly legal basis he is entitled to win.

In every first degree murder case, a jury should and must be polled. Some judges have allowed very broad latitude in examining the jury as to whether or not a talesman would follow the charge of the court on presumption of innocence, proof beyond reasonable doubt, premeditation, and credibility of witnesses.

In examining the juror on the voir dire, one should inquire whether the talesman, if accepted as a juror, will be prejudiced by an occurrence which had nothing to do with the merits of the case to be tried. For instance counsel may represent a client who has a criminal record which may be used for the purpose of attacking his credibility during the trial. This should be brought to the attention of the juror, and inquiry should be made as to whether the prospective juror would be so prejudiced by the introduction of the criminal record that he will not be governed by the evidence and the law in the case.

Direct Examination

In conducting direct examination, counsel should bear in mind the intelligence and education of the witness whom he is interrogating. If he has a witness on the stand who is illiterate and ignorant, he will not understand the attorney if questions are propounded in high-sounding language. He must frame his questions so that they are understandable to the particular witness who is being interrogated. I recall some years ago the late Judge Wolfe's admonishing a young man who had just graduated from law school not to use high-sounding phrases in questioning a witness who apparently was having difficulty in understanding the questions. The simpler the phraseology, the better for the witness, the jury, and the examining attorney.

The evidence should be presented in orderly fashion. If a man is building a house, he does not start from the roof; he commences by digging the cellar and laying the foundation; and then he goes to the first floor, the second floor, and so on. Thus in every case, the evidence should be arranged and presented so that a picture is being unfolded as to what actually transpired.

An attorney is really, in trying a case, describing to a court or jury just what occurred at the time and place in question. Every bit of evidence introduced should add color and life to the picture so that at the conclusion of his case the attorney can stand back like an artist and point to a glowing, vital representation. If, at the conclusion of an attorney's presentation, the court and jury do not have a complete understanding of what actually happened according to that attorney's claims, then he has not submitted the facts of his case properly.

Witnesses who are unaccustomed to court proceedings should be advised to be in attendance at court before the time they will be needed, since they may become less nervous about testifying if they are better acquainted with their surroundings.

It is wise to begin with an excellent witness whose testimony will be very effective, and to end the presentation of the case in chief in the same fashion. An attorney thus at the outset impresses the court and jury with the merits of his case; and, when he has had his last witness on the stand, he leaves the jury and court with the same kind of impression.

A weak witness should not be placed on the stand at the commencement of the direct examination or at the very end. Usually, it is necessary to place a weak witness on the witness stand because failure to call such a witness would cause the jury or court to draw an unfavorable inference. Such a witness should be placed in the position where he does the least damage.

If counsel is examining an expert such as a doctor, or economist, he should insist upon giving the qualifications to the jury. As a general rule, some attorney will volunteer the statement that he waives proof of qualifications of the witness. Such a magnanimous gesture should be rejected because the jury is entitled to and should receive the benefit of the cultural and educational background of the witness from the witness himself.

If a witness testifying observed the accident, counsel should, after leading the witness up to the time of the collision, ask him to tell his story in his own way as to what he observed at the time and place in question. Such a witness should not be interrupted once he begins his story, except under exceptional circumstances. If he speaks in a coherent and impressive manner, he will have more effect with the jury or court than if the story is dragged out of him piece-meal.

Where a witness's memory fails him, his recollection may be refreshed through the use of documentary evidence; or, if his memory is exhausted on a certain point, there are ways of refreshing his memory by referring to specific occurrences. It must be remembered, however, that counsel will always be confronted with objections on the ground that the questions are leading.

Hence, it is better to have the witness well prepared so that he may recall all of the testimony.

I am, of course, only touching upon the highlights of direct examination, but I would be quite remiss if I failed to discuss proof of redundant facts. Unnecessary evidence serves merely to cloud the issues and may result in substantial harm. By prolonged and unnecessary direct examination, an attorney may open the door to injurious evidence that would otherwise have been inadmissible.

Questions as to Damages

The questions with respect to damages should be prepared in advance. Loss of use and depreciation of an automobile, for instance, are difficult to prove; and, therefore, the proper questions should be framed beforehand. If counsel is trying a personal injury case, it is not sufficient that the physician who is testifying for the plaintiff state that the plaintiff sustained a fracture of the skull or a concussion of the brain, or a fracture of the tibia or fibula, or any injury of that character. The doctor should be asked further to define for the benefit of the jury the significance of a concussion of the brain or any of the injuries above stated. It is more important, of course, that the injuries be more fully developed to a jury than to a court, since the court as a rule knows the significance of a fracture of the skull or a concussion of the brain; whereas, the jury is not so conversant as the court with those terms.

Disclosing Weakness in Case

If counsel has a weakness in his own case of which opposing counsel are probably aware, he should bring it out himself. It is much more damaging when brought to light by the cross-examiner. Where the client or witness has a long criminal record, that fact should be brought out immediately. The jury will put more credence in a man who tells the whole story on direct examination and who does not conceal the unsavory facts concerning himself. In one instance the state's attorney was in possession of a confession made by the accused. The accused's attorney, knowing that the state's attorney would use this confession on cross-examination, requested it from the state's attorney, presented it in evidence himself, and thus destroyed much of its effect.

Cross-Examination

Cross-examination is one of the most delicate arts that a successful trial lawyer must master. Fraught with perils for the novice, it offers the experienced trial attorney a potent weapon with which to blast away an apparently invulnerable case.

Is it necessary to cross-examine every time a witness is on the stand? Not at all. If a witness has testified to no material fact against counsel, he should let him alone, since cross-examination may bring out additional evidence that is damaging. When an attorney knows a witness is telling the truth, he is likely to hurt himself by cross-examining. The wisest course to pursue when confronted with a truthful witness is to let him alone unless counsel can establish some contradiction in his testimony.

When an attorney is confronted with a lying witness who lies intelligently, he should approach that witness cautiously, ask him a number of immaterial questions, and gain his confidence. When his confidence has been gained, then the attorney may catch him off guard and trap him.

Each witness presents a problem for the cross-examiner. Such witnesses as those who resort to hyperbole are almost *sui generis.* In a case recently tried, a plaintiff testified at great length about her pain and suffering—to such an extent that her end appeared imminent! Instead of attacking this witness on cross-examination, the defendant's attorney slowly and methodically took the plaintiff through her paces again. On several occasions, he asked her if she was certain about various pains, to which, of course, he received a vehement, if not extravagant response.

At the conclusion of her testimony, the jury appeared obviously amused and apparently discounted the better part of her story. In short, with such witnesses, it would seem to be sound policy to cause them to exaggerate further, rather than to minimize their claims.

When confronted with a speech-making witness, an attorney should keep a firm rein on him. He should be checked step by step, and told so far as possible to answer the question "yes" or "no."

An accomplished trial lawyer invariably acquires certain fundamental techniques, which may be grouped and described under the classification of trial tactics. In propounding questions to a witness, an effective trial lawyer will never remain slouched over in his seat, but will rise and assume an easy but firm posture.

There appears to be a difference of opinion as to the advisability of taking notes while a witness is testifying. It would seem to be the better policy to take a few essential notes, but for the most part to forego detailed note-taking so as to permit counsel to scrutinize the witness. A careful study of the witness's face as he testifies will often indicate wherein his story is weak and wherein he is lying. Where trial counsel has an assistant, he can, of course, devote all of his time to observation of the witnesses while his assistant takes copious notes.

During the trial of a case, counsel should attempt to be scrupulously fair to his adversary and to all witnesses. The court and jury are likely to react unfavorably to a cause the proponent of which is unfair in its presentation. Everyone likes good clean sportsmanship and everyone likes good clean trying. It is important to be courteous to witnesses, to the bench, and to one's adversary. The jury has a great deal of respect for the court, and the lawyer who shows any disrespect for the court is doing his cause great damage.

If a trier, whether it is a court or jury, reaches the conclusion that an attorney is either taking unfair advantage of his adversary or is not fair in the presentation of his case, the deliberations of the trier will be unconsciously influenced by the attorney's conduct. On the other hand, if a trial lawyer is fair, the jury will be impressed by his conduct to the advantage of his client. As a general rule, witnesses must be handled in a very courteous and polite manner. A court or jury looks with disdain upon a trial lawyer who is badgering a truthful client. Most witnesses are subpoenaed to court, much against their will and to their financial detriment. They are in the majority of cases attempting to tell what they actually observed or what they know about the merits of the matter in issue; to attack viciously a witness because he has taken the witness stand for the opposing party is something that the court or jury will not tolerate. The same rule applies in the treatment of the bench and of opposing counsel.

Judge John J. Parker of the Circuit Court of Appeals has said:

"A trial is not a game of skill but an inquiry into truth in order that justice may be done. If the courts are to sustain themselves in the opinion of the public, the important business in which they are engaged must be conducted with dignity and efficiency."

While this statement is true, nevertheless, many cases are won or lost through the manner in which counsel for either side has conducted himself during the course of the trial. As a general rule, a jury is very vigilant and watchful as to the acts which are indulged in by the respective attorneys. Any move which may be interpreted as unfair and uncalled for by a jury will result disastrously to the cause represented by the lawyer who indulges in such tactics.

Counsel must be exceedingly careful about his demeanor during the trial of a case. No one likes a person who has a perpetual scowl on his face; a jury or a court, likewise, is favorably impressed with a cheerful person. When a witness gives evidence injurious to his case, the attorney should not demonstrate by any expressions that he has been dealt a telling blow. He should beware of showing his discomfiture, as is frequently done, by immediately conferring with his associates, and should proceed as if nothing had happened.

Some years ago a lawyer was trying a murder case and placed on the stand for the defense a witness who came from New York State to testify as to the character of the accused, who was on trial for shooting a police officer. The usual preliminary questions were asked and answered in the affirmative. The next question, with a great deal of gusto, was propounded by the lawyer, "Now, what is this man's general reputation?" The witness responded with an equal amount of gusto, "He was known everywhere as a straight shooter!" The judge, despite his dignity, could not restrain his laughter, in which counsel, of course, joined. Then he propounded the question, "What you mean is that he is a very square person?" The witness replied "yes."

Time after time excellent cross-examiners will run into pitfalls, since in the cross-examination of witnesses trial counsel invariably encounters something he never anticipated. Under such circumstances he cannot scowl, look disgusted, or go into a huddle with his associates. He must look as if he wanted that answer even though he did not. That is part of the trial of a case which the able tactician will meet in an unruffled manner.

A trial lawyer who conducts himself in a sullen manner certainly knows nothing about trial tactics. If he goes through the trial of an action, smiling, or, if he indicates that he has a sense of humor when he receives a telling blow through an answer given by a witness, if he can retain what is commonly known as a "poker face," or even if he can go on as if he expected the answer which injured him, these tactics are very helpful in a trial of an action. It is very unfortunate for a trial lawyer, who hears a witness testifying against his client's cause and receives a response which is very unfavorable, to show that he does not like the type of answer, or that he is embarrassed by the answer, or that there is something wrong with the case because of the answer. If he shows that he is discontented at any time or that there is something wrong with the case, the feeling is immediately transmitted to the jury.

Cross-Examination of Experts

Cross-examination of experts is a matter that merits special attention. Experts, of course, are far more conversant with the field in which they are testifying than is the cross-examining attorney. For that reason cross-examination of experts is dangerous and requires the utmost care upon the part of counsel. Consultation with other experts who can suggest points that should be brought out by the attorney is the most effective way to prepare to examine such witnesses.

Without such special training and preparation, an expert is very likely to make counsel appear ridiculous. One of the usual questions asked by trial counsel to establish that an expert's testimony is not entirely impartial is "Are you being paid to testify?"

Where a physician who has examined a plaintiff on only one or two occasions attempts to minimize his injuries in a suit for personal injuries, the effect of his testimony may be destroyed by emphasizing the meagerness of his examination and by pointing out that the physician who examined him regularly is in a much better position to tell about the man's condition. It is, of course, advisable in all cases to offset the testimony of experts by producing experts to testify on the other side of the question.

Frequently in the examination of experts, counsel must propound hypothetical questions. These questions should be carefully prepared beforehand so as to include all of the evidence favorable to his cause that counsel anticipates will be produced on the trial of the case.

Rebuttal

One of the problems that perplexes many lawyers is whether to use certain evidence in presenting the case in chief or to save it for rebuttal. For example, in a case where one of the parties to the action has made damaging admissions to another person, the question arises as to whether to use the person who heard these admissions in presenting the case in chief or to hold his testimony in abeyance for rebuttal.

The policy followed by most trial lawyers is to inquire of the party when he testifies as to whether or not he spoke to the person who heard the admissions, and to ask him whether or not he made those statements. If the party denies, as he generally will, that he made such statements, then the witness should be put on in rebuttal testifying as to the nature and extent of the admissions he has heard. Where an attorney has documentary evidence such as a letter or memorandum which is damaging to the opposing party, that evidence should be brought out in cross-examination of the party, for to confront a witness with such evidence is to destroy the effectiveness of his testimony.

Interrogatories

Despite the value which interrogatories may have in many cases, attorneys use them infrequently. In many cases the effect of a general verdict could be avoided by the propounding of interrogatories. For example, where an attorney is representing a defendant in a case where it is claimed that the defendant is guilty not only of negligence but also of wanton misconduct, he should submit interrogatories to ascertain whether or not the jury finds the defendant was guilty of negligence or of wanton misconduct, since the plaintiff may be guilty of contributory negligence as a matter of law and the defendant may be precluded from raising this point on an appeal if he allows the jury to render a general verdict in favor of the plaintiff. In a case, moreover, where there are three separate counts, it would seem to be sound policy to propound interrogatories as to each count.

Requests to Charge

In the ordinary negligence case, attorneys need not submit requests to charge, for the court has at its command pertinent law and rarely needs any enlightening. Where, however, the case contains a novel point, or it is at all unusual, counsel should assist the court in search of the law by submitting requests to charge. In such cases the court welcomes and appreciates such assistance. In drawing up requests to charge, counsel should number each paragraph and state a single proposition of law at the conclusion of which the authority therefor should be cited.

Closing Argument

At the conclusion of the trial of a case, it is, of course, necessary for counsel to restate and recapitulate in argument his claims and the evidence that has been introduced by him in support of these claims. The plaintiff's attorney in his opening argument should give a clear, logical statement as to why the jury or the court should render a verdict in his favor, but at the same time he must be careful not to expose any of the weak points of his case to an attack by counsel for the defendant.

If counsel in his opening argument discusses the evidence at great length, he renders his argument more susceptible to blasts from defense counsel. The safest and most effective kind of argument is one that covers briefly the highlights of the evidence in support of plaintiff's claims and recites briefly the law applicable to the facts as presented with the statement by counsel that the jury will, of course, take the law from the court and disregard the law as stated by counsel insofar as it does not accord with the statements of the law made by the court.

Counsel must say enough as to his claims in his opening argument to prevent his being precluded from discussing some new matter with reference to those claims in his closing argument. If he fails to touch upon certain claims in his opening argument, it may later be objected, if he attempts to discuss them in his closing argument, that he made no such claims or statements in his opening and hence gave the defense counsel nothing to rebut with reference to that point.

The defense counsel, likewise, in his argument should give a clear, logical, concise review of the evidence with a view to establishing that there is no liability on the part of the defendant and should refute all claims made by his adversary in his opening argument. It is customary, moreover, for defense counsel to anticipate some of the claims that will be made by the plaintiff's counsel in his closing argument and thus take the sting out of them.

In his closing argument, counsel should restate the issues and again review the evidence briefly and meet all claims made by defense counsel.

No argument should contain repetitious and long-winded statements, for the court or jury is interested in hearing only the highlights of the case and may become bored not only with counsel but with counsel's cause if he harangues the court and jury at great length.

In most cases, moreover, the jury has decided a case after hearing the evidence and before the beginning of argument. Such tactics as are engaged in by some counsel in flattering the jury by telling them that they are intelligent jurors would seem to provoke an unfavorable reaction on the part of the jury. No one likes obvious sycophancy. Simplicity in statement of claims and in review of the evidence is of paramount importance.

Conclusion

In a general way, I should like to discuss briefly some of the things to remember in certain types of cases examples of which follow.

In case (a), A, B and C were passengers in an automobile owned and operated by D in a northerly direction along the Danbury-Newtown road. D was proceeding at a rate of speed of 50 miles per hour and a collision occurred between the automobile operated by D and one operated by E which was proceeding in the opposite direction. Just prior to the collision, E and F both proceeding in the same direction, were racing each other, and as E was in the act of passing F, he collided with D, as a result of which A and B were fatally injured and C sustained severe and permanent injuries. The administrators on the estates of A and B retain Attorney X to represent them on their claims.

How should X proceed in representing the estates of A and B?

In this type of case it is important to join as party defendants every person who could be responsible for causing that accident.

Hence, in this case D, E and F should be made parties defendant, so that it cannot be claimed by any one of the defendants that one of the parties involved in the collision who was not sued was liable. In presenting this type of case to a court or a jury, counsel should put all the defendants on the witness stand and let them dispute among themselves as to who was responsible for the collision. Then the whole picture is placed before the court and jury, and a verdict is almost certain to be rendered against at least one of the defendants, if not all.

In case (b), A is a gratuitous passenger in an automobile owned and operated by B in a northerly direction along Main Street, a public highway of the City of Bridgeport. It appeared that A and B had been drinking intoxicating liquor before said automobile left Main St. and Fairfield Ave. to proceed to Trumbull, but not a sufficient quantity to impair the faculties of A or B. As B proceeded along Main Street, an automobile operated by C in a southerly direction along Main Street at a high and excessive rate of speed collided with the automobile operated by B, causing B to sustain fatal injuries and A severe and permanent injuries.

At the time of the collision, B was proceeding along the extreme right hand side of the highway at a moderate rate of speed. A and the estate of B consult X, an attorney, to represent them in their actions against C. Actions are instituted by the estate of B and by A against C, and the defense of contributory negligence is filed by counsel for C in the action instituted by the estate of B setting forth in said defense that at the time of the collision B was under the influence of liquor.

How should X try this case in view of said special defense?

This is one case where a jury should certainly be polled to inquire whether or not any one of the talesmen has a prejudice against a man who drinks intoxicating liquor. After being questioned as to prejudice against one who drinks intoxicating liquors, the jury will expect a great deal of evidence to be presented in support of the claim of intoxication. When the jury finds that there is little evidence to support that claim, it is likely to react quite favorably for the plaintiff.

There are, of course, many phases of the trial of a case that I have been unable to touch upon in the time and space allotted to me. As I conclude my remarks, I fully appreciate that an attorney who endeavors to speak or write about how a case should be tried is treading indeed upon dangerous ground. I trust, however, that what I have said will be regarded as I intend it, that is, merely as a group of suggestions.

This article was adapted from 3 Schweitzer, Trial Guide 1440, Baker, Voorhis & Co., Inc., New York (1945), which was adapted from the Connecticut Bar Journal, Vol. 14.

A Practitioner's Guide to the Use of Exhibits and Expert Testimony

By Wayne E. Stichter

UPON EFFECTIVE HANDLING of exhibits and expert testimony may depend the outcome of the trial. The growth and change of science and the economic system, complicating business and other transactions have necessitated changes in trial technique. No longer can an ordinary witness testify, from personal knowledge, to all the transactions of a large business. Nor, because of specialization, can an ordinary person testify accurately in scientific matters involving many technical details and knowledge. These changes, accentuating the importance of exhibits and expert testimony, have loaded new duties and responsibilities upon the practitioner.

This article is concerned with the practical problems of presentation of exhibits and expert testimony rather than being a dissertation upon the law governing their presentment. However, in discussing the mechanics of presentation it is necessary to keep in mind the rules of evidence.

Exhibits

Statutes Relating to Exhibits

Preliminary to a discussion of these problems, mention should be made of the main Ohio statutes which the trial lawyer should examine if he knows that he is going to deal with exhibits in the trial of a case. Section 154-18 provides for the admission in evidence of an authenticated copy of a record, official paper, or certain other instruments of any executive department of the state of Ohio. Section 11500 makes similar provision for certified copies of papers, books and records on file with either state officers or with the executive department of the United States government.

Sections 12102-26 to 12102-30 make admissible in evidence reports made by officers of the State of Ohio, or certified copies thereof, dealing with matters within the scope of their duties. Section 4235 provides that by-laws, resolutions, minutes of proceedings and ordinances of a village or city may be introduced in evidence by use of certified copies. Although many lawyers call the city clerk to prove the existence of an ordinance, clearly this is no longer necessary. If an attorney has a certified copy, one that is properly authenticated, and it is material and relevant to the case, all that is necessary to be done is to have it marked exhibit 1, (or whatever it may be) and simply tender it in evidence.

In dealing with a Michigan, Illinois, or Indiana guest case, or with the law of any other state, it has been necessary in the past to introduce evidence as to the statutory law of that other state. This was customarily done either by calling in someone familiar with the law of that state, or by stipulating with opposing counsel as to what the foreign statutes provided. Now, however, under the Uniform Judicial Notice of Foreign Law Act as recently enacted in Ohio,[1] a trial court is required to take judicial notice of the statutes of every state, territory, or other jurisdiction of the United States. The act, however, refers only to statutory law, excluding common law.[2]

With respect to the adjudicated cases that comprise the latter body of law, Sec. 11499 provides that the common law of any other state or country may be shown by parol evidence, or by books of reported cases adjudicated by the courts of such other state or country. The customary method of getting those reports in evidence has been through stipulations with opposing counsel. It has been the writer's experience that nearly always counsel will stipulate that the decisions in the library sets of the Reporter system, or the official state reports, may be used to show the common law of the state in question. Usually a stipulation can be had to the effect that tender of the volume in evidence is unnecessary, a typed copy being sufficient. Frequently opposing counsel will stipulate that it will not even be necessary to type out the foreign decision and physically tender it in evidence, or attach

1 Ohio Gen. Code 12102-31 — -37.

2 See Hallen, *Uniform Evidence Acts in Ohio,* (1939) 6 Ohio St. L. J. 25, note (1941) 7 Ohio St. L. J. 451.

it to the bill of exceptions; but that the trial court, or any reviewing court, may refer to the reports which are in the law library for a study of the decision offered in evidence. In such event, all that is necessary is to say, "I offer in evidence the case of *Waters v. Andrews,* 117 Mich., 225," leaving to the trial and reviewing courts appropriate reference to the decision. If stipulations of this character cannot be obtained, however, then it becomes necessary to secure someone to prove the decision. That may be done by calling a lawyer from the State of Michigan, for example, to prove that the particular reported decision is the official report of that particular state.

Ohio General Code, Secs. 12102-17 to -21 make admissible in evidence a composite written report of a finding of facts prepared by an expert and containing conclusions resulting wholly or partly from written information furnished to such expert by the cooperation of several persons acting for a common purpose. These are important provisions, with respect to both exhibits and expert testimony, obviating as they do the calling as witnesses of the persons furnishing such information and the production of the books or other writings on which such report and finding is based. Because there are no reported cases dealing with these new sections, it is impossible to say what interpreting limitations, if any, will be imposed by the trial courts, but it is a matter worthy of the practitioner's attention.

In the past, lawyers have had a great deal of difficulty in getting business records in evidence, because of the failure to bear in mind the requirement of the best evidence rule that original entries, for instance, and not some summary or copy must be introduced. The problem has been simplified somewhat by Ohio General Code, Secs. 12102-22 to -25, recently enacted. These sections make business records admissible to the extent that they reflect the usual course of doing business.[3] Clearly, of course, any record that is made for the purpose of a lawsuit, or any report of some special investigation that may be made because of some dispute or some litigation, would be excluded, as not made in the ordinary course of business conduct.

Other sections frequently overlooked include Ohio General Code, Sec. 11550, which may be utilized for the purpose of

[3] But see note, *Admissibility of Hospital Records,* (1940) 7 Ohio St. L. J. 248.

proving the genuineness of a document. Under that section, there is created the right in advance of trial to exhibit a document to opposing counsel and to demand admission of its genuineness; if that admission is refused the party so refusing is compelled to meet the expense to which the offering counsel is put in proving genuineness. Ohio General Code, Secs. 11551 *et seq.*, provide for the production of certain books and writings and for the right of inspection and reproduction.

Mechanics of Offering Exhibits

Certain preliminary steps should be taken before offering an exhibit in evidence, whether it be a photograph, letter, or X-ray plate. The proper thing for the lawyer to do, when he wants to offer it in evidence, is to hand it to opposing counsel, allow that counsel opportunity to inspect it, and then hand it to the court reporter and have him mark it as an exhibit. These preliminaries over, place the exhibit in the witness's hand and proceed in this fashion: "Mr. Brown, I hand you a paper here purporting to be a letter (or photograph, *etc.*) marked exhibit 12, and I ask you to state what this is." To which Mr. Brown will reply, "It is a letter from so-and-so." Many times it is advisable, almost necessary, to substitute a copy for the original exhibit. Usually, consent of opposing counsel can be obtained for this. In that event it is advisable to have the court reporter make up a copy and have it compared by counsel on each side, and then have the copy marked as an exhibit, with the stipulation in the record that this copy is to be used and substituted for the original. Upon identification by the witness the exhibit may then be offered; and if material, competent and properly identified, it will be received in evidence.

The exhibit should not be shown to the jury until it has been thus received. Many times in the trial of cases counsel will proceed to exhibit to the jury a letter or other exhibit prior to this time. That is improper, for the jury has no right to see any exhibit until it has been received in evidence. If the exhibits are photographs of a damaged car, or several photographs of the scene of a collision, time may well be taken to pass them along to the jurors for their inspection. After reception of an exhibit in evidence is also the correct time for objections by opposing counsel on the ground of insufficient identification or because of immateriality, or for any other reason. If the party offering the exhibit asks of the witness a number of questions, the answers to which would require the exhibition of that exhibit to the jury, opposing counsel should insist upon a ruling on its admissibility before any such exhibition takes place.

Should the court have some doubts as to its competency or identification, he may, before ruling on the offer, give permission for cross-examination of the witness as to the exhibit and particularly as to its identification. If, before the receipt of an X-ray exhibit in evidence, the court permitted the offering counsel to ask the witness to point out to the jury what the X-ray plate shows and to question him about it, objection later to its reception in evidence would not undo the damage already done. If the exhibit happens to be a letter or any other document, opposing counsel has the right, and it is entirely proper for him, after the exhibit is offered in evidence, to read it then and there.

When dealing with an opponent's exhibits, insist upon this right to see them before they are handed to the witness. As there may be something in them that is helpful to your client and harmful to the opposing case, it is well to examine them very carefully. If questions suggest themselves as to the qualifications of the witness who has made the exhibits, be he a photographer, a surveyor, or an X-ray man, or if there is some objection to their identification, objection should be made to the exhibits being received in evidence until opportunity has been had for cross-examination of the witness with respect to them.

To challenge the admissibility of an exhibit offered in evidence, a general objection is sufficient to cover any question of identification, competency, or materiality. However, if the court requests the ground of objection, it is the duty of opposing counsel, of course, to state whether the objection goes to the method of proof, that is, to the manner in which it is identified, or whether it is made on the ground of materiality. If several objections are offered at one time, it is well to act separately as to each. The writer recalls one Court of Appeals case some time ago in which certain exhibits *A* to *L* had been offered in evidence at the trial in the Common Pleas Court. Objection had been made in this form: "I object to their being received in evidence"; the trial court had overruled the objection, and all had been admitted. The Court of Appeals found that among those exhibits two were not admissible, but held that the overruling of the general objection as to *A* to *L* was not sufficient to constitute error.

On direct examination it is ordinarily best to offer an exhibit immediately upon its identification by the witness testifying. Especially is this true where the witness is to be asked a number of questions which will require him to use the exhibit and to display it to the jury. However, inasmuch as the offer of exhibits in evidence may be made at any time after proper identification, they may be saved until conclusion of the direct examination. But it must be remembered that a delay until the witness has been excused may result in a court ruling that the exhibit has not been sufficiently identified, or that it has not been shown to be material.

It may develop that an exhibit, although fully identified, is not admissible in evidence because it has not been sufficiently connected up with the issue. For instance, in the case of a photograph or a diagram of the scene of an accident, the photographer or the surveyor may identify it as a correct representation of the intersection at the time he made the photograph or made his measurements, but it may be inadmissible because it has not been shown that the intersection was in the same condition at the time of the accident. In such an event, the court will exclude it. Later, after adequate connecting up, the exhibit should then be re-offered in evidence. If material, the court will then probably admit it.

In the handling of exhibits several practical problems arise. Thus a lawyer often has to face the question whether or not a number of exhibits should be offered as a series or separately. Certain exhibits will be desired in evidence as a series or not at all, where harm can be done if only some are admitted although all together they would be helpful. Thus if they are offered separately, and several of them taken alone may be helpful to the opposing party, the court may on opposing counsel's objections exclude a portion only, admitting those affording the opposing party information and help; whereas if all had been admitted they would be helpful to the offering party. Again, when an exhibit, such as a letter or document or statement, consists of several pages or parts, it is well to have them numbered 1, 1-a,

1-b, *etc.,* so that the record will clearly show how many pages comprise the exhibit. And once an exhibit has been introduced and first reference had to it, further questions or statements concerning it should always be in terms of the exhibit number or mark, rather than "this picture," "this paper," or "this letter." Otherwise, in the event of a later appeal, the reviewing court may reject a contention that the trial court should have allowed certain questioning regarding the exhibit, simply because, with the record speaking only of this or that letter or photograph, it cannot determine what exhibit is involved.

When the exhibit speaks for itself, counsel is not permitted to ask the witness for explanation. For instance, where a witness has presented to him a self-explanatory letter, he cannot properly give his opinion or conclusion as to its contents. He may, however, state that it is a letter dated so-and-so and addressed to so-and-so. In order to get in evidence a photograph of a scene of an accident, it is necessary to show that the photograph is of the particular intersection involved. Consequently, the photographer may be asked about it; and he is permitted to say that it is a photograph of the intersection and to describe the position in which it was taken. But ordinarily he cannot be led into a description of what the picture discloses, when the picture speaks for itself. If it is a picture of a car, the photographer may properly say, "That is a picture of Mr. Jones' car," but he may not say, "That shows that the left front fender has been bent and the frame knocked out of line." Yet where an attorney finds that certain changes or alterations have been made in the exhibits which he wishes to offer, it is well and competent to allow the witness to account for those interlineations and erasures, rather than to open them up to an attack by the other side.

Often an exhibit is admissible only for a very limited purpose. For instance, it may develop that a picture taken of an intersection is not admissible for all purposes because the condition at the time of the accident was different from what it was at the time the photograph was taken, yet the picture will accurately show an obstruction to the view, the very condition which existed at the time of the accident; or perhaps the picture will show the location and wording of a stop sign as the same existed at the time of the accident. In such event, the picture is admissible to present such limited features. If an exhibit is wanted in evidence for a very limited purpose and a general tender is refused, the court should be apprised of the limited purpose of the offer and the record made to show that fact. The court may then admit it for that limited purpose. Where, on the other hand, the opposing counsel offers in evidence an exhibit which is admissible only for a limited purpose, and the court admits it on that limitation, care should be taken that the court instructs the jury on this fact either at that time or in the general charge.

If in the trial of a case counsel identifies a great many exhibits and at the close of his presentation of evidence he is not sure whether or not all that are wanted in have been offered, it is advisable to re-offer them. As a general rule, the court reporter will keep an accurate record of those which have been actually offered and those which have been received, but where there are many of them it is well to guard against any possible omission or error on his part. It also sometimes happens that some exhibits have been rejected because they have not at the time of their offer been properly connected up with the matter in issue. If later that connection has been made, it is then advisable to make another offer at the close of one's case, of those which have been rejected.

Identification of Specific Exhibits

In identifying a letter from the opposing party to one's own client, the fact that it is on his stationery is not sufficient. Proper identification may be had by calling the opposing party to prove his signature, or by showing that the letter is in answer to one of your client's. In the latter case it would be necessary to prove the correspondence which prompted the answering letter. To do this the other party may be called upon, either before or at the trial, to produce that correspondence. If not produced, a copy of the letter, upon a showing by the stenographer that it was dictated to her and by her typed out and mailed addressed to the other party, is sufficient. In that way it is shown, prima facie at least, that the opposing party received it; the reply letter will then be established as having been written by the opposing party. Clearly, letters or exhibits sent by one's own client are not admissible if self-serving; they can be used only where part of a series of correspondence between the parties.

A diagram should be checked for accuracy inasmuch as admissibility of this type of exhibit may depend upon various aspects of this factor. Pertinent, for instance, is the question whether it reveals all the objects which are within the area that is shown; whether it is drawn to scale; whether it constitutes a true representation; what the skid marks and lines indicate; and whether it shows the condition as it existed at the time of the accident. To be admissible a diagram does not necessarily have to reveal every object within the area, but it should be a fair representation of the situation. Considerable discretion is lodged with the trial court in the determination of whether it is fairly representative, only after which is it admissible.

Recent years have seen considerable relaxation of the rules of evidence with respect to X-rays. Formerly the X-ray expert was required actually to have been present when the X-ray was taken, and either to have himself developed it or to have had it developed or marked in his presence. But while the rule has been relaxed in many jurisdictions so as to permit it to be identified by one under whose supervision it was taken, identification should still be carefully made and opposing counsel required properly to identify his X-rays. In general, the witness should state the manner in which the X-ray was taken, the position of the subject, the position of the X-ray machine, showing the angle of the view, the length of exposure, the type of machine, and the fact that it was in good working order.

The matter of the angle of the view is very important. The writer tried a case recently in which certain X-rays of the skull were offered in evidence by the opposing counsel as proof of the existence of a fracture. In refutation it was contended that although certain lines appearing in those X-rays were identified as fracture lines, they were not fracture lines at all, but on the contrary were mere suture lines in the back part of the skull. The pictures had been taken through the mouth and in such position as to show those suture lines and make it appear as if there was a fracture of that part of the skull through which the spinal cord passes. The doctor who so testified on the basis of the plates also produced other X-rays of the same part, taken, however, through the top of the skull. From this angle no fracture lines appeared, thus confirming that the pictures taken through the mouth simply showed the suture lines as fracture lines. Regardless, then, of the extent to which rules of evidence have been or will be relaxed, it is important in handling X-rays to know the position of the machine and the angle from which the picture was taken.

Photographs, like X-rays, are apt to be deceiving. Thus photographs of an intersection may show an apparent obstruction by a hedge, when in fact the hedge did not obscure the view at all. The writer recalls one situation in his practice where the claim that a hedge obscured the view constituted a rather important issue in the case. The hedge having been cut down shortly after the accident, the question of obstruction consequently depended on oral testimony and on photographs of earlier date. One picture presented showed such an apparent obstruction as to have made it impossible for one to see an approaching automobile; it appeared that the hedge ran out to the sidewalk, and that the hedge was high enough to obscure the view of any vehicle except a high truck. But it developed on cross-examination that the camera had been placed about one foot or eighteen inches above the ground. A photograph taken five or five and one-half feet off the ground, at the height of the eyes, showed no obstruction whatever. A lawyer should, therefore, carefully check the background of photographs offered by opposing counsel; at the same time he should take care that his own are fair pictures, for if not, discovery may harm his case.

Also important in photographs are the focal length of the lens and the type of the film. People familiar with photography know that the shorter distance between the lens and the plate, the greater is the view across laterally and the shorter the view longitudinally. Thus with a picture of a street taken looking toward an intersection at, say, one hundred feet back from an intersection, a normal focal length lens will quite accurately reflect the distance from the camera to the intersection and the width of the street; whereas an abnormally short focal length lens will make the same distance appear to be about 15 feet while exaggerating the width of the road, thereby creating a false impression. Difference in film is important, for one film will show black and red to be exactly the same; while another will give a difference in shades of gray between the two colors. If there appears to be some trickery about a picture, it is well to ask for the production of the original film rather than accepting a print. It is not always necessary, in order to get a photograph in evidence, to call the photographer or other person who took the snapshot. Considerable discretion is allowed the trial court in such matters. The test is whether it is a fair, accurate representation of the condition which it purports to show.

Pleadings may be used as exhibits, and sometimes are important. The writer recalls one case he defended where there was involved an injury occurring to a doctor while he was crossing an intersection. He suffered some broken bones, but there was some question about the extent of his disability and the permanency of it. It was just by chance that I discovered that about six months before that same doctor had had another accident in an adjacent city. The plaintiff's pleadings in that case carried allegations regarding trouble with the left leg, that he suffered constant headaches, which continued up to the date of the filing of the petition, and that he had permanent scars on his face. In the later case the same things were alleged; yet the petition in the earlier action had been filed after the second accident.

The plaintiff did not know or even suspect that the defense had any knowledge of the other accident. I succeeded on cross-examination in getting the doctor well committed to the proposition that all the complaints mentioned at the time of trial for the second accident were traceable to it. Then he was confronted with the petition in the Fremont case, a certified copy of which was offered in evidence and received. On further cross-examination the plaintiff tried to lead the jury to believe that the injuries received in the other accident were minor and of little consequence. But the other case having been already tried, he was then confronted with a transcript of the record therein which he had testified at great length about the suffering he had endured as a result of the accident in Fremont, not mentioning in that case the Toledo accident, and blaming the Fremont accident for all his physical ills. Upon denial of this testimony, the Fremont Court Reporter was called to prove the correctness of the transcript and of the answers which the plaintiff had given in that case. The plaintiff was thereby so completely discredited that, while the case took eight days to try, the jury was out only eight minutes and returned a unanimous verdict for the defendant.

In presenting a weather report in evidence, the proper procedure is to call the United States Weather man, and develop from him what records are kept in the ordinary course of business, and that the record that he has brought along with him is the true record that was kept. The report is then ready to be introduced in evidence. Whether it will be admitted will depend somewhat on the relative locations of the weather bureau and the place of the accident. A weather report for Toledo would not be good for Fremont.

Judicial notice of mortality tables is usually taken by courts. In those which do not, it is advisable to offer the tables in evidence. It may be advisable in any event in order that the jury will learn about them. Statistical books or almanacs giving the time of sunset, sunrise, logarithms, weights, measures, computations of interest, and so forth, are admissible in evidence. Texts, however, on medicine or surgery, or any of the inexact sciences, are generally held not admissible in evidence as proof of the facts which they contain. However, excerpts may be admissible to impeach a doctor or expert who has testified as to what a particular text states.

Expert Testimony

Expert testimony has taken an important place in evidence presentation. In its infancy the idea was a very good one, growing out of the not infrequent necessity of admitting in evidence certain deductions from observed facts, to make which requires scientific or specialized knowledge or experience not possessed by the jury. For instance, jurors cannot from their general common sense and experience judge as to cause and effect in the medical field. With the triers of the facts thus unable to perform their peculiar function in such areas, provision is made for its performance by those capable of doing so. The general rule of evidence against opinion testimony is thus relaxed to admit the "expert," who has been variously defined as a man of science, a person cognizant or possessed of science and skill respecting the special subject-matter at hand, or one who has made the particular subject a matter for especial study, practice or observation. Abuses in the use of this type of testimony have, however, become so frequent and so great as to precipitate a very serious discussion among lawyers and laymen regarding the desirability of imposing some limitation on the practice. The central evil, of course, is that an expert or so-called expert can be found to testify to any opinion which a client or his lawyer may wish. Of the four types of expert, the dangerous one, clearly, is the dishonest but well qualified witness. Such a person knows his subject, he can handle himself well on cross-examination, and he is unscrupulous in his resort to lies and trickery if seemingly required to get his ideas across to the jury.

Selecting, Preparing and Qualifying the Expert

Many times the expert will in effect have been selected before the attorney is retained. An illustration especially in point is the case of the client's attending physician in instances of personal injury litigation. When such is the situation one must make the best of it. Where, however, counsel has control of the choice of an expert desired for particular testimony, the matter of selection is of such importance as to merit his great care. A personal recollection from the writer's own practice will again serve to illustrate. Successful in securing a new trial in a case involving an alleged defect in the manufacture of a ladder, after experiencing an unfavorable verdict for $25,000, I went out in search of an expert. The search ended at the Forest Products Laboratory, in Wisconsin. The wood expert found there was so well informed that on the retrial defendant received a unanimous verdict. This authority on woods was a real expert, the very one, it turned out, to testify later in the Lindbergh kidnapping case.

In considering the educational background of a possible expert, it is well to inquire into the extent of his practical experience as well as the particulars of his formal training. Further, his reputation among other experts in the same field, and the repute which he enjoys among the laity, are important. Not only does a high standard of ethics impel the attorney to avoid the dishonest expert; it is the best policy, for such a person will eventually reveal himself for what he is. Of great importance also is the ability of the expert to make a good witness. Extensive practical experience and other seemingly favorable qualifications will go for naught if he is unable effectively to impart his special knowledge in such a way as to convince the jury.

The expert who is chosen by the above tests should be informed of all the facts concerning the matter in relation to which he is to testify. Moreover, he should be made acquainted with related matters as well; thus a medical expert who is retained to testify as to cause and effect in the case of an injury to the head should know the facts regarding other injuries suffered by the client. Let the expert be the judge of what is material and what is not; he is in a much better position to judge than is the attorney. Review with the expert the questions it is proposed to ask him, and ascertain the answers he will give. Often it will be profitable to have him assist in the preparation of questions. Some lawyers used this latter technique with hypothetical questions, while others themselves prepare them for advance submission to the expert. In either event, where the expert is to be asked a hypothetical question counsel must know what the tenor of his answer will be if all chance of unfavorable response is to be eliminated. With question and answer worked out in advance of trial, it sometimes develops that the factual basis assumed in the question is not borne out by the evidence later presented. The expert should be informed of the rephrasing of hypotheticals necessitated by this variance; otherwise he may think the refashioned question calls for an opinion different from the one actually wanted.

Make sure in connection with question preparation that all interrogatories to be directed at the expert are couched in language which the jury can understand. Many doctors go on the stand and testify in very technical language. They talk about a comminuted or a compound fracture, a thrombosis, or an ecchymosis—terms wholly meaningless to the jury. It is for the attorney, if representing the party calling the expert, to make sure that the jury is enlightened, through the use by the expert of ordinary English, as to what the situation is, and to see that the questions and answers present to the jury a logical, forceful case. But important as is this factor, it is not the only one compelling the careful attorney to be thoroughly prepared in the area of *expertise.* For even though he does not expect to call an expert, the other party may. In any case, therefore, where expert testimony is a possibility, counsel should thoroughly familiarize himself on the subject in hand by a study of the literature available. In the preparation of the ladder case, previously mentioned, the equivalent of a week was spent reading literature on the subject. Not that the attorney can hope to know as much as an expert, but at least he can talk intelligently on the subject. He should also supplement his reading by discussions with experts. There are times, of course, when from the financial aspect a case doesn't warrant the expenditure of any large amount of time and effort; but if a case is to be won, study had better be spent whether remunerated or not.

If the expert to be called hasn't had much court experience, he should be advised as to what should be his manner and bearing in court towards the judge and jury and toward opposing counsel. He should be advised how to state his various qualifications without appearing to be boasting or bragging. Some expert witnesses simply destroy themselves by telling about their experience and background in such a way as to make it appear they believe they know more than anybody else in the world. Proper cautioning of the inexperienced expert should prevent this.

To qualify the expert upon his taking the stand, he should first be asked to state his name, his present address and how long he has lived there, and his profession. This preliminary over, his background should then be brought out. Generally, this is best done on a chronological basis. Thus with a doctor the questioning would pass from his pre-medical education to where he had received his professional training, where he had interned and for what period of time, how long he had been engaged in the general practice, and whether he followed any specialty. If he is a specialist the nature of this special capacity should be explained to the jury. Description of post-graduate work, hospital connections and medical association membership concludes the qualifying picture. It is then for the judge to determine whether the witness is an expert; clearly, he himself is not qualified to decide this question but only to state the facts upon which the court can reach a reasoned conclusion. With wide latitude accorded the trial judge on this matter of the qualification of experts, his ruling is generally conclusive. However, he must act upon the basis of the evidence put in as to the witness's educational background and experience; he cannot rely upon his own acquaintanceship with the witness. The expert can be qualified only by sworn testimony.

Sometimes opposing counsel will waive qualification. It is not always advisable to accept this proffer. For instance, if the opposing party has used a so-called expert who has not made the best impression, it is good tactics fully to qualify an expert of opposite view as an aid to convincing the jury of the soundness of the contrary opinion. There is a right to show, and the jury has a right to hear, what the opposing expert has to say regarding his authority to speak. In that way judge and jury are enabled to place reliance where it belongs.

The Course of the Expert Testimony

There are two methods by which the expert's testimony is to be elicited. He may be one who, in the case from the start, has had something to do with the situation and is therefore in a position to review the facts as well as to offer his opinion. With an attending physician on the stand, for instance, there should first be introduced in evidence the facts to which he can personally testify. His opinion as to disability and permanency of injury may then be asked. Having treated the party involved, it is proper to request him directly, without the use of a hypothetical case, to give his opinion, if he has any, on those questions. Use, however, of the expert witness who has never treated or examined the plaintiff, but who is called merely to give his opinion as to cause and effect, calls for employment of hypothetical questions. Basically, this technique involves a request of the expert that he give a judgment based upon certain facts which have been testified to by other witnesses and which are brought to his attention specifically by the hypothetical question.

A wide range is ordinarily given to counsel in the putting of such questions. The questions may be short, or they may be long. In one case, within the writer's knowledge, there were put to three experts two identical questions comprising 36,000 words, and taking four hours to read. The trial court has considerable discretion with respect to a hypothetical question, as to whether or not it is confusing to the witness or the jury, is unnecessarily long, or a response to it is likely to be of any material help to the jury. The court may, if he wishes, direct that the hypothetical question be reduced to writing, so that he can properly pass upon it. Or a witness may ask to have it written out for careful study; and the court will ordinarily accede to such a request, because an expert witness should not be required to give an opinion until he knows the assumed facts. The witness may even ask for an hour or two, or a day for that matter, to study the question.

In the framing of hypothetical questions, the question must fairly reflect the pertinent facts. It need not contain all the proven facts to the case. It may omit entirely certain facts, or it may completely ignore, in whole or in part, the testimony of certain witnesses, but it may not omit a material fact which is essential to an intelligent opinion. Each fact which is incorporated in the hypothetical question must be supported by sufficient evidence to warrant the submission of such fact to the jury. If the evidence in support of certain claimed facts is weak, inclusion of those facts in the question should be omitted, if this can be done and the question still elicit the answer wanted, because if such facts are assumed and the jury disbelieves them, then the answer falls. If any fact assumed is not proved, the jury is obligated to disregard the opinion answer.

In stating the hypothetical question to the witness, it is not wise, and in fact it is generally held objectionable, to say to him, for example, "John Jones has testified so-and-so in this case," or "William Brown has stated such-and-such in this case," or "The evidence in this case discloses so-and-so." The better form is this: "Doctor, assuming that on the 14th day of January, 1939, a collision occurred between a truck and the person of John Jones, and that as a result of the collision John Jones received a fracture of the skull, and that subsequently thereto, on the blank day, and so on and so forth, his right arm became paralyzed and since then he has not been able to use it, and so on: Doctor, do you have an opinion as to whether such collision was a direct producing cause of the paralysis?" When he says he has an opinion, then he may be asked to state it.

Do not ask an expert to give his opinion in this fashion: "Doctor, you have heard the testimony in this case; what is your opinion as to so-and-so?" The expert should not be asked to give an opinion in such manner, because to do so not only burdens him with the necessity of recalling all the testimony in the case, both material and immaterial, but also requires him to determine the truth or falsity of the testimony of certain witnesses. In effect, he is asked to judge as between witnesses who have related conflicting testimony. However, if the testimony in the case is very brief and uncontradicted, it has been held that, upon making sure the expert has paid attention to the testimony which has been given, his opinion may be asked. But the expert witness should never be expected to pass upon conflicting testimony.

If the question is purely hypothetical, the answer must be based solely upon it and not upon the expert's personal knowledge of the matters involved. But the expert may be asked a question based in part upon his knowledge of the facts and in part upon the hypothetical facts, provided, of course, that the matters which are within his personal knowledge have been brought to the attention of the court and jury. The expert may, if he wishes, use a text to support his opinion, although, if he does, opposing counsel of course has the right to employ that text in an effort to impeach him.

It is a general rule of evidence that the expert is not permitted to give an opinion as to the ultimate fact in issue. However, the rule is about as much honored in the breach as in its observance; certainly in some cases that type of opinion is permissible. In a malpractice case against a physician, if someone is called as an expert to show that the doctor was guilty of malpractice, the expert will not be permitted to testify that the treatment in question was negligent treatment. Nor, in an action for damages based upon defective construction of a building, could the expert ordinarily say that the framework was negligently constructed. But the doctor, as an expert in a malpractice case, would be permitted to say whether or not the particular treatment given by the defendant was in accord with the usual and customary method of treating that injury in that vicinity. And in the building case, the expert would be permitted to say that the method of construction was or was not a recognized, customary method of construction. On the other hand, in an action on an accident insurance policy where the issue is whether death was due to natural causes or to an injury, most courts would permit an expert to give his opinion as to whether the death was or was not the result of the accident. Such cases are admittedly an exception to the general rule.

Cross-Examination

Even greater care is required on cross than on direct examination, for here there is lacking the cooperation existent in the other situation. The first issue to be decided—and an important one—is this, Should the witness be cross-examined at all? The answer depends largely on the impression made by the expert in advance of trial or on his direct examination. Prior to the time for cross-examination, therefore, opposing counsel should inquire into his general ability, his weaknesses, his foibles, his peculiarities, and whether he classifies as one honest and qualified, dishonest and qualified, honest and unqualified, or dishonest and unqualified. Observe the impression that he is making on the jury during the direct examination—his apparent attempt to cover up something, or exaggerate something, or to avoid certain facts in the case. Observe his indulgence in generalities, or his failure to be specific in anything. In other words, study him carefully just as one would any other witness. If these criteria raise a doubt whether to cross-examine, it is wise to refrain.

Many times the situation is such that if the expert is not cross-examined, defeat appears inevitable. When that is the case, cross-examine, but proceed cautiously. As a general rule, avoid cross-examining as to matters with which the expert has dealt at length, and as to which he has come to court fully prepared; it is often preferable to confine the cross to details which may reveal a source of weakness in the expert's verbal artillery. Thus if a physician-expert seems weak on anatomy, questioning along this line may produce favorable results. The writer recalls in this connection his defense of a malpractice suit in which several doctors testified for plaintiff in the capacity of experts. The defendant doctor remarked of one of these men, "This doctor is notoriously weak on anatomy." Consequently, on cross-examination that witness was asked questions which to most physicians would be quite elementary. He did become confused, unable to say, for instance, whether it is the tibia or the fibula that contacts and makes the joint with the femur, or whether the candyles are to be found on the femur rather than the tibia. The result was that this supposed expert became so completely at sea that the jury evidently did not pay a bit of attention to his testimony. Where the client is not, as he was here, himself a doctor, it is at times an effective step to call in a doctor to sit at the trial table and assist on the cross-examination of an opposing doctor. It should be cautioned, however, that in resorting to the kind of questioning just suggested, a lawyer should avoid giving the jury the impression that he is showing off his own knowledge.

If bored with one of those doctors who think it their duty to fight their patients' legal battles, it will often be wise to interrogate him regarding matters having nothing to do with his patient's immediate treatment. The writer, as defense counsel in a case involving injury to a boy on a bicycle, once found this procedure successful in such a situation. It was admitted that there was no tail light on the bicycle at the time of the collision; and the question was whether or not the accident happened in the night season. On this issue the testimony was very much in conflict. Counsel for plaintiff elicited from this doctor testimony not only on the medical phase of the case but also on the issue of whether the accident occurred during daylight. As to that he had said that someone telephoned him to come to the hospital to treat this boy and that he had arrived at the hospital before dark. Since all the rest of plaintiff's witnesses had testified that it was daylight when the accident occurred, presumably the doctor thought it was safe for him to follow suit. But in doing so, he committed a grave error. For it so happened that the defense had both a record of the exact time at which the boy was admitted to the hospital, and the testimony of police, who were at the hospital before the doctor arrived, that it was quite dark when he did come. While that testimony did not determine necessarily that it was dark at the time of the accident, it so completely destroyed the doctor that the jurors refused to believe his testimony. Nor would they believe the similar testimony of plaintiff's other witnesses. The trial resulted in a verdict for the defendant.

Sometimes information valuable for cross-examination of a doctor, especially where he is not altogether honest, frank or fair, can be had by looking at his records. Often his own records will not bear out the diagnosis, the extent of treatment, or the disability to which he has testified. Illustrative is one case in which plaintiff's doctor came in with about 16 X-rays and testified at great length without any interruption by counsel. To each X-ray he had attached a slip of paper containing his reading of it. It so happened that on direct examination he had testified, by way of introduction, that he didn't know until the previous day this case was coming up in court, and therefore had not had much opportunity to familiarize himself with it. On cross-examination, instead of going into a lot of matters dealing with his opinion, he was asked the purpose of the papers attached to the X-rays. "Well," he said, "that's to help the jury; it's much better if the jury can have before them the X-ray and the reading." On being queried whether this was customary, his reply was, "Only when I know I shall have to testify. I always do it when I know the case is coming up in court. I learned of the case yesterday, so I told my secretary to make those up." After being questioned as to how many times he had previously testified in court, he was dismissed. Offered in evidence, the slips were shown to carry the date when typewritten, in each case a date six months prior to the trial. The effect on the jury was quite apparently to make it feel that this doctor was trying to "pull a fast one."

Conclusion

These suggestions are offered, not as absolute guides, but as practical matters for consideration in trial preparation and practice. Arising out of actual experience, they are passed along to other lawyers, young and old, in the hope that they will be found valuable to them in their practice.

This article was adapted from 3 Schweitzer, Trial Guide 1459, Baker, Voorhis & Co., Inc., New York (1945), which was adapted from the Law Journal of Ohio State University, Vol. 8.

Conduct of Negligence Case for Plaintiff

By William J. Brock

The handling of a negligence case, which includes all the steps leading up to and including the trial, contains certain imponderable situations, at times unforeseeable and unpredictable, which may turn the case from victory to defeat or the reverse. It is counsel's duty to strive for the elimination of those unpredictable, startling, and sometimes fatal, events to his own case.

These questions occur to all lawyers and particularly to the plaintiff's lawyers. What are the things to do? What are the things not to do? There is no definite formula. We know that each case varies with the facts, but there are some rules that may apply generally. Whether they do apply depends upon the picture then confronting the trial lawyer.

Preparing the Case

How shall the case be prepared, handled and presented? As you can well see this requires planning, work and effort. In these days of staggering and unbelievable world events, we have become conscious of military problems.

The handling of a case can be likened to a military problem. We know that a campaign must be planned carefully and meticulously. The amount and type of material and men, not only of your side, but the resources of the opposition must be considered. The strength and capabilities of each side must be evaluated. Where can the opposition's lines be pierced, and where will the opponent attempt to strike, and how can this threat be met in the trial of a lawsuit? The bulletin and ammunition in a lawsuit are facts. How to present them involves the problem of strategy. Planning as you see, is of vital importance.

What facts shall you bring out first and through whom? Should there be constant repetition of the one basic and simple issue or can it be obvious? That requires touch, a fine, delicate, almost insensible hunch or feeling, which tells the lawyer what the effect of the story is upon the jury. And again that requires planning; planning requires work, effort and preparation.

That touch or intuition is developed or acquired through experience and study.

I shall try to demonstrate the ideas that I have just expressed as we go along. The client unless specifically referred to as female will be considered in the masculine gender.

Let us assume that you have a plaintiff's negligence case. Like the military commander who must prepare his campaign for the actual combat, you must immediately prepare and aim for trial; for the day when you will face the Court and Jury, keeping in mind the various psychological factors and situations that are bound to or may arise. The various steps will now be considered. (1) Investigation—(a) of the facts, (b) of the occurrence, (c) of the injuries and medical problems; (2) Evaluation of the case; (3) Negotiations with the defense; (4) The trial.

Investigation Generally

Let us consider the first problem—investigation. I believe that it is the concensus of opinion among trial lawyers that the importance of investigation in the handling of a negligence case as compared to all the other steps is 50% and upwards. Here I must say and repeat again and again, that work, constant effort is essential and if I repeat this admonition in other parts of my discussion, you will understand that I hope to impress its importance upon you.

The first step in investigation is the interview with your client. He should be advised not to sign any statements. He should be advised that he must not talk with anyone. It should be explained to him that a statement made orally or in writing as to some fact, whether he deems it important or insignificant which he may have carelessly or inadvertently stated, may damn him and destroy his case.

From the time of your retainer all reports made by him should be made in your presence and with your knowledge and copies kept. The fallibility of the human mind and memory is well known. Facts and impressions are forgotten. You should know exactly what he has stated or what written statements he has signed before he is placed on the stand.

Carefully go over the facts, favorable and unfavorable, of the accident, and if possible reduce these facts in writing. Avoid courtroom surprise. Explore and question him closely as to all details, even those that may appear to be insignificant or that may be hearsay or rumors. What to your client may appear to be insignificant may ultimately be vital and decisive, a turning point in the case. Did he talk to the defendants? Who are the witnesses or the possible witnesses?

Advise him to be on the alert for leads as to facts and to report them to you immediately when he hears of them. Do not accept or take for granted the plaintiff's version of the facts. A person's story is but the relation or impression of a series of photographic mental impressions and one in these series of impressions may be erroneous. You must, not only examine him, but cross-examine him. He may more readily understand the significance and importance of his impressions of the facts if he is informed as to the law of negligence and contributory negligence applicable to his case.

The Injuries

With reference to the injuries, carefully follow the inquiry through with the same meticulous, painstaking effort. Frequently in describing injuries after a short lapse of time your client will dwell upon the more important injuries and disregard what appears to him to be the less important injuries. This may be true, not only of the client, but of the physician, and the hospital records.

The injury that appears to be insignificant to the client, doctor or hospital nurse or physician, may be important and may form the basis for the most serious claim for damages. Failure to recite all those injuries to the physician for the defense may prove harmful upon the trial. Testimony by the defense physician that a specific complaint or history was not obtained may leave an adverse impression upon the jury.

I can cite an example where a seemingly unimportant injury proved of the greatest importance. A plaintiff was riding in an automobile, which was struck by a streetcar. He sustained a chest injury and rib fractures together with other minor bruises. He described those bruises to me. One was a slight bruise on the angle of the jaw. The statement was reduced to writing and signed by the client. After a lapse of approximately 12 or 13 months, I was informed that my client died. The physician attending him assumed that it was a case of pneumonia.

I requested that an autopsy be performed. The autopsy revealed that it was not a pneumonia but a septicemia that caused his death. The autopsy showed that at the exact point where the client received the blow to the jaw that the bone became infected, pus formed which finally broke through the sac, entered into the blood stream, caused septicemia and ensuing death, giving symptoms which might well justify diagnosis of a pneumonia or chest condition.

The hospital record was silent except as to "numerous bruises" containing no statement as to specific injury to the jaw. The family physician had but a dim recollection of injuries in the region of the jaw. The wife and members of the family remembered the injury; remembered that the client more or less continuously rubbed his jaw; that it seemed to be sore, but that he paid no particular attention to it, and occasionally complained to them of a funny feeling or a pain in the jaw. The signed statement proved of inestimable value. You practicing attorneys have frequently had cases in which your client was impressed with the seriousness of a bruise which overshadowed seemingly unimportant other bodily injuries. The painful bruise disappeared but the other apparently insignificant injuries persisted. The patient may even have neglected for a considerable period to mention that injury to his own physician.

Investigation of Facts

In the investigation of the facts all leads must be followed. Obtain a copy of the police report, of all motor vehicle reports, of operator's license, of ownership of the vehicles, reports from the Sheriff's office or State Trooper's if any. Interview quickly and without delay and obtain statements in writing, if possible, of all witnesses, whether they appear to be important or not. You will find that witnesses frequently hesitate to become involved in the case by making statements. They should be told that they may some day find themselves in the same predicament as your client and justice denied them because some witnesses hesitate to give evidence. Although witnesses cannot be paid to testify, they can, however, be paid for the lost time.

Photographs should be taken as quickly as possible showing skid marks and physical conditions. A change of physical conditions may occur. Signs or obstructions may be removed, proof of the presence of which may be of value. Take several views of the scene of the accident and of the vehicles involved. A diagram should be made of the location of the accident. You will find this of great assistance in understanding the merits and value of the case.

If possible interview and obtain a statement of the defendant. This can ethically be done before the defendant appears by an attorney. You know that your plaintiff will be interviewed and a statement obtained, if possible, by the defendant's representative. You know that a statement so obtained can and frequently does affect your client's case.

Investigation of Injuries

View as much of the injuries as with delicacy you can. Indeed have such injuries photographed as will show by photograph. Talk to the doctor in the presence of the patient, if possible, going over all injuries, both important and those of apparent insignificance.

Impress upon the physician the importance of having all those details placed upon his record and in a report to you. If you think it is important or desirable, suggest that an expert or specialist be called to back him up and to prove your case. Care must be exercised at this point, that the physician be not offended; that he does not feel you lack confidence in his ability. The average physician will welcome additional medical proof by well-known able and worthy specialists.

Frequently the average family physician thinks in terms of economy and hesitates to have X-rays. The importance of X-rays cannot be overestimated in proof of injuries. The failure to take X-rays, it may be argued by the defense, is an indication that the injury was of little consequence.

On the other hand, the revelation by X-rays of a fracture or other condition may clinch the proof and make it unanswerable. The expense involved is small indeed as compared to the benefits obtained or to be realized. It would be well to discuss the injuries, not only with your client, but with members of his family or close and intimate friends, who may recall or more effectively describe injuries which your client may have overlooked and not mentioned.

The physician should keep a complete record of the complaints and calls, which he may refer to or which may be examined by opposing counsel at the trial. Plaintiff is entitled to have all facts presented so that he may receive full payment for the damage sustained.

The client should from time to time come to your office and give information bearing upon the factual as well as the medical side of the case. This should be reduced to writing. It will prove useful to round out the picture at the time of preparation for trial. The client should keep a record and receipts of all expenditures occasioned by the accident and forming part of the claim. Receipts which are placed in evidence are far more effective and impressive to a jury than mere oral testimony on the subject.

Settlement Negotiations

We now come to the subject of evaluation. Lawyers frequently consult with each other as to the settlement value of their case. The evaluation of a case involves so many elements, many of which are imponderables and of a vague nature, that can hardly be expressed or explained but which nevertheless play or have a part in the evaluation of the case.

Not only the injuries, expenses, lost time and facts of the accident must be considered, but the type of witnesses that you have, that the opponent has, their appearances, the impressions they are apt to make. One of the elements, which unfortunately must be considered and faced, is the nationality of the parties. In these days when democracy is rocking on its heels, when ideals are at stake, undemocratic suggestions are unpleasant to deal with or discuss, but as prejudices do exist they are important and must be considered.

A lawyer must be practical and look the situation squarely in the eye. Yet a jury may be brought to the realization that such a condition should not and must not exist, and react in the fine, traditional American manner, doing even justice to all.

I think that a further consideration is, and this may surprise you, although it should not, who is the defense counsel.

The value of your case is affected by the kind of opposition you may expect, just as the general in conducting his military campaign must consider the type of command opposing him.

One of the most difficult problems which confronts the plaintiff's lawyer is to satisfy his client, as to the amount of settlement. Pressure upon the client to accept settlement sometimes creates doubt and mistrust. You must convince gently that you honestly believe that a figure other than the one the client has in mind should be accepted.

If the client feels that you are afraid to try the case, stop further discussion with the statement that you are prepared to try it. I have found it effective to write my clients in some cases after such a discussion, making it a matter of record that I have advised settlement in a specified figure and calling to the client's attention that if an adverse result is obtained that it was due to the decision of the client and not mine. This has been productive of a change of mind on the client's part.

I find that in settlement negotiations the same broad principles apply as in ordinary business affairs. If your statements and dealings with claim adjusters and attorneys are found to be truthful, reliable and reasonable, you will gain the respect of the defendant's representatives. That is good business. You will find that the majority of claim adjusters will attempt to match you in fairness. You will learn who are reliable, truthful and fair, and you will learn the method to be employed with each claim adjuster.

I think it important that you should allow an early medical examination of your client. This will impress the opposition with your fairness. The defense will see the injury while the wounds are fresh. They will have an opportunity to properly evaluate the case and so report to their home office or superior authority and this will ultimately have a bearing on the value or amount of settlement.

At the time of this examination, however, your physician should be present and if possible you should be present and make notes of the proceedings. The client should be advised not to discuss facts of the accident to the opposing physician.

In the settlement negotiations you must remember that the adjuster or the defendant's representative probably knows as much about this case and of the law and facts generally and the handling of cases as you do. Don't underestimate his intelligence. Discuss the facts fairly without revealing or giving a lead to the names of witnesses. Don't bluff. Once you are caught bluffing or misstating facts, you will for all time have lost the confidence of the opposition.

If your opponent suggests a different set of facts, check on that version. I find it desirable to advise my clients, preferably in writing, of the various steps in the negotiations. Your client will understand your problems and will appreciate more readily your efforts.

Now we come to preparation for trial. Your client should be examined by his physicians approximately 2 or 3 weeks before the trial. Then have the client come to your office, go over the facts and medical history with him; then interview the physician or physicians placing these facts before him or them.

Now we come to the actual trial. What to do and what not to do? Here again I say there can be no general rule that applies to all situations.

Selection of Jury

You are about to select a jury. Here is a great mystery. It almost involves mind and character reading and study of human nature. A jury list will be helpful with a record of the results of the case in which each juror was a member, but such a list may be erroneous. The juror's reaction may be entirely different in one case than in another.

Here hunch or that intangible feeling or touch plays its part, and—you may be wrong. The plaintiff hopes to have a jury that has human understanding. Is that juror the type that would sympathize with or understand your type of client or case? I would think that a plaintiff would prefer an elderly juror as against a youthful juror. Youth has not yet been mellowed by age and by the problems of life and may be harsh. You want a genial type. Occupation influences a juror's understanding and leanings. The bartender, the barber, salesman, carpenters, city employees; and generally people that have known adversity; the working man, brokers of life and liability insurance companies appear to be desirable types for the plaintiff.

What types should you avoid? Generally, but again with exception, superintendents, owners of large businesses, general insurance agents, bankers, stockbrokers, people who pay large taxes and large insurance premiums, people that have been subjected to claims. Avoid, if possible, the youngsters who appear to be smart alecks, or those that have a tough, harsh expression, who are tightlipped, have set, stern expressions.

Let us consider the juror that has been through a serious accident and has received little or nothing for his injuries. May he not measure the value of your client's case by his own experiences and reason that your client should likewise receive such a sum? Would he react differently and have the necessary understanding to award an adequate verdict to the other fellow? The guess or hunch is yours.

Women as Jurors

And now we come to the question of women jurors. Women, God bless them, have ever been to man the profoundest of all mysteries. The same rules apply to them, but there are some added considerations. Are not women apt to be critical, more critical than men, particularly in a woman's case? Is the prospective woman juror a reformer? Does she belong to civic clubs? Is she the suffragette type? Does she belong to the upper crust, so to speak?

Jury service to them is a new experience. They have read of large verdicts. They do not learn of the small and inadequate verdicts and of the large percentage of no cause verdicts. Aren't they going to show these men? Aren't they going to do the job better?

Women generally are the receivers of income from their husbands. They hold and have to watch the purse strings. Generally they do not see or deal with large sums of money. They are in the paying-out department and may have to pinch pennies. The money earner, their husband, striving to increase his earnings, is apt to have the more generous viewpoint. The observations, of course, do not apply to all women jurors.

Women jurors are, I think, acute, sharp and intelligent, and will with continued experience as jurors develop into and become the same jurors as the male type. Large demands are made in the complaint; the plaintiff's lawyer is in a quandary. If the jury should, in an infrequent case, award more than the verdict the attorney is embarrassed by his client for failing to have asked an adequate sum. If the sum demanded seems exorbitant to a juror, it reacts unfavorably in the case. Make the demand adequate, but not too large.

The Opening Statement

Win the jury in the opening with your frankness and openness; anticipate the opponent's statements, have in mind the opponent's style, and remove the sting of the opponent's opening. They should be reminded by you, as you know they will be by the defense counsel, that the attorney's statement is not evidence and they must keep an open mind until the evidence is given.

Explain to them what evidence is. State the facts carefully and logically. Point out the vital, important facts. Give them a general, but yet fairly extensive statement of the injuries. Show how the facts will apply to the law so that they may mentally apply them to the law involved as the evidence is unraveled.

Developing the Proof

Try to make the issues at the trial simple and clear. Bring out the facts so that the least intelligent of the jury will grasp them. That rule which has been known to trial lawyers for generations is now being employed by the master propagandists. While you are trying to reach the least intelligent, try, however, to impress the strongest member or members of the jury.

Here again is involved the question of touch. Watch the effect of the testimony upon the jury as it goes in. Don't bear down too hard. While it is difficult to judge when a case is being overtried, remember that overtrying a case is less desirable than undertrying it.

The first witness should be the best witness. The first impression is frequently lasting. The last witness should be the second best witness. If you have a number of witnesses, alternate the less with more effective witnesses. While you must be certain that all essential facts are brought out in direct examination, leave out some details which your opponent may bring out on cross-examination. If that does not occur, bring them out in redirect. Here the surprise element is important. If your witness has a record of conviction, you should bring it out first.

Don't swear a witness who isn't frank with you or who is hostile. Where your witness has been shaken, you must estimate the damage and the possibility of repair. If it can be overcome by the facts, other witnesses or other evidence, perhaps it is best to drop the witness. Here again is involved the nicety of judgment and balance and that thing called "touch."

Don't at all costs indicate your chagrin by face or gesture. Go along smoothly and evenly impressing the jury with your faith and confidence in your case. After he has been destroyed, you should ask the witness another question on another subject and then veer back: The explanation of an apologist may be more harmful. Does the witness still appear to be honest? What is the reaction on the jury? Can he extricate himself from the trap into which he has fallen? If you are in doubt and have other evidence, I say drop him. The succeeding witnesses will see the trap into which the witness on the stand has fallen and they will be prepared for it and avoid it. Have your witness answer the questions politely without argumentation and yet with firmness. Prepare the witness for the type or style which the opposing attorney has. Describe the method and demeanor employed by the attorney.

I have in mind a case in which a lady was the plaintiff. She was advised that the defense counsel, whom we shall call Mr. Jones, was the aggressive attacker type. She approached the ordeal on the stand with fear. I advised her to be polite. Each question by the defense counsel contained an intimation of doubt as to her integrity and implied dishonesty. Her reply was either a prompt and respectful "Yes, Mr. Jones," or "No, Mr. Jones," until the attorney in exasperation asked her to never mind or forget the Mr. Jones. The effect upon the jury was not adverse to her.

If on cross-examination opposing counsel misquotes or misstates the meaning of an answer and proceeds to another misstatement or misquotation, an objection would be proper, pointing this out. Your witness, who is under pressure on the stand may believe he did so state when he did not, and the practice will be exposed to the jury.

Throughout the entire trial the issues, the theme of the lawsuit, both on direct and cross-examination must be again and again pointed out or referred to. In order that it may not appear to be overdone, it must each time be presented in a different form.

You cannot hope to answer in summation all the defendant's arguments which appear to be on their face palpably incorrect. You will find that your time in summation will be limited and you wish to present views of your own concerning the theory of your case instead of merely answering arguments or points raised by opposing counsel. Expose these points during the trial as they occur for the jury may not be able to reason the fallacies of these various arguments while they are engrossed in attempting to following the testimony. They should be set right on the spot. The mere statement by counsel or implications of his statements may be considered evidence by the jury, if you do not expose the fallacy instantly while the matter is fresh.

If the opponent injects his personality, can you match him with your personality? Does he overstep? Then if he does, should you remain in the background letting the jury understand and see it? Should you point out such a possibility to the jury during jury selection or upon opening or summation? Should you do it directly or indirectly? Here again is involved that old question of "touch," and a study of the technique of the opposing counsel.

Proving the Injuries

What are the psychological considerations? First—the jury does not know anything about the injuries. They must be shown. There is almost a presumption of exaggeration. In the ordinary case it is fallacy to assume that the jury's sympathy is with the plaintiff.

The jury may have been impressed by past wide, paid publicity and propaganda that all claimants are exaggerators. It is, therefore, important that your client appear not to exaggerate. A small amount of unintentional exaggeration, which may be normal to a person that has been subjected to injury, may assume mountainous and gross proportions and be fatal. The British have found understatement to be the most effective method. Would it not be effective if he understated and then have the witness upon cross or direct spout spontaneously some additional facts which prove that he has not exaggerated, but has understated his claim? If this does not occur then upon redirect you should bring out these additional facts.

Your doctor, who may be an excellent physician, may not have the gift of vividly and adequately describing the effects of the injury. His bill should be shown to be reasonable. A slight exaggeration or apparent exaggeration in amount might be extremely harmful. It is well to give a hypothetical statement giving all the facts. Not only do you obtain the opinion as to permanency, but a complete resumé is stated and restated before the jury of the relevant facts, which need not be restated in summation. Repetition, not overdone, cannot be harmful and should be helpful.

There is no more effective way of presenting injuries to a jury than by lay evidence. The jury is thereby brought into the home and into the home life of the plaintiff. He sees the type of people that the plaintiff associates with and gets the picture and the story from lay people like the juror himself as to the effect of the injuries upon the plaintiff.

The Mortality Tables should be introduced in evidence whenever advisable. The employer should aid in presenting the picture as to the effect of the injuries upon the plaintiff. This will have its influence upon the jury, who will understand or reason that the employer has some regard for the plaintiff and that the plaintiff is or has the attributes of a good, decent workman.

Cross-Examination

Volumes have been written on this subject by authors of eminence. How and when and when not to cross-examine involves the question of touch. These books and authorities can be read with profit by the practicing trial lawyer.

There are few simple observations that I should like to discuss. They are: Don't labor too greatly with the witness. When you score a direct hit, don't grind it in. If you think the witness can't extricate himself, repeat it with a little different approach. Don't, as plaintiff's attorney, appear cruel or harsh. This may excite sympathy for the witness. It may arouse the same feeling of cruelty and harshness in the jury and those are not the reactions which are desirable to a plaintiff's case.

If you cannot destroy a witness by frontal attack, can you attack him at the flank or from the rear? Should you smile or be angry? What is that jury thinking? It is a question of touch. Don't ramble; it indicates hopelessness and may lead you into a serious hole. That, of course, doesn't mean that you should not pick openings. Don't repeat harmful evidence. Make your examination brief and crisp, if possible. A good witness for the defense may improve for the defense under cross-examination.

Your witness upon cross-examination has made a statement either before or during trial which contradicts him. What shall you do? Don't let it unhorse you. Touch only briefly and lightly upon the subject of the statement and then ask him again what the facts are, statement or no statement. Here again is the question of touch. Can the witness handle himself? Is he honest? Was he careless in making the statement? Was he led into making it? How does the rest of the case look? What will its effect be on the other evidence?

Cross-examination of the doctor—It is desirable to point out that the doctor frequently testifies in the defense of negligence cases. If you know your subject and have medical authorities at hand, make him admit those things which are medical verities. He will admit that medicine is not an exact science and if he denies those which are medical verities he may be destroyed. If he admits them, you are so much to the good.

He should be pressed for the admission, for example, that the pain and other subjective conditions may exist without any objective sign or symptom and that he cannot deny their existence and would not swear that they do not exist in this case.

Summation

How much should you devote in answering defendant's arguments? Generally not as much time as in presenting your own facts, theories and ideas, but it is always important to show any misstatement of fact or law made by opposing counsel. The preponderance of your talk should deal with your own favorable evidence; the salient facts that make your case. The recollection of the jury may be refreshed as to those facts and be carried into the jury room. The jury should be made to feel that they have lived through the experience that the plaintiff has; that you are unable to adequately describe the experiences of the plaintiff over the period of time past and for the period indicated by the Mortality Tables. They should be made to feel that payment for injuries in a negligence case is equally as legal and moral an obligation as the amount due and owing on a commercial account or under a promissory note.

To summarize and to state briefly. The plaintiff's lawyer may well follow this rule—(1) As to preparation—work, work, you can't overwork, you can't overdo it. As to trial—Don't overdo it.

Adapted from 3 Schweitzer, Trial Guide, 1479, Baker, Voorhis & Co., Inc., New York (1945).

Handling the Medical Witness

By Dr. W. Webber Kelly

It is not my intention to attempt to discuss in detail the exhaustive subject of expert medical testimony. Such a detailed discussion lies within the province of one trained in the law. My purpose is merely to set forth some of the personal experiences and impressions gained from 35 years of continued and frequent attendance in court as a medical witness.

Expert Testimony

The original purpose of expert testimony is obvious. It is permitted in order to aid in the elucidation of certain issues in the case, which elucidation is only possible by the testimony of witnesses possessing special knowledge not to be obtained from the average individual. The general rule is that opinion evidence is not admissible;[1] in other words, the witness must testify to facts within his knowledge or those derived from his own perception. While it is true that from necessity the conclusions of certain witnesses are admissible in matters of identity, quantity, value, time, distance, velocity, heat, cold and others; as well as questions concerning various mental and moral aspects of humanity; namely, temper, anger, fear, excitement, intoxication, veracity and general character: such testimony is conclusive evidence and based upon evidentiary facts.

The general rule of opinion evidence is flagrantly broken in the case of expert medical testimony. Such testimony permits the consideration and credence by the jury of opinions and conclusions based upon facts not necessarily within the knowledge or observations of the expert, but introduced in evidence by other witnesses and presumed to be true. Its limitations appear to be very broad. Once having qualified and while his competency

[1] Mundo, *The Expert Witness*, p. 1; Jones, *Evidence*, § 1242, p. 2283.

remains unchallenged, it permits the witness by hypothesis and assumption of facts either testified to at the time of his direct examination, or upon promise of later proof, an expression of opinion not only as to the injury or episode being the proximate cause of the present disability and a belief as to the permanency of the litigant's present condition; it also allows statement of belief as to the probable or even possible future onset of remote effects.[2]

At this point, therefore, medical expert testimony enters the field of prophecy. It has appeared to me that this matter of prophecy is at times permitted to go too far. Belief as to probable exacerbations or remote results in the individual's mental and physical state without evidence that such a development is already apparent, appears unreasonable and is obviously double speculation.[3] Thus, to say that any nervous disorder resulting from an injury or shock may at some distant future time probably or possibly result in insanity, is to assume the role of prophet. Medicine is a changing and progressive science, and the last word in therapeutics today may not be the last word tomorrow; however such speculation appears to be permissible.

Hypothetical Question

Webster defines hypothesis as "A tentative theory or supposition provisionally adopted to explain certain facts, and to guide in the investigation of others." This definition defines the mechanics, at least, of hypothetical inquiry. As I understand it, the theory and supposition must be in the case, and the facts supporting them must have been testified to, before a basis may be established for the propounding of the hypothetical question. The groundwork for such question is, of course, a simple matter for the attorney whose purpose it is to offer it later in the trial. In framing such an interrogation a great deal of care and effort must be spent. To attempt to recite extemporaneously the facts desired is often a confusing and unsatisfactory method of handling it. While in court I usually hear two constant objections

[2] Block v. Milwaukee Street R. Co., 89 Wis 371, 61 NW 1101 (1895); Hanton v. Omro, 122 Wis 337, 99 NW 1051 (1904); Faber v. Reiss Coal Co., 124 Wis 554, 102 NW 1049 (1905); Sundquist v. Mad. R. R., 197 Wis 83, 221 NW 392 (1928).

[3] Schweitzer, *Negligence Actions,* p. 376, n. 1; Griswold v. N. Y. etc. R. C., 115 NY 61, 21 NE 226 (1889).

by opposing counsel to the hypothetical questions submitted to me.

First, that the question recites facts not shown in the evidence, and second, that the question does not contain all of the facts in the case. A promise to introduce the missing facts later in the case appears to be sufficient to invalidate the first objection. As to the second, it would appear that the question need not include any particular number of facts, it may assume any one or more facts whatsoever, and need not cover all of the factors which the questioner alleges in his case. The questioner is entitled to the witness' opinion in any combination of facts that he may choose.

It is often convenient and even necessary to obtain that opinion upon a state of facts falling short of what he or his opponent expects to prove because the questioner cannot tell how much of the testimony the jury will accept; . . . For reasons of principle then, and to some extent of policy, the natural conclusion would be that the questioner need not cover in his hypothesis the entire body of testimony put forward on that point by him or by the opponent, but may take as limited a selection as he pleases and obtain an opinion on that basis. Such is the orthodox doctrine as applied to most courts.[4] On the other hand, other authorities are of the opinion that generally speaking a hypothetical question should state all the facts relevant to the formation of an opinion . . . there is no exclusive formula . . . and the matter of form is largely discretionary to the trial court.[5]

At this point may I, as a layman, offer a word of caution as to the length of the hypothetical question. Often one hears a question covering several pages of foolscap and containing so much material that the attorney himself cannot remember it. Under these circumstances it is difficult to believe that the jury at its conclusion is in any better position. Limited to essential facts, clearly and intelligently cited, upon which the jury may know the premises upon which the opinion is to be given, it appears to be more effective. One prominent trial lawyer tells me that he adopts the rule of writing the question carefully and as concisely as possible, committing it to memory and then tearing up the written version. His argument is that unless he can remember it, he is certain that the jury cannot do so.

---

[4] 1 Wigmore, *Evidence,* § 682, p. 778.

[5] 3 Jones, *Evidence,* p. 2427-28.

The effect of medical expert testimony upon the jury has intrigued me. After speaking to many jurors, I am now convinced that its effect is greater than I formerly believed. This, of course, depends a great deal upon the manner in which this evidence is given, and is concerned with the apparent honesty of the witness, the firmness of his conclusions and, above all, his employment of language as intelligible as possible to laymen serving as jurors. Many expert witnesses forget that the jury exists, and address their answers to the questioner. His replies should be directly aimed at the jury, and he should, if necessary, change his position in the witness chair in order that they may hear distinctly what he says.

At this point let me discuss that individual who is at once the trial and despair of judges and opposing counsel, and the white haired boy of the trial attorney who engages his services.

The Expert Witness

It must be borne in mind that a physician who qualifies as an expert must expect to be judged by a different standard than the physician who gives evidence as an ordinary witness. By this is meant that from the latter we have no right to expect more than average knowledge of the issues in the case. From the former we have a reason to demand an opinion based upon a larger personal experience and scientific familiarity with the issues involved.

An interesting point occurs in connection with this latter statement. Objection may be raised to an expert witness as to the bookish source of his knowledge; first, because it implies a lack of skill and experience as affecting his expert capacity for judgment; and second, because it involves accepting as a knower of a given fact one who has not really observed it for himself, but is trusting in the opinions of others. In other words, it is an objection against the witness' experience on the quality of his knowledge.

To deny the competency of a physician who does not know his facts from personal observation in similar cases is to reject medical testimony almost in its entirety. . . . Medical science is a mass of transmitted data; general relations are rare which are the result of one man's personal observations exclusively; and the law cannot expect its petitioners to obtain these rare persons.[6]

There appears to be no precise general rule as to how the skill of a witness must be acquired. According to decisions in Michigan a witness may express an opinion upon certain matters even if his knowledge is derived from study alone.[7] Wigmore agrees with the above rule, feeling apparently that the knowledge however acquired is a question relating only to the weight of the evidence given.[8]

The Supreme Court of Wisconsin holds that the opinion of an expert must, in addition to knowledge, be derived from experience. The logic of this position is that since books themselves cannot be read in evidence, extracts from them should not be permitted from the lips and memory of the expert.[9] I raise this question because of an occurrence in a personal injury suit within my knowledge. The question involved a case of a rare pathological condition of the eye in which an expert from Milwaukee was called to testify by the plaintiff. Upon admission that the witness had never seen a similar case in his experience, a plea of lack of competency was upheld and the witness was not permitted to testify. The decision of the trial court as to competency lies within its own discretion, and unless founded upon some error of law, serious mistake or abuse of discretion, its ruling is not reversible.[10]

Another difficulty encountered by the expert witness is the objection that his opinion given as the result of his examination of the plaintiff or defendant, as the case may be, is in part based upon hearsay; in that he must rely upon the patient's own statements as to the history and symptoms and that such hearsay testimony is not valid. Such limitation is apparently the rule in Wisconsin, although in other states the rigidity of this practice does not pertain.

As Wigmore logically states, the exclusion of information so obtained and its basis in the formation of the expert's opinion does in strictness exclude all medical testimony based upon per-

6 1 Wigmore, *Evidence,* § 687, p. 782.

7 People v. Thacker, 108 Mich 652, 66 NW 562 (1896).

8 1 Wigmore, *Evidence,* § 569.

9 Soquet v. State, 72 Wis 659, 40 NW 391 (1888); Zuesdorf v. Grotsky, 195 Wis 253, 218 NW 186 (1928).

10 3 Jones, *Evidence,* §§ 1317, 1318.

sonal examination.[11] Thus the witness is confined in testifying only as to the objective symptoms. A qualified expert can, however, overcome this handicap by enumerating many of the subjective findings and by increasing his powers of observation and giving proper expression to them. It would appear to be a case of much ado about nothing as an experienced attorney can readily present the history, symptoms and any other missing facts in hypothetical form for the expert's conclusions.

Prerequisites for the Medical Expert

It goes without saying that he should be absolutely honest and unbiased in his testimony, and thoroughly familiar with the medical aspects of the case in which he is testifying. This should be done by preparing himself by looking up the general literature on the matter and for his own information familiarizing himself with the opinions of authorities who may have written upon the subject.

To this must be added his professional background and standing in the community in which the action rests, or his medical reputation throughout the state if he is from the outside. He should display ready understanding and even anticipation of the questions propounded, and possess sufficient ability to take care of himself as far as possible without protection from the attorney engaging his services. He must, however, avoid the delusion that he is a medical jurist. He should at all costs retain great composure and control of his temper, and be definitely courteous and patient under cross-examination. He should, as previously stated, speak distinctly and slowly, and in terms as intelligible as possible to the jury.

Technical terms, unless explained, are lost upon jurors and nullify the effect of his testimony. In enumerating the qualifications I would emphasize preparation. To my mind this is very essential. One should never enter a lawsuit as an expert witness without thoroughly acquainting himself not only with the gross medical facts involved, but with the anatomy, physiology and other allied subjects connected with them. My personal prepara-

[11] 1 Wigmore, *Evidence,* § 688, pp. 783, 784 . . . "Those who object to testimony of the sort where considered must expect to surrender the medical witness stand to veterinary surgeons exclusively."

tion includes an effort to anticipate the possible questions that may be asked me by the opposing attorney.

Needless to say most of these questions are never asked, but should they be, I expect to be in a position to have a ready answer. It may appear paradoxical, but it is nevertheless true that many intelligent and well-educated physicians fail to make good witnesses. This results from shyness, fear, or lack of ability to express themselves logically. On the other hand, many physicians of mediocre attainments, with alert minds and plenty of self assurance may make a good showing. The danger in the latter case lies in the possibility of disaster at the hands of an attorney who is well prepared medically and with experience in this type of cases.

Wisecracking and other forms of subtle humor should be strictly avoided by the witness. On the other hand an attitude of abject humility or what may be termed the "Uriah Heap complex" is equally to be deplored.

The Question of Partisanship

The question of partisanship, as evidence by the invariable conflict of opinion by experts on both sides of the case, has often been discussed. A physician should refuse to testify in cases where any doubt exists in his mind as to the correctness of the position assumed by attorneys or other medical witnesses. I am glad to say that having advanced my views and objections to the medical theory of the case, no attorney has ever insisted in his demands for my services or attempted to influence my convictions or decisions to testifying.

As a general rule no one has a right to question the honesty of the medical witness. It is true that one may unconsciously become partisan, due, no doubt, to the fact that he is certain that whatever conclusions he testifies to will be contradicted by the doctor testifying on the opposite side. There may be, and are, many honest differences of opinion in medical matters, and it is very hard to get away from one's own convictions. Some witnesses become dogmatic and are unwilling to admit that any opinion other than their own can possibly be correct. The contradictory form of expert testimony as evidence by those testifying on opposite sides of the case has become proverbial, and several suggestions have been made for its correction.

Under some statutes, the judge of the trial court in criminal cases may, after notice to the parties and a hearing, appoint one or more disinterested qualified experts, not exceeding three, to testify at the trial. Under this section, these experts are required to subscribe to a special oath and their compensation is fixed by the court and paid by the county upon the court's order constituting a part of the costs of the action. They are, of course, subject to cross-examination by both parties who may also summon other expert witnesses at the trial. Why this practice cannot be extended, even in modified form, in civil cases is hard to fathom.

For many years efforts by eminent members of the bar and the several professions have endeavored to have enacted by the various legislatures, laws authorizing the court to appoint its own experts, especially when there appears, as is frequently the case, wide differences between the experts for the plaintiff and defendant, differences which tend to completely confuse and confound both the court and the jury.

In certain foreign countries, the expert is chosen by the court from a list of scientific and highly qualified members of the various professions. A penalty is attached for disregarding the summons, and the commonwealth provides a moderate, fixed compensation, together with expenses, for appearance and testimony in court. The medical expert's position becomes thereby an official one; in fact he is thus made an officer of the court. It is regarded an honor and distinction to be so designated, and there is attendant on the office every courtesy and dignity to which its responsibilities entitle it. The utmost care is observed in the selection of physicians and surgeons as official experts, so that only men of known special scientific attainments, personal integrity and possessing the ability to clarify complex problems, are chosen.[12]

Section 1871 of the California Code of Civil Procedure provides: "When it shall be made to appear to any court or judge thereof, either before or during the trial of any action or proceeding, such court or judge may, on motion of any party, or on motion of such court or judge, appoint one or more experts to investigate and testify at the trial of such action or proceeding

12 California State Bar Journal, May, 1937.

relative to the matter or matters as to which such expert evidence is, or will be, required, and such court or judge may fix the compensation of such expert." The commission on the administration of justice in New York State has proposed similar legislation, and it would appear that the trend is definitely in the direction of the appointment of experts by the courts.

Qualifications Admitted

I believe that many attorneys err in failing to emphasize the qualifications of their expert. "Qualifications admitted" has come to have a familiar sound to me. This short cut method of qualifying an expert has two principal objections.

First, the counsel whose witness you are misses an opportunity to impress the jury with any qualifications including medical training, membership in recognized medical societies, period of practice, general experience; as well as familiarity with the issues in similar cases.

Secondly, "It must be borne in mind that once having stipulated the witnesses' qualifications the opposing attorney is barred from later attempting to impeach the competency of the expert and complaint cannot be made on appeal that he was not qualified."[13]

Cross-Examinations of Experts

Unless properly prepared the average attorney is gambling with odds in the cross-examination of a competent medical expert insofar, at least, as the technical medical details of the case are concerned. Attorneys frequently engaged in personal injury cases are of course an exception to this statement. Proper preparation with the aid of some competent medical man prior to the cross-examination is imperative. I do not mean by this that the opposing attorney should entirely refrain from cross-examination. Inconsistencies and contradictions and conclusions clearly illogical should be questioned and questioned severely.

"Yes or No"

The medical witness is frequently instructed to answer a question "yes" or "no." Compliance with such a demand may be

[13] McGuire v. Baird, 9 Cal(2d) 353, 70 P(2d) 915 (1937).

impossible. If such is the case, the witness should so state. If ordered by the court to do so without being permitted to give the reasons for his answer, it is a simple matter for counsel to ask him on redirect to give the reasons for such an answer, and to explain the conclusions or premises which required him to do so. Such an opportunity cannot be withheld.

The common-law rule is that scientific books may not be read to the jury as evidence, because the statements therein contained are wanting in the sanctity of an oath, are made by one not present, and who is not liable to cross-examination. While the common-law rule has been modified by statute in many states to allow certain scientific books to be received in evidence, the rule of exclusion still prevails as to medical books.[14]

Mortality Tables for estimating of the probable life of a party, the given age, chronological tables, tables of weights, measures and currency and the like, are admissible to prove facts of general notoriety and interest in connection with such subjects as may be involved in the trial of a cause.[15] But medicine is not considered as one of the exact sciences: it is of the character of inductive sciences which are based on data which each successive year may correct and expand, so that what is considered a sound induction last year may be considered an unsound one this year.[16]

In some jurisdictions it has been held that the medical witness may reinforce his opinion from a stated condition by showing that certain textbooks upon the subject are in accord with his views.[17] Such a practice in my opinion is dangerous, for the witness may be discredited upon cross-examination from extracts read from such authorities and contradictory statements or those subject to varying interpretations are to be found in the same textbooks. It is generally held, however, that the use of medical texts to prove a fact in issue is improper. It has been my lot on several occasions to face attempts by opposing counsel to read statements from textbooks by authorities about whose standing there could be no question, and then requested to state whether I agreed or disagreed with the theories they embrace.

---

14 Mundo, *The Expert Witness,* p. 87.
15 Wagar v. Schuyler, 1 Wend 553 (1827).
16 Wharton, *Evidence,* § 665.
17 Louisville R. Co. v. Howell, 147 Ind 266, 45 NE 584 (1896); Pinney v. Cahill, 48 Mich 586, 12 NW 862 (1882).

A competent witness will refuse to be drawn into any such trap. Counsel must be expressly limited in references to only such treaties as have been used or referred to by the witness upon his direct examination.[18] The witness may refresh his memory by referring to X-rays, charts made by him or under his direction and notes taken by him at the time when the matter was fresh in his memory.

The rule respecting notes is that the witness is allowed to refresh his memory by anything written by himself or under his direction at the time when the fact occurred, immediately thereafter or at any time when the fact is fresh in his memory. Unless necessary, notes should not be used. If notes are used, they must be produced so that the adverse party may see them and cross-examine the witness upon them as he chooses. They may be read to the jury.[19]

Before leaving the subject of expert testimony, may I suggest the abandonment of a policy which I think is undesirable. I have reference to having counsel's own medical witness sitting behind him and coaching him during the examination of the other attorney's medical expert. Physicians regard this as not being strictly ethical, and there is no question in my mind that it has a distinctly injurious psychological effect upon the jury. Not only is it unsatisfactory in technique, but it is an admission of counsel's own weakness, and gives the impression of not being good sportsmanship.

The Lawyer From the Layman's Viewpoint

May I begin by saying that collectively and individually I hold the members of the legal profession in the highest regard. In my contacts with them throughout the state, I have been impressed by their high character and honesty of purpose. This is in great part due to the judiciary, for the character and ability of the judge reflect upon the members of his circuit. Among lawyers there appears to me to be a great degree of consideration for each other and a large absence of the petty jealousy that exists in other professions, including the medical fraternity.

---

[18] Schweitzer, op cit., pp. 386, 387, n 1, 388, 389.

[19] Mundo, op cit., p. 47; Braxten v. Brown, 197 Minn 511, 267 NW 489 (1936); Wright v. Upsilon, 303 Ill 120, 135 NE 208 (1922); People v. Schepps, 217 Mich 406, 186 NE 508, 21 ALR 658 (1922).

Personally, I have experienced nothing but courtesy and kindness from the Bar as a whole, and while I know that to many of them I have at times been very trying, they have never failed to treat me with respect and consideration. Therefore, anything that I may say will indicate no desire on my part to be disrespectful or unkind. It is sometimes interesting, however, and even profitable to see ourselves as others see us. Hence these observations of a layman.

Preparation

One thing is apparent with some attorneys, and that is their lack of preparation. This arises either from the fact that they are too busy and have insufficient help, or from neglect. They enter court without definite strategic plans and even familiarity with the legal angles involved, as well as an absence of understanding as to what their own witness will testify to.

In some cases cross-examination has all the earmarks of a fishing expedition and some of them should be members of the Isaak Walton League. Many attorneys of mediocre ability can make a confrere with definitely greater legal experience look sick by the simple expedient of thoroughly preparing his case. The most successful members of the Bar of my acquaintance are usually those with whom preparation is a ritual. I would much prefer not to be associated with the attorney who calls me up the night before a case to discuss the important matter of the medical testimony. On the other hand, it is a joy to work with one who is sufficiently interested to discuss these details two or three times before putting me on the witness stand.

Over Examination

Another matter that has intrigued me greatly is the yen some attorneys possess for over examination. How frequently one sees witnesses tied up completely and with the record in excellent shape, only to have the effect of their answers destroyed by continued questioning. Having obtained an answer that is entirely satisfactory to his case, some attorneys persist in asking the same question in several different forms, until finally the answer is so modified as to be hardly recognizable.

A satisfactory answer is an asset worth preserving. Why attempt to paint the lily? Equal danger appears to lie in failing to sufficiently examine the witness. This was brought forcibly to my mind in a murder case in which I was retained by the state. An eminent psychiatrist and excellent witness was on the stand. In spite of advice to the contrary, the prosecutor read to him two long detailed hypothetical questions, and instructed him to answer "yes" or "no" to both. His strategy was then to turn him over to counsel for the defense in the full expectation that he would be cross-examined, and in this way enabled to elaborate his answers. These were the only two questions asked him.

The result was unfortunate. The attorney for the defense simply said, "No questions, doctor" and the witness left the stand. Thus the testimony of an outstanding expert, brought many miles for the specific purpose of tearing the defense apart, was completely thrown away. Moral: don't depend on the other fellow to try your case.

Another thing that is noticeable to an onlooker is the eternal leading that goes on in the examination of witnesses. My rough guess is that a large majority of the questions asked are leading. This has become such a habit with some attorneys that when they are called on it, they are often at a complete loss to frame the question in a non-leading manner, and are often aided by the court in their dilemma.

Conscientious Objectors

A psychological understanding of the judge, as well as the jury would appear essential. Many attorneys acquire psychological knowledge from experience, but often at the expense of many disasters that might have been avoided. No doubt legal psychology is a part of the curriculum of every law school. If not, it should be, and also emphasized. Some attorneys seem to have an affinity for objecting and objecting eternally. To one who is not versed in legal lore, most of these objections appear to be trivial.

An experienced trial attorney of my acquaintance, when asked by me why he did not object to a certain question, informed me that no matter how irrelevant or immaterial, he never objected so long as the question did no harm to his case. He felt that he got along with the judge a great deal better by following this rule. It is used by some attorneys to confuse and confound opposing counsel.

Whether this is effective or not I do not know. It is not only the constant objections which delay the trial and tire the judge, but the exceptions to the judge's ruling one occasionally hears that are irksome and annoying. Since exceptions are, in this state deemed taken to adverse rulings, they are unnecessary—why rub his Honor's fur the wrong way?

With the passing of the years, it has been noticeable that the explosive and noisy type of oratory is gradually fading from the scene; it seems to have disappeared with crinoline and the political torchlight parades. Occasionally one still hears it, but it has lost much of its former effectiveness. Side remarks made by one attorney to another, remarks that are intended to be humorous but which are frequently bitter and vindictive are still with us. Beyond causing momentary amusement, they have little favorable effect upon the average juror. This type of vaudeville would never be permitted in an English courtroom. It tends to lower the dignity of the court. Some judges, strange to say, are very tolerant in this regard.

Cross-Examination, Material and Otherwise

An expert witness needs a long memory, for one is not infrequently confronted with prophecies made at previous trials. A somewhat amusing, but nevertheless tragic, incident occurred a short time ago which illustrates this point. It occurred in federal court in a case with which I was associated.

One of the witnesses for the government, an eminent and distinguished professor of one of our large universities, was on the stand. The opposing counsel (with no textbooks in sight) read to him a long statement which he had written on his scratch pad. The question covered a theory closely related to the issue in the case. When he had finished he asked the witness whether he did not believe that the statement was a fair one, and covered the situation thoroughly. The witness could hardly wait for the completion of the statement and question, and immediately replied, "I utterly disagree with that theory—in my opinion it is not correct." The attorney looked at him intently for a moment and then said, "You are sure, doctor, that you disagree entirely with that statement?" The witness answered, "Yes." "That is strange, doctor, because that is an exact copy of a paragraph contained in a textbook of which you are the author, and which is in general use among medical students and practitioners." The judge immediately called for the book, which was produced, and the witness was required to read the paragraph in question and state whether it did not coincide word for word with the excerpt which had been read to him.

I have had my full share of questions that are irrelevant and immaterial. It has often amazed me not only that these questions should be asked, but that they should be permitted by the trial judge. Some of them call for a facetious answer, although this should be avoided if possible.

The classic answer of Dr. Joseph Collins of New York is an example:

> Q—"As a matter of fact, doctor, you are an alienist pure and simple?" A—"Yes, an alienist moderately pure, but not simple." Let me quote one or two irrelevant queries which come to my mind.
>
> Q—"You testify in all of Attorney Jones's cases, don't you doctor?" A—"I am not in a position to answer that question intelligently, because I am not aware of how many cases Attorney Jones has."
>
> Q—"How far North, how far South, how far East and how far West have you traveled to testify for Attorney Smith?" Where is the relevancy in a question of this type?
>
> Q—"You are a personal friend of the attorney on the other side, are you not doctor?"

The implication in such a question is obvious, and the answer equally illuminating. The question as to the size of the fee the expert witness expects to get in a given case, while not frequent, occasionally presents itself. Its object is evidently to demonstrate interest and bias, and in that respect is, of course, proper.

In the majority of cases, the matter of compensation has not been discussed between the attorney and the witness at the time of the question, but an answer to this effect does not appear to be sufficient.

Then comes the query, "How much are you in the habit of receiving for testifying in court?"

This would appear irrelevant, as the compensation received in some previous trial has certainly no bearing on the present case. The best way to handle this question is to answer it frankly and responsively, and let the matter end there.

Occasionally one runs into trick questions and the witness must be on his guard. In a certain case I had testified that in my opinion the injury in question was permanent, and I knew of no treatment or operation that could correct it. On cross-examination the opposing attorney asked me these questions—"You say, doctor, that nothing can be done to cure this man?" My answer was "Yes."

"You don't believe that Christian Science could do anything for him?" My answer was—"I really couldn't say, for though I have a deep respect for Christian Science, I am not familiar with its operation in conditions of this nature." This apparently did not satisfy him.

"Will you say positively that Christian Science could not cure him?" My answer was—"I would make no such statement, because as I have already stated, I am not familiar with it, although I have heard of some remarkable results that it has accomplished." As I stepped down from the stand and passed the attorney I whispered to him—"How many Christian Scientists have you on the jury?" He smiled and answered—"Only two."

This was a clear case of fishing, but my legal friend had forgotten the repeated admonition and cardinal rule for fishermen, enunciated by the late Isaak Walton,—"First, know your fish." (—the gentleman apparently mistook me for a sucker.) The question was, of course, improper and should have been objected to. No expert of one school of healing can be questioned about any other school with which he is unfamiliar.

My purpose in presenting this paper has been to record some of the experiences, impressions and reactions derived from a close observation of court procedures over a period of many years. It is only proper that a medical expert witness should be concerned with those phases of the law regarding competency, the use of medical texts, opinion evidence, hypothetical inquiry and other legal questions which directly affect him as a witness. Such knowledge, even though lacking in profundity, is in my opinion necessary to enable a medical expert to perform his function intelligently and effectively provide his services, and to aid the court and jury in promoting justice.

This article was adapted from 3 Schweitzer, Trial Guide 1494, Baker, Voorhis & Co., Inc., New York (1945), which was adapted from Marquette Law Review, June, 1943.

Trial Technique

By W. D. Vance

The term or word "Trial" at once suggests many things—it may well be preliminary or final in character. It may be objective or subjective—a test of strength of body or mind—the development of a motive, plan or ultimate fact. Something carried out for elimination of the least worthy—or to put an end to further contest or quibble as to the matter or question involved.

"Technique" may best indicate the means employed—the skill with which the test is made—the ultimate fact developed—the various steps or stages used in reaching the end of the contest—the goal for which the trial is intended.

In short, it is the adaptation of knowledge, skill and personality to the subject matter of the trial.

To limit the discussion to the actual process of the trial—stripped of the labor and basic matters necessarily involved from the inception of the occurrence or question, down through the stages leading to the actual lining up for the test, would indeed result in leaving a narrow, and to me uninteresting, field for discussion.

Basically—there are many elements that enter into, and are primarily essential to, the application of proper trial technique.

Fundamentally, there must be all of the following elements in at least some reasonable measure, if a trial before the court, or court and jury, is to be conducted successfully:

(a) The attorney must have natural ability—not acquired or borrowed.

(b) He must know people and have the genius of recognizing facts, and distinguishing them from pretentions.

(c) He should be a logical thinker, and understand the value of correct arrangement of facts—such as will impress the most, and lead to clearness of understanding and effect.

(d) Perhaps more important than all else, he should be able to anticipate the probable claims and contentions to be made by his adversary.

(e) Avoid the rut of believing his own client in the face of patent probable facts, where reason and common knowledge require discounting the claims made by him.

(f) Let no fact detail escape attention in the preparation of a cause for trial—that apparently insignificant fact may be the turning point of the issue to be decided.

(g) Thoroughly prepare your facts first—this to be done on the basis of adhering to the true facts, so far as humanly able to get at the facts—then turn to the law for the rules to which the same are properly to be applied.

(h) It is of course appreciated, that to first find the rule of law, and to then make the facts fit the rule, is not to be done by the man who properly regards his oath of office—the ethics of his profession—and the natural fairness and justice to which everything else should be subservient.

(i) There is even more than a suspicion in my mind that all trial lawyers do not fairly follow the rule of conduct last above suggested. This is one kind of dishonorable conduct all loyal citizens condemn.

(j) Having made the preparation of the facts and law, as outlined—and finding support for the contentions as pleaded—the trial attorney can be a firm believer in the cause he represents.

(k) Unless one firmly believes in his cause, he enters upon the actual trial with the way dark, or possibly exhibiting the weakness of his cause by his every word and act—a sorry spectacle to the discerning trial judge and jurymen.

(*l*) Having what one feels is a just cause, and being adequately prepared, the trial attorney goes into court at the assigned hour for trial—in a condition of mind such as will enable him to give of his very best—his cause is half or more won in such a situation.

(m) In the courtroom, his natural course of conduct will be, first and over all, courteous, yet dignified; he will proceed with dispatch, be as thorough (avoiding boring and unnecessary duplication of fact and contentions) as his cause reasonably requires—always remembering logic and simpleness of statement (avoiding the use of language only intended to show special knowledge of intricate terms or rules) and remembering when to quit.

(n) Keep in mind that it is frequently well to anticipate the things your adversary will most probably present, to see to it that the court or jury is shown in advance the inaptness of the contentions to follow—that is, remove the sting if possible before it is allowed to settle too deeply in the body of the cause with added injury.

(o) No difference what may happen—how much your adversary or others may depart from the rules of proper trial conduct—maintain your poise and do not stoop to the lower levels; the advantage thus to be gained often proves to be the turning point in favor of a cause that may have had a losing aspect as the trial had progressed.

(p) Always remember that for the time being at least the trial court is right—this is especially true in jury trials—more frequently than not, the jury is greatly impressed with the rulings and expressions of the trial judge (and this is as it should be), so to argue too much with him will most generally be to lose ground for your cause.

(q) In the examination of witnesses, do not embark on an uncharted sea. Generally, if you do not know what a witness will say, do not ask the question; and as a general rule, long and persistent cross-examination leads to disaster—better allow the first impression to remain, even though adverse to your contentions, than to help the unfriendly witness to further impress the court or jury with the claims made by him.

(r) I believe the best rule is for the trial lawyer to be himself—if he has the natural talent and personality to be a successful trial practitioner, since his knowledge, ability and fairness will be thus best shown; if his is specially bright, if he has made a success in his profession, that impression will develop without effort on the part of the individual himself.

(s) The one rule that should always be applied is: To exert every ounce of sincere effort in the representation of a client's cause that is possible; never let down until the task is complete and, even then, be thinking of the future action necessary to make effective the contentions espoused.

What has been said thus far is even a poor beginning, since the subject being discussed is so comprehensive that it is impossible to cover it within the time limit for this discussion. No doubt, as presented, it will appeal to but a limited number of those within hearing, or who may read this paper.

Then, too, there is properly so much individualism among the trial attorneys that any set rule of procedure is of small value. To succeed he must be himself—no one can guide him in the processes of a trial—but the average one can certainly profit by the experience of others.

I trust that the actual passing of the showman in trial work is about complete. There is no real place for him in our ranks. Appeals to the sentimentalist, to the prejudices which blur or blot out the real issues, have no place in our legal system. It is within our power to further discount these practices—to help raise the standards of trials to the high plane the ethics and real justice among men demands.

There is a place of high importance for the trial judge in the trial of issues. He can so direct as to make for the high standards we want to maintain, or he may render it impossible for the best results to be obtained. (Infrequently though it may be that the latter failure is present, it is still for the most part inexcusable.)

Of course, cooperation on the correct basis as between counsel and the court is a necessity—to the end that proper technique in trial work may be applied. Finally, may it be repeated that one must prepare thoroughly—must be of logical mind—must believe in his cause—must be actually and practically ethical—must be able to meet, to know, to understand people of all classes and kinds of employment. He must love his profession, believe in its high purposes and place in the scheme of things. Without these in full measure, successful trial practice is not possible.

This article was adapted from 3 Schweitzer, Trial Guide 1511, Baker, Voorhis & Co., Inc., New York (1945), which was adapted from Journal of Bar Association of Kansas, February, 1943.

Examination of Medical Witnesses

BY CLAYTON SMITH, ESQ.

THE PROPER EXAMINATION of medical experts is probably one of the most difficult phases of trial work. There is a wide diversity of opinion as to the technique to be employed. Consequently, there can be no specific rules for our guidance. I feel that the most you can hope to get from this discussion is a few suggestions which may at some time be of benefit to you.

If you have a case of possible liability then from the standpoint of either plaintiff or defendant the manner in which you conduct the examination may spell victory or defeat. If a plaintiff, it is defeat if you have not obtained a result which adequately compensates your client for the injuries sustained.

Choice of Expert

The first thing to be considered is the choice of your expert. If you represent the plaintiff you may find yourself handicapped because of the fact that you have had no choice in the selection of an attending physician. You have inherited him with the case.

Not infrequently does the plaintiff's attorney find himself saddled with an unimpressive or indifferent medical witness. Your own experience tells you that many doctors abhor coming to court. After all, they must anticipate an attack upon their general knowledge, skill or ability. Take it home to yourself, how would you like to be questioned before a jury on general legal procedure or specific propositions of law? How would you like to have your fund of legal information spotlighted?

I believe that seven out of ten physicians go through the ordeal unwillingly. Psychologically, this unwillingness gives the cross-examiner the advantage. On an equal footing we must concede that our knowledge of medicine or human anatomy is not to be compared with that of the ordinary medical expert. But in the courtroom we are not on an equal footing. That is our workshop. That is the place where the unwilling witness feels the least at home and as an inquisitor you have a distinct advantage.

The witness has to face the possibility of your showing him to be inadequately informed. If, by your attitude, you are able to get this idea across you will have paved the way for a profitable cross-examination. If, in addition, you assume an attitude of fairness in the style of your examination and the form of your questions, it is reasonably certain that the witness will at least to some extent support the theory which you are attempting to develop.

A medical witness either nervous or not exactly sure of himself will always welcome your apparently generous inclination to make the ordeal comparatively easy even though the obtaining of that relief has resulted in weakening, to some extent, the plaintiff's medical proof.

Keep in mind, however, that you can effect such a result only with certain types and even then you must at the outset convey the idea that you are the master of the situation.

Types of Medical Witnesses

But suppose you are not so fortunate as to be confronted with one of the seventy per cent who dread the ordeal or find it embarrassing. You may then find yourself called upon to cross-examine one of two types. The first, anxious to impress but lacking in fundamentals. The second, really skillful and speaking with authority.

These two types make for a very interesting examination. Failure to handle either of them properly may result in a complete loss of confidence of your ability to control the situation. The effect will be quickly transmitted to the jury to your detriment.

The Over-Anxious Witness

The first type requires special handling. You must feel your way along. You are dealing with a witness who is anxious to tell what he knows. Do not afford him that opportunity.

The attempt to impress is in reality a defense measure instituted for the avowed purpose of smoke screening his lack of ability. He is really very vulnerable. Ask him a few perfunctory questions.

Let your questions lull him into a feeling of security which will eventually lead up to some unguarded moment.

Witnesses of this type are long on general and broad statements, but short on details. Assume for the purpose of illustration that the most serious injury which the plaintiff received was a concussion of the brain, and assume that you have subpoenaed the hospital record. He probably has neglected to read the nurse's chart. My experience has been that that very valuable record containing the nurse's daily report is not infrequently neglected by doctors in the course of their preparation to testify.

I will assume that you have examined the chart, and that you have found therein a number of days shortly after the plaintiff's admission to the hospital indicating that the condition is generally good. Take your witness and go over that part of the chart with him day by day, have him admit that the pulse, temperature and blood pressure, if such is the fact, are recorded as normal.

In other words, it is done something like this. The chart indicated to the doctor that the plaintiff's pulse three days after the accident was between 70 and 80, the temperature 98.6, children 99.2, the blood pressure 110/70. That is within normal range in each instance. He will have to admit that it is. In going over the daily report with him you are preparing yourself for the general question which is to follow, and the one which will elicit the answer you are looking for. Here it is:

"Well, doctor, if that is so is it not true that the shock of accident had almost entirely disappeared?" The answer must be "Yes."

"And if the shock had disappeared then the injury was not severe enough to produce anything but temporary shock, is that not a fact?" If he answers no then follow up with this question.

"If it had been a severe concussion, is it not true that the effects would have persisted much longer?" The answer must be "Yes."

If by these questions you have succeeded in eliciting a favorable answer be satisfied. Know when to stop and do not spoil the result obtained by any further excursions into a field which will give him an opportunity to destroy the effect.

The Confident Witness

The very able type of medical expert knows his business and has little to fear from your questioning. He has a supreme air of confidence and quickly conveys the impression that he is master of the situation and not you. Treat him gently and tenderly.

His success has undoubtedly resulted in his acquiring some degree of vanity. Play up to it. Make him feel that you realize that his opinion is to be respected. Such a course on your part will incline him to be conciliatory. Whatever conciliations or admissions he makes, you make them count. They may be few but play them up for all they are worth.

Be satisfied with small results in examining a witness of this type. Above all do not butt your head against a stone wall by frantically attempting to break down his testimony. Any effort to show that he is not telling the truth or does not know what he is talking about must fail.

You will not only make yourself ridiculous but the result will be to emphasize the testimony which he has already given. Do not, under any circumstances, review his direct examination in detail, pick out the favorable, and emphasize its importance later.

Developing the Proof

The development of your medical proof is something which would receive serious consideration and attention before you go into trial. Let us consider it first from the plaintiff's angle.

You have a medical witness not of your own choice and to that extent your situation is unlike that of a defendant. If your witness' medical knowledge is basically sound and he is well able to handle the subject, your way is comparatively smooth. But if he lacks either of these two qualities, a difficult task lies before you.

If he is an indifferent practitioner and in your opinion incapable of doing justice to the case, then you owe it to your client to suggest that his testimony be supplemented with that of someone who is more experienced; not to build up your medical proof but merely to have it presented by a witness who inspires confidence.

Any attempt to build up insignificant injuries in this manner is unethical and should be deplored. Too often have we heard defendant's counsel during the course of the trial refer rather caustically to the fact that the plaintiff's lawyer has injected some doctor other than the attending physician.

It has been my experience that those who make these charges and work themselves into a veritable frenzy, on that account, are the very ones to have handpicked their own experts solely for two reasons; first, because of recognized ability, and second, because of the convincing manner in which they deliver their testimony.

Preparing the Medical Witness

If you would develop your medical proof properly do not do as a number of counsel very often do, that is, to phone their doctor at the time of trial and trust to luck that he will deliver himself creditably. In order to properly develop your medical proof, spend a few hours with him in the course of the preparation for trial.

Give him the advantage of knowing just what you expect to develop. Harmonize your client's claims, not only as to his injuries but also his present condition at the time of trial.

You are courting trouble if previous to trial you have failed to afford your doctor the opportunity to reconcile the client's claims with his conclusions. Not only that, but you may have inexcusably and unnecessarily left your client open to the charge of making claims unsupported by medical proof.

Go over the details in advance, not only of the injury found but also the condition that it is expected will result. Have him evaluate the conclusions which you have reached. Get the advantage of having him set you right in order that you may present your material not only clearly but also convincingly. In this way, and in this way only, will you get the most benefit out of the medical proof.

My experience has been that doctors welcome such conferences because to a certain extent they need you as much as you need them, and a thorough understanding previous to trial of what they may expect by way of questioning is conducive to a smooth and impressive examination.

It will help the witness to avoid many of the well-known pitfalls of cross-examination which so often result from lack of coordination between the attorney and the medical expert.

Qualifying the Witness

The next step is the manner in which you develop your medical proof on direct examination. The qualification of the doctor is not to be treated lightly. It has the advantage of satisfying the jury that he speaks with authority and is a witness on whose testimony some reliance can be placed.

With a certain type of juror too much qualification of a defendant's medical expert sometimes acts as a boomerang because it labels him as a professional witness and testifier. Some jurors resent doctors who lay too much stress on their training and experience. You will have to be the judge of the extent to which that subject should be pursued.

Do not place too much reliance in the hope that you are going to overwhelm your opponent with the impressiveness of your medical expert. The good old family doctor by the very simplicity of his manner many times finds that his conclusions are accepted in preference to those of highly paid experts. In such a case it is neither the skill nor lack of skill which counts, but the simple straightforward manner of delivery.

The Direct Examination

The direct examination of a medical witness should be accomplished by questions which are simple and uninvolved. Avoid the use of highly technical terms except where necessary. Do not attempt to inject yourself into the picture to such an extent that the jury may be distracted by your familiarity with medical terms rather than impressed with the testimony of your witness.

I have observed many plaintiffs' counsel purposely stumble over involved medical terms well known to them simply to put themselves on the same plane with the jurors and make them feel that they know as much about it as he does.

This may be good technique as a plaintiff's counsel. My advice is do not attempt it when you are on the defense. While the defendant's counsel should avoid too much show of impressiveness, still he should at all times let the jury know that he has his subject well in hand and is thoroughly conversant with the matter in hand.

Any indication of lack of knowledge of medical terms may result in a complete failure by the jurors to accept his analysis of the medical testimony during his summation simply because he has not put across the idea that he knows what he is talking about. As a defense counsel you must of necessity give all you have and you cannot convince anybody unless they gain the impression that you know whereof you speak.

These statements sound as though I felt that the plaintiff's road was very easy and the defendant's difficult. That is not so, for as a trier of the facts on either side I know that the plaintiff's road is not an easy one. I do feel that in a personal injury case many jurors naturally lean toward the plaintiff's side of the case until otherwise convinced. If that is their attitude it is reasonable to expect that they will overlook the shortcomings of the plaintiff's lawyer, at least to some extent, but on the other hand they may be inclined to be critical of the counsel for the defense.

Examining Witness' Notes

Is it good technique on cross-examination to attempt to pry into the notes or reports which your opponent's medical expert may be using on the stand? That is a debatable question. For the purpose of contradicting him on the facts such as the condition of the plaintiff on the occasion of one of his examinations, I feel that it is proper.

But any attempt to disclose to the jury that part of his report which contains his conclusions and suggestions to your opponent is in my opinion improper and should not be done. It is no different than requesting your opponent to let you see a copy of a statement taken from a witness. These matters are of a confidential nature and should be respected.

Hypothetical Questions

As to hypothetical questions—keep in mind that the answers which they elicit are no better than the facts on which they are based and your efforts should be directed to showing that if the facts are not as stated then the answer of necessity would not be the same.

You must remember that most hypothetical questions include subjective symptoms which are merely the complaints or statements made by the plaintiff and in giving his conclusions a doctor must of necessity take them into consideration. If they are not true or not reasonable then the conclusion based on them must be erroneous.

Hospital Records

It is generally assumed that the purpose of admitting hospital records into evidence is to show the condition of the patient at the time of admission, treatment and discharge. Beyond that I feel that the contents have no place in the deliberation of the jury.

However, these records are subpoenaed by both sides and in many instances it develops they are in court not to support the plaintiff's medical experts as to the nature and extent of the injury, not to assist the cross-examiner in an attempt to show that a favorable result has been obtained, but for the sole purpose of getting before the jury statements contained therein which are wholly irrelevant and improper.

Whichever side you represent you should examine such a report very closely and take care that you are familiar with its contents. The very first page inside the cover is usually called the Admission Sheet. Many times this contains statements of how the accident is supposed to have happened. If the statement comes from the plaintiff, of course, it is competent, if it in any way contradicts his testimony. If, however, it comes from others who have no firsthand information, who are not charged with making a report or reporting the information entered, then, of course, it is incompetent and should be excluded.

Summary

In conclusion, may I offer these few suggestions. Let your questions on cross-examination be as limited as your knowledge of the subject with which you are dealing. Never overstep. Know and appreciate your own limitations. Make the best of what you know and understand.

Never open up a gap which you are unable to close. Insist that the witness confine his answer to the question and under no circumstances invite or permit your opponent's medical expert to give a discourse or lecture supporting his theories. Avoid any show of antagonism. Accept adverse testimony with all the composure at your command. Be ever on the alert for inconsistencies and misstatements.

Keep in mind that we may not know medicine or surgery but we are supposed to be able to marshal facts and draw the reasonable inferences which will best subserve our client's interest.

Adapted from 3 Schweitzer, Trial Guide 1515, Baker, Voorhis & Co., Inc., New York (1945).

The Expert Witness

By Max W. Ball

Bench and bar have said a great deal about the expert witness, some of it judicial, a little of it complimentary, and much of it that could not safely be mailed, but so far as I know the expert witness has had little to say about himself. Something may be gained, therefore, by letting an expert witness take the stand and present his views as to what the lawyer should expect of him and what, more searchingly, he should expect of himself. The lawyers may then cross-examine if they wish.

Speaking solely for myself (and I have no brief to speak for anyone else), I find the giving of expert testimony one of the most challenging and stimulating of professional experiences. The reason is simple: A man's work either stands up or is shown up on the spot. If the cross-examination is informed and skillful—and heaven help the witness who expects anything less—he will know when he steps down from the stand whether he has done a good job or bungled. The sharp and searching test of his knowledge and presentation, and the immediacy with which he can taste pride of accomplishment or shame for failure—these make the expert's day in court exciting and on occasion satisfying. They also make it advisable for him to consider seriously what qualities he requires to pass the test and to taste pride more often than shame at the end of it.

Need for Sincerity

To begin with, he must, of course, be honest. If he will testify to what he does not wholeheartedly believe he is not an expert, he is a prostitute, and the sooner he is thrown out of the case the better for both counsel and client. He is not likely to convince judge or jury of that of which he himself is doubtful, no matter how renowned or fluent he may be.

Nor is a mere negative honesty enough; his sincerity of belief should be complete and positive on his client's behalf. If, within the field in which he is qualified as an expert, there is any important phase of the case about which his candid opinion would be harmful to his client, he should not accept employment or, having accepted and later learned of the adverse phase, he should step out of the case. There is nothing that a judge or jury or commission will sense more quickly than a lack of frankness and conviction, nothing more damaging than the slightest suggestion of evasiveness. Good expert testimony is rooted in sincerity so profound that it will not evade or cover up.

For such sincerity the client may have to pay a price. In spite of the expert's most careful study and preparation, an unforeseen set of facts may be sprung on him while he is on the stand. His sincerity should be such that he will give his opinion in the light of the unforeseen facts as straightforwardly as he has given his previous opinions, even though he hurts his client's case and incurs his client's displeasure. This is a risk the client takes in retaining him, but it is a risk that in most cases will pay off handsomely in the conviction that sincerity carries. The client can and should minimize the risk by making every material fact known to him available to the witness. Holding out on one's own expert is not the way to win a lawsuit.

The wise witness, by the way, will not let solicitude for his sincerity make him an easy mark. An astute cross-examiner may try to focus the witness' attention so sharply on the obligation to be honest that the witness will neglect to examine critically the statements the cross-examiner is making. Such an attempt should not succeed. True sincerity is ingrained and its owner need not stand guard over it. He can devote himself to realistic examination of the facts being presented and to answering truthfully. He is not being honest if he lets thought for his honesty keep him from an honest application of every faculty to his job of serving his client.

For honesty and sincerity do not imply that the expert should take a detached or disinterested view of the case. Before deciding to accept employment he should do so, until he has fully convinced himself of the righteousness of his client's cause, but having convinced himself and accepted employment, then his detachment should end and he should give everything he honestly can to winning the case. Once he enters the case he should cease to be an observer and become a partisan; unless he does so—unless he makes his client's cause his own—he will not be worth his fee. He should not let his partisanship affect his judgment or his perspective or lead him to distort facts or to draw too favorable conclusions from them—to do so would be a poor service to his client and might lead to disaster in court—but his heart should be in his client's honest success.

Familiarize Witness with Case

If he is an enthusiastic partisan, as he should be, he will not be content to sit silently on the side lines until waved into the game and then when his own special play is completed race off to the showers. He will want to participate in as much of the planning and playing of the game as his qualifications permit. He will not rest with the thorough preparation of his own testimony or even with the most complete possible understanding of the other testimony to be offered and its interrelationship with his own; he will also want to know as much as he can about the underlying theory of the case.

I have known a witness to hold that his job was confined to giving certain facts and opinions, and that the law of the case, or for that matter its conduct or even its objective, were no concern of his. Such an attitude is on all fours with that of the workman who drops his tools when the whistle blows, heedless of what the sudden interruption may do to the job in hand. An expert witness is not retained to present facts and opinions in the abstract; he is retained to present facts and opinions in their relation to and as part of a case that his client is trying to establish. It is his business—and obligation—to try to shoot his testimony into the net, and how can he do it unless he knows the rules and the strategy of the game as well as what can be expected from the other players?

Perhaps a word of warning is needed at this point. However much he may know or think he knows about the case, the expert witness should remember that the ultimate responsibility is with the lawyer, and that counsel's word is final as to the conduct of the case. Let the expert present his views as forcibly as he may in the preliminary conferences; let him argue and plead to the point of being a pest if he wishes; but when the lawyer's final decision has been made, it must and should govern. The lawyer is the coach; the expert, after all, is merely a player on the team. He should never let himself forget it.

Selection of Witness

We have been taking it for granted that the expert is qualified and competent. We may continue to do so, else why would he have been retained? Would it be presumptuous, however, to make a suggestion or two to counsel?

First, if you must choose between thorough knowledge of the particular subject-matter and a big reputation, take the knowledge rather than the reputation—and take both if you can get them. I doubt that judges or juries are as much impressed as lawyers sometimes think by big names as such, but reputation is usually accompanied by the breadth of knowledge and the varied experience that properly give weight to opinion. If the case is sufficiently important, a man with wide experience and an established reputation is likely to be a good investment, either to carry the main burden or to supplement and confirm the testimony of the men who lack the reputation and experience but have more intimate knowledge of the facts. But if a choice must be made, take the man who best knows the facts, even though he has less renown.

Second, if a man is brought in from outside, give him time to become thoroughly familiar with the particular case, so that his opinions will be based on facts before the court instead of being theories from hypothetical assumptions. If the basic factual evidence is being prepared by other men, call him in, if possible, in time for him to participate in its preparation. The conviction that will be added to his testimony should more than pay for any additional cost.

Clarity of Expression

Returning to what the expert witness should require of himself: Next to sincerity, professional competence, and loyalty to his clients I would put clarity of presentation. Expert testimony is offered to inform and persuade those before whom it is given, whether judge, jury, commission, or investigating committee, and to be either informed or persuaded one must understand. Unless expert testimony is understood, at least the essentials of it, it might as well not be given. And the key to understanding is simplicity.

The expert should remember that he is not addressing a meeting of his fellow scientists or technologists or even lecturing to graduate students. His job is to make something clear to men to whom the subject is new and strange, and about which they are likely to have the skepticism and antagonism that most of us feel toward things beyond our comprehension. He must bring his subject-matter within their comprehension, and must do it so simply and with such freedom from condescension that their skepticisms and antagonisms will be replaced by interest and then by belief.

The art of doing this is the art of all good exposition, namely, putting oneself in the other fellow's position. Consciously or unconsciously the expert witness should say to himself, "If I were Judge A or Commissioner B or Juror C, what would I know about this subject; what foundation would I have on which to build an understanding of it; what facts and what form of presentation would build that understanding most easily and quickly; what symbols and analogies would make it most vivid to me?" From the time he starts preparing his material to the time he steps off the stand, everything he does should be checked against the query, "If I were in his place, would I be getting this?" If the answer is no, the witness should promptly back up and put in whatever material or explanation is necessary. Telling a man something he doesn't comprehend is worse than wasting time; it is all too likely to create hostility.

This involves thorough preparation and digestion of the material to be presented. Simplicity and clarity should not be left to extemporization; they should be planned. This does not mean, of course, that the testimony need be written out or memorized or rehearsed; it does mean that the witness should so master his material and so break it down into its simplest terms that he can present his testimony and answer any question simply, clearly, and without going beyond the depth to which he has already taken his audience.

Illustrate and Simplify Wherever Possible

In planning his presentation he should not forget that most of us grasp things new and strange more quickly by eye than by ear. Graphic presentation, by means of charts, diagrams, maps, sketches, and photographs, properly explained, is often the most effective presentation. Here again simplicity should be the watchword. Most of us are prone to make graphs that only our professional brethren can grasp; graphs from which a number of facts or factors can be read. Graphs for presentation in court should be as clear and simple as a newspaper war map. If a number of factors need presentation, give a graph to each, and be sure that they start with A and come out with X, so that in reading them the reader is never more than one step beyond what he has already learned. And every graph should be big enough and bold enough so that everything on it can be easily seen by everyone concerned.

How about technical terms? The expert should use them, by all means. He is talking to grown men, not children. Men recognize the need for special terms to convey special concepts, and they will appreciate being let in on their use, provided the terms are used to clarify and not to mystify. The witness who uses technical terms to impress a jury will impress them, all right, but not in the way that he hopes. The expert should use whatever technical terms will help his hearers to comprehend his testimony, and not one more. Whatever terms are used must, of course, be explained, and as a rule it is better to describe the thing or concept first and then give the technical term, rather than to use the technical term and then attempt to define it.

If a man really puts himself in the shoes of those he is expected to convince, he will avoid the biggest sin an expert witness can commit, the sin of "talking down." If because of his special knowledge in his own field he thinks himself Mr. Big among the pygmies, he may come off the stand feeling like Mr. Martyr among the lions. He is not Teacher talking to the first grade; he is talking to intelligent men who may be as good in their specialties as he is in his. They happen not to have been educated in his branch of knowledge any more than he has been in theirs. It is his job to pass on to them some of his special education, as he would want them to do with him if the positions were reversed, without condescension or mental arrogance. A decent humility is as becoming in the witness box as it is anywhere else.

Conclusion

These, then, it seems to me, are the things that a man should require of himself if he goes on the stand as an expert: Honesty so sincere that it will permit no evasion, wholehearted partisanship in his client's cause, interest in every aspect of the case in which he is qualified to be helpful, readiness to abide by the decisions of counsel, such thoroughness of preparation and such ability to put himself in the position of judge or juror or commissioner that he can make his evidence clear to them, and such freedom from condescension or arrogance that he creates friendliness rather than hostility toward his client's case. These requirements do not seem impossible or immoderate; they should be within the capacity of every professional man of reasonable ability and experience. Why, then, are so many hard words said about the expert witness? I do not know. Perhaps all of them are said by opposing counsel.

Your witness, gentlemen.

This article was adapted from 3 Schweitzer, Trial Guide 1524, Baker, Voorhis & Co., Inc., New York (1945), which was adapted from the American Bar Association Journal, December, 1943.

Defense Psychology in Negligence Cases

By Harry J. Kelly

The title of my discussion is given as "Defense Psychology." It is always well to define and limit our terms. Psychology is generally defined as the science of the mind; systematic knowledge and investigation of the powers and functions of the mind. After analyzing this definition, I find that it doesn't exactly express the idea that I shall try to convey to you today, so with your permission I will substitute the term "strategy" for "psychology."

While some of the suggestions which I am about to advance apply generally to the defense of all types of actions, most of them apply specifically to the defense of negligence actions. The trial of a negligence action does not commence when you enter the jury room to select your jury. Much less after the jury has been selected and you have opened your case to the court and the jury. The trial of a negligence action commences at the very moment that you are retained. I appreciate that ninety per cent of the negligence actions that are tried in our courts are defended by attorneys representing insurance companies. I appreciate further that the defense attorney seldom gets the case until it has been well investigated by trained insurance investigators.

Probably the first knowledge the defense attorney has of the action is when the summons and complaint, together with the investigation file, is delivered to him. Occasionally, however, the attorney is retained directly by the defendant. Such retainers, however, will become less frequent in some States because of the Financial Responsibility Acts which, while not compelling the motorist to take out insurance, yet make such a step almost indispensable for proper protection.

The strategy of defending the individual or personal client will not differ materially from that used in defending the insurance-covered case, save in one respect, and that is in the preliminary investigation and marshalling of facts.

Investigation

A client calls you on the telephone and advises that he has had an accident resulting in injuries to third persons, and states that he has no insurance or that his insurance has lapsed. He probably has put off consulting you until he has been served with a summons and complaint. You have him come to your office immediately.

From this point to the day of trial the work of the defendant's lawyer is very similar to that of the plaintiff's lawyer. Take a complete statement from the defendant and have him sign it. Don't take your client's word that he has witnesses who will testify to such and such a state of facts. Make him produce those witnesses, reduce their statements to writing, and have them sign those statements.

Above all, one of the perquisites of proper preparation is that the defendant's lawyer, as soon as possible, visit the scene of the accident, familiarize himself with the landmarks and familiarize himself with the geographical layout. I know of nothing so demonstrative of poor preparation as to have an attorney get up in court and question a witness and not know which street runs north and south and which runs east and west. He should know the locality. He should take his witnesses with him to the scene and have them point out to him where they stood and what their position was when the accident happened. Measurements should be made in the presence of the witnesses and if possible the witnesses should personally make notes to refresh their recollections at some future date.

Before dismissing the client and witnesses they should be instructed not to give any statements concerning the accident and above all not to discuss it with some pleasant person who may be accompanied by a stenographer who will take the entire conversation in shorthand. One thoughtless statement, taken in shorthand and transcribed, may, upon cross-examination, ruin an otherwise perfect defense.

Examination of Pleadings

Next in importance is to examine the pleadings. Be sure that the plaintiff has stated a cause of action, and if you are not satisfied that he has stated sufficiently definite facts concerning the alleged negligence of your client, then consider a demand for a bill of particulars as to the specific acts of negligence, as to the ordinances and statutes, and any other laws it is claimed that your client violated.

Carefully prepare your answer, admitting such allegations of the complaint as are immaterial, or which in honesty should be admitted, try to reduce the issues as narrowly as possible. If your client was injured or suffered property damage, by all means interpose a counterclaim on his behalf. You thereby anticipate and refute an argument often advanced by attorneys for the plaintiff, that if defendant honestly felt that he was not negligent and that plaintiff was, why didn't he counterclaim for his damages?

Injuries

Two perplexing questions present themselves in connection with injuries. First, should you have the plaintiff examined by an expert medical witness? There are many instances in which you have definite information of the nature and extent of the injuries. You know the attending physician to be ethical and scrupulously honest.

Try to obtain from the plaintiff's attorney a copy of the attending physician's report. If it corroborates your previous information it behooves you not to have an examination, for by doing so you only tend to emphasize the injuries and perhaps call attention to symptoms and conditions that might otherwise be forgotten.

The second question to be answered is, should a bill of particulars of the injuries and special damages or monetary losses be demanded? If your information on these questions is meagre and unsatisfactory and the pleadings are verified, the answer is yes. It is, however, to be remembered that when the plaintiff's attorney prepared the bill of particulars he isn't going to leave anything out of that bill of particulars.

He will put in a great many things that perhaps the plaintiff himself or herself had forgotten about, trivial injuries that have passed away, but with the bill of particulars everything is put in down to the last twenty-five cents spent for a box of Band-Aids. During the trial of the action the plaintiff's attorney has before him that bill of particulars, and if the plaintiff neglects to testify as to any of these items, you may rest assured that the attorney can't forget them because they are right there in writing before him.

Trial Memoranda

Of paramount importance is the preparation of a trial memorandum for the court, a brief statement of your facts, a memorandum pointing out the statutes, the ordinances, whether they are the Vehicle and Traffic Law, Labor Law, Tenement House Law, whatever statutes or ordinances are applicable to your case—include them in your memorandum of law. Cite the leading cases in support of your contentions.

Months may pass between the time you prepare the trial memorandum and the time the case reaches trial. During that time read the new decisions. It is no task every week or every two weeks to pick up the reports of the new decisions and read through them; if there is a case in point, make a note of it, and place it in your file, and bring your memorandum down to the date of trial. It is surprising how much these memoranda of law are appreciated by the trial courts.

There are some judges who may require and request you to submit to them all the statutes and all ordinances which you claim have any application. I admonish you that if you have failed to give those statutes and ordinances to him, and at the conclusion of his charge you make a request that he charge with respect to certain statutes and ordinances not included in your memorandum, that your request may be granted but not in a manner which will be very helpful to your cause.

Witnesses

You are advised by your clerk that the action will be reached for trial in a few days. Again visit the scene of the accident. Bring in your witnesses, and discuss the case with them. I like to make it a practice of having the witness tell me what he remembers of the accident before showing him his statement. I like to test his memory.

I like to test his ability to describe certain facts without reference to the written word, because if it isn't written out by the client or the witness, the verbiage of the man who takes the statement creeps in. Permit your clients and witnesses to describe things in their own way and if they have omitted some salient features, why then give them their statements and let them read them, and, above all, before you go to court instruct your witnesses that if they are asked if they have ever talked about the case to say "yes," that they have given you a statement, and if they are asked if they have read the statement, let them say "yes," truthfully, because you have given them the statement to read when they are in your office.

You have your witnesses before you and you try to evaluate the effectiveness of their testimony. How are you going to place them on the witness stand? Again I repeat that your strategy is very similar to that of the plaintiff. Use a good witness first. I like to keep the best witness for the last, because his is the final impression that you are going to leave with the jury, and if possible make him a disinterested witness. S. Burton Heath observed, "By the time a modern trial gets into the law books, all the juice has been squeezed out, and little remains of the human warmth and affection and sympathy and indignation."

It is with this human warmth, sympathy, affection and indignation that you must present your client's cause to the jury so that it may be viewed in the light of human understanding rather than as a cold legal abstract entity.

I remember years ago when I first started the practice of law that most defendants' trial attorneys were trying their cases for the books. Exceptions were taken to everything; at the least little deviation from the hard and fast rules of hearsay testimony, leading questions, conclusions, etc., whether of materiality or no, there was an immediate objection and exception. The records were rife with these objections and exceptions.

What shall I do with my witnesses? Shall I bring them to the courtroom with me from the commencement of the action? Shall I let them sit there and listen to what the plaintiff and his witnesses have to say? You know that some people are very impressionable. If you find that you have a witness who tells a fair story, but you are afraid, perhaps, that if he sits in the court and listens to the plaintiff's case, he might be impressed and perhaps falter, keep him out of the courtroom until you are ready to go on with your direct case.

On the other hand, you may have a witness who is not too enthusiastic about the case, probably resents having been called down to appear and testify, yet who on paper gives a version favorable to your client. Bring him over and let him listen to the statements and the story told by the plaintiff's witnesses, and if they differ from his, he may take it as a personal affront to his honesty and make for you a very much stronger witness.

Selection of the Jury

The time has come to select the twelve men and women who are to decide whether or not your client did or failed to do any or all of the things charged by the plaintiff and if so, the amount he shall be called upon to pay to the injured party.

You have before you a list of the jurors from which the selection is to be made. It is a common practice among lawyers for both plaintiffs and defendants, to keep records of past performances of the individual juror. I question very seriously the efficacy of such records. Your record may show that John Jones sat on a jury which rendered a verdict of $20,000 in favor of a plaintiff. Should you, representing the defendant, excuse him? He may have consistently voted a very small amount of damages. Again the case in which the verdict was rendered may have been worth considerably more. Your record shows none of these things and therefore does not furnish adequate information upon which you may base a sound judgment as to the individual juror's qualifications.

Your examination of the jurors is your first opportunity to impress them with your own personality and the merits of your client's cause. Listen most attentively to the questions asked by the plaintiff's attorney. Listen attentively to the answers given, so that when it comes your turn to question these jurors you won't have to repeat the questions, and won't have to ask them to repeat the answers which they may have previously given.

If possible, try to remember the names of your jurors. You have time to do it while the plaintiff's attorney is examining, and I know of nothing that makes a better impression on a jury than to address each by name without referring to any list. If you have impressed the jury with your ability to remember, the jury is more apt to accept any statement you make in summation concerning the testimony of a witness than they are that of your opponent who has not exhibited the same facility of memory.

Jurors appreciate humor and witticisms. Never practice humor or attempt witticisms at the expense of a juror. If your opponent attempts to be humorous with you, don't try to be just a little bit funnier. If anything, go to the other extreme and show the jury that this to you is a serious matter, not to be trifled with.

Before you question your individual jurors, tell them briefly what the case is about, what type of an action it is, where it happened, the date, parties involved and names of the doctors, and refrain from questioning the jurors before giving them this background. They will be able to answer your questions much more intelligently.

The less involved your questions are to the jurors the better. Do not ask them if they are in accord with certain principles of law, or if they believe that such and such a principle of law should be upheld. They would not have qualified as jurors unless they had taken the oath to uphold and support the laws of the State.

Neither should a juror be asked directly if he is prejudiced against a certain type of action, or class of people. No juror wants to admit a prejudice. It is more diplomatic if you know a prejudice exists in the mind of a juror to ask him if he would rather not sit on this type of case without inference of prejudice.

There are no hard and fast rules for accepting or excusing jurors. There are some general propositions, however, which do apply. If you are trying a case involving a pedestrian and an automobile driver, excuse from your jury anyone who has never driven a car. If you are representing a trucking concern, keep any juror who is directly or indirectly engaged in the transportation business. In the event that your client is a corporation, reject bank tellers and bank clerks, accountants, or any person who is accustomed to handle large sums of money on behalf of others.

Certain characteristics are common to people of the same nationalities. The Irishman is generous and sentimental, the Scotsman is thrifty and close, the Italian is emotional and liberal. Whether you will accept a juror with whose national characteristics you are familiar depends largely upon the nature of the case you are trying and the personalities involved.

When the proposition was advanced to qualify women for jury service, I believe most defense attorneys anticipated the event with some misapprehension. Any that they may have had should by now be dispelled. When a woman accepts jury duty she does so voluntarily; as a result our women jurors are for the most part of more than average intelligence and have a keen sense of their responsibilities. I have found that women listen very attentively to all of the evidence and are much quicker to discover the false note than are men.

Women base their verdicts upon the evidence and upon the literal charge of the court. I have found them to be more patient than men, less inclined to permit sympathy or prejudice to influence their verdicts and more inclined to debate a proposition fully than to take the easiest and quickest way out by compromise. Many men who have sat on a jury with women are high in their praise of the reasonableness with which women approach a question, and it is my opinion that a beneficial influence has been reflected in verdicts by mixed juries.

The Trial Proper

The plaintiff opens his case. Listen to the opening. Make notes of what the plaintiff expects to prove. It is your turn to open. Just what shall you say in your opening? Again I say, make your opening statement on your opening clear and concise. Don't divulge too much of the evidence that you expect to produce. You may have some very important evidence with which you are quite certain the plaintiff's attorney is not aware. Don't disclose it in your opening. A clever plaintiff's attorney will have an answer to that before he has finished his case. Save it until the last.

You have had two opportunities to address the jury. You have talked to them once while you were selecting them, and you have talked to them in your opening. You will have another during summation. In the meantime, forget your jury. Don't look at your jury every time a strong point comes out in the testimony and don't address your questions to the jury. Address all of your questions directly to the witnesses. It is the answer of the witnesses and not your questions which are to decide the law suit.

Cross-examination

Probably no part of trial procedure is more overdone than cross-examination. Make your cross-examination as brief as possible. You know whether or not a witness is telling the truth.

You can perhaps tell it from the information that you have in your file. Leave a truthful witness alone.

Don't have him repeat over and over again for the benefit of the jury the very telling statements which he has made on his direct examination. If you can obtain from him the admission of but one fact that you want or expect to prove, drop him there. Leave that last impression with the jury. He has testified to something in favor of the defendant. It may not be terribly important, but nevertheless it is very helpful.

Your file may contain evidence that the plaintiff or one of his or her witnesses has been convicted of a crime involving moral turpitude. This evidence can be used for the sole purpose of attacking the credibility of the witness. Hesitate a long time before you use it. Bringing it to the attention of the jury may have the very opposite effect.

None of us are such paragons of virtue that we would relish having our past fully disclosed to our fellowman. Because a man has transgressed the civil law or the Ten Commandments does not necessarily make him unworthy of belief. The pain that he suffers, the money that he pays out to doctors, hospitals and nurses and the wages that he loses are the same as pain suffered and the money paid out or lost in wages by the saint.

I recall a case that was tried only a short time ago. The plaintiff, a lady, had a record of three divorces. The defendant's attorney on cross-examination and in summation made much of these three divorces, inferring that something must be radically wrong with such a woman. Unfortunately for the defense there was sitting in the jury box a lady who had just completed her third divorce and taken on a fourth husband.

It is not necessary to make use of all of the information contained in your file.

I had a very sad experience in this respect about a year and a half ago. A kindly old Irish lady had been injured in a street car accident and her case was being tried. She had had two previous claims against the Street Railway Company. Her subjective symptoms following each of the three accidents were identical. The objective injuries sustained in the accident that we were trying didn't amount to very much. She complained of a strained knee, shock and a few minor bruises, all of which had cleared up, but the memory lingered on, and it appeared to me that she was grossly exaggerating her complaints.

On cross-examination to demonstrate to the jury that she was claim-wise, I examined her concerning her previous claims, one of which, ten years prior to the trial, had been settled for $500. The file reflected that on that occasion she had sustained a wrenched shoulder which had cleared up at the time of examination by a physician for the company.

The cross-examination was about as follows: "Well, Mrs. Murphy, this isn't the first time you have made a claim against the International Railway Company, is it?" She answered, "No, sir." "You have had two previous accidents, haven't you?" "I know, I know, yes. One little one." "You had one about ten years ago, didn't you?" and she said, "Yes." "You got $500.00 for that accident, didn't you?" And with that she ripped open her shirtwaist and cried, "Sure, and look what they done to me." And at the top of her shoulder was a cyst as large as a football. Her doctor had been on the stand and hadn't mentioned the presence of the cyst. The examining physician for the company, who had a splendid reputation, testified that he had seen the cyst when he examined her and that it had no relation to an accidental injury. The harm had been done, she obtained a verdict three times the true value of her actual injuries. Beware of the nature and extent of your cross-examination.

Protect your own witness as far as possible from an unfair cross-examination, but do not give the jury the impression that the witness needs protection. You may hear what you think is a misquote on the part of the plaintiff's attorney in questioning your witness on testimony given by him on direct examination. Unless you are positive that the plaintiff's attorney has misstated the testimony, don't make a point of it, because I know of nothing more harmful than to have the plaintiff's attorney say, "Well, if your Honor please, may the stenographer read back that testimony?" You score another hit for the plaintiff if the reading of the testimony proves you to have been in error.

You have had a physical examination of the plaintiff. Should you call your doctor to testify as to his findings? If the attending physician has been fair and honest in his testimony and there is little discrepancy between his prognosis and that given by your doctor in his written report it is better that your doctor be left off the stand, for his testimony will be but a repetition of that given by plaintiff's physician and will only tend to emphasize the nature and extent of the injuries.

I had not forgotten that at the close of the plaintiff's case it is customary for the defendant to move for a nonsuit. I delayed discussion of this move so that it could be considered in connection with the defendant's motion for a direction of a verdict. Make your motions to save your exception, but unless you have good and sufficient grounds for your motions refrain from arguing at too great length lest the denial of the motions by the court in the presence of the jury may detract from the effectiveness of the same arguments made on summation.

The Summation

In summation, once more you hold the center of the stage. Like your opening, let your summation be brief. Do not try to review the testimony in detail. Make certain that any quotation of testimony made by you is correct. Select the strength of your case and the weakness of your opponent's, argue these points, drive them home by repetition. They may be perfectly clear to you but this may have to be presented to the jury from several different angles before each of the individual jurors is fully cognizant of the logic of your reasoning. Anticipate as far as possible the arguments of your adversary, thus placing him on the defensive. The more time he is obliged to take in answering your arguments, the less time he will have to dwell on his affirmative case.

Don't attempt to half-heartedly explain away testimony obviously harmful to your contentions. Rather pass it over altogether, lest you emphasize your weakness rather than your strength.

No one can hope to attain even a modicum of success as a trial lawyer by reading books or listening to speeches, any more than one can hope to attain success in baseball through reading Spaulding's Baseball Guide or hearing Babe Ruth lecture on how to hit a home run. Success can be obtained only through practice and personal experience. Do not ape the mannerisms of Clarence Darrow or Max Steuer. Be yourself, make use of such natural gifts as have been bestowed upon you. If it is your nature to fight, well then, fight. If, on the other hand, a conciliatory manner more becomes you, that very manner may spell success for you.

Nothing that is contained herein should be construed as a hard and fast rule to be followed in every case. No matter how careful and complete your preparation, always be prepared to meet the exception to the rule. Judge Story, many years ago, summed up in a few lines advice that it behooves us all to follow:

"Spend not your words on trifles but condense;
Strike with the mass of thought, not drops of sense;
Press to the close with vigor, once begun
And leave (how hard the task!) leave off when done."

Adapted from 3 Schweitzer, Trial Guide 1531, Baker, Voorhis & Co., Inc., New York (1945).

Appellate Briefs and Oral Argument

I INSPIRATIONAL AND INTRODUCTION

Advocacy Before the Supreme Court: Suggestions for Effective Case Presentations

BY ROBERT H. JACKSON

MORE THAN TEN YEARS AGO, John W. Davis, in a wise and stimulating lecture on "The Argument of an Appeal," shared with our profession the lessons of his own rich experience. He suggested, however, that such a lecture should come from a judge—from one who is to be persuaded, rather than from an advocate. With characteristic felicity, he said: "Who would listen to a fisherman's weary discourse on fly-casting . . . if the fish himself could be induced to give his views on the most effective method of approach?" I cannot add to the available learning on this subject. I can only offer some meditations by one of the fish.

Let me confess that, when dangling bait before judges, I have not always practiced what I now preach. Many lessons that I pass on to you were learned the hard way in the years when I was intensively occupied with presentation of government litigations to the Court. And if I appear to overrate trifles, remember that a multitude of small perfections helps to set mastery of the art of advocacy apart from its counterfeit—mere forensic fluency.

Importance of Oral Argument Is Decisive

Lawyers sometimes question the value of the relatively short oral argument permitted in the Nation's highest Court. They ask whether it is not a vestigial formality with little effect on the result. In earlier times, with few cases on its docket, the Court could and did hear arguments that lasted for days, from such advocates as Webster, Pinkney, and Luther Martin. Over the years the time allotted for hearing has been shortened, but its importance has not diminished. The significance of the trend is that the shorter the time, the more precious is each minute.

I think the Justices would answer unanimously that now, as traditionally, they rely heavily on oral presentations. Most of them form at least a tentative conclusion from it in a large percentage of the cases. This is not to say that decisions are wholly at the peril of first impressions. Indeed, deliberation never ceases and there is no final commitment until decision actually is announced. It is a common experience that a Justice is assigned to write an opinion for the Court in accordance with a view he expressed in conference, only to find from more intensive study that it was mistaken. In such circumstances, an inadequate argument would have lost the case, except that the writing Justice rescues it. Even then, his change of position may not always be persuasive with his colleagues and loss of a single vote may be decisive. The Bar must make its preparations for oral argument on the principle that it always is of the highest, and often of controlling, importance.

Who Should Present the Argument?

If my experiences at the Bar and on the Bench unite in dictating one imperative, it is: Never divide between two or more counsel the argument on behalf of a single interest. Sometimes conflicting interests are joined on one side and division is compelled, but otherwise it should not be risked.

When two lawyers undertake to share a single presentation, their two arguments at best will be somewhat overlapping, repetitious and incomplete and, at worst, contradictory, inconsistent and confusing. I recall one misadventure in division in which I was to open the case and expound the statute involved, while counsel for a government agency was to follow and explain the agency's regulations. This seemed a natural place to sunder the argument. But the Court perversely refused to honor the division. So long as I was on my feet, the Justices were intensely interested in the regulations, which I had not expected to discuss. By the time my associate took over, they had developed a lively interest in the statute, which was not his part of the case. No counsel should be permitted to take the floor in any case who is not willing to master and able to present every aspect of it. If I had my way, the Court rules would permit only one counsel to argue for a single interest. But while my colleagues think such a rule would be too drastic, I think they all agree that an argument almost invariably is less helpful to us for being parceled out to several counsel.

Selection of leading counsel often receives a consideration after the case arrives at the high Court that would have been more rewarding before the trial. But when the case is docketed in the Supreme Court, the question is, shall counsel who conducted the case below conduct its final review? If not, who shall be brought in?

Convincing presentations often are made by little-known lawyers who have lived with the case through all courts. However, some lawyers, effective in trial work, are not temperamentally adapted to less dramatic appellate work. And sometimes the trial lawyer cannot forego bickering over petty issues which are no longer relevant to aspects of the case reviewable by the Supreme Court. When the trial attorney lacks dispassionate judgment as to what is important on appeal, a fresh and detached mind is likely to be more effective.

No lawyer, otherwise fairly equipped for his profession, need hesitate to argue his own case in the Supreme Court merely because he has not appeared in that Court before. If he will conform his argument to the nature of its review and his preparation to the habits of the Court, he has some advantages over a lawyer brought in at that late stage. Sometimes even his handicap will work out to his advantage. Some years ago, a country lawyer arguing a tax case gleaned from baffling questions from the bench that his case was not going well. He closed by saying, "I hope you will agree with me, because if you don't, I certainly am in wrong with my best client." Such a plea is not enough to win a decision, but its realism would assure a most sympathetic hearing from any judge who can still remember what it is to face and explain to a defeated client.

Many litigants, and not a few lawyers, think it is some advantage to have their case sponsored by a widely known legal reputation. If such counsel is selected because of his professional qualifications, I have nothing to say against that. Experience before the Supreme Court is valuable, as is experience in any art. One who is at ease in its presence, familiar with its practice, and aware of its more recent decisions and divisions, holds some advantage over the stranger to such matters. But it is a grave mistake to choose counsel for some supposed influence or the enchantment of political reputation, and, above all, avoid the lawyer who thinks he is so impressively eminent that he need give no time to preparation except while he is on a plane going to Washington. Believe me when I say that what impresses the Court is a lawyer's argument, not his eminence.

On your first appearance before the Court, do not waste your time or ours telling us so. We are likely to discover for ourselves that you are a novice but will think none the less of you for it. Every famous lawyer had his first day at our Bar, and perhaps a sad one. It is not ingratiating to tell us you think it is an overwhelming honor to appear, for we think of the case as the important thing before us, not the counsel. Some attorneys use time to thank us for granting the review, or for listening to their argument. Those are not intended as favors and it is good taste to accept them as routine performance of duty. Be respectful, of course, but also be self-respectful, and neither disparage yourself nor flatter the Justices. We think well enough of ourselves already.

The time may come when you will be sought out to argue a case for other lawyers. In that event, you should consider whether it is not due yourself to insist on full responsibility for its presentation. Divided command is as disastrous to a litigation as to a military campaign. Either you will be in control of the litigation or someone else will be in control of your professional reputation. Some of the wisest leaders of the Bar decline to participate in a case, even with most amiable and reputable associates, unless they are given undivided command.

The claim recently was given publicity that leading members of the Bar refused professional employment in support of the

Communist challenge to the constitutionality of the Smith Act. Every accused person has a constitutional right to counsel and there is a correlative duty on the part of the Bar to see that every accused, no matter how unpopular, is represented competently. In addition to this sense of duty, many eminent lawyers would welcome the professional challenge involved in that case. Knowing this, I examined with care the allegations filed in the Supreme Court that the Communists could not get counsel. They did not disclose that any so-called leader of the Bar had been asked, or would be allowed, to assume full responsibility for argument of the case. The most that appeared was that they were asked to associate themselves with attorneys who were in control of it and whose conduct of it already had resulted in a sentence for contempt. No American lawyer is under a duty to become the tail to another lawyer's kite, or to submit himself to control of counsel or clients whose tactics in the case he does not approve. No lawyer becomes too eminent to consult and cooperate with other members of our brotherhood, but those who, by a lifetime of hard work and fair dealing, earn enviable reputations at the Bar rightly reject any employment that will impair that independence of judgment and freedom of action which becomes an officer of the Court. He is not obliged to become anyone's mere hired hand.

Selection of Questions Is Test of Discriminating Advocate

One of the first tests of a discriminating advocate is to select the question, or questions, that he will present orally. Legal contentions, like the currency, depreciate through over-issue. The mind of an appellate judge is habitually receptive to the suggestion that a lower court committed an error. But receptiveness declines as the number of assigned errors increases. Multiplicity hints at lack of confidence in any one. Of course, I have not forgotten the reluctance with which a lawyer abandons even the weakest point lest it prove alluring to the same kind of judge. But experience on the bench convinces me that multiplying assignments of error will dilute and weaken a good case and will not save a bad one.

If you are called in after assignments of error have been filed, or feel impelled to raise many in your brief, at least forego oral argument of all but one or two. The impact of oral presentation will be strengthened if it is concentrated on a few points that can be simply and convincingly stated and easily grasped and retained.

The successful advocate will recognize that there is some weakness in his case and will squarely and candidly meet it. If he lost in the court below and needs appellate relief, that fact alone strongly suggests some defect in his position. If he is responding to a writ of certiorari, he should realize that several Justices have been tentatively impressed that the judgment below is dubious or in conflict with that of other courts, otherwise certiorari would not have been granted. The petitioner should never dodge or delay but give priority to answering the reasons why he lost below. The respondent should ask himself what doubts probably brought the case up and answer them. Each will then be covering the questions that the Justices are waiting to hear answered. To delay meeting these issues is improvident; to attempt evasion of them is fatal.

The order and progression of an argument are important to its ready comprehension, but in the Supreme Court these are not wholly within the lawyer's control. It is difficult to please nine different minds, and it is a common experience that questions upset the plan of argument before the lawyer has fairly started. I used to say that, as Solicitor General, I made three arguments of every case. First came the one that I planned—as I thought, logical, coherent, complete. Second was the one actually presented—interrupted, incoherent, disjointed, disappointing. The third was the utterly devastating argument that I thought of after going to bed that night.

Justices Are Much Given To Interrogation of Counsel

I can offer no formula that will guarantee unbroken argument, for the Supreme Court is much given to interrogation. Perhaps the opening argument will have the best chance for an uninterrupted interlude if counsel will begin with a concise history of the case, state the holding of the court below and wherein it is challenged. He should follow with a careful statement of important facts, and conclude with discussion of the law. Argument for a respondent is more variable. Sometimes it may be necessary to restate the case and establish justification for the decision below. At other times it may be more effective to strike a few selected weak spots in appellant's attack upon the judgment.

Most Contentions of Law Are Won or Lost on Facts

For whichever side he appears, the choice of his materials and arrangement of its sequence will test the skill of the most experienced craftsman. The purpose of a hearing is that the Court may learn what it does not know, and it knows least about the facts. It may sound paradoxical, but most contentions of law are won or lost on the facts. The facts often incline a judge to one side or the other. A large part of the time of conference is given to discussion of facts, to determine under what rule of law they fall. Dissents are not usually rooted in disagreement as to a rule of law but as to whether the facts warrant its application. Sometimes facts are best unfolded chronologically, and at other times it will be more effective to assemble them about particular topics. The presentation is sometimes aided by maps and charts, which counsel is at liberty to use. Courage to drop irrelevant or unimportant details and to avoid becoming entangled in interesting or hotly contested questions which do not go to the result is an aid to clarity.

Counsel must remember that the function of the Supreme Court is to decide only questions of law. If the appellant, or petitioner, attempts, or so puts his facts that he appears to be attempting, to reargue a verdict or findings of fact, he will meet with an embarrassing judicial impatience. Both sides should strive so to present the questions of law that it will be clear they are not depending upon a reweighing of conflicting evidence.

Oral argument may be simplified by integration with the brief. Some issues are technical and must be resolved by study of exact language in statutes, patent claims, or the like. Such precision is more readily communicated if the eye of the judge is called to the aid of his ear. Some counsel meet this problem by making a brief general statement of their ultimate contention and requesting the Court to consult the brief for the close analysis in its support. Others fully expound their contention orally, reading the decisive language, requesting the Justices to follow it for themselves, and pointing out the page in the record or briefs where it is to be found.

In discussing questions of law, the advocate must sometimes hazard a guess as to how much of the law applicable to his case the judges already know. He is too polite—and discreet—to enter upon a long legal exposition that will insinuate a lack of judicial acquaintance with elementary propositions. On the other hand, it is his duty not to risk omission of the many matters that judges are presumed to know but often do not.

It does not seem to me safe ever to assume that a judge is able to recall exact words of a statute or a document, even if he is known to be familiar with its general terms. Statutory language is artificial, elusive and difficult to carry in mind. Dates, relationships to the case of persons named, and other details escape memory.

But I should make the contrary assumption about the Court's own precedents, particularly its recent precedents. I can think of no more dismal and fruitless use of time than to recite case after case, with explanations why each is, or is not, applicable. If the authority for your contention is a decision, of course you must make clear its meaning and application. But if the one or two best precedents will not convince, a score of weaker ones will only reveal the weakness of your argument. I always look with suspicion upon a proposition with a page full of citations in its support. And if the first decision cited does not support it, I conclude the lawyer has a blunderbuss mind and rely on him no further.

It would surprise you to know how frequently counsel undertake to expound a recent decision to the very men who made it. If the exposition is accurate, it adds nothing to the Court's knowledge and if it is not, it discredits counsel's perception or fairness. My advice is to presume judicial familiarity with recent decisions, accept them at full face value and read nothing more into them, and thereby avoid entanglement in any disagreements that may have occurred within the Court when they were written.

Now and then a lawyer invokes or quotes a dissent in aid of his cause. By identifying his contention with a recent dissent, he may close some minds to the rest of his argument. Of course, majority decisions are sometimes overruled and dissents become the law, but usually after considerable time has elapsed. If the overruling of a decision is all that will save you, go about asking it directly and candidly. But if your case can be supported by

Court decisions, it will not be wise to confound it with even a good quotation from a dissent. Sometimes counsel is confronted with the dilemma of inconsistent lines of authority where the Court has recently overruled its own not-very-old decision. In such cases, the sitting Justices are apt to be sharply divided as to which rule will apply to slightly varied facts. I have no advice to offer in this situation—you will just have to get out of that dilemma by your own wit.

Whether one will invoke extrajudicial writings or speeches of a sitting judge is a matter of taste—usually, I may say, of bad taste. I do not recall any instance in which it helped. A collegiate court entertains as many different views as it has colleagues. Individual expressions, such, for instance, as this lecture, may or may not accord with the views of other Justices, and reliance upon controversial writings of one Justice may alienate others. But if an individual judge is to be quoted, by all means let it be in matter-of-fact fashion and without tossing compliments to the writer, for nothing depreciates one's position more certainly and quickly than to fawn upon one of the judges whom he appears to think he can capture by flattery, and nothing is less welcome to the judge.

Regard for his professional standing will deter the lawyer from intentional misleading, but it is twice prudent not to quote out of context or ascribe a strained meaning to writings of a sitting judge. I have been, and I have seen other Justices, indignant at the distortion of some writing. It is hard to retrieve the confidence forfeited by seeking such an advantage.

The rules permit opening counsel, after making a fair opening, to reserve time for rebuttal. I would not say that rebuttal is never to be indulged. At times it supplies important and definite corrections. But the most experienced advocates make least use of the privilege. Many inexperienced ones get into trouble by attempting to renew the principal argument. One who returns to his feet exposes himself to an accumulation of questions. Cases have been lost that, before counsel undertook a long rebuttal, appeared to be won.

Aids to Delivery of the Argument Are Widely Varied

The manner of delivery must express the talents and habits of the advocate. No one method is indispensable to success, and practice varies widely. Few lawyers are gifted with memory and composure to argue a case without papers of any kind before them. It is not necessary to try. The memorized oration, or anything stilted and inflexible, is not appropriate. Equally objectionable is the opposite extreme—an unorganized, rambling discourse, relying on the inspiration of the moment. If one's oral argument is simply reading his printed brief aloud, he could as well stay at home. Almost as unsatisfying is any argument that has been written out and is read off to us, page after page. We like to meet the eye of the advocate, and sometimes when one starts reading his argument from a manuscript he will be interrupted to wean him from his essay; but it does not often succeed. If you have confidence to address the Court only by reading to it, you really should not argue there.

The first step in preparation for all exigencies of argument is to become filled with your case—to know every detail of the evidence and findings, to weigh fairly every contention of your adversary, and to review not only the rule of law applicable to the specific issue but the body of law in its general field. You never know when some collateral or tangential issue will suddenly come up.

My practice was to prepare notes, consisting of headings and catch words rather than of details, to guide the order of argument and prevent important items from being overlooked. Such notes help to get back on the track if one is thrown off by interruptions. They will tend to limit rambling and irrelevance, give you some measure of confidence, and at the same time let you frequently meet your judges eye to eye.

Do not think it beneath you to rehearse for an argument. Not even Caruso, at the height of his artistic career, felt above rehearsing for a hundredth performance, although he and the whole cast were guided and confined by a libretto and a score. Of course, I do not suggest that you should declaim and gesture before a mirror. But, if you have an associate, try out different approaches and thrash out every point with him. Answer the questions that occur to another mind. See what sequence of facts is most effective. Accustom yourself to your materials in different arrangements. Argue the case to yourself, your client, your secretary, your friend, and your wife if she is patient. Use every available anvil on which to hammer out your argument.

If one is not familiar with the Court and its ways, it may be helpful to arrive a day or two early to observe its procedure, to see how the Court deals with counsel and how counsel gets on with the Court.

When the day arrives, shut out every influence that might distract your mind. An interview with an emotional client in difficulty may be upsetting. Friends who bear bad news may unintentionally disturb your poise. Hear nothing but your case, see nothing but your case, talk nothing but your case. If making an argument is not a great day in your life, don't make it; and if it is, give it everything in you.

By all means leave at home the associate who feels constantly impelled to tug at your coat tails, to push briefs in front of you, or to pass up unasked-for suggestions while you are speaking. These well-meant but ill-conceived offerings distract the attention of the Court, but they are even more embarrassing and confusing to counsel. The offender is an unmitigated pest, and even if he is the attorney who employed you, suppress him.

I doubt whether it is wise to have clients or parties in interest attend the argument if it can be avoided. Clients unfortunately desire, and their presence is apt to encourage, qualities in an argument that are least admired by judges. When I hear counsel launch into personal attacks on the opposition or praise of a client, I instinctively look about to see if I can identify the client in the room—and often succeed. Some counsel have become conspicuous for the gallery that listens to their argument and, when it is finished, ostentatiously departs. The case that is argued to please a client, impress a following in the audience, or attract notice from the press, will not often make a favorable impression on the Bench. An argument is not a spectacle.

You should be warned that, in acoustical properties, the Supreme Court chamber is wretched. If your voice is low, it burdens the hearing, and parts of what you say may be missed. On the other hand, no judge likes to be shouted at as if he were an ox. I know of nothing you can do except to bear the difficulty in mind, watch the Bench, and adapt your delivery to avoid causing apparent strain.

The time allotted to you will be one hour ordinarily, and half of that if the case is on summary docket. Time is sometimes, though rarely, extended in advance if the case appears to require it, but seldom do we find extended time of much help to the Court. In any event, do not waste time complaining that you do not have enough time. That is a confession of your own inadequacy to handle the case as the Court's experience indicates it should be. Keep account of your own time or, if you cannot, have an assistant do so. Some lawyers ask, and some even ask several times, how much time they have left and wait for it to be calculated. Why will a lawyer interrupt his effort to hold the attention of a Court to his argument in order to divert its mind to the clock? Successful advocacy will keep the Justices' minds on the case, and off the clock.

This, above all, remember: Time has been bestowed upon you, not imposed upon you. It will show confidence in yourself and in your case, and good management of your argument, if you finish before the signal stops you. On the other hand, if the warning that your time has expired catches you in the middle of an argument, the chances are that you have not made good economy of your time.

Agility and Diplomacy of Counsel Tested by Questions from Bench

The Supreme Court, more than most tribunals, is given to questioning counsel. Since all of the Justices gave the case preliminary consideration when certiorari was granted or jurisdiction was noted, tentative opinions or inquiries are apt to linger in their minds.

Questions usually seek to elicit information or to aid in advancing or clarifying the argument. A question argumentative in form should not be attributed to hostility, for oftentimes it is put, not to overbear counsel, but to help him sharpen his position. Now and then, of course, counsel may be caught in a cross-fire of questions between differing Justices, each endeavoring to bring out some point favorable to his own view of the law. That tests the agility and diplomacy of counsel.

Some lawyers feel an ill-concealed resentment at questions from the Bench. It is not hard to see that if they had the wit they would have the will to respond as did a British barrister in an incident related to me by Arthur Goodhart, K.B.E., K.C.: The judge said, "I have been listening to you now for four hours and I am bound to say I am none the wiser." The barrister replied:

"Oh, I know that, my Lord, but I had hoped you would be better informed."

A Justice may abruptly indicate conclusions which tempt a lawyer to reply as one did long ago in a local court in the country where I practiced. He had barely stated his contention when the judge said: "There is nothing to your proposition—just nothing to it." The lawyer drew himself up and said: "Your Honor, I have worked on this case for six weeks and you have not heard of it twenty minutes. Now, Judge, you are a lot smarter man than I am, but there is not that much difference between us."

But I always feel that there should be some comfort derived from any question from the bench. It is clear proof that the inquiring Justice is not asleep. If the question is relevant, it denotes he is grappling with your contention, even though he has not grasped it. It gives you opportunity to inflate his ego by letting him think he has discovered an idea for himself.

When I was at the Bar, it seemed to me that I could make no better use of my time than to answer any doubt which a judge would do me the favor to disclose. Experience in the Court teaches that a lawyer's best points are sometimes made by answers to pertinent and penetrating questions. A lively dialogue may be a swifter and surer vehicle to truth than a dismal monologue. The wise advocate will eagerly embrace the opportunity to put at rest any misconception or doubt which, if the judge waited to raise it in the conference room, counsel would have no chance and perhaps no one present would have the information to answer.

Some lawyers complain that questioning is overdone; and sometimes colloquy between Court and counsel is undoubtedly carried too far. If cases were uniformly well presented, perhaps the best results would be obtained if few questions were asked. Generally, an argument that from its very outset shows that it will be well-organized and thorough tends to ward off questions. At all events, nothing tests the skill of an advocate or endangers his position more than his answer to questions, and in nothing is experience, poise, and a disciplined mind a greater asset.

I advise you never to postpone answer to a question, for that always gives an impression of evasion. It is better immediately to answer the question, even though you do so in short form and suggest that you expect to amplify and support your answer later.

Counsel should be prepared to deal with any relevant question, but, if he is not, he ventures less by a frank admission that he does not know the answer than by a guess. Counsel need not fear that he will be prejudiced by declining to be drawn into a discussion of some proposition that is irrelevant to his case. To refuse might seem like a rebuff to the inquirer, but it may delight eight colleagues.

Many Counsel Adhere to Custom of Formal Morning Attire

It may seem a trivial matter, but I am told that one of the questions most frequently addressed to the Clerk's Office concerns the apparel in which counsel must, or should, appear. Formal dress is traditional and I understand once was required.

Some amusing stories of those days linger among Court attachés. It is said that Chief Justice Taft once refused admission to the Bar to a candidate who appeared without necktie or waistcoat, with the suggestion that he renew his application when properly attired. The Marshal's Office kept in active service, and still keeps in moth balls, one or two cutaway coats to lend to counsel in need. Apparently he was expected to be equipped with his own trousers.

Those days have passed away, but the tradition remains that appearance before the Court is no ordinary occasion. Government lawyers and many others, particularly older ones, adhere to the custom of formal morning dress. The Clerk's Office advises that either this or a dark business suit is appropriate. But the informality which permeates all official life has penetrated the Court. It lays down no rule for its Bar.

No toleration, however, can repeal the teaching of Polonius that "The apparel oft proclaims the man." You will not be stopped from arguing if you wear a race-track suit or sport a rainbow necktie. You will just create a first impression that you have strayed in at the wrong bar. For raiment of counsel, like the robe of the judge, is taken as somewhat symbolic of his function. In Europe the advocate, as well as the judge, is expected to robe for his appearance in court. The lawyer of good taste will not worry about his dress, because instinctively it will be that which is suitable to his station in life—a member of a dignified and responsible profession—and for an important and somewhat formal occasion.

What Remedies Are Open to Disappointed Lawyer?

In most courts the folklore of the profession gives the aggrieved lawyer a choice of remedies: One is to appeal, the other is to go down to the tavern and cuss out the court. He may, and usually does, pursue both simultaneously. But the tavern cussing of the Supreme Court has to be stronger than usual, to compensate for the lack of any appeal. In Washington it will be easy for a disappointed lawyer to find sympathetic companions. We are never surprised nor angered when disappointed counsel avails himself of the one relief left to him. Sometimes one or more dissenting Justices would like to join him.

I think it was Mr. Justice Brandeis who said that a judge often must decide a case as if he were 100 per cent convinced one way or the other, although usually he is not more than 55 per cent convinced. Many decisions prevail by a narrow margin of Justices and the decisive Justices admit a large margin of doubt. More than a few court opinions represent a compromise of reasoning, if not of result. While I recognize the annoyance to the Bar of dissenting and concurring opinions, I think they are the lesser of evils. A court opinion which puts out a misleading impression of unanimity by avoiding, or confusing, an underlying difference is a false beacon to the profession. Far better that the division be forthrightly exposed so that the profession will know on what narrow grounds the case rests and can form some estimate of how changed facts may affect the alignment in a subsequent case.

If you are inclined to think the Court has given too little time to your case, or too superficial consideration to your contention, it may be some comfort to know that in most cases I, for one, would agree with you. Few decisions are handed down to which I do not wish it were possible for me to give more time and study. From the viewpoint of the Bench, yours is but one of a dozen cases to be argued in the same week; it is but one of over two hundred cases to be decided on the merits during the term and is but one of a thousand or twelve hundred cases in which we have to pass on petitions for relief during the year. The printed pages filed in these cases are several times those which any judge, if he could give twenty-four hours a day to the task, would be able to read.

Some of the most thoroughly prepared men, by learning and practice, who have come upon the Supreme Court bench have found it necessary to "scorn delights and live laborious days" to satisfy their own sense of duty. Justices Brandeis and Cardozo were almost as retired as hermits and Chief Justice Hughes withdrew from all social engagements, except one night a week which he allowed Mrs. Hughes to bestow on their friends. Judges practicing self-denial under such pressure may well be impatient of surplusage, irrelevance, and professional incompetence.

The Art of Advocacy Is an Exacting One

So long as controversies between men have to be settled by judges, proficiency in the art of forensic persuasion will assure one of first rank in our high calling. In the judicial process, as practiced among English-speaking peoples, the judge and the advocate complement each other, for, as Thoreau said, "It takes two to speak the truth—one to speak and another to hear."

But if not a lost art, advocacy is an exacting one. When he rises to speak at the Bar, the advocate stands intellectually naked and alone. Habits of thought and speech cannot be borrowed like garments for the event. What an advocate gives to a case is himself; he can bring to the Bar only what is within him. A part written for him will never be convincing.

If you aspire to such a task, and I address particularly the younger men at the Bar and in the schools, do not let your preparation wait upon a retainer. There is not time to become an advocate after the important case comes to you. Webster, when asked as to the time he spent in preparing one of his memorable arguments, is said to have replied that his whole life was given to its preparation. So it is with every notable forensic effort.

The most persuasive quality in the advocate is professional sincerity. By that I do not mean that he believes in his case as the Mohammedan does in his Koran. But he must believe that under our adversary system both sides of every controversy should be worthily presented with vigor—even with partisan zeal—so that all material for judgment will be before the Court and its judgment will suffer no distortion. He must believe with all the intensity of his being in law as the framework of society, in the independent judicial function as the means for applying the law, and in the nobility of his profession as an aid in the judicial process. He will feel equal disdain for a judge partisan in his favor and one partisan in his opposition. The opportunist, the lawyer for revenue only, the cynic, will never reach the higher goal.

The effective advocate will not let mastery of a specialty foreclose that catholicity of interest essential to the rounded life and the balanced judgment. He will draw inspiration not alone from the literature of the law, but from the classics, history, the essay, the drama and poetry as well. It is one of the delights and intellectual rewards of the legal profession that it lays under tribute every science and every art. The advocate will read and reread the majestic efforts of leaders of his profession on important occasions, and linger over their manner of handling challenging subjects. He will stock the arsenal of his mind with tested dialectical weapons. He will master the short Saxon word that pierces the mind like a spear and the simple figure that lights the understanding. He will never drive the judge to his dictionary. He will rejoice in the strength of the mother tongue as found in the King James version of the Bible, and in the power of the terse and flashing phrase of a Kipling or a Churchill. And the advocate will have courage—courage to assert his conviction that the world is round, though all about him men of authority say it is flat. Most memorable professional achievements were in the face of opposition, abuse, even ridicule.

The advocate may be summoned often to other forums, but he will appear in the Supreme Court of the United States only when that tribunal has been satisfied that decision of his cause is important to the body of federal law. Emphasis on the public interest in a just and uniform legal system has submerged emphasis on special equities and individual interests which properly prevail in trial and intermediate courts.

Adequately and helpfully to present a case—as it is about to be transformed into a precedent to guide future courts, to settle the fate of unknown litigants, perhaps to become required reading for a rising generation of lawyers—will challenge and inspire the true advocate. Decisional law is a distinctive feature of our common-law system, a system which can exist only where men are free, lawyers are courageous and judges are independent. To participate as advocate in supplying the basis for decisional lawmaking calls for vision of a prophet, as well as a profound appreciation of the continuity between the law of today and that of the past. He will be sharing the task of reworking decisional law by which every generation seeks to preserve its essential character and at the same time to adapt it to contemporary needs. At such a moment the lawyer's case ceases to be an episode in the affairs of a client and becomes a stone in the edifice of the law.

As I view the procession of lawyers who pass before the Supreme Court, I often am reminded of an old parable. Once upon a time three stone masons were asked, one after the other, what they were doing. The first, without looking up, answered, "Earning my living." The second replied, "I am shaping this stone to pattern." The third lifted his eyes and said, "I am building a Cathedral." So it is with the men of the law at labor before the Court. The attitude and preparation of some show that they have no conception of their effort higher than to make a living. Others are dutiful but uninspired in trying to shape their little cases to a winning pattern. But it lifts up the heart of a judge when an advocate stands at the Bar who knows that he is building a Cathedral.

Adapted from Vol. 37, American Bar Association Journal (1951).

What Price Success on Appeal?

By Jacob Morgan

This is a brief review of the trials and tribulations of a successful appellant. There is a saying quite frequently voiced by both classes of litigants, winners and losers, victors and defeated, that "If you win, you lose; and if you lose, you win." There is considerable justification for this statement, more so now than in past years. In these days of long and expensive transcripts and printed briefs, appeals have become a luxury, available as a successful remedy or relief principally to those of financial means and ample patience, and to those who become disgruntled with a burdensome decision of a trial court or the verdict of guilty by a jury in a criminal case. The losing attorney upon hearing the fatal decision is greeted by his justice-seeking and innocence-asserting client with this practical question: How much will an appeal cost? The defeated client having been informed of the probable cost of the appeal, then manages to raise the necessary money therefor and authorizes his counsel to proceed with an appeal "to the highest court of the land if necessary."

The Question of Time

After being convinced of the injustice and error of the decision or verdict the indignant litigant propounds the following interrogatory to counsel for the prospective appellant: How long will it take to appeal the case and obtain a favorable decision? This question must be answered with care and caution. After informing his inquirer that court reporters are busy—extremely busy—in the daily and constant war-like litigation of persons engaged in peaceful occupations—and that it will take several weeks for the completion of a transcript of the evidence (written outside of the hours during which trials must be reported), the wondering and somewhat bewildered client is then informed there will be further delay occasioned by writing for a certified copy of all the proceedings had or pleadings and papers filed in the case. Upon completion of these transcripts and their approval by the trial judge, the venturesome but justice-seeking litigant is told that his counsel must have those documents indexed and bound and each page renumbered and marginal notes written thereon so that the court on appeal may know at a glance the purported contents of each page and thus save the wheat from the chaff.

Then it is that the lawyer must acquaint his almost perpetual client (for he will have this client for a long time pending the appeal) that it will take many days—and nights too—of the time of his advocate while not trying cases or not being engaged in more important work, to create a brief properly, and efficiently, sufficiently presenting to the court on appeal the story of his client's defense, alibis and excuses, and setting forth with accurate precision and skill (in the manner required by the highly technical rules of the court) the many grave charges of error and misjudgment on the part of the trial judge, backed and supported by decisions of the highest courts of the state, the nation and of foreign countries, together with quotations and statements of principles from various text books and eminent legal authorities.

Virtues of a Printed Brief

The client then learns that a printed brief is easier to read than a typewritten one, and that printed briefs receive greater consideration from the courts and do not blur; and besides he can have some copies for circulation among his business associates, relatives and friends so that "they who run may read" and thus learn how he was "robbed" or "persecuted" (as the case may be). Naturally, the client seeing himself about to be made the hero of a new best-seller, yields to the wise counselor's advice, and after many visits to the office of his busy legal adviser, he receives a number of printed copies of the latter's able efforts produced in a finished state after months of labor and research, and forthwith the appellant proceeds to increase the circulation of the paper-bound book which has reached its first and only edition.

Serious Purpose of Brief

But the undistributed excess number of this valuable and individually unpriced book are destined for a more serious and useful mission, free from personal interest or adornment of library tables. A dozen of their number are placed on file in the office of the clerk of the court of appeals, after notices of the appeal have been issued or served, and thereupon in company with his counsel who also files the transcript (a massive and impressive stenographic achievement), the humble appellant seeking only justice and complete vindication finds himself lifted to the heights of hero of a new story bearing a prison-like serial number and duly catalogued and indexed under his name in the permanent archives of the court and state. In due time the case is fully briefed and argued orally by both sides (without the presence of the appellant or appellee) and then waits its turn for final decision by the august tribunal which likewise has before it for similar disposition, a varied assortment of appeals involving almost every statute or principle of law.

After making prompt disposition of most of the copies given and paid for by him, our anxious client reads his advocate's final appeal for mercy and justice, and is greatly impressed and eminently satisfied with the author of his own choice. He learns for the first time that if not an angel, he is at least a law-abiding citizen, incapable of harming anyone, particularly society, while he remembers the prosecutor's thundering charge to the jury that the defendant was a hardened criminal. Or, if it be a civil case, involving a breach of contract, for instance, the appellant reads of himself as being an honorable and upright business man and citizen, dealing fairly and squarely with everyone whether his contract be expressed by pen or voice, and that the possibility of breaking a contract was to him unthinkable. The appellant goes on, his chest expands and a pleased look gleams from his eyes when he recalls the closing argument of the plaintiff's lawyer accusing him of being a slick trader, a crook, a man whose signature to a contract was meaningless and a waste of ink; a man who intended to perform his contract when it appeared beneficial to himself but who dodged it when a storm approached and a slight loss seemed imminent. How well did the appellant remember the mean look of the opposing attorney when making those nasty and caustic remarks to the court, nor could he forget the quick, cutting and puzzling questions propounded to him which caused him to blush, then turn colors, then squirm around in the witness chair, and hesitate frequently before answering the rapid and searching cross-fire of his enemy's counsel. He remembers he finally lost his head completely and blurted out meaningless and confusing answers. Those uncomfortable minutes had been as so many hours of torture.

The appellant laid down the book-brief, wearied of technical terms and phrases, for after all he was human; he did not like to see an unpleasant play a second time nor read a story twice. He wanted to forget and not be reminded of the battle in the past. He fell asleep, and after a long rest so it seemed, (but it was years later) he awoke to learn from the press reports that his case had been reversed by the court of last resort, a fitting climax to the noble work of his counselor-at-law.

Advice of Counsel Remembered

The appellant remembered the advice of his attorney concerning appeals: Faces of witnesses before the court or jury are in time obliterated; their testimony becomes dimmed and hazy and is eventually blurred and re-shaped into printed or typewritten words; the peculiar conduct of witnesses on the stand becomes invisible and disappears; if a witness takes a second, a minute or two minutes or more to answer a puzzling question, the answer in printer's ink does not so indicate because a stop-watch is not part of the reporter's equipment. If a witness evidences hostile looks to the court and jury, those looks fade away forever and do not show up in the transcript. If a witness displays guilty characteristics while testifying and his actions belie his words, his words prevail in the typewritten record of his conduct as well as in the printed record and briefs, for no records on appeal contain photographs or motion pictures except patent cases. If a witness answers distasteful questions in an equally distasteful or boisterous manner, his distaste or manner never reach the transcript except as mere words identical with those of the most polished gentleman. If a witness does not impress the court or jury with his candor or truthfulness, the court on appeal nevertheless holds that *all* witnesses must be believed, if possible, and will not weigh the evidence. If a witness testifies while drunk and the reporter (because of his proximity) smells liquor on his breath, the reporter not being called as a witness cannot include his knowledge of the drunken condition of the witness in the transcript. If the defendant in a liquor case says he never took a drink in his life but staggers to the witness chair and gives incoherent answers and the court and jury know he has not fully recovered from the drink mentioned in the indictment, the jury's knowledge vaporizes into thin mist and is not apparent of record, and the stagger is merged and becomes entirely lost in the printed straight and steady lines of the record.

The appellant feels that the dead have been buried and buried well. To summarize, how magical is an appeal to the wronged and injured litigant. His real character may truly be submerged. The astute counsel said that while the presumptions on appeal as to the correctness of the trial court's decision (or the guess of the jury) are with the appellee, yet he felt a reversal could be had and *some* of the bad features of the case obliterated on appeal because the higher court does not *see* the parties and does not *hear* the evidence, but merely *reads* the record and briefs. Naturally, it was not difficult for the appellant to see the advantages of an appeal.

What the Court Decided

On calling at his attorney's office the latter's stenographer reads to him the opinion of the highest court of the state, from which the successful appellant ascertains with certainty that he won his case for the following reasons: because the trial judge should have sustained a demurrer to the seventh paragraph of the third amended complaint; or because the trial judge in charging the jury in a criminal case had stricken out a few essential words in one of the instructions tendered by the defendant's counsel.

Then the stenographer reads "Cause reversed with instructions to the trial court to grant defendant's motion for new trial." When informed that this meant that he, though successful in his appeal, would have to go through the ordeal of another trial, the appellant realized that the mask had been snatched from his face, that his true character would again be proclaimed, that the highest court of the state had reversed the case only upon reaching the first reversible error without proceeding further with the other errors assigned in the briefs, that the court on appeal never decided whether he was guilty or innocent, right or wrong—*the merits of the case had not been determined.*

The appellant then came to life. He saw his own ghost walk . . . and he collapsed.

Adapted from Vol. 3, Indiana Law Journal (1928).

The Argument of an Appeal

BY JOHN W. DAVIS

IF A LECTURE ON THE well-worn subject assigned to me is to be given in this series, no one knows better than the Chairman of your Committee on Post-Admission Legal Education that he and not I should be the person to give it. This is true in the first place because of the fact that in his lecture on summary judgment he has given the perfect example of what these lectures ought to be —informative, scholarly, helpful—and has set a standard which it is unfair to ask others to rival. And in the second place a discourse on the argument of an appeal would come with superior force from a judge who is in his judicial person the target and the trier of the argument than from a random archer like myself. Or, supposing fishes had the gift of speech, who would listen to a fisherman's weary discourse on fly-casting, the shape and color of the fly, the size of the tackle, the length of the line, the merit of different rod makers and all the other tiresome stuff that fishermen talk about, if the fish himself could be induced to give his views on the most effective methods of approach. For after all it is the fish that the angler is after and all his recondite learning is but the hopeful means to that end.

I hope I may not be charged with levity or disrespect in adopting this piscatorial figure. I do not suggest any analogies between our reverend masters on the Bench and the finny tribe. God forbid! Let such conceits tempt the less respectful. Yet it is true, is it not, that in the argument of an appeal the advocate is angling, consciously and deliberately angling, for the judicial mind. Whatever tends to attract judicial favor to the advocate's claim is useful. Whatever repels it is useless or worse. The whole art of the advocate consists in choosing the one and avoiding the other. Why otherwise have argument at all?

I pause for definition. Argument, of course, may be written as well as oral, and under our modern American practice written argument has certainly become the most extended if not always the weightier of the two. As our colleague Joseph H. Choate, Jr. recently remarked, "we have now reached the point where we file our arguments in writing and deliver our briefs orally." Yet it was not always so and in certain jurisdictions it is not so today. In England, for instance, where many, perhaps most cases are decided as soon as the argument is closed, counsel are not expected to speak with one strabismic eye upon the clock and the other on the court.

I recall that I once visited the chambers of the Privy Council in London hoping to hear a Canadian friend argue a Canadian appeal. When I arrived his adversary had the floor and was laboriously reading to the Court from the open volumes, page by page and line by line, the reported cases on which he relied. Said I to the Clerk, "How long has he been speaking and when will So-and-So come on?" "He has now been speaking," said the Clerk, "for six consecutive days and I doubt if he concludes today." I picked up my hat and sadly departed, realizing into what an alien atmosphere I had wandered.

In the old days, when not only courts but lawyers and litigants are reputed to have had more time at their disposal, similar feats were performed at the American Bar. It has been stated, for instance, that the arguments of Webster, Luther Martin and their colleagues in *McCulloch v. Maryland* consumed six days, while in the *Girard will case* Webster, Horace Binney and others, for ten whole days assailed the listening ears of the Court.

Those days have gone forever; and partly because of the increased tempo of our times, partly because of the increase of work in our appellate tribunals, the argument of an appeal, whether by voice or pen, is hedged about today by strict limitations of time and an increasing effort to provoke an economy of space. The rules of nearly every court give notice that there is a limit to what the judicial ear or the judicial eye is prepared to absorb. Sometimes the judges plead, sometimes they deplore, sometimes they command. The Bar is continuously besought to speak with an eye on the clock and to write with a cramped pen.

Observing this duty of condensation and selection I propose tonight to direct my remarks primarily to the oral argument. I begin after the briefs have all been filed; timely filed of course, for in this matter lawyers are never, hardly ever, belated. I shall assume that these briefs are models of brevity, are properly indexed, and march with orderly logic from point to point; not too little nor yet too much on any topic, even though in a painful last moment of proof-reading many an appealing paragraph has been offered as a reluctant sacrifice on the altar of condensation.

I assume also that the briefs are not overlarded with long quotations from the reported opinions, no matter how pat they seem; nor over-crowded with citations designed, it would seem, to certify to the industry of the brief-maker rather than to fortify the argument. A horrible example of this latter fault crossed my desk within the month in a brief which, in addition to many statutes and text-writers, cited by volume and page no less than 304 decided cases; a number calculated to discourage if not to disgust the most industrious judge.

I assume further that they are not defaced by *supras* or *infras* or by a multiplicity of footnotes which, save in the rare case where they are needed to elucidate the text, do nothing but distract the attention of the reader and interrupt the flow of reasoning. And I remark in passing that these are no more laudable in a judge's opinion than they are in a lawyer's brief.

I assume that there is not a pestilent "and/or" to be found in the brief from cover to cover; or if there is, that the court, jealous of our mother-tongue, will stamp upon the base intruder.

And finally I assume as of course that there has been no cheap effort to use variety in type to supply the emphasis that well-constructed sentences should furnish for themselves. It may be taken as axiomatic that even judges, when they are so disposed, can read understandingly; and I should think that where the pages of a brief begin conversationally in small pica, nudge the reader's elbow with repeated italics, rise to a higher pitch with whole paragraphs of the text—not mere headings—in black letter, and finally shout in full capitals (and such have been observed), the judge might well consider that what a well-intentioned effort to attract his attention was in reality a reflection on his intelligence.

So it is with our briefs brought to this state of approximate perfection that we approach our oral argument. Much has been said pro and con as to the utility of this particular exercise. The appellate court which I most frequently encountered in my early days at the bar made no secret of the fact that it regarded the time spent in hearing cases as a sheer waste; and the announcement "Submitted on briefs" always won an approving nod from the bench. Fortunately, I think, that was an idiosyncracy which has passed away even in that tribunal. There is much testimony, ancient and modern, for the contrary view.

Says Lord Coke, "No man alone with all his uttermost labors, nor all the actors in them, themselves by themselves out of a court of justice, can attain unto a right decision; nor in court without solemn argument where I am persuaded Almighty God openeth and enlargeth the understanding of those desirous of justice and right." Agreeing with this pious sentiment, we lawyers sometimes think nevertheless that "God moves in a mysterious way, his wonders to perform." Judge Dillon in his lecture on the Laws and Jurisprudence of England and America, declares that as a judge he felt reasonably assured of his judgment where he had heard counsel and a very diminished faith where the cause had not been orally argued; for, says he, "Mistakes, errors, fallacies and flaws elude us in spite of ourselves unless the case is pounded and hammered at the bar." Chief Justice Hughes is on record to the effect that "The desirability of a full exposition by oral argument in the highest court is not to be gainsaid. It is a great saving of the time of the court in the examination of extended records and briefs, to obtain the grasp of the case that is made possible by oral discussion and to be able more quickly to separate the wheat from the chaff." With all this most judges, I think, will agree, always provided that the oral argument is inspired as it should be with a single and sincere desire to be helpful to the court.

Professing no special fitness for the task, I have ventured accordingly to frame a decalogue by which such arguments should be governed. There is no mystical significance in the number ten, although it has respectable precedent; and those who think the number short and who wish to add to the roll when I have finished, have my full permission to do so.

At the head of the list I place, where it belongs, the cardinal rule of all, namely:—

(1) Change places, in your imagination of course, with the court. Courts of appeal are not filled by demigods. Some members are learned, some less so. Some are keen and perspicacious, some have more plodding minds. In short, they are men and lawyers much like the rest of us. That they are honest, impartial, ready and eager to reach a correct conclusion must always be taken for

granted. You may rightfully expect and you do expect nothing but fair treatment at their hands.

Yet those who sit in solemn array before you, whatever their merit, know nothing whatever of the controversy that brings you to them, and are not stimulated to interest in it by any feeling of friendship or dislike to anyone concerned. They are not moved as perhaps an advocate may be by any hope of reward or fear of punishment. They are simply being called upon for action in this appointed sphere. They are anxiously waiting to be supplied with what Mr. Justice Holmes called the "implements of decision." These by your presence you profess yourself ready to furnish. If the places were reversed and you sat where they do, think what it is you would want first to know about the case. How and in what order would you want the story told? How would you want the skein unraveled? What would make easier your approach to the true solution? These are questions the advocate must unsparingly put to himself. This is what I mean by changing places with the court.

If you happen to know the mental habits of any particular judge, so much the better. To adapt yourself to his methods of reasoning is not artful, it is simply elementary psychology; as is also the maxim not to tire or irritate the mind you are seeking to persuade. And may I say in passing that there is no surer way to irritate the mind of any listener than to speak in so low a voice or with such indistinct articulation or in so monotonous a tone as to make the mere effort at hearing an unnecessary burden.

I proceed to Rule 2—

(2) State first the nature of the case and briefly its prior history.

Every appellate court has passing before it a long procession of cases that come from manifold and diverse fields of the law and human experience. Why not tell the court at the outset to which of these fields its attention is about to be called? If the case involves the construction of a will, the settlement of a partnership, a constitutional question or whatever it may be, the judge is able as soon as the general topic is mentioned to call to his aid, consciously or unconsciously, his general knowledge and experience with that particular subject. It brings what is to follow into immediate focus. And then for the greater ease of the court in listening it is well to give at once the history of the case in so far as it bears on the court's jurisdiction. And sometimes there may be, I am not sure, a certain curiosity to know just whose judicial work it is that the court is called upon to review. For judges, like other men, judge each other as well as the law.

Next in order—

(3) State the facts.

If I were disposed to violate the rule I have previously announced against emphasis by typography, I would certainly employ at this point the largest capital type. For it cannot be too often emphasized that in an appellate court the statement of the facts is not merely a part of the argument, it is more often than not the argument itself. A case well stated is a case far more than half argued. Yet how many advocates fail to realize that the ignorance of the court concerning the facts in the case is complete, even where their knowledge of the law may adequately satisfy the proverbial presumption. The court wants above all things to learn what are the facts which give rise to the call upon its energies; for in many, probably in most cases when the facts are clear there is no great trouble about the law. *Ex facto jus oritur,* and no court ever forgets it.

No more courteous judge ever sat on any bench than the late Chief Justice White, but I shall never forget a remark which he addressed to a distinguished lawyer, now dead, who was presenting an appeal from an order of the Interstate Commerce Commission. He had plunged headlong into a discussion of the powers of the Commission, and after he had talked for some twenty-five minutes, the Chief Justice leaned over and said in his blandest tone, "Now, Mr. So-and-So, won't you please tell us what this case is about. We could follow you so much better."

Of course there are statements and statements. No two men probably would adopt an identical method of approach. Uniformity is impossible, probably undesirable. Safe guides, however, are to be found in the three C's—chronology, candor and clarity: Chronology, because that is the natural way of telling any story, stringing the events on the chain of time just as all human life itself proceeds; candor, the telling of the worst as well as the best, since the court has the right to expect it, and since any lack of candor, real or apparent, will wholly destroy the most careful argument; and clarity, because that is the supreme virtue in any effort to communicate thought from man to man. It admits of no substitute. There is a sentence of Daniel Webster's which should be written on the walls of every law school, courtroom and law office: "The power of clear statement," said he, "is the great power at the bar." Purple passages can never supply its absence. And of course I must add that no statement of the facts can be considered as complete unless it has been so framed and delivered as to show forth the essential merit, in justice and in right, of your client's cause.

(4) State next the applicable rules of law on which you rely.

If the statement of facts has been properly done the mind of the court will already have sensed the legal questions at issue; indeed they may have been hinted at as you proceed. These may be so elementary and well established that a mere allusion to them is sufficient. On the other hand, they may lie in the field of divided opinion where it is necessary to expound them at greater length and to dwell on the underlying reasons that support one or the other view. It may be that in these days of what is apparently waning health on the part of our old friend *Stare Decisis*, one can rely less than heretofore upon the assertion that the case at bar is governed by such-and-such a case, volume and page. Even the shadow of a long succession of governing cases may not be adequate shelter. In any event the advocate must be prepared to meet any challenge to the doctrine of the cases on which he relies and to support it by original reasoning. Barren citation is a broken reed. What virtue it retains can be left for the brief.

(5) Always "go for the jugular vein."

I do not know from what source I quote that phrase but it is of course familiar. Rufus Choate's expression was "the hub of the case." More often than not there is in every case a cardinal point around which lesser points revolve like planets around the sun, or even as dead moons around a planet; a central fortress which if strongly held will make the loss of all the outworks immaterial. The temptation is always present to "let no guilty point escape" in the hope that if one hook breaks another may hold. Yielding to this temptation is pardonable perhaps in a brief, of which the court may read as much or as little as it chooses. There minor points can be inserted to form "a moat defensive to a wall." But there is no time and rarely any occasion in oral argument for such diversions.

I think in this connection of one of the greatest lawyers, and probably the greatest case winner of our day, the late John G.

Johnson of Philadelphia. He was a man of commanding physical presence and of an intellect equally robust. Before appellate courts he addressed himself customarily to but a single point, often speaking for not more than twenty minutes but with compelling force. When he had concluded it was difficult for his adversary to persuade the court that there was anything else worthy to be considered. This is the quintessence of the advocate's art.

(6) Rejoice when the court asks questions.

And again I say unto you, rejoice! If the question does nothing more it gives you assurance that the court is not comatose and that you have awakened at least a vestigial interest. Moreover a question affords you your only chance to penetrate the mind of the court, unless you are an expert in face reading, and to dispel a doubt as soon as it arises. This you should be able to do if you know your case and have a sound position. If the question warrants a negative answer, do not fence with it but respond with a bold *thwertutnay*—which for the benefit of the illiterate I may explain as a term used in ancient pleading to signify a downright No. While if the answer is in the affirmative or calls for a concession the court will be equally gratified to have the matter promptly disposed of. If you value your argumentative life do not evade or shuffle or postpone, no matter how embarrassing the question may be or how much it interrupts the thread of your argument. Nothing I should think would be more irritating to an inquiring court than to have refuge taken in the familiar evasion "I am coming to that" and then to have the argument end with the promise unfulfilled. If you are really coming to it indicate what your answer will be when it is reached and never, never sit down until it is made.

Do not get into your head the idea that there is a deliberate design on the part of any judge to embarrass counsel by questions. His mind is seeking help, that is all, although it may well be that he calls for help before he really needs it. You remember Bacon's admonition on the subject in his Essay on Judicature:

> "It is no grace to a judge," he says, "first to find that which he might have heard in due time from the bar, or to show quickness of conceit in cutting off evidence or counsel too short, or to prevent information by questions though pertinent."

On the other hand, Chief Justice Denison of the Supreme Court of Colorado puts the matter thus:

> "A perfect argument would need no interruption and a perfect Judge would never interrupt it; but we are not perfect. If the argument . . . discusses the truth of the first chapter of Genesis when the controlling issue is the constitutionality of a Tennessee statute it ought to be interrupted. . . . It is the function of the Court to decide the case and to decide it properly. . . . The Judge knows where his doubts lie, at which point he wishes to be enlightened; it is he whose mind at last must be made up, no one can do it for him, and he must take his own course of thought to accomplish it. Then he must sometimes interrupt."

Judges are sometimes more annoyed by each others' questions than counsel, I have observed. I remember a former Justice of the Supreme Court much given to interrogation who engaged counsel in a long colloquy of question and answer at the very threshhold of his argument. In a stage whisper audible within the bar Chief Justice White was heard to moan, "I want to hear the argument." "So do I, damn him," growled his neighbor, Justice Holmes. Yet questions fairly put and frankly answered give to oral argument a vitality and spice that nothing else will supply.

(7) Read sparingly and only from necessity.

The eye is the window of the mind, and the speaker does not live who can long hold the attention of any audience without looking it in the face. There is something about a sheet of paper interposed between speaker and listener that walls off the mind of the latter as if it were boiler-plate. It obstructs the passage of thought as the lead plate bars the X-rays. I realize that I am taking just this risk at present, but this is not a speech or an argument, only, God save the mark, a lecture.

Of course where the case turns upon the language of a statute or the terms of a written instrument it is necessary that it should be read, always, if possible, with a copy in the hands of the court so that the eye of the court may supplement its ear. But the reading of lengthy extracts from reported cases or long excerpts from the testimony can only be described as a sheer waste of time. With this every appellate court of my acquaintance agrees. A sentence here or a sentence there, perhaps, if sufficiently pertinent and pithy, but not I beg of you print by the paragraph or page.

There is a cognate fault of which most of us from time to time are guilty. This arises when we are seeking to cite or distinguish other cases bearing on our claims and are tempted into a tedious recital of the facts in the cited case, not uncommonly prefaced by the somewhat awkward phrase "That was a case where," etc. Now the human mind is a pawky thing and must be held to its work and it is little wonder after three or four or half a dozen such recitals that not only are the recited facts forgotten but those in the case at Bar become blurred and confused. What the advocate needs most of all is that his facts and his alone should stand out stark, simple, unique, clear.

(8) Avoid personalities.

This is a hard saying, especially when one's feelings are ruffled by a lower court or by opposing counsel, but none the less it is worthy of all acceptation, both in oral argument and in brief. I am not speaking merely of the laws of courtesy that must always govern an honorable profession, but rather of the sheer inutility of personalities as a method of argument in a judicial forum. Nor am I excluding proper comment on things that deserve reprobation. I am thinking psychologically again. It is all a question of keeping the mind of the court on the issues in hand without distraction from without.

One who criticizes unfairly or harshly the action of a lower court runs the risk of offending the quite understandable *esprit du corps* of the judicial body. Rhetorical denunciation of opposing litigants or witnesses may arouse a measure of sympathy for the persons so denounced, while controversies between counsel impose on the court the wholly unnecessary burden and annoyance of preserving order and maintaining the decorum of its proceedings. Such things can irritate; they can never persuade.

(9) Know your record from cover to cover.

This commandment might properly have headed the list for it is the *sine qua non* of all effective argument. You have now reached a point in the litigation where you can no longer hope to supply the want of preparation by lucky accidents or mental agility. You will encounter no more unexpected surprises. You have your last chance to win for your client. It is clear therefore that the field tactics of the trial table will no longer serve and the time has come for major strategy based upon an accurate knowledge of all that has occurred. At any moment you may be called on to correct some misstatement of your adversary and at any moment you may confront a question from the court which, if you are able to answer by an apt reference to the record or with a firm reliance on a well-furnished memory, will increase the confidence with which the court will listen to what else you may have to say. Many an argument otherwise admirable has been destroyed because of counsel's inability to make just such a response.

(10) Sit down.

This is the tenth and last commandment. In preparing for argument you will no doubt have made an outline carefully measured by the time at your command. The notes of it which you should have jotted down lie before you on the reading desk. When you have run through this outline and are satisfied that the court has fully grasped your contentions, what else is there left for you to do? You must be vain indeed to hope that by further speaking you can dragoon the court into a prompt decision in your favor. The mere fact that you have an allotted time of one hour more or less does not constitute a contract with the court to listen for that length of time. On the contrary, when you round out your argument and sit down before your time has expired, a benevolent smile overspreads the faces on the Bench and a sigh of relief and gratification arises from your brethren at the Bar who have been impatiently waiting for the moment when the angel might again trouble the waters of the healing pool and permit them to step in. Earn these exhibitions of gratitude therefore whenever you decently can, and leave the rest to Zeus and his colleagues, that is to say, to the judges on high Olympus.

Before I obey this admonition myself, may I say, Mr. Chairman, how painfully conscious I am that I have offered nothing new concerning the subject in hand. I have not even been able to cover old thoughts with new varnish. How could I have hoped to do so? The process of appeal from one tribunal to another is very old in the history of human justice. No matter in what form it is carried on the essentials of an appeal are always the same, and there is nothing very new to be said about it. The need for an appellate process arises from the innate realization of mankind that the human intellect and human justice are frail at their best. It is necessary therefore to measure one man's mind against another in order to purge the final result, so far as may be, of all passion, prejudice or infirmity.

It is the effort to realize the maximum of justice in human relations; and to keep firm and stable the foundations on which all ordered society rests. There is no field of nobler usefulness for the lawyer, for him who in the splendid words of Chancellor D'Aguesseau, belongs to an order "as old as the magistracy, as noble as virtue, as necessary as justice."

Adapted from American Law Institute (1952) which was adapted from Vol. 26, American Bar Association Journal (1940).

Forensic Persuasion

BY ARTHUR T. VANDERBILT

THERE ARE TWO DISTINCT parts in the lawyer's work in court. The first is the presentation of evidence on direct, cross and redirect examination, a great art in itself, but the evidence alone would often fail to attain full significance without the other phase of the advocate's work, skill in forensic persuasion which enables him to make the most of the evidence. These matters are the heart of the lawyer's work. His client's life or liberty or his property interests depend on his ability to do both tasks well. Nor is this all; on his skill in the presentation of his case in court the course of the development of the law may turn, for the courts must necessarily rely largely on the research of counsel in reaching their decisions. Yet, oddly enough, the arts of forensic persuasion are not taught in any of our law schools. So hard pressed for time are we in imparting knowledge of the law and in teaching skill in legal reasoning that the acquisition of the great arts of the advocate is left to chance as if there was neither art nor science in the matter.

I hope to be able to demonstrate to you that there are some very definite laws prescribed neither by the courts nor the legislature that govern the effective presentation of every case in court quite as much as if they were written in the statute book or embodied in the rules of court. These laws may seem to vary as one moves from the opening of a case to the summing up after all the evidence is in. They may seem to differ when there is a jury present from what they are when the judge sits alone as both the trier of the facts and the arbiter of the law. There may seem to be little resemblance between such an opening and summation on the one side and the remarks that counsel addresses to the court on objections to the reception of his adversary's evidence or on a motion for a nonsuit at the end of a plaintiff's case or for a directed verdict at the close of the entire case. There may also seem to be little in common between any of these steps in a trial and a motion for a new trial after a jury has come in with an adverse verdict. Even more set apart may seem to be the argument of an appeal from the judgment below to a reviewing court, which is everywhere deemed to be the crown of the advocate's work. Yet in all of these various types of forensic persuasion there is an essential unity; the outward differences merely reflect either differences in the tribunal addressed or the purpose for which it is addressed. This essential unity springs from the nature of the human mind. In each step we are dealing with the impact of one mind on another in an effort to resolve a controversy between human beings according to certain very definite rules of fair play that have for their grand objective the substitution of reason for force. When the process works, we achieve justice; when it fails, we must write it down as a failure of your profession and mine.

Most of these successive steps in the forensic presentation of a cause emphasize the constructive phase of the advocate's activities; he is endeavoring to synthesize the facts and the applicable law from his client's point of view and to make the most of them. It is work that often reveals the lawyer at his best. The pleadings, his trial brief, even his appellate brief may seem cold and detached as by their inexorable logic he seeks to demonstrate to the judicial mind the soundness of his client's position, but from the very fact that lawyers and judges and jurors are men, every word that the advocate utters in the courtroom, whether in opening to the jury or in arguing to the court of last resort, will inevitably be permeated, for better or worse, by the influence of his personality, however much the wise advocate may seek to subordinate it to the facts and the law of his case. Every word that the lawyer addresses to the court or the jury is intended not merely to convince, but to persuade—to move the court or the jury to take a desired action, action I may add that is always at the expense of the adverse party. The competitive spirit of the trial court or of the appellate tribunal, although always restrained within the limits of forensic decorum, cannot fail to quicken the pulse of the true advocate and to give him an exhilaration and glow—win, lose or draw—that cannot be equaled by any other intellectual activity of our profession.

The arts of forensic persuasion are especially important in an era such as the one in which we are living, when the velocity of social change is greater than anything hitherto known to the common law and where the course of the law, to a much larger degree than most of us suspect, depends upon the way facts and the law are presented to the court by counsel. Indeed, not long ago I received a letter from one of our most distinguished professors of law, lamenting the fact that the law had become so complex that it was difficult, if not impossible, for even the judges to know it and suggesting therefore that the primary obligation of the law schools might well be to teach their students the arts of persuasion. While I am sure John Randolph Tucker would have never accepted this concept of the aim of a law school nor, I suspect, would my friend if faced with the necessity of making a choice, I feel certain that Dean Tucker would have heartily approved of the study and the practice of the art of forensic persuasion, which his own career exemplified in such a high degree.

The Six Factors in the Work of the Advocate

Before proceeding to discuss in some detail the various types of forensic persuasion to which I have already alluded, it will be helpful to enumerate and then to comment briefly on the six factors that are involved in the work of the advocate. As I proceed, you may find it interesting to take personal inventory of your own stock in hand by way of preparation for becoming an advocate:

1. The capacity for grasping all the facts of a case in all of their interrelations and implications quickly and comprehensively.

2. A thorough understanding of the fundamental principles and rules of law and the ability to apply them to the facts of a case.

3. An understanding of human nature and an ability to get along with people generally.

4. A comprehension of the economic, political, social and intellectual environment of modern litigation, for cases are never tried in a vacuum.

5. The ability to reason concerning the facts, the law, the personalities involved in a litigation, and the environment of a case in such a way as to solve the pending problem in the most satisfactory manner possible.

6. The ability to express one's self clearly and cogently, orally and in writing.

The temptation is strong to delve into a thorough-going analysis of the part that each of these factors plays in a lawyer's life, but I must content myself with a brief comment on each.

1. Every experienced advocate will tell you that *mastering the facts* of a case is the most difficult part of his work. There are likely to be as many different versions of the facts of the case as there are witnesses and parties in interest, and it is by no means improbable that these versions may change materially—and quite without any intentional dishonesty, such is the frailty of human memory—from the time the witnesses are first interviewed to the day of trial. It is the lawyer's duty to know as many of these different versions of the facts as he possibly can before he comes to court, either from interviewing his own witnesses or through pretrial examinations of his adversary's witnesses, and to anticipate in his inauguration those hostile versions of the facts that for one reason or another he is unable to ascertain in advance of trial. This effort to obtain a comprehensive grasp of the facts of the case from his client's point of view and to anticipate his adversary's case is seldom a routine matter; it often calls for a high degree of constructive imagination in which a knowledge of human nature that is at once broad and deep is required. This diversity of views as to the facts means that he must keep a tentative attitude toward the facts of the case that are disclosed to him, realizing full well that at the trial he will learn things that he has never dreamed of before. By knowing or anticipating the story of each witness he will often be able to explain away seeming contradictions and point up the truth. On crucial items he should be able to repeat the story of each of the witnesses in their own words, and on the argument of an appeal he should be able to tell where every statement of fact appears in the record and to refer to it quickly. Such skill rarely comes by grace; one's faculties for organizing and remembering facts must be arduously cultivated. Fortunately, it is our privilege—nay, our duty—to forget the facts of a case as soon as it is over, for otherwise the advocate's mind would soon become an intellectual junkyard.

Though the lawyer must know all of the facts of his case and everybody's version of them, it is essential that he should not harbor the notion that he is bound to tell either the trial court or the appellate tribunal all that he knows. Indeed, there could be no surer way of losing a case. Knowing all of the facts, he must confine his presentation to those which are most cogent and persuasive. His power of selection, of arrangement and of emphasis will be the measure of his genius. He will do well to remember the force that inures in the concrete instance in contrast to vague generalities and he will never forget the wisdom of Macaulay's dictum in presenting a picture to either jurors or judges: "Logicians may argue about abstractions, but the mass of men must have images."

Not infrequently in complicated cases counsel will be called upon almost overnight to learn about an entire art or industry with which he may previously have been totally unfamiliar. Thus, years ago I was called upon to defend some insurance companies that were being sued for the loss of certain paintings which the plaintiff described as the works of certain old Italian and Dutch masters. The defense was that they were not the old masters they were represented to be, but fraudulent reproductions. The preparation and trial of the case called for a thorough knowledge of the paintings of the Italian and Dutch artists in question, of the characteristics and techniques of each of them, of the kind of canvas on which each worked, and the chemistry of the pigments each used, in contrast with the canvas and pigments disclosed by the charred remains of the pictures that had been insured. My investigation required not only much study of books but conferences on art, on canvas, and on pigments, matters with which I was blissfully ignorant before being called into the case. Every experienced trial lawyer has scores of such experiences.

2. Little need be said about the second element in the advocate's work, because the acquisition of a thorough understanding of the fundamental principles and rules of the *law* is one of the chief aims of every law student. To understand the law, however, in its proper perspective to the other factors in the lawyer's work we would do well to remember that in contrast to the facts of a case, which tend to be specific and concrete, the rules of law always are abstract and they deal with the relations between persons or between persons and things. It is therefore most important to form the habit of noting to one's self throughout every step of a case and in dealing with every one of the many versions of the facts, the rules of law that apply thereto. The advocate will, of course, be interested not only in the controlling rules of substantive law and the principles underlying them, but also in the rules of pleading by which issues

are presented to the court, and of evidence by which they are proved there. This process of applying the law, substantive and procedural, to the facts of the case is the converse of the process that the student is accustomed to use in the study of cases, but it will give him no difficulty if he has done his law school work thoroughly.

3. The third element in every law suit, and quite as important as the facts and the law, is a *knowledge of human nature* and an ability to get along with people. I am referring not only to the lawyer's client and his witnesses, but also to his adversary and his client and his witnesses, and the judge, the jury and everyone with whom he has to deal in the conduct of the suit. Each of them is a unique personality. Their variety is infinite. A single mistake in drawing a jury may cost the plaintiff his case, while at the same time a single deft choice may mean victory for a defendant. "The proper study of mankind," says Pope, "is man." And of no one is this more true than of the trial lawyer. He must learn to judge character as much by the voice and by a man's manner as by what he sees in his face and what he says. It is a difficult art but a fascinating one. The prospective advocate may learn much through observation, more through conversation, but most from daily contact with people. He should school himself to make his study of human nature a lifelong habit. He may learn much through the study of the world's great literature, notably the Bible and Shakespeare, that he will not be able to discover elsewhere.

4. Next the advocate must know the economic, political, social and intellectual environment of his case and the *trends of the times*. He must know whether he is working with or against what Dicey has well called "the assumptions of the age":

> "There exists at any given time a body of beliefs, convictions, sentiments, accepted principles or firmly rooted prejudices, which, taken together, make up the public opinion of a particular era, or what may be called the reigning or predominant current of opinion. . . . It may be added that the whole body of beliefs existing in any given age may generally be traced to certain fundamental assumptions, which at the time, whether they be actually true or false, are believed by the mass of the world to be true with such confidence that they hardly appear to bear the character of assumptions."

All this calls for a knowledge of the social sciences in the broadest sense of the term as well as of the humanities and for insight in forecasting the trends of the future. As a profession we have been slow to recognize this responsibility. Indeed, I suspect that even you may think I am speaking not as a practical man of the law but as an erstwhile educator in urging on you desirable but not essential attainments. The matter is so vital that I cannot permit any doubt of your responsibility for preparation in this field to linger in your minds. I summon to my aid two of the great corporation lawyers in the country. Said Edward F. Johnson, General Counsel of the Standard Oil Company of New Jersey:

> "Unless the lawyer is keenly sensitive to such [social] trends, advice acted upon today is likely to fail to meet the test of judicial scrutiny years later. . . . To statute and decisions has been added a new legal dimension—the dominant public interest. A lawyer's advice based upon a two-dimensional study of the law is likely to result in as great a distortion of reality and to be as flat as a two-dimensional painting without depth or perspective. A sound lawyer—sober, hardheaded and realistic craftsman that he is—pays heed to every relevant fact, whether or not that fact is to his liking."

Hear also William T. Gossett, General Counsel of the Ford Motor Company:

> "The lawyer representing business today, if he is to live up to the challenge of his new responsibilities, . . . will be alive to the social, economic and political implications of the time; he will avoid a narrow, shortsighted approach to his client's problems; he will act with due regard for the social responsibilities of the enterprise; he will have the courage to advise against a business program or device which, although legally defensible, is in conflict with the basic principles of ethics. Failing this, he not only will be ignoring his obligations to society, he will be doing a disservice to his client, who may find himself in the position of winning a legal battle but losing a social war.

5. The fifth factor in a lawyer's work is the *ability to reason* concerning the facts, the law, the personalities involved in litigation and the environment of the case in such a way as to solve a controversy in the most satisfactory way possible. There is little need to talk to law students about this, for the great educational

achievement of our modern law schools has been in training their students to think as lawyers think. It is the necessity of reasoning about concrete facts, abstract law, complicated personalities, and the complex social scene that calls for such a variety of traits in the trial lawyer and that in turn makes his work so absorbing. While the lawyer thinks both inductively and deductively in the preparation for trial and the courtroom, it is important to observe here that in forensic persuasion he uses largely the deductive approach.

6. Finally, the advocate must be able to *express himself* in words. He must master the use of words or they will be likely to master him. He must cultivate the arts of both written and spoken expression until their use becomes second nature to him. I do not have in mind any tricks such as sometimes masquerade under the guise of semantics. Many a case is won or lost according to the skill of counsel in translating his points into language that may be grasped by his particular audience. After he has completed his study of the facts, the law, the people of a case, and the environment, after he has exhausted his powers of reasoning, he will still have the problem of making himself so clearly and so forcibly understood as to be able to persuade his hearers. They must feel—and he must be able to make them feel—that he is uttering realities and not mere words. Self-expression is, indeed, a lifelong adventure.

The law student will note that with the exception of the second factor in the advocate's work, an understanding of the law, and the fifth, the art of legal reasoning, all of the elements that enter into his work are those of the educated and enlightened good citizen. They are not narrowly professional. The more the student has learned and the more he has trained his faculties in each of these fields, the easier will be his initiation in the arts of advocacy.

All advocacy involves conflict and calls for the will to win. But the conflicts of advocacy proceed under very definite rules, the first of which is that the contestants must be gentlemen. They must have character. This means that they have certain general standards of conduct, of manners, and of expression that are so habitually theirs that they do not have to stop in an emergency to argue with themselves as to whether or not they should conform to them. The prospective advocate, moreover, may learn much from a study of the functions of the several steps in forensic persuasion and of the different kinds of tribunals he will be called upon to address, so that in his hour of testing he will not have to stop, when his mind should be on the merits of his case, to debate with himself the intricate questions of trial or appellate tactics. Nothing, of course, will take the place of actual experience in developing his own skill, but a study of the problems inherent in the various phases of advocacy and of the experience of others may save him from making a multitude of unnecessary mistakes. The prospective lawyer must also learn that hard work is his daily lot. As Lord Chancellor Eldon graphically put it: "I know of no rule to give them but that they must make up their minds to live like hermits and work like horses." But the reward is great. To quote Judge Cardozo, "What we give forth in effort comes back to us in character. The alchemy is inevitable." Character, capacity for hard work, the will to win, and a study of the methods of the advocate round out the requirements for preparation for the art of advocacy.

Adapted from Vol. 7, Washington and Lee Law Review (1950).

In the Matter of Oral Argument

By Biggs, *Chief Judge*, and Maris, Goodrich, McLaughlin, Kalodner, Staley and Hastie, *Circuit Judges*

Goodrich, *Circuit Judge*.

A good lawyer asked me the other day, "What is there to say in oral argument when I have put everything I have to say in my brief, and said it as carefully and clearly as I can?" A good question, which deserves a thoughtful answer, especially since every now and then an appellate judge will tend to deprecate the value of oral presentation of appeals.

Here is one quick answer. Some people get ideas better by hearing than by reading. President Eisenhower is said to be one of them. Statistics are lacking to show how prevalent this preference is among judges; likely on the whole they tend to be bookish men. But an appellate judge who has had trial court experience has of necessity learned to understand law points made orally often unaided by a brief. So oral argument gives counsel a chance to appeal to the ear-minded judge.

Futhermore, oral argument plus brief gives the lawyer a chance to make both eye and ear attack for his case. Surely two weapons are better than one. Advertising people know that; note the skill with which a television commercial is presented. You may not like the style, nor the article. The extravagant claims for it may make you sick. But you are left in no doubt of the advertiser's position about what the advertiser wants you to do.

A brief can do something that oral argument cannot, if, as in most courts, the time given counsel for oral argument is limited. The brief can develop points in detail; it can marshal authorities; it can quote from court opinions and text writers—it constitutes an argumentative text book—on the particular points involved.

Oral argument, to be good, must be much less detailed. No judge's memory is good enough to remember a lawyer's minute and detailed line of decisions, and the distinctions among them. A great deal of appellate time is wasted because lawyers do not seem to believe that judges, unlike elephants, can forget.

The same caution goes for detailed discussion of facts. The judge may know some of the precedents of his own or other courts if the field is one in which litigation is frequent. He certainly will not know the factual history of a particular case which he is learning about for the first time on appeal.

The first thing for the advocate to accomplish is to bring the court to understand the problem. This may be simple, as it is in many tax cases. Is a given expenditure by a taxpayer to be given a deduction as a business expense, or is it to be regarded as capital? Is a payment to a retiring pastor of a church to be treated as a gift or taxable income? One could put a dozen instances as fast as he can write. The fact that the problem can be simply stated by counsel and easily grasped by a judge does not, of course, indicate that the answer is clear, simple or easy. It may be, or it may not. But if the problem can be simply stated, it certainly should be, for such a statement lets a court move at once to the suggested answer.

But often facts are complicated. Patent cases are a notable instance of this. A court must be made to understand what the claimed invention does, itself a hard thing to comprehend in the case of devices with the technique of which the layman is wholly unfamiliar. Radio and television patents are examples. The court must understand both the presently claimed invention and the prior art before it is in a position to pass any judgment at all. An oral explanation of his case by a skillful patent lawyer is a beautiful thing to listen to. And by skillful is meant, of course, not skill in engineering techniques or in framing an application for the patent office, but skill in so stating a complicated problem that a court, hearing about it for the first time, can understand what the problem is which must be solved to decide the case.

Assume, then, that counsel's skill has brought to the court a comprehension of his case. What then? An oral argument can hardly win a case, unless it is so clear that it is apparent that there is everything to one side and nothing to the other. But successful argument can make the court want to decide the case counsel's way. Here is the chance for the advocate to use his own personality to impress the court with his case. He certainly should not read to the judges either from his brief or a prepared paper. He should refer to his notes only when he must. He should refrain from histrionics. They will bore or maybe disgust his hearers. But straightforward talk to the bench by a man who knows his record and can tell why the court should decide for him may go a long way to win the appeal.

McLAUGHLIN, *Circuit Judge* (concurring).

Since, as of now, in oral argument advocates are facing a condition which more and more has become the order of the day for all appellate courts, it might just as well be so accepted and dealt with accordingly.

This does not make it an unmixed blessing for lawyers. Generally speaking it is of no help to a really weak contention for if the other side fails to break through the thin spots chances are the court will. Even so if the attorney has lived up to the *sine qua non* of this top branch of his profession, meticulous preparation, he won't do bad. He will make his argument in the best possible fashion. He will know and discount its weaknesses and not evade the inevitable queries regarding them. He will not let his case down or run from it; far more desirable that he give a substitution if for whatever the reason he is unable to function sincerely and zealously on behalf of his cause.

On the other hand a sound case can hardly be ruined by oral argument. Nor will the latter ever be overwhelming unless justified by the facts and law behind it. Assuming that the brief is adequate or at least that the right of the appeal can be ascertained from the record, the appellate court as a rule will be able to dredge it out.

It is when the question is confusing or close or both that oral presentation can be of prime value to the parties, the advocates and the court. A direct incisive presentation of the particular position does assist amazingly in not only clarifying the view urged but in bringing alive its strength. It is worthy of note here that on occasion problems and their answers seemingly outstanding in briefs fade to insignificance under close discussional scrutiny.

Therefore, necessarily accepting the proposition that oral argument is with Bench and Bar as a fact, let the advocate never forget that the merit of the cause is the sole interest of the court. Prominence or power of the lawyers, personal quarrels, enlargement of difficulties are unimportant. Overargument, facile or otherwise, is a mistake and exhausting to a tribunal completely concentrated as it is on the appeal at Bar. Emphasis should be placed on the fewest possible valid points and this benefit retained by ruthlessly eliminating weak issues.

The advocate should be dedicated to his case; saturated with a thorough knowledge of it. He should make an adult lawyerlike argument; accurate, fair, in good taste. And if he does, though because of the nature of basic questions involved he may not be able to persuade the court finally, he can rest assured that he will be listened to closely and with respectful regard.

KALODNER, *Circuit Judge* (concurring).

Oral argument is the seasoning to the brief. Effectively presented it makes more palatable to the judge the dish of controversy served to him by the opposing parties. Like all seasoning it must be discriminately used.

As far as I am concerned, oral argument and the brief are "indispensable parties." Briefs read prior to the oral argument serve to acquaint me with the nature of the controversy, its factual phases and issues of law. Oral argument serves to bring into sharper focus the critical aspects of the case. In a sense, oral argument is a "close-up" view of the controversy. It makes more intimate and personal the case itself and all of its facets. It brings into sharper outline the more impersonal aspects of a brief. It serves too, to stimulate both counsel and judge. It enables counsel to parry and to thrust with respect to the brief and oral argument of his adversary. Additionally, it affords counsel an opportunity to present their respective views anent any question which may trouble the judge. Because they are traditionally cautious, lawyers all too often in their briefs go a-huntin' with a shotgun loaded with buckshot. In oral argument they could more profitably use a single chamber rifle and direct their fire to the vulnerable part of their target.

Oral argument is most effective when it succinctly states the critical facts, the issues of law and the impact of legal principles on both. The statement of facts should be brief—the issue or issues should be pin-pointed—and the discussion of legal principles or precedents should always be relevant. Questions from the bench should be answered when they are asked and not met with the answer "I'll come to that later." "Later," alas, too often proves to be too late!

STALEY, *Circuit Judge* (concurring).

I have only two notions to add to those of Judge Goodrich.

The first springs from the obvious fact that a brief is impersonal and formal, while oral argument is personal and less formal. At oral argument judges and counsel are face to face. In a loose sense, counsel has been admitted to the conference room. Assuming that the court reads the briefs before the argument, as our court does, I think one real advantage of oral argument is that it gives counsel the chance to discover what are the important issues *in the judges' minds*. This is no small matter, for the judges are the ones who are going to decide counsel's case, and, while his brief may be otherwise excellent, its whole thrust may bear on a matter on which the judges are already convinced. They may be bothered by an issue not mentioned or not fully developed in the brief. Pointed questions from the bench will show counsel where he should direct his argument, thus giving him a chance to resolve doubts in the minds of the judges, a chance that is too often forfeited by evading the question or seeking to postpone the answer. Of course, counsel may think that the point on which the judges are bothered has nothing to do with the case, but unless he can make the irrelevancy clear, his case is in jeopardy. Oral argument gives the opportunity to do this. Furthermore, this works both ways. Oral argument gives counsel the chance to exploit those gaps in his opponent's brief that he may have overlooked but that have been brought out by the court.

Finally, I think that the fact that only a limited time is allowed for oral presentation is itself a blessing. There is no doubt in my mind that that argument is best that goes to the jugular of the case. The time limitation forces a verbose advocate to restrain himself and stick to the vitals. He must squeeze into those minutes allowed only those points that are really worth telling the court about. An intelligent selectivity on this score insures presentation of what is really important by both eye and ear attack and leaves the relatively minor matters for the brief.

HASTIE, *Circuit Judge* (concurring).

It is my observation that oral argument on appeal is a very important aid to judicature.

This is not to deny that there are all too many arguments of the type which led one Justice to note how often "It is only when argument ends that search for truth begins." Then too, there are many cases in which it is so easily determined what the decisive issues are and how they should be decided under our regime of law that the best argument does not much facilitate, nor the worst much confuse judicial inquiry into the merits of the matter in controversy. In this category I would place almost all of the thirty per cent of our appeals which result after argument in summary per curiam disposition, and some others as well. But over-all, to the extent that individual experience is a criterion, it seems a reasonable approximation that at least half of the time appellate judges hear competent advocacy in cases which are sufficiently difficult to analyze and analogize, and seem to present troublesome enough conflicts of relevant considerations, so that argument time is not wasted.

The characteristic values of oral advocacy are familiar. That argument is particularly useful which clarifies, simplifies, or selectively emphasizes the written presentation of the appellate brief. Briefs, belying their name, tend to contain everything the lawyer thinks it may be useful to place before the court. But in effective argument counsel, having decided which is his best foot, puts it forward. He stresses the considerations which should be decisive in his favor and hammers away at what seem to him the essential weaknesses of the opposing presentation. It is this selectivity which simultaneously focuses attention on the matters counsel would have the court appreciate and makes the essence of his position clear.

In addition, we should not minimize the importance of the opportunity which argument gives the court to cause opposing counsel to join issue squarely. Opposing briefs often do not discuss the same things. The oral argument is the court's one chance to invite counsel to meet head-on what seem to be the strongest opposing contentions. It is noteworthy that this can most effectively be done when judges themselves come into court with such over-all comprehension of the case to be argued as is afforded by the reading of briefs and the scanning of records in advance.

The oral argument certainly influences me in many cases and enables me to be more confident thereafter that the matter is being decided correctly.

BIGGS, *Chief Judge* (concurring).

If I had to decide between eliminating written briefs or oral argument I would be hard put to reach a conclusion. Fortunately, such a dilemma does not face me for like most courts we employ both briefs and oral argument as essential courtroom tools. It is the practice of our very efficient Clerk to have in the hands of the judges comprising the panel—or in those of the court en banc—the briefs of the cases to be heard from ten to five days prior to the day of argument. Appendices which are part of the briefs set out the essential evidence. It is the custom of our judges to study the briefs, and in many instances the appendices as well, some time prior to argument. It follows that when the judges comprising the panel come into court they know—or think they know—what the issues are.

But oral argument enormously sharpens those issues and sometimes develops new ones. If, for example, a judge thinks that counsel has missed the point of the case the judge can discuss what he thinks is the point and get counsel's immediate reactions or answers, and, if necessary, another brief.

So many of the issues which come before the United States Courts these days present original or, to commit an Irish bull, nearly original questions. The ramifications of some of these are extremely difficult to grasp. Without the aid of oral argument the difficulty in resolving such questions would be very great indeed.

Without oral argument the work of an appellate tribunal would be deadly dull. One would never see counsel or enjoy the clash of minds and wits. We like to think that the attorneys enjoy arguing before us. Certainly we like to hear members of our Bar. If oral argument were dispensed with I personally should have the feeling that I was sitting in the rear of those dispensing slots in a cafeteria, dispensing some kind of cafeteria justice. I hope the day will never come when oral argument is dispensed with.

MARIS, *Circuit Judge* (dissenting in part).

I am not one of those judges referred to by Judge Goodrich who gets ideas better by hearing than by reading them. To me the well prepared brief is much more useful than the best oral argument unless, indeed, the latter is taken down stenographically and thus made available for later reading and study. Accordingly if I had to choose between having briefs and oral argument for the decision of a case I would unquestionably choose the former. And during my earliest days upon the court before we adopted the practice of reading the briefs in advance of argument I must confess that to me the oral argument was in most cases almost completely a waste of time. It was extremely difficult for me to follow the oral presentation of complicated facts with which I had no prior familiarity and when, a month later (as our practice then was), we came to conference and the preparation of opinions the oral argument had gone almost completely out of my mind so that my reliance had to be on the briefs alone in most cases.

The present practice of our court to read the briefs in advance of oral argument and to hold a conference each afternoon upon the cases heard during the day does, however, give the oral argument a vital function in assisting me in the process of decision. This is not so much in its presentation of a resumé of the issues and points of argument which I have already read in the briefs although it does help to fix them in my mind. Its primary value to me is to afford an opportunity for the judges to pose to and secure from counsel answers to the questions which have arisen in our minds after the preliminary consideration which we have given to the briefs. This is of real help to me in getting down to the basic issues between the parties and in bringing out the points which may prove decisive. Oral arguments which thus in effect have become conferences between court and counsel have many times proved extremely helpful.

Adapted from Vol. 1, The Practical Lawyer (1955).

Appellate Practice and Advocacy

By Hon. George Rossman

Appellate practice, even in cases involving small sums, may offer attractive returns. The decision announced in a case argued today will outlive the attorney and carry his name into eternity. His brief, when bound together by the law librarians with others argued during the same term, may be an enduring memento of his skill. When an attorney writes such an excellent brief that some of its passages make their way into the eventual decision, he experiences a sense of gratification, and if the decision becomes a part of a law school casebook, where it will school future generations of lawyers, he will deem that his efforts were well rewarded. It is reasonable to infer that if better briefs are written the courts will produce better decisions. Better decisions yield better law. The decision in a case settles, not only the rights of the appellant and the respondent, but also the rules governing similar controversies which may arise in the years to come between unknown persons. Accordingly, even though a case involves only a small amount, its outcome may yield satisfactions of an enduring nature.

Appellate work is divisible into two parts. One consists of compliance with the regulations that govern the prosecution of an appeal. Counsel for both the appellant and the respondent must render themselves familiar with the rules and statutes which govern appeals. The regulations create, in part, time schedules which are exacting.[1] The other phase of appellate practice is more alluring to counsel and affords him greater opportunity to display his art. It consists of appellate advocacy and is utilized, in this instance of counsel for the appellant, in planning skillfully a line of attack upon the decree or judgment which the circuit court entered. It is also employed in brief writing and again when counsel addresses the court. That final period, if employed effectively, can be the decisive moment in the case.

1 See, especially, ORS §§ 19.070 and 19.100.

The two phases of appellate work are different and call for talents that are dissimilar. The one demands that counsel acquaint himself intimately with the statutes and court rules which prescribe the course that must be taken to transfer the case from the trial to the appellate court. The work is mechanical in nature. Upon the other hand, to discern in a case which was lost in the trial court the rulings which are most susceptible to attack, and to cast aside all others, requires of the lawyer skill and courage. Then to present the well chosen assignments of error to the appellate court in such a manner that the attention of the bench is arrested, the minds of the judges are drawn to counsel's point of view, and all become eager to examine the record under an apprehension that the challenged judgment is wrong, exacts of the attorney a degree of ability which some term an art.[2]

When To Learn Appellate Procedure

Many cases that were defeated in the trial court were lost there irretrievably because counsel for the defeated party failed to lay the basis for a successful appeal. The time for counsel to familiarize himself with the rules which govern appellate review is before the trial in the circuit court begins. This paper is not concerned primarily with the phases of trial court procedure that contract or expand, accordion-like, the scope of eventual appellate review; however, mention will be made of some of the rules of practice which reveal the necessity for counsel to study trial procedure before he begins litigation. One section of Oregon laws prescribes the objections which must be made in the circuit court to the instructions given to the jury if it is desired to challenge them upon appeal.[3] Another outlines the course which a party must take in the trial court if he desires to present upon appeal issues which stem from the findings of fact.[4] A rule of practice requires counsel to make an offer of proof when an objection is sustained to a question which he propounded to a witness; otherwise, the appellate court may decline to consider the merits of his objection.[5]

[2] "My underlying thesis is that Appellate Advocacy is an Art." Prettyman, *Some Observations Concerning Appellate Advocacy,* 39 Virginia Law Rev. 285, 20, Journal of District of Columbia Bar Assn. 197.

[3] ORS § 17.510; Poulsen v. Johnson, 182 Or 297, 186 P(2d) 521.

[4] ORS § 17.430; Consolidated Freightways v. West Coast Fast Freight, 188 Or 117, 212 P(2d) 1075, 214 P(2d) 475.

[5] O'Brien v. Dunigan, 187 Or 227, 210 P (2d) 567.

Still another requires the aggrieved party to challenge the regularity of the verdict while the jury is still in the box under threat that if he neglects the opportunity he may not avail himself of it upon appeal.[6] The rules of practice known as the Theory of the Case[7] and Law of the Case[8] may restrict materially the scope of appellate review. Appeals from rulings made by administrative agencies which disappoint the appellant sometimes result from an injudicious choice of the remedies which are available to those who wish to gain judicial review of administrative action.[9]

Oral vs. Written Notice of Appeal

When counsel has decided to appeal to the Supreme Court he has a choice, if his case is a civil one, between two methods of giving notice of appeal. He may avail himself of an oral notice of appeal given "in open court * * * at the time the judgment, decree or order is made[10]" or he may "within 60 days from the entry of the judgment, order or decree" give written notice of appeal.[11] A written notice of appeal must be properly signed; it must describe the challenged judicial order and it must be served upon all adverse parties. An oral notice of appeal enables the appellant to escape the hazards which have tripped some would-be appellants who attempted to employ a written notice of appeal.[12] A glance at the annotations to the sections of our laws which make provision for written notice of appeal possibly indicates that if the unsuccessful appellants had employed an oral notice they would have succeeded.[13]

The Undertaking

The undertaking upon appeal usually creates no difficulties for counsel for appellants, but occasionally a problem presents itself

6 Fischer v. Howard, 201 Or 426, 271 P(2d) 1059.

7 Edwards v. Hoevet, 185 Or 284, 285, 200 P(2d) 955.

8 Quinn v. Hanks, 196 Or 283, 248 P(2d) 832; Kingsley v. Jacobs, 194 Or 394, 241 P(2d) 115; Simmons v. Washington F. N. Ins. Co., 140 Or 164, 13 P(2d) 366; 5 C.J.S., Appeal and Error, § 1964.

9 Inland Navigation Co. v. Chambers, 274 P(2d) 104; Wadhams & Co. v. State Tax Comm., 273 P(2d) 440; Bechtold v. Wilson, 182 Or 360, 186 P (2d) 525, 187 P(2d) 675.

10 ORS § 19.030, subd. 1.

11 ORS § 19.030, subd. 2.

12 See, for example, Temminick v. Doering, 97 Or 145, 191 P 348; In re Water Rights of Burnt River, 116 Or 525, 241 P 988; Northwestern National Insurance Co. of Milwaukee, Wis. v. Averill, 149 Or 672, 42 P(2d) 747.

13 1953 Annotations, ORS § 19.030.

as to whether a cost bond[14] affects the operation of self-executing orders.[15] The difficulty arises from the fact that after ORS § 19.040 has segregated into paragraphs several categories of cases, ORS § 19.050 says: "In cases not provided for in such paragraphs, when an appeal is perfected, with an undertaking for the appeal only, proceedings shall be stayed * * *." Notwithstanding those words it has been held that an order, which, in addition to refusing to appoint as executor a party nominated in a will, appointed another as administrator with will annexed, was not stayed by a cost bond.[16] The decision deemed the challenged order as self-executing. Orders for the custody of children are generally regarded as self-executing and not affected by cost bonds.[17]

Assignments of Error

Oregon appellate practice employs assignments of error. Prior to 1899 the requirement for their use was legislative.[18] Since that year it has been court rule.[19] Notwithstanding the rules' plain demand for assignments of error, some appellants in law actions fail to submit in their briefs any assignments of error and meet with motions to strike.[20] In some cases the Supreme Court has ordered the appellant to reprint his brief and include in it assignments of error. In one instance the brief was stricken. The courts of some other states deal with offending appellants in a more rigorous manner by affirming the challenged judgment when the appellant failed to submit any assignment of error.[21]

An assignment of error based upon a ruling pertaining to the reception of evidence must be followed by the pertinent data, such as the question, the objection, the answer given, or, if the objection was sustained, by the offer of proof. Otherwise, the purported

14 ORS § 19.040.

15 The nature of self-executing orders is expounded in 4 C.J.S., Appeal and Error, § 632.

16 In re Workman's Estate, 156 Or 333, 65 P(2d) 1395, 68 P(2d) 479.

17 Sakraida v. Sakraida, 192 Or 217, 217 P(2d) 242, 233 P(2d) 762; Blair v. Blair, 199 Or 273, 247 P(2d) 883, 260 P(2d) 960.

18 Buel v. Mathes, 186 Or 160, 197 P(2d) 687, 205 P(2d) 551.

19 Rules and 13, Rules of the Supreme Court. A historical treatment of assignments of error is given in Sunderland, *Improvement of Appellate Procedure,* 26 Iowa Law Rev. 3.

20 Buel v. Mathes, 186 Or 160, 197 P(2d) 687, 205 P(2d) 551.

21 4 C.J.S., Appeal and Error, § 1220; 3 Am.Jur., Appeal and Error, § 700.

error will not be considered.[22] Analogous material must accompany assignments of error pertaining to the instructions.[23]

A rule of the Oregon Supreme Court says: "Assignments of error presenting the same legal question are to be avoided."[24] By avoiding multiple assignments of error, each presenting the same legal question, the appellant's brief is shortened and expense is saved. Some attorneys do not seem to discern the advantage of restricting the assignments of error to as small a number as the nature of the case permits, or possibly they lack the quality which John W. Davis terms "courage of exclusion."[25] One court, speaking of an excessive number of assignments of error, said: " 'Such interminable assignments, instead of impressing the court with the thought of an imperfect trial, rather cast discredit upon the worth of any of them.' "[26]

Since it is the appellant, not the respondent, who prepares the assignments of error, it is the appellant's privilege to select the battleground upon which the case will be fought in the appellate court. If he includes in it assignments of error which the respondent can readily explode, he weakens his case.

The Limited Powers of an Appellate Court

Let us now consider brief writing. One who writes a brief in a law action should perceive clearly the nature of the service to justice which an appellate court performs. Upon appeal, the court does not retry the case. Appeal is not a return engagement for the case. The purposes served by appeal are not to afford the appellant a second chance to win his cause. An appeal accepts as done everything disclosed by the record, and in law actions searches the record for error, but only for error. In law actions the appellate court does not attempt to determine whether the challenged judgment is just and right. If the appellant is unable to point to error, the search stops and the challenged judgment is affirmed.[27] But

22 Hallowell v. Bird, 193 Or 254, 238 P(2d) 217.

23 Edvalson v. Swick, 190 Or 473, 227 P(2d) 183.

24 Rule 13(A), subd. 3, par. a.

25 Justice Robert H. Jackson, *Advocacy Before the United States Supreme Court,* 37 Cornell Law Quar. 1, 5, makes some valuable observations upon the desirability of reducing the number of contentions.

26 Chicago Great Western R. Co. v. McDonough, 8 Cir., 161 F 657, 659, 88 CCA 517; Rutledge, in *The Appellate Brief,* 28 American Bar Assn. Journal 251, after mentioning briefs which contain twenty or thirty assignments of error, said: "That kind of brief may be labeled the 'obfuscating' type."

27 Sunderland, *Improvement of Appellate Procedure,* 26 Iowa Law Rev. 3, 7.

if the court finds error, the judgment is reversed, unless the error was nonprejudicial. Such is the nature of the work performed by an appellate court in law actions. In equity cases, the appellate court does not search for error, but determines whether or not the challenged decree is just. Error, normally, is immaterial in equity cases. It is frequently said that appellate courts "retry" equity cases.[28] The statement may be misleading. Such courts receive no new evidence and are generally forced to defer to the trial judge's superior advantages in judging the witnesses.

Brief Writing is Advocacy

Brief writing is advocacy. The administration of justice depends upon the adversary system, and the latter in turn is dependent upon advocacy.[29] Advocacy is not adapted for use in trial courts only. It can reach its very meridian in an appellate court. When an attorney appeals a case he should never forget that he is an advocate. The adversary system cannot serve its purposes unless counsel for both the appellant and the respondent make the most of their respective sides of the case.

A brief should manifest conviction. Unless counsel for the appellant believes in good faith that the trial court committed reversible error, he should not appeal the case. When he accepts the responsibility of appealing the case, he should write a brief which will impress its readers with the thought that the writer believes that the challenged order wrongs the appellant. The problem out of which the case arose should not be stated as if the writer were preparing a question for a bar examination. It should be portrayed in such a graphic manner that the court will view it as one of life's human problems. If the facts are important, the dry record should be made to spring to life, and the witnesses should not appear as mere names. Accordingly, the primary rule governing brief writing is: Brief writing is advocacy.

It is virtually impossible for a brief to create an impression of conviction if it contains an excessive number of quotations[30] or is larded with numerous citations to the authorities. Short quotations sometimes clinch a point, but long ones fail of that objective. Deviation from the rule just suggested not only deprives

28 ORS §§ 17.440 and 19.120.

29 Jackson, *The Advocate,* 36 American Bar Assn. Journal 607.

30 Pittoni, *Suggestions on Brief Writing and Argumentation* 30, 37.

the brief of an atmosphere of conviction, but hinders the reader and impedes the continuity of thought.

Generally, if an appellant has two grounds upon which to seek reversal he should first set forth his strongest. If one of his grounds is based upon the merits and the other upon a purported violation of procedure, it is best to offer first the contention which stems from the merits, for courts prefer to rest their decisions upon the facts as distinguished from procedure.

The facts of a case, even when free from controversy, are important, and counsel, in writing his brief, should see to it that the court correctly understands them. An attorney cannot hope to create in the minds of the judges an image of the case unless he has completely captured the facts himself. Therefore, before writing his brief, he should make himself master of the record.

The Brief Writer Must Know More than Facts and Law

Appellate court advocacy involves discrimination and discernment; it demands of the lawyer a keen understanding of the period in which we live.[31] Although we think that the courts are concerned only with the law, at times they are called upon to determine matters which can properly be termed policy. Such was the situation in the *Erie Railroad Company* case, and possibly it was also present in the recent *Race Segregation* case. In some cases the courts must display an element of statesmanship. Such was true in *Marbury v. Madison* and *McCulloch v. Maryland*. *McPherson v. Buick Automobile Company* is also worthy of note. In presenting cases of that kind, counsel must possess a knowledge of the economic, political and social problems of the day. The *Brandeis Briefs*[32] set a new pattern appropriate to the issues which this period of administrative law presents to the courts. The full

31 Vanderbilt, *Forensic Persuasion* 8; The 1950 John Randolph Tucker Memorial Lectures.

32 Muller v. State of Oregon, 208 US 412, 419, 52 LEd 551, 28 SupCt 324, gives an epitome of the material which Mr. (later Mr. Justice) Brandeis set forth in one of his briefs. Judge (later Mr. Justice) Rutledge says in *The Appellate Brief*, 28 American Bar Assn. Journal 251: "The brief, as Justice Brandeis showed, is the instrument for bringing to the court's attention and knowledge facts not of record, but of which it may take judicial notice. Judges often are vastly ignorant of facts they know judicially. There is a wide difference between judicial knowledge and actual knowledge. In some, perhaps only a few, cases these are the crucial facts. This statement is not intended to invite a deluge of Brandeis briefs. But there should be more of them, * * *."

effect of the Field Code was long delayed because the courts did not sense the propelling motive which had influenced the legislative bodies. Although the Commissioners on Uniform State Laws have achieved for their measures uniformity of legislation, uniformity of law has not resulted, possibly because counsel, in the cases to which the uniform laws are applicable, has failed to stress the need for uniformity of interpretation. Lord Mansfield, by correctly interpreting the spirit of his time, enriched the common law with the Law Merchant. Sometimes the man on the bench needs to possess broad understanding, but back of him, and prompting him, is always the advocate who writes the brief. A good brief writer needs to know something more than law and facts.

Some "Musts"

In preparing a brief, counsel faces many "musts": (1) He must learn and follow the rules written by his court upon the subject of brief writing; (2) he must understand the facts of his case and see to it that he sets them forth in such lucid style that the court, too, will understand them; (3) he must stay in the record and, under no circumstances, stray from it; (4) he must understand the law which governs his case; (5) he must express himself in an easy, clear, forceful style; (6) he must give to the court accurate citations to the record and, in order to make certain that his citations are accurate, recheck them; (7) he must see to it that his citations to the authorities are correct; (8) he must be honest; he must not mislead, overstate or in any other way deceive.

The Index

Every brief, more than twenty pages long, must begin with an index.[33] If a brief contains several assignments of error or many citations to authority, an index is very useful. If the brief's portrayal of the facts or of the issues segregates the material into subdivisions with appropriate headings, the index's usefulness will be enhanced by including in it the headings. If, instead of using headings, such as Deceit, Negligence, or Laches, counsel employs barbed headings, such as Defendant Employed Fraud, The Evidence Established Negligence, etc., his argument will begin with the index if he includes in it the headings.

[33] Rule 13(A), subd. 1, Oregon Supreme Court.

Statement of the Case

The next part of an appellant's brief is the statement of the case.[34] This must be succinct, impartial, nonargumentative and informative. It should enable the judges of the court to gain a ready grasp of the case. Discussion, reasoning and editorializing must be excluded from the statement of the case. All cases fall into categories; for example, they involve the constitutionality of a statute, the construction of a statute, the application of the rules of evidence, or the application of a principle of law upon which the parties agree to a set of facts which is in dispute. It would be helpful to mention in the statement of the case the category in which the case belongs. Likewise, if the case is one of first impression for the court, that fact should be disclosed by the statement of the case. The local court has at times elucidated the requirement which calls for a statement of the case.[35]

Question Presented

The next division of briefs, especially in law actions, presents the first assignment of error. Mention has already been made of the fact that it is desirable to restrict the assignments of error to as small a number as possible. Someone has admonished counsel to "strike for the jugular vein." Whoever originated the phrase performed a good service for counsel. If the assignments of error are restricted to a small number, appellant's counsel can add to their effect by accompanying each with Question Presented.[36] The latter complement and strengthen the assignments of error. Assignments of error are frequently devoid of penetrating effect. The Question Presented, when well phrased, confronts the court directly with the problem that must be solved. It performs the additional function of bringing the brief writer to grips with the problem which he must brief and argue. The appellant's brief in *Youngstown Sheet and Tube Company v. Sawyer,*[37] prepared by that master of appellate practice, John W. Davis, reduced to

34 Rule 13(A), subd. 2, Oregon Supreme Court.

35 In re Miller's Estate, 269 P(2d) 524.

36 Pittoni, *Suggestions on Brief Writing and Argumentation* 46; Stern and Gressman, *Supreme Court Practice* 280. Although the Rules of the Oregon Supreme Court do not require the use of Questions or Issues Presented, they do not prohibit their use.

37 343 US 579, 96 LEd 1153, 72 SupCt 863, 26 ALR(2d) 1378.

three the issues which were presented to the United States Supreme Court in that case of historic importance. Each of the three was phrased in the form of Question Presented, and each of the latter submitted, in compelling language, the problem that awaited solution.

Each assignment of error should be succeeded immediately with the citations, if any, which counsel wishes to submit. An undue number of citations should be avoided. The best should be given and for the remainder the brief should refer to a digest, textbook or encyclopedia where they can be found. Authorities should not be cited merely because it is conventional to find them in briefs, but because counsel believes that those which he cites possess value and will aid the court. If the lawyer has found two or three authorities which are well reasoned and are verily in point, their importance will be diluted if a score of additional decisions of indifferent quality are added merely because briefs generally submit many citations. Following the citations to the authorities, counsel should argue that specific assignment of error.

The Facts

A review of the evidence should pursue a pattern which will enable the court to envision the episode or controversy out of which the lawsuit stemmed. No less an authority than John W. Davis has pointed out that "A case well stated is a case more than half argued." It is seldom useful to review the evidence by setting it forth in this manner: "Witness Smith testified," succeeded by a condensation of Smith's testimony, after which the brief abridges in like manner the testimony of the other witnesses, one by one. Such a course is little better than handing the court the transcript of the evidence. The brief writer should treat the evidence in a manner that will enable the court to grasp the truth and catch an image of the controversy which led to the litigation. Many attorneys who write good briefs, in making their summaries, narrate the facts chronologically. When that is not advisable, they summarize the evidence upon a basis of topics or subjects.[38] At times it is well to give the main facts first and follow them with the details. Briefs filed by appellants in criminal cases sometimes begin their review of the evidence by mentioning facts which tend

[38] Stern and Gressman, *Supreme Court Practice* 280.

to cast doubt upon the defendant's guilt or that direct attention to the excellent reputation which he bore as a law-abiding citizen.

The statement of the facts should never run on into a paragraph covering many pages. It is a common experience to be deterred from reading a decision or other writing when one encounters a lengthy paragraph. Long passages should be broken into smaller parts. Paragraphs of interesting length, preceded by good subheadings, tempt the reader on. Short sentences can create the impression of action and strength, but, if employed in unbroken sequence, produce a staccato effect.

Plain, Direct, Forceful Language

Lawyers who have a mastery of the English language have a splendid facility for brief writing. The late Mr. Justice Jackson, in speaking of the advocate, said: "He will stock the arsenal of his mind with tested dialectical weapons. He will master the short Saxon word that pierces the mind like a spear and the simple figure that lights the understanding. He will never drive the judge to his dictionary. He will rejoice in the strength of the mother tongue as found in the King James version of the Bible, and in the power of the terse and flashing phrase of a Kipling or a Churchhill."[39] Another pre-eminent advocate declared: "If the advocate is to add to his purely legal equipment, the mighty weapon of the well-stored mind, knowledge of every kind cannot be too highly commended, and for my own part I believe that from wide reading in the realm of books comes something not to be acquired elsewhere. The affinity between law and letters is really very close."[40] Lincoln's Gettysburg Address and Bacon's Essays are good examples of the power of simple, chaste English.

Briefs should avoid the use of terms "infra" and "supra". The rules of at least one appellate court[41] forbid their use. Likewise, they should shun words of a scholastic nature and expressions which appear to be cute. Plain, direct, forceful language should be employed. Winston Churchill vouches for this sage advice: "Short words are best and the old words, when short, are best of

39 Jackson, *Advocacy Before the United States Supreme Court*, 37 Cornell Law Quar. 1.

40 Birkett, *Law and Literature: The Equipment of the Lawyer*, 36 American Bar Assn. Journal 891.

41 United States Court of Appeals, Seventh Circuit.

all." The terms "appellant," "respondent" and "cross-appellant" frequently require the reader to turn repeatedly to the brief cover to identify the parties. When a writer sees that the use of those terms will lead to difficulties he should consider the use of such identifying words as "plaintiff Smith," "defendant Jones," "appellant-defendant," "the owner," "the insured." Simplicity and clarity should be the objectives of those who write briefs. All competing objectives should be spurned. Mr. Davis has spoken of "the rule of the three C's," chronology, candor and clarity. It contains excellent admonitions.

Arguing the Law

The secret of writing a good brief upon the law is a simple one: The lawyer should render himself thoroughly familiar with the principles of law under scrutiny. To render oneself thoroughly familiar with a rule of law is a big task, but it is the secret of good brief writing, just as it is the secret of good decision writing. The mastery of a rule of law is not always gained by spending a few hours, or even days, in the companionship of law books. It is acquired only when the lawyer has made himself so conversant with the rule of law under consideration that he is able and willing to discuss it upon reason and principle. The best briefs upon the law are those which stress principle and reason rather than those which insist upon authority.

In preparing his brief, the lawyer should always bear in mind the first rule with which we began; that is, he is an advocate. The courts want from him argument, reason and the material out of which a good decision can be written. Abstract discussion had better be omitted. Fervent pleas and a denunciation of the opponent are out of place in briefs. It is useless to assert that hornbook law and the basic principles of Anglo-Saxon justice support counsel's position. The brief should distill from the record the facts and help the court to discern correctly the controlling principles of law.

In presenting his contentions as to the law, the attorney should realize that the court may not correctly discern the legal principles which govern the case if he submits that issue as though all that the court need do is to compare the facts of his case with those in the decisions which the brief cites and then select the law in a manner resembling that of a painter who matches color cards.[42] Good law is not developed in that way. It is more likely that the court will discover the law correctly if the briefs argue principle and aid the court in evaluating the available decisions. The value of every cited case is dependent upon the question which it decided, the facts of that particular case and the reasoning which the court employed. Normally, a decision is not deemed controlling in another case unless it adjudicated a similar question involving corresponding facts and employed reasoning which appears to be sound. Briefs perform their greatest service for the court when they argue principle and analyze the available authorities in such a way that their merit, or lack of it, is divulged.

When an attorney analyzes a precedent and submits to the court a principle of law for its acceptance, he should realize that rules of law are not independent of one another and separated from each other like the stars in the sky. When a court adopts or rejects a principle of law, it has in mind all related principles and wishes them to fit in together so that they will create a harmonious body. Consequently, when a brief argues for or against some rule, its author should show the court how the principle under contemplation will fit into the state's jurisprudence.

Possibly it was Judge Cardozo who said that a judge convinces himself fifty one percent and then writes the decision as though he were one hundred percent satisfied. Before concurring in an opinion written by the member of the court to whom the case was assigned, his colleagues may entertain doubts, but the decision, upon being pronounced, gives the impression that the court was thoroughly satisfied. In appraising the value of a decision, the writer of a brief may wish to bear in mind the observation which Judge Cardozo made.

A brief which argues a question of law should not attempt to make the entire outcome of the case depend upon a single word or sentence which it quotes from a precedent. When the court wrote that passage it had in mind the facts of that particular case and the entire body of law. It did not attempt to cram into that word or passage all of the law.

The Oral Argument

Justice Raymond S. Wilkins, referring to the oral argument, made this pertinent observation: "It is a mild euphemism to aver

42 Cardozo, *The Nature of the Judicial Process* 20.

that this opportunity is sometimes not fully realized."[43] In view of the masterly address made upon the subject of oral argument by John W. Davis,[44] little remains to be said.

The oral argument and the written brief have in common the function that each seeks to persuade the court, but in all other respects they are dissimilar. The oral argument must be concentrated, its length being limited to thirty minutes, but the brief's treatment of the case, since it is unlimited in length, can be devoted to many contentions. The oral argument is of a personal nature, with the attorney facing the judges, whereas the printed brief, written in a law library, is impersonal. The oral argument must be "caught on the fly"[45] and leaves behind only an impression, whereas the printed brief lies upon the desk of the judge when he writes the opinion. The printed brief, like a cold transcript of evidence, lacks life, but an oral argument affords counsel opportunity to make his case lucid, vivid and graphic. A courtroom clash may cause an idea to spark which no amount of brief writing could have created. The colloquy between court and counsel during the oral argument may disclose to the lawyer doubt in a judge's mind and enable him to dispel it, whereas his printed brief was written in ignorance of the doubt-creating feature. Thus, although the objectives of brief writing and oral argumentation are the same, their means of inducing persuasion are dissimilar.

Since the oral argument and the printed brief are materially dissimilar, it should be unnecessary to state that counsel should never read his brief to the court. An error in tactics only slightly less ill-advised occurs when a lawyer reads a typewritten argument to the Bench.[46] The best impressions are made when the lawyer looks the judges in the eye during his oral argument and engages in what Chief Justice Hughes termed "oral discussion." To prepare an argument for which only thirty minutes is available is often a more difficult task than to write a brief. In the organization of a brief, selection and choice of material are important, but in the preparation of an argument for which only a half hour is

[43] 33 Cornell Law Quar. 40.

[44] Davis, *The Argument of an Appeal,* 26 American Bar Assn. Journal 895.

[45] Prettyman, *Some Observations Concerning Appellate Advocacy,* 20 Journal of District of Columbia Bar Assn. 197, 39 Virginia Law Rev. 285.

[46] "Never read your argument. Talk to the court instead. For once you begin to read, whether from a formal written brief or from an informal brief which constitutes your text for argument, you raise a curtain between yourself and the court." Wiener, *Oral Advocacy,* 62 Harvard Law Rev. 56.

available, the lawyer is forced to display discrimination that subjects his skill to the supreme test. Many attorneys for appellants reserve some of their precious thirty minutes for rebuttal. In most instances, the attorney does his best in his opening period and, since the rebuttal is unorganized, it may have the effect of an anticlimax. When counsel for the appellant arises at the close of respondent's argument and confines himself to a terse statement that he sees no occasion for rebuttal, he gives an impression of confidence that reinforces his opening argument. Such a statement may be a superior rebuttal.

Good presentations take place when counsel has prepared his argument in a flexible manner and needs the help of nothing except a few notes. To deliver an argument of that kind demands that counsel, before coming to the lectern, master not only the facts but also the applicable principles of law. "There is something psychologically persuasive about a man who comes before an appellate court unburdened by a lot of legal paraphernalia."[47]

Although the suggestion was made that counsel should depend upon nothing except a few notes, it is often helpful in aiding the court to grasp the case to use a chart, a map, or an enlarged photograph which is among the exhibits. Those objects should be placed upon an easel. If a short passage from a statute, deed or will is the subject of the argument, it may be helpful to have the pertinent words enlarged upon a chart and set the latter upon an easel where all can look at it while counsel centers attention upon the passage.

Questions From The Bench

In appellate courts, the members frequently ask counsel questions during the oral argument. Some attorneys do not like this practice, but, since it is employed, the questions should be willingly answered. Those who prefer to speak without interruption may wish to consider this observation which was made by Mr. Justice Jackson: "A lively dialogue may be a swifter and surer vehicle to truth than a dismal monologue." Although no one can devise a method whereby the speaker can be assured that no questions will be asked, one which may yield good results is for counsel, after stating the nature of his case, to make such a

47 Morison, *Oral Argument of Appeal,* 10 Washington and Lee Law Rev. 1.

clear outline of his intended discourse that the bench will see that he has the mastery of his case and will discuss the controlling issues adequately. How to answer effectively questions that are asked from the bench is an art that some attorneys have failed to sense and cultivate. Attorneys who are active in appellate work declare that a substantial percentage of cases are won during the questioning period. It not infrequently occurs that a lawyer makes his best point in the interpellation. The facts just mentioned possibly intimate that since questions are asked from the bench, lawyers will do well to welcome them and acquire the skill to participate effectively in the colloquy.

The Lawyer and His Personality

Mr. Justice Jackson declared: "When he rises to speak at the bar, the advocate stands intellectually naked and alone. Habits of thought and speech cannot be borrowed like garments for the event. What an advocate gives to a case is himself; he can bring to the bar only what is within him. A part written for him will never be convincing."[48] Every man has an interesting personality and must always be himself. Nothing will be gained, but much will be lost, if the young advocate disparages his own personality and wishes to exchange it for that of another. All that he can give to his cause when he approaches the lectern is himself, but he must give all of himself to the cause. If he is honest, intelligent, sincere and has the mastery of his case, his voice and personality will serve his cause well.

Make An Enduring Impression

Since counsel is allotted only thirty minutes to present his case, he should plan carefully his argument. Some attorneys attempt to give the court a panoramic, or bird's-eye view of the case. Such presentations frequently are sketchy and inconclusive. Other attorneys, upon approaching the lectern, delve at once into the heart of the case. They "go for the jugular vein." However, before rushing into the controlling issue, it is always advisable to make certain that the bench is familiar with the case and its facts.

The goal of an oral argument should be to create in the mind of every judge such a favorable impression of counsel's contentions

[48] Jackson, *Advocacy Before the United States Supreme Court,* 37 Cornell Law Quar. 1.

that it will do battle for his cause while the case is under advisement. The decision may not come forth for many months and, hence, the impression will have to have enduring qualities. The impression must be lodged not only in the mind of the judge to whom the case will be assigned, whoever he may be, but also in the minds of the other judges who will be asked to concur in the decision when it is drafted. Experience shows that an impression gained from the argument can have enduring qualities and can put up a vigorous fight even if many months pass before a tentative decision is prepared. But such an impression can rarely be made if the attorney scatters his efforts upon many assignments of error or discusses the details of the facts. Likewise, it is most unlikely that an effective impression can be made in oral argument if the attorney endeavors to distinguish the cases cited in the briefs from the one at bar. The way to make a vivid impression is to concentrate upon the heart of the case. If the facts are important, and generally they are, the lawyer should portray clearly those that are controlling. If the law is important he should argue principle and reason. Above all things else, his constant aim should be to lodge in the mind of every man upon the bench an impression of the case which will do battle for him at the crucial hour.

Petitions For Rehearing

Lawyers sometimes question the efficacy of petitions for rehearing, and yet, pardoxically, they rarely fail, upon losing a case, to file such a petition. Obviously, if the briefs were well written, if the oral argument was of good quality, and if the court itself is competent, not many decisions requiring reversal upon rehearing will be announced. Yet all courts make provision for petitions for rehearing.[49]

If a decision was reached by a vote of four to three, and one of the majority judges dies before the mandate is issued, a petition for a rehearing may yield a good result.[50] If a decision is announced by a court which is evenly divided and then a judge becomes available before the decision has become final, a petition

49 Rule 58, United States Supreme Court, 28 USC; Rule 20, Oregon Supreme Court; Stern and Gressman, *Supreme Court Practice* 327, discusses reversals upon rehearing in the United States Supreme Court.

50 Eastern & Western Lumber Co. v. Patterson, 124 Or 112, 258 P 193, 264 P 441.

for a rehearing may be granted.[51] If a decision construing recently enacted statute, of important social or industrial implications, provokes enlightening discussion after its announcement, a petition for a rehearing may succeed.[52]

Conclusion

A good decision which enriches jurisprudence is often the joint product of an able brief and the hard work of a man who is worthy of the place upon the bench which he occupies. Win or lose, in cases of that kind, the advocate will experience a sense of satisfaction in his realization that he gave his best. Let us return to our thesis: Better briefs yield better decisions. Better decisions produce better law. The latter is the greatest reward for the efforts of both bench and bar.

---

[51] Gray v. Powell, 312 US 666, 85 LEd 1111, 61 SupCt 824; Id., 313 US 596, 85 LEd 1550, 61 SupCt 938; Id., 314 US 402, 86 LEd 301, 62 SupCt 326; Halliburton Oil Well Cementing Co. v. Walker, 326 US 696, 90 LEd 410, 66 SupCt 482; Id., 327 US 812, 90 LEd 1037, 66 SupCt 677; Id., 329 US 1, 91 LEd 3, 67 SupCt 6.

[52] Lamm v. Silver Falls Timber Co., 133 Or 468, 277 P 91, 286 P 527, 291 P 375; Varrelman v. Flora Logging Co., 133 Or 541, 277 P 97, 286 P 541, 290 P 751; Sprague v. Fisher, 184 Or 1, 197 P(2d) 662, 203 P(2d) 274.

Adapted from Vol. 16, Federal Rules Decisions (1955).

Some Observations Concerning Appellate Advocacy

BY E. BARRETT PRETTYMAN

ALMOST ALL LAWYERS WHO HAVE presented causes upon appeal, and all judges who have sat on an appellate bench, have notions as to the desirable and the undesirable in appellate presentations. I am no exception; hence this paper. The observations thus made do not purport to be expert advice. They are merely personal notions gleaned from a long-time interest in the subject.

My underlying thesis is that appellate advocacy is an art. It is not a scientific process. It is not a mathematical formula. There are no compounds or elements which react with certainty to produce a predetermined result.

It is a process wherein one human mind attempts to propel three other human minds into a certain channel to a certain result. Dealing with the vagaries of human minds is not a fixed routine but is a matter of imponderables, unknowns, and many delicate maneuvers. We can suggest the brushes, the canvas, and the paints; we can teach the fundamentals of color combinations and line impressions; but the production of an oil painting is a matter of individual performance. So we approach the subject with this thought in mind: How does one persuade three human minds to think as he does upon a given topic?

I stress all this because so many members of the Bar seem to think that an appeal is an occasion for making a speech, like a preacher in a pulpit, or a teacher on a rostrum, or a Memorial Day orator. Many others seem to think that an appellate brief is a document in which one assembles more or less relevant quotations from texts and cases so as to make a pretty picture. Those are not accurate ideas. Appellate advocacy is a task of persuasion.

Let us begin with a correct conception of what an appellate proceeding is. It is a proceeding for the correction of errors. An appellate court is not a tribunal for a general review of proceedings in a trial court or before an administrative agency. Many lawyers seem to think the appellate court is just that. They tell the appellate bench how they should have won their case and how iniquitous the trial judge or the agency was. Every losing lawyer thinks that. But the place to win lawsuits is in the trial forum. The purpose of an appeal is to correct errors of law. The appeal is not a repeat performance of the trial. Recognition of two propositions will save you a lot of difficulty: (1) The place to win lawsuits is in the trial court. (2) An appellate court is for the correction of errors of law made by the trial tribunal, and for nothing else.

The task upon appeal is to persuade the three appellate judges that the trial judge made a mistake. The first problem for appellate counsel is: What mistakes did the trial judge make? Cold-bloodedly, objectively, with utter detachment, the appellate advocate should make up his mind—not his heart or his emotions, but his intellect, his mind—as to what mistakes the trial judge made.

If the case has been properly tried, with full preparation, counsel knows when the trial concludes, and even before the result is announced, what errors he thinks the trial judge has made. He will have either anticipated or recognized each and every crucial step in the trial and will already know the correct answer, or the answer which he thinks is correct. He will have carefully protected his client's side of the controversy at each of these critical steps. Moreover, it is a universal rule, almost without an exception, that you cannot ask an appellate court to correct an error unless the error has been called to the attention of the trial court and that judge has been given a fair chance to correct it. The foundation of sound appellate advocacy is laid in the course of the trial proceeding. If the lawyer is one of the tribe who try lawsuits out of their hats, without preparation or without knowing the critical points of law in the controversy, he will not be a good appellate advocate; nor is he a good trial lawyer either, for that matter.

Trial judges make relatively very few errors. If a lawyer is prepared, as he ought to be prepared, to try a case, and if he is ready to direct the trial judge to the authorities or to submit persuasive reasoning upon each critical point as it arises, the chances of a trial judge making a mistake are numerically infinitesimal. The District Court in the District of Columbia, which is the trial court of general jurisdiction, disposes of about ten thousand cases a year. Our court has about three hundred and fifty cases from that court. We reverse about one-sixth of those appealed. So the numerical percentage of errors appears on the face of the records to be about one-half of one per cent. But trial judges do make mistakes, or at least their brethren on the appellate court, after weeks or months of cogitation and research, sometimes do not agree with their opinions on legal points. These errors may occur because trial lawyers are not prepared to submit to the trial judge authorities or reasons, and that judge has no time to wait around while the lawyers prepare the case. The trial judge must shoot from the hip, as it were. Sometimes a brand-new question comes up, such as the meaning of a new statute or the proper application of old principles to brand-new factual situations. Sometimes the trial judge, like every other human being, including those sitting on appellate courts, simply makes a mistake.

Assuming that counsel knows clearly what errors he thinks the trial tribunal has committed, his next step is to state those errors. Believe it or not, this phase of appellate advocacy is one which calls for the greatest degree of skill and is the one most usually botched by counsel. I had an amusing experience in this connection. Some years ago a friend of mine, who had practiced in Pennsylvania, called my attention to the rule in that state which requires counsel to state on the flyleaves of their briefs the questions presented. I was telling him of our difficulties in that respect. I picked up three sets of briefs at random from a pile on my table, and I challenged him to ascertain from reading the statements of points in those briefs what questions the court had to decide. He read them and shook his head in amazement. By and large—not universally, but more frequently than not—the appellate court has to read the whole of both briefs and match them one against the other to ascertain where they conflict, in order to find out what the disputed question is. A primary task of appellate counsel is to state the question he wants the court to decide; describe the error the trial tribunal is alleged to have made. The task requires consummate skill, and it also requires careful, painstaking labor.

There are ways and ways of stating questions. But there are two simple fundamental rules. First: State the question clearly. The lawyer's greatest weapon is clarity, and its whetstone is succinctness. Clarity in stating a question has two essentials. The lawyer must have a clear idea of what the question is, and he must be familiar with the briefer forms of expression in the English language. I sympathize with lawyers who write backwards, as I habitually do that myself. I am inclined to say, "When so-and-so and such-and-such, is plaintiff entitled to a hearing?," instead of much clearer "Is plaintiff entitled to a hearing when so-and-so and such-and-such?" The attainment of clarity of expression is a delightful and a profitable achievement. It can be done by constant practice.

Second: State the questions accurately. Some eminent authorities advise that one should so phrase the question that upon reading it the court will be inclined to answer it favorably to the view desired by counsel. They do warn that if the court detects the purpose of this tactic it may react to the disadvantage of counsel. Apart from the professional ethics of such practice, my own experience is that one's opponent is usually not sufficiently asleep to pass such a statement unchallenged, and the challenge can be completely devastating. Moreover an appellate court is less than likely to be deceived by so infantile a maneuver. The judges examine the briefs of both sides. When they see a question twisted out of shape they get the impression either that the lawyer does not know what the case is about or that he has so bad a case that he seeks to avoid the actual issue. After all, red herrings are red and can be seen quite clearly.

It is an odd fact that despite honest efforts to be clear and accurate, opposing counsel rarely agree upon what the question in the case is. In our court we require that the "Question Presented" be stated on the frontispiece of the briefs. In almost every case the appellee deems it necessary to restate the question. An appellate court must not only decide the question presented but often probe to ascertain what that question is.

If a lawyer states clearly and accurately the question he wants a court to decide, he has laid a firm foundation upon which to proceed with his task of persuasion.

The Preparation of Briefs

Appellate counsel have two opportunities to persuade the court to reach the desired answer to the question presented. One opportunity is in writing and the other by word of mouth. The two are different. The written brief and the oral argument are not two variations of one weapon; they are two weapons. A brief is not a printed speech. An oral argument is not the reading of a written document.

There are many technical essentials in the preparation of briefs, but I shall not touch upon them. I do offer a few observations, perhaps suggestions.

Generally speaking, an appeal is one of a few types. It may involve merely the application of an established rule to the facts of the instant case. Or it may involve a law question of first impression in the jurisdiction where the case is pending, though the question has been answered elsewhere. Or it may involve a question of first impression in any jurisdiction. The task of counsel differs in these three types of cases, and he is well advised if he keeps in mind which type of problem he has. Moreover, he is well advised to tell the court as early as possible which type is involved. Thus wise counsel will say early in his brief, "This case involves no new principle of law. It involves merely the question whether the doctrine of 'last clear chance' applies to the facts in this case." Or he may say, "This case involves a question of first impression in this jurisdiction. It has been decided, however, in ten [or fifteen or twenty] states, the decisions being divided. We shall maintain that the opinions of the Virginia, North Carolina, South Carolina, and West Virginia courts are the better reasoned and that the rule there established is correct." Or he may say, "This case presents a question of first impression in this or any other jurisdiction. It concerns the meaning of Section 198 of an Act of Congress of June 10, 1948, known as the XYZ Act."

The whole brief and argument take on shape and character from the type into which the case falls. If no new rule of law is involved, counsel should briefly describe the established rule, with an authoritative reference or two, and then devote his main effort to applying that rule to the facts of his case. If a new rule for the jurisdiction is involved, discussion of the facts in the instant case should take second place to an analysis and comparison of the pertinent cases in other jurisdictions and an ultimate evaluation of the reasonings in the divergent schools. If a brand-new question, not yet decided by any court, is presented, counsel must devote a major effort to basic reasoning or analogy, or, in the case of statutes, to context or to legislative purpose and history.

In cases of the latter two types, it is important that counsel remember that the appellate judges must not only decide his case but also write an opinion. That opinion should contain the reasons for the decision in the case in which it is written, but that is not its chief importance. It should be useful as an authoritative reference work in the libraries of both Bench and Bar. Under our system of jurisprudence, controlling law is expected to be found in the opinions of appellate courts. Therefore, when I write the reasons for a decision in a given case presenting a new question, I am actually writing a rule of law for unknown numbers of cases which may arise in the indefinite future. In future days counsel will say to the trial courts and to the appellate court in an unascertainable number of cases: "If your Honor please, this case is governed by the decision of the Court of Appeals in the *Delsnider* case [or the *Kelly* case, or *Kephart v. Kephart,* or *Johnson v. Matthews*]." Or, in another jurisdiction, counsel will be saying, "If Your Honor please, the rule in the District of Columbia is thus-and-so, as shown by the opinion in *Curley v. United States* [or *Billeci v. United States*, or *Hitaffer v. Argonne Co.*]" and other courts will be saying, "In a well-reasoned opinion the Court of Appeals for the District of Columbia held so-and-so"; or "Although the rule in the District of Columbia is so-and-so, the view which seems to us better reasoned is that of the Court of Appeals for the Fourth Circuit."

These necessities in the writing of appellate opinions highlight *desirata* in the writing of briefs. A brief should be written to be read and also to be studied. This latter is of great importance. The judge looks at the brief in his own time and in atmosphere of his own chambers. It will not be considered in the atmosphere of the courtroom, or in the presence of adverse counsel, or under the pressure of a time limitation. The judges look to the brief to supply the material, or references to it, with which to formulate a decision. A properly prepared brief will be so meticulously prepared, so complete, that the judge will be neither forced nor tempted to do his own research, either through the record for facts or through the library for cases. This function of the brief is too often forgotten.

If an appellate judge can find in the briefs the material from which to fashion the opinion he must write, he is very happy about it. If he cannot find it there, he must search for it in the record or in the lawbooks. Therefore it often happens that in the written opinion of the court there is to be found little that is in the briefs. That is the fault of counsel. Judges do not yearn for this extra work. However, they are aware that the reasons they state as propositions of law will be used in contexts foreign to the current one. I believe that Judge Learned Hand is credited with saying that the decision of a case on a point not briefed or argued is a reproach to the lawyers rather than a tribute to the court's inventiveness. Astute counsel therefore put in a brief dealing with problems of first impression the material, or references to the material, which not only persuades the court to a given conclusion but also serves as the basis for an opinion which will bear the judge's name. If they do that, they avoid the possibility that the judge, in the course of his own independent research, will come up with something exceedingly unpleasant.

A brief contains, first a statement of the questions presented, a matter we have already discussed. Thereafter a brief has two parts, the facts and the argument. What facts should a lawyer put in his brief? The answer is simple: Enough but not too many. The preparation of the statement of facts is the exercise of an exquisite art. The statement should contain all the material facts. I would emphasize "material" rather than "all" in that sentence. Do not bury the point of the case in a sand of minutiae. The statement should not omit the unfavorable facts, lest one's opponent seize upon that omission to condemn the whole argument. It should also contain enough background facts to give a suitable atmosphere to the bare outline. It should be simply and clearly written. It should be literate. It should avoid long sentences. (I once read in a brief a sentence two and one-half printed pages in length.) The statement should give the court a quick summary and then a detailed fill-in. It should be rewritten and rewritten and rewritten, until at last it is the very best that counsel can do.

The facts should be written so that they are readily understood. To be specific, don't keep saying "appellant" and "appellee." By the time the reader gets to the third page he becomes completely confused as to which is which. Those two words have no meaning except a technical, procedural one. Say "the husband" and "the wife," or use names or some descriptive expressions that have some meaning in the context of the controversy. Say "the insured," "the contractor," "the company," "the employee," "Smith," "Miss Jones," "the father," "the Government," "the corporation," "the X Company," or some such descriptive term. We recently had a brief in a case involving two radio stations. The sentences, with the letters changed to prevent identification, ran in somewhat this fashion: "Acting on the WKML petition, the Commission made a grant to WLTK upon condition WLTK would not interfere with WKML so long as WKML did not disturb WLTK." From twelve to twenty times a page those call letters appeared for many pages. I was confused.

After the statement of facts comes the argument. The argument is supposed to be an argument. That sounds like a silly truism. But it is important, because in many briefs we find no argument. We find discussions, pleas, questions, characterizations, and references aplenty to "basic principles of Anglo-American jurisprudence," but no argument. Of course discussion, etc., may be proper parts of an argument. However, despite popular conceptions to the contrary, appellate judges are not persuaded to hold a trial court in error by a pointless general discussion of some topic, by the characteristics, good or bad, of the parties, or by the passion of a plea for reversal. The appellate judge wants to know from the appellant what the alleged error was and why it was an error, and from the appellee the contrary. And so he wants to be supplied with reasons and material. From the standpoint of counsel, that means an argument, which in better phrasing means a process of persuasion.

The process of persuasion may be from authority, usually decided cases, or may be by reasoning alone. Appellate counsel ought to be conscious of which method he is attempting to use. Sometimes, of course, he must use a combination of methods. In broad outline he may be proceeding by a syllogistic progression, but he may establish each premise by drawing from the authorities. But whatever he does, he ought to be conscious of the fact that he is doing it.

What I am trying to say at this point is that the arguments in many appellate briefs are wholly without any recognizable form or shape. They begin nowhere, proceed along meandering lines, and end nowhere. They quote a sentence or two from a court opinion, make a couple of collateral remarks, posit a general principle, refer to a fact or two, quote some more, and end with a conclusion that the trial court was in error. The judge reads such a brief, rereads it to make sure he did not drowse the first time, and then tosses it aside as useless, turning to the opponent's brief in the hope that it will reveal sufficient strength or sufficient weakness to support a conclusion one way or the other. When a lawyer prepares the argument in a brief, he ought to recognize in his own mind what the nature of the argument is, and then he ought to cast it in that form.

I know of no expression more completely damning to a written argument than to say that it sounds as if it had been dictated. Sometimes as you read you can almost see the lawyer walking up and down before his secretary, dictating, declaiming, gesturing, changing his mind, striking out some portions, stopping to take a telephone call or to see a visitor, adjourning overnight, and repeating long passages of the previous day's dictation when he resumes the next morning. In such an argument you usually find the nub of the lawyer's contention buried in the next-to-the-last sentence of the last paragraph. Such a document is a waste of paper. We once had a brief in which, about halfway through the argument, the printed page suddenly said, in effect: "At this point it occurred to counsel that maybe so-and-so had happened at the trial. He therefore suspended preparation of this brief and went to the courthouse to look at the record. There he found so-and-so to be the case. Therefore, counsel now rests his appeal upon the following point." Believe it or not, that lawyer did not even take the trouble to discard what he had already dictated or even to rearrange his argument.

To write a good argument you must first master the subject of the lawsuit. Master the legal topic before you begin to compose the argument. That takes time and work, no matter how tiny the topic's scope. You ought to be willing to read fifty cases in order to use one. Go back to the Yearbooks if necessary. When you are master of the subject, select and discard the material; then select and discard again, and then again. When you finally make your selection, arrange and rearrange it; then arrange and rearrange it again, and then again. When you have finally arranged your material begin to write your argument, then rewrite, and rewrite again and again. Do not be disturbed if the number of drafts exceeds a dozen. All this work pays dividends, not only in the courtroom but in your office, in client appreciation. If you simply go to a digest and pick a couple of cases to support your side of the argument and let it go at that, you will probably get nowhere. Your opponent will cut you into pieces, and the court is likely to ignore your briefs and tear you to pitiful ribbons on oral argument.

It is not bad practice to include in a brief minor points or contentions. Indeed it is frequently very good practice. You must exercise some degree of selectivity. The appellate court is not impressed if you assert that the trial judge made a mistake every time he made a ruling. And, moreover, many errors are so relatively minor that they are washed out in the whole of the evidence and the trial. A recent brief before us described sixteen errors as having been committed at the trial and stated sixteen questions upon the appeal. When questioned at oral argument, counsel abandoned fourteen of those points. The remaining two-sixteenths of his brief was, of course, inadequate for the discussion of those two points. But often there is more than one point in a controversy, and, although there may be one or two outstanding contentions, which to counsel seem conclusive, there may be several other sound contentions of comparatively lesser moment. It is good practice to put them in the brief. I skip ahead of the story to say, however, that the same advice does not apply to oral argument. In oral argument stern, courageous selectivity is a necessity, diffusion is fatal.

A question sometimes arises as to how far counsel should go in stating and establishing elementary principles of law. The answer is that it depends upon the nature of the case and the experience of the court. If the case is in a field familiar to the court—crimes, negligence, statutory construction—knowledge of established principles can usually be assumed. If the case is in a specialty field—taxes, radio, air, utilities—it is wiser to make at least adequate references to principles already established. In the brief it is wise not to take chances on fundamentals. In the oral argument counsel must use his judgment.

I would say a word or two about the use of cases as authorities. A decided case has four parts: (1) the question, (2) the facts, (3) the decision, and (4) the reasoning. The correct use of a decided case as an authority recognizes these several parts. The case is authority for the decision there rendered upon the question there presented in the light of the facts there involved, and it is persuasive for the validity of the reasoning used. Wise counsel approach the use of a decided case as an authority with an analysis of that sort.

I would speak one emphatic, although trite, negative word. Never rely upon a quoted extract from an opinion, unless it accurately sums up the decision upon the point. Sentences out of context rarely mean what they seem to say, and nobody in the whole world knows that better than the appellate judge. He has learned it by the torturing experience of hearing his own sentences read back to him. When in a brief counsel merely say, "The such-and-such court said 'So-and-so'," the appellate judge is put on his guard. He may use the reference as an incentive to get the case and read it. But an unexplained quoted extract is of no use to him; at least it ought not to be. I must admit that a great deal of extremely bad law has been made by appellate judges doing precisely what I am now saying they do not do. Decision by epigram is one of the worst of our judicial evils. However, whether judges do it or not, they ought not to do it, and counsel ought not to help them do it.

One further somewhat obvious word upon case authorities; Never cite a case in a brief without running it down in a reliable citator.

Whatever else you are in your brief, be accurate. Be accurate in your references to the record. Be accurate in your references to the authorities. Be accurate in your references to statutes. Be accurate in your quotations, of whatever sort they may be. It is not an easy task. In the preparation of opinions in my office, three of us—my secretary, my law clerk, and I—check and recheck every item for accuracy, but, even so, once in a long while to our horror somebody comes up with an error in a published opinion. But flagrant inaccuracy is inexcusable. We have had some strange experiences along that line. We have had cases cited which do not remotely approach the problem at hand. We have had statutes misquoted. We have had counsel in oral argument rely upon a cited case as the leading authority on the point he was arguing when he had the wrong facts, the wrong court, the wrong volume, and the wrong page. My advice is: The least a lawyer can do in his effort to persuade an appellate court is to be accurate in what he says to it.

Judge Arthur Vanderbilt, in his Tucker lectures at Washington and Lee University, emphasized the manner in which a judge reads briefs. I agree with what he said. So far as I am concerned, before the oral argument I read over the briefs and some material parts of the records, in somewhat cursory fashion, enough to know what the points in the case are and what the positions of the opposing parties are. When the oral argument is over, the answer to the controversy is sometimes indisputably clear. But in most cases it is not and a real study is in order. Usually I first read both parties' statements of the questions presented; then I read the appellant's statement of the general nature of the controversy. Then I look at his outline of argument to see what points he makes. Then I look at the appellee's outline of argument to see what he is going to do in reply. Then I go to the joint appendix to see what the trial court or the administrative agency did. Then I read the appellee's statement. Thereafter I examine the two briefs one point at a time, first the appellant's and then the appellee's, on the first point; then both briefs on the second point, etc. If the point is an obvious one, or if one side or the other seems to be wholly without strength on it, I do not spend too much time on that point in my first study. On the really contested points I study both sides, read the cases, and, if the facts are critical, check the record references. The briefs on the critical points are often reread and reread. If the briefs and the authorities there cited stand up in our search, we can relax and rely upon them. But, if our first examination shows that the surface of the subject has not been scratched by the lawyers, we really have to settle down and plow. In such instances, it often happens that the briefs must for all practical purposes be discarded and the judge must proceed on his own. Sometimes, when I get weary with working on such a presentation, I threaten to write an opinion saying: "On the briefs as presented, the appellant wins. I have gone no further than the facts and authorities presented to me in the briefs and arguments. Whether the answer I have reached in this manner is correct or not, I have not the slightest idea." On the other hand, of course, many briefs bring delight to the judge's heart. A carefully prepared, carefully stated, lawyer-like written argument is a work of art and a joy forever.

In this connection let me remind you of what Mr. Justice Jackson pointed out in his address on this subject, published in the *Cornell Law Quarterly*.[1] An appellate judge must render an answer which is a flat "Yes" or "No" on each point before him. Unless the case be severable the judgment below must be either affirmed or reversed. He cannot say "I think this contest should be declared a draw." And he cannot say "I haven't the slightest notion what to do with this case." Judge Wilbur K. Miller likes to refer to a judge who, when in that predicament, suggested to his brethren that they return the appellant's filing fee of two dollars and tell him to take his case somewhere else. But, although the appellate judge must announce a "Yes" or "No" just exactly as though the matter were 100 per cent right or wrong, very frequently he is far from feeling that way. Very often he finally comes out 55 per cent one way and 45 per cent the other, but on balance he has to decide flatly for the preponderant weight as it lies in his mind. Appellate counsel do well to remember this in close cases. If in dealing with a close question they point out the pros and cons each way and then point to a proper balance, they make more impression than if they urge complete and unqualified virtue in their own side of the case.

One further word on briefs in general. I have a great contempt for that form of advocacy which consists of a combination of means and methods calculated to result satisfactorily to the advocate regardless of actual merit. Of course, an advocate should press his side of the controversy with every honorable means at his disposal. Our system of adjudication contemplates that each adversary will advance every existing fact and argument in his favor. The judges, being thus furnished with the utmost available on each side of the dispute, have the duty of weighing, evaluating, and reaching a decision upon the conflict. But to be an aggressive, competent, forceful, fighting advocate is not to be a slick, cute, tricky one. I have read advice that questions be slanted so as to produce a satisfactory answer, that facts be stated so as to lead a busy court to reach an answer favorable to that party, that irrelevant factors be introduced and emphasized with the object of leading the judges into misapprehension of the real dispute; in sum

[1] Jackson, *Advocacy Before the United States Supreme Court,* 37 Cornell Law Quarterly 1 (1951).

that, short of actual misstatements, tactics be designed for the sole purpose of winning the lawsuit.

My contempt is in part upon moral and ethical grounds. Our jurisprudence rests upon no foundation except right and honor and justice. Those who are purposely antagonistic or even merely supercilious toward those fundamentals ought to be barred from masquerading as its officers. But I think my contempt may be even greater because of the stupidity of the course suggested. We can sometimes bear with an amiable knave, but a fool has no place in a profession such as ours. In the first place, an advocate who intentionally misstates by what he deems imperceptible slanting, insults his adversary. What better opportunity does an opponent want than the chance to point out that a lawyer fears to meet the true issue? To assume that an opponent is so stupid as not to take advantage of so patent an opportunity is the epitome of folly. The suggestion is equally insulting to the court and in that respect even more laden with self-destruction. Appellate judges are, at the very least, professionals at dissecting argument and at exploring propositions hurled at them. To suggest that they may be tricked by inaccurate phrasings of such features as the questions presented and the facts is an unbelievable arrogance. The advocate who follows that course will, I assure you, soon be trying to figure out why he is never on the successful side of an appellate proceeding. Whatever else you do, don't try to be cute with your opponents or with the judges.

The Oral Argument

Now we turn to the oral argument. This is a different form of opportunity for persuasion. Whereas each statement in the brief can be examined and studied and re-examined by the judge, the statements in oral argument, once made, are gone forever except in the memories of those who heard them. Whereas the brief can be expected to convey the precise meaning intended, no such guarantee can be attached to the oral word, which must be caught on the fly amid difficulties. Whereas the brief is an impersonal print, personalities pervade and color the oral argument. Whereas the brief is to be examined when counsel are absent, at oral argument counsel come to actual grips with the mind of the judge and can seek to ascertain and deal with the judge's trend of thought on the problem. Oral argument is your opportunity to make sure that the essentials of your position pass at least once through the minds of the judges. If you cannot convince them, at least you can make them read your brief.

The oral argument should be an oral argument, not a verbal rendition of a brief. The two are different in purpose, in nature, and in form.

I think I could do no greater service in respect to oral argument than to urge you to read the classic on the subject, the address delivered some twelve years ago by the great master of appellate argument, John W. Davis, and published in the December, 1940, issue of the *American Bar Association Journal*[2] and just recently reprinted by the American Law Institute. With apologies to Mr. Davis I epitomize his decalogue:

Rule 1: "Change places (in your imagination of course) with the Court." The judges, he pointed out, "are anxiously waiting to be supplied with what Mr. Justice Holmes called 'the implements of decision.' " The lawyer should imagine to himself what he would want done were he in the judge's place, how he would want the problem stated, the skeins unraveled.

Rule 2: "State first the nature of the case and briefly its prior history."

Rule 3: "State the facts." This, to Mr. Davis, is the great and important rule. ". . . [T]he statement of the facts," he says, "is not merely a part of the argument, it is more often than not the argument itself." He gives three guides for a statement of facts, the three C's—chronology, candor, and clarity. Charts and pictures are often great aids in oral argument.

Rule 4: "State next the applicable rules of law on which you rely."

Rule 5: "Always 'go for the jugular vein.' " By that is meant that upon oral argument the lawyer should pick the nub of the case and go for it. " . . . [T]he quintessence of the advocate's art" Mr. Davis calls the ability to pick one single point and drive it home as the only worthy topic in the case. If you are superbly courageous you can concede impossible and even dubious points. It is an effective maneuver whence an advocate says, "My op-

[2] Davis, *The Argument of an Appeal*, 26 American Bar Assn. Journal 895 (1940).

ponent is correct when he says so-and-so. He is also correct when he says thus-and-so. And he is correct in contending this-and-thus. But . . . ."

Rule 6: "Rejoice when the Court asks questions." Mr. Davis emphatically urges a positive answer, warns against evasion, shuffling and postponement. He condemns the familiar "I am coming to that" as merely irritating.

Rule 7: "Read sparingly and only from necessity." I add this comment: reading is the most deadly soporific of the courtroom.

Rule 8: "Avoid personalities."

Rule 9: "Know your record from cover to cover."

Rule 10: "Sit down."

I add an observation or so, gleaned from the listening side of the bench. Mr. Davis did not mention specifically the statement of the questions to be decided. In argument Mr. Davis did not fail to state the problem; he wove the problem in as he went along. But less proficient technicians should not trust to that form of skill. My advice is that early in an oral argument, after the first sentences, counsel ought to state to the court succinctly and accurately the problem or problems posed by the appeal.

Another bit of advice I would add is that counsel outline to the court in the very beginning the general program of argument he intends to follow. Counsel complain bitterly about interruptions from the bench. I would not attempt to justify much of the interruption I have seen and heard. I would not attempt to justify many of the interruptions I myself have perpetrated. But I have analyzed my own behavior and know why, generally speaking, I do or do not interrupt. If counsel makes a preposterous statement or advances what is patently an unjust proposition, I am impelled to interrupt from irritation. If he makes an inaccurate statement, I am inclined to interrupt for the same reason. On the other hand, if he obviously is capable and knows what he is talking about, I often interrupt to get help on some phase of the case that troubles me. Having read the briefs before I go on the Bench, I often want to learn something further upon some point. I may have in mind the idea that counsel will strengthen a tentative impression I have in his favor, or I may expect a revelation of weakness in his position. Again, when counsel apparently has nothing particular in mind to discuss, no arrangement or argument, no clear view of what the questions in the case are, I have an irresistible urge to make him help us in spite of himself, and suggest topics, in the form of inquiries, for him to express his views upon.

I believe that much merely harassing questioning—not all of it, but most of it—can be avoided if counsel shows in the beginning of his argument that he understands clearly and precisely the points he wants to make, and if he shows that he has prepared a line of treatment of those points. The court is then inclined to let him proceed except for real inquiries seeking aid in understanding. Of course, judges may be impatient and irritable and "ride" counsel; but that is the exception and not the rule. By and large, I think judges ask questions for the same reasons I do.

At this point I insert a word about the court. Sometimes the judges read the briefs before the oral argument. Sometimes they do not. To the lawyers preparing and making an oral argument the difference is a material one. If the briefs have been read he can proceed immediately to the point or points in dispute and devote his allotted time to an argument at the nub of the controversy. If the briefs have not been read, he must spend a large part of his time informing the court of the nature of the case, the disputed points, the facts, and the prior proceedings. It is my firm conviction that every appellate court should have an announced custom in this phase of its proceeding. Counsel should be allowed and expected to assume that the announced custom has been followed. If perchance one judge is out of step, through misadeventure in the particular case, that judge should let the customary course of argument be followed without interruption for his individual benefit.

Conclusion

I said at the outset that appellate persuasion is an art. But it is an art which, like many other, can be learned. One need not be born a genius to succeed at it. How does a lawyer acquire proficiency at this art? The answer is quite simple. It is: By work. I have said this at other times in other places. There is no other road to success at the law. Work. More work. Then more work. Sad though the fact is, it is true that the vast majority of young lawyers do not and will not work; hence many young lawyers do not succeed.

What do we mean by "work"? We mean several things. I mention four.

First: Learn to write. I say this to young lawyers, and I say it to the older ones too, even to those as ancient as I. Can you write a sentence in English—a sentence in which a thought is stated so clearly and simply that it is easily understood and cannot be misunderstood? Rarely is ability to write such sentences a natural gift. It is acquired. You write, and rewrite—four, six or eight times. Those crystal-clear sentences that you sometimes see are rarely flashes of genius. They are the product of long, weary trying, and trying, and trying—either on the particular sentences or in years of constant cultivation.

Second, "work" means: Probe facts. Spare no effort to learn the most minute detail in every problem you undertake.

Third, "work" means: Exhaust the authorities on every legal problem you undertake. I meant *exhaust,* not merely examine, or cull, or find.

Fourth: Learn to speak. A good rule for a young lawyer is never to decline an invitation to speak—schools, service clubs, community drives, Sunday School, political meetings—anywhere on any subject. In learning to teach a Bible lesson to a Sunday School class of high school students, one learns much of value for pleading a case to a jury, arguing a point to a court, stating a proposition to a conference, or maintaining a position in a negotiation. Speaking effectively in our day is an art acquired only by hard work. The "gift of gab" is a hinderance rather than a help. Glib talk sounds well, but it is not effective in this middle of the Twentieth Century. A lawyer should speak as often as he can. He will learn something new about the art every time he speaks.

The foregoing are merely a few suggestions as to what we mean by Work. They and others like them, not natural brilliance or personality or bluff, are the touchstones of success at appellate persuasion—and at the practice of the law in every phase.

Adapted from 20 J. of D.C.B. Assn. 197 which was reprinted from 39 Virginia Law Review, April 1953.

The Argument of an Appeal

By Raymond S. Wilkins

THE ARGUMENT OF AN APPEAL is, in most cases, the last, and frequently the most important step in the trial of a lawsuit. In the appellate court, a case which up to that point has been lost, may still be won. On the other hand, a case which has been carried thus far with success may nevertheless be lost. Anyone can cite numerous examples from the myriads of decisions which are authority for this truism. If it be thought that, occasionally at least, some cases have been wrongly decided, and that still other cases may yet be, this should be a further incentive to appellate counsel to assist the court. And in these days when divided courts may be more common the challenge to appellate counsel is even greater.

Upon this very old subject I have no delusion that I may present any new thought. Nor do I have any notion that I might fall within the rule of property once laid down in verse by James Russell Lowell:

> "Though old the thought and oft exprest,
> 'Tis his at last who says it best"

What I hope to say, although admittedly not new, has—to speak conservatively—been demonstrated so thoroughly to have eluded general mastery and to have failed to receive uniform application that repetition is not only justified now but undoubtedly will be throughout the predictable future.

At the outset it should be appreciated that a great change has occurred in appellate practice in the last one hundred years. In the early years of the Supreme Court of the United States the oral arguments consumed hours and, in some cases, days. This could only have been with the approval and encouragement of the judges, who must have felt that this assisted them. As time progressed, changed conditions vastly increased the case load of the courts, and there is now a marked tendency to the other extreme of restricting greatly the time permitted for oral argument. Judges think that this method will best assist them in their work as a whole. No disapproval of the principle of oral argument is involved. It means merely that in these days less rather than more talking on both sides fits in better with the scheme of things judicial.

Let us begin with a few words about the record, which is, or should be, the tangible reproduction of the case. In my State the printing of the record is in the hands of the clerk. What it should contain is settled by statute, by rule of court, and by decision. It is most prudent, however, to confer with the clerk to make sure that the record contains everything that one is entitled to have included, and, what is equally important, that it is not cluttered with anything which there is a right to have omitted and which neither counsel intends to use. Those moments are most wearisome which are devoted to arguments and discussions arising out of belated discoveries of avoidable shortcomings of the record.

Once the record is printed and received, counsel must adhere to the fundamental rule which permeates the whole subject of appeals: Know the record! Its substance must be mastered in order to prepare the brief, and, for the most effective oral argument, this mastery must be retained and alertly supplemented by a geographical familiarity—that is, by page and line—with its every nook and cranny as perfect as was the knowledge of Nydia of the smoke and cinder filled streets of Pompeii. Failure to know and to understand a record sometimes results in the argument of a different case than is in fact or in law before the court.

Once a case has reached the appellate court the procedure, I suppose, does not differ much throughout the country. Essentially it is this. Upon the basis of a printed record there must be prepared a printed or written brief, the length of which usually is not, but nevertheless may be, limited by rule. This may be, and usually is, followed by an oral argument, the length of which is rigorously limited by rule. This means that one should make the best use of each of his two weapons, the written and oral argument. The argument in the brief may be extensive, but the oral argument must be intensive.

The brief should be drawn with an eye toward creating a favorable first impression in the judge's mind. It should be able to weather oral assault by an opponent, who will surely have read it before the arguments. It should contain everything which is worth arguing in the case, and should cover with finality questions like those of evidence, which can at most merely be adverted to orally. On the other hand, whatever, upon mature deliberation, is considered unworthy of argument should be frankly and expressly waived. This was Abraham Lincoln's method, and it was a good one. It is a practical recognition of the rightness of Cardozo when he wrote, "Analysis is useless if it destroys what it is intended to explain."

The preparation of the brief should proceed in the knowledge that it is timeless and tireless in its ability to speak. Owing to the case load of each judge and the number of working days in the year there is no secret in the disclosure that an opinion may take form under tremendous pressure. It is also true—at least it is with me—that at some moment in the consideration of a great many cases the scent suddenly becomes very hot. The physical processes —the hand if you write, or the tongue if you dictate—struggle to keep pace with the mental. The excitement may be genuinely great. I recall a cartoon in a leading periodical of a hunter riding alone who without warning came upon three foxes. His ejaculation, "Tallyho for goodness' sake," becomes the apogee of understatement in comparison with the judicial sensations at the moment to which I refer. The brief maker should take all this into account. On that indefinite future day, perhaps weeks after the arguments, when the writer of the opinion, in the solitude of his lonely room, starts work on the case, the brief with all its merits and all its shortcomings is there before him to read if he will. And he most certainly will read it on the issues material to the line of reasoning of the projected opinion. In fact, he may re-read it a score of times, particularly if it be the brief of the side which at the moment appears to have the worse of the argument on the point under consideration.

In aiding this cloistered workman, the advocate should realize that he is aiding his own cause. Hence, he should make sure that his brief is appropriate, and neither too long nor too short for the particular case. The facts must be fittingly set forth with supporting references to the record which are accurate and explicit. Nothing will forfeit the confidence of the court more effectively than the misstatement of the record or the statement of a fact off the record. The latter failing is especially pernicious, as it sends the writer of the opinion on a wild-goose chase hardly calculated to enhance his estimate of the soundness of the legal principles of him who brought it about.

The statement of facts should be succinct but at the same time full and complete as to the material issues. Such a statement is not easy to prepare, but it probably is the most important single thing appeal counsel has to do. Facts tend to complexity and often are double-edged blades. Two great figures, one in English, and one in American, literature, were both right, when they respectively said many years apart, "Facts are stubborn things," and "Facts are contrary 'z mules."

If a statute, city ordinance, town by-law, or rule of some court or administrative body is involved, it should be quoted accurately and in full. The places in the record where the questions of law arose should be meticulously cited. The newspaper headline format is out of place and constitutes self-confessed ineffectiveness of expression. The brief should be logically arranged by topic with reasonable citation of authorities, so that, when the three foxes sooner or later appear, the judicial huntsman will not lose too much time in hurdling any hedges in the reasoning, or be led off the scent through citations which may not be in point or which may be unreasonably numerous or incorrectly given. The citations should be selective and support the respective propositions of law. Citations are not merely conventional, like marks of punctuation, nor are they like architectural embellishments added for no utilitarian purposes but solely for adornment. The suggested purpose will not be attained by listing the first cases remotely in point which are discovered, much less by transcribing on faith directly to the brief an uncensored galaxy of citations clustered in the footnotes of some digest or other stock of prefabricated material. The members of a court need no indiscriminate ticket of admission to the library stacks. If no case in point be found, it is better to cite none, and to emulate the frankness of the English counsel, immortalized in one of the case books I used in law school, who, when asked by the court what authority he had for his statement, responded, "None, my Lord, but I submit that it must be true on principle." If your brief is long, and you have cited a large number of cases, an index is desirable, even though the rules of the particular appellate court may not require it. When you cite the Federal Reporter, give the name of the court in parenthesis. It may be important to indicate whether it is a decision of the Court of Appeals of the Second Circuit or of a District Court judge deciding a case in the first instance. Don't cite the arguments of counsel, which are sometimes printed in the law reports, unless, on rare occasion, you mean to do so and refer to them as such. Don't cite cases which have been overruled unless, on rare occasion, you mean to do so and refer to them as such. Mr. Shepard will help you here. If you quote from a decision in another case, quote it absolutely accurately. Should you omit from the quotation parts of that decision which you deem immaterial, carefully indicate any omissions. Above all, take care not only to avoid garbling the quotation but to avoid the least appearance of doing so. Do not use those disconsolate inadequacies, *supra* and *infra*. They border on the discourteous unless the point referred to is but a few lines away, and in that event they are not needed.

I shall leave this topic by saying that I do not believe that the brief can be proofread too often or too carefully. It should be checked with the record and with the original law reports, not with your own draft. Such reading crystallizes knowledge of the issues. It is the best preparation for the oral argument. And it should utterly eliminate typographical errors. One or two undetected misprints may be excusable in these days of post-war printing, but any considerable number tends to destroy confidence in the substance of the brief itself and in the conscientious thoroughness of its preparation.

The other weapon of contending counsel on appeal, the oral argument, affords a great opportunity. It is a mild euphemism to aver that this opportunity is sometimes not fully realized. Appellate argument resembles general literature. Almost anyone has some critical competence, but only the few achieve a standard of performance which the many sense. Although appellate argument is a common occurrence and represents the culminating competitive effort in the legal contest, it is probably a fact that this is the least qualitative accomplishment of the bar as a whole. This continues true notwithstanding that there have been delivered highly distinguished exhortations on the subject, many of which have been published and are easily available.

A bench of appellate judges is commonly composed of just so many ordinary men. If it is not, there is something wrong, something non-human, about that particular bench. That the Bench and the Bar are sprung from a common fungible source is illustrated by the statement of a distinguished Pennsylvania lawyer who declined appointment to the bench because, as he has been quoted as saying, he would rather talk to fools than listen to them. Counsel should never forget this identity of origin, and in their arguments should try to enlist the sympathetic interest of their fellow humans, the judges. This calls for a supreme effort to make the presentation as attractive as possible, both in substance and in form. The vital point or points should be exposed and attacked incisively. This calls for careful deliberation in advance. The manner of speaking should be varied to attain the proper degree of impressiveness. A monotonous intonation should be avoided. In this connection it is constructive to think of the baseball pitcher who has a good change of pace.

I have already said that the oral argument must be intensive, and it has to be, in order to achieve, within the limited time, effective fire power upon the fleeting target. Counsel wants the court to understand the case, and, at the same time, to understand it his way. The right method of doing this is simple: Tell the judges about it. Give them the facts, and begin by giving them the facts. The very first sentence should focus attention upon the general nature of the controversy. It should settle, once and for all, whether the subject at hand is a murder, a taking by eminent domain, a divorce, or the application in a will of the rule against perpetuities. No matter how interesting—to counsel—the points of law may be, they should be merely indicated and not argued until the essential facts have been stated, even if this requires reliance upon the brief for much of the law. This means that there should be a budgeting of the allotted time and, except in emergency, a rigid adherence to it.

To the court every new record is a mystery. Sometimes it is also a labyrinth. Whatever their legal qualifications judges usually are neophytes as to the facts of a particular case. In my experience it is seldom that there has been an opportunity before the arguments to study the records or the briefs. Even on rare occasion when a judge is able to do this, he does not acquire from the cold record the grasp of detail and the perspective of the facts which counsel always should, and usually do, possess. In my earlier days, while traveling in Europe, before striking a new town, I always studied a street plan, so that I might later find my way about without contemporaneous consultation of a guidebook. By analogy, the oral argument could be the introduction and guide to the record and briefs. It is advisable if possible, during the argument, to induce the judges to make on their copies of the record and of the briefs, as many pencil marks as may be reasonable to indicate facts or authorities favorable to the contentions. Counsel should give them his view of the mystery, and if there be a labyrinth, he should guide them his way to the place where the Minotaur is to be found. Likewise, if there are important plans, photographs, or documents, not printed in the record but incorporated by reference, this information should be called to the attention of the court early in the argument. What a futile sensation it is when a somewhat blind argument makes this revelation almost by way of peroration!

If, notwithstanding every conscientious act of thoroughness, errors have been discovered in the record or in your own brief, bring them to the court's attention by page and line early and before the argument really gets under way, but preferably not as the topic sentence. If you find similar errors in your opponent's brief, tell him privately, so that he may correct them on his time and not on yours.

A statement of facts should contain the facts, all the facts, and nothing but the facts. Statements off the record are just as bad in the oral argument as in the brief. The inevitable dénouement may or may not be close at hand, but its effect, whenever it occurs, will be equally baleful. Equally devastating is the suppression of a vital fact. In a certain case of the Sherlock Holmes type, the defendant's counsel argued his full time without mentioning anything remotely connecting his client with the crime. The presentation differed from Poe's truncated *Murders in the Rue Morgue* only in not being admittedly fragmentary. The prosecuting attorney in a few moments then supplied the omissions which rendered the whole evidence as cogent as that which satisfied Robinson Crusoe that he was not alone on the desert island. A delay of one hour in the full exposure of the facts is hardly worth while. To entertain an expectation that such exposure may not occur is sheer chauvinism.There was a wise saying in the Field Service Regulations of the United States Army which went something like this, "Always attribute to the enemy the same intelligence as your own even though he may not possess it." This is equally applicable to an argument on appeal. I believe it must have been this sort of thing which Thomas More had in mind when he wrote in his *Utopia*, "They have no lawyers among them, for they consider them as a sort of people whose profession it is to disguise matters."

An inevitable and valuable part of the arguments is the questions by the court. Although often so regarded, they usually are not a manifestation of unfriendliness. Nevertheless, a question may be. There is the instance in that delightful book, "Philadelphia Lawyer," where the judge's question was met by the response, "Your Honor, I am addressing myself exclusively to those members of the court who do not make up their minds until the conclusion of the argument." Of course, no advantage lies in feeling, much less in betraying, annoyance. There is the occasion of the counsel who had closed his argument without damage from his own efforts or those of his opponent only thoroughly to be discomfited at the last moment by an interrogation from the bench. He then turned to the spectators and inquired, "Is there anyone else present who would like to ask any questions?"

Questions by the court most often spring from a yearning for the facts. They sometimes are means of communication to a colleague on a distant part of the bench, perhaps in reply to a question of his to counsel. In the main, they serve to advise the advocate of the issues to which at least one judge is directing his attention, and as such are a coöperative effort to make the best use of time, and thus expedite a just determination of the cause.

It often happens that a question is asked which relates to a matter which counsel intends to consider at a later point in his argument. The best way to handle the situation is for counsel to state briefly what the answer is to be and say that he will cover the matter more fully before he closes. But should he follow this course, or should he feel that to give an answer on the spot would require too long a digression and that he wishes to be excused temporarily from answering, under no circumstances should he omit to carry out his promise. To fail in this respect evokes judicial speculation as to the reason. Was it an oversight? Was it ignorance? Was it evasiveness? Or was it something else? And if so, what was it, and what is its bearing upon the merits of the case?

One situation which occasionally arises in questions from the bench is beyond the control of counsel. It may be that a judge may put a formidable question before counsel scarcely has begun to speak or to have had a fair opportunity to state his position. In that unfortunate plight the most that counsel can do is respectfully and tolerantly make the best answer he can, and trust to good fortune that he will be able to resume stride without losing too much precious time.

Like every speaker on this subject, I have a few favorite "Don'ts." The brief reader may be dismissed with an anecdote. Wearied by the futile consumption of time by a lawyer who was droning through his brief, a helpless judge wrote on a piece of paper, "A brief reader is the lowest form of living animal," and then passed it to a colleague. The latter read it, took a pencil, wrote, "He is a vegetable," and passed it back.

A brother of the half-blood to the brief reader is the counsel who instead reads a prepared statement. The only difference to be observed is that it is harder to guess the probable length of the ordeal when, unlike with the brief, there is no copy in one's own hands. Regardless of what is read, the very act of reading draws an iron curtain between counsel and the sympathetic attention of the court.

Do not relate the facts of cited cases in painful detail. They are too many to be absorbed from oral presentation. It wastes time that can be utilized to better advantage. In the average case it is sufficient to announce that you rely on such and such cases. The court, before deciding the case, will read them just as carefully as have counsel if they are even remotely material to the reasoning of the opinion.

One should never volunteer the statement that he did not try the case below. It is at most a defensive remark, and is too suggestive of "*Sauve qui peut.*"

If extra time is allowed for the argument, this should not be regarded as an offer by the court to a unilateral contract to be accepted only by speaking performance which persists till the last grain of sand has run out of the hourglass. The words that remain unspoken under such conditions beget much good will, particularly with the attending members of a bar awaiting their turn to address the court. This principle applies to all arguments. In an earlier court generation one youthful counsel, who asked how much time he was permitted, was told, "You have half an hour to talk, but you do not have to talk half an hour."

It is just as important to close as it is to open. The argument should not be a one-way ticket to nowhere. Upon reaching the predetermined destination, one should alight. In other words, he should make clear his final point, stop talking, and be seated. And in so doing expressions of gratitude or thanks to the court for their attention are most unhappy. Such a rhetorical anti-climax is, at best, none too pleasing to the judicial ear. Some years ago such a conclusion more than once evoked a judicial reminder that listening was the very minimum of the duties of the office of the faithful performance of which all the members had been duly sworn.

There is sometimes the problem whether to argue orally or to submit on briefs. If the record is complicated, my advice is not to lose a golden opportunity to set forth the facts in the presence of those who must understand them before they can decide the case. If the record is not complicated, and if you prevailed in the court below, and if your opponent is going to submit, it may be wise to rely on your brief provided you are still satisfied with it. But if you were unsuccessful below, or if you were successful and your opponent is going to argue orally, it is my belief that allegiance to the cause calls for oral argument on your part. General rules without exception applicable to every case cannot be laid down, and what I say is only the view of one judge of one court, and not the result of any Gallup poll.

One may wonder how it is possible, in a half hour or in an hour, to make an oral argument upon appeal and yet do justice to a case which may have taken days, or even weeks, to try in the lower court. One answer is that the judges have a profound familiarity with the law of their own jurisdiction. They are also experienced listeners, and are alert to detect wherein the argued case resembles decided cases. With a skillful oral statement of the salient facts and with the brief to rely upon, it is seldom necessary to do more than guide their minds from the cornerstone of fact to the structural outline of the legal principles believed applicable. It is not uncommon that when a case is called for argument, counsel in tones approaching despair proclaim their inability to argue within the prescribed time limit and beg for an extension. It is my observation that, aside from capital cases, counsel, more often than not, fail to give the court assistance commensurate with any additional time allotted.

In my early days of practice, I asked a leader of my local bar what he considered the best method of learning to try a case. He responded, "Try and try and try, and get licked over and over again." I do not think it is indispensable to taste exclusively of the cup of defeat in order to acquire proficiency in appellate argument. But experience is the only guide, and that means an experience based upon a planned course designed to avoid mistakes, and, after mistakes inevitably occur, to avoid their repetition. In this, as in other fields of the legal profession, the successful practitioners are not men—if there be such—who never made a mistake, but are men who undismayed do not repeat them.

I believe I have demonstrated how difficult it is to disclose any really new aspect of this very old human relationship, the argument of appeals. It is fortunate perhaps that discoveries in this field are unlikely, because the old has proved more than adequate to test the mettle of both judge and advocate. In the great *nisi prius* case of *Shylock v. Antonio*, the plaintiff asked one question which at the time did, and usually would, provide its own answer, "Woulds't thou have a serpent sting thee twice?" As an aspect of the argument of appeals there may be more than one view as to the proper answer to that question. At all events, I trust that I may be accorded pardon for any superfluous sting.

Adapted from Vol. 33, Cornell Law Quarterly (1947).

Oral Argument of Appeal

BY H. GRAHAM MORISON

I HAVE BEEN REQUESTED to distill from experience some helpful principles to be observed in the oral argument of appeals. In candor, I confess that this is like asking a mountain fiddler to explain to a music society the principles of harmony that came to him by instinct and ear. Truly you deserve a Beethoven, but I hope that you will tolerate a Carson Robertson.

I shall probably violate every principle of forensic statement I am about to declare, but that is chargeable to that special type of poetic license granted to the advocate.

It is like the lawyer who won a signal court victory on a certain point of law in one case, and who argued a case the following day before the same judge taking the opposite side of the same point of law. When questioned by the Bench as to how this could be, he explained, "Your Honor, it occurred to me, as it might have occurred to you, that my legal logic was so unassailable in the other case that my peculiar talents should, in all propriety be pitted against the principle—lest the law become fixed and immovable in the iron box of *stare decisis*."

It is, then, the oral argument of the appeal that is our concern. We shall assume that the brief, adequate in all respects, has been filed.

I shall, without further ado, get into the middle of the problem. But I can not refrain from flexing a few preliminary professional muscles to show you I have been in the ring. I shall divide my proposition into logical categories, in the same way Chief Justice Taft reported that a lawyer addressed the Supreme Court, stating that he proposed to divide his argument into three parts. "In the first," he said, "I shall state the relevant facts; next, I shall propound the applicable principles of law; and, third, I shall make a lunge at the passions of the court."

Some General Principles

Like the stilling of music of the mountain waterfall by the power dam, the grandeur of legal oratory untrammeled by time limitations has given way to the necessities of our modern age. As a lover of waterfall symphonies and of sweeping oratory, I bitterly resent what the modern age has imposed, but as a modern man I reluctantly bow to the community need for electricity and, as an up-to-date advocate bent upon winning my case, I adjust my oral approach to doubting appellate judges in conformity with the necessities of modern appellate courts.

Where, in another day and time, appeals were argued for weeks on end, now only the most urgent public necessity will bring an appellate court to grant additional time for argument. Thus, brief, compact argument, powerful in impact, is the instrument that must be used in modern appellate argument. The rifle is the weapon to use—not the shotgun.

In this day, appeals are won or lost upon oral argument. The judges of every appellate court in the land with which I am acquainted could not, reading 24 hours a day, read and digest all of the printed material that is currently filed in their courts. Even with the able assistance of clerks and secretaries, it is impossible for judges to adequately cover the material.

This means that appellate judges must depend upon oral argument as the indispensable vehicle for "knowing" the cases that come before them. It means that appellate judges rely upon the vigorous advocacy of each side to light up every corner of the controversy. The court becomes the anvil and the advocates the hammer. To appellate courts, the brief is but an introduction to the problem, a guide during the course of argument and a source of after-argument reference when decisions are prepared. Oral argument, then, is a prime instrument for decision.

Is it not clear, then, that the oral argument is of essential and fundamental importance? Thoreau said, "It takes two to speak the truth—one to speak and one to hear." It is thus in the oral argument that the truth shines most clearly, if you will but sharpen your oral presentation.

All who have written about the oral argument of appeals are unanimous in saying that, in such argument, the lawyer has the opportunity to bring into play all of his resources of mind and heart and spirit. It is the highest art of the legal profession and truly serves to "separate the men from the boys."

The argument of an appeal in many ways depends upon rudimentary principles of salesmanship, drummed into every Fuller Brush salesman. The first of these principles is to "know your prospect" and in the case of the appellate advocate, to "know your judges."

I would advise you to read the opinions of judges who will hear your appeal to learn their inclinations in the broad principles you will espouse. Try to determine their mental attitudes as revealed by what they have done and what they have said in their opinions, speeches and published articles. Then look at your case in the eyes of each of those mental attitudes.

Do your best to surmise what questions each judge will ask and why he will ask them. What doubts will each judge have from a quick reading of your brief and from his memory of the external brush with the issues which he had when you applied for an appeal?

Determine, as best you can, which of the judges you believe will be with you, which will be against you, and which will be neutral! Map your argument so as to win over those who may be against you, carry the neutrals, and give no offense to those who are with you!

Keep in mind the factors which necessitate placing time limits on oral argument. If you would put yourself in the shoes of the judges, you would find you are tired physically and mentally most of the time, that you no longer have a social life or the opportunity to pursue hobbies and avocations, and that every waking hour is consumed in its entirety by the necessity of going over the flood of papers dealing with appeals. If you lived that life, think how grimly you would react to a verbose, time-consuming argument that wandered all over the lot and wasted the precious time of a court so heavily burdened. On the other hand, consider what a joy it would be to hear an advocate argue his case with an economy of words, in a style that combined clarity with spice, who said his piece in a clear but modulated voice and, most of all, who brought to the argument that intangible thing of the heart that touches every word with gold—passionate sincerity.

Preparation for Oral Argument

Be liberal in the time you provide yourself for preparation of your oral argument. It is a great fallacy to asume that because you have tried the case in the trial court or written the brief that it will be a simple matter to prepare the oral argument. The only appellate argument I ever undertook in which I had adequate time for preparation was the first one I made in 1934. I took two months to prepare my argument simply because in those days I had nothing else to do. Even so, on the day of argument I felt hollow and inadequate.

Unless you are lucky enough to be selected to argue an appeal in your very beginnings when time hangs heavy on your hands, or unless you are at the top of your profession so that all of your partners and associates bear the burdens of the legal work, there is no Patmos to which the average lawyer may retire to devote himself to the important task of preparation, without interruptions. Thus, I reiterate, set aside *twice* as much time as you judge will be necessary for the preparation of the argument.

If you wrote the brief or made a major contribution to its preparation, you have the advantage of a familiarity with the record and the principles of law involved in the case. This advantage is almost nullified, however, by the fact that your point of view may have become fixed and stubborn as a result of your prior work. The only answer in either situation is for you to wipe your mental slate clean and start at the beginning and read the record, pleadings and exhibits with great care and thoroughness.

It is my practice first to read the record in this fashion without taking any notes and then to go back and reread the record, taking careful notes as I go along. You will be surprised how many points are overlooked in the first reading and how often your point of view changes after the second careful reading.

Having thus taken careful notes covering the essential points of fact, you are now ready to nail down the elusive principles of law *which govern* the case. There is no rule that I can give you as to how far your legal research should take you. Each man must satisfy his own appetite. I can only say that I have never been impressed by preparations that gave over-lengthy citations nor with the appellate advocate who attempted to buttress his point by citing a long list of cases. If there is one thing which the practice of law teaches the advocate, it is that there is no decided case which precisely fits another and the art of appellate advocacy is to distill broad principles of law convincingly so that the justice and equity which he seeks are properly reinforced by these principles.

In all that I have recommended, I have tried to say that you must *saturate* yourself with your case. First, the facts, then the law, and from this, the broad equities of your proposition. When you have accomplished this, you should then have the confidence which comes from thorough preparation and which is so essential to the plan for the attack upon that citadel of doubt—the appellate court.

So far as my own experience demonstrates, and my opinion is fortified by the concurrence of every great appellate judge that I have ever talked with, the most important single element of successful oral argument is the ability to select the heart of your case —the hub—the core, upon which all else depends. If you have saturated yourself with your case as carefully as I recommend, you should be able to make this decision easily.

In making this fundamental decision, however, do not be afraid to take your problem to older practitioners. Most of them will be delighted to give you their advice and help. You may also want to consult the lawyer who tried the case below and others associated in the case. But in the end you, *and you alone*, must decide what is the heart of the case.

When you have decided this basic issue, then you have the task of laying out your argument on that central point, tearfully giving up all of the interesting by-roads that are so enticing and all of the subsidiary arguments intended to be security points on the long pull. This is where you become the generalissimo and make the technical legal decision of where the fight will be made.

From that point onward, a great deal of your task becomes mechanical. I suggest that you write out what you propose to say, and in writing it I suggest the elimination of all fancy phraseology and involved sentences. Stick to good Anglo-Saxon words and phrases, make your sentences pithy, distill your thoughts into simple language, and if you *can,* be vivid; but, *above all else, be brief.*

After you have satisfied yourself with the first draft, cut it in *half* and when you have done this, go over it again and cut it about *one-fourth.*

In your preparation of these drafts, I suggest the following:

First, state whom you represent and where your client is located.

State the nature of your case—that it is a tort, a question of constitutional law, or whatever it may be.

Make a brief statement of the court's jurisdiction. A lawyer now deceased, whom I knew and respected as a great advocate, argued one case in the Supreme Court before he died. In argument, he launched headlong into his case and when the Chief Justice asked him, "How did you get here?," he replied, "I came up on 42, Southern Railroad."

Next, *state the facts*. Daniel Webster said that "the power of clear statement is the great power at the bar."

It is at this point that John Davis' recommendation of the "Three C's" of appellate argument should be borne in mind: "Chronology, Candor and Clarity."

State the rules of law which you rely upon and be prepared to meet any challenge that may come to your position. Keep in mind the heart of your case and, even though questions may momentarily take you away from the main road, diplomatically avoid any extensive treatment of such issues and return to the hub of your case.

Now, reduce what you have written for oral argument into bold headnotes easy for you to read at a glance, and preferably on a very few pages.

Begin to rehearse your argument out loud. Whatever you do, avoid committing to memory your purple passages. You will need flexibility and, if you memorize, you solidify the mind.

Time the length of your argument so that you can finish it in no more than two-thirds of the time allotted. As you continue your rehearsal, plan to cover your essential argument in *half* the time, for the court's questions may prevent you from employing over half of the time.

If you have an associate or a partner in the case, have him assist you in your rehearsal by interrupting you with searching questions that you anticipate the members of the court may ask you, and rehearse your answers to those questions.

Now, you are prepared for the argument.

Argument

Try to go to the court a day or so ahead of your case and take time to make a friend of the clerk or one of his deputies. You will find these people most helpful in advising you of the peculiarities of the court and its rules as it pertains to oral argument, and in telling you something about the individual preferences of each of the justices. If you can, listen to the argument of a case the day before you go on, so that you can get the feel of the court at work.

Do your best to anticipate what your opponent will say about your argument and be prepared to meet it *if* he says it. But, whatever you do, do not take precious time to anticipate what your opponent may say.

If your client will stand it, get a room in a hotel where you can work in comfort and seclusion. On the day of the argument, leave behind associates, wives and clients whose presence in the courtroom may tend to distract you from your important task.

Dress conservatively, not in slavish conformity, but because the dignity of the process in which you are engaged is not the place for the individualism found in gaudy raiment.

Leave behind all your multitude of law books and papers. By this time, you should not need them.

The essential things to have with you are, first, your notes for argument; second, the record tabbed appropriately for purposes of ready reference, should that be necessary; and, finally, your brief.

There is something psychologically persuasive about a man who comes before an appellate court unburdened by a lot of legal paraphernalia.

Remember the limitations of time which are so important to the court and to the strategy of your argument. If you are interrupted by questions, be prepared, within the limitations of time remaining, to revert to the heart of your case and cover its major aspects.

As you address the court, look its members in the eye. Avoid reading *anything* unless it is absolutely essential and, in that event, confine it to those things that are in the record so you can, by reference to page and paragraph, have the court read it at the same time you are reading it.

Joyfully embrace the questions of the court. Many of my friends among appellate lawyers are convinced that appeals are won or lost in the handling of the questions from the Bench.

Above all, never avoid a question or postpone it. Answer with sincerity and complete frankness, even if your answer is against you. Use the court's questions to return to the central heart of your case.

Avoid rebuttal simply because the time is there. Oftentimes greater emphasis is given to your proposition and to your confidence in its correctness by refusing rebuttals. Avoid it if you are convinced the court understands your proposition.

Above all, learn to sit down. If you have said your piece as you planned it and if you have covered the essential points, the court will be grateful to you if you will sit down.

Finally, do not be afraid of your inadequacies. You will find the court will exhibit its instinctive desire to help you and, if you have truly immersed yourself in your case, you will never be inadequate.

If you know your case, you should not be afraid. Once you are swimming in the stream I promise that you will forget all of your doubts and worries.

The essence of all great advocacy is sincerity. If you hammer your points with righteous zeal, your sincerity will shine through and add dignity and life to your cause. The court will be grateful for your sincerity, and even though they may not decide with you, you will have done justice to your cause.

Adapted from Vol. 10, Washington and Lee Law Review (1953).

Preparation and Presentation of Cases in Courts of Review

By Orrin N. Carter

Every lawyer wishes to present his case to the court so as to bring the best results. No fixed rules can be laid down with reference to this matter. I know of no book discussing this question and have never had my attention called to any magazine article on it. The law dictionaries sometimes devote some pages to discussing the preparation of briefs. A few suggestions drawn from years of experience on this subject may be of assistance to lawyers in the preparation and presentation of their cases in courts of review. Courts of review usually require the filing of briefs and arguments to assist the court in passing on the issues involved in any case. The Supreme Court of Illinois also requires a printed abstract. In some courts the abstract is not required, but the court goes directly to the record. It is a great saving of time for the court, when there is a large record, if a printed abstract is prepared by the lawyers and presented with the briefs. It enables the judges to become familiar with the facts and issues of the case much more easily, because each judge then can have a copy of the abstract, whereas, if the record only is available and must be searched in order to find the facts, only one judge can have access to it at a given time. The principal assistance given to a court of review in deciding a case, necessarily, is the briefs and arguments prepared by counsel. The lawyers who best understand the facts and the law applicable thereto, everything else being equal, will prepare the best briefs and arguments. The question of the preparation or lack of preparation in presenting cases in a court of review is very noticeable. Many cases are won in courts of review, as they are in trial courts, because of the thorough preparation of the counsel. The methods of preparing and presenting briefs and arguments are governed in a general way by the rules of each respective court, and necessarily the rules of such court must be studied by the lawyers in order to prepare the brief for such court, but a few general rules can be laid down that will apply to all courts of review.

Printed Briefs and Abstracts

Doubtless all courts of review in this country, at the present time, require printed briefs to be filed in every case, unless by special order counsel, on account of the financial condition of the client, is permitted to file a typewritten brief, or one written with pen and ink. For example: in a criminal case where the accused has no means to pay for the printing of a brief—doubtless all courts, on such question being presented to them in proper form, would permit a typewritten or pen-written brief to be filed for such person. All courts, however, do not require, even in this day, printed abstracts. In the supreme courts of some of the various states in the country, I understand the practice is for the judges to go to the record itself in order to ascertain the actual facts and issues in a given case. There can be no question but that the printing of abstracts, if properly prepared by counsel, will greatly facilitate and lessen the work of the members of the court in ascertaining the issues in a given case and the facts necessary to be understood to fairly decide it.

In most courts, the rules permit, and sometimes require, oral arguments by counsel in the cases presented to the court for its decision. Of course oral arguments may be of great assistance to the court in properly deciding a case, but printed arguments are essential, with the present volume of litigation in various jurisdictions, to enable the court to reach anything like satisfactory results.

The rules of the court in most jurisdictions attempt to lay down some general directions as to the preparation of briefs. The rules of the Supreme Court of this state require that a printed brief shall be filed by each party in three subdivisions, viz: (1) statement of case, (2) brief, (3) argument. The brief of appellant or plaintiff in error should first contain a short and clear statement of the case, including, first, the form of the action; second, the nature of the pleadings sufficiently to show what the issues were, and to present every question subject to review arising thereon; third, in cases depending upon the evidence, the leading facts which the evidence proved or tended to prove without discussion, argument or detail; fourth, how the issues were decided and what the judgment or decree was, and, fifth, the errors relied upon for a reversal. Appellee's, or defendant in error's brief should be prepared in a similar manner, except that if the statement of the case already made by opposing counsel is satisfactory, there is no necessity for restating it.

Few lawyers seem to possess the faculty of making a statement of a case so clear, concise, and full, that the judge, on reading it, can clearly and fully understand the questions at issue. Unless counsel themselves fully understand the case and have in mind, clearly, what it is about, it certainly will be difficult to write a statement in the brief that the court will understand. The word "brief" is often used to include "statement," "brief" and "argument." The statement proper in the brief should contain only a recital of the actual facts. If there is any controversy as to what the record shows as to the facts, this can be suggested in the statement, but without attempting to argue which side finds support in the record. The question of argument should be taken up in that part of the brief and argument technically known as the argument proper. Using the terms in a technical way, the statement, brief, and argument should each be kept separate and distinct one from the other, and this applies with particular force to the statement of the case. I know of nothing that is of greater assistance to the court than to have the statement in the brief clearly and logically set out the story of the case and the issues involved, without any attempt to argue as to the writer's views on the issues in controversy. It is a rare thing to find any brief in which counsel have been able to resist the temptation to inject an argument into the statement of a case in support of their viewpoint. The most helpful statement is one that gives a clear story of the case, letting the actual facts speak for themselves. The maxim frequently repeated by Judge Tuley, one of the greatest trial judges that ever sat in the courts of Chicago, was, "Out of the facts springs the law." It is a maxim that cannot be kept too steadily in view by all lawyers in the preparation of briefs. I have known briefs to be prepared and presented in certain cases by lawyers of great experience and more than ordinary ability which contained no statement of the case of any kind. Then I have known other briefs in which the statement was found near the close of the brief and argument. The lawyers who prepare briefs in such a manner have no correct conception as to the purpose and value of a good statement of the case.

The brief proper should be inserted after the statement of the case and should not attempt to set out any of the facts or make any argument. Its peculiar province is to cite, under proper headings, the authorities relied on, and possibly to show their proper application. The shorter these headings, the better, provided they are clear and to the point. Sometimes a certain fact or argument is found in identical language, set out in the statement of the case, again in the brief proper and a third time in the argument. Ordinarily such a repetition is unnecessary and not helpful. The practice of citing too many authorities in the brief is a growing evil. While no hard and fast rule can be laid down on this subject, it needs no argument, it seems to me, to prove that if many authorities are cited that are not in point, as is frequently the case, the members of the reviewing court cannot be blamed if they do not examine all the authorities at length. The court will always be greatly assisted if a careful selection of appropriate authorities is made of the cases and text books and then only those are cited in the brief that are in point and apply the most closely to the facts in the given case. In these days of publication of opinions of all courts, both nisi prius and the appellate, by the reporter system and in legal periodicals, it is comparatively easy to find many cases on any given question. I do not wish to be understood as intimating that lawyers ought not to look up cases and authorities in all jurisdictions, but to cite the decisions of nisi prius courts is ordinarily of little value. A dozen well selected authorities from courts of standing are of far greater assistance than several hundred selected on the "hit-and-miss" plan.

The argument proper should take up and discuss the points in the same order in which they are printed in the brief. While it is helpful to have a subdivision and classification of the points, both in the brief and argument, some lawyers divide and subdivide and subhead briefs and arguments until the subdivision becomes a burden to the court. I recall a case in which no great principle was under discussion and the amount involved was small, and yet the brief contained fifteen subdivisions and some resubdivisions. Two subdivisions would have fully served the purpose and would have been much easier to understand and follow. In this connection it may be stated that lawyers frequently make the mistake of relying on too many objections. Many criticisms of the record are frequently thrown indiscriminately into the arguments and briefs, without any logical arrangement, and frequently as much stress is laid upon the minor points, as upon the important questions which may be fairly open to debate and discussion. The far-sighted lawyer understands the chief points in the case and will make his main argument upon those points and touch only briefly, if at all, upon those of minor importance.

The authorities relied on should be cited in the brief, but the important ones may be referred to afterwards in the argument, if it is desired to quote from them, or, if for any reason, it is wished to emphasize the points claimed to be supported by the authorities in question. If the questions raised in the briefs are all fairly equal in importance, then, ordinarily, it is advantageous to take them up in the briefs and arguments in the order in which they arose in the trial itself. But here again no hard and fast rule can be laid down to be followed. If a lawyer has questions that he thinks are vital to the decision of the case, they may be first raised and considered in the briefs and discussed in that order in the argument and the minor points taken up afterwards. It is sometimes thought necessary, by opposing lawyers, to review each of the authorities cited by other counsel. This is generally not wise or helpful. If the authorities of opposing counsel are deemed not in point, they can easily be classed together in the brief in a few sentences stating that fact and if deemed necessary to refer specifically to a given authority, but many of them need only a brief mention. Perhaps in no part of the brief and argument can more skill and good judgment be shown than in carefully classifying and commenting in the argument on authorities of opposing counsel.

The rule of the Illinois Supreme Court provides that the abstract shall not set out at length the evidence in the record by questions and answers. It may well be questioned whether it is ever a good practice for counsel in their briefs to set out the evidence at any length by question and answer. If there is some vital point in the case that can best be shown by question and answer, a very brief quotation with a few questions and answers might be proper, but such quotation ought never to extend over half a page or a page at the most. If it is desired to have the court read the questions and answers, it would be better practice to set them out in the abstract, and then refer in the briefs to the place in the abstract where they may be found. Ordinarily, it is not wise to set out at length the questions and answers either in the briefs or abstract. If counsel think it is advisable to have the questions and answers before the court, they can make that statement in the brief and refer to the special pages of the abstract and record, where the questions and answers will be found, giving briefly in the argument their reasons why the court ought to read the questions and answers in order to get the point counsel is trying to make.

A brief should not contain statements disrespectful to the trial judge, the opposing counsel or the court in which the brief is filed. Reasonable and fair criticism of the court or counsel is always permissible, and much latitude should be permitted if the remarks of counsel are applicable and pertinent to the subject under inquiry. No court attempts to claim infallibility; it is subject to error as is every other human agency. Judges need the assistance of counsel in order to reach right conclusions, but in no case should a brief be used as a vehicle for conveying hatred, contempt, insult, disrespect, or professional discourtesy of any nature to the court of review, to the trial judge, or to opposing counsel. Courts usually strike briefs from the files if their attention is called to such language, and often do it of their own motion.

Citation of Authorities in Briefs

In my experience in the work of the Supreme Court it has often occurred to me, as it has to my associates on the bench, that lawyers, carelessly, perhaps, make mistakes in their briefs in their method of reference to and quotation from the decisions and authorities.

Of course no definite and settled rule can be laid down that will apply in all cases and in all briefs, as to just how many authorities should be referred to or quoted from. But some general suggestions can readily be made that will certainly be helpful to the court if followed, and may be of great assistance to the lawyers in presenting their cases. In these days, with the hundreds of authorities that are readily accessible to all attorneys, and with the stenographer and typewriter always at hand, the temptation is to cite too many authorities and quote from them at too great length in the briefs. A few authorities especially applicable on a given point will be of greater assistance to the court, and are much more apt to influence it in favor of the attorney who cites them, than the citation of numberless authorities taken from all jurisdictions, many of which may not have any special application to the point under discussion. I recollect a personal injury suit in which the lawyer cited in his brief, of course expecting the court to refer to and read them, over a thousand authorities. Now, any one at all familiar with personal injury law knows that there are only a very few legal principles involved in any case in such an action, and even if the Supreme Court had time to read over or refer, even hurriedly, to all of the thousand authorities, so many cases might tend to becloud the real issue rather than assist. How much better in such a brief to refer to and quote from a comparatively few authorities that are especially or peculiarly applicable to the facts in the given case.

Then, too, attorneys in their briefs often use very poor judgment in quoting from the various authorities. It is rarely of any benefit to me to have a lawyer quote at great length in a brief from any given decision or authority and I doubt if it is to any other judge. What is helpful to me is to have the lawyer quote a sentence, more or less, from a given authority that has particular application to the point under discussion, giving the exact page of the book from which the quotation is taken; for instance, *Johnson v. Jones,* 291 Ill. 119. If the attorney, as is frequently the case, only refers to the page of the book upon which the opinion begins, and the decision is of any length, it may require a good deal of time to find the exact place in the opinion quoted from. Ordinarily, in my judgment, it is not helpful to the court for a brief to quote at length from the decision of any court, and this suggestion applies particularly to the decisions from the Illinois Supreme Court. If I am to read at length from any opinion as bearing on the question under consideration, I would much prefer to see the case itself, rather than read a long quotation from it, and, of course, the decisions of our own state court are always easily referred to by any judge when he is studying briefs. This rule as to limiting the quotation, should possibly not be as strictly followed when the attorney is referring to an authority not readily accessible to the judge as the decisions of the Supreme Court of this state; but most of the members of the court have at hand not only decisions of this state, but the decisions of most of the states published in the West Reporter System, and the Supreme Court Library at Springfield contains all authorities.

The mistake also is frequently made, if a part of an opinion bears on the question under discussion to quote parts of the opinion that do not bear directly on the question. The temptation always is in quoting from an opinion that is in point to begin too far from the real point of the quotation and continue the quotation too far. Of course it is much easier for a lawyer to do that than simply select just the parts of the opinion to quote that bear directly on the point at issue. Only the part of the opinion that bears directly on the point should be quoted in the brief.

In this connection attention may be called to the citing of an authority the second time. Some attorneys seem to think it is necessary in the argument proper to set out and refer to every authority that they have cited in the brief proper. Of course this is not necessary, and often not wise, though it may be stated that it will save the judge much time in a long brief, when referring in the argument to an authority cited in the brief, to give the full title of the authority, with page and volume, and not to print, as is often done by lawyers, "supra." For example: "*Brown v. Smith,* supra." Instead of that, in my judgment, the attorney should always, in writing a brief, when referring to the authority the second time, give the volume and page. For example: "*Brown v. Smith,* 290 Ill. 319," because if the word "supra" is used instead, it may frequently, in a long brief, take considerable time to look up the information in the former part of the brief and argument. I am aware that the Supreme Court opinions generally use "supra," and usually refer only to the first page of an opinion, but that practice does not necessarily apply to the writing of briefs. Moreover, such practice in a long opinion is undesirable.

It may well be doubted whether the lawyers, in citing any of the several encyclopedias of law that are in general use at the present time, ought to cite the text without looking up the authorities cited in support of that text, to see if they are really in accord with the text, and this suggestion applies to a judge in writing an opinion in a case. I have more than once found, in comparing the authorities cited in support of a given text in encyclopedias of law, that they do not support the text, but are simply given as bearing on the point under discussion.

In Citing Authorities, Should Preference Be Given to Cases or Text Books?

The question has often been asked me whether the citing of a case involving a principle under consideration, or the citing of a text book discussing the same principle, will best assist the court. No positive rule can be laid down in regard to this matter; it depends very much upon the character of the text book cited. The text book is supposed to base its doctrine upon the rules and principles laid down in many cases, and to be written after an exhaustive study of the various cases and authorities by the author of the book. The same is true, to a certain extent, of every opinion —that it is a condensation of the writer's opinion with reference to the principles of the law, as found in many cases, applied to the facts of a given case. Many text books written in recent years are often little more than digests of many cases, hurriedly collected by the author under the pressure of preparing copy for the printer. The citation of such a text book is ordinarily not as valuable as the citation of a well considered opinion in a case, and often, unfortunately, the text in the so-called encyclopedia is wrong and is gathered so hurriedly that the doctrine laid down in the text cannot be safely followed without an original and an independent investigation of the cases relating to the principles involved. I am gratified to state that the encyclopedias of law that are being recently published are more accurate in their statements in the text than some of the earlier editions of similar classes of work. This result is a reasonable and natural one, because the writers in the recent books on any given subject have the advantage of all the information gathered in the former encyclopedias of law, and necessarily use freely the results of the work of former writers on the subject under consideration. If a text book, whether in the form of an encyclopedia of law or an ordinary single volume on a given subject, is prepared with the care and investigation that Kent, Blackstone, Greenleaf, Bishop, or Story gave to the preparation of the text books which bear their names, then a citation from such a text is always valuable, and especially if it is an encyclopedia of law, because along with the text in the book are the citations of many authorities which can be readily looked up if the investigator is in doubt about the correctness of the text. If, however, the text does not correctly state the principles of law contained in the authorities cited, then it is misleading and not helpful. I have repeatedly had occasion to state that the text of an encyclopedia of law should not be cited, either by counsel or judge, without an investigation of the authorities cited as bearing out the text. The crux of the whole question in the citing of authorities is to cite something that is really in point, and the more consideration that has been given by the author of the opinion or book cited to the principles discussed and the authorities referred to, the more valuable will the citation be to the judge who is writing the opinion.

The following of any given rule, plan, method, or suggestion, or any set of rules, will not produce the best briefs, or even briefs of a high class. Such rules or methods may aid in their preparation. What is a good plan or method of preparation of a brief in a given case may be a poor plan of preparing the brief in another case of an entirely different character. The best brief must be mixed with brains, and no good brief can be written in any important case without long-continued, systematic, and exhaustive work on the part of counsel. Of course a knowledge of the law of the case is helpful in the preparation of any case, but it is usually as important, and sometimes far more important, to have an accurate knowledge of the facts of the case and the ability to state in a manner that the reader can understand, without study or independent investigation, all the important facts of the case.

Oral Arguments

The question of oral arguments in courts of review has often been discussed. In all courts, so far as I am aware, the privilege is granted under the rules to argue a case orally if counsel desire. In my judgment, oral arguments in a court of review are always helpful. Lawyers frequently waste much time unnecessarily in their oral arguments, but even a poor oral argument is helpful to the court. No lawyer should attempt to make an oral argument without special preparation for it. Counsel should not attempt in such an argument to read at any length from the printed brief and argument or to state everything found in the points made in the printed briefs. In the oral argument as well as in the printed brief and argument, it is important to state to the court just what the case is about, and the errors complained of, but ordinarily in oral arguments the facts should be stated with less detail than in the printed brief—only the most prominent being mentioned—and these in chronological order. In oral arguments it is even more important than in the printed brief that the statement of the case should be made clearly and concisely and without an attempt, while making such statement, to argue as to the force of the facts. It has more than once been said to me in discussions with lawyers as to oral arguments, "Of course, in an oral argument one should not state any points that are argued in the printed brief and argument." Necessarily such a conclusion is erroneous. The printed brief, if fairly and correctly prepared, should cover every point relied on by counsel. The oral argument should attempt to state in much briefer, and perhaps more vivid form, the points made in the printed brief and argument. The oral argument should only touch the high points in the case—the mountain peaks or possibly the hilltops—of the lawyer's side of the case. The practice in the Supreme Court of Illinois is not to permit the reading from briefs or the reading at any length from decisions of the court or any other authority. This practice, I am sure, is a wise one, because a lawyer reading from an authority rarely ever prepares himself with such care as to know precisely where to begin reading and where to end, and usually he takes so much time in finding the place to read from, that he wastes the time of the court. A lawyer should never read, on such an argument, from an authority, more than a sentence or two at a time and then only that part of the authority that bears directly on the point being argued, and he should be able to turn to the part of the decision or authority that he desires to quote and read without a moment's delay. The mistake is also frequently made, even by the best of lawyers, of attempting, in an oral argument, to read at length from a long contract, or ordinance, or other document they wish to have considered by the court. The better plan is to state the substance of the instrument and refer to a page of the abstract or brief where it is set out in full. Then, if counsel desires, it is very helpful to the court to refer to various sentences in the document, reading possibly the important ones and commenting on them as the argument progresses. The court can quickly take in the whole connection by glancing over the printed document as the argument is proceeding. Much time is wasted in the court, on oral argument, by counsel reading a mass of details from documents which have no especial bearing on the particular question about which there is a disagreement. The lawyer who makes the best oral argument rarely ever attempts to read from an authority, even to the extent of a sentence or two. The best oral arguments are made by those who have made careful preparation, not by having a speech learned by rote, but by becoming fully familiar with all the facts and the legal points in the case, and who then—with perhaps typewritten memoranda to serve as headings and as reminders, of their main points—proceed to make the oral argument forcibly and briefly. Under the rules of the Illinois Supreme Court, when both sides are present, each side is permitted an hour in which to make the oral argument. In the hundreds of cases that have been argued since I have been a member of that court, there have been scarcely a dozen that could not have been wisely argued in less than an hour on a side. The shorter the argument in a busy court, provided the points are covered clearly, the better for counsel and the court and for the right decision of the case.

Counsel frequently think that the oral argument is especially helpful to the judge who writes the opinion. Of course if the case is argued well orally, it is a help to the writer of the opinion, but if the case is properly presented in the printed briefs and arguments, the great benefit in a court of review from a good oral argument, is the assistance it gives to the members of the court who do not write the opinion. The judge who writes the opinion necessarily becomes familiar with all the facts and the law in the case from a study of the briefs, but a good oral argument will save very much labor, especially to the members of the court who do not write the opinion. Petitions for rehearing are sometimes filed asking for the rehearing largely on the ground that the judge who wrote the opinion did not hear the oral arguments. If the printed briefs and arguments are prepared as they should be, such an argument for granting a rehearing is practically without merit.

I have known lawyers who strongly objected to the members of the court asking them questions while they were making an oral argument. Such lawyers have said to me, "I have studied the case much more carefully than have the members of the court at the time of making my oral argument and I should be permitted to present my views without interruptions." Of course the members of the court may ask too many questions, but the purpose of any fair question is to get at the real issues of the case and necessarily every lawyer wants to have the court understand the questions in dispute. If the judges have not been clearly shown what the real questions are which are in dispute, in no other way can the lawyer be of greater assistance to the court and his cause than by making clear what are the crucial questions to be decided. I have known judges to ask too many questions. I am quite certain that in some oral arguments I have asked too many myself, and have made the mistake sometimes made by members of courts of review, of attempting to argue the questions with the lawyers during the oral argument, forgetting, as a great English judge once said, that it is unwise to try to convince a lawyer who is arguing a case. He is hired to convince the court that his client's side is right, and it is impractical to try to convince him—or at least to make him admit—that he is in the wrong.

The practice of the Illinois Supreme Court is never to permit interruptions by opposing counsel during oral arguments. My experience leads me to think that this is a wise practice, because such interruptions usually serve to throw very little light upon the case and are apt to cause a great waste of time. Moreover, the lawyer for the appellant or plaintiff in error usually has an opportunity of making a reply and can answer any questions or points that have been raised by the other side which he has not discussed in his opening speech.

Personally, I am very strongly in favor of oral arguments, but like every one else, sitting in a busy court, crowded with work, I sometimes get impatient at the time wasted because of lack of preparation or lack of experience by counsel in making oral arguments. This impatience with wasting time and not getting anywhere, now and then, will cause the members of the court to make statements or ask questions of counsel that should not be made or asked. Not long since, after a very busy and uncomfortable day of oral arguments in the Illinois Supreme Court, one of the lawyers said to another at the adjournment of court, he didn't see how a helpful oral argument could be made in this court, because one of the judges told him, while he was making his argument that day, that he must not talk about the facts, and another one had told him from the bench that he must not talk about the law. He wanted to know what he was to talk about if he didn't talk about the law or the facts. I have no doubt that there may have been some force in his criticism.

When several lawyers are in a case, it is not usually wise or helpful for more than one on the same side to argue a given case orally. It seems almost impossible for the lawyers to divide the points; so that if more than one attempt to argue the case on the same side, both lawyers will argue the same point in much the same way. This is particularly true when more than one counsel attempt to argue the case for appellee or defendant in error. It is not so difficult for the appellant's or plaintiff in error's side, because the lawyer who speaks last is speaking in reply and the province of the reply is only to answer anything that has been said by opposing counsel that it seems necessary to answer.

Had I the power, in any court of review of which I was a member and time permitted, I would require every case to be argued orally, but I would insist upon a careful preparation by the lawyers before the argument was made. Indeed, some lawyers who are familiar with the work insist that only lawyers of trained experience in that class of work ought to argue cases orally in courts of review. Under our system of government and jurisprudence, with our social ideals of equality, such a rule doubtless would be impractical in most of the courts of this country, but I think much can be done to educate the lawyers as to the right methods in the preparation of cases for presentation to courts of review, especially as to oral arguments. Frequently lawyers argue cases in such courts who have never argued a case before, and may not for years argue another, and they are somewhat embarrassed; but a lawyer who has thoroughly prepared for the argument generally acquits himself with credit, for if he is embarrassed, the members of the court soon see that, and will make an effort to help him out and assist in relieving his embarrassment. Of course, an oral argument cannot be made to advantage by reading from printed or typewritten manuscript; such an argument is not "oral," in the right sense of the term. All the force and effect which come from the properly presented points of a spoken speech, are lost to the court if the argument is read from manuscript. With careful preparation, a brief, clear, and forcible statement as to the facts and the issues of the case, with his views as to the application of the law on the disputed points, can be made by almost any lawyer with careful preparation, and such an argument is always helpful, and wastes no time of the court.

Notwithstanding the well-known practice of the Illinois Supreme Court not to allow interruptions by opposing counsel, they are sometimes made and are occasionally very amusing to all the listeners, if not to the participants. Quite a noted lawyer in the central part of the state, who had served for years on the circuit bench, a few years ago was arguing a case orally in the Supreme Court and cited a certain decision as upholding his position. When opposing counsel rose and replied, he showed clearly to the court that the authority cited sustained his side rather than that of counsel who had first cited the authority. As the argument of counsel proceeded and grew more and more forcible in showing that the authority in question was not in point for the other side, the former judge, who had cited the authority, grew restive, attempted two or three times to rise and interrupt counsel, and finally did interrupt, saying to the court: "Your Honors, I cited that authority through mere inadvertence!"

It is always unwise in an oral argument to attempt to state, in detail, what the different witnesses have testified to on the trial of the case. Such a practice cannot be helpful, because in many of the cases argued in a court of review, it is impossible for the judges, without referring to the briefs, abstracts, and record, to remember from the oral argument all the details. This same statement may be made with reference to printed briefs and arguments. There should be no attempt in the statement of the case or in the argument in such printed briefs to set out, at length, the testimony of every witness. Far better to set out the substance of the evidence and refer to the page of the abstract or record where such evidence can be found, so that the court can turn to that page, if it is desired to do so when reading the brief, and read just what the witness testified to.

I believe so strongly in oral arguments in a case that if I were to return to the practice of law I would argue every case orally that I was interested in before any court of review, provided I could get the other side to argue it orally; and then I would plan and study to make my argument just as short as possible and cover the main features of the case. I would not take the entire hour simply because the rules permitted it; and I would hesitate before I would ask in any case, no matter how important, that more than an hour should be allowed for the oral argument. Not that any good lawyer cannot in most cases consume an hour in a good oral argument; but in the crowded condition of the dockets in courts of review in the large states, much more effective oral arguments can be made by hitting only the high spots and condensing the argument into as brief a compass as possible, rather than to take the entire hour or more and make such an argument as ought to be made, to understand the points in the case, if there were not printed briefs covering carefully every point raised. The aim should be in every oral argument in a court of review to leave out all minute details, to waste no time in any way in reading from the briefs or at length from any authority. In a word, to make the oral argument as short as possible and give the court a clear picture of the issues and your view of the proper application of the law to the facts. If you can do this in forty-five minutes, it is better for you and your side of the case to take only forty-five minutes rather than to take an hour; and if you can do it in thirty minutes rather than forty-five, far better take only thirty minutes or less, if possible, than to use forty-five minutes.

Adapted from Vol. 12, Illinois Law Review (1917).

II. FORM

Briefs and Arguments That Help the Courts

BY HU C. ANDERSON

I RECOGNIZE AMONG THOSE PRESENT a number of the ablest advocates at the bar. I do not expect that anything I may say will add to their knowledge of the subject with which I am to deal. My appearance on this program can be justified only by the possibility that the younger members of the profession may be impressed with the importance of an adequate presentation of a case in the appellate court and induced to pursue the subject further by recourse to authoritative articles dealing with it.

It is perhaps true that all lawyers do not agree about what constitutes a good brief or a good argument; nor do all judges. Hence, what I say must be regarded as my personal views only. It must be understood also that my purpose is to suggest rather than to dogmatize, for there are no fixed, inflexible rules of universal application for preparing a good brief or making a good argument, written or oral. Differences in the inherent nature of cases and in questions presented for decision necessarily influence to some extent not only the content but the method of presentation. Moreover, my remarks are to be regarded as referring to the presentation in the Court of Appeals, since my experience with the judicial viewpoint is limited to service in that tribunal.

Briefs and arguments are a very important part in the appellate process. One of the most satisfactory and pleasing experiences of an appellate court judge is to deal with the record in a case that has been ably briefed and argued. Well prepared briefs are not only helpful as a means of persuasion and an aid in the investigation necessary to a decision, but are highly useful in the sometimes burdensome task of preparing the formal opinion of the court. I, of course, do not mean to intimate that the opinion should be, or ever is, a mere servile adoption of the brief of the prevailing party, but to say that from the briefs of both parties the member of the court who is assigned the duty of preparing the opinion should be, and in the case of a well-prepared brief is, able to state the contention with respect to every question to be decided substantially as they were formulated by counsel for the respective parties without being compelled to analyze the whole or a large part of the brief and argument in an effort to ascertain the position of counsel. In this connection, it is perhaps appropriate to point out a distinction that is not always recognized in brief-writing. This is, that a statement of the issue presented in a case is not the same thing as a statement by the respective counsel of their contentions as to why the issues should be decided in their favor. A thorough understanding and recognition of this distinction is of no little importance in a logical presentation.

I think it fairly accurate to say that the principal function of a brief is to, first, present in logical form the questions for decision, and then the reason they should be decided in a certain way. But a brief is scarcely less important as a vehicle of attack on the contrary position. The material that goes into the brief is, of course, vital, but from a standpoint of persuasiveness, as well as from a standpoint of helpfulness to the court, the material must be arranged and presented in an orderly and logical form to be most effective. Clarity and precision in the formulation and presentation of the determinative questions and of your position with respect to each are of prime importance.

In the rules of both the Supreme Court and Court of Appeals there are to be found general directions for the preparation of briefs and assignments of error which can be followed with profit both to the brief-writer and the court. These rules are founded on long experience. They are supposed to be mandatory, but too often are only partially observed, resulting not necessarily in a wrong decision but in no little inconvenience to the members of the court in the consideration of the case.

Insofar as they relate to my subject, the rules of the Supreme Court and the Court of Appeals are substantially the same. Their purpose is to secure a logical and orderly presentation. They provide that the assignments of error shall contain, in the order stated, a statement of the nature and purpose of the case, the precise points raised by the pleadings, the substance of the verdict and judgment, or judgment without verdict, or decree, a statement of the errors of fact or law relied upon to review or modify the same, showing specifically wherein the action complained of is erroneous and how it prejudiced the rights of the appellant or plaintiff-in-error. Detailed directions are given for the manner in which errors must be assigned upon certain specific rulings, such as those involving the action of the court upon preliminary motions, demurrers, or pleas, the admission or rejection of evidence, the charge of the court, and the report of the master.

The assignments of error must be accompanied by a brief which shall state precisely and specifically the propositions of law and fact, without argument or elaboration, relied upon by the appellant or plaintiff-in-error to sustain the several errors assigned for reversal of the trial court. The brief may be combined with the assignments of error or filed in separate form, but there must be a brief in the one form or the other.

The reply brief must be of like character with that required of the plaintiff-in-error or appellant except that no specification of error is necessary and no statement of the case unless that already filed is controverted. Each assignment of error of law and fact must be answered in the reply brief.

In dealing with these rules, Mr. Gibson in his classic work on Suits in Chancery, Sections 1303, 1307, makes a number of valuable suggestions illuminated by forms which can be profitably considered by the young practitioner. It will be observed that the supposed case used by Mr. Gibson as an illustration is a relatively simple one. From a standpoint of helpfulness to the court, I do not think it advisable to deal with complicated cases in as brief and summary a manner as that indicated in the forms. These nevertheless furnish a very clear interpretation of the minimum requirement of the rules with respect to a brief combined with the assignments of error and with respect to a reply brief, which I have no doubt will prove of considerable aid to the novice. However, I think it is not too much to say that the rules, the application of which is demonstrated thereby, are to be regarded as providing the minimum rather than the maximum requirements with respect to the contents and arrangement of briefs.

The manner in which errors shall be assigned is perhaps the most important provision in the rules. The first essential of a well-formulated assignment is that it show upon its face clearly and accurately the ruling complained of so that the question for decision raised thereby can be readily ascertained by an inspection of the specification alone without recourse to any other part of the brief. But this, by itself, is not sufficient by any means. From a standpoint of helpfulness to the court, little is accomplished unless immediately following each specification of error there be a statement in concise form of the reason or reasons which you insist make the ruling erroneous. These may be either of law or fact or both. Too much emphasis cannot be placed upon this feature of the brief. It is not enough for the court to know that you think the ruling erroneous. It is equally important that you give the court the why of your position, and it seems to me the logical place to do this is in immediate connection with the statement of the ruling about which you complain. I do not mean that at this point in the brief you should make an argument or elaborate upon your reasons, but that you should give them in a simple, concise form; not in academic generalities, but in terms of the facts, if any, involved in the particular ruling and of the law as applied to these facts. The elaboration and argument may be appropriately made later.

Notwithstanding that it is required by the rules of the court and those of logical arrangement as well, a failure to follow the specification of error immediately with the reasons relied upon to sustain it, is one of the most common defects to be found in briefs filed in the Court of Appeals. Where this is the case, the court is frequently compelled to turn to and analyze the propositions of law and of fact that generally accompany the assignments of error in written form, and the argument as well, in an effort to figure out from the whole, the why of the insistence that the challenged rulings are erroneous. I think it cannot be gainsaid that where this is true the effectiveness of the brief as a logical presentation and as a help to the court is greatly impaired.

But it is not enough to show merely that the ruling challenged by a specification of error was erroneous. You must also show how the error prejudiced your rights. This requirement is likewise frequently ignored. It is perhaps true with respect to some rulings that the resulting prejudice is so obvious that a statement with respect thereto seems unnecessary, but an assignment of error to be good in form or to be of much help must always show prima facie not only that the ruling complained of was erroneous but was prejudicial as well, and, as the rule makes clear, the place to make this showing is in immediate connection with the particular specification. Where there is no effort to do this, the court is left to find out for itself just how the rights of the complaining party were affected and may overlook a viewpoint which you could have presented.

I have already pointed out that the filing of a brief of the law and facts in support of each error assigned is mandatory, and that the rules permit the brief to be combined with the assignments of error or filed separately. The form given by Mr. Gibson, to which I have referred, provides a good illustration of a brief combined with the assignments of error, and, in my opinion, this method is to be preferred in most cases. I say this because it seems to me that it makes for a desirable compactness and cohesion that is otherwise lacking. Each specification of error including the reasons assigned and supporting propositions of law and fact is then a complete unit in itself in the sense that it shows prima facie, without it being necessary to resort to any other part of the brief, that the particular challenged ruling was both erroneous and prejudicial.

If you choose to file a separate brief, then I think it helpful to clearly indicate by appropriate headings the particular assignments of error to which the propositions of law and fact relate. Following this designation, there should be stated all of the propositions of fact, if any, relied upon in connection with that particular assignment, followed by the pertinent propositions of law applicable to the particular question. Where this method is followed, there will be found, grouped under an appropriate heading, all the propositions of law or fact or both relied upon to sustain your position with respect to a specifically designated question. Each assignment of error should be treated in the same manner. This method, I think, is to be preferred to the common practice of stating all the propositions of fact insisted upon in one group, and all the propositions of law relied upon in another. This seems to me to be more logical.

By a brief of the facts is not meant quotations from the evidence, nor is it intended that the brief should consist of generalities. To be helpful it should be made up of propositions of subordinate facts claimed to be shown by the requisite quantum of evidence, which, taken together, establish the ultimate facts necessary to show prima facie that the particular ruling to which they relate was erroneous. At no place are citations to the record more helpful. The reference should be to the specific page or pages where the evidence relied upon to sustain the propositions in connection with which the citation is made may be found. To simply say, as is sometimes done, "See record, pages 50 to 100 inclusive," is of little or no value.

The rule requiring a brief of the law does not mean long quotations from authorities, but a statement of legal principles applied to the particular situation contemplated by the challenged ruling to which they are intended to relate. In citing authorities, it is perhaps needless to point out that those in this jurisdiction are of prime importance and should be cited first. Indeed, I may say that where such authorities exist and directly support the principle relied upon, it is of little use to cite in a brief file in the intermediate appellate court authorities from other jurisdictions. The purpose of that court is primarily to ascertain whether the applicable principles of law have been declared by the Supreme Court, and if so, to apply such principles to the facts of the case in hand. Only where there is no precedent in this state can it venture to promulgate a rule, and generally speaking, in such cases only are authorities from other jurisdictions of much value. There is this exception, however; in some instances such decisions are helpful in furnishing illustrations of the application to the facts of a principle already established in this state where the factual basis of the decision in the cited case is analogous to that in the case being briefed.

So far, I have been talking principally about briefs filed in connection with assignments of error. As I have said, the rules of both courts also deal with a reply brief which must be filed by the appellee or defendant-in-error. They require this brief to be of like character as that expected of the opposite party, except that no specification of error is necessary and no statement of the case is required, unless that already made is controverted. The most important requirement with respect to a reply brief is that it shall contain an answer to each assignment of error of law or fact with appropriate references to the record and authorities. From a standpoint of helpfulness to the court, it is important that the answers be specific and not left to implication.

Here again logical arrangement is of great help. The contents of a reply brief should be so arranged so as to leave no doubt about the particular question in the opposing brief at which each proposition of law and fact is directed. This can be most effectively done by taking each assignment of error separately and in the order in which they appear first stating the question involved in the particular specification and then your position and reasons therefor, followed by a brief of the law or facts or both to support your views. Some excellent brief-writers eliminate all uncertainty as to the target at which they are shooting by repeating the assignment of error substantially as it appears in their opponent's brief or the question raised thereby, and following this with an affirmative statement of their own position with respect to the particular question involved. This process is repeated with respect to each assignment of error. The issues are thus sharply drawn and made readily apparent in a compact form without its being necessary to look elsewhere.

I wish to emphasize again the importance of giving reasons. It is of little help to say in a reply brief that a challenged ruling was correct without giving the reasons for that insistence. It is no less important that each reason advanced by your adversary with respect to a particular error should be answered by a counter-statement of a specific nature. Generalities are worthless wherever they appear. For instance, it is of no benefit to say, as is sometimes done, that the contention of your adversary is not sound in law, or that it is not supported by the evidence, or that it is not applicable, or that it is immaterial, without undertaking to show why.

Occasionally, there is to be found in the briefs of one party or the other, statements something like these: "The assignments of error do not lend themselves readily to separate treatment and will be discussed generally"; or, "It seems expedient to discuss the assignments generally rather than to treat them separately." This method is ill-advised for it conveys the idea that you either do not grasp the full import of the questions presented or have no adequate answer for, at least, some of them and in lieu thereof, wish to leave it to the court to find the answer.

One thing that the court rules do not in terms require in the brief proper, which I think may be helpfully incorporated, is a statement of the factual background of the case. I do not mean a detailed, evidentiary statement, but something in the nature of a thumb-nail sketch, setting forth the important and material facts and circumstances which gave rise to the controversy. Such a statement will often enable the court to better grasp immediately the full purport of the questions presented for decision, and I think it would be no offense against logical order to put it in the brief immediately after the result of the trial is given, or following a statement of the questions presented for decision where, as is sometimes true in excellent briefs, that formula is used in lieu of a statement of the precise points raised by the pleadings required by the rules. But as a precaution, I suggest that neither is an appropriate place to discuss the evidence or argue controverted issues of fact. That may be done later.

In connection with briefs, I should like to draw attention to a rule that has prevailed in Pennsylvania for many years. It requires, in substance, that the appellant shall, on the first page of his brief, without any other matter appearing thereon, set forth separately each question involved in the case in general terms and without names, dates, amounts or particulars of any kind, and that whenever possible each question must be followed immediately by an answer stating how it was resolved in the court from which the appeal was prosecuted. To compel conciseness, it is required that the questions and answers in their entirety shall not ordinarily exceed twenty lines and never exceed one page. If an appellee thinks the appellant's statement inaccurate, or that it does not present the points for decision in a proper light, he may submit a counterstatement. The rule is regarded as mandatory in the highest degree, admitting of no exception. A substantially similar rule has been adopted in a number of other states, and I understand that the formula prescribed has everywhere given great satisfaction both to the bench and the bar.

While I am not disposed to advocate at this time the adoption of the Pennsylvania rule as a mandatory requirement, I have no doubt that a voluntary observance or substantial compliance with the theory of it would be of great help to both the court and to counsel, especially in the presentation and consideration of the oral argument. In fact, a number of the more experienced practitioners already use substantially this method in writing briefs for the Court of Appeals. Apart from the aid given the court, younger members of the profession will find it a profitable practice from their own standpoint, because, more effectively than any other means with which I am acquainted, it compels that thorough study and analysis of the case which we all know is essential to the preparation of a good brief and the making of a good argument. There is no better test for determining whether you really know your case. I concede, and those trying it will find, that the formulation of such issues is not always a simple task. It cannot be accomplished with the nonchalance and ease which sometimes apparently attend the drafting of pleadings and the like in these days. Inevitably, there must be in some cases a number of attempts, coupled with re-writing and polishing off before the desired degree of success is attained. Nevertheless, when you have written and re-written, and then thrown everything away and started all over again a number of times until you are finally satisfied with the job, you will find that the brief is more than half-way done. The remainder of it will frequently prove a comparatively simple matter.

I should say in this connection that such a statement of the questions for decision is not meant to take the place of assignments of error. These are still required in Pennsylvania and serve a different purpose. The difference is too obvious to require elaboration.

Those interested in the working of the Pennsylvania rule will find a most informative discussion of its value, illuminated by concrete examples taken from briefs, in a law review article by Chief Justice Robert von Moschzisker.[1]

The rules do not require that a written argument be filed, but, for my part, I regard such an argument as one of the most important parts of the appellate process. It provides an opportunity to demonstrate the validity of the reasons assigned in the brief in support of the position therein taken, and to attack those of your adversary. If it has not been given elsewhere, I think it helpful and not inappropriate to begin the written argument

[1] *A Time-Saving Method of Stating in Appellate Briefs the Controlling Questions for Decision,* 34 Yale L. J. 287 (1925).

with an outline of the important facts and circumstances giving rise to the controversy. Thereafter, the argument should follow the brief closely, for the brief is really the frame-work of an argument. An outline of the facts having been given in one place or another, the next thing required, by logical arrangement, is to deal with each question raised by the assignments of error in the order in which they are made. Whether in support of a particular assignment or in refutation of the contention of your adversary, the proposition to be argued should be first stated. This is essential from a standpoint of logical presentation for the same reason that the first step in a joint debate is a statement of the proposition to be debated. The discussion should follow immediately and should be confined to the proposition stated. If the point be one of fact, the effort should be to demonstrate that the evidence supports the position taken with respect to the proposition involved. An analysis of the evidence with respect to its probative value is frequently helpful. Too often counsel are content to refer merely to the testimony, without utilizing legitimate inferences. In many cases inferences are determinative. When legitimate, they are evidence in themselves, no less so than direct testimony. They are legitimate when they logically attend a given fact or facts.

Having demonstrated the factual basis for the stated proposition, the argument should proceed to a discussion of the applicable rule or rules of law, with appropriate references to the authorities. This does not necessarily mean that all of the cases cited in the brief should be discussed. If the proposition be an elementary one, about which there is no controversy, it needs no discussion at all. But the application of the law to the facts assumed to have been shown is an art and a highly useful process, wherein lies an excellent opportunity for skill and ingenuity coupled with a nice sense of discrimination.

Some cases present questions of law that occur but infrequently. It is no reflection on the court to assume that these are less well known. A discussion of the legal principles involved in such questions is always helpful.

As I say, it is seldom necessary to discuss all of the cases cited in the brief. For this purpose leading cases, those that are best reasoned, should be selected and discussed with a view of demonstrating the principle upon which you rely and its application to a particular state of facts. In doing this, a thumb-nail sketch of the determinative facts in a cited case is important. Quoting statements of academic principles without reference to the facts is not of much help.

Occasionally a case will present a question that has not been decided in this jurisdiction. Where this is true, a discussion of the authorities is always in order and appreciated, especially where they are conflicting. Here, your effort is to persuade the court to adopt the view favorable to your contention. An argument directed to this end should discuss underlying principles. What the court wants to know is, which view is the soundest and more nearly in keeping with the general policy of this state as evidenced by judicial decision and statutory enactments. Here breadth of learning, coupled with skill in analysis plays a conspicuous part.

Some questions involve the construction of statutes, and here again an argument can be employed to good advantage. Canons for statutory construction are of course settled and well known. The argument should consist in the application of these canons to the particular statute in question. To simply quote the statute and then quote the rules of construction is a waste of time. What the court wants to know are your reasons for thinking that the application of the canons to the statute will produce the result contended for. This is a matter of demonstration. Here, there is room to point out the reasonableness of your view upon the one hand, and the dire consequences which in conceivable situations you contend will result if your adversary's view be adopted.

In connection with statutory construction, the history of the statute and the circumstances which brought about its enactment are often highly important and sometimes overlooked. It happens not infrequently that the true legislative intent, the object sought to be accomplished by the particular statute, cannot be ascertained without reading its language in the light of a knowledge of the conditions prevailing at the time of the enactment. These considerations are a fertile field for helpful argument in connection with statutory construction.

A written argument may be used for still another purpose, which I regard as of first importance. As I have said, it provides an excellent opportunity not only to discuss your own side of the case, but to refute the contentions of your adversary with respect to the facts and the law, where both are involved. While it is of course not expected that you should undertake to present your opponent's side of the controversy, it is altogether appropriate to state your understanding of his position with respect to each determinative question. Indeed, there is no better way of giving point to your own contention with respect to an issue than to state that of your adversary. I think it is well to do this with respect to each question immediately following the statement of your own contention. The issue is thus brought into sharp relief.

Every arguable case in the appellate courts has two sides; otherwise, it would not be there. A discussion devoted to one side only leaves the case but half argued. It is no less important to undertake to show why the authorities relied upon by your opponent should not control the particular question in connection with which they are cited than it is to show that those relied upon by you should do so. It is a rather common thing to find in a written brief that the author has been so engrossed with the view of the case favorable to his side that he can see no merit in the contentions advanced in support of the other side, and, therefore, makes no effort to answer them. Occasionally counsel on both sides have this attitude. The result is a gap in the argument which the court must close for itself. In such case the court is very likely to get the impression that you have no answer for your opponent's views. To this, a novice representing an appellant or plaintiff-in-error might unthinkingly respond that, since the reply brief of his adversary had not been filed when he prepared his assignments of error and brief, he did not know just what contentions would be made by the opposition. Such a reply would be not a reason but an excuse, and a poor one at that; one that a cagy, battle-scarred practitioner would never find necessary to make. If, by the time your case reaches the Court of Appeals, you do not know every contention that your opponent could possibly make, you do not know your case.

The answering part of your brief is not to be confined to contentions expressly made, but should go to every one that could be reasonably made under the law and facts disclosed by the record, whether actually made or not; for, even if your adversary overlooks a theory favorable to his position, the chances are that if it is determinative the court will make the discovery, and should it be adopted as a basis for the decision you will be confronted with an adverse result based on a view about which you have not been heard. If this occurs, you will have only yourself to blame. Limited only by procedural rules that long experience has proved essential, the court sits to decide questions as rightly as may be, and not to turn out conclusions that reflect merely the comparative skill and ability of counsel.

Do not be content with simply stating that the adverse citations of law are not in point. What the court wants to know is why you think so. Here again reasons are important. To give them where a point of law is involved requires in the first instance an understanding of the rationale of the case cited and an ability to distinguish it either by showing that the facts which control the decision are not present in your case; or, if an analogy is relied upon, that it is not a true one; or that the principle of the decision is not sound if it has been cited in connection with a question of first impression in this state.

Likewise, it is important not to omit an assault upon your adversary's factual position. To be sure you should give adequate attention to the evidence that is favorable to you, but do not dodge that which is against you. Admit its existence and attack it from every possible angle and with all of the weapons at your command. To fail to do so will avail nothing because, if by any chance the significance of such evidence escapes your adversary, it is not likely to escape the court, and your opportunity to present your views in opposition will have been lost.

Finally, I wish to talk about oral argument, which I think is a most important and valuable part of the presentation of a case in the Court of Appeals. Limitations upon the time allowed, as well as other considerations, make an oral argument a very different thing in important respects from a written one. It must, in the nature of things, have an elasticity not required of its written counterpart. The first essential is, of course, careful preparation. Occasionally, an argument will be opened by a statement that the advocate has not lately seen the brief and the record. By this, the court knows at once that little help will be forthcoming. It is hardly to be expected that such a statement should not discourage rather than attract the attention of the judicial mind.

To be effective, it is essential that you shall have given considerable thought not only to what you will say in your oral argument, but as to how. It is to be assumed that, through preparation of the brief and otherwise, you have become thoroughly saturated with the facts and law of your case. You are then confronted with a limitation of time allowed for oral argument, which will very likely prevent you from covering all of the ground contained in the written presentation. Hence, if you are wise, you will give long and careful thought to the particular points which you wish to present, selecting them with a view to their relative importance. Determining what should be left out is no easy task. I think it was Sam Jones, the great evangelist, who said that he would require four weeks' notice to prepare for an address of twenty or thirty minutes on any subject in his particular field, two weeks if allowed an hour, one week if given an hour and a half, but that if offered unlimited time he was ready to speak at once. This is frequently true at the bar, and the better the lawyer knows his case, the truer it is.

Having determined which points you will discuss, the next thing to be considered is the manner of the presentation from a standpoint of logical arrangement. The introduction is of primary importance as a time-saver. The nature of the case, the result of the trial under review, and the questions to be argued, are the things that the court wants to know first in every case. Sometimes there is an effort to first give an analysis of the pleadings, and sometimes a chronological history of the facts. When this is attempted, the court is left very much in the position that an audience attending a joint debate would be in, if the discussion got under way without a statement of the subject being debated. You can get a good idea of the mental agony which the judicial mind is subjected to an argument without being first informed as to the issues to be decided if you can imagine yourself in attendance at a debate where the audience is left in that plight.

This phase of an argument is so important from the standpoint of the court that, for the benefit of the young members of the profession, I am persuaded to yield to the temptation to give an illustration of one appropriate way to open an oral argument in a typical negligence case. Thus: "This is an action for damages for personal injuries sustained by a pedestrian when he was struck by an automobile while crossing a highway. The verdict and judgment were for the plaintiff. The questions for decision are: First, whether there was any material evidence to warrant the conclusion that defendant was guilty of actionable negligence; second, whether plaintiff was guilty of contributory negligence as a matter of law; third, whether the judge erred in charging the last clear chance doctrine; fourth, whether he erred in overruling an objection to evidence to the effect that defendant was notoriously a reckless driver." The factual background in the form of a thumb-nail sketch of important facts may appropriately follow.

By such a statement, the case is put before the court in two minutes or less, and the argument can proceed from point to point in an orderly and logical manner. Of course, not every case can be so simply stated, but there are few which cannot be gotten before the court by following the method indicated, in less time than would be otherwise required.

Having stated the first question you desire to argue, the next logical step is to state your contention with respect to that quesion, and then that of your adversary, unless it be so obvious as to make that course unnecessary. Having gotten this far, it is of the utmost importance from the standpoint of all concerned that you get clearly before the court the factual basis for your contention. If you must leave out anything, do not leave out the facts material to the issue. You may safely assume that the court is at least familiar with the principles of law which it is constantly called upon to apply. But the court does not know the facts of your particular case, or those material to the questions to be discussed, and these are what it desires to hear about in the oral argument, assuming that the nature of the case and the questions for decision have been clearly stated.

There may be some cases presenting unusual legal questions or involving nice distinctions in which it is profitable to discuss authorities in an oral argument, but, in my opinion, they are very few in number. Generally, such a discussion merely consumes a valuable part of the limited time that could better be employed in getting before the court your views with respect to the facts and in combating the contentions of your adversary. Unless it is so well known as to make even this unnecessary, it is generally sufficient to state the principle relied upon and apply it to the particular facts which give rise to the question or proposition you are discussing, if facts are involved. You should bear in mind, both in the oral and written arguments, that the court is not only interested in the academic principles of law upon which you rely, but in how you think the principles apply to the particular facts of your case.

I do not wish to be understood as suggesting that the manner of presentation I have sketched should be followed in all cases or inflexibly adhered to in any case. I have attempted only what is perhaps an overly-simplified outline of some features of the oral presentation of the average uncomplicated case. My purpose has been primarily to provoke thought on the part of the young practitioner concerning what, I know from my own experience, is more or less an ordeal for him on his first appearances.

As is true with the brief-writer, there is sometimes an apparent reluctance on the part of the advocate to state in the oral argument his opponent's contention with respect to a question being presented. He will readily state his own, but sometimes shies from that of his adversary. I think this is a mistake. As I have said, there is no better way to bring into sharp relief an issue which has been adequately stated then by a clear, concise statement of the contentions pro and con. Nothing so quickly prepares the judicial mind for the discussion to follow. This is the reason why there is frequently an inquiry from the bench as to the contrary contention.

This naturally brings to mind the rather controversial subject of interruptions from the bench in the course of oral arguments. Like most everything else, there are two sides to this question. You are thoroughly familiar with one side. My purpose is to invite your consideration of the other.

I readily concede that questioning can be overdone, but I am equally convinced that, when conducted fairly and with moderation, the members of the court, in many instances, are thereby enabled to expedite the hearing, and get a better grasp of the determinative issue or issues than would be true if they remained sphinx-like during the presentation.

I venture to say that the majority of questions from the bench come about through the failure of the advocate to clearly state the nature of the case, the questions for decision and the contentions both pro and con. The purpose of an oral argument is to enlighten the court. It should proceed upon the presumption that you have presented the case in your brief in what you think the most logical manner. It seems to follow that it would be an advantage to know, first, whether those whom you are trying to persuade have grasped the questions for decision, and, second, how your presentation strikes them, so that you may have a chance to combat any tentatively hostile views. It is without doubt true that sometimes the nature of the inquiry shows clearly that the questioner is off the track completely. But it seems to me that, even so, the interruption should not be regarded as altogether unwelcome, because you are thereby afforded an opportunity you would not otherwise have to get the wayward judicial mind back on the right road. You can rest assured that if your presentation raises an unasked question it will not be forgotten. Upon the contrary, unless answered, it will recur in the course of the investigation and consultation that will take place when you are not present. Your brief may not contain an adequate answer or deal with the particular aspect of a question which has occurred to the would-be interrogator. So, if you regard it as an advantage to be heard upon a point not covered in the brief that has intrigued the mental processes of the judge whose interest has been thus aroused, it would seem that the opportunity afforded by a question in the course of the argument should be welcomed. When you come to think about it, a question from the bench demonstrates that your argument is being measurably successful, for it could hardly be made clearer that you have caught the interest of your audience, and that is a good part of the battle insofar as the oral argument is concerned.

Many interruptions will be avoided if you will remember that from the moment you get on your feet the judicial mind is groping for the nature of the case, and the points of difference between you and your adversary with respect to each question presented for decision. If these be not made clear in the very beginning, they must be discovered by the listeners either by a question or by examination or by examination of the briefs, if they are immediately available, or by mere surmise, before there is anything to which your remarks can be referred by the mental processes of those whom you are trying to convince. To thoroughly realize this, you have only to again imagine yourself a member of an audience at a joint debate where the subject of discussion and the positions of the debaters with respect thereto have not been clearly stated before the argument begins.

One other thing remains. Though I am happy to say that the occasions are very rare indeed, an overzealous advocate will sometimes seek to belittle the learning or ability of the judge or chancellor who tried the case. Nothing could be in poorer taste, more futile, and less helpful. Such attempts leave a bad impression, and are never made by an astute lawyer. Apart from other reasons that are too obvious to be given, to attack one who is not present to defend himself offends the typical American sense of fair play. Such tactics have never been tolerated in the appellate courts of Tennessee, so far as I am advised. Nor have unwarranted remarks reflecting adversely upon opposing counsel. I do not, of course, mean that improper conduct, if any, disclosed by the record, must, or necessarily should be ignored, but only that a sense of fair play implemented by courtesy and good manners is no less important and effective in the presentation of a law suit than it is in the other pursuits of life.

Adapted from Vol. 17, Tennessee Law Review (1943).

Presenting Your Case to The Court of Appeals

By Watson Clay

As Albert J. Beveridge once observed, every man's problem is how to be effective. In any court this problem, in endless form and hue, constantly confronts you as the practicing lawyer. Before the Court of Appeals your creative talent meets a sharp challenge, and the plan of presenting your case not only measures your ability but often may mean the difference between winning and losing. Dredged from the mistakes of others, you may find the following practical suggestions will materially contribute to your effectiveness in that Court.

You may rashly assume from the title that this article is for beginners only. It is not. Just the other day one of the older, most competent and experienced attorneys in this Commonwealth committed what approaches an unforgivable sin in an oral argument before the Court of Appeals. He was asked from the bench a pertinent and specific question concerning an important issue in the case. His answer was substantially as follows: "Now, Judge, that point is covered somewhere in my brief, and I expect to discuss it later on in this argument." Such an answer is tactless and unsatisfactory. It punctures the enthusiasm of the enquiring judge, and may blow a hole a mile wide in the lawyer's case.

This incident, and many other good examples of bad oral argument and brief writing, prompted this article. There was an important contributing factor. By recent amendment to its Rules, your Court of Appeals has aspired to encourage more and better oral arguments and the submission of better briefs.

By and large the oral argument and the brief are fundamentally the same thing. *Their sole objective is and should be to persuade the Court to take favorable action in the lawyer's cause.* It is positively astounding how many attorneys seem unable to grasp what this concept involves, or to exert their best efforts in its realization.

I am reminded of the barb tossed by a university coed at her elderly mathematics professor. One day he was standing in his bathing suit at the edge of a swimming pool on the university campus when this beautiful coed accidently dropped her camera off the deep end. She called to the professor for help. He said he would be glad to dive after the camera, but first wanted to know how she happened to choose him when there were so many handsome young men in easy reach to do the job. She answered: "Professor, you have apparently forgotten me, but I am in your statistics class. I have found that you can go down deeper, stay down longer, and come up drier than anyone I know." Lawyers can be that way too.

Seriously, the matter of inducing a favorable decision is one of overwhelming importance in every lawsuit. This is so obviously self-evident that it seems rather ridiculous to state the proposition. Yet you would be surprised to hear the many arguments and read the many briefs in the Court of Appeals demonstrating that the lawyers involved had become so imbued with petty facts, or wholly inapplicable principles, or their own verbosity, that they had completely lost sight of their objective. Such efforts show a distressing lack of appropriate preparation.

The proper pattern for presenting a case effectively, either orally or in writing, may be found in almost any good book on public speaking. Personally I think our law schools are sadly deficient in failing to emphasize adequately, as an important part of their curriculum, the principles and practice of this art. Even if a lawyer never opens his mouth, sometime or another he must learn to think persuasively.

Cicero aptly delineated the five essentials of good public speaking, which are likewise the five requisites of acceptable brief writing. They are: (1) determining exactly what one should say; (2) arranging the material, with good judgment, in the proper order; (3) using well-chosen words and carefully phrased sentences; (4) fixing the entire presentation in mind; and (5) delivering it with dignity and grace.

I have already given one example of an improper approach which tended to sap the persuasive tendency of an oral argument. It constituted a lack of good judgment in the arrangement of the lawyer's materials. He wanted to put last an issue which a member of the Court considered should come first. Under such circumstances it is, if nothing else, discreet to accede to the judge's wishes.

I remember a true story told so effectively by Mr. Edmund F. Trabue. In an argument before a Federal Circuit Court of Appeals a gentleman whom we shall call Smith was vigorously presenting his client's case. One of the judges said: "Mr. Smith, we have read the brief in the case and are generally familiar with the background you are discussing. Will you please give us your views on proposition No. 3?" Mr. Smith responded: "Your Honor, I will come to that." A few minutes later the same judge made the same request and received a similar answer. Somewhat later the judge again asked the lawyer to discuss proposition No. 3. The latter again replied: "I will come to that." Thereupon the judge, with excusable emphasis, said: "Mr. Smith, you are there *now*!"

It is sometimes difficult to understand why a lawyer will hesitate to tackle a prominent issue in his case. Perhaps the reason is that he cannot successfully meet it. At least that is the natural reaction of his hearers. But he should always bear in mind the words of Mr. Justice Robert H. Jackson*: "To delay meeting issues is improvident; to attempt evasion of them is fatal."

Here is another example of what should be avoided. We have all seen it happen. A judge on the bench asks the advocate what he considers a very pertinent question. The latter, instead of undertaking to answer the query, says: "Your Honor, let me ask *you* this question." Personally, I think that is the most classic of all "famous last words." For an attorney to honestly believe that by such conduct in an oral argument he is still on the objective track of persuasion is fantastic.

Many lawyers seem overly infatuated with the "background" of their case. By this I mean introductory aspects, preliminary events, side issues, or circumstances which suggest that his client is a good fellow. Before a jury this "background" discussion may serve an excellent purpose. It should be remembered, however, that judges have been pretty well immunized to the afterclap of a jury argument. The fact is, like the lady in "Mr. Pettibone," they have been up against that same sort of thing *so* many times.

The damaging aspect of wandering in the byways is that, in using up so much time trying to draft the sympathy of the court,

* This, and a later quotation, appear in *"Advocacy Before the Supreme Court,"* an earlier article, p. 189, to which your attention is invited.

the advocate cuts himself out of the opportunity to present adequately the real questions involved. I will give you another true example, because these things which seem to ring the wrong bell really do happen. Not long ago an attorney was given thirty minutes within which to present his argument. At the end of twenty-five minutes he asked the Chief Justice how much time he had left. (This in itself is a mistake.) The Chief Justice advised him he had five minutes. The lawyer, aghast, exclaimed, and I quote: "Good Lord, I haven't come to my main point yet!"

One final observation with respect to oral argument may be ventured. The Court has other work to do and lots of it. When an hour and a half is set aside for the hearing of an argument (assuming the full membership of seven judges and four commissioners are present), the lawyers are given, then and there, sixteen and one half man-hours of the Court's time. That is the equivalent of more than two full days of one judge's time, devoted exclusively to hearing you and opposing counsel argue your case. Since the Court is loaning you its undivided attention for so long, it is only fair that you should have devoted a proportionate period to the preparation of your case so that your presentation will make a material contribution to a proper decision. It is an unjust imposition on the Court, the Commonwealth, and other litigants for you to waste its time.

What has been said above is equally applicable to the writing of briefs if not more so. Here we may restate our objective, which is to induce favorable action by the Court. We have the same old problem of persuasion, and the lawyer's job is to devise the very best method of effecting it in his particular case. It should be apparent that writing a good brief is easier than making a good oral argument for the simple reason that in the latter instance the lawyer speaking extemporaneously must depend upon the immediate acuteness of his wits; whereas, in writing his brief, he has ample time to rework and rearrange his material and to endlessly edit his work until it approaches perfection. Therefore, while a poor argument may be understandable, a poor brief is inexcusable.

I would like respectfully to direct the reader's attention to section 1.340 of the Rules of the Court of Appeals. I would like you to reread that rule. I would like to see every lawyer in the Commonwealth restudy it. Your brief could be stricken for non-compliance, but that, to my mind, is not its most important aspect. This rule sets forth an excellent pattern for the presentation of your case in the most persuasive manner. Many lawyers overlook its requirements or ignore them. That is a mistake.

The rule directs the briefing lawyer to do what, if he gave the matter a smidgen of thought, he would do anyhow. It says in substance that he shall classify the questions which he wishes to discuss; that the facts, pleadings, and principles raising an issue shall be clearly stated; and that the authorities in support of the points raised shall be appended. In other words, the requirement is simply that the brief have an orderly arrangement so that the argument shall proceed from proposition to pertinent fact to applicable authority. Is there anything difficult or oppressive about such a requisition?

To some, systematic and effective collocation seems an intolerable burden. I have seen any number of briefs which fail to state at any point what issues are involved on the appeal. Some briefs even neglect to indicate whether the suit is at law or in equity, involves contract or tort, or arises out of negligence, a contract, a will, a trespass, or a rape.

Suppose you were the judge initially considering an appeal. When you picked up the briefs, what would you first want to know? Obviously the nature of the action. What next? Surely it would be helpful to be informed who won and what sort of judgment was entered. What next? Doubtless you would appreciate being advised of the significant questions you were called upon to decide.

Such an introductory arrangement of a brief is not only logical but it is most helpful. At the very outset it gives the Court a picture of your case, so that when your argument is considered the judge knows what he is looking for. Some depressing briefs start off with a discussion of the evidence introduced and continue the recital to the bitter end. Without knowing what question or questions are involved, it is impossible to evaluate the significance of particular facts. One might just as well recite the story of "The Three Bears" if he does not give the judge a key to his case. The same criticism may be made of an unnecessary exposition of the pleadings.

This introductory aspect of the brief cannot be over-emphasized. Not only is it important to the Court, but it is important to you in developing your argument. If, right at the beginning, you grasp the correlative force of your contentions, and accurately put down on paper what are the principal and subordinate issues involved, the pattern of your brief should almost automatically unfold your best argument.

Do not discourage the Court about your case. It is possible, as witness this preposterous opening statement in an appellant's brief:

> "At the outset, we desire to apologize to this Court for the statement of this case because of the fact that we do not think it possible to make an intelligent statement of this case. Rather, we must insist that the Court read the entire record before it can have a reasonable and fair understanding of this case."

This approach has about as much persuasive effect as hitting the judge in the head with a shovel.

It is true a lawyer may become lost in the later portions of his brief. Often this is due to the fact that he has not evaluated the relative importance of the various points he wishes to raise, and will waste time trying to prop up a weak point instead of swinging the sledge hammer on his strong ones. Recently I saw a lengthy brief which had listed under its "Points and Authorities" twenty-two different propositions. They all appeared of equal dignity; that is, they were numbered I through XXII. There were no sub-propositions. Throughout the brief those twenty-two points were given approximately the same quantitative treatment. The normal reaction of one reading such a brief is that it just cannot be true. There could honestly not be twenty-two good solid grounds for reversal. Such treatment obviously impairs the proper consideration of the significant issues. Here again I would like to quote Mr. Justice Jackson:

> "Legal contentions, like the currency, depreciate through over-issue. The mind of an appellate judge is habitually receptive to the suggestions that a lower court committed an error. But receptiveness declines as the number of assigned errors increases. Multiplicity hints at lack of confidence in any one. Of course, I have not forgotten the reluctance with which a lawyer abandons even the weakest point lest it prove alluring to the same kind of judge. But experience on the bench convinces me that multiplying assignments of error will dilute and weaken a good case and will not save a bad one."

What has been said with respect to an abundance of propositions carries over into endless citation of cases. Perhaps nothing could be more non-persuasive. An avalanche of law is likely to smother the judges considering the case. To be perfectly frank with you, in the ordinary course of events, neither the Court nor any member thereof is going to read all the cases you can cite. Each judge has an adequate supply of law books in his office to read in his spare time. (He hasn't any.)

As a general rule, one or two cases should support adequately a particular proposition, and if the question involved is of sufficient importance, a brief exposition of the case, with possibly a quotation, should be given. If you have one or two strong cases in point, it is a waste of your time, the Court's time, and your stenographer's time to throw in some extra citations for good measure.

Whether it be by unnecessary citations, or repetitious coverage of the same proposition, or simply general observations on the state of the universe, a lawyer is laboring under an unfortunate delusion if he thinks he can improve his position by padding his brief. He should remember, as once observed: "He who uses many words for explaining any subject, doth, like the cutlefish, hide himself in his own ink!" Perhaps to those fellows, who apparently love the tinkle of a typewriter, was addressed these words:

"They do not write in verse or prose:
They simply lay their words in rows.
The self-same words that Webster penned,
They merely lay them end to end."

Quite often a judge gathers the impression that the lawyer, writing a long and loose brief, has dictated it principally for the purpose of impressing his own stenographer. You can just see him with his feet propped up on the desk, a balmy breeze blowing through the window, and an empty afternoon before him. The sound of his own voice is charming. Every little thought that crosses his mind must be recorded for posterity. He covers as much territory as possible, and then starts his dogs through it again. He doesn't miss a rabbit.

This sort of thing in itself should not be hastily condemned. The real crime this lawyer may commit will be in his failure to read what his stenographer has transcribed, and then go to work on it. More effective arrangement can almost certainly be made. A great quantity of drippings may be cut out and thrown in the wastebasket. The language can be sharpened. Only after such careful editing will the brief be truly presentable.

It is hoped by some members of the Court that the day will come when all briefs are printed. There are two good reasons. The first is that the written word will be more readable. The second is that it will almost necessarily require the lawyer to edit his work with painstaking care. If the lawyer and the client both realize that the printer demands a price for each page, there will be fewer and better pages.

It is surprising what good briefs the Court of Appeals receives in the form of Petitions for Rehearing. Usually they are models of brevity and directness. They indicate that the losing attorney had finally realized that he must shake the heart out of his case. But by then it may be too late. Why not do the hard work in the beginning, when you have a greater promise of more certain dividends.

In recent months your Court of Appeals has developed a system designed to improve the quality of its opinions. Lawyers may contribute materially to this planned improvement by themselves adopting and adhering to accepted methods for the better presentation of their cases. Ofttimes, after you have lost your appeal, you may be disheartened by the seeming inadequacy of the opinion. If you will stop and consider the calamity objectively, perhaps you will discover that the emaciated characteristics of the opinion but reflect the quality of your own presentation.

Adapted from Vol. 16, Kentucky State Bar Journal, (1952).

Is Brief-Making A Lost Art?

BY ALFRED C. COXE

A BRIEF, AS ITS NAME IMPLIES, should be short and concise. The lexicographers define it as "an epitome, a statement in few words, an abridgement of a client's case, a statement of the heads or points of a law argument."

In England, the name is applied to the document furnished by the solicitor to the barrister to enable the latter to present the cause understandingly to the court. In the United States the word has come to have a more restricted meaning, and, especially as applied to appeal cases, it means the statement of law and fact filed for the information of the court and opposing counsel. "The grand rule to be observed in drawing briefs, consists in conciseness with perspicuity."[1]

"A brief, in addition to an abbreviated statement of the case, should contain a summary of the points or questions involved, with a citation of the authorities relied on, and an argument based upon both which should be characterized by perspicuity and conciseness."[2]

The Supreme Court in 1872 amended Rule 21[3] stating the requisites of a brief filed in that court, and the rule has remained substantially in that form until the present day.

These requisites are:

I. A concise abstract, or statement of the case, presenting succinctly the questions involved, and the manner in which they are raised.

II. An assignment of the errors relied upon, which, in cases brought up by writ of error, shall set out separately and specifically each error asserted and intended to be urged, and, in cases

1 *Tidd's Practice*, p. 774.
2 Anderson v. Neal, 88 Ind 320.
3 14 Wallace, xi.

brought up by appeal the assignment shall state, as specifically as may be, in what respect the decree is alleged to be erroneous.

III. A brief of the argument, exhibiting a clear statement of the points of law or fact to be discussed, with reference to the pages of the record, and the authorities relied upon in support of each point.

The Circuit Courts of Appeals and the Appellate Courts of the states have adopted similar rules. The key-note of every definition of a brief is brevity, abridgement, conciseness.

The courts not only in their rules, but not infrequently in their opinions, oral and written, have emphasized the importance of these characteristics and have directed, requested and almost implored counsel not to disregard them. That they have been disregarded to such an extent that a brief—namely a concise perspicuous statement of fact and law—is becoming a *rara avis,* cannot be gainsaid.

The twentieth century lawyer, to paraphrase Bulwer Lytton's language seems to think that—

> In the lexicon of law, which fate reserves
> For courts and judges, there is no such word
> As—*brief.*

Half a century ago, when the law was more of a science and less of a business than it is to-day, the lawyer took a personal pride in presenting to the court the best product of his brain which hard and conscientious labor could produce. He did not delegate this work to stenographers, clerks and office boys. He did not patronize law factories where briefs are quoted at so much per dozen with a liberal discount for cash. He sat alone in his library, often at night, and did not abandon his task until he had reduced the facts to their last analysis, stated the principal questions of law and had cited, one or perhaps two, leading authorities in support of those propositions which might be regarded as debatable. Occasionally there was a short quotation from a report or text-book, but generally the judges were expected to examine the authorities at fountain head. Those having an indirect bearing or based on doubtful premises were ruthlessly cast aside; it was the survival of the fittest. The single purpose of the brief was to put the court in possession of the salient features of the case in as few words as possible. The writer of the brief did not waste his time and energies in arguing inconsequential and technical exceptions. He knew that "judges are people," and that even the most careful and conscientious judge can hardly avoid being prejudiced against a case where the most trivial points as well as the most weightly are given the same prominence.

A federal judge in one of the western circuits had before him a motion to dismiss a pleading. After listening to the first point, which was that the paper was not properly folioed, he surprised counsel by announcing: "The point is overruled and the motion is denied." "But your Honor," exclaimed the excited lawyer, "I have eight other points which I wish to present." "I think it will hardly be necessary," replied the judge, "as I invariably deny a motion that *begins that way.*" Somewhat arbitrary and abrupt, no doubt, and yet, considered from the view point of common sense, there is much that may be urged in support of the judge's position. It is, to say the least, quite possible that a lawyer who brings such trivialities to the attention of the court has no substantial grievance of which to complain.

The wheat is lost in the bran, and one who has been detected in offering bran to those in search of wheat, must not be surprised if he be regarded with suspicion even when he proffers the genuine article.

The brief of fifty years ago contained little that was counterfeit, it was the product of hard, intellectual labor, labor freely and enthusiastically bestowed, it was honest thought distilled and crystallized. Such a brief is before me as I write. It was used over a quarter of a century ago by one of the leaders of the bar of New York in arguing a cause before the Supreme Court of the United States which involved a large amount of money and several important and novel questions. *Imprimis,* it occupies but forty-seven printed pages. The writer of the brief did not assume, as is often the case to-day, that the court knew by intuition the names of the parties, the character of the action and the result in the court below. He prefaced the brief with a short "preliminary statement" setting forth these facts.

Next follows a "statement of the case" in which the testimony is sifted and condensed until the contents of a record containing over six hundred pages is clearly and succinctly stated in less than ten pages.

The contention of the parties is then stated generally and the errors complained of are set out. No member of the court having read the first twelve pages could fail to appreciate the salient facts and the exact nature of the dispute regarding them.

A lawyer who has never held a judicial office does not, I think, fully appreciate the importance of getting the principal facts and the main contention between the parties firmly fixed at the outset in the mind of the court. When he has done this, his labor is half over. When he enters upon his argument, the judge is able to give him calm discriminating attention instead of hunting with nervous haste through the record to find out how the controversy arose.

I recall hearing a cause argued before Judge Blatchford when he was circuit judge. The counsel for the complainant was one of those fuliginous debators, a breed not wholly extinct, who deem it wise to plunge directly into the heart of the argument without putting the court in possession of the facts upon which the argument rests. In vain the judge pleaded for information but without result. After arguing for three hours the counsel resumed his seat, leaving the judge in a maze of cryptic problems from which there seemed to be no exit. The counsel for the defendant was one of the leaders of the patent bar, noted for the clearness and candor of his statements. As he rose to address the court he was met by the following inquiry from the Bench: "Mr. ——, will you kindly tell me what this case is about?" Evidently embarrassed, Mr. —— endeavored to avoid the task thus thrust upon him, saying: "I much prefer, your Honor, that you should receive a statement of the facts from my learned adversary." "I appreciate your reluctance," replied the judge, "but I have not the slightest idea what this controversy is about and I would deem it a favor if you would inform me."

Thus challenged, there was no alternative but to proceed and in fifteen minutes he had made the case so clear that it was understood, not only by the judge, but by all who listened to the lucid explanation. The pity of it was that the complainant's case was made so plain that judgment was ordered in his favor.

Returning to the brief in question, the "points," eight in number, are stated, the facts bearing on the point under discussion are briefly reviewed with citations to the folios of the record where they appear in full and the authorities, few in number, bearing on the proposition debated, are cited. Occasionally a sentence or two is quoted from a peculiarly apposite statement found in a syllabus, or an opinion, but the brief is not loaded down with page after page of quotations either from the authorities or the record. In conclusion, the court was asked to reverse the decree. It was reversed.

Such briefs are sometimes met with at the present time but they are the exception, not the rule. The age of combinations, bureaucracies, telephones and stenographers is at hand, but is still in its infancy. Some of us may yet live to behold a machine where the pleadings and proofs are inserted in a condensing hopper, passed through a solution of text-books and syllabi and from there to a drying chamber, to be deposited finally in a receiver attached to the clerk's desk, in the form of a completed brief.

It is to-day as difficult to find a hand-made brief as it is to find a hand-made shoe.

The prevailing characteristics of the modern brief are discursiveness and prolixity. In the courts of the United States a brief under thirty pages is the pleasing exception and there are authentic instances where they have exceeded eight hundred printed pages. *Valde deflendus!*

What is true of the federal courts, is, I am informed, also true of the state courts. It seems to be thought that quantity and not quality is what will most surely convince the courts.

A few years ago a cause was tried before the writer where the points in controversy were so sifted at the argument that but one simple question was reserved for decision. Counsel united in requesting that they be permitted to furnish briefs. In vain the court suggested that such a course was unnecessary as there was no dispute upon the facts and he only desired to examine an authority or two on the law. At last the court yielded and permission was given upon the express understanding that the briefs were not to aggregate more than ten pages. In due course the briefs arrived, there were but ten pages, it is true, but in one of the briefs they were royal octavos; and printed thereon in agate type was matter enough to cover forty pages of ordinary size. No notice was taken of the imposition, the court feeling that any fine imposed upon the author of the brief as a juggler should, in all fairness, be returned to him as a reward for his pre-eminence as a humorist.

Few men can resist the temptation to argue every question which the record presents, no matter how inconsequential. They forget that in all probability the cause will ultimately turn upon one fundamental proposition and that he will succeed who has the ability to discover and present this proposition in the clearest light.

Mr. Webster was retained to argue in the Supreme Court a cause which had gone decisively against the plaintiff in the court below. When the cause was about to be reached, Mr. Bosworth, the attorney, came to Washington for a consultation. Mr. Webster sat with half-closed eyes as the attorney droned on from one hopeless position to another. At last he paused, saying: "Well, Mr. Webster, that is the case with a single exception; there is another point which we did not argue in the Circuit Court, but I think I should call your attention to it." As he unfolded the discarded point, Webster's interest became more and more intense and when it was fully explained he sprang to his feet, his great eyes flashing with triumph, and exclaimed: "Mr. Bosworth, by the blood of all the Bosworths who fell on Bosworth Field, that is *the* point in the case!" And it was.

Of course the ability to seize the strategic point, whether in the forum or on the battle-field, is given only to the "divinely gifted man."

The Websters are always in command, the Bosworths always in the ranks.

From Aristotle to the present day human minds have been divided into two classes, the rifle and the shot-gun types. The former use a bullet; they do not always hit, but when they do, they bring down big game; the latter use bird shot; they always hit something, but never kill anything.

Why is it that the art of brief-making has declined? There is more average ability in the profession to-day than ever before. The twentieth century lawyer is as able and industrious as his brother of a half century ago. What, then, is the reason? May it not be found in the changed environment and the intense activity of modern life? To keep pace with the age, the lawyer is compelled to resort to modern methods. Where there was one report to examine there are now a hundred; where there was one statute to construe there are now fifty; where there was a page of testimony to review there is now a volume. Small wonder that the lawyer of to-day seeks the assistance of digesters, stenographers and typewriters. The result is not a carefully thought-out argument; it is a digest. Everything bearing on the issue is found in the modern brief—somewhere. It is, however, so hidden in the wilderness of quotations from record and reports that it is apt to escape the attention of the most careful reader. At almost every term of court several of these bulky volumes appear.

Contemplate the cruelty of asking a judge, who has to dispose of several hundred cases annually, to study a printed book ten inches long, seven inches wide and one and a half inches thick. The mere physical act of reading it understandingly will occupy a week. It is an example of "man's inhumanity to man." In contemplating such a document one is forcibly reminded of Macaulay's review of "Nares's Memoirs of Lord Burghley." After stating the dimensions of the book and the weight of the paper consumed, he says: "Such a book might, before the deluge, have been considered as light reading by Hilpa and Shallum, but unhappily the life of man is now three-score years and ten, and we cannot but think it somewhat unfair in Dr. Nares to demand from us so large a portion of so short an existence."

There surely is no necessity for quoting *ad infinitum* from the record and the authorities. The judge must read the testimony and to insert it in the brief compels him to read it twice. If a leading case be cited it is fair to assume that the judge is familiar with it, and, if it be an ordinary case, no careful judge will rely on the quotation without examining the context. And yet the modern brief is often filled with quotations which have become household words alike of the judges and the counsel. These quotations have done such yeoman service that they are often used to identify the case. No member of the patent bar, for instance, will fail to know what is meant when the *Advancing Wave Case*,[4] or the *Nose of Wax Case*[5] is referred to, and every admirality lawyers knows well what is meant when the *Refrigerator Case*[6] is mentioned.

A cause was recently presented to a federal court, in which several parties were interested, involving many perplexing questions of fact and law. Eight counsel appeared and every statement made was disputed by one or more of the opposing counsel. Recess arrived while yet the case was in an impenetrable fog. When the court reconvened the judge held up the eight briefs aggregating a volume an inch and a half in thickness and exclaimed: "I have

4 Atlantic Works v. Brady, 107 US 192, 27 LEd 438, 2 SupCt 225.
5 White v. Dunbar, 119 US 47, 30 LEd 303, 7 SupCt 72.
6 The Southwark, 191 US 1, 48 LEd 65, 24 SupCt 1.

been endeavoring to find out what the truth about this case is from an examination of these briefs. It is impossible; it would take a week to read them. Counsel who present such briefs to a busy judge should be disbarred." For a moment there was consternation in the court-room, but the senior counsel relieved the situation by saying: "We have to thank your Honor for the impartiality of your ruling; we are all treated alike; we all go over the bar together." The laugh which followed was joined in heartily by the judge. The remark of the judge was not made in anger. It was, in a way, the expression of a feeling of resentment that he should be required to struggle through such a mass of conflicting statements to get at the truth which might have been made so clear. It was the unpremeditated protest of one who had suffered mental agony in trying to fathom the mysteries of the modern brief. To adopt the words of the translator of the Inferno, it was "the passionate outcry of a soul in pain."

What is the explanation of this unquestioned tendency to prolixity? In a word, it is due, I think, to the ease with which speech can be converted into type by modern methods. Human beings like to discourse. It requires no great mental or physical exertion to lean back in one's easy-chair and pour out floods of erudition into the ears of a stenographer, whose rapid pen catches and holds captive the inspired thoughts until they are embalmed forever in imperishable type. While the modern brief-maker is lying back in ease the ancient brief-maker was bending over his desk and laboriously writing down each sentence. Is it not the change from one method to the other which has produced such Brobdingnagian verbosity in pleadings, proofs, briefs and opinions? It is so easy now-a-days to fill page after page with "words, words, words."

At a country club near New York I once met a lawyer and invited him to a game of golf. In reply he said: "I suppose I should stay here; I have an expert inside, dictating to a stenographer, but I will run in and ask him another question and I will have time to play at least nine holes before he finishes his answer." The joy of the game was marred somewhat by the reflection that sometime in the near future I might be required to read that answer.

The dictated brief begets the dictated decision with the result that the reports are filled with opinions, many of them wholly unnecessary and many of the necessary ones are, in length, entirely out of proportion to the unimportant question involved. It is at least debatable whether, in the matter of time, the dictated brief and opinion are economical. The dictated brief saves the time of the bar at the expense of the bench. The dictated opinion saves the time of the bench at the expense of the bar.

I fully realize that any one who advises the abolition of dictation will be regarded as a hopeless reactionist, but I submit that its uses should be greatly curtailed in the preparation of opinions and briefs. This should be so, at least, until the habit of putting thought into the fewest possible words has been acquired by a careful apprenticeship with the pen. Undoubtedly it is more luxurious to talk to a human writing machine than to bend over the desk, pen in hand, but can there be a doubt as to which produces the best results? Is it not certain that the forty-page opinion and the four hundred-page brief would disappear, if in their preparation the pen were substituted for the mouth?

Dictation is the enemy of clear, logical thought; it leaves no time for deliberation and condensation; the tongue must wag; there is no speed limit.

It is impossible to imagine that the Second Inaugural, the speech at Gettysburg, Webster's argument in the *College Case* or *Erskine's plea* in the Stockdale Case, were produced by such a process.

The pen is a great analyzer and a superb logician, unconsciously and almost mechanically it punctures the sham and specious argument, discovers sound reasoning and forces it into the light. Many of the tedious and unconvincing dissertations which now disfigure briefs would never appear if the author had attempted to formulate them with pen and ink. Let any skeptic test the truth of this assertion by a simple experiment.

A complicated bill in equity is before him, he is for the defendant and wishes to know if a demurrer will lie to the bill. He reads it over with care but is in doubt. He calls his stenographer and attempts to dictate an abstract, but the causes of action are so complicated and interlock at so many points that his doubt is still present. He then dismisses the stenographer, runs his pen through repetitions, substitutes for the language of pleading the language of common sense, strikes out conclusions of law and reduces the statement of fact to its lowest terms, and lo! the true pleading stands revealed—a moribund creature, without sufficient vitality to stand alone. Or suppose he is asked for his opinion as to the constitutionality, scope and meaning of one of the many thousand laws annually turned out by the forty-six statute works of this country which are running over time to create ill-considered legislation, much of which, whatever the motive of the lawmakers, results in perplexing commerce and retarding trade. Is the law constitutional, how much of it is new, what part of the old law is repealed, what portion of it remains in force? Let him subject it to the pen test, strike out redundant matter and unnecessary verbiage and rewrite what remains in simple language. He will then be able to get as near to the legislative intent as is possible for a merely finite mind.

It is freely conceded that the foregoing has been written from the view point of the bench. It is altogether probable that a member of the bar would trace the true cause of the difficulty to long and rambling opinions so prevalent of late.

If both judge and counsel have fallen into careless habits it is but another reason why both should return to methods which, though slightly antiquated, will in the end lighten the intellectual labors of the profession.

The law student should start right, the habits which he acquires at the school will go with him through life. He can follow no better rule than this—never dictate brief or thesis. And let him adhere to the rule after being called to the bar, at least until the habit of condensing and clarifying thought has been acquired by long apprenticeship with the pen.

Adapted from Vol. 17, Yale Law Journal (1908).

How Lawyers Should Argue Cases on Appeal

BY HENRY T. LUMMUS

HOW SHOULD A LAWYER about to argue before the full court proceed? The first thing he should do is to put himself *in imagination* in the place of the court. You remember the story of the farmer's boy who was very successful in finding lost cattle. When asked how he did it, he said he tried to think where he would go if he he were a cow and got loose. The lawyer ought to imagine himself a judge, and ask himself what sort of argument would really help him decide a case. He would find that oratory of the old-fashioned type would not help, that he would wish to get the facts clearly, without suppression or distortion, and that he would wish to know the state of the established law, the current trends of the law, and the practical consequences of the adoption of the competing rules for which counsel are contending.

I think that is the main secret of good and bad arguments. Take a simple instance. At every sitting we notice that many counsel about to make a motion in a case on the list do not put themselves in our place sufficiently to make the motion properly. They rise and say:

"In the case of Jones v. Smith, No. 4711, I wish to make a motion."

About that time the Chief Justice says, "Where is the case?" And then they fumble around with the list and finally discover on what page the case appears. By that time we have forgotten the name of the case which was stated in the first place, and some time is spent in finding it. Whereas, if the lawyer should put himself in our place he would see that he should say:

"In a case on page 12 of the list, the third case down from the top, No. 4711, Jones v. Smith."

As soon as he had said that the court would have the case before it. It is just want of imagination that makes trouble even in such a trifling thing as that.

The same want of imagination is the cause of a good deal of bad argument. I suppose the prime necessity in arguing a case is the making of an orderly, clear, uncolored statement of it. It really is surprising to see what a small percentage of the bar appears capable of that. Not only in our court but in every court there is nothing so necessary to an advocate as the ability to state a case in an orderly, plain, uncolored fashion.

You remember the story of the English judge. Counsel was stating the case. He began in the middle and jumped from one end to the other until the judge became exasperated and said: "Mr. So-and-So, I wish you would adopt some order in the statement of the case. The chronological order is ordinarily the best, but for Heaven's sake have some order, even if it is only an alphabetical order."

Statement of Case Is Vital

I do not believe there is anything that will so well repay a practitioner as the study of the art of stating a case. I remember when the late Mr. Rackemann came up before us to argue the constitutionality of the declaratory judgment law. We opened the papers and began to skirmish around through them trying to find what the case was about. That is a necessity in many of the cases argued before us, for otherwise we should not know what they were about. Mr. Rackemann said:

> "May it please the court, if the members of the court will refrain from examining the papers in the case and will give me their attention, I think I can put them in possession of the facts in much shorter time than they otherwise could learn them."

I must say for Mr. Rackemann that he made good that promise. It is not every counsel who might say those words who would be able to make them good, but he did. He stated the case beautifully.

Statement is the first thing. So many counsel make an inadequate or an untrue or colored statement of the case, and then rush into what they conceive is their argument. They would do much better to state the case well and then sit down than to state the case badly and then go on with the best argument that could be made on a bad statement of the case. After all, a case well stated, assuming that the court knows its business at all, is two-thirds argued as soon as the statement of the case is finished.

In the statement of the case some counsel are tempted to distort the facts a little their own way or omit troublesome facts. I think there is nothing more irritating to a judge than to have counsel purport to state a case and then state it untruly. It is very bad psychologically, because omitted facts stand out conspicuously when the counsel on the other side call attention to them or the court discovers that they exist. They are much more conspicuous than they would have been if they had been stated properly in the first place.

Brief Must Contain Everything

When the case has been stated comes the argument of it. I assume that your briefs are going to be full. The brief, after all, is the thing that stays with the court when the oral argument is forgotten. Everything must be in the brief. The brief should contain all your citations. By the way, speaking of citations, I begin to be a little suspicious of counsel when sometimes they ask me if the judges have to read all the cases that they cite in the opinion. I usually answer that as a rule the judges read about ten times the number of cases they cite. Such questions make me doubt whether counsel always study carefully all the cases they cite. I have known counsel to go to some book like the Encyclopedia of Law and find a principle that they can use, and then, instead of citing the Encyclopedia for what it is worth and letting us find the cases, they just take out of the book half a dozen or a dozen cases the names of which look pretty good and throw them in, and sometimes omit to name the Encyclopedia from which they got them. Then the court finds itself just a bit irritated at discovering that the cases cited do not support the proposition at all, and especially when it discovers how they were collected. The counsel really were putting their worst foot forward, because if they had cited the Encyclopedia they could lay it to the Encyclopedia if the cases didn't support the principle. Counsel who cites a case impliedly warrants that he has read and studied it and that according to his judgment the case supports the proposition for which it is cited.

Now, as to the argument. The court is not much interested in citation-chopping in argument; counsel assuring us that in this case such a thing was decided and in another case something else was decided. The court ordinarily is not familiar with those cases unless they are great leading cases, or recent cases in this jurisdiction. If they are minor cases or cases from other jurisdictions, the court usually does not know them, and does not know what counsel are talking about when these cases are discussed.

What you are aiming for in the argument is to get the first impression of the court in your favor. The ultimate study will be made with the use of your brief. The argument, like shock troops, may take the trench. Your brief, coming up afterwards, may hold it. You want to get the court headed right. To do that you should discuss principles and very seldom refer to cases unless there is some case that directly controls the point or unless the proposition for which you contend is an inference from some important case.

Quite as common as citation-chopping is another bad habit, and that is brief-reading. Many counsel open their briefs in front of them and proceed to read. When a judge finds that counsel is doing that, once he has determined the case in miles an hour at which the lawyer reads, he can go out and stay ten minutes and know the exact place where the lawyer will be on his return.

Reading Brief Annoys Judges

Such reading is dull and depressing. It does not accomplish anything. It simply tries the court. The court is going to have your brief. I think there has never been a case in the history of Massachusetts where a man has been chosen for the supreme judicial court who could not read for himself. You are just wasting your time by reading the brief. To be on the safe side and to shun temptation, you had better put the brief in the seat of a chair and let someone sit on it, or else leave it in your bag. If you are not familiar enough with your case to argue it without aid from your brief, you would better not argue at all. If you do argue, stand up and look at the court. Don't be looking down reading something. Tell the court in plain words, first, the case; second, the reasons why you contend that the decision should be your way. When you get through with that, sit down.

Don't try to argue orally everything that may be in your brief. There are cases that come before us not on one point, but on twenty points. It would be silly to try to argue the twenty points. Some of them are minor and some of them may be of more importance.

There is no use in arguing orally a miscellaneous collection of points. Confine yourself to the points that you can argue with force and effect, and simply say to the court that you submit the rest of your case on the brief. *In fact you do not have to say that, because you do not waive anything that is in your brief, whether you say anything about it or not.*

There is another mistake that you frequently see made. Usually it is accompanied by an inadequate statement of the case. A lawyer will make a sort of fragmentary statement of the case, and before the court can grasp it at all he will begin to get excited and emotional and to become denunciatory of the other side. You might just as well put on a Punch and Judy show as to argue a case in that way. The court cannot share the emotions of counsel when it does not yet know what the case is about. If there has been a great fraud perpetrated on your client and you state the case plainly and unemotionally, the court can see the fraud as clearly as you do. If it is real fraud, the judges are just as likely to get indignant about it inside if you keep calm.

Another fault that is common is arguing outside the record. Frequently, the argument consists of a mixture of things, some of which are in the record and some of which are not. Of course we pay no attention to things that are not disclosed by the record, and if we find counsel stepping in and out of the record we begin to doubt whether much of what he says is supported by the record.

Lastly, on the question of brevity. Sidney Bartlett was one of the great lawyers of Massachusetts, especially in argument before the full court. He was always brief. He stated the case well, he argued a few matters of principle, and then he sat down. Sometimes he sat down when the court wished he would go on. But his sole purpose was to get the court headed right, and that really is the purpose of an argument.

Some counsel seem to have the idea that no matter how small the point they must use up the allotted time. That is bad policy, even in jury cases. Some of the most successful jury lawyers make brief arguments. Surely before the full court, which is supposed to be able to see a question of law once it is clearly presented, to keep on with an oration beyond the point where the court is being educated is absurd.

I do not wish to appear condemnatory of the entire bar. There are quite a number of lawyers, some of whom I see before me, whose arguments are models to be followed. But I really think there are many men at the bar who ought to put themselves in imagination in the place of the court, and if they do so, I think they will revise some of their methods.

Adapted from Vol. 26, Journal of the American Judicature Society (1943).

Essentials of an Effective Appellate Brief

BY FREDERICK BERNAYS WIENER

IT IS REALLY NOT PROFITABLE to discuss an effective brief in terms of abstractions. Too many otherwise excellent discussions of brief-writing are of very little use except to the expert, simply because they are abstract; and *ex hypothesi,* the expert does not need them. What follows, therefore, will be concrete and detailed.

Most of the examples discussed will, necessarily, be taken from my own practice.[1] For extended research, the best sources are the libraries of courts, bar associations, and law schools, many of which preserve the records and briefs in appellate cases. There is no better guide anywhere to good brief-writing than the examination and study of briefs written by leaders of the bar and (generally) by such government agencies as handle extensive litigation. Briefs in those categories are highly instructive as to form, substance, and technique.

Essentials of a Good Appellate Brief

The really essential features are—

(1) Compliance with rules of court.

(2) Effective statement of facts.

(3) Good, forceful English.

(4) Argumentative headings.

(5) Appealing statement of the questions presented.

(6) Sound analysis of the legal problem in argument on the law.

[1] This choice is dictated by convenience, not by egocentricity. Of course there are plenty of other, and, I have no doubt at all, better examples. But the briefs discussed here are the ones that arise out of the cases with which I have wrestled; these are the ones which I have personally sweated out. Nevertheless, while the examples chosen are thus limited, I have sought to select, not esoteric specialties, but topics of general interest and techniques of general application.

(7) Convincing presentation of the evidence in argument on the facts.

(8) Careful attention to all portions of the brief.

(9) Impression of conviction which allays the reader's doubts and satisfies his curiosity.

1. *Compliance with rules of court.*—This requirement is put first, because even if one should succeed in writing that dream brief, the clerk would not permit it to be filed if it exceeded the permitted length. So—first essential—familiarize yourself with the rules of the court in which your brief is to be filed, and comply with them. The only safe procedure, if you are new at the game or are writing a brief for a strange court, is to read the rules, check with the clerk or an older practitioner, and examine and follow some briefs that have already passed muster.

Here I shall not even attempt to classify the types of rules. But it may be pertinent to note that, in the federal courts, every circuit except the 5th and 9th limits the lengths of the briefs which may be filed without prior leave of court, and that similar limitations are becoming popular in other courts.

There is no limit on the length of briefs in the Supreme Court of the United States. But a brief in support of a petition for certiorari must be "direct and concise," and the petition may be denied for noncompliance with that requirement.[2] And briefs on the merits filed by eminent—and no doubt highly-paid—counsel have been ordered stricken when they contained "burdensome, irrelevant, and immaterial matter."[3]

[2] "The petition for writ of certiorari in this case is denied for failure to comply with par. 2 of Rule 38 of the Rules of this Court. The brief filed in support of the petition is not 'direct and concise' as required by that rule." Zap v. United States, 326 US 777, 90 LEd 470, 66 SupCt 265, (1945). The original supporting brief had been 83 pages long. Thereafter, issuance of the order denying the writ was stayed, 326 US 692, 90 LEd 407, 66 SupCt 268, (1945), and on rehearing certiorari was granted. 326 US 802. Zap's conviction was affirmed, 328 US 624, 90 LEd 1477, 66 SupCt 1277, (1946), and a petition for rehearing was denied. 329 US 824, 91 LEd 700, 67 SupCt 110, (1946). But, at the next Term, a second petition for rehearing was granted and the indictment ordered dismissed, because of the absence of women on the grand jury which had indicted—Mr. Zap. 330 US 800, 91 LEd 1259, 67 SupCt 857, (1947).

[3] See *Journal,* U. S. Sup. Ct. Oct. T. 1928, p. 101: "It is ordered by the Court that this case be restored to the docket for reargument on January 14, 1929, with the same limitations as to the time of argument and the number of counsel as in the original hearing; that complete new briefs be filed, and that the old briefs heretofore filed shall not be used; that the new briefs shall conform to the rules of this Court, be compact, logically arranged with proper headings, concise, and

2. *Effective statement of the facts.*—In many respects, the Statement is the most important part of the brief.

The greatest mistake any lawyer can make, after he has written a fine brief on the law, is to toss in a dry statement of facts and send the thing off to the printer. Thanks to the guidance of able teachers, I learned the great lesson that, in writing a brief, the facts should first be studied, mastered, sweated over—and written out into an acceptable draft before the rest of the brief is even touched.

For courts are not automatons; the constantly repeated demonstration that "hard cases make bad law" is living proof of that proposition. The real importance of facts is that courts want to do substantial justice and that they are sensitive to the "equities." Consequently the objective of the advocate must be so to write his statement that the court will want to decide the case his way after reading just that portion of the brief.

First of all, when you write a statement of facts, you must remember that you are assisting another person's mind, and that knowledge is cumulative. Therefore, state the case as you yourself would wish to read it—the introductory summary first, the details later.

Above all, avoid the lazy kind of statement that says, "The witness Quackenbush testified that ———; that ———; that ———," and so on *ad infinitum* and *ad nauseam*. Any literate stenographer can do that; most lazy lawyers do it; but it isn't very helpful to the court.

Similarly, it is a mistake to set out the testimony in the invariable order in which it was presented at the trial. The trial lawyer must take one witness at a time, and develop what witnesses X, Y, and Z know about incidents A, B, and C. There is generally no other way in which he can get such evidence into the record. But the appellate lawyer writing the statement should marshal his evidence, not according to witnesses, but according to topics. True, it takes more work, which is why so often it is not done, but the topical arrangement is really the only effective one.

---

free from burdensome, irrelevant, and immaterial matter; . . ." The record contained 2023 pages, the briefs first filed extended to 1924 pages, and the briefs on the second argument contained only 789 pages. The case was Gilchrist v. Interborough Rapid Transit Co., 279 US 159, 73 LEd 652, 49 SupCt 282, (1929). See Frankfurter and Landis, *The Business of the Supreme Court at October Term, 1928* (1929) 43 Harv. L. Rev. 33, 57.

Once the basic arrangement has been blocked out, with proper topical introduction, and with the facts arranged in the logical order—and generally the chronological order is the most logical one—it is time to consider the next step, which is, succinctly, to incorporate the atmospheric trimmings.

Here the task is to present the facts, without any sacrifice of accuracy, but yet so as to squeeze the last drop of advantage from your case—and that is a task which in a very literal sense begins with the first sentence of your statement and continues through the last one (in which you set forth the opinion or judgment below). Examples of how to do it and of how not to do it are considered below; here will be noted some of the general principles.

First and foremost, you must be accurate. You owe that to the court, and, equally, you owe that to your client. And, for the same reasons, you must be candid.

Second, grasp your nettles firmly. No matter how unfavorable the facts are, they will hurt you more if the court first learns them from your opponent. To gloss over a nasty portion of the record is not only somewhat less than fair to the court, it is definitely harmful to the case. Draw the sting of the unpleasant facts by presenting them yourself.

Next, never argue or editorialize in your statement. Always be straightforward; indicate the conflict in the evidence, gain whatever advantage you can out of the order of its presentation, but save your argument for the body of the brief. The temptation to slip in a sly remark is sometimes pretty strong; let it go into an early draft, if you must, and get what fun you can out of it; but be sure it is out of the final product.

In short, present your facts accurately, candidly—but always favorably, and always strive to make the most favorable impression with the facts that you have.[4]

---

4 I may perhaps be pardoned for quoting from a reply brief which passed over my desk within the year:

"An appellant does not often use much space in a reply brief to praise a brief for the appellee. Here, then, though we think commendation due, a few words may seem enough.

"In general, the appellee's brief recites the evidence fairly. Of course, quite properly, the statement is of that most favorable to the Government, but there is little at which to quibble * * *.

"The argument seems to us to say all that can be said for the Government on the points raised, and to say it with great skill; *e.g.*, how much more effective the connotations of the words in the brief * * * than those in the indictment. * * *.

Examples of Effective and Ineffective Statements

It remains to illustrate the foregoing generalizations with specific and concrete examples.

(a) Courts dislike to referee ideological contests, or to be asked to umpire disputes which exude even the faintest suggestion of mutual zeal to get a question decided,[5] or to assist the litigant who goes to law to vindicate a principle rather than a substantial legal right. The problem in such cases is to make the court aware of what is going on—which obviously cannot be done by calling one's opponent a strike-suitor or his cause a cooked-up case. Generally, the facts of record speak for themselves, and all the advocate need normally do is to set them out, without comment.

An example that comes to mind is that of a bitterly contested proceeding involving a tract of public land which was of no possible value except as a source of rock for a nearby breakwater. If the claimant succeeded in obtaining it, the neighboring municipality would of necessity have had to pay handsomely for the stone it wanted. In order to convey the desired impression, the brief for the public official commenced its statement as follows:

> Whaler Island is a small rocky island in the harbor of Crescent City, California, some 3.65 acres in extent (R. 17-18). It is without value for agricultural purposes, is not adapted to ordinary and private occupation, and is of utility only in connection with the improvement and development of the harbor (R. 31).
>
> This is the land for which the appellant Lyders seeks a patent (Bill, pars. V, XVIII; R. 4, 15-16).[6]

In that case, the matter was dropped with its mere statement, and was not further pursued. There was nothing to argue about, because the circumstances in question were atmospheric only, and legally

"We do not suggest that the choice of words employed in the brief for the appellee goes beyond the license of an advocate * * *.

"Our praise of the appellee's brief is, therefore, tempered with a note of caution. Its art is in its color, not applied in crude daubs, but with restraint that sometimes requires scrutiny to perceive its fundamental flaws * * *."

[5] *Cf.* United States v. C.I.O., 335 US 106, 92 LEd 1849, 68 SupCt 1349 (1948).

[6] Lyders v. Ickes, 65 AppDC 379, 84 F(2d) 232 (1936). For earlier stages in the Whaler Island litigation, see West v. Lyders, 59 AppDC 122, 36 F(2d) 108 (1929), and Wilbur v. Lyders, 61 AppDC 202, 59 F(2d) 877 (1932); for the sequel, see Lyders v. Del Norte County, 100 F(2d) 876 (CCA 9th, 1939), certiorari denied, 308 US 562, 84 LEd 472, 60 SupCt 73 (1939).

irrelevant. In other cases, however, facts going to the infirmity of a party may become relevant, in which event they are properly taken up for subsequent argument. Then the problem is to distinguish between the Statement and the Argument, to keep the first absolutely straightforward, and to put the editorializing and characterization where they belong, viz., in the portion of the brief designated as Argument.

Examples of the second category arise in situations where review by a higher court is discretionary and not as of right, and where accordingly the appellate court must be convinced, not so much that the decision below is correct or incorrect, but rather that the question is important and one which deserves or requires review. In such a situation any fact tending to show that a litigant is more interested in obtaining an advisory opinion than in vindicating his legal rights becomes not only relevant but important, and, it may be, controlling.

A recent case arising out of a war-time removal order, but coming up sufficiently long after V-J Day to be of essentially academic interest, illustrates the point. The plaintiff had been individually excluded, by force, from the sensitive West Coast area after having been convicted of conspiracy to commit sedition.[7] He sued the Commanding General for damages, a judgment in his favor was reversed on appeal, and he petitioned for a writ of certiorari to review the result. The statement in the Commanding General's brief opposing the petition therefore pointed out that—

> The complaint asked damages in the sum of $3500, but subsequently petitioner filed a waiver of all damages in excess of $100 (R. 83, 291, 296, 303).

In the portion of the General's brief headed "Argument," he reverted to this fact and argued that—

> . . . the circumstance that, after bringing suit for $3500 (R. 11), petitioner subsequently stipulated that he would waive all damages over $100 (R. 83, 291, 296), strongly suggests that the object of this proceeding for damages was not so much redress for injuries sustained as the obtaining of

[7] Distinguish the mass exclusion orders considered in Korematsu v. United States, 323 US 214, 89 LEd 243, 65 SupCt 193 (1944), and Hirabayashi v. United States, 320 US 81, 87 LEd 1774, 63 SupCt 1375 (1943).

> abstract pronouncements from the courts as to respondent's authority. This he cannot have. . . .

Certiorari was denied,[8] and the factor just mentioned may well have contributed to that result.

(b) It is a commonplace that a very bad man may have a very good case. But judges are human, they want to do substantial justice, and therefore in close cases they are, more or less unconsciously (depending on the individual judge), bound to be influenced by the character of the litigant, particularly when he appears before them as a crusader for the right. Consequently, the real function of the statement in a brief in a criminal case is to indicate something of the party's guilt or innocence. If you represent the prosecution, your aim must be to convey the impression that the convicted man is just as clearly guilty as he can possibly be; if you represent the defendant, you must strive to show that he has been greatly wronged—and this is true in both instances not only when the question concerns the sufficiency of the evidence to support the verdict, but whatever the question is, quite regardless of the formal issues raised on the appeal. "Courts delight to do substantial justice."

A striking instance for the employment of this technique was presented by the recent sordid *Restaurant Longchamps* tax fraud case. Three of the convicted persons appealed without success and then petitioned for a writ of certiorari. At the trial and again in their petition these defendants indicated that there was no denial of the tax frauds charged, and raised only issues arising out of their alleged disclosure prior to the Treasury investigations, and out of the use of their admissions and of the books of their corporations.

Notwithstanding the admission of the tax frauds thus made in the petition, the government's Brief in Opposition to the granting of certiorari discussed the facts relating to the fraud in as great detail as if the issue had been the sufficiency of the evidence in the Circuit Court of Appeals rather than the importance of petitioners' questions for purposes of review of their case by the Supreme Court. All the shabby details were set out, the evidence relating to the alleged disclosure was discussed at length, and the

[8] Wilcox v. Emmons, 67 FSupp 339 (S. D. Cal. 1946), reversed *sub nom.* De Witt v. Wilcox, 161 F(2d) 785 (CCA 9th, 1947), certiorari denied, 332 US 763, 92 LEd 349, 68 SupCt 68 (1947).

facts bearing on the credibility of one of the defendants on his contradiction were stated *in extenso.* (This individual had made the grave mistake, *inter alia*, of testifying to a meeting with the Collector of Internal Revenue, alleged to have taken place at the precise time when that official was in fact meeting with eight very substantial and prominent fellow-citizens in connection with the affairs of the Governor Smith Memorial Fund). Moreover, the findings of the District Court, to the effect that the alleged disclosures were neither full nor frank nor voluntarily made, were not simply summarized, but were quoted in full.

The consequence was, not so much that the Brief in Opposition was able to brush off the questions sought to be raised as never having been reached, but that there was necessarily generated a feeling in the mind of any reader that, whether the questions were reached or not, these petitioners were so clearly guilty of such a particularly outrageous crime that jail was doubtless much too good for them.[9]

(c) No matter how long or short a Statement of Facts may be, it should always be written so as to advance the cause of the party on whose behalf it is prepared. It must not argue or editorialize; its strength lies in selection and juxtaposition, without of course ever appearing to involve the irrelevant.

Frequently a Statement will be long, particularly when the record is long. In that event it should not be written as one continuous screed, but should be divided up, through the use of sub-headings, so that the reader can more easily grasp the relevance of what he reads.[10]

---

[9] United States v. Lustig, 163 F(2d) 85 (CCA 2, 1947), certiorari denied, 332 US 775, 92 LEd 360, 68 SupCt 88 (1947), rehearing denied, 332 US 812, 92 LEd 390, 68 SupCt 160 (1947).

[10] Here are examples of subdivisions of statements in two recent cases, one civil the other criminal.

(a) Federal Trade Commission v. Cement Institute, 333 US 683, 92 LEd 1010, 68 SupCt 793 (1948).

The Federal Trade Commission's complaint.
The findings of the Commission.
The cement industry and respondents' position therein.
Absence of competition in the industry.
Respondents' multiple basing-point delivered-price system.
Collective action to prevent competition and to maintain respondents' pricing system.
Effects of respondents' combination.
Violation of Section 2 of the Clayton Act.
The Commission's conclusion and order.
The decision of the Circuit Court of Appeals.

And, when the Statement is long, it is even more necessary to write it so that the reader's interest will never flag, but will always be held, and will always be carried in the direction that the advocate wishes it to go. And that endeavor must never be permitted to sag, even at the end, when the proceedings in the court below are being discussed.

It is a mistake to write simply, "The court below affirmed (R. 74)," when you could have written, "The court below affirmed on the ground that the evidence amply justified the jury in finding petitioner guilty as charged (R. 74)." Frequently the Statement can be, as it were, neatly buttoned up by a juicy quotation from the findings or opinion below: If you are appealing, summarize or quote the opinion below when it seems pretty obviously wrong, or summarize or quote from the dissenting judge, or both. If, on the other hand, you are for the appellee, spread the conclusions or the apt quotation from the majority opinion, or do the same for the dissent when it seems unsound on its face.

In short, write your statement of facts from beginning to end, from the first paragraph to the last, with this one aim always before you, to write your Statement so that the court will want to decide the case in your favor after reading just that portion of your brief.

Examples of Matters That Must Be Avoided

The four outstanding horribles in brief-writing are: Unprofessional inaccuracy, unsupported hyperbole, unwarranted screaming, and personalities and scandalous matter.

Most of these unpardonables crop up in portions of the brief other than the Statement; and, at least in my experience, even

---

(b) Chandler v. United States, — F(2d) — (CA 1, 1948).

A. Appellant's activities prior to Germany's declaration of war against the United States on December 11, 1941.

B. Appellant's broadcasting activities in Germany, 1942-1945.

C. The substance of appellant's broadcasts and his intent to betray the United States.

D. The overt acts submitted to the jury.

(i) Arranging for and making recordings.

(ii) Participating in conferences for the improvement or formulation of broadcasts.

(iii) Participating in conferences for the resumption or continuation of broadcasting activities.

E. Appellant's apprehension and his return to the United States in custody.

F. Appellant's alleged insanity.

the most unprofessionally unprofessional inaccuracy is generally met with in the argument portion of the brief (after the writer's ardor has really been inflamed).

Apart from those, which are really beyond the pale, the outstanding fault in too many Statements is a tendency to editorialize and to argue.

3. *Good, clear, forceful English.*—This is the next essential, though I shall do little more than state it. But the observations which follow may be suggestive, and possibly helpful.

First, clarity is more important in a brief than literary excellence. Next, what you write should be grammatical. A lawyer is a professional man, in whom poor English should not be tolerated. I know that a good many brief-writers do not (perhaps because they can not) use good English, but there is really no excuse for any such performance. Offhand the only justified departure from the rules of grammar for a lawyer is the split infinitive, "to specifically perform." In that instance alone, the English Department is of no help to the equity practitioner.

I think, also, that a lawyer should be at pains in his briefs (whatever may be the case in pleadings and contracts) to minimize legal formalisms such as "the said," "hereinbefore," "thereinafter," and the like; nor is it any longer a sign of learning to encumber a brief with excerpts from the Latin—unless they are very pat indeed.

The Statement, as has already been indicated at length, should be straightforward, without embellishments and with a minimum of adjectives. It is not until the Argument portion of the brief is reached that you change the pace, so to speak, of your prose, and, if I may mix a metaphor by mechanizing it, really turn on the steam. From then on, you *argue*! Of course, it is well not to press too hard at your own weak points, for frequently the skill of the advocate consists in skating deftly where the ice is thin (or even where there isn't any ice at all). A good many situations will call for what has aptly been called "walking violently on eggs." But you can't write an Argument without arguing, and therefore statements which in law review articles might well be preceded with the professorial "it would seem" must be introduced in briefs by "it is therefore abundantly clear," or, at the very least, by "it necessarily follows."

Moreover, when you really get to the heart of the case, don't be afraid to hit hard, and don't hesitate to write a fighting brief. There is nothing in brief-writing quite so fallacious as what, for want of a better term, I like to call the striped-pants complex, namely, the notion that it is somehow undignified to make a strong hard-hitting argument. That idea is really on a par with the view that an advocate should be impartial, or has any business being so.

Style is of course an individual matter. It may be that the Frenchman was right who said that style is the man himself. Certainly there is full opportunity in this field for the exercise of individual and personal judgments, since many different styles of writing may be equally effective.

Ideally, the raw material for such a discussion in the present field would be a library full of briefs, with representative examples of good, bad, and indifferent extracted and compiled within the covers of a single casebook. But there are no such casebooks, and the available libraries are few and necessarily inaccessible to many practitioners. Therefore I have selected my examples from opinions by former members of the Supreme Court, which are of course readily available in the reports. The portions of such opinions which follow the statement of the facts and issues are generally written in a more or less argumentative style, and thus are helpful here; and it may be noted that, since dissenting opinions are normally written with more zeal (if not indeed with somewhat less restraint), dissents are an even more valuable source of forceful legal writing.

In terms of familiar opinions, my own view—and I put the matter in terms of personal preference because it very largely comes down to that—my own view is that the most effective argumentative style is one like that of the late Chief Justice Hughes, with possibly a touch of Holmes for the snappers at the ends of significant passages. There is something powerful and inexorable about a Hughes opinion—I cite a few at random in the footnote.[11] Read those opinions, get the feel of the pulsating,

[11] *E.g.*, Apex Hosiery Co. v. Leader, 310 US 469, 514 (dissent), 84 LEd 1311, 60 SupCt 982 (1940); Labor Board v. Jones & Laughlin, 301 US 1, 81 LEd 893, 57 SupCt 615 (1937); United States v. Wood, 299 US 123, 81 LEd 78, 57 SupCt 177 (1936); Morehead v. N. Y. ex rel Tipaldo, 298 US 587, 618, (dissent), 80 LEd 1347, 56 SupCt 918 (1936); Retirement Board v. Alton R. Co., 295 US 330, 374, (dissent), 79 LEd 1468, 55 SupCt 758 (1935); Sterling v. Constantin, 287 US 378, 77 LEd 375, 53 SupCt 190 (1932).

rhythmical, irresistible argument rolling on towards its predetermined end, and you will appreciate the force of really argumentative writing. Chief Justice Stone also wrote some good strong opinions, notably in dissent; those collected below seem to me outstanding, and to merit reading and rereading.[12]

Other judges have their admirers also—but, I repeat, these are personal preferences. Cardozo, J., wrote beautiful English, but his opinions are too limpid and too lyrical to constitute the most effective argumentation. Holmes' opinions are generally too epigrammatic for brief-writing, except as to the snapper sentences; a judge can rest on neatly phrased assertion, an advocate needs something more. The judge needs only to decide; the advocate must persuade.

Some lawyers and judges urge that a brief should always contain short sentences. It is true that excessively long sentences result in turgidity. The force of Chief Justice White's later opinions was very perceptibly marred by this quality, though assuredly they rolled onward to powerful conclusions.[13] But the constant use of short sentences to the exclusion of longer ones imparts a staccato quality to prose writing which also detracts from the final results. Mr. Justice Brandeis' opinions always seemed to me to fall into that category; they were, however, crystal clear and wholly devoid of verbal embroidery.[14]

4. *Argumentative headings.*—Headings should always be argumentative rather than topical or even assertive. For instance, say "This suit is barred by laches because brought twenty-five years after the issuance of the original certificate" rather than "This suit is barred by laches." The first gives the argument in a nutshell, the second does not—though certainly the second as-

[12] *E.g.,* Girouard v. United States, 328 US 61, 70, (dissent), 90 LEd 1084, 66 SupCt 826 (1946); Schneiderman v. United States, 320 US 118, 170, (dissent), 87 LEd 1796, 63 SupCt 1333 (1943); United States v. Darby, 312 US 100, 85 LEd 609, 61 SupCt 451 (1941); Helvering v. Gerhardt, 304 US 405, 82 LEd 1427, 58 SupCt 969 (1938); Morehead v. N. Y. ex rel Tipaldo, 298 US 587, 631, (dissent), 80 LEd 1347, 56 SupCt 918 (1936); United States v. Butler, 297 US 1, 78, (dissent), 80 LEd 477, 56 SupCt 312 (1936).

[13] *E.g.,* Selective Draft Law Cases, 245 US 366, 62 LEd 349, 38 SupCt 159 (1918); Minneapolis & St. Louis R. R. v. Bombolis, 241 US 211, 60 LEd 961, 36 SupCt 595 (1916).

[14] *E.g.,* Ashwander v. Tennessee Valley Authority, 297 US 288, 341, (concurring opinion), 80 LEd 688, 56 SupCt 466 (1936); Louisville Bank v. Radford, 295 US 555, 79 LEd 1593, 55 SupCt 854 (1935); New State Ice Co. v. Liebmann, 285 US 262, 280, (dissent), 76 LEd 747, 52 SupCt 371 (1935); Wan v. United States, 266 US 1, 69 LEd 131, 45 SupCt 1 (1924).

sertive heading is infinitely more effective than the merely topical, "The question of laches." Similarly, say "Appellant had notice of the defect and therefore is not a holder in due course" in preference to "Appellant is not a holder in due course" or to "Appellant's contention."

Sub-headings should likewise be argumentative rather than topical or merely assertive, primarily because all are collected in the index at the beginning of the brief, and are thus frequently read first by any judge who wants to get the argument in abbreviated compass. You lose a lot, therefore, if your sub-headings are not precise and specific. If your headings and sub-headings are properly argumentative, your argument starts at page i of the brief, and the court will not need to go beyond that point to catch the gist of your position at a quick glance.

Collecting all the headings and sub-headings in the index has also this important incidental advantage: it discloses whatever lack of uniformity may have crept into them in the course of your writing, and so provides a convenient opportunity for strengthening revisions (and, it may well be, for catching misprints and the almost inevitable juxtaposition of "appellant" and "appellee").

Perhaps this is as good a place as any for the admonition that a main heading should never be followed by just a single sub-heading. If a proposition cannot be divided into more than one part, it is being restated. Therefore, if you find yourself unable to work out more than one sub-heading, the difficulty is that your main heading is improperly formulated; you had better rewrite it.

Here is an example of some argumentative headings and sub-headings, taken from the index page of the prevailing brief in a fairly celebrated case,[15] which are sufficiently detailed and precise to give the reader the very heart of the party's contentions:

1. It has always been held that one of the incidents of a lawful arrest is the right to search the premises under the control of the person arrested for the instrumentalities of the crime of which he is accused, and that such a search is a reasonable one within the Fourth Amendment.

15 Harris v. United States, 331 US 145, 91 LEd 1399, 67 SupCt 1098 (1947).

A. The cases in this Court prior to 1927 establish that the right to search premises for instrumentalities of crime is an incident of a lawful arrest therein.

B. There may be an exception permitting search of the premises for evidentiary papers incident to a lawful arrest in the cases where a crime is actually being committed in the presence of the arresting officers.

C. The *Go-Bart* and *Lefkowitz* cases have been uniformly understood to hold that a search of premises incident to a lawful arrest has as wide a scope as a search authorized by a search warrant, and is limited to the objects for which such a warrant could issue.

D. The right to search premises under the accused's control for instrumentalities of crime as an incident to his lawful arrest is of ancient origin, and its recognition by the courts represents not an encroachment on constitutional protections but rather a reaffirmation of their original boundaries.

You may read all this and disagree, and certainly later decisions have substantially whittled down the propositions established in the particular case;[16] the point here is that, after reading these detailed, specific, and argumentative headings, you know precisely the substance and scope of the argument.

Here is another example, likewise taken from the prevailing brief in a recent case,[17] which also sets forth a party's arguments, in this instance in step-by-step progression:

1. The railroads' refusal to make direct delivery of livestock to sidings located on their line is a breach of their legal duty to the public as common carriers, which the Commission had power to remedy by its order.

A. If Track 1619 were owned by the New York Central, then clearly the Interstate Commerce Act has been violated, and the Commission's order would be unassailable.

16 See McDonald v. United States, 335 US 451, 93 LEd 153, 69 SupCt 191; Trupiano v. United States, 334 US 699, 92 LEd 1663, 68 SupCt 1229 (1948); Johnson v. United States, 333 US 10, 92 LEd 436, 68 SupCt 367 (1948); *cf.* United States v. Di Re, 332 US 581, 92 LEd 210, 68 SupCt 222 (1948).

17 United States v. Baltimore & Ohio R. Co., 333 US 169, 92 LEd 618, 68 SupCt 494 (1948).

B. In view of Section 1(3)(a) of the Interstate Commerce Act, the situation is not altered in any respect by the circumstance that Track 1619 is owned by a non-carrier.

C. Nor is the situation altered by reason of the New York Central's contract with the Stock Yards which provides expressly for discrimination against livestock, since common carriers cannot by contract relieve themselves from their duties to the public.

D. The Stock Yards' right, if any, to compensation from the New York Central for the use of its land has no bearing upon the validity of the Commission's order requiring the railroads to perform their duties to the public.

There were additional points, but the foregoing was the nub of the argument. Again, the reader is left in no possible doubt as to the substance or the progression of the propositions presented.

Here is another example, this time of reasonably argumentative headings, but of only topical sub-headings:

1. Section 266 of the Judicial Code, requiring the hearing and determination by three judges of applications for certain interlocutory injunctions, is not applicable to this case. Therefore the three-judge trial court convened pursuant to section 266 was without jurisdiction to issue the interlocutory injunction and abused its discretion in doing so.

No state statute involved.

As to order of administrative board or commission.

——————— v. ——————— discussed and distinguished.

Section 266 inapplicable where order affects only particular district and is of limited scope.

Conclusion.

* * * * * * * * * *

3. This action is a suit against the State of ——— ———, of which the Supreme Court has exclusive jurisdiction awarded in section 233 of the Judicial Code. Being without jurisdiction for this reason, the trial court abused its discretion in granting the interlocutory injunction.

Statutes.

Officers' authority as to state court suit.

Grounds for state court suit.

As to agreement discharging liability.

This is a suit against the State.

Quite apart from any substantive aspects, the main headings are weakened by being divided into two sentences, and of course the force of the sub-headings is almost completely lost by being rendered topical; the reader does not and cannot obtain any clue to the party's position from reading them. Specifically, "——— v. ——— discussed and distinguished" would have been much stronger had it been rendered as, "——— v. ——— is not controlling because ———," going on to indicate briefly why not controlling. "This is a suit against the State" is assertive rather than topical, but, since it does not go on to say why the suit is one against the state, it is not argumentative. "Section 266 is inapplicable where order affects only particular district and is of limited scope" is the best of the lot—but it would have been even better if instead of "where order" there had been written "because the order here." Then the sub-heading would have read, "Section 266 is inapplicable because the order here affects only a particular district and is of limited scope"—and then it would have been a good, thumping, argumentative sentence.

Perhaps it should be added, with reference to the main heading under 3, that if the trial court really was without jurisdiction, its issuance of an interlocutory injunction would have been somewhat worse than an abuse of discretion—the latter expression being one that implies the existence of jurisdiction. It is therefore not a good heading. A heading should, at the very least, be consistent with itself, and should not generate disbelief or opposition on a first reading.

Possibly there is one situation where merely topical headings are justified, namely, when you are simply analyzing the authorities, and are presenting them in a spirit of sweet reasonableness, i.e., where it doesn't make much difference which of several lines the court will take since they all lead to the same result. But with perhaps that single exception, failure to set off the various stages in the Argument portion of the brief with full and detailed argumentative headings detracts materially from the brief's effectiveness.

5. *Appealing formulation of the questions presented.*—By "appealing" in this connection is meant a phraseology which most

effectively impels the reader to answer the question posed in the way that the writer wants him to answer it. Consequently this is an extremely important item, particularly since by stating well the question presented you are really choosing the battleground on which your litigation will be contested. And the formulation of the question is particularly important whenever review by a higher tribunal is discretionary, as for example certiorari in the United States Supreme Court and appeal by leave of the higher court in numerous other jurisdictions. In that situation permission or refusal to go higher frequently depends in very large measure on the framing of the question. On behalf of the petitioner or appellant you induce review by making the question appear important and the result below wrong; contrariwise, when the object to be obtained is the denial of review, the question should be framed so as to minimize the importance of what is involved.

Two forms will fit almost every case. The first and more usual form is to use a sentence beginning with "whether," e.g., "Whether post-mortem declarations are admissible." The second, usually appropriate only for the more complicated cases, is to state the salient facts and then to add, "The question presented is whether in these circumstances the later proceeding is barred by the earlier judgment." This second method may also be appropriate whenever the simple statement of the question does not make the case appear to be sufficiently interesting or appealing.

In using the first form, the essential technique, generally, is so to load the question with the facts of the particular case or with the relevant quotations from the statute involved, *fairly stated*, that you can practically win the case on the mere statement of the question it presents. Please observe the caveat: *fairly* stated. If an excess of zeal leads you to state the question unfairly, the thing will boomerang and explode in your face—which is to say, in your client's case.

Let me take up some examples:

First is a tax case, involving a very wealthy father in the surtax brackets, who owned certain gilt-edged bonds. Before the coupons matured, he clipped them and gave them to his son as a gift. When the coupons matured, they were cashed by the son who returned the proceeds as income on his return. The revenue officials undertook to tax the father for the income from the coupons.

How phrase the question? The Commissioner of Internal Revenue could have stated it as "Whether a man is taxable on income which his son receives"—but that would hardly have induced any court to say "Yes." So he stated the question as follows (first example is from the petition, second from the brief on the merits):

> 1. Whether the owner of coupon bonds should include in his gross income the amount of coupons which he detached and gave to his son several months prior to maturity.
>
> 2. The taxpayer owned coupon bonds. Several months prior to maturity of the interest coupons he detached them and gave them to his son, retaining the bonds themselves. Is he relieved of income tax with respect to such interest coupons?

Both are well-formulated questions. The second is probably a shade the better because it stresses that the taxpayer retained the bonds and then asks on top of that whether he is relieved from tax. The Supreme Court, by 6 to 3, held that he was not.[18] Note also the change in the form of the question presented, from the one-sentence "whether" form to the fact-statement-plus-question form, all in the direction of adding appeal. The significant point is less the result in the particular case than the way it illustrates to what extent phrasing the question may be a problem in applied semantics.

Another example is taken from the case of the Week-End Sailor—the member of the Temporary Reserve of the Coast Guard who patrolled the waterfront in his spare time and then insisted that he was entitled to veterans' preference in subsequent federal employment. Here again, the question stated the case, and here again, certiorari was granted and the decision below, which held such an individual to be a veteran, was promptly reversed.[19] The question as stated:

> Whether members of the Volunteer Port Security Force, a branch of the Temporary Coast Guard Reserve, who were assigned duty periods (here, of less than six hours a week) in order to interfere as little as possible with their hours of regular civilian employment during their enrollment, who could be disenrolled at their own request upon representation that their

[18] Helvering v. Horst, 311 US 112, 85 LEd 75, 61 SupCt 144 (1940).
[19] Mitchell v. Cohen, 333 US 411, 68 SupCt 487 (1948).

> duty assignments conflicted with such civilian employment, who were not subject while on duty to transfer away from their homes without their consent, and who remained at all times subject to the draft provisions of the Selective Training and Service Act, 1940, are entitled to preference in federal employment as "ex-servicemen . . . who have served on active duty in any branch of the armed forces of the United States, during any war," within the meaning of the Veterans' Preference Act of 1944.

It should be remembered that these techniques are equally applicable to every kind of case, and are not in any sense limited to the somewhat esoteric public law cases which fall to the lot of government counsel to handle. Here is an example involving a real estate title which could well arise in any country lawyer's office at the courthouse square; the question as phrased was—

> Whether a lost grant of a fee simple title may be presumed when there has been only spasmodic possession at long intervals, where the original grant and the first mesne conveyance in a complete chain of title disclose the defect in the claimed title and show that only a five-year lease was granted by the sovereign, and where no record of a grant from the sovereign appears although the law required records of such grants to be kept.

There's your chain of title—and your case—in a nut-shell. And that is an example of almost universal utility, since a land-title dispute could and does arise anywhere.[20]

Additional Examples

It goes without saying that not all situations are adapted to the loading-with-facts technique of formulating the question presented. But the question presented in any case can be clearly and appealingly stated—or, contrariwise, unclearly and unappealingly. It will probably be helpful to set out here as examples the questions presented in other cases. The first statement in each instance is the petitioner's formulation of the question, the second

[20] This particular one arose in Hawaii; the Ninth Circuit decided it twice, once for one side and then for the other; and the Supreme Court split 5-4. United States v. Fullard-Leo, 331 US 256, 91 LEd 1474, 67 SupCt 1287 (1947).

is the respondent's. As it happens review was denied in each instance, but nothing turns on that for present purposes. The significant point for the student of the process is to inquire which of the rival statements is more effective, and why; and whether in his judgment the parties could have stated the problem for their purposes more effectively than they did. (For convenience in reference, the citations to the opinions below are included in the footnotes.)

(A) *Petitioner:*

1. Is the Petitioner a native, citizen, denizen or subject of a "hostile nation or government" liable as such "to be apprehended, restrained, secured and removed," as an alien enemy?

2. Is the Petitioner a citizen of the Third German Reich or the German Nation or Government?

Respondent:

Whether an alien, born in Bohemia, then a part of the Austro-Hungarian Empire, in 1905, who later became a Czechoslovakian citizen when the place of his birth was included in that country after World War I, and who, after the Munich Pact of 1938, while in the United States, petitioned to be and was recognized as a German citizen, is now a citizen or subject of an enemy country within the meaning of the Alien Enemy Act of 1798, despite the reocccupation of the territory of his birth and former residence by Czechoslovakia.[21]

Petitioner's questions are too generalized to be informative. Respondent on the other hand has set forth the facts in his question, through use of the "loading" technique, and has framed it in such a way that there is but little doubt of the answer.

(B) *Petitioner A:*

The question presented is whether or not a retired United States District Judge is entitled to increased compensation at the rate of $15,000 per year provided for District Judges by the Act of July 31, 1946 (Public Law 567, 79th Congress), in lieu of the salary of $10,000 per year currently being paid.

Petitioner B:

[21] United States v. Carusi, 157 F(2d) 732 (CCA 3, 1946), certiorari denied, 330 US 842, 91 LEd 1288, 67 SupCt 1081 (1947).

1. Whether the new salary law applies to retired judges of whom petitioner is one; whether it is open to construction and legislative history to impose upon it an implied exception of "retired" judges and petitioner from it and the increase of salaries granted by it to all district judges.

2. Whether the so-called retirement law is "a special reference" or "specific aspect" or consideration of salaries of "retired" judges and "fixing" the same; whether exercise of the privileges or options of said law is acceptance of an offer on condition that "he should continue to draw the salary he was receiving when he retired" and restricting him thereto despite the subsequent new salary law and its increase of salary, whether it operates as an implied exception imposed on the new salary law to exclude "retired" judges and petitioner from the grant thereof; and whether the "retirement" law is of any *legal* effect save to conditionally authorize appointment of additional judges without permanent increase in the number thereof, and in all else futile, superfluous verbiage affecting the status and salary right of petitioner not at all.

Respondent:

Whether petitioners, who had retired as United States District Judges prior to July 31, 1946, are entitled to be paid at the rate of $15,000 per year, as provided by the Act of July 31, 1946, for "each of the judges of the several district courts" when the judges' retirement act provides for payment to a retired judge of "the salary of which he is . . . in receipt" at the time of retirement, and when the salary received at that time was $10,000 a year.[22]

Petitioner A has stated the question clearly and without trimmings; Petitioner B's statement is—well, not very helpful; while respondent by quoting the two statutes in his question has made it pretty plain that the judges retired prior to 1946 were just out of luck—which is what was held.[23]

Additional examples are legion. But the principle is always the same, that the most appealing statement of the question is

[22] Bourquin v. United States, 108 CtCl 700, 72 FSupp 76 (1947); certiorari denied, 332 US 762, 92 LEd 348, 68 SupCt 66 (1947).

[23] Subsequently Congress changed the law, so that the retired judge now gets the benefit of salary increases occurring after retirement. 28 USC (1948) § 371; FCA 28 § 371.

always the one which most effectively impels the reader to want to answer it as the writer of the question wanted him to.

6. *Sound analysis of the legal problem in argument on the law.* —We come now to the body of the brief, the argument proper. If and to the extent that a question of law is to be argued, then the essential for an effective brief is that the legal problem involved be carefully and soundly analyzed. Here the basic problem for the brief-writer is to determine which are the principal questions and which the subsidiary ones; what to do when there are alternative propositions, any one of which is sufficient to prevail; and in which order the points on which one relies should be presented.

These are, obviously, not matters as to which one can profitably be dogmatic, but a good rule of thumb is to put one's best foot forward.

(a) Where there are no alternatives, *i.e.,* where you must prevail on every point in order to win, the only solution is to set forth your points in logical step-by-step progression. This is subject to the qualification that, if there is no particular logical sequence, the point which goes to the very heart of the matter, that strikes the jugular, should always be argued first.

Let me take some examples:

(I) In the *Harris* search-and-seizure case,[24] the officers arrested Harris under a warrant, then searched his apartment for the instrumentalities of the crime for which he was arrested, and in the course of that search found the contraband for the possession of which he was tried and convicted. In order to sustain the conviction, it was first necessary to show that the officers had a right to search, next that this right extended to all of Harris' apartment, and finally that they could retain any contraband discovered in the course of that search. The point first mentioned was basic and hence it was argued first; the others followed logically thereafter. Here was the sequence of points:

1. It has always been held that one of the incidents of a lawful arrest is the right to search the premises under the control of the person arrested for the instrumentalities of the

[24] Harris v. United States, 331 US 145, 91 LEd 1399, 67 SupCt 1098 (1947).

crime of which he is accused, and that such a search is a reasonable one within the Fourth Amendment.[25]

2. The search was not a general exploratory search for evidence of crime.

3. The search was not improper because it extended beyond the precise portion of the premises where petitioner was arrested.

4. The seizure of the Selective Service documents and their introduction in evidence were proper.

(II) In the *Hackfeld* Alien Property case,[26] the facts, briefly, were that Hackfeld's Hawaiian property had been seized during the first War; that it was returned to him, pursuant to an Executive Allowance signed by the President, on a determination that he was an American citizen; that thereafter he sought a further recovery, after which the government brought a cross-action for the return of alleged overpayments, asserting that Hackfeld had never been an American citizen as a matter of law, and that he had, through his fraud, induced the determination that he was one.

The trial judge directed a verdict in favor of the government on the sole basis that Hackfeld had always been a German and that the additional payments had in consequence been made without authority of law; Hackfeld's estate appealed.

On the appeal, the government had to show first, that the court had properly gone behind the Presidential allowance; next, that a certain tax proceeding was not *res judicata* as to Hackfeld's citizenship; third, that the trial judge was right as a matter of law in ruling as he did; and, finally, that the facts of record as to Hackfeld's fraud were sufficient for alternative support of the judgment. So the brief filed in the Second Circuit presented the main points in that order:

1. The Executive Allowance in No Way Constituted a Bar to This Action.

2. The Federal Estate Tax Proceeding is No Bar to this Action.

---

[25] For the subheadings under this point see pp. 366, 367, *supra*.

[26] United States v. Rodiek, 117 F(2d) 588 (CCA 2, 1941), re,hearing denied, 120 F(2d) 760, (CCA 2, 1941), affirmed by an equally divided court, 315 US 783. See also Rodiek v. United States, 100 CtCls 267.

3. Hackfeld Never Became An American Citizen.

4. The District Court Should Have Directed a Verdict in Appellees' Favor on the Ground of Fraud.

It is proper to note, however, that these last headings are assertive and not argumentative, and therefore not to be commended as headings.

(b) When you have alternative grounds, place the most appealing one first—and by "most appealing" in this connection is meant the proposition which evokes the least judicial sales resistance.

(1) For instance, in cases involving judicial review of administrative action, when you are appearing for the agency, show that the agency was right before you start to argue that, right or wrong, its determination is not subject to judicial review. The other order may be more logical, but it involves substantially more judicial reluctance; courts don't like to be told that their jurisdiction to review is limited.

Thus, in the case which involved the scope of a railroad's release under the Transportation Act of 1940,[27] the two main headings in support of the administrative action giving that release full effect were as follows:

1. Claims to lands granted by the Acts of 1874 and 1904 in lieu of lands granted by the 1866 Act and thereafter relinquished were extinguished by the release here executed pursuant to the Transportation Act of 1940.

2. Apart from the merits, the Secretary's construction of the interrelationship between the Acts of 1866, 1874, 1904, and 1940 involved the exercise of discretion, was reasonable, has not been shown to be clearly wrong, and thus is impregnable to mandamus.

As it happened, the Court went directly to the merits and upheld the Secretary,[28] but the same technique employed in

[27] Krug v. Santa Fe P. R. Co., 329 US 591, 91 LEd 527, 67 SupCt 540 (1947).

[28] *Id.* at p. 597. "We agree with the District Court. We think, as it held, that the Secretary of the Interior's construction of the 1940 Act was clearly right. Therefore, we do not discuss the Government's contention that, since the Secretary's construction was a reasonable one, it was an allowable exercise of his discretion which should not be set aside by injunction or relief in the nature of mandamus. See Santa Fe P. R. R. v. Work, 267 US 511, 517; *cf.* Santa Fe P. R. R. v. Lane, 244 US 492."

similar cases may well lead to decisions resting on non-reviewability.[29] In any event, courts are much more inclined to withhold their hand after first being convinced that the administrative officer was right—which is simply another illustration of the principle that courts delight to do substantial justice or, at the very least, that they are perceptibly influenced by "the equities."

(II) Similarly, where one alternative involves distinguishing away a recently decided case while the other has a clear path not thus obstructed, put the latter first to avoid the reluctance which courts always feel when asked to reshape their recent precedents. Asking a court to overrule or modify a case but lately decided, after full consideration and over strong dissent, always involves a heavy uphill pull.

(III) It may happen on occasion that correct analysis and effective presentation require the broader and more difficult proposition to be argued first. A striking illustration of such an instance was the case which involved the refusal of the Rhode Island courts to enforce treble-damage actions for overcharges in violation of OPA ceilings, on the ground that these were actions for penalties based on the statute of a foreign sovereign![30]

Two questions were involved, one being whether such a proceeding was really an action for a penalty, and the other whether, even if it was, it could be maintained none the less. The argument for the plaintiff (joined by the Price Administrator as intervenor) was that, under the federal rule, the action was not one for a penalty, but that, even so, the state courts were bound to enforce it. Which point should be argued first? The quotation is from the first argument paragraph of the prevailing brief:

> We assume *arguendo* at the outset that the present action—a consumer's action for treble damages under Section 205(e) of the Emergency Price Control Act as amended—is an action for a penalty even though the actual recovery here was limited

[29] *Cf.* Wann v. Ickes, 67 AppDC 291, 92 F(2d) 215 (1937); Lyders v. Ickes, 65 AppDC 379, 84 F(2d) 232 (1936). It is not clear how far the "impregnable to mandamus" rule, which reached its highest flowering under the fostering care of the most conservative judges (Wilbur v. United States, 281 US 206, 74 LEd 809, 50 SupCt 320 (1930) (Van Devanter, J.); Riverside Oil Co. v. Hitchcock, 190 US 316, 47 LEd 1074, 23 SupCt 698 (1903) (Peckham, J.)), may have survived the judicial review provision of the Administrative Procedure Act, 60 Stat. 243 (1946), 5 USC 1009; FCA 5 § 1009 (1946). See Snyder v. Buck, 75 FSupp 902 (D. C., 1948).

[30] Testa v. Katt, 330 US 386, 91 LEd 967, 67 SupCt 810 (1947).

> to the amount of the overcharge plus an attorney's fee. We make that assumption in order to bring more sharply into focus our contention that, since the courts of Rhode Island are open to actions for penalties founded upon state law, they cannot consistently with the Supremacy Clause of the Constitution refuse to take jurisdiction of similar actions founded on federal law. Thereafter, once the basic question of discrimination against a federal cause of action is disposed of, we proceed to show that, since the consumer's action under the Emergency Price Control Act is a federal right, its nature must be judged by federal standards, and that, under the decisions of this Court, it is clearly a remedial action and not one for a penalty, even though multiple damages plus an attorney's fee may be recovered. That being so, *a fortiori* the Rhode Island courts cannot refuse to entertain such actions.

The Court followed this approach, assumed without deciding that the section in question was a penal statute, and then held that the state courts were not free under Article VI of the Constitution to refuse enforcement of the claim.[31]

(IV) The advocate's problem is underscored by the comparison of example (III) above with examples (I) and (II): When is it appropriate to argue the easier point first and when the harder one? The only honest answer, of course, is "it all depends" —because there just isn't any ironclad rule which will fit every case. Normally it is sound technique to start on the line of least resistance, but occasionally a situation will call for grasping the nettle firmly, for arguing the really difficult point at the outset. The last example discussed illustrates such a situation—and it's

[31] "For the purposes of this case, we assume, without deciding, that § 205(e) is a penal statute in the 'public international,' 'private international,' or any other sense. So far as the question of whether the Rhode Island courts properly declined to try this action, it makes no difference into which of these categories the Rhode Island court chose to place the statute which Congress has passed. For we cannot accept the basic premise on which the Rhode Island Supreme Court held that it has no more obligation to enforce a valid penal law of the United States than it has to enforce a penal law of another state or a foreign country. Such a broad assumption flies in the face of the fact that the States of the Union constitute a nation. It disregards the purpose and effect of Article VI of the Constitution which provides: 'This Constitution, and the Laws of the United States which shall be made in Pursuance thereof; and all Treaties made, or which shall be made, under the Authority of the United States, shall be the supreme Law of the Land; and the Judges in every State shall be bound thereby, any Thing in the Constitution or Laws of any State to the Contrary notwithstanding.'" *Id.* at p. 389.

simply up to the lawyer handling the case to decide which approach is more likely to succeed. There is no ready-made rule of thumb to save one from the pain of choosing which course to pursue—but once you decide, adhere to the approach you have selected, and don't wobble back and forth as though you still couldn't decide.

Matters to Be Avoided

(a) *Weak propositions.* Perhaps the most important admonition under this heading is to avoid arguing weak questions or any in which you have no faith; their inclusion only serves to weaken the rest of your argument, and may well result in serious prejudice to your case.

I have had in my own recent experience an object lesson in this proposition, in the *Di Re* case.[32] There the question, stated most favorably for the prosecution, was, "Whether, when officers have been informed that contraband is to be transferred at a certain place, and their observations reasonably justify the conclusion that a transfer has taken place in an automobile at such place, they are justified in searching and arresting a third person present in the automobile about whom they had no previous information." In the petition for certiorari it was urged, first, that Di Re's search could be justified without regard to the validity of his arrest, under the principle that a vehicle may be searched by officers having reasonable cause to believe that it is being used to carry contraband;[33] and, second, on the ground that, in any event, probable cause existed for the arrest.[34]

After the petition was granted, and in the course of working on the brief on the merits, I was beset with doubts as to the soundness of the first proposition, because after all it is quite a step from searching the automobile to searching the people who ride in it. In the end, we reversed the order of the points in the brief, arguing first that "The search of respondent was justified as incident to a lawful arrest," and second, that "Alternatively the

32 United States v. Di Re, 332 US 581, 92 LEd 210, 68 SupCt 222 (1948).

33 See Scher v. United States, 305 US 251, 83 LEd 159, 59 SupCt 166 (1938); Husty v. United States, 282 US 694, 75 LEd 629, 51 SupCt 240 (1931); Carroll v. United States, 267 US 132, 69 LEd 543, 45 SupCt 280 (1925).

34 Judge Clark had said, dissenting below, ". . . police officers cannot be held unreasonable in declining to view as a mere bystander one who accompanies a criminal to a crime rendezvous." United States v. Di Re, 159 F(2d) 818, 820 (CCA 2, 1947).

search of respondent was justified as incident to the search of a moving vehicle reasonably believed to be carrying contraband." At the oral argument I simply stated the alternative point, and did not in any sense bear down on it. But my real mistake was in leaving it in at all. It was a weak point, I had no faith in it, and yet it colored the entire case. We lost, and the Court's opinion took up and demolished our weak ground first. By the time that was disposed of, the Court was in a fine frame of mind to do execution on our strong point—and it did just that.

The weak point, then, didn't help; it only undermined the good point. I don't mean that we would necessarily have prevailed on the stronger point, but at least it would have been considered and disposed of in a more favorable setting. So I say, with the conviction derived of painful experience, avoid arguing questions in which you have no faith.

(b) *Hornbook generalizations.* Another sound caution is to avoid emphasizing or relying upon elementary or hornbook propositions. Any time, for instance, that a lawyer goes all out on the presumption of constitutionality, it all but indicates that he very much doubts the validity of the statute on which he is relying. Similarly, any time a brief dealing with a question of statutory construction cites *Holy Trinity Church v. United States*, 143 US 457, 36 LEd 226, 12 SupCt 511 (1892), an astute court at once recognizes that it is being asked to rewrite a law in the way the legislature should have done but didn't.

There are other indicia of last resort arguments also, points that should simply not be made because to make them amounts to giving the court a signal that your case is hopeless—and that you know it is hopeless. In this category fall most of the equal protection clause contentions in constitutional matters,[35] and, in criminal appeals, arguments that the indictment was duplicitous or that the court erred in not granting the motion for a bill of particulars.

(c) *Requests to overrule cases.* Another line of argument which it is usually desirable to avoid is the out-and-out request

35 "But, it is said, however it might be if this reasoning were applied generally, it fails when it is confined to the small number who are in the institutions named and is not applied to the multitudes outside. It is the usual last resort of constitutional arguments to point out shortcomings of this sort." Buck v. Bell, 274 US 200, 208, 71 LEd 1000, 47 SupCt 584 (1927), *per* Holmes, J.

that a governing precedent be squarely overruled. Lower courts can't overrule cases (although, believe it or not, they are on occasion asked to do so),[36] and the courts of last resort are reluctant to do so. This is true even in that most open-minded of tribunals, the Supreme Court of the United States as now constituted. It is always easier, particularly when the precedent in the way is of fairly recent vintage, to suggest distinctions and differentiations, and frequently an effective technique is to talk around the offending case and give it a form of silent treatment, by emphasizing the principles which lead to a different conclusion. At the very least, this technique may result in a favorable decision on another ground.

Of course there will be instances when a lawyer must ask for a case to be overruled. The progress of constitutional law from 1937 to 1946 is full of instances where old precedents were squarely overruled, generally at the request of counsel.[37] But the

[36] This is perhaps subject to the qualification that on occasion lower courts or lower court judges correctly divine that a decision of a court of last resort is about to be overruled. See Barnette v. West Virginia State Board of Ed., 47 FSupp 251 (S. D. W. Va. 1942), where the court, *per* Parker, Circ. J., correctly foretold the impending demise of Minersville School Dist. v. Gobitis, 310 US 586, 84 LEd 1375, 60 SupCt 1010 (1940); and United States v. Girouard, 149 F(2d) 760, 764-767 (CCA 1, 1945), where Woodbury, Circ. J., dissenting, accurately predicted the early end of the Schwimmer (279 US 644, 73 LEd 889, 49 SupCt 448 (1929)) and Macintosh (283 US 605, 75 LEd 1302, 51 SupCt 570 (1931)) cases. See note 37, *infra*.

[37] West Coast Hotel Co. v. Parrish, 300 US 379, 81 LEd 703, 57 SupCt 578 (1937), overruling Adkins v. Children's Hospital, 261 US 525, 67 LEd 785, 43 SupCt 394 (1923); Helvering v. Producers Corp., 303 US 376, 82 LEd 907, 58 SupCt 623 (1938), overruling Burnet v. Coronado Oil & Gas Co., 285 US 393, 76 LEd 815, 52 SupCt 443 (1932), and Gillespie v. Oklahoma, 257 US 501, 66 LEd 338, 42 SupCt 171 (1922); Erie R. Co. v. Tompkins, 304 US 64, 82 LEd 1188, 58 SupCt 817 (1938), overruling Swift v. Tyson, 16 Pet 1, 10 LEd 865 (1842); Graves v. New York ex rel. O'Keefe, 306 US 466, 83 LEd 927, 59 SupCt 595 (1939), overruling Collector v. Day, 11 Wall 113, 20 LEd 122 (1870), and New York ex rel. Rogers v. Graves, 299 US 401, 81 LEd 306, 57 SupCt 269 (1937); O'Malley v. Woodrough, 307 US 277, 83 LEd 1289, 59 SupCt 838 (1939), overruling Miles v. Graham, 268 US 501, 69 LEd 1067, 45 SupCt 601 (1925); Madden v. Kentucky, 309 US 83, 84 LEd 590, 60 SupCt 406 (1940), overruling Colgate v. Harvey, 296 US 404, 80 LEd 299, 56 SupCt 252 (1935); United States v. Darby, 312 US 100, 85 LEd 609, 61 SupCt 451 (1941), overruling Hammer v. Dagenhart, 247 US 251, 62 LEd 1101, 38 SupCt 529 (1918); United States v. Chicago, M., St. P. & P. R. Co., 312 US 592, 85 LEd 1064, 61 SupCt 772 (1941), overruling (in part) United States v. Lynah, 188 US 445, 47 LEd 539, 23 SupCt 349 (1903); Nye v. United States, 313 US 33, 85 LEd 1172, 61 SupCt 810 (1941), overruling Toledo Newspaper Co. v. United States, 247 US 402, 62 LEd 1186, 38 SupCt 560 (1918); California v. Thompson, 313 US 109, 85 LEd 1219, 61 SupCt 930 (1941), overruling Di Santo v. Pennsylvania, 273 US 34, 71 LEd 524, 47 SupCt 267 (1927); Olsen v. Nebraska, 313 US 236, 85 LEd 1305, 61 SupCt 862 (1941), overruling Ribnik v. McBride, 277

basic reluctance to overturn what was once decided is still present,[38] so that it is well, when the request must be made, to make it at the end of the brief after a full demonstration that logical consistency requires such a step. I discuss in the footnote which follows the details of three recent requests for overruling of prior precedents at a single term of court; it may be significant that all three failed.[39]

US 350, 72 LEd 913, 48 SupCt 545 (1928); Alabama v. King & Boozer, 314 US 1, 86 LEd 3, 62 SupCt 43 (1941), overruling Panhandle Oil Co. v. Knox, 277 US 218, 72 LEd 857, 48 SupCt 451 (1928), and Graves v. Texas Co., 298 US 393, 80 LEd 1236, 56 SupCt 818 (1936); Graves v. Schmidlapp, 315 US 657, 86 LEd 1097, 62 SupCt 870 (1942), overruling Wachovia Bank & Trust Co. v. Doughton, 272 US 567, 71 LEd 413, 47 SupCt 202 (1926); State Tax Comm. v. Aldrich, 316 US 174, 86 LEd 1358, 62 SupCt 1008 (1942), overruling First National Bank v. Maine, 284 US 312, 76 LEd 313, 52 SupCt 174 (1932); Williams v. North Carolina, 317 US 287, 87 LEd 279, 63 SupCt 207 (1942), overruling Haddock v. Haddock, 201 US 562, 50 LEd 867, 26 SupCt 525 (1906); Board of Education v. Barnette, 319 US 624, 87 LEd 1628, 63 SupCt 1178 (1943), overruling Minersville School Dist. v. Gobitis, 310 US 586, 84 LEd 1375, 60 SupCt 1010 (1940); Smith v. Allwright, 321 US 649, 88 LEd 987, 64 SupCt 757 (1944), overruling Grovey v. Townsend, 295 US 45, 79 LEd 1292, 55 SupCt 622 (1935); Girouard v. United States, 328 US 61, 90 LEd 1084, 66 SupCt 826 (1946), overruling United States v. Schwimmer, 279 US 644, 73 LEd 889, 49 SupCt 448 (1929); United States v. Macintosh, 283 US 605, 75 LEd 1302, 51 SupCt 570 (1931); and United States v. Bland, 283 US 636, 75 LEd 569, 51 SupCt 569 (1931).

The foregoing list does not include any earlier cases which were not squarely overruled during the period in question, but were "distinguished," limited or simply whittled away.

38 See particularly, for a recent example, United States v. South Buffalo R. Co., 333 US 771, 92 LEd 1077, 68 SupCt 868 (1948). See also, United States v. Willow River Co., 324 US 499, 506, 89 LEd 1101, 65 SupCt 761 (1945).

39 (a) In the South Buffalo case, just cited, the Government asked that United States v. Elgin, J. & E. R. Co., 298 US 492, 80 LEd 1300, 56 SupCt 841 (1936), be overruled, but the Court, by a vote of 5 to 4, declined to do so, on the ground that Congress had specifically refused to overturn the earlier case by legislation.

(b) In Williams v. Fanning, 332 US 490, 92 LEd 95, 68 SupCt 188 (1947), which involved the question whether, in an action for an injunction against a subordinate public officer, his official superior was an indispensable party, the Government argued that Gnerich v. Rutter, 265 US 388, 68 LEd 1068, 44 SupCt 532 (1924), and Webster v. Fall, 266 US 507, 69 LEd 411, 45 SupCt 148 (1925), were utterly inconsistent with Colorado v. Toll, 268 US 228, 69 LEd 927, 45 SupCt 505 (1925); it urged, therefore, that the latter case be squarely overruled. The Court held that the cases were consistent on their facts and that, in the situation presented—action to restrain a local postmaster's enforcement of a mail fraud order issued by the Postmaster General—the superior officer was not an indispensable party. Nothing was overruled—except, silently, the language and reasoning of Gnerich v. Rutter.

(c) In United States v. Line Material Co., 333 US 287, 92 LEd 701, 68 SupCt 550 (1948), and United States v. U. S. Gypsum Co., 333 US 364, 92 LEd 746, 68 SupCt 525 (1948), the Government urged the Court to overrule United States v. General Electric Co., 272 US 476, 71 LEd 362, 47 SupCt 192 (1926), and its doctrine that price-fixing pursuant to a patent license did not constitute a violation of the Sherman Antitrust Act. The Court declined to do so, and decided each of the two cases in favor of the Government on the basis of their particular facts.

7. *Effective presentation of the evidence in argument on the facts.*—This is really a problem of so marshalling your evidence as to make it thoroughly convincing to the reader. Basically, three steps are necessary: assertion, presentation, and conclusion. First you state what you intend to show. Next you set forth the evidence, using pertinent quotations from documents and testimony, stressing any inconsistencies in the case against you and making full use of that most deadly of all comparisons, the parallel column technique. Finally you conclude, generally by restating your original assertion.

Whenever the case is at all complicated, it is well to divide up the several points you are making, and to make liberal use of argumentative sub-headings, so that the direction of your thought is clear. Remember that what you are aiming at is to leave conviction in the minds of your readers, and remember also that no characterization, however apt, ever has the stark impressiveness of verbatim extracts from damaging testimony or from letters that the writer later wishes he had never written. And I repeat: stress the inconsistencies in your opponent's documents and testimony, bear down on every self-contradiction in the record. For while of course it is the law that "A very bad man may have a very good case," none the less courts are human and nobody loves a liar.

Bear in mind, however, that the technique of *arguing* facts is very different from that appropriate for *stating* facts. In writing the Statement the aim is to state the facts appealingly but straightforwardly, so that the effect derives from the selection and juxtaposition of the facts. Once the Argument is reached, however, the facts should be frankly argued, commented on, and editorialized. The only limitations are those dictated by good taste and professional standards and by the caution that on occasion a restrained argument may be more effective than one which seems to shout too much.

In the Statement, you get your color from the facts themselves; in the Argument, you get your effect either from arguing inferences from the undisputed facts or from frankly arguing to a conclusion from disputed facts. You do not add comments of your own in the first instance, you do in the second.

8. *Careful attention to all portions of the brief.*—Just as it is a mistake to toss in a dry statement of facts on top of a good argu-

ment on the law, and thus to mar the finished product, perhaps with irreparable injury to the case, so also it is a mistake to neglect any other portion of the brief. The circumstance that these other portions are easier to write or may be less important still does not warrant giving them so little attention that they pull down the quality of the whole. Three parts of a brief, too frequently given but little care, are considered here.

(a) *Summary of argument.* The rules of many courts require that all briefs, or all except the very shortest ones, contain a summary of the argument. Some courts prescribe in detail just how such a summary is to be constructed, and require that it contain a citation to every authority relied upon in the argument proper. What follows is addressed only to the usual situation, not to the specifically prescribed forms.

First of all, consider the importance of the summary. It is required in order that the court may have a bird's-eye view of your argument, in somewhat more elaborate form than that available from the index (which last of course simply sets forth your headings). And, mark this, the summary is one of the portions of the brief read at the outset. You will in consequence be well advised to make your summary as appealing as possible, rather than dry-as-dust, and, generally, to expand it substantially over a mere repetition of your headings.

Therefore, within the space at your disposal, don't be afraid to make it long enough to be effective. The real secret of a good summary is to go beyond mere assertion, because the farther you get beyond that, the more convincing the summary will be to the reader. And, while a summary normally should not cite many cases, except when specifically required by rule of court, it is a very good idea to sprinkle your summary with a few of the leading authorities on which you rely.

One caution to be added is that the summary should not deviate from the Argument proper; it should be a synopsis of the Argument, not a novel or different train of thought.

(b) *Conclusion.* Generally the conclusion should be pretty formal, as for example:

The judgment below should be affirmed.

For the foregoing reasons, the judgment below should be reversed, with directions to dismiss the petition.

Or, in a supplemental brief—

For the foregoing additional reasons, the judgment of the district court should be reversed, with directions to enter a judgment granting appropriate relief to the United States.

On occasion, it is helpful to expand the conclusion somewhat, and to summarize the nub of the argument. Thus, in the case which involved the refusal of a state court to entertain an action based on a federal statute,[40] the conclusion of the plaintiff's brief read,

> The decision below is based upon a misconception of the nature of the federal system. The judgment should therefore be reversed with instructions to enter judgment on the verdict.

And, in the *Haupt* treason case,[41] a long brief was concluded as follows:

> Petitioner was convicted of treason after a sober, careful, and eminently fair trial, on the basis of evidence clearly establishing by the required two witnesses a number of legally sufficient overt acts of aid and comfort to the enemy, and clearly showing intent to betray. Reversal of the judgment below can be supported only by artificial refinement and technicalities which find no support in the treason clause of the Constitution. We therefore respectfully submit that the judgment below should be affirmed.

It is not generally profitable to extend a conclusion further; it loses its effectiveness if it is made too long or if it is turned into a peroration.

One caution: never fail to indicate just what kind of relief you want in addition to reversal, *viz.,* reinstatement of the judgment of the trial court, or release of the appellant from custody, or dismissal of the indictment. Be specific so that the court's order will likewise be specific, and be sure to ask for the relief to which you are really entitled, else there will be mistakes and a lot of very red faces all around.[42]

---

[40] Testa v. Katt, 330 US 386, 91 LEd 967, 67 SupCt 810 (1947).

[41] Haupt v. United States, 330 US 631, 91 LEd 1145, 67 SupCt 874 (1947).

[42] In a fairly recent case, the Court of Claims entered judgment in favor of the plaintiff in the sum of $3,227.93, and the government petitioned for certiorari, assigning as error the entry of judgment for $1,877.93 in respect of a particular item, as to which it was contended that the contracting officer's determination was final. John McShain, Inc. v. United States, 88 CtCls 284 (1939), certiorari granted,

(c) *Appendix.* This is not the so-called Appendix Record required by the rules of some Federal circuits, pursuant to which counsel print as an appendix to their briefs pertinent portions of the record (which is not separately printed), but is the Appendix to the brief which contains the collection of statutes involved and similar materials, whenever such matter is too long to be set out in the brief proper.

The basic cautions, so far as statutes are concerned, are to quote from the original statute, and, whenever amendments are pertinent, to show clearly and unmistakably the development of the statute through successive amendments.

Remember, with reference to federal statutes, that the United States Code is only *prima facie* evidence of the law, except where particular titles have been enacted into positive law.[43] Thus, Title 26 (Internal Revenue Code), Title 28 (Judiciary and Judicial Procedure), and Title 18 (Crimes and Criminal Procedure), among others, have now been enacted into law, the last two effective September 1, 1948.[44] In the absence of such enactment, you will frequently do better to rely on the Statutes at Large.

I know that when I was primarily a state practitioner, I felt that the Code was all that counted, but I soon found out, after beginning to feed at the public trough, that the experts in the various federal specialties never used Code citations except for purposes of parallel reference; they always talked about section

---

307 US 619, 83 LEd 1499, 59 SupCt 1043 (1939). The single item was the only one in issue, but the government concluded by saying, "It is respectfully submitted that the judgment of the Court of Claims should be reversed, and the cause remanded with instructions to enter judgment in favor of the United States." Less than three weeks after argument the Supreme Court entered a memorandum *Per Curiam* in the precise language of the conclusion in the brief, viz., "The judgment is reversed, and the cause is remanded to the Court of Claims with instructions to enter judgment in favor of the United States [citing cases]." United States v. John McShain, Inc., 308 US 512, 84 LEd 437, 60 SupCt 134 (1939). This deprived the respondent of the sums admittedly due, with the result that, four weeks later, the Court had to amend its order to read: "The judgment is reversed to the extent that it includes the $1,877.93 alleged to be due from the United States in paragraphs XIV through XXIV of the petition to the Court of Claims, and the cause is remanded to the Court of Claims with instructions to enter judgment in favor of the United States with regard to this item. [citing cases]" United States v. John McShain, Inc., 308 US 520, 84 LEd 437, 60 SupCt 134 (1939).

43 Citation should be to the re-enacted title; see note 44. 1 USC § 204(a); FCA, § 204(a); 61 Stat. 633 (1947).

44 Title 26, 53 Stat. 1 (1939); Title 28, 62 Stat. 869 (1948); Title 18, 62 Stat. 683 (1948); also Title 1, 61 Stat. 633 (1947); Title 3, 62 Stat. 672 (1948); Title 4, 61 Stat. 641 (1947); Title 6, 61 Stat. 646 (1947); Title 9, 61 Stat. 669 (1947); Title 17, 61 Stat. 652 (1947).

so-and-so of the National Defense Act, or of the Mineral Leasing Act, or of the Puerto Rican Organic Act, or of Sections thus-and-so of the Revised Statutes. Consequently I learned, or thought I did, to use the Code primarily as a secondary and parenthetical citation, citing the statute in the first instance as it appeared in the Statutes at Large.

I say, "or thought I did," because in one case I didn't check the Appendix carefully, and the statutes involved were printed there as they appeared in the Code, namely, amended up to date. Now the case involved the effect of successive amendments to the governing statute, and while I was up on my feet, Chief Justice Stone complained in open court that he didn't like the Appendix because it didn't show him the statute before and after. There are, I can assure you, more comfortable courtroom experiences than that one. So—

1. Always show the statute before and after, whenever something turns on the amendment.

2. If the statute has been amended from time to time, but the case isn't affected thereby, print the statute as it was at the time in question, *e.g.*, when the offense was committed.

3. Use any available typographical aid to point up the amendments—italics for the new portions, brackets for the old ones, explanatory footnotes, etc. And—

4. Check your Appendix carefully; you just can't afford to let it go with a once-over lightly. (I know!)

Of course an Appendix is not necessarily restricted to statutes. In appropriate cases, it should set out executive regulations; texts of administrative rulings; legislative materials whether excerpts from debates or from committee reports; opinions in cases either unreported or not yet reported; forms of conveyances or of relevant documents; explanation of related proceedings; identification, by way of *dramatis personae*, of the individuals involved in the case (as for instance in complicated antitrust proceedings involving many corporate defendants, each having many individual officers who are referred to in the brief); lists of exhibits; and the like. Include whatever is relevant or whatever may be of assistance to the court in understanding the case and its background.

9. *Leaving an impression of conviction with the reader and satisfying his curiosity.*—If a case is a close one, even the most

experienced and learned judges will be in doubt after having read the briefs on both sides. But no one should be left either in doubt or with curiosity unsatisfied after reading the brief on only one side. If any one is, then that particular lawyer hasn't written an effective appellate brief.

I have left this element for the end, not because it is the least important, but because it is really the sum-total of what you are driving at when you sit down to write a brief. At the very least, the brief must be convincing by itself. At the very least, your brief should be in such shape that, if the other side filed nothing, a judge reading your brief would understand the case and be persuaded that you should prevail.

Analytically, here are some of the elements which contribute to a brief's unsatisfactory character:

(a) Inadequate analysis—problem not thought through.

(b) Tangential discussion, as a main point, of a question not really reached on the record.

(c) Extensive discussion of a prior decision, urging that it be not extended, without fully stating its facts or holding.

The last is what I have in mind when I speak of unsatisfied curiosity: in order to understand the discussion, it was necessary to get the volume down from the shelf and read the case. But it shouldn't be; a brief should give the reader enough of any case which is discussed at length therein to enable him to know what that case holds and why it is either applicable or inapplicable in its present context, without having to look it up in the library. I don't mean for a moment that a judge can escape reading the case when he sits down to write the opinion, but I do insist that he shouldn't have to do so when he first reads the party's brief in order to be convinced by that brief.

And any tangential thoughts which a reasonably learned lawyer may have as he reads a particular brief should likewise be satisfactorily answered, *in the brief*, as he reads along—why, for instance, the case isn't governed by *Schmaltz v. Commissioner,* just recently decided, or why it isn't affected by the statute passed last year, or why the claim in question isn't barred by limitations. The brief-writer must be sufficiently aware of all such potential questions, not only to be able to answer them, but also to make sure that they are answered in the brief which he is writing.

The Final Accolade

Perhaps it is unduly pragmatic to say so, but after all the real test of whether a brief has been effective—the ordeal by fire—is whether it wins the case. True, there are many good briefs that don't win cases, and assuredly there are poor ones (including some exceptionally poor ones) that do. But a good brief, however close to perfection it may come, that didn't win, just wasn't an effective brief; it didn't persuade the court, so it lapses into the realm of "fine try" and "well played." The lawyer needn't be ashamed of it, but the client lost the case. The pat story in this connection concerns a Northern gambler who cleaned out all the local talent in a little Southern town, after which the home town boys gathered round in a somewhat menacing manner and insisted that he tell them whether in his opinion Grant or Lee was the better general. The slick Yankee thoughtfully considered the question, gave even more thoughtful consideration to the group around him, and then answered, "Well, gentlemen—they paid off on Grant." So here: clients don't pay off on good losing briefs.

However, when the winning brief is inadequate, and forces the court to do a lot of independent research, and the opinion relies on cases not discussed or even cited by counsel and flatly rejects the proposition advanced by the prevailing side, then that wasn't a very effective brief either: it didn't persuade.

So I conclude with this proposition, that really an effective brief is one that (a) wins your case, and (b) persuades the court to follow your analysis of the problem and to rely on your authorities.

I never get the same pleasure out of winning a case when the court goes off on a tack of its own as when it follows the analysis which I have labored over and set out in the brief. And I must confess to feeling the ultimate in forensic satisfaction when the opinion uses an analogy which I devised[45] or incorporates into the

[45] (a) "The analogy suggested by counsel for the appellant seems apposite: namely, that of a defendant who commits a crime in Canada, escapes to the United States, and then returns to Canada; he cannot defend on the ground that between the offense and the trial he was beyond the jurisdiction of the Canadian court." United States v. Malanaphy, 168 F(2d) 503, 507 (CCA 2, 1948), certiorari granted, 335 US 842, 93 LEd 392, 69 SupCt 66 (1948).

(b) "The Government makes the reasonable contention, and we so hold, that the district into which the accused is first taken under custody and landed is the district into which the accused is 'first brought' within the meaning of § 41 of the Judicial Code [now 18 USC (1948) § 3238; FCA 18 § 3238]; and this was the

study of those portions which bear most directly upon the issues to be presented to the appellate court. Counsel who has properly devoted his energies to the task of knowing the record will have not only a knowledge of its contents but also a familiarity with the *actual physical location* of the material in the record. Such a "geographical" grasp of the record is helpful in briefing the appeal and is vital in connection with the oral argument.

System of Indexing

In cases where the record on appeal is rather lengthy, it is an excellent idea to *tab* the record, i.e. use of cardboard or composition tabs to indicate the physical location of pleadings, testimony of the various witnesses, exhibits, and, in some cases, it may even be desirable to tab important portions of the testimony of certain witnesses. In the tabbing process, counsel cannot help obtain greater familiarity with the physical location of the contents of the record which will save much time in the process of briefing and avoid embarrassing moments during the oral argument. One can observe all too often in appellate courts the disastrous results which flow from the failure of counsel to know the contents and location of material in the record. For example, in the course of oral argument, one of the judges asks counsel where a particular exhibit, to which he wishes to refer, is located. Whereupon counsel begins to thumb frantically back and forth through the pages of the record, mumbling apologies and making promises that he is sure he can find it for the court in just a moment. Meanwhile his client, sitting on the sidelines, justifiably becomes restive and the court becomes impatient. His adversary, however, who is well prepared and knows his record, turns unhesitatingly to the elusive exhibit and comes to the rescue by informing the court exactly where it can be found. Such a display has the inevitable effect of undermining the confidence of the court in counsel who is presenting the argument and of indicating to the court that counsel for the opposing party is probably the person upon whom the court can best rely in obtaining any information it may need during the argument.

One word of warning to the trial lawyer who is also handling the case on appeal. Don't assume that because you gave birth to the record during the trial below, you know your record on appeal.

There is no doubt that there is a tendency on the part of a trial lawyer to assume that he knows his record on appeal without studying it as carefully as would counsel who had no familiarity with the case prior to the appeal. Such an assumption is dangerous because, as the trial lawyer, he is familiar with all of the background of events at the trial, many of which are not in the record, and it is impossible for him to recall which matters of evidence were admitted, which were excluded, what testimony was stricken, etc. So, Mr. Trial Lawyer, study the record on appeal as diligently as if you had never heard of the case before. If you do, the fact that you also tried the case should give you an edge over your adversary who was simply brought in to prosecute the appeal.

Once counsel has faithfully performed the task of completely familiarizing himself with the record on appeal, he is in a position to evaluate the significance of the material in the record in relation to the legal questions involved. He can now begin to formulate the legal theories which will form the basis of the appeal in the light of the evidence available to support them.

Preparation of the Brief

At this point counsel is ready to enter the second phase of presentation of a case on appeal—the brief. The brief should be prepared with an eye to the fact that it represents a continuing source of reference for the appellate court until the appeal is decided, whereas the oral argument serves the function of giving the court a quick grasp of the facts and issues which are before it and the opportunity for the court to clear up in its own mind any questions regarding such facts and issues which may occur to it during the course of the argument. As the court's constant source of reference, the brief cannot be too carefully and painstakingly prepared.

What are some of the guideposts in preparing a brief? I think the first and most important rule is that a brief should be just that—brief. Probably the most common failing of appellate lawyers is the tendency to submit briefs which are far too lengthy. Such documents—it hardly seems right to call them briefs—impose on the time of the over-burdened appellate courts and fail, through prolixity and repetition, to accomplish the purpose of persuading the appellate court to the cause of the client. Remember that yours is not the only case the appellate court has to consider. Most appellate court dockets are crowded. The time of the judges is limited. So a ten page brief which covers the same ground as a thirty page brief submitted by your opponent will not only be appreciated by the court but also is more apt to win the case for you.

One of the principal causes for lengthy briefs is failure to organize one's thoughts before actually starting to write the brief. Close analysis of the exact issues of fact and law which are to be presented to the appellate court must be made before starting to draft the brief. Also, careful study of the most effective means of organization and presentation are essential. Preparation of a careful and somewhat detailed outline of the various points to be presented in the brief before preparing the first draft is an excellent method of insuring sound analysis, logical organization and effective presentation. With such an outline as the framework, the appropriate facts and points of law can be more skillfully knit together to fill out the entire form of the brief in the drafts which are to follow.

Another cause of lengthy briefs is failure by counsel to be *selective* in deciding what should be included in the brief. There is seldom an appeal which does not involve more issues, more facts and more possible points of law than can possibly be presented effectively to the appellate court. Counsel's task is to select only those facts and issues which will lead to the most effective presentation—excluding all else. Far too many appellate briefs, however, lack brevity and thus sacrifice effectiveness because counsel did not have the courage to limit himself to the vital facts and issues. Such briefs usually compound issues upon refinement of issues, bury essential facts in a forest of trivia, and make every possible legal argument confused by ridiculous assumptions arguendo and needless attacks upon straw men. It is small wonder that such briefs, while they contain everything, accomplish nothing because all emphasis upon the real importance of the vital facts and issues is lost in a morass of detail.

Other Guideposts

While I am inclined to feel that the matter of brevity, which can only be accomplished by careful analysis and organization together with judicious selection of issues to be presented, is probably the most important factor in the preparation of an appellate brief, there are a number of other guideposts which must definitely be borne in mind. One point to be remembered is to strive diligently to construct an opening paragraph in the brief which contains a succinct statement of how the case came to the appellate court and a concise statement of the issues involved on the appeal. With the use of some imagination and considerable redrafting and rephrasing, an opening paragraph should be achieved which accomplishes these ends and, at the same time, piques the curiosity and interest of the court in the subject matter of the appeal. Such an opening will create a good first impression on the court which should work to your advantage as the court studies the rest of the brief.

Another guidepost—spare no effort in organizing a clear and persuasive statement of facts in the brief. Remember that the court will usually be a complete stranger to the facts of your case. Because you have become completely immersed in the facts contained in the record, don't fall into the error of stating the facts as if the appellate judges had the same head start. If you err in this regard, the statement of facts in your brief will be presented in such a shorthand way as to give the court an incomplete or even inaccurate impression of the overall picture of the facts and issues on the appeal. When stating the facts try to put yourself in the position of the court. If you were reading the facts for the first time, what would you want to know first? What facts would you deem most important? What other facts would you need to fill out and complete the picture in order to have an intelligent grasp of the issues involved? What facts would you feel could be omitted without loss of effectiveness? If you prepare the statement of facts in the brief with this attitude in mind, they will be presented effectively and persuasively.

Your statement of the facts will, of course, be carefully documented with references to the record on appeal. Such references are of great assistance to the court if they are accurate and explicit. For this reason great care and attention should be given to the checking and rechecking of the record references for accuracy as well as fidelity to the facts contained in the record. There is no quicker way to undermine the confidence of an appellate court in the merit and sincerity of an appeal than misstatement or exaggeration of the record facts or the inclusion of facts which are completely outside the record.

In briefing the law pertinent to the appeal, the organization should be as logical as possible without, however, sacrificing emphasis on a particularly important point of law simply for the sake of logical arrangement. There are times when some point of law may be of sufficient importance to the appeal that counsel will wish to highlight the point by presenting it first—even though, from the standpoint of logical arrangement, it would normally fall into another part of the legal argument. In most cases, however, a logical arrangement is the best arrangement. Do not burden the points of law with too many citations of cases. Remember that the court is not so impressed with the *number* of citations as it is with the *applicability* of the cases cited. Select only those authorities which have a true bearing on the legal problem involved and make an accurate application of those cases to the point which you are urging. If there are no authorities which support a particular proposition, don't cite any. Don't place a strained or far fetched interpretation on a case simply so you will have an authority to cite for a particular point. It is usually better not to cite any cases and simply to argue the point as a matter of principle than to stretch the holding of a case. Check local court rules to be sure of the rules or practice regarding the form of citing cases. If there are no such rules or practice, be uniform in your method of citing cases. Don't cite the official state reporter some of the time and regional reporters other times.

When the final proof of the brief is prepared, all record references, quotations from the record, citations of cases and quotations therefrom should be carefully checked from the record itself and from the original case reports. The entire brief should then be thoroughly proofread in order to achieve mechanical perfection and accuracy.

The Oral Argument

Having now completed your brief, which, I am sure, will be the soul of brevity, clarity, accuracy and persuasiveness, let us turn to the last phase of presentation of your case to the appellate court—oral argument. It has become a matter of common and somewhat embarrassing knowledge among lawyers that appellate judges generally feel that the most neglected and poorly handled phase of presentation of cases on appeal is the oral argument of the appeal. Many lawyers, I am sure, are inclined to excuse their fumbling efforts on oral argument on the theory that one must be naturally gifted before he can make an effective oral argument. The attitude that orators are born, not made, is no excuse for a sloppy preparation and ineffective presentation of oral argument. There is no reason why any attorney who is able to brief a case effectively cannot learn to carry through the oral phase of the presentation of his case effectively and persuasively. The poise, confidence and adaptability which are necessary for an effective oral argument can only be learned by experience. The appellate lawyer who prepares a competent brief on appeal and then at the last moment submits rather than going through the agonies, to his way of thinking, of an oral argument is doing not only his client but also himself a disservice. Only by gaining experience by participating in oral argument can you prepare yourself to render the fullest service to your clients in appellate work. Certainly everyone will make mistakes and perhaps, at times, feel a bit foolish as a result of the mistakes made in the course of oral argument. Such mistakes are excusable, however, if the lawyer honestly is making an effort to school himself in the art of oral argument. If he makes such an effort you can be sure that the same mistakes will not occur again and again. If more lawyers were to regard the oral argument of an appeal as a golden opportunity to drive home to the appellate court the righteousness of their client's case rather than a fearsome duty to be performed with the least possible pain and embarrassment, the quality of oral arguments, I am sure, would generally improve.

Oral argument affords each lawyer an opportunity to give the appellate judges their first look at the case and a grasp of what must later be faced by the judges in reflection and study before reaching a decision. It stimulates questions which, if not answered on oral argument, might otherwise puzzle the judge and remain forever unanswered. It affords the opportunity of corralling the judges' thinking within the real area of conflict between the parties and serves to focus their attention with exactness upon the issues involved.

One of the problems of oral argument in these days of increased pressure of work in appellate courts, is the stringent limitation of the time allotted for oral argument. Gone are the days of *McCullough v. Maryland* where the argument before the Supreme Court of the United States took six full days and of the *Gerard Will* case in which the argument to the same court lasted for ten days. Thirty minutes is more apt to be the amount of time allotted to you on an argument today with one hour being generally regarded as liberal. No matter what the time limitation may be, it is your duty to adhere strictly to it. And if, by chance, you don't need your full time—sit down. Don't go rambling on. Because of the strict limitations on oral arguments in appellate courts, the argument must be prepared most carefully. There will seldom be a situation in which you can discuss every issue you would like to present in the time allotted. For that reason, care should be exercised in selecting only those issues which you feel may be most troublesome to the court. Being troublesome they should have the benefit not only of the argument presented in your brief but of whatever persuasive force can be brought to bear upon them through oral presentation.

First Impression Important

In planning the oral argument do not, by all means, neglect the importance of an effective opening. The entire temper of an oral argument may well depend upon the impression you create with the court during the first two or three minutes of argument. As an artist is able to sketch the recognizable outlines of his subject with the first quick strokes of his crayon, your opening statement should sketch, in an understandable and interesting way, exactly how the case arrived in the appellate court and the essential issues involved on the appeal. Indicate to the court as soon as possible that you have a definite objective in mind which you intend to accomplish by your argument. If the opening is effective, the court's attitude will generally be one of interest in hearing your further remarks for the court *wants* to understand your case just as you *want* it to understand the case. If it sees from your opening that you give promise of being able to help it get a grasp of the problems involved, you will have kindled an interest which you should be able to carry throughout the rest of the argument. If the opening statement is ineffective, however, the court is apt to sit back in indifferent resignation to the confusion which generally follows such an inept beginning.

Immediately after the opening statement, counsel should proceed with a careful and cogent statement of the facts. Remember that the ignorance of the court is complete with regard to the facts of the case whereas it will have a broad legal background to aid it in understanding the legal significance of the facts as they are unfolded. It is safe to say that in the limited time ordinarily allotted for oral argument, a persuasive statement of the facts in relation to the issues involved is actually the entire argument. There is seldom time to argue the law in detail. In stating the facts, do not start nibbling at the fringes. Instead drive to the very core and present the most essential facts first. Then begin to fill in, logically and persuasively, the other facts which are necessary to a complete understanding of what the case is about. As when you were writing the brief, it will be helpful if you put yourself in the position of the court and imagine what facts you would want to know and how you would feel the story should be told if you were hearing it for the first time. If the statement of facts is presented with persuasive candor and clarity, you will have progressed a long way toward converting the strangers on the bench into the well-informed friends of your client's side of the case.

One word of caution is in order. In stating the facts, you must be careful not to go outside the record nor to misstate or exaggerate the facts in the record. Also the statement of facts should contain all the facts. Oftentimes there are some facts which are not favorable to your client's case but which are essential to a clear understanding of the case. Do not neglect to state these facts to the court for you can rest assured that, if left unstated, an unfavorable reaction will be caused when your adversary makes them known to the court, as he inevitably will.

If your statement of the facts is not cogently presented, you can be sure you will fall victim to the embarrassing fate of so many appellate lawyers who, after having rambled on ineffectively concerning the facts of the case for 5 or 10 minutes, are suddenly stopped by a not too patient inquiry from the bench such as: "Now just a minute, counsellor. Would you please tell the court just what the question is that you are presenting to the court and what relief your client wants?" Or, as sometimes happens, you will hear the following devastating inquiry from the bench: "Before you go any further, counsellor, would you please try to tell the court just exactly what the facts are in this case?" In a final desperate effort the court may even try to pry the facts out of counsel by a literal cross-examination. Your job as appellate counsel is to guide the court through the maze of facts to the conclusion that the appeal *must* be decided in favor of your client. Don't force the court to attempt to lead you by the hand through your argument. Such an incident should happen to an appellate counsel only once. If it occurs more often, counsel should begin to commune with himself in an effort to discover the error of his ways in preparing and presenting an oral argument.

In most cases there should be little need to argue points of law in detail. If the facts are well presented, the court, with its general legal background, will have an understanding of the legal issues involved, and, in most instances, probably will prefer to study your brief for detailed application of the law to the facts. If you feel, however, something more than a general indication of the points of law involved is necessary, you certainly should not begin to relate the facts of individual cases upon which you rely in tedious detail. Never read quotations from cases in your brief to the court. The cases are treated in your brief and can better be absorbed by the court from a study of the brief rather than wasting the court's time with such material in oral argument.

Questions from the Bench

Now, what about the matter of answering questions put by the court? And I don't mean the questions born of desperation to which I have previously referred. I mean questions which stem from a genuine interest aroused through effective oral argument. Some lawyers are inclined to regard questions from the bench as a necessary evil which interferes with their orderly plan of oral presentation. If counsel has such an attitude, the court's questions are usually ineffectively answered, if at all. I say you should be encouraged by questions. They indicate the court is interested and is following your argument. Questions are a guide to the court's initial reaction to the case and point out the particular problems which seem to be troubling the court. With questions as indicators, the effective appellate lawyer will be able to adjust his presentation to give greater force and emphasis to matters in which the court seems most interested and about which it seems to be troubled.

The most important admonition with regard to questions from the bench is not to postpone answering the question. The psychological time to answer is now. It is the time when the court's interest in that particular point is keenest and the time when the court will probably be most receptive to an intelligent attempt to satisfy its curiosity. Delay in answering risks loss of the inquiring judge's attention which may be diverted to something far afield or concentrated on another point by the time the answer is belatedly given. Delay in answering risks loss of the interrogating judge's attention in subsequent parts of your argument while he sits and ponders the problem posed by his question which you have not answered. Delay in answering risks the possibility that the judges will gain the impression that it is futile to seek your help in informing them on matters which are troubling them and will sit back throughout the balance of your argument without attempting to elicit further information from you by way of questions no matter how puzzled they may be. Delay in answering also risks the possibility that you will forget about the question at a later stage of the argument and will leave it unanswered. The judges are then left to speculate whether the failure to answer was the result of lack of a satisfactory answer or something else.

If, as is rarely the case, you are up against a particular judge who is a natural debater and tends to consume too much of your time in technical debate of one particular point, you usually will find that the presiding judge, who is aware of his brother's tendencies, will discreetly halt the debate and give you an opening to proceed with the rest of your argument.

Do not let awe for the court intimidate you in answering questions. Stand up to the court with a respectful conviction. If you answer questions timidly and inconclusively, the court may conclude that you are not even convinced of the point yourself. If, on the other hand, you give your answers intelligently and with honest sincerity of purpose and conviction, the court, even though inclined to disagree with you, will be impressed with your conviction and with the desirability of giving the position which you have taken every possible consideration and study.

Avoid Written Argument

Another important trait which should be developed by the appellate lawyer is adaptability in oral presentation. While the argument should be carefully and thoroughly prepared, I think it is a mistake for it to be written out. A written argument may be a great solace to you personally as insurance against "forgetting your lines," but it tends to result in flat presentation, lack of imagination and complete inflexibility when it is necessary to adapt yourself to the situation as it develops during the argument. Questions by the court often anticipate arguments which are to be made at a later point in the oral argument. If counsel is following the text of a written statement, he is very apt to find himself making a point from his written argument which he covered earlier in answer to questions from the bench. Furthermore, the use of a written text makes it difficult to telescope your argument as is often necessary when there have been considerable questions from the bench.

Adaptability in presentation will make it possible to fit your argument more adequately to the needs of the moment as they are indicated by the reactions of the court. For example one proposition may get immediate indications of approval from the court. In that event, leave it alone. To belabor the point may well do more harm than good. Or the court may seem inclined to resist acceptance of another of your propositions. In that event your argument should be flexible enough to allow you to spend more time and emphasis in attempting to bolster it.

If you represent the respondent on appeal, you should be alert to the reactions of the court during your adversary's argument. It may appear obvious from the court's questioning of your adversary that it is not likely to accept his position on a particular point. In such case, you will be well advised to touch lightly upon the point yourself. The court by its persistent questioning of your adversary has put itself in the position of an advocate of your point of view. To belabor the subject in your own argument usually will detract rather than add anything. Valuable clues will appear as to the court's attitudes and reactions to the case during your adversary's argument which should indicate to you the questions which are really bothering the court. You should then be adaptable enough in your argument to spend some extra time informing the court as to such questions.

In the foregoing comments, I realize I have offered nothing which has not been said in slightly different ways many times before. After all, the art of persuading human beings—including judges—has remained pretty constant through the years. However, while not much can be added to the subject, it can never be studied and considered too often by lawyers interested in mastering the art of effective presentation of cases to appellate courts.

Adapted from Vol. 29, Michigan State Bar Journal (1950).

The Form and Organization of Briefs

BY HERMAN F. SELVIN

THERE IS SOMETHING MORE to the writing of an appeal brief than assembling the relevant facts and making an argument. The facts and the argument must be so put together as to be conveniently usable by one who, knowing nothing of the case, is required to become fully familiar with it in a limited period of time. A brief may be complete and readily understandable to one steeped in the details of the case. It may still be less than fully effective with the court because of difficulties which its organization and arrangement put in the way of full appreciation of its content.

Pitfalls

Incomplete and even inaccurate summaries of the pertinent facts; failure to bring into early prominence the basic facts and questions involved; abstract case citations not specifically related either to their own facts or the facts of the appeal; inadequate references to the record; cross-references which do not pinpoint the place intended—these and other faults of like kind tend to consume an undue part of the court's time in unnecessary analysis and supplementation of the presentation made. By thus limiting the time available for study of the determinative questions, and by interrupting thought and concentration on those questions, they impair the persuasive force of the brief.

Basic Goals

Generally speaking, the form and organization of a brief ought to conform to two rules: First, it should be so complete within itself that reference to extrinsic sources will not be needed to learn anything that needs to be known about the case, but only to confirm the accuracy of the presentation. Second, the presentation should be such that it may be grasped and understood by the court without the expenditure of unnecessary effort or time. What follows in this article is intended to be of some assistance along these lines.

Court Rules

Form, organization, and even typography of a brief are usually prescribed by court rules, which vary considerably from jurisdiction to jurisdiction. These are always the starting point. Any suggestions for brief writing must, of course, be adapted to meet the applicable rules lest the brief be stricken, the appeal dismissed, or the judgment affirmed. See, e.g., *Drummond v. West,* 212 Cal. 766, 767, 769-770, 300 Pac. 823, 824 (1931) (dismissing appeal for failure, inter alia, to comply with rule requiring each point on appeal to be separately stated under heading showing the question to be presented).

History

It is obviously desirable that a judge reading a brief should learn as soon as possible what it is that he is being called upon to decide. In the very beginning, therefore, a preliminary or introductory statement is essential. That statement should be short but still long enough to describe the position of the parties on the record, the nature of the judgment appealed from the basic question or questions raised, and, in general terms, the factual context in which they arise.

Facts

It is equally desirable that the judge should be apprised of *all* of the questions raised. The statement of those facts ought to include the bad as well as the good; and it should be as objective and non-argumentative in form as possible. That is not to say that the statement must be nonpersuasive. To the contrary it should so be arranged—by logical and dramatic development of the story, by appropriate juxtaposition of telling evidence, and by judicious choice of language—that the facts will speak for themselves. Frequently, understanding of the significance of any fact can be facilitated by footnote comments pointing out their place in the argument to follow. But the statement itself should not be an argument except as its content produces its own persuasive effect.

Every assertion in the statement of facts *must* be supported by an appropriate reference to the record where the evidence or other material establishing it may be found. Those references, to the extent that the form of the record permits, should be precise; that is, they should refer the reader to the exact page and to the folio, paragraph or line, as the case may be, at which the material appears. Nevertheless, the statement should be so complete and fair in itself as not to require any revision or emendation by the court after the references have been checked. As a rule, a narrative statement rather than a verbatim reproduction of the transcript conduces to ease of reading. If direct quotations from the testimony are thought desirable they can be placed in a footnote if not overlong, or in an appendix if lengthy.

Summary of the Argument

When the brief itself is long or the issues complex, a summary of the argument is a valuable aid to understanding. It may well be included in most briefs, even when not prescribed by rule. Its purpose is not necessarily to persuade by itself but rather to give to the court a preview of the argument which is to come. It should be something more than a bringing together in one place of the section headings and subheadings; and by the same token it should not be a repetition in extenso of the detailed argument.

Cross-References

Where assignments of error are required, it is helpful to supplement them by a reference to the section of the argument in which they are discussed. Similarly, the section headings of the argument should be cross-referenced to the assignments of error to which they relate.

In fact, the development and use of some practical system of cross-referencing the entire brief can be of great aid in advancing the writer's purpose—which should be to inform and, by informing, to persuade. References back and forth from statement of facts to argument and from one part of the argument to another are needed to achieve clarity, emphasis, and logical development of one's point. A practical method of making such references enables the writer to avoid unnecessary repetition; and it saves the court the troublesome experience of being unable to find with ease some "*supra*" or "*infra*" reference.

The best method, of course, is to refer to the exact page of the brief to which attention is being directed. But, in printed briefs, this requires page proofs and subsequent resetting of the lines of type at which the page numbers are inserted, thus adding expense and time. In most cases the same result can be achieved by identifiable subdivision of the brief. For example: the statement of the case may be divided into lettered sections and numbered paragraphs; the argument into numbered and lettered sections and subsections. Cross-references would then read something like this: "[See, *Statement of the Case,* B, Par. 4 *supra*]"; or "[Point I, A, 1, *First, infra*]."

Descriptive Headings

Each separate point made in argument should be preceded by a descriptive heading; and the subsections under each point similarly prefaced. These headings may be topical, declarative, or argumentative. The latter form is generally perferable. It relates the legal principle involved to the actual problem before the court instead of being merely a statement of some abstract proposition of law. It serves as a summary of, or topic sentence for, the argument which it introduces. And when the headings and subheadings are collected in a table of contents, they not only facilitate cross-reference but serve, as well, as another outline or summary of the case as a whole.

Citations

Citations to reported decisions ought to be to the official report and to the National Reporter System; the latter at the very least for cases from other jurisdictions. A court can usually be expected to have its own official reports readily available, but not necessarily those of other jurisdictions. It is almost certain to have the Reporter System. Too, judges who find the standard working day not long enough may read briefs at home. There it is not likely that they will have any reports other than the volumes of the Reporter System which the publisher supplies to all appellate judges.

In addition to the conventional reference to volume and beginning page, it is a good idea also to give the page or pages on which appears the discussion for which the case is cited, e.g., *Doe v. Roe,* 25 Cal. 2d 892, 922-924, 186 P. 2d 345, 360-361. If, because of prevailing law review practice, it is feared that such a citation will convey the impression that the reference is to a dictum, that impression can be avoided by a general caveat footnoted at the beginning of the argument, or by labeling a dictum reference as such. The advantage of the so-called internal citation is that in long opinions deciding several points, only one of which is relevant to the case at hand, the court is directed at once to the pertinent part of the opinion. The court can then read as much or as little of the remainder of the case as it desires.

On repeating a citation, a mere "*supra*" after the title is not enough, unless the repetition comes within a few lines of its first mention. The volume and at least the internal citation should be given, thus: *Doe v. Roe, supra,* 25 Cal. 2d at 923, 186 P. 2d at 360. It can be quite annoying to have to search back through many pages or go to a table of cases for the book and page reference to a citation which the reader wants to look at right then.

The manner in which cited cases are handled is of first importance. On the basic or definitive questions the decision relied upon is best presented in context; that is, by an appropriate brief quotation evidencing its holding, accompanied by an abstract of its facts so as to show the factual application of that abstract holding. Extensive cumulation of parallel decisions is generally not necessary. It may be done, however, to show the well-settled nature of the rule invoked or its manifold applications to differing sets of facts. When this is done, each citation should be followed by a brief or catch-line statement of the holding in specific rather than abstract terms. For example, "*Doe v. Roe,* 25 Cal. 2d 892, 922-924, 186 P. 2d 345, 360-361 (holding that a state university is a 'charitable institution' within the meaning of the mortmain statute)" is preferable to "*Doe v. Roe,* 25 Cal. 2d 892, 922-924, 186 P. 2d 345, 360-361 (holding that 'charitable' in its legal sense includes 'educational')." Another method is to preface the list of cases with a statement of the general principle for which they are cited and catch-lining each citation with a description of the factual situation to which that principle was applied.

On collateral or incidental propositions which develop or lead up to the main argument, citations should be supplied even though the propositions are familiar or well-settled. Here, however, cumulation is hardly ever necessary. The leading or latest case or two is enough. Not infrequently, a large number of decisions is cited throughout a brief. Abstracting or quoting from these may unduly interrupt the logical or rhetorical flow of the argument. When that is the situation, a convenient device is to place abstracts and quotations in an appendix, to which the reader may readily refer. An appendix is also helpful for handy reference to cited material which is not otherwise readily available. In this category come statutes from other states, administrative rules and regulations, decisions and rulings published only in specialty reports, and the like.

When several or many authorities are cited to the same proposition, they should be presented in the order of their appositeness to the case at hand. The strongest and most nearly similar case will naturally come first. To this general proposition there is one exception: "Prime" authority for any court is generally one of its own decisions. When one is available it will usually head the list even though other cases may be somewhat more directly in point or more clearly illustrative of the principle relied on.

The adverse authority, like the unfavorable fact, should never be ignored. If the brief writer was able to find it there is no reason to suppose that his opponent or the court cannot do as much. Like it or not, the decision will in all probability be before the court. It is, then, obviously good tactics (to say nothing of ethics) to refer to the case and to have before the court at the outset the countering comments. Similarly, it is generally good policy to anticipate and answer the opposition's reply. Regardless of how convinced the advocate may be of the soundness of his side of the case, there is usually something to be said in opposition. The opposing argument is not met or eliminated by refusing to recognize its existence. Since it is certain to be put to the court, the opportunity for gaining whatever benefit lies in making the first impression ought not to be given up.

Use of Special Type

Italic, bold-face, or underscoring, when sparingly used may serve to signal an important point. When used indiscriminately and frequently they destroy effectiveness by bringing major propositions down to the level of minor ones. It is generally better to err on the side of conservatism in this regard.

Reply Brief

Reply briefs should meet the opposition argument head-on. The particular point being met must be adequately identified and, for the court's convenience, its location in the other side's brief ought to be set out. The answer to it must be specific. If the argument is irrelevant, that fact may be noted and the reasons stated; but it is well to answer the argument on the merits too. The court may not agree that it is irrelevant. If an argument is based on erroneous or incomplete factual assumptions, the defects should be spelled out. If it is unsupported by or distinguishable from the authorities cited, the particulars must be specified.

In the nature of things, courts do not have the detailed or quickly remembered knowledge of a case which the lawyers have or ought to have. Nor do they have the same time for extended research. Judges, therefore, not only have the right, but are frequently required, to lean heavily on counsel's industry and his resulting familiarity with the case. As a consequence, a point not made may be treated as a point not worth making. By the same token, a point which seems obvious to one fully familiar with the record, may not be so readily apparent to one not similarly situated. For these reasons a reply brief ought to be specific and complete. For the same reasons the right to file a reply or answering brief should seldom if ever be waived, regardless of how patent the answer may seem to be.

Literary Style

The literary style of a brief, of course, is important. But style is so individualistic a matter as not to admit of many safe generalizations. This much can be said — few of us have the ability to write in the manner of Holmes, Cardozo or Learned Hand. Even if we had, their epigrammatic and elliptical style takes too much insight for granted to be effective in argument. The effort to imitate them generally succeeds only in producing a bad case of "elegant" writing which obscures meaning and distracts attention from content.

So, too, the stilted cliches of pleading and conveyancing are out of place in a brief. The "aforesaids" and "hereinbefore stateds" and the cumulated synonyms which abound in so-called legal drafting engender merely dullness in a written argument. The simple word, the short sentence, and a moderately informal rhetoric make for the most readable briefs.

Perhaps, the main objective in developing style, is to have it bespeak sincerity and individuality. If fully developed in the written word, these qualities tend to carry over to the spoken word at the argument. They make the brief and the oral presentation ring true. They impart conviction. Coupled with a fully developed and mechanically clean brief, they make an argument strong. And, after all, a strong argument is its own best advocate.

Adapted from Vol. 2, The Practical Lawyer (1956).

III CONTENTS

Judges and Briefs

By Robert N. Miller

Judges have to be on their guard in reading briefs, because they know briefs are one-sided by their very nature, both as to statements of fact and of law. How can briefs be best written so as to overcome this handicap of known partisanship?

Considerable help toward answering that question is found in the views expressed and put into practice by the late Sewall Key, who served for years as a Department of Justice specialist in criticizing and drafting certain types of Federal appellate briefs. He profited by an unusual opportunity to observe over a long period what kind of brief seems to succeed with judges and what kind does not. It is well at the outset to review some ideas which he emphasized in talks with his associates and with lawyers like me, in outside practice.

Separating Statement-Material from Argument

A brief has two functions—(1) that of giving the court a reliable statement as to what the dispute is about and as to what the salient facts are as disclosed by the record, and (2) that of presenting arguments of counsel. The part of the brief which performs the first-named function is generally accepted at par by judges unless it has been confused by including material not easily checkable from the record—doubtful conclusions, for instance. It is the other part of the brief—presenting the arguments of counsel —to which the handicap of partisanship mainly attaches. Not infrequently, also, a judge examines the statement part of each of the briefs—the part which purports to be objective—before he looks at the arguments in any of them. He does this because he wishes to form at the outset his own reaction to the facts of the case, uncolored by the views of counsel. With this purpose in mind, he looks at the statements to inform himself as to the bare bones of the controversy. This is, of course, before his final conclusion is formed and long before he begins to consider what reasons or citations should be put into an opinion.

All these considerations make it important (1) that the draftsman of a brief shall make it very clear that he has carefully separated statement-material in the brief from argument-material and from merely partisan conclusions, and (2) that he shall use special judgment, patience, and ingenuity in presenting the statement-material.

As to the part of the statement which presents the facts, it can generally be drafted in any one of several different ways, not one of them contrary to the record. In stating facts, Key was careful, first of all, to make sure that any fact which might prove a turning point in his client's favor was not only clearly stated in the non-argumentative part of the brief, but was given such a prominent position there—disregarding logical order when necessary—that the court could not fail to grasp it.

Stating the Issues

Illustrating how ingenuity can draft the nonargumentative part so effectively that it prepares the way for the arguments is the approach used by the late John W. Davis in the *Couzens* case, 11 B.T.A. 1040, tried in 1927 in the Board of Tax Appeals, predecessor of the Tax Court. The taxpayer had sold Ford Motor Company stock, and computation of the resulting profit depended on the March 1, 1913, value of the stock. Prior to the sale, the Commissioner of Internal Revenue had, at the request of the seller, made an independent investigation as to that value and a determination of it; the tax so indicated had been duly paid. Later, another Commissioner having taken office, a deficiency of more than $9,000,000 was computed by using a lower March 1, 1913, value, and the taxpayer sought a redetermination by the Board. Both sides called many value witnesses, and the trial, before three members of the Board, lasted about two months.

Mr. Davis spoke somewhat as follows as to the nature of the controversy, preliminary to his discussion of the merits:

> We contend first, that one Commissioner is bound by the value determination of his predecessor; the Government disputes this, there is no deficiency; but if the Court disagrees with us, we merely come to the second question; we say that when it is admitted by the second Commissioner, as it is here, that neither any new fact nor any new principle was considered in the revaluation, the succeeding Commissioner cannot substitute his value judgment for that of his predecessor. The Government disagrees; if we are right, there is no deficiency. Only if we are wrong on each of these positions of ours do we come to the question as to what the value was as of March 1, 1913.

It is clear that this statement avoids any admixture of argument, but it manages to put the Court on guard against too heavy a reliance on the action of administrative officials. At the same time, it states alternative contentions without weakening any one of them.

The Court decided against the taxpayer on each of the issues except the final value-issue, but it fixed a March 1, 1913, valuation even higher than the one adjudicated by the earlier of the two Commissioners, so that instead of paying a deficiency the taxpayer received a refund of more than $1,000,000.

Minimizing Rebuttals

Another of Key's convictions was that rebuttals must be kept to a minimum because their defensive quality weakens the positive tone essential to a good brief, and because they may arouse suspicion that the writer misguidedly hopes to win on the weakness of his adversary's case. Whether the brief-writer's client is the bringer of the action or the defender, the appellant or the appellee, the main task of a brief is to show direct reasons why the client should win—a strictly affirmative task which must be accomplished whatever the weakness of the other side. The policy of minimizing rebuttals is well served when the nonargumentative part of the brief is so presented that a judge, when he reads the adversary's brief, will be equipped to see for himself the weaknesses in it, without help from anybody's argument.

Rebuttals were by no means absent from Key's briefs, but foundations for them were so clearly laid in the statement part of the brief that even a condensed treatment of rebuttals could be readily grasped by the reader.

Common-sense Aspects of the Controversy

In drafting the nonargumentative part, serious and separate thought ought always to be given to this question: Does the case involve any feature which, from the viewpoint of the man in the street who is ignorant of legal rules and decisions, seems to favor my side? If so, the brief must make that feature particularly clear. The reason is that in various fields—notably the interpretation of tax laws and regulatory laws—a judge is often confronted with conflicting lines of argument neither of which can be held legally unsound or wholly inapt. In that situation, all he can do is to consider which line ought to weigh heavier in the instant situation. This choice is almost certain to be made by considering which one of the lines of thought leads to the more reasonable and sensible result.

To put aside technicalities in that way is harder for lawyers than for other people; will power and close application are needed to overcome the technical habits of thought which the lawyer has been trained to use—sometimes he is overtrained.

Having analyzed the case from the common-sense point of view, the writer of the brief must next construct the nonargumentative part of it so that anybody reading that part could not fail to be influenced merely by seeing the fact-statements themselves, in the direction of their common-sense aspects. If this result is achieved, less space need be given in the argument part to expressing the brief-writer's views as to how the judge should rule.

Forecasting the Judge's Reaction

What has been said about principles as to which Mr. Key expressed helpful views must not divert our attention from one of the affirmative virtues of a good brief—the virtue of emphasizing those aspects of the case which the judge is likely to consider most important—as distinguished from the aspects which most appeal to the brief-writer. To forecast the judge's reaction is difficult, because he will have a different background from the lawyers in the case and will have far less knowledge of the special situation. But this difficulty does not diminish the necessity of making the forecast; perhaps the most useful skill of a great lawyer is that of guessing where the judge is likely to think the jugular vein of each issue lies.

Confidence-Impairing Weaknesses

Experienced judges tell us that briefs often fall short of commanding confidence not merely because they fail to take advantage of such affirmative principles as have been mentioned, but because they violate some simple principles of briefwriting.

1. *Confusing the Issues.* This involves failure squarely to acknowledge and meet the true issues either of fact or of law. While the judge must look through the briefs of counsel to the record itself, he should be able to rely to a considerable extent on the briefs. But he cannot rely on a brief which fails to show that the writer knows exactly where the real issues are, or which purposely evades them.

In reading some briefs one gets the impression that the writer believes in the gullibility of judges. Such briefs suggest the rhyme:

Brian O'Lynn had no watch to put on,
And he tuke him a turnip to make him a wan,
And he tuke a black cricket and put it within,
"They'll think it's a-tickin," said Brian O'Lynn.

The Brian O'Lynns of the profession often deceive themselves as to how the judge will think, but seldom deceive the judges.

2. *Personalities.* If a brief takes the position that the adversary's brief contains statements which are erroneous, the judge expects this to be demonstrated in a certain way—by references to the record or to the authorities—certainly not by *ad hominem* arguments. Personalities shake the judge's confidence in any brief, because they suggest that the writer thinks he can win on the alleged weakness of the other side instead of on the merits, or that the writer is giving way to his emotions and is therefore in a mood which cannot be relied on for straight thinking. In contrast, a fair and friendly tone toward the adversary establishes confidence.

There is also an *ad hominem* attitude toward the judge himself which must be avoided, however tempting—that of prominently relying on a case previously decided by the same judge. The judge recognizes it as an attempt to make it hard for him to give to the question the freshness of attention which it is his duty to give. Who knows, also, but that the judge had serious doubts when he wrote the previous opinion, and has changed his mind, as he should do if he was wrong?

3. *Confused Organization.* Only by separating clearly in his own mind the different elements and arguments in his case can a brief-writer compose a brief which a court can feel is reliable. Each of the various arguments should be clearly separated from the others; once made, an argument must not be repeated elsewhere in the brief, even with different language, unless by way of very short summary. A disordered brief indicates that the writer's analysis has been a muddy one—and it wastes the judge's reading time. Repetitions are less likely to occur if headings and subheadings as to each important element of the facts and of the argument are employed. They are important, too, because a judge, after reading all the briefs, very often wishes to go back and reread something he remembers; proper subheadings help him to find promptly what he wishes to review.

4. *Prolixity.* Fact-statements can be spoiled by including factual elements which are immaterial; arguments can be spoiled by including material which is overhistorical and overanalytical, and by case citations which are unnecessary because the judge does not need to be reminded of them. A prolix brief dilutes the effect of its most impressive features.

One kind of prolixity involves citing too many court decisions. A conscientious judge who feels obliged to read all the cited cases will be unreasonably burdened, unless there is a sound reason for including each citation. Along the same line, it is not wise to quote extracts from opinions which when carefully examined prove to be distinguishable on the facts, or otherwise unhelpful.

Somewhere in every brief the judge should be able to find a sharp clear paragraph or two—not too long—showing just why the writer thinks his side should win.

Conclusion

Experienced lawyers have always recognized the soundness of the various ideas reviewed here. Why, then, do judges so often see briefs which fall short because these ideas have not been applied?

In some instances I suggest that the explanation may be that they are seeking to please insistent clients who are under the mistaken impression that—as is sometimes true in jury trials—cases are won by demolishing the lawyer on the other side. But in general the reason may be that most of us, when we meet with opposition, do not deny ourselves the selfish gratification of showing how forcible we can be in direct controversy, written or oral. In that mood we are in danger of forgetting that while a judge must rely to a considerable extent on the lawyers who write briefs and make arguments, he knows that a human being is least reliable when his thinking is colored by emotion or self-interest. If a brief is so drafted that if the judge were to use its language in an opinion, the opinion would have the temperate and objective quality which opinions must have, the brief is entitled to and is likely to get the respectful attention of the judge.

Almost everybody develops a habit of sizing-up each person he has occasion to deal with: Is he honest? Is he intelligent? Has he been willing to do the necessary work on the matter in hand? Judges, consciously or unconsciously, form similar conclusions as they read each brief. A brief has a character of its own, and good character will carry it a long way. A brief which does not stand the character test is handicapped just as is an individual of poor character.

Finally, while a lawyer is bound to present his client's case with all the force and skill at his command, and so has a partisan duty, the lawyer has just as compelling a duty to the court, as one of its officers. Experience, happily, shows that the client's interest is best served by a lawyer whose briefs and whose general conduct indicate loyalty to both of these duties.

Adapted from Vol. 1, The Practical Lawyer (1955).

The Advocate as a Lawmaker: The Advocate in the Reviewing Courts

BY WALTER V. SCHAEFER

TODAY'S SURVEY OF THE LIFE and times of the advocate shows him to be indeed a ubiquitous and versatile fellow. We have seen him in many familiar places and in many familiar roles. When I received Dean Harno's invitation to be here today, I saw the word "Advocate" and the words "Reviewing Courts," and I assumed that what was called for was a discussion of the familiar theme of appellate advocacy. That is not a very difficult undertaking for a judge of a reviewing court. It is certainly no secret that most of us have such a speech readily at hand.

And so I saw myself delivering that old reliable stand-by—sparkling with wit and wisdom, both largely borrowed from my betters. But while the reviewing court is one of the advocate's familiar haunts, his role in connection with the law-making function of such a court is another cut of cloth indeed. And because I looked a second time at my assigned subject, and saw then the implications which I should have seen before I undertook this venture, you will miss those gems of wit and wisdom, and sit uncomfortably while I deal inadequately with a difficult subject.

The subject assigned to me makes two basic assumptions: first, that reviewing courts make law; and second, that advocates have a part in that lawmaking process. Not so long ago neither assumption would have been made, for it was thought that the job of a reviewing court was simply to apply ready-made, pre-existing legal principles to the case before it.

While both assumptions are correct in my opinion, it should be pointed out that by no means do reviewing courts make law in every case, or even in most cases. There are no statistics, and I doubt that there ever will be any, for the shadings are too delicate for statistical analysis. But it is clear the great bulk of the work of reviewing courts does involve an application of existing principles of law to the facts of the case, or a selection between competing principles.

I take it that our concern today is not with that great bulk of the cases, but rather with that much smaller group in which a new doctrine is evolved, or an existing one is overturned, expanded, or contracted. The number of such cases is small, but their importance is not measured by their volume, for it is in these cases that the common law demonstrates its capacity for growth and adaptation.

To isolate and analyze just what it is that the advocate is doing, or should be doing, in this class of cases is difficult because we do not know with any great degree of certainty what the courts are doing. There have been very few studies of the operation of the judicial process in this area. For a number of reasons, the opinion of a court does not always tell you why the court reached the result it did. In part, this is due to the prevailing style of opinion writing. However great the doubts with which the judge has wrestled in the process of reaching his decision, almost invariably those doubts fail to appear in his opinion. When he writes, he becomes an advocate. He does so, I think, less because he wants to persuade his colleagues or the bar to the inevitability of the result he has reached, than because that style has been and is the accepted practice in opinion writing.

Typically, his colleagues will share his views with varying degrees of certainty. The absence of dissent or special concurrence does not indicate an absence of doubt, for neither the dissent nor the special concurrence is a response to doubt. They stem from certainty, but in a direction other than that taken by the opinion of the court.

To find out what the judges are doing on the frontiers of the law, therefore, we must look beyond their opinions. And that terrain is not well mapped. I can by no means fix all the boundaries and fill in all the contours of that intriguing and important area. My difficulty is not lack of time. It is rather that I lack the ability, and so, I think, do other judges, and perhaps all other men, to describe accurately the process by which a decision is reached. There is comfort, if not full satisfaction, in William James' observation that, "when the conclusion is there we have already forgotten most of the steps preceding its attainment."[1]

[1] James, *Principles of Psychology* 260.

What I can do, and all that I can do, is to suggest some matters that my own brief experience indicates an advocate should think about and do when he is working on the frontiers. And in the process, of course, I shall be suggesting indirectly some of the factors that in my opinion influence courts in deciding whether existing doctrine is to be contracted or expanded.

First of all, it seems to me, the advocate must capture the interest and the imagination of the court. This he should try to do in any case, of course, for in a reviewing court each case is almost always competing with many others for the attention of the court. But it is particularly important in the class of cases we are considering, because judges are lawyers, and so by training and habit are a conservative lot. Inertia, therefore, weighs heavily in favor of existing precedent. If there is to be change, the court must be sufficiently stimulated to overcome its underlying preference for the law as it is.

The principal stimulus, of course, comes from the facts of the case. The interaction between fact and law is close and continuous. Twenty years ago Chief Justice Stone suggested the interrelation in this picturesque way: "The law, itself," he said, "is on trial quite as much as the cause which is to be decided."[2] Each decision of a court measures the existing body of legal doctrine against the particular facts before the court. Once rendered, the decision becomes itself a part of the existing body of precedent. Its adequacy, in turn, is measured by the impact of the facts of future cases. The process is a continuing one, and it is that process which gives vitality to the common law, and makes it able to adapt itself to changed conditions.

Because of this interrelation of fact and law, the advocate must also identify for the court the problem involved—not as an isolated thing, but in its relation to the body of the law generally. And, if the court is to be induced to make a change, it must then be shown that the existing law as applied to the facts of the case will produce an incongruous result. And I must hasten to say that I do not mean incongruity as measured by the standard of the advocate. To some lawyers, any doctrine which militates against their position smacks of incongruity. I mean incongruity by objective standards. In the last analysis, of course, the determinative standard is that of the court which decides the case. But the court's standard is not al-

[2] Stone, *The Common Law in the United States*, 50 Harv. L. Rev. 4, 10 (1936).

together, or even primarily, subjective. The views of the legal profession, as expressed formally in treatises and law reviews and the opinions of courts of other jurisdictions bear heavily upon the question. So, indeed, does the opinion of any informed group. Witness, for example, the impact of the views of psychiatrists on the tests for determining sanity in criminal cases as announced in *McNaghten's Case*.

A court's conviction of the unsatisfactory operation of a legal doctrine may stem not just from the result in the case at hand, but from cumulative impact of earlier results. For example, the application of the rule of *Swift v. Tyson*[3] to the facts in *Erie Ry. Co. v. Tompkins*[4] would not have involved an extension more dramatic than many others that had been made. And more recently, the case in which the California Supreme Court rejected its rule that evidence illegally obtained was nevertheless admissible in a criminal prosecution did not differ greatly from those in which the discarded rule had been consistently applied over the years.[5]

In each case, it seems to me, the existing doctrine fell because its vitality had already been weakened by the accumulated pressure of the many cases to which it had been repeatedly subjected over the years. Incidentally, in neither of these cases, as I understand it, was the change due to the efforts of the advocates. In each instance, however, the case history of the doctrine showed a number of strong dissents preceding its ultimate demise. But I suppose not even the dissenters could have predicted just when their appeal to the conscience of the future would be heard, and so the lawyers can hardly be blamed for their failure to diagnose accurately.

Assuming the presence of the requisite ingredient of incongruity of result, the advocate must consider the quality of the change he is urging. While it is true that courts make law, they do not engage in the business on a large scale. They "legislate interstitially," said Holmes.[6] They are restricted to movement of the particles and may not move the mass. And as the same author pointed out, "A common law judge could not say I think the doctrine of consideration a bit of historical nonsense and shall not enforce it in my court."[7]

---

3 41 US (16 Pet.) 1 (1842).

4 304 US 64, 82 LEd 1188, 58 SupCt 817 (1938).

5 People v. Cahan, 44 Cal (2d) 434, 282 P(2d) 905 (1955).

6 Southern Pacific Co. v. Jensen, 244 US 205, 221, 61 LEd 1086, 37 SupCt 524, 531 (1917).

7 *Ibid.*

Before a court will modify a legal doctrine, it must be able to see the consequences of the step it is taking. It does not choose the precise problems with which it deals, nor even the general area of law in which it is to work. The materials with which it works are those churned up by the chances of litigation. It lacks a legislature's capacity to grasp an entire problem, and to deal with all its ramifications.

So the likelihood of a change in legal doctrine depends upon the degree to which the doctrine in question is interrelated with others. Mr. Justice Brandeis expressed the thought in *International News Service v. Associated Press.*[8]

> "Court are ill-equipped to make the investigations which should precede a determination of the limitations which should be set upon any property right in news or of the circumstances under which news gathered by a private agency should be deemed affected with a public interest. Courts would be powerless to prescribe the detailed regulations essential to full enjoyment of the rights conferred or to introduce the machinery required for enforcement of such regulations. Considerations such as these should lead us to decline to establish a new rule of law in the effort to redress a newly-disclosed wrong, although the propriety of some remedy appears to be clear."

In point of fact, the Court in the *International News* case did establish the new rule of law. But the limitation described by Mr. Justice Brandeis is nonetheless a real one, and the advocate must be prepared to demonstrate, so far as it is possible, the point at which the change which he advocates will cease to have a direct bearing upon other legal doctrines.

The advocate who seeks to persuade a court to depart from precedent must also reckon with the reluctance of courts to disappoint the expectations of those who have relied upon existing law.

In a sense courts might be said to have a greater freedom in this respect than legislatures, for the overruling decision does not encounter constitutional *ex post facto* clauses. While the judicial decision operates retrospectively, it has been regarded in theory as announcing the law as it has always existed, and so as merely correcting a previous error. But the court which is being asked to make the change is not itself deluded by any formal theory, and so moves

[8] 248 US 215, 267, 63 LEd 211, 39 SupCt 68, 82 (1918).

slowly and warily where there is a possibility that reliance upon precedent may be disappointed. Of course the influence of reliance upon judicial precedent in shaping human conduct is easily exaggerated, as Cardozo has pointed out.[9] There are large areas of the law in which reliance upon precedent is necessarily non-existent. But there are other areas in which it may exist, and so courts will continue to take account of it.

The possibility of reliance and the fact of reliance are thus to be considered by the advocate. But there is also available here a counter-technique of decision, and hence a theme of advocacy which may be useful. A few courts confronted with the combination of reliance upon an unsatisfactory decision plus the normal retroactive operation of a judicial decision, have solved the problem by adhering to the existing precedent for the case at hand, while announcing that a different rule will be applied in the future. Wigmore mentioned the technique in 1917.[10] Kocourek, in 1931, proposed to embody it in a statute providing that a supreme court should not decide any case under a prior rule if the court believes that rule unjust, unless the former rule had been the basis of a reasonable and justified reliance by the litigant or by other persons not before the court.[11] Then in 1932 the Supreme Court of the United States sustained the action of the Montana court which had applied the existing rule to the case at hand while announcing that a different rule would prevail in the future.[12]

From the point of view of most advocates the technique may not be attractive, for it presupposes the loss of the case at hand, and the advocate, I suspect, has a livelier interest in present victory than in prospective, and hence academic, improvement of legal doctrine. But there are volume litigants, both in and out of government. And for them the value of the technique is far from theoretical.

More frequently available to the advocate is another line of argument which is seldom used. Twenty years ago Chief Justice Stone pointed out as a defect in the common law its habit of re-

---

9 Cardozo, *The Growth of the Law* 122 (1923).

10 Wigmore, *Introduction,* in Modern Legal Philosophy Series, *The Science of Legal Method* xxviii (1917).

11 Kocourek, *Retrospective Decisions and Stare Decisis and a Proposal,* 17 AB AJ 180, 182 (1931).

12 Great Northern Ry. Co. v. Sunburst Oil & Refining Co., 287 US 358, 77 LEd 360, 53 SupCt 145 (1932).

garding a statute as "in the law but not of it."[13] Any judicial decision, however poorly considered, is a potentional point of departure in the common-law process of reasoning. Statutes are not generally so regarded, though they be preceded by the most thorough legislative investigation. Chief Justice Stone looked forward to the day when statutes, like judicial decisions, would be used as social data, or points of departure, in the common-law process. He spoke of "the ideal of a unified system of judge-made and statutory law woven into a seamless whole by the processes of adjudication."[14]

That ideal has not materialized, but there are many instances in which radiations from statutes not directly applicable have influenced or shaped judicial decisions. The most dramatic illustration, it seems to me, is the influence of the Married Women's Acts, which, about the middle of the last century, gave married women the right to own their separate property, to contract, and to sue and be sued. Many common-law doctrines, in criminal law, evidence, torts, and other areas, had rested to a greater or lesser degree upon the incapacities of a married woman as they existed at common law. And across the country those areas of law are responding to the statutory removal of common-law incapacities. That removal plays a part, for example, in determining whether one spouse is competent to testify against the other, whether they can conspire together to commit a crime, whether the husband is liable for the torts of his wife, as he was at common law, to mention only a few of many instances.

There are other illustrations, although in no other instance, I think, has the influence of a single statute been so pronounced. In the Chinese sovereignty case last year the question was whether or not a counterclaim could be asserted against a sovereign government.[15] No statute dealt directly with counterclaims as related to sovereign immunity, but the decision which allowed the counterclaim was based upon a policy distilled from many statutes relating to counterclaims generally.

In a statutory construction case decided by our court a term or two ago, construction of the particular pension act before us

---

13 Stone, *supra* note 2, at 14.

14 Stone, *supra* note 2, at 12.

15 National City Bank of New York v. Republic of China, 348 US 356, 99 LEd 389, 75 SupCt 423 (1955).

was based upon an analysis of what the legislature had provided in other, unrelated pension acts. And in another statutory construction case now awaiting decision the court showed a lively interest in the provisions of other statutes dealing with the same problem in other areas of government. We have pending another case in which the question is the availability of injunction to restrain the violation of a regulatory statute. Some other regulatory acts expressly authorize the issuance of an injunction, but the one in question does not. In a similar case, the New York Court of Appeals acted upon the legislative policy in favor of extending the equitable remedy which it found to have been expressed in other statutes.[16]

When we think of advocacy in a reviewing court, we think ordinarily of the advocates before the bar, and not of those on the bench. And we think of advocacy as ended when the case has been submitted for decision. Actually, of course, advocacy does not end; it moves from the courtroom to the conference room.

Much has been written of Marshall during the past year. What I suppose is the orthodox view pictures him as successfully writing the doctrines of the Federalist party into the decisions of the Court, even though most of his colleagues belonged to a different party. Another view is that Marshall's career was a long and stubborn rear guard action in defense of the Constitution as it was meant to be read. Nevertheless, the story goes, he was continually forced into compromise and defeat, the cumulative effect of which amounted to a transformation of the Constitution. It does not matter which view is correct, for both of them underscore Marshall's role as an advocate inside the Court.

That advocacy should exist in a reviewing court is as inevitable as that it should exist in any other situation in which a group judgment is being reached. The extent to which it exists in any court depends in part, I suppose, upon the temperaments of the individual judges, and their capacity.

The techniques of intramural advocacy do not differ fundamentally from those of formal advocacy. Courtroom formality is shed, of course, inside the conference room, but otherwise what is good advocacy in court is good advocacy in the conference room. There is, however, a significant difference. Relationships inside

16 People v. Laman, 277 NY 368, 14 NE(2d) 439 (1938).

the court are personal and they are continuing. The case at hand is one of many awaiting decision. It does not stand isolated from those which have gone before or those which will follow.

No single member of a reviewing court can have every opinion the way he wants it, and that is as it should be. The result is that he must focus his fire on the significant, letting the details go. There is thus a unique tactical quality about conference room advocacy that is lacking in the more formal type. A judge's influence with his colleagues is a sensitive thing, which could readily be impaired. The balance is delicate in a court which has a large volume of business. In such a court, it seems to me, an important problem for the judge is that of deciding where he is going to concentrate his energy.

The underlying basis of sound courtroom advocacy is emphasized by a consideration of the way conference room advocacy operates. Judges are not overawed by the words that are written in the reports. They are more conscious than others, I suspect, of their own limitations. Cardozo's description of the process of judicial disillusionment can not be improved upon. "A brief experience on the bench was enough to reveal to me all sorts of cracks and crevices and loopholes in my own opinions when picked up a few months after delivery, and reread with due contrition. The persuasion that one's own infallibility is a myth leads by easy stages and with somewhat greater satisfaction to a refusal to ascribe infallibility to others."[17]

Judges are interested, of course, in what has been said and what has been decided, and the traditions and formal ritual of courtroom advocacy encourage lawyers to pitch their arguments on that ground. In most cases that may be enough. But in any case it is desirable that the thrust go deeper, and in cases on the frontiers of the law a deeper thrust is imperative. Those cases are not decided just upon the ground that "it was so held" in such and such a case. They are decided upon a consideration of why it was so held and upon an appraisal of the results of that holding in actual operation plus the anticipated consequences of an expansion or curtailing of that holding. This is the level upon which conference room advocacy operates. It is also the level upon which the most effective courtroom advocacy operates.

---

[17] Cardozo, *The Nature of the Judicial Process* 29-30 (1921).

Adapted from *Readings in Oral Advocacy*, Harvard Law School (1953).

The Appellate Brief

By Wiley B. Rutledge

Briefs are as varied as the lawyers who make them and the cases with which they deal. Consequently there can be no rule of thumb for writing them. But with the variables of author and case, there are recurring patterns and some constant elements. Judges present another variable in the total function of the brief. They and lawyers approach and use briefs differently, because their functions differ. It is not only the difference of reading and writing. It is the difference of advocacy and sitting in judgment. Some impressions of briefs and briefing from the judge's viewpoint may be helpful to the bar, which does not always know or fully comprehend what goes on behind the bench. That is the reason for this paper. But, as with all impressions, those given here can be helpful only if taken as such, not as "the law and the gospel."

The Oral Argument

These are days of the functional approach, an overworked but still meaningful term. It is proper therefore to start with the function of the brief. Because they are all part of the appellate process, that must be related to, though not identified with, the functions of the record and of the oral argument.

There is a clear difference between the function of the oral argument and that of the briefs. Lawyers, and clients, place much emphasis, and properly, on the former. The function of the oral presentation is controlled by two factors. One is its brevity. The other is the preparation with which the judge comes to it. That is determined, of course, by whether he has read the briefs, or them and the record, before the argument. If he has not done so, and unless the case is very simple, the argument generally can perform two functions.

One is to give the judge a bird's-eye view of the important facts. In this there is frequent failure. Often the argument becomes so clouded in a hodgepodge of basic facts and intricate factual detail, much of it irrelevant, that the judge who has not previously dug out the essential ones, cannot see the forest for the trees, the bushes, and the trailing arbutus. For him, this kind of argument is a total loss.

The other function, closely related to the first, is to bring out clearly the controlling issues in the case. This, in my judgment, is more than half the battle. But often it, too, is lost at the argument because the lawyer brings so many points to the court's attention. The result is he gets it for none. And occasionally the argument serves rather to confuse than to clarify the issues, not merely because of their number, but because the lawyer has not thought his case through to the real questions involved. If he had done so, there would not be so many. If the attorney succeeds in getting to the court a clear picture of the essential facts and in drawing out the real issues, his argument is a success. Occasionally he will be able to add to this something beyond casual reference to the pertinent authorities. But in the main not much can be done, especially by appellant's attorney, toward thorough discussion of previous decisions. In that situation, therefore, the time which remains after stating the facts and elucidating the issues is better devoted to discussion of them on controlling principles, with reliance on the brief for detailed substantiation.

An entirely different type of argument could be had, even in the short time allowed, if all the judges should come to the hearing thoroughly prepared on the facts and the law by previous reading of the record and briefs, and study of the issues and authorities. Then the statement of the facts could be omitted or highly skeletonized. The greater portion of time, on both sides, could be given to analysis of issues, discussion on principle, and argument from authority.

But presumably the "bird's-eye" type of argument is the more prevalent, and therefore the one for which, in general, preparation must be made. This has some consequences for the brief.

One is that the brief is the real presentation. If it does not have your case, the court is not apt to get it from the oral argument or otherwise, except in very sketchy form. That leads directly to the function of the brief as the most important element in the appeal, saving only and perhaps doubtfully the record. This has a direct relation to the function of the appeal itself, and the part of the record in it.

The Record

The proper purpose of an appeal is to secure a decision "whether or not one or the other of the parties has been ill used under the law."[1] This should be modified to say "so ill used under the law that the judgment should be reversed." For not every error is prejudicial or sufficiently so to require reversal. The purpose of the record on appeal is to tell the appellate court what happened at the trial and other previous stages of the litigation. It is to present "an authenticated story of the action and trial between John Doe and Richard Roe from their coming into court until their appeal to the higher court."[2] But, except rarely, it need not tell everything. It should tell enough, and seldom more than enough, to bring before the appellate tribunal a general view of the case as background or setting for the issues and a clear comprehension of the facts or incidents with respect to which it is claimed prejudicial error was made. With the practice recently adopted in the District of Columbia and previously in the Third and Fourth Circuit concerning printing of the record,[3] much of the formerly existing difficulty in this respect has disappeared. The appendices, together with the statements of fact in the briefs, generally give an adequate picture of the previous phases of the litigation. The bar has cooperated in this. Some lawyers have gone farther by submitting cases upon agreed statements of fact. These greatly relieve the court's burden. It is to be hoped the day has passed when, as was true with at least one case heard before the new rule took effect, the judges had to wade through ten volumes of printed record and index, each three inches or more thick. It is part of the lawyer's job, if he wants real and favorable consideration for his client's case, to have not only consideration, but some mercy, for the court. When he designates and prints such a mass of irrele-

---

[1] Stone, *The Scope of Review and Record on Appeal,* at page 4, found in Judicial Administration Monographs, Series A, No. 16, prepared under the auspices of The Special Committee on Improving the Administration of Justice of the American Bar Association.

[2] *Ibid.*

[3] Rule 17 of the General Rules of the United States Court of Appeals for the District of Columbia provides in part: "Unless ordered by this court, it shall not be necessary to print the record on appeal or on petition for review of or enforcement of an order, except that appellant shall print as a part of the appendix to his brief the pertinent pleadings and pertinent docket entries, the judgment or order appealed from or sought to be reviewed or enforced, together with any findings of fact, conclusions of law and opinion or charge of the court, board or commission."

vant material he is simply loading or unloading on the court's shoulders a task he is too lazy, too busy, or too lacking in perspective to do. Yes, judges do read the record—and the briefs. But occasionally they do it muttering through their teeth things they could not say aloud in Sunday School.

This criticism must be guarded. It is better to overload the record than to leave out something vital. At times that occurs. The lawyer, if he must err in this respect, should do so on the side of his client, rather than that of relieving the court. But this is a different thing from throwing in everything on the chance the court itself may fish out something the lawyer may miss. This shotgun practice may be a boomerang.

The Fact Function of the Brief

Now to turn to the brief. What is it supposed to do, how should it do it, and what should it not do? There are both "do's" and "don'ts."

Laying aside the formal requirements of the rules, the brief has several functions. Its basic one is to get to the court the lawyer's picture of the facts, analysis of the issues, and application of the law. If it does this, he wins. I should like to consider each of these phases separately, and at the outset with reference to the "do's."

First then, the lawyer's picture of the facts. The case is greatly simplified for all when the facts, or the essential ones, are not disputed. The agreed statement is appropriate for this situation. There are also many cases in which factual difference is limited to a few things—the bulk of the evidence is not controversial. In such cases an agreed statement, so far as it can go, likewise is helpful. I suspect it would be as much so to the lawyers as to the court if in every case they would approach the appeal in the spirit of the question, "How much can we agree upon?" rather than "How much can we fight about?"

But when the facts are generally and highly in dispute, whether because of conflicting evidence or because of conflicting inferences and interpretations, the fact function of the brief becomes important. It is so in any case where there is not either formally or substantially an agreed statement. This, in several respects.

In the first place, the appellant's attorney (or appellee's, if necessary) can set forth a connected statement of the essential facts. Here the brief can perform a "bird's-eye" function. It is a valuable one, especially when the record or appendix is long and complicated. Since the more detailed facts appear of record, the brief-writer does not fear that by failing to mention those he regards as immaterial or subordinate he will prejudice his client's cause. So he can freely and truly summarize. This often, and especially when well done, may be the most helpful, if not also the most important part of the brief. It cuts the brush away from the forest; it lifts the judge's vision over the foothills to the mountains. It enables him to read the record with an eye to the important things, intelligently, in true perspective.

Second, this phase of the brief gives opportunity for placing emphasis, that is, where the writer thinks it should be. What are not only the facts in bird's-eye view, but the most important facts? What are the Pike's Peaks and the Mount Pisgahs?

Again, what are the true facts? The jury and the trial tribunal have the major function here. But there are times when appellate tribunals must exercise some judgment about it. Perhaps for them it is most important in the matter of inferences and interpretation. How are the proven facts to be regarded? What other facts may be drawn, permissibly or rightly, from them?

Finally, and this is related to all the foregoing, what color shall be given to the facts? There are times when color, which is more than emphasis, more than truth, more than the bare fact itself in proof, gives meaning concealed or dimmed without it. In what light is this or that fact to be regarded? How is it affected by this or that other one or by the general complex? The brief gives the legal painter his chance. But it is a dangerous one if he attempts to apply color which is not on the palette of the case.

There is one thing more. The brief, as Justice Brandeis showed, is the instrument for bringing to the court's attention and knowledge facts not of record, but of which it may take judicial notice. Judges often are vastly ignorant of facts they know judicially. There is a wide difference between judicial knowledge and actual knowledge. In some, perhaps only a few, cases these are the crucial facts. This statement is not intended to invite a deluge of Brandeis briefs. But there should be more of them, and they need not all be long ones.

Mechanically, I have only one suggestion in respect to the factual portion of the brief. That is for accurate reference to the appendix (or record) for every statement of fact. The statement is worth that if it is worth making, and doing it is a great time saver for judges.

Analysis of the Issues

It is hard to generalize upon analysis of the issues. But I regard it as next in importance to stating the facts accurately, sufficiently and succinctly. If the real issues are not drawn out, or this is done only confusedly, the remainder of the brief becomes almost a total loss, except for the possibility that some case or other authority which gives light may be cited accidentally.

There is no way for one person to tell another how to analyze. In a large percentage of our briefs we have excellent analysis. But there are still too many in which it is only half or two-thirds done. There are a very few in which it amounts to less than that.

Two dangers may be selected for comment. The first is overanalysis. When a judge finds a brief which sets up from twelve to twenty or thirty issues or "points" or "assignments of error," he begins to look for the two or three, perhaps the one, of controlling force. Somebody has got lost in the underbrush and the judge has to get him—or the other fellow—out. That kind of brief may be labeled the "obfuscating" type. It is distinctly not the kind to use if the attorney wishes calm, temperate, dispassionate reason to emanate from the cloister. I strongly advise against use of this type of brief, consciously or unconsciously. Though this fault has been called overanalysis, it is really a type of underanalysis.

In the second place, a fairly common danger is concentrating so fully and completely on one's own picture of the facts and issues that one misses the big one or cannot see the merit of the other lawyer's. Occasionally this is done by the lawyers on both sides. The result is an argument in hiatus, and the gap may be the hole where the big issue is hiding.

So much for analysis, though one thing more may be added. If the case presents several issues regarded as important, it aids to indicate which are thought the more important. Again, this is a matter of emphasis for the brief.

The Argument

The third function of the brief is to apply the law—in other words, the argument proper. Given the facts, given right and true analysis, two functions remain, argument on principle and argument on authority.

Having been so long a teacher, the writer has a predilection for principle, though that does not imply a contempt for authority. Enlightenment in the former respect is absent more frequently than in the latter. Perhaps my own major criticism of briefs, apart from that relating to analysis, would be the lack of discussion on principle. Some cases are ruled so clearly by authority, directly in point and controlling, that discussion of principle is superfluous. But these are not many. It has been surprising to find how many appealed cases present issues not directly or exactly ruled by precedent. That is as it should be. The novel case is the one most appropriate for appeal, and on the whole the bar appears to exercise excellent discrimination in selecting such cases for appeal. In a large percentage of cases, therefore, there is room for discussion and thought as well as for citation.

Discussion on principle is related directly to analysis of facts. If that is clearly and fully made, the former follows almost automatically. What judges want to know is why this case, or line of cases, should apply to these facts rather than that other line on which the opponent relies with equal certitude, if not certainty. Too often the *why* is left out. The discussion stops with assertion that this case or line of cases rules the present one. Assertion is not demonstration. Beyond the amount necessary for statement of position and emphasis it may weaken both or indicate that the lawyer is doubtful of his position. "The lady doth protest too much." The argument which stops at this point may give judges the lead it is desired they follow. But it is bobtailed, nevertheless. The lead may be the wrong one, or the judge may think it such. The attorney's reasons for thinking it the right one may keep the judge out of error, if he can be saved. In a close case, where the authorities pertinent by analogy are conflicting and especially when they are equally pertinent and numerous on both sides, the discussion of the underlying principles as related to the present application counts heavily to swing the scales. In this connection a suggestion made later concerning the use of legal periodicals is apropos.

Finally, the authoritative function of the brief will be stated as shortly as possible.

1. When available, the cases in point—on all fours—are the ones courts want. If they are available, your way, and in quantity to settle the law,[4] citation and discussion of others waste your time and the court's.

There is one exception. That is when the law is settled the wrong way and one thinks he can play legal Don Quixote successfully. This has become a legal sport more popular in recent than in former years. But it is still a mountain-climbing, if not a windmill-tilting, sport and when one tries the climb perhaps anything goes, principle, law review articles, Brandeis briefs, what not. The climb is not recommended for everyday exercise.

2. When the case is not ruled directly by precedent, analogy must take over the functions of persuasion and decision. This is where much waste occurs. The cases most approximate are the ones needed. But approximation is always a matter of judgment and degree. It is the old question of "When is far too far?" When using cases by analogy (as well as otherwise) and relying heavily upon them, it is always wise to give, in one's own words, a brief *and* accurate statement of the facts. Half or more of the meaning of the case is lost unless this is done.

3. Referring again to what has been said about discussing principle, I suggest quite earnestly the more frequent and general citation of law review materials. By this is meant the notes and comments as well as the leading articles. When material pertinent to the case can be found, and it will seldom be lacking entirely, the legal periodicals have several distinct advantages for citation in the brief intended to win on appeal.

First, if a leading article or a good note or comment is in point on the case or on an issue, it will cite more pertinent cases than the average busy lawyer is likely to find through the digest or Corpus Juris. Its strictly authoritative value therefore is first-rate. But this presupposes citation of periodical material with the same dis-

[4] There is not space for digression to discuss pet theories of *stare decisis*. But one decision doesn't always give set to the law. Perhaps it seldom does. It was nearly fifty years before the law as to the scope of interstate commerce and Congress' power over it assumed sufficient stability to be reliable as precedent in matters of federal power to regulate business activities, particularly in manufacturing.

crimination used in citing cases; in other words, it is the article in point, or closely sold, which is helpful. For assistance in locating it, the Index to Legal Periodicals is available.

Again, an article or comment in point does something more than any single case can do. A case is an incident in the history of a principle or principles. It indicates or illustrates, but it does not define or comprehend a trend. It is merely a link in a chain. A good article gives one, in addition to good citations, the history of an idea, the background of an institution, the evolution of a principle, and lines of discrimination for its application. In a recent case in which case authority was scarce, involving difficult questions of administrative law and procedure, the writer found more help in three law review articles than in all the case law and the statutes. They gave the legislative history of the agency and the administrative history of its functioning. These could not have been secured from the strictly authoritative materials. Nor could one have found them otherwise without weeks of investigation, which a busy judge often does not have to give and perhaps would not feel free to make if time were available.

Finally, though other advantages might be mentioned, law review materials, especially leading articles and notes, give superior analysis of problems and discussion of their legal disposition on principle. The "professor" still gets the raspberry. Too often it is more rasp than berry. The "college-boy" editor or author still supplies sport for the practical man of the law. But the professor is by way of becoming respectable in law in this country, somewhat as his European colleagues were before academic freedom, and with it the great influence of the universities, disappeared from the Continent. Regardless of whose "hot dogs" they may be, the college-boy lawyers and law teachers are showing every day briefs and oral arguments as able as any courts read and hear. This is due in part to their mastery and use of law review methods and materials.

Miscellaneous Suggestions

There are a few "do's" and a few "don'ts" for further mention, which may assist in disclosing something of the judge's point of view.

1. Be brief, that is, concise—but not too brief. By this is meant being as brief as one can consistently with adequate and clear presentation of his cause.

2. Be candid. That applies to both facts and law. Nothing, perhaps, so detracts from the force and persuasiveness of an argument as for the lawyer to claim more than he is reasonably entitled to claim. Do not "stretch" cases cited and relied upon too far, making them appear to cover something to your benefit they do not cover. Do not try to dodge or minimize unduly the facts which are against you. If one cannot win without doing this—and it is seldom he can by doing it—the case should not be appealed. It is equally bad to give evasive answers to questions at oral argument. Conversely, few things add strength to an argument as does candid and full admission, whether as to facts or law, of the factors which are clearly against one. When this is made, judges know that the lawyer is worthy of full confidence, and every sentence he utters or writes carries force from the very fact that he makes it.

3. It helps to break the monotony of the printed legal page to add a bit of life now and then. Recently a brief characterized an opponent's argument as "splitting a legal hair the wrong way." That gave me a kick for a day. Now and then there is a bit of unconscious humor. It is better, from the judge's viewpoint, to have that than not any.

A few "don'ts" may be mentioned, some already touched upon.

First, as to quotations from prior opinions. I am tempted to say simply, "Don't." But that would be going too far. Generally the long ones should be omitted. Judges, too, can read the opinions, particularly if they are cited. Again, generally speaking, leave out the abstract ones. By this is meant quotations from opinions usually are meaningless, or nearly so, unless accompanied by thumbnail sketches of the important facts of the case. Meaning then becomes concrete and definite. The case takes point from the facts. Without them, to paraphrase Holmes, it is "brooding ambiguity in the skies." "Thumbnailing" is an art, and all too uncommon.

Again, avoid overstatement and repetition, except for the proper uses of emphasis. Frequently judges are able to understand the statement after the third reiteration, that is, if it is understandable.

Finally, avoid as much as possible stilted legal language, the "thereins," "thereofs," "whereinbefores," "hereinafters," and what-have-you's. Use English wherever you can express the idea as well and as concisely as in law or Latin. A healthy respect for the robust Anglo-Saxon appeals more than does the Latin, whether or not it is Anglicized. The home-grown product in this case is better than the imported, not to say smuggled, one. But law has its vocabulary and that has its proper uses. Technical legal terms and phrases often shorthand ideas otherwise to be stated only with circumlocution and loss of meaning. Then one should "talk like a lawyer." But the abuse comes when good, simple English will do the work of the term of art just as well. The readability of Holmes and Cardozo is due in part to their mastery of the native tongue and subjugation of the acquired language of the law.

All that has been said comes down about to this, make your briefs clear, concise, honest, balanced, buttressed, convincing and interesting. The last is not least. A dull brief may be good law. An interesting one will make the judge aware of this. The real way to discuss briefs profitably would be to exemplify them. The brief, and its merit, are always relative to the particular case. It is the rare brief that leaves judges uninformed, confused (more than before they read it), or irritated. Happily, the general effect makes one proud to be a member of the profession, though as a judge separated somewhat from its most active life. Through lawyers as lenses judges see the causes of their clients. If they fail to see them truly, as often as not it is their vision, not the lens, which is defective. But in unison, vision and lens reflect the picture of the life they serve and, may we hope, guard to some extent from the dangers which sweep over and throughout a storm-tossed world. Lawyers too are judges of the people.

Adapted from Vol. 28, American Bar Association Journal (1942).

Tactics in Appellate Briefs

By John Alan Appleman

If there are any general rules which would serve as a general rule to the attorney having his first case upon review, they would, I am sure, be the following: (1) be brief; (2) be specific; (3) be courteous; (4) be persuasive. Other matters are important also and worthy of consideration, but these four rules are indispensable landmarks.

It is a truism that two men cannot write a single brief. It must be considered and integrated as a unit. There may be two or 12 counsel upon a single case, but they cannot divide the responsibilities with each writing a separate portion and combining them for printing as many lawyers attempt to do. No such attorney then has a complete grasp of the entire effort. The contents and styles are frequently inconsistent, and the brief is always shapeless and sprawling. It is not the best possible work.

One attorney must demand and receive full responsibility for the brief. His must be the approach adopted. His must be the hand which shapes the result. A brief should be a work of art simple to the point of concealing art—but conceived, directed and polished by a single artist. Can one conceive of a single landscape painted with the brushes of many masters? With their varying approaches, points of view and techniques the resulting canvas would be disclaimed by the merest art student. And most attorneys, even those appearing in higher courts, are scarcely "artists" in their profession.

If there are co-counsel, they still may examine the brief prior to printing. Their comments, suggestions and criticisms may be of help to the one who labored. He should be patient of such comments and recall that like reactions may occur to the judge of the reviewing court, and in an even less favorable vein, since he is not a protagonist. But if a conflict in views develops, the one who has assumed the responsibility must retain it even to the point of overruling the family attorney. The expert cannot guarantee success, of course. He can almost assuredly guarantee failure if ill-advised views are followed. He has no right to jeopardize the client's cause nor his own reputation by deferring, through courtesy or otherwise, to bad judgment.

The situation will frequently arise where one is called into a case to be reviewed following its trial by another attorney. He labors, therefore, under a double handicap. First, he is concluded by the record established by such counsel—his theories, pleadings and failure to object properly or to make required motions. In short, he is called upon to shape the roof of a house which another has erected. Second, an attorney must know the case so well and intimately that it is part of him. This is difficult to do with another's case where one has not seen the witnesses, heard the evidence or shared in the heat of battle. Yet he is no more handicapped than are the reviewing judges to whom it is also an alien matter. In that respect he has the advantage of viewing the case with dispassion, and gleaning that which is worthwhile from the cold language of the record by which the higher court will also be restricted.

But the reviewing attorney must become thoroughly cognizant of every matter in the record. He cannot fumble in his briefs. He cannot equivocate upon oral argument. He must know everything which is in the record, whether favorable or adverse. He must be in a position to admit freely that which is adverse but immaterial. He must be in a position to select that which constitutes the meat of the appeal, to form conclusions as to the direction of attack of defense, and to crystallize a point of view which is logical, understandable and appealing. These things he cannot do by a cursory examination of any transcript.

Legal Research

Patience marks the appellate lawyer, even as it does the trial court advocate. He must study the law exhaustively, not only to determine that which is favorable and that which is adverse, but to determine the reasons which underlie the doctrines which he will urge. My conception of legal research differs from that of many lawyers. It does not consist, I feel, of assembling a vast body of quotable precedents, but the selection of worthwhile authority which supports the logic or justice of a position urged. Perhaps this sounds confusing. If so, let me make it clear.

Every doctrine in law stems from a fundamental root or underlying principle. Frequently, loose thinking or tangential reasoning incubated by resort to precedent cited without study has produced some fabulous offshoots from the original root. Therefore, I recommend in all cases that one study not only the most recent cases, but that he see what leading cases that court relies upon and go to those older cases and trace the doctrine down through the English common law, if necessary, or even to the Roman law. It clarifies one's own thinking. It does not require a vast body of precedents for citation to the reviewing court. However, a tracing of the historical development showing where the tangent abruptly developed, and how a rule grounded in logic suddenly became illogical, will frequently result in bringing the court back to a re-establishment of the original doctrine.

For another reason I like to go back to very old cases. Whenever the construction of a statute or a question of constitutionality is involved, I find it most helpful to search the ancient and scholarly legal digests for that state and to trace down the first three decisions which dealt with the provision at issue. Those judges, faced with a question of first impression, were forced to reason out the fundamental meanings of that law. Such reasoning frequently is most helpful to the appellate lawyer.

But I do not believe in limiting research wholly to the old cases. I want to know what are the most recent authorities in the field, including the very latest decisions in the advance sheets. One may construct a beautiful house of cards, only to have it demolished by the court's latest pronouncement.

In this study of the law, it is a great mistake to search only for that which is favorable. One should search out adverse authorities as well. Then he must compare the facts of favorable cases with those of unfavorable ones and see what constitutes the line of demarcation. Until he finds the dividing line and realizes what makes a case fall upon one side or the other, the appellate attorney cannot possibly adopt a successful theory of the case. He cannot create a logical line of approach. Nor is he in any position to rebut his adversary until he can understand the reason underlying the opposing authorities. And he need not think wishfully that his opponent will find no such cases. He must anticipate the most able opposition. Even if his opponent is befuddled, the court may not be.

This exhaustive study is necessary for even a most basic comprehension of the law. Most attorneys read words—they do not read the history of our civilization as written in the pages of those decisions. Frequently they do not even check the statutes to see what changes have occurred therein which might account for a changing attitude of the courts, nor do they check the procedures to see how a new and apparently inconsistent line of authority developed.

As a brief example of such a situation, Illinois jury instructions which refer to the issues made by the pleadings are now held erroneous, unless an instruction is given expressly defining the issues. Many attorneys have been deluded into a contrary belief by old cases which held reference to the pleadings unobjectionable. But a study of courtroom procedure at that period of judicial history discloses that the pleadings were then sent to the jury room, along with exhibits and instructions, so that a reference to the pleadings created no confusion. This custom having changed, the reason for the judicial rule altered and the permissible instructions are, accordingly, varied.

Changing uses, social customs and economic conditions likewise create new judicial approaches. What was sound law to Charles Evans Hughes may appeal differently to Felix Frankfurter, with both of them acting in highest good faith. Like it or not, lawyers must realize that courts do not operate in a vacuum. Social thinking definitely affects judicial results. If they expect to win litigation, lawyers must be aware of the social, economic and political consequences of their contentions. Blinding themselves to these factors neither demonstrates intelligence nor wins lawsuits.

The element of predictability enters along this line of research and adoption of a theory of procedure. Seldom are courts in a fixed juridical channel. Usually the jurisprudence in any area is in a state of flux. I have often compared it to the swing of a pendulum. Usually it is either rising or falling. The last appropriate decision may not have gone far enough or it may have gone too far. Courts, like lawyers, have human frailties. Either they are too timid and approach the logical by little nibbles, or they overthrow an old principle with great abandon and then cautiously retreat.

One must determine which way the pendulum is swinging, and help to move it in the right direction.

Bearing these various elements in mind, including the purpose of research, I suggest finally that the appellate lawyer also read leading law review articles and textbooks bearing upon his subject. To my mind, this study should remain until near the last. It is too apt to formulate one's own thinking and to mold it irrevocably to the point where original thought is no longer possible. This result I deem bad, particularly since some books and articles written today are ground out by the editorial staffs of some law publishers which are comprised of young lawyers who have lacked practical experience in the legal field in question. There are, of course, scholarly books—Scott's *Trusts and Trustees* is one—and astute articles by experts in a given field, or even those written by nonspecialists who, nevertheless, are thoughtful attorneys aware of the importance of the problem. While one should not burden a court with a mass of such references, a single cogent article or a statement of a recognized authority will carry great weight.

Last, in the matter of research, is the statutory law. One must check carefully to be certain that no vital statutory reference has been omitted. Frequently, a single statute which is directly in point will dispose of a dozen speculations. An attorney must learn how to use statutory indices, and to search every potential word-lead in order to find the available law. He must be able to trace the history of legislation in order to study the discussions and learn the purpose intended and the legislative desire. Then, he must search out the meanings of the words employed, through such works as *Words and Phrases*. He must fit himself to think as a lawyer, to reason as a man of wisdom, and to express himself so persuasively that men will listen to his words and be persuaded by them.

Selecting Angle of Attack or Defense

Lawyers tend to act too quickly and to think too little. It is necessary, before writing a brief, first to reason out fully the exact attack the appeal should take. Every appeal, or defense of an appeal, must revolve around one key point—with possibly two or three important, but subordinate, secondary lines of attack or defense. If one has reasoned through his case prior to the filing of suit in the lower court, these lines may have been crystallized except for such errors as may have occurred upon trial. Largely, however, one approaches an appeal with new eyes, and must gaze upon the problems as if he were a stranger interested in them only academically. He must twist and turn each point so that its facets gleam in the light to catch any reflected flaw. He must meditate upon the case, seek out weaknesses and determine the path of approach. The ultimate theory must be simple, logical, accurate and appealing to one's sense of equity. Then he is ready to begin serious thinking about the drafting of the required documents.

But this does not mean gazing upon the main point with such fixation as to induce self-hypnosis. The research and muttering meditation one has done doubtless has raised many questions in his mind. One must use his ingenuity, imagination and resourcefulness to be certain that he comprehends every possible avenue of attack and reasons out the worthiness of every approach. For example, many statutes have been held valid against attack over periods of decades. Then, suddenly, a new line of attack upon them is presented and invalidity is declared.

For example, a few years ago in a case of first impression I raised two points upon appeal: (1) that the State of Illinois could not recover in a case because it had already been reimbursed; (2) that a statute which had many times been held valid had become unconstitutional by reason of certain amendments and changes in judicial construction. The court evaded the second question to hold me on the first. Another attorney, a few months ago, having no other avenue for attack, limited himself to an attack upon constitutionality and succeeded by a five-to-two decision.

Once one has determined his procedure, from that moment on he cannot equivocate. *Alea acta est.* He must isolate the important point. He must make it crystal clear. He must refuse to be led off upon tangents and not permit a court to be so misled.

Weeding Out the Immaterial

But one must not employ any self-delusion in determining what constitutes the controlling issue. He must face the weaknesses of his case squarely. Few cases presented to a trial court are perfect. As a general rule, they do not improve in a higher court. The adversary's case may have weaknesses also, but one seldom gains a victory merely by punching holes in the case of the opposition.

The appellate attorney will, at least 85 per cent of the time, win upon the strength of his case rather than upon the weakness of the opposing case. Therefore, it is better not to be unduly alarmed over the fragmentary weaknesses which may exist or to try to hide them. Their uprooting by the opponent will magnify their size and betray your alarm. It is far better to expose the weaknesses casually and candidly—then point out how they are met, either factually or as a matter of law, and demonstrate their inconsequence in view of the bulwark of the case.

For the same reason, one must be willing to slough off petty or immaterial differences, to concede the unimportant and to waive the trivial. One who speaks at length about 20 minor errors which would not be of reversible character takes the sharp focus of attention away from a matter of major concern. A single error is all that is required. One who uses either a shotgun attack or defense is felt to be acting in desperation, or else to be beclouded in his approach—if indeed, the judges do not regard him as pettifogging. Therefore, the immaterial error made by one's opponent in stating facts and the inconsequential mistake of a court (a minor deviation upon a tangential issue) should be waved aside and, if possible, with magnanimity which is observable. Of course, one must be careful never to waive any matter nor to stipulate as to any fact which is so crucial to his case as to require his defeat.

Pursuing a similar line of reasoning, one must recognize that justice could lie with the cause of his adversary, were certain material facts slightly different. One who is incapable of appreciating the position of his opponent is a dullard. Mere stubbornness will not persuade courts of review, nor will dogged reiteration of a hornbook principle necessarily convince judges that an applicable situation is presented in the instant case.

As previously pointed out, one must recognize where the line of demarcation arises which separates a case upon one side of a proposition from one reaching a contrary result. He must select out and point up the material facts which cause his case to fall upon the desired side. He must be prepared to concede graciously that the general principle for which his opponent contends is a proper one and, if only these particular facts were different, he would be in accord with his opponent's views. But, because of these certain facts (spot-lighting them), the case is brought within some doctrine which directs a contrary result.

Judges, being lawyers, are by nature argumentative. They are repelled by flat and obstinate contentions. Subconsciously, they begin to find for themselves the flaws in such reasoning and to dig out the limitations of such doctrines. But a logical and precise exposition which recognizes the limitations of the applicable doctrines and focuses attention upon the controlling facts is appealing to the judges. They follow the reasoning of such an attorney with interest. They are persuaded that he is a lawyer of discernment, and are usually convinced that he is right—which he will be, unless his analysis is a purely specious one.

As a result of his preliminary analysis and the more final approach the attorney has weeded out worthless contentions from his brief. He will not advance something which the court has no authority to decide. For example, he will not urge a question which has not been preserved properly for review. Where the authority of an intermediate court is limited so that it cannot pass upon constitutional issues or freehold questions, he will not waste its time by discussing these issues. In the Supreme Court of the United States, where the review is limited to questions of law, he will not argue that the court of appeals was in error upon the facts, but will accept the facts as stated in its opinion as correct. By eliminating false issues, the attorney does three things: (1) He avoids wasting his own energies and those of the court upon false issues; (2) he brings into sharp focus the vital questions which the court has power to decide; (3) he avoids a "loss of face" in the eyes of the court by knowing the extent of its jurisdiction.

These are not trivial or unusual mistakes. Almost every advance sheet I pick up is replete with cases where attorneys have been guilty of such errors. It is as grave a mistake as if a physician opened an abdominal cavity to remove a pair of tonsils. The lawyer who realizes he cannot file an injunction suit with a policy magistrate should be equally familiar with the jurisdiction of his courts of review. No court wants to commit error, and a reviewing court would have little feeling of confidence in rendering a decision in favor of an attorney so little astute as to be unaware of the questions proper for that court's consideration.

One must approach the court with frankness, as well. If a case presents a question of first impression, say so candidly and say it immediately. Instead of reaching grotesquely for a wealth of attentuated authority and reasoning by ill-chosen analogy, inform the court in the inception that whatever its ruling may be it is about to create new law in that jurisdiction. It will quicken the interest of the court. It will bring a certain excitement to those who have to paddle around with bare feet daily in the puddles of muddled precedent.

Similarly, if it is absolutely essential to your success that a particular case be overruled, be candid in that regard as well. Nine times out of ten such drastic action will not be necessary. If it is vital, it is usually better to precede the request with an orderly development of the situation that leaves no alternative in logic and justice but to grant the final request. Then, if the precedent is absolutely indistinguishable, a court will respect the honesty of the lawyer who admits that fact and who states bluntly that the case represents bad law. There are many poor decisions upon the books today. Courts do not hesitate to overthrow them if necessary. However, I must confess that as many or more bad decisions are being rendered daily, and possibly we as lawyers are responsible for many of them.

Human Aspects of Appellate Practice

To my mind, the most important single aspect in successful appellate practice is what I would term the "human" aspect or approach to a case upon appeal. This may be a trifle difficult to explain, but I consider it of such great importance that I want to spend some time upon it. If there is any single "secret" of appellate practice, it lies in this factor.

When I was younger and more scholarly, I wrote masterly appellate briefs and lost my cases. I exhausted the law and the judges. The briefs were lengthy, literate and cold. Then, suddenly, one day I made a great discovery which altered my entire approach to appellate practice. I discovered that judges were human beings.

This is not intended to be a facetious statement. Those of us who practice law, and particularly younger lawyers, are too prone to regard appellate court judges as remote beings in some far-off firmament, unapproachable and distant—invested with different types of minds with a queer type of reasoning mechanism studded with scalpel-like edges which automatically cuts out the meat of relevant decisions for use in an appropriate situation. Thus, we would pour in a volume of their raw meat—that is, *stare decisis*—

and wait for the wheels to spin around and the knives to start cutting. To our disappointment, the diet was inadequate and the opinions seemed undernourished.

Other lawyers besides myself have been guilty of this cardinal error. The case which glowed with life before a jury undergoes a strange mutation upon appeal and becomes as dry as Death Valley. Perhaps 12 men and women upon a jury and a trial judge saw it not as dry and uninteresting, but as a warmly human story, gripping in its interest. They saw a need for justice. They felt a "rightness" about it which made it, to them, more than merely an article of legal machinery.

Then why approach the judges of higher courts differently? They are merely jurors with legal training. They are merely your trial judges elevated to a higher court. They are still charged with the same passions, sympathies, emotions and reactions which denote them as men. When they doff the judicial robes and sit in the bar at the country club or sit in the grandstand rooting at a baseball game, no one looks askance at them as being strange or unusual. Being human beings and normal men, they must be approached the same as one would approach any other judge or juror from whom he is asking justice.

I ask that the reader apply the principle I am about to expound with some seasoning of common sense, bearing in mind the formal restrictions of printed briefs. But, subject to that limitation, forget that you are talking to a court of estimable men of great stature. Think of them as a jury. Then bring to your presentation the same points of appeal, the same persuasion and the same heart-stirring factors that you would present to a jury. Nine times out of ten, legal factors being somewhat equal, if the jury would be persuaded the higher court will be as well.

This is, perhaps, because both approaches rest upon the same basic or fundamental principles of salesmanship. These principles are simple. First, one must capture attention immediately. He must then kindle interest in his case. Last, he must induce conviction. That is the art of persuasion, whether it be a jury or a higher court which is the audience.

This means that the lawyer must inspire his audience with a powerful feeling of rightness or wrongness—either that his cause is eminently fair and that justice will permit only a result favorable to his client, or that there is something so wrong in his adversary's position that a holding for his adversary would result in a flagrant miscarriage of justice. All law is directed fundamentally toward the goal of achieving justice. If it does not, there is some shortcoming resulting from the efforts of either those who have created the law or those who have construed it. In these days, with law and equity irretrievably intertwined and with citations available to support almost any conceivable side of a case, the opinion will almost invariably go to the one upon whose side justice seems to rest.

Corollary to this, it should be recognized that judges are also motivated by fears. To achieve a successful result, one must prevent any of these fears from consciously or unconsciously interfering with a favorable decision. He should also, wherever possible, stimulate one or more of such fears into action against the result sought by his adversary. Since these elements are self-explanatory, I will not examine them in detail, but will merely list them: (1) the fear of working an injustice to a party to the case; (2) the fear of appearing absurd by misconstruing or misapplying the facts; (3) the fear of misunderstanding or misapplying the law; (4) the fear of creating an absurd or embarrassing precedent; (5) the fear of untoward social or economic consequences.

Preparing the Brief

Bearing these general principles in mind, there is perhaps one word which signifies to me the most important attribute which an attorney must bring to his case. That word is "sincerity." To induce conviction in others, one must himself be convinced. No contention will bear the close scrutiny of intelligent men which is not advanced with complete honesty. This does not mean that one should become so thoroughly the advocate that he becomes unfair or dishonest either in the discussion of facts or in his analysis of controlling law. To the contrary, it requires frankness with the court, an ability to recognize that which is unfavorable and honest reasons for believing justice is with one's cause despite such factors. I have seen honestly mistaken lawyers win cases upon appeal by the ardor of their conviction, but I do not personally recall ever having seen a successful appeal conducted by an attorney with tongue in cheek.

In this regard there are several common types of errors, at least one or more of which will occur in 75 per cent of briefs filed upon appeal, which, if not fatal to the chances of success will at least diminish the possibilities of victory. They are as follows:

(1) Inaccuracy. In this category I would include such matters as an inaccurate or grossly biased statement of the facts in issue either which the court will discover for itself or which opposing counsel will seize upon with gusto, to the detriment of the guilty lawyer. Omission of vital data, misquotation of the evidence and distortion of occurrences in the proceedings must be so classified. Similarly, the citation of cases for propositions which they will not support upon scrutiny, the quotation of evidence or of the language of cases out of context and similar conduct must necessarily breed distrust of the attorney attempting to better his position through such perversions.

(2) Exaggeration. This error is closely related to the first point, but is distinguishable from it in that the conduct is a matter of degree, rather than of total misrepresentation. It has long been evident that stage or cinema performers who underact walk off with the laurels in preference to the chronic ham. A customer instinctively distrusts the overeloquent salesman who puts on the pressure, and tends to deal with the diffident salesman who knows the worth of his product but leaves some discretion as to purchasing with his customer. So it is with higher courts who are asked to "buy" upon the lawyer's presentation. Unwarrantable exaggeration of either the facts or the law, the overcoloring of a situation presented, overemotionalism, hysteria, or screaming either at a lower court or at opposing counsel predispose the reviewing court toward one's adversary.

(3) Loss of personal or professional dignity. Above all, a lawyer, as an officer of the court, is supposed to be a gentleman. Gentlemen do not engage in verbal brawls more suited to alleys than to the rostrum of a court of last resort. If one's adversary has grossly misrepresented the facts, a proper showing of the facts will confound him. It adds nothing to characterize him as a perjurer or trickster. The higher court will draw its own conclusions. Nor does a bitter attack upon a trial judge, who is helpless to defend himself against such attack, advance one's cause. It will create only sympathy in the hearts of his brethren upon the appellate tribunal. Even if a brief is not stricken for libelous, scurrilous, profane, in-

sulting or unpleasant language, or for a resort to personalities, it still has not advanced the cause of such counsel. Indeed, the psychological reaction is such that if the adversary has even a modicum of support from the law and evidence he is almost certain to succeed.

To add briefly to the foregoing rules, there are certain other general principles which it is well for lawyers to remember in their brief-writing. In referring to any case relied upon as authoritative, it is well to give the facts of such case to show that it is apropos. There should be no deliberate or even inadvertent omission of a detrimental fact, or one which would alter the applicability of it as a precedent. The case should not be quoted out of context, nor language omitted which would destroy the effect of the quotation. It then becomes a thrice-fold dangerous weapon in the hands of one's opponent. At no time should one ever attempt to mislead the court. Not only will it lead to a loss in the particular case, but it will stamp such attorney with a brand which will jeopardize his chances in all future cases before that court. Particularly is it not clever to distort the language of recent decisions rendered by that tribunal. The justice writing such an opinion will become righteously indignant, and an implacable enemy may sway the judgment of several others having a passive belief in the soundness of your position.

Creating an Interesting Brief

The lives of appellate court judges are not enviable ones, considering the dry cases which come before them and even drier briefs which they must peruse. Nor can attention be more than half focused upon a boring brief. Even if it seems to be somewhat logical, it will seldom leave the judge with any compelling urge to decide the cause in the manner urged.

For that reason, I lay down a first commandment: "Make your brief interesting." There is no reason why it must be dull. Determine that the court will enjoy your brief, that it will become interested in your side of the controversy and that it will be sympathetic with your client. Fiction writing, it is said, depends little upon plot. It depends, rather, upon characterization—the creation of believable persons in whose problems the reader becomes engrossed, in whom he is interested and whom he wants to see emerge triumphant. If the same general reaction can be produced in the breasts of the judges, the case is half won. If no other results follow such a presentation will incline the judges to your side of the controversy for the simple reason that you have stimulated them—that you have created an oasis in the desert of pedantry.

Of course, to determine what will produce a favorable emotional reaction upon the part of judges one must consider their backgrounds and temperaments as reflected by their past decisions and actions. Pierce Butler and McReynolds, for example, were ultra-conservative. The cries of invasion of the Constitution, the tearing down of tradition, the creation of new and dangerous precedents and the destruction of laissez faire would have produced a rather favorable reaction. On the other hand, Justice Hugo Black and the late Frank Murphy reflect powerful convictions of the sanctity of personal liberty, constitutional safeguards and due process. If the case shows any overreaching of the rights of the individual, that would constitute the key to their judicial doors. Justice Jackson is extremely rational and logical. He would be repelled by glittering generalities and insist upon correct facts, exact logic and precise law. Justice Frankfurter would demand a lucid explanation of the position of that case in the historical development of the applicable jurisprudence, considering the overtones and implications of decisions not wholly consistent with each other.

It may be that you cannot wage war upon all fronts simultaneously. By doing so, one might lose the interest of all members of the court. It may well be that it is better to realize precisely which judges will be attracted by your factual or legal situation, and to slant your presentation in an effort to woo those particular judges, hoping to capture enough others to secure a majority. While the temperaments of judges vary from state to state, a lawyer practicing in any state will shortly be able to deduce rather accurate conclusions which may stand him in good stead by keeping abreast of his advance sheets and noting the language and reasoning of his local judges.

Irrespective of the situation presented or of the question of judicial temperament, it is still possible to make a brief interesting to all persons. Short sentences (not to the point of a staccato style but to the extent of clarity), short paragraphs, well organized material, frequent section headings and simple but exact words are all conducive to read interest. In addition, there is the use of simple dramatic art in one's expression. For example, instead of starting out with a lot of rigamarole in the statement of facts concerning the pleadings, how much more effective it would be to start off simply: "Upon April 16, 1948, John Smith stopped at the corner cigar-store. It was closed. He started across the street and died under the wheels of defendant's car." One can expand from that beginning, but the court visualizes the scene; you have its attention.

Then, once one has attracted the court's attention, interest must be maintained. To this end, the key point (the direction of attack) must be kept constantly in mind. It must be isolated so that the court is not bewildered by trying to follow an attorney who ducks through mazes and back alleys in driving toward his objective. Stay away from tangents. Neither introduce them nor permit yourself or the court to be led astray upon them. Recognize them for what they are. As any golf pro will tell you: "Keep your eye on the ball."

There are courts of last resort which are absolutely bound by the factual determinations of intermediate courts. Our United States Supreme Court is one of such courts. In such event, one of the most common tangents or rabbit-trails which attorneys pursue is to argue an error upon the part of the intermediate court in its statement of facts. One must bow to the inevitable. It is easier to walk around a boulder than to bump one's head against it and expect it to give way. When no purpose is to be gained by arguing something which has been concluded, rightly or wrongly, it is better to argue something upon which one has a chance of success. Not only is much energy conserved, but the court is not given an initial negative impression of the limitations of counsel's knowledge.

Stylistic Matters

Insofar as it is possible, an identical order should be followed in presenting the issues in the case, propositions of law, and argument. In each instance, it is conducive to a logical presentation to break the questions down and to identify them by the use of Roman numerals, letters and Arabic numbers if subheadings are necessary. Thus, if II A in each section of the brief is the same heading, it becomes simple for the court to find related discussion and authorities. While this is not always possible, it is a good goal to strive for.

Rather than have many pages of discussion upon unrelated issues, it is desirable to stop each discussion at a dramatic point and place a different subject under its appropriate heading. Usually one will find no subdivisions, in the average brief, under either statement of facts, points and authorities, or argument. The court necessarily approaches the reading of such a brief with a sigh. It appears to be long and boring. But, if each portion is broken down into relatively short segments with explanatory and persuasive headings, the reading of such a brief induces pleasure. It also induces conviction.

For the same reason, it is desirable to avoid paragraphs which ramble on for pages. Modest-sized paragraphs make a more readable page. They permit a greater continuity of thought by stopping at the close of one idea and starting a new approach in a separate grouping. They add emphasis, which invariably falls upon the first and last sentences in any paragraph.

Lengthy sentences should be avoided. This does not require a resort to a choppy style, but it does require simplicity. It is difficult to retain the sense of a single sentence for a hundred words. The mere fact that the English system of punctuation permits the use of commas and semicolons does not require the omission of periods. Both the brief-writer and the court require a second wind from time to time.

Even a short sentence may not be clear, and clarity is of the utmost importance. For example: "The plaintiff pushed the defendant, and a struggle ensued in which he was injured." To whom does "he" refer? The attorneys may know, but this is an alien controversy to the court. Lawyers are habitually vague, and their chronic use of dangling parenthetical expressions, in accurate use of diction and disregard of fundamental principles of punctuation result in considerable confusion which could easily be avoided. It would be well, prior to the printing of any brief, to have it read critically for clarity by a high school rhetoric teacher or by a newspaper editor. The resulting red pencil comments frequently would require a complete revision.

From a stylistic point of view, it is well occasionally to use an odd but accurate sentence structure, an epigrammatic expression, or an unusual word which requires the court to stumble and stop for greater emphasis. Too great fluency may cause the court to skim material which is deserving of greater consideration. An artificial device of this type should be used seldom, but it may have occasional value. In this category I would place the rhetorical question. Used once, it may be splendid; twice it is of lesser value; three times, and out.

Quotations either from the transcript or from cases must necessarily fall into a similar category. If longer than a single sentence, they should always be indented. First, they shorten the textual paragraph; second, they break up the page for greater readability; third, they attract attention. Of course, too many sign posts confuse the traveller.

Upon the questionable side of attention catchers, must be placed the twin demons of inexperienced brief-writers—italics and bold face. Most of us, in adolescence, received love letters from equally immature girls which read somewhat as follows: "My *darling,* you *know* how *much* I *miss* you."

The brief studded with italics and bold face seems equally immature. Certainly, there is a key word which is the crux of a situation, attention may be directed to it by some unusual device. But one should not use bold face to indicate that he is raising his voice, nor use as a sledge to hammer home his points. It is better to let the subject matter or the manner of approach and discussion create the emphasis without artificial aids.

Personally, I have a different tool which I believe is much more valuable as an aid to clarity. I believe strongly in visual appeal. The better trial lawyers make extensive use of demonstrative evidence—charts, diagrams, photographs, X-rays, skeletons, blackboards, motion pictures and any other possible visual devices to create understanding visually. If used with extreme moderation, similar devices may be equally effective in higher courts, particularly if forceful in character. Perhaps a single enlarged photograph, comparing two disputed signatures, inserted directly in the brief or in an appendix may swing the result. A few charts illustrating graphically the opposing contentions of the parties and the result which would follow in each instance may be of assistance. The comparison of the problem to a single algebraic formula, substituting elements in the legal problem for that in the mathematical, may produce a *reductio ad absurdum.* The ingenuity of counsel will suggest other methods. The tests to apply are: (1)

simplicity; (2) clarity; (3) good judgment; (4) dramatic impact.

One must, on the other hand, avoid interrupting the train of thought of the reviewing court when it is hotly pursuing the theory advanced by him. Interruption at such a time, is most dangerous. Going off upon a tangent is one such danger to which attention has already been called. Another is by using such expressions as *supra, infra, ibid.,* and neglecting to repeat a citation. That is one method of creating increased blood pressure upon the part of the interested judge. In such an instance, it is always well to indicate that the case has been cited previously, but always repeat at least the official citation. Such reference would then read: "Smith v. Jones, *infra,* 106 U. S. 204 at 210."

Last, one cannot overemphasize the importance of vocabulary. It has frequently been said by psychologists that the size of one's vocabulary expresses his degree of intellect. The point is not to display one's erudition by employing polysyllabic expressions, but to use exact words conveying the precise meaning intended to be conveyed. Careless expressions, sloppy diction and inaccurate words all contribute greatly to the misfortunes of lawyers attempting to present points of precision. Usually, these are evidences of loose thinking. If the guilty attorney in such instance should succeed, despite himself, it is usually due to either pressure upon the court from overwork or poor footwork by his adversary. When not due to loose thinking, such inaccuracies usually may be blamed upon an inadequate vocabulary. No man who works with words as tools the way a lawyer does should be satisfied with less than an excellent vocabulary. A good carpenter could not use a saw of which half the teeth were broken, nor could he smooth a board properly with a dull plane. A lawyer's tools, also, should be adequate for their task.

Delicate Nuances of Brief Writing

A successful brief will 90 per cent of the time reflect courtesy, respect, dignity and calm—not only as pertains to the court of review, but to the lower court, the parties and the adversary. The inner attitude of the attorney will invariably control the style of the discussion.

Assuming the attorney has learned the art of restraint, proper organization and style as suggested in the prior material, this still does not place the stamp of "artist" upon him. True, he will be an able craftsman (which is more than are 90 per cent of the lawyers presenting cases upon appeal) but to transform a brief from an able presentation to one which includes, let us say, a higher degree of finesse, it must include something further.

Some would term it the "stamp of counsel's personality." I prefer to think of it as a blend of the personalities of the attorney and the presiding judges—or, perhaps, the personality of the counsel as affected or modified by the personalities of those before whom he appears.

In every brief there is a peculiar opportunity for the apt expression, the remark which is particularly apropos, to drive home a crucial point. This may be done in several ways—by use of maxims, proverbs, quotations or humor—within reasonable limits. Some attorneys possessed of unlimited resourcefulness create their own epigrams or even verse. But usually it is the truism which demonstrates the truth—the familiar which brings recognition of the unfamiliar. So often a verbose presentation of one's adversary (or our own) which is filled with pomposity can be punctured by a deft quotation familiar to all the judges.

There are a couple of cautions which must be here observed. Wit should, at least, appear spontaneous and should be used but sparingly. Facetiousness or heavyhanded humor and blunt ridicule or ill-mannered jocularity are always in bad taste and may subject the attorney to criticism. Again, vulgarity will never bring a nod of approval. The occasion must call forth the comment. The comment must serve a sharp delineating purpose, or else have a definite constructive effect as to one's own case or a destructive possibility as to the case of one's opponent.

In speaking of the familiar, I certainly do not intend to convey the thought that one is limited to the Bible or Shakespeare. In fact, Biblical quotations are dangerous. What would strike one judge as apropos might seem to another judge to be frivolous or blasphemous. Proverbs of many lands, familiar maxims, or such widely scattered sources as Confucius, Omar Khayyam, Pope, Browning, Voltaire, Thackeray, Gilbert and Mother Goose may strike the precise note necessary for true artistry. Or even a timely illustration from daily work or some recreational activity may shed light upon a confusing problem. The aim is always simplicity, to reduce difficult problems to such elementary equations that only one logical result can follow. If such device so assists the court, it has served its function.

Again, in this regard, it is well to know as much as possible concerning the personnel of the court. What hobbies do they pursue? What are their recreational activities? What authors and poets do they read? What philosophers have influenced their thinking? What judges of the past do they admire? Whose reasoning do they emulate? Whom are they prone to quote? Some of these things one can learn from a study of their opinions, or, in the cases of particularly prominent judges, from biographies. Some of these matters one will learn from social conversations with the judges or with their clerks or secretaries.

The illustration may then be made more apt by connecting it up with something which will have particular significance or appeal to one or more justices without giving offense to others. The impact will then bear particular force. But as in all other stylistic matters, one must use delicacy and restraint; it must not be apparent that he is gunning for a particular court member, or the reaction will be more detrimental than the desired effect.

There are hundreds of possible illustrations which could be given. To use merely one recent example, I might first give the background leading to its use. Justice Jackson, in his opening statement as prosecutor before the International Military Tribunal at Nurenberg, made it clear that he was not seeking the death penalty for all defendants but preferred, like the Mikado, to let the punishment fit the crime. So, an automatic mental note was registered that at least one justice of our highest court is fond of Gilbert and Sullivan.

A few years ago, in a brief in the Supreme Court, the following comparison was used to spotlight a legal issue:

> "If something is a nullity, it is nothing. It is as if it had never happened. *Ergo post propter hoc,* it never happened and the obligation exists as before. We apologize if our language sounds strangely reminiscent of Ko-Ko in the Mikado, 'Consequently, that gentleman is as good as dead—practically, he is dead—and if he is dead, why not say so?' "

It is seldom that one can point to a particular illustration such as this and say "this helped to turn the tide," particularly when courts will seldom quote, in their opinions, anything of humorous bent. But so long as offense is not given and the illustration does help to clarify the question and one continues to win his cases, it is well to continue the same technique.

Every brief, of course, is in its basic essentials an argument. But let us understand clearly, it is an argument with one's adversary, perhaps to some extent an argument with an erring trial court, or an argument with certain erroneous principles of law or precedents. It is never ("no, never,"—quoting the Captain of the Pinafore) an argument with the reviewing court. The task of the attorney is to induce conviction, to advocate and to persuade. At no point does he gird his loins to do battle with the court itself.

One does not induce conviction by bludgeoning, threatening or intimidating anyone. Least of all does he possess any chance for success with a higher court, by employing such methods. After all, they are the bosses; he is the applicant for the position of successful counsel. Right or wrong, the justices are the lawyers having the "last guess" upon the matter at issue. The attorney must induce them to guess his way, and persuasion is far more effective than any force or pressure.

For this reason, I prefer never to tell a court it "must" do something. After all, it doesn't have to do so and probably will not, if it gets its back up. Nor is it wise to accuse a court of stupidity if it should fail to accord with one's reasoning. Resentment could produce an undesired result. Nor does it always pay to draw too-obvious conclusions. If the background is completely laid forth for the drawing of certain inevitable conclusions and the reasoning steps are pursued by counsel, it is sometimes well to permit the court to draw an inference or two for itself. Particularly is it unnecessary to keep battering home, time and time again, some perfectly obvious point which the court caught the first time it was mentioned. A little natural resentment may arise at the resulting inference of stupidity.

I do not mean that an attorney should leave his conclusions dangling in mid-air, nor should he hesitate to drive home his points with conviction. But I do suggest that he exchange his bludgeon for a scalpel, that he use sincere, earnest persuasion in lieu of a violent or brutal approach. It will be more conducive to success.

Reflections on Brief Writing

By Arthur C. Bachrach

In the last ten years legal literature has been increasingly concerned with trying to find out how judges really decide cases—a most difficult and ambitious undertaking. A number of writers have been trying to study the "nature of judicial process" from the point of view of what the courts *really do in fact* when they decide cases.[1] Their investigation is characterized by an attempt, first, to free themselves of all preconceptions; second, to observe carefully and accurately what they see and then to describe the process in clear, simple language; language which attempts to leave behind the traditional terminology, used in describing the nature of judicial process, which they think may by its vague ambiguities frustrate both accurate observation and description. Judging from the literature thus far, it seems highly improbable (if not impossible) that the process can ever be completely analyzed and understood in any genuinely scientific sense.

---

[1] Cardozo *The Nature of Judicial Process.*

Hutcheson *The Judgment Intuitive: The Function of the "Hunch" in Judicial Decisions* (1929) 14 Cornell L. Q. 274.

Frank *Law and the Modern Mind.* See also by same author: *What Courts Do in Fact* (1932) 26 Illinois Law Review 770, *Are Judges Human?* (1931) 80 U. Pa. L. Rev. 17, and *Mr. Justice Holmes and Non-Euclidean Legal Thinking* (1932) 15 Cornell L. Q. 568.

Green *The Duty Problem in Negligence Cases* (1928) 28 Col. L. Rev. 255. See also by same author *Judge and Jury* (1930).

Pound *The Theory of Judicial Decision* (1923) 36 Harv. L. Rev. 641; *The End of Law as Developed in Legal Rules and Doctrines* (1914) 27 Harv. L. Rev. 195; *The End of Law as Developed in Juristic Thought* (1914) 27 Harv. L. Rev. 605, (1917) 30 Harv. L. Rev. 201; *The Call for a Realistic Jurisprudence* (1931) 44 Harv. L. Rev. 697.

Dickinson *Legal Rules: Their Function in the Process of Decision* (1931) 79 U. Pa. L. Rev. 833; *The Law Behind the Law* (1929) 29 Col. L. Rev. 1014; also see (1929) 29 Col. L. Rev. 313.

Llewellyn *A Realistic Jurisprudence*—The Next Step (1930), *The Bramble Bush* (1931).

Cohen *The Ethical Basis of Legal Criticism* (1931) 41 Yale L. J. 201.

Arnold *The Role of Substantive Law and Procedure in the Legal Process* (1932) 45 Harv. L. Rev. 617.

Moore and Sussman *The Lawyer's Law* (1932) 41 Yale L. J. 567.

Gavit *Legal Conclusions* (1932) 16 Minn. L. Rev. 378.

Indeed, these writers themselves (each in varying degree) seem to suggest that the process cannot be mastered. All lawyers will agree that "opinionating" is far from being an exact science; that the result of most law suits cannot be predicted with certainty; that where a contest on the facts exists uncertainty is greatly increased; that whether the facts will be contested or not cannot be known at the time the opinion is given by the lawyer.

Some of the literature, however, holds as true and stresses the following: that the judges in deciding cases choose between "competing principles of the law"; that in this choice the peculiar facts of each case (even where undisputed) themselves have an emotive content; that the emotions of the judges (who are human beings) are a much more potent factor in deciding the applicability of the competing principles of law than is generally consciously recognized; that the process of deciding cases is far from being a matter of pure deductive logic; that the assumption is not correct, that judges first carefully ascertain "the facts" and *then* determine, as a separate activity, which principle of law is applicable to such facts so found; that the principles of law announced by the courts in their opinions are frequently not the "causes of the decision"; that it just appears so; that the decision is reached by a "hunch" or intuition after "brooding" over the case; that the principles of law stated in the opinion are only the "apologia" for the decision.[2]

Judge Hutcheson[3] in describing his own method of arriving at a judicial decision tells us that he examines all the available material at his command and duly cogitates upon it and gives free play to his imagination

> "and brooding over the cause, waits for the feeling, the hunch —that intuitive flash of understanding that makes the jump-spark connection between question and decision and at the point where the path is darkest for the judicial feet, sets its light along the way . . . *In feeling or 'hunching' out his decisions, the judge acts not differently from but precisely as the lawyers do in working on their cases,* with only this exception, *that the lawyer, in having a predetermined destination in view—to win the law-suit for his client—looks for and regards only those hunches which keep him in the path that he has chosen,* while

2 These viewpoints are not all consistent with each other, and are not all held by the same writers.

3 *Supra,* note 1.

the judge, being merely on his way with a roving commission to find the just solution, will follow his hunch wherever it leads him . . . I must premise that I speak now of the judgment or decision, the solution itself, as opposed to the apologia for that decision; the decree, as opposed to the logomachy, the effusion of the judge by which that decree is explained or excused . . . The judge really decides by feeling and not by judgment, by hunching and not by ratiocination, such ratiocination appearing only in the opinion. The vital motivating impulse for the decision is an intuitive sense of what is right or wrong in the particular case; and the astute judge, having so decided, enlists his every faculty and belabors his laggard mind, not only to justify that intuition to himself, but to make it pass muster with his critics. Accordingly, he passes in review all of the rules, principles, legal categories, and concepts which he may find useful, directly or by an analogy, so as to select from them those which in his opinion will justify his desired result."[4]

Frank writes:[5]

"Roughly speaking, then, the task of the lawyer may be summarized thus:

"(1) A lawyer tries to predict and anticipate future enforceable court decisions (i. e., judgments, orders or decrees) in specific cases.

"(2) A lawyer tries to win specific cases; that is, to induce courts in specific cases to render enforceable decisions (i. e., judgments, orders or decrees) desired by his clients. . . .

"*The lawyer's task, then, becomes this: The determination of what produces the judge's hunch. . . .*

"Let us here take stock. (1) Specific enforceable decisions (i. e., judgments, orders and decrees) in concrete cases are of the essence of the lawyer's work. All else is subsidiary. (2) *Specific decisions are the result of the judge's hunches. (3) To predict or bring about decisions, one should know something about what produces judicial hunches. (4) The so-called legal rules and principles are some of the many hunch producers.* (5) Whatever may be the stimuli to the making of those hunches, those stimuli must operate through their effects on what may loosely be described as the judge's personality. (6) Neither the

4 Italics applied for emphasis by Illinois Law Review.

5 *What Courts Do in Fact*, *supra*, note 1.

background stimuli nor the congeries labeled 'judge's personality' are stated or statable in terms of the conventional legal rules and principles. (7) The failure to recognize the composite nature of this hunch and the artificial breaking up of the decisional process into 'rules' and 'facts' accounts in part for the delusion of the formalist as to the exclusive value of the 'rules.' (8) The formalist errs also in overlooking the circumstance that it is impossible to predict what cases will be 'contested' and the subjective nature of the 'facts' of a 'contested' case and the resulting unchallengeability of the judge's statement of those 'facts'."

Dean Leon Green says:[6]

"When we say in a particular case that the plaintiff had a right or the defendant was under a duty, and the like, this but means that we have already passed judgment . . . The process has been concluded in some unknown way; the result is merely being vocalized . . . As lawyers we constantly delude ourselves and likewise delude others by insisting that those delightful word jousts we call opinions are dependable guides to the workings of the judicial processes. When that stage is reached, the action has already been fought. An opinion is but the smoke which indicates the grade of mental explosive employed. Somewhere behind the curtains of legal expression lie the laboratories of our intellect. They are not legal. They comprise all that we are. Perhaps our judgments on the least item of the day are given shape there in the same way as our most solemn decision in a law suit."

Gavit says:[7]

"It is not true that 'Hard cases make bad law.' Hard cases usually make good law, and one who would subscribe to the opposite doctrine is interested in the form of the law and not in its substance; in its metaphysics and not its reality. The essence of the idea expressed in the generalization is simply that the court has used an old word or phrase for a new concept; it has put new wine in an old bottle and neglected to change the label; reality has triumphed over theory. For it is usually agreed by the exponents of the view that 'Hard cases make bad law' that the result reached is a desirable and just one, and the

[6] *Supra,* note 1.

[7] *Supra,* note 1.

quarrel is simply with the name the court has given to the new concept."

We need not concern ourselves, however, with the correctness of all of the above views. It will be sufficient for the purpose of this paper to assume as correct that the judge's emotional reaction to the facts of the case will be a strong factor in his selection of the principle of law applicable thereto. This view probably will be readily accepted by almost all experienced trial lawyers and brief writers.

How the courts decide cases directly concerns the two principal functions of lawyers; firstly, predicting decisions, and secondly, securing favorable decisions in litigation.[8] Since the review courts' "reactions" to both the facts and the law are produced largely by the briefs (and briefs are the "neck of the bottle" through which all important litigation must flow), hence, the problems discussed by the above writers and some of their conclusions may vitally affect the development of the technique of brief writing.

Brief writing differs essentially and fundamentally from all the other work in the office routine. To give legal opinions to our clients, to draw ninety-nine-year leases, mortgages and the like of course require the most careful study, thought, and sometimes legal research. But lawyers feel that brief writing involves a functioning which is radically different from drafting mortgages and the like, however difficult, boring, and irritating the latter may be. This difference is dimly felt to be a matter of more than merely greater difficulty, effort, or greater concentration. The task of brief writing is approached with distinct feelings of uneasiness and inadequacy and doubts not only as to how but whether it can be done at all. This doubt, of course, we do not admit to ourselves and generally only become aware of its existence when we have advanced far enough in our task to "see daylight." We then sometimes experience a relief so great as to prove the existence of the previous doubt.

To tell a lawyer thus already so sorely perplexed that the task of brief writing is a "creative" one similar to that of artists—novelists, dramatists, and poets—would at first blush seem only to be putting "salt on his wounds" (whatever may have been his secret artistic ambitions in the past).

[8] See quotation from Frank *What Courts Do in Fact, supra.*

Nevertheless, it is the central theory of this paper that brief writing is essentially a creative function in just as real a sense as writing dramas, novels, poems or short stories;[9] that the greatest and most lasting satisfactions in life can be gotten from truly creative work; that thus really understood brief writing can become the most desirable and satisfaction-giving activity of the lawyer; further, that to the lawyer with the necessary equipment (principally a clear, emotional, as well as intellectual, understanding of the truth of this statement) the job will be attacked with pleasurable anticipation and zest.

The courts would doubtless frown upon a brief written in the manner of *Mourning Becomes Electra,* if that were possible; many of the devices employed by the writer of short stories would obviously be out of place; briefs cast in poetic form would be stricken by the court sua sponte; but it does not follow that a study of the literary arts may not (a) render real practical assistance to the brief writer in approaching his task, and (b) enrich the existing technique of brief writing so that it will furnish a more articulate technique for self-criticism.

It may be well worth while for the profession to consider, first, whether the present technique of brief writing can be made more articulate and effective and, to that end, it may be interesting to make inquiry to ascertain whether such technique is concerned with any problems essentially the same as those involved in writing a drama, a short story, etc.

It may at once be conceded that there are certain outstanding differences between the two techniques because of certain limita-

[9] When writing briefs I have always experienced the feelings, which I imagined creative artists felt, when they wrote a drama or a short story. Other lawyers have told me that their reaction was similar.

It is interesting to note that Mr. Walter in his book on *Brief Writing and Advocacy* states that the brief writer (in his statement of facts) "is telling a story" in just the same sense as a writer of fiction. Mr. Walter, however, dismisses the idea because he thinks the element of suspense—"always a merit in fiction"—is a demerit in brief writing where the object is "to get to the point without delay." Mr. Walter thinks that the technique of a newspaper reporter is more nearly like that employed in a statement of facts. His book is praiseworthy and competently discusses the technique of brief writing. His preoccupation with so many other phases of brief writing and advocacy perhaps explains his failure to pursue this idea further.

It is also interesting to note that a writer on the technique of playwriting (Arthur Edwin Krows *Playwriting for Profit* at page 91) in explaining the construction of a play, uses the idea of the structure of a lawyer's brief.

The pride lawyers take in their printed briefs seems in excess of their pride in drafting mortgages and other documents; this suggests the pride of artistic creation.

tions inherent in brief writing which are absent in the case of the art technique. The principal limitations are, first, the rules of court prescribe certain definite conventions; and, second, the dramatis personae are not a matter of choice but are furnished to the brief writer; and third, the "plot" apparently is "given" to the brief writer.

Now, it may be thought that where the artist has foisted upon him *both* the dramatis personae and the plot there is not left much room for artistic creation or creative functioning. While these limitations must be recognized, still the brief writer can function as an artist. He must accept the dramatis personae given by the record but can so portray them, by a permissible use of the process of selection and rejection of facts, as to secure the desired effect. As to the plot: here again we must recognize that the brief writer functioning as an artist can use only the facts and incidents disclosed by the record. He can invent neither facts nor situations. But this by no means implies that he cannot, within the limitations mentioned above, write his own plot.

Before discussing the question of the applicability of the technique of the arts to brief writing, let us first consider the basic function of brief writing. The object of the brief writer is, of course, to secure a decision in his favor. The document—the brief—is the mechanism which is to be read by the court.

A writer of a drama—a poem—or a short story, wants "to win *his* case," i. e., to move his audience emotionally in a very specific manner. The artist wants—not any response—but a very definite response to his art product. He is an artist, first, in being able to divine or conceive beauty and, secondly, insofar as he is able to convey the artist's emotion to his audience (human beings). *Hence we will be concerned also with this second: the artist's conscious mastery of his materials to produce or evoke the desired emotion.*

It may be urged that a brief is not intended to and does not call for an emotional response; that it does and should appeal to the intellect, the intelligence of the audience (the human beings who are now functioning as judges); that so functioning they are not to be pleased aesthetically or to be moved emotionally; that their process is a cold, reasoning one in which the emotions are left out entirely. It is fashionable to pretend that this is true.

Of course, the intellect—logic—enters into the process. The intellect should guide, check and perhaps control the emotions. For a penetrating insight of how judges must and do choose "between competing principles of the law" see *The Nature of Judicial Process* by Cardozo, and *The Intuitive Judgment* by Judge Hutcheson. Mr. Justice Cardozo points out quite clearly how judges, in deciding cases, have to determine what *weight* is to be given to the historical factor, the philosophical factor, the sociological factor, etc. When not being highbrow or formal, members of the bar in appraising various judges sometimes speak of a judge having a "feel" for the law.

Logic—intellect—can list factors and perhaps determine their relevance (although this also is possibly, at least partly, emotional); but neither logic nor intellect can determine *what weight* to give to the various factors. Call the process what you will, it realistically is *a leap in the dark,* and is emotionally determined. The intellect carries us up to a certain point. From then on "intuition," "instinct," "hunch," "a sixth sense" and the like come into play.[10] Indeed, where intellect begins and emotion begins, it is impossible to say; exactly what is meant by intellect and exactly what is meant by emotion is not clear. The judges react to all external stimuli with all the equipment they possess. When we say that a judge should not be emotional in his judgment and should decide the case upon "reason," all that is meant is (or all that should be meant is) that his emotions should be controlled and checked by self-discipline; that logic and reasoning should be used to list the factors and possibly to determine their relevance. Like or dislike of one of the parties, the fact that one is rich and one is poor, prejudices against any legal defense like gambling, usury and so forth, are illustrative (and, of course, by no means exhaustive) of what the judges are expected to rule out; but this by no means implies that a judge in understanding and reacting to the facts of the case (or in choosing between "competing principles of the law") should not do so, and does not do so, with all of his faculties including his emotions.

On the other hand, the critical playgoer or short story reader will at all times keep a careful watch over his emotions to see to it by means of his intelligence that his emotions have not been cheaply or sentimentally or otherwise dishonestly aroused. Indeed,

---

10 For a comparison of the respective abilities of intellect and intuition to understand life and life situations see statement in Appendix B on Bergson's *Creative Evolution.*

it is the function of critics and the writers on the literary arts to make articulate the principles which at least in some degree will make the art appreciator conscious of aesthetic principles so that the appreciator can make an informed response—which will be a composite of the intellectual and the emotional.

There may be differences between the response to an art product by the audience and the response to a brief by the judges; but it would be wrong to assume that the responses in each case do not involve the emotions. The tyro for decades has been told never to antagonize the judge; never to interrupt; never to contradict the court directly; but to point out tactfully not that the court is in error, "but that the court does not really mean to include the tyro's contention within their statement just made, etc."; these and many others. It is true that perhaps the above may concern merely "good manners."

It is our theory, however, that apart from those matters which may be included under the phrase of "good manners," the judges respond emotionally in very essential matters, viz.: (1) the facts, (2) the legal principles, (3) arguments in respect to both. These three items constitute in every jurisdiction the structure of a brief, namely, (1) the statement of the case including the facts, (2) points and authorities, and (3) argument.

Let us consider these three parts of the brief, then, in the order stated.[11]

"THE FACTS"

For the purposes of this discussion we will assume that in the first third of the brief the brief writer presents the facts. The record may consist of fifty to three thousand pages with an infinite number of documentary exhibits; or the facts may be compressed into a stipulation of facts and appear to be very few. What are "the facts"

[11] The cases considered by the reviewing courts may, for purposes of discussion, be roughly classified as follows: (1) chancery or law cases where the sole question involved is the sufficiency of a pleading; (2) a chancery decree or a law judgment which is made upon a finding of facts and an application thereto of principles of law; (3) a judgment upon a jury verdict; (4) cases in which it is claimed that (a) there is no evidence to sustain the verdict, (b) the verdict is against the weight of the evidence, (c) there are errors in admission or rejection of evidence, (d) there are errors in instructions. The above, of course, is not exhaustive, but is sufficiently representative for this discussion. In some of the above cases it is clearly apparent that the brief writer will have to deal with the facts. In most, if not all, of the others, it will, upon reflection, be seen that the facts must also be dealt with.

in any given case? For that matter, what are the facts in respect to any inclusive life situation such as a street car accident, a marriage, a death, a divorce, a birth, the coming of spring, a golf game, or a bridge game? What are "the facts" about anything? What is this thing called "relationship between facts"? How are relationships determined?

It is far from the intention of this writer to enter the metaphysical plane here. For the purposes of this discussion it is conceded that there is such a thing as cause and effect, by which is meant invariable sequence, and that under certain conditions when one fact is shown to exist it is possible to predict the occurrence of a second factor at some time thereafter. In other words, we are not denying scientific predictability nor do we deny that facts have relationships for certain purposes. But a scientist who even after a lifetime of work has discovered an invariable sequence between two facts has not for any other human purpose exhausted those two facts. Those two facts still enter into and have millions—nay, an infinite number—of relationships with all the other facts in the universe. Milk may be used to make ice cream but milk may also be used for many other purposes.

The narrow range of the activity of the average person is such as to make him completely unaware and oblivious to any but a very small number of relationships of any given fact, thing, or event. The relationships which exist may exist concerning a thing, fact, or event. They will be viewed and perceived differently by the various departments of science, anthropology, ethnology, and the rest. The relationships, then, of any two or more facts which will be made known or discovered will depend upon the specific practical interest or criterion of the particular scientist or human being who makes the inquiry. Once given a criterion, relationships doubtless become more or less fixed but until the specific special interest of the investigator is definitely determined, each fact radiates its multitudinous relationships to all the other facts of the universe.[12]

Of course, the above is not new. It is mentioned here merely because it is contrary to the conventional attitude of lawyers generally which is such as to result in a fixed preconception in this matter. Lawyers speak about the facts in a case as if they did

12 For similar views on this point see the very interesting book Karin Stephenson *Misuse of Mind* and particularly that portion which deals with "The Facts."

possess, with respect to each other, very definite and fixed relationships; that there are certain true relationships of facts in a case; that all other relationships are pseudo and false; that these "true" relationships can be discovered and that they will be ultimately announced by the court of last resort, and that then it will appear that those who held contrary notions (namely, the losing lawyer and his client) were just wrong; that courts have an infallible omniscience in these matters.

It is our theory that the facts of the case and the relationships between them (subject to the one limitation that they must come out of the record) are whatever the lawyer can persuade the court they are; that the very existence of the facts and their relationships to each other are, in a manner of speaking, constantly in a state of flux during the period of the writing of the brief, during the oral arguments, during the consideration of the case by the court, and until the court finally makes its decision. Furthermore, every record contains many facts; some contain thousands. We speak of certain facts as relevant and others as not. We speak of certain facts being evidentiary facts and other facts being ultimate. The rules of some of the courts with respect to briefs say that the "leading facts" should be stated. Of all of the facts, which are "the facts"; and which relationships are to be set forth and described by the writer? Obviously the brief writer must do exactly what every artist does. He must select and reject facts; he must select and reject relationships; he must from the depths of his own inner being determine the basis or criteria upon which he makes these selections and rejections.

To all of the above it may be urged that this is all very fine for the artist; the artist may roam in the process of selection and rejection, in whatever direction and over whatever road his fancy leads. But not so the brief writer. The brief writer, notwithstanding all of the above, must (it may be urged) be governed by something very definite—something very rigid—an ironclad rule—which really leaves only a very small area for either rejection or selection of fact or relationships, that this principle is that the facts and their relationships must all be selected or rejected with respect to the principles of law which apply to "the facts"; that when this is perceived it must be admitted (it will be urged) that conformity to this principle must result in a foreclosure of the use of any facts or relationships except those that are relevant to the principles of law applicable to "the facts."

To this we make the following reply: We will not know which of the various competing principles of law will be applied by the court of last resort to "the facts." Secondly, we will not know until the final decision as to whether the record contains facts which may, in the instant case in the opinion of the court of last resort, give rise to an entirely new principle of law, which will control the decision in the case; or perhaps to base thereon a new exception to some previously existing principle of law. Enough has been said to indicate the writer's point of view.

But, it may be then urged: Even granting that in most or even all cases (which is not true), the "doors are wide open" for the selection of facts, because (a) of the presence of the possibility of choice between "competing principles of law," or (b) the presence of the possibility of urging a modification or overruling of an existing rule or the creation of an exception to an old one, nevertheless the range of choice as to facts is quite limited; namely, either to those facts showing the application of *one* (because the brief writer must *ultimately* select only one) principle of law; or to business or sociological data, constituting the basis for urging a change in the common law.

The above observation is partially correct. Of course, in the case of (a) facts *must* be set forth so that the desired principle of law can be seen to be applicable, and in the case of (b) the basic data sufficient to warrant a change in the common law must be set forth. But this does not preclude the brief writer from *adding* thereto (if he can find them in the record and if he knows what they are) facts which are "hunch-producers" (i. e., virtually decision-makers).

"Hunch-producers"

A hunch-producer may consist of one or many facts (and their relationships). These facts may (a) be the same or (b) different from or (c) overlap with the facts which "prove" the applicability of the desired principle of law. Which facts are *such* facts cannot be known before the decision and usually not even afterwards. What is a hunch-producer for one judge obviously may not be so for another. Doubtless brief writers also will frequently disagree as to which facts have this quality. Adequate description of hunch-producers is impossible. Yet experienced brief writers feel, and take considerable pride in their belief, that in a specific case they can recognize and state in their brief the hunch-producers. They will be less tolerant of criticism of their brief which attacks this belief. And (is it because of a creative feeling akin to that of the artists?) they are usually not fully conscious of dealing with facts as hunch material and perhaps don't want to be?

If as Judge Hutcheson[13] says: "The final motivating impulse for the decision is an intuitive sense of what is right or wrong in the particular case," then we have some clue for our search for a criterion of recognizing hunch-producers. A principle of law itself may be one. All the facts (as selected and when arranged in a certain manner) may, for no logical or articulate reason be felt to be another. The recognition of such hunch-producers is largely intuitive; logic and intellect may and should be employed to "check" or verify them; the final decision of the brief writer will again, however, be reached in the main intuitively. Even though no description of "hunch-producers"[14] can be adequately given, we can now, in a rough and very general way, describe the brief writer's process as to how he goes about getting a hunch.

The Hunch Process

In describing this process, we find it convenient to make use of the terminology employed by Graham Wallas in his book *The Art of Thought,* making our own application of his theory to brief writing. He calls his first step Preparation—"the stage when the case is investigated in all directions." The brief writer begins by first reading and studying his record and abstract until he knows all "the facts." Through condensation or reabstracting the abstract, he gets rid of all superfluous material which he is sure he has no use for. He then ponders the facts and their relationships. He considers the "law." Does an abstract principle of law readily suggest itself as being probably or possibly applicable?[15] He reads law. He reads "all around" the specific question involved. He returns

13 *Supra,* note 1.

14 For an interesting and suggestive description of "hunch-products" see Jerome Frank *Law and the Modern Mind* pp. 104-117, from which the phrase "hunch-producers" is borrowed; see also his article *What Courts Do in Fact, supra* note 1; see also quotation therefrom, *supra.*

15 For some concrete and practical suggestions see Hadley *Law Teaching and Problem Analysis* (1932) 38 Case and Comment No. 3.

to the record. Certain facts begin to emerge as being somehow more prominent—more striking. He studies perspective. He tries to get a bird's-eye view. He projects in imagination various "arrangements" of facts and tests these arrangements against various principles of law. Do any of the various arrangements manifest an affinity for any principle of law? Do "the facts" produce a feeling of "what is right or wrong in the particular case"?

The second stage is called Incubation. This process is a sort of dreaming—undirected thinking. The process is in essence the "natural" one of association of ideas. There are "risings and fallings" of consciousness during this period. The writer may proceed to other business or perhaps recreation. The process, however, continues automatically and non-volitionally.

The third stage is Illumination. This stage at first automatically and imperceptibly grows out of the second. There comes a rising awareness or consciousness of a train or trains of associations. Wallas uses the term Intimation to describe a sudden inner warning of the approach of the "flash of success" which first occurs in the Illumination period. Here Wallas warns us to be careful lest we interfere by conscious effort (before the train of associations is complete) with the automatic process and lose this feeling of Intimation. He quotes from a poem by Mr. Robert Graves called *A Pinch of Salt* thus:

> "When a dream is born in you
> With a sudden clamorous pain,
> When you know the dream is true and lovely,
> With no flaw nor stain,
> Oh, then, be careful,
> Or with sudden clutch you will
> Hurt the delicate thing you prize so much."

This "fringe consciousness" lasts up to the "flash" instant. Apparently when the flash occurs *you just know it.*

The fourth stage—Verification—is self-explanatory. The validity of the idea, or the hunch, is tested, this time of course consciously, using both intellect and intuition.

The above is an oversimplified and greatly condensed statement of Mr. Wallas' description of the creative thought process, with the writer's own application to the process of brief writing. The exact order of each stage, the amount of effort, how much is unconscious, and all the rest, of course varies among all persons (artists or otherwise). The above is most emphatically not intended as anything more than an attempt merely to suggest the *nature* of the hunch process.[16]

To summarize: The brief writer after studying the record facts and legal processes having possible application to "the facts" eyes the record facts letting his mind dwell on them; certain facts begin to emerge; relationships begin to suggest themselves; arrangements of facts are rejected, discarded and altered as to position or emphasis. Finally comes the "click" of harmony; the facts in "this" arrangement seem to fit or belong. The writer feels this. The lawyer has thus "detected the pattern" in the record facts; the pattern thus created has come to the lawyer (after much "brooding" by himself and "divining" it) through repeated testing of various arrangements of the facts with projected applications of the various principles of law, until he seems to bring life to the facts in the form of a pattern. The lawyer then "feels" that this is the pattern. This feeling is then checked consciously by the intellect and intuition against all possible factors—the attitude of the courts generally and specifically—past experience in similar cases—past experience in life. The whole personality (including all his past experiences whether conscious or not) functions through the intellect and intuition and makes the final decision as to whether the hunch is good. The hunch or flash may not come until after several drafts of the statement of facts have been written. On the other hand it may precede even the first draft which then may require (although this is most improbable) only slight "polishing."

This description of the actual thought process which occurs in brief writing appears haphazard, accidental, dreamy and emotional; it will doubtless be disappointing to lawyers who think of this process as being cold, intellectual and precise, and having to do *solely* with deductive logic or thinking of the mathematical type, but an attentive bit of introspection will quickly show that deductive or intellectual thinking (except for checking hunches) is pretty largely a myth; or at any rate, it is not the largest part of the thought process involved in writing a brief.

---

[16] For an amplification of this process see an extremely interesting essay *The Difference Between Art and Science in Their Relation to Nature* in Alfred E. Cohen *Medicine, Science and Art* (1931).

We have seen that the brief writer's process has a great deal in common with the artist's first function: to detect a pattern or a design in facts which are apparently unrelated aesthetically; and (to mix our metaphor) the artist, like the brief writer, by arranging facts, supplies the connective tissues.[17] The second function of the artist, to produce a specific emotional response by conscious control of his material, remains to be examined to see whether his technique may be of practical assistance to the brief writer.

Let us briefly consider the techniques involved in the writing of a drama, a short story, and a poem. We shall see that (insofar as they deal with the employment of material to produce specific emotional responses) each has special problems peculiar to each, which brief writing does not have; that the *remaining* problems which they have in common with each other *and with brief writing* are by no means the exclusive property of the arts; that it is primarily the artist's solution of the latter problems which may assist in solving the brief writer's problems. More specifically, a comparison of the problems of the arts with that of brief writing, revealing differences and resemblances may result in a more vivid intimate, and empathic appreciation of the problems of brief writing.

The Special Problems of the Drama, the Short Story, and the Poem

Playwriting has as its own peculiar problem that of "crisis." This is the significant factor which dominates its form. Its construction —all its parts—have meaning only with reference to the crisis. The drama, after the preliminary explanation (the exposition), is a gathering of emotional tension, slowly at first, then increasing into minor crises, which in turn give way to the principal crisis and then a disbursement of tension—namely, the resolution. Suspense and its creation culminating in a crisis is the essence of drama. Hence, practically all of the dramatic rules can be properly understood only with reference to their part in the production or resolution of the crisis. In this sense it must be frankly admitted that a brief has no "crisis." But the dramatist does employ the process of selection and rejection of material. He must employ

17 For an excellent discussion of certain phases of the process employed by the novelist and related problems see Joseph Wood Krutch *The Critic's Dilemma* published in The Nation in three installments, December 2, 1931, January 6, 1932, and April 3, 1932.

this process in working out problems peculiar to the drama and more difficult than those involved in writing a brief (and which are absent in the case of brief writing). This very difference should bring home a keener appreciation to the brief writer of the significance of the process. The other difference is due to the necessity of writing only in dialogue. This burden is also fortunately escaped by the brief writer.

The short story writer is not limited to dialogue. A short story of course has the problem of suspense and indeed may be said to have a crisis which rules out the technique intended to solve problems relating directly or indirectly thereto. The problem of interest, however, in brief writing is important and differs only in degree from that of suspense.

The poem, apart from its idea-content, is intended to please the ear. The poet is concerned then, with word patterns, meter, rhythm, number of lines to a stanza, and so on. The use of vowels and certain consonants and alliteration all have to do with the question of creating pleasurable sounds. (Their value to brief writing is not further considered herein, solely on account of space.) The chief contribution which poetry can make is the use of its visual imagery by the use of certain words or by the use of apt metaphor or simile. (Obviously poetic license will not be tolerated by courts except within the established conventions.) In brief writing the importance of stating facts attractively and vividly by the use of words which will carry with them a keen and vivid appreciation of the facts is of tremendous importance; a study of poetry will be a genuinely practical help to the brief writer.

The above then is a rather brief statement of the problems peculiar to these three arts. All three arts and brief writing have, however, certain problems in common which we shall now consider. Apart from the problem of crisis and suspense the drama and the short story have in common other problems of importance. These artists must portray human beings each with different personalities, some vastly different, others subtly different. The artist is primarily concerned—not in resemblances—but with just those intangible factors of a personality which distinguish it from all others; in conduct partly determined by their environment and partly by the force of the personality.

All human activity occupies the artist; human desires, imaginations, aspirations, dreams, commonplace routine conduct, social relations, business relations, together with their resultant conflicts, disputes, and controversies. These three arts basically are engaged in portraying some one or more phase of life, some one or more personality, some human conduct. They have as their common problem the task of doing so in such a manner as will enable the audience vividly to "understand," "appreciate," and "realize" the subject portrayed. The effect of empathy, actual identification by the audience with the characters, sufficient to result in an adequate understanding "from within" must be produced. This then is the basic function of these arts.

The additional problem of crisis (in drama and perhaps the short story), of meter, rhythm, and sound values (in the case of poetry) merely increases the difficulties inherent in these three arts, but should not obscure their basic function. For their basic function, within limits, is the basic problem of the brief writer, namely, to present in three-dimensional form, certain conduct of the parties or others (which is the subject of the judicial investigation) so as to enable the court as best it can to "understand," "appreciate" and "realize" it correctly and adequately. (If both opposing lawyers use this technique successfully, the court should then be able to understand from "within" as well as from "without" the respective positions of the two partisan advocates and can thus choose efficiently between them.[18]

The hunch-producing material (which as noted above may include the entire statement of facts) should be presented in form so as to give a three-dimensional effect, and in a manner that will secure for it a vivid understanding, appreciation, and realization. The understanding, appreciation, and realization are empathy process the same as in the arts. It is a composite of the intellect and intuition.

We believe that further than this the "rules" and "principles" of dramatic or short story technique, cannot take us;[19] but this is quite a "lift on the journey." From this point onward the writers

[18] One judge whose decisions have a splendid reputation for their "fairness and justice" described his initial attitude in the decision process as follows: "I first imagine myself in the plaintiff's shoes and then try to understand his claim from that vantage point; I then identify myself completely with the defendant in the same manner; I then *feel* better able to decide where justice lies."

[19] It should never be forgotten that these pretentious "rules" and "principles" are nothing more than common sense suggestions or guides; they are obviously the product of trial and error. They are, however, sometimes stated in books on playwriting with all of the solemnity of a Cosmic Law.

can point out merely what "not to do"; and then give examples both ways. This they do.

Writers on brief writing have apparently not considered these matters. For example, they content themselves with suggestions of this type: "Every case has a set of facts out of which the controversy arises—these should be stated"; the statement of facts should be "direct," "precise," "interesting," "clear," and "fair"; the statement should be attractive and in a narrative form; not too much detail nor too little; there are suggestions as to when to use sub-headings; "Yes, it is literally true that a brief writer preparing a statement of facts is telling a story just as a contributor to a short story magazine."[20]

We believe, therefore, that the modern technique of brief writing may well include a consideration of the problems of the arts common to them and to brief writing and the means employed by these artists to solve them;[21] and that this will bring home to the brief writer a more thorough understanding of his problems.

There is another important distinction between the drama (and, for that matter, all of the arts) and brief writing which is as follows: it is the purpose of all art forms to produce what is called an aesthetic emotion. The amount of literature on this subject is of course vast and this writer has no intention to attempt here any definition of aesthetics. It is the brief of the writer, however, that it is universally conceded that no emotion can be an aesthetic one in which the audience feels a practical interest. In other words, it is the glory as well as the function of art that the appreciator should be able to preserve an emotional detachment. This detachment is absolute in the sense that the purpose of the artist is to produce in his audience an ability to "enjoy," understand, and appreciate emotionally *without* having to take any practical attitude with respect thereto whatsoever. Rembrandt's portraits of old women illustrate the point. In real life we would have to take a practical attitude towards an old woman begging on the street corner or selling newspapers. On the canvas we feel no obligation or impulse to

20 In *Brief Writing and Advocacy* (1931) Walter devotes eleven pages to the chapter *Stating the Facts*. In the appendix he gives model briefs illustrating the use of his suggestions. (Brief writers will find this book competent; it contains many valuable suggestions.) He does not deal nor purport to deal with the central subject of this article, however. We do not consider our viewpoint at all antithetical to this book and indeed heartily recommend its use by the bar.

21 For examples of suggestions made by writers on playwriting see Appendix C.

do anything about it. Freed from all practical interests, we are now enabled to respond aesthetically. Other numerous and better illustrations will readily occur to the reader.

The brief writer does not want to provoke a purely aesthetic response. He does not want the court to preserve towards the facts a purely detached attitude. He wants to produce in the court a desire "to do something about it," i. e., a desire for action—and particularly action favorable to the brief writer. This, by no means, implies that, it is wise or permissible (whether from the selfish viewpoint of the brief writer or from a social viewpoint) to resort in brief writing to the use of perfervid rhetoric and appeals to prejudices. It would be harmful socially and the courts would quickly resent any attempt on the part of a brief writer to arouse prejudices, angers, or hostilities and the like. Courts should expect (and rightfully) that both presentation and discussion should be calm, temperate, and dispassionate. The emotional reactions (always guided, disciplined and checked by the intellect) should be in response to an emotional-intellectual understanding of the facts reached slowly and without any excitements engendered by dishonest and collateral stimuli. It is difficult, as Mr. Justice Holmes has frequently remarked (in other connections) to know where to draw the line. The fact that there may be borderline cases which are doubtful does not disprove the point that the distinction in the majority of cases in this respect is quite clear. Brief writers know from experience how to discriminate between the use of meretricious appeals to the emotion and appeals which are legitimately engendered by an honest deep understanding of the facts in their case. So much for the "Statement of Facts."

Points and Authorities

This is no perfunctory task. Considerable time, thought, and study are necessary for a clear and effective statement of points and authorities. In accordance with the theory of this paper we suggest that the points be stated so as to make the judges "feel" that they belong to the facts and that the facts belong to them.

Argument

Basically, the real contest in brief writing is competition between patterns or arrangements of the facts. If we can get the court to feel the "validity" and the truth of our arrangement of the facts, usually success is achieved. We must be prepared to convince the court emotionally as well as intellectually, that of all the competing principles of law in existence the one which should be adopted is the one desired by the brief writer. The ground for this has already been prepared by the Statement of Facts and the Points and Authorities. The Statement of Facts must be non-argumentative. The brief writer has to rely upon subtlety of presentation to picture them as the "true" arrangement. The brief writer, however, can now make explicit that which was only implicit in the Statement of Facts. The brief writer will do this by the Argument. This does not mean mere repetition. It means the process of throwing the searchlight upon that portion of the facts which the brief writer believes has emotive content. The relative importance of the facts will be argued—relationships will be pointed out and made vivid. More specifically the attention of the court will be focused upon the hunch-producer.

Argument is an advantage which the brief writer has over the dramatist. After the dramatist has written his play he will not be heard to explain, argue, interpret, or point out relationships. This he must do (at his peril) in the exposition or during the action of the play. True, he may point out relationships—of cause and result—psychology of his characters—through the lips of the actors. He may not, however, resort to ex post facto argument as the lawyer may do.

Disputes in testimony, argument with respect to circumstantial evidence, and the rest of the familiar problems are beyond the scope of this paper.

The handling of case material is of course quite important. Mr. Walter[22] makes many excellent suggestions with respect to this. In the last analysis an understanding of authorities, although obviously involving the exercise of the intellectual faculty, rests at bottom upon a "feel" for distinctions and similarities between *factual situations* and involves an understanding of life and the relations between men. The weight of an authority must be determined emotionally as well as by the intellect. The consideration of each authority cited (of course we have not the time actually to do this) theoretically involves the same process of understanding as that presented in this paper with respect to writing a brief.

[22] *Supra,* note 19.

Conclusion

If the judicial process is a hunching process (and we sincerely believe it is) then the technique of the brief writer should be to capitalize hunch-producers,[23] bearing in mind that one hunch-producer may be nothing more nor less than the entire arrangement of the facts. An actual study and comparison of the technique of the literary arts may help to know how to discover hunch-producers and how to present them.

Appendix A

Mr. Justice Cardozo says:

"What is it that I do when I decide a case? To what sources of information do I appeal for guidance? In what proportions do I permit them to contribute to the result? In what proportions ought they to contribute? If a precedent is applicable, when do I refuse to follow it? If no precedent is applicable, how do I reach the rule that will make a precedent for the future? If I am seeking logical consistency, the symmetry of the legal structure, how far shall I seek it? At what point shall the quest be halted by some discrepant custom, by some consideration of the social welfare, by my own or the common standards of justice and morals? Into that strange compound which is brewed daily in the caldron of the courts, all these ingredients enter in varying proportions. I am not concerned to inquire whether judges ought to be allowed to brew such a compound at all. I take judge-made law as one of the existing realities of life. There, before us, is the brew. Not a judge on the bench but has had a hand in the making. The elements have not come together by chance. Some principle, however unavowed and inarticulate and subconscious, has regulated the infusion. It may not have been the same principle for all judges at any time, nor the same principle for any judge at all times. But a choice there has been, not a submission to the decree of Fate; and the considerations and motives determining the choice, even if often obscure, do not utterly resist analysis." * * * * * "All their lives, forces which they (the judges) do not recognize and can-

23 As to the importance of knowledge about "hunch-producers" in (a) predicting decisions and (b) in bringing them about, see Frank *What Courts Do in Fact; supra,* note 1.

not name, have been tugging at them—inherited instincts, traditional beliefs, acquired convictions; and the resultant is an outlook on life, a conception of social needs, a sense in Jame's phrase of 'the total push and pressure of the cosmos,' which, when reasons are nicely balanced, must determine where choice shall fall. In this mental background every problem finds its setting. We may try to see things as objectively as we please. None the less, we can never see them with any eyes except our own."

Appendix B

Bergson, the French philosopher, advanced the theory that life evolved by following the two divergent paths of intellect and instinct; that as they developed, they diverged more and more, but never entirely separate from each other, and because of their common origin, still interpenetrate; that "all concrete instinct is mingled with Intelligence as all real intelligence is penetrated with Instinct"; that intellect is only a partial and local manifestation of life; that it "feels itself at home among inanimate objects" and "triumphs in geometry"; that intellect and instinct constitute two different modes of knowing—the former possess only an "external knowledge" of objects and deals with relationships, whereas the latter is *innate*; that "intelligence and instinct are turned in opposite directions—the former towards inert matter, the latter towards life"; that they both "represent two divergent solutions, equally fitting, of one and the same problem"; that intellect is incapable of presenting "the true nature of life, the full meaning of the evolutionary movement," that on the other hand, "it is to the very inwardness of life that intuition leads us—by intuition, I mean, instinct that has become disinterested, self-conscious, capable of reflecting upon its object and enlarging it indefinitely."

Appendix C

It is surprising how applicable to the problems of brief writing, are some quotations from a typical book[24] on playwriting. For example:

"A successful dramatist first determines the special thing he wants to say. Then he selects only those portions of his material

[24] *Supra,* note 9.

that help him to say it. And finally he arranges these for the most effective statement of the whole."

* * * * *

Aristotle explains that in a single plot:
"the structural union of the parts is such that, if any one of them is displaced or removed, the whole will be disjointed and disturbed."

* * * * *

"In a well-made play, in which the subject is single and the successive incidents are merely its ramifications, the audience is imperceptibly led along the smooth and consistent course that some master intellect would follow spontaneously. The pleasure of the theater is very largely the stimulating pleasure of clear, logical thinking without the spectator's effort to originate. I think that this probably is the principal reason why an audience prefers unity of a play's action."

* * * * *

"So we cut the unsympathetic side to the bone, to its absolute essentials, and correspondingly enlarge, develop, the sympathetic side whose fortunes the spectators have come to witness."

* * * * *

"Adroitness in selecting the high spots of a story, and in making all the complementary parts essential, too, gives the spectator the feeling that his time is not being wasted. He is there only when something vital is happening; he is 'in at the death,' as it were. This ability to present just the cream of a dramatic action truly is characteristic of the most successful craftsmen. It proves the trained, discriminatory eye. Suppose you were called upon to write the story of Jack and Jill. Could you state it much more pungently than in the form already sung in the nursery?

"Jack and Jill
Went up a hill
To fetch a pail of water.
Jack fell down
And broke his crown,
And Jill came tumbling after."

* * * * *

"Continued interest implies progress, an increase of knowledge about the object of attention—never a diminution. Moreover, the progress leads necessarily to an improved understanding on the part of the audience."

* * * * *

"It is not enough that the unity of the subject be clear in the analytical diagram; it must be clear in the presentation itself. Emphasis should be placed so as to bring out the force of the major proposition. If this is not done, the proposition will be valueless in establishing unity, and will itself be destroyed."

Adapted from Vol. 27, Illinois Law Review (1932).

A Case on Appeal—The Advocate's Point of View

BY CLARENCE A. DAVIS

THIS IS A SUBJECT which so distinguished an advocate as John W. Davis has characterized as "well-worn," and if there can be any justification for my discussing it with you today, it must lie in such applicability as I may make to our local courts in Nebraska, or in such things as I may say to the younger lawyers who have not yet had the time (or to the older ones who have not had the diligence) to read some of the tremendous literature that exists on the subject. When Judge Goodrich, John W. Davis, Mr. Justice Jackson, Chief Justice Arthur Vanderbilt and the late Chief Justice Charles Evans Hughes have written profusely on a subject, there is certainly nothing additional that I can contribute to the discussion. Those things which I shall say represent only an appropriation of ideas, I hope with consent, from these and other distinguished barristers.[1]

Wiener remarked that "Counsel defeated in the trial court—the licked lawyer—is recognized as having twin rights: (1) he may go down to the inn at the county seat, or to his club in town, and cuss the court and/or jury; and (2) he can take an appeal."[2]

This is one of the few places in which I suspect that verbal monstrosity "and/or" may have been appropriately used.

So we have lost our case and have perfected our appeal. Our appeal is docketed in the Supreme Court and we now have thirty days in which to write our brief. And this does not mean that our

---

1 I am deeply indebted for the substance of these remarks to the observations of many friends of the Nebraska Bar, some of whom are long since departed. More formally I am indebted to the following: Davis, *The Argument of an Appeal,* 25 ABAJ 895 (1940); Goodrich and Carsons, *A Case on Appeal,* A.L.I. Series (Aug. 1952); Jackson, *Advocacy before the Supreme Court,* 37 ABAJ 801 (1951); Simmons, *Behind the Scenes,* 22 Neb. L. Rev. 39 (1943); Vanderbilt, *Forensic Persuasion* (1950 Tucker Memorial Lectures at Washington and Lee University); Wilkins, *The Argument of an Appeal,* 33 Cornell L. Q. 40 (1947); Wiener, *Effective Appellate Advocacy* (1950).

2 Wiener, *Effective Appellate Advocacy* 3 (1950).

briefs should be prepared between the twentieth and thirtieth days —an admonition that too frequently is appropriate.

The Briefs

We have some rules promulgated by our Supreme Court, and all other courts have their rules, too, about the preparation of briefs.

My first admonition is to read the rules. I assume that most lawyers are sufficiently competent to read, but I am also informed that the number of them who do read and follow what are perfectly clearcut instructions as to the preparation, sequences and style of handling material in a brief casts some doubt on my assumption.

There is nothing complicated about the rules of our own Supreme Court. They have been evolved out of long experience to promote efficiency and save the time of the Court, to make it possible to readily locate points, authorities and argumentative material, and to reduce what might otherwise frequently be rambling discourses to some semblance of legal order.

First, therefore, read the rules, and no matter how many briefs you have already written, I suggest they be read again. Memory is a tricky thing. The lawyer who relies on his memory of a statute is courting disaster, and so may he who relies upon his memory for the form and style of a brief.

I shall not deal with the rules in detail. I assume you can and will read. I shall deal with some general suggestions under the suggested sequences.

Statement of the Questions Involved

The requirement is that there shall first be a "Statement of the Questions Involved," and it is here, on line one of the brief, that the outcome of litigation may be determined. It is an unusual lawsuit, especially in our State courts, that involves more than two or three really important questions worthy of note, except in those cases, perhaps, where the Court makes an original review of the facts. Yet I have seen briefs with as many as fifteen to twenty questions, involving all kinds of argumentative statements and factual statements submitted as part of the statement of questions. They testify largely to the inadequacy of analysis of counsel and muddled thinking. They are apt to create an impression in the beginning that if counsel has not analyzed his lawsuit any more clearly than is evidenced by his "Statement of Questions Involved," the chances are his later statements of the errors of the trial court are likely to be equally confused.

A "Statement of Questions Involved" should be a statement of those propositions of law about which there is disagreement between appellate counsel and the rulings of the trial court.

Statement of the Case

We are next directed to make a "Statement of the Case," and here, again, it is a rare occasion indeed that one or two sentences, properly phrased, will not convey to the Court exactly what the lawsuit is all about. Under this heading we are further directed to outline the issues as set forth in the pleadings and state how they were decided. It is not necessary or proper to recopy a long and involved pleading. After all, the Court can read the transcript, if detailed matters of pleading are involved, or they may be quoted at length in the argument if they are critical.

What the Court wants to know is the material allegations of the petition, what, in substance, are the defenses pleaded in the answer, and how the trial court determined the issues.

Assignment of Errors

This brings us then to the "Assignment of Errors." It is at this point that we must take a look backward to the trial record. After all, we can't assign errors in an appellate proceeding unless we can point out the errors in the trial court record. I cannot emphasize too strongly the absolute necessity of tying down supposed errors in the course of the District Court trial. I think many of us have a tendency to feel that our record is better than it is. In rulings made by the trial court we are apt to read hopefully into the record the look of the judge, the tone of his voice, the manner in which a statement is made, all those undefinable things that create an impression. For appellate purposes the only things worthwhile are the actual words as transcribed by the reporter. Therefore, it seems to me that in the trial of cases, when complicated and sometimes foggy situations develop as to exactly what counsel has offered by way of evidence or as to exactly what ruling the trial court has made, that counsel should be extremely careful, even asking a question of the Court, if necessary, to make clear in the record the ruling of the Court.

Then the question arises as to how many errors should be assigned, whether to stand on only the most important and vital ones, or all of them. I tell you frankly there are two schools of thought. I know that some of the finest lawyers have adopted the plan of raising only two or three of the assignment of errors in an appellate brief, or at least of arguing and discussing only these few, feeling that unless the two or three most obvious errors will stand up, there certainly is no use to argue the others.

On the other hand, I have known many equally good lawyers who have told me that it was amazing how many times, by raising a multitude of issues, they have succeeded in securing reversals on points in which they themselves had little confidence, while the Court disregarded the major errors on which counsel at least thought the case should have been decided. This is the theory, of course, of the more hooks, the more fish (no odious reflections intended). But I do give the admonition that nothing is more disgusting to an appellate court than to have a tremendously long list of assignments of error, in many of which there is obviously no merit, and I have always had the feeling that a cause was weakened by the assertion of a multitude of doubtful propositions, no matter how much merit there might be in a limited number of others.

Propositions of Law

That brings me to the "Propositions of Law." In the "Propositions of Law" counsel are supposed to state what they believe to be the law that governs the appeal. As a minimum, it seems to me, those propositions should be stated in lawyer like—Supreme Court like, if you wish—language that could appropriately be a headnote of the case in the event the appeal is successful. Therefore, purported propositions of law which undertake to state the facts of the particular litigation, which undertake to make reference to particular documents in the litigation and such matters of a limited nature, are not truly propositions of law. They are simply statements about the individual case.

Citations

And now let me discuss for a moment the matter of citations. Our rules are definite on this point, and yet they are repeatedly violated. Quite apart from the rules, certainly a proper respect for our own Court would require that the citations given be referred to the volumes of our own Court's opinions. Certainly, as has been well remarked, the collection of a page of miscellaneous citations, while it may testify to the industry of the brief writer, may also indicate a shotgun approach to a proposition. On matters on which our own Court has passed, especially where they have passed two or three times, it would appear that citations from other Courts are superfluous, unless the validity of the proposition is under direct attack, in which case the Court may wish to find itself fortified by similar decisions of other Courts.

Statement of Facts

We come now to the most important part of the brief, that is, the "Statement of Facts." It has been said that the power to collect and summarize facts in a clear and logical manner is the greatest attribute of the lawyer. The facts should be reduced to narrative form. They should be made readable; they should be related, so nearly as possible, in consecutive order of their occurrence, and there is certainly no rule against making the statement of facts interesting. Above all, every statement of fact in the brief ought to be documented to the page and question number of the Bill of Exceptions from which it is taken or summarized. This is a laborious job in a big bill of exceptions, and that is especially true where several witnesses in different volumes of the bill of exceptions have testified about the same thing. A job such as this can represent dozens of hours of effort which will never be apparent to anyone except to opposing counsel and the judges of the Supreme Court, but if all of the testimony on each factual statement made can be collected from each witness and brought together, the impact of the factual statement made is tremendously more impressive than if it is scattered throughout the testimony of a dozen witnesses over eight or ten separate pages, even though it be accurately cited in connection with each one of them.

We are all familiar with the old maxim that "A case well stated is a case half won." Our Court hears many cases. This maxim is perhaps more applicable to the oral argument than it is to the brief, but nevertheless, since the Court and the individual judge working on an opinion may have a half-dozen matters under consideration at the same time, it is just as important that a clear consecutive, documented, factual statement be in the brief as in the oral argument.

Argument

This brings me to the argument in the brief. Personally, I feel that the argument in the brief should be complete and all inclusive. While the oral argument may cover all the points, after all, it is always possible that its delivery might be interrupted, the Court's attention temporarily distracted or it might just be forgotten, and, therefore, the argument on both the facts, if they are involved, and the law should be adequately set out in the brief. At this point may I give some admonitions:

If you value your lawsuit, if you value your reputation, don't ever—ever—misquote a citation, garble a quotation, or take excerpts of only part of an opinion which is weakened or nullified by the remainder of it; never misquote and never mislead.

I have heard it said many times by the judges of many appellate courts that one such trick—or slip—and only one, may ruin a lawyer's entire future. I know of a large firm whose standing at the Bar is supposed to be great, and yet whose briefs are never accepted by appellate courts without checking every citation and every quotation. The man who has acquired that sort of reputation has at least one strike on him whenever he appears to argue another appeal.

It is sometimes a great temptation to quote favorable parts of an opinion and ignore the rest. When they say what we want them to say and say it convincingly, the temptation to quote only that part is almost irresistible, but I repeat, it is most deadly of all sins if we omit anything to the contrary.

Let me relate a little experience with one of the large law firms in Denver a few years ago. They had a very important piece of litigation in the Supreme Court of the United States. The case had been argued and submitted. One of the propositions of law was obscure. They had a fine staff, with one of these typical bookworm lawyers who had worked for months upon it and had finally found two cases in all of English and American law that were in point on his proposition. He had said in the brief, "These are the only cases on the subject," which incidentally is a thing one never should say. I went into that office one afternoon to find him substantially in tears, embarrassed and humiliated. He had by accident found another case. It was partially in his favor, but he was writing a letter to the Clerk of the Supreme Court of the United States, citing the case and apologizing for the rashness of the statement he had made. That represents the highest type of appellate court practice and the highest level of legal integrity.

In this same connection, let me comment on the use of quotations from the Digests, particularly from Corpus Juris and similar texts. I am sure we all realize, first, that it is never safe without reading them to quote cases which are summarized in the texts of these encyclopedias, and furthermore, that there is hardly a proposition on which there is not conflicting authority cited in the same encyclopedia. Some of the volumes, it is true, are authorized by outstanding legal scholars whose opinion as to the weight of authority makes the text itself of some value; others are not. Certainly, therefore, except upon the most elementary and well settled proposition, a quotation of digests of that nature lends little weight to a brief and has slight convincing quality with the appellate court, except only and solely as it has been checked and the cited cases read. A digest citation of course is helpful if used only to direct attention to the general discussion of the field of law involved.

Next, the question of how extensive excerpts from other cases should be set forth in the brief. I find myself one of the worst sinners in this connection; when a court in California or New York has spent a page beautifully arguing the proposition which I am trying to sustain, I find it almost irresistible to copy that portion of the opinion into the brief. I like to have it there; I hope the Court will read it; but I also remember that in many respects I am insulting the Court. I am practically saying to the Court, "I don't believe you will read this case if I cite it, because I think you are too busy or too lazy to get the book and read the opinion, and, therefore, I will quote what it said." I have found several times, however, that the Court is not content with the happy little quotation which I have given, but that they have gotten the book and have studied the entire opinion of which I gave them such a long, and I may add, expensive, excerpt. I am sure we all could save many dollars of the printer's bill if we only convinced ourselves that the Court is not going to rely solely on any particular excerpts which we quote. They are still going to read that original opinion, and the only real purpose that our excerpt serves is possibly to excite curiosity to the point where the opinion will be read more carefully than it might otherwise have been.

So much for some suggestions about the preparation of briefs. Certainly the composite should be in such form that the Court, if they had never heard of the case before, by reading the brief from cover to cover should be advised what the legal issues are, exactly what the case is about, exactly what the facts are, exactly what the law is governing that set of facts, followed by the most persuasive argument of which the writer is capable, to induce the Court to apply the law as he sees it to the facts as he has honestly stated them. The test is this: if the Court had no other information before it, is the brief so clear and so convincing that in the absence of an opposing brief, the Court would inevitably find for the writer? Unless the brief is of that nature, the lawsuit is obviously half lost before it is ever argued.

So the briefs have been finished and filed—we hope on time. At any rate, it has been done, and your opponent has filed his brief. If you have done an adequate job in the first instance, you have already expressed your views of the principal issues in the case. If your analysis of the case is correct, there is not much reason for a reply brief. Alas, however, your opponent very likely has evolved some brilliant theory of which you were completely unaware. Perhaps he has discovered authorities which you have overlooked; perhaps he has committed some other sins which, of course, you would not have committed, but which for some reason your opponent always persists in committing. Perhaps you don't even meet on common ground on the issues of the case. Perhaps the record is misstated by your opponent. Under some of those circumstances, of course, a reply brief is essential. Certainly nothing is to be gained by reiterating the propositions of the principal brief. Certainly the reply should be confined to those matters not previously discussed; to correction of the record, if necessary; to the answering, if able, of propositions raised by an opponent, illogically, we hope, but nevertheless of sufficient plausibility to disturb you. In hard fought litigation the temptation to write reply briefs and say it all over again is a difficult one to forego. Let us remember, however, that repeated reiteration can ultimately exhaust the Court and make everyone begin to wonder whether you were not trying to make up by repetition that which your argument lacks in merit. In any event, you have replied or not, as the circumstances indicated.

You have received the Clerk's notice that you are on the final call, and on such and such a day and hour your case will come on for hearing, at which time you will be allowed thirty minutes to present your side of the controversy.

The Oral Argument

The skillful argument of Appellate causes has been denominated by many lawyers as the highest form of the advocate's art. It involves not only making the convincing and plausible argument which meets the ear, but if it is well done, it involves vast preparation which does not meet the eye.

First of all, for a successful oral presentation one should know the Court. There are courts and there are courts. An argument which may be highly effective in the Supreme Judicial Court of Massachusetts may be an utter failure in the Supreme Court of Kansas. An argument before most of the high courts of our states is not appropriate in the Supreme Court of the United States, and vice versa. The lawyer, therefore, presented with a problem of oral argument of a case on appeal needs everything by way of background that he can possibly learn. He needs, if possible, to know the judges, not personally but something of their manner of thinking, the manner in which their court is conducted, of their background, of their viewpoint if expressed in opinions, of their eccentricities, if any, of their mode of thought. After all, the task of the advocate is to convince appellate judges of the correctness of his position, and to that task he will bring every art of persuasion of which he is capable, and he will have to try to bring it under what have grown to be somewhat adverse conditions.

First, he will be talking against time limitations. The good old days in which counsel might argue for six days before the Supreme Court of the United States as in *McCulloch v. Maryland* or ten days as in the *Girard Will* case are long since gone. The day in which a lawyer can move from one case to another and orient himself to his argument as he goes along is gone. Crowded dockets and the tremendous multiplicity of authority on most propositions still further complicate his task. The question is, how and what to do and say in a limited time to an overburdened court.

There are still as many styles and manners of oral argument on appeal as there are lawyers. It is not possible for most of us to bring to the Bar that facility and succinctness of expression, that whimsical humor, that extreme earnestness of purpose on critical matters which can be brought by a man of the caliber of Hughes, John Davis, George Wharton Pepper, and others. All we can do is to generalize about the do's and dont's, and most of us can profit by following even such simple rules as would be apparent to all of us if we stopped and thought the matter through.

Mr. Davis says, and rightly, that the first thing in the arguing of any Appellate cause is to mentally change places with the court. Suppose you, as a total stranger who had never heard of the case, were sitting there waiting for someone not only to explain it to you but to convince you of the righteousness of his cause. What would you like to hear? It must be remembered that appellate judges are honest, impartial, earnestly trying to reach a correct conclusion. It must be remembered that, in only about half of the appellate courts of the United States do the judges read the briefs before argument. Our own Chief Justice is authority for the statement that on our own court, some of the judges do and some do not read the briefs before argument. Therefore, we must approach the matter on a presumption that the court has never heard of the causes before we stand up and say, "May it please the Court." Our impressions on the Court begin even before we open our mouths. Chief Justice Vanderbilt has well summarized it as follows:

> "In the few seconds that it takes after his case is called for the advocate to rise from the counsel table, gather his papers and approach the lectern and utter the magic words, 'May it please the Court,' he will be giving the Court a preview of his entire argument. If he stumbles over his chair as he leaves it, if he bundles his books and his papers, his glasses and his pencil in his arms like a schoolgirl, if he waddles to the scene of action, if he puts on his glasses and then takes them off before he starts to talk, the Court will know just about what it is in for."[3]

Is it not obvious that we must begin by a statement of the

3 Vanderbilt, *Forensic Persuasion* 32 (1950 Tucker Memorial Lectures at Washington and Lee University).

nature of the case and briefly state its prior history? The case which is so well known to us and with which we have lived for months and perhaps years, the Court has never heard of. We are frequently emotionally wrought up, not to mention nervous. We are well aware of the critical points. We sometimes are writhing under what we think is gross injustice of the trial Court. The temptation to plunge into the middle of the argument is great, and it is so great that it has overcome men even in the Supreme Court of the United States, who, after an opening ten or fifteen minutes, have had to be asked, "Will you please tell us what this case is about." I regard the opening sentence of an oral argument and the opening five minutes of a oral argument as its critical point. The middle section may be filled with plausible argument. The conclusion may sound very convincing, but, if I have not aroused interest, have not stated my facts and noted my disputed propositions of law with absolute clarity so that they are completely understood by every judge on the Bench, then my argument is wasted and my logical conclusion goes for nought. It is here that the maxim previously quoted, that a case well stated, convincingly stated, and argumentatively stated, is half won. I am indebted to George Turner for the story of a member of our Bar, long since deceased, who fumbled to the lectern and exploded his case before the Court with the startling sentence, "This is the case about the rent." Contrast that, if you will, with the opening statement, in a denaturalization case before the Supreme Court of the United States in which counsel said, "the issue is whether a good Nazi can be a good American."[4]

By way of further preparation before the argument is begun, the universal command is to know your record. After all, the record, the transcript of the pleadings, and the bill of exceptions is all that the Appellate Court will ever see, or all that they will ever know about. Whatever play of conduct or emotion may have transpired in the trial, however much the jury may have been influenced by their general knowledge of the parties, or the scene of the accident, or the community understanding, will never appear in the appellate record. You will stand or fall by what is within its binders. Your statements must be substantiated and you must know your record so well that (without fumbling for five minutes) you can put your finger on the testimony relating to any question that may be asked about the lawsuit. This is no mean task. It is not ac-

[4] Knauer v. United States, 328 US 654, 90 LEd 1500, 66 SupCt 1304 (1946).

complished by skimming the record the evening before an argumen or by reading it while sitting in the waiting room. If there is merit in your argument it can be substantiated from the record at every point. It is an insult to the Court to say, "It is somewhere in the record," or, "I just can't put my finger on it."

So the question arises, "What do you say to the Court?" It is here that the true skill of the advocate has full play. It is here that no mechanical process can quite replace a native gift for stating facts and arguments plausibly, sincerely, and convincingly.

Pause a little and consider the circumstances under which you appear before an Appellate Court. "The presentation of a case to an appellate court, like any other instance of advocacy, is an exercise in persuasion: You seek to make the judges decide in your favor. Everything must be bent to that end—every sentence in the brief, indeed every footnote; every sentence in the oral argument; every mannerism, every gesture, even the advocate's attire. Every form of oral advocacy involves the impact of one personality on others. In an appellate court, it is the impact of the lawyer on three, five, seven, or nine judges. Though the number on the Bench may vary, the advocate's aim remains the same: He must always, persistently, constantly, unflaggingly seek to persuade a majority of his listeners to agree with him.

"That being so, he does not help his cause if he antagonizes his judicial audience—or any of them. One never persuades by antagonizing. You may take a dim view of a particular judge, or of a particular decision . . . but when you appear before the judges on behalf of a client, your job is to win that client's case, not to tell them off, or any of them. . . ."[5]

The frequency with which counsel fight a court or show in their mannerism the contempt for a judge or the contempt of a previous opinion always amazes me. That is not one of the ways to "win friends and influence people." Lawyers afflicted with that irrepressible desire "to tell off the court" or abuse its previous decisions should all be required to take a course with Dale Carnegie.

Many techniques have been tried in the argument of Appellate causes. Some have tried writing an oral argument and committing it to memory, but, unfortunately, a question from the Bench may be completely devastating, not only to memory but to the logical

[5] Wiener, *Effective Appellate Advocacy* 232 (1950).

sequence of that which has been memorized. Others have tried to write an oral argument which they can follow at the lectern. Here again the same problems arise. Others rely on following the points in a brief. But, after all, the Court can read a brief. There is nothing more conducive to a loss of interest by the Court than to stand and read excerpts from a brief which some of the judges have read before and which others are capable of reading long after you have departed thence. The oral argument that is convincing and effective is the one that is spontaneous, which flows along smoothly from point to point, never in the language of the brief except and only as it states propositions of law and authorities generally, but which is such an argument as you would address to a friend whom, in all sincerity, you were endeavoring to convince of the righteousness of your cause.

I repeat, there is no substitute for the natural endowment that some people have in this connection. I think it is now generally agreed that an oral argument of an appellate cause should be made from not more than a single page of notes or perhaps if you have glasses trouble, two or three pages if the writing is in half-inch letters. How many times have we seen lawyers addressing appellate courts, trying to follow typewritten manuscripts that were single spaced or written with a dim ribbon that draws the eyes of the speaker to the manuscript till he finds himself reading instead of speaking. He not only loses all of the convincing qualities of his manner and voice but he is actually liable to lull everyone into a state of sleepiness. Are there any of us being addressed who don't wish a speaker to look at us, to talk to us straight from the shoulder as though he meant what he said and believed every word of it? Certainly, a man adequately prepared to make an oral argument needs, at most, careful study of the two or three points that he is going to cover. If he has a dozen assigned errors (which are probably too many in the first place) he stands no chance of covering all those errors adequately in the time allotted to him by the average State Court. If he has pay dirt in his brief, he had much better take one, two, or three, at the most, of his telling points and argue those fully and completely and pray that the others will be adequately examined in the brief if they have merit.

When I was first admitted to this Bar, Judge John J. Sullivan, who had been Chief Justice of this Court, had a very extensive practice in Omaha. Judge Sullivan was a fine lawyer with a tremendously large practice. His technique in all appeals was extremely simple. The Court used to tell me that Judge Sullivan rarely used over 10 or 15 minutes in the presentation of a case. His technique when he was appellant was simply to take one, or two at the most, of the principal points, lay them out clearly and convincingly, and say to the Court, "On this ground there is error in this record and this cause must be reversed. There are other grounds which your Honors may consider at your leisure." After all, it only requires one substantial point of error to secure a reversal, and that one is worth more than the other ten if it is adequately and convincingly made.

Next, so far as I know, there is no law prohibiting people in oral arguments being reasonably entertaining. Of course, it entirely depends on the case. I don't know of very much that can be said of an entertaining nature about corporate litigation or real estate titles. And yet I sometimes suspect that by draping a little of the human element over them, they are given life and vitality they would never have as cold legal propositions. After all, the advocate of an Appellate cause is entitled to all of the "tricks of the trade" of the public speaker. He is entitled to employ all the modulations of the voice, all of the effects of emphasis, all of the rhetorical questions, and all other devices which make his argument effective. How many of these he will use and how appropriate they may be will have to depend entirely upon the Court to which the argument is addressed and may have to depend even upon the particular circumstances of the moment of the argument. Appellate judges, sitting as they frequently do for four to five hours at a time, being human like the rest of us, cannot but appreciate the appropriate clever aside or the entertaining witticism that comes out of a play on words, or any other device that a speaker uses to hold his audience, always remembering, however, that he is trying to convince and not entertain, and that there is a time and a place for all things.

I need hardly say that the day of the courtroom orator is passed, and that is especially true of appellate causes. The Supreme Court is not a jury, and a harangue is not only distasteful but ineffectual. On the other hand, occasionally on grave questions involving great social and economic consequences, restrained oratory has still not left the Appellate courtroom.

One of the most moving statements made in the Supreme Court of the United States, according to many persons who heard it and according to the results that it achieved—was the closing of Senator George Wharton Pepper in the AAA case in which he said:

"My time is fleeting and I must not pause to sum up the argument I have made. I have come to the point at which a consideration of delegation is the next logical step, and that is to be dealt with effectively by my colleague, Mr. Hale. But I do want to say just one final and somewhat personal word.

I have tried very hard to argue this case calmly and dispassionately, and without vehement attack upon things which I cannot approve, and I have done it thus because it seems to me that is the best way in which an advocate can discharge his duty to the Court.

But I do not want our Honors to think that my feelings are not involved, and that my emotions are not deeply stirred. Indeed, may it please your Honors, I believe I am standing here today to plead the cause of the America I have loved; and I pray Almighty God that not in my time may 'the land of the regimented' be accepted as a worthy substitute for the 'the land of the free.' "[6]

In our court, counsel are not bothered so much as in many others with running fire questions from the Bench. Many lawyers are terrified or at least thrown off balance when their train of argument is interrupted by a question. On the contrary, a well prepared lawyer should welcome the questions. It shows the judge is interested in his case. If his case is so weak and his knowledge of the record so frail that he is devastated by a single question from the Bench, he will probably not prevail in any event. Whereas, if his knowledge of the record is perfect, his examination of the law involved and related fields is adequate, a question from the Bench is a magnificent opportunity to continue the argument in the language of the judge who has asked the question. It exposes completely the judge's own thinking, is a guide to that which should be said or not said, and a question completely and convincingly answered may do more to attain the ultimate objective than fifteen minutes of uninterrupted argument when the

[6] *Ibid.* at 218.

speaker has no idea whether the court is agreeing with anything that he says or not.

There are a great many very simple do's and don'ts that can be rapidly condensed. For instance, don't do those things which distract the court's attention from that which you are saying. Don't fuss with papers on the rostrum, don't read, don't make unusual or distracting gestures, don't appear in dress that is unusual and distracts attention, don't interrupt opposing counsel, don't make disparaging remarks about opposing counsel unless they have invited it in the presence of the court and even then its worthwhileness is doubtful, don't show irritation with the Court because of interruption, don't interrupt co-counsel by passing up notes unless it is extremely critical, unless he has misstated the record or seriously misspoken himself, don't cast aspersions on the trial court. The fact that you have appealed is adequate notice to the Supreme Court that you don't think much of the trial court. Don't follow the classic example of saying, "This is an appeal from a decision of Judge So-and-So and there are other reasons also for reversal" no matter how enticing such a wisecrack may seem.

To summarize: know your record, know your court, so far as possible know your judges, know your law thoroughly and completely, and be prepared to discuss it, and then approach your oral argument as you would to a total stranger, telling him of your wrongs and the reasons they should be set right. Do it earnestly, do it sincerely. Never do it hypocritically, never do it casually, and when you have finished telling your story in the best manner you can, then stop, whether that is fifteen minutes, twenty minutes, or thirty minutes. There is no more you can do. Repetition or half hearted closing sentences have ruined many a good argument. You have done your best.

Permitte divis cetera—for the benefit of you commoners, your lawsuit is in the lap of the Gods.

The Motion for Rehearing

After all of the preparation and all of the skill and persuasiveness that has gone into our brief and argument, suppose the blankety blankety so and so's, because of their innate stupidity and all of the other curses which afflict the human race, have rendered an opinion against us. What in the world do we do?

What in the world do we say to the client, and more important for these purposes, what do we say to the court?

I have been very much in favor of greatly extending the time within which to file Motions for Rehearing. I still insist that temperatures do not return to normal within the short space allotted by our rules!

After we have explained the stupidity of the court to our client, and after we have told every other lawyer within the sound of our voices what we think of the court and the judge who wrote the opinion in particular, and how we are certain that he never read the brief and he must have been looking out of the window when we made the oral argument, and besides that, we never thought he liked us anyhow, and all of the other alibis that disappointment can engender, we are still confronted with the practical situation of whether or not we should file a Motion for Rehearing. After all, by filing a Motion for Rehearing, we can at least get ten minutes of oral argument in which we have the rare privilege of telling the Court exactly what we think about them. This is a privilege not easily foregone by one who is still quivering under the sting of defeat.

My advice, which I confess is hard to take myself, is that we had better take a careful second look at the situation. There is always a possibility, you know, that the seven judges on our Court might be more nearly right than we who have been hypnotizing ourselves for months in advance with the idea that our position was unassailable. I would suggest, first, that some of our associates or our friends at the Bar be asked to carefully read the opinion, and if not in fear of their lives, to tell us what they honestly think of it. Second, we should ourselves return, painful though it is, to the scene of the slaughter and most carefully analyze why we lost the lawsuit. My guess is that if those two simple rules were followed, the number of Motions for Rehearing might materially decrease.

I can imagine no more senseless conduct in the world than for a lawyer to write a motion and brief for rehearing in which he abuses the Court and the original opinion. One would think that enlightened self-interest, if nothing else, would prevent that sort of thing. After all, we might have another case some day! Do we hope to win friends and influence people by abusing them or being sarcastically critical of an opinion which has represented hours of effort on the writer's part? Surely, common sense should tell us that a motion for rehearing should never be filed unless there is, for instance, a divided Court, indicating some possibility that the advocate has another advocate inside the conference room, or the court has misunderstood the facts, which not infrequently happens (and which, by the way, is usually the fault of counsel), or unless the Court has been led into a misstatement of a legal proposition.

Under those circumstances a carefully restrained Motion for Rehearing, an argument bearing more a tone of regret and disappointment than abuse and cocksureness, does occasionally, as we know, result in a rehearing and sometimes in a withdrawn opinion.

I think sometimes we miss the boat in complicated litigation when we file blanket motions for rehearing and attack the entire proceeding, when we might gain at least a part of our objective by asking reconsideration of some portion of the opinion that is really vulnerable and which may have an effect on the ultimate disposition of the case.

If I may personalize a little, many years ago I had one matter in our own court in which I filed four successive motions for modification of opinion, each of them attacking particular language which would inevitably have an effect when the cause was remanded, as it had been. Each of those four motions was sustained in part, and by the time the process was complete, we had removed from the opinion language which might have resulted in an instructed verdict against us on the second trial below.

Human nature being what it is, I am reasonably confident we would not have progressed to that point if we had started the Motions for Rehearing by telling the court, in more or less refined language, that they were all wrong and didn't know what they were talking about.

Certainly the vast majority of the cases decided by our own court, to me as an outsider in reading them, indicate that a Motion for Rehearing is actually a waste of time. The box score on the allowance of such motions indicates that at least the Court feels similarly.

On the other hand, we must recognize that courts are human, are subject to errors; that they make mistakes like the rest of us; that they have certain pride of opinion; that they are earnestly seeking to render justice between the parties as best they can, and that if a true error can be pointed out, embarrassing as it may be and reluctant as the Court may be, they will correct that error. Certainly, to have a Motion for Rehearing allowed, one must shoot with a rifle and not with a shotgun. The complaint must be pin-pointed, must be accurate, it must be forceful, it must not be insulting. If it is not all these, I think we have learned that the little postcard, "Motion overruled" is very apt to follow after the next conference of the Court.

Adapted from Vol. 33, Nebraska Law Review (1954).

Practical Hints in the Preparation of Briefs

By John F. Dillon

It is, of course, impossible fully to go into this subject within the limits of a short paper. It is but practicable to outline some of the more material points. I propose to give a few hints only concerning the preparation of briefs. Much of what may be said is equally applicable to oral arguments. Indeed, an oral argument is usually based upon the brief which it may, according to circumstances, either expand or abridge.

The first essential to either mode of presenting a cause to a Court is a minute study and thorough understanding of the facts and the law of the particular case. Not some other case, but *the* case in hand. Cases presenting to superficial observation the same general features, are often found, upon more careful scrutiny, to contain elements or to be wanting in elements which make them essentially distinguishable. The same state of facts often give rise to different principles, depending upon the character or relations of the parties to the controversy. A very common fault is found in the failure to take into consideration *all* the facts upon which the legal duty or liability arises. But perhaps the most difficult function of the lawyer is to determine which of the facts are essential and which are non-essential; to eliminate the latter and to show, against the possible contention of the opposing counsel, their immateriality. The facts of a given cause may be and often are numerous. But many, perhaps a majority, of cases turn upon one or two controlling points. Study and careful discrimination are necessary to select from the mass of facts those that are controlling; to select from the storehouse of the law the legal principles which justly apply to the controlling facts. In the study of a cause, after the controlling facts are ascertained, I have found it to be a most useful general inquiry to make: *What is the intrinsic justice of this case?* If it is clear that right and justice are on my client's side, I can prognosticate with great confidence a favorable result. But if they are on his adversary's side, and I have to rely upon the provisions of an uninterpreted statute, or upon some reported case which I suppose to be in point, the reliance generally, and I may add, rightfully fails.

If the *right and justice* of a case are clear, the counsel may feel assured that, with rare exceptions, right and justice are coincident with the true principles of the law applicable to it. If a legal principle is asserted, which is subversive of justice, it is quite certain either that there is no such principle, or what is, perhaps, the more common error, the principle, though sound when rightly applied, is inapplicable to the case in hand.

The careful study of a cause such as I am insisting upon as being absolutely essential, will necessarily lead the counsel to form his theory of his cause, and, so far as he may, the theory of his adversary. This done, the work of formulating the brief may be begun, and here the first step is the

Statement of the Case

Not only the first step, but the most important. Not only the most important, but it may perhaps surprise the legal reader to add *the most difficult.* As a result of large observation and experience, I feel obliged to say that comparatively few lawyers understand the art of stating a cause to the Court. Some have no plan at all. Some begin in the middle. Others fail to discriminate between what is essential and what is immaterial. Others are verbose and rambling. You here perceive the value of what is said above as to the necessity of a careful study of your cause, and the formation of your theory of it. The statement of the case consists in the regular and logical exposition of the material facts, and, where necessary, showing that other facts are immaterial. The importance of a concise but complete statement of a cause is found in the fact that perhaps nine cases out of ten are practically decided when the case is stated; and your case may be lost if you have omitted the controlling of even material facts in your presentation of it.

The late Mr. Justice Curtis of the Supreme Court of the United States was remarkable for his felicity and power of condensed but complete and accurate statements. His reported judgements both on the Circuit and in the Supreme Court may be profitably studied, as examples of the mode of properly stating a cause, as well as for their legal learning, and as models of judicial style.

Having stated the facts of the cause, the next question is, *What is the law of the cause?*

And here the first impulse of the average lawyer is, "Is there any case in point?" If the lawyer proceeds carefully he will first inquire and make sure whether there is any constitutional provision, Federal or State, applicable to the case stated. Next, whether there is any statutory provision applicable to it, and whether and how it has been judicially construed. Failing to find his case controlled either by constitutional provisions or statutes, his next inquiry should be what legal duty or liability arises on this state of facts—in other words, what are the true legal principles applicable thereto? To determine this, he naturally and properly has recourse to his books—Elementary Treatises and Reports. Textbooks of acknowledged merit may of course be used. There is, however, much difference in their value; too many are worthless and unreliable. A statement of the law by writers such as Sugden, Byles, Benjamin, Mr. Justice Lindley, Chancellor Kent and some other authors of recognized merits, carries with it a very strong presumption of its correctness; and often more force than the mere statement of the law in an isolated case in a book of reports. But the highest evidence of legal principles is, as we all know, to be found in the Reports, which not only state the principle but show its applications.

The most common defect I have observed in the argument of causes next to faulty "statements" is *the missuse of reported cases.* No lawyer is justified in citing a case in his brief which he has not carefully read and studied. What does this mean? It means that without a careful reading and study of the case cited it can not be seen that it is applicable to the case in hand. Concerning the proper use of adjudged cases and their missuse in other respects, I may say something hereafter. But if the lawyer conscientiously pursues the course above indicated, viz., to cite no case upon his brief until he has read it so carefully that he could himself make an accurate syllabus of it, he will avoid a most prevalent and mischievous practice—the loose, careless and inconsiderate citation of cases. A citation of a case under a given proposition ought, unless distinctly otherwise stated, to be equivalent to an implied professional certificate that, in the writer's judgment, the case cited is an express authority in support of such proposition.

Adapted from Vol. 14, American Law Review.

A Case on Appeal—A Judge's View

By Honorable Herbert F. Goodrich

It must be apparent that no one can provide another with a chart to bring him success upon an appeal.

Shouldn't a judge be able to do it? In the course of a few years he hears hundreds of appeals and writes scores of opinions on a great many different questions. But most judges sit only in one Appellate Court. The judge knows, as well as one person can, his own mental processes. If he is observant he knows fairly well those of his colleagues. But he and his colleagues, as compared with all the appellate judges in the country, comprise a very small fraction of the number. Members of federal Courts of Appeals get about somewhat and sit with each other in different Circuits. But even with this additional means of widening experience the material on which to found a generalization about appellate judges and appellate procedure still remains limited.

What about the practicing lawyer? Many lawyers argue, over the years, a great many appellate cases. Some they win and some they lose. But out of that experience it is pretty hard to give generalizations as to what wins a case. Many cases well briefed and well argued are lost and many others neither well briefed nor well argued are won. Indeed, some lawyers say they tremble with apprehension when their opponent is highly incompetent because of the fear that a court, in its effort to make sure that the client does not lose because of the incompetence of his lawyer, will unconsciously become an advocate for the party who is badly represented. However that may be, neither lawyers nor judges would recommend to one who has an appeal that his best chance of success is to secure the poorest lawyer he can find to present his case in the hope that the court will fight his battle itself.

Does An Appeal Lie?

Many things may happen in the course of a trial which counsel may feel are erroneous maybe even outrageous. They may arise any time, from start to finish. It may be a ruling on a motion regarding the pleadings, or it may be refusal of postponement of the trial. It may be a ruling on evidence. It may be the qualification of an expert, or it may be the judge's charge or his failure to charge the jury as counsel wishes. Some of these adverse rulings at an early stage of the trial may influence the whole course of the litigation thereafter. Well, then, why not appeal? Why should the parties be compelled to go through a long and expensive trial when at the very start there was an error which counsel feels was so deep and far-reaching that the whole course of the litigation was thrown off the track? On the other hand, how much of the course of a particular piece of litigation should be interrupted by trips to an Appellate Court to correct errors which may wash out in the final result? After all, no matter how many errors a trial court has committed in a litigant's case, if he has final verdict and judgment notwithstanding, he has no occasion for spending time and money on appeals.

The question, when may an appeal be taken, is one which is the subject of much argument[1] and upon which the practice varies. In the federal courts the general rule is that an appeal lies only from a final judgment or order with certain specified exceptions.[2] This sounds easy if you say it fast. But the determination of what is "final" involves both trial and Appellate Courts in troublesome questions every year.[3] Practice in some states is much more liberal on the matter of appeals before final judgment.[4]

Which is the best course to follow we need not discuss, much less pronounce upon here. The first and obvious thing for a

[1] See Clark v. Taylor, 163 F(2d) 940 (2nd Cir. 1947) and Libbey-Owens Ford Glass Co. v. Sylvania Industrial Corp., 154 F(2d) 814 (2nd Cir. 1946).

[2] 62 Stat. 920 (1948), 28 USC §§ 1291-2; FCA 28 §§ 1291, 1292 (1950 Supp), "The courts of appeals shall have jurisdiction from all final decisions of the district courts of the United States . . . except where a direct preview may be had in the Supreme Court." Other exceptions are listed in the next following section.

[3] See United States v. Sineiro, 190 F(2d) 397 (3rd Cir. 1951); David v. District Columbia, 187 F(2d) 204 (D. C. Cir. 1950); Kam Koon Wam v. E. E. B'ack, Ltd., 182 F (2d) 146 (9th Cir. 1950).

[4] See 12 Purd. Pa. Stat. Anno. §§ 1091-1107 (1949); 60 Kan. R. S. § 3303 (1949), ". . . an order affecting a substantial right . . ."; Minn. Stat. (1949), c. 605, § 605.09(3), ". . . from an order involving the merits of the action or some part thereof."

lawyer, who feels himself aggrieved by the trial judge's action, to do is to find out if an appeal lies at that point. If it does, he asks the question whether the appeal is worth taking. If it does not, the most that he can do is to make sure that his point is properly made in the record and get along about the other business of the trial.

This last statement deserves mention, although not much discussion now, so far as concerns the "properly made" requirement. In federal courts, and in most state courts, there is no longer necessity for the old fashioned "exceptions" with the sealed "bill of exceptions" as the basis for his record on appeal. Nowadays an objection is sufficient to preserve one's rights if it is timely made and clearly enough made so that an Appellate Court can see that the trial court had the point before it and actually ruled on it. Generalizations are dangerous on matters of local practice. The lawyers should be advised as to what is necessary to make the record so that an Appellate Court may consider a party's objection in argument.

Is an Appeal Worth-while?

Appeals are expensive. Lawyers have to be paid; stenographers have to be paid; printers have to be paid. If the case is a small one it may well be that an appeal, even if successful, costs more than what it brings the litigant even with costs awarded to him as a successful appellant. That is too bad. A man should not have to lose a meritorious case because victory costs too much. But perhaps in a completely perfect world people would be so reasonable that there would be no need for litigation. And that is no kind of world for lawyers to live in for they would have nothing to do.

Appeals are sometimes used as a basis for helping to induce settlements. How successful a means to this end they are a judge is hardly in a position to say. But that settlements come after appeals is known to every appellate judge. Sometimes they even come after a case has been submitted. Usually settlements between the parties may come at any time at the will of the parties themselves. There are some rules, however, regulating the matter where the lawsuit involves, not only the one litigant who wants to settle or dismiss, but others as well. That is a matter to be watched for. Sometimes a court must give its permission as well as the parties.[5]

Sometimes a timid litigant will lose a notable victory by settlement after submission. Our Court had a case a few years ago in which an appellant was about to win a smashing victory. A draft of an opinion was all written and the judges, in an unusually careful conference, had agreed on the result and almost decided the language by which the result was to be expressed. Then came word that appellant had accepted a settlement and asked for a dismisal of the appeal. The appeal was dismissed and the distinguished contribution to the law embodied in the tentative opinion went into the waste basket. Neither litigant nor lawyer ever knew what he had lost.

This is as definite as the matter can be put. Whether an appeal is worth taking is a matter of judgment for each case. Unless there is really serious error in the trial an appeal is inadvisable unless there is something to be gained by delay or leverage for settlement. Judges do not like small points. No long trial can go through without something to which a party or his lawyer can technically object, but if the whole record looks fair and satisfactory a small technical point is likely to be an annoyance to an Appellate Court instead of an advantage to the litigant. This is not always so. If the case is a criminal one and constitutional rights are involved, the Appellate Court must be very astute to see that they are fully protected. If not, the Supreme Court will.[6] But if the trial record contains error and the error seems substantial and the case is worth appealing, the Appellate Court should, and probably will, hear it patiently and gladly. That is what it is there to do.

The Stairs Up

How does one get to the Appellate Court from the trial court? The answer is simple: follow the rules. For instance, an appeal is usually started by filing with the clerk of the trial court a "notice of appeal" within a prescribed period of time after filing of the judgment or order to be appealed.[7] In some cases the clerk may then notify opposing counsel and in others it may be the duty of

[5] See Fed. R. Civ. P. 23 (c): "A class action shall not be dismissed or compromised without the approval of the court." See Webster Eisenlohr, Inc. v. Kalodner, 145 F (2d) 316 (3rd Cir. 1944); May v. Midwest Refining Co., 121 F (2d) 431 (1st Cir. 1941); Cohen v. Young, 127 F (2d) 721 (6th Cir. 1942).

[6] See United States v. Hoffman, 341 US 479, 95 LEd 1118, 71 SupCt 814 (1951); Upshaw v. United States, 335 US 410, 93 LEd 100, 69 SupCt 170 (1948); Thiel v. Southern Pacific Co., 328 US 217, 90 LEd 1181, 66 SupCt 984 (1946).

the attorney to notify them himself. It may also be necessary to secure and file an appeal bond and perhaps also a supersedeas bond if it is desirable to stay execution on the judgment or order until the appeal has settled the controversy.[8] Filing fees are usually required with some of these papers and should be paid promptly to avoid unnecessary difficulties.

Getting The Case Ready for Submission

One need not develop the proposition that after counsel has got his case properly in an Appellate Court he must decide what he is going to present to that court and how he is going to present it. Laymen seem to assume that it is enough to come with a story something like that of the apocryphal appeal to the chancellor's conscience: "I am a poor devil and I can't get justice." However easy a modern Appellate Court may want to make the procedural path for litigants and their lawyers, the orderly conduct of appellate business requires something more precise than the client's statement that he was robbed in the court below in order to get his grievance considered. Let us then start consideration of that "something more."

Points to Be Urged for Reversal

Probably every court rule or statute requires the appellant to set out the points he relies upon to show error in the trial of his case. The statement of the rules varies somewhat, but their purpose is a common one. The appellant must set out in orderly fashion the reasons why he thinks his adverse decision was incorrect.[9] This requirement does not admit very much discussion. Legal argument in this respect is the same as argument of any other kind. Any debater makes at least an attempt to set out his side of a proposition in a one, two, three order. So does the lawyer's son when the lad is late getting home with the family car. A few matters of advice may be relevant.

---

7 See Fed. R. Civ. P. 73(a) and 63 Stat. 104 (1949), 28 USC § 2107; FCA 28 § 2107 (1950 Supp.).

8 See Fed. R. Civ. P. 73(c).

9 *E.g.*, ". . . a statement of the questions involved, setting forth each question separately, in the briefest and most general terms. . ." Rule 24(2) (b) of Rules of U.S. Third Circuit Court of Appeals. See also Code of Iowa (1950), Rules Civ. Proc. 344(a) for a similar and typical state rule.

First. The points should be clear. Sometimes appellants tend to criss-cross them and point three sounds so much like point two that it is hard to find any difference, even if they are cross-read with the judge watching text and his secretary reading aloud the other point. The end product may often be an inconspicuous distinction which makes no difference. Solicitors drawing claims for the patent office frequently put in a great number of claims with only minute differences between them so as to cover all possibilities for the invention claimed. That may be the effective way to draft patent applications. But it is very confusing to judges on appeal. The more clearly the point is made, and the more distinctly it stands out, the more easily the judge will understand it and, it may be hoped, in understanding it, appreciate its significance.

Second. There should not be too many points on appeal. A case with two or three points clearly stated and vigorously argued is much better than one filled with a dozen bases of complaint. If a court goes through a half dozen points which it regards too small to be material it is likely to become a little impatient concerning the possibilities of the rest. Furthermore, a long, long list of points to be urged on appeal is in danger of creating the impression in the judges' minds that "the trial couldn't possibly have been so bad as that." If one of the grounds for complaint is that there were erroneous rulings on evidence, perhaps it will be possible to group them together so that one point becomes erroneous rejection or acceptance of evidence, and the individual instances can serve as examples rather than each one constituting a main point on appeal. One error in rejection or omission of testimony is, on the whole, not likely to procure a reversal unless the point was critical. [For example of a critical point see US v. Augustine, 189 F(2d) 587 (3rd Cir. 1951)]. It can be classed as "harmless error."[10] But the cumulative effect of a series of unfavorable erroneous rulings may convince the Appellate Court that the litigant did not get fair treatment.

Third. The order of the points may make some difference in presentation, both orally and in the brief. For the appellant the

[10] "On the hearing of any appeal or writ of certiorari in any case, the court shall give judgment after an examination of the record without regard to errors or defects which do not affect the substantial rights of the parties." 28 USC § 2111; FCA 28 § 2111 (Supp. 1951).

best rule is to bring up the strongest point first and hit it as hard as it can be hit. It is the first point which necessarily gets first the attention of the men in the black robes while their attention is at its highest. If unimpressive and smaller points are discussed before the biggest ones are taken up, the impression will be that this case does not amount to much. But if a good strong point is effectively presented, the smaller ones may fall into place as clinching arguments to support the conclusion already indicated by the strong first point.

The Record or Abstract Thereof

Here is the place where the printing costs mount up. If the Appellate Court is going to review the action of a trial court, a commission, or an official, obviously it must be informed as to what went on in the proceeding it is asked to review. How is it going to find out? Assuming that there was testimony taken in the hearing which is the subject of the review, and assuming the testimony was transcribed, one way, and a simple way, to find out what went on in the hearing, is to get the original papers before the Appellate Court along with a transcript of the testimony. But that would give only one copy of the relevant material. Appellate Courts are composed of panels of three to nine, and sometimes even more judges. Even then, they could pass the papers around and sometimes they do. But it is not an efficient way of doing court business. Some material is almost certain to be lost and the delay occasioned by successive instead of simultaneous consideration of the material would be unfortunate for all litigants. One of the objectives to be attained by good appellate procedure is reasonable expedition. And that would be defeated by one-copy methods. Therefore, some practice swings to the opposite extreme and requires the appellant to print the "whole record."[11] This has two disadvantages. One is that it is exceedingly expensive. And in days of mounting printing costs it may prevent an appeal. The second objection is that it brings to the Appellate Court a large amount of unnecessary and irrelevant material in many instances. In almost no case is the entire record necessary for consideration of whatever points the appellant has to make. In some cases the relevant points on appeal are shown by a comparatively small amount of all the

[11] See *e.g.,* 12 Purd. Pa. Anno. Stat. §§ 1110, 1132, 1134 (1949); 231 Mass. Stat. Anno. § 135 (1949).

things said, done and written that went before the tribunal of first instance.

This matter of the bulk and expense of a record has had thought by those interested in providing quick and inexpensive justice. Sometimes records are shortened by requiring an "abstract" of testimony.[12] In some of the federal circuits the rules provide for an "appendix" to the brief. The appendix method is designed to ease the burden and expense of getting an appellate case ready. The object of the appendix is to give the court what counsel think the judges should know to understand the case and its problems.[13]

If the appellant's appendix leaves out something the appellee thinks the court should have, the appellee may prepare an appendix of his own. If that appendix bulks too large the result may be that a conscientious court is pushed to the task of hopping from book to book to find the pieces of testimony in which it is interested. This, of course, is not good. A joint appendix by the lawyers for the opposing parties is the ideal solution. But it is not always that the situation between the parties and their lawyers permits this common sense method of handling the matter to be submitted in connection with the appeal.

Court rules will probably provide that the material brought up as the record or appendix be printed on a definitely named size of paper. Why? Lawyers are grown-up people and should, perhaps, be allowed to choose pages of the size they like. And judges are grown-up people and ought to be able to handle books of any size within their physical strength. The rule restricting size is one for purely practical convenience. Most courts bind briefs and appendices and keep them permanently in their libraries. Uniformity is desirable. That is the only reason for the rule. Two other small points are worth mentioning in connection with this matter of the record. Some courts are now allowing various substitutes for the

---

12 See 12 Okla. Stat. § 957 (1941); Code of Iowa (1950), Rule Civ. Prac. 340.

13 See Rule 24(2)(e) of Rules of U. S. Court of Appeals for the Third Circuit: "An appendix (which may be separately bound) which shall contain the relevant docket entries below arranged chronologically in a single column, any relevant charge or opinion of the court, agency, board or commission below, the judgment, decree, order or decision appealed from or sought to be reviewed or enforced and such other parts of the record material to the questions presented as the appellant or petitioner deems it essential for the court to read in order to decide those questions."

standard type of printing in an effort to cut down the expense.[14] Others will do so in the future. Also, it may be remembered that if the client is without funds there probably will be some provision for getting a case up on a typewritten brief and appendix. There is some formality required in connection with this although occasionally the court orders it of its own motion.[15]

The Brief

Now we come to the heart of our discussion. Timely notice of appeal has been given. Whatever record required has been prepared, and is in the hands of the printer. Within a given period fixed by court rules the appellant must file his brief. This question of date is worth noticing. A definite time limit on the filing of a brief is universally required. Additional time can be had, in accordance with court rules, when needed. Unless one is in a fearful jam he had better not ask for more time. It is better to have the case move on as scheduled.

It is hard to overstate the importance of the brief on an appeal. Oral argument will be discussed later. It is important, too. But it is made only once in nearly all instances and it is inevitable that some of its effect will be lost in the interval between the time the argument is made and the court opinion appears. The longer the opinion-writing judge takes to produce an opinion the hazier the points of the oral argument become. And there is nothing which counsel can do to hurry the opinion-writing judge. That will have to be left to his colleagues. But the brief speaks from the time it is filed and continues through oral argument, conference, and opinion writing. Sometimes a brief will be read and reread, no one knows how many times except the judge and his law clerk. Indeed, the statement is sometimes made that some judges lift a portion of the successful party's brief and incorporate it into the opinion of the court. Whether this is a compliment to the lawyer or a stricture upon the working habits of some judges need not be enlarged

14 Rules of United States Court of Appeals for the Third Circuit 24(7), as amended, 1951, ". . . Such printing may be done by ordinary typographic methods or by the process of offset duplicating."

15 28 USC § 753(f); FCA 28 § 753(f) (1951), ". . . Fees for transcripts furnished in other proceedings to persons permitted to appeal in forma pauperis shall also be paid by the United States if the trial judge or a circuit judge certifies that the appeal is not frivolous but presents a substantial question. . . ." See also Rules of U. S. Court of Appeals for the Third Circuit 26(2), "The court may also, if the facts warrant, permit any such petitioner to file briefs in typewritten form."

upon here. Certain it is that the brief is the most important thing about an appeal, although oral argument may be the most fun.

Mention has already been made that there is probably a court rule about the typography, size of paper, index, list of citations, and the like. They are readily found in a court rule. Even if not in terms required, an index and table of citations is something a careful writer will put in anyhow. And, if he is a careful writer, he will check his citations in proof just to be sure they are accurate. An inaccurate citation will probably not lose a case, but the presence of very many of them shows sloppy work.

There is probably a page limit to the brief, a limit which may be extended by permission if counsel really thinks he needs more pages to tell his story. Usually he will not need more pages. A brief is more likely to be hurt by too many pages than too few. Of course, it is easier to tell a long story than a short one. The page limit not only makes less reading for judges, but it compels the lawyer to get his thoughts into clearer shape. Therefore, the page limit rule really helps the lawyer to present his case clearly. The effect on the judge's eyesight is interesting to him but not important, generally.

How should a brief be written? The general principle is the same as that of any good writing or speech-making and is contained in the King's instructions to Alice in *Alice in Wonderland*: "Begin at the beginning and go on till you come to the end: then stop." But there are some technical points about arrangement and the like which are especially applicable to brief writing and these should be talked about here.

The Tax Division of the Department of Justice has a skeleton outline for its brief on appeal which was worked out under the direction of Mr. William D. Mitchell when he was Solicitor General of the United States. It is really very useful and will apply to nearly every case, although not quite all. Here are the heads:

Opinion Below
Jurisdiction
Questions Presented
Statute and Regulations Involved
Statement (This is a statement of what the brief-writer considers the relevant facts.)
Statement of Points to Be Urged

Summary of Argument
Argument
Conclusion

In many cases, of course, some of the points in this outline may be omitted. Not every case involves statutes or regulations, although all tax cases do. Not every case has an opinion filed by the court below, although the fact that no opinion is filed is relevant information for the Appellate Court too. A conclusion is often a formal paragraph saying that for the foregoing reasons the judgment should be reversed or affirmed as the case may be. The "Summary of Argument" is not as good a device as theoretically it might be thought to be. If the brief-writer must put his various arguments in summary form before they have been made *in extenso* he must necessarily be peremptory in his method of statement. Otherwise he repeats the argument to be made later. Peremptory conclusions on points, before the reader of the brief has had a chance to go along and see how the points are developed, is premature. The statements often raise great doubt and sometimes opposition in the mind of one who is just getting acquainted with the case. It would be better to have the summary of the argument and the conclusion of the brief writer put in one section, following the extensive argument, as a sort of recapitulation of the whole. The point just made is not directed to the presence of a paragraph telling the court what the propositions to be argued are, but refers to an attempted synopsis of the argument prior to its being made. With that exception the outline is very serviceable and moves the Appellate Court on from point to point with no lost motion.

The brief-writer has his points to be urged to the court as a reason for reversal or affirmance. That was discussed in this paper earlier. It was suggested there that the points be stated so that the strongest one or two come first. The same applies in briefing. If the strong points are urged with great vigor the smaller ones will either disappear or become additional reasons for a conclusion reached on the main point. Again, it should be repeated that there should not be too many reasons for reversal.

The Statement of the Case

The lawyer knows all about this case, presumably. But the judges know nothing. The lawyer's first job is one of exposition.

He must tell the court in the shortest possible fashion what his case is about. And in telling what it is about he must keep in mind that it is not a general background in which the court is interested; it is the very points involved in this appeal.

In preparing the statement the writer should be meticulously accurate. Of course, he will state it sympathetically for his side. But he must not tell a half truth by putting in partial statements. Quotations or paragraphs from the testimony should be followed by a parenthetical reference to the record or appendix where the statement is to be found in full. When a judge reads the statement of facts he should see what the background of the appeal is. If the important questions on appeal are fact questions they can and will be developed in the course of the brief. The initial statement is to give the judge his bearings.

The Points on Appeal

A brief is not poetry. But there is no reason why it need be dull reading. The first virtue it must have is clarity. Attaining clarity is a painstaking effort. If one thinks clearly one can write clearly if he puts enough work into what he writes. There is no reason why one should have to read a sentence in a brief, or anywhere else, three or four times before he understands what it says. Lawyers frequently use long sentences. They would write more clearly and effectively if they would chop those sentences into shorter pieces. One good way to see how the material runs is to read it aloud to somebody else, a junior in the office or, if she will listen, one's wife. There is no reason why legal propositions cannot be stated so that they can be understood by any intelligent listener. Of course, when the material is highly technical, as in a tax case or patent case, the hearer may be troubled because he or she does not have enough technical background to know the terms. But even then, a great deal more clarity is possible than is frequently attained.

One should write logically as well as clearly. Perhaps this is simply the other side of the shield. If one writes clearly the development will probably proceed from point to point. What all this adds up to is to say that brief writing is much like any other writing in which one seeks to explain something to another and convince him that the explanation is accurate. If a man writes a good letter he should be able to write a good brief.

Authorities

How much material should one put in a brief? There are lawyers who boast that they give a court every decision on every question. If they do they make a lot of unnecessary work for themselves.

This business of the use of authorities is worth a little talk. What is a citation good for anyway? Perhaps we can classify citations into three types. One is the citation of the authoritative decision which binds the court in which an appeal is heard. The second is the citation of a decision on the same point by a court which does not bind this court. And the third is the citation of a case which is analogous or distinguishable either by the present Appellate Court or some other.

All would agree that the ruling by the superior tribunal is conclusive. In fact, if the appellant has one of these against him in a case he is in a bad way. But there are not very many situations in which this happens, really. If the Supreme Court of the United States has ruled on a constitutional question that ruling binds all the state courts and all the federal courts. But a state court is not concluded by a federal court's decision on state law, even by the Supreme Court. Lower federal courts are, of course, bound by Supreme Court rulings on non-constitutional questions such as, for instance, the Labor Relations Act and the taxing statutes. But one need hardly add that it is frequently open to argument whether a given case does conclude the question now before the court. If it does not, the presence of dicta or intimations looking opposite to the appellant's view need not scare him out. Passing dictum may be seized upon and made the foundation for decision in a later case. Or, if the court as now constituted does not care for it, it may be explained away or passed over in silence.

If the appellant is confronted with a decision from another court which is contrary to his position he need not be too badly frightened. If the case is directly against him he will do well to say so and not try to distinguish the indistinguishable. He can attack it as incorrectly decided and proceed to show his reasons why it is not correctly decided. If the court before whom he argues has the courage of independence of judgment, here is a place where that judgment can very well be exercised. If the court thinks the cited decision is right it will take the holding as a guide for itself. If the court thinks it to be wrong, it will not.

Finally, what about analogous cases? How useful they are depends upon the kind of point the court has before it. All courts make some law. But they do not make it in great jumps, but only in short steps. Every court by nature and training wants to keep itself in line with the development of the law as a whole. If it has a new point it will be helped in deciding that new point in seeing how problems close to that which is before it have been met. A good instance is found in the cases arising under the new Federal Tort Claims Act. Here is a new piece of legislation which starts without any precedents whatever. It is most helpful to a court with a problem arising under that Act to see how judicial brethren in other courts have developed the points arising under the Act. On the other hand, if the case is one involving local negligence law, where every point has been contested through many cases, analogous propositions must be sifted very carefully before they need be cited. They may tend only to confuse rather than clarify.

Some brief writers throw in an enormous number of decisions as if by mere numbers an Appellate Court can be impressed. Some of the government agencies are offenders in this respect. This point is best illustrated by several examples from briefs on file in the library of the United States Court of Appeals for the Third Circuit. For instance, here are some from the National Labor Relations Board briefs. The lawyers for the Board know their jobs. They are well prepared; they know their cases. But they do love citations. Note the following:

Proposition: Disproportionate hiring of non-union workers permits an inference of discrimination. 9 cases cited at pp. 19-20 of Board's Brief in N.L.R.B. v. Clausen, 188 F(2d) 439 (3rd Cir. 1951).

Proposition: Where employer is guilty of illegal discrimination among employees, it is immaterial that his motive may have been to benefit them. 8 cases cited at p. 20 of Board's Brief in Cusano v. N.L.R.B., 190 F(2d) 898 (3rd Cir. 1951).

Proposition: Right to control result of work and means and manner of accomplishment is general test of employer-employee relation. 12 cases cited at pp. 17-18 of Board's Brief in N.L.R.B. v. Nu Car Carriers, Inc., 189 F(2d) 756 (3rd Cir. 1951).

In the *Nu Car Carriers* case, the Board's brief contains citations to eighty-five cases and the problem involved there is largely one of factual analysis, the legal problem being only whether the relation between the parties was employer-employee or that of independent contractor.

Now, what is the purpose of all these citations? Is a judge going to read all these decisions? If counsel thinks so he is more naive than counsel should be expected to be. Courts do and can read briefs and they can and do read opinions of other judicial brethren. But unless a case is of critical importance in a new field it is to be very much doubted whether anybody is going to read all the decisions to write an opinion in one Labor Board case which turns largely on facts anyhow.

Two or three decisions directly in point are worth a dozen which are not, or, in most cases, a dozen which are. Lawyers know good opinions when they see them. There is no reason why the selective process should not be exercised by the brief writer. Of course, if one can find a case directly in point from the very court now hearing an appeal, that is well worth citing even if it is not a model of good writing. Courts hesitate to depart from their own decisions much more than they do to go contrary to the decisions of another court.

A word might be said about law reviews. What about citation of law review material? The time was when law review editors were pleased and proud to see a court deign to recognize them by citing law review articles or notes. That time has long since gone. Student notes are worth citing; considered articles by scholarly writers are almost a must. One is tempted to leave out the word "almost." If counsel do not cite the articles, the judge, especially if he has a law clerk to help him, will almost certainly see if there is not something on the point written by an expert to help him reach a conclusion, particularly if the point is new. What is just said will not apply with run of the mine negligence cases resulting from automobile accidents, which constitute so much of the burden in so many courts.

This caution should not be necessary but since it is sometimes disregarded it is well to note it here. Are the cases relied upon still the law? Have they been modified, distinguished or even overruled?

It is not hard to trace what has happened to a given decision. The lawyer who cites the decision without knowing its subsequent history is leaving himself open to the possibility of being put in a very embarrassing situation. If his relied on authority or an intermediary case has had a subsequent reversal by a higher court of appeal, his failure to know it stamps him as too careless a workman to be relied upon.

All of this has been talked pretty largely from the standpoint of the appellant, his appeal and his brief. This is necessarily so. The appellant is the man who has to set the pace. The appellee meets the appellant's points as best he can. He can set up his brief on the appellant's outline. After all, he won below and all he has to do is to show that there is nothing substantial in what the appellant presents. What is said about authorities is applicable to each.

In neither case should either side indulge in personalities about the other unless it is absolutely necessary. If a lawyer can and needs to show that his opponent or his client is a lying rascal, then it becomes his duty to do so. But courts are not interested in controversies between lawyers and if counsel wants to accuse his opponent of untruths he had better be prepared to prove it. Nor is a court likely to be impressed by counsel depicting his client as being angel white and his opponent as black Satan. This does not always hold true, of course. Sometimes litigants are miserable wretches and ought to get what miserable wretches deserve. But a lawyer who comes to court always with spotless angels opposed to Satan in various forms is likely to amuse rather than arouse the sympathies of the court.

General talk is often helped by concrete example. The example selected is lifted from a very strong brief in the case called *Williamson v. Columbia Gas & Electric Corp.* reported in 186 F(2d) 464. This happens to be from an appellee's brief. No unfavorable comparison is intended with appellant's brief in the same case which was also good nor from other briefs which have come over the desk from time to time. Please note in reading over the material which follows how the argument marches along and how clearly the separate points stand out so that the reader senses the arrangement the first time through. The whole brief is good but the one point here selected will serve as well as anything else for illustration of what has been said above.

PART ONE
Res Judicata

POINT I

THE CAUSE OF ACTION ASSERTED IN THE COMPLAINT DISMISSED IN 1939 WAS THE SAME CAUSE OF ACTION THAT WAS ASSERTED IN THE COMPLAINT HEREIN.

A. Both Actions were Brought Under the Same Section of the Same Statute—38 Stat. 731, 15 USCA § 15 [FCA 15 § 15] (Clayton Act § 4).

Both Complaints asserted, in identical language (Par. 4 of both) that this was an action brought under 38 Stat. 731, 15 USCA § 15 [FCA 15 § 15], commonly known as Section 4 of the Clayton Act. That Section provides:

> "Sec. 4. Any person who shall be injured in his business or property by reason of anything forbidden in the antitrust laws may sue therefor * * *, and shall recover threefold the damages by him sustained, and the cost of suit, including a reasonable attorney's fee."

B. Both Actions were Based on the Same Alleged Injuries Caused by the Same Alleged Forbidden Acts.

Both Complaints alleged exactly the same injuries to the same business and property by reason of the same alleged acts of Columbia. Had it not been (they both alleged) for Columbia's wrongful acquisition of control, suppression of the projected Detroit pipe line, institution of receiverships and domination of the Receiver, Inland—which had theretofore always operated at a loss—would have turned into a profitable operating company. In setting forth these injuries, both Complaints alleged, in an identical narrative sequence, and in identical circumstantial detail, the same monopoly by Columbia, the same threatening "project", the same acts by Columbia to protect the monopoly, viz., the same acquisition of stock control of Inland and Kentucky Fuel, discontinuance of the Detroit line, institution of receiverships, and domination by Columbia of the receiver, Lockhart, to prevent expansion of Inland and Kentucky Fuel markets and to prevent disaffirmance by Lockhart of the burdensome gas contracts. And finally, both Complaints enumerated the identical items of damages, in identical principal amounts, for which three-fold damages were sought.

In dismissing the Complaint in the instant action the District Court said, in its opinion

> "In the present cases, the facts alleged are substantially the same as those that were alleged in the dismissed actions. The damages sought are substantially the same. In addition the right violated and the legal wrong are the same. . . . I am of the opinion, therefore, that under the generally accepted tests there is identity of causes of action between the pending suits and the dismissed suits." (Pl's App. 129a)

C. The Assertion of Different Statutory Grounds for the Illegality of the Same Alleged Acts (Conspiracy Under the Sherman Act in One Complaint and Violation of the Clayton Act in the Other) Does Not Make the Causes of Action Different.

(i) This has Been Expressly Held, for Purposes of Res Judicata, in a Civil Treble Damage Action Under the Anti-Trust Laws.

It is clear that plaintiff's two Complaints alleged the same injuries from the same alleged wrongful acts. In essence, the distinction which plaintiff attempted to make between the two Complaints was to allege that the acts were wrongful for different reasons—in one wrongful because pursuant to a conspiracy in violation of the Sherman Act; in the other because in violation of Section 7 of the Clayton Act.

F. L. Mendez & Co. v. General Motors Corporation, 161 F(2d) 695 (CCA 7th), cert den 332 US 810, is directly in point. The substance of the decision is stated in the first headnote as follows:

> "Successive actions by automobile dealer against manufacturer based upon same wrongful cancellation of dealer's franchise, involved same causes of action though the first action was brought under Sherman Anti-Trust Act and the second action under Clayton Act, and hence judgment for defendant in first action was res judicata in second action."

The Court stated the grounds of the decision as follows:

"* * * The primary right of plaintiff alleged to have been injured was its contract right to purchase automobiles. The wrong of defendant, as asserted by plaintiff, was wrongful cancellation of that right. The fact that in one case defendant's repudiation of the contract was alleged to have been wrongful for one reason and in the other for another reason does not alter the fact that the cause of action was for the same injury, —wrongful cancellation of the franchise. * * * (p. 697)

"* * * We are dealing with a civil suit in which the private right of plaintiff has been, as it says, unlawfully taken from it. It has one right and one only; the right to enjoy its contract. It complains of one wrongful act, namely, deprivation of that right. Its action is not for recovery under the Sherman Act or for recovery under the Clayton Act but for recovery for the wrongful cancellation of its property right. The gist of its action is its injury arising from alleged wrongful deprivation of its contract right.

"Whether the cancellation was caused by any one or more allegedly illegal acts is a question which must be litigated and determined fully in one suit and not in separate suits. * * *" (p. 698)

(ii) A Cause of Action is the Wrongful Invasion of Plaintiff's Right, and Not the Grounds of Illegality.

The Mendez case, *supra,* applied to the particular situation presented by successive treble damage suits, a long established principle: that a cause of action consists of the act invading plaintiff's right and not of the grounds of its illegality, and therefore all "media concludendi" will be bound by the judgment.

In Baltimore S. S. Co. v. Phillips, 274 US 316, the court held that a judgment in an action for personal injuries arising from defendant's negligent failure to provide safe equipment and a safe place to work (a ship) barred a second action in which the negligence charged was the incompetence of officers and employees in charge of the ship and appliances. The Court said:

"A cause of action does not consist of facts, but of the unlawful violation of a right which the facts show. * * * The mere multiplication of grounds of negligence alleged as causing the same injury does not result in multiplying the causes of action. 'The facts are merely the means, and not the end. They do not constitute the cause of action, but they show its existence by making the wrong appear. "The thing, therefore, which in contemplation of law as its cause, becomes a ground for action, is not the group of facts alleged in the declaration, bill, or indictment, but the result of these in a legal wrong, the existence of which, if true, they conclusively evince." ' Chobanian v. Washburn Wire Company, 33 R. I. 289, 302" (p. 321; italics in the original).

Since the grounds of alleged illegality are not themselves the cause of action, a plaintiff is required to set forth at one time all of the grounds upon which he rests his claim. Authority and statements to this effect are very numerous. Grubb v. Public Utilities Comm., 281 US 470, 478-9:

> "The thing presented for adjudication in the case in the state court was the validity of the order, and it was incumbent on the appellant to present in support of his asserted right of attack every available ground of which he had knowledge. He was not at liberty to prosecute that right by piecemeal, as by presenting a part only of the available grounds and reserving others for another suit, if failing in that. * * *"

Justice Holmes, in United States v. California & Ore. Land Co., 192 US 355, 358:

> "* * * But the whole tendency of our decisions is to require a plaintiff to try his whole cause of action and his whole case at one time. He cannot even split up his claim, Fetter v. Beale, 1 Salk. 11; Trask v. Hartford & New Haven Railroad, 2 Allen 331; Freeman, Judgments, 4th ed. §§ 238, 241; and, a fortiori, he cannot divide the grounds of recovery. * * *"

Werlein v. New Orleans, 177 US 390; Magnolia Petroleum Co. v. Hunt, 320 US 430 and many others are to the same effect; see Freeman, Judgments (5th ed.), §§ 681, 682, RESTATEMENT OF THE LAW, JUDGEMENTS, § 63 (1942).

Now the brief is written. It is as clear as crystal; it has the force of a battering ram and it is written as elegantly and gracefully as the lawyer knows how to write. A good brief is a beautiful piece of craftsmanship.

The Argument

This is the part of the appeal that is the most fun. For that reason it is what senior partners love to do. And, likewise, what senior partners like to write about. There is good literature on the subject. If an advocate could learn and do all the things mentioned in the excellent discussions by highly successful advocates the life of an appellate judge would be even more interesting than it now is. If successful brief writing is comparable to a science good appellate argument is certainly to be classified as an art. In fact, substantial support could be found for the proposition that a well made appellate argument is one of the most beautiful things in judicial life.

There is, however, some difference of opinion as to whether appellate argument is worthwhile. The position is taken that what determines the outcome of an appellate case is the study of a brief, the analysis thereof and the considered conclusion reached thereafter. The oral argument, this view explains, is simply an opportunity for the lawyer to strut his hour upon the stage like Macbeth's poor player.

With the above point of view this writer is in complete disagreement. It may be granted that oral argument seldom settles an appeal. But if it is well done it can go far in helping a court to understand the case. It can also leave the court with the impression that the side presenting this good argument deserves to win. Of course that impression may be dispelled by subsequent study. But certainly, to start that study with the highly favorable impression of the case thus described is a noteworthy advantage for the man who has created that impression.

Who should argue the case? Now we skate on thin ice. If a junior has tried the case below and has written the brief he is the logical person to make the argument. He knows the record. He knows what happened and where the account of any incident is to be found. He knows the facts of the case and he knows the law of the case. Even if he is not so eloquent an advocate as some members of his firm, his lack of eloquence will largely be compensated by the plenitude of his knowledge. But if the senior partner wants to argue the case all these considerations will, presumably, have no weight. It is to be hoped, however, that if a senior partner is to argue the case which his junior has tried and briefed he will take the time fully to inform himself about it. There used to be a story current about "Congressional Limited" lawyers. These were, supposedly, senior partners from New York offices who took the Congressional Limited in the afternoon to argue a case before the Supreme Court the next day. Their preparation consisted of a reading, during the journey, of the brief which had been placed in their hands as they left the office for the station. Whether the story was completely apocryphal or whether pressure of Supreme Court questioning caused a change in practice, the authorities do not say.

A rather considerable amount of money has been spent by some clients who lost cases below in hiring a big name lawyer to argue the case on appeal. Where a case has been badly tried, it may be a good investment to get an experienced appellate lawyer to help prepare the appeal and to make the argument. But to bring in the big name to make an argument on another man's brief, because of the supposed impression on the bench, is not an advantageous expenditure of money. Courts are impressed by a good argument. But no court worth its salt is much impressed by the appearance of a good name lawyer who does not know the case. Perhaps this is wasted printer's ink because clients may not believe it. But nevertheless it is true.

The time for oral argument will probably be limited by court rule. The time may be an hour, it may be three-quarters of an hour, it may be half an hour. This is really no hardship. The old statement about few souls being saved after fifty minutes of a sermon applies almost equally well to legal argument. At any rate, hardship or not, the rules stand. While courts will give counsel extra time if the case seems to justify it, his effort should be in the direction of conforming to the limit rather than in getting the time limit extended. It is amazing what a good man who has thoroughly and thoughtfully prepared his argument can do in half an hour. Counsel should watch his time. If there is a clock on the wall in front of him, so much the better. If not, he can use his own watch. If he gets too oblivious of his time he may find it expired when he really has something important to say. If he watches his clock too closely he will not make so good an argument. He will have to meet this dilemma as best he can. Overcoming difficulties makes a good advocate, just as it makes a good athlete.

What shall the advocate do with his time, whatever it may be? Perhaps it is good to start out by saying one thing which he should not do. He should not read his brief to the court. Over and over again one may hear it said from the appellate bench "Please do not read us your brief, Counsel. The court may not be able to think but it certainly can read." The argument should go along the lines of the brief but it should be different. Quotations should very seldom be read. But they may be paraphrased to give the court the substance of what somebody else has said. The protest against brief-reading goes also to a somewhat lesser extent to the reading of any prepared manuscript. Surely a lawyer doing court work can learn to talk to a court from notes without having to put a paper between himself and his judicial audience.

The way in which a case is presented will be guided somewhat by the familiarity which the court has with the cases before the Advocate gets on his feet. Some judges read the briefs before the argument is made. Some do not. There is a difference of opinion among judges on the question of whether such pre-argument reading is a good thing. To those of us who do read briefs ahead, the question of the desirability of such reading seems too clear for argument. The argument against it is said to be that the judge is likely to make up his mind before the argument. He does not, as a matter of fact, unless the appellant's case is so lamentably weak that the lack of substance in it shows itself when the brief is read. The great advantage in this advance reading is that it gives the court a background of the controversial points on appeal and enables it to direct questions to those points which seem to the judges really a matter of concern. It also helps counsel in (a) shortening the time to tell about his facts and (b) letting him hammer hard on the various facts which he deems the most important.

To sum this up then: If the court has read the briefs, the counsel's task is going to be lightened if he is one who can join in the give and take of discussion. He will be able to make more out of his period of argument and leave a stronger impression of his case in the minds of the judges. If the court has not read the briefs, counsel will be compelled to tell his story from the beginning; he stands the danger that some impatient judge will start shooting questions on matters which previous reading of the brief would have cleared up completely. There is nothing counsel can do about all this. He cannot make courts read briefs ahead of time nor can he keep them from doing so. But he can find out from the clerk what the practice of the judges in a particular court is.

Whether the judges have read a brief or not, the first thing which counsel must do is to acquaint the court with the facts of the case. If the brief has been read this may be simple. But in any event a refreshing of the court's mind on the most important facts is called for. If the case is largely a factual one this may take a good part of the time allotted for argument. *If the facts are presented clearly and the counsel's position about them is right, they almost constitute proof of the proposition of law to be urged.* In technical cases as, for example, those involving engineering patents, factual preparation is by far the most important part of the argument. It is a delightful experience to watch a skillful counsel go step by step through an elaborate, complicated, and difficult piece of mechanical or chemical process and make the case so clear that a court unlearned in the subject matter can either understand it, temporarily, or thinks it can. Here, again, as in the writing of the brief, one of the best elements of persuasion is clarity.

If the court has by now an understanding of the facts it can turn to the legal questions presented. The strongest one should come first. It will hit the hardest because the court knows the background and its interest is fresh. The general question is: Why should the facts already presented call for the results which counsel asks for? Judges who are any good want to know the why of it. True, if they are confronted by the decision of a superior court or one of their own previous decisions directly in point, they will be inclined to rest on that without asking why. Obviously, in case of a decision by a superior court the why virtually disappears. If what confronts counsel is a previous decision by the court before which he argues he will have a hard job getting a decision overruled. But it has been done. It will take a bit of demonstrating, however.

Legal arguments need not be long. If the court has the facts it will sense the law point pretty fast. It is not helped by a meticulous and detailed discussion of many decisions or the differentiation between them and some other decisions. If the case involves some point of technical law, as for instance a tax question, there may be two or three decisions that are directly in point or nearly directly in point and which may determine the question on review. Then discussions of individual decisions is relevant and helpful. But for a counsel in oral argument to talk about ten or fifteen different cases is a waste of time. The court cannot possibly remember the distinction made and the argument gets duller and duller. If the advocate will tell the court why the result he argues for is right and then just point to the authorities in his brief, the argument will be much more interesting and the impression he makes much more lasting.

The court is likely to break into his argument with questions. These may bother a lawyer reciting a prepared speech. Sometimes a question or two is asked by the presiding judge just to help the advocate feel at ease and get into a discussion in the nature of a conversation about the points being argued on appeal. It is very difficult to argue to a dead-pan panel and if counsel can be made to feel at ease and to sense the interest which the individual judges have in his case, the argument is helped. But most of the questions will be directed to something the judge wants to know. Maybe it has already been answered in the previous part of counsel's argument. Maybe it is something which counsel intends to come to later. But if the judge wants to know something, it is highly advisable for counsel to tell him the answer as well as he can. He should not postpone answering his judicial questioner and he certainly should not evade him. An evasive answer does not fool anyone and if the judge has been on the bench for any length of time he has had the same kind of an experience as that of one who has conducted a school room through the years. All the tricks that students can try have been tried before.

The questions really open up to counsel what is in a judge's mind and it is into the judge's mind that counsel wishes his argument to penetrate. So the opportunity to argue the case through answers to questions presents a great opportunity which a man who is at all quick thinking hurries to embrace. Many a case has been cleared up by the excellent way in which counsel removed real or feigned confusion in the judge's mind by the answers. It should not be necessary to add, but it will be out of abundant caution, that the answer should be pretty frank. The slightest misstatement of fact or misquotation of a case will do worlds of harm. That does not mean that there cannot be honest differences of opinion about the effect of judicial decisions and, even more, about facts. Sometimes an advocate may think that he has not been able to present his case because he has been so much interrupted by the court. Under those circumstances the court of its own motion will frequently extend his time. Even if it does not he has probably done much better than he thought, if he has answered his questions well. So long as there are silly judges there will be silly questions. This should not be the despair of counsel. If he can clear up petty difficulties his progress is just as great as though the questions were more searching. And a vote against him by a judge who misunderstands the question does just as much harm as one based on a thorough understanding of the case. So, to repeat: Questions from the court present the opportunity for the advocate to get in some of his best work. He should welcome them, he should meet them fairly and squarely. To meet them fairly and squarely he must know his record and the decisions he relies on.

Now the facts have been stated and the points argued. Time is about up. If the appellant has a choice between a fervent peroration and a brief opportunity for rebuttal he had better choose the latter. When the time is up counsel should quit, and quit promptly. It is an imposition on the court and everybody else with a case in court that day if he insists on talking longer. Furthermore, he will probably exasperate the presiding judge.

The appellee's argument, like the appellee's brief, will be based on what the counsel said. If he thinks the facts are not clearly stated or if more need to be added, his argument will open with such a statement. He should not accuse his adversary of a conscious misstatement unless (1) such accusation is necessary and (2) it can be proven. Here again as in brief writing judges are not interested in rows between counsel. They want to know about the case. An appellate argument is in this report something like a golf game played with due regard to propriety. The outward manifestations are punctiliously polite whatever inward urge one may feel against an opponent.

When the appellee is through, the appellant, if he has any time left, may answer. Nearly always the time spent in rebuttal is not very well spent. Lawyers are inclined to get down to small points, so small that half an hour later the court will not have the faintest recollection of what was said. In the presentation of an appeal which has been carefully briefed, there is not nearly the necessity or desirability for closing remarks that may be found in purely extemporaneous argument. Each side here knows about what the other is going to say. The man who opens has the greater advantage in presenting his side first. He must be careful not to lose it by letting his rebuttal get down to exasperating trivia.

End of the Road

The case is now submitted. Each side believes in the correctness of his own cause. Each side thinks or hopes he will win. Obviously one must be wrong.

It is to be hoped that party and counsel will not have to wait too long to find out what the court thinks. Counsel can do nothing about that. The time between submission of a case and the time opinion appears is dependent upon: (1) The amount of previous work the judges have on hand when they hear this case; (2) The speed with which the judge to whom the case is assigned for opinion can write his opinion and get it approved by his colleagues. Some judges work very fast. Others who do just as good work do it much more slowly. Counsel will not know which kind of a judge has the opinion to write; (3) The degree of diligence exercised by the opinion-writing judge. Counsel cannot affect that either. All he can do is wait.

When the opinion comes down somebody is going to be disappointed, of course. It is highly improper for the disappointed client or counsel to try to talk the matter over with the judge who wrote the opinion. He can, if he thinks it worthwhile, ask for rehearing by filing a petition for it. Most petitions for rehearing are nothing but a rehashing of the argument on appeal. It is quite clear that if the court has worked through a case thoughtfully and rejected a certain line of argument it is not going to change its mind by hearing the argument made again. But every once in a while a case appears where the court has mistaken the facts or misconstrued the point of a case. In that sort of a situation it may grant petition for reargument. For judges, while they exasperate lawyers a great deal, really want to do the right thing. But let it be repeated, these instances of mistake based on fact or misconception of the case are few. The only other thing disappointed counsel can do is to ask the Supreme Court of the United States for certiorari. If the trial court was a federal district court and the Appellate Court a United States Court of Appeals process is well defined and fairly simple. If the Appellate Court is a state court the kind of question which will be entertained on certiorari is much more limited and this paper is not the place to discuss it.

There we end the appeal. The clerk will tax the costs. If counsel has won he will undoubtedly be very happy. If he has lost, well, part of a lawyer's business is to become accustomed to taking defeats with good grace.

Adapted from A. L. I. Series 1 (1954).

The Oral Argument on Appeal

BY HAROLD R. MEDINA

THE SUBJECT OF THIS PAPER is so wide in its scope and has so many implications that it seems fitting at the outset to prescribe the limits within which the discussion will be confined. No effort will be made to differentiate between the various appellate courts before which oral arguments may be made. Nor will any attempt be made to treat the philosophical phases of the subject which have been so much discussed during the past year and which relate to the functions of judges, the nature of the judicial process, the aberrations of the judicial mind, and so on.

The point of view from which this paper will approach the subject is that of the advocate. And, in this connection, there should be an understanding about certain fundamentals. The duty a lawyer owes his client is a peculiarly sacred one. No lawyer has a right to take a client's money when he knows that there is no possibility of giving the client anything in return. No lawyer has any right to take a client's money without giving him full value in services rendered in return for the fee. There is accordingly not the slightest excuse for a lawyer accepting a retainer on appeal or otherwise unless the side on which he is to be retained has merit. He has no right to take the fee unless he is prepared to fight to the last ditch and to use every weapon in his arsenal in order to win the case.

To say that the case must have merit does not exclude so-called technical points or points of practice and procedure. If there is some technical flaw which deprives the court of jurisdiction, it is the duty of the lawyer for the respondent to bring about a dismissal of the appeal, whatever may be the equity of the case or the merit of the controversy between the parties. So, also, as to other mistakes or defects in the procedure adopted by the other side. No lawyer should feel himself open to criticism for taking advantage of rules of law which benefit his client. If the rule of law should be changed, that is the business of the Legislature or of the courts.

Preparation

It is perhaps surprising to know that a considerable number of appeals are bungled because of inadequate preparation. This is sometimes due to the inexcusable practice of having the brief written by some junior assistant and handed to the lawyer as he rushes to court to argue the case. More frequently the lack of preparation is due either to an absence of that careful, general training for advocacy which is indispensable to those doing this work or to a misconception of what is the proper preparation for the argument of a particular case.

It is often said that the art of oratory is dead and that all a man has to do now is to get on his feet and say what is on his mind. It is true that formal oratory, following a set plan such as described by Cicero, and the rhetorical, emotional and highly colored efforts which one reads about in connection with the arguments before the Supreme Court of the United States in the first thirty or forty years of its existence, are gone. It would be absurd for anyone to attempt such flights of eloquence today, whether in or out of a courtroom. With rare exceptions, the arguments and even the trials of important cases today lack that element of the public spectacle which was formerly commonplace. In almost every instance the argument proceeds under conditions of repose and calm. Appellate calendars are now so crowded as to make the element of time a matter of pressing significance. One must be brief and to the point; there is little or no opportunity for embellishment or emotionalism. It does not follow, however, that the function of the advocate is any easier under these conditions. On the contrary, his task becomes all the more difficult. Pressed for time and with judges whose minds are occupied in the consideration of hundreds of cases, it is more necessary than it ever was to spend years of arduous toil and the most constant application to develop what may be truly called the art of persuasion or advocacy.

Such matters as proper posture and voice modulation are extremely important. Some lawyers deliver their arguments shouting incessantly at the tops of their voices. This creates an atmosphere of extreme discomfort for their hearers. It becomes literally impossible for the judges to concentrate on what such lawyers are saying, so great is the distraction caused by the noise. On the other hand, certain lawyers make it a point to speak in almost a whisper, their contention being that in this way the judges become more intent upon what they are saying. They claim that in this way they get a better dramatic effect. It would seem that both methods are equally to be condemned. One should be as careful as possible to speak in a clear and distinct voice with as little harshness or discordancy as possible. At the same time a certain amount of rise and fall by way of contrast and emphasis is most desirable. These things usually do not come naturally. They require practice and experience.

A general consideration having to do with preparation which is of even greater consequence relates to the making of a clear and understandable statement of the facts of the case. In listening to lawyers in appellate courtrooms one often finds the greatest difficulty in knowing what they are talking about. In many, if not most cases, this is due to faulty preparation and carelessness. The lawyer is so full of the facts of his case that he unconsciously acts upon the assumption that the members of the court know as much about it as he does. Or, perhaps, he is so anxious to interject irrelevant matters which he thinks may prejudice the judges in his favor that he mixes everything up in a confused hodge-podge. In many cases, although there is a complete absence of any of these irrelevant details and the lawyer really knows the facts down to the last detail, his arrangement of them is confusing. He is so eager to get down to his points of law that the statement of facts becomes a hopeless mess.

The answer to these difficulties lies in careful preparation. There is a certain art in the telling of any story, and every law case is a story in itself. The secret of the method to be employed lies in putting one's self in the other man's shoes. This is one of the most difficult things to do and yet it is literally indispensable if one is adequately to argue an appeal in open court. This applies not only to the facts but to the law, about which more will be said hereafter.

A good way to get training and experience in stating facts is to practice upon one's relatives and friends. The idea is merely to tell someone else that here was a case in which the facts were so and so and to ask him what he thinks about it. If this is tried again and again and again, after a while there will come a certain sense of balance and order of statement from which there naturally evolves a method of telling the story so clearly and above all so briefly that anyone can grasp it. Insofar as the facts are concerned, it is not necessary that the listener be a lawyer or have any legal training. If one can describe a complicated set of facts in such a clear and simple fashion as to make them intelligible to a layman, they will be even more intelligible and plain to the trained mind of an appellate judge.

It is impossible to place too much emphasis upon the statement of the facts. These must be told in an interesting way. And nothing arouses the interest of others so much as the interest and animation of the man who is telling the story. There is no point in a cold, clammy recital of the facts. Some people seem to think that it is unethical or undignified to appear interested in and aroused by the cause of one's client. There is no basis for any such feeling; and the lawyer who shows a keen interest in his client's cause generally makes a much better impression.

The notion that the facts, whether simple or complicated, speak for themselves is sheer nonsense. In reality there are as many ways of telling the story of any case as there are fleas on a dog. Subtleties of arrangement and emphasis; the selection of particular words or phrases; and innumerable little twists and turns all play their significant part and are worthy of study.

Prior to the argument of a case it is advisable to read the whole record over again carefully, not relying upon the brief or upon previous study of the record. It is also advisable to review orally the argument about to be made. This does not mean memorization of the argument. Nothing could be more fatal than that. The process should be in no sense a rehearsal. The point is that an oral statement made *viva voce* tends to clarify one's thoughts, leads to the most appropriate arrangement of the facts and law points, and generally helps to whip the case into shape in a way that no amount of silent study will do.

It is inadvisable to prepare notes to refer to in the course of the argument, or to write out notes during the argument of one's opponent to remind one of the points to be taken up for the respondent or in reply. Some lawyers come into court with thirty or forty pages of yellow paper covered with handwritten notes, folio numbers and references of one kind or another and one can see them during the argument of their adversaries busily engaged in scribbling out several additional pages of similar notes. This practice is distracting in the extreme and does more harm than good. In order to do work of this sort capably one must have a good memory. Memory is largely a matter of training and experience. If from the first a lawyer accustoms himself to retain in his memory rather than on pieces of paper the different points and references that he thinks may become important, he will find that his argument will greatly benefit from the practice.

Argument for the Appellant

An appellant should always argue, except perhaps where the appeal is from some unimportant interlocutory order relating to a field thoroughly familiar to the court, such as bills of particulars. The fact that a large number of oral arguments are futile and a mere waste of time is beside the point. If the appeal is to be presented in as clear, convincing and attractive a manner as possible, argument should supplement the brief, no matter how good a printed brief may have been submitted on the appellant's behalf. The judges are human beings and not mere machines. If their sympathy or their interest is aroused, as they should be by a proper oral argument on behalf of the appellant, the effect is bound to be of advantage.

Getting down to the argument itself, the very first consideration for the appellant's counsel is making the facts clear to the court. This can best be done by a simple chronological statement, just as though the story were being told to a friend. It is well to try to anticipate the thoughts and questions that might occur to the judges as they listen to the recital of the facts. No gaps should be left which would be likely to make some of the judges wonder whether or not some essential and harmful circumstance had been omitted. Where there are certain facts which are helpful to the other side, they should be met squarely without any attempt at evasion and without, in the first instance, going into any lengthy explanations or excuses. Every case contains factual matters which are embarrassing and difficult. These must be met head-on, face to face and without any dodging or straddling. Nothing can ruin an oral argument so completely as the slightest tendency toward evasion, concealment, straddling or running away from the facts.

It is similarly important for the appellant to state the facts with the utmost precision. Most of the charges of misrepresentation of the record and falsification of the facts heard so frequently in the appellate courts are due to carelessness on the part of the lawyers under attack. Little variations are seized upon by the other side, however irrelevant they may be, with the result that the court is left in an atmosphere of confusion and suspicion. The only way to avoid this is to state the facts with absolute accuracy. If a witness testified in a certain way, his exact words should be repeated. If a document contains certain phraseology that has some important bearing on the case, the phraseology should be memorized or the record should be turned to.

Many of the most important appeals turn on questions of fact. In such cases the matter very often resolves itself into characterizations of the evidence by either side. A lawyer will say, for example, there is absolutely no evidence that the plaintiff looked before he crossed the street. He may simply mean that such evidence as exists is, in his judgment, no evidence at all. The more advisable procedure for a lawyer to follow is frankly to state to the court that it is his view that there is no evidence on such a point, that such and such proof, to be found at such and such a folio, is insufficient and when so regarded there is no other evidence in the case to supply the defect. Nothing whatever is to be gained by dealing in unexplained characterizations. They should be dissected and clarified in every instance.

Then there is the problem of how to deal with disputed facts. Almost every case involves a certain number of sharply contested issues on which the witnesses on either side testify differently. It is not practicable to give a clear and connected chronological story of the case and keep stopping every minute or two to explain all the contradictions in the evidence. An attempt to do this usually results in confusion. It is hard to lay down any very general rule, as cases differ so in this particular. Very often it is possible to give a fairly connected account of the facts with some incidental reference to the existence of one or two disputes on vital points which will be explained a little later. Then when the chronological sequence has been concluded and the court has a definite view of the basic facts, it is easy to describe the character of the evidence on the disputed points. Where the facts are relatively simple it is sometimes possible to interrupt the connected story by elaborating on the character of the disputed evidence as one goes along. The substance of the matter is that one should explain to the court in some way what facts are conceded or undisputed and what facts are in dispute either by direct contradiction in the evidence or by conflicting inferences to be drawn from the evidence; and that this should be done in a way which will not so confuse or interrupt the general trend of the statement of facts as to make it unintelligible.

With reference to the use of mechanical aids and models, they are to be placed generally in the same category with reading excerpts from cases or text books. Some lawyers will come into an appellate court with several assistants carrying models and a pile of books and these will be spread out on a counsel table with what the lawyer may regard as great dramatic effect. Usually the effect on the judges is just opposite to the one desired. No matter how the event occurred, or how complicated the facts relied upon may be, it is possible, by a carefully prepared an artful oral presentation, to paint the picture orally and to explain the matter without reference to any models or books. Nothing is more tiresome than the reading of quotations from briefs or from books or from the record. The presiding judges of most appellate courts will immediately stop counsel, and this interruption almost always spoils the effect.

A case involved a suit on a burglary policy against an insurance company. The company claimed that the burglary was a fake and they relied largely upon the proof of the size of the hole in the ceiling through which the burglar was supposed to have entered, their claim being the hole was too small for any human being to get through. Counsel for the company, as appellant, had in court a piece of wood with a hole cut in it of precisely the dimensions referred to in the testimony. He was rather a small man and he waved the board in the air, claiming that it was perfectly obvious that no one could crawl through such a small hole. After he had done this for some little time one of the judges said, "Why, Mr. X, you can get through that hole yourself. Just try and see if you can't." In some embarrassment he wriggled around, sticking his head and one of his shoulders through the hole, and claimed that he could not get through. From the standpoint of a spectator it was a question of whether or not he was really trying to get through. In any event, the general effect of the use of the exhibit was very bad and quite contrary to the one intended.

There is another feature fully as important as are the mechanical details above outlined. In order to absorb the factual atmosphere and to produce a natural effect it is always well to go and see the places involved in the case where the facts relate to some physical factors, such as a building, a ship, a certain neighborhood and so on, and also carefully to study the technical nomenclature applicable to the subject. In almost every instance it is possible with a little extra labor to immerse one's self, as it were, in the technical jargon of the particular field. The wisdom of this course is most apparent when the members of the court show themselves to be already thoroughly familiar with the particular field and appreciative of the use of language having a precise and particular connotation in that field.

The next consideration is the method of arguing the law. It is always helpful at the very outset of the argument to make a clear statement of the nature of the appeal, indicating the power of the court to entertain the appeal, together with a very short summary statement of the character of the points which will be argued. This is a difficult thing to do, but it is quite necessary so that the judges may follow the statement of facts and prepare themselves for the more detailed description of the law points in due course. A little practice and experience will make this method an easy one to follow.

In discussing the law, certain things are definitely taboo. Many lawyers in their oral argument run on something like this: "The point we make was sustained by this Court in the case of *Brown v. Shyne,* 242 N. Y., page 176, as well as by the older cases of *Haffey v. Lynch,* 193 N. Y., page 67, and *Hubbard v. Matthews,* 54 N. Y., page 43." This reference to the names and citations of cases is futile. There is not one chance in a thousand that the members of the court are going to remember the names of these old cases, and the rigmarole of cases and citations is boring in the extreme. The lawyer should be able to talk in terms of his point of law and if the court of last resort has really already decided that question, it is enough to say that it has been decided. If some case is referred to by way of analogy, counsel should state in a clear and direct fashion the facts of the case, show how the analogy exists and make his argument without any reference to names and citations. They confuse the court and spoil the continuity of the argument. As a result of care, ingenuity and experience it is possible to make the discussion of the law points just as interesting if not more interesting than that of the facts, however dramatic the latter may be.

In his argument of questions of law, it is suggested that in general the most strategic procedure for counsel to follow is to select the one big central point of law on which he hopes to obtain a reversal, to concentrate on that and so to arrange the various phases of his argument that this point will be fully and clearly understood in every aspect. Peppering away with a lot of miscellaneous points of more or less importance is apt to leave the court without any very definite impression that the judgment or order should be reversed. If the forces are marshalled so as to deliver one good, solid blow, the appellant's chances are greatly enhanced. Naturally, the selection of this point requires considerable skill and judgment. Furthermore, it is not a rule of universal application, as some cases are of such a character as to make it possible and advisable to argue two or more points with almost equal force. In other cases, however, the points are of a more or less contradictory character so that it is absolutely indispensable to decide on one and hammer away at that, leaving the rest to be studied by the members of the court when they read the appellant's brief.

Just as there are difficult and embarrassing factual matters in every case, so also are there difficult and embarrassing features of the law. As a general rule these difficulties should be met head-on just as with respect to matters of fact. Where the law points are simple and wholly lacking in complications, this method is the only admissible one to be followed.

On the other hand, cases arise not infrequently where the law points in their various aspects, including all the various analogies, are legion. In such instances it is generally a mistake for counsel for the appellant to go out of his way to elaborate upon some incidental legal feature of the case which he regards as difficult or impossible to answer. In such cases it is generally better to say little or nothing except by way of reply after one's adversary has concluded his argument.

In general, when the case is complicated and the questions of law are numerous, the best policy is to try so to arrange the argument as to get your adversary to discuss the legal points which favor your contentions. It is a matter of emphasis, but it must be realized that the case may ultimately be won or lost as the emphasis is shifted from one to another of the legal phases of the controversy.

Argument for the Respondent

If the appellant submits, it is generally bad strategy for the respondent to argue. To do so puts him upon the defensive and generally has a bad effect. Where the case is frankly a borderline case, however, and there is no denying the fact that the court may well decide either way, it would seem much better strategy to take the bull by the horns and argue the case fully, even though the appellant has submitted.

Some lawyers feel that when they argue for the respondent it is necessary for them to go over all the facts again, even though their opponent has already stated them clearly and accurately. This is definitely bad procedure. If the appellant has stated the facts fully and accurately, there is no point whatever in the respondent talking about the facts at all. He should get down to his law and present his side of the case without delay. A long, repetitious rehashing of the facts bores the court to distraction and is apt to put the judges in a frame of mind where they pay very little attention to the really important part of the respondent's argument.

Both with respect to the respondent and the appellant it is very inadvisable to interpolate any irrelevant matter. The judges are quick to sense this irrelevancy and to draw the inference that counsel is trying to pull the wool over their eyes and draw their attention away from the real issues. The effect is frequently disastrous, even though it may be pleasing to one's client or his friends sitting in the courtroom listening to the argument. The same is true to a greater degree of reference to matters outside of the record. This is an indefensible practice and never does any good.

Just as counsel for the appellant should try to guide the interest of the court and the discussion by his adversary to phases of the case favorable to the appellant, so it is equally important for counsel for the respondent to checkmate strategy of this sort and guide the discussion into channels favorable to the result desired by the respondent. Nothing could be a more serious mistake than merely to answer the arguments made by counsel for the appellant. These arguments may be skilfully designed to lead counsel for the respondent off into the woods or they may lead him there unintentionally. The proper line of attack for counsel for the respondent to adopt is to proceed to demonstrate by his discussion of the law and the facts that the judgment is right and that it should be affirmed. All other considerations are secondary.

There are several special difficulties which frequently arise from the respondent's point of view and which need rather careful treatment. The first is, suppose the appellant makes a perfectly wretched presentation of the case so that the court, with an inadequate understanding of the facts, has indicated by various questions and statements that it is definitely against the appellant and for affirmance. What should the respondent do? The old gag about saying nothing when the judge is with you is, generally speaking, a good rule, as it is easy to keep on talking until the judge changes his mind and decides the other way. The course to be pursued depends a good deal upon the nature of the case. If the respondent's position is really a strong one, it is probably better to go through a purely perfunctory argument and let it go at that. Where the case is a close one, however, counsel for the respondent should frankly state that the facts have not been made clear and then proceed to open up the entire matter, stating the facts fully and making sure that the court understands the points the respondent has to meet. He should then proceed to meet these points squarely so that the court will understand what the issues are and get the beneficial effect of as good an argument as the respondent can make.

Another important consideration from the viewpoint of the respondent is how to treat the situation when the appellant has either garbled or misstated the facts. It is a mistake to charge one's adversary with trying to mislead the court. The instances are rare when a lawyer deliberately tries to mislead the court. By far the better course to follow is to say that due to some misunderstanding the facts have become a little confused and then to proceed with care and deliberation and with appropriate reference to portions of the record to tell just what the true facts are. This is the gracious and proper way to handle the situation. An appellate court is no place for a cat and dog fight, and the man who begins making charges of fraud and falsification is very apt to find himself holding the short end of the stick. Such tactics naturally antagonize the court.

Then there is the problem of how to handle surprise points suddenly brought up by counsel for the appellant in his oral argument but not referred to in the appellant's brief. Sometimes these points are entirely new and sometimes they are merely a clarification of some obscurity in the appellant's brief which made very little impression. These points are the most dangerous of all, as they catch the respondent unawares. The proper course for the respondent to pursue is to state at the very beginning of his argument that such and such a point is new, that it does not strike him as being very important in view of the fact that it had never been brought up before, but that he should like to have a few days to put in an additional brief in case he feels there is something special he wants to say about it. In this way all confusion and embarrassment is eliminated and the point may well be lost in the shuffle.

Questions from the Bench

This brings up the most delicate and beyond question the most difficult task of the advocate.

Questions and remarks from the bench fall into a large number of categories. It is obvious that, whatever the nature of the questions, the lawyer should retain his poise and composure and under no circumstances lose his temper or become impertinent or disrespectful. Whatever the aggravation and however unfair the question may seem to be, there is no possible justification for impertinence or disrespect.

Sometimes judges have a misguided sense of humor and ask questions merely for the purpose of poking a little fun at the lawyer or perhaps of easing the tedium of a boresome session. In such cases the only thing counsel can do is to try to see the humorous side of the situation and fall in with it without becoming unduly disturbed. If the interruption is repeated or followed by other similar questions, there is nothing to do but answer them in good grace, coming back to the relevant facts of the case and the points which one has to make.

In this connection, and with reference to all advocacy, it is quite important for the lawyer not to take himself too seriously.

It is so easy to become pompous or self-important or in some way to take offense at something said by some member of the court or by one's adversary. This should never be done. The effect is always bad.

Another difficult situation to handle involves questions by the court requiring a direct and unequivocal answer upon a matter which counsel had planned to discuss at some length later on in his argument. The following would seem to be the best course for counsel to pursue. He should first try to have the matter held in abeyance so that it can be taken up in the ordinary course. If this effort is unavailing there is absolutely no alternative other than to go into the whole subject thoroughly and completely and to do it in a way that involves no criticism or reflection upon the judge who asks the question. In other words, what he should do is to say something like the following: "Judge, you have put your finger right on one of the very important phases of this case and the evidence on it depends upon the characterization which I put on this evidence on the one hand and that which my adversary puts on the other hand, and that evidence is as follows," and then go ahead and explain the whole thing. It is quite important that this be done in a way that is acceptable and pleasing to the judge who asks the question, rather than antagonistic to him.

Sometimes a judge will question counsel upon some matter to which the latter has not given mature consideration. In such a case counsel should frankly say that he has never considered the point before and that he does not feel that any haphazard thoughts that might come to him in the course of the argument would be of any value. To adopt the other course and merely to guess or try to reason the matter out on the spur of the moment only leads into difficulties and perhaps into admissions which may prove harmful on some other aspect of the case.

A problem of considerable difficulty is presented when the judges begin to talk among themselves and are apparently paying no attention to the argument. In some courts this is done a great deal and in others almost not at all. In such instances some lawyers will stop their argument entirely and remain silent until one of the judges directs them to proceed. The better course to pursue would seem to be to go right ahead with the argument, looking at the judge or judges who happen to be disengaged and who are apparently listening. To remain silent is bound to be interpreted as a criticism of the judges who are conversing together and it is apt to irritate them, as in almost every instance the judges are discussing some phase of the case on argument and they naturally feel that counsel should make no objection to their doing this. On the whole, there is no single feature of an appellate argument which causes more mental anguish to the lawyer than these conversations between the judges. Whether they are talking about the case or not, the effect upon the lawyer is bound to be extremely embarrassing.

Many years ago a symposium was held by the Bar Association of the City of New York on the subject of the oral argument of appeals, different views being presented by Austin G. Fox, Clarence J. Shearn and Francis M. Scott. The discussion was most illuminating, as these men represented the very best in the bench and bar and they spoke their minds with frankness and sincerity. One of the outstanding suggestions was that the whole matter could be summed up by saying that he who serves the court best serves his client best. This is indeed true and should always be borne in mind. All resort to chicanery and subterfuge, garbling of the facts and argument of specious points of law reacts in the end to the disadvantage of the client.

Next in importance is the handling of the cases in such a way as to appeal to the natural human instincts of the judges on the bench. The justice of the cause from the standpoint of the ordinary man in the street and the good conscience of the community as a whole is never a mistake. It is sometimes said that there is more law to be found in the musty volumes of the cases marked affirmed without opinion than in all the published opinions of all the courts in the land. Whether or not this be true, no one can doubt that substantial justice has been done in innumerable cases where it might be difficult to formulate the principles of the decision in a written opinion. Finally, an abiding sense of humor and an attitude of humility are all but indispensable. After all, the issues at stake in the administration of justice are too sacred and the subtle forces at work too imponderable to warrant anyone in approaching the task of the advocate in an egotistical spirit.

Adapted from Vol. 20, American Bar Association Journal (1934).

The Argument of an Appeal From the Judge's Point of View

BY NEWELL JENNINGS

THE RATHER CLUMSY TITLE conveys the idea that this is a sequel to an article entitled *How to Try a Case in the Trial Court from the Judge's Point of View* which appeared in this publication a few years ago.[1] The subject is not new but my experience has indicated that a fresh presentation even of old ideas may not be amiss. Chief Justice Maltbie's *Oral Argument on Appeal*[2] and his Connecticut Appellate Procedure, § 160 et seq., discuss many phases. There are philosophical works like Cardozo's *The Nature of the Judicial Process* as well as technical treatises.[3] Speakers before bar association meetings have frequently discussed the subject.[4] The purpose of this article is further to assist lawyers in the effective presentation of their cases in the Supreme Court of Errors of Connecticut. Needless to say, it represents only my personal views. The oral argument will be considered first and, as stated in the title, from the judge's point of view.

The degree of the judges' familiarity with the record at the time of the argument varies with the personal methods of the judge and the time of his disposal. It is fair to assume generally that the degree of familiarity is slight. The first purpose of the opening oral argument should therefore be to acquaint the court with (1) what the case is about, (2) the main issues to be argued, and (3) the facts. The first two should be covered by the opening statement in the brief.[5] This is about the only part of the brief which should be read but even this will be presented more effectively orally, possibly with some amplification. The facts should then be stated as concisely and clearly as possible. The method of

1 Conn. B. J., Vol. 14, p. 112.
2 Conn. B. J., Vol. 11, p. 163.
3 *Brief Writing and Advocacy,* Walter; *Brief and Law Finder,* pp. 371 et seq., Spelling; *From Writ to Rescript,* Little, Brown & Co., 1941, pp. 268 et seq.
4 See, for example, *The Argument of an Appeal,* by Hon. John W. Davis, 26 A. B. A. J., p. 895.
5 Conn. App. Proc., § 166, App. I; 34 Yale L. J. 287.

their presentation will vary with the type of appeal. If the object of an appeal is to upset or defend a verdict, they must be stated as favorably to the appellee as the evidence permits; if to test a charge, the finding is the guide. In presenting an appeal from a trial to the court, the appellant should make clear whether he is relying on the finding as made or on the finding as he seeks to have it corrected. When the issue arises on a demurrer or the like, the contents of the pleadings involved should be stated. Whatever the form of presentation, no pains expended on this phase of the case will be wasted. Clearness, conciseness, and a conscientious adherence to the printed record are the chief disiderata.

The next step is the consideration of the assignments of error. These may be, and usually are, numerous. A proper statement at this point is to the effect that while no assignments pursued in the brief are waived, the main points to be discussed orally are as follows: and they should then be described.

There are various types of discussion that are unprofitable, for the reasons so clearly pointed out in Chief Justice Maltbie's article, *supra.* Among these are detailed discussions of corrections in the finding; reading from the record, briefs, or cases; going outside the record to create atmosphere. The latter is improper and militates against the offender. The former are simply a waste of time. The record, including the evidence when printed, and briefs will be read with care and the citations studied and analyzed. The time for this, however, is when the opinion is being written, not when the case is being argued. What then should be talked about?

The subject of the argument should be the main points of the appeal selected for oral presentation. Examples are: Taking the evidence in its aspect most favorable to the plaintiff, the jury could not have found for him. Why? The plaintiff could not recover without proof of a contract. The only evidence to prove it was so and so. This evidence should not have been admitted. Why? The only foundation for the second defense on which the defendant's judgment was based is a statute. The statute is unconstitutional or should be construed not to apply to the facts found. Why? The charge was erroneous or defective in the following respects. Why? An essential element in any argument is to establish that its validity affects the judgment rendered so as to make the latter erroneous. This court is not interested in what Judge Hinman calls "flea hunting."

This subject matter is to be presented orally. At this stage of the proceedings this oral presentation is the principal source of information as to the claims of the parties available to the court. It follows necessarily that no argument will be effective to accomplish its purpose unless the judge can hear and understand it. One of the tags of information I brought away from college is that clear articulation alone will hold the interest of the hearer, regardless of content. If logical arrangement and relevancy to the point being discussed are added, perfection in argument is being approached. This is no treatise on elocution, but there are few more tiring tasks than straining to hear what is being said or having your eardrums assaulted by a flood of words delivered in a piercing monotone. The conversational method is customary and acceptable but that does not mean that the attorney should talk to himself only. Finally, although the purple peroration is doubtless outmoded, the argument should end rather than peter out.

The oral argument is based on the written argument, the so-called "brief." Thorough familiarity with the record is essential for the preparation of the latter. It should be full and complete. Each assignment of error that the appellant desires to pursue should be treated therein. The importance of the opening statement has been stressed. The study of the brief will be facilitated if the assignments of error are treated in logical order. Where their nature permits, they should be grouped. The smaller the number of subdivisions, the more effective the brief, speaking generally.

This court is primarily interested in Connecticut law. In construing a statute, its legislative history as well as its judicial construction should usually be stated. When it is claimed that a point has been settled here, extensive citation of cases from other jurisdictions is generally unprofitable. Exceptions to this principle occur when it is desired to call attention to some particularly clear exposition of a rule; when a case substantially "on all fours" can be found; when it is claimed that a Connecticut holding should be reconsidered in view of a weight of authority to the contrary; when one of the so-called uniform state laws, like the sales act, is being construed; when, as stated above, the Connecticut rule is not clearly or completely set forth in our own decisions. Probably there are other exceptions. It remains true, however, that this court aims to state the law clearly for the guidance of Connecticut citizens and that that statement of the law is based primarily on our own cases. There is no objection, as the opinions show, to noting the fact that the Connecticut rule is in harmony with the general current of authority or to showing how it has been applied in other States. A pertinent decision of the Supreme Court of the United States is always relevant and may be controlling. The decision as to the number of cases to which reference should be made should be governed by common sense. It goes without saying that one good case is worth a hundred poor ones and that the occasion justifying a great mass of citations is rare.

Two minor but practical points remain to be noticed in connection with the citation of authority. Briefs differ, but, again in general, the citation of authorities is very properly extensive. All of these must be examined. That examination will be materially facilitated by reference to sub-pages where the precise point is treated and to particular notes when referring to sections in a digest, text book, or law journal article. If this method is used, extensive quotation from the authorities is rarely necessary. The reference is sufficient. Most bulky briefs will be found to be made up largely of quotations from the cases and from the record. As between official and unofficial citations, the former are preferred. Both should be given when they are available.

The final question is, what should an attorney do who comes before the court with a carefully prepared argument who is subjected to questions from the bench which interfere with its presentation? In the first place, the only object of the court is to get a clear picture of the legal claims of the attorney in relation to the facts. There is certainly no desire to embarrass counsel. The questions are generally prompted by failure to grasp the full import of the opening statement or because, in violation of some of the canons of proper procedure, the attorney appears to be spending his time unprofitably as far as the understanding and determination of the main issues are concerned. This may be due to the fault of the attorney, it may even be due to the fault of the court. In either event, no question of improper motives is involved since both have the same object in view, the legal and proper determination of the issues before the court. Since this is so, the attorney should give the same attention to questions asked by the court as he gave to questions which arose during the preparation of his brief and oral argument. Mr. Davis' discussion of the question is so clear and complete that I venture to quote from the article cited, p. 897: "Rejoice when the Court asks questions. And again I say unto you, rejoice! If the question does nothing more it gives you assurance that the court is not comatose and that you have awakened at least a vestigial interest. Moreover a question affords you your only chance to penetrate the mind of the court, unless you are an expert in face reading, and to dispel a doubt as soon as it arises. This you should be able to do if you know your case and have a sound position. If the question warrants a negative answer, do not fence with it but respond with a bold *thwertutnay*—which for the benefit of the illiterate I may explain as a term used in ancient pleading to signify a downright No. While if the answer is in the affirmative or calls for a concession the Court will be equally gratified to have the matter promptly disposed of. If you value your argumentative life do not evade or shuffle or postpone, no matter how embarrassing the question may be or how much it interrupts the thread of your argument. Nothing I should think would be more irritating to an inquiring court than to have refuge taken in the familiar evasion 'I am coming to that' and then to have the argument end with the promise unfulfilled. If you are really coming to it indicate what your answer will be when it is reached and never, never sit down until it is made."

To sum up, the purpose of the argument of an appeal is to place before a court that has not more than a superficial knowledge of the record a clear and concise statement of the issues and of the arguments in favor of the attorney's contentions. If that purpose is kept in mind, the brief and argument should be satisfactory. The object of this article is to make some practical suggestions for attaining that desirable result.

Adapted from Vol. 20, Connecticut Bar Journal (1946).

Appellate Court Practice—Briefs and Oral Argument

By Emmet H. Wilson

It is the statutory right of a defeated litigant to appeal to a higher court in which he may present for review any alleged error claimed to have been committed by the trial court and obtain a final adjudication of his rights, whether his life, his liberty or his property rights are in question.

It is said in the Canons of Professional Ethics that "it is the duty of the lawyer to do whatever may enable him to succeed in winning his client's cause. * * * The lawyer owes his 'entire devotion to the interest of the client' * * * to the end that nothing be taken or withheld from him, save by the rules of law, legally applied." The client is entitled to the benefit of every remedy and every defense that is authorized by law. With this in mind, the lawyer should not be deterred from appealing a case, though the chances of reversal may seem small, if he is conscientiously of the opinion that the lower court has erred in some particular in the application of the law or of the facts. This right of the litigant and this duty of the lawyer, however, is not a license for prosecuting frivolous appeals.

In deciding whether a case should be appealed the duty of the lawyer is the same as that in determining at the outset whether an action should be commenced. The 30th Canon of Ethics, relating to justifiable and unjustifiable litigation, may be paraphrased to apply to appeals and as so paraphrased the lawyer is advised not to appeal a case when the appeal is "merely to harass or to injure the opposite party or to work oppression or wrong," but when the attorney has determined that an appeal is justified it becomes his duty to appeal from an adverse judgment and to present the legal merits of his client's claim to the highest court to which the action may be taken. The fact that the appeal is taken "should be deemed equivalent to an assertion on his honor that in his opinion his client's case is one proper for judicial determination" by the higher court.

When an appeal is contemplated in which questions of fact are to be argued I cannot emphasize too strongly the rule that an appellate court does not weigh the evidence. In case of a conflict and there is substantial evidence in the record, or reasonable inferences may be drawn from the evidence, supporting the judgment, an appeal on the ground of the insufficiency of the evidence to sustain the findings or the judgment would be a useless waste of the client's money and of the time of both the attorneys and the court. In few cases is the evidence relied on to sustain the judgment so incredible, improbable and unbelievable that an appellate court will grant a reversal on that ground.

Before appealing a case the attorney should familiarize himself with the statutory provisions relating to appeals and with the rules on appeal so that his record and his briefs may be prepared in the manner there prescribed. He should acquaint himself with the time schedule provided by law and by the rules for the taking of all steps in an appeal from the entry of the judgment in the trial court until the final disposition of the case in the appellate or supreme court.

It is the duty of the lawyer to present the record on appeal and his written and oral arguments with candor and fairness. He should not knowingly misquote the pleadings or the evidence, nor should he misquote or knowingly misapply the language of decisions or text books which he cites. He should not cite a decision that has been overruled or modified except where the case is cited for the purpose of illustrating his argument, and then the fact that the decision has been overruled or modified should be clearly stated and the reason for its citation should be made plain. The same rule applies to the quotation of or reference to statutes that have been repealed or amended.

Since brevity is more appealing and generally more compelling than prolixity, the best briefs are usually the short ones.

If in the discussion that is to follow I go into somewhat minute detail it is because so many briefs that we are required to read are so ineptly constructed that an unnecessary and unwarranted burden is placed upon the court.

The clerk's transcript of the pleadings, findings, judgment, and other portions of the record requested by counsel to be transmitted to the appellate court, and the reporter's transcript of the evidence having been filed, the duty then rests upon counsel for the appellant to prepare his opening brief. The brief should be in three parts: (1) A statement of the case; (2) a short statement of the questions raised; (3) the argument. At the outset a full and fair statement of the pleadings should be given, with a short review of the findings and judgment, so that the court may know the issues presented to the trial judge and how he decided them. If no questions are raised other than those based on the pleadings, no reference need be made to the evidence. If it is claimed that the evidence is insufficient to sustain the findings of the court, or the verdict where the case is tried by a jury, or if assertions of error are predicated upon the admission or rejection of evidence or upon the giving or refusing to give instructions to the jury, a sufficient amount of the evidence should be stated to enable the court to rule on the questions raised.

The statement of facts, either those derived from the pleadings or from the evidence, should not be one sided. If the statement is complete and fair, giving not only the facts favoring the appellant's position but all the facts in the case, it will not be necessary for the respondent to present a counter-statement. A single correct statement of facts will make the work of the court much lighter than if the justices are required to read two statements and to check the record to determine which, if either, is correct. Each statement of fact should be followed by a reference to the page and line of the transcript where the record may be found.

Next in order in the brief should appear a statement of the questions raised by the appeal in order that the court may have a complete picture of the entire case before commencing to digest the argument. This need not be, and in fact should not be, an extended narration but should be succinct. The details will be appropriately elaborated at the proper places in the argument. Then follows the formal extended argument. Each point raised should be set forth in a black type heading and the argument of each point should be completed before another is begun. It has been the unfortunate experience of the justices that in too many briefs several questions have been discussed in such a jumbled and confused manner that it has been difficult to ascertain when the discussion of one subject has ended and another has commenced.

Under each heading there should be a discussion of the applicable law and facts, with appropriate references to the pleadings and the evidence, directing the court to the page and line of the transcript at which the record may be found.

In the respondent's brief the court expects first a statement of such facts as are necessary to a decision of the case that do not appear in the appellant's statement, followed by an appropriate reference to page and line of the transcript. It will be helpful if the respondent answers the appellant's points in the same order in which they have appeared in the latter's brief. However, if the respondent's counsel finds that his views of the case may be more logically presented by arguing the questions in a different order he is at liberty to do so. If the respondent's counsel desires to raise questions that have not been presented in the appellant's brief, it is immaterial whether the discussion of such points precedes or follows his answer to appellant's argument. The attorney must judge for himself where it should logically appear and where he believes it will be most effective.

The appellant's reply brief is confined to answering the respondent's argument. New questions should not be raised except by leave of court, and if leave be granted the respondent will be given an opportunity to reply. A repetition of the arguments found in the appellant's opening brief is superfluous, although they may be referred to briefly for emphasis on the questions argued in the opening brief.

The court will be aided in the expeditious disposition of appeals by attention to a few details in the preparation of briefs. Reference should be made to the page and line of the transcript where we may find the exact text of the record supporting each quotation or paraphrase of the pleadings or the evidence. Applicable citations of authorities should be made, and in so doing not only the page on which the opinion begins but the page on which the court discusses the particular point should be stated. If this suggestion is followed much of the court's time will be conserved, especially when a long opinion is cited. Short quotations from opinions are not objectionable. It is permissible to quote as much as may be necessary to illustrate or emphasize the argument. Since we read the cases cited long quotations are not desired. If a judge is unwilling to read a cited case it is reasonably certain that he will not read a long quotation in the brief.

When it is necessary to refer to a statute it need not be quoted at length except where a logical argument seems to make it necessary. In citing general laws reference should be made to the official statute books, since many inaccuracies have been found in some of the unofficial publications.

Search well for authorities and cite a sufficient number of them to demonstrate the rule under consideration. A long list of citations is unnecessary unless the courts of different jurisdictions are in disagreement. Select the best and give us the benefit of them. Do not follow the example set by the writer of a brief recently before us in which he said that there were hosts of authorities for his contention but he failed to cite any of them.

A decision should never be cited unless it has been carefully checked for the purpose of ascertaining whether it has been overruled, modified or limited; nor should a statute be cited until it has been determined that it has not been repealed or amended, or that it has not been declared unconstitutional or its effect limited by judicial decision.

An exception to the foregoing suggestion is recognized where it becomes necessary in the elucidation of an argument or in the interpretation of a statute to refer to decisions that have been overruled or limited, or to statutes that have been repealed or amended. In such case a reference to them may properly be made if accompanied by a statement that they are no longer in force and by a citation of the decision or the statute which has eliminated them as authority.

The term "supra" in connection with a citation is an abomination and is a lazy person's aid in writing a brief or an opinion. It should be shunned except where the case or statute has been cited on the same or the immediately preceding page. It is conceded that the omission of the book and page of a citation that is successively referred to possibly saves time for the writer, but much more time is lost by the readers when they are compelled to turn back several pages in an effort to find the proper reference to the case or the statute.

It is not only unnecessary but sometimes confusing to insert the date of the decision along with the citation of the book and page. There is one exception to this suggestion, and that is where a statute is involved the date of the decision with reference to the date of the statute should be provided so that the readers may know which one preceded the other. Upon citing text books, law reviews and references other than reports of decisions, the date of the publication should be given and in the case of a text book the edition, whether first or otherwise, should be stated.

Under the rules on appeal counsel have the right to argue their cases orally, and this right should not be denied or curtailed. You may be assured that the justices of appellate courts read the briefs carefully and familiarize themselves with the decisions cited. In making an oral argument a mere repetition of the matter found in the briefs is of no aid to the court. An argument should be presented with a view of amplifying the matters appearing in the brief and of making more graphic and vivid, if possible, the points found therein. When the arguments have been printed their oral repetition is unnecessary.

Lest my caution against verbose and diffusive briefs may lead you to the other extreme and cause you to omit necessary matters from your briefs, reference is made to the case of *Bell v. Germain,* 12 Cal App 375, in which counsel for the appellant had reduced his brief to ultra simplicity. The court said on page 378, "It is apparent that counsel for appellant has been somewhat misled in the preparation of his brief by the repeated requests of the supreme court and this court for brevity and succinctness in the presentation of cases. . . . The simplicity of presentation desired is that which avoids prolixity, verbosity and repetition; which omits theoretical disquisitions on abstract principles of law, needless presentation of questions of fact as to which the action of the trial court is final, the citation of innumerable authorities indicative of an examination of the subject which has never passed the digest stage. . . . When briefs fail altogether to present the matters mentioned, the court must elect between acting as counsel for the appellant, or passing upon only such questions as are sufficiently presented for consideration by the brief, and in accomplishing the purpose mentioned, to wit, the dispatch of business, the latter course has generally been adopted."

This quotation is an admonition to make the briefs brief, but not to the point of omitting matters that are of significance in presenting the questions necessary to a decision.

The foregoing, I believe, presents an outline of what the appellate courts desire and expect of the lawyer. If he is candid and fair with himself he must of necessity be candid and fair with opposing counsel and with the court. We demand nothing more and we expect nothing less.

Adapted from Vol. 22, Cal. S. B. J. (1947).

Brief Writing

By Howard C. Westwood

In view of the part they play in forming the courts' opinions, it is somewhat disturbing to discover the low estate to which most briefs descend. The simplest criteria for helpful and persuasive presentation are ignored. Some reference to the more glaring faults may not be amiss.

A cardinal feature of the brief is the statement of points. The importance of the device is manifest. The judge wants something that will enable him with a glance to see not only what the case is about but also how the argument is shaped. Whether or not he examines the brief before oral argument, such an index assists him to grasp the argument more easily and sympathetically, to be more patient with the presentation, and to concentrate upon those portions on which he particularly needs enlightenment. Yet all too frequently, despite rules of court, the statement is either omitted or fails to fulfill its function. How often must the harried judge sigh at reading a statement containing only such noncommittal points as, "The decision below is contrary to principle," and "The decision below is contrary to authority." Even an otherwise incomprehensible argument may be saved by a patient judge if he has before him a serviceable statement. And the lawyer himself will benefit greatly by the discipline and the form imparted to his presentation if he has properly worked out his points.

Closely associated with the statement of points is the statement of the questions to be decided. There is the risk of losing content through over generalization, but if this is avoided the tactical value is great. Point is at once given the argument and, if the questions are included beforehand, the statement of facts is incalculably aided by significant focus. It is unfortunate that briefs usually do not include this feature. Those of the Office of the United States Solicitor General demonstrate with what peculiar skill it may be employed.

The summary of the argument also serves somewhat the same function as the statement of points. The difference, however, is not sufficiently kept in mind: it is to sum up, rather than to guide. It should include the complete argument, stating it once and for all in the most persuasive manner. Here, if ever, the syllogism or dilemma can be put compellingly and the rhetoric of the epigram, hazardous elsewhere, has its place. Whether it should be included at the beginning or the end of argument depends upon courts' rules and lawyers' tastes, but it is very effectively employed at the end, for there the emphasis it affords is especially strategic.

The argument itself is a problem individual to each case and lawyer. But there are certain matters of style that demand attention. The extent to which standards of concision and brevity are violated is alarming. It is impossible to tell how this affects the decision of cases, but one would think that professional pride if nothing else would curb the rambling discourse that fills so many pages. The evil obtains even where there is specific admonition from the court to maintain appropriate bounds, notably as in the United States Supreme Court rules for petitions for certiorari. It is amusing that usually not only the coherence but the merits of the argument vary inversely with the size of the brief.

At some time the thought apparently went abroad that the ideal brief is one that will disclose the full argument upon any single page, and many lawyers adhere strictly to the principle. Yet if the argument is adequately organized and summarized there is little excuse for repetition. And there is never excuse for repeating the same argument under differently entitled points; that simply throws doubt on the strength of the case.

The briefs emanating from the Office of the United States Solicitor General are an admirable example of efficient restraint. In petitions for and in opposition to certiorari, they very rarely exceed ten or fifteen pages and adequacy is not sacrificed. Such a treatment inspires confidence.

Aside from being brutally long-winded, the most common failings of the argument are the "digest method" and the "record method" of writing. The former consists of confining argument largely to extracts from the digests—or so it appears; the latter of copying pages from the record. Properly this is not argument at all. Of the petitions for certiorari in the United States Supreme Court, which furnish the best available cross section of the American bar's product, almost every third one is guilty of these faults.

There is little or no analysis, and nothing is less reliable or more suspicious than the mere invocation of a series of cases, even when adequately stated, or the bare quotation of an arid record.

The use of authority presents a vexing problem. The chief difficulty is that it has not yet been sufficiently impressed upon the bar that law is not found but is made by the judges. The first question in deciding how to employ precedent should be whether the particular court will be likely to adhere to precedent simply because of the principle of stare decisis. There are some instances where it is very probable that a court will be concerned only to maintain a position strictly in accord with past decisions, as in the interpretation of standardized clauses in certain types of contracts, such as insurance policies, or in dealing with a technical or a more or less unfamiliar subject, such as patent or admiralty law. Beyond such relatively few categories, most appellate courts are ready enough to take a fresh view of justice and want only constructive aid. To that end the use of authority has two functions; illustration, and the definition of decisions which will serve as a foundation.

One would guess that the former function would be commonly employed, schooled as lawyers are in analogizing and in the "supposing" of the class room. Yet the fact is that in his brief the lawyer seems oppressed with the feeling that his reasoning must be the servant of his authorities, with the result that his argument often becomes heavy from forced subordination, when it might be lightened by using the cases merely to illustrate, like pictures in a book.

The second function is familiar enough. The difficulty is that the definition is not sufficiently precise. Of course a lawyer wants to milk a case for all it is worth. But some cases are dry, and some will give precious little; and one may as well be frank about it. No matter how prone the judges are to write opinions as though "the point is settled by authority," it must be apparent that they have not forgotten that cases can be distinguished; and of all the weaknesses that a brief can present to a wary opponent the most telling is that of an authority-foundation which has not allowed for the embarrassing facts that lurk in every case.

An annoying detail is that of citing numbers of cases. It is sometimes justifiable in footnotes to provide the court with a large share of the authority. But the string citation should be sparingly used.

The brief that contains two pages of citations with the lazy statement that "the following cases are in accord" gives a ludicrous appearance. Strangely enough, some textbooks on brief-writing contain model briefs which fall into such an error. The least that should be done, if a large number of cases is to be cited, is to make some classification. And even if the facts of the cases are recited there is danger of giving the impression of the "digest method." The key number may be a useful tool for research, but it will not write a brief.

An equally grievous and very common use of authority is the quotation. Instances where quotation is justified are rare. Now and then a judge has made some pithy statement that may be quoted to advantage. Occasionally a dictum is of peculiar import and bears reproducing. But typically quotation is meaningless without a statement of the facts of the case, and with the facts it is likely to be needless repetition of a point already made and more neatly clinched otherwise.

Evaluation of authority is not often attempted. Yet it is very helpful. The relative value of most cases is apparent on their face. But now and then extraneous factors give a case peculiar significance. The local standing of the judge, local disputes that have evoked special consideration, a unique position in a line of cases, notice and elaboration received in legal periodicals and casebooks, and in other jurisdictions—such factors should be disclosed to an unfamiliar court.

Non-case material has been treated disparingly by most brief-writing texts. Briefs themselves rarely resort to it, and usually when they do it is only to the extent of citing some encyclopedia or compilation which has little value save as a supplement to digests. It is perfectly legitimate to give a clue to further sources of case material. But the law review is generally just as fruitful in this respect as the better compilation; and it has the added value of containing keener analysis and more discriminating use of cases than can be found in the encyclopedia. It is particularly unfortunate that student work in the reviews is so much neglected in the brief. The student work in a number of the reviews is, on the whole, more helpful than leading articles. It is alert to new trends, it is concentrated, disciplined, original. And for research purposes it is far superior to the stultifying digest. The judge should be given the benefit at least of the citation.

The law schools have recently given considerable prominence to the use of economic material, recognizing that in many cases which get to the appellate stage there is an element of doubt that may best be resolved by some effort at economic analysis. As yet the bar has not attempted, to an appreciable extent, to articulate such analysis with the legal presentation in the brief. Even in matters of public law, where the peculiar place of the American judiciary should make economic considerations vital to decision, the judge is usually left to rely upon his own investigation if any is to be made. It is not infrequent that a lawyer at the bar of the Supreme Court flounders hopelessly when some Justice seeks information. During the last term there were at least three unusually important constitutional cases which turned upon the economic consequences of questioned legislation but in which the lawyers gave not a word of advice on the crucial issues. And there are numberless matters of private law where neglect of economic material leaves the judge to the exercise of uninformed judgment.

Any effort to cope with this inadequacy is commendable, for a technique must be developed. However, there is one serious weakness discernible to some of the few economic treatments that have been made, a tendency to maintain the economic rigidly separate from the legal analysis. This may be carried to the extent of adopting, in the former, a different language, one unfamiliar to the ordinary judge, and, more serious, of failing to make a lawyer-like application to the facts of the case. Where this occurs it is probably due to leaving the economic analysis entirely to a specialist. Specialism has had sufficiently unhappy consequences in the law without carrying it to this extreme.

The statement of the facts of the case is the heart of the brief, and draws most heavily upon the skill of advocacy.

The first requisite is most frequently ignored, that of shaping the recital to make absolutely clear upon what points the litigant relies. It is usually necessary to depart from the chronological history, and it is difficult to do so without sacrifice of continuity and coherence. Yet if the lawyer has not succeeded in making his points plain from his statement of facts, no matter how well he may have made his statement of points, it is probable that his case will be obscured for it is rare that his argument can be given the attention demanded to supplement adequately a recital of facts that has not itself brought the points into sharp relief.

The lawyer must also depend upon his statement of facts to convince the court of the importance or unimportance of the issue presented for decision. As is particularly true on petition to the Supreme Court for certiorari, most appellate courts, either by inclination or because of the prescription of statute, will go to great lengths to leave undisturbed such determinations below as do not have general significance. But what has been determined is defined by the facts; significance must come from the facts themselves, not from some general statement of doctrine supposedly involved. A temptation commonly yielded to is that of leaving some crucial fact out of the statement and of consideration in order to color the issue with importance. Even when the lower court has pitched its decision upon a broader ground, the narrowest issue which all the facts present must be the one calling for primary consideration and it is in the statement of facts that everything involved must be shown. Over and over again a brief is rendered virtually useless because a persistent opponent succeeds in using an ignored fact to reduce the question to unimportance.

It is likewise tempting to leave out of a statement those facts which support the opponent's argument. To do so is a blunder. The moment it becomes likely that the opponent's argument is to derive peculiar strength from this or that fact, that fact becomes of supreme importance in the statement. In the first place there is nothing like frankness to inspire the confidence of the judge. And in the second place only through skill in the initial statement can the lawyer present the view of the whole case he wants the judge to take. Relevance, perspective, the delicate adjustment of conflicting implications: there must be the light of all the facts, and if the lawyer does not show them in his statements he has finally crippled his argument.

Scarcely less important is the problem of making the statement interesting, particularly when it is long and complex. The beneficent effect of providing a labored judge with a good story is apparent. The facts, after all, will be the material for building the decision and opinion, and laying bare with a novelist's art the drama that has produced dispute is paramount. Of all the brief, this statement will most surely be read, and carefully, and must be referred to repeatedly. This demands that there be more than arrangement and proportion; the telling itself must catch and hold attention. But so many lawyers, seemingly steeped in the law of real property, insist on writing as though the statement were a mortgage; indeed it is not infrequent that in paraphrasing relevant documents the stilted jargon of the formal papers is mercilessly adopted.

But of all offenders, the worst is he who drones on indefinitely, cluttering his pages with facts that can have nothing to do with the case and interest no one, until the reader gives up in sheer exhaustion.

Writing the statement is not easy. It requires time, imagination, and care. But it is the vital job. Nine times out of ten it determines the case.

The brief is as peculiar and exacting as the sonnet. The busy lawyer, prone to dictate, does not often find time to cultivate an art which should be the pride of his profession, and for some reason the law schools seem to have neglected it. However the Office of the Solicitor General of the United States under Mr. Mitchell and Mr. Thacher developed an admirable technique which should serve as a model for lawyers the country over. It would be a great service to the bar if the product of the Office could be made more readily accessible.

Adapted from Vol. 21, American Bar Association Journal (1935).

The Argument of an Appeal in the Court of Appeals

BY JOHN T. LOUGHRAN

I WANT TO BEGIN WITH A WORD or two about the admirably happy discourse upon the present topic that was presented two years ago in this room. You cannot have forgotten the picture of the fisherman to which I owe the part I shall now attempt to perform. On the theory that such an argument is a conscious and deliberate angling for the judicial mind, you were asked to fancy certain advantages that might ensue "if the fish himself could be induced to give his views on the most effective methods of approach."[1]

As I play this part of the fish in the picture, I take for granted your understanding that I speak for myself alone, and only from my own point of view, and that, in the nature of things, there is no judicial dogma on this subject. With your leave, then, I shall candidly do my best to turn the picture 'round and let you look at it from the back. As a preliminary, something must be said respecting methods of the work of appellate tribunals in general.

A few years ago, I was told by an Australian judge that an appeal in his court was argued in this fashion: After the facts were stated, counsel on either side was permitted to cite three cases and no more in support of each of his points. The reports of these cases were then and there examined on the bench, after which all hands discussed the issues in the light of the cited authorities until a de-

[1] Davis, *The Argument of an Appeal* (1940) 26 ABAJ 895; a lecture delivered by John W. Davis, before the Association of the Bar of the City of New York, October 22, 1940: "And in the second place a discourse on the argument of an appeal would come with superior force from a Judge who is in his judicial person the target and the trier of the argument than from a random archer like myself. Or, supposing fishes had the gift of speech, who would listen to a fisherman's weary discourse on fly-casting . . . and all the other tiresome stuff that fishermen talk about, if the fish himself could be induced to give his views on the most effective methods of approach. For after all it is the fish that the angler is after and all his recondite learning is but the hopeful means to that end."

cision was reached. Such an oral analysis of all the difficulties would probably be generally accepted as the perfect method of arguing any appeal. My Australian friend, however, told me also that so detailed a dissection often took two days or more to do, and that consequently the process was almost too much, even for a tribunal which heard but fifteen appeals at a session of four weeks.

Of course, no routine of that extended order would be possible in our affairs. During the eight years I have been in our Court, six hundred or more appeals have been disposed of every year. Sometimes we take in as many as a dozen cases on the order calendar in one afternoon. The weekly grist runs on the average anywhere between twenty-five and forty cases. The conditions of our work were once described by Chief Judge Crane with characteristic directness. I borrow from him these words:

> "The majority of us dine together every day of the session. Every Tuesday, Wednesday and Thursday we are in consultation from half-past nine in the morning until one, followed by the court session from two until six. In the evening, it has been customary for members of the court to work in their chambers in the courthouse until late at night.... By tradition the consultations of the court are an outstanding feature of main importance to the work. They are quite formal. The judge to whom a case has fallen is expected to report fully upon all questions involved, and while making his report it is the duty of the Chief Judge to see that he is not interrupted, no matter how long he may take. When he is through, the matter then passes to the next associate in rank who is accorded like treatment."[2]

In his lectures on the Supreme Court of the United States, Chief Justice Hughes sets forth the different practice employed in that tribunal. He says:

> "At the conference, it is the practice for the Chief Justice, unless he desires otherwise, to be the first to state his opinion with respect to the case to be decided; he gives his opinion first and votes last. After a decision has been reached, the Chief Justice assigns the case for opinion to one of the members of the Court that is, of course, to one of the majority, if there is a division and the Chief Justice is a member of the majority. If he

[2] Minute of the Court of Appeals, 278 N. Y. V, VI (1938).

is in a minority, the senior Associate Justice in the majority assigns the case for opinion."[3]

As to whether either of these divisions of labor is superior to the other, I shall have nothing to say. My point about the matter is simply this: There is nothing in the idea that a case in the Court of Appeals is likely to fall to one judge rather than to another merely because of the nature of the controversy. The assignment of cases among its judges does not depend at all on any supposed expertness of some member of the bench in a given field, common as the contrary impression may have been. The medium of assignment, as Judge Crane said, is an affair of rotation and nothing else.

But whatever the merits of either of the practices described, there has been in some appellate courts another practice which has been roundly condemned—that is to say, the practice of assigning a record on appeal to one judge to write an opinion without previous consultation by the whole court. "This course," said Judge John F. Dillon, "ought to be forbidden, peremptorily forbidden by statute."[4] There is no such practice in the Court of Appeals. On the contrary, every appeal—and every motion for that matter—is in the first instance freely and openly discussed in the conferences of the court until all are satisfied. Except in emergencies, our opinions are written and circulated among us when the court is in recess. During a recess we also exchange written reports upon all cases that were left undecided at the end of the conferences of the last session. These opinions and reports are the first things taken up for discussion at the start of the following session and are then voted upon. There will also be at that time a number of motions to be got out of the way before the current calendar becomes the order of the day in our conferences. Meantime, the oral arguments have been going on each afternoon in the courtroom with the result that the first case argued at any session does not come up at the consultation table earlier than the following week. Moreover, this gap constantly widens as the session runs along, for in the conference debates—as Judge Crane put it—"every man is afforded full opportunity for self-expression and the indulgence of his own peculiar method of approach or attack."[5]

---

3 Hughes, *The Supreme Court of the United States* (1928) 58-59.
4 Dillon, *The Laws and Jurisprudence of England and America* (1895) 192.
5 Minute of the Court of Appeals, 278 N. Y. V, VI (1938).

The bearing of all this upon questions as to the effectiveness of any argument, oral or written, cannot be left out of account, if the advocate would in imagination change places with the court, as I assume he has already been persuaded to do by a cardinal rule of his own. With so great a volume of work to be done in time so limited, it must be clear that the judges approach every case with a strong feeling of the necessity for prompt and exact grasp of the issues to be determined at the consultation table. Note this one point, if no other: the chief end—nay, the sole end—of every argument of counsel is to equip the judges for the work of their conferences.

Next I take this question: Do the judges ordinarily look into a case in advance of the oral argument? At the beginning of my apprenticeship eight years ago, the kindly gentleman who at that time was clerk of the court tried to convince me of the benefits of getting a head start by examining over the summer the records and briefs in the cases that were filed for the autumn session. Laudable as that advice may have been, it was not suited to me. You may decide for yourselves upon the validity of my reasons, which were these: It must be to any advocate a disenchanting thing to have to work out the pattern of his oral argument before an auditor who gives evidence of having already gone below the surface of the thing for himself. Again, such antecedent diligence of an auditor might make it necessary that some pre-acquired notions be rubbed out of his mind before anything else could well be put in, inasmuch as nothing is more important to the average man than his own little discoveries. Go back for a moment at this point, if you will, to the figure of the angler and consider his trouble in this last predicament. See how he is now forced to follow, not only his own purpose, but also some unanticipated notions of the fish as well. Behold the change in his ordered plan, as, in a single cast, he now launches two or even three flies instead of one. I pass to another question.

Can anybody read all the records in so many cases within the available time? The whole record is read scrupulously in cases of murder in the first degree, and usually when there is exercise of the jurisdiction to review new findings of the Appellate Division. In many other situations a great part of the record is nothing to the purpose. One or two commonplace examples will be enough to make this sufficiently plain. You would probably be surprised to find how many are the negligence cases in which the story of the accident will be but a minor fraction of a record which bulks big in medical expert testimony and other items of proof of damage which are no longer in the case, since the facts have now been finally determined. So the mass of a record in a condemnation proceeding may at this last stage present no more than the single question whether the correct measure of damage was applied.

But however many the cases in which the review may thus be limited—whether the pages to be read are few or many—a judge must at all events bring with him to the conference an accurate and ready knowledge of all matters of fact that are relevant to the points open to discussion. If he is industrious, he will, perforce, gather technique and perhaps wisdom in this indispensable business of getting into and out of a record. Be that as it may, every word of an argument which helps him on his way in that direction will fall pleasantly on his ears. Hence the primary importance to the court that the advocate have sure knowledge of every nook and corner of his record. It sometimes happens that a judge will disclose some misapprehension respecting the facts you have stated. Be ready then with chapter and verse to put him back on the track —for his own good, I mean—and to your profit also, because you may lose much of his interest should you fail him in such a moment. I pass now to something of almost equal importance.

The main facts are the pivot on which most cases turn, and it is not in the power of man to state them too clearly. Unless the appeal is before the court by its own leave, the judges will probably know very little about the controversy before the argument begins. Let the main facts be adequately brought forward and they will vitalize the whole discussion as it proceeds thereafter. Let the main facts be clouded by a slipshod statement of them and the rest of the argument is as good as lost. In truth, it is a personal confession that the charm of a lucid fact presentation seems one of the best arguments of all.

I have been speaking of the statement of the facts themselves; the argument of questions of fact is quite a different thing. You often hear it said from the bench that the court will not hear extended discussion of questions of fact. I have already given you the reason: the work at the consultation table is always a week or more behind the arguments of counsel. During this hiatus, usually twenty-five or more other cases have been argued and inevitably the subtleties of the oral argumentation of a case a week old will, to a great extent, have been forgotten. This is the reason why the court calls out, "Give us the high-lights," when for example, the argument is whether there is any evidence to support a finding of fact. The record alone can in that instance supply the answer and whether or not that record constitutes any evidence is a matter of individual interpretation. Yet it is remarkable how frequently the time and attention of the court are taken up by lengthy arguments on this very point, which always involves on one side the proving of a negative. The development of such arguments, as I believe, is more wisely made the office of the printed brief.

And now what of questions from the bench during argument? Not so long ago, Lord Justice Atkin of England delivered himself on this subject in forthright fashion:

> "There are times in our courts when it is rather difficult to know whether the argument is proceeding or whether the Court is delivering a series of interlocutory judgments. I remember one case, when I was a junior at the Bar, which excited great interest, a case as to whether you could obtain an interlocutory injunction against an alleged libel. The Court sat, and, the argument having proceeded all day, about a quarter to four the presiding judge said to counsel: 'I suppose, Mr. Cozens-Hardy you have about concluded your argument?' He said, 'My Lord, I have not begun yet. The Court has taken the whole time.' "[6]

This seems to me to go to the heart of the problem. Questions from the bench are well enough so long as the oral argument is not too much disturbed. In my personal opinion, such questions should be directed solely to the speedy and precise exposition of the thing to be decided.

A moment ago I remarked that nothing was more important to the average man than his own little discoveries. Now judges are average men and, if in the course of your argument there should occur to one of them some theory which would do you no good, it is better you should know it through a question from him than that it should remain a masked battery for your possible undoing. When you are faced by such an unexpected question, it is far more to the judge's satisfaction either that you meet it head-on or frankly concede your present unreadiness to answer. In the latter case, do

[6] Atkin, *Appeal in English Law* (1927) 3 Camb. L. J. 1, 8-9.

not hesitate to ask for time for the submission of some further memorandum; never risk the weakening of a well-constructed argument by attempting an out of hand response to a question raising an undigested difficulty.

Tonight I have said a good deal about oral argument and the thought may arise whether an exhaustive brief really requires the aid of oral presentation. Again the answer must be a personal one. I know that I experience a feeling of distinct disappointment when on the call of a case that falls to me, I hear the clerk say, "Submitted." When the briefs in a submitted case are picked up at the end of a day that has told heavily they are dead things. Under those circumstances, it is hard for a judge not to feel a diminution of his ardor. The printed word of the ablest advocate, to me at least, falls far short of the same arguments when heard face to face through his living voice.

The phrasing of my feeling in this aspect is difficult; but you may take my word for it, oral address may breed an intimacy between advocate and judge that can never come out of a printed page. Even an expression lacking in grace and of no great profundity often conveys a hidden appeal to the feelings of the court. I shall not easily forget the counsel who, just before our tired closing hour, half-complainingly but with grave earnestness said this: "Now, your Honors, before I sit down, I want to say a word about a brief that has been filed against us by an *amicus curiae.* I have to talk about that brief because, if the man who wrote it is a friend of this court, he certainly is no friend of mine." He instantly had the attention of the whole court.

I remember another who argued an appeal in a capital case. Every transition of his thought was introduced by the phrase, "Now, gentlemen, I expect to show." After he had repeated this phrase a dozen times, he pulled himself up and humbly said to the court: "I beg your Honors' pardon. This is my first time in this court. You see I am used to talking to juries." Chief Judge Crane thereupon broke in: "Why did you tell us that? We would never have known you were not here before. You talk like an old-timer, and, if you want to call us gentlemen, it's all right with us. I hope we are." After that lawyer had concluded, the Chief Judge said to him: "When you come here again may you be fortunate enough to make as good an argument as you did today; and the best part of it is that you were yourself."

Simple incidents like these, and all I have said before, are meant to convey the truth that the advocate is indeed at all times the instructor of the court. Professor James Bradley Thayer, in the prefatory note to his Cases on Evidence, said, and on this note I close: "In law, as in other things, every teacher has his own methods, determined by his personal gifts or lack of them,—methods as incommunicable as his temperament, his looks or his manners." On that basis, I give you as a final word this blunt but kindly admonition of Chief Judge Pound to a young lawyer on his first appearance in our Court: "Don't forget that you are talking to seven ordinary men like yourself."

Adapted from Vol. 12, Fordham Law Review (1943).

Suggestions About Briefs and Arguments

BY STANLEY E. QUA

PRESIDENT THOMAS M. A. HIGGINS: The next gentleman has agreed to write an article on the preparation of briefs. When that is written each member of this Association will have a copy of it. The gentleman whom I am about to present to you was a practicing attorney in Lowell. He was an able member of our Lowell Bar. I saw him as he went about his daily tasks. I saw him as a conveyancer. I saw him as a trial man. He was a good man then. He has developed into a Judge whom we respect and whom his colleagues on the bench respect—the Honorable Stanley E. Qua.

The Address

Mr. President and Members of the Middlesex Bar. I did not know that I had agreed to write that article. If you do not receive it according to the promise just made it will be proof that I have not agreed to write it.

I did, however, know that I was expected to say something tonight. I am not getting out of that. I will be honest to that extent. I will go a little further. I regret it as much as you do. I do not quite know why, but I did make up my mind that I would have my notes large enough so that you could all read them. Well, the truth is I picked this stuff out of a drawer. I do not know what is in it exactly, although I put it there once. I do have a notion that I might cull a few choice excerpts from it for a few minutes.

When I first learned I might be here tonight, I got to reminiscing, as I do on such occasions, a sign of advancing age, no doubt. I have been on the bench for approximately 26 years. If I live three or four months longer it will be 26 years, if my arithmetic is still good. It had occurred to me that I might perhaps say something along the line of judicial confessions. It occurred to me Rousseau wrote his confessions before he was quite as old as

I am. His were different from mine. If I pursued that line you might be disappointed.

Well, then, it seemed to me that, perhaps, I should indicate something in the natue of Nestorian advice. Your president was kind enough to ask me if I would say something tonight about the presentation of cases before the full bench. Now that request involved two assumptions, first, that you did not know how to present a case to the full bench, and secondly, that I did. I suspect that there is very little truth in either of those assumptions.

I have been on the receiving end of the battery for so long now that I do not know as I ought to try to coach the pitcher. Probably I ought to devote my time to coaching the catcher. But, if I were to assign any subject to my few remarks tonight it would be the invisible curtain, not the iron curtain, but the invisible curtain.

When I say the invisible curtain I mean the curtain that sometimes seems to fall between the bar down on the floor and the bench up on the platform. I have wondered whether in pursuance of the suggestion of your president I might be able to make a few suggestions to you tonight that might, perhaps, be helpful in the matter of the presentation of cases. Inasmuch as I have already intimated that I am talking from a one-sided view, you will be able to judge from the other side how much attention you may pay to what I have in mind. I think that there are a few suggestions that could be followed out that might help materially in the presentation of cases before our Full Court.

I think such difficulties as exist are due to the fact that the members of the bar for the most part have never sat upon the bench and the members of the bench, although they have at a certain age been at the bar, have perhaps forgotten a good many of the trial difficulties that they had to face in the days when they were there.

Let me make my first suggestion. Suppose you have a case you are going to present to the full court. You are the appealing party, we will say. I wonder if it would not be a pretty good idea when you are the appealing party to see to it that you get a proper record of the case you are going to take up. I suspect that most of you do what I did when I was at the bar. I left it to the clerk. The clerk probably did a better job on the whole than I would have done if I had done it alone. And yet it is our experience that there is an occasional case that comes to us on an inadequate judicial record where if the appealing attorney had carefully gone over the material that was being prepared, he could have seen to it that we had a full and complete presentation.

To take just one instance; as you know, a great many cases depend upon the exhibits. Documentary proof is probably the highest form of proof. Many cases depend entirely upon the documentary proof at the trial. Yet we get case after case in which the exhibits that were the mainstay of the appeal, do not come to us in such form that we can be sure we can make any use of them. If you have a bill of exceptions, you can refer to the exhibits in the exceptions. There are present rules that they need not always be printed. The judge below can make a statement or certificate that it is not necessary to print them. If the certificate is made and incorporated into the record the exhibits can be presented at the argument.

But I think you would be surprised how often an attorney in appealing a case will come in with photographs that have been most persuasive before the jury or the judge and not have them made part of the record. They may not even be in the courtroom. A last minute attempt is made to make them part of the record by getting the consent of the opposing counsel. All of this is in the absence of the trial judge.

My first suggestion to you is when you have a case, especially if you are the appealing party—if you are not, more or less the same thing applies—see to it that we get the record that you are willing to stand by, a record that contains everything that you want to put up to us, so that we will not take exhibits, and when we get them at our desks behind the scenes and begin studying the case, find after it is too late that there is some exhibit you argued about and referred to in your brief which under the rules that govern our proceedings, we cannot even look at.

Now let me pass on. Suppose you have a good record. Your exhibits have all been taken care of. All your material is in the right form for us to use. May I suggest a second step? I think the next thing to do is to make up your mind what is open to you to argue upon and then argue on that. Now you might think that having the record before you, it is self-evident, all you have to do is use that record. I think that is not quite true. Let me take an instance or two. Suppose first that an action of law has come up. Suppose it was tried on agreed facts in the court below. Wait a minute. *Was* it tried on agreed facts or on a case stated? Do you know which it was? Whether the agreement on which you tried the case was a case stated or whether it consisted only of facts agreed as evidence, does not depend upon the title. It depends upon the substance.

What difference does it make, you say, whether it is a case stated or agreed facts? Well, suppose we are talking about an action at law. If it is a case stated, the full court by statute can draw inferences of fact from the facts agreed upon. If it is a case presented on agreed facts and is not a case stated, all inferences of facts are for the trial court. The full court cannot draw inferences of fact.

Let me ask you, does that make a difference or does it not in that which is open to you to argue? What may happen to your case if you argue a case as if it were a case stated when in fact it is not?

Well, take an auditor's report. It is still the law, of course, that if the auditor's findings of fact were to be final, it is a case stated. Do not ask me why it is. It is. I might have difficulty in explaining why. I can cite you cases, but we have to take it as it is. The full court in that case can draw inferences of fact. Of course, if the findings of fact of the auditor are not final, even if there was no other evidence introduced, the situation is different. You would have a case where the auditor's findings are *prima facie* evidence, but that is all.

Now, suppose we pass on. I am still trying to suggest to you the importance before you write your briefs or prepare your arguments of finding out exactly what is open on the kind of record that you have. In equity cases either the evidence is reported or it is not reported. If the evidence is not reported and there are no findings of fact by the judge, what is open to you on that record? Practically nothing. The only thing open is whether such a decree as was made in the court below could be made on the pleadings. That question may be of some consequence. Usually it is not. Usually you would have practically nothing to argue in that kind of case. You had better not come in with it at all. It is not always true. Everything I say in this, as in other instances about the law, is subject to exceptions.

Suppose there *are* findings of fact. I am still supposing the evidence is not reported. The trial judge has made findings of fact. Now you have another question you must ask yourself. Has he made a complete findings of all the facts on which he made his decision, or has he found only certain facts as explanatory of the course he took? What difference does it make? It makes this difference, that if he has made a set of findings of fact designed and intended as a statement of all the facts on which the decision is based, then it was his duty to state facts enough to support that decision. The facts are assumed to be all the facts. If you cannot stand on those facts without any other facts, the decree will be reversed. But suppose the findings of fact of the judge were not intended to be all the facts. What happens then? In that case there is a presumption that he has found other facts, all other facts which under the pleadings could be found that would be sufficient to support the decree he made. If you were the appealing party, you would be up against it. You might win. You would have a heavy burden. You would have to know what your burden was. You would have to be prepared to carry it. Of course, if the judge has found the facts under the statute, the statute applicable to the Superior Court in equity or the corresponding statute applicable in the Probate Courts, in response to your request for findings of material facts, the findings expressly made will always be deemed to be all the findings. It is then said that there is no room for any presumption that any further findings entered into the decree.

Another instance, still in equity. Suppose your case comes up on a master's report. There is a summary of the evidence you have asked for and obtained under Rule 90 of the Superior Court rules or the corresponding rules of the other courts. What use can you make of that evidence? Can you use that evidence to prove that the master's findings were wrong? No. That rule and the evidence reported under it are designed solely to bring up questions of law. You can use a summary of evidence under Rule 90 to check the master's rulings on evidence or otherwise in the progress of the hearing before him to see whether they were erroneous or not. You can also use it in presenting the question of law, whether there was any evidence to support a finding which he made, which is a question of law. You cannot use that summary of evidence to show that his findings of fact were wrong as findings of fact.

Now, I do not say that it is desirable that all of these distinctions should exist. I suspect that appeal procedure will always be technical. I suspect that if we were to attempt now, as some people want us to do, to rewrite the appeal procedure in this Commonwealth—the net result, unless it was done with extraordinary skill and after assiduous study, would be, merely, that we would have to make a fresh start. It would become necessary to construe the new statute and all we would have would be another series of decisions. They would look just as technical as those we have now. If our appeal procedure is to be revised, it is my most earnest hope that the revision be done with the most extreme care, because I know it would be entirely possible to muddy it still further and it would be a great deal easier to do that than to clear it up.

Well, let me suggest something else. Suppose you have a good record. It contains everything you need. You have analyzed that record so that you know just what is open to you to argue. I think your next step is probably to decide whether you are going to argue the case orally or whether you are going to submit it on briefs. Now, how are you going to decide that? Well, you cannot lay down any general rule that fits every case. I am myself a believer in the oral argument. I believe in oral arguments only if they are good ones. I do not believe a poor oral argument ever won a case that could not have been won by submitting the case on a brief.

The relative positions of the brief and oral argument have I take it changed within the last few generations. I think that originally the brief was intended to be, as its name implied, a sort of synopsis of the oral argument and the oral argument was looked upon as the main thing and the brief as a secondary aid in the process of remembering the oral argument. I think that situation has changed today. Today the brief, as we call it, is the primary argument in the case. It is a written argument. It is more than a brief. I think, commonly, it should be more than a brief. I do not think it should be spun out at great length. It should be as compact as possible, but I think it should be the principal argument.

One thing I want to say before I forget it,—do not be afraid that you are going to waive any point you have argued on your brief even if you say nothing about it in your oral argument. It is not necessary in your oral argument to say you do not waive points you do not talk about. If you have argued them on your brief, that preserves them and the court will decide all questions and will stand on the brief. It will not do, of course, just to say on your brief you do not waive a point if you do not argue it. We expect you to argue the point in the brief, at least to some extent, if you want us to hear you.

To get back for a moment; are you going to argue the case orally or submit it on briefs? If you submit the case on briefs, it will as a rule go before the judges who are sitting in the quorum at the time. Every judge on the quorum will have a copy of the record and the briefs. He will read your briefs and as much of the record as he can.

Now again I am going to approach a confession. I do not know what my associates will say. I see they are alarmed. If there is anything that a Supreme Court judge is afraid of, it is his associates. Right now they are more afraid of me than I am of them, because they don't know what I am going to say.

I remember the first year or two of my being on the Superior Court. Every junior judge went to Fall River. I went to Fall River. I did not see anything the matter with Fall River except that it was a long way from home for me. I liked it down there. I had a good time there. It was no penance for me to be sent to Fall River. I thought they had a good bar down there. Especially do I remember old Simeon Borden. If you are not a Bristol County man, perhaps you did not know him. You missed something. When I first went there in 1921 Simeon Borden, if I remember correctly, had been Clerk of Courts for 52 years. I will not vouch for the exact figure. I get him confused with Robert O. Morris of Springfield. Their terms of office were more or less co-existing. Borden told me a story. He said that the last time the full court came down to Fall River, or Taunton, to be more exact, he had not come in to greet the Chief Justice. This was Chief Justice Rugg. He said it had been an immemorial custom there, and he supposed in other counties, for the clerk to come in just before they came into the courtroom and say "Good Morning" to the Chief Justice and the justices assembled there. He said he did not have time to do that. He was busy about something. He had gone right into the courtroom when the opening hour arrived. They had the sitting. When the sitting was over, the justices were in the consultation room. Borden had a call. They wanted to see him. He said he went into the consultation room and the Chief Justice arose and said, "How do you do, Mr. Borden?" Mr. Borden took the lesson and went out.

That is aside from my point. I have wandered a bit. It was at the same time Borden told me, and I have always remembered it and felt it since, that one of the most extraordinary things about the Supreme Court was how afraid all the judges were of each other. Well, to come back to my near confession, I have supposed you submitted your case on briefs. I have told you, and told you truthfully, that every member of the quorum will read the briefs and as much of the record as he can, very likely all of it, but perhaps, not.

I am going to ask you for just a moment to consider, when you remember some of our records run into hundreds of pages and and we have generally 300 or more cases a year, whether, if you were a judge, you could read all those records all the way through. The answer is you could not do it in a twenty-four-hour day, taking no holidays and no Sundays. So when you submit a case on briefs, you have a certain advantage in that every judge has quietly read those briefs. But you cannot be sure every judge has read every word of that record.

There could be something in the record you would like to talk about face to face with the court. The advantage of the oral argument is that you can do that. Now I do not mean to suggest that a case is less well considered when it is submitted on briefs. Sometimes I have thought that on the whole they were more considered. But it is true that you have lost the opportunity to talk face to face with the court about some particular thing you may think you can express orally better than you can get it across in any other way.

On the other hand, if you argue your case orally, the judges, sitting there on the bench, have to grasp that case from your oral argument with such snatches of the brief as they can get in the meantime. There is not the same leisurely opportunity to grasp the case in the first instance by the whole quorum as when they are submitted on briefs. Probably they wash out about the same, but the nature of the case ought to be the deciding factor.

I see time goes on. I want to make just one more point and then I will finish. I am talking now about oral argument. You are not going to be able to believe what I am going to say, because I find that as I talk to lawyers, some of them are polite enough to remain silent, but in general they do not believe what I am now about to say. You have a limited time for argument, half an hour. The thing not to do is to hurry your statement of the case in order to get to your argument about the case. If you are the appealing party, you have to do two things in an oral argument. First, you have to state the case and then you have a line of reasoning about that case you would like to present and have the court follow. As between these two things in an oral argument, the important thing is the statement of the case and not the reasoning about it.

Now again, put yourself behind the invisible curtain. Suppose you are seated on the bench. You are a little bit slow-witted, as I am. It is a little hard for you to listen sometimes. You do not orient yourself too rapidly from one environment to another. You may hear anywhere from four to fourteen cases a day. They flash before you rather fast. They run the whole gamut of every possible kind of litigation that can exist. One moment you have a divorce case. The next moment you have a workmen's compensation case. The next moment it is a suit in equity and then an action in tort. You may have an appeal from the Department of Public Utilities and so on.

You have oriented yourself. You know what your case is about. You have thought about it. You have arranged it. You know the law about it and all the statutes. The judge has not the benefit of any of that. He has not the slightest idea what your case is. Until you begin to tell him, he does not know whether it is a divorce case or what it is. So you can see the advantage of a statement of facts that will get across and that will go through the curtain. If you make a clear-cut statement of facts you are going to argue orally with a segregation of the issue from the mass by which it is always surrounded and encrusted, so that you can take that issue and hold it up and look it over, as it were, and see its facets and its shape and its form and if you can make the judge see that issue that way, then you have made a successful oral argument.

When you have done that, you can go on to the reasoning about the thing that you want to present. If you hurry over your statement of facts in order to get the reasoning you have lost the chief advantage of oral argument. You might as well submit the case on briefs, and better so, I think. That point is one I want to make with all the emphasis I can, because if you think about it, you will realize, as I say, that its importance can be seen only when you have crossed to the bench and got behind the curtain. Every man on the bench knows when you sit down and the court adjourns for the day, that he has to go at once into a consultation room. He has to give an opinion about that case and about ten or twelve other cases. He must first find out what the point is. If you do not clearly state that point, he must try to discover it for himself, and he cannot very well listen to your argument while he is doing that.

This is another confession. Every man on that bench knows that he has to face the ordeal of the consultation room. Being as afraid of his associates as I tell you he is, he is not going to go in there and not know what the case is about. Therefore, if he is not getting a clear statement from you, he is going to shuffle the papers and read the briefs. It will appear he is not listening to your argument. He may listen more than you think. But there is nothing that will engage him and get the attention of the Court more thoroughly than a clear-cut statement of facts at the beginning.

Well, gentlemen, I think I have taken as much time as I ought to take. I could go on endlessly, but I am not going to. Just one thing I will say. Our rules require that statutes which are the subject of the case should be printed in the briefs. It may be one statute, one section. More often, perhaps, it means that you have to print several sections which may be needed for comparison. There again, put yourself behind the curtain. We on the bench do not remember all the statutes. Some of us do not. I do not doubt that some of my associates could repeat the statutes from memory, or the Bible or the Dictionary, but, so far as I am concerned, I could not repeat a single statute of Massachusetts to save my life.

Once when I was studying law I remember a barber of my acquaintance who always struck up a conversation when I was covered with lather. One day he said, "You have to work very hard." I said, "Yes." He said, "How many laws do you have to learn in a day?" I said, "About ten." "Well," he said, "that must be hard."

Well, now, if you have not printed anything and if you have only read a statute, that is just so many words wasted. I do not get it unless I have it before me. I cannot understand your argument. You might just as well not make the argument as far as I am concerned. Of course, my associates, I do not speak for them again, but may I ask for myself that, when you prepare your briefs, you follow the rule. We do not always like to throw a brief out because it has not observed a rule. I suppose we ought to. I think we agree we do not want to be fuss-budgets in the Supreme Court. You can get away with a good deal. I am going to leave as my parting shot the suggestion that you do not try to get away with arguing a statutory case and not printing the statutes.

I thank you very much for your patience in listening to this rambling discourse. It will have achieved its object if I have, perhaps, put across through the invisible curtain one of the suggestions I have tried to make.

Adapted from Vol. 32, Massachusetts Law Quarterly (1947).

A Time-Saving Method of Stating in Appellate Briefs, the Controlling Questions for Decision

BY ROBERT VON MOSCHZISKER

LAW IS A SCIENCE, but its administration is an art; diligent pursuers of this art devise methods by which they achieve success, and when these successes present developments in practice which may be made of common use, they are as much the concern of others engaged in the same field of endeavor as are advances in the science itself. With these thoughts in mind, it seemed to the writer that, in view of the constant complaints of the law's delay, a plan which has materially aided one of our busiest appellate tribunals in bringing its work up to date[1] may well be considered a subject of general interest. The Supreme Court of Pennsylvania has accomplished this desirable result very largely by confining oral arguments in each case to one-half hour a side; but, to make the short-argument plan effective, additional rules were required, and one of the chief of these provides that a concise statement of the controlling questions for decision, drawn according to strict regulations outlined in the rule, must be included in the brief of every appellant. These regulations have proved so useful in operation that a discussion of their origin, terms and advantages appears to be warranted.

The court had long required a statement of the "history of the case," and, originally, it was intended that this should show, in narrative form, without unnecessary details, not only the nature of the controversy and the steps taken in the court below, but

[1] By "bringing its work up to date," I mean that, when the last session of the Supreme Court of Pennsylvania [1925] opened, all cases which were ripe for argument and decision had been heard and disposed of by opinions filed, and the lists are now in such condition that, where desired, cases can be, and many are, set for argument within seven weeks from the perfection of the appeal, or in less time where both sides are prepared and agree to the advancement.

also the points to be determined on appeal. Counsel, however, fell into the habit of inserting so many details as to obscure the controlling questions: as a result, hope of obtaining this information through the medium of the history of the case was abandoned, and, in 1900, new rules were promulgated requiring appellants to insert in their briefs a separate "statement of the questions involved."

At first the regulation on the subject read thus: "The statement of the questions involved is designed to enable the court to obtain an immediate view of the nature of the controversy. It must state the question or questions in the briefest and most general terms, without names, dates, amounts or particulars of any kind whatsoever. It should not exceed six or eight lines, and must not, under any circumstances, exceed half a page. For any violation of this rule the paper-book will be suppressed and the appeal *non prossed* . . . . This rule is to be regarded as in the highest degree mandatory and admitting of no exception." Realizing the natural tendency to particularize, the court provided further that "It shall be optional with counsel to add such particulars as may be thought necessary in his history of the case."

The rule governing "the statement of questions involved" has been changed twice. In 1911, it was amended to read that the statement "should not ordinarily exceed ten lines," as compared with the "six or eight" at first prescribed, but the maximum allowance was still half a page. In 1923, the rule was made to read "it should not ordinarily exceed fifteen lines," and the maximum was extended to one page. This increase was to cover occasional cases where more space might be needed than was before permitted; not to allow the insertion of details.

The intention is that the statement of questions involved shall be framed in such a manner, that by reading it, the court, without being compelled to examine the argument of counsel or any other part of the brief or record, may quickly see the nature of the legal issue, and in a general way, what points it will be called on to decide. As an aid to this end, the latest rule requires appellant to print the statement on the first page of his brief, and to put nothing else thereon.

If an appellee thinks appellant's statement inaccurate, or that it does not present the points for decision in a proper light, he may submit a counter-statement as well as a counter-history of the case. Counsel for appellees avail themselves of this privilege in about fifty per cent of the appeals, though quite often appellant's statement is so satisfactory that the court, in writing its opinion, takes up the questions involved just as they are stated and follows that order throughout. This is the best proof of their value, for it shows that they have served as an aid both on oral argument and in reaching the final decision of the case.

The rule is now firmly established to the satisfaction of all concerned, and there have been so many decisions explaining its meaning that the profession in Pennsylvania has comc thoroughly to understand it; for the benefit of those outside the state, who may desire further information than is given in this article, some of the leading authorities on the subject are mentioned in the footnotes. These cases and others of their kind have now reached the point where they form a body of constructions representing an established system, which may be taken advantage of in other jurisdictions.

The cases show a steadfast determination that the new requirement shall not be frittered away, as the old one concerning the history of the case had been; accordingly, from the beginning, the rule was rigidly enforced. The first year following its adoption, an appellant's brief was presented which contained no statement of the questions involved, and the appeal was *non prossed.*[2] Many other appeals, for the same reason, suffered a similar fate.

It was likewise insisted that the statement be kept within the prescribed limits. In an early case, appellant's brief contained a statement exceeding the permitted length; this was condemned as being "worthless for the purpose for which it was intended, viz., to enable the court to obtain an immediate view of the nature of the controversy," and the profession generally was admonished to adhere strictly to the rule.[3] In keeping with this admonition, later appeals were *non prossed* because of the undue length of the statement of questions involved;[4] and some appeals were quashed

2 Fifth Ward B. & L. Assn. v. Boylan (1901) 198 Pa 250.

3 Van Sciver Co. v. McPherson (1901) 199 Pa 331, 335, 40 A 73.

4 Green v. Sumby (1915) 248 Pa 120, 93 A 868; Duffee v. Bankers' Surety Co. (1915) 247 Pa 17, 93 A 17.

at bar.[5] One opinion goes so far as to say that this penalty may be inflicted for violations of the rule "even in murder cases."[6]

The decisions have made it plain that counsel assume great risks to their clients either in disregarding the requirements of the rule or in permitting printers to do so. Thus, in one case where the statement took up a page and a half, but was printed in large type and double spaced, suppression of the brief was avoided solely on the ground that the matter would not have exceeded half a page had it been printed in the ordinary way.[7]

A too lengthy statement is invariably due to the insertion of unnecessary details; it is attributable almost never to the fact that the questions involved could not be set out satisfactorily within the prescribed limits.

A recent case in the Superior Court of Pennsylvania, having the same rules as the Supreme Court, furnishes an excellent example of a statement of the questions involved which could have been materially condensed and made more clear by omitting details of dates, etc. As prepared by counsel, it read: "The question involved is, whether the plaintiff, who signed an application for a policy of insurance upon his dwelling house, in the Mutual Life Insurance Company of Annville, Lebanon County, Pa., about five o'clock p.m., Saturday, June 10, 1905, and paying simply the application fee of $2.50, and there being no mail from that community by which the said application could be sent to the company for its acceptance or rejection until about eight o'clock a.m. of June 12, 1905, and before the application could be sent the premises for which the application had been made was destroyed by fire, of which the agent who was authorized simply to receive applications for insurance, was duly notified, can recover for the loss? Was there any negligence on the part of the company, or its agent, because the agent did not forward the application, after he had knowledge of the destruction of the premises by fire, before it was possible to have forwarded the application by mail, simply to have the company reject the application *pro forma,* as would bind the company and make it liable?"

Some such statement as the following, omitting all particulars which do not aid in outlining the legal question involved, would

5 H————v. T———— (1904) 208 Pa 233, 57 A 562.

6 Com. v. Strail (1908) 220 Pa 483, 484, 69 A 866.

7 Buckman v. Phila. & Reading Ry. Co. (1911) 232 Pa 351, 354, 81 A 332.

permit a readier grasp of the problem: Request for insurance against fire was signed by applicant and insurance company's agent, who accepted application fee. Agent had authority only to receive and not to pass upon applications. Before the request could be mailed to company for approval or rejection, the premises were burned down. On receiving notice of the fire, agent tendered return of the fee and did not forward the application to company. Approval of application was later refused. Was there a contract of insurance on which company is liable?

From the rule that, in the absence of a statement of the questions involved no part of the appeal will be considered, it was but a logical step to say that, where a particular point urged on appeal is not included in or suggested by the statement of questions involved, the point will not be determined; this is now the established practice.[8] It has been held in several cases that such matters are not properly raised[9] and, therefore, are not before the court,[10] the authorities saying that only those questions which are in the statement,[11] or are relevant to and suggested by it,[12] will be reviewed. The court does not go beyond the statement of questions involved,[13] for by it counsel limit the matters to be considered,[14] and this limitation is binding on appellant.[15] Questions which could be raised should be included if counsel want them decided,[16] for the court has held that, by his statement, appellant "specifies

[8] Murphy v. Ahlberg (1916) 252 Pa 267, 270, 97 A 406; Spang v. Mattes (1916) 253 Pa 101, 103, 97 A 1026; Hopkins v. Tate (1916) 255 Pa 56, 62, 99 A 210; Yeager v. Anthracite Brewing Co. (1917) 259 Pa 123, 130, 102 A 418; Huntington v. Supreme Commandery (1918) 261 Pa 168, 172, 104 A 498; Silver v. Edelstem (1920) 266 Pa 531, 532, 109 A 679; Garvey v. Thompson (1920) 268 Pa 353, 355, 112 A 82; Haughney v. Gannon (1922) 274 Pa 443, 447, 118 A 427; Friedline v. Friedline (1923) 275 Pa 463, 467, 119 A 545; Lane v. Dickson (1923) 276 Pa 306, 309, 120 A 264.

[9] Lenox Coal Co. v. Duncan-Spangler Coal Co. (1920) 265 Pa 572, 576, 109 A 282.

[10] Bethlehem Steel Co. v. Topliss (1915) 249 Pa 417, 423, 94 A 1099; Pramuk's Appeal (1915) 250 Pa 45, 51, 95 A 326; Kennedy v. Rothrock Co. (1918) 261 Pa 580, 588, 104 A 746; Knobeloch v. P. H. B. & N. C. Ry. Co. (1920) 266 Pa 140, 143, 109 A 619.

[11] Kanawell v. Miller (1918) 262 Pa 9, 14, 104 A 861; Philadelphia v. Ray (1920) 266 Pa 345, 347-48, 109 A 689; Blough v. Lochrie (1923) 275 Pa 491, 496, 119 A 654.

[12] Felin v. Philadelphia (1913) 241 Pa 164, 170; Collingdale Boro v. Phila. Rapid Transit Co. (1922) 274 Pa 124, 129, 117 A 909.

[13] Furman v. Broscious (1920) 268 Pa 119, 121, 110 A 736.

[14] Keck v. P. H. B. & N. C. Ry. Co. (1922) 271 Pa 479, 482, 115 A 824; Etnier v. Pascoe (1923) 275 Pa 308, 310, 119 A 406.

[15] McIlvaine v. Powers (1921) 270 Pa 341, 343, 113 A 365.

[16] Lincoln v. Wakefield (1912) 237 Pa 97, 107.

all matters [he] desires to have reviewed,"[17] and that those so contained are the only ones "on which [he] is entitled to be heard,"[18] the theory being that counsel does not deem questions omitted worthy of attention.[19] The court has said also that, to call for consideration, a question not expressly set forth must be plainly suggested[20] or clearly comprehended by reference or direct implication[21] in the statement of the questions involved.

The above pronouncements are from cases construing the rule as at first written; the present rule, following previous decisions, expressly provides that "ordinarily no point will be considered which is not set forth in the statement of questions involved or suggested thereby." The authorities have always held, however, that it is within the discretion of the court to pass on issues which rightly belong to the case, though not brought forward by the statement of questions involved, and this is done when deemed proper.[22]

Although each point appellant desires determined ought to be included in the statement of questions involved, yet every one so included is not necessarily entitled to consideration; again, the declaration that a particular question is involved does not cure defects or omissions in other parts of the appellate procedure. For example, the legal issue urged by an appellant must ordinarily have been raised in the trial court, or it will not be reviewed on appeal;[23] and a case will not be considered on a theory different from that advanced in the court below,[24] even though the point or new theory is put forth in the statement of questions involved. Exceptions to the rulings complained of on appeal must have been taken in the court below, for, unless the trial judge's attention has

17 Hanlon v. Davis (1923) 276 Pa 113, 118, 119 A 822.

18 Stephens Adamson Mfg. Co. v. Armstrong (1914) 245 Pa 552, 553.

19 Yeager v. Gateley & Fitzgerald (1919) 262 Pa 466, 471, 106 A 76.

20 Sullivan v. Baltimore & Ohio R. R. (1922) 272 Pa 429, 436, 116 A 369.

21 Vulcanite Paving Co. v. Philadelphia (1916) 252 Pa 600, 602, 97 A 928.

22 Ferguson v. Pittsburgh & Shawmut R. R. Co. (1916) 253 Pa 581, 585, 98 A 732; Clark v. Butler Junct. Coal Co. (1918) 259 Pa 262, 267, 102 A 952; Compton v. Hoffman (1919) 265 Pa 257, 264, 108 A 626; Palkovitz v. American Sheet & Tin P. Co. (1920) 266 Pa 176, 182, 109 A 789; Com. v. Smith (1920) 266 Pa 511, 517, 109 A 786; Opening of Parkway (1920) 267 Pa 219, 227, 110 A 144; Crumley v. Penna. R. R. Co. (1922) 272 Pa 226, 231, 116 A 152; Pittston Twp. School Dist. v. Dupont Boro. School Dist. (1922) 275 Pa 183, 191, 118 A 308; Clapp v. Hunt (1923) 276 Pa 127, 129, 119 A 818.

23 Woodward & Williamson's Assessment (1922) 274 Pa 567, 570, 118 A 501; Maisel v. Patrick Corr & Sons (1923) 277 Pa 331, 333, 121 A 61.

24 Saxman v. McCormick (1923) 278 Pa 268, 273, 122 A 296.

been called to such matter, the appellate courts, if the error is not basic and fundamental, will not consider it[25] even when included in the statement of questions involved.

The rule requiring a statement of questions involved does not relieve appellant from filing formal assignments of error;[26] though assignments which are not in effect comprehended by the statement will ordinarily be dismissed.[27] Alleged errors not specified in the assignments or not otherwise properly before the court have no place in the statement of the questions involved,[28] and will not be determined even though found there.[29] The questions stated should not be in form "merely a repetition of the specifications of error;"[30] if that only were desired, there would be no necessity for this extra part of the brief. Several assignments of error may involve only one question of law, because there may have been many alleged errors committed, in different ways and at different times, as a result of a supposed misapprehension of one legal principle; all such assignments must be embraced by one question. Where the main questions have been stated and other subordinate ones are assigned for error, these lesser questions, if they directly relate to the main ones, may be stated in an abstract way which ordinarily would be insufficient if they stood alone and unconnected with other questions involved. Thus, following the statement of the main questions, "Correctness of instructions as to the effect of non-production of certain testimony, and concerning the condition and conduct of plaintiff after accident; rulings on admission and rejection of testimony," will indicate sufficiently the nature of the other points raised. If, however, these minor questions are "necessarily involved in or suggested by the principal questions stated," then their recital as separate questions is "not required or desired."[31]

When the statement contains practically self-evident propositions to which a negative answer would be immediately given,

25 Rahm's Estate (1912) 233 Pa 602, 608; Stone v. Stone (1923) 277 Pa 277, 278, 121 A 500; Saxman v. McCormick (1923) 278 Pa 268, 273, 122 A 296.

26 Thompson's Estate (1916) 253 Pa 394; Schuylkill Ry. Co. v. Pub. Serv. Com. (1919) 265 Pa 451, 452, 109 A 151.

27 Smith v. Lehigh Valley R. R. Co. (1911) 232 Pa 456, 462; Garvey v. Thompson (1920) 268 Pa 353, 355, 112 A 82.

28 Com. v. Snyder (1918) 261 Pa 57, 61.

29 Haddock v. Plymouth Coal Co. (1912) 237 Pa 37, 40; Citizens Bank v. Lesko (1923) 277 Pa 174, 180, 120 A 808.

30 Creachen v. Bromley Bros. Carpet Co. (1906) 214 Pa 15, 17.

31 Smith v. Lehigh Valley R. R. Co. (1911) 232 Pa 456, 462.

unless those propositions really control the case, appellant has done nothing to advance his cause or to assist the court.[32] If self-evident propositions are involved, they must have some application to the facts of the particular case, and, if the dispute concerns their application, then the statement should show the question of applicability.

Framing a statement of the questions involved requires the cultivation of the art of eliminating immaterial details; but, after a lawyer has gone over the case with his client and witnesses, prepared his pleadings, and tried it in the court below, he should be able to state in a very few words the points which will control the decision on appeal, and this is all that the rule requires. If in writing a brief, one focuses his attention on the controlling points, it should be easy to state them within narrow bounds; should there be failure in this respect, however, and the error be discovered only after the briefs are prepared, it may be remedied by inserting a corrected page in the printed books. If the briefs have been filed already, counsel may ask leave to amend accordingly; attempts to rectify prolix or indefinite statements by filing typewritten corrected ones have been held to be bad practice.[33]

While the rule requires that the statement be in the "most general terms," this means that the particular question should be stated in terms of generality, not that the statement may be vague, indefinite or uncertain. For example, to say that a question involved is the "charge of the court," does not suggest what legal proposition is in dispute;[34] nor does "the correctness of answers to certain of defendant's points," or "portions of charge specially assigned as error."[35] The statement of the questions involved must show the precise point of substantive law at issue and its applicability to the fact in hand. Statements such as, "sufficiency of the affidavit of defense."[36] "Did the affidavit of defense raise questions of fact which should have been submitted to a jury?" and "Did the court below err in the entry of judgment?"[37] are too indefinite to comply with the rule. Again, merely raising a question of power does not ask the court to determine whether there has been

32 Swisher v. Sipps (1902) 19 Pa. Super. Ct. 43, 47.
33 Rowan v. Com. (1918) 261 Pa 88, 90, 104 A 502.
34 Com. v. Coccodralli (1920) 74 Pa. Super. Ct. 324, 328.
35 Jones v. Matheis (1901) 17 Pa. Super. Ct. 220, 221.
36 Devers v. Sollenberger (1904) 25 Pa. Super. Ct. 64, 69.
37 Internat'l Sav. & Tr. Co. v. Kleber (1905) 29 Pa. Super. Ct. 200, 202.

an exercise of it. Thus, "Can a husband transfer his personal estate in payment of his debts, regardless of coverture?" does not put the question of whether or not he did so in the particular case.[38]

The following examples of badly stated questions involved, taken from briefs in recent cases, are illustrative of inadequate attempts to comply with the rule:

"Should the court below have entered a nonsuit?" This fails even to suggest what questions are involved.

"Whether the gift to Danforth Phipps Wight lapsed by reason of his death before death of testatrix, and whether Barrington Wight was not entitled to three-eighths of the residue instead of one-fourth?" This statement suggests that the construction of a will is involved, but little else.

"Is there sufficient competent and relevant testimony in this record upon which to base an award for compensation?" Such a question as this is involved in every workmen's compensation case; to put it forward as the point in a particular controversy is useless for the purpose intended to be accomplished by the rule under consideration.

"Action prematurely brought; misjoinder of parties defendant; vacation of street on city plan by action of municipality; absence of allegations of acts by defendant which would constitute an interference with public use of a street; negotiations inducing plaintiffs to purchase are merged in their deeds; absence of any averments of facts constituting a violation of any covenant entered into by defendant with plaintiffs; absence of privity of contract beween plaintiffs and defendant; restrictions must run with the land to bind defendant; effect of failure to record plan of which defendant had no record or actual knowledge or notice; laches of plaintiffs in failing to have plan recorded; plaintiffs' cause of complaint not cognizable in equity; plaintiffs have adequate remedy at law." This rambling statement presents no intelligible problems, only argumentative suggestions.

"(1) Does the evidence disclose such breach of contract on the part of defendant as to justify binding instructions for plaintiff for the amount of damages claimed? (2) In plaintiff's defense to defendant's counter-claim, was the testimony offered by plaintiff as to market value of steel ingots, competent and properly ad-

[38] Duncan v. Duncan (1920) 265 Pa 471, 473, 109 A 222.

mitted?" No judge could understand the true meaning of these questions without reading the notes of trial or history of the case; the statement is faulty in that it does not take specific questions from a field of possible ones and state them for decision.

The following properly stated questions involved, from briefs in recent cases, are good examples of compliance with the rule:

"Where a court of equity has entered a decree ordering a husband to pay a certain sum of money under the terms of a separation agreement and he fails to make payment, has the court power to attach the person of the husband?"

"The liability of a subscriber to telephone service to pay at the rate prescribed in the company's schedule of tariffs filed with the Public Service Commission for service actually received, when the contract between the company and the subscriber provides that it is to be effective only in the event of a certain number of telephones being installed in a community and the required number never were installed."

"Is the process of making roasted coffee from green coffee a manufacturing process which exempts the proceeds of the sale of roasted coffee, delivered from the place where the process is carried on, from a mercantile license tax, under the terms of section 11 of the Act of April 22, 1846 (P. L. 489)?"

"Where a testator provides as follows: 'Item. I give . . . unto my beloved wife . . . the house in which I may reside at the time of my decease, should said house belong to me, but in case said house should not belong to me then I give . . . to my said wife the house I now reside in, she to have, hold and enjoy the same during all the term of her natural life, and upon her decease, I order and direct that the same shall go into and form a part of my residuary estate to be disposed of as is hereinafter directed,' and at the time of his death the house in which he resides does belong to him, does his widow take a life estate or a fee simple title in and to said property?"

"Does the conversion of private dwellings into apartment houses by additions thereto violate a restriction that there shall not be erected on the ground a building or buildings designed for any purposes other than a private dwelling house and that no such building erected thereon shall be occupied or used for any purpose other than a private dwelling?"

"Is the cleaning and sprinkling of streets and collection of refuse by a municipality a governmental function exempting it from liability for the negligence of its employees in the performance of such work?"

"(1) Whether a widow living separate and apart from her husband at and before his death, not being supported by him, and not dependent on him, is entitled to compensation as his widow under the Workmen's Compensation Act; (2) Whether step-children, not part of decedent's household at time of his death and not dependent on him, are entitled to such compensation."

"(1) Has execution defendant who claims no ownership in goods sold, power to petition to set aside sheriff's sale? (2) Should the court permit actual owner of goods to intervene to set aside sale? (3) Should sheriff's sales be set aside because of gross inadequacy of price, where prospective bidders on premises leave scene of advertised sale, on suggestion of sheriff's auctioneer, because of failure of sheriff to appear at the hour fixed for sale?"

"Should a juror be withdrawn and the cause continued on the application of defendant, where members of the trial jury were present in another court room, during a recess in the trial, listening to the delivery of forcible arguments, and to the reading of newspaper articles, referring to the particular offense for which the defendant is on trial?"

"(1) Where a son, not a member of his father's family, who has a family of his own, renders services to his father, at the latter's request, of such a character as would not ordinarily be rendered gratuitously by a son so situated for a parent, what is the measure of proof required to establish a contract to pay for such services? (2) Where a son has been emancipated and has engaged in business for himself, living at a remote distance from his father's residence, is there a presumption of gratuitous service where the son leaves his family at this father's request, goes to his father's home and takes care of his father and mother, where the father is able to pay?"

"If A, a manufacturing corporation, and B, an individual, make a parol agreement that, in consideration of B doing certain things, A will furnish B with a certain commodity as long as A does business in its then present location; B carries out his part of the contract; A also, for a period of seven years, carries out its part of the contract, when, without any reason except that B has had 'service long enough,' A refuses further to furnish B with the commodity; what is the measure of damages?"

"Where a partnership doing a general banking business hires a safe deposit box to two of its patrons who leave a key thereto with the cashier, a partner, and he enters their box; removes bonds therefrom; sells the same; deposits the proceeds, with other funds, to the credit of the partnership bank in a bank where it kept a general account, and made deposits almost daily, which were mingled generally with other funds; and thereafter the partnership bank makes a general assignment for the benefit of creditors, can the said patrons treat the fund realized from the sale of their securities as a distinctive trust fund and compel the assignee to pay the said amount to them in preference to general creditors?"

In the beginning of this article, it is stated that one of the things chiefly responsible for the success of the system of restricted, or half-hour arguments, which has enabled the Supreme Court of Pennsylvania to bring and keep its business up to date, is the rule here discussed, requiring a concise statement of the controlling questions to appear on the first page of the appellant's brief in every case. The above examples of properly stated questions involved, show at once the value of this requirement, both to the court and to the barrister. When the rule is efficiently followed, as it is in the great majority of cases, the court can, at a glance, perceive, at least in a general way, the points for determination, and, with this accomplished, the judicial mind can better concentrate on the argument; while the advantages to the barrister are equally as great, for the obligation to formulate a statement of questions involved[39] compels concentration on the main or controlling points in the case both in the preparation and delivery of the argument, so that in most instances lawyers brought up under the rule are able to present even complicated cases within the limited time allowed for oral argument,[40] depending, of course, on

---

39 Rules of the Supreme Court of Pennsylvania, 42 and 43, require appellants' briefs to contain statements of the questions involved and expressly permit counter-statements by appellees.

40 *Ibid.* Rule 72 provides that appellant and appellee shall each be allowed thirty minutes in which to present his side of the case, and reads: "If two or more appeals are from the same judgment or decree, but raise different and unrelated questions, counsel for each appellant will be allowed thirty minutes and counsel for all the appellees thirty minutes, to be divided between them as they may decide, and subject to an extension if the presiding justice shall consider more time necessary."

the printed history of the case[41] and the argument in their briefs for the detailing of noncontrolling facts, discussion of minor matters, elaboration of legal points, and application of cited authorities. Thus the oral argument performs its true function of briefly introducing the case to the court and affording the judges who are to decide it an opportunity to make inquiry of counsel, and the latter to enlighten the court, on points which may suggest themselves in course of the presentation. Another advantage is that this enforced segregation of and concentration on the main points in the case enables counsel, in preparing their briefs, readily to eliminate from the record and testimony matter not relevant to the actual questions involved on the appeal as required by another very useful rule of court.[42]

---

[41] *Ibid.* Rule 51 provides: "The history of the case must begin with a statement of the form of action, followed by a brief reference to the pleadings, or papers in the nature thereof, upon which the case was tried or heard in the court below, and to any other pleadings or papers which were passed upon by it, if its order or judgment thereon is assigned as error or they are pertinent to the questions raised on the appeal; must include a brief statement of any prior decision of this court or of the Superior Court, in the same case or estate, and a reference to the place where it is reported; must give the names of the judges whose rulings are to be reviewed; must contain a closely condensed chronological statement, in narrative form, of all the facts which are necessary to be known in order to determine the points in controversy; and must briefly state the verdict and judgment, order or decree appealed from; but must not contain any argument, or quotations from the testimony"; and *Ibid.* Rule 47 permits appellee to print a counter-history of the case, providing that, if he fails to do so, or, in his brief, otherwise to challenge the statement of facts in appellant's history, "it will be assumed he is satisfied with them."

[42] *Ibid.* Rule 55 provides that: "Evidence which has no relation to or connection with the questions raised by the assignments of error, must not be printed; nor must deeds or long documents, the construction or validity of which are not in issue, but only such parts thereof as are necessary for a proper consideration of the case. In order effectually to carry out the foregoing requirement, appellant shall file in the court below, before he commences the printing of the Record, a brief statement of the questions he intends to argue on the appeal and of the evidence he does not intend to print, and shall serve copies thereof on appellee, together with a written notice that consent will be presumed if no objections are made within ten days thereafter, unless the court below, on cause shown, shall grant an extension of time. If objections are made, the court below shall forthwith fix a time for hearing them, and shall then decide the dispute in accordance with, and subject to the provisions of the Act of May 11, 1911, P. L. 279 [legislation permitting, and setting up judicial machinery to carry out what this rule requires]. In passing on the materiality of evidence, the inquiry shall not be whether the court below deems the evidence substantial, but whether it refers to the particular contentions made by the litigant."

Adapted from Vol. 34, Yale Law Journal (1925).

Defining the Issue on Appeal

BY JAMES CRAIG PEACOCK

THE ALMOST INESTIMABLE VALUE of pleadings in defining the issue to be passed on by judge or jury in a court of first instance has been long and fully recognized by the legal profession. A century or more ago the common law had already developed a comprehensive system of pleading which in its exactness and meticulousness has probably never been equalled in any similar line of endeavor. Equally complete although in many respects differing systems of pleading have been developed over the years in practically every American jurisdiction. With this heritage and background it is strange indeed that so little progress has been made along analogous lines in our appellate procedure where the need for an accurate definition of the precise question to be considered by the appellate court would seem to be equally as great.

Specifically, there is in mind the far too frequent lack of agreement in the briefs of appellant and of appellee as to the exact question or points to be presented for the court's consideration. In case after case the appellee's brief will present both the question and the argument in an entirely different form from that of the appellant's brief, and the court is handicapped rather than helped in its effort to grasp the real issue.

In the course of many years of active practice in the higher federal courts the writer has become more and more impressed with the utterly unnecessary burden of additional labor carried by the judges of those courts in attempting to find out precisely what is the issue in a large proportion of the cases which they must decide. True it is that many of them through long experience have learned how to separate the wheat from the chaff and get to what appears to be the issue. But why should they have to wade through all that chaff in so many cases? Or why should they so often be subjected to the risk of being given a wrong impression of the exact nature or scope of the question involved? In a word, why should that be made hard for them which could be made so much easier by recourse to one of the most fundamental and time-honored principles of their own profession? Far more serious is the fact that the present system, or rather lack of system, not merely wastes time and effort and thus adds to delay and congestion but inevitably tends to impair the value of many of the resulting decisions as permanent contributions to the body of American case law. Courts must necessarily depend and rely to a great extent upon counsel, who after all are "officers of the court," and if the argument is not clearly and soundly presented the opinion cannot fairly be expected to be much better.

The matter has been touched upon by the present Chief Justice of the United States in his recently much-quoted lectures at Columbia University. In his discussion of the actual working of the Supreme Court may be found such comments as that the progress of civilization is but little reflected in the processes of argumentation and a vast amount of time is unavoidably wasted in listening to futile discussion, and that although oral arguments have been compressed by a time allowance, briefs are not, and the judges have to contend with their diffuseness. His further references to what happens when the judges apprehend the precise question to be decided cannot fail to bring to mind only too many briefs, especially those filed by appellees, which have made it hard rather than easy for the judges to quickly grasp the real question in issue.

It has been suggested that the assembling and making available in an article such as this of certain pertinent facts as to this fundamental inadequacy in modern briefing, together with some information as to the progress which has been made in a few jurisdictions toward remedying this situation, might be of real and constructive value to the profession and to the courts. It is by no means true that all of the waste of time of the courts in listening to futile discussion is unavoidable, and there are two suggestions in particular which are commended for further consideration.

Those suggestions will, however, be better appreciated if the reader first has clearly in mind some concrete illustrations of how the matter under consideration is or can be handled in the average brief. To facilitate this the writer has briefly surveyed a run of the mine list of cases with which he was already somewhat familiar. He has taken from his office docket the fifteen most recent cases in which the client was appellant (or petitioner) and the fifteen similarly most recent cases in which the client was appellee (or respondent). These thirty cases, taking us as they do into the Supreme Court of the United States and six federal circuit courts of appeals and participated in altogether by some seventy different attorneys, should afford a typical and representative cross-section of the practice in this respect in typical appellate courts in widely separated sections of the country.

In order to better emphasize the points in which we are specially interested, the group of *appellee* cases will be first considered. It is gratifying to the writer to find that in only two instances were he or his associates guilty of restating without explanation the question already stated in appellant's brief, and in both cases the restated question was phrased concisely in three and a half lines and hence it is hoped did not contribute greatly to confuse the court. In several other cases the question was also restated, but in each instance with a short explanation of perhaps six or eight lines as to why the question as stated in appellant's brief was seriously inadequate or misleading. (In at least two cases the appellant's statement of the question naively assumed as a conclusion of law the very issue which was to be considered on the appeal!) In other cases are found such statements as that "the question is presented correctly enough although somewhat abstractly stated" in appellant's brief but "it might facilitate a quicker appreciation of the real issue to restate it more concretely in terms of the language used in the statute . . .", or "the statement at pages 1-3 of appellant's brief while substantially correct is slightly inaccurate and inadequate in certain particulars which will be noted to avoid possible misunderstanding." While by no means satisfied that the issue was as clearly defined in all of these cases as it should have been, it is nevertheless felt that even this brief summary of what can be done may prove a small contribution toward placing this whole matter on a sounder basis.

Especially so when the need for some such improvement "in the processes of argumentation" is apparently as great as would appear from our analysis of the briefs in the group of fifteen *appellant* cases. In those cases the briefs filed in behalf of the appellees bore the names all told of more than thirty different opposing counsel coming from almost as many states, and hence may reasonably be assumed to be fairly typical of appellee briefs the country over. In practically every one of those briefs the question, although already stated in appellant's brief, was completely restated in entirely different phraseology. In each case this was necessarily confusing to a greater or lesser extent and in a number of instances any restatement at all was obviously unnecessary. In those few cases where appellee may possibly have been justified in raising a new question or a new aspect of a question already raised, there was no explanation to aid the court in grasping that fact. Indeed, in not a single case was there any criticism, helpful or otherwise, of the statement of the question in appellant's brief, or any explanation of why a restatement was necessary. An analogous situation would be afforded if defendants would customarily file lengthy answers repeating in paraphrased wording all the averments of the declaration or complaint, including those not controverted as well as those which might be in dispute. This existing lack of system in defining the issue on appeal is an utterly unjustified imposition upon our appellate judges as well as an appreciable cause of delay in the administration of justice, and it is difficult to estimate how much time and effort is as a result uselessly wasted by judges in the nearly one hundred appellate courts in this country.

The writer has not made an exhaustive study of the rules of all of those courts, but after considerable inquiry he has been able to learn of only a very few instances in which any real effort has been made to take care of this situation in the rules of court or otherwise. The nearest approach is probably Rule 50 of the Supreme Court of Pennsylvania, the principle of which, however, had at latest reports been followed only in about half a dozen other jurisdictions. That rule requires counsel to set forth on the first page of the brief and without any other matter appearing thereon a concise statement of the question involved. It further requires that the statement

> "must set forth each question separately, in the briefest and most general terms, without names, dates, amounts or particulars of any kind, and whenever possible each question must be followed immediately by an answer stating simply whether it was affirmed, negatived, qualified or not answered by the court below. . . . The questions and answers in their entirety should not ordinarily exceed one page, and must always be printed in type at least as large as point 10 . . . This rule is to be regarded as in the highest degree mandatory and admitting of no exception."

A very illuminating article on the history of and practice under this rule by Chief Justice von Moschzisker will be found in 34 Yale Law Journal at page 287 (1925). He emphasizes the purpose that the statement of the questions involved should be so framed that the court, without having to examine the argument or any other part of the brief, may quickly see the nature of the legal issue and the points which have to be decided.

The Pennsylvania rules further provide that appellee's brief need contain only his argument "but he may add . . . a counter-statement of the questions involved; unless he does so, or in his Brief otherwise challenges those of appellant, it will be assumed he is satisfied with them." While, as indicated below, the writer might prefer an even more specific rule with respect to appelleee, it appears that the spirit of the Pennsylvania rule is so thoroughly established and so well understood by the bar that anything further may be unnecessary in that state. In a few of the states which have followed Pennsylvania the rules as to appellees are even more pointed. Thus the Supreme Court of North Carolina in Rule 27½ provides for a counter-statement only "in case of disagreement as to the exact question or questions presented for determination" and further emphasizes that "no counter-statement need be made unless appellee thinks appellant's statement is inaccurate, or that it does not present the points for decision in a proper light."

Chief Justice von Moschzisker says that in Pennsylvania counsel for appellees avail themselves of the privilege in only about 50 per centum of the cases, and that quite often appellant's statement is so satisfactory that the court follows it in writing the opinion. This suggests that much has been accomplished, and that appellants have been taught to be more careful in stating the question, and appellees to be more restrained in unnecessarily restating it, than is true in appellate courts generally. All of which concentration on properly stating the question inevitably makes for briefs which in turn are more concise and to the point.

Closely related to what has just been discussed is another practice which is equally unsound and is indulged in even more commonly. An appellee's brief almost invariably presents its argument under points or headings entirely different from those in appellant's brief. If the latter is deemed worthy of consideration at all, it would seem that the court should be entitled to have the benefit of the appellee's comments—or silence—on each of its specific points as such. A judge may frequently be impressed by or interested in some particular point made by appellant, and yet it is seldom that he can turn to any one place in appellee's brief and find quickly and conveniently whether the latter has been able to develop any serious answer to that point. To the extent that the appellant's presentation of any given point is wrong the court is entitled to have it clearly and conveniently pointed out, while to the extent that it is right the appellant himself is entitled not to have it obscured by a smoke screen such as has not infrequently been thrown up for that very purpose. There has come to our attention only one instance in which this matter has been even touched upon in a court rule. That is Rule 22-9 of the United States Circuit Court of Appeals for the Seventh Circuit where it is provided with respect to appellees' briefs that

> "the points shall be discussed, so far as practicable, in the order in which they appear in briefs for appellants, with page references to appellant's brief where the proposition is discussed."

It would seem that this is a decided step in the right direction, and that general adoption of a similar rule would be most salutary.

To sum up. The writer has no desire dogmatically to urge upon appellate courts throughout the country the adoption of new and more or less arbitrary or uniform rules along the lines here suggested. He fully realizes that differing conditions and long established practices in one jurisdiction may make impractical or undesirable something which is entirely practical and greatly needed in another. He also realizes that he has but scratched the surface, and that there may be much more, both pro and con, which can be said about what has been discussed. He does feel, however, that the work of our appellate courts would be facilitated, and the standard of their decisions and opinions even further improved, by a more general attention to and insistence upon two working rules which are fundamentally sound. One is that the appellant should be required to make at the very outset a clear and concise statement of the questions involved, and the appellee should be discouraged from restating it unless there is a real reason for so doing—in which event, at least in the judgment of the writer, he might well be required to also indicate the reason. The other is that so far as practicable the appellee in his argument should be required to first dispose of or answer *seriatim* the appellant's points or headings with of course the privilege of continuing with such further points, if any, as might still remain necessary.

Adapted from Vol. 23, American Bar Association Journal (1937).

Stating the Issue in Appellate Briefs: A Matter of Legal Strategy

BY FRANK E. COOPER

IT IS SOMETIMES SAID FACETIOUSLY that the most important paragraph of a judicial opinion is the last one (announcing affirmance or reversal). This is true, if at all, in only a limited sense. But in every sense of the word—and in all seriousness—it can be said that the most important paragraph in a brief is the first one, in which appears counsel's formulation of the issues presented for decision.

It is by this brief statement that the case is introduced to the court. Many appellate judges commence their study of a case by comparing appellant's and appellee's statements of the issues involved. The judge's initial impression of the merits of the case often is formed on the basis of these preliminary statements.

Judges have frequently spoken of the vital role which this short statement has in influencing the ultimate decision in the case. It not only gives a bird's-eye view of the entire case, but it focuses attention on those particular aspects of the case which counsel believes will control decision. In drafting his statement, counsel is choosing the battleground on which the case will be fought out. If an attorney can so draft his "statement of the issues" that (1) it summarizes the essence of the case in capsular form, and (2) the mere reading of the statement will subtly suggest to the court that the question should be answered as the lawyer contends throughout the balance of his brief, then the lawyer has made a most successful beginning.

Stating the Issue in Terms of the Facts

From the court's viewpoint, the first of these two purposes—acquainting the court with the general outlines of the case—is most important. This is the first requisite of the statement of issues involved.

Adequate introduction of the case to the court requires that the statement of the issue involved do more than state a legal question in a vacuum. It is essential that the question be phrased in terms of the facts on which it arises, for it is commonplace that the facts control decision.

Thus, if plaintiff's complaint has been dismissed on motion in the trial court, and plaintiff appeals, counsel for defendant will utterly fail to accomplish his purpose of introducing the case to the court if he asserts that the issue involved is:

> Does the complaint state a cause of action?

The court will have a much better idea of the nature of the case —and be much better prepared to appraise the significance of the argument, as it develops—if counsel for appellee phrases the question:

> In an action for the purchase price of 1,000 carburetors, under a sales contract which provided that the buyer's obligation to pay the agreed purchase price was conditional upon the carburetors' passing certain tests, is the complaint sufficient where it fails to allege either that the carburetors had passed those tests, or that they could have passed the tests?

If defendant in an automobile accident case contends that the action should have been dismissed because plaintiff was guilty of contributory negligence, the issue might be stated:

> Was plaintiff guilty of contributory negligence?

But how much more it would mean to the court if the statement read:

> Where plaintiff admits that he could not have stopped his car within an assured clear distance ahead, is he chargeable with contributory negligence, to bar his claim for physical injuries suffered when plaintiff's car struck the rear of a car operated by defendant, who had made an emergency stop without signalling?

Subtly Suggesting the Desired Answer

No great art is required to draft statements which satisfy this initial requirement of letting the court know how the issues arise out of the facts of the particular case.

The advocate's art must be employed, however, so to phrase the question as to suggest—ever so subtly, for obvious attempts at argumentation will defeat the whole purpose—that the apparent answer to the question is the one which will win the brief-writer's case.

How the initial statement may compress into a brief phrase enough of the heart of the case to attract the interest and sympathy of the court, is illustrated in the brief of counsel for the Tennessee Valley Authority in *Ashwander v. T.V.A.*, 297 U. S. 288 (1936):

> The sole substantive question is whether the Federal Government may dispose of the surplus water power necessarily created by Wilson Dam and may authorize generation of electric energy and acquisition of transmission lines as a means of facilitating this disposal.

Unless counsel states the issues briefly, he cannot attain any of the objectives for which he must strive in formulating his description of the question involved.

One aspect of this problem of brevity involves the necessity of making an intelligent choice among the many issues which could be selected. Counsel for appellant can almost always find many instances of what he deems aggravated errors on the part of the lower court. To cite them all, however, is poor strategy. Asserting many errors is not only tiresome, but is commonly taken as a confession that counsel has no great confidence in any of his assignments of error.

Courage and determination must be employed to pare down the possible "issues involved" to the minimum compatible with a proper presentation of the case. Nothing of real importance should be overlooked, for in many courts counsel are not permitted to argue matters not specified or fairly implied in the statement of issues involved. On the other hand, nothing should be included that can reasonably be dispensed with.

When counsel has finally selected (after great inner turmoil) the issues to be pressed, his final task is to determine the order in which they shall be set forth—the strongest first, ordinarily; although occasionally, if it appears that the court's interest may be more readily caught by a brief, provocative statement of a subsidiary point, this may precede the statement of the longer (and necessarily somewhat complicated) major issue.

The Statement Should Be Readily Comprehensible

The lawyer who proceeds on the theory that the easiest way to tell what a case is all about is to tell all about the case, usually succeeds only in making the reader wonder what the case really is all about. The inclusion of unnecessary detail is one of the most common errors in drafting the statement of issue involved. It is also one of the most difficult to avoid.

Justice von Moschzisker, in the law review article above cited (34 *Yale Law Journal* 287) pointed out this example of what to avoid:

> A recent case furnishes an excellent example of a statement of the questions involved which could have been materially condensed and made more clear by omitting details of dates, etc. As prepared by counsel, it read: "The question involved is, whether the plaintiff, who signed an application for a policy of insurance upon his dwelling house, in the Mutual Life Insurance Company of Annville, Lebanon County, Pa., about five o'clock p.m., Saturday, June 10, 1905, and paying simply the application fee of $2.50, and there being no mail from that community by which the said application could be sent to the company for its acceptance or rejection until about eight o'clock a.m. of June 12, 1905, and before the application could be sent the premises for which the application had been made were destroyed by fire, of which the agent who was authorized to receive applications for insurance, was duly notified, can recover for the loss. Was there any negligence on the part of the company, or its agent, because the agent did not forward the application, after he had knowledge of the destruction of the premises by fire, before it was possible to have forwarded the application by mail, simply to have the company reject the application *pro forma,* as would bind the company and make it liable?"

Overly Abstract Statements Are Ineffective

Paring down the statement, by omitting irrelevant detail, is but the first step. It is only the *unnecessary* detail which should be pruned out. If one goes too far and omits all factual detail, not mentioning even those which lend life and color and "equity" to the case, the result is likely to be a cold, lifeless, unpersuasive statement.

An extreme example appeared in a brief filed not so long ago, wherein appellant advised the court that the controlling issue was: "Did the Court err in granting defendant's motion to dismiss?" It may fairly be presumed that this was a very accurate statement of the ultimate question before the court. But can it not be just as fairly asked whether the court, after receiving this information, had any idea at all as to what the case was all about?

The difference between a dry-as-dust, abstract statement of the issue (which gives the court only the faintest glimmer of light) and an intriguing, factually informative statement of the same issue, can be illustrated by the briefs filed in connection with an application for certiorari seeking a review of the decision in *United States v. Carusi* (CA 3, 1946) 157 F(2d) 732. Counsel for petitioner in certiorari advised the court that the issue was:

> Is the Petitioner a native, citizen, denizen, or subject of a "hostile nation or government" liable as such "to be apprehended, restrained, secured, or removed as an alien enemy?"

Opposing the petition for certiorari, counsel for the Government restated the issue as follows:

> Whether an alien, born in Bohemia, then a part of the Austro-Hungarian Empire, in 1905, who later became a Czechoslovakian citizen when the place of his birth was included in that country after World War I, and who, after the Munich pact of 1938, while in the United States, petitioned to be and was recognized as a German citizen, is now a citizen or subject of an enemy country within the meaning of the Alien Enemy Act of 1798, despite the reoccupation of the territory of his birth and former residence by Czechoslovakia?

The court denied the petition for certiorari, 330 US 842. Do you suppose the mere reading of the statements of issue involved may have inclined the court in the direction of its ultimate decision?

In the above case, counsel for appellee cleverly corrected the vague abstractness of appellant's statement.

Sometimes, unfortunately for the court, neither counsel succeed in capturing the essence of the case, in their statements of the issues involved. Consider the following example, again from a federal court of appeals:

Appellant's statement of questions involved:

1. May one obtain possession of premises fraudulently and retain possession under the protection of rent control law?

2. Does a trespasser have the protection of the rent control law?

Appellee's counterstatement of questions involved:

1. Was there substantial evidence to support the trial Court's Findings of Fact that the housing accommodations here involved were used by tenants only for dwelling purposes, and that appellant, the landlord, knew or should have known that the accommodations were so used?

If (as some jurists do) the judge assigned to the above case had begun his work by comparing the statements of the respective parties, to see what the case really involved, would you blame him for heaving a deep sigh?

Aside from being dull and unimpressive, a statement couched in abstract terminology can easily become confusing. Witness the following example from a brief filed in the Appellate Division in New York:

> Whether a "current account" so intended and so labeled, rendered as a basis of subsequent liquidation by an employee employed by these defendants, can or has in this case by acceptance by plaintiff to whom it was rendered become an account stated so as to entitle this plaintiff to the credit balance shown in cash, when such effect is contrary to and in derogation of the express terms of a written contract existing between the plaintiff and defendants, and when it has the further effect of crediting plaintiff, who is entitled under the contract only to net profits, with book profits which to the knowledge of both plaintiff and defendants had been turned into losses by shrinkage in the inventory value of accounts receivable on the basis of which the profits had been computed?

Self-Evident Propositions Are Not Helpful

In their attempts to so phrase the question on appeal as to make sure that the mere reading of the question will incline the court to their side of the case, counsel sometimes go too far and formulate a statement which suggests that the only issue involved is a plainly self-evident proposition. There is rarely, if ever, a case taken before an appellate court where the facts and law are so clear that there could be but one possible outcome; and when the statement of the issue involved makes it appear that such a case has at last been discovered, the court is apt to be a bit cynical, if not outright distrustful.

It does not pay to adopt some self-serving, self-evident proposition and try to make the court think that the issue involved is that simple. It never is.

Furthermore, there is the everpresent danger that counsel for the other side will point out, to your embarrassment, that the case is not nearly so simple as you had tried to pretend. In one case, counsel for appellant tried too hard to win his case on the opening sentence of his brief. He described the issue by asking:

> Is a final decision of the Board of Tax Appeals binding and res judicata upon the same question and between the same parties?

Perfectly simple, wasn't it?

But counsel for appellee spoiled it all, by offering the following counterstatement:

> In response to a determination by the Commissioner of a deficiency in income tax for 1937 against "Louisville Property Co., H. C. Williams, Assignee", a petition was filed with the Board of Tax Appeals by "H. C. Williams, Successor Assignee in Trust for the Benefit of the Creditors and Stockholders of the Louisville Property Company, Petitioner." The Board dismissed the petition for lack of jurisdiction. The question is whether the doctrine of res judicata is applicable here and makes the dismissal of this suit obligatory.

State the Question So That Opponent Must Accept It

It goes without saying that the statement of the question involved must be scrupulously accurate. If opposing counsel can point out to the court that appellant's statement of the question involved is unfair, or that it overlooks an issue which might be controlling of the decision, then appellant has lost the confidence of the court at the outset and this is often fatal.

Counsel for appellant can win some advantage by careful formulation of the issue involved. If his statement is brief, comprehensible, informative, intriguing, subtly persuasive, and at the same time scrupulously accurate, he has succeeded in his first aim of being able to fight the battle on a terrain which is favorable to him. Often, counsel for appellee would prefer to shift the court's view to some other aspect of the case, but it is difficult if not impossible to do this where appellant's statement fairly presents an issue which he is entitled to have the court consider.

Counsel for appellee must hesitate in submitting a counterstatement of the issue involved where appellant's statement is precise, comprehensive and fully accurate. If appellee's counterstatement appears to be mere quibbling, the only result is to strengthen in the court's consciousness the importance and apparent merit of the question urged by appellant.

On the other hand, where appellant's statement seeks to conceal a real weakness in his case, counsel for appellee can most effectively direct the court's attention to the vital omission, and then restate the question with telling force.

Thus, in one case involving a suit on a life insurance policy, counsel for appellant overlooked several matters that might have been deemed of controlling importance, when he phrased as follows his statement of the question involved:

> Is a change of beneficiary effected where the policy of life insurance provides that the insured may designate a new beneficiary by filing at the home office of the company a written designation of beneficiary and the insured on January 7, 1946, three months before his death, writes the agent of the company a letter which states "Marital difficulties since my return have made it necessary to again change the beneficiary of my policy. I therefore request that the usual procedure be instituted making the present beneficiary Miss M.E.R. (my sister) the recipient in the event anything happens to me," and the agent forwards the original letter immediately to the home office of the company, where it was received on January 11, 1946, and remained at all times thereafter?

Counsel for appellee effectively pointed out to the court that the case was not nearly so simple, and that the court would surely desire to consider the following additional facts, set forth in appellee's counterstatement:

> When a life insurance policy permits the insured to designate a new beneficiary by filing at the home office a written designation of beneficiary, which in no case shall be effective until the date upon which it is so filed, and the insured is an educated man who, having twice before effected a change of beneficiary under this same policy, is thoroughly familiar with the procedure required to effect a change of beneficiary, and the insured writes to the agent to request "that the usual procedure be instituted" to change the beneficiary, and pursuant thereto the agent sends to the insured duplicate forms of the same type that the insured had previously executed on other occasions with instructions as to their execution and return, and the insured retains these forms unexecuted in his possession until the time of his death some three months later, during which period he makes statements that he does not intend to change the beneficiary, and there is no evidence that the insured is incapacitated or for any reason unable to complete the forms and return them to the insurance company before his death, the correspondence and conduct of the insured do not designate a new beneficiary of said policy.

Another instance in which a counterstatement can profitably be employed occurs when appellant's statement does not sufficiently inform the court as to the facts on which the question arises.

Thus in one automobile accident case, appellant stated the question involved in this form:

> Where defendant's truck became disabled on the highway at night, and defendant's driver placed lighted flares upon the highway as required by statute, did fact that one or more of said flares went out just before accident, constitute such gross and wanton negligence as to preclude the defense of contributory negligence of the plaintiff from being submitted to the jury?

In his counterstatement, appellee pointed out to the court that the above statement did not fully inform the court as to the controlling facts. He restated the question by saying:

> Was defendant's truck driver guilty of gross negligence to deprive defendant of right to rely upon plea of contributory

negligence where driver knowingly left a disabled truck standing on the highway blocking northbound traffic in Tennessee at 10:00 o'clock at night, the atmospheric conditions being very bad all night and the driver violating Tennessee statute in failing to place rear flare in center line of northbound traffic and further violating the statute in failing to keep flares burning until one-half hour before sunrise and the driver going fifteen miles away from truck and there sleeping all night without knowing how long the flares he claimed to have placed out would burn, and plaintiff having been injured by reason of the absence of statutory signals?

While leaving something to be desired, perhaps, from the viewpoint of literary form, this counterstatement at least succeeded in effectively placing before the court important facts which appellant had inadvisedly chosen to ignore.

Adapted from Vol. 39, American Bar Association Journal (1953).

IV THE USE OF ENGLISH

The Disorderly Conduct of Words

BY ZECHARIAH CHAFEE, JR.

HUGH AND PATRICIA were an attractive couple on the permanent plateau of prosperity, but Hugh had much more money than was good for them. They drifted apart and in the spring of 1929 came the divorce. Hugh placed a large block of government bonds in the hands of trustees. The settlement directed the trustee to pay the income to Patricia for life and the principal to her children, but "if she remarries" then the income is to go to the children at once. Next October Hugh's remaining investments suddenly shrank. As he was walking along Fifth Avenue feeling very blue, whom should he meet but Patricia in a new hat and more charming than ever. At her suggestion they went to her apartment for tea, and he soon found himself pouring his troubles into her sympathetic ears. Tea prolonged itself into dinner and dinner was succeeded by breakfast. After visiting the City Hall, Hugh and Patricia departed for a second honeymoon. While they were disporting on the beach at Waikiki the market crashed again. Whatever Hugh had left was wiped out, but Patricia said, "Never mind, darling, we can live on what you generously gave me while you are getting a fresh start." Soon came the expected long envelope from the trustees, but inside instead of the usual check was a formal letter stating that since she had "remarried" the trustees were now obligated to pay the income from the bonds to her children. And so, the story goes, Hugh and Patricia hurried home to be supported by their boys and girls.

This unreported case is a fair example of the problems presented by law and language combined. Observe that the difficulty is caused, not by any long commaless legal jargon, but by one plain word—"remarries." The trustees were merely echoing the joyous outcries of the couple's friends—"Have you heard the latest—Patricia and Hugh have remarried"!

Yet I have a strong guess that a court would not uphold the trustees' interpretation of "remarries." Why? Possibly the judge would declare: "The parties did not intend 'remarries' to include this eventuality." Yet, when the spouses signed the settlement on the bitter eve of divorce, nothing was farther from their thoughts than being reunited. The truth is, the only person who had any intention about not applying "remarries" to the present situation is the judge himself. Whither should the judge go for help? That is the question to which I shall keep returning.

Words are the principal tools of lawyers and judges, whether we like it or not. They are to us what the scalpel and insulin are to the doctor, or a theodolite and sliderule to the civil engineer. So we need to know more about their imperfections. Several books have appeared recently about a new science of language called Semantics. Best known in the United States are *The Meaning of Meaning* (1936), a technical and difficult work by C. K. Ogden and I. A. Richards, and *The Tyranny of Words* (1938), a popular discussion by Stuart Chase. I have gone to these for help, to see whether they supplement the efforts of judges and lawbooks to solve problems of legal interpretation.

I

The first lesson I have learned is, that language is not used solely for the communication of thought. That purpose is uppermost in our minds when we write opinions or briefs or law review articles, and hence we lawyers easily forget that words are frequently employed with quite a different object—to make somebody do something. Ogden and Richards stress this emotive function of language as distinguished from its communicative function; and illustrate this by printing Malinowski's observations on the speech of children and savages.[1] They do not employ language, he says, as a condensed piece of reflection and a record of fact or thought, as does the author of a book or inscription. With them, language functions as a link in concerted human activity, as a piece of human

[1] Malinowski, supplement to Ogden & Richards, *Meaning of Meaning* (4th ed. 1936) 309-321 *passim.*

behavior. It is a mode of action and not an instrument of reflection. For example, among primitive people:

> A word, signifying an important utensil, is used in action, not to comment on its nature or reflect on its properties, but to make [the utensil] appear, be handed over to the speaker, or to direct another man to its proper use.

It takes only a little thought for us to realize that among civilized adults language is largely employed for the same emotive purpose. One instance will suffice—the young wife who complained, "When I ask Charles if he loves me, he acts as if I were asking for information."

What bearing has this emotive function on law? More than we like to admit. The clerk's prelude to the session of court,—"Oyez! oyez! oyez!"—aims to produce an attitude of seriousness and wrench us out of the careless moods of everyday life. The lawyer's address to a jury is only in part an attempt to organize the evidence clearly. In large measure, he seeks to evoke emotion and action, namely, a favorable verdict. Nor can we say that the emotive function is always absent from the lawyer's argument before an appellate court. When Mr. Joseph Choate told the United States Supreme Court in 1895 that a 2 per cent income tax had "scattered to the winds the great fundamental principle of private property,"[2] he was not aiming to give accurate information but to create judicial hostility to the statute. Indeed, some experienced advisers consider that the main purpose of appellate argument is to make the judges want to decide your way. It is even said that the citation of authorities is a solemn pretext. My own view is quite different, but here too action is the end desired—a decision for one's client —and not merely the transmission of clear ideas.

When one gets into this vein, he discovers the emotive function operating in almost all speech and writing. The communication of facts and thoughts seems never completely separated from the desire to make somebody do something or feel somehow. Nothing appears sterilized from emotion except a quitclaim release. Even when the informative purpose is very strong as in a law-book, the author wants to write so that a publisher will print it and lawyers will buy it. Although a law review article gets no compensation,

2 See Pollock v. Farmers' Loan & Trust Co., 157 US 429, 39 LEd 759, 15 SupCt 673 (1895).

it may produce academic promotion or esteem among the elect. Most audacious of all is the idea that a judicial opinion is more than pure thought. Does not the judge hope thereby to win over a hesitating colleague, to reconcile the losers to their fate, and perhaps to make courts in other states eager to follow his views?

Why worry? It's one of the things language is for. Probably the distinction between the communicative and emotive functions is only a matter of degree. The transmission of information and the creation of an attitude in the listener are dual purposes in most speech, though in varying proportions. Because we believe reason to be our best guide, we must exert ourselves in legal expression to make our thoughts fit things and our words fit our thoughts, to keep down the emotional element, and above all to pick and choose among possible emotions. The evocation of a sense of fairness may be within the emotive function as truly as the stimulation of hatred and greed, but it is a much more legitimate aim.

However, our major concern as lawyers is with the communicative function of language, to which my remaining observations will be devoted. My next main point is that *The Meaning of Meaning* gives us much help in understanding the true relation between a word and the object for which the word stands. (I use "object" loosely to embrace persons and abstract ideas as well as tangible things; the semanticists use instead the technical word "referent").

To start with, the word is not the same as what it points to. Obvious as this statement may seem, the contrary belief is constantly cropping up; that words have existence and power, that they are equivalent to the things and persons they denote, or nearly so. It is something like the relation assumed by primitive or superstitious minds between the god and the image. A Harvard professor fell into conversation with a peasant in the Campagna, who asserted defiantly that there was no God. "I suppose you don't believe in the Devil either." Quick as a flash the peasant crossed himself and looked behind him with terror.

Although this identification of the word with the object is avoided by more sophisticated minds, they often slip just one peg down into the deeply-rooted notion that the word inevitably and unalterably belongs to a particular thing or person. A name is like a label chained around the object by God's order, which nobody must presume to detach. "And whatsoever Adam called every living creature, that was the name thereof."

An Englishman was lunching in a Paris restaurant. He knew no French, the waiter little English. They engaged in the friendly task of giving names in their respective languages to things at which the Englishman pointed. Eventually he pointed at the bread. "Pain," said the waiter; and the Englishman burst out laughing. "What you call it, M'sieur?" "Bread"—and the waiter laughed. At this the Englishman got angry. "M'sieur," expostulated the waiter, "you laugh when I say 'Pain,' I laugh when you say 'Bread'." Back came the Englishman, "But it *is* bread, you know."

Lawyers and judges are highly susceptible to this notion of an indissoluble link between the word and the thing. A sense of the inherent potency of words is natural with us. Words are the effective force in the legal world. In statutes, they result in heavy fines, long imprisonment or even death. In contracts, deeds, or wills, they transfer large amounts of property. Hence the persistent feeling in our profession that the right words must be used. You must in the old days say "A and his heirs" to give a fee, not "A and his descendants" or "A and his successors."

Nor can we flatter ourselves that we have wholly outgrown this tendency to believe that a word points to this object and only this, and that no other word can point to it. Look at a case in the House of Lords in 1914.[3] A testator who had spent all his life in Scotland bequeathed £500 to "The National Society for the Prevention of Cruelty to Children." These words corresponded to the charter name of a London society, which did no work in Scotland and of which the testator had never heard. Near his home was a branch office of The *Scottish* National Society for the Prevention of Cruelty to Children, whose activities he knew. Which charity should get the £500? The Scotch courts awarded the bequest to the Scottish society, as the testator pretty clearly intended. Yet the remote charity in London got the money, because the Law Lords said that "he had by name designated" the London society; that it was "the possessor of the name mentioned in the will." Lord Dunedin declared: ". . . the question for a Court of law is, . . . what is the meaning of the words used?"

Here the Law Lords clung to the notion that the Scottish society had only one name, which the testator must use to reach that

[3] National Society v. Scottish Nat. Soc., [1915] A. C. 207.

society just as Ali Baba couldn't open the door without saying "Open Sesame". Doubtless, a corporation should use its corporate name in formal documents for conveying land, *etc.,* but a moment's reflection makes it clear that the corporation may have other names too. Think of the names we give our pet charities in conversation and letters. We call government corporations R. F. C., H. O. L. C., and T. V. A. We specify railroads as the Big Four and the Soo. I work for an institution whose corporate name is the President and Fellows of Harvard College, but is that its only name? Most of the time people call it Harvard College, Harvard University, or Harvard. My guess is that many Scotchmen used the same name as the testator for the Scottish society, and that the Scotch courts were sensible in recognizing that fact.

Then, when the House of Lords said that its award to the London society was following "the meaning of the words," what did "meaning" mean? Not the intention of the testator, not common usage, not the opinion of the average reasonable Scotchman under the circumstances. Many American courts would speak of "the single plain meaning" of the words, and reach a similar result defeating the testator's intention.[4]

The need for analysis of this word "meaning" is obvious. Ogden and Richards constantly insist that words are only symbols of objects. These symbols do not arise from the nature of the objects, but are created by human beings for purposes of convenience, just like buoys and traffic-signals. So far there is nothing new. Wigmore, for example, has an admirable presentation of the symbolic quality of words.[5] But now comes a big contribution from Ogden and Richards. The relation of the word to the object is only indirect. Between these two factors a third factor always intervenes, the thought of some person. Thus the object causes a thought in the mind of a speaker or writer, and he uses a word to express his thought. In listening or reading, the process is reversed. The word brings about a thought which refers to the object. The authors diagram their theory by a triangle. The word and the object are at the two base angles; the thought is at the apex. We never go directly across the base of the triangle, from word to

[4] *E.g.,* Tucker v. Seaman's Aid Soc., 7 Metc. 188 (Mass. 1843); *See* Mann v. Mann, 1 Johns. Ch. 231, 236 (N. Y. 1814). *Cf.* Thomas v. Stevens, 4 Johns. Ch. 607 (N. Y. 1820).

[5] 9 Wigmore, *Treatise on Evidence* (3d ed. 1940) § 2459.

object or *vice versa,* but always travel the long way around through somebody's thought at the top of the triangle. Of course, we telescope this process in popular parlance by saying that the word stands for the object, but in careful analysis we must always remember the whole series: object to thought to word, or word to thought to object.

The value of this analysis to law can be realized only after a full consideration of Ogden and Richard's book. I shall speak of only one application, to the problems of Mistake. Since the relation between the word and the object involves two steps, two different kinds of mistakes may occur. First, the thought may not adequately represent the object, as when parties buy and sell a racehorse which is in fact dead. This type of mistake I call Error. Second, the word may not correctly express the thought. For example, a deed describes the "east" half of Blackacre when the parties intended the west half to be conveyed. This I call a Mistake of Expression. This distinction is important, because the usual remedy for Error is to call the bargain off (rescission), and for Mistake of Expression is to remould the writing to the actual intention (reformation).

Another big contribution of Ogden and Richards is their demonstration that this word "meaning," which we lawyers and judges use so blithely as if it were a clear path out of our tangles, is really a network of paths in which we are likely to get worse lost than ever. The authors list sixteen different main definitions of "meaning" and nine sub-variations, all derived from reputable sources. I mention only a few of these, as apt to occur in law: the other words annexed to a word in the dictionary; what the user of the word intends to be understood from it by the listener or reader (intention of the testator, etc.); that to which the user of the word actually refers; that to which the user of the word ought to be referring (this is common usage, the view held by Mr. Justice Holmes, who insists on "the ordinary meaning of the language in the mouth of a normal speaker situated as the party using the language was situated");[6] that to which the interpreter of a word refers; that to which the interpreter believes himself to be referring; that to which the interpreter of a word believes the user to be referring.

[6] Violette v. Rice, 173 Mass. 82 (1899). To the same effect is Holmes, *The Theory of Legal Interpretation* (1899) 12 Harv. L. Rev. 417.

When a lawyer or judge speaks of "the meaning of the word used," he needs to know clearly which of these numerous definitions is applicable. Sometimes a case on the interpretation of a will or contract or statutes shows the judge employing "meaning" in three or four different senses and sliding unconsciously from one sense to another in a single sentence of his opinion.

I have spoken of two lessons for law to be gained from the writers on Semantics—first, the varied functions of language; second, the analysis of the relation between the word and the object. We now come to a third lesson, that words are very imperfect means of communication. A word doesn't stay put. It wabbles and slides around. This is illustrated by the migrations of "meaning," just discussed. Hundreds of examples arise in daily life. We pay dues to a golf-club and use a golf-club to hit a ball. Then we invite our fair partner to a ball at the clubhouse.

When the objects for which a single word stands are thus widely separated, no harm results except an occasional excruciating pun, from which even the law is not free. A Massachusetts doctor charged with procuring an abortion argued to the Supreme Judicial Court of Massachusetts that he was protected by the Statute of Frauds—no one should be held for the debt, default or "miscarriage of another" unless evidenced by some memorandum in writing.

However, when the same word signifies two ideas which are close to each other or overlap, confusion and obscurity are probable. The writer may fall into the terrible crime called the utraquistic subterfuge, of using the word in both its senses during the same discussion. This is said to be a frequent crime among philosophers. For example, "knowledge" may be used for both the content of what is known and the process of knowing. Such an error occasionally creeps into judicial opinions. For example, a case involves a serious misstatement of fact, but it is not clear that the speaker knew of the falsehood or intended to deceive. The judge begins by calling innocent misrepresentation "constructive fraud." After a while "constructive" drops out. Later on he cites a number of cases of intentional misrepresentations which stress the wickedness of "fraud." "Fraud" is an emotive as well as a communicative word, and the judge begins to warm up. Before long the speaker's knowledge of the falsehood is treated as irrelevant, and the judge concludes that an innocent misstatement should be heavily penalized because "fraud" is a vicious quality.

If words were perfect instruments of communication, such difficulties could be avoided. Ogden and Richards lay down as the first requirement of a satisfactory system of symbols, "One symbol stands for one and only one referent." ("Referent," as already stated, is their word for my "object,"—what one's thought refers to). Unfortunately, this requirement can only rarely be fulfilled. In mathematics, we have a specially devised system of symbols of such a character; *pi* always means the same thing. The natural sciences approximate this ideal. Our colonial ancestors used "robin" for an English relative of the sparrow and an American relative of the thrush, but an ornithologist calls each bird by a different Latin name. But it would be impossible to impose such precision on ordinary language, for it would go to pieces in the wear and tear of everyday intercourse. "Thus it constantly happens that one word has to serve functions for which a hundred would not be too many." Some attempts to introduce a specially devised symbolism into law have not been successful, as we shall see later. For the most part we must be content to let words remain imperfect symbols.

It is some consolation to realize that other kinds of symbols often possess the same difficulty. Stuart Chase would have us go back to gestures as far more accurate than words, but has he never been perplexed by the ambiguity of the arm motions of a traffic policeman? A red light symbolizes the rear of an automobile, a pile of dirt, a railway crossing, a fire alarm box, the port side of a steamer, and (on a lighthouse) the presence of rocks and shoals. Probably nobody has ever confused the port light of a boat with a moving automobile, but a lowered railway gate has been mistaken for such an automobile with disastrous consequences. Ordinarily we are able to attach the proper significance to the red light because of the environment, just as a word which is in itself ambiguous can often be understood in the light of the context and surrounding circumstances. But this is not always possible.

We find abundant examples in law of the trouble caused by a word which is capable of standing for two or more different objects, like "remarries" in the divorce settlement. Are canary birds subject to a tariff on "live animals"?[7] A life insurance policy makes the company not liable for death while "participating in aeronautics"; does the phrase apply when the insured is killed while a passenger in a commercial plane which crashes?[8] This quality of words was described by Mr. Justice Holmes in the first *Stock Dividend* case, where he made it plain that "income" in a revenue act did not necessarily mean exactly the same as "income" in the Sixteenth Amendment:

> A word is not a crystal, transparent and unchanged, it is the skin of a living thought and may vary greatly in color and content according to the circumstances and the time in which it is used.[9]

Less familiar legal examples appear outside documents and cases on interpretation. Thus we very frequently say that a particular decision is "wrong" or "unsound." When we do this, it is well to bring ourselves up with a round turn and ask ourselves what the word signifies. Conceivably it means: (1) The decision offends our sense of justice. (2) It does not fit into the logical symmetry of earlier cases. (3) It is likely to produce undesirable social consequences. (4) It is likely to be overruled or disregarded in later cases. (5) It has already been overruled or disregarded by courts. (6) Our client lost. The method just adopted of thinking up conceivable meanings of a doubtful word complies with a very useful piece of advice given by Ogden and Richards.[10] When we have completed such a list, we may discover that the various senses have no common denominator and that the single word is a sort of ashcan into which many different kinds of objects have been thrown during the course of years.

Of late years lawyers have been urged to stop concentrating on metaphysical reasoning and devote more attention to collecting facts. A thirst has grown for all sorts of legal statistics. The best known instance is the lists which appear frequently in the newspapers of "crimes known to the police" in various large cities. These contain surprising conclusions. Thus in one year Philadelphia was stated to have only a quarter as many thefts for its size as Toronto and only a fifth of the thefts of Washington, D. C. Miami

7 Reiche v. Smythe, 13 Wall. 162 (1871).
8 Note (1938) 23 Corn. L. Q. 335.
9 Towne v. Eisner, 245 US 418, 62 LEd 372, 38 SupCt 158 (1918).
10 *The Meaning of Meaning*, 131.

in another year reported three hundred times as many robberies per hundred thousand inhabitants as Lowell. Newark reported twenty-four times as many burglaries proportionately as New York.[11] This illustration shows how the elastic nature of words can easily render legal statistics almost valueless. Two items may not be comparable although they bear the same verbal label. Thus "thefts" as reported by the police in two cities may have quite a different scope, because the legal definitions of the crime differ from state to state, *e.g.,* in omitting or including temporary borrowings of automobiles by joy riders, because automobiles are reported as stolen merely to escape fines under parking regulations, or because some police faithfully list every offense sent in while others patriotically cut down the list to correspond to the number of arrests made in order to give a pleasing picture of activity. Plainly, before any inferences can be safely drawn from legal statistics, great care must be taken by somebody to insure that the standards of classification and the accuracy of reporting are approximately uniform. Utraquistic subterfuges may as easily occur in identical statistical headings as in judicial opinions and old-fashioned law-review articles.[12]

A fourth and final lesson is taken from a Polish exile Korzybski. This I call the hierarchical nature of words. All words are symbols, but some of them are much nearer than others to the five senses. Thus, at the bottom level we have "John Marshall," "Ford sedan No. 1,207,643" and "26 Broadway." On a higher level come generalized words for persons and things, like "judge," "automobile," "office-building." Above these are "men," "chattels," "real estate." Still higher come abstractions like "mankind" and "property." Some writers, especially Stuart Chase, stress the dangers that we run as we get up on the heights. The more abstract the word, the greater the risk that any proposition in which it is used will not be true of all the persons and things within the class denoted by the word, and the more liable we are to forget that at bottom we are talking about persons and things. An ardent advocate of female rights will assert that "Women are oppressed by men" re-

---

[11] 1 Reports of National Commission on Law Observance and Enforcement (Wickersham Commission), No. 3, *Report on Criminal Statistics* (1931) 39; Warner, *Crimes Known to Police* (1931) 45 Harv. L. Rev. 307, 312.

[12] See Dr. F. G. Crookshank's account of the breakdown of English official classification of supposed different types of infantile paralysis, in supplement to *The Meaning of Meaning,* 347-354.

gardless of several hen-pecked husbands she knows. With this inexactness of abstractions goes another danger, their emotional quality. Men are stirred to frenzy by words like "democracy," "un-American," "New Deal" without taking the trouble to specify to themselves the individual persons and practices which they purport to admire or hate.

Similar dangers exist in the legal use of abstractions. "Property" is a striking example. It includes a great range of things from my home to my interest in a free access to prospective customers and employees. Suppose that an official, acting under a statute, is compelling me to bargain with a union or alter my management of a holding company in which I have majority control. Because he is restricting my "property," I begin to feel and talk as indignantly as if I were turned out of my home or forbidden to cruise in my own sloop. Mr. Justice Holmes, who has given as much thought to the meaning of words as any American judge, recognized this danger in *Truax v. Corrigan.*[13]

> Delusive exactness is a source of fallacy throughout the law. By calling a business "property" you make it seem like land, and lead up to the conclusion that a statute cannot substantially cut down the advantages of ownership existing before the statute was passed.

Some kinds of property like a home or a savage's spear and canoe would be owned even though there were no courts and legislatures, under

> The good old rule, the simple plan,
> That they should take who have the power,
> And they should keep who can.

But an owner cannot control other kinds of property, like contracts and corporate shares and good will, just by fighting for them. He must have the help of legal process. What the law gave, it can to some extent take away. It can abridge or regulate or fail to protect such intangible property within wider limits than is permissible in the case of the immediate instruments of life.

However, it is one thing to say that abstractions must be used cautiously, and quite another to urge, that, unless they can be

[13] 257 US 312, 66 LEd 254, 42 SupCt 124 (1921) (dissenting opinion). See also White-Smith Music Pub. Co. v. Apollo Co., 209 US 1, 52 LEd 655, 28 SupCt 319 (1908).

verified by the methods of the natural sciences, they must not be used at all. The higher ranges of the hierarchy of words are indeed dangerous, but so are high buildings and high voltages. Modern life would be hampered without these; and every department of intellectual activity including law would be slowed down almost to a standstill if we did not employ shorthand expressions to denote great masses of related facts.

As part of this attack on abstractions, widely sold books are persuading the lay public that "negligence," "good faith," "reasonable" and the very word "law" are weasel words which do not really serve to settle disputes. Precedents are marked for slaughter, for if universals are to be abandoned we should admit that we live in an atomistic world where one legal case lacks any significance for another legal case. The proposed substitute for "law" is very simple. Get the sort of judge "who can wisely decide situations in a real world, now, using whatever practical rules may be necessary." Man would be "willing to take his decision, if he were a good judge, without the ornament of citations."[14]

As an antidote to this frequently held layman's ideal of leaving everything to the common sense of judges, we lawyers need to bestir ourselves and popularize numerous aspects of John Adam's principle of "a government of laws, not men." One can begin by pointing out that the substitute just described embodies abstractions far removed indeed from the five senses. When is a case "wisely" decided? Cynics say it is when your side wins. What rules are "practical"? What we agree with is apt to seem practical, and what we dislike theoretical. Who is the "good" judge? It depends on the point of view. Judge Jeffreys was a good judge to James II.

The evils of abolishing general phrases in law will become clearer to laymen if they be led to consider its effect upon the kind of law with which they are most familiar—criminal law. The substantive definitions of crime would disappear. For example, treason would not consist only "in levying war against the United States or in adhering to their enemies, giving them aid and comfort" and be further limited by centuries of judicial precedents. Instead, the government would be at liberty to imprison or execute anybody if a tribunal decided that he was an objectionable person or not sufficiently enthusiastic about the policies of the

[14] Chase, *Tyranny of Words* (1938) 321, 327.

administration. Our law would be like that of Germany, where a man can be punished without having committed any defined crime, merely because his conduct is considered not to be "according to healthy public sentiment."[15] Harold Laski tells a story about the Round Table Conference that met in London to draft the new Constitution of India. The Conference was at work on the Bill of Rights and had reached the provision that *habeas corpus* should not be suspended. One of the native princes asked what this clause signified. After listening to a lengthy explanation, he asked, "Do you mean I shan't be able to put a man in prison when I wish, except for committing some specific crime?" "That's exactly what it means." "Well," said the Maharajah, "I don't want anything like that in my dominions!"

Even if judges should give up their abstractions and swear never to create any more, the law will still be crowded with concepts imposed by statutes, like "restraint of trade" in the Sherman Act, "unfair methods of competition" and "unfair or deceptive acts or practices" in the Federal Trade Commission Act, "gifts in contemplation of death" and "income" in Tax Acts, "advocate the overthrow by force or violence of the Government" in the Deportation Act, and "obscene" in the Tariff and Postal Acts.

The need for general words is plainest to laymen in the many important statutes which are mainly enforced by government officials, so that it would be impossible to rely merely on the "common sense" of judges and juries. Examples are the Internal Revenue Acts, the Interstate Commerce Act, and the National Labor Relations Act. The standards laid down by such a statute for the officials to apply to ordinary citizens must be framed in pretty broad terms in order to embrace the varied situations which may arise and which cannot possibly be all foreseen so as to be listed by the legislature in concrete terms. The resulting lack of precision gives rise occasionally to amusing problems, whether hen's eggs are "bird's eggs" within the free list of a tariff act, or whether tomatoes are "vegetables" or "fruit" under a similar statute.[16] These legal jokes, we are told, render the whole system of laws ridiculous. Of course, a few such borderline cases are bound to arise and prove nothing. Precision cannot be attained in

[15] See McIlwain, *Government by Law* (1936) 14 Foreign Affairs 185.

[16] Nix v. Heddon, 149 US 304, 37 LEd 745, 13 SupCt 881 (1893), ridiculed by Arnold, *Symbols of Government* (1935) 78.

the administrative process until its final stage—the ruling of an official on a given set of facts. Detailed statutory wording would fetter official action, while the total omission of prescribed standards from statutes would leave government employees free to deport and regulate and tax us and seize our property as they pleased. A citizen would soon come to understand all this, if there were more readable books on law, based on wisdom rather than wisecracks.

This long reply to the superficially tempting plan of dropping general concepts out of the administration of justice does not take the position that all such concepts are now satisfactory or that they are all wisely handled. Every sensible judge or lawyer or law teacher is well aware of the fact that these legal phrases are not accurate measures like the yardstick in the Bureau of Standards. They can more fairly be compared to a chart of colors, which is constructed to give some indication of the differences between scarlet and crimson, and so forth, in spite of the fact that its maker knows that every color shades by imperceptible degrees into every other. Furthermore, judges and law teachers should be constantly engaged in the task of making these phrases fit present conditions better. We need a big spring cleaning to see which terms embody useful principles like "good faith," and which are enough worn out to throw away like "malice" and "conclusive presumption." Finally, I shall be sorry if my argument sounds like a pharisaic belief that laymen have no right to question legal doctrines and practices. Surely the common man who feels the impact of law has the best of rights to point out its imperfections, and he can often call attention to matters which professional habit makes us overlook. We should be glad indeed to have the help of able economists and journalists in our task of improving and modernizing the concepts which have been handed down to us. But the fact that the houses in which we live happen to be ugly or inconvenient is no reason for tearing them down and sleeping in the woods.

II

Thus far I have talked of the help we men of law can get from the writers on Semantics. Now I want to speak briefly about the help they can get from us.

Our case-law provides a vast storehouse of examples of the imperfect symbolism of language. It offers four centuries of reflection by judges on the meaning of words, some of it very acute. Long before the problem of interpretation received systematic attention from nonlegal writers, it was explored by such able lawyers as Hawkins, Holmes, Thayer, Wigmore, and Williston.[17]

There are strong practical reasons why the contributions of law to the problem of language are very carefully thought over. First, when a judge is confronted with a word whose meaning is not clear, he must force himself to understand it if this be possible. An ordinary listener could let the word slide by him as not worth bothering about, but the judge has to try and apply the word to real life. To use the terminology of Ogden and Richards, the judge must find referents (objects) for the verbal symbol. Secondly, a lawyer who is drafting an important document also acts under compulsion in just the opposite direction. He searches for words to fit objects. He must probe his client's mind to ascertain his wishes for all the contingencies that are likely to occur, and then do his best to put into the document a phrase which describes the persons or things the client desires—every one of them and no more. Furthermore, the lawyer must be sure that when the document later gets before the court, the judge will reverse the lawyer's process and go back from the phrase to those very persons and things. Thus the lawyers who wrote wills or contracts and the judges who interpreted them have acted under a very heavy responsibility.

At times lawyers have found common speech inadequate to their purposes, especially in dealing with real property and trusts, and have made some use of technical terms, which form "a specially devised symbolism," resembling so far as it goes the method employed by mathematicians and chemists in making up

[17] Wigram, *Extrinsic Evidence in Aid of the Interpretation of Wills* (3d ed. 1840); Hawkins, *On the Principles of Legal Interpretation with Reference Especially to the Interpretation of Wills* (1860) 2 Jurid. Soc. Papers 298, reprinted in Thayer, *op. cit. infra,* 577; Nichols, *On the Rules which Ought to Govern the Admission of Extrinsic Evidence in the Interpretation of Wills* (1860) 2 Jurid. Soc. Papers 351; Elphilstone, *The Interpretation of Formal Documents* (1867) 3 Jurid. Soc. Papers 251; Thayer, *Preliminary Treatise on Evidence* (1898) 390-483; Holmes, *The Theory of Legal Interpretation* (1899) 12 Harv. L. Rev. 417; Phipson, *Extrinsic Evidence in Aid of Interpretation* (1904) 20 L. Q. Rev. 245; 9 Wigmore, *Treatise on Evidence* (3d ed. 1940) §§ 2458-2478; 3 Williston, *Treatise on the Law of Contracts* (1936) §§ 601-603. For recent collections of legal materials, see Morgan and Maguire, *Cases on Evidence* (1934) 891-899; Gardner, *Cases on Contracts* (1939) 211-250; Leach, *Cases on Future Interests* (1935).

a language that is more accurate than regular English words.[18] Unfortunately, in some of the situations that call for such special symbols, the client either writes the document himself or hires an incompetent lawyer, leaving it for others to struggle with the inadequate symbols drawn from everyday speech. "The jolly testatrix who makes her own will" supplies remunerative semantic investigations for the bar.

The fact that judicial insistence on technical language in such situations will often defeat the intention of the parties has prompted the courts to sheer away from the special symbolism exemplified by "A and his heirs," and adopt a liberal construction. In so doing, they lose exactness by giving effect to non-technical phrases which are capable of several different meanings. I am by no means sure that this is to be deplored. Indeed, my previous adverse criticism of the Scottish charity case stressed the disadvantages of extreme precision. Years ago James Bradley Thayer emphasized the hopelessness of the ideal which lawyers have long cherished, of treating all the language in legal documents as a specially devised symbolism:[19]

> The Chief Justice [Holt] here retires into that lawyer's Paradise where all words have a fixed, precisely ascertained meaning; where men may express their purposes, not only with accuracy, but with fulness; and where, if the writer has been careful, a lawyer, having a document referred to him, may sit in his chair, inspect the text, and answer all questions without raising his eyes. Men have dreamed of attaining for their solemn muniments of title such an absolute security; and some degree of security they have compassed by giving strict definitions and technical meanings to words and phrases, and by rigid rules of construction. But the fatal necessity of looking outside the text in order to identify persons and things, tends steadily to destroy such illusions and to reveal the essential imperfection of language, whether spoken or written.

For the most part, the language of lawyers is likely to possess a good deal of the indefiniteness of the language everybody speaks. It is significant that the technical terms suggested by Wigmore and Hohfeld to clarify legal discussion, like "autoptic proference"

[18] See Cohen and Nagel, *An Introduction to Logic and Scientific Method* (1934) 119-120.

[19] Thayer, *A Preliminary Treatise on Evidence* (1898) 428-429.

and "no-right," have not been widely accepted by the bench and bar or even by law schools.

Let me describe a few legal difficulties about non-legal words, which seem of value to the writer on Semantics. Few of these have to do with abstractions of high order. Most of the worries of Ogden and Richards are about words like "beauty," "meaning," "knowledge," "good," where the user of the words had no specific objects clearly before his mind. Judges and lawyers worry a great deal about words on the lower levels of the verbal hierarchy such as "children" or "issue," where the person who wrote down the words was thinking of something pretty definite, but it is hard later on to know what it was.

The first group of cases involve ordinary concrete words in a document which were intended to indicate just one person or thing, but the interpreting tribunal discovers that the words are conceivably a symbol for two persons or things. To which shall they apply? The Scottish charity case is an illustration. Here proper names cause great difficulty though they are not abstract at all. Suppose a will leaves a large legacy to "my nephew Joseph Grant"; two Joseph Grants claim it, the testator's nephew and his wife's nephew, with whom he was much more intimate.[20] Enemies of Senator Norris of Nebraska almost succeeded in putting the name of a mute, inglorious George W. Norris of Broken Bow on the ballot along with the Senator's name, to leave the voters hopelessly confused between two identical symbols.[21]

In a second situation the writer had several persons or things or acts in mind and used one generic word to describe his intention, but uncertainty subsequently arises as to the exact limits of the class. Thus "remarries" in my opening illustration was obviously intended to include possible remarriages to many different persons; the only doubt was whether union to the writer of the word was within the class of forbidden acts. Many cases turn on the limits of "children" and "grandchildren."[22] For example, after a life estate a fund is given " to my grandchildren." Does this include a lawful child of the testator's illegitimate son? An illegitimate child of the testator's lawful daughter? Her adopted child?

20 Grant v. Grant, L. R. 5 C. P. 727 (1870).

21 State ex rel. Smith v. Marsh, 120 Neb 287, 232 NW 99 (1930), see (1931) 9 Neb. Law Bull. 467-468.

22 See Casner, *Class Gifts—Definitional Aspects* (1941) 41 Columbia Law Rev. 1.

Grandchildren born after the testator's death? Grandchildren who died before the distribution of the fund? Grandchildren born after that date?

A third problem is suggested by a recent New York case.[23] A former Wellesley professor had written a book on education containing a chapter entitled "Words and Their Meaning." Thereafter she wrote her own will. Among other gifts, some money was bequeathed to Arthur Garfield Hays "to use at his discretion in promoting the ends of justice." A serious controversy followed as to the extent of the legacy to Mr. Hays. The testatrix undoubtedly had in mind some portion of her property, but did not clearly say what portion. She left it uncertain whether the benevolent purposes she mentioned were to absorb the bulk of her estate, or only a small fund. Here, there was a need for the special symbols devised by lawyers to indicate a rather complex process. Words of common speech proved inadequate. However, the courts managed to find sufficient evidence to give the bulk of the estate to Mr. Hays to promote the ends of justice.

Finally, we have the interesting situation where the writer employs a usual word in an unusual sense. May "a thousand" be construed to mean twelve hundred as it does in the rabbit business?[24] Can the court take "white" for "black" in a contract about "white selvage," as the trade calls something definitely dark?[25] Here Sir George Jessel declared to counsel that "nobody could convince *him* that black was white"; but the Court of Appeals reversed him. Even if we are thus willing to ignore the usage of ordinary speech and derive our system of symbols from the special language of a trade or profession, what shall we do with a testator who writes a will in his own peculiar code or a business man whose contract employs words in a sense unfamiliar to the other party? The difficulty of this problem of the divergence between ordinary and special meanings has caused sharp conflict of opinion between such great thinkers as Dean Wigmore and Mr. Justice Holmes.

One important warning must be given to non-legal students of words who resort to law for material. The information which can be employed by a legal tribunal during interpretation is somewhat

23 Matter of Hayes, 146 Misc 660, 263 NYS 730 (Surr. Ct. 1933), aff'd, 263 NY 219, 188 NE 716 (1934).

24 Smith v. Wilson, 3 B. & Ad. 728, 110 Eng. Rep. 266 (K. B. 1832).

25 Mitchell v. Henry, 15 Ch. D. 181 (1880).

limited by rules based on tradition or policy. When we lawyers are dealing with an operative document like a will or deed or contract or judicial decree or statute, we have a special purpose. As Hawkins says, "We desire not solely to obtain information as to the intention or meaning of the writer . . ., but also to see that that intention or meaning has been expressed in such a way as to give it legal effect and validity."[26] We must not let our attention wander far away from what has been properly authenticated by the formalities required by law, such as a seal for a deed or witnesses for a will or the execution of a written contract or a lease by both parties.

For example, if an office holder writes a letter which makes some obscure statement about his not running again, political columnists can elucidate his meaning by all his oral references to the subject. But if a testator makes an obscure disposition in his will, his contemporaneous oral statements about his intention cannot ordinarily be collected to explain the will, because they are not surrounded with the safeguards imposed by law—writing and execution in the presence of witnesses. There is danger that to some extent we might be setting up an oral will.

Again, if A offers in writing to rent a house to B, a stranger, for "fifty-nine dollars" a month and B accepts, B can have it for that amount even though dozens of witnesses testify that ever since the United States went off gold A has been accustomed to use the words "fifty-nine dollars" to describe $100 in bills. Yet if A uses the same phrase in a political speech, his friends can afterwards explain his arithmetic by telling about his verbal whim. To introduce this private joke into the lease would be unfair to the tenant and deprive him of the safeguards offered by the writing on which he relied.

A considerable portion of the judicial opinions and writings on legal interpretation are concerned with this question of preserving proper safeguards and of enforcing the document rather than something else. In this respect they may not be very helpful toward solving the question what words mean.

[26] Hawkins, *op. cit. supra* note 17, reprinted in Thayer, *Preliminary Treatise on Evidence* (1898) 580, 581.

III

In concluding, I should like to draw together a good deal of what I have been saying into a few suggestions about two unsolved problems of interpretation. I am not pretending to be able to solve them, but perhaps I can bring the solution a bit nearer.

It is high time that I wound up the case of Hugh and Patricia. It touches the broader problem—what part does the user's intention really play in the determination of the legal effect of words? My first suggestion is, that we should firmly resolve never to speak of the intention of a testator or other writer on a given point except after we have carefully convinced ourselves that that point was actually in his mind when he wrote the words in question. For example, we will never say "He intended this result" when we merely think that if he had foreseen the present contingency (which he didn't) then he would have intended this result. That consideration may be helpful, but it is not his intention. Again, what the judge would have intended in the circumstances of the writer or what a reasonable man would have intended or what the normal speaker of English would have intended may also be helpful, but they have even less to do with the mind of the man who used the words. My guess is, that if we stick by this resolve, we shall soon find that his intention is a much less important factor in the decision than the frequent uncritical use of the word in judicial opinions and law books would lead us to suppose. Once in Providence the relatives of a testator contested his will and eventually all the parties interested agreed on a compromise will, which under the Rhode Island statute was probated as *the* will of the testator. Subsequently a dispute arose about a clause which the contestants had put into the compromise will, so they had a suit to construe that will, during which the judge frequently referred to "the intention of the testator."

Ogden and Richards give dire warnings about the obscurity of defining "meaning" either as what the writer intends to be understood from the words by the reader, or as that to which the reader believes the writer to be referring.[27]

To clarify the problem, go back to my earlier statement that legal interpretation is a passing from the word to the object through somebody's mind. Whose mind? Not that of the author

[27] *The Meaning of Meaning,* 195, 208.

of the document. Indeed, if it be a will he is dead. It must be the mind of the judge. Although his mind may be influenced by what he believes the testator or other user to have thought, the mental operations of the two men cannot fully correspond. Other important factors beside the supposed intention of the testator, *etc.*, contribute to the thought which the judge ultimately frames before applying the words to the outside world.

Therefore, my next suggestion is that the "meaning" of language in operative documents is a combination of several of the different senses in which judges use "meaning," only one or two of which involve the intention of the writer; and that the relative importance of his intention varies considerably with the type of document under consideration. It is most important in a will, which Lord Blackburn called "the language of a testator, soliloquizing."[28] It is less important in a contract, where the fair expectation of the other party has to be given effect. "It makes not the least difference," says Judge Learned Hand, "whether a promisor actually intends that meaning which the law will impose upon his words. The whole House of Bishops might satisfy us that he had intended something else, and it would make not a particle of difference in his obligation."[29] Intention is even less important, I venture to say, in the interpretation of a statute, in writing which hundreds of persons participated with widely varying degrees of attention and with very little chance of envisaging the contingencies that have arisen later. This important point was cleared up by Morris Cohen years ago,[30] so that a single illustration must suffice.

Years ago I drafted an intestacy act for the Rhode Island Bar Association. After hearing my explanation, the Association accepted the draft and had it introduced in the legislature. At the committee hearing I again explained the bill. The legislature enacted it, largely because the Association recommended it. Later the Rhode Island Supreme Court had to decide whether the words

28 Grant v. Grant, L. R. 5 C. P. 727, 728 (1870).

29 Eustis Mining Co. v. Beer, Sondheimer & Co., Inc., 239 Fed. 976, 984 (S. D. N. Y. 1917). See the same judge in Hotchkiss v. Nat. City Bank, 200 Fed. 287, 293 (S. D. N. Y. 1911).

30 *Legal Theories and Legal Science* (1915) 38 Rep. N. Y. St. Bar Ass'n 177, reprinted in revised form in his Law and the Social Order (1933) 112ff. See also Gray, *The Nature and Sources of the Law* (2d ed. 1921) 170-188; Chafee in America Now (1938) 310-312.

"real estate" in the statute included a peculiar interest in land.[31] Both sides wrote me to learn my intention. In two identical replies I said that I had never thought of this point before, but that I now considered the interest to be "real estate" within the act. Both lawyers offered to read my letter to the court, which very properly refused to listen to it. So the intention of the only person who had given prolonged thought to the bill was ignored, and in fact he had no intention on this point. The court decided the case according to my subsequent view, and said that this construction was "not inconsistent with the manifest intent" of the legislature. As Gray writes, "When the judges are professing to declare what the legislature meant, they are in truth themselves legislating to fill up *casus omissi.*"

My last suggestion is that a judge faced with an interpretation case may wisely follow Ogden and Richards' plan of listing all the senses in which he employs "meaning," that is all the factors which he proposes to use in forming his thought-picture in reacting to the disputed words. Then when he comes to write his opinion, it will be very profitable if, instead of jumbling these factors, he takes them up one at a time, always making it clear what he is doing at the moment.

So I venture to put myself in the place of a judge deciding Hugh and Patricia's suit against the trustees. First, the actual intention of the parties when signing the settlement is considered and rapidly dismissed, since the possibility of reunion to Patricia was out of Hugh's mind, and equally out of hers.

Next, other clauses of the settlement are examined for help. For instance, there might be a clause expressly mentioning a reconciliation between spouses. Nothing is found.

Then common usage is invoked and dictionaries are pulled down, but they merely sanction both proposed interpretations. Holmes' "normal speaker of English" would sometimes use "remarries" to apply to a new marriage between the same persons and sometimes only to a new marriage with a new spouse. Indeed, I suspect that common usage is much less important in this kind of litigation than Holmes maintains. There are of course thousands of occurrences out of court every day when members of a family or business men or administrative officials settle the effect of a

31 Fischer v. Scott, 44 RI 368, 117 A 417 (1922).

document by common usage. But for the most part, it is only when this kind of arbitration fails that litigation begins. The disputants don't usually start suing each other except when, as here, each party can find a dictionary definition which backs up his side of the case. For example, how useless "good use" is in all the will-cases about "children" and "grandchildren." Common usage resembles the banks of a river. The court must keep within it, but it doesn't tell where the proper channel lies.

Sometimes a rule of construction established by statute or prior decisions gives a presumptive meaning to a phrase, especially if it be technical—the specially devised symbolism already mentioned —but "remarries" has, I assume, not been thus defined.

At last I am thrown back to a device judges frequently use and rarely admit. To be frank, the parties have left a hole in the instrument and the court must fill up this hole with the plan that will work most fairly to all concerned under the circumstances. It is something like invisible mending, except that the hole was there from the start; the same requirements prevail,—the hole must not be a big one and the added material must fit into the old pattern. Hugh and Patricia did not say what was to happen if they were reunited, so the court must draft its own clause to cover the situation. There would be some sense in preventing a second husband from living off Hugh's bounty, but that contingency has not arisen. To give the money to the children, now that their parents are reconciled, serves no useful purpose, so the trustees were wrong. What then? Perhaps the fund should go back to Hugh, on the ground that the life of the trust ends with the life of the divorce. But I am apprehensive that the marriage once broken may not be very well mended, and I should like to keep the trust alive awhile to take care of a possible second smash-up. This may be too strong-armed an exercise of judicial power, although the continued supervision over alimony is analogous. At any rate, I direct the income to be paid to Patricia until the court decrees otherwise, and shall not be unduly grieved if Hugh ungraciously appeals and I am reversed.

In short, what is commonly called "the intention of the parties" is in large measure the intention of the judge, subject to all sorts of traditional restraints on his range of choice. When all is said and done, the court of last resort in an interpretation case can echo quite a bit of the famous boast of Humpty Dumpty:

> "When I use a word," Humpty Dumpty said, in rather a scornful tone, "it means just what I choose it to mean—neither more nor less."
>
> "The question is," said Alice, "whether you can make words mean so many different things."
>
> "The question is," said Humpty Dumpty, "which is to be master—that's all."

Still more complex is the problem of interpreting a document written many years ago, like the Constitution of the United States. Some critics of the Supreme Court like to demonstrate that words like "commerce" had a different meaning for the framers than for us, in view of the great changes in economic and social conditions since 1787. And "due process" was always a vague phrase. So they go on to the conclusion that, apart from the rules of the Constitution for governmental machinery, "its power today is largely ritualistic, and so without much useful meaning for practical problems."[32] One of two consequences seems logically to follow. First the Supreme Court justices might frankly exercise an unlimited veto power over statutes, without professing any longer that they are obligated to do so by a document which, we are told, was written to surmount a crisis that was surmounted more than a century ago. Or secondly (what these critics probably prefer) the justices might recognize every federal or state statute as valid. Either way, most of the Constitution would have the same historical interest as the Declaration of Independence and the same lack of present legal effect.

Here again the problem is far less simple than these writers make out. No doubt we are forced to broaden our conception of the "meaning" of a word, when we are dealing with language which is applied many years after it was originally written. Those who used the word knew of definite persons or things which fell within its terms. Many of these tangible realities have long since disappeared. Others have come into existence of which the writers never thought. But must we necessarily say that the word has now become meaningless? Permanence and change are not always inconsistent. Even a solid object like a table, as Eddington tells us,

32 Chase, *Tyranny of Words,* 316.

is not really the same from one instant to another, for there is an ever-shifting dance of molecules or electrons. Yet for all the practical purposes of life, we can say that the same table stands there year after year. Or take a river. The drops of water that compose it pass steadily on, but something stays there which is distinct from its physical constituents.

> I see what was, and is, and will abide;
> Still glides the stream, and shall not cease to glide;
> The Form remains, the Function never dies.

Indeed the ever-changing Tiber has outlasted all the buildings that once stood motionless along its banks.

> Disce hinc quid possit fortuna; immota labascunt;
> Et quae perpetuo sunt fluitura, manent.

An even closer analogy to an enduring phrase is found in a human individual. He is considered to be the same person from birth until death, although his tissues replace themselves, his mind develops, and his external relations may be completely altered. Gladstone, whom Macaulay in 1839 called "the rising hope of those stern and unbending Tories," was not a different person from the man who was too radical for half of the Liberal Party in 1886. Some kind of identity persists through changes that startle even the person concerned. As the old lady exclaimed when her mind went askew,

> If I be I, as I think I be,
> Then will my little dog know me!

Therefore it is not correct to say, with Stuart Chase, that "we cannot expect the meaning of written constitutions to survive extensive changes in culture." Of course a clause acquires new significations as external conditions alter and many cases are decided. It becomes applicable to more tangible objects or to fewer. It grows like a human being, or like a university, which has a continuous life although older professors and students are gradually replaced by younger men. Thus the study of words raises one of the deepest philosophical problems, that of identity, which the Greeks expressed in the paradox of the Argo: Was the ship still there though all the timbers had been renewed? It is the small boy's "same old jack-knife with six new blades and five new handles."

The problem of long-enduring words extends far beyond constitutions. Even if courts could disregard constitutional phrases limiting the national government at the risk of disrupting the federal system, they would not be equally free to reject the responsibility of interpreting words in old statutes (some of them long antedating the Constitution, like the Statute of Frauds of Charles II's reign) and old contracts and deeds. In 1933 a United States court had to interpret the gold clause in a lease of water power executed just before the Civil War.[33]

Nor is it always sufficient to determine what objects the words were applied to at the time they were written. A grant of the dramatic rights in a popular novel, given before the invention of motion pictures, may conceivably include screen rights; and few will follow the lawyer who wrote a book to prove that Congress could not regulate railroad rates under its powers over "commerce" because the only transportation in 1787 was by boats and wagons.[34] When those who used words contemplated their long continued application, these words must eventually acquire a new content, especially when, as Marshall said, "It is a Constitution that we are interpreting."

Let me end with a story about Robert Browning. Toward the close of his life he received a letter from Professor Hiram Corson of Cornell, asking whether one of his early obscure poems meant what Corson supposed it did. Browning replied, "I didn't mean that when I wrote it, but I mean it now."

---

[33] Holyoke Water Power Co. v. American Writing Paper Co., Inc., 68 F(2d) 261 (CCA 1, 1933). See also Nashua Hospital Association v. Gage, 85 NH 335, 159 A 137 (1932) (construing deeds executed in 1850).

[34] Prentice *Federal Power over Carriers and Corporations* (1907).

Adapted from Vol. 41, Columbia Law Review (1941).

Language and the Law

BY GLANVILLE WILLIAMS

LANGUAGE IS PERHAPS the greatest of all human inventions. Most people think of it merely as the chief means of communication, but it is much more than that: it is the chief medium of thought. Almost all thinking, above a very primitive level, is in words. A person congenitally deaf, who of course cannot think in vocables, can hardly think or reason at all (that is, by civilized standards), until he is taught or develops a gesture-language, or until he is taught to speak or read, after which he is able to think in manual or oral gestures or in symbolic pictures. Exactly how far there can be thought without words, or without symbols of some sort, is a controversy into which it is not necessary to enter. Köhler's apes apparently thought without words, and so, perhaps, does a chess player or architect. One writer (Rignano) has argued that all reasoning is a series of operations or experiments performed merely in thought, that it does not require words, and that even insects, reptiles, and others are in some degree capable of it. However this may be, it can be confidently asserted that without words we are hardly capable of forming and manipulating general notions; and Rignano himself admitted as much.

For lawyers language has a special interest because it is the greatest instrument of social control. Lawyers are perhaps apt to regard law as the sole, or chief, means of social control, forgetting that the law is only a special department of language and that, whereas the application of law is limited, language is all-pervasive. From nursery days words like "coward," "decency," "manners," "fairness," help to stimulate conduct considered socially desirable and to repress conduct considered undesirable; in later life words like "success," "blackleg," and "patriotic" perform the same function. The law, with its verbal apparatus of "rights," "duties," and "wrongs," is merely a particular application of language as a means of social control. It has, of course, special features.

Coming down to the more narrowly professional point of view, words are of central importance for the lawyer because they are, in a very particular way, the tools of his trade. Words occupy the lawyer's attention in the drafting and interpretation of statutes, wills, contracts and other legal documents. Other specialists, such as engineers, surgeons, and painters, are also concerned in part with words (namely, the words in which they communicate their ideas to each other), but not to the extent that lawyers are.

Such is my excuse for writing a paper the object of which is twofold: to explain the modern theory of the function of language, and to show the importance of this theory for the lawyer and the student of jurisprudence. The study with which I shall be concerned is sometimes called the study of symbolism, or meaning; an alternative title is "semantics." Semantics studies the meaning of words—not, indeed, the meaning of this or that particular word, but the nature of meaning in general. It also considers the general conditions that must be satisfied before a word can have meaning; the influence of words upon thought; and the non-symbolic (emotive) function of words. The subject is not an entirely new one, for it has long been nourished in the womb of philosophy, the mother of the sciences. Its birth as a distinct science may be attributed to C. K. Ogden and I. A. Richard's work, *The Meaning of Meaning,* first published in 1923, now in its sixth edition, and already a classic.[1]

1 Bibliography. The following are the principal works on semantics in English, excluding periodical literature. The chief predecessors of Ogden and Richards were the philosopher Locke (*Essay Concerning the Human Understanding,* 1690, hereafter referred to by book, chapter, and sometimes, section), and two opponents of traditional logic, Alfred Sidgwick (various works, particularly *The Use of Words in Reasoning* (London, 1901)) and F. G. S. Shiller (*Formal Logic* (London, 1912)). It was apparently a Frenchman, Bréal, who coined the word *sémantique,* and his work on the subject (1897) was translated into English in 1900 under the title "Semantics." This is, however, more a work on philology or comparative grammar than on symbolism as Ogden and Richards understand it.

Works subsequent to the first edition of Ogden and Richards are: Ralph M. Eaton, *Symbolism and Truth* (Cambridge, Mass., 1925); A. N. Whitehead, *Symbolism, Its Meaning and Effect* (Cambridge, 1928); B. B. Bogoslovsky, *The Technique of Controversy* (London, 1928); Gustaf Stern, *Meaning and Change of Meaning* (Göteborg, 1931); Susan Stebbings, *Modern Introduction to Logic,* 2nd ed. (London, 1933), Chapter 2; John Dewey, *How We Think,* new ed. (Boston, etc., 1933); G. H. Mead, *Mind, Self and Society* (Chicago, 1934); I. A. Richards, *Interpretation in Teaching* (London, 1938); C. W. Morris, *Foundations of the Theory of Signs* (International Encyclopedia of Unified Science, Chicago, 1938); L. Bloomfield, *Linguistic Aspects of Science* (*ibid.,* Chicago 1939). A popular exposition is Stuart Chase, *The Tyranny of Words* (London, 1938).

For the Logical Positivists see below § 9.

The opinion is steadily growing that semantics is an important prolegomenon to the study of philosophy and of the so-called "inexact" sciences, such as psychology and the social sciences. In the past philosophers have tended to mistake the structure of discourse for the structure of the universe, and a training in semantics helps to prevent this error. In psychology and the social sciences it is coming to be recognized that one of the greatest difficulties is the difficulty of statement, and that many disputes are due to the imperfections of language. Lawyers, perhaps, are not in such need of having the imperfection of language impressed upon them; for every case on construction is an object-lesson in it. Still, even they are not immune from error, as I shall seek to show. Jurisprudence, too, is in my opinion badly in need of semantic analysis. It is ridden with disputes, and many of them turn out on examination to be disputes not as to matters of fact or of value-judgment but purely as to the use of words. A student of jurisprudence who comes to the subject armed with an understanding of what is a verbal dispute, will find that his knowledge enables him to pare off the unprofitable matter from his subject. It helps him, in Locke's words, to clear the ground a little, and to remove some of the rubbish that lies in the way of knowledge.

In the present paper I shall (1) state Ogden and Richard's doctrine as succinctly as possible, (2) supplement it by the work of others, in particular by the work of certain unorthodox logicians and of the philosophical school known as the Logical Positivists, and (3) intersperse the discussion with remarks on its relation to law and jurisprudence. These remarks are, I fear, on very diverse topics; for semantics touches law and jurisprudence at many points, and I am anxious to show the range of its importance

---

Among the many works on the psychological side are W. B. Pillsbury, *Psychology of Reasoning* (New York, 1910) and *Psychology of Language* (New York, 1928); Bertrand Russell, *Analysis of Mind* (London, 1921); Eugenio Rignano, *Psychology of Reasoning* (London, 1923); H. L. Hollingworth, *Psychology of Thought* (New York, 1926); J. F. Markey, *The Symbolic Process* (London, 1928); Frank Lorimer, *The Growth of Reason* (London, 1929).

The work of Ogden and Richards is certainly not unknown among academic lawyers, but so far it seems to have had little effect upon legal literature, at any rate on this side of the Atlantic. In America it has had a greater vogue; it was used by Jerome Frank in writing his Law and the Modern Mind (New York, 1930) (though I think he misapplied its doctrine, as I hope to show elsewhere), and more recently it has inspired an entertaining article by Professor Chafee in the Columbia Law Review: "The Disorderly Conduct of Words," (1941), 41 Col. L. Rev. 381, reprinted (1942) 20 Canadian Bar Review 752. Chase, *The Tyranny of Words* (above), also has a chapter on the law.

even at the risk of making my paper seem disjointed and rambling.

The Use of Words as Symbols.

The use of words as symbols is well explained by Ogden and Richards. These writers were not the first in the field, for they were anticipated in many important particulars by Locke. But it is to Ogden and Richards that we must look for a modern statement of the subject.

The core of their theory is as follows. In themselves words are nothing; or at least they are (as an old time lawyer expressed it) "no other than the verberation of the air."[2] Their importance consists in the fact that they are a kind of symbol, which is itself a kind of sign. Sign is the genus, symbol the species, and word the sub-species. Let us consider first signs in general. Skating over the difficulties of definition, the nature of a sign can best be explained by an example. Suppose a person sees smoke coming from a chimney: he promptly thinks "There is no smoke without fire," and so concludes that a fire is burning underneath. Here the smoke is a sign of the fire. The ability of any particular person to interpret a sign that comes into his consciousness—*i.e.*, to find meaning in it—depends upon his past experience, in this case his past experience that smoke is a consequence of fire.

Symbols are a special class of signs. There are other signs than symbols; thus smoke is a sign, but it is not a symbol. A symbol is a conventional sign; it is a sign that is consciously designed to stand for something.

Words are a special class of symbols. There are other symbols than words, such as a traffic sign, a wink, and a numeral. But words are much the most important kinds of signs used in ordinary thinking and communication.

A word or other symbol is generally used to refer to an object or situation in the real world. It is convenient to have a technical term for this object or situation, and Ogden and Richards coin the term "referent" to indicate it.[3] Words and phrases, then, are

---

2 Per Saunders, arg., in Partridge v. Strange, 1 Plowd. 83.

3 Stebbings, *Modern Introduction to Logic,* 2nd ed., 13, n. 2, suggested that this term was unhappily chosen, because "referent" was already in use among logicians as a technical term with another meaning. She accordingly suggested instead the term "referend." Ogden and Richards have not themselves adopted this suggestion, and it has not been adopted by other writers.

symbols that stimulate mental references to referents. The referent is that which is signified. The relation between a symbol and its referent is always indirect; between them there always intervenes the thought of some person. If there were no minds there would be no symbols and so no words.

This theory sounds and is so beautifully simple that there is danger of its revolutionary implications being missed unless they are expressly pointed out. In the next section I shall consider some errors in the use of language, particularly in connection with law, in order to indicate how much we have to mend our ways if we adopt the gospel of semantics.

Some Common Errors.

There are some errors in relation to the function of words that are so frequently committed that we must suppose them to be natural ways of thinking. Two of them will now be considered. (a) One is the idea that words are somehow important of themselves, and irrespective of their symbolic function. (b) Another is the supposition that real distinctions exist where in fact the only distinction is between two forms of words. In law this takes the form of making legal results depend upon purely verbal distinctions.

(a) The tendency to attach importance to words as such assumes its extreme form in the age-old tendency to identify words with things, and to suppose that words are in some way parts of things or always imply things corresponding to them. Somewhat similar is the supposition that words have immediate power over things. Among primitive peoples these ideas result in many forms of word-magic and word-taboos. Names, for instance, are regarded as part of the personality. Hence, among some primitives, a new-born infant is not regarded as a complete child until he has got a name. The name given to him is that of some ancestor, and the name is regarded as the soul of the ancestor. If two persons are given the same name, they have a certain identity. Some other primitive peoples, however, taboo the name of a dead man and refrain from applying it to any person or property that bears it, evidently out of fear of death. Again, there is a widely held belief that by means of the name injury may be done to a man. One can harm an enemy by making an effigy of him, giving it his name, and performing operations upon it. The same result can be achieved by giving his name to an animal captured in the chase, and then proceeding to mutilate it. Even merely alluding to a name is the same thing as assaulting the person who bears it. The consequence is that people conceal their "real" names and go about under an alias, which is regarded as not really belonging to the man. What is true of the names of human beings is equally true of the names of animals and things; one avoids speaking of snakes, leopards, etc., because to pronounce their names is to invoke the presence of the animals so named, and is fraught with grave danger.[4]

The superstitions so prevalent among the primitive peoples studied by anthropologists are also to be found, to some extent, in the earlier civilizations. Witness, for example, the elaborate curses pronounced by the priests in Deuteronomy upon anyone who should break the law.[5] A clear illustration of the reification of words is the story of Isaac's blessing of his son.

> "Jacob secures by fraud the blessing intended for Esau, and once given, the blessing cannot be withdrawn. It is quite comparable to a piece of goods made over once for all and not to be resumed. The most Esau can hope is that the store may not be exhausted—'Hast thou not reserved a blessing for me?' 'Hast thou but one blessing, my father?' Yet if the blessing were the true expression of the father's loving gratitude won by good service, Jacob should rather have had a curse for his deceit."[6]

I have thought it desirable to start with these ancient illustrations in order to win the reader's agreement before venturing on the more modern, and therefore more controversial, instances of word-superstition. Let me begin these more modern illustrations with the royal title. In 1521 the title of *Fidei Defensor* was conferred by Pope Leo X upon King Henry VIII. But when the quarrel with Rome was in full swing, Pope Leo's successor de-

[4] Lucien Lévy-Bruhl, *How Natives Think* (Les fonctions mentales dans les sociétiés inférieures) (London, 1926) 50-4, 346-7; same, The "Soul" of the Primitive (London, 1928) 208-10; same, L'Expérience mystique et ies symbols chez les primitifs (Paris, 1938) 236-8; J. G. Frazer, *Golden Bough*, abridged ed. (London, 1922), ch. 22; L. T. Hobhouse, *Morals in Evolution* (London, 1906) i 46; Enc. Brit. s.v. "Magic".

[5] Deut. xxvii 15-26; cp. Hobhouse, *op. cit.* ii 52.

[6] Hobhouse, *op. cit.* ii 53; Gen. xxvii 36-8. See also Hobhouse, *op. cit.* ii 69-70 (Egyptian Book of the Dead), 102 (Laws of Manu).

prived Henry of the title. His Majesty retaliated by procuring the passing of an "Act for the ratification of the King's Majesty's Stile," which insisted upon the Sovereign's right still to be described, both in Latin and in the vulgar tongue, as "Defender of the Faith." This last Act was "repealed, made frustrate, void and of none effect" by a statute passed under Philip and Mary, but was restored under Elizabeth.[7] All this controversy centred on a mere empty form of words. Whether Henry was a Defender of the Faith depended upon what one meant by "Faith"; the word had not the same meaning for Henry as for the Pope. If Henry was a Defender of the Faith, no amount of denial by the Pope could alter the fact, and if he was not, no Act of Parliament could make him one. But the parties to this dispute were not using words to convey meaning; they were using them as though they were of importance in themselves.

It may be thought that this childish concern over the royal title is a thing of the past. But look at the preamble to the Statute of Westminster, 1931. In this it is gravely recited that the assent of the Dominions shall be required not only to any alteration in the law touching the succession to the throne (which is a comparatively important matter), but also in any alteration in the law touching the royal style and titles (which is a mere empty form of words). It is not impossible that a constitutional crisis might occur through Great Britain taking it upon herself to change His Majesty's title without the assent of the Dominions.

If word-fetishism had stopped at this it would not have been a very momentous error, but it did not. Perhaps its worst effect in the law has been in connection with offences having a religious or supernatural basis. The imaginary offence of witchcraft, for instance, was at one time a felony punishable with death[8]; and the belief in the existence of witchcraft was partly due to the belief that evil effects could be produced by words. The crime of blasphemy, too, was originally based on the same kind of logophobia as the primitive taboo; the god was supposed to be personally

[7] 1 & 2 Ph. & M. c. 8, s. 20; 1 Eliz. c. 1. I owe these details to Theobald Mathew's *For Lawyers and Others,* 201.

Even the names of private individuals have sometimes occupied the attention of the Legislature; cp. the Scots Act of 1600 stamping out the name "Ruthven," and the Act compelling Irishmen to take English names: Linell, *Law of Names* (London, 1938) 46.

[8] See 1 Jac. 1, c. 12. Earlier statutes were 33 Hen. 8, c. 8, and 5 Eliz. c. 16.

offended by the desecration of his name. Even in the reign of Henry VIII a boy was put to death by burning because of some idle words he had chanced to hear respecting the sacrament, which he ignorantly repeated.[9] Nowadays, however, the maintenance of the crime of blasphemy is to be justified on a more rational ground, namely, the emotive power of words. Blasphemers are now punished not because they desecrate sacred formulae or because they revile Christianity, but because they may cause respectable Christians to break the peace.[10] This emotive power of words will be considered later (§ 7).

The only surviving offence that is still, to my mind, based largely on word-fetichism is bigamy. Bigamy became a felony by an Act of 1608[11] (it is perhaps not without significance that this Act immediately precedes on the statute book James I's notorious Witchcraft Act). At first punishable with death, bigamy is now punishable with a maximum of seven years' penal servitude.[12] The reason for punishing bigamy is frankly stated by Kenny: it is "the broad one of its involving an outrage upon public decency by the profanation of a solemn ceremony".[13] Consider what this means. If *A* deserts his wife and lives with a mistress he commits no crime, either in deserting his wife or in committing adultery. But if he tries to make the position appear more regular by going through a form of marriage with his mistress, then, even though the marriage is totally null and void (as it necessarily is), so that the whole ceremony is a mere empty form of words, and even though he never thereafter cohabits with the woman, he commits a felony. And this simply because he is "profaning a solemn ceremony." The ceremony may have taken place in a Registrar's office, but that makes no difference to its solemnity in the eye of the law.

Suppose we were to press for a reason why this profanation of a ceremony should thus entail a liability to seven years' penal servitude. Is it because the wrath of the Deity needs to be appeased in this manner? That may have been the idea underlying the

9 Pike, *History of Crime in England* (London, 1876), ii, 56 (quoted by Ogden and Richards).

10 The change dates from R. v. Ramsay and Foote (1883) 15 Cox C. C. 231. See further Nokes, *The Crime of Blasphemy* (London, 1928).

11 1 Jac. 1, c. 11.

12 Offences against the Person Act, 1861, s. 57.

13 *Outlines of Criminal Law,* 15th ed. (Cambridge, 1936), 361.

Act of 1603[14]; but it can hardly justify the continuance of the offense in modern law.[15] For one thing, it involves an Old Testament conception of the Deity; for another, we now think that an act should not be made a crime unless its commission involves harmful social consequences. What are the harmful social consequences of bigamy? The answer that would probably be given by one who supported the present law is that bigamy often involves the practising of a grievous deceit upon an innocent woman. This is true, but then the law is not confined to this case. It frequently happens that a male offender has told the woman before the ceremony that he is already married. A ceremony performed in such circumstances is no more than a pathetic attempt to give a veneer of respectability to what is in law an adulterous association. Yet not only does the man remain guilty of the felony of bigamy, but the woman becomes guilty of it as well, as a principal in the second degree. It is therefore clear that the crime does not consist in the deception of the other party to the bigamous marriage.

A second possible reason for punishing bigamy is that the offender by procuring a marriage certificate to which he is not entitled has in a way committed forgery. But forgery proper involves an intent to defraud or deceive,[16] whereas a person can be branded of the felony of bigamy although he honestly believed that his first marriage was at an end and thus that his second marriage was valid.[17] Even if the bigamy were intentionally com-

---

14 The preamble declares that bigamy involves "the great Dishonour of God, and utter undoing of divers honest Men's Children, and others." It may be suggested that the second reason is a make-weight; it is difficult to see how the mere celebration of a void ceremony can "undo" children.

15 I do not want to offend susceptibilities, but when the sanctions of the criminal law are used to inflict suffering upon those who offend against the religious beliefs of others, persons holding such beliefs must expect to find them made the subject of discussion. It is, therefore, fair to ask those who consider the law of bigamy to have a religious justification, how they reconcile this view with the recognition of divorce by the secular authorities. If a bigamous marriage be regarded as sinful, while a second marriage after a secular divorce is not sinful, this must be because the State authorities have divine sanction to dissolve marriages. In other words, the enormous red-tape of our divorce law is part of the law of God. For my part I cannot see how an intelligent person can believe this. It was this absurdity that gave point to Maule J.'s famous satirical address to the poor prisoner convicted of bigamy: see R. Walton, *Random Recollections of the Midland Circuit* (1869) i 154-6; Heard, *Oddities of the Law* (London, 1921) 48; Foss, *Lives of the Judges* (London, 1864) ix 225. Cp. (1932) Law Notes 3, where Rowlatt J. is reported to have said that in many bigamy cases "it was a pity that the law could not look another way."

16 Cp. Forgery Act, 1913, s. 3 (2).

17 R. v. Wheat and Stocks [1921] 2 K. B. 119.

mitted, the precise nature of the intent to defraud or deceive needs to be considered. Where both parties to the bigamous marriage have the guilty intent, their object in going through the ceremony is generally to hold themselves out to the world as man and wife. This is certainly an intent to deceive the world at large; but is anyone necessarily the worse for it? (It must be remembered that I am putting aside as irrelevant the desertion of the lawful spouse, which, though often a cruel moral wrong, is not in itself a crime, and am considering only the deception of the world at large.) Many petty deceits are practised in life without any punishment being assigned for them; why do we single out this one for punishment? Also, it is to be noted that where the intent to deceive the public exists without the bigamous ceremony having been performed—where a man and woman living in adultery declare to their friends that they have been married—no crime is committed, unless of course property is obtained by the fraud. On the other hand if the bigamous ceremony is performed, even though only in private, without any use being made afterwards of the marriage certificate, the crime of bigamy is committed.

The only anti-social consequences that are necessarily involved in the mere celebration of a bigamous marriage are (1) the falsification of the State records, and (2) the waste of time of the Minister of Religion or Registrar. But as to (2), though one must not minimize the dishonesty of making false statements in order to procure a bigamous ceremony, or the affront to the feelings of the celebrating officer, it hardly seems justifiable to protect these feelings by penal sanctions, at any rate by the sanction of imprisonment; and as to economic loss, if the parties have made the usual disbursements on marriage, it may be thought that the economic loss is theirs rather than the celebrating officer's or the State's. As to (1), the falsification of the State records, I personally cannot regard it as a very important matter[18]; certainly not one deserving more than a moderate fine.

To sum up, the crime of bigamy as it now stands (having regard to the severity with which it is or can be punished) does not make

18 Nor does the State itself seem to do so, for it allows a man to marry ten of his nieces, one after another, without making any provision for his punishment (if the nieces are over the age of consent). Such marriages are not bigamous because there is no initial valid marriage to found upon; yet the falsification of the State records is the same as in bigamy. This anomaly is inconsistent with any theory of bigamy whatever.

sense except on the supposition that the marriage ceremony is a magic form of words that has to be protected from profanation at almost any cost in human suffering.

I should perhaps add that in writing the above I am not unaware of the tremendous social importance of the marriage ceremony. It is this ceremony that, through the force of tradition, maintains the institution of monogamy and keeps families stable. Punishment is perhaps justifiable if it is necessary to preserve such an important institution; but we should first make quite sure that it is necessary, and that monogamy can be maintained in no other way. What I contend is that the sanction of nullity is enough to prevent bigamous marriages in most cases, and that the exceptional cases where bigamy is committed are not (quasi-rape apart)[19] harmful enough to deserve anything more than a moderate fine on summary conviction. Where the bigamous ceremony has been performed merely in order to gain "respectability," the sanction of a fine plus the attendant publicity is obviously enough to neutralise the "respectability" gained by the ceremony; and it should be enough to keep the offence within bounds.

(b) The second error in relation to the function of words is the supposition that real distinctions exist where in fact the only distinction is between two forms of words. Judges have said more than once that "there is no magic in words"[20] but unfortunately this is not the case. That there is legal magic in words was admitted by Chitty J. when he said that "a difference in the mere form of words does in several cases make a difference in law".[21] For instance, if *A* lends money to *B* on mortgage, and stipulates that the interest shall be 5 per cent., but if not paid promptly 6 per cent., the latter part of the provision is void as a penalty. Thus *B* need pay only 5 per cent., even if he does not pay promptly. Yet if *A* had provided that interest should be 6 per cent., but if paid

[19] Where the "second wife" did not know the ceremony to be bigamous, the case is of course altogether more serious, for morally it may be tantamount to rape. But I think we should distinguish between (1) cases where both the man and his "second wife" wish to be faithful to each other, and (2) cases where he deserts her. In (1) it should be borne in mind that any punishment imposed on the man is an aggravation of the suffering of his victim.

[20] Per Lord Kenyon C.J. in R. v. Inhabitants of North Nibley (1792) 5 T. R. 24; per Lord Romilly M.R. in Lord v. Jeffkins (1865) 35 Beav. 16; per Jessel M.R. in Re Caplen's Estate, Bulbeck v. Silvester (1876) 45 L. J. Ch. 280 at 281.

[21] Dean v. Dean [1891] 3 Ch. 150 at 155.

promptly 5 per cent., the whole would have been good.[22] Lord Hatherley, with that reluctance to condemn a rule outright that seems to be a characteristic of the legal mind, called this a "fine distinction"[23]; whereas actually it is not a distinction at all, except in words and in legal results. For the objective situation that is contemplated, the referent of the two forms of words, is the same in each case: namely, the situation in which *B* has to pay 5 per cent. interest if paid promptly or 6 per cent. if not paid promptly. If this situation is one in which it is thought that *B* is unfairly penalized for delay in paying, a change in the word-symbols used to refer to the situation cannot make any difference to the fairness or unfairness of the situation.

Another case where the law has become lost in mere words is in the famous distinction between "but if" and "until"—a distinction that an Irish judge considered to be "little short of disgraceful to our jurisprudence."[24] If *A* gives property on trust for *B*, "but if *B* marries then for *C*," the gift to *C* is struck out, because it tends to induce *B* to remain unmarried, and the procreation of legitimate children is regarded as a public interest. Thus on this form of words *B* will take absolutely. But if the words used were "on trust for *B* until he marries and thenceforth for *C*," the gift over would be valid and *B* would lose the property if he were to marry.[25] The difference is supposed to be between a gift subject to a condition subsequent and a determinable limitation. Yet the intention in each case is that *B* shall enjoy the property until he marries and that thereafter *C* shall enjoy it. Thus the referent is again the same. If the referent is the same the meaning must be the same. And if it is against public policy to tolerate the situation when one form of words is used, it must necessarily be against public policy to tolerate the same situation when the other form of words is used. No amount of subtle distinguishing between the emotional *nuances* of the two forms of words can affect this proposition.

22 Strode v. Parker (1694) 2 Vern. 316. Cp. Wrigley v. Gill [1906] 1 Ch. 165.

23 Wallingford v. Mutual Society (1880) 5 App. Cas. 685 at 702.

24 Per Porter M.R., in Re King's Trusts (1892) 29 L. R. Ir. 401 at 410.

25 See Underhill, Trusts, 9th ed., 78-80; but see the cases collected in (1943) 59 L. Q. R. 353, n. 36. There are other legal distinctions between "but if" and "until," all equally verbal: see Re Randell, Randell v. Dixon (1888) 38 Ch. D. 213; Re Bowen, Lloyd Phillips v. Davis [1893] 2 Ch. 491; Re Talbot, Jubb v. Sheard [1933] Ch. 895 (all on the perpetuity rule); Whigham v. I. R. [1941] 2 K. B. 18 (Finance Act, 1922); (1943) 59 L. Q. R. 352-3 (repugnancy).

Again, a covenant in a deed to pay an annuity of £1,000 free of income tax is illegal (by the terms of the Income Tax Act); but a covenant to pay such a sum (not mentioned in figures) as, after deducting income tax, would leave £1,000, is perfectly good.[26] Here again the law is simply playing with words. One can put it more strongly and say that the cases allowing the second form of words are a repudiation of an express provision of an Act of Parliament, namely, the provision that "every agreement for . . . annual payment in full without allowing any such deduction [of tax] shall be void."

Another illustration: if *A* agrees to give the whole of his time to the service of *B*, this necessarily means that he will not serve anybody else during the period of his employment with *B*. But if *A* breaks his contract and enters into the service of somebody else, no injunction will be granted against him to prevent him from doing so. If, however, *A* had expressly agreed *totidem verbis* not to serve anybody else, an injunction will be granted to prevent him from doing so.[27] The granting of the injunction depends not upon the actualities of the case nor upon the intention of the parties as shown by their words, but upon the particular words chosen to express that intention.[28]

While I think that the foregoing are verbal distinctions, it must be admitted that the judge's lot is not always a happy one when he is faced with some ingenious attempt to drive a coach and four through a statutory or common law rule. It may not be at all easy to decide in a particular case whether a suggested distinction is purely verbal or whether it has some basis in fact or in distinct

26 Income Tax Act, 1918, rule 23 (2) of General Rules of All Schedules; Konstam, Income Tax, 9th ed., 181; per Greene M. R. in Re Horlick's Settlement Trusts, Colledge v. Horlick [1938] 4 A. E. R. 602 at 606.

27 Mortimer v. Beckett [1920] 1 Ch. 571.

28 Other examples of verbal distinctions: (1) In the law of charitable trusts a gift "to my country England" is a good charitable trust; a gift "for patriotic purposes" is not: Re Smith, Public Trustee v. Smith [1932] 1 Ch. 153; A. G. v. National Provincial Bank [1924] A. C. 262; but see Albery in (1940) 56 L. Q. R. 49. (2) In the law of restraint of trade a compound covenant worded as a single covenant if partly bad is wholly bad (Attwood v. Lamont [1920] 3 K. B. 571), but if worded as several covenants may be partly bad and partly good (Putsman v. Taylor [1927] 1 K. B. 637 741). And this on a matter of public policy! (3) It has been suggested that the Courts would draw verbal distinctions under s. 4 of the Statute of Frauds: see Lord Wright in (1939) 55 L. Q. R. 206. (4) A release of one joint debtor or tortfeasor discharges the other; but a covenant not to sue does not: Hutton v. Eyre (1815) 6 Taunt. 289. (5) A verbal distinction has been suggested as to options to purchase in a mortgage deed: (1944) 60 L. Q. R. 191.

legal result. Even if the distinction is not purely verbal, the judge still has to decide whether the transaction is so glaringly *in fraudem legis* that it must be upset. To take an illustration, consider the rule that a person intending to make a testamentary disposition can do so only by an instrument that complies with the Wills Act. Suppose that *A* orally or by an unattested writing declares himself a trustee of his chattels for himself for life with remainder to *B* absolutely, reserving a power of revocation by instrument under hand, etc. If cunningly worded this transaction might (unless defeated by the Courts) achieve all or almost all the results of a will; yet it is in the form appropriate to a transfer *inter vivos.* Would it be defeated as an infringement of the Wills Act? A Court before whom the question came would first have to decide what it meant by a "testamentary disposition," and having settled that it would have to decide whether the impugned transaction bore the marks of one. There is always the danger, in the absence of very clear thinking, that a verbal distinction will emerge.[29]

Even when the law has not gone so badly astray as in some of the foregoing examples, it does not always escape the charge of verbalism. At common law it was not at all infrequent for certain technical expressions to be required for effecting certain results, particularly in conveyancing and pleading. An obvious illustration is the requirement of the words "to *A* and his heirs" to pass a fee simple. Occasionally a case can be made out for technicalities of this sort, but usually they are no more than irksome absurdities.

The case is of course different with technical terms or formulae that bow to an indication of contrary intention; the attaching of a "fixed" meaning to such terms or formulae, in the absence of contrary intent, may be quite rational. An illustration or two may, however, show the fineness of the line that separates verbality from reason. A person with no knowledge of the law would probably see no difference between a tenancy at £52 a year payable weekly and a tenancy at £1 per week; yet the period of notice required by law for the first is at least six months, while for the second it is only a week. In a way this is a verbal distinction, but in a way it is not, for these forms of words have become established for indicating the period of notice that is required. The rule is not like those criticized above, for whereas the latter allow the evasion

29 Cp. (1935) 13 Can. B. R. 324 ff.

of fixed rules of law by the mere turn of a phrase, the present rule results from a genuine attempt to ascertain the intention of the parties, where the intention is all that matters. A second illustration is the rule that if two articles are given as one gift, the donee cannot disclaim one and accept one; whereas he can if they are given as two gifts.[30] Here, again, the Court is doing its best to guess what the donor would probably have intended, although the *indicia* of intention on which it is obliged to proceed are very slight.

The Process of Abstraction.

A famous medieval controversy that was largely concerned with the problem of meaning was the dispute over the reality of universals. This dispute split the scholastic world into two camps (with many divergent divisions within each camp), called the "realists" and the "nominalists." The question was raised by Plato, but the medieval dispute is generally regarded as starting from a question of Porphyry (died 304), who asked whether classes (called by logicians genera and species) exist outside the mind or only in the mind. The question can be stated in simple language as follows. Very early in our lives we begin to notice that individual things have common characteristics and consequently a common name. We notice, for instance, that different individual flowers resemble each other, and we learn to call them by the name "rose." Perhaps one of the characteristics of these particular roses is a certain colour, which we learn to call by the name "red." Similarly we learn that Tom, Dick and Harry are all "man." The question to be decided is whether there is any objective reality corresponding to our concepts of "rose," "redness," "man" and so on. Are there such things in the universe as "rose," "redness," and "man," or are there simply individuals, such as individual roses, individual red things, and individual Toms, Dicks, and Harrys? If the latter, what are we to make of our concepts of "rose," "redness," and "man"? Are these words without meaning—*i.e.,* without referents? Or, if these words have referents, what are these referents if they have no objective reality?

In the Middle Ages those philosophers who (following Plato) argued for the "reality" of the concepts of quality and relation

30 Re Joel, Rogerson v. Joel [1943] Ch. 311.

(such concepts being called "universals") came to be known as "realists," their opponents as "nominalists"; but as I have said there were many variations of opinion within each group. Broadly speaking, the argument of the realists was this, that as Socrates is (at one time) real, and as Socrates is a man, man is real; then as man is real, and man is a rational animal, rationality and animality are real. In the same way it could be asserted that redness, heaviness and justice were real. From this the conclusion was drawn that humanity, animality, rationality, heaviness and the like existed in the world independently of their concrete manifestations. Against this view the nominalists contended that the only reality consisted of individuals with certain attributes, and that there could be no heaviness apart from heavy things, no justice apart from just acts. Heaviness and justice were simply names given to certain qualities, and had no special non-empirical mode of real being.

Such was the famous controversy, and to us it may seem incredible that it attracted so much attention. Partly this was because it had theological implications. On the whole it was the doctrine of the nominalists that finally attracted the greatest support, largely through the writings of William of Ockham; but the controversy has not wholly died in philosophical circles even at the present day.

The view of the semanticist may perhaps be stated as follows. All universals are arrived at as a result of a process of abstraction. (The same is true of individuals, as will be shown in the next section.) Abstraction may be defined as the imaginative selection of some one characteristic of a complex situation so that it may be attended to in isolation.[31] We are all familiar with this process from childhood; it is bound up with our earliest efforts to learn our mother tongue. Imagine a baby in whose household there is a terrier called "Caesar." The baby will be taught to call this dog "bow-wow," because "bow-wow" is easier to say than "Caesar." If he sees another dog he will guess or be told that this other dog is to be called "bow-wow" as well. At first this transference of the word from one individual to another may well be due merely to the infant's inability to discriminate differences: one dog will be

[31] Stebbings, *op. cit.* 7. Cp. Locke, *op. cit.* 2, 11, 9; 3, 3, 5, 6; Schiller, *op. cit.* 22-3; Ogden and Richards, *op. cit.* 212-4; Russell, *op. cit.* Ch. 11.

the same to him as another.[32] Later, however, when he comes to distinguish between the two dogs, his continued use of the same name for both of them, and his extension of it to other dogs that he knows to be different again, will be the result of abstraction. Abstraction is, in short, the perception of similarity in spite of differences.

The importance of abstraction in our thinking cannot be stressed too much. "Without abstraction there can be no recognition of similarity; without the recognition of similarity there can be no advance in knowledge."[33] But the process has its dangers. The danger is particularly present when we objectify ("hypostatize") our abstractions. As a matter of linguistic convenience we are accustomed to hypostatize words expressing qualities or properties, thus speaking of (say) "justice" or "redness" as though these things were part of the stuff of nature. But semantically there is no difference between the adjectives "just" and "red" and the nouns "justice" and "redness"; the difference is only in grammatical form. Qualities like these are not to be found by themselves anywhere; they are simply "phantoms due to the refractive power of the linguistic medium."[34] In real life there are simply people or things or conduct or events to which the qualities in question are applicable.[35] To speak of redness apart from red things is like speaking of the grin without the Cheshire cat. It is the same with words expressing relation. When we appear to speak of relations we are merely using the words as tools, which does not involve actual referents corresponding to them. All such words, then, are merely symbolic accessories, apparent symbols, which, though

32 Thus James Ward (*Psychological Principles* (Cambridge, 1918) 304) denied that the formation of concepts was the result of abstraction: "the same name is applied to different things or events [not out of conscious disregard for their differences but] because only their more salient features are perceived at all." This may be true, but it does not affect the proposition that when class-names are continued in use by a person who has come to perceive individual differences, their use is a case of abstraction.

33 Stebbings, *op. cit.* 7.

34 Ogden and Richards, *op. cit.* 96.

35 The view of a scientist on this matter is not without interest: "The idealist philosopher Plato gave abstract nouns like 'justice' an existence independent of the social circumstances of the people who describe a social action as just or unjust. Plato's curious views about such words were closely connected with his curious views about numbers. Both were wafted into his firmament of universals which the scholastic theologians believed to be as definite a place as hell itself. Modern science began when men like Roger Bacon and Francis Bacon rejected the world of 'universals' and set about making words describe the solid earth of human experience"; Hogben, *Mathematics for the Million* (London, 1936) 78.

indispensable as machinery, have often proved to be dangerous impediments to straight thinking.[36] As Ogden and Richards drily remark, the consequences of supposing that such words symbolize real entities eternally fixed in the order of nature "are sometimes called Philosophy."[37] Philosophers of the so-called "realist" school, from Plato onwards, have mistaken for a fundamental characteristic of reality what is merely a characteristic of language. But it is not only the philosophers who have the unfortunate habit of hypostatizing abstractions. "How popular and how influential is this practice may be shown by such a list of terms as the following: Virtue, Liberty, Democracy, Peace, Germany, Religion, Glory. All invaluable words, indispensable even, but able to confuse the clearest issues, unless controlled."[38] Such words are to be fought and died for; yet we do not always have a clear realization of what we mean by them. If these words mean anything it can only be a meaning in relation to the actual lives of individuals. By themselves they are simply abstractions, and many of them are abstractions on the meaning of which there is little agreement. The way to control such words is in every case to discipline ourselves to find the lower-order referent in the world of real life—that is, to find the real object in which the quality is conceived as inhering. Unless the speaker and his listener can agree on some such concrete referent for the word in question, a proposition relating to that word cannot be intelligently discussed.

At this point I must again interrupt the exposition of semantics by trying to show the bearing of this branch of it upon the law. Chiefly, I think, it is important in jurisprudence; but it is also of some value in the work of the Courts. The consequences of failing to reduce an abstract word to its lower-order referent can perhaps be illustrated from the law of charitable trusts, and in particular from the cases on trusts for the promotion of sport. In *Re Nottage*

[36] Ogden and Richards, *op. cit.* 63-4, 93-101, 133-4, 188-9. My account of the authors' views is slightly simplified, for I have avoided reference to the "levels of interpretation" and to the "contraction" of symbols.

[37] Ogden and Richards, *op. cit.* 93. Cp. *ibid.* 29: "The persistence of the primitive linguistic outlook not only throughout the whole religious world, but in the work of the profoundest thinkers, is . . . one of the most curious features of modern thought. The philosophy of the nineteenth century was dominated by an idealist tradition in which the elaboration of monstrous symbolic machinery (the Hegelian Dialectic provides a striking example) was substituted for direct research, and occupied the centre of attention."

[38] *Ibid.* 133-4.

(1895)[39] a bequest to provide a cup "to encourage the sport of yacht-racing" was held by the Court of Appeal to be not a charitable trust, Lindley L.J. saying that "a gift for the encouragement of a mere sport" could not be charitable. Taken in itself this sentence may mean either of two things: (1) that no gift for the encouragement of sport is charitable, or (2) that no gift for the encouragement of sport "as such" is charitable, but that a gift to encourage human beings to take part in sport is (or may be) charitable. If Lindley L.J. meant (2), the distinction is clearly verbal. The referent of "sport" or "yacht-racing" is not a metaphysical entity *sport* or *yacht-racing* in the abstract, but is a number of actual yacht races (or other sporting events) by human beings. Actually, however, it seems that Lindley L.J. meant (1); according to the tenour of the rest of his judgment, no trust for the promotion of healthy sport can be charitable. Lopes L.J. was more cautious, for in one part of his judgment he said merely that "a gift, the object of which is the encouragement of a mere sport or game primarily calculated to amuse individuals apart from the community at large, cannot upon the authorities be held to be charitable, though such sport or game is to some extent beneficial to the public." This seems to contemplate *some* sports the promotion of which would be a charitable object. But it is not a very satisfactory statement, for in drawing a distinction between individuals and the community it must not be forgotten that the community consists of individuals. The phrase "a sport calculated to amuse individuals apart from the community at large" means "a sport that amuses some people but not all." Now of course no sport amuses all people. Perhaps what Lopes L.J. meant was that the individuals amused by yacht-racing constituted a minority of the community. If this was the *ratio decidendi,* it implies that a trust to encourage a popular sport would be charitable. But, again, I do not think the learned judge meant this, for he went on in the rest of his judgment to assert the contrary.

Re Nottage thus appears to rest chiefly on the Victorian principle that *mens sana* is more important than *corpus sanum,* and it cannot itself be cited as an instance of the error under consideration. However, the principle laid down is not satisfactory, and the wording of the judgments is sufficiently unclear to tempt a twen-

39 Re Nottage, Jones v. Palmer (1895) 2 Ch. 649.

tieth-century judge to verbal distinguishing. In *Re Gray* [1925][40] Romer J. held that a gift to provide sport for a regiment was good, the chief reason being that it was in the public interest that soldiers should be physically fit. The learned judge purported to distinguish *Re Nottage* on the ground that that was a gift for the encouragement of sport, whereas the present gift was for the benefit of a regiment. It follows from what has already been said that this was a misleading way of expressing the distinction. The true contrast is not between "sport" and "a regiment" but between "those who take part in yacht-racing" and "the members of a regiment." Apparently the distinction means that the health of those who take part in yacht-racing is unimportant to the community, while the health of the members of a regiment is important to the community. The unsatisfactory nature of this distinction will be appreciated as soon as it is realized that those who take part in yacht-racing themselves form a section of the community.

More recently, the question has twice been raised whether a trust for the promotion of foxhunting is charitable, the answer of the judges being that it is not.[41] In the second of the two cases Lawrence J. said: "The main purpose of the appellant society's activities is to benefit foxhunting, not to benefit the community." Here again a translation into the lower-order referent destroys the sharpness of the verbal distinction. There being no metaphysical entity *foxhunting* that is capable of being benefited, and the object of foxhunting not being to benefit foxes, it must surely be admitted that a so-called benefit to foxhunting is in fact a benefit to those human beings who take part in foxhunting. These persons constitute a section of the community. It is true that they do not constitute the whole of the community, but it is not necessary to a charitable trust that it should benefit everyone. One may add, if the fact is of any relevance, that foxhunting is no longer the pastime exclusively of the upper classes.

Turning to jurisprudence, the denial of the independent reality of universals is important chiefly because it necessitates a theory of law that will not assume law to be some entity mysteriously existing on its own account, independently of the external world and of

40 Re Gray, Todd v. Taylor (1925) Ch. 34.

41 Re Thompson, Public Trustee v. Lloyd [1934] Ch. 342; Peterborough Royal Foxhound Show Society v. I. R. [1936] 2 K. B. 497.

the world of mind. Such a theory has been well stated by Professor Olivecrona in his book *Law as Fact.* He writes as follows:—

> "We are dimly conscious of a permanent existence of the rules of law. We talk of them as if they were always there as real entities. But this is not exact. It is impossible to ascribe a permanent existence to a rule of law or to any other rule. A rule exists only as the content of a notion in a human being. No notion of this kind is permanently present in the mind of anyone. The imperative appears in the mind only intermittently. Of course the position is not changed by the fact that the imperative words are put down in writing. The written text—in itself only figures on paper—has the function of calling up certain notions in the mind of the reader. That is all.
>
> In reality, the law of a country consists of an immense mass of ideas concerning human behaviour, accumulated during centuries through the contributions of innumerable collaborators. . . . The ideas are again and again revived in human minds, accompanied by the imperative expression: 'This line of conduct *shall* be taken' or something else to the same effect."[42]

Some philosophers will not have this common-sense solution. They will go on endlessly trying to make some independent "reality" out of the universals. Take, for instance, Dr. Joad's discussion of what is in effect the same problem, namely, the "reality" of Shakespeare's play *Hamlet.* Joad argues that *Hamlet* is in some way a subsistent object with an independent being (he would, I suppose, argue the same for *law*), and he discusses and rejects a number of alternative opinions. One opinion that he rejects is that *Hamlet* consists of "ideas in our own minds, and in the minds of all those who are performing, or seeing, or reading the play, or at any time have performed, or seen, or read it and remember what they learned, saw, or read." This, it will be observed, is much the same opinion as Olivecrona holds concerning the concept *law.* Joad rejects it on the following grounds (he is considering in particular the meaning of the sentence "*Hamlet* is a great play").

> "(1) It seems most improbable that we are in fact referring to all these minds and experiences, most of which are unknown to us, when we make the statement "*Hamlet* is a great play." (2) If we were referring to them, we should, in so far as our

[42] *Law as Fact* (Copenhagen and London, 1939) 47-8.

own experience is concerned, be paying a totally undeserved compliment to ourselves. . . . (3) If all those who are seeing and reading, and have seen and read *Hamlet,* were abolished, it would, if this view were true, cease to be a great play. I doubt if anybody who has really admired *Hamlet* believes this. (4) When we make this assertion about *Hamlet,* it certainly seems as if we are purporting to speak and we certainly believe ourselves to be speaking not about our own or about anybody else's experiences, but about something which is *the cause of* these experiences. Now this something is not, at least *prima facie,* itself an experience."[43]

All these difficulties seem to me to disappear if we say that "*Hamlet*" means either or both of two things—(a) a certain collection of symbols capable of evoking ideas and emotions, and (b) the ideas and emotions themselves. There seems to me to be no reason whatever to conclude, as Joad does, that *Hamlet* is "a member of the class of subsistent objects which are neither mental nor material but are, nevertheless, constituent factors of the universe possessing being in their own right." To answer Joad's particular arguments, as to his argument numbered (1), we are referring not to other people's ideas but to the symbols and their meaning for us; as to (2), we pay the compliment not to ourselves but to the man who had the genius to put the symbols together in that way; as to (3), it is true that *Hamlet* would cease to have meaning if all beings capable of understanding the languages in which it is now written ceased to exist—whether *Hamlet* would then itself cease to exist is a question not admitting of a simple answer in the affirmative or negative; it would exist only as a number of marks on paper; as to (4), we are in fact speaking in part of something that is the cause of our experiences, namely, the marks on paper, or the general effect produced on the stage.

By the same analysis, "the law" is a collection of symbols capable of evoking ideas and emotions, together with the ideas and emotions so evoked. We need not dispute whether it is primarily symbol or primarily idea or primarily emotion; sometimes one, sometimes another aspect may be predominant, but usually all three are inseparably connected.

[43] C. E. M. Joad, *Guide to Philosophy* (London, 1941) 269.

Ambiguity; Central and Peripheral Elements in Meaning.

This section will be concerned with two different types of obscurity of meaning. The words that are commonly recognized to be obscure in meaning and consequently to give rise to difficulty of interpretation are the ambiguous or equivocal ones, the words of multiple meaning. It is not so generally appreciated that even "univocal" words prove without exception to be extremely fractious when one comes to apply them to the facts of experience. I shall first make a few remarks on ambiguous words, and then pass to the larger subject of fringe meaning.

(1) *Ambiguity.* It was said at the outset of this article that language is perhaps the greatest of man's inventions. But it is an invention that he is a poor hand at improving. Language shows a most remarkable maldistribution of words, a great unevenness of density; for some ideas are expressible in a dozen different words and others have to be lumped together under one. The result is much false reasoning. As C. S. Peirce put it, "The woof and warp of all thought and research is symbols, and the life of thought and science is the life inherent in symbols; so that it is wrong to say that a good language is *important* to good thought, merely, for it is the essence of it."[44] Philosophy stands out as the striking example of the flatulencies that may gather round the unacknowledged puns of language.[45] On the whole lawyers have appreciated the danger, and have been at pains to construct and preserve a moderately precise technical language. Oddly enough, it is least precise in its most fundamental parts. We use the word "right" in some half-dozen different senses and often pass insensibly from one to the other, of course with disastrous results upon our reasoning. We use the phrases "*in rem*"—"*in personam*" in four different meanings. It was through confusing together two of them that Langdell and Maitland came to compose a famous fallacy, which has been exposed by Hohfeld.[46] "Ownership" has two distinct senses, called by Salmond "corporeal" and "incorporeal"—*i.e.,* ownership of things and ownership of rights; and the word "estate" should be similarly differentiated, for it bears a different

[44] C. S. Peirce, *Collected Papers* (Cambridge, Mass., 1932) ii, 129.

[45] Some examples are given by Adrian Coates, *A Basis of Opinion* (London 1938), 42-3.

[46] *Fundamental Legal Conceptions* (New Haven and London, 1923), 69, 106-10.

meaning when we speak of an estate in land from its meaning when we speak of an estate in a right. This last ambiguity makes havoc of section 1 of the Law of Property Act, 1925. "Property" has at least seven different meanings, "acceptance" four, "special damage" three, and "specific," "condition," "warranty," and "implied contract" at least two each. "Chose in action" is a well-known chameleon expression. The division of animals into "tame" and "wild" (*mansuetae naturae* and *ferae naturae*) is in fact not one classification but two, one in the law of property and quite another in the law of tort.

Notwithstanding these defects in our vocabulary, we are at best timid in our measures of reform and frequently oppose even timid reforms. When Hohfeld wished to sort out four meanings of the word "right" and to give them (together with their correlatives) distinguishing names, he felt obliged to defer to conservative feeling to the extent of using only words already current. In two instances the only words that he could find were words ("liability," "immunity") that were already in use with quite different meanings. The unfortunate result was that, while freeing the word "right" from equivocation, he created new equivocations for the two words so transferred. Notwithstanding this, Hohfeld deserves great praise for the way in which he accomplished his main task, the clarification of the word "right." Pollock's comment does him less than justice, and indeed, in my opinion, praises him for his only defect. "I do not doubt," wrote Pollock, "that the late Professor Hohfeld was a learned and ingenious man, and he seems to have had at least the merit of not inventing new words. But it is strange how many rational beings believe the ultimate truths of the universe to be reducible to patterns on a blackboard."[47] One must not treat a remark in correspondence, as this one was, as a considered opinion; but I must say that I have not seen anything in Hohfeld's work to suggest that he regarded himself as doing more than improving our symbolism, which seems to me to be a worthy purpose in itself.

The ambiguity of words gives trouble to lawyers not only in manipulating their own technical language but also in the construction of non-legal language in documents. Many words change their meaning in the course of time: (1) some become restricted,

47 Pollock-Holmes Letters (Cambridge, 1942), ii, 63.

(2) some widened, and (3) some transferred by metaphor, the original meaning either remaining or disappearing. To illustrate: (1) "asylum," originally any refuge, now means in particular a refuge for those mentally diseased; but the old meaning has not quite disappeared.[48] "Accident" etymologically means anything that happens, and this meaning is preserved in the remarkable judicial determination that murder is an "accident" within the Workmen's Compensation Acts;[49] but generally the word means only damage not caused intentionally, or (even more narrowly) damage not caused by fault. (2) "Committee" originally meant one individual to whom something was committed, the stress being on the last syllable. Both this meaning and this pronunciation have survived in some contexts, *e.g.,* in lunacy law; but generally nowadays a committee is not one person but a body of persons, and in this meaning the stress is shifted to the middle syllable.[50] "Animal" has undergone both processes: originally any creature with breath, it became widened in scientific circles to include all non-vegetable forms of life, *e.g.,* fish, and also became narrowed in popular use to include only quadrupeds.[51] Another instance of divorce between popular and scientific meaning is in the word "fish," where the popular meaning (any animal—in the scientific sense—living in water) is wider than the scientific meaning (cold-blooded vertebrate with gills, etc.).[52] (3) "Spirit" once meant breath, "person" meant a mask, "governor" meant the steersman of a ship; so frequent are these changes that language has been well called a dictionary of faded metaphors. When the native meaning of a word has quite disappeared, as in the last examples, it does not vex us; but often the meaning is in a transitional state and then it does. Thus words like "asylum," "committee," and "animal," when they appear in legal instruments, are capable of giving great difficulty of construction, and have in fact done so. Occasionally judges seem to be unduly slow to abandon an older literary meaning in favour of a newer popular one. There are two reasons for this: the first, that judges are often men of letters, and are through their reading more familiar with the older meaning than the

48 Dilworth v. Stamps Comr. [1899] A. C. 99, at 107-8.

49 Nisbet v. Rayne [1910] 2 K. B. 689; Trim School v. Kelly [1914] A. C. 667.

50 O. E. D., s.v.; Burrow's Words and Phrases, s.v.

51 O. E. D., s.v.; Burrow's Words and Phrases, s.v.

52 Cp. Leavett v. Clark [1915] 3 K. B. 9, where winkles were held to be "fish" —adopting the popular meaning.

ordinary person; the second, less creditable, that they are influenced by the "proper meaning" fallacy, which is to be discussed in § 6. In general it may be said that words ought not to be given an archaic meaning that the parties, situated as they were, would probably not have intended them to bear. One other general observation may be made before passing on: with modern works of reference, a draftsman usually has no excuse if he uses ambiguous words in an ambiguous context. If, for instance, the draftsman of a statute uses a word like "accident" or "animal" without defining it, it cannot be said that he is properly discharging the duty of his office.

(2) *Fringe meaning.* Some words, though not equivocal in the sense of having two or more distinct definitions, are yet obviously vague in their meaning, as for example "about," "near," "more or less." Such words, which ought generally to find no place in legal documents, give considerable trouble when they do occur.[53] What I am concerned to demonstrate in this section is that not merely some but all words are capable of occasioning difficulty in their application.[54] This is perhaps implicitly recognized in legal works on interpretation, but it is well to make it explicit. I shall consider in turn (*a*) words indicating qualities of continuous variation, (*b*) class-names, (*c*) names suggesting unity, (*d*) mathematical terms, and (*e*) words uncertain in their time-reference.

(*a*) Consider words for opposites like "white" and "black," "night" and "day," "open" and "shut," "good" and "bad." At first sight opposites like these may seem to be mutually exclusive. "A door," says the French proverb, "must be either open or shut." Similarly we may in our less lucid moments be tempted to think that it must always be night or day, and cannot be both at the same time. So obvious did this seem to the founders of logic that

[53] See Burrow's *Words and Phrases,* s.v.; 44 E. & E. Dig. 146-8. In the Labrador Boundary dispute (1927) the Privy Council had to determine how wide is a "coast": 137 L. T. 187.

[54] This topic is not discussed by Ogden and Richards. Non-legal writers on it are three heretical logicians: Sidgwick, *op. cit.;* Schiller, *op. cit.;* Bogoslovsky, *op. cit.* Cp. Locke, *op. cit.* 3, 5-6; Russell, *op. cit.* 197-8; Stebbing, *op. cit.* 62, and Cohen and Nagel. Introduction to Logic and Scientific Method (London, 1934), 118. Legal writers are chiefly Wurzel, "Methods of Juridicial Thinking," in Science of Legal Method (New York, 1921), basing himself upon Wundt's Logik; also Frank *op. cit.;* Chase, *op. cit.;* Clarence Morris, *How Lawyers Think* (Cambridge, Mass. 1938), 78-9.

they erected it into one of the three "laws of thought": a thing, they said, cannot be both *A* and not-*A*.

This theory, which once seemed patently true, is now held by a school of heterodox logicians to be just as patently false. A door can be, in a sense, both open and shut, or neither open nor shut; for it may be ajar. If "white" be defined as the property of reflecting all light, and "black" as the property of absorbing all light, then nothing is completely white and nothing is completely black, but every so-called "black" thing has elments of "whiteness," and every so-called "white" thing has elements of "blackness." Whiteness and blackness are therefore matters of degree. In fact, all words of the type instanced are simply the first and last members of a continuous series, and the extremes may be purely notional, having no existence in the world of sense-experience.

The difficulty of fixing the frontiers of words in situations like these was well brought out in the sophism of the schoolmen concerning the "heap." The sophism consisted in propounding the question: Does one stone make a heap? If the person questioned answered in the negative, the questioner then asked: Do one hundred stones make a heap? If this received an affirmative answer, the questioner asked similar questions for two stones, ninety-nine stones, three stones, ninety-eight stones, and so on, until he pinned his victim down to some such apparently absurd proposition as that eight stones do not make a heap but that nine stones do. The same game was played by asking how many hairs make a beard, or how many sheep a flock. The only sensible way of meeting the difficulty is to say that there is an area of uncertainty between the number of units that certainly do and those that certainly do not make the aggregate in question.

When one comes to consider them, one finds that these words for qualities of continuous variation exist in the language in altogether unsuspected numbers: and the fact of variation is obscured by the sharpness of the words used to describe the extremes. "Sane" and "insane," "drunk" and "sober," "democracy" and "dictatorship" are sharply contrasted words; but no chasm sunders the two states in the world as we know it.

Some logicians have pointed out two fallacies to which these polarities may give rise.[55] The first, which is much the commoner

[55] R. H. Thouless, *Straight and Crooked Thinking* (London, 1930), chap. 9; cp. L. S. Stebbing, *Thinking to Some Purpose* (Harmondsworth, 1939), 142-5.

of the two, has been called "the fallacy of white or black." It consists in supposing that every object must be white or black, without allowing for the possibility of its being something in between. As applied to the words "white" and "black" the fallacy is obvious; but as applied to such words as "good" and "bad," "honest" and "dishonest," "intelligent" and "unintelligent," it foments much needless controversy.

The second fallacy consists in arguing that black is white because there is a range of half-tones in between. For instance, if it is desired to prove that 5,000 stones do not make a heap, this can be proved by assuming that one stone does not make a heap, and that the addition of one stone, in itself, does not convert that which is not a heap into that which is a heap. This was the argument of the man who broke his camel's back by heaping straws upon it one at a time, thinking that a single straw could not break a camel's back. The fallacy is an ever-present danger in law and ethics, for it is often hard to see the objection to an argument of the "if this why not that?" type, which, if allowed to be pressed far enough, will make every exception swallow up the rule.

The difficulty of using such words as these does not press upon the ordinary man because it usually does not matter to him whether, for instance, he calls a number of stones a "heap" or not. All that matters is that he should make his meaning clear enough for the purpose on hand. Suppose that a housewife is following a cookery book which tells her to add a pinch of mustard to a particular dish. She cannot tell how many grains make a pinch, but she can guess what is meant by a pinch and if she puts too much, or too little, her palate will in due course discover her error.

With law it is different, for in law we make sharp consequences hang upon these words of gradation. The question whether a man is left in freedom or detained in a mental institution depends on whether he is judicially classified as sane or insane,[56] as also does the question whether his dispositions of property are upheld or not.[57] Whether a man is punished or acquitted may turn simply and

[56] See, *e.g.*, Lunacy Act, 1890, ss. 4, 28, and Sch. 2, Form 8.

[57] "The difficulty to be grappled with arises from the circumstance that the question is almost always one of degree. There is no difficulty in the case of a raving madman or a drivelling idiot in saying that he is not a person capable of disposing of property. But between such an extreme case and that of a man of perfectly sound and vigorous understanding, there is every shade of intellect, every degree of mental capacity. There is no possibility of mistaking midnight for noon;

solely upon whether an attempt to commit a crime was sufficiently "proximate", or upon whether a statement that he falsely swore was "material" to a judicial proceeding; and in a murder case it may be literally a question of life or death whether the accused intended to hurt by means of an act "intrinsically likely to kill."[58] Well may a convict echo the words of the poet—

> "Oh, the little more, and how much it is!
> And the little less, and what worlds away!"

In tort we have one rule for reservoirs, another for duck-ponds; and the Court somehow has to draw the line between the two. A libel is in "permanent" form and a slander in "transient" form; but permanency is a matter of degree. In the law of negligence and nuisance the defendant pays full damages or nothing according as the Court puts his conduct at the "reasonable" or "unreasonable" end of what is in fact a continuous gradation. So also with remoteness of damage. The law of vicarious liability abounds in such puzzles; thus (*a*) the employer of an independent contractor is not liable for him merely because he is employed to do an ordinarily hazardous act, but is liable for him if he is employed to do an extra-hazardous act[59]; (*b*) the distinction between a servant and an independent contractor rests on the infinitely variable matter of control; (c) the master of a servant who exceeds his authority is responsible for some excess, but not for excessive excess;[60] and (*d*) the master of a vanman who deviates from his route and negligently injures a pedestrian is liable if the deviation is a slight one but not if the deviation is such that every yard he goes is a yard away from his employment and not to it[61]—no precise angle being laid down. A contract to be valid must be "certain in its terms," and certainty of meaning is, as it is the object of these pages to show, a question of degree. The "lodger" shades off into the "lessee of a flat"; yet somehow the Courts must draw a line between them, because the relative law is different. In some parts of the law, such as copyright and charities, we must distinguish

---

but at what precise moment twilight becomes darkness is hard to determine": per Lord Cranworth L.C. in Boyse v. Rossborough (1857) 6 H. L. C. 2 at 45, quoted by Hannen J. in Boughton v. Knight (1873) L. R. 3 P. & D. 64 at 67.

58 The terminology is that of Kenny (Outlines of Criminal Law, 15th ed., 155); but the word "intrinsically" seems to be meaningless in this context.

59 Honeywill & Stein v. Larkin Bros. [1934] 1 K. B. 191.

60 Poland v. Parr [1927] 1 K. B. 236 at 243.

61 Pollock, Torts, 14th ed., 70-1.

between a thing that concerns "the public or a portion of the public" and a thing that concerns "private individuals," this resulting in innumerable perplexities.

Judges refuse to be frightened by these difficulties. They are not intimidated from saying that the case is on one side or the other of the line merely because they discover that the line is difficult to draw. Thus in one of the cases working out the limits of the rule against remoteness, where a limitation was upheld as not infringing the rule, Lord Nottingham said: "It hath been urged at the bar, where will you stop if you do not stop at *Child and Bayly's Case*? I answer, I will stop everywhere when any inconvenience appears, no where before":[62] Blackburn J. observed of the rule in *Hadley v. Baxendale*: "It is a vague rule, and as Bramwell B. said, it is something like having to draw a line between night and day; there is a great duration of twilight when it is neither night nor day; but on the question now before the Court, though you cannot draw the precise line, you can say on which side of the line the case is."[63] "Courts of Justice," said Chitty J., "ought not to be puzzled by such old scholastic questions as to where a horse's tail begins and where it ceases. You are obliged to say, 'This is a horse's tail,' at some time."[64] Similarly Lord Coleridge C.J.: "The Attorney-General has asked where we are to draw the line. The answer is that it is not necessary to draw it at any precise point. It is enough for us to say that the present case is on the right side of any reasonable line that could be drawn."[65] And Lindley M.R.: "It is urged that it is difficult to draw the line. I admit that it is extremely difficult. . . . It is always a question of degree. It may be asked, What is the difference between one cart and two, and so on? You cannot draw the line in that way. Nothing is more common in life than to be unable to draw the line between two things. Who can draw the line between plants and animals? And yet, who has any difficulty in saying that an oak tree is a plant and not an animal?"[66]

[62] Duke of Norfolk's Case (1681) 2 Swans. 454 at 468; 3 Chan. Cas. 14 at 36.

[63] Hobbs v. L. & S. W. Ry. (1875) L. R. 10 Q. B. 111 at 121. Cp. Scrutton L.J. in The San Onofre [1922] P. 243 at 253.

[64] Lavery v. Pursell (1888) 39 Ch. D. 508 at 517. See also Pollock C.B. in White v. Bluett (1853) 23 L. J. Ex. 36 at 37: "By the argument a principle is pressed to an absurdity, as a bubble is blown until it bursts."

[65] Mayor of Southport v. Morriss [1893] 1 Q. B. 359 at 361.

[66] Att.-Gen. v. Brighton & Hove Co-operative Supply Assn. [1900] 1 Ch. 276 at 282. Cp. per FitzGibbon L. J. in Gregg v. Fraser [1906] 1 Ir. R. 545 at 578-9:

So also, judges are not always deterred in framing new legal rules by the consideration that they may be hard to apply. In the words of Bowen L.J.: "It is not a valid objection to a legal doctrine that it will not be always easy to know whether the doctrine is to be applied in a particular case. The law has to face such embarrassments."[67] In the *Pollock-Holmes Letters* Holmes writes: "People in the law as elsewhere hate to recognize that most questions—I think I might say all legal questions—are questions of degree. I have just sent back an opinion of one of our JJ. with a criticism of an argument in it of the 'where are you going to draw the line' type—as if all decisions were not a series of points tending to fix a point in a line."[68]

Despite these brave words, it is to the interest of legal certainty that, other things being equal, the rules of law should be as clear of application as possible. Some words have a wider fringe of uncertainty than others, and for legal purposes those with the narrowest fringe are generally the best. Rules relating to "dangerous things," "extra-hazardous acts," and "excessive excess," are *prima facie* objectionable, because they require so many cases to be litigated. But the difficulty is to know whether other things *are* equal, *i.e.,* whether other needs are sufficiently strong to counterbalance the need for legal certainty. An illustration or two will show how the Courts have veered in this matter. In *Winterbottom v. Wright* (1842)[69] Alderson B. expressed himself thus: "The only safe rule is to confine the right to recover to those who enter into the contract; if we go one step beyond that, there is no reason why we should not go fifty." This was the kind of reasoning that Holmes disapproved, and in fact *Winterbottom v. Wright* was restrictively distinguished in *Donoghue v. Stevenson* (1932).[70] Similarly in *Colgate v. Bacheler* (1602)[71] it was held that all contracts in restraint of trade were void; "for as well as he may restrain him for one time or one place, he may restrain him for longer times and more places, which is against the benefit

"This is in each case a pure question on the construction of a written document, whether the case lies on the one side or on the other of a definite line in the mathematical sense—a line without breadth—every case must lie on one side of that line or on the other . . . and 'line balls' are barred."

67 Dashwood v. Magniac [1891] 3 Ch. 306 at 364.

68 Pollock-Holmes Letters (Cambridge, 1942), ii, 28.

69 10 M. & W. 109 at 115.

70 [1932] A. C. 562 at 588-9, 610.

71 Cro. Eliz. 872, Owen 143.

of the commonwealth." This rule also has been abandoned, and the Courts now essay the difficult task of drawing the line between reasonable and unreasonable restraint.[72] Thus an argument based on the difficulty of drawing a line is not a strong one; but, as already said, it is not altogether without force.

As an illustration of a legal distinction that is both misty and unnecessary, consider the distinction between contracts of sale of goods and contracts for work and materials. This distinction is made in popular speech but is not at all precise. One speaks, for instance, of "buying" a bottle of medicine from a chemist but not of buying one from a doctor. One "buys" a tailor-made suit but not false teeth. An amateur photographer who has his prints made by a chemist would not be very certain whether he was "buying" the prints or not; and one who orders a dog kennel to be specially made would probably not speak of "buying" it: he would speak of "getting a man to make it." In ordinary life these verbal distinctions do not matter; but lawyers, having created a needless legal distinction between contracts of sale and contracts for work and materials, have found themselves bogged in the uncertain borderland between them.

It is next to be observed that the situation in which a judge refuses to draw a precise line and determines simply whether a particular case is on the one or the other side of it is not always satisfactory. It appears to be satisfactory only because the same judge is not presented with a series of cases identical in all their facts except the variable fact under consideration. Take, for instance, the present rule as to deviation by servants driving vehicles in the course of their employment. At first sight this rule, which leaves everything to the judge's discretion, appears less arbitrary than a rule laying down a definite test of the employer's liability, *e.g.*, by fixing a precise angle, say forty-five degrees, as the maximum angle of deviation consistent with the employer's liability, or else by fixing the maximum proportion (*e.g.*, 50 per cent.) that the extra distance occasioned by the deviation must bear to the distance authorized by the master. But suppose that, with the law as it is, the same judge has to decide a series of cases involving the same vanman's deviation from the same line of his employment, the angle or proportionate length of deviation becoming

[72] Holdsworth, H. E. L. viii, 58 ff.

greater and greater in each case. It is clear that he would have to fix on some angle, or to draw some line on the map, as marking the watershed between what is a mere deviation and what is altogether outside the course of the employment. The line so chosen would be an arbitrary one. If the same judge had to decide many groups of such cases, he would probably fix upon some one angle or proportion which he would apply to all of them as a rough rule of thumb. Decisions given in pursuance of this rule of thumb would not be any more arbitrary than those now rendered without any rule at all; but the arbitrariness would be announced beforehand, which would facilitate the settling of cases without litigation.

There are many branches of the law where this process of settling a line has in fact taken place. Precise periods of time are commonly laid down in statutes. Instances are the statutory periods of limitation, which, though arbitrary, are preferable to a vague rule that laches defeats rights. At common law the definition of "night-time" for the purpose of the law of burglary was whether there was sufficient sun-light to discern a man's face[73]: by statute this was changed to the fixed period 9 p.m.—6 a.m.[74]

Sometimes fixed times are even laid down in the common law. A good illustration is the age of majority. The age of twenty-one was originally fixed by custom as the age of majority of tenants by knight's service. Pollock and Maitland, basing themselves on Bracton, suggest that it was the age at which heavy armour could be borne.[75] Other classes had their own rules: thus the young burgess was of full age when he could count money and measure cloth.[76] How the rule for tenants by knight's service became generalized we do not know; it may well have been the work of the judges. However it arose, the rule is clearly more satisfactory than one which bids us inquire whether the particular individual has attained the ability to look after his own affairs. Again, the judges have recognized or created earlier ages for particular purposes. Ideas as to the average age of puberty yielded the ages for consent to marriage—twelve for a female and four-

73 Hale's P. C. i. 550-1.

74 See now Larceny Act, 1916, s. 46. For another statutory definition see Night Poaching Act, 1828 (c. 69), s. 12.

75 P. & M., 2nd ed., ii, 438-9; Bracton, f. 86b.

76 P. & M. *loc cit.*

teen for a male,[77] and also the minimum age at which a boy could be convicted of rape (fourteen).[78] Children under seven were given complete exemption from criminal responsibility and those under fourteen a qualified exemption.[79] The period of minority became incorporated in the rule against remoteness,[80] and more recently in the rule against perpetual duration.[81] When the Court of Chancery wished to give extended protection to infants in respect of their ratifying contracts obtained during infancy by undue influence, it named one year as the extended period. "In the Court of Chancery," said Lord Cranworth, "we are obliged to cut the knot as to the question of time, by naming some time."[82] In the law of bills of exchange, definite times have been laid down as the limit of what is normally a reasonable time for the presentation of cheques[83] and the giving of notices of dishonour.[84] So, too, the Courts, following the practice of conveyancers, fixed sixty years as the period of title in general required to be shown under an open contract of sale[85]; later this period was successively reduced by statute to forty[86] and thirty[87] years. Another example of definite times being laid down by the judges is in the law of evidence. When the rule was first invented that ancient documents "prove themselves," no fixed meaning was assigned to the word "ancient." "But a more definite standard naturally became desirable. Since the lack of living witnesses to the document was the justifying fact, and since such witnesses might be assumed to have been at least of age at the time of execution, they would presumably have disappeared from the stage of life after the lapse of forty or at most fifty years. Accordingly the period of forty years came, by the 1700s, to be taken as the time when a document was treated as 'ancient' under this rule. But the reckoning was too strict, because the witnesses were

---

77 Co. Lit. 78b (following the canon law); see now Age of Marriage Act, 1929.

78 Hale, P. C. i, 630; Archbold, 31st ed., 12, 1021. At the other end of life, there is no fixed age at which a woman is taken to be past child-bearing: Wigmore, *Evidence,* 3rd ed., § 2528.

79 Hale, P. C. i, 25-8; see now Children and Young Persons Act, 1933, s. 50.

80 Holdsworth, H. E. L. vii, 226-7.

81 Re Hooper [1932] 1 Ch. 38; Nathan, *Equity Through the Cases,* pp. 163-5.

82 Smith v. Kay (1859) 7 H. L. C. 750 at 772.

83 Byles on Bills, 20th ed., 18, 19.

84 *Ibid.* 261-3.

85 Williams, *Vendor and Purchaser,* 4th ed., 112-5.

86 Vendor and Purchaser Act, 1874, s. 1.

87 Law of Property Act, 1925, s. 44.

more likely to have been mature persons, and therefore at least thirty years of age; and another thirty years would suffice to bring them near the end of their span. Ever since the second half of the 1700s, therefore, the period of thirty years has sufficed to constitute an 'ancient' document; except under special statutory rules."[88] It may be added that although the period was originally fixed by reference to the likelihood of the attesting witnesses being dead, the Courts now hold that it applies even though the witnesses are alive and in Court.[89]

Occasionally times have been fixed by analogy to a statute; that was how the year 1189 came to be hit upon for the period of prescription and custom,[90] and the period of seven years' absence as the period for presumption of death.[91] The former is a good example of the harmful nature of the fiction that judges do not make the law. Had the origin of the rule been frankly recognized, the rule might have been kept up to date by adopting the analogy of later statutes of limitation fixing new periods. As it was, the limit of legal memory was regarded as irrevocably settled, and it has become steadily more ridiculous with the passage of years.

There are other ways in which the common law has tied itself down to more or less precise rules. There is the forty-five degrees rule as a rough test of infringement of ancient lights.[92] The Statute of Forcible Entry, 1381, forbids an entry "with multitude of people," and Coke reports the opinion that a multitude consists of ten or more people—*multitudinem decem faciunt*; but he adds that he does not himself share this opinion, holding that the precise number is at the discretion of the judges.[93] Superficially this may sound the more reasonable view, but it is suggested

[88] Wigmore, *Evidence,* 3rd ed., § 2138. The period is reduced to twenty years by the Evidence Act, 1938, s. 4.

[89] Phipson, *Evidence,* 8th ed., 515.

[90] Holdsworth, H. E. L. iii, 166; vii, 343-5.

[91] Originally perhaps, the number seven was chosen as a magic number. As a rule of English law the rule first appears, in special applications, in James I's Bigamy Act, 1603, and in an Act of 1667 (19 Car. 2, c. 6). The general seven-year rule was first laid down, on the analogy of these two statutes, in Doe d. George v. Jesson (1805) 6 East 80. See Thayer, Preliminary Treatise on Evidence (London, 1898), 319-24.

Apart from absence there is no fixed period for the presumption of continuance of life; nor is there a fixed period for the presumption arising from the possession of goods "recently" stolen.

[92] Colls v. Home & Colonial Stores [1904] A. C. 179 at 204, 210; Davis v. Marrable [1913] 2 Ch. 421 at 430.

[93] Co. Lit. 257a.

that if in one case ten persons are held to constitute a crowd, there can be no reason why in another case it should be held that eleven persons do not constitute a crowd; and so for other figures. It will be recollected that in the similar offence of unlawful assembly, an assembly is defined as a meeting of three or more persons.[94] In my submission this fixing of precise times and amounts is in every way a desirable one, and should be extended.

Another method of meeting the difficulty caused by continuous variation in nature is to provide a continuous variation in legal results. This can be done in some cases by giving the judge a wide discretion as to damages or punishment. A good illustration is *Kiddell v. Burnard* (1842),[95] where it was argued that a horse was not unsound within the meaning of a warranty if the unsoundness were slight. Parke B. said: "An argument has been adduced from the slightness of the disease and facility of cure; but if we once let in considerations of that kind, where are we to draw the line? A horse may have a cold, which may be cured in a day; or a fever, which may be cured in a week or month; and it would be difficult to say where to stop. Of course, if the disease be slight, the unsoundness is proportionably so, and so also ought to be the damages." Another illustration is the Admiralty rule, now to be applied by statute to non-maritime cases, allowing apportionment of damages in cases of contributory negligence. There is no necessity to adopt an "all or nothing" rule as the common law does in these cases; the damages can be made to vary according to degrees of fault.

Where perfect elasticity of legal consequence is impossible, something can be done to mirror nature by multiplying categories. Thus the Mental Deficiency Act, 1927, subdivides the class of mental defectives into idiots, imbeciles, feeble-minded persons, and moral defectives. But there is still a great gulf fixed between this class as a whole and the class of so-called normal persons. One day we may recognize that the class of "normal" persons itself needs subdivision, for it includes neurotics and others needing therapeutic treatment and special economic assistance.

(*b*) Hitherto in this section we have considered chiefly pairs of words that indicate the poles of a continuous variation. We are

[94] Dicey, *Law of the Constitution,* 9th ed., 562-3, 8th ed., 501; Field v. Receiver of Metropolitan Police [1907] 2 K. B. 853 (riot).
[95] 9 M. & W. 668.

now to consider class-names, which we shall find show much the same characteristic.

Classes are sometimes divided into two sorts, natural (*e.g.*, lions), and artificial (*e.g.*, buildings). Taking artificial classes first, it is obvious that very great difficulty may be found in determining what falls within them. "The imperfection of human language", said Byles, J., in *Stevens v. Gourley* (1859),[96] "renders it not only difficult, but absolutely impossible, to define the word 'building' with any approach to accuracy. One may say of this or that structure, this or that is not a building; but no general definition can be given; and our lexicographers do not attempt it." Many other instances of the difficulty of putting metes and bounds to artificial classes will be found in the reports. For instance: is an album a "book"?[97] Is a bicycle a "carriage"?[98] Is a flag a "document"?[99] Is a flying-boat a "ship or vessel"?[1] Are household goods "money"?[2] Is ice-cream "meat"?[3] Is sandstone a "mineral"?[4] And so on.

These difficulties in the case of artificial classes are familiar enough to lawyers; but it may come as a surprise to learn that much the same puzzles are found in dealing with the so-called "natural" classes.

One aspect of the medieval "realist" theory was the idea that "natural" classes exist in nature, ready-made, with clear-cut edges. The world was full of lions and tigers, trees and apples, gold and silver, and all that man had to do was to learn their names. This is still the attitude of the child. Even when it came to be admitted that words were of human invention, it was still thought that the classes to which they applied existed in nature, fixed and immutable.

Modern scientists and some modern philosophers reject this view. Their arguments run along two main lines, which may be called the logical and the evolutionary.

96 7 C. B. (v. s.) 99 at 112.

97 Burrow's *Words and Phrases*, s.v.—no.

98 *Ibid.* s. v.—yes.

99 Phipson, *Evidence*, 8th ed., 524—no.

1 Polpen Shipping Co. v. Commercial Union Assurance Co. [1943] K. B. 161—no.

2 Perrin v. Morgan [1943] A. C. 399—yes.

3 Slater v. Evans [1916] 2 K. B. 403—no.

4 North British Ry. v. Budhill, etc. Co. [1910] A. C. 116; cp. Lord Macmillan, *Law and Other Things* (Cambridge, 1937), 155-7.

(i) Class-names being the result of abstraction, agreement upon class-names requires agreement upon the qualities that are regarded as essential to the class. Suppose that all the individuals hitherto regarded as belonging to a class possess the qualities a, b, c and d. It may come to be thought that these qualities are essential to qualify for the class-name. But now suppose that a new individual is found possessing qualities a, b and c, but not d. The question may then arise whether the former definition is to be maintained, resulting in an exclusion of a new-found individual from the class; or whether it is to be modified, allowing of his inclusion. A vivid illustration is that of the black swans of Australia: so imbued were zoologists with the idea that whiteness was a property of swans, that when black swans were discovered in Australia it was at first determined to allot them not to the genus *Cygnus* but to the genus *Chenopis.* Even to-day ornithologists are undecided whether to class bearded tits as tits; they possess some, but not all, the characteristics common to the other birds called tits. The question is, of course, a verbal one; but that it can be raised at all shows the artificiality of class-distinctions.

(ii) Astronomers, geologists, biologists and physicists combine in their different ways to prove the truth of the Heraclitan idea that reality is in a flux. To go back to the beginning, the earth was once a flaming mass, and life started with elementary forms. The classes that now seem to be so fixed in nature can be traced in large measure to an undifferentiated origin; nor can we be confident that the process of change has stopped. This is particularly evident in biology.[5] Take as an illustration the class *man,* symbolized by the word "man." In most of its applications the meaning of this word is clear. But the man has developed out of the lower animals, and there is no serious break between him and the amoeba. At what point in the line of Adam's ancestors shall we first refuse to apply the label "man"? Clearly our limit must be an arbitrary one. We may even find difficulty in applying the word to present-day situations, if, for instance, we are asked to consider a foetus or a corpse.

The difficulty that thus confronts us with the word "man" is also experienced with other class-names, and indeed with all general

5 "The concept of species has lost all the quality of immutability originally postulated by Linnaeus. As a result of Darwin's work, the idea of change has supplanted that of changelessness in regard to all biological groups:" Huxley, Haddon and Carr-Saunders, *We Europeans* (Harmondsworth, 1939), 95.

names. There are no words for a class, quality or relation the application of which to concrete instances is not capable of giving rise to difficulty. It is not that similarities and differences do not exist in nature; they abound in nature. The difficulty is in drawing firm lines around or between them.

It is true that the likelihood of trouble in the case of some classes is so small that it may be ignored; or, as Sidgwick put it, "some classes are, for all practical purposes to-day, conspicuously definite and unlikely to need any change of definition to-morrow."[6] But this is a matter of probability, not of certainty; and with the advance of science the scientist has become more and more reluctant to dogmatize on class-boundaries.

In the case of both artificial and so-called natural classes there are certain special elements of difficulty. One difficulty, already noticed in the case of natural classes, is in deciding when a thing begins and ends as a member of a class—when the egg becomes a chick, when coal becomes cinder, and so on.[7] A second difficulty arises from "impurity"; thus "water" is rigidly defined by the chemist, but one can put a progression ranging (say) from sea-water to cabbages in which the extent of application of the word will not be at all clear. In regard to biological terms, nature is continually inventing hybrids to puzzle and confuse us in our nomenclature.[8] A third difficulty is that of saying whether a part of an individual thing is entitled to the class-name enjoyed by the thing as a whole: for instance, whether an anchor is part of a "vessel," so as to make a collision with an anchor a collision with the vessel to which the anchor is attached.[9] A fourth, felt particularly in the law, is the difficulty of distinguishing between "land" and "chattels." Take any heavy article (*e.g.,* a piece of trade machinery) and imagine it screwed down; is it still what it was before—"trade machinery"—or is it now "land"?[10]

6 Sidgwick, *op. cit.* 155. A good illustration is the distinction between living and dead things. But even this distinction is not absolutely sharp: see Bogoslovsky, *op. cit.* 63-5.

7 Cp. Thomas W. Ward Ltd. v. Waugh [1933] S. L. T. 619, where the question was whether a ship that was being broken up was still a "vessel."

8 Cp. Heath's Case (1801) 2 East P. C. 609-10, where it was held that "any red or fallow deer" included the cross breeds, such as a bastard menald, bred from a menald buck and a fallow doe. ("Fallow"—light brown; "menald"—dappled chestnut.)

9 Re Margetts and Ocean Accident, etc., Corpn. [1901] 2 K. B. 792—yes.

10 In re Yates, Batcheldor v. Yates (1888) 38 Ch. D. 112 (held, land).

The upshot is that the words we use, though they have a central core of meaning that is relatively fixed, are of doubtful application to a considerable number of marginal cases. In general, we try in our language to sharpen our distinctions beyond what is warranted by the facts of the case. It is a necessary feature of language that we should have to make this effort, and thus it is inevitable that our linguistic distinctions should constantly break down.

Once again it must be remarked that the ordinary man is not usually troubled with these perplexities. It does not matter to a seaman whether an anchor is or is not called part of a "vessel." A chemist does not need to answer the question, yes or no, does a rolled-gold watch come within the description "gold"? Biologists may find difficulty with their classifications, but nothing turns on the question whether they classify a creature under one heading or another; it is simply a question of verbal expediency. With the lawyer it is different. The lawyer, like the theologian, is faced with a number of texts that he regards as authoritative, and that are supposed to settle any question that can conceivably arise. Each text was at one time drawn up by someone who presumably meant something by it; but once the document has left its author's hands it is the document that matters, not any unexpressed meaning that still remains in the author's mind. For the lawyer the words of the document are authoritative as words, and there is generally no possibility of obtaining further information from the author, either because the author is dead, or because of rules of evidence precluding reference to him, or because a reference to the author would infringe a rule requiring the document to be in a certain form. It is this inability to refer to the author, coupled with the inherent vagueness of language, that makes interpretation such a perennial source of legal difficulty.

Before leaving the subject of classes, a few remarks may be made on some rules of law that refer explicitly to classes or kinds. One such rule is to be found in the law of remoteness of damage, or at any rate was to be found there before the decision In *Re Polemis* (1921).[11] The general principle was that if the consequence was not foreseeable by the defendant in kind, he was not responsible for it either in contract or in tort; but "when it is found that a man ought to have foreseen in a general way conse-

11 [1921] 3 K. B. 560.

quences of a certain kind, it will not avail him to say that he could not foresee the precise course or the full extent of the consequences, being of that kind, which in fact have happened."[12] Upon this distinction a wag once inquired whether the difference between a difference of kind and a difference of degree is itself a difference of kind or a difference of degree. The answer that will be gathered from the foregoing pages is that it is a difference of degree. A difference of kind is merely a violent difference of degree.[13] The impossibility of drawing a sharp line between kind and degree is clearly evidenced by the cases. If I push a man down, I can foresee that he may be hurt but I cannot foresee that he will die; yet if in fact he suffers from an egg-shell skull, a fatty heart, or haemophilia, and so unexpectedly dies, it was clear even before *Re Polemis* that I am liable for this consequence.[14] Thus, to save the rule, death must be regarded as a consequence of the same kind as pain; though many might think it a consequence of an altogether different kind. Sometimes the kind-degree distinction seems to be applied not to the ultimate harm but to the way in which the harm is brought about. If my quiet horse strays on the highway and kicks a child, the consequence before *Re Polemis* was too remote,[15] apparently because it was unforeseeable in kind. But if the horse strays and, being frightened by a boy, takes to flight and injures a child in its headlong career, inflicting precisely the same injury as in the previous instance it inflicted when at a standstill, the consequence (given an initial breach of duty[16]) was probably not too remote.[17] The damage is the same; it is only the causal sequence that is supposed in the first case to be different in kind from what could have been foreseen. When distinctions like these are drawn it may not seem altogether a bad thing that in *Re*

[12] Pollock in (1922) 38 L. Q. R. 167; Smith v. L. & S. W. Ry. (1870) L. R. 6 C. P. 14 particularly per Blackburn J. at 22-3; Goodhart, "The Palsgraf Case," Essays in Jurisprudence and the Common Law (Cambridge, 1937), 129.

[13] I recently asked a well-known biologist if he could give me from the whole field of biology one clear example of a difference which scientists would unequivocally agree upon as a difference in kind, and another which they would agree upon as a difference in degree, so that there would be no longer any doubt about the precise meanings of the two words. He was unable to give the required examples. I have since put the query to a number of other scientists and psychologists with no better luck: R. A. Wilson, The Miraculous Birth of Language (London, 1941), 81.

[14] Per Kennedy J. in Dulieu v. White [1901] 2 K. B. 669 at 679.

[15] Cox v. Burbidge (1863) 13 C. B. (n.s.) 430; cp. Williams, *Liability For Animals* (Cambridge, 1939), 159 ff.

[16] Cp. Deen v. Davies [1935] 2 K. B. 282.

[17] Cp. Patterson v. Fanning (1901) 2 O. L. R. 462; Williams, *op. cit.* 170, 382.

Polemis (1921) the Court of Appeal purported to abandon the test of reasonable foresight as a rule for remoteness of damage. According to this decision, damage is not too remote merely because the defendant could not have foreseen it in kind. The new rule, however, has difficulties of its own, and it is still not at all certain how far it will be applied. *The Edison* (1933)[18] casts doubt on the extent even of the rule than damage is not too remote merely because unforeseeable in degree. In that case the plaintiffs recovered damages for the loss of use of their dredger during a normal period of replacement, but not for loss of use during the extended period of replacement necessitated by their own poverty. It might have been thought that this was a mere difference in the degree of damage, for which the defendants were liable. Contract cases are in an equally puzzling state; some of them seem to apply the rule that the defendant is liable for an unexpected difference of degree,[19] but most do not.[20] Some sort of reconciliation can perhaps be made by distinguishing between remoteness of damage and measure of damages; thus it may be said that *Re Polemis* regulates the question whether the defendant is liable for the loss of the ship, while *The Edison* regulates the amount of damages that he must pay in respect of the ship if he is held to be liable for its loss, *i.e.,* it regulates the way in which the physical loss is to be translated into terms of money. But this distinction is itself a very unclear one, for it varies according to the loss that is being attended to. If in *The Edison* we consider the loss of the ship, the question whether the plaintiffs can recover for their loss in respect of their dredging contract appears as a question of measure of damages for the loss of the ship. But if we consider directly the loss in respect of the dredging contract, and inquire whether the defendant is liable for it, we turn the question into one of remoteness of damage.

18 [1933] A. C. 449.

19 Phillips v. L. & S. W. Ry. (1879) 4 Q. B. D. 406 (plaintiff compensated for loss of income on basis of actual income, although unusually large; but Cockburn C.J. seemed to indicate that the damages might be reduced if "the attempt to award full compensation in damages might be attended with ruinous consequences to defendant"); Great Lakes S.S. Co. v. Maple Leaf Milling Co. (1924) 41 T. L. R. 21 at 23 ("If grounding takes place in breach of contract, the precise nature of the damage incurred by grounding is immaterial").

20 E.g., Hobbs v. L. & S. W. Ry. (1875) L. R. 10 Q. B. 111 (recovery for inconvenience of having to walk home in the rain, but not for catching cold in consequence—surely more a difference of degree than the difference between pain and death, which is settled to be one of degree); The Arpad [1934] P. 189.

All things considered, it seems that the best we can hope for in this part of the law is a number of detailed rules regulating as precisely as possible the situations that occur in practice. It seems evident that the effort to bring all cases under a very few broad principles is doomed to failure, or at best can result in nothing but the palest of generalities.

Comparable to remoteness of damage in civil law is transferred malice in criminal law. The rule is that malice may be regarded as "transferred" where the harm done is of the kind intended, though not otherwise. It is settled that for the purpose of this rule an injury to *A* is of the same kind as a similar injury to *B*,[21] but an injury to the person is not of the same kind as damage to property.[22] To give an illustration of the difficulties met with in working the rule, suppose that the prisoner has intentionally (*i.e.*, in technical language, maliciously) set fire to chattels in a house, the fire then unintentionally spreading to the house; is the prisoner's malice transferred to the house? On the rule above stated, the answer depends on whether damage to chattels is regarded as being of the same kind as damage to a house (both being species of the genus "damage to property"), or whether it is of a different kind. The answer given by the judges is that it is of a different kind.[23] Clearly the answer might just as well have been the other way. Similar verbal jugglery is possible in working the *ejusdem generis* rule.[24]

Consider again, the law of *non est factum*. This operates as an exception to the salutary general principle that a person who signs a document without taking the trouble to read it is liable on it, and cannot plead that he mistook its contents; it also operates as an exception to the general rule of estoppel. The exception is that if the defendant thought that the document he signed belonged to an entirely different legal category from that to which it in fact belonged, he can plead *non est factum* and escape liability although he did not trouble to read the document and although he misled the plaintiff into supposing that he was agreeing.[25] The exception

21 R. v. Latimer (1886) 17 Q. B. D. 359.

22 R. v. Pembliton (1874) 2 C. C. R. 119: Kenny, *Outlines of Criminal Law*, 15th ed., 170, 189-90.

23 *R. v. Child* (1871) 1 C. C. R. 307; *R. v. Nattrass* (1882) 15 Cox 73.

24 Williams, "The Origin and Logical Implications of the *Ejusdem Generis* Rule," (1943) 7 The Conveyancer, 119.

25 On the question whether negligence alters the case see Anson in (1912) 28 L. Q. R. 190 and Underhay in (1930) 8 Can. Bar Rev. 661.

is nothing but an archaic and irrational survival; it is objectionable on the score of policy, and it is also open to practical objection as involving the Courts in the difficulty of distinguishing between a mistake of terms and a mistake of legal category. A good illustration of the difficulty is *Howatson v. Webb* (1908).[26] A solicitor asked his clerk to take a conveyance of certain property at E. as his nominee, and the clerk complied. Later the clerk was asked by the solicitor to execute certain deeds "transferring the E. property"; this he did without reading them, supposing them to be conveyances on sale. One was actually a mortgage containing a covenant by the clerk to repay the principal money and interest. The Court of Appeal, affirming Warrington J., held that the clerk was liable on the covenant. In the view of Warrington J., which was approved by the Court of Appeal, the mistake was merely "as to the contents of the deed, not as to the character or class of the deed."[27] This seems to mean that a conveyance on sale and a mortgage belong to the same legal class, namely, "conveyance." But the Court might easily have taken the opposite view, that conveyance on sale and mortgage were different types of transaction, as indeed most lawyers would suppose them to be.

A case in which it was held that the document signed belonged to a different class from that supposed is *Foster v. Mackinnon* (1869).[28] The defendant was induced to endorse a bill of exchange on the assurance that it was a guarantee; it was held that he could plead *non est factum* even against a holder in due course. This is puzzling, for in law the endorsement of a negotiable instrument *is* a guarantee, though one of a special kind. It is therefore difficult to see how the Court could hold, as it did, that the contract was "of a nature altogether different from the contract pretended to be read from the paper."[29]

Howatson v. Webb and *Foster v. Mackinnon* afford good illustrations of the emptiness of a rule referring to classes when the

---

Landon in (1935) 51 L. Q. R. 274 points out that the plea of *non est factum, eo nomine,* was confined to actions of covenant brought upon deeds, the analogous pleas for simple contracts in writing being *nil debet* and *non assumpsit.* But it is convenient to have the single name "*non est factum*" for all cases, and this extended use of the expression is allowed by modern usage.

26 [1908] 1 Ch. 1 (C. A.), affg. [1907] 1 Ch. 537.

27 [1907] 1 Ch. 537 at 549.

28 L. R. 4 C. P. 711.

29 Cp. the criticism on this score in (1921) 37 L. Q. R. 514 and (1923) 39 L. Q. R. 131.

classes are not specified in detail. Both decisions were unpredictable by means of this rule, and they have done little to establish a basis of prediction for new situations.

An understanding of the artificial nature of classes should help English lawyers to avoid importing into their system the complexities of the Roman law of *specificatio,* which was largely a product of erroneous Greek philosophy. According to the Greeks, every tangible thing was supposed to be a combination of matter (substance) and form. The purely linguistic character of this distinction was not perceived, and, to make matters worse, the Greeks disputed as to the relative importance of the two supposed elements. Aristotle and the peripatetics thought that form was primary, while the stoics gave primacy to matter. These differences (in reality verbal, like the root distinction from which they sprang) were thought by Roman lawyers to have important legal consequences. Two schools of thought sprang up corresponding to the two schools of philosophy. The Proculians, following Aristotle, held that a person who gave a thing a new form thereby created a new thing and acquired a new property in it, even though he did not own it before the change. The Sabinians, following the peripatetics, denied this. The Proculian view, which was partially adopted by Justinian, gave rise to any amount of subtlety on the question what was a change of form—*i.e.,* of species.[30] In the majority of cases the rule meant that merely altering a thing in such a way as to alter its name conferred property.

So far there is no conclusive authority compelling English lawyers to tread the same path. Bracton, indeed, gives a partial statement of the Roman rule, but very briefly and without discussion.[31] In the Year Books the question is discussed not as a question of *specificatio,* the making of a new species of thing, but on the distinctively English basis that ownership is lost when the marks of ownership are lost, *i.e.,* when the chattel becomes unrecognizable as the same chattel. It was for this reason that, in a case of 1489/90, it was held that the making of leather into shoes did not change the ownership, and the owner of the leather was

[30] See generally Cornil, Droit Romain (Brussels, 1921), 201; Buckland, Text-Book of Roman Law, 2nd ed. (Cambridge, 1932), 215-8; same, Main Institutions of Roman Private Law (Cambridge, 1931), 136-8.

[31] F. 10a: *"Adquiritur etiam nobis per specificationem, ut si quis de alienamateria speciem fecerit aliquam, dominus erit speciei qui fecit";* cp. Azo in Maitland's Bracton and Azo (S.S.), 122-4, and see *ibid.* xx. So also Bl. Comm. ii, 404.

entitled to recapt[32] the shoes.[33] In a case of 1559, shortly after the end of the Year-Book period, the rule is given in a slightly "philosophical" form by saying that notice—*i.e.,* the means of recognition—is not lost so long as that which remains is "the principal part of the substance—*major pars substantiae.*"[34] Here the philosophy seems to be rather that of the stoics than that of Aristotle; if pushed far enough it would result in a denial of any change of ownership in cases of *specificatio.* The actual decision in the last case was that where trees were wrongfully cut and turned into timber, the owner could recapt the timber—for this there was Year-Book authority; but the Court added, apparently *obiter,* that the owner could have exercised his right of recaption even if the trees had been cut into boards. The latter remark appears to be inconsistent with the recognition theory, for trees can hardly be recognized after they have been cut into boards.[35] It seems, therefore, that the case, while paying lip-service to the recognition theory, shows a tendency to abandon it in favour of a theory of continuance of "substance." Another mixture of medieval legal ideas with philosophical notions is to be seen in

---

32 This useful word is not in the dictionaries. Future dictionary-makers should give the credit for its invention to Professor Hollond, who uses it in his lectures.

33 Y. B. (1489/90) H. 5 H. 7, 15b, pl. 6. "And as to the cases of grain taken and malt made from it, the party cannot take it, because the grain cannot be known. And so it is with pennies or groats, where one piece is made of them, it cannot be taken, because of the pennies one cannot be known from another. And so it is if a man takes one piece, and strikes pennies from it at the mint, the party cannot take the pennies, because the pennies cannot be known one from another. And so of all like cases. And also in the case of the building of a house, now the timber is altered, for now it is freehold, and for this reason he cannot take it. But in every case where the things themselves can be known, there the party can take them, notwithstanding that some chattel is joined or mixed with them. As if a man takes a piece of cloth and makes a cloak for himself, the party can take it back well enough, because it is the same thing and not at all altered. And so it is in the case put, if one cuts a tree and squares it, the party can take it well enough, because the tree can be known well enough, notwithstanding. And so it is of iron, where a smith makes of it a bar, etc. And so it was held by the whole Court." The same doctrine was stated in Y. B. (1520) M. 12 H. 8, 9b, pl. 2, where it was held that the killing of a hart did not change the property, and the owner was entitled to retake the corpse from the killer. "Although it is dead and has lost its name (for *bos mortuus non est bos*), still it is the same thing as was taken out of my possession, and so it is lawful for me to retake it": *per* Eliot J. at f. 10b. "But if it be roasted or baked, then I cannot take it, for I have lost the notice of it; as if one takes my silver cup or my gold chain and melts it, I cannot take it, for I cannot have notice of it": *per* Brudnel J. at f. 11a.

34 *Anon.,* Moore (K. B.) 19, pl. 67.

35 But it will be recalled that in the case of 1489/90 (last note but one) it was said that a tree can still be known although it is squared, and iron although it is made into a bar. I should say that as a proposition of fact this is false.

Doderidge J.'s *English Lawyer,* published posthumously in 1631.[36] Doderidge begins by stating the Year-Book doctrine. He says that if a man steals my barley and makes it into malt, I cannot recapt the malt because I cannot distinguish it as mine. Similarly if my ox is killed, I cannot take the flesh because I cannot distinguish it: but if the ox be found hanging in the skin, whereby the mark may appear, I may seize it. This is good medieval law, but immediately afterwards Doderidge, who had a reputation as a civilian, gives it a philosophical twist.

> "Inasmuch as the forme giveth the essence, it was said of Ulpian the Romane Lawyer, out of the rules of Logicke, that *mutata forma prope interimitur substantia rei*:[37] for so in the former examples wee see, that if a man take my Barley and make Malt thereof, it cannot be seised by the former Owner; and yet neither matter, quantity nor outward forme is lost, but is become a thing of another nature and use, because the inward forme (to speak as Morall Philosophers) whereof dependeth the use, is changed; for Morall Philosophy doth not so curiously observe the naturall causes as Naturall Philosophy; but according to the information of manners."[38]

In Doderidge's statement of the law, then, we can detect two distinct strands: (1) the medieval English rule, originally perhaps a rule of evidence but become a rule of substantive law, that ownership is lost when the thing itself cannot be recognized, and (2) the Proculian rule, based on the philosophy of Aristotle, according to which a thing that has been so altered as to deserve a new name becomes a new thing capable of new ownership. In the background, not consciously avowed but perhaps helping to maintain these technical rules, there may possibly be (3) some very

36 Pages 126-7, 132-3.

37 Dig. 10, 4, 9, 3: *Mutata forma prope interemit substantiam rei*—not on *specificatio* and evidently quoted by Doderidge from memory.

38 Doderidge goes on to give other analogous rules. (1) If the bailee of a whole piece of cloth cuts it up and offers it back in this condition, this is no lawful restitution. This seems to mean that detinue lies. (2) A bequest of wool is adeemed if after the date of the will the testator converts his wool into cloth. (3) A common of estovers for a dwelling-house is lost if the dwelling-house be destroyed, even though another be built at another place near, or in another form; *aliter* if another house be built upon the same foundation, and in the same form. (4) A man has a water-corn-mill with a right of watercourse over a neighbour's land. If he changes the corn-mill into a fulling-mill he still has the right of watercourse, "for that it did not belong unto the Corne-mill, as specially unto a Corne-mill, but it did belong unto it generally as unto a mill going on or driven with water, and not otherwise."

slight tinge of an idea of fairness or public policy, according to which a person who has worked upon another's chattel, at any rate if he has acted in good faith, ought to be recompensed. But it must be admitted that the rules as stated give hardly any effect to this idea.

What is the law to-day? It is submitted that rule (2) is the result of an erroneous philosophy. There is no sufficient authority for saying that it has ever been made part of English law: at most there is the bare statement of Bracton, obviously copying Roman sources, and Doderidge's self-contradictory exposition in a didactic work. Rule (1) was the law once, but it is submitted that it has become obsolete with the decay of the idea that ownership depends upon the marks of ownership.[39] Thus, at the present day, the mere fact that a chattel has been changed beyond recognition, or has been so changed as to entitle it to a new name, does not create any new ownership in it. Nevertheless, as Salmond pointed out, over and above the question of ownership there arises the question of restitution.[40] It is this question that gives scope for the working out of (3) the idea of fairness and public policy. If *B* wrongfully takes *A's* chattel and does work upon it, *A* cannot get an order for specific restitution save at the discretion of the Court, and the Court will probably give him it only on terms that he pays for *B's* work, at any rate if *B* has not acted dishonestly. If *A* sues for damages, his damages will be based on the value of the article at the time when *B* took it, not upon its value in its embellished state.[41] The only trouble arises over recaption, and it is submitted that on this the medieval authorities are unsatisfactory. Recaption ought not to be permitted in any case where the defendant or a person through whom he claims has increased the value of the thing.

Another rule that may let in the subtleties of *specificatio* is the rule that while the destruction of a thing grounds trover, damage to a thing does not. Salmond suggested that "the test of destruction, as opposed to mere damage, is presumably the disappearance of

---

39 It is, however, uncritically repeated in Williams on Personal Property, 18th ed., 26.

40 Salmond, Torts, 10th ed., 316-7, § 82, 3.

41 Reid v. Fairbanks (1853) 13 C. B. 692, approved by Bramwell B. in Chinery v. Viall (1860) 5 H. & N. 288 at 295; Caxton Publishing Co. v. Sutherland Publishing Co. [1939] A. C. 178 (where the plaintiffs recovered the value of the sheets which were their fictional property but not the value of the books into which they had been bound): Mayne, *Damages,* 10th ed., 378 ff.

the identity of the article. Grapes are presumably destroyed when they are turned into wine, cotton when it is woven into cloth, corn when it is ground into flour."[42] It is submitted that, on the contrary, the test of destruction is whether the defendant's act has made the thing practically worthless. To admit Salmond's suggestion would be to introduce into the law the subtleties of classification that Salmond himself expels from it in his discussion of *specificatio*.

A similar question arises in the law of carriage by sea. The rule is that the shipowner cannot claim freight if he does not deliver the goods contracted to be carried, but can claim it if he does deliver them, notwithstanding that they are in a damaged condition (in both cases he may, of course, be liable in damage). The question arises whether the shipowner can claim freight where the goods have, in the current phrase, "lost their identity," as "where a valuable picture has arrived as a piece of spoilt canvas, cloth in rags, or crockery in broken shreds, iron all, or almost all rust, rice fermented, or hides rotten." The test suggested by Willes C.J. was "to ascertain from the terms of the contract, construed by mercantile usage, if any, what was the thing for the carriage of which freight was to be paid, and by the aid of a jury to determine whether that thing, or any and how much of it, has substantially arrived."[43] This test is open to objection as depending merely upon the verbal classifications of things; nor has it been uniformly acted upon by the Courts. Thus in *Garrett v. Melhuish* (1858),[44] bricks were shipped and were found on arrival to be reduced to dust, which was afterwards sold for a very small sum. Stuart V.-C. held that freight was payable. It is submitted that this decision is consistent with the proper rule, which is that freight is payable notwithstanding that the goods carried have become so changed that we apply a new name to them, and is not payable only if they have become substantially worthless. The only doubt as to *Garrett v. Melhuish* is whether on the facts of that case the goods had become substantially worthless; but the fact that they were saleable at all seems to indicate a negative answer. In *Duthie v. Hilton* (1868)[45] the cargo was cement which became hardened

[42] Torts, 10th ed., 294, § 74. 11.
[43] Dakin v. Oxley (1864) 15 C. B. (n.s.) 646 at 667.
[44] 4 Jur. (N.S.) Part I, 943.
[45] 4 C. P. 138.

into solid masses by the action of water. It was held that no freight was payable, Keating and Brett JJ. saying that the goods had been destroyed and Montague Smith J. saying that they had "ceased to exist as cement." It is submitted that the proper reason for the decision was not that the goods no longer deserved the name "cement" but that they were worthless. In the next case *Asfar v. Blundell* (1895)[46] the question arose in particularly neat form, there the cargo consisted of dates, which were sunk and later raised; it was then found that the dates were inedible but of considerable value for the purpose of distillation into spirit. The Court of Appeal unanimously held that no freight was payable. Lord Esher M.R. said: "The first point taken on behalf of the defendants, the underwriters of the freight, is that there has been no total loss of the dates. . . . The ingenuity of the argument might commend itself to a body of chemists, but not to business men. . . . The test is whether, as a matter of business, the nature of the things has been altered. The nature of a thing is not necessarily altered because the thing itself has been damaged; wheat or rice may be damaged, but may still remain the things dealt with as wheat or rice in business. But if . . . the thing . . . is so changed in its nature by the perils of the sea as to become an unmerchantable thing, which no buyer would buy and no honest seller would sell, then there is a total loss." This statement is open to severe objection. The words in the last sentence "which no buyer would buy" must mean "which no buyer would buy under the original name of the article unless the nature of the damage were stated by the seller at the outset." The words cannot mean what they say without qualification, for the dates in the case at bar were actually sold for the not inconsiderable sum of £2,400; yet there was held to be a total loss. But if the words are given the meaning first suggested, they fail to point a contrast with the damaged wheat or rice: for no buyer would buy, and no honest seller would sell, damaged wheat or rice unless the nature of the damage were stated before the contract; yet a buyer might buy them, and an honest seller might sell them, if such damage were stated and the price reduced accordingly.

Thus while *Asfar v. Blundell* must be taken as introducing the linguistic test into the law of freight, it should be regarded as an

[46] (1896) 1 Q. B. 123.

unfortunate decision, and the hope may be expressed that it will one day he overruled by the supreme tribunal.[47]

These cases on liability for freight are really part of the law of failure of consideration. A somewhat similar question of failure of consideration arises in the law of sale of goods. To take the classic illustration of Lord Abinger,[48] if there is a contract to sell peas and the seller delivers a different thing, *e.g.,* beans, this is a non-performance of the contract. It is not a question of warranty, nor (it seems) is there any need to speak of an implied condition. The delivery of the beans is altogether beside the point, just as much as the delivery of an elephant; the fact is that the seller has not delivered peas. There is thus a failure of consideration for the buyer's promise to pay, or for his actual payment.[49] On the other hand if the seller delivers peas, though inferior to the ones that the buyer was entitled to expect under the contract, there is no failure of consideration (unless indeed the proper quality of the peas was a condition—not a mere warranty—in the contract, and unless the buyer validly rescinds for breach of the condition). It is fortunate that this distinction is, in view of the provisions of the Sale of Goods Act, of small practical importance,[50] for numberless cases can be put in which it becomes a very difficult one. On a contract to sell a Singer car with a sliding roof, is the delivery of a Singer car with a fixed roof the delivery of a different thing, and so a quantitative failure in performance, or is it a mere failure in the mode or quality of performance? Questions like these show that the distinction between quantity and quality, like the distinction between kind and degree, is one of degree. It is submitted that the solution of the difficulty is different from that suggested for the law of freight: in sale of goods, the rule should be that any departure by the seller from the contract description is a quantitative failure of performance and therefore a failure of consideration. The reason for the difference of rule is that in the law of freight the goods are, to start with, agreed upon, and the law should not

[47] Cp. the criticism on a rather different ground in Scrutton, *Charterparties,* 14th ed., 410 n. (t).

[48] Chanter v. Hopkins (1839) 4 M. & W. 399 at 404.

[49] J. L. Montrose in (1934) 5 C. L. J. 275; Williams in (1941) 57 L. Q. R. 494-6; Williams in McElroy, *Impossibility of Performance* (Cambridge, 1941), 117.

[50] The question arises chiefly where the contract excludes conditions implied by the Sale of Goods Act. It seems that the law of failure of consideration is not excluded by such a clause.

tangle itself in verbal questions of *continued* identity; in the law of sale of goods, where unascertained goods are sold by description, no specific goods are agreed upon and the question is not one of continued identity but whether the goods tendered conform to the description. Translated in this way, the question when a thing is a "different thing" loses most of its terrors.

(c) Modern philosophy perceives that just as classes are artificial, so is singleness. There is no "single" fact in nature otherwise than as we choose to consider it so. "Singleness" is always singleness for the particular purpose that we have on hand. This subjectivity of singleness may be shown in three ways. In the first place, every fact that we choose to regard as a unity can also be regarded as itself made up of unities, or else as being part of a larger unity. Second, many such facts have uncertain boundaries, and we are not certain how much can be added to or subtracted from them without affecting their notional unity. Third, every empirical fact that we regard as a single fact is also, if regarded temporally, a changing process. To illustrate: Nelson was verbally an individual and was "the same" individual from his birth to his death. But (1) this individual Nelson was a society of individual living cells; (2) Nelson lost an eye, and might have acquired a glass eye and false teeth, have lost his memory and become mad, without affecting his "individuality"; (3) the Nelson of actual fact was, like everything else, a process: his origin was in two cells belonging to two other individuals; he became a baby, a youth, and a man; the physical constitution of his body changed several times—all without affecting the notional unity that we impute to him.[51]

It should not be necessary to add that the above argument is not a denial of the individuality of Nelson in the sense in which it may be said that Nelson was a different person from Napoleon. What is asserted is simply that individuality is always individuality for a purpose, individuality in a context. Like classification it results from abstraction, for it results from our perception of simi-

[51] "In the expression 'Nansen skates,' Nansen is a grammatical proper noun and may therefore be supposed to stand for a particular and not a universal. But, as Stout points out, it is really a universal. Nansen perceived must be Nansen eating or Nansen sleeping or Nansen skating. The individual Nansen is a universal, as a connecting link of his own manifold and varying states, relations, qualities, and activities. We cannot *see* the individual Nansen except through this universal": W. M. Urban Language and Reality (London, 1939), 142.

larities or relationships between the parts composing the individual notwithstanding differences between those parts, and of similarities between the manifestations of the individual at two points of time notwithstanding differences between those manifestations.

Although things are constantly changing without this affecting our notion of their unity, and so without its affecting our names for them, a change may be so striking that we regard it as placing the thing in a different category, and as entitling it to a different name. We have already seen that this gives rise to the pseudo-philosophical problem of continuation of identity, to the Roman law of *specificatio,* to a certain unfortunate suggestion as to the English law of trover, and to an actual decision in the law of carriage by sea. The problem arises in an even more nebulous form with regard to the continuation of identity of unincorporated associations, such as charities. Suppose that a charity to which property is left by will changes in constitution or situation either before the testator's death or afterwards; does the gift fail or not? The test suggested by Professor Keeton is whether the charity "may be regarded as having so far survived the changes . . . as to be capable of being identified with the institution named and contemplated by the testator."[52] This test appears, with respect, not to advance the solution of the problem, for the answer to it must be purely subjective. It would be better to say that the gift goes with the rest of the charity's property to the "new" charity, provided that the "new" charity has objects similar to those of the "old" charity that it has replaced.

Realization of the notional character of unity helps one to understand the difficulty experienced by the Courts in applying rules that presuppose unity—for instance, in fixing the precise temporal limits of an "operation," "work,"[53] or "transaction"[54] or the precise spatial limits of a "house";[55] in deciding whether several purchases made at the same time are one contract or several contracts;[56] or whether a part of a written contract, in form one

[52] Keeton, *Trusts,* 3rd ed., 150; Re Watt, Hicks v. Hill, [1932] 2 Ch. 243.

[53] Kent County Council v. Folkestone Corpn. [1905] 1 K. B. 620 at 629.

[54] Phipson, *Evidence,* 8th ed., 52, 55 (res gesta); Underhill, *Trusts,* 9th ed., art. 92.

[55] Burrow's *Words and Phrases,* s.v. See also Re Nielson, Cumming v. Clyde (1929) 73 S. J. 765 (bequest of "my law library in my room in the Temple" where some volumes were not in the room at the time of death); Jarman, *Wills,* 7th ed., 1233-4.

[56] Benjamin, *Sale,* 7th ed., Bk. 1, Pt. II, ch. 3.

clause, is one promise or several promises;[57] or whether, when a contract is altered by a later agreement, the later agreement is a mere variation of the previous agreement or amounts to a rescission of the previous contract and a new contract substituted for it;[58] or whether an interruption in a contract is "so long as to destroy the identity of the work or service, when resumed, with the work or service when interrupted,"[59] or in deciding where the "repair" of a building stops and "renewal" or "reconstruction" begins.[60] Decisions on questions of this sort are often unpredictable, because the Court is not determining facts but is simply deciding upon the attitude that it wishes to adopt towards facts.

(*d*) It is sometimes thought that in mathematics, at least, one reaches a haven of security in the use of words. "Except in mathematics," said Grove J., "it is difficult to frame exhaustive definitions of words; they must be construed with reference to the subject-matter to which they are applied."[61] Now it is true that the words used in mathematics are sharply defined; but this does not mean they are easily applied to the world of experience, or that they are immune from the general necessity of being construed with reference to the subject-matter. In applying mathematical terms it is just as necessary to decide questions of degree as in applying other words. Euclidean geometry, for instance, starts from notions of points and lines which, having no size, are not objects of sense; thus the figures constructed from these notions are not objects of sense either. Even if we modify the definitions by allowing points to have magnitude and lines breadth, we are still faced with the difficulty that the figures of geometry, such as the circle, are supposed to conform perfectly to definition, while we do not find such perfect figures in nature. No straight line that science finds is straight, nor do perfectly parallel lines exist in fact; indeed, on one occasion the House of Lords allowed the sides of an object to pass as "parallel" although they fell far short of the ideal ex-

57 Putsman v. Taylor [1927] 1 K. B. 637.

58 The cases on the importance of this distinction are in some confusion, the latest being Bessler, Waechter, Glover & Co. v. South Derwent Coal Co. [1938] 1 K. B. 408; cp. Phipson, *Evidence,* 8th ed., 576.

59 Per Lord Dunedin in Metropolitan Water Board v. Dick, Kerr & Co. [1918] A. C. 119 at 128.

60 "A covenant to repair a house is not a covenant to give a different thing from that which the tenant took": per Lord Esher, M.R. in Lister v. Lane [1893] 2 Q. B. 212 at 217; Woodfall, *Landlord and Tenant,* 24th ed., 699-701.

61 Wakefield Local Board v. Lele (1876) 1 Ex. D. 336 at 343.

pressed by the word.[62] The numerals seem to be clear because they are precisely defined in terms of each other; but apply them to facts and the clarity ends. A big pea and a little pea may be regarded either as two peas or as one and a half peas according to the purpose in hand. Again, few words would seem at first sight to be so precise as the words of measurement. Every precaution has been taken to fix the length of an Imperial yard by an Act of Parliament making reference to certain bars of gun-metal lodged at the Board of Trade and other places;[63] and other distances, such as miles, are precisely defined in terms of yards. It would be the merest pedantry to deny that, as units of measurement, yards and miles are very exact when we choose to use them exactly. But in ordinary speech we do not always use them exactly. "A yard of cloth" is probably only an approximation to the legal yard; how close an approximation is a question of degree. Again, difficulty can arise in determining what it is that is to be measured. Sometimes we measure distances in a straight line, sometimes not. Thus, on a covenant not to carry on a trade within a mile of a specified place, litigation may arise on the question whether this means a mile "as the crow flies" or a mile by the nearest practicable road.[64]

(*e*) The last type of uncertainty to be noticed is uncertainty in the time to which words are to be applied. Does the word "convict" or "felon"[65] include a person who was a convict or felon once but who has served his sentence? We have touched upon this difficulty in discussing class-names; but further illustrations may be given. Property lawyers are familiar with the difficulties of interpreting such phrases as "die without issue," or "leaving no issue," and with the complicated rules that have had to be developed on the questions when a class "closes." In interpreting a statute it is frequently difficult to know whether the words are to be applied to a situation at the passing of the Act, or to a situation that arises afterwards.[66] Again, suppose that a compulsory-purchase statute requires the authority to resell any land "not required for

[62] Clark v. Adie (No. 2) (1877) 2 App. Cas. 423.

[63] Weights and Measures Act, 1878 (c. 49).

[64] Mouflet v. Cole (1872) L. R. 8 Ex. 32 (held to mean the former). Cp. Langley v. Wilson [1943] 2 A. E. R. 213 ('radius'). So also the question has arisen whether "five miles square" refers to geometrical symmetry or merely to area: Robertson v. Day (1881) 5 App. Cas. 63 (held the latter).

[65] Leyman v. Latimer (1878) 3 Ex. D. 352—no.

[66] Brighton Parish Union v. Strand Union [1891] 2 Q. B. 156; White & Hales v. Islington Corpn. [1909] 1 K. B. 133.

the purposes for which it was acquired"; does "not required" mean "not immediately required," or "not required in the future"?[67] Illustrations of this sort could be multiplied.

It will be noticed that the difficulties discussed above under the heading of "fringe meaning" are very different from the difficulties caused by words of multiple meaning. In the first place, the difficulties here discussed cannot be cured by definitions, unless of course, the definition makes express provision for the particular difficulty that has arisen. If, for instance, it is found difficult to determine whether some early ancestor of man, such as *Pithecanthropus erectus,* is to be called "man," it does not help in the least to remember that "man" is a rational animal. For the two elements in this definition have their own difficulties, rationality being a quality of continuous variation, and "animal" being a class-name carrying the same type of difficulty as the word "man."

In the second place, such difficulties cannot be cured by the adoption of a technical language. A technical language is useful to prevent equivocation; but it cannot cause "univocal" words to become clear of application to the facts of experience.[68]

It is hard to state a case without exaggerating it. When Shakespeare wrote: "Words are grown so false I am loath to prove reason with them," he put the remark into the mouth of a clown. However imperfect our symbolism we must use words in reasoning, because in general we cannot reason otherwise. Also, words *in contexts* are usually clear enough for practical purposes. Were it otherwise, language would be useless.

One way in particular in which context helps to give meaning to a word is in indicating the word to which the word in question is being opposed. Failure to recognize that words change in meaning according to the word to which they are being opposed leads to much idle controversy. For instance, the word "freedom" has no single meaning. Freedom versus imprisonment; freedom versus legal duty; freedom versus deprivation of the franchise; freedom versus imposition; freedom versus economic bondage; freedom versus determinism; freedom versus licence—all these are different

---

67 Att. Gen. v. Teddington U. C. [1898] 1 Ch. 66.

68 This appears to be ignored by Morris R. Cohen in (1916) 29 H. L. R. 634. He seems to argue that the adoption of a technical language would get rid of the difficulties in applying phrases like "direct tax," "interstate commerce," "restraint of trade." But the trouble does not arise from the fact that these words have a popular as well as a legal currency; it arises from the fact that they all have a

meanings.[69] Political philosophers who dispute with one another upon "the meaning" of liberty, or "the nature" of liberty, are wasting their time, unless indeed they begin by agreeing upon the contrast under discussion. Other chameleon words are "democracy," "law," "state," "right," "ownership," "property," "interest," "possession," "agency,"[70] and so on. Numberless attempts have been made to squeeze these words into the four corners of a single definition, but such attempts are mistaken insofar as they assume that each word represents a single unvarying concept.

A good illustration of the necessity for attending to context is the phrase "the common law." In practice this phrase is used, like the word "layman" or "alien," in a negative or residuary sense, meaning that which is left after the subtraction of something else. Thus the phrase may mean, according to context, the law that is not local law, or the law that is not statute law, or the law that is not equity. In the second of these senses it may include equity, in the third it may include statutes. This is a statement of the way in which the phrase is actually used. Observe, however, the treatment of it in Salmond's *Jurisprudence.* Salmond supposes that the phrase "the common law" must represent a single, invariable concept, and thus he defines it as the whole of the law of England except statute law, equity, and special law in its various forms. Salmond expressly refuses to admit that its meaning varies with the context. "The term always, in its proper sense, excludes statute law, equity, and all the forms of special law; but sometimes the particular contrast intended to be expressed is that between common law and statute law: sometimes it is that between common law and equity; and sometimes it is that between common law and special law."[71] It is significant that when, later in the book, Salmond has occasion to use the phrase "the common law," he uses it in one of the senses that he condemns as "improper," namely, as including equity and perhaps special law, and excluding only statutes.[72]

wide penumbra of uncertainty. Merely changing the symbol would not eliminate this uncertainty. Cohen elsewhere admits that "even in scientific language there is a fringe of uncertainty as to the limits of the denotation or application of names:" Cohen and Nagel, *op. cit.* 118.

69 Cp. Bogoslovsky, *op. cit.* 121. Bogolovsky says that some of the above are different aspects of the single concept *liberty,* but it would seem better to say that there is not one concept but many.

70 Cp. Morris, *How Lawyers Think,* 102-3.

71 *Jurisprudence,* 7th ed., § 24.

72 *Ibid.* § 46.

Salmond is unable in his own writing to keep the concept to the singleness that he himself desires.

Should the reader think that this discussion of the phrase "the common law" is of merely academic interest, let him look at section 62 (2) of the Sale of Goods Act, 1893, which saves "the rules of the common law" relating to the sale of goods, except in so far as they are inconsistent with the express provisions of the Act. In view of this opposition between "the common law" and the Act, it seems clear that the phrase "the common law" is meant to include equity. But if Salmond's idea of the "proper" meaning of "the common law" were applied, it would not include equity.

* * * * * * * *

I have already pointed a number of legal morals in the course of this section, but some general conclusions of legal interest remain to be drawn.

(1) In the first place, the theory here advanced destroys completely and for ever the illusion that the law can be completely certain. Since the law has to be expressed in words, and words have a penumbra of uncertainty, marginal cases are bound to occur. Certainty in law is thus seen to be a matter of degree. (2) Correlatively, the theory destroys the illusion that the function of a judge is simply to administer the law.[73] If marginal cases must occur, the function of the judge in adjudicating upon them must be legislative. The distinction between the mechanical administration of fixed rules and free judicial discretion is thus a matter of degree, not the sharp distinction that it is sometimes assumed to be. This is not to say that judges have an unlimited legislative power. A judge has a discretion to include a flying-boat within a rule as to ships or vessels; he has no discretion to include a motor car within such a rule.

If it be recognized that a judge when operating within the fringes of meaning is not interpreting a pre-existing intent but is exercising a legislative power, the conclusion ought to be that less attention should be paid to dictionary meanings and more to legislative policy. A good example of the proper approach to inter-

[73] The illusion has, of course, been destroyed many times, notably by Dickinson, "The Law behind Law" (1929) 29 Col. L. Rev. 113, 285. But it has extraordinary vitality. One still sees discussions among international lawyers upon the respective merits of legal tribunals and tribunals deciding *ex aequo et bono,* without any express statement by either side that the distinction is one of degree.

pretation is the recent case of *Watkinson v. Hollington* (1943),[74] where it was held that distress damage feasant is not "distress" within the Courts (Emergency Powers) Act, 1939. Verbally, distress damage feasant is by its very name a form of distress; moreover at common law it is procedurally similar to distress for rent. Nevertheless (i) it is a comparatively unusual form of distress, so that probably it was not present in the mind of the draftsman of the Act of 1939; and (ii) to apply the Act to it would be absurd. On a proper understanding of the nature of meaning, the decision of the Court of Appeal excluding distress damage feasant from the operation of the Act was not more legislative than the decision of the Court below including it; but it was much more sensible.

Substance and Quality.

As we have seen, the philosopher's belief that the universals have some mode of existence independent of their concrete manifestations is due to the false idea that reality follows grammatical form. There is another danger lurking in the grammatical construction of language. It is this grammatical construction that leads us to distinguish between substance and quality, a distinction corresponding to the subject and predicate of the sentence. We say that this individual table now before us is wooden, or is square, or is brown, as though in nature there were two things: the substance, and its quality. Philosophers have now come to realize that this distinction is simply a matter of linguistic convenience and does not exist in nature.

The chief importance of this conclusion for lawyers is in connection with the distinction made in the law of contract and elsewhere between mistake of identity and mistake of attribute ("attribute" being another name for "quality"). To discuss fully the exact nature of this last distinction would make the present section inordinately long and would take us too far away from the main theme of the paper. It is therefore left for discussion elsewhere.[75]

Interpretation.

This is a convenient heading under which to gather some remarks on interpretation in general and certain matters connected

74 [1944] K. B. 16.

75 Williams, *Mistake as to Party in the Law of Contract* (1945) 23 Canadian Bar Review, 271 ff.

therewith. These will concern (1) the "proper" meaning of words, (2) definition, (3) intended, comprehended and ordinary meaning, (4) logical implication, (5) literal and ulterior meaning, and (6) the transition from implied terms to rules of law. Considerations of space forbid detailed discussion of the legal rules of interpretation.

(1) *The "Proper" Meaning of Words.*

There is a famous passage in *Alice Through the Looking-Glass* (Chapter VI), where, to Humpty Dumpty's claim to use words in unusual senses, Alice made what may seem to the ordinary person to be an unanswerable objection. "The question is," said Alice, "whether you *can* make words mean different things." "The question is," replied Humpty Dumpty, "which is to be master—that's all." Humpty Dumpty's theory was that supported by Locke, who laid it down that the significance of all words is perfectly arbitrary, and that every man has an inviolable liberty to make words stand for what ideas he pleases.[76] This admirable statement has fallen on many deaf ears, and Ogden and Richards have again to deplore "the curious instinctive tendency to believe that a word has its own true or proper use."[77] Scientifically speaking, words have no true or proper meaning, except in two senses. First, words have an ordinary—*i.e.,* commonly-accepted—meaning. The ordinary meaning need not be current among the community as a whole: it may be confined to a particular section of the community, such as educated persons, business men, scientists or lawyers. (For instance, a lawyer may say that the proper meaning of the word "contract" does not include contract bridge, meaning that it does not include it in the technical language of the law.) Second, the particular person who uses a word may assign to it a special meaning; the "proper" meaning of the word for his purpose is then this assigned meaning. Apart from such ordinary or assigned meanings words have no "actual," "correct," "essential," "grammatical," "legitimate," "literal," "natural," "necessary," "rational," "real," or "reasonable" meaning (all of which adjectives are com-

[76] *Essay Concerning the Human Understanding* 3. 3. 8. B. Russell (Analysis of Mind 189-90) denies that words are conventional, but all he means is that language is part of the environment in which we grow up: we do not deliberately adopt it. This is true, but not a contradiction of the proposition that there is no connection between words and referents save in the mind.

[77] *The Meaning of Meaning* 123; cp. *ibid.* 206-7.

mon in legal literature). Similarly, "historical," "etymological," "wide," "narrow," "strict," "metaphorical," "technical" and "legal" meanings are all varieties of ordinary or assigned meaning. Historical or etymological meaning is simply the ordinary meaning of the word, or of the parts from which it is compounded, at some period of the past. It is an unreliable guide to the present meaning of a word, because meanings change.[78] "Technical" (including "legal") meaning is that current among a special class of persons; "legal" meaning may also indicate a determination on the part of lawyers to read words in a particular way although they know that the user did not intend them to bear that meaning. "Strict," "narrow," and "wide" refer to the denotation of ambiguous words, again as a matter of use. "Proper" as contrasted with "metaphorical" means the original meaning of a word as opposed to its transferred meaning; the expressions are acceptable provided that it is remembered that metaphorical meaning may overshadow or even wholly oust "proper" meaning and so become the chief or only meaning. For example, many words for non-empirical facts or for values began as words for empirical facts; and it would be pedantic to assert that the "proper" meaning of all such words is an empirical one (*e.g.*, that "right" and "wrong" properly mean straight and twisted). As one writer puts it, "if we started on the principle of restricting words to their so-called proper meaning, and pursued this theory to its logical conclusion, we should ultimately reduce language to the few inarticulate ejaculations from which it began."[79]

If a writer uses the phrase "proper meaning" otherwise than in the sense of ordinary or assigned meaning, past or present, he must be using the phrase not scientifically but emotively, to express what he considers *ought* to be the ordinary meaning. Thus if a lawyer writes: "The proper meaning of 'implied contract' is contract implied in fact, not quasi-contract," he does not express what is now the invariable usage of lawyers (for in fact their usage does not always conform to this), but simply states what in his view should

[78] This was recognized by Kindersley V. C., when he said: "It is not necessary to go into the derivation of the word, for that sort of reasoning would not assist in the administration of justice": Barrett v. White (1855) 24 L. J. Ch. 724 at 726. "[Nephew] is derived from the Latin *nepos*, signifying a grandchild, but it is clear that such an interpretation could not now be given to the word": *per* Lord Cranworth L. C. in Crook v. Whitley (1857) 7 De G. M. & G. 490 at 494-5.

[79] George Willis, *The Philosophy of Speech* (London, 1919) 167.

be the usage. The writer thus dresses up an expression of emotion to make it look like a proposition of fact, for he avoids the use of the optative "ought" and uses instead the apparently factual "is." We all use this device, and it is often successful in winning agreement; but it is also the source of much fruitless controversy. For the mode of statement often tempts others to dispute the suggested "proper meaning" as though it were a matter of fact, instead of a mere matter of choice of words.

It may be added that we may sometimes stigmatize a phrase as "improper" because it seems to indicate that the species denoted by it belongs to a genus to which the species is not in fact regarded as belonging. Thus the phrase "involuntary bailee," though much used, is "improper" in the sense that an involuntary bailee is not a bailee *simpliciter.* So, a void contract is not a species of contract, a warranty *ex post facto* is not a species of warranty, and a service tenancy (in one sense of that phrase) is not a species of tenancy. We can call such phrases "improper" or "misnomers" without implying that words have inherently-proper meanings.

The worst form of the proper-meaning error is the supposition that words have not merely proper meanings but single proper meanings. On this view, every ambiguous word necessarily has one of its meanings "proper" and one "improper," and the task of science it to find out which is which. It is submitted that an example of this error occurs in Sir John Salmond's discussion of ownership. Salmond points out, correctly, that we speak sometimes of owning a right and sometimes of owning a thing; these two senses of the term he distinguishes by the useful names "incorporeal ownership" and "corporeal ownership" respectively. He then proceeds: "If we look, therefore, no deeper than the mere usages of speech, it would seem as if the subject-matter of ownership were sometimes a material object and at other times a right. This, of course, would be a logical absurdity. Ownership may conceivably be in all cases a relation to a material object; or it may in all cases be a relation to a right; but it cannot be sometimes the one and sometimes the other."[80] The author evades the supposed difficulty by saying that incorporeal ownership is ownership in the proper sense and that corporeal ownership is only a figure of speech, a metonymy. The truth is, however, that the difficulty does

[80] *Jurisprudence* (7th ed.) 279, § 87.

not arise. The supposed difficulty appears to arise from an assumption that there is some single entity in the universe, *ownership*, which cannot be defined in contradictory ways. This is an error. "Ownership" is a word symbolizing an idea, and this idea, the meaning of the word, may and does vary according to context. There is therefore no logical absurdity in defining the word "ownership" in two different ways. It may be added that Salmond's mode of escaping from his self-made difficulty is particularly unfortunate because it seems to suggest that incorporeal ownership is the original idea and corporeal ownership an extension of it, whereas the reverse is the case.

Realization of the fact that words have no inherently-proper meanings has great importance for the student of jurisprudence, because it enables him to write off almost the whole of the vast and futile controversy concerning the proper meaning of the word "law,"[81] as well as many others of less magnitude. In the realm of constitutional law, not only students but law lords need to be headed off the verbal question whether Canada is properly called a federation.[82] In the law of wills, a rule that badly needs attention from the semantic point of view is the rule stated by Wigram in the following words: "Where there is nothing in the context of a will from which it is apparent that a testator has used the words in which he has expressed himself in any other than their strict and primary sense, and where his words so interpreted are sensible with reference to extrinsic circumstances, . . . the words of the will shall be interpreted in their strict and primary sense, and in no other, although they may be capable of some popular or secondary interpretation, and although the most conclusive evidence of intention to use them in such popular or secondary sense be tendered."[83] It will be seen that this rule does not merely prefer the strict and primary meaning of the words to some special meaning adopted by the testator alone: it even prefers it to the "popular" meaning of the words, which is another kind of ordinary meaning. Hence the rule amounts to a statement that one kind of

---

81 The controversy is discussed in an article to be published in the British Year Book of International Law for 1946.

82 The hare was started by Viscount Haldane L.C. in Att.-Gen. for Australia v. Colonial Sugar Refining Co. [1914] A. C. 237 at 252-3, contrasting what he called the "loose" sense of the word "federal" with "the natural and literal interpretation of the word."

83 Wigram, *Extrinsic Evidence in Aid of the Interpretation of Wills*, Proposition II.

ordinary meaning is automatically and as a rule of law to be preferred to another kind, without regard to the particular meaning that was probably intended by the testator, and this merely because the former kind is supposed to be the "strict and primary" meaning. It is assumed that the two kinds of meaning can be separated clearly enough for the purpose of applying the rule. Enough has already been said to indicate that the distinction is not nearly so clear as the wording of the rule would seem to suggest; also, recent cases indicate that the authority of the rule is less secure than was formerly supposed.[84]

A somewhat surprising challenge to Humpty Dumpty's assertion of human mastery over words came recently from no less a judge than Lord Atkin. This was in *Liversidge v. Anderson* (1941),[85] where the question was whether the words "If the Secretary of State has" in a statutory regulation could be read as meaning "If the Secretary of State thinks he has." Lord Atkin said: "I know of only one authority which might justify the suggested method of construction." He then quoted Humpty Dumpty as being this one authority, and added: "After all this long discussion the question is whether the words 'If a man has' can mean 'If a man thinks he has'. I am of opinion that they cannot, and that the case should be decided accordingly." With all respect to Lord Atkin, this rejection of Humpty Dumpty's doctrine is not happily phrased. It is not true to say that the one phrase cannot mean the other. If, for instance, the regulation had expressly stated that the words "If the Secretary of State has" as used in the regulation meant "If the Secretary of State thinks he has," then the one phrase would mean what is ordinarily meant by the other. Again, if the regulation had used the phrase "If the Secretary of State thinks has" several times, and then, in the crucial clause, used the phrase, "If the Secretary of State has," it might be clear from the general context that no change of meaning was intended. What Lord Atkin probably meant to convey was that the one phrase did not normally mean the same as the other, and that there was nothing in the regulation to lead to the conclusion that their meaning was intended to be the same. The majority law lords took the opposite view on the latter point.

---

84 See, e.g. Perrin v. Morgan [1943] A. C. 399.
85 [1942] A. C. 206 at 245.

The denial that words have a proper meaning, independently of ordinary, assigned and desired meaning, is liable to be misunderstood unless certain qualifications are expressly stated. It is not denied that a writer ought generally to take meanings as he finds them. An important function of language is to communicate thought, and it can serve this function only if there is a general measure of agreement upon the meanings of words. Humpty Dumpty laid himself open to the charge of vexatiously and quite unnecessarily changing in his own speech the ordinary meaning of words. Even where some change in established usage is called for, it is not desirable to give a word a new meaning so divorced from its traditional meaning as to make the new use of the word aesthetically offensive to many people. Still less is it justifiable to debase the language by turning words of precise meaning into mere synonyms for other words, as, for instance, in the schoolgirl's use of the word "chronic."

(2) *Definition.*

The function of definition is to explain the meaning of words. We do not learn the meaning of all words by definitions, for definition presupposes the existence of an understood language. In childhood we learn the meaning of such words as "red" by being shown the objects to which they are to be applied; and in fact the names of colours remain indefinable throughout life. Most words, however, admit of being replaced by groups of other words. This process is called definition. As Ogden and Richards put it, definition is the substitution for the symbol to be defined of a symbol or symbols that can be better understood. It involves the selection of known referents as starting-points, and the identification of the referent of the *definiendum* by its connection with these. For instance, a referent may be located by its similarity to another referent, by its relation in space or time to another referent, or by its being the cause or effect of another referent.[86]

This view of definition throws overboard the theory initiated by Aristotle and widely accepted after his day. The latter theory supposes that there is only one true definition of every unambigu-

[86] Ogden and Richards, *op. cit.* 110, 113 ff. (The authors give a special heading to "legal relations" (p. 120), but the treatment is not helpful.) For a previous statement of a similar view see Locke, *op. cit.* 2. 3. 10.

ous word, namely, *per genus at differentiam.*[87] The view now accepted is that words have no "true" definition and that it is possible and permissible to define variously, one definition being proper for one purpose, another for another. Genera and species are no longer regarded as an objective and rigid ordering of nature; they are seen to be no more than subjective conveniences of classification. Being man-made they are mutable, and it is possible to regard the same thing as belonging to distinct genera. Thus "man" may be defined not only as a rational animal (the classical definition) but as a rational biped. Or, altering the *differentia,* he may be defined as a talking animal, an acquisitive animal, an imaginative animal, an artistic animal, a moral animal, a laughing animal, a weeping animal, or a superstitious animal. None of these definitions explains perfectly all uses of the word "man," for the word may be applied to a lunatic, a deaf mute, a pauper, a philistine, an egoist, a hypochondriac, and so on. Conversely, these definitions may to some extent fit some of the lower animals. This trouble with words has already been observed: there is always the possibility of dispute as to the limits of their application, and no definition can get rid of this possibility.

The above view as to definition also involves a rejection of Aristotle's doctrine of essences. Aristotle taught that essences are fixed in nature, and that a definition is a phrase signifying this essence. On this view it is possible to dispute about "true" definitions as though they are matters of fact. We now know that "essence" simply means "important feature," and that what is important is a subjective or emotional matter. No definition ever states the sum total of the qualities that seem to go to the being of a thing; it always involves a selection from those qualities, and the exact selection made depends very much upon the purpose of the definition.

These considerations reinforce the conclusions previously advanced in the discussion of "proper meaning." Every definition of a word is a definition of (i) its ordinary meaning, or of (ii) its specially-assigned meaning, or of (iii) its desired meaning. The only scientific dispute over definitions is a dispute over (i). Obviously there is no point in disputing (ii), and a dispute over (iii)

[87] *I.e.* by stating the genus of which the word to be defined is the species, and then stating the difference between this species and others of the same genus. Thus "man" is (genus) animal, (difference) rational: man is a rational animal.

is, except to the extent that common premises are agreed, a conflict of value-judgments, not a scientific dispute. As to (i), it is frequently possible to settle the dispute by taking a number of admitted referents of the word and abstracting from them enough of their common features to explain the use of the word. It must, however, be remembered that the number of features abstracted must often be a matter of choice, that words may have two or more ordinary meanings, and that every word is of doubtful application in marginal cases. Those who dispute about definitions and forget these points are wasting their time.

It is next to be observed that many questions and disputes that seem to be concerned with the empirical world are in fact concerned only with definitions. For instance, every question in the form "What is . . .?," or "What is the nature of . . .?," or "What is a . . .?," or "What is the nature of a . . .?" (followed in each case by the name of a class, quality or relation) is a request for a definition of a word. It is not a request for information about the empirical world, except to the extent that such information may happen to be furnished in the course of the definition. Examples of such questions are: "What is an atoll?" "What is a unicorn?" "What is cause?" "What is the nature of law?" "What is possession?"[88]

Similarly, every inquiry into "the nature of" (or, "the essential nature of," "the fundamental nature of") a class, quality or relation is a search for a definition; and every dispute about "the (essential, fundamental) nature of" a class, quality or relation is a dispute about a definition. It is not an inquiry into, or dispute about, facts, except to the extent that it concerns the ordinary or assigned meaning of words. If this were generally realized the world would be saved much pseudo-philosophy.[89]

---

[88] It is true that the answer to the question "What is an atoll?" does not merely supply a definition of the word "atoll"; it also gives information about part of the earth's surface. The context in which the question is asked and answered implies an understanding that atolls exist—*i.e.* that the description of an atoll is true of part of reality. But the context in which the question "What is a unicorn?" is asked and answered would not, usually, imply an understanding that unicorns exist, and if it did the understanding would be false. Comparing these two questions, it is evident that a question of this form is invariably a request for a definition but not invariably a request for information about the empirical world. It is the latter only if the word in question happens to symbolize an empirical fact.

[89] See, generally, Ayer, *Language, Truth and Logic,* 64-5; Richards, *Interpretation in Teaching,* 354-5.

The only exception to the foregoing propositions is where the word in question is independently defined, so that there is no dispute about its application. Thus an inquiry into the nature of atolls, if there is no dispute as to which territorial formations are denoted by this word, would be a scientific investigation, for there are data to be observed. But an inquiry into the nature of atolls, or of law, or of possession, if the word in question is not independently defined, is not a scientific or factual inquiry, except to the extent that it is an inquiry into verbal usages.

Lest all this be thought to be tilting at windmills, it may be well to consider in greater detail a specific example of confusion between definitions and non-verbal facts. Let us take the usual legal or jurisprudential discussion of "the nature of" possession. As already stated, this discussion is in reality a discussion of the definition of the word "possession." This, however, is not the way in which the participants usually regard it. They seem to think that in discussing "the nature of" possession they are discussing, at least in part, some non-verbal fact. This assumption underlies the division of possession into "possession in fact" and "possession in law." Although the meaning of "possession in fact" is variously interpreted, the usual assumption is that possession in fact is, as the name implies, possession that is somehow visible in the facts of the case. Let us consider how far this assumption is true. To start with, we may picture a situation that raises difficulties in applying the idea of possession. In describing this situation it will be necessary to use words, but the reader is asked to imagine the scene in a non-verbal way, in order to reproduce as nearly as possible the raw material with which we have to deal. *A* has a pocket-book containing his name and address and some bank-notes. He unknowingly drops it on the street and walks on. Many people pass, and eventually *B* finds the pocket-book and forthwith decides to keep it for himself. *B* gives it to his son *C* to hold for him, but shortly afterwards *C* is pursued by bandits, who succeed in wresting the pocket-book from him. This is the factual situation, and we have to apportion the possession of the pocket-book between *A, B, C* and the bandits. In doing this, since we are speaking of possession in fact in the sense above described, we have to do without the various rules that have been developed on the subject by different legal systems. Probably it will become clear after a moment's thought that the difficulty in the way of determining who at any moment has possession of the pocket-book is not a difficulty in ascertaining facts, for the material facts are practically all given, but is a difficulty in knowing what is meant by the word "possession." "Possession" is an abstract word of somewhat vague meaning. A theory of "possession in fact" seems to be one of two things: either a statement of the way in which, in the view of the writer, the word "possession," or the phrase "possession in fact," ought to be used (which is not a statement of fact at all, but a value-judgment), or else a statement of the way in which the word "possession" is ordinarily used by non-lawyers (which is a statement of fact only in the sense that it is a statement of verbal usage). If the particular theory of possession in fact is intended as the latter, a statement of the layman's meaning of "possession," the writer ought, if he is honest, to recognize that his theory is incapable of solving any of the difficult problems that arise in law-suits, for the simple reason that the layman has no clear idea of what he means by "possession."

Consider, in the light of this analysis, Sir John Salmond's treatment of possession. His treatment is singled out for discussion because the well-deserved esteem of the work in which it appears has made it the usual student's introduction to the theory of possession. Salmond begins by distinguishing between possession in fact and possession in law, and supposes that possession in fact is "the truth of things"; it is possession "in truth and in fact"; it is "fact" in contrast to "law."[90] Having rubbed this well into the reader, Salmond suddenly calls possession in fact a "conception." This it certainly is, and of course a conception is a fact, so that the learned author is perhaps safe from the charge of self-contradiction. But it may be doubted whether he is safe from the charge of having misled the unwary reader. For if possession in fact is a conception, and so a fact, possession in law is also a conception, and so also a fact. Thus the contrast of "law" and "fact" breaks down.

One way of restoring it would be to say that possession in fact is the conception found among laymen, while possession in law is the conception found among lawyers. If this is the meaning, one would expect a work on Jurisprudence to be concerned with possession in law, that is, with possession as a technical legal term.

90 Salmond, *Jurisprudence* (7th ed.) § 94.

Yet Salmond professes to concern himself only with possession in fact. It may also be noted that his discussion of it is far richer and more precise than a layman's discussion of it would have been.

To add to the perplexity, Salmond expressly denies that there are "two ideas of possession, a legal and a natural." He admits that "were this so, we could dispense altogether with the discussion of possession in fact"—because then it would be our duty as lawyers to pay attention to the legal meaning only. But in reality, he says, "there is only one idea, to which the rules of law do more or less imperfectly conform. There is no conception which will include all that amounts to possession in law, and will include nothing else, and it is impossible to frame any definition from which the concrete law of possession can be logically deduced. Our task is merely to search for the idea which underlies this body of rules, and of which they are the imperfect and partial expression and application." When Salmond says that there is no legal idea of possession, his statement is true only if the word "idea" be taken to mean a single, neat, compact idea, capable of being expressed in a short sentence. It is perfectly true that there is no legal idea of possession of this kind. A complicated legal idea of possession there certainly is, though it varies from one branch of the law to another, and even within the same branch of the law, according to the purpose of the particular rule. It comes to this, therefore, that Salmond's theory of possession in fact is really a simplified and idealized theory of possession as he finds it in the legal system. It is the legal theory of possession with its inconsistencies smoothed away. Such a theory is not an adequate statement of the law, and it is very improperly called a statement of fact. It is either an elementary statement of the law, perhaps useful for the beginner but misleading if not carefully stated, or a statement of the ideal towards which in the writer's opinion the law ought to develop.[91]

[91] The confusion above considered runs throughout Salmond's treatment of possession. Thus in § 95 (7th ed.) he debates the question whether incorporeal possession is possession "in truth." In § 104 he takes objection to Savigny's theory that possession at its commencement and possession in its continuance are made up of different elements, appearing to think that this is somehow a logical impossibility. "Savigny's theory . . . tells us, at the most, how possession begins, and how it ceases; but we wish to know what it essentially and continuously *is*." In § 101 he distinguishes between immediate and mediate possession; on his own previous statement this is a discussion of "possession in fact"; yet he declares that "a test of the existence of a true mediate possession is to be found in the

(3) *Intended, Comprehended and Ordinary Meaning.*

Ogden and Richards seem to treat meaning as though it were a single relation. But "meaning" is a word of many meanings, and to search for *the* meaning of meaning is (if it be not undue temerity in a lawyer to say so) to fall into error from the start. In the present division of this article it is proposed to examine three important varieties of meaning, and to show their importance for the work of the lawyer. They are: (1) the intended meaning, the meaning intended by the speaker or writer; (2) the ordinary meaning, the meaning that would be attached to the words by the ordinary hearer or reader; and (3) the comprehended meaning, the meaning actually attached to the words by a particular reader or hearer, *e.g.,* one to whom the words were particularly addressed. Where misunderstanding occurs, (1) differs from (3).

(1) It is not often that the law addresses itself purely and simply to meaning in the first sense, the intended meaning. It does so, however, in the law of deceit, for here the requirement of a fraudulent state of mind means that the Court must, where the words are equivocal, look to the sense actually intended.[92] It is submitted that meaning in sense (2), the ordinary or "reasonable" meaning of the words, is not in issue, except as evidence of what the defendant probably intended and what the plaintiff probably understood. For, on the one hand, a defendant who has "paltered in a double sense" cannot excuse himself by showing that the meaning applied by the plaintiff to his words, being the meaning that he hoped the plaintiff would apply, was an "unreasonable" one.[93] And, on the other hand, however reasonable the

operation of the law of prescription." To a casual reader it is most confusing to be informed that rules of law are a test of what exists in fact.

92 Per Lord Blackburn in Smith v. Chadwick (1884) 9 App. Cas. at 201; per Bowen L.J. in Angus v. Clifford [1891] 2 Ch. at 472; per Atkinson J. in Halifax Building Society v. Salisbury [1939] 4 A. E. R. at 452.

93 Contra, Winfield, *Text-Book of the Law of Tort* (3rd ed.) § 116, who lays it down that "if the statement is ambiguous, the true interpretation of the authorities seems to be that the plaintiff must prove (i) that the statement was reasonably capable of bearing the meaning which he attached to it; (ii) that he understood it in that sense; and (iii) that the defendant made use of the ambiguity with the express purpose of deceiving the plaintiff." This implies that a plaintiff cannot succeed in deceit although the defendant meant him to understand the statement in the way in which he did understand it, unless he shows also that the statement was reasonably capable of bearing the particular meaning. It is respectfully submitted that there is not this requirement. Of course, the Court may be slow to believe that the defendant meant or hoped that his words would be understood in an "unreasonable" way, and it may also be slow to believe that the plaintiff did understand them in an "unreasonable" way. But if the evidence is clear, the

plaintiff was in attaching the untrue meaning to the defendant's statement, if the defendant did not intend his words to be taken in that sense, there is no deceit because there is no guilty mind.

In wills, statutes, deeds, written contracts and other formal documents, the general theory is again that the Court is concerned with the meaning of the author or authors, but this is seriously qualified by a refusal (in general) to look at certain classes of extrinsic evidence (that is, evidence outside the document itself) for the purpose of ascertaining the author's intention. The result is a tendency to look only at the meaning of the words *as words*—that is, not at the actual personal meaning of the author but at the usual meaning in which the words that expressed the actual meaning are commonly employed. But it is always the duty of the Court, within the limits set by the law of evidence, to go behind the dehumanized dictionary-meaning to what the assertor was actually trying to express. As F. C. S. Schiller put it (he was not speaking of legal interpretation, but his words have a strong interest for the lawyer):—

> "It is the desire to communicate meaning which dictates the choice of the words used, and ultimately controls their meaning. For the original compilers of dictionaries get the word's meanings from an examination of the passages in which it has been used in print. Nevertheless, the meaning (or meanings) as formulated in a dictionary never can be an absolute and infallible guide to actual usage. It represents merely the *average* meaning, with which the word has been used in the past, and the probable meaning, with which it will be used in the future; but it cannot prohibit its modification. To understand any particular sentence, we may have (as every schoolboy translator has painfully to discover) to go beyond anything we find in our dictionaries, and in any case we have to select the 'right' meaning from those given, and to adjust their *dicta* to our special problem. No critic of a bad translation would allow the excuse that the wrong meanings given to the mistranslated words had been found in a dictionary."[94]

question what was the reasonable interpretation of the words is surely irrelevant. What matters, ultimately, is what the parties in fact intended and understood respectively, not what a reasonable man would have intended or understood. The words of Lord Selborne L.C. in Smith v. Chadwick, 9 App. Cas. at p. 191, are, it is submitted, not inconsistent with this view.

94 Formal Logic 17. At one place Ogden and Richards seem to deny that meaning in one sense of the word is a personal matter, for they say (p. 103)[3]

On the whole the Courts realize pretty well the dangers of blind adherence to dictionaries. Thus it is laid down as one of the governing rules of interpretation that words are not to be looked at in isolation but their meaning is to be gathered from their context: *noscitur a sociis.* Moreover, in the case of wills and contracts, evidence is admissible, within certain limits, to show that words were used in a special meaning that is not their ordinary one. There are instances, however, where the Courts fall far short of the ideal of interpretation as the ascertainment of meaning. A striking case of this sort is *Re Gale* (1941),[95] where the testator, who had lived with an unmarried woman and had had four children by her, died leaving her certain property "during her widowhood." Farwell J. held that the gift failed, because a woman who had not been married could not be anyone's "widow." This astonishing refusal to exercise intelligence in the construction of language cannot fairly be said to represent the customary attitude of judges; yet, though not the rule, it may be said, without disrespect, to be too frequent an exception.

(2) There are some cases where the Court is concerned solely with the ordinary meaning of words, and frankly disavows any intention to look at the meaning of the speaker or writer, or even at the understanding of those to whom the words were intended to be addressed. Illustrations occur in the law of defamation, but the precise rules are too complicated to be gone into here.

(3) We pass to the third kind of meaning, the meaning attached to language by the hearer or reader. There are several situations in which this is the kind of meaning that is important in law. Thus, the question whether an offer is made or acceptance given depends, at least in part, on the question what the other party reasonably understands. So also do the questions of innocent misrepresentation and estoppel. In such cases there are two matters to be considered: first, what the hearer understands by the words, and second, whether his understanding is "reasonable" —*i.e.,* whether it conforms to what the ordinary person, or the judge himself, would have understood in the circumstances. Thus, this type of meaning is a compound of senses (2) and (3).

"A symbol refers to what it is actually used to refer to; not necessarily to what it ought in good usage, or is intended by an interpreter, *or is intended by the user* to refer to." It is probably my deficiency, but I do not understand this, and the discussion that precedes and follows it seems in my humble opinion to confuse meaning with truth.

95 Re Gale, Gale v. Gale [1941] Ch. 209.

To say that the Court in a particular case is concerned with the ordinary meaning of words (sense (2)) does not solve all difficulties, for the Court may have to select between different ordinary meanings current in different circles; or, in the case of phrases, it may have to select between the meaning built up from a consideration of the words taken separately, and the meaning of the phrase as a whole. Good illustrations are supplied by two cases decided on the Merchandise Marks Act, 1887. By section 2 (1) (*d*) of the Act it is an offence to apply "any false trade description" to goods; and similarly, under section 2(2) it is an offence to sell goods to which a "false trade description" has been applied. Now before a description can be pronounced to be true or false its meaning must be ascertained, and the ascertainment of meaning may depend upon the group of people whom one takes as interpreting the words. This is illustrated by *Lemy v. Watson* (1915),[96] where the Court had to choose between a meaning current among vendors and a meaning current among purchasers. The facts were that small fish caught off the coast of Norway were sold in tins under the description of "Norwegian sardines." The word "sardine" had come to England from France, being the French name for a pilchard. English usage had confined it to small fish, *i.e.,* young pilchards. There were no pilchards in Norwegian waters, and the so-called Norwegian sardines were brisling. This was well known in the trade, but was not known to the purchasing public. The public was unaware that the fish so sold were different from the French sardine, and for the most part did not know that the French sardine was a pilchard. In these circumstances, was the epithet "Norwegian sardines" false as applied to these fish? It was held that it was, and that an offence had been committed.

It is hardly necessary to point out that the decision is not an authority for saying that French usage, the usage of the country of the word's origin, is to be preferred to English usage, or that original usage must be preferred to current usage, or that the meaning built up from the words taken separately is necessarily to be preferred to the meaning of a phrase taken as a whole. All that the case decides is that under the Merchandise Marks Act the buyers' usage must be preferred to the sellers' usage. If this be the *ratio decidendi,* a *dictum* of Lord Reading C.J. in the course of his judgment is open to some objection. Referring to the fish

96 [1915] 3 K. B. 731.

sold under the name of Norwegian sardines, he said: "They were not sardines in fact because they were not the small pilchard which is the sardine proper, and even with the prefix 'Norwegian' it was false in fact to say that these fish so prepared were Norwegian sardines. It is true they were Norwegian, but they were not sardines." In criticism of this it may be said that when there is a conflict of linguistic usage, as there was in this case, it is begging the question to assert that the goods were or were not something or other. The question whether the goods were or were not *x* is, in the absence of an agreed definition of *x*, a verbal, not a factual question, and it can be resolved only by deciding which usage is to prevail. Nor did it help to say that the goods were not sardines "in fact," or not sardines "proper," because this was true only on the assumption that the French (*i.e.,* the buyers') usage was to be adopted in preference to the sellers' usage. Finally, it was misleading to suggest that goods that are not "sardines" *simpliciter* may not be "sardines" qualified by an epithet like "Norwegian." They would be, if that were the understanding of the buyers. As Darling J. put it:

> "There are many erroneous terms consecrated by common use. One which has been mentioned in the course of the argument, a glaring instance, is the term 'Bombay ducks' as applied to an Indian fish, and it is agreed that if anybody ordered Bombay ducks and somebody supplied him with ducks from Bombay the contract to supply Bombay ducks would not be fulfilled. Another obvious instance is eau de Cologne. Whatever eau de Cologne may be, as to which I know nothing, it certainly is not water from the Rhine. If eau de Cologne were ordered and you simply supplied a gallon of water from Cologne that would not fulfill the contract. Another instance where anybody would understand what was meant is if you spoke of Roman pearls. They are not pearls with which any oyster has anything to do, nor do I know that they are Roman. They indicate something which is probably neither Roman nor a pearl, just as it was said by a well-known historian that the Holy Roman Empire had for its chief characteristic that it was neither holy nor Roman nor an empire. One other instance occurs to me of a term consecrated, if I may say so, by common user which does not indicate the true fact, and that is when

people speak as they commonly do of the judicial ermine, meaning merely any white fur when worn by a judge. These expressions have become conventional terms, and are, I think, instances of a trade description lawfully and generally applied."[97]

In the other case, *Fowler v. Cripps* (1906),[98] the substance sold possessed the qualities indicated by the descriptive words taken separately, but the description was nevertheless misleading to the ordinary purchaser. The facts were that Glauber's salt was sold under the name of "soda crystals." It was proved in evidence that both Glauber's salt and washing soda are salts of soda in crystalline form; but the description "soda crystals" was by the usage of the trade of manufacturing chemists applied only to washing soda. It was therefore held that an offence had been committed. Wills J. said: "The fact that a description as applied to particular goods is scientifically correct will not prevent it from being a false trade description." While respectfully agreeing with this, it must be pointed out that the words "scientifically correct" mean only "in accordance with the linguistic practices of scientists." They do not mean that a scientist can pronounce upon the "correctness" of ordinary verbal conventions.

Similar problems arise under the Food and Drugs Act, 1938, s. 3 (1), whereby it is an offence to sell food that is not of the nature, substance and quality demanded. At first sight it may appear that the question whether an article of food is of the nature, substance or quality demanded is wholly a scientific one, for are not "nature, substance and quality" matters of objective fact? But on further reflection it will be seen that the question is only partly scientific, being in part linguistic. The question "What, in ordinary language (including scientific language) is the description of the article that has been sold?" is a scientific one, to be settled by examining the thing that has been sold. But the question "What is the meaning of the words used by the purchaser, and does the thing sold (as already examined) conform to this meaning?" is linguistic. In practice, the difficulty that the judge experiences in deciding cases under the Act is always on the linguistic question, for the scientific one can be accurately answered by the evidence of analysts.

97 [1915] 3 K. B. at 752-3.
98 [1906] 1 K. B. 16.

Particularly interesting as illustrations of the linguistic difficulty are the "cordial" cases of the war now ended. Before the war it was the almost invariable practice of manufacturers of the drinks called cordials to put into them substantial quantities of sugar. It appears that the word "cordial" originally signified what is now called a liqueur, but in the course of time it came to be applied to non-alcoholic beverages containing this substantial quantity of sugar. The sugar took the place of alcohol in giving the beverage the stimulating effect that justified its name. After the outbreak of the war, when sugar became scarce, so-called cordials were put on the market that contained no sugar or alcohol, being sweetened with saccharin, and the question accordingly arose whether they could properly be sold as "cordials." This question illustrates three of the perennial problems of interpretation. (1) In the first place, it illustrates the difficulty of choosing between "essence" and "accident" in definition. It was open to the vendors of the so-called cordials to admit that a very large proportion of the drinks sold as cordials before the war did contain sugar, and yet to argue that this fact was a logical accident, the essence of "cordials" (as the term was understood immediately before the war) being that they were sweet; on this view a drink sweetened with saccharin is a cordial. (2) Second, it illustrates the difficulty caused by an incipient change of meaning. At the outbreak of the war a drink containing a large percentage of sugar was clearly a cordial, although that was not the original meaning of the word. Had the practice of selling saccharin "cordials" gone on long enough without legal proceedings being taken, it would have been easy to hold that the word "cordial" had undergone yet another change of meaning. The difficulty arose from the fact that the attempt to change the meaning of the word was nipped in the bud. (3) The third difficulty, which if satisfactorily solved might also for legal purposes solve the other two, is the difficulty of evidence. It is clearly settled that the question of the meaning of a word like "cordial" in cases under the Food and Drugs Act is not one of law to be decided exclusively by the judge's own view of language, but is a question of fact to be decided (chiefly) by evidence. It is true that the judge is entitled to use his own knowledge of the meaning of words, even if that knowledge is a specialized one;[99] also, he may look at dictionaries. But, in addition, it is always open to the parties to give evidence on the meaning of the words. What kind of evidence, then, is to be tendered? This is the crux of the difficulty in cases under the Food and Drugs Act. To formulate more precisely the question for decision in cases under the Act, it is what the hypothetical purchaser who demands (say) "cordial" expects to receive. To begin with, it would seem that the question is not what a particular actual purchaser expected to receive, for, on the one hand, his expectation may have been quite "unreasonable," *i.e.,* unusual, and, on the other, he may not have realised the full implications to the ordinary person of the word he was using. He is entitled to expect an article that he can himself properly resell as "cordial," and the fact that he does not know the ordinary meaning of the word, and is himself quite satisfied with what he gets, is immaterial. The question, then, turns on the expectation of the hypothetical purchaser. But the hypothetical purchaser is an abstraction, who cannot be put into the witness-box. How is the judge to be made to understand the mind of this abstract entity? Scientifically, the proper thing to do would doubtless be to issue a questionnaire to some hundreds or thousands of people who are likely to buy the commodity in question, carefully selected so as to be representative of the community as a whole, and to ask the judge to go by the majority of their answers. This method has not hitherto been suggested in a Court of law, and would quite possibly be regarded as violating the rules of evidence. An alternative method, less accurate but more in accord with ordinary Court practices, would be to draw a number of witnesses at random from the newest Clapham omnibus; but again no attempt has been made to do this. In practice, the only evidence to which the Court listens is that of a few so-called experts. Thus, in *Sopers v. Johnson* (1944),[1] which was a civil action for breach of a warranty of compliance with the Food and Drugs Act, the judge listened to evidence of the meaning of the word "cordial" tendered by (among others) a public analyst and a manufacturer of "soft drinks." Neither of these persons can well be regarded as representing the ordinary member of the buying public.

[99] R. v. Field (1895) 64 L. J. M. C. 158; cp. Bell, *Sale of Food and Drugs* (11th ed) 97.

[1] [1944] 2 A. E. R. 42, affirmed ibid. 586.

In prosecutions under the Act a particular difficulty has arisen. By section 81 (1), "in any proceedings under this Act, the production by one of the parties of a document purporting to be a certificate of a public analyst in the prescribed form . . . shall be sufficient evidence of the facts stated therein . . ." It might be thought that this provision was confined to statements of scientific fact made by the analyst, resulting from investigations that he has been trained as a scientist to make. However, the Courts have extended it to opinions given by the analyst as to the proper (*i.e.,* ordinary) use of words, such as the question whether a particular product is properly called a cordial.[2] One cannot help feeling that this is a confusion between the scientific and the verbal question. The question what such-and-such a product contains is a scientific question, with which the analyst is fitted to deal; but the question whether, given the composition of the product, it is properly called by a certain name, is a verbal question, to answer which the analyst has frequently no better training than the ordinary educated person. Further complexity is caused by the decision in *Collins Arden Products v. Barking Corporation* (1943),[3] where it was held that the certificate of the analyst may be contradicted by witnesses, and that in the event of this happening the Court is left to frame its own opinion of what an ordinary person who goes into a shop would mean by the words under consideration in the case (*e.g.,* the word "cordial"). Unfortunately, the type of evidence adduced in these cases frequently fails to provide an answer to this question.

(4) *Logical Implication.*

One of the apparent puzzles of mathematics, which a philosopher is called upon to explain, is the almost uncanny way in which its pronouncements, if accurately worked out from correct premises, are verified by the facts of experience. The interior of a box measures 6″ x 6″ x 6″. It is desired to fit 1″ wooden cubes into this box. A mathematician, on being given these facts, predicts that 216 cubes, and no more, will fit into the box. Upon the

2 Broughton v. Whitaker [1944] 1 K. B. 269, following Bowker v. Woodroofe [1928] 1 K. B. 217, where Avory J., at p. 225, characterized an analyst's certificate that a particular article was not a meat and malt wine as a "statement of fact." It is submitted that it was not a statement of fact except in the sense that it was a statement (whether true or not) of the ordinary use of words.

3 [1943] 1 K. B. 419, distinguished in Broughton v. Whitaker, last note.

experiment being performed, the prediction is invariably found to be correct. The mathematician is not surprised, for he asserts that, given the accuracy of the premises, by no possibility can his prediction ever be found to be wrong.[4] This looks like a standing miracle. What is the explanation of it? The answer is that the mathematician's prediction, if his reasoning has been accurate, is invariably correct because it was already contained in the premises from which he started. So long as the premises remain constant the conclusion must follow, because the conclusion is merely a restatement, complete or partial, of the premises. This holds for all mathematical deduction, and indeed for logical deduction in general. Statements of deductive logic are necessarily true for the simple reason that they are tautologies.

The interesting thing is that a person may be aware of certain premises, and understand their immediate "meaning," without realizing the logical implication that, in fact, is necessarily contained in them. Thus, a person may know the dimensions of a box and know the dimensions of the cubes that are to go into it without knowing how many cubes will fit into the box. The logical deduction, when drawn, may come as a psychological surprise. Yet the proposition deduced was, in a sense, already contained in the known premises.

In some cases logical implication yields quite remarkable consequences. Illustrations of this occur in geometry, where the acceptance of a few simple axioms involves acceptance of a complicated logical structure. To take one example: a circle is defined as being bounded by a line, every point in which is equidistant from a certain point within the circle. It is not an obvious consequence of this definition that the length of the circumference bears a constant ratio to the length of the diameter of 3 14159 to 1; yet such is the case. Similarly, it is not obvious to a person who knows the English language but has no mathematical knowledge that every triangle with sides in the proportion 3, 4, 5 is necessarily right-angled. In such cases the consequence follows from the premises

[4] Cases are sometimes put in which the mathematician's result seems at first sight to be falsified in practice, but it will be found that the falsification is only apparent. For instance, it may be admitted that pouring a pint into a pint jug that is already full does not yield two pints in the jug; but the mathematician does not say that it will. He says only that the addition of one pint to one pint will, assuming the continued existence of both pints, result in a total of two pints somewhere.

and cannot be rejected without self-contradiction; yet the consequence is not, to an ignorant person, psychologically obvious from a bare statement of the premises.

This element of psychological surprise in logical implication is capable of presenting some awkward legal problems, particularly in the case of contracts, where the Courts are accustomed to reject the defense of unilateral mistake. For instance, suppose that *A* offers to employ *B* for a term of five years, commencing at £1,000 a year, with a rise of £100 every year. *B* considers this offer and then counters by proposing that he be paid by the half-year, starting at £475 for the first half-year and rising by £50 every half-year. *B* knows the mathematical implications of this, but shrewdly suspects that *A* does not. The suspicion is well founded, for *A* thinks, as most people would, that the counter-offer is substantially the same as the original proposal, and that the difference relates merely to the time of payment. *A* accordingly accepts the counter-offer. Actually the counter-offer is very much more beneficial to *B* than *A* thought, for it turns out that, by a freak of arithmetic, a rise of £50 every half-year is equivalent to a rise of £200 every year.[5] At the end of five years *B* will have pocketed £1,000 more under his counter-offer than he would have done under the original proposal. Will the Court hold the contract to be void for mistake on the part of *A*? An even more serious question arises in the case of a trick played with geometrical progressions. In *James v. Morgan* (1663),[6] a horse was delivered in return for a promise to pay a barleycorn for the first nail in the horse's shoes, doubling it for every nail to the total of thirty-two nails. This amounted to 500 quarters of barley, which was doubtless much more than the promisor expected. On action being brought for the non-delivery

5 The amounts work out as follows:—

	A's offer	*B's* counter-offer		
		January-June	July-December	Total
	£	£	£	£
1st Year ..	1,000	475	525	1,000
2nd Year ..	1,100	575	625	1,200
3rd Year ..	1,200	675	725	1,400
4th Year ..	1,300	775	825	1,600
5th Year ..	1,400	875	925	1,800
Total	£6,000			£7,000

6 1 Lev. 111; 1 Keble 569. Cp. Thornborow (Thornborough, Thornburgh) v. Whitacre (1706) 2 Ld. Raym. 1164; 6 Mod. 305; 3 Salk. 97, where the plaintiff accepted a similar recompense by way of compromise, and no judgment was given.

of the barley, Hyde J. held the contract to be good, but directed the jury to give only the value of the horse as damages. This solution means in effect that the contract is undone, for the so-called damages amount merely to quasi-contractual recovery in protection of the restitution interest. It is submitted that this is the desirable result, and that mistake as to the logical implications of a contract, if known to or suspected by the other, ought to have the same effect as a slip of the pen or of the tongue,[7] and render the contract void; at any rate, where the logical implication is substantially different from what was expected by the party under the mistake.

Exceptional cases apart, the Courts will enforce consequences logically implied in the terms expressed in contracts, statutes and other legal documents and transactions, as though they had been expressed *totidem verbis.* Also, consequences may be logically implied not only from the terms of the document taken alone but from those terms taken in conjunction with propositions of fact or rules of law. Thus, speaking of wills, Lord Westbury declared that implication may be founded upon "a direction to do something which cannot be carried into effect without, of necessity, involving something else in order to give effect to that direction, or something else which is a consequence necessarily resulting from that direction."[8]

(5) *Literal and Ulterior Meaning.*

In division (3) of this section we considered the distinction between (1) the intended meaning, (2) the ordinary meaning, and (3) the comprehended meaning. Another distinction must now be made between (*a*) the literal or primary meaning of the words, and (*b*) the ulterior meaning, *i.e.,* the meaning, other than the literal meaning, intended to be conveyed by the speaker when he uttered the words, or the meaning, other than the literal meaning, attributed by a hearer to the speaker.

In some cases ulterior meaning may coincide with logical implication; but the meaning of the two phrases is different. Ulterior meaning is a matter of psychology, not of logic. On the one hand, the logical implication of statements may lie hidden for years, as did the truths of mathematics before they were discovered. On

7 Webster v. Cecil (1861) 30 Beav. 62; Hartog v. Colin [1939] 3 A. E. R. 566.
8 Parker v. Tootal (1865) 11 H. L. C. 143 at 161.

the other hand, the ulterior meaning of a proposition need not be logically entailed in its literal meaning.

The distinction between literal and ulterior meaning applies to each of the three meanings of "meaning" stated in division (3), this resulting in six possible combinations. For example, a tactless host looks out of the window and says to his guest: "It has stopped raining." The guest mistakenly takes this to be an oblique hint that he is desired to leave. Here it may be said that while the meaning of the words to the host is "It has stopped raining" (intended literal, 1*a*), the meaning to the guest is both this (comprehended literal, 2*a*), and also "Please go" (comprehended ulterior, 3*b*). If the host meant his guest to make this implication, there would be a fourth "meaning," namely, an intended ulterior meaning (1*b*). The facts are too scanty for a pronouncement on whether the ordinary onlooker would make the implication (ordinary ulterior, 2*b*), but he would of course understand the literal meaning (ordinary literal, 2*a*).

It may be contended that so-called ulterior meaning as explained above is not meaning at all. In support of this contention it may be said that when the guest reads (or thinks he reads) his host's mind from his words, he might equally have read it from his host's non-verbal acts, like the expression on his face or the impatient tapping of his toe. This kind of meaning is, therefore, not confined to symbols. Also, it may be said that the sentence "It has stopped raining" does not mean the same as the sentence "Please go." In reply, it may be said that although the objections are true in a way they do not affect the proposition that the intention of the host (the state of affairs that he desires to bring about by his words) when he says "It has stopped raining" may be the same as when he says "Please go." Whether or not ulterior meaning is called meaning is simply a question of words.

Ulterior meaning—or, as Wyclif called it, "ghostly understandynge"—has given rise to a distinct literary form, namely, the parable or allegory. In legal matters it figures prominently in the defamatory innuendo and the construction of documents. To discuss the former in detail would take us off into too specialized a branch of the law, but something may be said upon the latter.

It has already been remarked that the Courts will generally enforce consequences logically implied in the language of contracts, wills, statutes, and other legal documents and transactions. The point now to be noticed is that the legal doctrine of implied terms goes much farther than this. Judges are accustomed to read into documents and transactions many terms that are not logically implied in them. As an academic matter non-logical implication may be classified into three kinds: (i) of terms that the parties (the plural shall throughout include the singular) probably had in mind but did not trouble to express; (ii) of terms that the parties, whether or not they actually had them in mind, would probably have expressed if the question had been brought to their attention; and (iii) of terms that the parties, whether or not they had them in mind or would have expressed them if they had foreseen the difficulty, are implied by the Court because of the Court's view of fairness or policy or in consequence of rules of law. Of these three kinds of non-logical implication (i) is an effort to arrive at actual intention; (ii) is an effort to arrive at hypothetical or conditional intention—the intention that the parties would have had if they had foreseen the difficulty; (iii) is not concerned with the intention of the parties except to the extent that the term implied by the Court may be excluded by an expression of positive intention to the contrary.

Concerning the three kinds of non-logical implication there are the following special remarks to be made. First, the name "non-logical implication" is intended to indicate that this sort of implication has no *necessary* connection with logic. In any particular case it is possible for a term to be implied both logically and by what is here called non-logical implication. Second, although the line between the three cases can be made sharp as a matter of definition, in practice they merge imperceptibly into each other, because the distinguishing factor, that of probable intent, is a matter of degree. Third, only in case (i) does the implication amount to a declaration by the Court of ulterior meaning in the sense already defined; in the other two cases the so-called implication is in reality an addition by the Court to the meaning of the parties. The present discussion of ulterior meaning will therefore be concluded with some remarks on the attitude of the Courts towards non-logical implication of type (i).

Generally speaking it may be said that whenever the Court comes to the conclusion that the meaning of the parties has been incompletely expressed, and that the unexpressed meaning can be gathered from what has been expressed (simply because in the circumstances it is improbable that the parties meant their words to be a complete statement), the omitted words will be supplied. As Lord Westbury put it, "implication may arise from an elliptical form of expression which involves and implies something else as contemplated by the person using the expression."[9] But there are some few cases where the Court may refuse to make this form of implication: for instance, it may be excluded by a presumption. An important exclusion of it in the law of wills is in the rule that a will confers no interest by mere implication. Thus, in *Scalé v. Rawlins* (1892),[10] a testator devised property to his niece during her life, and after her death "(she leaving no child or children)" he gave the property to his nephews. The niece died leaving children. It was argued that the intention of the testator must have been that if the niece left children they were to have the property, for otherwise there could be no possible reason for making the gift over to the nephews depend upon the niece's not having children. However, it was held by the House of Lords that since no gift to the children was expressed in the will, effect could not be given to any unexpressed intention of the testator. The policy of this strict rule of construction may be doubted, and there is at least one case where it is departed from. If a testator leaves a sum of money "after the death of *A*" to *B*, the person who would be entitled to the money if the testator died intestate, the Court will imply a life interest in *A*, for otherwise the testator's evident intention to postpone *B's* enjoyment of the property would fail of effect.[11]

(6) The Transition from Implied Terms to Rules of Law.

We pass to a consideration of non-logical implication of types (ii) and (iii). It is common form among judges to deny that they ever read into a contract or other document anything other than what, in their view, the parties actually intended;[12] and occasionally they have even gone so far as to say that the implication must

9 Parker v. Tootal (1865) 11 H. L. C. 143 at 161; cp. Jarman, *Wills* (7th ed.) 601 ff.

10 [1892] A. C. 342.

11 Jarman, op. cit. 606 ff.

12 "An implied warranty, or, as it is called, a covenant in law, as distinguished from an express contract or express warranty, really is in all cases founded on the presumed intention of the parties and upon reason": *per* Bowen L.J. in *The Moorcock* (1889) 14 P. D. 64 at 68; and see the same judge in Lamb v. Evans

be collected from the words of the document itself.[13] These statements cannot be taken seriously. It is true that the declaration of presumed actual intention is the commonest form of implication; but it is not the only form. Courts frequently import into a document terms that are not logically implied in it, and that the parties probably did not think about: or, to say the least, such terms are imported whether or not in the particular case it is probable that the parties thought about them. Examples of such terms "implied" into contracts by rules of law are the implied conditions of reasonable fitness and merchantable quality on a contract of sale of goods, the rule that payment and delivery of goods are concurrent conditions, the implied warranty of seaworthiness, the implied condition on the letting of a furnished house that it is reasonably fit for habitation, the implied promise by one who agrees to build a house that the house will be reasonably fit for habitation, the implied promise by a servant not to disclose secret processes, not to hand over to a rival written work completed for the master, and not, while still in his master's employment, to solicit the master's customers to transfer their custom to himself, the implied promise by an employer (in some cases) to furnish

[1893] 1 Ch. 218 at 229. "The Court has no right to imply in a written contract any such stipulation, unless, on considering the terms of the contract in a reasonable and business manner, an implication necessarily arises that the parties must have intended that the suggested implication should exist. It is not enough to say that it would be a reasonable thing to make such an implication": per Lord Esher M.R. in Hamlyn v. Wood [1891] 2 Q. B. 488 at 491; and see the same judge in Emanuel v. La Compagie Fermiére de l'Etablissement Thermal de Vichy [1889] W. N. 150 at 151. "Implied obligations in a contract must be governed by the common intention of the parties": per Lord Loreburn in Lyttelton-Times Co. v. Warners [1907] A. C. 476. "The Court ought not to imply a term merely because it would be a reasonable term to include if the parties had thought about the matter, or because one party, if he had thought about the matter, would not have made the contract unless the term was included; it must be such a necessary term that both parties must have intended that it should be a term of the contract, and have only not expressed it because its necessity was so obvious that it was taken for granted: per Scrutton L.J. in Re Comptoir Commercial Anversois and Power [1920] 1 K. B. 868; and see the same judge in Reigate v. Union Mfg. Co. (Ramsbottom) [1918] 1 K. B. 592 at 605, and Guaranty Trust Co. v. Hannay [1918] 2 K. B. 625 at 664. "Prima facie that which in any contract is left to be implied and need not be expressed is something so obvious that it goes without saying; so that, if, while the parties were making their bargain, an officious bystander were to suggest some express provision for it in their agreement, they would testily suppress him with a common 'Oh, of course!' At least it is true, I think, that, if a term were never implied by a judge unless it could pass that test, he could not be held to be wrong": per MacKinnon L.J. in Shirlaw v. Southern Foundries, Ltd. [1939] 2 K. B. 206 at 227, affd. [1940] A. C. 702.

[13] E.g. per Lush, J. in Churchward v. R. (1866) L. R. 1 Q. B. 173 at 211. Contra, per Bowen L.J. in Lamb v. Evans [1893] 1 Ch. 218 at 230; per Vaughan Williams L.J. in Krell v. Henry [1903] 2 K. B. 740 at 749.

work, the implied duty of care in the carriage of passengers and in looking after bailed goods, and the implied promise by a banker not to disclose the state of his customer's account.

The view may perhaps be held that this particular process is not very happily called "implication." It is not so much the interpretation of a pre-existing and expressed intent as legislation amending or supplementing the expressed intent. Terms so read into the contract might better be called "constructive" than "implied."[14] However, this is simply a question of nomenclature; and in any case no fixed nomenclature can be maintained in practice, because terms of classes (i) (ii) and (iii) merge into each other. There is no legal difference between the three classes, and the only practical difference is that the Courts are more ready to imply terms of class (i) than of classes (ii) and (iii). Terms of classes (ii) and (iii) are mainly of specified types and are comparatively rarely added to, though it is always open to the Court to add to them.[15] Also, implication of type (iii) is generally confined to the interpretation of bilateral or multilateral private transactions like contracts. Generally, it is not applied to the interpretation of wills, for the Courts disclaim any jurisdiction to reform wills,[16] except in the exercise of statutory powers. Generally, also, the doctrine of separation of powers prevents the Courts from interfering with legislation otherwise than by declaring the probable or (at most) hypothetical-probable intent of the Legislature. However, in declaring the probable or hypothetical-probable intent of a testator or Legislature the judge naturally tends (however much he may deny it) to go upon his own ideas of policy, convenience or justice. Further, there are certain rules of construction of wills and statutes that may, if desired, be thought of as implied (constructive) terms, such as the rule that "children" does not include illegitimate children, or

[14] So Restatement, Contracts, § 253; Williston, Contracts (revised ed.) § 668; Patterson, "Constructive Conditions in Contracts" (1942) 42 Col. L. Rev. 903. There is much confusion of terminology. In Re Cadogan and Hans Place Estate, Ltd., Ex p. Willis (1895) 73 L. T. 387, Rigby L.J. seemed to say that terms of class (i) were express, and those of class (iii) implied. Cp. Salmond and Williams, Contracts, 2nd ed. 24. In Williams v. Burrell (1845) 1 C. B. 402, Tindal C.J. recognized that the phrase "implied covenant," in one meaning, applied to terms of class (i), though he held that it differed in no respect from an express covenant.

[15] Thus in Aerial Advertising Co. v. Batchelor's Peas [1938] 2 A. E. R. 788, on a contract to advertise by an aeroplane towing trailers, there was held to be an implied promise not to fly during the two minutes' silence on Armistice Day.

[16] Per Knight Bruce V.-C. in Bird v. Luckie (1850) 8 Hare 301 at 306-7.

that statutes do not bind the Crown in the absence of express words or necessary implication. No doubt the ordinary lawyer would dislike hearing these referred to as implied terms, but they differ in no way from implied terms of classes (ii) and (iii).

This brings me to my last point, which is that it is a matter of taste whether implied terms of classes (ii) and (iii) be styled implied terms or rules of law. They are in fact merely rules of law that apply in the absence of an expression of contrary intent:[17] whether we choose to call them implied terms or not is simply a matter of terminology. Our terminology as we now have it is not consistent, for there are some rules of law that are indistinguishable from implied terms in their practical effect, yet which are never called implied terms. Such, for instance, are the rules of interpretation. So, also, we do not say that the rule that a contract is voidable for innocent misrepresentation is an implied term,[18] although it can be derogated from by agreement; yet some judges and writers have been known to declare that the law of frustration,[19] the duty to disclose in contracts *uberrimae fidei*,[20] and even part of the law of mistake in contract,[21] rest upon implied terms or conditions. With all respect to those who hold a contrary opinion, it is submitted that the question is purely terminological and has (or should have) no practical importance. This submission may be stated a little more fully for the first two of the three departments of law just mentioned.

17 Exceptionally, the rule that the Crown can dismiss its civil and military servants at will, though said to be a term implied into contracts of employment with the Crown, seems to be incapable of being excluded by contrary agreement. See D. W. Logan, "A Civil Servant and his Pay" (1945) 61 L. Q. R. at 255, 262; Rodwell v. Thomas [1944] 1 K. B. 596. It would be better not to call it an implied term.

18 See per Luxmoore L.J. in Merchants' and Manufacturers' Ins. Co. v. Hunt [1941] 1 K. B. 295 at 318; and cp. Pennsylvania Shipping Co. v. Compagnie Nationale de Navigation (1936) 155 L. T. 294.

19 For a review of the dicta see L. J. Sturge, *The Doctrine of Implied Condition* (1925) 41 L. Q. R. 170. Lord Wright has rejected the language of implied condition in frustration cases: Denny, Mott & Dickson, Ltd. v. Fraser [1944] A. C. 265 at 275-6; cp. his address in *The Future of the Common Law,* 112.

20 Per Parke B. in Moens v. Heyworth (1842) 10 M. & W. 147 at 157; per Lindley L.J. in Blackburn v. Vigors (1886) 17 Q. B. D. 553 at 578; on appeal, per Lord Watson (1887) 12 App. Cas. 531 at 539-40, but see per Lord Halsbury L.C. ibid. at p. 536; per Atkinson J. in Zurich Ins. Co. v. Morrison [1942] 1 A. E. R. 529 at 535. Contra, per Fletcher Moulton L.J. in Joel v. Law Union and Crown Insce. Co. [1908] 2 K. B. 863 at 886.

21 Lever Bros., Ltd. v. Bell [1931] 1 K. B. 557 at 584, 595-6, per Scrutton and Greer L.J.J.; on appeal [1932] A. C. 161 at 224-7, per Lord Atkin.

(*a*) A problem that may seem at first sight to give practical importance to the issue in the law of frustration is one concerning the interpretation of an arbitration clause. Suppose that a contract contains a clause referring to arbitration all disputes arising "under" the contract, and suppose that a dispute arises over the question whether the contract has been frustrated: is that a dispute arising "under" the contract within the meaning of the arbitration clause? In *Hirji Mulji v. Cheong Yue S.S. Co.* (1926)[22] the Privy Council held that it was not, but this decision was doubted, *obiter,* by the House of Lords in *Heyman v. Darwins* (1942),[23] and Viscount Simon L.C. put his dissent on the ground that discharge for frustration rested upon an implied term in the contract, "If, . . . when parties have entered into a contract, circumstances arise before the performance of the contract is completed which, in the view of one party, bring the contract to an end by frustration, and, therefore, discharge both parties from further performance, but the other party does not agree, this is a difference about the applicability of the implied term, and is just as much within the arbitration clause as if it were a difference about an express term in the contract."[24] Lord Wright, however, though he concurred in doubting the *Hirji Mulji* Case, expressly said that his criticism of it did not depend upon the implied term theory of frustration.[25] It is respectfully submitted that this is a perfectly tenable view. It can be held that a dispute as to frustration is a dispute arising "under" the contract, because it is a dispute concerning the application of the law of frustration to the contractual situation; there is no need to bring in the implied term theory.

Although, as already said, the question is (or should be regarded as) purely one of terminology, there are certain reasons for rejecting the terminology of implied term in cases of frustration. In the first place, although the rubric "implied term" is a convenient heading for some comparatively minor rules of law, like the implied conditions and warranties on a contract of sale of goods, it is not convenient as a matter of classification to include under it such a large subject as frustration. In the second place, to speak of the discharge of *both* parties on account of frustration as

22 [1926] A. C. 497.
23 [1942] A. C. 356.
24 At p. 367.
25 At pp. 382-3.

resting on an implied term or condition conceals the fact that their discharge is governed by different principles of law. The discharge of the party whose act becomes impossible of performance rests on the law of impossibility of performance or undue delay; that of the other party rests on the law of failure of consideration. That the principles are different is seen from the fact that sometimes one party is discharged and not the other.[26] A terminology that slurs this over cannot be accounted satisfactory. In the third place, the phrase "implied term" (or "condition") has a threefold signification. It is now clear that as applied to the law of frustration it refers to implication of type (iii), but there are some older *dicta* that make it seem to refer to implication of type (i), and this tends to create doubt and confusion in the law. For instance, it is sometimes suggested that a contract is discharged for frustration only where the frustrating event was not contemplated by the parties, for if it was contemplated by them, and yet not referred to in the contract, no term relating to frustration can (according to this argument) be implied. This argument was rejected by Goddard J. (as he then was) in *W. J. Tatem v. Gamboa* (1939),[27] it is submitted rightly. Discharge for frustration, if we must state it as a matter of implication, rests upon constructive implication, not genuine implication.

(*b*) There appears to be only one case in which a practical consequence was purported to be attached to the so-called "rule" that the duty to disclose in contracts *uberrimae fidei* rests on an implied term. This was the case of *Pickersgill v. London, etc., Insurance Co.* (1912),[28] where the question arose whether an insurer's defence of non-disclosure by the assured was a defence "arising out of the contract" within the Marine Insurance Act, 1906, s. 50 (2). Hamilton J. held that it was, on the ground that the duty to disclose arose out of an implied condition in the contract. It is submitted that the decision is right but the reason unsatisfactory, for, granting that the duty to disclose can be said to be an implied condition, the implication belongs to type (iii), and is simply another name for a rule of law. The proper reason for the decision is that, on the construction of the section, a defence

26 Williams, The Law Reform (Frustrated Contracts) Act, 1943, 26-7.

27 [1939] 1 K. B. 132. Criticisms of this decision are considered by Williams in McElroy, Impossibility of Performance, 246.

28 [1912] 3 K. B. 614.

arising out of the combined effect of the contract (*i.e.,* the agreement) and the rules of law relating to the contract is a defence "arising out of the contract." Were the construction otherwise, the section would have no application, for every defence arising out of a contract is at the same time a defence arising out of a rule of law applicable to the contract, even if it be only the rule of law that a defence expressly given by the contract shall be a good legal defence.

In *Merchants' and Manufacturers' Insurance Co. v. Hunt* (1941),[29] it was argued that, on the assumption that the duty to disclose is an implied term, it is superseded by an express term covering the same ground as (or being inconsistent with) the implied term.[30] The Court of Appeal did not finally pronounce upon this argument, but Scott L.J. said: "I am not satisfied that [the] argument on principle is sound. I realize that there are several reported cases in which judges have, in the course of their judgments, expressed an opinion that the duty of disclosure may be regarded as resting on an implied term, but I do not know of any case where the point has come up for actual decision." It is submitted that in any event the argument has no bearing on the conclusion sought to be deduced from it. Whether or not the law of non-disclosure is stated in the language of implied term, it is evident that the parties are able, if they wish, to contract out of it; and whether they have so contracted out of it is a matter of construction that need not be affected by the terminological question whether or not the law is stated as an implied term.

29 [1941] 1 K. B. 295.

30 Cp. the somewhat similar argument raised and rejected on the law of frustration in the Fibrosa Case [1942] 1 K. B. 12 at 25-6, affirmed on this point [1943] A. C. 32.

Adapted from Vol. 61, Law Quarterly Review (1945).

English as She is Wrote

By William L. Prosser

At the time that these remarks are written, I have just finished reading and grading a set of two hundred and twenty-five law school examination papers. The young men who wrote them for me are all graduates of accredited high schools in half a dozen middle western states. All of them have attended some presentable college for at least two years; rather less than half of them have documents under the seal of some institution of learning which attest that they are Bachelors of Arts. Approximately two-thirds of them have come into my hands from a large, and on the whole rather eminent state university. They are all educated young men, and—since the law school's standards are known to be high, and the work is notoriously difficult—it may reasonably be supposed that they are a selected group.

The examinations which I have inflicted upon them are very old-fashioned and not at all in accordance with the dictates of modern pedagogy. The department of education and the department of psychology assure me with vehemence that they are all wrong, and I am in no position to gainsay them. In the first place, they are of the "essay" type, in which the student is required to set forth whatever ideas he may have in his own words, instead of placing a cross in one of many squares on a paper, which a clerk may then grade with a stencil. In the second place, they are four hours long—a fact which occasionally leads to something approaching nervous prostration from the sheer strain of thinking for that length of time. But what is infinitely worse, they do not even inform the victim as to what the problem is but leave him to discover it for himself. The questions consist of a set of facts of the sort which may wander into any lawyer's office, and to these facts he is expected, in his own words, to apply the law.

One such question may serve as an illustration:

Defendant, the owner of an apartment building, left the door of an elevator in the building open and unguarded. Plain-

> tiff and her children were visiting a tenant in the building. When they left the tenant's apartment, the children ran ahead of plaintiff toward the elevator, and without any fault on the part of plaintiff, entered the elevator and set it in motion. Plaintiff, seeing the elevator ascend with the children, was much frightened, and suffered a miscarriage. The elevator stopped automatically at the top, and the children were not harmed in any way. Has plaintiff an action against defendant?

Any teacher of Torts will at once recognize the case of *Cohn v. Ansonia Realty Co.* Any attorney who has dealt to any extent with negligence cases will recognize the legal problems—the responsibility of a landlord for the safety of common passageways, the obligation to protect meddling children against their own propensities, the possibility of recovery for injuries caused by fright at the peril of another.

I have before me the answer of one young man to that question. Verbatim, it reads as follows:

> Defendent should be libel for the freight. Children are all ways foreseible by a reasonable man the fear of children and their consequences freight is all ways to be antissipated from a woman. Wimmen are afrad of children and she could forsee when he left the elevator open that there might be children and she might be freightened and have a miscarage. The owner of a bilding is required to keep the premaces safe for people who come to visit the tennents and when he causes fear of children and a miscariage he should pay for the freight.

The author of this grotesque and scandalous bit of writing is a graduate of a high school of excellent reputation, in a city of more than three hundred thousand people. He has been exposed to a one-year course in English composition in the state university to which I have referred. He is seeking to enter what is, after all, one of the principal literary professions. One might hazard the supposition that the average lawyer in the course of a lifetime does more writing than a novelist. He must draw contracts, wills, and pleadings, write opinions, briefs, and letters, and set thousands of words on paper where the most meticulous accuracy is of supreme importance, and the use of "effect" for "affect," of "except" for "accept," of "heirs" for "legatees," or of "may" for "shall," may conceivably bankrupt a client. He must use that double-edged tool, the English language, with all of the precision of any surgeon handling a scalpel. When I look upon this candidate for such a life of literary endeavor, I am reminded of nothing so much as the cry of the late Henry van Dyke to the boy who did not like to read: "Poor child! Who crippled thee?" He is of course gone from our law school; yet when I think of the wills that he might have drawn, I cannot mourn his departure.[1]

The example I have chosen is of course extreme. Not many of my embryo counselors at law involuntarily introduce the doctrines of Margaret Sanger into questions dealing with legal liability for emotional disturbance. Not many of them are really good for a laugh. But very, very many of them are hopelessly, deplorably unskilled and inept in the use of words to say what they mean, or, indeed, to say anything at all. Of the two hundred and twenty-five there have not been more than a dozen who write really well, choosing the apt word and saying the thing effectively, so that it is a pleasure to read the paper. Few can turn a phrase. I still recall with affection the graduate of five years ago who reduced *Sassoon v. Lindsay, Bendix & Co.* to one sentence worthy of Macaulay: "A nation which is proud to insist that clothes do not make the man clings nevertheless to the belief that it is the label which makes the liquor." There is all too little of that in these papers. Once past my dozen, perhaps less than half of the remainder are capable of writing a simple essay, in English unadorned, to convey a plain meaning that he who runs may read. The rest shade off into varying degrees of floundering incoherence, stammering repetition, and murky confusion of thought, until we reach a few lost souls like my friend above.

One might perhaps pass over all the bad spelling, although it goes rather against the grain to graduate from any major law school men who after three or four years still write "negleganse," "defendent," "arest," "sueing," "priveledge," and "assaut and batery." I have been told, and I do not question the statement, that there are many well-educated persons who are constitutionally incapable of learning to spell. It does seem odd that so many of them should congregate, year after year, in our law school.

1 When last heard of this particular individual was a guest of the State of Minnesota for an extended term, in one of its more prominent institutions.

Surely there is something wrong when twenty papers, selected entirely at random, yield the following spellings of common, nontechnical words:

two [for too]	speshal	probly
haveing	hazerdous	distinkt
chanse	titel	vishius
rite [for right]	tresspas	oposit
ommission	judje	loose [for lose]
thret	rong	delaid
too [for to]	alledge	mallus [for malice]
dammege	attact	pleeding
alright	weppon	deceipt
ofer	permision	lible [for liable]
criminial	useing	bargan
forsee	recieve	bussines
beleaf	gilty	layed
insolt	writeing	persue
heith [for height]	fense	

I am given to understand that reading is taught by the "word" method nowadays in the primary grades and that very little attention is given to spelling—which may account for the foregoing list. But after all, I suppose that this may not be very important. Perhaps it is too much to ask that an attorney, an officer of the court and a gentleman, shall not be illiterate, so long as he can find a stenographer who can spell.

One might also overlook all the bad grammar, although it is difficult not to wince at "could of been," "hadn't ought to of," "not done nothing," "had went," "when he done same," "these cases is," and the like, on the part of college men seeking to enter a learned profession. I am told that the schools do not bother greatly about grammar now and I can readily believe it. Perhaps it does not matter; if no one uses grammar except the professors, an attorney may possibly do very well without it.

But it is not so easy to dismiss the appalling lack of ability to organize a paragraph or even a sentence, to say simply and clearly what is meant. For weary hours I have struggled profanely through dismal swamps of incoherence, of which the following is a fair, by no means exaggerated, sample:

> The buyer has an action for breech of warenty if he has gave notice to the seller in a reasonable time Uniform Sales Act sec. 48 after he knows of the defect there is a trade name here but he does not give such he has an action no action for breech of warenty also after he reasonably ought to of known the warenty would be implied warenty of merchentable quality here thirty days is too long. You could not bring fitness for the purpose here because there is a trade name Holden's Beer is a trade name buyer took initiative in asking for it so reliance on seller's skill and judgment not here but merchentable not excluded according to Cardozo if this is sale and not service I think it is sale and merchentable quality in spite of trade name but no notice and so no action for breach of implied warenty of merchanteble quality in spite of trade name.

With due allowance made for the fact that the examination was written under pressure of a time limit and under considerable nervous tension, I suggest that the author of this passage is still not competent to write his native tongue. In sixteen years of education, through grade school, high school, and college, he has not acquired the ability to think through what he has to say, organize it coherently, and write it down. It is not his memory of the law which is at fault; the answer to the question is there, if one excavates deeply enough. He simply never has learned to think in terms of his own written language—which is certainly a very elementary skill, consisting of little more than the power to plan what is to be written and to see that there is some orderly connection between the ideas set down. He has traveled a long educational road to plague my June evenings with *sukiyaki* like that. To the end of his days he will remain convinced that he was not treated fairly on the law examinations, because he knew all of the answers, but "didn't know how the faculty wanted them written." He, too, is gone from our law school; and when I consider the contracts that he might have concocted, he remains unwept, unhonored, and unsung. In a greater or less degree, he is typical of a hundred others who are on our hands. Poor child, who crippled him?

It is not for me to say where the responsibility for all this may lie. It is easy to leap to the conclusion that there must be astonishingly low standards in any college English department which has passed these students on. Certainly all is not well. But I do not believe that the fault lies primarily with the colleges. I have great respect and the utmost sympathy for my harassed, overburdened colleagues who are charged with the labored, tedious task of teaching English composition. Confronted with an entering class of a thousand in all stages of literary deficiency, they can do little more than require a daily theme and deal savagely with the blunders. It is a rare student who, given twenty-four hours with his attention fixed on the writing and a fraternity brother to help, cannot produce something which will pass muster. Once the unpleasant chore is out of the way and he has rendered unto the English department those things that are English, he relapses into his own written language, which resembles nothing unless it be Mark Twain's German. Those who teach college English must be reminded constantly of that phrase of Bolivar's that he who fights for liberty in Spanish America has plowed in the sea.

One may question seriously whether the rudiments of writing can be taught in college. It is too late. The most that can be done is to put a roof on the structure already begun. One learns to write, I think, for better or worse, in high school or even before that. The last real opportunity for drill in the fundamentals is in the secondary schools. Whether the explanation is the great increase in the size of classes or the slow lowering of all standards to the level of the weaker students who are flooding in upon the high schools, I do not know; but for whatever reason and however the job is being done, it is apparent that the product is not one of which anyone can be proud.

I am very sure that the high school which I attended in those halcyon days before the war would never have tolerated for one moment the kind of writing which is offered me today by Bachelors of Arts. One wrote decent, intelligible English there or failed to pass until he did. There are high schools today which teach their students how to write. I know, because I have papers from their graduates. There is one in a neighboring city whose graduates consistently are outstanding in their ability to express themselves. One of its old teachers told me why. It was agreed there years ago that any student who could not spell common words, who used wretched grammar, who was unable to frame a series of simple sentences to say what he meant, should fail. As a result of this revolutionary program, the graduates of that high school, every one of them, can write the English language. It seems almost worth the effort.

At the risk of invoking the wrath of those twin departments of education and psychology, I might venture the suggestion that the almost universal use of the "objective" type of examination question, from grade school through college, has done nothing to further the cause of literacy. The very obvious labor-saving convenience of presenting the student with a mimeographed, predigested set of answers, on which he places a check mark after "true" or "false," selects one out of a multiple set, or writes a single word to complete a sentence, so that the whole may be graded by any assistant janitor who has the key—this, together with the comforting assurance that he is either right or wrong, that no element of individual judgment can enter into the final grade, and that there can be no unfairness and no argument about it afterward—has thrust far into the background the much more difficult method of requiring the man to tell you what he knows. It is no uncommon thing for a bewildered and angry freshman, confronted with his initial law examination, to complain bitterly that this is the first time in his life that he ever has been asked to write down his own knowledge and his own thoughts about a problem in his own way and that such questions are damnably unfair—how is he to know what we want him to say?

Without being an educational psychologist, one may concede the merits of the objective question. But where, if not in school, should one gain practice in organizing his own ideas in answer to a question? How useful is knowledge if it cannot be put into a coherent, intelligible statement on paper? Is everything well with an education, when sixteen years of it lead only to utter consternation at the prospect of a little original writing?

What is to be done about all this? I wish that I knew. There is little enough that we can do in the law school, except to be pretty brutal and to see that the professional gates are guarded well. The damage has been done long ago. Standing close to the end of the road and looking back upon an entire educational system, it is easy to see that in one respect, at least, it might be improved. I wish that these people could be taught to write English. Or, failing that, I wish that they would not come to study law.

Postscript. These observations were written in 1938. Any law professor will of course recognize the frame of mind of a man who has just finished reading nine hundred hours of examination handwriting. There is, however, nothing in my subsequent experience that would lead me to alter what is said. It was all unhappily true. I should like merely to add the following mature reflections and comments.

At California in 1954, the situation is not as bad as it was at Minnesota in 1938. I do not attribute this to any particular difference in the literacy of the population of the two states, or in the quality of the pre-legal education of the two groups of students. I am inclined to explain it entirely on the basis of the difference in the admission policy of the two law schools. Minnesota in 1938 admitted any applicant who had completed two years of any college with a minimum passing average. California in 1954 requires a degree of A.B. or its equivalent, and an average of at least 1.5 (middle *C*); and in addition it takes into account the standing of the college from which the student comes, and his score on the Princeton "aptitude" test, and on that basis refuses admission to a good many students with averages ranging from 1.5 to 2.0. The result is that California in 1954 would probably reject rather more than half of the students whom Minnesota admitted in 1938.

Deficiency in writing English is, I think, very largely identified with low college grades. I do not know whether this is because the college instructors, consciously or otherwise, do take bad writing into account in their grading, or whether it is because any one who has reached college age and has not by that time attained a decent minimum of literacy is simply an intellectual lame duck with no brains who never has learned to think. It is an interesting question, on which some one in the department of education may some day do a thesis. However that may be, I am sure that the correlation is there. There may of course be good and sufficient reasons, as there were at Minnesota in 1938, for admitting marginal students to a good law school which will fail them out rather than turning them away into the hands of poor ones which will pass them; but I am convinced that their elimination at least gets rid of much of our trouble with crippled English. What the situation must be in some of the bad law schools which subsist only upon marginal students is a thing I shudder to contemplate.

This is not to say that matters are entirely satisfactory in California today. The deficiencies are still there, although they are displayed by fewer students, and they are not so extreme as the foregoing paper would indicate. The difference is one in degree only, and not in kind.

I am not so disposed as I was in 1938 to absolve the college English departments of all responsibility, and to shoulder all of the blame upon the earlier schools. The task of the English department is a discouraging one, and it is entitled to all due sympathy and allowance; it cannot be expected to make silk purses out of the ears of pigs. But there is still a good deal that it can do, particularly if other departments are willing to cooperate. The Lehman committee experiment on the Berkeley campus initiated a program under which the readers of examinations or other papers in all departments were expected to report serious deficiencies in English, and special study was arranged for the students so reported. A recent meeting of deans agreed that this had been quite successful and should be continued, but agreed also that it was not a complete solution.

I still think that this is a matter of real concern to the law schools, and that there is very little that the law schools themselves can do. I am still quite certain that for the protection of the public these poor unfortunates should never be allowed to graduate from any law school; and that the professional gates should continue to be guarded well.

Adapted from Vol. 7, Journal of Legal Education (1954).

The Language of the Law

BY URBAN A. LAVERY

I.

WHEN SHAKESPEARE made Hamlet say to the grave-digger:

> Why may not this be the skull of a lawyer?
> Where now be his quiddities, his quillets,
> His cases, his tenures, and his tricks?

he was paying the profession a real compliment; and a compliment none the less because it was intended as a slur. A quiddity is defined by Webster as a "trifling nicety," and the word quillet is another form of "quibble." Both words seem to have been in fairly common use three hundreds years ago and Shakespeare used them to express the sharpness of the lawyer and his facility in the use of words even in that day and time. For the ability of the lawyer to confuse others by the use of words has long been the subject of proverbs. The reasons for this distinction—or if you prefer, for this reproach—are not hard to find; they lie in the lawyer's training and in the work he is called upon to do. And yet, no matter what else may be said of him, the lawyer, in his field—even as the physician and the priest in theirs—remains the last resource of other men and women. When the wisdom of common men fails them and disaster is at hand, when the layman's brain is overworked till his mental fuse burns out, when the motor car of "Business" blows out its tires and piles up in the ditches of insolvency, when the human derelict is finally tossed upon the rocks by the stormy seas of life, then the lawyer is sent for and his "quiddities" and his "quillets" are more than welcome; then the myriad complexities of human frailty, and the baffling chicanery of men, test out all "his cases, his tenures, and his tricks."

And yet it is not the purpose of this paper to praise the linguistic nimbleness of the lawyer, but rather to consider some of his defects. It is to ask: Why is it that the lawyer, who thinks and speaks the King's English better than his fellows, falls below them when he writes it? Why does the lawyer seem to lose his mastery of words when he puts his pen, instead of his tongue, to the task of expressing them in statutes, in judicial opinions or in legal documents? For it is an ancient charge that the lawyer, as compared to other writers, is prolix and muddy in his literary style and is unduly given to the over use of words.

But discussing such a subject is no easy task. For teaching others the art of writing—and especially is it true of writing laws—has ever been recognized as a difficult and dreary job; difficult and dreary alike for both teacher and scholar. Moreover, he who undertakes the task is likely to be marked down as an Egoist for his pains; he runs the risk of being called a pedantic preacher. Especially does he run this risk in this day and time, when the world is full of preachers and nobody stops to listen; when everybody gives his neighbor advice on every topic under the sun and nobody pays the slightest heed. Just as a current example one might mention the fact that almost more books have been written about the war than there were soldiers who fought in it; while the River of Ink about the Treaty and the League of Nations flows on and on even though all those who were the real actors in the great drama have silently gone back to work.

There is another point about our task which must be kept in mind; it must be carried out with a nice delicacy and a subtle sense for the Egotism of others. For it is quite true, as the grammarian Goold Brown has said:

> It is even impertinent to tell a man of any respectibility that the study of his native language is of great importance and interest; if he does not from the most obvious considerations feel it to be so, the suggestion will be less likely to convince him than to give offense.[1]

Nevertheless, this most laborious and exhaustive of all students of English grammar proceeds in more than a thousand pages of fine octavo print to tell his fellow men how important the study of their native English really is. Indeed, in spite of the difficulty and delicacy of the task a great many others have done the same thing, for the list of books on the Art of Writing is endless. There are books on writing poetry, there are books on writing prose, there are books on writing scientific English, on writing

[1] *Grammar of English Grammars,* 10th Ed., 1881, p. 94.

business English, on writing orations, on writing plays,—on writing every kind of English except (so far as I know) on writing legal English. Everybody seems to have assumed that all lawyers write good English, even though everybody knows pretty well that they do not. One of the purposes of this paper is to call attention to the lack of such a book rather than to supply it. And if in discussing the subject, this paper too should seem to preach, it is done with fear and trembling; for although words are to be loved when they are well used, yet even more does the active man love deeds best.

And so without further explanation or introduction let us come to grips with our subject.

William Caxton was not only our first English printer, but he was also an observant and careful writer and one of the first English authors to be interested in keeping pure the style of his mother tongue. In the year 1490 he published a translation of the Aeneid from the French and in the preface to his book he refers to the literary style of some of the writers of his time, and says:

> . . . For in these days any man that is in any reputation in this country will utter his communication and matters in such manner and terms that few men shall understand them; and some honest and great clerks have been with me and desired me to write the most curious terms that I could find. And thus, between plain, rude and curious, I stand abashed.[2]

These words were written before the discovery of America, and yet the reader will notice how clear the meaning is and how entirely the words are written in the English of today. For the purpose of getting a good sample of the legal English of that time I turned to the Acts of Parliament, passed during the seventh year of the reign of Henry VII, which was also the year 1490, and there I hit upon an Act to provide for "The penalty of a captain or soldier retained to serve the King in his intended wars, not doing their duties." The purpose of the Act as thus stated is clear and concise; but the statute goes on:

> For as much as it is notoriously known that the King, to his great costs and charges, hath sent his ambassadors to Charles his adversary of France, to have had convenient peace with

[2] Quoted in *Words and Their Uses,* by Richard Grant White.

> him, and to have his right without effusion of Christian blood, which was refused; wherefore the King, by the grace of God in whose hands and disposition resteth all victory, hath determined himself to pass over the sea into his realm of France, and to reduce possession thereof by the said grace to him, and to his heirs, Kings of England, according to his rightful title . . .[3]

This quotation gives less than a third of the first sentence of the statute. The sentence goes on and on in terms and phrases strangely like those of modern legislators, until we come finally to the real business intended, where it is said:

> BE IT THEREFORE ORDAINED by the authority of this present Parliament, THAT any captain . . . etc.

One can hardly help wondering if the "great clerks" of whom Caxton speaks were not the lawyers of his time; and if that author —in referring to the men who "uttered their communication and matters in such manner and terms that few men shall understand them"—did not have in mind the gentlemen who sat in Parliament.

A hundred years after Caxton we find Shakespeare speaking of the lawyer in the manner shown by the quotation already given, and we realize what was thought about the literary style of the lawyers in the Golden Age of Elizabeth. Two hundred years more pass, and we come upon the name of Blackstone—a very great lawyer, but a lawyer who was an exception to the rule, for he wrote in a clear and fascinating style, so much so that laymen have read him with unceasing interest for over a century and a half. Blackstone himself often criticized the language of lawyers. Speaking of the lawyers who wrote the Acts of Parliament he said:

> To say the truth, almost all the perplexed questions, almost all the niceties, intricacies and delays (which have sometimes disgraced the English as well as other courts of justice), owe their origin not to the common law itself, but to innovations that have been made in it by Acts of Parliament, "overladen," as Sir Edward Coke expresses it, "with provisos and additions and many times of a sudden penned or corrected by men of none or very little judgment in the law."

[3] Statutes at Large (Cambridge, 1763), Volume 4, p. 51.

This indictment is pretty severe; though lawyers no doubt will find their alibis. It is easy to think some up; and yet they are not wholly good—for the lawyers *are* responsible for the wording of the written law.

In my work for the Illinois Constitutional Convention I have read and used many books on the subject of drafting laws; but one book, though it is hardly more than a pamphlet, stands alone (in some respects) for its philosophic treatment of the subject. It is called "Legislative Expression,"[4] and was written by George Coode, a member of the Inner Temple, and submitted in 1843 as a part of a report presented to Parliament. The words of Coode are so pat for the subject now in hand, they can hardly be omitted, for he says:

> There is apparently a notion among amateurs that legislative language must be intricate and barbarous. Certain antick phrases are apparently thought by them to be essential to law writing. A readiness in the use of "nevertheless," "provided also," "it shall and may be lawful," "is hereby authorized, empowered and required," "nothing in any act or acts to the contrary notwithstanding," etc., etc., seem to constitute the qualifications for drawing Acts of Parliament.

The author here lays his finger on a defect which somehow always persists. It appeared in the old statute of Henry VII, and it may be observed in this year of grace at Washington, at Springfield, or wherever the work of our modern legislators is considered. And yet, as this critic truly says:

> It is, however, a clear mistake to think that this absurd style, prevalent as it is, and much as we sacrifice to adhere to it, has the sanction of written authority . . . It is to be observed that after all nothing more is required than that instead of an extended and incongruous style, the common, popular structure of plain English should be adhered to.

These criticisms of Blackstone and Coode seem fair enough, and the lesson to be learned is obvious. Yet the form and style and wording of our statutes have been changed but little—to say nothing of being improved—in five hundred years.

4 Printed in *Law Library,* Vol. 29; also found in Brightly's Purdon's Digest, 1873 (Pa.).

This matter of drafting laws is really a large part of our subject and it may well concern our thoughts. Indeed, it may be truly said that the form and style of our written laws make up a chief cause for complaint against the language of the lawyer. For laws, like the poor, are not only always with us, they are above us and around us and almost reach within us. They must be read and obeyed—and therefore understood—by laymen as well as lawyers; since ignorance of the law excuses no man. For obvious reasons therefore, laws should be as clear and simple as possible. Yet, strangely enough, it is in this matter of writing laws that the lawyer often reaches and surpasses the limits of human capacity. If you take up the present Constitution of the State of New York you may read a single sentence from Article 8, Section 10, beginning:

> "All certificates of indebtedness or revenue bonds issued in anticipation of the collection of taxes," etc.

which covers a full page of print. The sentence is far too long to quote, for it contains 462 words without a single break; it is more than five times as long as the entire Ten Commandments, which have altogether 91 words.

Modern law books are full of examples of a like kind, for indeed our constitutions and statutes seem to vie with each other in a race to be longwinded and complex. Two further examples will suffice. The first is from Section 34 of Article 4 of the Constitution of Illinois. Here is to be found a single sentence containing 494 words. Yet the sentence is concerned with a complex and difficult subject matter which would be hard to understand if stated in the simplest terms. This sentence would occupy more than one-third of a column of an average newspaper, and consequently it defies being understood even when read over and over again. The Constitution of Oklahoma has many illustrations of this character; it is full of sentences containing from one hundred to four hundred words. What might be considered as the prize in this regard is found in Article 1, Section 7, of that Constitution, where a "proviso" clause to another sentence contains 237 words. Let the lawyers who read this indictment turn to these examples and answer if they can what is meant by the language used. Certainly no layman—absolutely not one— could ever be guilty of writing in such a style, no matter how difficult the subject or how involved the idea to be expressed. One must admit that this is strong criticism, but it certainly seems justified; because whatever else such examples may be called, they are not written in the English language.

It is not only in writing laws that the style of lawyers has been criticized, but in writing everything else. In order to prove the point let us take up at random two well known modern law books. In Branson's Illinois Forms, at Page 1109, there appears a lease for a dwelling house for a term of years, a form which is recommended for general use. One does not criticize its use; it is far too old and too much crystallized in the body of our law. But certainly the language there used proves the fairness of the criticism here made. One paragraph of the lease begins:

> Provided always that these presents are upon this condition, that if the said rent shall be in arrears . . .

What more do these words mean than if the paragraph began —"If the said rent shall be in arrears?" There seems no difference in meaning or legal effect; except that one form says in 18 words what the other says in 8. In a book written nearly one hundred years ago—and yet a book of the greatest help to the legislative draftsman in his special work—there is found the following quotation:

> From the manner in which lawyers usually multiply terms in order to express their facts *precisely,* it would seem that, with them, precision consists rather in the use of *many* words rather than a *few.* But the ordinary style of legal instruments no popular writer can imitate without becoming ridiculous.[5]

Certainly the language of this critic seems entirely fair if applied to the lease in question.

The other modern book referred to is Foster's *Federal Practice* (Fifth Edition), which will be recognized as a widely used and popular law book. In it there is given a set of forms for pleadings, and on page 2640 there appears a form for a Bill of Foreclosure of a Railway Mortgage. The third paragraph of this bill contains a single sentence which covers more than a half page of fine print; the sentence by actual count has 352 words. It has fifteen or sixteen main verbs and more than a score of modifying phrases and clauses. The fourth paragraph of the bill consists of a single

[5] Goold Brown's *Grammar of English Grammars,* p. 1064.

sentence, which again is very long, for it contains 261 words. Both of these examples (to repeat) are taken from modern law books; and yet it is quite true, as Goold Brown has stated, that no layman could imitate this style "without becoming ridiculous."

Of course, it may be said that counting words in sentences is a poor way to prove our case; and yet this matter of sentence length seems to be the "maxima culpa" of the lawyer. On this point a recognized and authoritative modern textbook says:

> The sentence is the basic unit of expression. We cannot so much as resolve to telephone a customer without forecasting it to ourselves in some sentence form . . . Sentence length in business messages demands consideration in order that the best results may be secured. As a general rule, sentences should be short, because short sentences are more quickly and easily understood than long sentences. A sentence containing not more than fifteen words is called a short sentence.[6]

If *fifteen* words is a short sentence, what then is to be said of the sentence of 494 words in the Illinois Constitution, or the sentence of 352 words in the Bill to Foreclose a Railway Mortgage?

In concluding the first part of this paper let us call—as an expert witness on the literary style of lawyers—an authority whose opinion carries weight. More than thirty years ago the late Barrett Wendell wrote his famous treatise on "English Composition." It has been called an "epoch-making book" and is a work that practical lawyers (as well as other men who write) may study with constant interest and profit. He refers at considerable length to the habit of judges of using interminable sentences in their written opinions. He speaks also of the prolixity of the style of the average lawyer and criticises the "appalling" manner in which legal English is so often written. He says:

> At one time it was my fortune to read a good deal of law; even after I had learned what the technical terms meant, I found the greatest trouble in understanding the books . . . Not long ago a friend sent me a sentence from a respectable legal periodical. He described it as a beautiful expression of legal English, and here it is:

[6] *Hand Book of Business English,* Hotchkiss and Kilduff, p. 58.

At the risk of being tiresome I am giving the sentence in full, because I believe Wendell is entirely fair in his implication that the quotation is a good example of modern "legal English."

> "The comparatively recent introduction of sleeping cars upon the great highways of travel, as a means of public conveyance, while it marks a new era in the history of common carriers of passengers, and signalizes the advancement of the age in the attainment of the luxuries of refinement and wealth, yet on account of the unique and peculiar features of the system as it exists, both with reference to the railroads that employ them, and to the traveling public that enjoy their superior comforts and facilities, there have arisen interesting questions of law, touching the responsibility of such companies, for the loss or theft of the goods, luggage, and valuables of passengers, upon which there exists, among the bench and bar, an undesirable, and, it would seem, needless amount of uncertainty, not to say, diversity of legal sentiment." (p. 225)

Wendell makes the same criticism of the opinions often written by judges and quotes a very long sentence from an English opinion written in 1842, and says, by way of conclusion:

> If the learned judge who laid down the law about pleas of set-off had given a little attention to the principle of unity he would have bettered his opinion without hurting his law; at all events, he would have said exactly what he did say, but in such a manner that an ordinary human being could understand that he was uttering something other than a string of technical words. If the gentleman who wrote about sleeping cars had given the principles of composition a tenth part of the consideration he gave the legal questions in hand, he might, by the simple exercise of good sense, have produced an essay that an ordinary human being could read.

You will read in that book of Goold Brown's to which reference has been made so many times, that Henry VIII, who seems never to have done things by halves, caused a law to be passed by Parliament commanding the English Grammar written by one William Lily to be everywhere adopted and taught. Indeed, the King went further, for he became in name at least one of the editors of the book which was called *King Henry's Grammar.* The privilege of publishing (and no doubt the profits too) was patented by the Crown. Goold Brown states that so far as he was able to learn when he wrote his book in 1832, the old act was still in force in England—at least it had never been repealed. It is not so easy in these days to do such things; nevertheless, we, as lawyers, still have a practical interest in striving for correctness in such matters.

II.

The first part of this paper concerns itself chiefly with some illustrations of the defects in the written style of lawyers. We come now to considering the why and the wherefore of these defects and—with grave modesty—to offering some suggestions as to their cure. It has been said that our subject has been called dreary, and yet it need not be dreary if it is properly presented. As a proof of this there may be cited an admirable modern book on rhetoric and style recently published by the Oxford University Press and written by two men who have largely helped to compile the great Oxford Dictionary. The book is called *The King's English,* and in the preface you will find both the reasons for this dreariness and the ways to avoid it clearly pointed out, for it is there said:

> It is notorious that English writers seldom look into a grammar or composition book; reading of grammars is repellent, because, being bound to be exhaustive on a greater or less scale, they must give much space to the obvious and unnecessary; and composition books are often useless because they enforce their warnings only by fabricated blunders against which every tyro feels himself quite safe.

It is "notorious," say these authors, that English writers seldom consult a book on grammar or composition. Is this not even more true of lawyers? How many lawyers who write briefs or other documents requiring unusually careful statement ever consult such a book once to the hundred times they consult their law books? How many lawyers, for example, know and apply in their writing the proper uses for those fundamentally different methods of expression—the loose and the periodic sentence? How often do they stop to consider questions of syntax, which is defined as "the construction of sentences;" or to consider the laws of good use which apply to adverbs, prepositions, to conjunctions, to participles and infinitives, to relative pronouns and to all the other parts of speech? These things, no doubt, *sound* academic and dreary; and yet when convincing argument is to the fore, or clearness of expression is desired, they are often more important than piled up citations of cases. In this book which has just been mentioned you will find proof that these things are not so dreary or so remote or so impracticable as they sound. The book is made up on an excellent scheme, for it consists almost entirely of what the authors call "Blunders that observation shows to be common." Accordingly, you will find in this book most of the great names of the last century—Emerson, Lowell, Thackeray, Balfour, Meredith—all quoted to show how bad English and bad grammar will sometimes be found in good company.

But our special concern here is with the characteristic faults of the literary style of lawyers, and some of these faults will now be considered in some detail. The chief fault of lawyers is certainly that of prolixity. Webster defines "prolix" as "extending to great length," and then in a note he says: "Prolixity is one of the worst qualities of style." There are, of course, deep and subtle reasons for the prolixity of what lawyers write—reasons which lawyers do not generally realize or understand. They lie chiefly in two ever present factors; a constant and inherent complexity of subject matter, and an impelling urge toward guarded and cautious language. It may be from experience, it may be from instinct—but the lawyer uses his pen as if it were an old-fashioned breech-loading musket; he is always afraid of the "kick" when the thing goes off. Lawyers who are intellectually honest will recognize this tendency toward prolixity in their own experience, and will constantly be on their guard against it.

A clear example of what is here meant is found in the life of Jeremy Bentham, a lawyer who is almost as famous in English law as Blackstone himself. Bentham has been called the greatest law reformer who ever lived in any country, and it is generally conceded that the form and style of the modern Acts of Parliament are largely due to his writing and his influence. He became famous by publishing in 1776 his celebrated *Fragment on Government,* and he continued to write voluminously for nearly sixty years until his death in 1832. He was constantly thundering against the prolixity of statute law. During his earlier years he wrote clearly and well, but as the years went by and he grew older, he gradually lost his sense of style, until his later works became most difficult to read. Ilbert, one of the leading modern writers on legislative drafting, who for many years has acted as parliamentary counsel to the British Treasury, in discussing Bentham's influence on legislative drafting, says:

> Bentham in his early years wrote admirable English, terse, lucid, vigorous, racy, pungent . . . but in his later years his eccentricities grew upon him until he became almost unreadable, except as interpreted and translated by such favorable disciples as Dumont.[7]

It was, no doubt, to take a fling at lawyers in general, rather than at one of the greatest of them, that made Fitzgerald exclaim:

> What would have become of Christianity if Bentham had had the writing of the Parables?

Bentham's case was exaggerated, but his faults in a less degree became the faults of many lawyers and judges. Their style becomes crabbed because they are excessively cautious, because they move so slowly as to make their readers tired, and because they insist upon explaining what needs no explanation.

What I am trying to convey here has been well expressed by John Stuart Mill, who was a great authority on rhetoric and the art of writing, as well as a famous critic of government and laws. He was also speaking of Bentham when he said:

> He could not bear, for the sake of clearness, and the reader's ease, to say as ordinary men are content to do, a little more than the truth in one sentence and correct it in the next. The whole of the qualifying remarks which he intended to make he insisted upon imbedding as parentheses in the very middle of the sentence itself. And thus the sense being so long delayed, and attention being required to the accessory ideas before the principal idea had been properly seized, it became difficult without some practice to make out the train of thought.[8]

Mill was a philosopher as well as a very learned critic and there is a wealth of meaning for lawyers in his words. Does he not here express a cogent criticism of most lawyers' writing? Do *they*

[7] *Mechanics of Law Making,* p. 96.

[8] *Dissertations and Discussions*—Bentham, J. S. Mill.

not also insist on "imbedding" their qualifying remarks in the middle of the sentence, before the main idea has been "properly seized?"

Professor Hill of Harvard, perhaps the greatest American rhetorician, discusses this subject of prolixity in a way to show its importance in writing. He speaks of lawyers and gives a famous quotation which seems still good advice for them, although more than 100 years have passed since it was spoken:

> "Mr. Jones," said Chief Justice Marshall on one occasion, to an attorney who was rehearsing to the Court some elementary principle from Blackstone's Commentaries, "there are some things which the Supreme Court of the United States may be presumed to know."

This quotation is taken by Hill from a textbook on *The Theory of Preaching,* and some of the advice of this book may well be taken to heart by lawyers as well as preachers. The quotation goes on:

> Be generous, therefore, to the intelligence of your hearers. Assume sometimes that they know the Lord's Prayer. Do not quote the Ten Commandments as if they had been revealed to you instead of to Moses. The Sermon on the Mount is a very ancient specimen of moral philosophy; do not cite it as if it were an enactment of the last Congress. The Parables are older than the "Meditations" of Aurelius Antonius; why then rehearse them as if from the proof sheets of the first edition? In a word, why suffer the minds of your audience to be more nimble than your own, and to outrun you?[9]

It is easy enough to be critical, but have we not all heard sermons and read lawyers' briefs—which reminded us of the well known quotation:

> You say an indisputed thing in such a solemn way!

Another chief defect in the writing of lawyers is the fact that they use circumlocution rather than straight, blunt speech. They prefer to go round a subject with their words rather than straight to it. In their use of language they prefer a steam shovel rather than a spade—and then they neglect to cast away the rubbish. Here again we can cite with profit an eminent modern authority,

[9] Hill, *Principles of Rhetoric,* p. 323.

Sir Arthur Quiller-Couch, the famous professor of English literature at Cambridge University. He has written much—novels, poetry and essays—but nothing better than his treatise on the *Art of Writing.* In that book he devotes a chapter—and any lawyer who has not read it is the poorer—to what he calls "Interlude. On Jargon."

I will not ask pardon for making extended quotations from this book because to do so will carry us on our way. The author seems particularly to have in mind the lawyer and the draftsman of legal English when he says, concerning Jargon:

> Cannon is its father, the instinct to save everything and especially trouble; its mother. Indolence. It looks precise, but is not. It is in these times safe; a thousand men have said it before and not one to your knowledge has been prosecuted for it. . . . It is becoming the language of Parliament; it has become the medium thru which boards of Government, County Councils, Syndicates, Committees, Commercial Firms, express the processes as well as the conclusions of their thought.

And he illustrates his meaning by an example which is certainly a common one:

> Has a Minister to say "No" in the House of Commons? Some men are constitutionally incapable of saying no; but the Minister conveys it thus: "The answer to the question is in the negative." That means "no." Can you discover it to mean anything less, or anything more except that the speaker is a pompous person?

It is in what Quiller-Couch calls "Jargon" that lawyers most offend. They have a cautious dragnet method about their work, and they carry the same method into their writing. To quote this author further:

> As a rule Jargon is by no means accurate, its method being to walk circumspectly around its target and its faith, that having done so it has either hit the bull's eye or at least achieved something equivalent and safer.

> Have you begun to detect the two main vices of Jargon? The first is that it uses circumlocution rather than short straight speech. . . . The second vice is that it habitually uses vague, woolly, abstract nouns rather than concrete ones.

By way of conclusion Quiller-Couch gives what he calls "two extremely rough rules to avoid Jargon:"

> The first is: Whenever in your reading you come across one of these words—*case, instance, character, nature, condition, pursuant, degree*—whenever in writing your pen betrays you to one or another of them, pull yourself up and take thought. . . .
>
> For another rule just as rough and ready but just as useful: Train your suspicions to bristle up whenever you come upon *"as regards," "with regard to," "in respect of," "in connection with," "according as to whether,"*—and the like. They are all dodges of Jargon, circumlocutions for evading this or that simple statement; and I say that it is not enough to avoid them nine times out of ten or ninety-nine times out of a hundred. You should never use them.

Under the first rule the author has in mind the "vague, woolly, abstract nouns rather than concrete ones," concerning which he has already spoken. A little thought will indicate how often such words are used by lawyers, and yet a little care will usually prove how these words may be avoided and the writing improved; for such words are mostly used because they are handy dodges of a tongue or pen, whose thought is itself not sharp and clear. Take the words "case," "instance," or "character"; they are all (usually) grab-bags into which we stuff rag ends of ideas whenever we do not care to be accurate and specific. Like Charity, they cover a multitude of sins; and hence they find frequent use. The phrases quoted by the author under the second rule are even less to be excused. It is seldom that such phrases as "in respect of," or "as regards" really help the meaning of what is written; they are usually a sort of spring-board, used for jumping from one idea to another. No doubt it will sometimes be necessary to use such words or phrases; but let the writer be frank with himself and recognize he is being vague rather than clear, that he is being abstract rather than concrete, that he is dealing with the general rather than the specific; or that he is using one or more of the phrases which Quiller-Couch condemns, as a sort of coupling-pin for his thoughts.

It will, of course, be obvious that the lawyer cannot always accept these suggestions. But where is the lawyer who can stand up boldly and plead "not guilty" to an indictment for using

"Jargon" as it is pointed out in these quotations? Where is the literary lawyer who will not improve his style if he keeps such things in mind?

It may be admitted—indeed it must not only be admitted but asserted—that the lawyer's problem in writing is a difficult one. Whether he has to write a statute, a deed, a will, or what not, the lawyer must do more than the average writer; he must make what he writes (as I have heard it put) "fool-proof." Indeed, not only "fool-proof" but "knave-proof." A lawyer must so word his document that it will be impossible to misconstrue it. The average writer does not have this problem; he need only write for the average reader. In other words, he so writes that his words *ought not* to be misconstrued; but the lawyer must so write that his words *cannot* be misconstrued. To put the matter another way, the average writer may expect and demand good faith—that is, an honest intention to get at the meaning of what is written—from his reader. The lawyer, on the other hand, must anticipate bad faith on the part of many of his readers and must guard against it; he must so write that the reader who is seeking some other meaning than the natural meaning of the words used, will be foiled in his purpose. Especially must the lawyer constantly anticipate the astute attack of other lawyers in an effort to destroy or muddle up the meaning of his words.

But conceding this, it is the major thesis of this paper—as will be inferred from what has gone before—that lawyers do not give due attention to the detailed business of what Quiller-Couch calls "Art of Writing." Every lawyer thinks that he can write good English, forsooth because he is clever with his tongue; but nimbleness with oral words is not enough. Roget, the famous author of the *Thesaurus of English Words,* called attention to this fact in the admirable introduction which he wrote to his book nearly three quarters of a century ago. There is no doubt that Roget had in mind writing as distinguished from speaking, when he said:

> However distinct may be our views, however vivid our conceptions, or however fervent our emotions, we cannot but be often conscious that the phraseology we have at our command is inadequate to do them justice. We seek in vain the words we need and strive ineffectually to devise forms of expression which shall faithfully portray our thoughts and sentiments. The

appropriate terms, notwithstanding our utmost efforts, cannot be conjured up at will. Like the spirits from the vasty deep they come not when we call.

It has already been said that lawyers use written words and sentences as if they were to be spoken orally; that is their chief mistake. Conversation is at its best when it is a hit and miss affair —often conveyed by a glance, a gesture, a tone, or even a pause. It is a truism to say that what is well spoken may have an abominable style if written. It is easy to apply a simple test; let anyone listen to the debates of a political assembly or a convention, and then let him read a stenographic report of the same speeches. What was clear and forceful when spoken will often appear disconnected, redundant and even ungrammatical when printed.

We must never forget the magic of the spoken word. It is as different from the written word as a man is from his photograph; indeed, the writing is after all but a picture for a word. The ancient Greeks, who were, and still remain, the great masters of the literary world, knew the deep difference between speech and writing. With them these two arts of oratory and rhetoric were carried to the highest point reached by man; and yet with them the two arts were always separate and distinct. Indeed this must be so. The spoken word is a living, breathing thing which fights for its life in the hurly-burly, and give-and-take, of talk. It is the natural, instinctive means of expression of the human being, compared to which the written word is highly artificial. In talk two or more personalities are always contending. On the other hand, writing is always what lawyers call an "ex parte proceeding"— there is only one side represented. There is no opportunity in writing, as in talk, for instantaneous question and reply. Moreover, the spoken word cannot easily be smothered out, or if it is, it bobs up again in a moment, to be repeated and repeated until its point is made.

If one listens to a heated argument—as an outsider—between even common men, what impression does one get? Particular words are stressed and repeated and repeated again, until all doubts of the speaker's meaning have been cleared up. The person spoken to can no more avoid the meaning intended than he could avoid getting wet if he stood out in the rain—he is drenched in a shower of words. But written words cannot be used so lavishly:

one by one they must pass before the reader's eye and each must make its point or fail, for there is no bringing up of reserves, as in a battle. Perhaps this point can be made clear by illustration. If an address is spoken, instead of written, the speaker—if he is experienced—will see from the faces of his audience the points they do not readily understand and will go back and cover the ground again. If a paper is read by the author to an audience, he can by emphasis and stress and voice control go part way in this direction. Finally, if the audience should read the same matter in type, they would probably be less impressed—certainly they would not get the same meaning or impression as if either of the other two methods were employed. Taken in the order of their effectiveness therefore, there are three grades of expression; first, the oral address; second, if the author reads what he has written; and third, if the reader does all the work and must interpret for himself.

It is just this difference between oral and written words which makes the dictated brief such an atrocity. That document is a mongrel which has speech for its father and writing for its mother; and it exhibits all the vices and none of the virtues of its parents. Such a document shows an utter failure to realize the technique which lies in the art of writing, for there is a technique in writing English, and especially in writing legal English, as this paper has tried to show. It is a technique which can only be acquired by persistence and effort and laborious attention to details; it does not come with the profession, as many lawyers think.

This paper is already over-long, but we are coming to the end. Its purpose was to show that lawyers in their writing overlook—as beneath notice—what have been called the "subtle and inconsiderable elements of style." I know what some of the lawyers who read this will be saying in their hearts; that it is all very pretty, but is academic and has very little to do with the everyday business of the lawyer. If this paper has not already made clear that these things of which we have been speaking are really of the greatest importance, it cannot do so by further argument.

One further opinion on the point will be given from a book written nearly two thousand years ago. The words are quoted from Quintillian, the greatest of Latin rhetoricians, he whom the Romans called "the supreme controller of the restless youth." He said:

> Wherefore they are little to be respected who represent this art as mean and barren; in which, unless you faithfully lay the foundation for the future orator, whatever superstructure you raise will tumble into ruins. It is an art necessary to the young, pleasant to the old, the sweet companion of the retired and one which in reference to every kind of study has in itself more of utility than of show. Let no one therefore despise as inconsiderable the elements of grammar.

Is not this statement as true now as it was in the days when Cicero was the leading lawyer of Rome, as well as the best grammarian of his time? And yet how many lawyers ever concern themselves with these "little things?" How many lawyers ever stop to parse a sentence? To repeat a question that has been asked before: How many lawyers ever consult once a book on grammar or on good use of English, where they consult a lawbook a hundred times? A short examination of what many lawyers write will answer these questions without further search. It must be admitted that the lawyer too often is a careless writer; and he, before all men, might write well if he but strove to do it. But he does not strive; he "dangles" his participles, he "splits" his infinitives, he scatters his auxiliary verbs, he leaves his relative pronouns and adjectives to die of starvation far removed from their antecedents; his various parts of speech are often not on speaking terms with their best friends. And when it comes to making sentences, he piles phrase upon phrase and clause on clause ("imbeds" them, as Mill has called it) until what he produces is as uninviting and as hard to penetrate as those rows upon rows of barbed wire, tangled deep with weeds, which used to stand before the outposts of Verdun. As a result, when he gets through a paragraph of a Bill of Equity, or a section of a statute, he is, as Wendell has pointed out, "far beyond where any human being retains the slightest idea of what all this means."

Adapted from Vol. 7, American Bar Association Journal (1921).

Improving Our Legal Writing: Maxims from the Masters

By Eugene C. Gerhart

"Nature's chief masterpiece," we are told "is writing well."[1] How do we lawyers rate in the literary field?

A few years ago Harvard Law School's Edward H. Warren[2] sounded his bugle for an assault upon current legal literary style with this clarion call:

> The literary style, or lack of literary style, of many judges, professors of law, and editors of, and contributors to, law reviews is deplorable (or, at least, it so seems to me). What is the trouble? Three sources of trouble may be mentioned: (1) sloppy thinking; (2) a love for "half-tones"; (3) a love for resounding words and expressions.[3]

Professor Warren's blast may have helped to rally a band of legal writers who have recently been organized. "Scribes" is the name of this new group. Two of the principal goals of the Scribes are:

First: To develop an interesting way of writing.

Second: To develop a clear, succinct and forcible style.

It would be presumptuous for any lawyer or group of legal writers to lay down *the formula* for legal writing. The reader may recall the story of the Persian philosopher. Upon being asked by what method he acquired so much knowledge, he answered, "By not being too proud to ask questions where I was ignorant." By adopting his attitude we may be able to find some valuable hints which will improve our own legal writing.

---

1 "An Essay on Poetry" in 1 *The Works of John Sheffield, Duke of Buckingham* (3d ed.; London: T. Wooton, 1740), p. 127.

2 Professor Edward H. Warren of Harvard Law School was affectionately known to his students, including the author, as "Bull." He was one who believed in discipline. He did not suffer fools gladly. He called his short review of the best of his life work, *Spartan Education* (Boston: Houghton Mifflin Company, 1942). President Conant of Harvard University said of him: "Your work has been unique and your fame as a great teacher and master of the science of law has extended throughout the English-speaking world." *Spartan Education* facing p. one.

3 *Spartan Education* p. 29.

To achieve the first goal of the Scribes, developing an interesting way of writing, we should first know what makes reading interesting. Rudolph Flesch in his recent book, *The Art of Readable Writing*,[4] gives us a clue. He states that "readability" means ease of reading *plus* interest. "Structure of words and sentences has to do with one side of readability, 'personal words' and 'personal sentences' with the other," says Flesch.[5]

Lawyers' language has long been regarded as the prime example of complex, unreadable, often unintelligible English. Such phrases as "legal technicality," "fine print," "lawyers' Mumbo-Jumbo," etc., should be a warning to legal writers. Maury Maverick summed it up in a new word he coined himself—"gobbledygook!"[6] If the function of writing is to inform or to persuade, the writer fails unless his words convey ideas to his readers. In the best writing the reader follows the author's ideas effortlessly, without being conscious of the writer's words. Complex words impede the transmission of the author's ideas to the reader's mind. Don't you think lawyers sometimes forget that the purpose of language is to *reveal* thought, not to conceal it?

"Short words are best and the old words when short are best of all," says Sir Winston Churchill.[7] He is no mean authority himself, since he won the Nobel Prize for Literature in 1953. Long words are notoriously hard to read. Fancy words are often merely evidence of pompous pride of knowledge. If we want our readers to find our legal writing interesting we must use plain language, and follow Carlyle's advice: "Be not the slave of Words."[8]

After words come sentences. Churchill tells us that he learned English under the tutored eye of a Mr. Somervell. "I learned it thoroughly," he says. "Thus I got into my bones the essential structure of the ordinary British sentence—which is a noble thing."[9]

We lawyers have dealt harshly with this noble thing. We stand accused of being the "one profession that thinks it can't live with-

---

4 New York: *Harper & Brothers,* 1949.

5 *Id.* at 145.

6 Flesch, *The Art of Plain Talk* (New York: Harper & Brothers, 1946) p. 123 ff. See also Lederle, "What the Public Has a Right To Expect of the Courts," 26 *N. Y. State Bar Bull.* 319 (October, 1954) at 321-22.

7 Coote, C. R., and Bunyan, P. D., Sir Winston Churchill: *A Self Portrait* (London: Eyre & Spottiswoode, 1954), p. 142.

8 *Sartor Resartus,* Book 1, Chapter VIII.

9 *A Roving Commission,* p. 17.

out long sentences."[10] The trouble with long sentences is that they become so complex that they are not readily understandable. If they are not readable, how can they be interesting? If you doubt me, take a look at Section 23(p) of the old Internal Revenue Code. The first sentence of that taxpayers' nightmare contained 438 words! Congress unfortunately has just expanded this literary monstrosity in the new Code to more than 450 words![11]

Flesch tells us that the average number of words in the standard English sentence is seventeen. Very difficult writing contains twenty-nine words or more per sentence. We must take more seriously Mr. Justice Cardozo's advice: "There is an accuracy that defeats itself by the overemphasis of details. . . . The sentence may be so overloaded with all its possible qualifications that it will tumble down of its own weight."[12] The French say that "The art of being a bore is to tell every detail."

Fine writing involves more than words and sentences. "Fine writing, according to Addison, consists of sentiments which are natural, without being obvious. There cannot be a juster and more concise definition of fine writing," wrote David Hume.[13] To this Shenstone adds: "Fine writing is generally the effect of spontaneous thoughts and a labored style."[14] Again Churchill summarizes my point well in these words:

> I began to see that writing, especially narrative, was not only an affair of sentences, but of paragraphs. Indeed I thought the paragraph no less important than the sentence. Macaulay is a master of paragraphing. Just as the sentence contains one idea in all its fullness, so the paragraph should embrace a dis-

---

10 Flesch, *The Art of Readable Writing,* at p. 111, and *The Art of Plain Talk,* p. 36. Legal literary writing must, of course, be distinguished from the drafting of legal documents. In statutes, conveyances, contracts, etc., certainty is the paramount aim of the draftsman rather than attractive legal style. "Drafting is more a science than an art; it lies in the province of mathematics rather than of literature, and its practice needs long apprenticeship." Gowers' *Plain Words: Their ABC.* (New York: Alfred A. Knopf, 1954, p. 18).

11 See Section 404 of I.R.C. revision of 1954. Lawyers must yield the palm to Nobel Prize winner (1950) William Faulkner, however. His latest book, *A Fable* (New York: Random House, 1950) contains one sentence which is more than a page and one-half long. Faulkner's sentence contains more than 690 words! pp. 50-52. Philosophers are just as bad! See Blanshard, "Philosophical Style," in the *Yale Review* (September, 1953), p. 547.

12 *Law and Literature in Selected Writings of Benjamin Nathan Cardozo,* edited by Margaret E. Hall (New York: Fallon Publications, 1947), p. 341.

13 Essay, *Of Simplicity and Refinement in Writing.*

14 William Shenstone, Essay, *On Writing and Books.*

tinct episode; and as sentences should follow one another in harmonious sequence, so the paragraphs must fit on to one another like the automatic couplings of railway carriages. . . . Each chapter must be self-contained. All the chapters should be of equal value and more or less of equal length. . . . Finally the work must be surveyed as a whole and due proportion and strict order established from beginning to end.[15] Sir Winston concludes that, "Good sense is the foundation of good writing."[16]

So much for our first point.

We lawyers realize we must adapt our style to our various audiences. But whoever our audience, a clear, succinct and forcible style is the ideal we aim at.

How shall we attain such a style?

Less Abstraction Is the Key to Clarity

Daniel Webster observed that "the power of clear statement is the great power at the bar."[17] Rufus Choate said that, "The best argument on a question of law is to state the question clearly."[18] Legal writers often deal in abstractions. Abstract concepts are usually vague because no word ever means exactly the same thing to two different people. Our writing cannot remain at the abstract level for long and still be clear. We find the remedy in the case method. We can guide our readers to the conclusions we have in mind if we put concrete cases as examples after our abstract statements. It is not amiss to recall that the Master Himself taught by parables. We lawyers might well give those ancient abstract litigants, John Doe and Richard Roe, more modern names. They would become more human and more interesting. Our old friends, *A, B* and *C* are hard to picture as flesh-and-blood men and women. Dickens has proved that symbolic and catchy names—even of

---

15 *A Roving Commission*, pp. 211-12.

16 *Id.* at p. 212.

17 Harvey, *Reminiscences and Anecdotes of Daniel Webster* (Boston: Little, Brown and Company, 1877), p. 118. "Mr. Matthew Arnold once said to me: 'People think that I can teach them style. What stuff it all is! Have something to say, and say it as clearly as you can. That is the only secret of style.' " Russell, G. W. E., *Collections and Recollections* (New York: Harper & Bros., 1898), p. 136.

18 As quoted by Judge Harley N. Crosby in his article, "Mistakes Commonly Made in the Presentation of Appeals," in Schweitzer's *Trial Guide* (New York: Baker, Voorhis & Co., Inc., 1945), Volume 111, p. 1546. John W. Davis agrees that clarity is the forte of the great advocate. John W. Davis to E. C. Gerhart, December 10, 1951.

legal characters—can be made to live indelibly in readers' memories. When we make our writing less abstract and more personal, we also make it clearer, more readable and therefore more interesting.

A clear style is one that is sincere, simple, coherent and direct. It results from exactness in the use of specific words. Richard C. Borden in his excellent work, *Public Speaking—As Listeners Like It!*[19] believes that clarity is the most important element. Says Borden: "If your speech phraseology is clear, you gain more than clarity. To be clear is also to be convincing."[20]

The Scribes have made succinctness another of their ideals of style. Many lawyers suffer from a literary disease called "sentence inflation." They love sesquipedalian words. Verbosity is their habit of mind and expression. Perhaps this is a hangover from those days in England when the master and his clerks were paid by fees and, as Holdsworth tells us, "every warrant, every copy, every report, indeed every proceeding carried its fee. . . . Then, too, we must remember that it was to the interest of everyone concerned to increase the length of all these documents, because increased length meant increased profit."[21] Dickens' *Bleak House* tells us that story well. The cure for "sentence inflation" is to stop being stuffy, legalistic, technical and overly precise in our writing for the general reader.

Mr. Justice Holmes once gave a long-winded lawyer some advice on succinctness. He interrupted the wordy advocate with this question:

"Counsellor, do you read French novels?"

"No, Your Honor. I do not," the lawyer answered.

"Well," replied Holmes, "I recommend them to you. You'll learn to say a lot by innuendo."

In his later years Holmes wrote his opinions *standing up,* commenting that, "Nothing conduces to brevity like a caving in of the knees."[22]

The third of the Scribes' ideals is a "forcible style."

---

19 New York: Harper & Brothers, 1935.

20 *Id.* at page 89. Professor Warren believed that "the best way to be persuasive is to be simple, clear, and terse." *Spartan Education* p. ix.

21 9 Holdsworth, *History of English Law,* pages 361-64. See also Holdsworth, *Dickens as a Legal Historian* (New Haven: Yale University Press, 1928), p. 99.

22 Bowen, *Yankee from Olympus* (Boston: Little, Brown & Company, 1944), p. 324.

Flesch tells us that: "Psychologists have used the ratio between adjectives and verbs for years to measure the forcefulness of writing; writing teachers have been preaching the gospel of the active verb ever since anybody can remember."[23] It seems that the inactive, the intransitive, the impersonal style is preferred by lawyers. Inactive style is not forceful: It is weak. Use active verbs. Watch your adjectives. Use a sharp-pointed blue pencil to strike out as many words as you possibly can without altering the sense, and you will increase tremendously the vigor of your style. Dr. Johnson's only rule for writing was this: "Read over your compositions, and when you meet with a passage which you think is particularly fine, strike it out."

If we are to be forceful we must avoid pedantic slavery to grammatical rules. Jefferson said that, "Whenever by small grammatical negligences the energy of an idea can be condensed or a word be made to stand for a sentence, I hold grammatical rigor in contempt."[24] To occasionally split an infinitive may enable you to better organize your material and to more effectively state your case. Otherwise you may be sacrificing sense to mere sound. Our English language gives us "the inestimable advantage of being able to put adverbs where they will be most effective, coloring the verbs to which they apply and becoming practically part of them. . . . If you think a verb cannot be split in two, just call the adverb a part of the verb and the difficulty will be solved."[25]

On Using Prepositions To End Sentences

Today English teachers believe that a preposition may be a good word to end a sentence with. And why not? When Churchill was criticized for such a prepositional "error," he snorted: "This is the type of arrant pedantry, up with which I shall not put." Neither will any other good Scribe!

Professor Warren did not limit his observations on legal literary style to caustic criticism. He left behind some genuinely construc-

---

23 Flesch, *The Art of Readable Writing,* p. 134.

24 As quoted in Palmer, *Self-Cultivation in English* (Boston: Houghton Mifflin Company, 1925), p. 18.

25 Frank W. Grinnell, Editor-in-Chief of the *Massachusetts Law Quarterly,* reprinted an interesting letter of the late Joseph Lee from which this quotation is taken, in 37 Mass. L. Quar. 65-66 (July 1952). Mr. Lee adds: "If you insist upon your Latin indivisible infinitive, you render the higher emphasis of English speech and literature impossible."

tive suggestions.[26] He estimated that he had written more than 10,000 printed pages during his years in the law. "There is nothing else that I have written that I so much desire should have a wide, enduring influence as the first two pages in the preface to the treatise on *Margin Customers*,"[27] he wrote in his legal testament, *Spartan Education.*

He advised legal writers to stop trying to impress people by the use of long words, or words with which the ordinary man is unfamiliar. We can all profit by the advice this legal disciplinarian gave his students on effective juristic style. Here it is:

1. Never dictate anything which calls for careful thinking. Write out everything (except quotations) in longhand. If you dictate, you are likely to get into a habit of using words of many syllables like "formulated" or "constituted." If you write in longhand you are likely to get into a habit of using words of one syllable like "made" or "was."

2. Make it a habit of life to spend ten minutes a day in reading something in the Psalms or Proverbs or Gospels; and treasure the short, terse, depicting, dynamic, devastating words and expressions.

3. See to it that not less than sixty-six per cent of your words are words of one syllable, and that not less than eighty-three per cent are words of one or two syllables.

4. Go over the drafts as they come back from the typist and rub and rub and rub again until you have massaged away every muddy word and every waste word.

5. If you are dealing with a tough juristic topic, lighten the strain from time to time. If one page has to contain a headache, balance it with another page that contains a smile. A joke may be the most effective of arguments, and the most dignified dignity is an unstilted dignity.

6. *But* avoid being "cheap" as you would shun the plague. You are living in a picture age; picturesqueness is the order of the day. All right, adapt yourself, be picturesque; but *never*

[26] Flesch, *The Art of Readable Writing,* pp. 136-37.

[27] He published his treatise, *Margin Customers,* in 1941. It was distributed by the Plimpton Press, Norwood, Massachusetts. The quotation above is from his *Spartan Education,* p. 30.

be cheap. And be keenly conscious of the fact that the line between the picturesque and the cheap is *not* a bright line.

7. Let learning be your servant, not your master; the deepest learning is the learning that conceals learning. The bread of an idea is worth more than a stone of information. Do not spread out in full your laboratory notes. Do not be *magis in operatione quam in opere.* Appraise your "productivity," not by quantity, but by quality. Read much, discuss much, ponder most, write a little.[28]

Sir Walter Scott's productive facility and his rapidity of writing amazed everybody. What he produced was excellent. A faculty for ready writing is valuable, but intense thought should precede rapid writing. "And herein truly lies the secret of the matter:" Carlyle confides, "such swiftness of mere writing, after due energy of preparation, is doubtless the right method."[29]

What is easily written is seldom easily read! Sheridan's well-known couplet is a constant warning to intellectuals:

You write with ease,
  to show your breeding,
But easy writing's
  curst hard reading.[30]

This is doubtless what led Professor Warren to confess that, "Before I finish a law review article, I sweat blood for a month."[31]

An excess of mediocre writing is a literary offense. No author envies the fate of the Etruscan writer, Cassius, who poured out two hundred lines before lunch each day and the same number after dinner. Horace tells us that Cassius "was burned on a funeral pyre made of his own books in their covers"![32]

Since perfection is unattainable, the indispensable art in writing is knowing when to quit; "how to get done," as Carlyle put it.[33] "Too much painstaking speaks disease in one's mind, as

[28] *Spartan Education,* p. 31.

[29] Essay, *Sir Walter Scott,* in 25 The Harvard Classics, 409 at p. 461.

[30] Moore, *Memoirs of the Life of the Right Honourable Richard Brinsley Sheridan* (3d ed.; London: Longman, Hurst, Rees, Orme, Brown and Green, 1825), Volume 1, p. 55. See also, Carlyle, *Sir Walter Scott,* 25 The Harvard Classics, at p. 460.

[31] 58 *Harv. L. Rev.* at 1115 (1945).

[32] Essay, "An Answer to Critics" in *The Complete Works of Horace* (New York: Modern Library, 1936), p. 39.

[33] Carlyle, *Sir Walter Scott,* in 25 The Harvard Classics, at p. 460.

well as too little. The adroit sound-minded man will endeavor to spend on each business approximately what of pains it deserves; and with a conscience void of remorse will dismiss it then."[34]

What is the reward the legal writer should seek in this finest of fine arts? Whom should the author seek to please? To what critic should he listen most attentively? Emerson's counsel is this: "The way to speak and write what shall not go out of fashion is to speak and write sincerely. . . . He that writes to himself writes to an eternal public."[35]

Here is the advice of a two-thousand-year-old Roman writer whose works are still published today by the Modern Library:

> You must make frequent use of the eraser if you want to write something that deserves a second reading. You must not be concerned for the admiration of the multitude, but must be satisfied with readers who are discriminating but few.[36]

Young Holmes liked Horace's advice. After his classic, *The Common Law,* appeared in 1881, Holmes wrote his friend Pollock: "I hope you will read my book. It cost me many hours of sleep and the only reward which I have promised myself is that a few men will say well done."[37]

Sleepless hours! Writing, like law, like art, is a jealous mistress. Literary fame is won by giving care and attention to those trifles which make for perfection. But perfection itself is no trifle!

> There is no luck in literary reputation. They who make up the final verdict upon every book are not the partial and noisy readers of the hour when it appears; but a court as of angels, a public not to be bribed, not to be entreated, and not to be over-awed, decides upon every man's title to fame. Only those books come down which deserve to last.[38]

Whatever literary fame may come to any Scribe, he should not ignore Holmes' caution: ". . . as long as one continues to write, the question is always of tomorrow and not of yesterday,

---

34 *Ibid.*

35 Emerson, Essay, *Spiritual Laws.*

36 *The Complete Works of Horace,* edited by C. J. Kraemer, Jr. (New York: Modern Library, 1936), p. 39.

37 *Homes-Pollock Letters* (Cambridge: Harvard University Press, 1946), Volume 1; p. 17; see Bowen, *Yankee from Olympus* (Boston: Little, Brown & Company, 1944) pp. 283-284.

38 Emerson, Essay on *Spiritual Laws.*

and tomorrow one may show what a fool one is. So one's head does not swell beyond the dimensions of one's hat."[39]

Perhaps the formula for legal writing is that there is no such formula. Writing itself is an art, not a science to be reduced to mechanical rules. The judge or advocate in the process of exposition, wrote Justice Cardozo, "is practicing an art."[40] Writing is like painting a picture or planning a battle. The techniques and the strategy will be governed by the facts and circumstances of each case. The best writers, like the best artists and the best generals, will achieve their results without being mastered by the rules. This is true because nothing takes the place of an intelligent judgment applied to a given set of facts. Were it otherwise, writing would be reduced to a drill-book exercise instead of the art that it is.

In conclusion, we can smile at old Ben Franklin's verse:

If you would not be forgotten,
As soon as you are dead and rotten,
Either write things worth reading,
Or do things worth the writing.

Writing is one of the few means by which we can respond to that innate desire we all have to be remembered. An art is best taught by example. Yet, lest we become mere imitators we must keep in mind Holmes' admonition: "The best style that a man can hope for is a free, unconscious expression of his own spontaneity, not an echo of some one else. Therefore, although one can learn by reading, the help is only indirect."[41]

If we are to leave behind something worth reading, we shall do well to analyze and emulate the best work of the best writers we know. Perhaps in that way we may leave some spark of inspiration to those who come after us, so well written that they shall not willingly let it die. That is immortality!

---

39 Homes-Pollock Letters, Volume 11, p. 211.
40 *Law and Literature in Selected Writings*, p. 356.
41 *Justice Holmes to Dr. Wu*, October 7, 1923.

Adapted from Vol. 40, American Bar Association Journal (1954).

Law and Literature: The Equipment of the Lawyer

By The Right Hon. Lord Justice Birkett

It was Dr. Johnson who once observed "To those who have been much together, everything heard, and everything seen, recalls some pleasure communicated or some benefit conferred." And I cannot renew this happy and fraternal association without acknowledging with a full heart, the lasting pleasure communicated, and the inestimable benefit conferred upon me, by the fortunate circumstances which first brought me across the Atlantic many years ago. It has been my good fortune to come to you on so many occasions now that the immigration authorities are beginning to look upon me with a little suspicion. Those of you who are familiar with the great lines of Emma Lazarus engraved on the Statue of Liberty may recall that they conveyed a warm-hearted invitation to come to these shores to all those who were unfortunate enough to be poor. Coming from England at this time, I should have thought my qualifications in that respect, at least, were beyond any challenge; and I anticipated that I should easily pass through what Emma Lazarus poetically called "The Open Door." But the immigration authorities, somehow, don't seem to know about Emma Lazarus. It does not appear to satisfy them when I state in writing that I am quite content with one wife, and that I have no intention of trying to embarrass either President Truman or Mr. Acheson. When they interrogate me, as they do, about the purpose of my visit, and I reply that my simple purpose is to bring a message of great good will from the Bench and Bar of England, their suspicions deepen visibly. The art of cross-examination is then seen at its best—acute, incisive, pungent and excessively unbelieving. When, under pressure, I deviate a little from the strict truth in my answers, I comfort myself with the observation made by Chief Justice Richardson a couple of centuries ago. When a disappointed litigant threw a book at his head as he was bending low over his desk, he straightened himself and said: "Now, had I been an upright judge I should have had it."

But, Mr. President, having survived that ordeal once more, I think that this joint meeting is perhaps the most memorable gathering in all the experience of the two Associations. One tiny fear still assails me. In the criminal courts of England, we are still governed by the Criminal Procedure Act of 1865 which allows a witness to be confronted with a statement made on a former occasion inconsistent with his present testimony. I have no particular fear of this, because on all my visits whether in war or peace, I have had virtually one theme only, and that was to say in one form or another that the best and surest hopes of all mankind lay in the closest alliance of our three great countries.

But there is some danger, perhaps, that I might say something tonight that I have said before either in America or Canada, and I have debated with myself whether I ought not to begin, as a young and brilliant friend of mine began a lecture the other night in London to a most distinguished audience by saying: "Ladies and Gentlemen, I have delivered this lecture once before. It was to the prisoners in His Majesty's prison at Pentonville. I must therefore apologize in advance if any of my hearers have heard me before."

History Is a Register of Mankind's Follies

But, Mr. President, I feel I need make no apology tonight if I say just one prefatory word on that theme of former addresses. When I first spoke at Indianapolis under the presidency of my good friend, Mr. Jacob Lashly, I like to recall that I spoke of the ties that bound us one to another—ties of blood, of language, law, and literature, and our unsleeping love of liberty—ties that have become immeasurably dearer since that night in the James Whitcomb Riley room, and are now sealed with the outpourings of our blood and treasure. It was Gibbon, of course, who said that "History is indeed little more than the register of the crimes, follies, and misfortunes of mankind."

The state of the world today gives a terrible and tragic force to it. All over the face of the earth there spread the dark and forbidding clouds of anxiety and apprehension. It is a great and an inspiring thing for an Englishman to come to this great country, conceived in liberty, to which all the nations who love that selfsame liberty turn in their distresses, and to this great gathering of American and Canadian lawyers. My own country, weakened and exhausted by the great exertions of war, will have reason to be grateful throughout its subsequent history for the understanding, the insight, the humanity, and the practical help so freely given by America, and by the loyal and magnificent support of Canada in every time of need.

Our purposes are the same; the ideals we cherish are the same; for in all our countries there is to be seen in the development of our institutions and particularly in the development of our law, sometimes confused and hesitating, but always there, the passionate attachment to freedom of speech and thought, based on the sure belief that only by such freedom can the mind of man itself develop and display its finest powers. In the year I spent at Nuremberg I saw with clear eyes the disaster which finally overcomes a great nation and a great people when the rule of law is disregarded and justice is set at naught. In the place of law, fear reigned; where justice had been, tyranny reared its menacing head. The courts were mere registering instruments of a dictator's will. The judges were the tools of the executive. The secret police were a law unto themselves. There was no place for the fearless advocate, no place for the fair trial, no place for the semblance of justice.

We Must Dedicate Ourselves to Preservation of Liberty

It is altogether right and proper therefore that in these troubled days of ours, we should reflect for a moment or two in all our deliberations on the great blessings we are so apt to take for granted—the supremacy of law and the freedoms which spring therefrom, and to dedicate ourselves afresh to the work of seeing that they do not perish from the earth.

Now, Mr. President, I have thought that I could best serve the interests of your two Associations if I forbore to speak further on the state of the world and devoted myself to some considerations affecting the lawyer's life and work, that might serve as a relaxation and possibly be of interest and value.

Thirty-five years' experience of the Bench and Bar of England have confirmed me in the view that the profession of the law, despite all its detractors, is one of the most honorable and dignified and responsible callings to which a man can consecrate his life, and that the true exercise of the profession demands that such a man should be very much more than a mere man of law. I do not wish to be understood to mean that all lawyers should engage in what Lord Morley once called "the eager and tumultuary pursuits of the life political." As one of our more daring counsel in England once said to a judge who had refused the postponement of a case to a rather distant date on the ground that all the judges on the Bench might be dead by then, "My Lord, that would be too much to hope for."

Lawyers Must Have Wider Outlook than Law

Many lawyers, particularly in America and in Canada, do take commanding positions in public life and therefore bring luster and prestige to the profession, and it is well that this should be so; but what I am to commend to you is that the lawyer in fitting himself for the work of the profession and in its practice should aspire to the wider outlook, the loftier range than the study of the law, by itself, can ever give. One of the greatest of the American Chief Justices, John Marshall, was of the opinion that no lawyer is justly entitled to the honorable and conventional title of "learned," if his learning is confined to the statutes and the law reports.

John Marshall was a great man of law and the value of the opinion I have quoted derives from that very fact; but he was also a considerable man of letters. It was from that wider field that he drew the strength and the inspiration and the judgment that make him a great figure not only in this country, but whereever lawyers foregather. In the course of his professional life the lawyer finds that he is called upon to deal with almost every form of human activity; and every form of knowledge, therefore, is of immense value to him. Not infrequently he will find that into his hands have been confided all that his clients deem to be most precious—reputation, property, even life itself—and it will be his duty to defend those rights and liberties from whatever quarter they may be assailed.

In his address to the Stanford University Law School, Mr. Justice Jackson, whom I am very proud and honored to call my friend, recently gave it as his opinion that while the scholarship of the Bar had been improving, the art of advocacy had been declining. Having spent the best part of my life in the exercise of the art of advocacy I should view any such decline with the very greatest regret. When I was first beginning at the English Bar, Edward Carson was at the height of his power. With his rich Irish brogue and his command of pathos he could move an English jury almost to tears. Indeed he could reduce himself to tears at times, and on such occasion, Tim Healy, his opponent, himself exercising one of the weapons of the advocate, said to the jury, "When I see my learned friend in tears, I reflect that it is the greatest miracle that ever happened since Moses struck the rock in the wilderness." I was myself in the chambers of the great Marshall Hall and I shall always remember that tremendous scene in court, in a great and dramatic murder case, when, speaking to the jury of the irrevocable effect of their verdict, he quoted from *Othello*:

> Put out the light, and then put out the light;
> If I quench thee, thou flaming minister
> I can again thy former light restore
> Should I repent me; but once put out thy light
> Thou cunning'st pattern of excelling nature,
> I know not where is that Promethean heat
> That can thy light relume.

There can be no doubt, I think, that the outward form of advocacy has undergone great changes, but I think it will always be one of the matters to which the profession would do well to give the closest attention. And if some of the younger members of the profession when reading the speeches of great advocates are apt to wonder wherein their power resided, it should be remembered what the younger Pitt once said when somebody expressed wonder at the enormous reputation of Charles James Fox: "Ah! But you have never been under the wand of the magician." The elements of advocacy are many—the advocate himself with his quick mind and understanding heart, his power of expression, his readiness and resource, his courage, the occasion with all its dramatic possibilities, the theme whether noble and lofty or tragic and pitiful, the form and manifestation of all these things—but my own view born out of a lengthening experience is that the most important element in advocacy is the man himself.

Nature and Quality of Lawyer Determines His Success

Knowledge of the law and assiduous training in its growing complexities is essential to any kind of success in the profession; but in the last resort everything depends upon the nature and quality of the man. The first Lord Rosebery, himself a great master of the written and spoken word, said of the oratory of Chatham:

> Assiduous study of words, constant exercise in choice language so that it was habitual to him in conversation, and could not be other than elegant in premeditated speech, this combined with poetical imagination, passion, a mordant wit, and great dramatic skill would seem to be the secrets of Chatham's oratorical supremacy. And yet it would be safe to say that a clever fellow who had mastered all these would produce but a pale reflection of the original. It is not merely the thing that is said *but the man who says it that counts,* the character that breathes through the sentences.

And James Russell Lowell, when speaking of the magic of Emerson, expressed the same view:

> Those who heard him while their natures were yet plastic, and their mental nerves trembled under the breath of divine air, will never cease to feel and to say:
>
> "Was never eye did see that face
> Was never ear did hear that tongue,
> Was never mind did mind his grace
> That ever thought the travail long;
> But eyes and ears and every thought
> Were with his sweet perfections caught."

It would be unreasonable to expect the same excessive care to be given to the art of advocacy in the present age as was bestowed upon it when the world was very much different. Both the Greeks and the Romans paid the very greatest attention to it. They ranked it with poetry, painting and sculpture in the pains taken to reach perfection. If advocacy can be taught, the ancient writers supply a complete code. Over eighteen centuries ago, Quintilian was discussing with amazing insight the qualities to be cultivated by the advocate in the exercise of his calling.

For example, it was he who pointed out the inestimable advantage of knowing your judges. He said: "For it will be desirable to enlist the temperaments of the judges in the service of our cause, where they are such as are likely to be useful, or to mollify them when they are likely to be adverse, just according as they are harsh, gentle, cheerful, grave, stern or easy-going." Could anything have been more tactfully expressed? The tradition that the advocate should try to laugh naturally or at least to smile appreciatively when the judge makes a joke, however feeble, is a survival of the teaching of Quintilian! Lord MacMillan, whose collection of essays *Law and Other Things* should be on every lawyer's bookshelves and to which I am so deeply indebted now and at all times, has developed this theme with his accustomed brilliance.

The Emphasis Has Changed in Our Day

But fashions change, manners change, all things change; and there has been a change in emphasis in our day. The spread of education, the astonishing development of journalism, the coming of the radio with its own special technique for public speaking—all in some measure have contributed to the decline of which Mr. Justice Jackson spoke.

But how rich are the rewards for care and pains in the art of advocacy may be seen, for example, in the speeches of Mr. Churchill during the last war. For let nobody suppose that those speeches were made without immense preparation and the care that ever Demosthenes gave to his orations, for of him it was said "he adopts no thought at random, but takes much care of both the arrangements of his ideas and the graciousness of his language." In the speeches of Mr. Churchill were to be seen thought and character inextricably intertwined, the man himself, and all that his experience and training had made him. There was the unrivalled power of exposition, the gift of enthralling narrative, and there of course was the noble and adequate theme and the sincere and impassioned mind which produced the eloquence that nerved the arm and fortified the heart.

It is true that the advocate is not likely to tread so exalted a stage; but the advocate can at least take notice of the exceeding great rewards which attend the pains taken in the preparation of anything he has to say in court or elsewhere. Great advocacy, I contend, is in the last and supreme analysis, the product of what the man is who produces it, and the plea I therefore venture respectfully to make is that the lawyer when devoting his life to the law, indeed consecrating his life to the law, should enlarge the sweep of his mental vision so that nothing that is human, or that affects humanity, should be to him common or unclean.

Affinity Between Law and Letters Is Very Close

Now with this in mind, I would ask you for a moment to look with me at the relation of law to literature. If the advocate is to add to his purely legal equipment, the mighty weapon of the well-stored mind, knowledge of every kind cannot be too highly commended, and for my own part I believe that from wide reading in the realm of books comes something not to be acquired elsewhere. The affinity between law and letters is really very close. In that moving and memorable conversation between Johnson and Jonathan Edwards, recorded by Boswell, Johnson said: "You are a lawyer, Mr. Edwards. Lawyers know life practically. A bookish man should always have them to converse with. They have what he wants." This famous and much-quoted passage conveys the impression that lawyers and bookish men are in some degree opposites; the lawyer concerned only or mainly with the mundane and practical affairs of the world, the bookish man immersed wholly or mainly in the world of ideas. The contrast is quite false and fantastic.

The association between books and lawyers has always been of the closest kind. It would not be too much to say that in the purely professional sphere of the law, or at the very least, in some portions of it, the work of the law is inextricably bound up with the world of books.

The lawyers of fiction who have become national characters are not perhaps very many, but Counsellor Pleydell in Scott's *Guy Mannering* is surely one of them. You will remember what he said when showing Colonel Mannering around his chambers in the High Street in Edinburgh. Pointing to the books on his shelves, described as the "best editions of the best authors" and in particular "an admirable collection of the classics," he said: "These are my tools of trade. A lawyer without history or literature is a mechanic, a mere working mason; if he possesses some knowledge of these he may venture to call himself an architect."

Lincoln Is Perfect Example of Lawyer as Literary Craftsman

But the great figure of Abraham Lincoln provides the perfect example of my theme. His place in history is now so great and so secure that we are apt to forget that Lincoln was in his beginnings an accomplished lawyer. It was from his lips that there came the noblest short speech in the history of the language. Ten sentences were spoken in five minutes but they will continue to reverberate in the world until the language dies. The simplicity of diction in that speech is perhaps the secret of all great oratory. But whence came this power of Lincoln's to express himself in simple and lucid English?

The popular view is that the great President uttered the Gettysburg speech in a moment of supreme inspiration after Mr. Everett, the orator of the day had spoken for nearly two hours; but the truth is that it was all written out and fashioned with the greatest care.

Lincoln, no doubt, had great natural gifts, but there can be no doubt that his habit of reading all his life gave to him that sense of style and that choice of words that have placed him among the immortals in this respect, too. We are told that as a boy he read everything that he could lay his hands on and some of the books were *Robinson Crusoe, Aesop's Fables, Pilgrim's Progress,* the Authorized Version of the Bible, Weem's *Life of Washington,* Burns and Shakespeare, and (Heaven preserve us) the Revised Statutes of Indiana. If these statutes were anything like those we have at home, they were certainly a great contrast to *Robinson Crusoe* and I shall say a further word about them in a moment. But I want to interpolate here another word about the Gettysburg speech.

Four and a half months before he made it, he had spoken of the battle of Gettysburg and had referred to the founding of the Republic as taking place "eighty odd years since." In the Gettysburg speech so carefully phrased, the famous opening sentence you will remember was "Four score and seven years ago, our fathers brought forth upon this continent a new nation conceived in liberty and dedicated to the proposition that all men are created equal."

Words in Right Order Have Magical Power

Now, words in their proper order are the raw material of the law, and words have a magic of their own; they have color and sound and meaning and associations. But choice words in the right order have a more magical power still. It was an English writer who said: "You take a few words, you put them together and in a way not explicable, they flash into life and you have not a sentence but a song, a revelation, a new creation, a joy for ever." The difference between "Great is Diana of the Ephesians" and "Diana of the Ephesians is great" is as wide as the difference between a revolution and a peaceful protest. "The Vision and the Faculty Divine" opens a window on the Infinite, but "Vision and the Divine Faculty" lets in no light upon us.

Lincoln was in possession of this secret and the contrast between "Four score and seven years ago" and "Eighty-odd years since" will not be lost on all those who wish to use language in its most acceptable and most attractive form.

I wish I had time to spend in a little detail upon Lincoln. Just let me add this and leave it. He was also, because of that reading, the author and composer of some of the wisest and pithiest and choicest sayings in the world. One only will I give you which I suppose is very familiar to you: "A woman is the only thing I am afraid of that I know will not hurt me."

Advocate Must Master Words if He Would Persuade

Now, then, the advocate, therefore, must have the faculty, innate or acquired of being able to use the right words in the right order, if he desires to be a master of the art of persuasion, and this could never come merely from reading the Revised Statutes of Indiana. The historian, Clarendon, when speaking of Coventry, the Lord Keeper of Charles the First's day, said, "He had in the plain way of speaking and delivery without much ornament of elocution, a strange power of making himself believed—the only justifiable design of eloquence." This comes, I must insist, primarily from the man himself and from the form and content of his expression.

Now, because the lawyer finds words to be the raw material of his profession, he must find the words appropriate to the occasion.

I spoke a few moments ago of the Revised Statutes of Indiana. For many purposes the law must avoid what I may call the literary use of words. It must be content to use language shorn of all color or ornament in order to gain clearness. No doubt it often fails of its purpose and the history of litigation in England is a continuing testimony to that failure. But on the occasions when these considerations are not paramount the law has many examples of noble English to show.

As an illustration, if you want to see language employed by the advocate in its simplicity and in its strength, let me quote to you what we regard in England as the finest opening by the counsel for the defense in a murder case ever known. It was by John Inglis, the Dean of Faculty, when he appeared in the great trial of Madeleine Smith.

> Gentlemen, the charge against the prisoner is murder, and the punishment of murder is death, and that simple statement is sufficient to suggest to you the awful nature of the occasion which brings you and me face to face.

And in many of the judgments of English judges it may be truly said that law and literature came into their own.

Connection Between Law and Literature Is Long and Honorable

There has always been a long and honorable connection between law and literature. The books which lawyers have themselves written of the law and about the law are of course very many. I am glad to have upon my shelves at home many such American and Canadian books. But it is of course the life of the law in England that I know best. Some legal books have become the possession of the world. Blackstone's *Commentaries on the Laws of England* first published in the years 1765 to 1769 was one of the great events in legal history, and marked the first beginnings of true legal education in England. Jeremy Bentham said that book first taught jurisprudence to speak the language of the scholar and the gentleman.

But quite apart from what may be called law books, the contribution of law to literature has been immense. I happen to be a Bencher of the Inner Temple, and whilst the former glories of the Inns of Court have in a large measure departed, some things abide throughout the centuries. Clarendon who wrote the history of *The*

Great Rebellion was a member of the Middle Temple; Bacon with the *Essays* and the outpourings of that noble mind, is the glory of Gray's Inn; Sir Thomas More with his *Utopia* is the great son of Lincoln's Inn; and John Selden with his *Table Talk* belongs to the Inner Temple. Henry Fielding wrote *Tom Jones* in Pump Court; Cowper of the lovely Olney hymns came from the Middle Temple (we had one in the Cathedral on Sunday, though that was written by Newton)—Burke, Sheridan, De Quincey, Thomas More, R. D. Blackmore and *Lorna Doone,* Thackeray and a hundred others.

Dickens' Books Might Be Legal Texts

Charles Dickens was steeped in the traditions of the law and some of his books might even be made textbooks. In the famous action of *Bardell v. Pickwick* you may remember that the presiding judge, Mr. Justice Stareleigh, always called Mr. Serjeant Buzfuz "Brother Buzfuz." This was because they both belonged to the ancient order of serjeants-at-law, and though serjeants-at-law are now abolished, if you walk into the Royal Courts of Justice in the Strand today you will hear the judges of the King's Bench Division still calling each other "Brother" as if the old order of serjeants-at-law still survived. Samuel Pepys had a very close connection with the Temple. In the famous diary for 1662 he records: "I walked an hour in the Temple Garden recording my vows which it is a great content to me to see how I am a changed man in all respects since I took them." And then he records the purchase of a very scandalous book from one whom he calls "my bookseller in the Temple," which book says he "is a mighty lewd book, but yet, not amiss for a sober man once to read over to inform himself of the villainy of the world."

It is not possible for us all to go to the great universities, to spend years in the study of history or the classics or literature generally; and yet we would fain aspire to the great role of the finished advocate. There have been many, denied the larger and more glorious opportunities, who have made themselves familiar with the cadences of the Authorized Version of the Bible, that unrivalled storehouse of majestic English, and some of the greater masterpieces of our literature who have found therein a great enlargement of the faculties. The native energies of the mind have been thereby liberated, and all the perceptions immeasurably quickened. To live in books with the great and wise spirits of all time is somehow to feel their virtue and mysteriously to share it; and all these things to the advocate in the exercise of his art are beyond rubies.

Let me end with a renewal of my heartfelt thanks to your two Associations, and to express my fervent good wishes for the years to come. The greatest need of this unhappy world is a return to the universal rule of law, and the spread of universal justice among all the nations.

"Who shall put his finger on the work of Justice and say 'It is there'? Justice is like the Kingdom of God—it is not without us as a fact; it is within us as a great yearning."

From this statement of George Eliot your two Associations are never likely to dissent, and though the age of universal justice may seem at times far off, the ideal is at least discerned, and the life of every lawyer, however circumscribed his sphere may be, lived in the light of that great ideal not only brings honor to the profession but also brings the day of attainment nearer.

We cannot kindle when we will
  The fire that in the heart resides
The spirit bloweth and is still
  In mystery our soul abides:
But tasks in hours of insight willed
  Can be through hours of gloom fulfill'd.
With aching hands and bleeding feet
  We dig and heap lay stone on stone;
Not till the hours of light return,
  All we have built do we discern.

Adapted from Vol. 36, American Bar Association Journal (1950).

Appellate Briefs and Advocacy

By Paxton Blair

I

The diversity of the products which he must be prepared to turn out is a feature of the appellate specialist's practice calling for remark at the outset of any discussion of his work. He is like an automobile manufacturer who must be able to produce a limousine, a sedan, a truck, or a tractor as the customer demands. To vary the metaphor and turn to another phase of his work, he is like an architect who must adapt the plans of the building to the ground he is building on; and here the ground is the Record on Appeal, upon which each brief is to be built and which very definitely conditions and controls its form and structure. It is an old saying that "out of the facts the law arises"; and no argument possesses pertinence that has not some fact in the record to warrant its utterance.

There is no use consuming time in an analysis of the principal implements of research to be found in any law library. It is more important to state that a resourceful and audacious lawyer may and will carry his researchers beyond the law library, and use non-legal authorities to add strength to his argument. This is common practice in cases where the constitutionality of police measures or of sociological legislation is under scrutiny. The practice is sanctioned by the fact that judges used it before lawyers thought of doing so,[1] though lawyers were quick to catch on and follow suit.[2] An article in *Fortune,* for instance, was employed to bolster up an argument that the City of New York could constitutionally employ powers of eminent domain in furtherance of slum clearance

[1] See Judge Vann's opinion in People v. Lochner, 177 NY 145, 69 NE 373, (1904), rev'd, 198 US 45 (1905).

[2] See the brief of Mr. Brandeis (as he then was) in Muller v. Oregon, 208 US 412, 52 LEd 551, 28 SupCt 324 (1908), abstracted in the footnote to p. 419.

projects;[3] and to repel an argument that an ordinance requiring dealers in second-hand articles to be licensed was unconstitutional as applied to dealers in used heavy machinery, there were appended to the brief for the prosecution transcripts of a dozen articles in the *New York Times* describing thefts of safes weighing up to three tons![4]

II

I have already adverted to the fact that an appellate specialist may be called upon to produce various types of briefs. Here are some factors of differentiation: Is the brief one for the appellant, seeking reversal, or for the respondent, seeking affirmance? Is it addressed to a court of last resort, or to an intermediate appellate court? This is an important factor, since the court of last resort can change the law of the State, whereas an intermediate appellate court cannot. If you are before a court of last resort, are you appealing from a judgment of affirmance or from a judgment of reversal? This is an important factor because on an appeal from an affirmance, the court of last resort cannot inquire into the facts; but on an appeal from a judgment of reversal, accompanied by new findings of fact, the court of last resort *may* inquire into the facts.[5] Another significant element to be noted is whether there was a free, *i.e.,* undirected verdict, or was the case taken away from the jury? It is a more serious undertaking to upset a jury's verdict than to upset a court's determination that there were no issues whatever to submit to the jury. Was the judgment appealed from entered after a trial or upon affidavits?

[3] At p. 25 of the respondent's brief in Matter of New York City Housing Authority v. Muller, 270 NY 333, 1 NE(2d) 153 (1936), there will be found a reference to Fortune for February, 1932, p. 61.

[4] People v. Tilford, 268 NY 557, 198 NE 402 (1935), respondent's brief, p. 24.

[5] In New York, if the reversal by the intermediate appellate court has been on the law only, the court of last resort cannot inquire into the facts, for they stand affirmed. It can, in this situation, reverse the intermediate appellate court and reinstate and affirm the judgment at *nisi prius.* Woicianowicz v. Philadelphia & Reading Coal & Iron Co., 232 NY 256, 133 NE 579 (1921); Cannon v. Fargo, 222 NY 321, 118 NE 796 (1918). If the reversal has been on the law *and* the facts, the court of last resort can inquire into the facts; but its disapproval of the judgment of the intermediate appellate court must be followed by an award of a new trial and not by the reinstatement of the judgment at *nisi prius.* Maguire v. Barrett, 223 NY 49, 119 NE 79 (1918); Constantino v. Watson Contracting Co., 219 NY 443, 114 NE 802 (1916). See also Tenth Annual Report of the New York Judicial Council 372 (1944). See, further, Scarnato v. State of New York, 298 NY 376 (1949).

There are, too, special types of briefs with characteristic features, *e.g.*, briefs in support of (or in opposition to) motions for leave to appeal or petitions for (or in opposition to) writs of certiorari; briefs in support of (or in opposition to) motions to dismiss for want of jurisdiction; and briefs as *amicus curiae.* Of these more hereafter.[6]

III

Let us now consider some of the fundamental requirements a lawyer should possess if he is to excel in appellate work.

First of all he should cultivate a good English style. The process is not easy. It will be comparatively easy if the lawyer has a thorough mastery of Latin and Greek. Translation from these languages into English, and vice versa, is a great aid to precision and to grace. Reading good authors is a help, and some good modern ones are listed in the footnote.[7] Nothing can ruin a man's style more readily than the reading of newspapers and weeklies to the exclusion of books.

An interesting observation on the difficulties of learning to write well is found in one of Sir Edmund Gosse's letters. He said:

> ". . . you will not think me disagreeable if I ask you whether you are not a little rash in supposing that you can, without training, at once write in such a way as to be successful. No one expects to be a painter or a lawyer or an engineer in a couple of months. These professions require long training and laborious attention: why should not literature? My own experience is that years and years of study, concentrated on the particular purpose of eventually learning to write well, are needed to result in anything like success. Now, I hope you will not be offended if I say that I was struck in your first letter to me by several indications of want of skill, of simplicity, even of correctness in the turn of the phrases. If you do not yet write a letter well, may it not be that you have not mastered the techni-

6 Special purpose briefs are dealt with in Topic 13, *infra.*

7 Here are some: Philip Guedalla, Max Beerbohm, Charles Morgan, Lewis Mumford, W. A. Orton, D. W. Brogan, J. L. Lowes, C. H. Grandgent, E. L. Woodward, Harold Butler, J. E. Tyler, Rachel Annand Taylor, Rebecca West, Virginia Woolf, Dorothy L. Sayers. Among living judges, one might include Justices Frankfurter and Jackson of the United States Supreme Court; Judge Learned Hand, of the United States Court of Appeals, Second Circuit; Judge Edmund H. Lewis, of the N. Y. Court of Appeals; and Lord Macmillan, one of the Lords of Appeal in Ordinary.

cal art of book-writing? I must not venture to say that this is the case; but if you are so very anxious to write, would it not be well to read much and study the manner of writing before you make another attempt on the publishers?"[8]

It should never be forgotten that in a law office you will find three English styles: (1) the style of a contract, a mortgage, a conveyance, etc.; (2) the style of a pleading; and (3) the style which should characterize briefs. A brief written in the other two styles is a monstrosity.

Having done a great deal of reading of scholarly works in my life, I have concluded that style has continuously declined. Read a page of John Addington Symonds[9]—he flourished in the last quarter of the nineteenth century—and then read a page of any best-seller in the nonfiction field. You will feel as though you had just put down a glass of rare old port and begun to sip a glass of ice water. English judges, by the way, have a far keener sense of style than American.

Some textbooks on style are listed in an appendix.

Secondly, the appellate specialist should learn the art of arranging thoughts in logical sequence. Thus if you are writing a brief on behalf of a person who has been run down by a bus, and are trying to secure an affirmance of the judgment in his favor entered upon a jury's verdict, you would not begin with the medical testimony. You would begin with the conduct of the bus driver. You would stress his speed, and factors—heaviness of traffic, or darkness of the street—tending to show it was excessive. Perhaps there was testimony that he had just taken on passengers, and was busy making change when he should have been on the lookout for pedestrians. You would then go on to show the plaintiff's movements and to negative contributory negligence. Only after all this would it be logical to take up the nature of his injuries, and other factors bearing upon the *amount* of the verdict.

Thirdly, a capacity for selection should be developed. The brief should not be a mere abstract of everything in the record. Select

---

8 *The Life and Letters of Sir Edmund Gosse,* edited by Evan Charteris (1931), p. 249. See also *The Unacknowledged Legislator,* by Bonamy Dobrée (1942), p. 30; Free Minds: *John Morley and His Friends,* by Frances W. Knickerbocker (1943), p. 217. Contrary views are entertained by the gay protagonist in Gentlemen Prefer Blondes, by Anita Loos (1925), p. 14, but probably not by anyone else.

9 Try his *History of the Renaissance in Italy.* Its style is superb.

the circumstances which bear directly on the correctness of the judgment below (if you are for the respondent), or select the most palpable errors in the conduct of the trial (if you are for the appellant). Avoid playing up features which common sense and experience gleaned from reading the cases tell you would not be likely to be made the *ratio decidendi* of an opinion in your favor. Mr. John W. Davis, formerly Solicitor-General of the United States, is fond of observing that lawyers should exhibit the "courage of exclusion." And it does require courage to overcome either the client's ignorant insistence on the inclusion of trivialities, or your own petty fears that the Court might pounce on something you left out. Unless you practice exclusion, there will be a dissipation of emphasis, and a foggy presentation of the issues to the appellate court.

IV

We come now to the form and contents of the brief itself. It is a good idea, by the way, for the author to proof-read the brief himself. By this means, he will detect many defects which would escape his clerk—for instance, repeating the same word or phrase only a line or two apart, or awkward and abrupt transitions, or inaccurate cross-references, or inconsistent capitalization, or misprints too subtle for detection by a layman, such as "casual" for "causal," or "abusive discretion" for "abuse of discretion," or "agreement" for "argument," etc.

It is well upon picking up a record for the first time to skim through it rapidly, and get a general idea of the issues framed by the pleadings, the trial, the presence or absence of technical questions dealt with by expert witnesses, the result below and the sort of relief demanded by the appellant. Talk to the trial man if you wish, though this is not necessary. Then as you write the brief, begin the intensive study of the record.

The use of longhand is advisable. It leads to greater conciseness of language, and it facilitates changes and improvements, and the citation of additional folios of the record where, for instance, a detail of one witness' story is corroborated by another witness later on, or where a narrative is not clear unless an exhibit (a map, a blueprint, a photograph) is called to the Court's attention at the same time.

The opening paragraph of the brief[10] should show how the case came up, and embody a statement of the issues in the fewest possible number of words. Here are three examples:

(a) On an appeal, to an intermediate appellate court, by a municipal corporation from an adverse verdict in a negligence case:

> "The defendant has appealed from a judgment in favor of the plaintiff in the sum of $10,146.88 entered after a trial in the Supreme Court, Kings County, before Nova, J., and a jury. Two jurors dissented. The cause of action alleged in the complaint arose out of an injury sustained in the yard of a public school which the plaintiff attended, when a ball, thrown by someone, possibly another pupil, hit him in the face, destroying the sight of one eye and impairing that of the other. Negligence on the defendant's part purports to be premised on want of supervision over the children at play. The answer is a general denial."[11]

(b) On an appeal to a court of last resort from a judgment of unanimous affirmance:

> "The case is here by leave of this Court. The defendant has appealed from an order of the Appellate Division, Second Department, and from the judgment entered thereon, affirming a judgment of the Supreme Court, Richmond County, entered after a trial before Norton, J., and a jury, and awarding the plaintiff damages for the flooding of cellars and other injuries to real and personal property, caused by the inadequacy of a certain drain or culvert. In seeking leave to appeal, we urged that the failure to file a notice of claim and of intention to sue, under Administrative Code, § 394a-1.0, should have been deemed a fatal defect requiring the dismissal of the complaint, and that compliance with this statute was not dispensed with by the circumstance that (since the trespass was a continuing one)

---

10 What is here said concerning the order of the elements in the brief should be checked against the rules of the court before which you are appearing. They may prescribe a different order.

In rare instances, the whole appeal may turn on questions of fact. In that event, there need be no preliminary narrative of the facts; they may be developed under headnotes devoted to them instead of to propositions of law. See the prosecution's brief in People v. Hidden, 263 AppDiv 534, 33 NYS (2d) 494 (1st Dep't 1942).

11 From the defendant's brief in Graff v. Board of Education, 258 AppDiv 813, 15 NYS (2d) 941 (2d Dep't 1939), aff'd, 283 NY 574, 27 NE (2d) 438 (1940).

the complaint asked for injunctive relief in the alternative. This is the only question of law in the case."[12]

(c) From the respondent's brief, where a judgment of unconstitutionality has been reversed by the intermediate appellate court:

> "The petitioner has appealed from an order of the Appellate Division, First Department, which, with two Justices dissenting, (1) reversed an order, in the nature of a mandamus order, of the Supreme Court, New York County (Bernstein, J.), directing the Commissioner of Public Markets to rescind the revocation of a petitioner's license as a live poultry dealer in the City of New York and to reissue the license and to refrain from revoking it for non-payment of poultry-grading bills, and (2) directed the dismissal of the complaint. The Special Term had held that New York City Local Law No. 32 of 1942, known as the live poultry law, was null and void because not authorized by the City Home Rule Law, and because it violated the due process and equal protection clauses of the State and federal constitutions. The Appellate Division upheld the Local Law in all respects."[13]

After the opening paragraph, the order I recommend is this:

Pleadings;

Facts (or, if you prefer, "The Trial" or "The Testimony");

Statutes involved (if any);

Opinion below (if any);

Outline of argument (the point-headings all grouped together for ready reference);

The points, one after the other;

Conclusion (preceded by summary if length of brief warrants it).

V

As to the treatment of pleadings, the first precept is: Paraphrase them in your own language. Remember what was said about the three English styles to be found in any law office. The pleadings, when abstracted in a brief, should therefore be recast in the English style appropriate to a brief.

---

[12] From the defendant's brief in Missall v. Palma, 292 NY 563, 54 NE (2d) 686 (1944).

[13] From the defendant's brief in Matter of Avon Western Corp. v. Woolley, 291 NY 687, 52 NE (2d) 587 (1943).

Adherence to a chronological order aids clarity of presentation. In analyzing the pleadings in a negligence action, for instance, state briefly how the accident is alleged to have occurred, and then state whether the answer is a general denial, or contributory negligence, or a release under seal, etc. Or if the action is by a seller of goods, demanding the purchase price, show whether the defense is breach of warranty, or delay in delivery, or rescission, etc.

VI

In presenting the facts, I recommend the "mosaic" method. By that I mean that you should take each essential fact—generally in chronological order—and piece together what each witness had to say on the particular subject, so that the appellate court can have in readily comprehensible form everything that the jury had before it, and thus be facilitated in determining whether the verdict was consistent with the evidence or not. If, as appellant, you are arguing that the verdict is against the weight of the evidence and are going to conclude by asking for a reversal and a new trial, then you may analyze the stories of both the plaintiff's witnesses and the defendant's. But if, on behalf of a defendant-appellant, you are asking for a reversal of the judgment *and the dismissal of the complaint,* then you must confine your argument to what the plaintiff's witnesses said, and ignore the defendant's witnesses,[14] for the premise is that the plaintiff failed to make out a *prima facie* case. What the defendant did or failed to do is irrelevant.[15]

If on behalf of a plaintiff you are seeking to reverse a dismissal at the close of the plaintiff's case, or a directed verdict for defendant at the close of the entire case, your burden is comparatively slight.

14 See the brief (unsuccessful, to be sure) in McGarry Contracting Co. v. Board of Education, 289 NY 706, 45 NE (2d) 459 (1942), where I was compelled to pass over in silence some 360 pages of testimony and 70 pages of exhibits on behalf of my client, the defendant-appellant.

15 A rare exception occurs where the defendant is in a position to show that his affirmative defense was fully established and never rebutted. But in attacking the sufficiency of the plaintiff's proofs you must not forget the possibility that, if you, as the defendant's attorney, did not rest when the judge denied your motion to dismiss at the close of the plaintiff's case, the plaintiff may rely on something in your case to fill in the chinks in his own. Dixon v. Smith-Wallace Shoe Co., 283 Ill 234, 243, 119 NE 265, 269 (1918); State v. Denison, 352 Mo 572, 577, 178 SW (2d) 449, 452 (1944); Sigua Iron Co. v. Brown, 171 NY 488, 64 NE 194 (1902); Costello v. City of New York, 273 AppDiv 992, 79 NYS (2d) 324 (1st Dep't 1948); 9 Widmore, Evidence § 2496 (3) (3d ed. 1940); 6 Carmody, Pleading and Practice in New York § 398 (2d ed. 1932).

All you have to do is to show there were questions of fact which should have been left to the jury.

In the average record, you can usually discern the pattern in the carpet after reading the first thirty or forty pages of the testimony, and you can perceive what facts are likely to have been responsible for what the court below did. You can orient yourself in the appellate court with these in mind, and, if you represent the appellant, attack their legal sufficiency to support a judgment, or, if you represent the respondent, argue for their adequacy.

Testimony hostile to your client should not be passed over in silence. You can try to palliate it by showing that the witness who testified to facts unfavorable to your position was (1) contradicted by other witnesses whose position enabled them to see more accurately what really took place;[16] or (2) distorted by interest; or (3) caught lying in other particulars.

You must exercise a capacity for selection in analyzing testimony. Do not waste the time of the court in describing factors or events having no direct bearing on the result. Confine yourself to those which will enable the appellate court to bring the issue readily into focus, and, after seeing what probably influenced the court below, to pass upon the legal sufficiency of it.

Long quotations from testimony should be avoided. Quotations should be broken up after twenty lines, and a short interpolation of your own language made before resuming the quotation, or a reference may be made to other testimony supporting, qualifying or refuting the passage quoted. The latter device is normal when you are adhering to the "mosaic" method referred to above.

References to the pages or folios of the record accompanying quotations of testimony should precede a direct quotation and should follow an indirect quotation.

VII

When statutes are involved in the case under appeal, they should be paraphrased in the English style appropriate to a brief, with, however, a direct quotation here and there of a crucial phrase, if necessary.

16 When, for example, the speed of a car is in issue, the estimate of someone in a following car is less likely to be accurate than that of a person standing on the sidewalk and viewing the moving car broadside.

Argumentative matter, such as the solution of problems of construing interlocking statutes, should be deferred to the law points of the brief.

VIII

The opinion of the court below should be abstracted briefly, dispassionately and without argumentative distortion. It is permissible however, for an appellant to insert, either in parentheses or in a footnote, brief citations to such parts of the testimony as may be direct and powerful in their capacity to suggest error on the court's part. Never treat with sneers or disrespect an opinion with which you disagree. There is an *entente cordiale* among judges, and the pertinacious or indiscreet criticism of a decision in counsel's brief may inspire the appellate judges to seek out fresh grounds for affirmance.

IX

Precept Number One, when it comes to headnotes, is: *avoid blind headnotes.* By this I mean avoid headnotes which are so unenlightening and undistinguished that they might fit any one of a hundred records, and therefore fail to give a clue to any of the propositions of law which inhere in this particular record alone and differentiate it from all others. It is bad to phrase a headnote thus: "The verdict was against the weight of the evidence." Or: "The verdict was proper and should not be disturbed." Or: "The plaintiff failed to make out a *prima facie* case." Here are examples of headnotes on adequacy of evidence which do not exhibit the vice of blindness:

> "The plaintiff having been caught lying in collateral matters on several occasions, and her supporting witness having told a story which was so inherently improbable and devoid of circumstantiality that it may well be doubted whether she was even present when the accident happened; the verdict in her favor was against the weight of the credible evidence."[17]
>
> "The shocking inconsistency between plaintiff's story on the stand and the story he told the hospital attendants immediately after the accident, and the inconsistency between his own assertion of loss of consciousness and the doctors' testimony of

[17] Schwartz v. Murray, 266 AppDiv 1025, 45 NYS (2d) 278 (2d Dep't 1943).

> conversations with him, show that the verdict was against the weight of the credible evidence."[18]

Or, on an appeal from a decree in equity reforming a contract:

> "The complaint being premised on a scrivener's error and mutuality of mistake, it should have been dismissed when the scrivener testified he did exactly as told, and defendant-appellant testified that the writing exactly embodied her conception of the contract."[19]

Or, where the respondent seeks to justify the dismissal of a complaint in negligence where the plaintiff failed to prove notice:

> "The plaintiff having failed to prove notice of the presence of the sputum on the stairway, and her witnesses having described the sputum as still wet at the moment of the accident, the Trial Court rightly dismissed the complaint for failure to prove notice."[20]

The order of the headnotes is important and should be chosen with an eye toward sequacity or logical inevitableness. They should exhibit a tendency to follow one another as the night the day, so that when read in sequence they resound with a note of inevitability, and tend to sweep the court into agreement with counsel's contentions.

To achieve this, you must try to put yourself in the court's shoes. Look at the brief objectively, and see whether the logic is smooth or fails to show consecutiveness. Headnotes prefaced by "even if" are permissible. They sketch a secondary line of defense, and follow after the strongest headnote. Courts generally do not regard employing "even if" headnotes as a sign of weakness, but often welcome them as affording an easier way out. Such headnotes may open the door to a decision your way by permitting the court to adopt a narrow *ratio decidendi,* rather than undertake the trouble of phrasing a broad proposition of law.

Considerations of policy, and not only considerations of logic, may affect the order of headnotes. Generally speaking, state first the proposition on which it would be easiest to decide your way. Integrate this principle with the principle that courts are reluctant

[18] Behnke v. Brooklyn & Queens Transit Corp., 263 AppDiv 737, 31 NYS (2d) 28 (2d Dep't 1941).

[19] Sargent v. Black, 270 AppDiv 828, 61 NYS (2d) 383 (2d Dep't 1946).

[20] Clark v. Murray, 289 NY 746, 46 NE (2d) 353 (1942).

to decide cases on technicalities which side-step the merits. Thus a jurisdictional point should be briefed first only if clear and strong.[21] And a point urging that the complaint against a municipality be dismissed because of a defective notice of claim should normally come in last, though here, too, exceptional strength may justify pushing it up ahead.

Headnotes should not exceed four in number. That is about the limit the court can bear in mind, both during the argument and during their ensuing conferences. Loss through dissipation of emphasis ensues if this rule is violated. Only the most extraordinarily long and complex record justifies a departure. I kept within the rule on a certain occasion where I had a five-volume record, dealing with titles from 1636 to 1937.[22] If you practice that "courage of exclusion" already referred to, and avoid wasting time and words on what reflection will tell you is unlikely to be a basis of decision, compressing the headnotes into four will not be difficult.[23]

When arguments are being addressed to an appellate court, you should be alert to avoid reflections on the intelligence of the court from which (and, *a fortiori,* of the court to which) you are appealing. Reflections on opposing counsel are likewise unwelcome in an appellate court. It is sometimes wise to refer in a complimentary way to the zeal or industry of opposing counsel to prevent hurting his feelings with your attack on the logical soundness of what he has said in his brief.

X

The treatment of authorities is a difficult matter upon which to make general statements. But three principles have recognized force and pertinence:

(a) Be absolutely sure of their accuracy. If you have before you a recent case in a *nisi prius* court or in an intermediate court of appeal, do not rest content with Shepardizing it. Shepard's Citations can never be right up to the minute. Inquire at the office

21 For an example of the successful use of this device in a respondent's brief, see Matter of Board of Transportation, 272 NY 52, 4 NE (2d) 214 (1936).

22 Matter of City of New York, 275 NY 456, 11 NE (2d) 294 (1937).

23 For an extreme example of compression into four headnotes where the record was bristling with a multitude of questions of law, see my brief in McGoldrick v. Gulf Oil Corp., 309 US 414, 84 LEd 840, 60 SupCt 664 (1940).

of the clerk of the next higher court as to whether an appeal has been docketed in the named case; and whether argument and decision have taken place.

(b) Never cite a lower court decision to a higher court. However, if you have a point which is *res nova* in the higher court but which is found among the decisions of a lower court, cite it with a suggestion of apology, viz.: "This is only a lower court decision but we feel its reasoning should commend it to this court."

(c) Go slow about relying on decisions of the Supreme Court of the United States in any but the federal field. That Court is not a court of law today so much as a court of policy. It is really the handmaid of the executive in effectuating, through judicial legislation carried beyond traditional bounds, changes in policy which the executive has been unable to persuade Congress to make. There was a time when the President went to Congress to change the law in order to circumvent reactionary decisions in the Supreme Court. Today (or up to April, 1945) the President has been, it would seem, going to the Supreme Court to have it change a proposition of law which he does not like but which Congress has not the power,[24] or else has not the disposition, to change.[25]

The trouble with changes made by judicial legislation is that they are retroactive,[26] whereas those made by legislative enactment are prospective.[27]

---

24 For examples of the change, by judicial fiat, of well established principles of constitutional law, see, *inter nonnulla alia,* United States v. California, 332 US 19, 91 LEd 1889, 67 SupCt 1658 (1947); New York v. United States, 326 US 572, 90 LEd 326, 66 SupCt 310 (1946); Graves v. New York ex rel. O'Keefe, 306 US 466, 83 LEd 927, 59 SupCt 595 (1939).

25 A discerning modern author has attributed the substitution of expediency for principle in the Supreme Court of the United States to the "increasing relativization and degradation of law and ethical norms." P. A. Sorokin, The Reconstruction of Humanity 48 (1948). I agree; but I also attribute it to the total want, in its personnel, of lawyers with enough experience in law practice to be aware of the importance of *stare decisis.* "What business men need is a rule of law which a lawyer can give them when they consult him, and upon which they can act with ease and certainty." J. H. Beale, *What Law Governs the Validity of a Contract,* 23 Harv. L. Rev. 260, 264 (1910). And see Pound, *Juristic Science and Law,* 31 Harv. L. Rev. 1047, 1053 n. 24 (1918).

26 See the dissent of Holmes, J., in Kuhn v. Fairmont Coal Co., 215 US 349 (1909); and see R. H. Freeman, *The Protection Afforded Against the Retroactive Operation of an Overruling Decision,* 18 Col. L. Rev. 230 (1918).

27 An example of a change in the law made by judicial legislation and grossly unfair in its operation on the parties to the proceeding is United States v. South-Eastern Underwriters Ass'n., 322 US 533, 88 LEd 1440, 64 SupCt 1162 (1944).

XI

Let me comment for a moment on the extent, if any, to which the remarks I have been making must be modified when you are writing a respondent's brief. You have already received the appellant's brief when the time comes to write the respondent's brief. Does this make a difference? My answer may stamp me as a heretic, but I say "No." The reason is that a respondent's brief in a court of last resort[28] must be complete in itself and must stand as solidly on its own foundation as an appellant's brief. I therefore persevere in heresy by saying that a respondent's brief should be completed in first draft from *before you even read the appellant's brief.*

Two strong considerations conduce to this result.

In the first place, the court of last resort, limited as it generally is to passing upon questions of law, does not much care what the court below did, or which side is appellant. It will weigh the opposing briefs in the scale and follow whichever most nearly accords with its views of what is, or should be, the law of the state. Identity of form with dissimilarity of contents makes the weighing process easier.

In the second place, the scope of your brief should not be affected by the scope of your opponent, the appellant's brief. You should not get your hopes up because of his sins of omission. It is your duty to call the court's attention to a hostile case which the adversary has overlooked.[29] Furthermore, your adversary's brief reflects the learning and industry in all probability of only two or perhaps three legal minds. But (if you are in the Court of Appeals) when the issues are discussed in conference, your opponent's

28 To only a slightly less extent is this true in an intermediate court of appeal.

29 In Glebe Sugar Refining Co. v. Greenock Harbour Trustees, [1921] Sess. Cas. (H.L.) 72, 74, Lord Birkenhead said: "It is not, of course, in cases of complication possible for their Lordships to be aware of all the authorities, statutory or otherwise, which may be relevant to the issues which in the particular case require decision. Their Lordships are therefore very much in the hands of counsel, and those who instruct counsel, in these matters, and this House expects, and indeed insists, that authorities which bear one way or the other upon matters under debate shall be brought to the attention of their Lordships by those who are aware of those authorities. This observation is quite irrespective of whether or not the particular authority assists the party which is so aware of it. It is an obligation of confidence between their Lordships and all those who assist in the debates in this House in the capacity of counsel." I am indebted for this citation (though he states the year of the volume incorrectly) to *Law and Other Things,* by Lord Macmillan (1937), p. 193. Note also the emphasis on candor in New York Central R.R. Co. v. Johnson, 279 US 310, 73 LEd 706, 49 SupCt 300 (1929).

position may be scrutinized by fourteen legal minds, *i.e.,* the minds of seven judges and the minds of seven bright young law secretaries. Therefore give your brief the strength to stand up under the powerful impact of all these minds, and not only against such forces as are manifest in the appellant's brief.

I therefore reject the advice, which I occasionally hear from lecturers on appellate practice, that when you represent the respondent, you may rest content with an attack directed toward your adversary's "jugular vein."

Of course after your adversary's brief has been studied, go back to your own and insert such passages of comment and correction directed toward his brief as may be required. Test the adequacy of your handling of what he seems to think are the strongest cases his way. But it is rare that on reading your adversary's brief you will find it proper to delete anything from your own.

It is always a good idea, in arguing before a court of last resort, to make it clear just how far the principle you are contending for should be carried. This will disarm the skeptical; and it will minimize the danger of its collision with other principles which are established and unassailable.

XII

It is clear that ornamentation, "purple passages," imported jewels of rhetoric alien to the context, are all out of place in a brief.[30] The court regards them as annoying interruptions, particularly when the brief is receiving the intensive study which precedes the report in conference. On the other hand, a paragraph of sum-

[30] Not without pertinence in this connection are the observations of Hon. Horace Stern of the Supreme Court of Pennsylvania, in *The Writing of Judicial Opinions,* 18 Pa. Bar Ass'n. Q. 40 (1947). He said (pp. 41-42): "There has apparently grown up of late a wide-spread passion for 'fine writing' but in this tendency there lurks grave evil, for, unless the pen be guided by the hand of genius, there is apt to result a sacrifice of legal sense to purely artificial verbiage. Form should fit substance, like clothes the well-dressed man which, when appropriate, never attract attention on their own account. An ornate, pretentious, grandiose style, replete with superfluous frills and rhetorical extravagances, can act only as an undesirable distraction. Nor is a judicial opinion a proper vehicle for the exploitation of pedantic learning or extraneous disquisitions." As to how good style adds power to expression, see Daiches, *A Study of Literature* (1948), pp. 33-34 and 98-100. See also Max Beerbohm's essay on Lytton Strachey (1943), p. 21: "Let us not ignore the virtue of form in literature. It is the goblet for the wine. Be the wine never so good, is not our enjoyment of it diminished if the hospitable vintner pours it forth to be lapped up by us from the ground with our tongues?" Beerbohm's little essay is itself a fine treatise on style.

mary toward the close of the brief is desirable if the record has been long, and sustained close reasoning has been necessary to make the ultimate objective clear. The summary should be worked over to make it epigrammatic, to eliminate triteness, and to contrast in neat antithesis the opposing contentions between which the court must decide. We may call such well-wrought passages "punch lines," for want of a better phrase, and here are some examples:

(a) A case in which the argument required the delineation of the boundary, between federal and state power where they tended to clash:

> "It was error, therefore, for the Courts below so to construe the Act of 1906 and the Special Acts of 1919 and 1921 as to make the permit from the Secretary of War (issued under Congressional authority) virtually a sword with which to flout State sovereignty, instead of regarding it as a mere shield against federal prosecution; and it was error to ignore the Joint Resolutions relating to the Port of New York Authority, and to hold the defendant railroad's conduct lawful though utterly subversive of the Congressional program of coordination. Only by a reversal of the decree appealed from can this Court carry out the legislative intent to give in 1906 renewed vitality to the criteria in the Act of 1899, and, by leaving them unaltered, to retain concurrent authorization of bridges by Federal and State Governments as an indispensable prerequisite to their legality."[31]

(b) A case where the instinctive feelings of the court, and its sympathy, are on the side of your opponent but the law is on your side. Here a child who had been ill was taken to a public playground by her mother, but fainted when she began to use a swing, fell fifteen inches to the cinder-covered ground and suffered lacerations leading to the amputation of an arm:

> "It is impossible to suppress a feeling of sympathy for the infant plaintiff. But the Trial Justice and the jury seem to have yielded too much to sentiment, and to have found negligence where none in fact or in law existed. To allow the judgment to stand would be to impose upon the City, in carrying on activ-

[31] From p. 86 of the (unsuccessful) brief for the appellant in Newark v. Central R.R. of N.J., 267 US 377, 69 LEd 666, 45 SupCt 328 (1925).

ities unattended by profit, a burden too severe to be borne. To fulfill the requirements of due care as interpreted by the Courts below would involve either a substantial increase in playground supervisors for each park (which would involve closing some playgrounds to counteract the extra expense), or the removal of all devices capable, in any conceivable circumstances, of causing harm to children rendered dizzy while at play. The requirements are a 'counsel of perfections,' beyond reasonable human attainments, and attended by public disadvantages which would nullify any gain capable of flowing from their adoption."[32]

(c) A case where an industrious opponent was fighting a losing battle against the trend of recent authority:

"The development of the police power in the past two or three decades has been impressive. We have seen *People v. Williams,* 189 N. Y. 131 (1907) overruled by *People v. Charles Schweinler Press,* 214 N. Y. 395 (1915), and *Lochner v. New York,* 198 U. S. 45 (1905), criticized with a universality which makes its citation as a precedent today unthinkable. Without meaning to be disrespectful to the able advocacy of our opponent, we may say that his brief is haunted by the ghosts of departed doctrines, and is untenanted by any living principle."[33]

(d) A case where it was necessary to justify the use of eminent domain in aid of slum clearance, even though that meant advancing the police power beyond familiar horizons:

"While the power to abolish old tenements is perhaps more clearly established than the power to spend public moneys in erecting new ones, nevertheless we feel this Court should not hesitate to sustain the law in its entirety. Surely the Housing Authority, in its war on filth and disease, is not limited to a *pax Romana*—'they make a solitude and call it peace.' The power must exist to make available new homes for those whose old habitations have been destroyed; and the legislative findings

[32] From p. 17 of the appellant's brief in Peterson v. City of New York, 267 NY 204, 196 NE 27 (1935). The brief just quoted was the subject of favorable comment in P. P. Fallon, *The Relation Between Analysis and Style in American Legal Prose,* 28 Neb. L. Rev. 80, 86 (1948).

[33] From p. 23 of the respondent's brief in People v. Tilford, 268 NY 557, 198 NE 402 (1935).

of the inadequacy of private enterprise to perform the task should be respected to the extent of upholding the repose of power in the Housing Authority."[34]

(e) A case where it was desirable to defeat a petition for certiorari, directed to a federal court, and stamp out a charge of disregard of applicable state law evidenced by a lonely decision in a lower court:

"A bold attempt is made, by seizing upon an inconsiderate recent utterance of a Justice at *nisi prius* to make out either a case of conflict between the instant case and that of the State Courts, or to show that the City's power to pass the tax law in question is shrouded in doubt. But the decision at *nisi prius* which is cited purported to construe the federal Constitution alone and not the State; and, standing in isolation, it is incapable of conjuring up that degree of doubt which is a prerequisite to the granting of certiorari by this Court.

"The decision referred to is what biologists call a 'sport,' and would more fittingly be enshrined in the annals of teratology than of law."[35]

At the extreme end of a brief should occur a short, laconic statement of what you want the court to do. Here are some illustrations:

"The judgment appealed from should be affirmed with costs."

"The judgment appealed from should be reversed and the complaint dismissed, with costs in all courts."

"The judgment of the Appellate Division appealed from should be reversed, and that of the Trial Term affirmed, with costs in all courts."

"The judgment appealed from should be reversed with costs, and the matter remitted to the Trial Term, there to be proceeded with according to law."

"The judgment appealed from should be reversed and a new trial ordered, with costs to abide the event."

---

34 From pp. 24-25 of the respondent's brief in Matter of New York City Housing Authority v. Muller, 270 NY 333, 1 NE(2d) 153 (1936).

35 From p. 5 of the respondent's brief in Southern Boulevard R.R. Co. v. New York City, 301 US 703 (1937).

XIII

A word or two about special purpose briefs. Motions for leave to appeal should be concise, clearly focused and arrestingly phrased. They should play up such elements in the case as may serve to give it public importance. If the case presents a non-recurrent situation, of interest to no one but the litigants themselves, it is a waste of time to try to take it to a court possessing discretionary jurisdiction. These same observations hold true of petitions for certiorari addressed to the Supreme Court of the United States, but Rule 38, Section 5, of the rules of that Court gives a clear indication of the prerequisites which a petition should possess than is found in the rules of state courts on corresponding applications.

Briefs seeking to take a case to a higher court with discretionary jurisdiction may be opposed by briefs showing the amplitude of supporting authority behind the decision below; or stressing the non-recurrent character of the questions raised; or pointing out that the decision below really turned on the resolution of questions of fact which the court of last resort could not go into even if the case were brought before it.[36]

Briefs *amicus curiae* command little attention in appellate courts save when they are filed by public law officers. They must deal only with the propositions of law present in the record, but their authors may go out of the record to show factual situations to which the principles under debate may apply, with a view toward persuading the court either to qualify or to extend what was held below. One who files a brief *amicus curiae* should show on its cover whether it is in support of affirmance or in support of reversal.

The limited scope of briefs in support of, or in opposition to, motions to dismiss for want of jurisdiction is self-evident without further exposition.

XIV

As to oral arguments, I urge that they be made and that, generally, counsel not rest content to submit upon briefs. If you are

[36] Lawyers appearing for respondents are not as conscious as they should be of the readiness with which an appeal to the Court of Appeals taken as of right (because the Appellate Division was divided) may be defeated by merely showing that the determinative questions are factual, and thus beyond the powers of inquiry possessed by the Court of Appeals.

present to argue orally, you can bring back into line a judge who, by his questions, shows he has gone off on a tangent. Furthermore, if all the judges have heard oral argument, the reporting judge in conference has to spend less time giving his brethren the background. They can proceed at once to their deliberations on the crucial questions of law and policy involved.[37]

Your very first objective, when you get up on your feet to argue, is to convince the court that you have a program, that you have thought out a logical order for the presentation of your points and that you are capable of adhering to it. This will diminish the number of questions from the Bench.

I have always held that the trial man is *not the best man* to handle the appeal, but may even be the worst. The point has been the subject of divergent views in some public law offices I have known. In the office of the United States Attorney, Southern District of New York, the trial assistant keeps the case through the United States Court of Appeals; if it goes further, the Solicitor-General takes over. In the office of the Corporation Counsel of New York City and in the office of the District Attorney, New York County, a case taken to an appellate court is handed over to what is known as the appeals division or appeals bureau, and briefed and argued by an appeals specialist.[38]

There are, to my mind, overwhelming advantages in this method of handling appeals. The appeals specialist views the case precisely as does the appellate court, through the little square window of the record, so to speak, and not as something viewed from the

[37] One of the strongest reasons in favor of oral arguments is set forth in F. B. Wiener, *Oral Advocacy*, 62 Harv. L. Rev. 56, 59 (1948): "Appellate judges, virtually without exception, say that a case should never be submitted without oral argument. . . . These expressions reflect the fact that the task of judgment is infinitely harder when counsel is not present to be questioned regarding his exact position or the limits of a principle he has argued in the brief." See also Judge Loughran, *The Argument of an Appeal in the Court of Appeals*, 12 Ford. L. Rev. 1 (1943). Oral arguments are mandatory in some appellate courts. See Rule 1: 4-1 of the rules of the New Jersey Supreme Court, as reorganized under the Constitution approved by the voters in 1947.

[38] I was chief of the division of appeals in the Corporation Counsel's office, New York City, from 1934 to 1943. My staff averaged eight men, and as we handled about 500 appeals a year, I had to assign some cases to competent lawyers outside of my own division. These were, themselves, often division heads—Real Property, Franchises, Contracts, Torts, Taxation, Workmen's Compensation, etc.—or sometimes just bright and reliable young men. Statistics which I kept showed that the men of the appeals division had almost twice as high a batting average in the appellate courts as their brethren from other divisions.

great outdoors. The trial man's mind cannot free itself of matters which entered it during preparation for trial but which did not get into the record, either because a witness he interviewed failed to respond to a subpoena or was not allowed to testify because of failure to establish qualifications. Or if the witness did testify, some important facts may not have been established because objections to questions were sustained.

Then, too, the style of oratory a trial man develops, through his constant appeal to a jury less learned than himself, is out of place in an appellate court. A calm, conversational style is there appropriate; and his hearers' learning exceeds his own, or at least he should conduct himself as though it did.[39]

XV

A lawyer often finds himself with several clients adversely affected by the same statute or ruling, and he may wish to take a test case to a higher court. My advice is, try to arrange to take your strongest case up first, and if you win try to get the principle extended to weaker cases. Don't take a weak case up first, for if you lose you will spend the rest of your life trying to distinguish it.[40]

Interlocutory appeals, by the way, are not to be recommended, unless a ruinous injunction *pendente lite,* or an outrageous receivership makes such an appeal unavoidable. If you lose the interlocutory appeal, you may be before the same court on appeal from final judgment, and their interest will then be diminished because they feel you are offering them a warmed-over dish.[41]

To sum up: style, sequacity, conciseness, and integrity are the qualities which should characterize appellate briefs; and he who argues orally must show an awareness of the atmosphere, qualities and orientation found in an appellate court (viz., dignity and learning, calmness and unhurriedness, concentration on points

39 Mr. Wiener in the article cited in note 37 advocates "an attitude of respectful intellectual equality," 62 Harv. L. Rev. 56, 72 (1948).

40 See in this connection Esther Lucile Brown, *Lawyers, Law Schools and the Public Service* 84-85 (1948).

41 The advisability of interlocutory appeals on questions of practice—*e.g.,* from orders on motions to strike defenses, motions to make a complaint more definite and certain, motions concerning bills of particulars—is too complex a matter for inclusion in this lecture.

of law rather than fact), and of the court's want of power to consider anything that is not in the printed record, coupled, nevertheless, with an appreciation on the judges' part that they are laying down principles whose application will extend beyond the case at bar.

Adapted from Vol. 18, Fordham Law Review (1949).

Expressing the Idea—The Essentials of Oral and Written Argument

BY EDWARD S. DORE

MANY YEARS AGO, long before the telephone, the telegraph, and radio, there was a lighthouse about five miles out to sea off Cape Breton Island, Nova Scotia, guarding a reef that was dangerous to shipping at that point. There was another lighthouse near the shore, and connected with the shore by a causeway, which guarded another reef at the entrance to the shipping harbor.

One night in the midst of a terrible storm the outer lighthouse keeper observed a ship in distress, and he knew that unless aid was summoned swiftly, the ship would be dashed to pieces during the night on the outer reef. But at the time he had no means of communicating with the man on the shore, who was hidden in the other lighthouse as he was hidden in the tower five miles out to sea. So, all he could do was to watch the destruction of the vessel, with loss of life and loss of treasure.

Thereafter, at the first opportunity, when he went ashore he and the lighthouse keeper on the shore worked out between them a code of signals by flashes of light and black-outs of light, by means of which they could transmit to each other ideas that one wished to send and the other wished to receive.

That image of the two men in the two lighthouses is, I think, an image of the whole problem of communication between man and man. No matter how close we seem to be, no matter how close we actually are, there is no direct communication between mind and mind. You don't see my mind. I don't see your mind. Both your mind and your idea, as my mind and my idea, are invisible, just as the man in the lighthouse was invisible, and the only way that we have of communicating is the way that they decided to communicate: namely, by outer signals; in their case, flashes of light; in our case, a code that we have all agreed upon —the English language.

If there were a highly intelligent man from the Orient in the first row, with perfect hearing, he would hear every sound that was uttered and understand nothing, because he did not know the code.

And, therefore, we communicate, not as we think, directly to each other, but indirectly and by means of signs. "Sema," "sematos" from the Greek, a signal; "semata" signals; hence semantics —words.

That is the great mystery of the art of communication; and it also suggests its difficulty: it is not a science; it is an art. And even in the vernacular, it is not congenital. Congenitally, we can make noises, of pain or of pleasure, but congenitally we don't learn to transmit ideas, any more than the art of painting is learned by being born.

Just as in painting, sculpture, architecture, or any of the arts, the art of transmitting ideas must be learned by long years of study and then a lifetime of practice.

Now, in our profession it is perhaps more necessary than in any other profession. The basic ideas as to how it should be done are the same, whether a man is selling soap or preaching the Gospel or trying to transmit an idea to five judges on an Appellate Court, to get them to act upon it. It is an art, and therefore it is subject to the laws of all art. What are they?

In the early part of the 16th Century, a man could be seen in the southerly part of Italy at a great marble quarry looking for a flawless piece of marble. When he found it, he ordered it taken out and sent to his studio. And there it stood, a great big meaningless piece of stone. And then he started to work; not first on the stone, but first in his mind.

He decided that he would depict a man; not a man in general —there is no such thing; every man is a specific, concrete individual man—and the one he picked out was one well known, whose achievements, whose character and intelligence were known to mankind.

And then he drew drafts of the proposed statute, and he sought to have a limiting purpose before he touched the marble. When he had formed that purpose, he began his actual work. And, by taking pieces away and adding nothing, by merely taking pieces of marble away, Michelangelo brought out of the center of that meaningless piece of stone the incomparable statue of Moses which is in the Church of St. Peter in Chains, at Rome. It is living, breathing stone, every line of it suggesting strength, physical strength, intellectual strength, spiritual strength. But that dominant result is there only because it was first in the mind of the maker before it was transferred to the stone.

I give that illustration of the art of sculpture because limitation is the first law of all art; but it is especially illustrated in sculpture which produces its results by adding nothing; but taking away, limiting more and more.

So much so is that, that in Rome in the old days, in the place where the sculptors had their studios, outside some of them you would see the sign "sine cera"—without wax. Why? Because, as you can see at once, if a man took too much away at any crucial place—he would only have two alternatives. An honest sculptor would destroy the whole statue and start all over again. A dishonest sculptor would add something; take a little wax, color it with the color of stone and sell it as a perfect piece of art. Of course, with time and change of temperature the flaw would appear. So, the sculptors put out the sign—"Sine cera"—and those two words are the derivation of our word "sincere"—whole, uncorrupted.

Now, the same law applies to the art of utterance in words, and it may be stated thus: Before you put a word on paper, before you utter a word orally, limit your topic in your own mind to one dominant purpose, suited to the material and suited to a particular audience.

Remember the man at the lighthouse. The first thing that caused the invention of the code was an idea; because he had an idea—not a vague, general idea; a particular, definite limited idea that desperately needed expression to a particular audience, to get that audience to act upon it—the code of light signals was invented.

And so, with all our utterance. The thing that starts it, the thing of greatest importance, of the first magnitude, is the idea, the limited idea; the audience is second, the word is last.

For example, if a man was intending to give a speech, let us say, against Communism; it wouldn't help him a bit just to think that his purpose was to speak against Communism. This is too vague, too general a purpose. It is not limited. But if he took a look at his audience, which is the first thing everyone should do, and he saw an audience composed of political and economic elements in America, he might make it his limiting purpose to show that Soviet Communism by its basic principles and all its acts denies the possibility of co-existence with any other form of economic order. As soon as he formed that limited purpose, thoughts begin to flow, ideas and sources are suggested.

Or, he might look at the audience and find it was a religious audience in America. Then, he might make it his limited purpose to show that Soviet Communism, by its basic principles and all its practice denies religion, denies God; that it is the first political system in the world that begins with atheism as a first principle.

As soon as he has a limited purpose, ideas, suggestions, examples come, and sources are suggested. And when he gets through, the audience will have what he has: one definite idea in their minds. They will have it because the speaker had one definite idea in his mind before he started to speak.

Now, strange to say, the same thing applies to practically every case we have to argue or to brief.

Speaking from this platform over ten years ago, that great lawyer whom we all reverence, admire and love, John W. Davis, gave a talk on oral argument, and he reduced it to what he called "Ten Commandments." And his fifth commandment was: "Always go for the jugular vein." He continued: "Rufus Choate's expression was: 'the hub of the case.'" And then he said, "More often than not, there is in every case a cardinal point around which lesser points revolve, a single fortress, which, if strongly held, will make the loss of all the other works immaterial." He then referred to a great lawyer, John G. Johnson, of Philadelphia, and stated that in Johnson's Appellate arguments he spoke always only to one point and usually not more than 20 minutes, but with compelling force. "And when he finished," says Mr. Davis, "it was difficult for his adversary to persuade the Court that there was anything else worthy to be considered in the case. This is the quintessence of the advocate's art."

It is; and I say it is the quintessence of the whole art of utterance: to have one limited, definite purpose. What does that mean in the concrete? It means to think before you talk. It means to define in your own mind, to delimit in your own mind the one particular, dominant idea that you wish to transmit to others.

Don't forget that "define" comes from "definire," and "finire" contains "fines," which means boundaries, limits.

That is the first thought to have in writing a speech, in making an argument. I suggest that you write the purpose out, because writing makes an exact man, as Bacon said; *e.g.,* purpose: To show what you aim to be the one dominant, controlling idea that you wish to transmit to your audience. Put it up before you like a bull's-eye.

And when, by thought, by discussion, by reading, you have sufficiently limited the purpose and thus written it out, you apply the second law of art: the law of selection:—*Select* specific material suited to the limited purpose and the particular audience.

Now, mind you, so far I have said nothing about words at all. We are dealing solely with ideas.

I suggest that, in gathering ideas, you use small slips of paper of uniform size, such as these I hold before you. Don't think, at this part of your preparation, of the *order* in which you are going to present your thought, or of the words that you are going to use. Ideas come to us, usually, in most amazing disorder. Jot them down as they occur. And think only of one thing: does that case, does that thought, does that example, does that idea suit my limited purpose? Does it shoot right at the bull's-eye I have before me? If it does, throw it into an envelope; if it does not, reject it entirely. And so you gather, gradually, as you would a pack of cards, a number of notes. And when you have enough of them, you apply the third law of art: arrangement.

A hundred years ago if you went to a quarry in Tuckahoe, you would have seen a pile of cut stone, just heaps of meaningless cut stone. Today, if you go to 50th Street and Fifth Avenue, you will see the same cut stone arranged in a definite order in St. Patrick's Cathedral to achieve a limited purpose. There are the two great spires pointing upward. There are all the small, little needles and flèches of stone, all pointing upward. You can't look at them without raising your eyes and your head. That arrangement suggests a spiritual aspiration. That is the limited purpose of the building. And it is achieved by stone, which is one of the heaviest and the most material forms of matter. But it is achieved by the form in which the stone is arranged, in the form of spires, in the form of points, that lift the mind as they lift the eye heavenward.

The same law applies to expressing ideas in words. You have *limited* your purpose. You have *selected* specific material suited to your purpose. You now *arrange* that material in one definite order. The order depends upon the material, the dominant purpose and the particular audience. The most common order is the order of time. Or, you may follow the order of analysis. Or, you may follow the order of importance:—Begin with things that deserve distinction; end with things that deserve distinction.

And make an outline, a skeleton outline, to force you to see for yourself the order in which you are going to present your ideas. Now, I will suggest to you the form of outline on the blackboard. It is an outline of what I have attempted to say so far.

But, instead of using the abstract words "introduction," "body," "conclusion," which don't help the author at all—and we are looking at all of this from the point of view of the author, the maker, the writer, the man in the agony of composition—I suggest that, instead of the "introduction," use the words "Take hold." Immediately you think of your audience; what type of people are they; where are they with respect to your idea; what will you begin with that will challenge them and alert them and hold their attention?

And I suggest always, when you are making an address, as distinguished from an argument in court, that you begin with a picture, with an image, with a story. I don't care how deep or profound your subject is, if you start with a picture, an image, or a story that fits the subject, you already have an entrance to the minds of the audience. You are talking to minds, but they are minds that are incarnate.

No one who understands scholastic philosophy would say it lessens the importance of the intellect, reason and will. And yet, one of the first theses of scholastic philosophy is:—"There is nothing in the intellect that was not first in the senses"—"Nihil est intellectu quod non fuerit prius in sensu"—not in the same form, of course, but coming through the senses.

And since you are talking to minds incarnate, make your words so by a picture or an image. Begin with a picture or an image; not any picture or any image; but one that suits the particular dominant purpose.

Now, at the outset I told you the story of the men in the two lighthouses because I think it illustrates the problem of utterance between man and man. It removes from us the delusion that we ever talk directly from mind to mind. It makes us realize that, as those men in the lighthouses had to use outward signals, so do we use outward signals—words; semantics—to transmit our ideas to other minds.

I therefore suggest "Take Hold" instead of "Introduction," "Transmit" instead of "Body" and "Drive Home" instead of "Conclusion." And I suggest this form of skeleton outline with Roman numerals for main headings, Arabic numerals for subheadings, and "a," "b," and "c" for sub-subheadings: all in hanging or indented paragraphs—so that the main things stand out clearly, and you will probably never use more than three or four main headings. If you attempt to make impressions with more than that, you will make impressions of nothing.

Therefore I suggest this form of skeleton outline: Take hold; transmit; drive home.

And I give that only because unless we force ourselves to write down our own outline, the order in which we are going to present our ideas to the audience, we shall be vague and if we are vague, the audience is bound to get a vague impression.

Now, thus far, in everything that I have said, I have been talking about *ideas,* not words. That doesn't mean that words are unimportant. Words are tremendously important because, as I said in my "image," in that symbol, in that story, it is only by these words, these outer signs, these signals, that we transmit our invisible ideas from our invisible minds to other invisible minds.

But now we must come to words, and that is the fourth suggestion I make: write and revise. And the basic law of art with regard to words is the same as with regard to everything else: be specific. A few suggestions perhaps may help, and the first one is a translation of "be specific." (1) Prefer the concrete, specific word to the general and the abstract word. What is the use of referring, in an argument, to "The Appellant," and "The Respondent"? There is always an appellant in an Appellate Court and there is always a respondent. The words are too vague. They don't throw any light on the specific relation of the parties.

How much better to begin as follows: "Plaintiff, landlord, appeals from judgment in favor of defendant, tenant, after a trial before the Court without a jury in an action for rent." There is the whole story. And, as soon as you say "landlord" and "tenant," instead of "Appellant" and "Respondent" you show the relationship of the parties. And don't forget we have Appellant-Respondent and Respondent-Appellant and three or four other variations. It is all right to use such technical terms in the headings, but don't use them in the argument, don't exclusively use them in the brief, and don't use similar abstractions in legal documents.

I wish we could pronounce a final anathema now, on the following awful abstractions in legal documents: "The party of the first part," "the party of the second part," and sometimes the "third part," and sometimes the "fifth part." And the weary reader turns back to the first page to see if somehow he can manage to find out what you are talking about.

Be specific, be concrete: "John Jones, *landlord,* hereby agrees with Thomas Smith, *tenant,* as follows:" That's all you need: colon, dash, Arabic 1, 2, 3, 4, or 5, whatever number of specific agreements you have. You designate the parties by their real relationship.

It may not be landlord and tenant; it may be employer and employee; husband and wife; principal and agent. Whatever their specific relation is, reveal that in the first sentence of the argument, and retain that designation throughout the argument, throughout the brief and throughout the legal document.

(2) Another suggestion will be helpful: avoid jargon and legal mumbo-jumbo. Now, every science, every profession has its own jargon. But I think, even with shy and bashful modesty that we of the legal profession have to admit that we are notorious for legal mumbo-jumbo or legal jargon.

Listen to this indictment and see if you can find out what the man is trying to say. I have no doubt he went to high school. I'm sure he went to college, and he must have gone to law school because he was a lawyer and a District Attorney. And this is what he says:

"With force and arms, in and upon one John Blank, in the peace of said people, then and there being willfully, feloniously and of his malice aforethought, did make an assault with a certain pistol"—you will notice he is not worried about the English language—"loaded with gunpowder and one metal bullet, which said pistol the said defendant"—God forbid you should think it was some other defendant—"in his right hand, then and there had and held"—it wouldn't do to say "held"; it had to be "had and held"—"to at and against and upon the said," etc., etc., etc.

I'll read no more. The man is under the conviction that when it comes to drawing up a legal document—and that's a very important one—you are not bound to reason, you are not bound to use the English language; you should use legal mumbo-jumbo.

Now, what was he trying to say? He was just trying to say that the defendant on the second of January, 1954, with a pistol deliberately shot and killed John Blank. Well, why not say it and be done with it.

I regret to announce that this litany of horrors could be multiplied indefinitely. But I'll just give you one more:

"I, John Jones, of the City of Blank, County of Blank, State of Blank, being of sound mind and disposing memory, and not acting under any fraud, duress, or any undue influence of any person whatsoever, do make, publish and declare this my Last Will and Testament, in the following manner, to wit, as follows"—

In English, if he used the English language, he would say:

"I, John Jones, hereby make my will." All the protestations against undue influence, or lack of disposing mind, if they in fact existed, won't help. In fact, it's unwise to make such reference, because you almost suggest the worst. One wit has expressed it as follows:

"Law is law: in such and so forth, whereas and whenas, wherefore and therefore, provided always, nevertheless, notwithstanding, and of course, because"—

Now, that man was satirizing what some of us do. I rejoice to say only some of us. And, strange to say, it is a perversion of the legal conscience. We want to make it "legal." So we make it what? Often illiterate.

One wag has expressed it as follows:

"We do not write in verse or prose.
"We simply lay our words in rows.
"The self-same words that Webster penned
"We merely lay them end to end."

That happens, if you *begin* with words. That is why from the beginning I said the first principle of all the art of utterance is limitation of the idea in your own mind first. If you begin with words, you deserve the comment the Great Bard uttered:—

"Words, M'Lord, Words."

Or what he said of another worthy speaker:

"He hath been to a great feast of language and stolen the scraps."

Now, I could multiply the examples but I have to have regard for your patience and your time.

(3) I do wish to mention one more fault to be avoided: Avoid the "that" disease. What is the "that" disease? It springs from the affidavits:

"John Jones, being duly sworn,"—they usually add: "deposes and says."

And, by the way, what does "deposes" mean? It means states "under oath." But haven't you just said "being duly sworn," and don't you follow with the word "says"? Why add "deposes"?

"John Jones, being duly sworn, says: No. 1, that"—for a whole page. For a whole page? For 30 pages sometimes and, all "that clauses," beginning with a capital letter and ending with a period. But they are not sentences; they are dependent clauses, "that" clauses.

Now, in modern English, to use a "that" clause, a dependent clause with no main clause in the same sentence, is illiterate. Nobody should be graduated from grammar school who would do that, because he doesn't know the difference between a sentence and a battleship.

However, having started the "that" disease with the affidavits, to make things "legal" many lawyers tend to extend it to other documents. I read, last spring, a complaint of 30 printed pages, every alleged sentence a dependent clause, beginning with a "That" at the head of it and a period at the end.

Of course, such form interferes with understanding; and I will tell you how it hurts us in the Appellate Division, in the First Department, at least, seriously. They have what they call "sea lawyers" in all the State prisons. These are gentlemen with plenty of time. They get law books, they read them and they see the lawyers putting in the "That," and they too want to make their briefs legal. As a result we have to read 20, 30, 40, 60, or more pages of typewritten briefs, every one of the alleged sentences dependent clauses beginning with "That."

That is the "that" disease. I regret to announce it is widespread at the Bar.

But, on the other hand we have at this Bar some of the greatest lawyers in the country, perhaps in the world, and their briefs and their affidavits are well nigh perfect, so far as the English language is concerned. They are utterly devoid of legal mumbo-jumbo, jargon, and the "that" disease.

Now, notice all I have said (1) limit your topic to one dominant aim; (2) select specific material suited solely to that aim; (3) arrange the specific material in a definite order and outline.

Then only you come to words and this is the fourth suggestion! (4) Write and revise. Now, you may either write *in extenso,* as you do in a brief, but in oral presentation, the paper always comes between you and the audience. It is preferable to memorize the sequence of the ideas, rather than the sequence of the words, to make a skeleton outline such as I have placed before you and to talk from the notes rather than to read the argument.

And, while I am speaking of words, please do not think I underestimate their importance. They are tremendously important. They are the main things by which we transmit our ideas, they are the external signs by which we send our ideas to other invisible minds. But note that in every example that I gave in which there was a mistake in the word, you will see at once that it stemmed from the failure to *think* before the word was uttered, the failure to define clearly in the writer's own mind what precisely he meant to say. Do you mean to say that a man would draw up an indictment such as the one I read, if he were not under the illusion that he had to make it "legal" by making it mumbo-jumbo or jargonesque?

Now, what is "jargon"? "Jargon" may be defined as the illegitimate child of indolence and timidity: indolence: unwillingness to think before you use the word; timidity: unwillingness to say directly what you are talking about, but using circumlocution, like the man who recently said in a brief: "With regard to the situation presented, if your Honors please, it may be said the Trial Court totally misunderstood plaintiff's contention." As soon as you see a circumlocution—"With regard to," "In the case of,"—beware of it. Beware of it in your own style. Beware of it in anybody else's style, because the writer may be unconsciously slipping into jargon.

The clerk wrote: "In the case of John Jones, deceased, his coffin was ordinary." Now, if John Jones' body was in a coffin, he must have been deceased; if his body was in a coffin, does it also have to be in a "case"? What he is trying to say is, "John Jones' coffin was ordinary." Why not say it without the circumlocution? And, note the passive voice: "It may be said." I say unto you, avoid the passive voice except in cases where it is absolutely necessary; and it seldom is. If you are trying to say that John Jones was brought home in an intoxicated condition, I think the passive voice must be used for there is nothing he could do in the active voice. However, why say "in an intoxicated condition"? That's an abstraction. Why use the vague verb, "was brought"? Why not say, plainly, "John Jones was carried home drunk"? Then you have avoided jargon.

However, as I said before, I cannot underestimate the importance of words. They are the material, they are the means of transporting our ideas. Where do you get them? Normally, there is only one way and that is my last suggestion: by reading the great books. (5) Read the great books for a lifetime. The authors are the men that had the greatest power of utterance in the history of our race. What they said was said so well, both in substance and form, that the human race has refused to let it die, and it has lived on. And it is by reading the great books that we learn the appropriate word.

But, as I will intimate later, we learn much more. As to reading I can make only a few suggestions:

First, read the Bible, Old and New Testament. Remember, what so many of us forget, that both the Old and the New Testament are filled with graphic narratives told with such definite words that they challenge and hold the mind.

Take the parables of the Divine Founder of Christianity; all are stories, and He didn't begin by saying, "I am going to tell you a story that will illustrate a moral." He began with the story directly: "A man went down from Jersualem to Jericho and fell among thieves." Immediately you say, what happened next?

So, I recommend the reading of the Scriptures, for that reason alone, although there are many higher reasons.

Secondly, I recommend the reading of the classics, the Greek and Roman classics, if not in the original—though, of course, that's preferable—then in translation; and they are great even in translation. You remember what Keats, who knew no Greek, wrote when he first opened Chapman's translation of Homer. This is what he said:

"Then felt I like some watcher of the skies
"When a new planet swims into his ken;
"Or like stout Cortez when with eagle eyes
"He star'd at the Pacific—and all his men
"Look'd at each other with a wild surmise—
"Silent, upon a peak in Darien."

The classics are great even in translation. And the translations I recommend to you are the Loeb Classics. Most of you are familiar with them.

Who was Loeb? Loeb was the son of Solomon Loeb, the founder of Kuhn Loeb & Company, the private bankers in Wall Street. Enormously wealthy by inheritance and by acquisition, when he was 34 years old, about fifty years ago, he said to himself, "What am I doing in life? I have already more money than I can use. Am I going to spend thirty more years adding to it?" He didn't. He sold out. He went to England. He looked around to see what a man with his money could do for the human race. Mr. Loeb was a learned and wise man and he saw clearly fifty years ago that the tendency to throw over the Greek and Latin classics was profoundly wrong for us of the West; he realized that whether men knew it or not culturally we derive from those great classical sources; that we live on them in literature, in law, in rhetoric, in poetry, in art, in all the humanities, in the studies that make men more human. And, therefore, he determined in an effort to resist that movement away from the classics, to give an enormous portion of his large fortune as a foundation for an encyclical translation of all the Greek and Latin classics in what is known as the "Loeb Classical Library." There are now over 300 numbers—of the whole of the Latin and Greek Classics, with a good original text on the left hand page in Latin or Greek and a good English translation on the right hand page. And some of you who are quite convinced at least that those two languages existed, may find that you will refresh your soul occasionally by looking at the original text on the left.

But, at all events, read the Classics; read them in Loeb's Classical Library, the books are inexpensive if they are small; they can be carried in a pocket, carried in a train or on a journey.

Next, I recommend that you saturate your minds with Chaucer, Shakespeare and Milton.

Out of reverence for your time and your patience—which is almost infinite, I see,—I will defer any illustration but one. You remember how Chaucer described a lawyer who was on his way to Canterbury to visit the Blissful Martyr's Shrine? This is what he said in one line: "No busier man there was then he, and yet he seemed busier than he was." How true that is in the middle of the 20th Century, as it was in the 15th Century.

If your patience could stand it, I could give you a dozen more examples from Shakespeare, a dozen from Milton.

I recommend that you reread Paradise Lost once every two years at least. It will keep alive in you the sense of the sublime, and your mind will wonder with delight at the perfect diction, the absolutely perfect selection of the word and the phrase that brings the image before your mind.

Next, remember, the modern English sentence was not invented until the 18th Century. The 16th and 17th Centuries, for the most part, are hard-going in English prose. Read the makers of the modern English sentence. Read Dryden, Pope, Sam Johnson, Addison, and Edmund Burke.

In the 19th Century, reread the masters of English prose who took the improvements of the 18th and made them still more perfect English prose: Newman, Arnold, Pater, Ruskin and the rest.

I am really inviting you to a feast of reason, to what Horace called "The Delights of Letters, the Nights and the Banquets of the Gods."

All I have tried to say can be reduced to five words. Limit, select, arrange, write, read. Now, the last two have to do with words. But, the method that I am attempting to suggest or barely to outline in the necessarily limited time that I have can be reduced to three words: limit, select, arrange. And the greatest of these is "Limit."

(1) Limit your topic to one definite, dominant purpose before you put a word on paper. Suit the purpose to the topic and to the particular audience that you aim at.

(2) Select specific material suited to the dominant purpose and the particular audience.

(3) Arrange the selected material in a definite order, and make an outline to compel yourself to see the order.

If you do those three things, no one of which has anything to do with words, you will follow the basic laws of utterance.

And then only you come to words.

(4) Write and revise; and finally

(5) Read the great books in order to get words, the best words, the most appropriate words.

Now, I must realize how inadequate, necessarily, it is to present the philosophy of utterance in one lecture and attempt to suggest a method. But, if I have violated some of my rules, I ask you to remember that profound paradox of Gilbert Chesterton: "Only the sinner can preach."

But I have attempted the impossible, deliberately because I was doing it under the auspices of this great Committee and only to spark this Committee into subsequent meetings, conferences, seminars, to meet the desperate need for our Bar in training lawyers in the art of oral and written utterance, transmitting ideas to others, in the use of the English language instead of legal mumbo-jumbo in oral arguments, in briefs, in affidavits, even in legal documents and in the absolute avoidance of legal jargon.

I think the purpose of this Committee and this its ultimate aim, are more important than any law reform that was ever suggested or invented.

I end, as I began. Each of us, before we start to utter a word, is like the man in the outer lighthouse. As he was, sealed up in a tower of stone that concealed him and his mind, so each of us is sealed up in a tower of a material body and no man directly sees what is in our minds. As he was able to send a message only by an outer sign or signal, so, the only way we transmit ideas to other men is by outer signs and signals: by semantics, words.

In suggesting that you read the great books, to get words, I suggest that they will do more than bring you words. Read them, not merely to get the words—though that's the chief way you ever will get them—but read them to inform your own mind, to elevate your mind. The great French stylist, said: "Style is the man himself." It is true. And, how can you improve the style unless you improve the man?

Therefore, the reading of the great books to supplement our lack of concrete language is a great opportunity in life. It opens before us the whole panorama of human existence as recorded in the great books. By the magic of the printed word, we can associate for the rest of our lives with the greatest minds that ever lived, with the finest intellects with the minds who had the finest power of utterance, whose power of utterance was so great that the human race has never permitted what they said to die.

Limit! Select! Arrange! And the greatest of these is "Limit."

Adapted from Vol. 9, The Record of the Association of the Bar of the City of New York (1954).

On Learning to Write: Suggestions for Study and Practice

By Harold G. Pickering

A PREVALENT LACK OF PROFICIENCY in the art of writing throughout the profession is attested by the frequency with which judges, law professors and mere lawyers write about it.

For the most part these writings have been concerned with legal writing, and for obvious reasons.

A recent survey by a committee of law professors disclosed the fact that a number of law schools have introduced courses in legal writing. A review of the survey discloses that these courses—many of them "noncredit courses"—are usually integrated with courses in legal bibliography, the moot court program and other established courses. Sometimes they include lectures on legal research and analysis, on the common law, on brief writing or on the determination of the *ratio decidendi* of a case and the submission of problems in these fields.

Certainly there is no room for criticism of either approach. Both the writings and the law school courses are of inestimable value.

Nor is there room for the assumption that the competent authors and teachers involved are under any illusion that their readers or students know how to write and are deficient only in the skill of legal writing.

The fact remains, however, that the affirmative results of the most competent exposition and of the most competent instruction must perforce be limited by the degree of the capacity or of the incapacity of the reader or student to write at all.

Neither approach reaches the root of the problem.

With these premises in mind, a lecture of the following tenure was delivered to the senior class of The Hastings College of Law of the University of California. The class was a class in trial practice. As an adjunct to the course the students were actively engaged in preparing, briefing and arguing motions and in trying cases in a practice court at the trial level. It was not the objective of the lecture to outline a program for the colleges of liberal arts, or for the law schools. The object was merely to indicate to the students how they might offset the deficiencies in their scholastic training by self-education.

This is not a lecture on brief writing. Before you can write a brief you must know how to write. The technique of brief writing is a step beyond the fundamental art of writing, an art in itself.

Proficient Public Speaking . . . But Writing Is More Important

For the lawyer, proficiency in the art of writing is much more important than proficiency in the art of public speaking. Unless you have thought about it you may wonder why.

Proficiency as a speaker is, of course, more important to the trial lawyer than it is to other members of the profession. However, whether you are appraising the work of the trial lawyer or that of the office lawyer you will be faced with an inescapable fact. That fact is, that measured in terms of bulk or quantity, and for this purpose that is a sound and scientific standard of measurement, by far the greatest proportion of the lawyer's product, the commodity in which he deals, the thing which he sells, if you please, is the written word.

A somewhat extended recital of specific products may be necessary adequately to demonstrate the verity of this statement. There are, of course: wills, trust agreements, contracts, corporate charters, by-laws, corporate minutes, corporate mortgages—or indentures—title certificates, legal opinions, registration statements, prospectuses, annual reports, letters to stockholders, proxies, proxy statements, letters, petitions, claims for tax refunds, bankruptcy claims, claims in probate, pleadings, notices, motions, briefs, orders, findings of fact, judgments.

The drafting of every one of these writings calls for the highest degree of writing skill to which any lawyer can attain.

To that end the lawyer should have a good vocabulary, not necessarily a large vocabulary, but a discriminating knowledge of the utility and value of a sufficient number of words—preferably simple words—which will enable him to use the right word in the right place and the most effective word for the place.

He should know how to put words together in simple, concise and grammatical sentences and orderly paragraphs, with a sufficient knowledge of the integrity of each to enable him to depart from the rules now and then for the sake of effect, without doing violence to the rules.

He should have an infinite capacity for clarity, the ability to make the theme of the writing crystal clear.

The editor of Macaulay's *Life of Johnson,* commenting on the "absolute clearness" of Macaulay's writing said: ". . . this . . . was a quality that he sought continually, sparing himself neither work nor pains." There is no gainsaying that in the world of letters there are innumerable men of genius whose skill born of talent, you cannot hope to equal, much less to excel. But you can learn to write; and it is encouraging to note that even the masters of English prose were aware that their native talents needed to be augmented by study and practice. Unlike the skills of the heroine of *Annie Get Your Gun* which were attained by "doing what comes natcherly," the stature of the great writers was the end result of hard labor, unstinted self-criticism, unremitting self-discipline and endless revision.

Searching Out the Facts . . . The Children of Imagination

Of course you can't think of writing without calling into play your talent for imagination. How are you to discover and choose the facts which you will want to array? Inquiry of obvious sources of information will be superficial. Facts are more elusive than that. They are not so easily unearthed and brought to light. You will need to imagine what facts must or might have been antecedent to the thing you want to discuss, to explain or to establish, or you will not have the vaguest idea of what facts to look for. Only when you have done this can you make an intelligent search for the facts. Facts are the children of imagination out of investigation. Then too, you must have a mental concept of the whole of your theme before you start to arrange it. You must see it in substance before you write it. To conceive of the substance of a thing before it materializes is to imagine it. You must imagine how the whole thing is going to stack up. You must have a mental concept of every detail of your theme before you start to express it. How are you going to pick and choose your adjectives, your adverbs, your similes and your metaphors unless you first have a mental image of the picture you wish to depict? You must have the feeling of what you want to say while feeling for the words with which to say it.

You will need also to think of the development of your theme in the terms of logic. A popular public speaker once pointed out that of all the factors making for the successful public presentation of a subject, oral or written, the most important is logic. His thesis was that, however low the intelligence quotient of the audience, the fact remained that the human mind responds more readily to logic than to illogic.

Another indispensable talent is narrative power; the ability to bind your sentences and your paragraphs with a continuous thread of thought which extends all the way to the point of your theme.

And finally there is required the ability to build the narrative up to a climax.

Perhaps you are thinking something like this:

> "The man is, or should be, speaking of legal writing. A discriminating choice of words, sound sentence structure, logic and clarity—I can understand their relevance. But whoever heard or dreamt of the stylistic qualities of imagination, narrative and climax in connection with the drafting of a will, the spelling out of the preferences of the first and second preferred stock on the back of a stock certificate, or the drafting of a contract for the sale of real estate?"

If that is what you are thinking, it is because you do not appreciate the influence of these qualities upon your writing.

In connection with legal writing I am not thinking of imagination in the sense of fiction, or of narrative in the sense of that gripping prose which would be characteristic of a story of stark adventure; nor am I thinking of climax in terms of that ecstatic moment when the tangled threads of the drama are at last untangled in a thrilling denouement.

But in the most drab of legal documents which you may be called upon to write you have an objective to be reached, you have a point to make. You have to accomplish it with words, phrases, sentences and paragraphs. In doing it, if you are doing a good job you are utilizing, albeit subconsciously, these qualities of imagination, narrative and climax. You play upon them in subduced tones, or paint them in lackluster colors, but they still are there, giving quality to your writing. And the intelligibility of your writing will be in direct proportion to the presence or absence of these qualities in your style.

A lawyer's style of writing should be pliable, flexible.

If you will review the list of things a lawyer is called upon to write you will be aware of the fact that each of them will require a different treatment. Drafting a will differs measurably from the writing of a brief in which the qualities of narrative and climax really come to the forefront in their true colors.

So, like a baseball pitcher, you must have a change of pace if you are going to achieve a shut-out. You will need to adapt your style to the job in hand. If you are going to do that you have got to know something about pitching—something about style.

All of which is by way of saying: If it is important that others should know what you want them to know, then you will need to know.

How To Write

You may think you know something about writing. But few of you do know anything about it. Assuming that you do know something about it, the bald truth is that you do not know enough. If you have had no instruction in the subject you may be self-critical enough to realize your incapacity. In either case the question arises as to what you can do about it.

To Develop Style . . . Study and Practice

There is a great deal that you can and should do about it. Teach yourself. Resort to practice and study; study and practice. Even the indolent Samuel Johnson was wont to read a classic essay or treatise, put it aside, write one of his own on the same subject, and then to compare the two for his own instruction. Surely such an exercise cannot be beneath you.

Whenever you have anything to write, think as much about the writing of it as you do of what you are writing about. Think of your reader. Is he familiar with the subject or ignorant of it? Envision his background, experience and environment. Ask you, yourself, whether he is likely to be prejudiced or open-minded. Imagine yourself as the reader. Ask yourself how you would like the subject presented; to what sort of presentation would you be the most hospitable mentally? Fix in your own mind whether the writing is to be informative, declaratory, expository, emotionally persuasive or argumentative.

With these considerations behind you cut your pattern to fit the cloth.

But you arc not yet ready to write. You merely are ready to read. Take from the shelf a book or two by one whose writing is exemplary of the style which you think is the appropriate medium for your pattern, and read and read and read until you feel yourself in the mood of the style. Then you will be ready to write. "It was not for nothing," wrote Lytton Strachey in discussing Gibbon's style, "It was not for nothing that he read through every year the 'Provincial Letters' of Pascal."

As you write make a study of the important words you propose to use. Look them up in the dictionary, trace them through the thesaurus and see if there may be a synonym that is more suitable, more expressive or more forceful. Use the best word you can find.

For this procedure you will need tools. You should have those tools in your law library. In assembling your law library these tools, which of course are books, are the first ones to acquire.

The first book you should acquire is a good dictionary.

Next in order is Roget's *Thesaurus,* or Hartrampf's *Vocabularies.*

After these you should have a few good books by masters of style, snatches of which you should read every day, and which you should read more assiduously from time to time as circumstances permit.

In this category there is a wide choice, depending on individual tastes and preferences. Of course the Bible and Shakespeare are standard. In the careers of many famous writers and speakers they are reputed to have been basic. I would include them. The choice is wide. However, I can suggest a few books which are worthwhile to have around, and the reading of which will pay dividends if you are disposed to cultivate style. And I mean books for your law library.

An excellent book in which to browse, one which begins to veer away from the lyric toward the ingenuous, is Walton's *Compleat Angler.*

For outright utilitarian prose I would recommend Macaulay's *Life of Johnson.*

For exquisite narrative I recommend that you include Mile's translation of André Maurois's *Disraeli.*

For a thorough-going lesson in the cogency of brevity, by all means have at hand a copy of Strachey's *Portraits in Miniature.*

At the risk of being charged with contributing to your delinquency I would say that it would be worth your while to peruse the pages of the most recently discovered papers of James Boswell.

For an informative example of thought-provoking paragraphs and pregnant clichés, a frequent reading of Claude Houghton's *I Am Jonathan Scrivner* will be a source of inspiration.

As a brilliant study in the art of bringing into focus the seemingly irrelevant facts of life to illuminate the theme with the klieg lights of clarity read now and then Mankiewicz's *See How They Run.*

For beautiful diction and expository excellence turn frequently to a reading of Rachel Carson's *The Sea Around Us.*

You are minded, perhaps, to have a few law books about. Well and good!

You will need first of all your state statutes and codes, a good book of forms, your state digest, and if you can afford it, your state reports. But a law library of several thousand volumes will be ever inadequate for research and the county libraries, the court libraries and the bar association libraries are always available. You cannot duplicate them.

What you need at hand are the means of learning how to get your learning across the plate, where the umpire is calling strikes and balls.

And with that in view, be sure to include in your law library for instruction in the dramatic portrayal of incidents and spectacular characterization in the vivid eloquence of sheer simplicity a copy of *Alice's Adventures in Wonderland.*

Adapted from Vol. 41, American Bar Association Journal (1955).

The Appellate Process and Judicial Opinions

The Writing of Judicial Opinions

By Horace Stern

It is curious that neither the bar nor the general public have ever fully realized that the writing of judicial opinions constitutes a distinctive art. It is apparently assumed that any lawyer transferred to the bench becomes, merely by reason of his new office, immediately capable of formulating his views of the law in a clear and well-stated manner. Nothing could be further from the truth. Profound erudition, legal ability, literary charm—none of these offers any absolute assurance that a judge can write a "brilliant" or even a moderately "good" opinion. For, to accomplish that feat, there is required not only years of practice but a special "knack" which, in my opinion, has been possessed by fewer judges in America, proportionately, than in England, where a judicial opinion is valued for its merit as such entirely apart from the soundness of the legal principles which it enunciates.

Technically a case consists only of the facts and the decision rendered thereon; those elements spell, in conjunction, the determination of the controversy, and, in accordance with the familiar system by which our law develops, they alone constitute the precedent. What, then, is the function of the judicial opinion, which is thus apparently superfluous, since it can neither increase nor diminish the actual effect of the decision itself? Obviously it is designed for the satisfaction of one or more of three critical tribunals. The first is the litigants and their counsel; certainly the defeated party cannot be expected to rest content with the bare conclusions of the court; he will be eager to learn the successive steps, the turns and twists in the pathway by which the terminus was reached; he will be desirous of checking the judge's assumptions of fact, correctness of reasoning and accuracy of legal knowledge, in order to ascertain at what point, if any, the processes of the judicial mind may have gone astray and thereby caused the result which he naturally deplores. If the case involves a new legal problem of importance the second tribunal to consider the opinion will be the members of the bar at large. The third will be the general public if great public interests are concerned, political, economic or social. But above and beyond these appeals to contemporary judgments there is served a much larger purpose, for the opinions handed down by the courts constitute, of course, the basic texts for all legal study and the quarry from which succeeding jurists draw their material.

Such being its function and the broad extent of its reach, what are the essential qualities of a judicial opinion? Obviously in the first rank are accuracy of legal statements and reliability of logical deductions, for upon those factors depends the integrity of the decision itself. Second only to them are organization, simplicity, clarity and style. In order to appraise the merit of an opinion there are two infallible tests. (1) Has it satisfied counsel for the losing party—assuming, of course, that he is reasonably open-minded and of at least average legal ability? (2) Can the official reporter, in preparing the syllabus, determine without difficulty the precise import of the opinion? If ill-reasoned it will fail to clear the first of these hurdles; if rambling, confused, discursive or ambiguous, it will falter at the second. As far as form is concerned, Cardozo, in his admirable essay on "Law and Literature," has graphically depicted the role which elegant language plays in the realm of judicial opinions. Who can hope to compete with his own limpid style, its rich beauty and delightful imagery, or with Holmes' sententious utterances, or with Sutherland's sonorous and well-rounded phrases? How clumsy their would-be imitators! How futile the attempts to ape those masters! There has apparently grown up of late a widespread passion for "fine writing," but in this tendency there lurks grave evil, for, unless the pen be guided by the hand of genius, there is apt to result a sacrifice of legal sense to purely artificial verbiage. Form should fit substance like clothes the well-dressed man which, when appropriate, never attract attention on their own account. An ornate, pretentious, grandiose style, replete with superfluous frills and rhetorical extravagances, can act only as an undesirable distraction. Nor is a judicial opinion a proper vehicle for the exploitation of pedantic learning or extraneous disquisitions.

Making all allowances for the well-known temptation to exalt the past in comparison with the present, one is nevertheless justified in believing that the art of opinion-writing has, in one respect, markedly deteriorated. For how superior are the sweeping, unconditional pronouncements of Marshall, or our own Tilghman and Gibson, to the cautious utterances that characterize the judicial opinions of today! Those jurists, and others of their time, spoke as with Jove-like authority—with the calmness, the dignity and the assurance born of a conscious sense of mastery and power. Where our tone is timid and guarded, theirs was bold and unafraid. They scorned equivocal statements and eschewed words creating impressions of uncertainty or indecision. Is the wary note in our own opinions due to a greater anxiety as to the effect of our pronouncements on the highly sensitive organisms of modern industrial life? Or is it because judges in the earlier stages of our country's history could write opinions formulating legal principles without the restrictions now imposed by an overwhelming multitude of precedents? With the myriad of decisions accumulated during the course of the years there are always scores of prior cases to be studied and analyzed, and the resulting necessity of explaining our reasons for accepting, distinguishing or rejecting these as controlling is perhaps the real reason why the judicial opinions of today tend to be more labored, more argumentative and, incidentally, more dull, than those of former judges who were less bound by the achievements or, it may be, the mistakes, of their predecessors.

One of the dangers that always confronts persons in public office is the lure of newspaper publicity, and from this the judiciary, unfortunately, is not wholly exempt. We are living in an age of journalistic sensationalism, and it is easy to realize that a judge, whose work and whose life are of necessity somewhat monastic, may occasionally be tempted to seek a greater measure of public recognition by opinions designed to catch the eye and invite the interest of the newspaper editor. It need scarcely be said that the inevitable result is a deterioration both in integrity of content and dignity of form. Moreover, an exaggerated desire for personal acclaim naturally leads to opinions exploiting views of the writer rather than expressing those of the court. It is well that judges, in at least our higher courts, have rarely been guilty of such lapses.

A truly great opinion cannot be written unless the subject-matter itself is of commanding importance. While questions such as those concerning mechanics' liens, executory devises, or others of a like technical nature, may be adequately disposed of by commendable discussions of applicable law, it is only some problem of constitutional interpretation, or some controversy of grave social or economic consequence, which can furnish the setting for an "outstanding" or "brilliant" opinion. The judicial opinions which stand the test of time and are recognized as great landmarks in the history of the law are few and far between, and it is only a small roll of distinguished judges who have written them.

As to that feature of opinions which lawyers apparently are most fond of criticizing, namely their length, nothing is less deserving of the quips and raillery indulged in by the bar. Parenthetically, a judge may be pardoned for observing that addresses delivered by *lawyers,* and briefs and articles written by *them* have never been particularly noted for brevity. The truth of the matter is that the length of a judicial opinion is not to be measured by any fixed rule or standard. When Lincoln was once asked by a wag what he thought was the proper length for a man's leg, he replied that it ought to be just long enough to reach the ground. So an opinion should be just long enough to cover the subject with which it deals, and therefore its length is necessarily dependent upon the nature of that subject; an opinion of two pages may be too long in some cases and one of ten pages inadequate in others.

I have referred to the impropriety of opinions that are unduly individualistic. If a judge is occasionally possessed of an uncontrollable desire to express his personal views instead of having them continually absorbed in the compromise pronouncements of the court, he may gratify that urge by the writing of concurring or, if so disposed, even dissenting, opinions. But a concurring opinion must justify itself by furnishing a different reason for the court's decision, and even then should not be resorted to unless the writer of the majority opinion refuses to accept and incorporate the suggested additions or amendments. A concurring opinion which merely says the same thing in other language is not only valueless as a contribution to the science of the law but is somewhat of a reflection on the colleague to whom was assigned the duty of explaining the views and conclusions of the court.

It is in dissenting opinions that some judges shine at their best, for here they are inhibited neither in thought nor in style and are able to express themselves with a freedom restrained only by the dictates of fairness and courtesy to the associates with whom they are in disagreement. The dissenter is responsible only to himself for what he says and the manner in which he says it, and, because his opinion is therefore apt to be bold, vigorous and dramatic, it is naturally likely to attract greater interest than the more staid and cautious utterances of the majority; moreover, sympathy usually expends itself on the "under-dog." But here again lurks the danger of seeking meretricious glory, and only when a judge feels a really irresistible compulsion to disassociate himself from the conclusions of the court should he employ so formidable a weapon as a dissenting opinion.

How ephemeral at best is the reputation of even a distinguished judge! How quickly is his personality submerged in the long annals of judicial history! How truly applicable to him is the melancholy thought in the colophon with which Longfellow concluded his "Outre-Mer": "To what end is all this toil? Of what avail these midnight vigils? Dost thou covet fame? Vain dreamer! A few brief days, and what will the busy world know of thee?" And how mournfully must he resign himself to the reflection that each of his opinions is probably "but a bubble on the stream; and although it may catch the sunshine for a moment, yet it will soon float down the swift-rushing current, and be seen no more!"

Adapted from Vol. 18, Pennsylvania Bar Association Quarterly (1946).

Law and Literature

BY BENJAMIN N. CARDOZO

I HAVE PLANNED to say a word to you tonight about law as literature rather than about law as law. The subject is too large to be traversed from end to end, however, imperfectly and hastily, in a fragment of an hour. A few desultory excursions here and there will have to satisfy our yearning for hill and dale and stream. I am told at times by friends that a judicial opinion has no business to be literature. The idol must be ugly, or he may be taken for a common man. The deliverance that is to be accepted without demur or hesitation must have a certain high austerity which frowns at winning graces. I fancy that not a little of this criticism is founded in misconception of the true significance of literature, or, more accurately perhaps, of literary style. To some a clearer insight has been given. There are those who have perceived that the highest measure of condensation, of short and sharp and imperative directness, a directness that speaks the voice of some external and supreme authority, is consistent, none the less, with supreme literary excellence. Henri Beyle, the French novelist, used to say that "there was only one example of the perfect style, and that was the Code Napoléon; for there alone everything was subordinated to the exact and complete expression of what was to be said". The poor man succumbed to its charm to such an extent that he was in the habit of reading a few paragraphs every morning before breakfast. I do not seek to substitute this regimen for the daily exercise in calisthenics. Some of us prefer our literature like our food in less concentrated tablets. I do no more than suggest that the morsel hastily gulped down may have a savor all its own for the discriminating palate. But I over-emphasize and exaggerate if I seem to paint the picture of any active opposition that is more than sporadic and exceptional to so amiable a weakness as a love of art and letters. A commoner attitude is one, not of active opposition, but of amused or cynical indifference. We are merely wasting our time, so many will inform us, if we bother about form when only substance is important. I suppose this might be true if any one could tell us where substance ends and form begins. Philosophers have been trying for some thousands of years to draw the distinction between substance and mere appearance in the world of matter. I doubt whether they succeed better when they attempt a like distinction in the world of thought. Form is not something added to substance as a mere protuberant adornment. The two are fused into a unity. Not long ago I ran across a paragraph in the letters of Henry James in which he blurts out his impatience of these attempts to divide the indivisible. He is writing to Hugh Walpole, now a novelist of assured position, but then comparatively unknown. "Don't let anyone persuade you—there are plenty of ignorant and fatuous duffers to try to do it—that strenuous selection and comparison are not the very essence of art, and that Form *is* not substance to that degree that there is absolutely no substance without it. Form alone *takes,* and holds and preserves substances, saves it from the welter of helpless verbiage that we swim in as in a sea of tasteless tepid pudding." This is my own faith. The argument strongly put is not the same as the argument put feebly any more than the "tasteless tepid pudding" is the same as the pudding served to us in triumph with all the glory of the lambent flame. The strength that is born of form and the feebleness that is born of the lack of form are in truth qualities of the substance. They are the tokens of the thing's identity. They make it what it is.

Up to this point at least, I have little fear of opposition—We shall most of us be agreed, I think, not merely that style is not an evil in the Sahara of a judicial opinion, but even that is a positive good, if only it is the right style. *There* is the disquieting condition which checks the forward movement of triumphal demonstration. What is to be deemed the right style, or the right styles if there are more than one of them? Do the examples of the great masters reveal some uniformity of method for the instruction of the tyro? If uniformity is not discoverable, may there not at least be types or standards? If types or standards do not exist, shall we not find stimulus and interest in the coruscations of genius, however vagrant or irregular? If at times there is neither stimulus nor interest, may there not in lieu of these be the awful warning of example?

I suppose there can be little doubt that in matters of literary style the sovereign virtue for the judge is clearness. Judge Veeder in his interesting and scholarly essay, *A Century of Judicature,* quotes the comment of Broughman upon the opinions of Lord Stowell: "If ever the praise of being luminous could be bestowed upon human compositions, it was upon his judgments." How shall his successors in the same or other courts attain that standard or approach it? There is an accuracy that defeats itself by the overemphasis of details. I often say that one must permit oneself, and that quite advisedly and deliberately, a certain margin of misstatement. Of course, one must take heed that the margin is not exceeded, just as the physician must be cautious in administering the poisonous ingredient which magnified will kill, but in tiny quantities will cure. On the other hand, the sentence may be so overloaded with all its possible qualifications that it will tumble down of its own weight. "To philosophize," says Holmes in one of his opinions—I am quoting him from uncertain and perhaps inaccurate recollection—"to philosophize is to generalize, but to generalize is to omit." The picture cannot be painted if the significant and the insignificant are given equal prominence. One must know how to select.

All these generalities are as easy as they are obvious, but, alas! the application is an ordeal to try the souls of men. Write an opinion, and read it a few years later when it is dissected in the briefs of counsel. You will learn for the first time the limitations of the power of speech, or, if not those of speech in general, at all events your own. All sorts of gaps and obstacles and impediments will obtrude themselves before your gaze, as pitilessly manifest as the hazards on a golf course. Sometimes you will know that the fault is truly yours, in which event you can only smite your breast, and pray for deliverance thereafter. Sometimes you will feel that the fault is with counsel who have stupidly misread the obvious, in which event, though you rail against the bar and the imperfect medium of speech, you will be solaced, even in your chagrin, by a sense of injured innocence. Sometimes, though rarely, you will believe that the misreading is less stupid than malicious, in which event you will be wise to keep your feeling to yourself. One marvels sometimes at the ingenuity with which texts the most remote are made to serve the ends of argument or parable. But clearness, though the sovereign quality, is not the only one to be pursued, and even if it were, may be gained through many avenues of approach. The opinion will need persuasive force, or the impressive virtue of sincerity and fire, or the mnemonic power of alliteration and antithesis, or the terseness and tang of the proverb and the maxim. Neglect the help of these allies, and it may never win its way. With traps and obstacles and hazards confronting us on every hand, only blindness or indifference will fail to turn, in all humility, for guidance or for warning, to the study of examples.

Classification must be provisional, for forms run into one another. As I search the archives of my memory, I seem to discern six types or methods which divide themselves from one another with measurable distinctness. There is the type magisterial or imperative; the type laconic or sententious; the type conversational or homely; the type refined or artificial, smelling of the lamp, verging at times upon preciosity or euphuism; the type demonstrative or persuasive; and finally the type tonsorial or agglutinative, so called from the shears and the pastepot which are its implements and emblem.

I place first in order, for it is first in dignity and power, the type magisterial or imperative. It eschews ornament. It is meagre in illustration and analogy. If it argues, it does so with the downward rush and overwhelming conviction of the syllogism, seldom with tentative gropings toward the inductive apprehension of a truth imperfectly discerned. We hear the voice of the law speaking by its consecrated ministers with the calmness and assurance that are born of a sense of mastery and power. Thus Marshall seemed to judge, and a hush falls upon us even now as we listen to his words. Those organ tones of his were meant to fill cathedrals or the most exalted of tribunals. The judicial department, he tells us, "has no will in any case. * * * Judicial power is never exercised for the purpose of giving effect to the will of the judge; always for the purpose of giving effect to the will of the legislature; or in other words, to the will of the law." The thrill is irresistible. We feel the mystery and the awe of inspired revelation. His greatest judgments are framed upon this plane of exaltation and aloofness. The movement from premise to conclusion is put before the observer as something more impersonal than the working of the individual mind. It is the inevitable progress of an inexorable force. Professor Corwin in an interesting book, "John Marshall and the Constitution," shows how even his contemporaries, the bitterest critics of his aggrandizement of federal power, were touched by this illusion. "All wrong, all wrong," lamented John

Randolph of Roanoke, "but no man in the United States can tell why or wherein." I have re-read a few of the most famous of his judgments: *Marbury v. Madison; Gibbons v. Ogden; McCulloch v. Maryland;* they are all in the grand style.

Listen to the voice of the magistrate in *Marbury v. Madison:* "The distinction between a government with limited and unlimited powers is abolished if those limits do not confine the persons on whom they are imposed, and if acts prohibited and acts allowed are of equal obligation. It is a proposition too plain to be contested, that the Constitution controls any legislative act repugnant to it, or that the Legislature may alter the Constitution by an ordinary act. Between these alternatives there is no middle ground. The Constitution is either a superior paramount law, unchangeable by ordinary means, or it is on a level with ordinary legislative acts, and, like other acts, is alterable when the Legislature shall please to alter it. If the former part of the alternative be true, then a legislative act contrary to the Constitution is not law; if the latter part be true, then written Constitutions are absurd attempts, on the part of the people, to limit a power in its own nature illimitable. * * * If two laws conflict with each other, the Courts must decide on the operation of each. So if a law be in opposition to the Constitution; if both the law and the Constitution apply to a particular case, so that the Court must either decide that case conformably to the law, disregarding the Constitution, or conformably to the Constitution, disregarding the law,—the Court must determine which of these conflicting rules governs the case. This is of the very essence of judicial duty." Nothing is here of doubt; nothing of apology; no blurred edges or uncertain lines. "There is no middle ground." The choice that is made is "of the very essence of judicial duty." The voice has pealed forth. Let the wicked heed it and obey.

One will find this same suggestion of sure and calm conviction in some of the judgments of Lord Mansfield. The slave Somerset captured on the coast of Africa, is sold in bondage in Virginia, and brought to England by his master. The case comes before Mansfield on the return to the writ of habeas corpus: "The state of slavery is of such a nature that it is incapable of being introduced on any reasons, moral or political, but only positive law, which preserved its force long after the reasons, occasions, and time itself from whence it was created, is erased from memory. It is so odious that nothing can be suffered to support it, but positive law. * * * I care not for the supposed *dicta* of judges, however eminent, if they be contrary to all principle. The *dicta* cited were probably misunderstood, and at all events they are to be disregarded. Villainage, when it did exist in this country, differed in many particulars from West India slavery. The lord never could have thrown his villain, whether *regardant* or *in gross,* into chains, sent him to the West Indies, and sold him there to work in a mine or in a cane field. At any rate villainage has ceased in England, and it cannot be revived. The air of England has long been too pure for a slave, and every man is free who breathes it. Every man who comes into England is entitled to the protection of English law, whatever oppression he may heretofore have suffered, and whatever may be the color of his skin. '*Quamvis ille niger, quamvis tu candidus esses.*' Let the negro be discharged."

It is thus men speak when they are conscious of their power. One does not need to justify oneself if one is the mouthpiece of divinity. The style will fit the mood.

I have said that in dignity and power there is no method that can be matched with the method which I have characterized as magisterial or imperative. A changing philosophy of law has tended, none the less, to the use of other methods more conciliatory and modest. The development of law is conceived of, more and more, as a process of adaptation and adjustment. The pronouncements of its ministers are timid and tentative approximations, to be judged through their workings, by some pragmatic test of truth. I find a striking statement of this attitude of mind in a dissenting opinion by Mr. Justice Brandeis, filed not many months ago. Arguing for the restriction of a rule which had proved itself unworkable, he says: "Such limitations of principles previously announced and such express disapproval of *dicta* are often necessary. It is an unavoidable incident of the search by courts of last resort for the true rule. The process of inclusion and exclusion, so often applied in developing a rule, cannot end with its first enunciation. The rule as announced must be deemed tentative. For the many and varying facts to which it will be applied cannot be foreseen. Modification implies growth. It is the life of the law."

One cannot face the law in this spirit of cautious seeking without showing the changing point of view in a changing style and form. Universals will be handled more charily under the dominance of such a philosophy than in days when the law of nature supplied us with data that were supposed to be eternal and unyielding. Yet there are times even now when the magisterial method is utilized by men who know that they are masters of their calling. It is still utilized in fields where some established principle is to be applied to new facts or where the area of its extension or restriction is fairly obvious or narrow. But alas! even then it is the masters, and no others, who feel sure enough of themselves to omit the intermediate steps and stages, and leap to the conclusion. Most of us are so uncertain of our strength, so beset with doubts and difficulties, that we feel oppressed with the need of justifying every holding by analogies and precedents and an exposure of the reasons. The masters are content to say, "the elect will understand, there is no need to write for others." Perhaps there are opinions by Mr. Justice Holmes in which this mood can be discerned. The sluggard unable to keep pace with the swiftness of his thought will say that he is hard to follow. If that is so, it is only for the reason that he is walking with a giant's stride. But giants, after all, are not met at every turn, and for most of us, even if we are not pygmies, the gait of ordinary men is the safer manner of advance. We grope and feel our way. What we hand down in our judgments is an hypothesis. It is no longer a divine command.

I pass to other types which run into each other by imperceptible gradations, the laconic or sententious and the conversational or homely. There has been no stage of our legal history in which these methods have been neglected. The Year Books are full of wise saws and homely illustrations, the epigram, the quip, the jest. Perhaps this is but a phase of that use of the maxim or the proverb which is characteristic of legal systems in early stages of development. Dean Pound in a recent paper has traced the growth and function of the maxim with all the resources of his learning. If the maxim has declined in prevalence and importance, now that the truths of the law have become too complex to be forced within a sentence, there has been no abatement of recourse to the laconic or sententious phrase, to drive home and imbed what might otherwise be lost or scattered. Who will resist Lord Nottingham's adjuration: "Pray let us so resolve cases here, that they may stand with the reason of mankind when they are debated abroad": Is there any armor proof against a thrust like the dictum of Lord Bowen's: "The state of a man's mind is as much a fact as the state of his digestion"? Next door to the epigram is the homely illustration which makes its way and sinks deep by its appeal to every-day experience. In the wielding of these weapons, the English judges have been masters. The precept may be doubtful in the beginning. How impossible to fight against it when the judge brings it down to earth and makes it walk the ground, the brother of some dictate of decency or of prudence which we have followed all our lives. Perhaps the kinship is not so close or apparent as it is figured. Who will have the hardihood to doubt the reality of the tie when it is so blandly assumed to be obvious to all? The common denominator silences and satisfies. The rule that is rooted in idendities or analogies of customary belief and practice is felt and rightly felt to be rooted in reality. We glide into acquiescence when negation seems to question our kinship with the crowd. Something must be set down also to the sense of fellowship awakened when judges talk in ways that seem to make us partners in the deliberative process. "I entirely agree with my right honorable and learned friend upon the woolsack." We seem to be let into the mysteries of the conference, the sacrosanct "arcana," to quote Professor Powell's phrase, to which "the uninitiated are not admitted." Given such an atmosphere, with point and pungency thrown into it, the product makes its way into every crack and crevice of our being.

I have scant time for illustration, yet I cannot resist it altogether. Take this by Lord Bramwell: "It does not follow that if a man dies in a fit in a railway carriage, there is a *prima facie* case for his widow and children, nor that if he has a glass in his pocket and sits on it and hurts himself, there is something which calls for an answer or explanation from the company". Take this by Lord Blackburn in *Smith v. Chadwick:* "If with intent to lead the plaintiff to act upon it, they put forth a statement which they know may bear two meanings, one of which is false to their knowledge, and thereby the plaintiff, putting that meaning upon it, is misled, I do not think they can escape by saying he ought to have put the other. If they palter with him, in a double sense, it may be that they lie like truth, but I think they lie, and it is a fraud."

One could cite other examples without number. What a cobweb of fine-spun casuistry is dissipated in a breath by the simple statement of Lord Esher in *Ex parte Simonds,* that the court will not suffer its own officer "to do a shabby thing." If the word shabby had been left out, and unworthy or dishonorable substituted, I suppose the sense would have been much the same. But what a drop in emotional value would have followed. As it is, we feel the tingle of the hot blood of resentment mounting to our cheeks. For quotable good things, for pregnant aphorisms, for touchstones of ready application, the opinions of the English judges are a mine of instruction and a treasury of joy.

Such qualities on the whole are rarer close at home, yet we have one judge even now who can vie with the best of his English brethren, past as well as present, in the art of packing within a sentence the phosphorescence of a page. If I begin to quote from the opinions of Mr. Justice Holmes, I hardly know where I shall end, yet fealty to a master makes me reluctant to hold back. The sheaf will be a tiny one, made up haphazard, the barest sample of the riches which the gleaner may gather where he will. Some hint of the epigrammatic quality of his style may be found in this: "The Fourteenth Amendment, itself a historical product, did not destroy history for the States and substitute mechanical compartments of law all exactly alike". In this: "We are in danger of forgetting that a strong public desire to improve the public condition is not enough to warrant achieving the desire by a shorter cut than the constitutional way of paying for the change". In this: "Legal obligations that exist but cannot be enforced are ghosts that are seen in the law but that are elusive to the grasp". And finally in this, words of solemn dissent, their impressiveness heightened by the knowledge that the cause has been already lost: "Persecution for the expression of opinions seems to me perfectly logical. If you have no doubt of your premises or your power and want a certain result with all your heart you naturally express your wishes in law and sweep away all opposition. To allow opposition by speech seems to indicate that you think the speech impotent, as when a man says that he has squared the circle, or that you do not care whole-heartedly for the result, or that you doubt either your power or your premises. But when men have realized that time has upset many fighting faiths, they may come to believe even more than they believe the very foundations of their own conduct that the ultimate good desired is better reached by free trade in ideas—that the best test of truth is the power of the thought to get itself accepted in the competition of the market, and that truth is the only ground upon which their wishes safely can be carried out. That at any rate is the theory of our Constitution. It is an experiment, as all life is an experiment. Every year if not every day we have to wager our salvation upon some prophecy based upon imperfect knowledge. While that experiment is part of our system I think that we should be eternally vigilant against attempts to check the expression of opinions that we loathe and believe to be fraught with death, unless they so imminently threaten immediate interference with the lawful and pressing purposes of the law that an immediate check is required to save the country".

There is another type or method which I have spoken of as the refined or artificial, smelling a little of the lamp. With its merits it has its dangers, for unless well kept in hand, it verges at times upon preciosity and euphuism. Held in due restraint, it lends itself admirably to cases where there is need of delicate precision. I find no better organon where the subject matter of discussion is the construction of a will with all the filigree of tentacles, the shades and nuances of differences, the slender and fragile tracery that must be preserved unmutilated and distinct. Judge Finch of the Court of Appeals of New York was an adept in the writing of opinions which carried with them this suggestion of precision and refinement. Occasionally, it shades into a faint and gentle sarcasm which is sometimes the refuge of the spokesman of a minority expressing his dissent. Again I must restrict quotation. As an illustration, let me quote from the dissenting opinion in *People ex rel. Sherwood v. Board of Canvassers,* an election controversy which in its day provoked no little warmth of difference. The majority had held that despite the provision of the Constitution making each house of the legislature the judge of the elections, returns, and qualifications of its own members, the courts would refuse affirmative aid to a claimant for such an office if it found him ineligible in its own view of the law. Judge Finch protested against this holding. "And so," he said, "I deny the asserted doctrine of 'invocation'; of a right to do evil that good may come; of excusable judicial usurpation; and if the doctrine has anywhere got its dangerous and destructive hold upon our law, which I do not believe, it should be resolutely shaken off. But let us not deceive ourselves. The excess of jurisdiction is not even excusable, for it has neither occasion nor necessity." A moment later, he has his fears that he has been betrayed into excessive warmth. His closing words are those of apology and deference: "If what I have said does not convince the majority of the court, nothing that I can say will do so. I have tried faithfully, and, I hope, with proper respect, for certainly I have not meant to be wanting in that, to point out the mistake which, it seems to me, they are about to make. Theirs, however, must be both the responsibility and its consequences."

Such a method has its charm and its attraction, though one feels at times the yearning for another more robust and virile. It is here that I pass into the type which I have characterized as demonstrative or persuasive. It is not unlike the magisterial or imperative, yet it differs in a certain amplitude of development, a freer use of the resources of illustration and analogy and history and precedent, in brief, a tone more suggestive of the scientific seeker for the truth and less reminiscent of the priestess on the tripod. One might cite many judges who have used this method with distinction. I think the work of Charles Andrews, for many years a judge and then the Chief Judge, of the New York Court of Appeals, is a shining illustration. I can best describe the quality of his opinions in the words of a memorial written upon his death: "The majesty of his personal appearance," it was said, "is reflected in the majesty of his judicial style, the steady and stately march of his opinions from established premises to inevitable conclusion." Such a method, well pursued, has a sanity and a clarity that make it an admirable medium for the declaration of considered judgments. The form is no mere epidermis. It is the very bone and tissue.

My summary of styles may leave a cheerless impression of the solemn and the ponderous. I would not have you believe that flashes of humor are unknown, yet the form of opinion which aims at humor from beginning to end is a perilous adventure, which can be justified only by success, and even then is likely to find its critics almost as many as its eulogists. The story is told by Bernard Shaw of a man who wished to consult the writings of the great naturalist Buffon, and who startled the clerks in the bookstore by the pompous and solemn query, "have you the books of the celebrated Buffoon?" One of the difficulties about the humorous opinion is exposure to the risk of passing from the class of Buffons where we all like to dwell and entering the class of the celebrated Buffoons. The transition at times is distressingly swift, and when once one has entered the new class, it is so difficult, if not indeed impossible, to climb over the fences and back into the old. None the less, there are subjects which only the most resolute have been able to discuss without yielding to the temptation of making profert of their sense of humor. A dog or a cat or a horse if it is the occasion of a horse trade has been the signal for unexpected outbursts of mirth and occasionally of pathos from judges slowly stirred to emotion by the cinema of life. Judge Allen's opinion in *Wiley v. Slater* on the "code duello" among dogs, was on the whole a fine success, but it has been responsible for the writing of some others that were not. There is an opinion by Baron Bramwell which deals with the propensities of pigs. A fence was defective, and the pigs straying did mischief to a trolley car. The decision was that the barrier should have been sufficient to protect the adjoining owner against the incursions, not of all pigs, but of pigs of "average vigour and obstinacy". "Nor do we lay down," said the learned Baron, "that there must be a fence so close and strong that no pig could push through it, or so high that no horse or bullock could leap it. One could scarcely tell the limits of such a requirement for the strength of swine is such that they would break through almost any fence, if there were a sufficient inducement on the other side. But the company is bound to put up such a fence that a pig not of a peculiarly wandering disposition, nor under any excessive temptation, will not get through it." Perhaps the humor of this ruling was more unwitting than designed. Some may agree with Sir Frederick Pollock that the decision is "almost a caricature of the general idea of the 'reasonable man.'" In all this I would not convey the thought that an opinion is the worse for being lightened by a smile. I am merely preaching caution. Other flights and digressions I find yet more doubtful than the humorous. In days not far remote, judges were not unwilling to embellish their deliverances with quotations from the poets. I shall observe toward such a practice the tone of decent civility that is due to those departed.

I have had in mind in this excursus a humor that was conscious and intended. Perhaps I should have classed the opinion that is humorous or playful as an independent type, but I have preferred to treat it incidentally since I am not aware that any judge has employed it consistently or except on rare occasions. Humor also that is unconscious and unintended may be dug out of the reports if we take the trouble to extract it. I once gathered together for my own edification and amusement some gems that I had unearthed from the opinions of one of our local courts in days when it had an appellate branch of its own and handed down opinions which were faithfully reported. Unluckily, I have lost my memorandum, but a few of the items are still vivid in my mind. The question to be determined was the extent of the amendment of a pleading to be permitted upon the trial. The decisive principle was thus expounded: "The bed that litigants make and lie in up to the trial, should not be then vacated by them. They should continue to lie therein until the jury render their verdict." I understand that the Modern Practice Acts have swept this principle away, and that the suitor, who seems to his adversary to be innocently somnolent, may now jump out of bed at the last moment and prove to be very much awake. This is the new doctrine, but where will you find a more vivid statement of the doctrine of an elder day which decried surprise and haste, and was satisfied that justice herself should have the privilege of a nap? I recall, too, a charge to a jury, never reported, but surely fit to be preserved. "In this case," said the trial judge, "I believe that Mr. A (the counsel for the plaintiff), knows as much law as Mr. B (the counsel for the defendant), and I believe that Mr. B knows as much law as Mr. A, but I believe that I in my judicial capacity know as much law as both of them together." Whereupon he forgot to tell the jury anything else, but said they were to consider their verdict and decide the case in accordance with the rules he had laid down. Well, his charge was sparse, but it enunciated an important truth. Our whole judicial system is built upon some such assumption as the learned judge put forward a trifle crassly and obscurely. This is the great convention, the great fiction, which makes trial in court a fair substitute for trial by battle or by casting lots. The philosopher will find philosophy if he has an eye for it even in a "crowner's" court.

I must not forget my final type, the tonsorial or agglutinative. I will not expatiate upon its horrors. They are known but too well. The dreary succession of quotations closes with a brief paragraph expressing a firm conviction that judgment for plaintiff or for defendant, as the case may be, follows as an inevitable conclusion. The writer having delivered himself of this expression of a perfect faith, commits the product of his hand to the files of the court and the judgment of the ages with all the pride of authorship. I am happy to be able to report that this type is slowly but steadily disappearing. As contrasted with its arid wastes, I prefer the sunny, though rather cramped and narrow pinnacle of a type once much in vogue: "We have carefully examined the record and find no error therein; *therefore* the judgment must be affirmed with costs." How nice a sense of proportion, of the relation between cause and effect, is involved in the use of the illative conjunction "therefore," with its suggestion that other minds less sensitively attuned might have drawn a different conclusion from the same indisputable premises.

I have touched lightly, almost not at all, upon something more important than mere felicities of turn or phrase. Above and beyond all these are what we may term the architectonics of opinions. The groupings of fact and argument and illustration so as to produce a cumulative and mass effect, these after all are the things that count above all others. I should despair, however, of any successful analysis of problems at once so large and so difficult within the limits of this talk. One needs a larger easel if one is to follow such a map. Often clarity is gained by a brief and almost sententious statement at the outset of the problem to be attacked. Then may come a fuller statement of the facts, rigidly pared down, however, in almost every case, to those that are truly essential as opposed to those that are decorative and adventitious. If these are presented with due proportion and selection, our conclusion ought to follow so naturally and inevitably as almost to prove itself. Whether it succeeds in doing this or not, is something about which the readers of the opinion are not always in accord. To gain a proper breadth of view, one should consult counsel for the vanquished as well as counsel for the victor.

The thought of the vanquished brings me to the opinion that voices a dissent. The protests and the warnings of minorities overborne in the fight have their interest and significance for the student, not only of law itself, but of the literary forms through which law reaches its expression. Comparatively speaking at least, the dissenter is irresponsible. The spokesman of the court is cautious, timid, fearful of the vivid word, the heightened phrase. He dreams of an unworthy brood of scions, the spawn of careless *dicta,* disowned by the *ratio decidendi,* to which all legitimate offspring must be able to trace their lineage. The result is to cramp and paralyze. One fears to say anything when the peril of misunderstanding puts a warning finger to the lips. Not so, however, the dissenter. He has laid aside the role of the hierophant, which he will be only too glad to resume when the chances of war make him again the spokesman of the majority. For the moment, he is the gladiator making a last stand against the lions. The poor man must be forgiven a freedom of expression, tinged at rare moments with a touch of bitterness, which magnanimity as well as caution would reject for one triumphant.

A French judge, M. Ransson, a member of the Tribunal of the Seine, wrote some fifteen years ago an essay on the art of judging, in which he depicts the feelings of a judge of the first instance when a judgment is reversed. I suppose the state of mind of one reversed is akin in quality to the state of mind of one dissenting, though perhaps differing in degrees. "A true magistrate," says M. Ransson, "guided solely by his duty and his conscience, his learning and his reason, hears philosophically and without bitterness that his judgment has not been sustained; he knows that the higher court is there to this end, and that better informed beyond doubt, it has believed itself bound to modify his decision. Ought we even to condemn him, if having done his best, he maintains in his inmost soul the impression that perhaps and in spite of everything he was right? *Causa diis victrix placuit, sed victa Catoni.*" Cato had a fine soul, but history does not record that he feared to speak his mind, and judges when in the minority are tempted to imitate his candor. We need not be surprised, therefore, to find in dissent a certain looseness of texture and depth of color rarely found in the *per curiam.* Sometimes, as I have said, there is just a suspicion of acerbity, but this, after all, is rare. More truly characteristic of dissent is a dignity, an elevation, of mood and thought and phrase. Deep conviction and warm feeling are saying their last say with knowledge that the cause is lost. The voice of the majority may be that of force triumphant, content with the plaudits of the hour, and recking little of the morrow. The dissenter speaks to the future, and his voice is pitched to a key that will carry through the years. Read some of the great dissents, the opinion, for example, of Judge Curtis in *Dred Scott v. Sanford,* and feel after the cooling time of the better part of a century the glow and fire of a faith that was content to bide its hour. The prophet and the martyr do not see the hooting throng. Their eyes are fixed on the eternities.

I shall be travelling away from my subject if I leave the writing of opinions and turn to arguments at the bar. A word of digression may be pardoned, however, for the two subjects are allied. Lawyers, young and old, are often curious to know what sort of argument is most effective in an appellate court. Shall it be long or short, terse or discursive? Shall it assume that the judges know the rudiments of law, or shall it attempt in a brief hour to supply the defects in their early training? Shall it state the law or the facts? Shall it take up the authorities and analyze them, or shall it content itself with conclusions and leave analysis for the study? There is, of course, no formula that will fit all situations in appellate courts or elsewhere. If, however, I had to prepare a list of "Don'ts," for the guidance of the novice, I think I would say that only in the rarest instances is it wise to take up one decision after another for the purpose of dissection. Such autopsies have their value at times, but they are wearisome and gruesome scenes. In my list of don'ts, I would add, Don't state the minutiae of the evidence. The judges won't follow you, and if they followed, would forget. Don't attempt to supplement the defects of early training. Your auditors are hardened sinners, not easily redeemed. Above all, don't be long winded. I have in mind a lawyer who argues the appeals for one of the civil subdivisions of the state. His arguments last about a quarter of an hour. He tells us his point and sits down. The audience in the rear of the court room may not applaud, but the audience in front does—at least in spirit—and as the latter audience has the votes, it is best to make your play for them. If you faithfully observe these cautions, let not your spirits droop too low when the decision is adverse, even though there be the added gall and wormwood of a failure of the court to crown your brilliant effort with the dignity of an opinion. Many a gallant argument has met the same unworthy fate.

Young men as they approach admission to the bar must sometimes say to themselves that the great problems have been solved, that the great battles of the forum have been fought, that the great opportunities are ended. There are moods in which for a moment I say the same thing to myself. If I do, the calendar of the following day is as likely as not to bring the exposure of the error. It is a false and cramping notion that cases are made great solely or chiefly by reason of something intrinsic in themselves. They are great by what we make of them. *McCulloch v. Maryland*—to choose almost at random—is one of the famous cases of our history. I wonder, would it not be forgotten, and even perhaps its doctrine overruled, if Marshall had not put upon it the imprint of his genius. "Not one of his great opinions," says Professor Corwin, speaking of Marshall's work, "but might easily have been decided on comparatively narrow grounds in precisely the same way in which he decided it on broad, general principles, but with the probable result that it would never again have been heard of outside the law courts". So, too, the smaller issues await the transfiguring touch. "To a genuine accountant," says Charles Lamb (Essays of Elia, *The South Sea House*), "the difference of proceeds is as nothing. The fractional farthing is as dear to his heart as the thousands which stand before it. He is the true actor, who, whether his part be a prince or a peasant, must act it with like authority." That is the spirit in which judge or advocate is to look upon his task. He is expounding a science, or a body of truth which he seeks to assimilate to a science, but in the process of exposition he is practicing an art. The Muses look at him a bit impatiently and wearily at times. He has done a good deal to alienate them, and sometimes they refuse to listen, and are seen to stop their ears. They have a strange capacity, however, for the discernment of strains of harmony and beauty, no matter how diffused and scattered through the ether. So at times when work is finely done, one sees their faces change, and they take the worker by the hand. They know that by the lever of art the subject the most lowly can be lifted to the heights. Small, indeed, is the company dwelling in those upper spaces, but the few are also the elect.

Well, I have finished my excursion, and must come down again to earth. I hope you will follow my classification, and adopt the method of exposition that seems to be the most appropriate, when next you have to deal with the explanation of a contract or the meaning of a statute.

Adapted from Connecticut State Bar Association (1925).

Some Reflections on Judge Learned Hand

BY JEROME N. FRANK

I WAS ASKED, ORIGINALLY, to speak of Great Judges. I objected. What, I queried, does one mean by "great"? I remembered my dispute with Professor Thorne and Justice Frankfurter about Lord Coke, once Chief Justice of England. I said Coke was a nasty, narrow-minded, greedy, cruel, arrogant, insensitive man, a time-serving politician and a liar who, by his adulation of some crabbed medieval legal doctrines, had retarded English and American legal development for centuries.[1] Thorne and Frankfurter replied that I proved their case, that the duration of his influence, no matter whether good or bad, made him a great judge. I think I lost that argument. But if that be the test, then we must put on our list of "greats" such men as Attila, Robespierre, and Hitler, although most of us consider them evil. And so too as to the great among legal thinkers, lawyers, and judges, consider Tribonian who contributed importantly to the Justinian codification of Roman law which mightily affected the legal systems of the western world. Who was Tribonian? A brilliant scholar but a corrupt judge.

I concede, indeed I insist, that great men, good or evil, have often helped to shape history. Carlyle's theory of history—that all history results from the deeds or thoughts of great men—is nonsense, of course. But I think equally nonsensical what I call the No-Man Theory of history, according to which men are but puppets of "social forces," or economics, or geography, or the "spirit of the times"—in short, non-human or un-individual factors which wholly account, deterministically, for all human events. I shall not here enlarge on that theme. I wrote a book about it in 1945 which I here incorporate by reference.[2] There I did by no means exclude accidents, but I included great men among the accidents.

1 For a very different appraisal of Coke, see Bowen, *The Lion and The Throne* (1956).

2 *Fate and Freedom* (1945).

The theme, "Great Judges," is, then, vast and important. Conceivably, one could write much of legal history—as Campbell, Pound, and Seagle have tried to do—by writing the biographies of great judges. But that would be a horrendous undertaking. Were I to accept the theme originally allotted to me, I would at least confine it to some of the great judges whose influence has been beneficent. Even so, how is one to decide what judges deserve inclusion in that category? Obviously, no objective yardstick exists. Estimates of such greatness differ. It all depends on one's notion of the desirable.

So I've decided to restrict myself principally to one judge whom I consider great: Judge Learned Hand. I shall not, however, attempt even a short biography. For one thing, all biographies are full of gaps. "No man is an island," said John Donne. That's a half-truth, a misleading metaphor because of what it omits. True, no man can be wholly apart from his fellows. But, if each of us is a promotory, yet the promotory reaches out beyond the social mainland to a point where others cannot intrude. Beyond that point lies an unexplorable lonesomeness, a unique privacy. It is a no-other-man's land, for others can't penetrate it, can't communicate with it.

If this be true of men generally, it is emphatically true of judges. The private life, the inner environment of a judge, his deeper motivations, usually become extraordinarily opaque, hidden from public gaze, after he ascends the bench.[3] No judge has had a Boswell, and none has ever left behind him a detailed intimate diary like Pepys'. Sometimes, after his death, we can read a judge's private letters.[4] But as Howarth said of Pepys' letters, with them, as distinguished from his diary, we are not "inside the man, looking through the window he made of himself on the world," we are only "peering through a curtained pane from without."[5] We see not his "private

[3] Cf. Frankfurter, *A Note on Judicial Biography,* in Of Law and Men 107 (Elman ed., 1956).

[4] Consult, e.g., Holmes-Pollock Letters (Howe ed., 1941); Holmes-Laski Letters (Howe ed., 1953). Even these have been screened. "In Holmes's published works, whether they be his essays, his opinions, or his letters, he has told us very nearly all that we shall ever know with certainty of his convictions. He was careful to destroy all papers within his control which recorded those events and moods that he considered private." Howe, Justice Oliver Wendell Holmes: *The Shaping Years,* 1841-1870 vi (1957).

[5] Howarth, in Introduction to Samuel Pepys Letters and the Second Diary vii (Howarth ed., 1932).

face," only his "public face." As another writer observed, "behind the formal reserve of a high official a great deal more often goes on than most people suspect."[6]

The Roman lawyers, affected perhaps by the etymology of the word, thought of a "person," for legal purposes, as a mask, and recognized that legally one man may contain several different persons, having different masks or roles, or personalities, or selves. That pluralistic notion is not to be confined to legal thinking. We are all various persons; and most of the persons constituting a judge are exceptionally well hidden. As no biography, I think, can pretend to adequacy unless it includes a psycho-biography, a judicial biography must be inordinately incomplete. And glib psychological analyses of men, exciting or amusing as they may be, are terribly misleading.

Not long ago, some writers remarked that, since we entrust to "the judicial conscience" the interpretation and enforcement of our laws and constitutions, significant and accurate data about the occupants of the bench should be of major importance. Yet few such data have been assembled. "We do not even have available reliable indices of the intelligence of judges, to say nothing of measures of their psychiatric traits." Until the time when, the writers added, "we can reduce temperament, wisdom and probity to a scientific formula, many will say that any study of judicial personnel is merely touching the fringes of the problem."[7] That time is surely not here.

To write a competent biography of Learned Hand would be singularly perplexing. For he is an exquisitely complex person, or, rather, a complex multitude of persons. As Whicher said of Emerson: "He can be summed up in a formula only by those who know their own minds better than his"; he is "impenetrable, for all his forty-odd volumes." Moreover, for all that Judge Hand is gregarious—a life-long friend says that "he is a man of moods, and does not like to be alone"[8]—he keeps inviolate, more than most of us, an enclave of reticent privacy which no one may enter.

Now and then, one comes on a man who has made of his life a work of art, like a novel written by himself. Such a man is

[6] The Times (London) Literary Supplement, 364 (July 1, 1955).

[7] Mott, Albright, and Semmerling, Judicial Personnel, 167 The Annals of the American Academy 143, 144 (1933).

[8] Burlingham, Judge Learned Hand, 60 Harv. L. Rev. 330, 331 (1947).

Learned Hand. His long life—he is now 83[9]—has enabled him to round out that novel. It is replete with poetry and contains many delightful chapters and interludes. But some portions of that novel he alone has read and will never publish. If it be true that "nothing, except everything, can 'explain' anything,"[10] I can't possibly explain Learned Hand. Although I have worked with him for fourteen years, I wouldn't dare to say I have even begun to know him. For that matter, who thoroughly knows any man, himself or any other? "Who," asked old Thomas Fuller, "hath sailed about the world of his own heart, sounded each creek, surveyed each corner, but that there still remains much terra incognita in himself?"

My principal aim, therefore, will be to give you some glimpses of Learned Hand's approach to his work as a judge; to suggest the genesis, the background, of that approach; and to compare him with some other great judges.

In all honesty, in order that you can make allowance for my partiality, I must begin by saying that no man do I esteem more highly. As I wrote him early this year: "No one else I've ever known has excited in me such admiration and affection. You are my model as a judge. More, you have influenced my attitudes in incalculable ways towards all sorts of matters, intellectual and others. For your eminence lies not alone in the singular nature of your mind, but in the manner in which you infuse your ideas with emotions, both noble and humorous. You are, par excellence, the democratic aristocrat." I am unabashed in my admiration. It is not unique. Repeatedly, and within the past few weeks, I have seen men leave his presence with a feeling of exaltation, lifted out of themselves to a vision of new horizons.

Many who have written of Learned Hand have lamented the fact that he did not become a Supreme Court Justice, a post for which no one else has ever been so well fitted. Yet I wonder. I think of Cervantes' advice: "Try to win the second prize. For the first is always by favor. The second goes for pure merit." The praises of Judge Hand have been earned, not by occupying the highest bench, but by pure merit. Nor has he sought these

[9] Judge Hand celebrated his eighty-fifth birthday this year (1957).
[10] The Times (London) Literary Supplement, 492 (August 26, 1955).

praises. So much the better, since, as the Scriptures say: "For men to search out their own glory is not glory." The praises are still being earned, through Judge Hand's unflagging efforts in still producing matchless opinions, despite his years.

Nor have Judge Hand's years abated his keenness or deprived him of a youthful resilience. In nowise does he resemble Kipling's old men who say: "And whatever we do, we shall fold our hands . . . and think well of it. Yes, we shall be perfectly pleased with our work, and that is the perfectest Hell of it." Judge Hand's legendary fame has not made him arrogant. "A man," says the Bible, "is tried by his praise." Judge Hand has stood that trial well. Nor does he exploit the trappings of office to afford him any factitious dignity. He chuckled when recently I quoted to him Montaigne's lines: "Sitting on the loftiest throne in the world, we are still sitting on our behinds." He treats bright young men with warm generosity, and enjoys it when they disagree with him. He invites a colleague who differs from one of his opinions to write a dissenting opinion. He wants no slavish disciples, no hero worship. His way of life recalls Plutarch's report of the Athenians' welcome to Pompey: "So far may you be deemed a god as you confess yourself a man." This trait of humility, of self-scepticism, is fortunate in one who has such wide influence. Lord Acton's famous statement, "Power tends to corrupt and absolute power tends to corrupt absolutely," did not end there. Acton added, "Great men are always bad men, even when they exercise influence and not authority. . . ." I think Acton's aphorism absurdly sweeping. But it does high-light the fact that great influence is great power, and therefore can be corruptly wielded. Learned Hand's influence, if he can help it, will never corrupt.

When younger, he took Justice Holmes as one of his most important mentors. Like Holmes, he delights in contriving generalizations while recognizing their pernicious character if not constantly in gear with particulars. Or, to paraphrase Kant, he knows that generalizations without particulars are empty and particulars without generalizations are blind. Both men have been sceptical of neat, closed, systems; like William James, they have sought the "wild facts" that escape any system. Often Judge Hand is compared with Holmes. Although Holmes too is one of my heros, I think that, in the comparison, Hand gets the better rating. For Hand has been more generous, more outgoing, more easily accessible to others, always interested in the events of the day, while Holmes led an essentially cloistered life, and boasted of not reading the newspapers. And Hand has been more willing to admit mistakes.

Holmes once said that in writing judicial opinions, "one has to strike at the jugular and let the rest go"; and, in his later years, many of his opinions disclose a lack of interest in all but the jugular. Not so Judge Hand. Always as a young judge, and increasingly as he grows older, he has delved into the many legal niceties of a case, frequently to the dismay of his brother judges. Judge Hand wrote of Cardozo's "anguish which . . . preceded decision . . . for again and again . . . he had to wrestle with the angel all through the night; and he wrote his opinions with his very blood. But once his mind came to rest, he was as inflexible as he had been uncertain before."[11] Learned Hand has experienced that same anguish. But often it does not cease when the opinion has been uttered. I have known him to brood disquietingly over decisions he rendered several years earlier.

I was most pleased to learn, soon after I joined him on the bench in 1941, that we shared an admiration for George Savile, Lord Halifax. In 1684, attacked as a political "Trimmer," Halifax replied in a tract that he delighted in that label. "This innocent word *Trimmer*," he wrote, "signifieth no more than this, that if men are together in a Boat, one part of the Company would weigh it down on one side, another would make it lean as much to the contrary: It happeneth there is a third opinion, who conceive it would do as well if the Boat went even without endangering the Passengers."[12] Halifax's definition of a Trimmer satisfies, in large measure, Judge Hand's definition (and mine) of a true liberal. Liberals, we both think, should be proud to be tagged as Trimmers, in that sense. But they should know that often the way of the liberal is hard. Often he will be denounced as a shameless appeaser. Seldom will he be backed up by a militant crowd. For, as the Bible reports, men do not follow an uncertain call into battle. Extremists on one side breed extremists on the other.

[11] Hand, Mr. Justice Cardozo, in *The Spirit of Liberty* 129, 131 (Dilliard ed., 2d ed., 1953).

[12] The Character of the Trimmer 3 (1689). See Foxcroft, *A Character of the Trimmer* (1946).

The true liberal will be wary of both. His function, however, is to acknowledge that frequently, although not always, the extremists on each side have a point, but one that is exaggeratedly stated; to perceive that these exaggerations foster undesirable ways by which each side pursues its aims; and, if possible, to discover some resolution of the differences which allow for whatever is sound in the respective polar positions. That does not mean that Judge Hand parts his mind in the middle, or that he resembles the Duke in one of Chesterton's plays who tried to show his impartiality by donating equal sums to both sides of every cause.

Learned Hand's Literary Style

Judge Hand's fame derives in some part from the manner, the style, of his writing. Judge Wyzanski says it is "characterized by the compression, the poignancy, the balance, the diction of a sonnet."[13] Let me read you a sample from an address delivered in 1952:

> Our nation is embarked upon a venture as yet unproved; we have set our hopes upon a community in which men shall be given unchecked control of their own lives. That community is in peril; it is invaded from within, it is threatened from without; it faces a test which it may fail to pass. The choice is ours whether, if we hear the pipes of Pan, we shall stampede like a frightened flock, forgetting all those professions on which we have claimed to rest our polity. God knows, there is risk in refusing to act till the facts are all in; but is there not greater risk in abandoning the conditions of all rational inquiry? Risk for risk, for myself I had rather take my chance that some traitors will escape detection than spread abroad a spirit of general suspicion and distrust, which accepts rumor and gossip in place of undismayed and unintimidated inquiry. I believe that that community is already in process of dissolution where each man begins to eye his neighbor as a possible enemy, where non-conformity with the accepted creed, political as well as religious, is a mark of disaffection; where denunciation, without specification or backing, takes the place of evidence;

[13] Judge Learned Hand's Contribution to Public Law, 60 Harv. L. Rev. 348, 369 (1947).

> where orthodoxy chokes freedom of dissent; where faith in the eventual supremacy of reason has become so timid that we dare not enter our convictions in the open lists, to win or lose. Such fears as these are a solvent which can eat out the cement that binds the stones together; they may in the end subject us to a despotism as evil as any that we dread; and they can be allayed only in so far as we refuse to proceed on suspicion, and trust one another until we have tangible ground for misgiving. The mutual confidence on which all else depends can be maintained only by an open mind and a brave reliance upon free discussion. I do not say that these will suffice; who knows but we may be on a slope which leads down to aboriginal savagery. But of this I am sure: if we are to escape, we must not yield a foot upon demanding a fair field, and an honest race, to all ideas.[14]

His words, you'll agree, have a beauty, a lovely cadence, a lilt; but they are not Swinburnian, so bemusing in sound that you forget the thought. They do not merely ruffle the surface of the imagination; they plunge deep into it. They do not bully but they do demand—and receive—the attention. They are never emolient. His writings—to borrow one of his own phrases—contain no clichés designed as "anodynes for the pain of reasoning."[15] They stir the emotions, but emotions disciplined by reason.

Because, I think, of his agility with words, he has a marked interest in verbal meanings. Illustrative of both his style and his theory of statutory interpretation is this passage from an opinion he uttered in 1945: "Of course it is true that the words used, even in their literal sense, are the primary, and ordinarily the most reliable, source of interpreting the meaning of any writing. . . . But it is one of the surest indexes of a mature and developed jurisprudence not to make a fortress out of the dictionary. . . ."[16]

I want now to digress to consider some aspects of the function of style in the activities of the legal profession. I promise you that the digression will be relevant to Judge Hand.

The literary critic, John Mason Brown has said: "Lawyers are excused from the necessity of interesting their readers, and all

[14] A plea for the Open Mind and Free Discussion, in *The Spirit of Liberty,* op. cit. *supra* note 11, at 274, 283-84.

[15] Commissioner v. Sansome, 60 F (2d) 931, 933 (CA 2, 1932).

[16] Cabell v. Markham, 148 F (2d) 737, 739 (CA 2, 1945).

too often—let's face the evidence—they take advantage of this enviable exemption." Alas, that's true of all too many lawyers, as I know only too well through having had to read a host of their briefs. It's even more true of judges, for they have captive audiences. But some judges, eager to interest their readers, do cultivate literary style—or what they think is style. Some few become masters of the writer's craft. Their opinions are oases in a vast desert of dullness. It does not follow that what they say has value. If it is a mistake, as it is, to confuse obscurity with profundity, it is no less a mistake to confuse brilliance of utterance with sagacity. Novel pithy phrases may induce the acceptance of shoddy ideas. Happily, some judges who write literature also express wisdom.

Without doubt, Cardozo was a most wise judge.[17] Many have extolled his style. I happen to disagree with that verdict. I admit that, in such matters, usually one wastes time in disputing matters of taste. But I dare to say that, to my mind, Cardozo's style is unpleasantly ornate, baroque, needlessly intricate, a barrier at times to understanding his meaning. I think that, had he not been a judge, literary critics would have criticized severely the style in many of his writings. Yet, since it was a relief to read judicial opinions not worded like a mortgage deed of trust or a section of the income-tax statute, his style received wide acclaim in lawyerdom.

Let me try to explain Cardozo's style.[18] He was a contradictory personality. Although a recluse, a retiring man, he devoted most of his life to public service, and was therefore constantly making a public appearance. Deeply hurt, in his youth, by a bitter personal experience—the exposed corruption of his father, a judge—he withdrew from the manner of living followed by most of his fellow men. Yet he did not seek refuge in morbid introspection or in an ivory tower. He did retreat from 20th century living. But he re-entered it—disguised as an 18th century scholar and gentleman. His observations of the contemporary scene were

[17] For testimonials, consult the joint issue of the Columbia and Harvard Law Reviews and the Yale Law Journal published in 1939, 39 Col. L. Rev. 1 (1939); 52 Harv. L. Rev. 353 (1939); 48 Yale L. J. 371 (1939).

[18] In the discussion of Cardozo's style which follows, I have borrowed heavily from my own article, published anonymously, under the title *The Speech of Judges: A Dissenting Opinion,* 29 Va. L. Rev. 625 (1943). The discussion there is, of course, much more extensive than what is reported here.

keen, but not quite the observations of a contemporary. He wanted, at one and the same time, to be in and yet out of what was happening in the America of his day.

He achieved a compromise. That compromise reveals itself in his style. It is neither 20th century nor American. It imitates 18th century English: he wrote of 20th century America not in the current American idiom but in the "King's English" of two hundred years ago. The result was not ugly. His writings do have grace. But it is an alien grace.

He tried, I think, to use a private time-machine to transport himself into a past alien speech-environment. In a much-quoted passage, he wrote: "Not honesty alone, but a punctilio of honor the most sensitive, is the standard of behavior." Or consider such phrases as "One may take leave to deny," or "The subject the most lowly," or "An officer must not pause to parley," or "The risk of rescue, if it be not wanton, is born of the occasion," or "So the concept be not abjuring," or "Due process is a growth too sturdy to succumb to the infection of the least ingredient of error," or "Income . . . is the fruit born of capital, not the potency of fruition."

In his own essay on the style of judges, Cardozo remarked: "Form is not something added to substance as a mere protuberant adornment."[19] Look at the form of this very sentence. Would it have been less effective if less decorative? One is reminded of Barney McGee who was "full of phrases of length and latinity, such as honorificabilitudinity." No wonder that those who adulate Cardozo's style do not compare him with our best 20th century American writers. Instead they say he was "rare enough to compare with Charles Lamb." My own guess is that Cardozo thought of himself as engaged in imaginary conversations with Dr. Johnson.

I stress the character of Cardozo's style for this reason: good writing is speech heightened in tone and polished in form. An Englishman who writes his talk—his daily speech—is close to what he writes. He can pass with ease from oral speech to writing. He talks and thinks and writes in English. He does not talk, and therefore think, in one language and then have to translate

[19] *Law and Literature* 5 (1931), reprinted in the joint law review issue referred to in note 17, *supra.*

it into another. Most Americans, however, talk and think not in English but in American. When they write, however, they attempt to write English—which is really another language. Heighten and polish up American as much as you will, it is still not English. We could more easily learn to think and write in some language we could not fail to recognize as foreign, such as French or German. The very fact that English is not obviously alien—that the differences between American and English are subtle—makes that effort the greater.

This was brought home to me when I visited an English appellate court. After the argument of a case, the judges conferred for a short time, and then the presiding justice orally delivered the court's opinion. I was astonished by its literary excellence. No American judge, I thought, could match that performance. "What an inferior lot our judges are," I reflected. But I soon changed my mind. For, all over England, I found that moderately well educated Englishmen, casually and without effort, could talk in a style that few Americans of great talent could equal in their best and most carefully prepared writing. You can see the process in reverse when an Englishman tries to write American, for example, Bernard Shaw in his play, *Blanco Posnet.*

Some American authors have written admirably in the American language. For examples of first-rate style in American, written with ease by American judges, look at the opinions of Justices Douglas and Jackson.

I come back now to Learned Hand's style. What impresses the reader is that he writes in a beautiful English, not American, style. He is one of the few living Americans, on or off the bench, who has done so. But he also speaks in English, not American, and therefore thinks in English. Judge Julian Mack said of him that he never knew a man whose writings so conveyed the life of his talk.

How this came about I cannot explain except to this extent: speech in English seems to have been common in his family, of English origin. (His grandfather, in 1848, in a letter to his sons, wrote: "A man may blow away like a cornet for a time," but "the charlatan soon finds his level. Or perhaps by impetus in his descent plunges a little below.") English ways—verbal, social and political—have always charmed Judge Hand. Add the fact that he has a fine ear and an amazing ability as a mimic. (You should hear him tell dialect stories.) Whatever the explanation, stylistically, his opinions might have been written by the best literary artists on the English bench.

Like Cardozo, he resorts often to metaphors. But Hand's metaphors quicken the thought, do not impede it as Cardozo's frequently did. You can tell much about a man from the metaphors he keeps. All of us employ metaphors. Everyday speech is made up of them; all symbols, all abstractions, all analogies, all generalizations, are metaphors, as-ifs. No one can think without them. Scientific thought has always been metaphorical. But most of us use dead or embalmed or half-dead or somnolent metaphors. Learned Hand's are alive and zesty.

Nor does he submit to the foolish admonition against mixing metaphors. Shakespeare's best are mixed. The point is that metaphors should be well mixed, not badly, as in the case of a cocktail. Judge Hand, an artist in making a martini, mixes his metaphors beautifully, knowing that every metaphor, since it is an as-if, should be handled with care, that it must never be taken as an absolute, but like a "fiction," must be used to aid thinking, not to befuddle it.

The poetry in his style signalizes the poet in the man himself, in the judge. You can be sure that Judge Hand is aware that, as Pascal the poetic philosopher said: "The heart has its reasons, which reason does not know. . . . We know truth not only by reason, but also by the heart. . . . And reason must trust these intuitions of the heart." In calling Judge Hand a poet, I don't mean that he is over-delicate. That is a false notion about poets, and surely false if applied to Learned Hand. He has an avid interest in all phases of life. As you probably know, he has made a recording of two old ballads; you can buy the platter from the Library of Congress. He is wonderful as a singer and actor of Gilbert and Sullivan. Some enterprising producer should hire him to play the Lord Chancellor in Iolanthe. As Rabelais is one of his favorite authors, you may gather that he little admires asceticism. Once, when we talked of a much respected judge with ascetic habits, he remarked, "I distrust a man who distrusts his senses." Judge Hand is not the kind of person described by Ellen Glasgow as one who, "in his long life, never committed a pleasure."

I have, as others have, made much of his style. I would not have you believe, however, that he would not have been a great judge, had he written in the dullest manner.

Learned Hand as a Trial Judge

For 15 years, until his appointment to the Court of Appeals in 1924, Judge Hand served as a federal trial judge in New York. Except for a few articles and some notable judicial opinions, he would have been known for his efforts in those years to few other than the New York Bar. He gave the reason in 1952,[20] saying that "it is open to doubt whether the work" of a trial judge "is to be best appraised by that part which is recorded"; the major part "takes place in the court-room and either slips away into anonymity, or remains only in the transient recollections of those who may be present."

Judge Hand has written little of his experience on the trial bench, but that little is invaluable. In 1926, reflecting on that experience, he remarked: "I must say that as a litigant I should dread a law suit beyond almost anything short of sickness and death."[21] That comment by a sagacious judge should destroy any smug satisfaction with the administration of justice.

I will attempt to explain a part of the cause of Judge Hand's alarming remark, and then to link it up with his precept that judges should endeavor to control their personal preferences.

The explanation must begin with a recognition that a trial judge has two major functions: (1) Like an upper-court judge, he must concern himself with the legal rules applicable to the particular facts of particular law suits. (2) Unlike an upper-court judge, he often has the responsibility of ascertaining those facts, i.e., in non-jury trials.

Now, although we speak of a trial judge "finding" the facts of a case, in truth he can't "find" them, ready-made, waiting to be discovered. The relevant events happened in the past, before any law suit began. The judge, therefore, never sees them happen-

20 The Record of the Ass'n of the Bar of the City of New York 182, 183 (1952).

21 *The Deficiencies of Trials to Reach the Heart of the Matter,* 3 Lectures on Legal Topics 89, 105 (1926).

ing. The facts, for purposes of judicial decision, are not what really happened, only what he believes—or guesses—to have happened. He forms this belief, or guess, by listening to witnesses who purport to have observed those past events when they occurred. Often the witnesses tell conflicting stories. Some of them lie; some are honestly mistaken in their original observations or memory. The judge "finds" the facts by choosing which witnesses he will believe. On this choice—the exercise of his fact-discretion, as I call it—depends the fate of the litigants. For in most suits, the entire or principal part of the dispute between the parties relates to the facts, not to the applicable legal rules, so that most law suits could be labeled "fact suits." Usually, for reasons I'll state later, the trial judge's fact-finding is accepted by the upper court on an appeal, if there is an appeal. Because of the incorrectible mistakes in the trial judge's findings (or guesses), innocent men go to jail,[22] and other men suffer defeat in civil law suits they ought to win, thus losing their property, their fortunes, their jobs or their reputations. On that account, the work of the trial judge in determining the facts—that is, in choosing some rather than other evidence as reliable—represents the most important part of the judicial process. And note that the decisions, in most law suits not yet commenced, can seldom be predicted because the trial court's findings of fact cannot be prophesied. No reading of precedents, no study of legal treatises, can overcome such obstacles to prediction.

This job of trial-court fact-finding is far more difficult, if well done, than that of making and applying legal rules. Yet it shows up, scarcely at all, in law school study of the courts, a study confined chiefly to examination and criticism of the legal rules as expounded in judicial opinions. Accordingly, in law school, students learn almost nothing about those trial judges who are truly great in performing the task of finding the facts.[23]

The most significant factor in trial court fact-finding is this: no one has ever been able to contrive any rules to guide the trial judge in making his choice of the believable witnesses. That

22 Consult Frank and Frank, *Not Guilty* (1957).

23 Those who knew Hand as a trial judge report that he was a most capable "fact-finder." Apparently Holmes was not. One who knew Holmes and Brandeis well recently wrote me that Brandeis once said that lawyers avoided trying cases before Holmes and that Holmes had often remarked: "I do not know facts; I merely know their significance." In 1930, Holmes had written me to the same effect.

choice, that exercise of fact-discretion, therefore escapes the discipline of rules. It is un-ruly. When the witnesses testify orally in the presence of the trial judge, as ordinarily they do, he is guided, in very considerable measure, by his observation of the witnesses' demeanor—their facial expressions, falterings, or glibness. As I once said for our court: "The demeanor of an orally-testifying witness is 'always assumed to be in evidence.' It is 'wordless language.' The liar's story may seem uncontradicted to one who merely reads it, yet it may be 'contradicted' in the trial court by his manner, . . . his grimaces, his gestures, and the like—all matters which 'cold print does not preserve' and which constitute 'lost evidence' so far as an upper court is concerned."[24] As Judge Hand put it: "The whole nexus of sight and sound . . . is lost in a written record. . . . The words that a witness utters . . . are again and again of no probative weight at all because of his address, his bearing and his apparent lack of intelligence."[25] He has also pointed out that, therefore, where the trial judge saw and heard the witnesses, his "finding is indeed 'unassailable.' "[26] There you have the reason for the incapacity of upper courts, in most cases, to disagree with or correct a trial judge's findings of fact: the upper courts can't observe the demeanor of the witnesses.

Had I the time,[27] I'd qualify somewhat my statement about the finality of trial court findings. The qualifications are not too important. By and large, the facts are cooked when a case reaches an appeal court. That's why only some 5% of cases are appealed and why, in those few, many trial court decisions are affirmed. A few years ago, Judge Hand spoke disparagingly of trial judges he knew "who thought they could tell, just as soon as a man comes into the court-room whether he is going to lie or not." "I used to try cases," he continued, "and God knows, I was very unsure about it." Any sensible judge would be unsure. For a witness' demeanor, while sometimes revealing, sometimes deceives: The careful, poised, perjurer may seem reliable; the

[24] Broadcast Music, Inc., v. Havana Madrid Restaurant Corp., 175 F (2d) 77, 80 (CA 2, 1949).

[25] Purcell v. Waterman S. S. Co., 221 F (2d) 953, 954 (CA 2, 1955).

[26] United States v. Aluminum Co. of America, 148 F (2d) 416, 433 (CA 2, 1945).

[27] A more extensive treatment of the subject may be found in my book, *Courts on Trial* (1949).

honest, timid witness, frightened by the ordeal of testifying, may seem to be prevaricating. Nevertheless, our courts—on the whole justifiably—set great store by demeanor evidence. But you see how tricky is this reliance on demeanor evidence: one trial judge will interpret it one way, another judge, another way. There exists no common or objective measure usable in choosing the reliable witnesses.

And now I come to a most disturbing aspect of fact-finding, one which alone would explain Judge Hand's statement about the fear-inspiring character of litigation: the trial judge's belief about the facts, based on his choice of trustworthy witnesses, results from subjective, undisclosed, un-get-at-able, private factors in the trial judge, i.e., his prejudices, for or against witnesses who wear glasses, or who are women, or blond women, or fat women, or Irishmen, Englishmen, Jews, Catholics, negroes, or red-headed men, or men with facial tics or who speak with a foreign accent or with a Southern drawl, etc., etc. It would be bad enough were those prejudices merely knowable by others. But the situation is worse than that: most of these prejudices are unconscious. That is, they are unknown to the trial judge himself.

Here we arrive at an unexplored phase of the problem of how far a judge evaluating "moral character" should resort to the attitudes of the community. The trial judge, in choosing the witnesses on whose testimony he relies, is evaluating the "moral character" of each witness. Not only does this evaluation entail the difficulty I shall mention later—i.e., the inadequate means available to any judge psychologically to probe deeply another's character—but there is this further difficulty inhering in the trial judge: if his unconscious, sub-threshold, hidden, idiosyncratic prejudices, for or against particular witnesses, were consciously entertained and publicized, they would spell out as evaluations consisting of the application of moral, or immoral, or amoral, standards or norms. They would then be open to criticism by others and by the trial judge himself through his "conscious conscience." Then he could check his standards or norms by comparing them with the publicly avowed moral standards or norms of the average members of the community. In many instances, the judge's norms would then appear to be morally far below the so-called "common conscience." But as the worst of biases or norms of which I'm now speaking are concealed, and unknown to the trial judge himself, neither he nor anyone else can compare them with the community standards. Nor can he restrain or rectify those prejudices. In this respect, the trial judge is self-willed beyond his own power of self-control, and beyond control by the upper courts.

Here is a major element, a most undemocratic element, in the decisional process. Can this problem be solved? I incline to think so, at least partially, by having each judge, with the assistance of a psychiatrist, engage in a voyage of self-exploration and so become conscious of those sub-threshold biases. But that problem will never be solved so long as it is ignored, shoved under the rug, as it has been and still is, by judges, lawyers, and law professors. Moreover, if the problem is insoluble, we but delude ourselves by disregarding its existence.

Judge Hand has not, to my knowledge, discussed this problem. He has urged that judges should try to prevent their personal preferences from governing their decisions. The preferences to which he refers relate to rules and to the policies they embody; such preferences—of an economic, social and political nature—are rather obvious to the judges and others, and consequently can be moderately well controlled. But a trial judge's choices of witnesses, his personal preferences of that sort (largely unconscious), involve no recognizable rules or policies. In trial court fact-finding, because it does involve un-ruly fact-discretion, the dominant factor consists of the "personal element," the unique, unknowable, inscrutable, uncontrollable components of the trial judge's personality. The problem becomes more baffling in a jury trial when you consider the uncontrollable, unknowable, unconscious components of the personalities of the twelve jurors.

I trust that you perceive some of the startling implications of all this:

(1) We denounce arbitrary and capricious judicial decisions. But the concealed prejudices concerning witnesses, which yield the facts found in law suits, and which thus yield most court decisions, are often arbitrary and capricious as judged by any rational test.

(2) A distinguished judge recently said,[28] "Of course, individual judgment and feeling cannot be wholly shut out of the judicial process. But if they dominate, the judicial process be-

[28] Frankfurter, John Marshall and the Judicial Function, in *Of Law and Men* 3, 19 (Elman ed., 1956).

comes dangerous sham." Yet concealed, unconscious prejudices do frequently dominate trial court fact-finding, the most important part of the judicial process.

I think now you'll understand some of the reasons for Judge Hand's remark that one should dread litigation beyond almost anything short of sickness and death.

Judge Hand had another reason. If, he said in a Kafka-like utterance in 1926,[29] you, as a lawyer, watch your client in the courtroom while his case is being tried, "you will . . . see in his face a baffled sense that there is going on some kind of game which, while its outcome may be tragic for him . . . is incomprehensible." He added, "About trials hang a suspicion of trickery and a sense of result depending upon cajolery or worse." These comments open up an immense subject of which I'll say no more than this: according to the present accepted working rules of the game, each lawyer owes a duty to his client to employ all sorts of wiles and stratagems which frequently prevent the trial judge or jury from getting as close as possible to the actual facts of a case. Our profession, I think, owes it to our society to eliminate many of those wiles and stratagems. But that is still another subject.

Once upon a time, and not so very long ago, most American judges and lawyers denied that judges ever legislated. The judges and lawyers exploited, and themselves largely believed, the myth that in the creation of the huge body of common-law legal rules, not enacted by any legislature, the judges had played no part. Judges never have made and never will make legal rules. These rules pre-existed all court decisions. The judges merely find or discover these pre-existing rules—just as Columbus, or whoever it was, discovered America. The courts no more invent new rules than Columbus invented the "new world" when he found it. If a rule announced in a former case is later rejected by a court, it is an error to say that a new rule has been contrived by the court. To speak correctly, one must say that the old, abandoned rule was a sort of false map of the "Law"—just as a pre-Columbian map was false. The judge who announced the erroneous rule in the former decision must have had bad eyesight, for he had made a mistake in trying to find the "Law." Calvin Coolidge was talking in terms of

29 *The Deficiencies of Trials to Reach the Heart of the Matter*, 3 Lectures on Legal Topics 89, 95-96 (1926).

the myth when he wrote: "Men do not make laws. They do but discover them. . . . That state is most fortunate in its form of government which has the aptest instrument for the discovery of laws."

This myth, criticized in 19th-century England, had a peculiarly strong and tenacious hold in this country because, in theory, our constitutions give our legislatures the exclusive power to legislate. If the judges acknowledged that they made new rules, they would apparently be admitting that they were violating the principle of separation of governmental powers. The myth, if believed, absolved the judges from a charge of unconstitutionally usurping power. The myth did deceive the public. But it also induced the judges to deceive themselves.

When Learned Hand, aged 22, entered Harvard Law School as a student in 1894, the myth still largely prevailed. However, in 1891, Ezra Ripley Thayer had published an article,[30] entitled *Judicial Legislation: Its Legitimate Function in the Development of the Common Law,* in which, with unusual boldness for an American lawyer of his time, he dealt the myth a grave blow. In another article, in the same year, James Bradley Thayer, one of Hand's most influential teachers, said, "It is impossible to exercise the judicial function without such incidental legislation."[31] But he cautioned that, in law-making, judges should act "with great caution." Before that, Holmes, in 1881,[32] had written that the "growth of the law," through judicial decisions, "is legislative. . . . It is legislative in its grounds," based on "considerations of what is expedient for the community. . . ."; and he had suggested that, in the present, judges "should openly discuss the legislative principles," or policies, "upon which their decisions must always rest." When I was a law student, in the first and second decades of the 20th century, it was still heretical to agree openly with James Bradley Thayer and Holmes. But today the myth has dissipated. Judges of our day candidly admit that past judges invented many rules and that present judges do the same.

Since the final interment of the myth in the 1920's, some law teachers and many law students have entertained an equally false

30 5 Harv. L. Rev. 172 (1891).
31 The Case of Gelpcke v. Dubuque, 4 Harv. L. Rev. 311, 318 (1891).
32 *The Common Law* 35, 78 (1881).

notion. They believe that a judge can, and usually a judge does,[33] contrive rules about as he pleases, without restraint. That is wicked nonsense. It represents a gross exaggeration of a partial truth. Judicial legislation, as Holmes put it, is "interstitial." Most law-making is legislative, not judicial.

Repeatedly Judge Hand has discussed this question. No one is better equipped to do so. No one knows better than he that judges do legislate. For no other single judge has invented so many new rules, modified so many old ones. In every legal province—contracts, torts, equity, conflict of laws, criminal law, evidence, admiralty, patents, copyrights, trade-names, taxation, statutory interpretation—he has shaped or reshaped the important doctrines. Everywhere in the judicial domain you can trace his handiwork. With his creative insights, his penetrating intellect, his imaginative experience, he has enlarged the legal universe; although he obeys the Supreme Court's decisions, many of those decisions have been based on rules of his making. When he whistles a Supreme-Court tune, frequently it is really his own. Even the English House of Lords has been known to follow him.

What, then, has this unusually creative judge said about the limits on judicial creativeness? As Judge Hand sees it, the judge faces a dilemma, being both bound and free. In 1939,[34] Judge Hand wrote of the self-contradiction "at the basis of a judge's work." For on the one hand, "his authority and his immunity depends upon the assumption that he speaks with the mouth of others: the momentum of his utterances must be greater than any which his personal reputation and character can command, if it is to do the work assigned to it—if it is to stand against the passionate resentments arising out of the interests he must frustrate" by his decisions. So the judge voices, not his own view, but the "dictates . . . of a communion which reaches" into the past "far beyond the memory of any now living." But then, Hand continued, one encounters this paradox: the common-law doctrines have grown. The judges, successively, have contributed to its growth, not merely repeating what their predecessors said, not always speaking with the "mouth of others." So a judge "must manage to escape both horns of this dilemma: he must preserve his authority by cloaking

33 Cf. Rodell, Nine Men (1955) (passim).

34 Hand, Mr. Justice Cardozo, in *The Spirit of Liberty* 129, 130 (Dilliard ed., 2d ed., 1953).

himself in the majesty of an overshadowing past; but he must discover some composition with the dominant trends of his time."

Judge Hand had considered this dilemma at least as early as 1916;[35] he then said that a judge may not properly decide cases according to his own idea of what will best serve the common good, or of what he thinks will represent democratic aspirations not articulated in some legitimate matter. The judge must not thus give rein to his "personal notions" of the desirable; he must bow to "the social will" when clearly set forth in "written word[s]." However, when the language of a statute or a precedent is ambiguous, the judge should not "frustrate his free power by interpretation to manifest the half-framed purposes of his time." If he does, he "misconceives the historical significance of his position and will in the end" become "incompetent to perform the very duties upon which it lays so much emphasis."

In even greater detail, Judge Hand discussed this dilemma in a more or less popular radio talk, in 1933, entitled *How Far Is A Judge Free in Rendering A Decision?*[36] Because this talk is so discerning and so balanced, I quote from it at some length.

He began by saying that there are two extreme views of a judge's role: some think he ought to look solely "to his conscience and follow its dictates," that he should not be bound by "what they call technical rules, having no relation to natural right or wrong. Others wish him to observe very strictly, reading it as though it were all to be found in written words, and never departing from the literal meaning." They are correct to this extent: a

---

35 The Speech of Justice, id., at 13, 14.

36 Id., at 103 et seq. When no statute applies to a case and precedents are absent, or when the wording of a statute delegates to the judges the job of filling in gaps, Judge Hand knowingly legislates. In a "legislature," he said in United States v. Associated Press, 52 FSupp. 362, 370 (S.D. N.Y., 1943), "the conflicting interests find their respective representation, or in any event can make their political power felt, as they cannot upon a court. The resulting compromises so arrived at are likely to achieve stability, and to be acquiesced in. . . . But it is a mistake to suppose that the courts are never called upon to make similar choices; i.e., to appraise and balance the value of opposed interests and to enforce their preference. The law of torts is for the most part the result of exactly that process, and the law of torts has been judge-made. . . ." He concluded that Congress had, under the anti-trust laws, left these particular controversies to the courts. Hand is aware, you see, that as a judge he must make choices on policy grounds, choices likely to be affected by their own preference. A judge is thus required to exercise more than skill in manipulating legal techniques; he is required to display ripe wisdom and experience, together with a lively imagination and a capacity for empathy. All these things Hand can do and do superbly in his struggle to accomplish justice.

judge "ought not to usurp the power of government, and they believe that to exercise his own judgment as to the justice of the cause would be just such usurpation." Judge Hand disagrees with both these views.

Understanding of the problem requires a definition of "law," he says. Some persons think it "includes the customs or usages which are generally current in a society." Judge Hand prefers, with reference to a civilized modern society, a somewhat Austinian definition of law as "those rules which will be enforced by the government"—"the conduct which the government . . . will compel individuals to conform to, or to which it will at least provide forcible means to secure conformity." So defined, "the law is the command of the government, and it must be ascertainable in some form if it is to be enforced at all."

Its commands are put in words; and in our kind of society "these are always written," whether in statutes or in "books which report what has been decided before by judges whom the government gave power to decide." The judges have "the duty of saying what the law means, that is, what the government has in fact commanded."

The government's commands cannot be put in precise terms like those of mathematics. To be understood by the persons who must obey, these commands must be stated in "terms of common speech." Nor can the commands be nicely precise, for no one can "provide for all situations which might come up," nobody can "divine all possible human events in advance and prescribe the proper rule for each." The law thus uses "vague command[s]" which the courts—judges or juries—apply in respect of "all the circumstances of the particular case."

"The judge must therefore find out the will of the government from words. . . . How does he in fact proceed?" He takes "the language before him, whether it be from a statute or from the decision of a former judge." He tries "to find out what the government, or his predecessor, would have done, if the case before him had been before them. He calls this finding the intent of the statute or of the doctrine." The men who used the language did not have any intent at all about the case that has come up; it had not occurred to their minds. Strictly speaking, it is impossible to know what they would have said about it, if it had. All they have done is to write down certain words which they mean to apply generally to situations of that kind. To apply these literally may either pervert what was plainly their general meaning, or leave undisposed of what there is every reason to suppose they meant to provide for.

"Thus it is not enough for the judge just to use a dictionary. If he should do no more, he might come out with a result which every sensible man would recognize to be quite the opposite of what was really intended; which would contradict or leave unfulfilled its plain purpose."

Judge Hand grants that: "When a judge tries to find out what the government would have intended which it did not say, he puts into its mouth things which he thinks it ought to have said, and that is very close to substituting what he himself thinks right. Let him beware, however, or he will usurp the office of government. . . . In our country we have always been extremely jealous of mixing the different processes of government, especially that of making law, with that of saying what it is after it is made. This distinction . . . cannot be rigidly enforced; but . . . it has a very sound basis as a guide, provided one does not make it an absolute rule."

The men who framed our Constitution "wanted to have a government by the people" and believed this could be done only "by giving the power to make laws to assemblies which the people chose. . . . They believed that such assemblies would express the common will of the people who were to rule. . . . They might have made the judge the mouthpiece of the common will, finding it out by his contacts with people generally; but he would then have been ruler. . . . Still, they had to leave him scope in which he in a limited sense does act as if he were the government, because, as we have seen, he cannot otherwise do what he is required to do. So far they had to confuse law-making with law-interpreting."

"So you will see that a judge is in a contradictory position; he is pulled by two opposite forces. On the one hand, he must not enforce whatever he thinks best; he must leave that to the common will expressed by the government. On the other, he must try as best he can to put into concrete form what that will is, not by slavishly following the words, but by trying honestly to say what was the underlying purpose expressed. Nobody does this exactly right; great judges do it better than the rest of us. It is necessary that someone shall do it, if we are to realize the hope that we can collectively rule ourselves."

I have several comments on Judge Hand's exposition in this paper:

(1) Discarding the myth, i.e., the Columbus-law-discovery-myth, Judge Hand recognizes that judges have considerable latitude for creativeness. A judge, like Learned Hand, no longer can deceive himself into believing that he never makes rules.

Judge Hand's discussion raises these questions: Did the self-deceiving myth actually restrain judicial creativeness? Does the destruction of the myth mean that judges now create more freely, that we have come nearer to judicial despotism? I think the answer to both questions is no. On the contrary, the old judicial self-deception often led the judges to engage in extensive legislation.

(2) Judge Hand maintains that, when a judge is called on to legislate, he must seek to balance competing social interests, i.e., "desires and values." Judge Hand concedes that such "desires and values are not quantitatively measurable, for," as he said in 1952, "they seldom have any common constituents, and without these they cannot be objectively compared." Many who have espoused this notion of adjusting such interests—in Europe, the members of the "jurisprudence-of-interests" school; in this country Pound and others—have not been as wise as Judge Hand in perceiving that it yields no panacea, no quick and easy solution of legal conundrums. At best, this idea brings home to the judge the nature of his task, prompts him to an awareness of interests he might otherwise neglect. But that awareness merely creates a problem; it does not solve it.

(3) In this 1933 paper, Judge Hand is discussing the judge's function with respect to legal rules, principles, doctrines, legal generalizations. He is not discussing the way trial courts find facts, and the much wider scope of their power in that respect, about which I have already spoken.

(4) With particular reference to statutes, Judge Hand has in mind the separation-of-powers doctrine: he stresses "government by the people," the making of laws by the people's chosen representatives in legislatures which "express the common will."

This last theme suffuses his thinking. I think it fairly clear that he derived it from Thayer. In all Thayer's teaching—whether on judicial legislation or evidence or constitutional law—Thayer underscored this democratic idea.

What we learn from some of our teachers may shape our basic attitudes for the rest of our lives. From such influences, future judges are not immune. A recent biography of Mr. Justice Sutherland shows that, when he went on the Supreme Court in 1922, at the age of 60, he was still in the grip of ideas he learned in his youth from Professor Maeser, who accorded that rugged individualist, Herbert Spencer, the "first place among philosophers," and in Michigan Law School from another of Spencer's idolators, Judge Thomas M. Cooley.[37] So it was with Thayer and Learned Hand.

Thayer, in his teaching and writings on "constitutional law," dwelt on the fact that, until 1886, the Supreme Court—especially in applying the "due process" clause to substantive legislation as distinguished from procedure—had usually held that there is always a powerful presumption in favor of the constitutionality of a statute, that the Court must uphold a statute if it could conceive of the existence of facts which would render the statute reasonable. The Supreme Court had said that such a presumption must be indulged unless invalidity "is proved beyond all reasonable doubt,"[38] or "a palpable error has been committed";[39] that "For protection against abuses by legislatures the people must resort to the polls, not to the courts,"[40] to "the ballot-box, not to the judiciary";[41] and that the "courts cannot, without usurping legislative functions, override the will of the people as . . . expressed by their chosen representatives," since the judges "have nothing to do with the . . . policy of legislation."[42]

But, so Thayer wrote in 1893[43]—the year before Learned Hand entered law school—a new judicial trend had developed. Now the courts were shifting the presumption, striking down statutes unless their reasonableness affirmatively appeared. Against this trend, Thayer inveighed. When courts so conduct themselves, he said, when they do not, except in most unusual instances, keep their hands off statutes, the people, "not being thrown back on themselves, on the responsible exercise of their own prudence, moral

---

37 See Paschal, Mr. Justice Sutherland 5-9 and passim (1951); Dunham and Kurland, eds., Mr. Justice 123-146 (1956).

38 Ogden v. Saunders, 12 Wheat. (US) 213, 270 (1827).

39 Terry v. Anderson, 95 US 628 (1877).

40 Munn v. Illinois, 94 US 113 (1877).

41 Powell v. Pennsylvania, 127 US 678 (1887).

42 Mugler v. Kansas, 123 US 623 (1887).

43 *The Origin and Scope of the American Doctrine of Constitutional Law,* 7 Harv. L. Rev. 129 (1893), reprinted in Thayer, Legal Essays 39 (1908).

sense, and honor, lose much of what is best in the political experience of any nation; and they are belittled, as well as demoralized. . . . Under no system can the power of courts go far to save people from ruin; our chief protection lies elsewhere," i.e., at the polls.

Thayer urged that, in so far as validity turned upon the reasonableness of a statute, a court should act as it does when asked to set aside a jury's verdict. That is, the court should set aside the statute, not on the basis of the court's private standard of what is reasonable, but only if it determines that no reasonable man could think the statute reasonable.[44] In a period when legislatures were combatting excessive and cruel economic laissez-faire, Thayer was arguing for judicial laissez-faire as a constitutional attitude in opposition to the acceptance of economic laissez-faire as a constitutional principle.

But Thayer had another purpose. In 1901, he wrote: "The power of the judiciary to disregard unconstitutional legislation . . . , even when unavoidable, is always attended with a serious evil, namely, that the correction of legislative mistakes comes from the outside, and the people thus lose the political experience, and the moral education and stimulus that come from fighting the question out in the ordinary way, and correcting their own errors."[45] If, for example, the Supreme Court had held the Legal Tender Act unconstitutional, "we should have been saved some trouble and some harm. But . . . the good which came to the country and its people from the vigorous thinking that had to be done in the political debates that followed, . . . from . . . the enlargement of ideas, the strengthening of moral fibre, and the growth of political experience that came out of it all,—all of this far more than out-weighed any evil which ever flowed from the refusal of the court to interfere with the work of the legislature.[46] The tendency of a common and

[44] Harv. L. Rev. 129, 149-50 (1893); 1 Cases on Constitutional Law 672 (1895).

[45] John Marshall 106-107 (1901).

[46] Thayer admired and cited Bagehot, who, in Physics and Politics (1869), had applauded "government by discussion" which fosters a "diffused disposition" toward weighing evidence, a conviction that much may be said on every side of everything which more fanatic ages of the world wanted. A "polity of discussion" tends to cure an inherited excess of human nature, said Bagehot, and leads to "animated moderation." It enlivens thought all through society, making people think no harm can come of thinking. Moreover, it has developed more kinds of people ready to use their mental energy in their own way than would a despotic government.

easy resort to this great function [of invalidating statutes] now lamentably too common, is to dwarf the political capacity of the people, and to deaden its sense of moral responsibility."

Thayer was saying, in effect, that our democratic constitutions contemplate an adult, mature society, in which no one will play father to the citizens, treating them like children. For only in such a society, where the citizens, after discussion, reach their own policy decisions, to be enacted through their chosen representatives in the legislature, can the citizens grow up politically.

The federal Constitution does, indeed, contain restrictions on governmental officials, including legislators. Where those restrictions are fairly specific, the courts, said Thayer, properly enforce them. Where, however, they are vague—e.g., "due process" as applied not procedurally but to substantive legislation—the courts, Thayer argued, should be most reluctant to interfere paternally, since the Constitution looks primarily to self-government, not to citizens in pupilage to the judges.

Where the opposite theory may lead, we can discern in Berman's recent discussion of Soviet justice, disclosing dictatorship in action. The "underlying assumption," he writes, is that the "subject of law, legal man, is not a mature, independent adult . . . but an immature, dependent child or youth, whose law-consciousness must be guided, trained, and disciplined by official legal rules and processes. . . . The Soviet lawmaker or judge is like a parent." The Soviet legal system "may best be characterized as a system of 'parental law' in which people are treated . . . as immature, dependent youths . . . for whom rights . . . are . . . gifts." The system is "dangerous not because it is lacking in law and justice, but rather because it is developing a new type of law which, while helping to satisfy men's need for justice in their personal and social relations, is reconcilable with political and ideological tyranny." For it rests on the basis that rights "are conferred by the state as a matter of grace."[47]

Before I go further in considering Thayer's influence on Learned Hand, it may be well to indicate my own attitude to Thayer's thesis, since it bears on my attitude towards Judge Hand. Some 25 years ago, and before I had read Thayer, I published a book in which I envisioned a mature society where emotional father-dependence would vanish after childhood, in which each grown-up

[47] *Soviet Justice and Soviet Tyranny*, 55 Col. L. Rev. 795, 803-806 (1955).

man would become, so to speak, his own father and thus eliminate the need for fatherly authority among adults.[48] This comes close to Thayer's thesis.[49]

Learned Hand and Judicial Review

If elsewhere Judge Hand has sometimes been steered by his own personal notions of justice, unquestionably, when it came to questions of constitutionality, he has been unwaveringly faithful to his creed about the limited role of judges in a democracy.

The undemocratic judicial destruction of social legislation, via unconstitutionality, criticized by Thayer in 1891, did not abate after Learned Hand became a lawyer. The courts, state and federal, largely regarded themselves as uncontrollable super-legislatures or, as Mr. Justice Clifford, protesting, had put it, "sovereign over both the Constitution and the people," converting "the government into a judicial despotism."[50]

The courts, Holmes said in 1897, were responding to the fear of socialism on the part of the "comfortable classes of the community" who no longer hoped "to control the legislatures" but looked "to the courts as expounders of the Constitution"; in "some courts," Holmes added, "new principles have been discovered," outside the Constitution, which might be "generalized into acceptance of economic doctrines which prevailed about fifty

48 Consult *Law and the Modern Mind* (1930). Consult also Bienenfeld, *Rediscovery of Justice* (1947), reviewed by me in 38 Calif. L. Rev. 351 (1950).

49 It is also close to a theme of Judge Hand's, who wrote in 1932: "And so when I hear so much impatient and irritable complaint, so much readiness to replace what we have by guardians for us all, those supermen, evoked somewhere from the clouds, whom none have seen and none are ready to name, I lapse into a dream, as it were. I see children playing on the grass; their voices are shrill and discordant as children's are; they are restive and quarrelsome; they cannot agree to any common plan; their play annoys them; it goes so poorly. And one says, let us make Jack the master; Jack knows all about it; Jack will tell us what each is to do and we shall all agree. But Jack is like all the rest; Helen is discontented with her part and Henry with his, and soon they fall again into their old state. No, the children must learn to play by themselves; there is no Jack the master. And in the end slowly and with infinite disappointment they do learn a little; they learn to forbear, to reckon with another, accept a little where they wanted much, to live and let live, to yield when they must yield; perhaps, we may hope, not to take all they can. But the condition is that they shall be willing at least to listen to one another, to get the habit of pooling their wishes. Somehow or other they must do this, if the play is to go on; maybe it will not, but there is no Jack, in or out of the box, who can come to straighten the game." Democracy: Its Presumptions and Realities, in The Spirit of Liberty 90, 99-100 (Dilliard ed., 2d ed., 1953).

50 Loan Association v. Topeka, 20 Wall. (US) 655, 669 (1874).

years ago, and a wholesale prohibition of what a tribunal of lawyers does not think . . . right."[51]

Holmes's analysis was justified. In 1889, Peckham, then on the highest New York court, and later to become a Supreme Court justice, said that a statute fixing the rates of elevators was "vicious in its nature, communistic in its tendency."[52] That statement echoed the sentiments of Tiedeman who, in an influential constitutional treatise published in 1886, wrote that Socialism and Communism were "rampant throughout the civilized world;" that the "conservative classes" in America were threatened by an "absolutism more tyrannical . . . than any before experienced by man, the absolutism of a democratic majority"; and that the Constitution was opposed to such "democratic absolutism."[53] In 1894, the Supreme Court, with the plaudits of most leaders of the bar, destroyed the federal income-tax law; some of the Justices deemed it communistic.[54] In 1905, in the famous *Lochner* case, the Supreme Court (per Justice Peckham) vetoed a state statute limiting the working hours of employees in bakeries.[55]

In 1908, aged 36, a year before he became a district judge, and after some twelve years at the Bar, Learned Hand, in an article on the constitutionality of state eight-hours-of-labor statutes,[56] boldly followed Thayer, and perhaps went even further. He agreed with what Shattuck (Thayer's former law partner) had written in 1891, i.e., that the courts had usurped power when they construed "liberty" in the due process clauses of the 5th and 14th Amendments to include "liberty of contract." Hand said that the Supreme Court at one time had held that the "legislature was free to act as it thought best" in legislation on matters which actually affected the "public good" or "public welfare," and that the Court would interfere only if it was obvious that the legislature had acted but colorably (i.e., dishonestly). He clearly indicated that, in his opinion, such was the proper outer limit of judicial review under the due-process clause as to regulatory legislation. He pointed out, however, that the Court later had held that it could and would

51 *The Path of the Law,* in Collected Legal Papers 167, 184 (1920).

52 People v. Budd, 117 NY 1, 71, 22 NE 670, 695 (1889).

53 Limitations of Police Power vii-viii (1886).

54 Pollock v. Farmers' Loan & Trust Co., 157 US 429 (1895).

55 Lochner v. New York, 198 US 45 (1905).

56 *Due Process of Law and the Eight-Hour Day,* 21 Harv. L. Rev. 495, 498 (1908).

examine the expediency of a statute. He thought such a standard unjustified. But, if one assumed its propriety, then (following Thayer) he urged that the Court should use the analogy of a judge reviewing a jury's "verdict on the facts": "Only in those cases in which it is obvious beyond peradventure that the statute was the result, either of passion or of ignorance or folly, can the Court say that it was not due process of law." Then (perhaps here going beyond Thayer), he questioned whether even such judicial power—i.e., to veto legislation "with whose economic or political expediency" the Court "totally disagrees"—can endure in a democratic state; in the end, the exercise of such a judicial veto "may demand some change, either in the Court or the Constitution." But until then, he declared, the Court should sustain as constitutional a statute limiting work to eight hours, unless the Court could not see "any reasonable relation to any purpose which reasonable men may think desirable for the public welfare"; it "must be shown that . . . no one could reasonably believe it expedient, in other words, that it was either absurd or oppressive." Pretty plainly, Learned Hand then believed that, concerning due process as to social and economic legislation, our courts should accept, substantially, the English principle of legislative supremacy.

The Supreme Court's decisions aroused the ire of ex-President Theodore Roosevelt. In 1912, he angrily complained that the judiciary had virtually closed "the path to industrial, economic and social reform." In the Bull Moose campaign of that year, in which he ran as a third-party candidate for the presidency against President Taft and Woodrow Wilson, Roosevelt came out for the "recall of decisions," an idea once suggested by John Marshall, i.e., the Constitution should be amended to provide in effect that, if the Supreme Court nullified a statute, then, if Congress re-enacted it, the statute would become valid despite the Court. In advancing this proposal, Roosevelt referred to Thayer's writings.

Although appointed a federal district judge by President Taft in 1909, Learned Hand lined up with Roosevelt. He had had sent to Roosevelt, while the latter was abroad, a copy of Herbert Croly's book, *The Promise of American Life,* which became the basis of much of the Bull Moose political platform. Judge Hand supported Roosevelt in the 1912 campaign. He was, I think, then in favor of the "recall of decisions." In 1913, Judge Hand himself ran (unsuccessfully) on the Bull Moose ticket for the post of Chief Judge of the New York Court of Appeals.

Three years later, in 1916, still a federal judge, he again expressed his indignation at undemocratic decisions, in an article, *The Speech of Justice.*[57] He warned the judges and lawyers to discontinue thwarting the will of those not possessed of "property" by adhering always to old precedents and by narrow interpretations of new statutes favorable to labor. Here Judge Hand, aged 44, once more disclosed himself as an eager advocate of the lesson he had learned from Thayer. He never forgot that lesson. It was underscored when, in the 1920's and early 1930's, the Supreme Court demolished statute after statute which obviously had wide public approval, some of them apparently indispensable to the very economic existence of the country.

Judge Hand, however, has been a doughty defender of the procedural provisions of the Constitution, whether contained in the Bill of Rights or elsewhere. Read, for instance, his dissenting opinion in the second Remington perjury case.[58] In particular, he has, in his decisions, enforced rigorously the Fourth Amendment's prohibition of unreasonable searches and seizures; our kind of society, he believes, cannot survive unless the courts prevent such incursions on the individual's privacy.

But, thanks to Thayer's teaching, Judge Hand has, I think, never except once—and then only because he felt bound by Supreme Court decisions—held unconstitutional any federal statute not dealing with procedure.[59] He has used his considerable ingenuity to avoid such a result.[60]

Repeatedly, he has said that, except in its procedural provisions, our Bill of Rights with its "imprecise" provisions, such as the First Amendment, contains no more than "moral adjurations," mere "counsels of moderation," sententious phrases, not like laws which courts can or should enforce. In 1930, in a judicial opinion, he described these as provisions representing "a mood rather than a command, that sense of moderation, of fair play, of mutual forbearance, without which states become the prey of faction."[61] Elo-

57 The Spirit of Liberty 13 (Dilliard ed., 2d ed., 1953).
58 United States v. Remington, 208 F (2d) 567 (CA 2, 1953).
59 United States v. A.L.A. Schecter Poultry Corp., 76 F (2d) 617 (CA 2, 1935).
60 See, e.g., Addison v. Huron Stevedoring Corp., 204 F (2d) 88 (CA 2, 1953).
61 Daniel Reeves, Inc. v. Anderson, 43 F (2d) 679, 682 (CA 2, 1930).

quently, he has spoken against the hope that courts, in anything they do, can be the saviors of democracy. You hear clear echoes of Thayer in his assertion, in 1942, that a "society so riven that the spirit of moderation is gone, no court can save; that a society where that spirit flourishes, no court *need* save; that in a society which evades its responsibility by thrusting on the courts the nurture of that spirit, that spirit in the end will perish." The "spirit of moderation" entails, he declaimed, a "faith in the sacredness of the individual." It "is idle to seek shelter" for that spirit and that faith "in a court room." They "cannot be imposed; . . . decisions will not maintain them."[62] Again in 1944, he said, "I often wonder whether we do not rest our hopes too much upon constitutions . . . and upon courts. These are false hopes; believe me, these are false hopes. Liberty lies in the hearts of men and women; when it dies there, no constitution, . . . no court can save it; no constitution, . . . no court can even do much to help it."[63]

Judge Hand's interpretation of Thayer's thesis relative to constitutional issues is not necessarily the sole interpretation, for others of Thayer's adherents have interpreted it differently. In many of the years when the Supreme Court was mowing down statutes, three Justices—Holmes, Brandeis and (after 1925) Stone—in dissenting opinions expressed the Thayer view. Most of those cases related to statutes affecting rights of "property." In those cases, Holmes and Brandeis insisted on the presumption of constitutionality, as did Stone after he became a Justice. But, when a statute invaded the province of free speech, or freedom of religious worship, they accorded it no such presumption.[64] Such questions usually arose under the Fourteenth Amendment, which, so the Supreme Court held, embodied the First Amendment's provisions forbidding the enactment of any law respecting the "free exercise of religion" or "abridging the freedom of speech or of the press." Holmes and Brandeis were charged with inconsistency, with applying a double standard.[65] Without doubt, they faced an apparent dilemma from which, verbally, they never exited.

62 *The Contribution of an Independent Judiciary,* in The Spirit of Liberty 155, 164 (Dilliard ed., 2d ed., 1953).

63 In The Spirit of Liberty, id., at 189.

64 See, e.g., Abrams v. United States, 250 US 616 (1919); Gitlow v. New York, 268 US 652 (1925).

65 Consult, e.g., Corwin, *Liberty against Government* 156 n.63 (1948).

It was Stone, after Holmes and Brandeis had left the Court, who found the verbal exit from the dilemma. Without mentioning Thayer, he invented a formula which I happen to think was clearly implicit in what Thayer had written. Thayer, you'll remember, had maintained that the vice of judicial demolition of legislation was that it prevented public discussion of policies, thereby keeping the people from attaining that political maturity which democracy required. Stone, in 1938, in the *Carolene Products* case, suggested that, as to any statute which would seriously impede the democratic process, there should be virtually a presumption of invalidity, that perhaps "legislation which restricts these political processes, which can ordinarily be expected to bring about repeal of undesirable legislation, is to be subjected to more exacting scrutiny . . . than are most other types of legislation."[66]

Stone developed that idea, in 1940, in his dissenting opinion in the first "flag-salute" case, involving the validity of a statute affecting, so Stone said, the Jehovah's Witnesses' freedom of religious worship. There, citing *Carolene Products,* he said: "We have previously pointed to the importance of a searching judicial inquiry into the legislative judgment in situations where prejudice against . . . minorities may tend to curtail the operation of those political processes ordinarily to be relied on to protect minorities." The specific character of the "constitutional guaranties of civil liberties" as to "freedom of speech and religion" meant that the courts must not permit a legislature the latitude which it must be allowed "when no question of civil liberties is involved." I cannot perceive, he continued, "that in prescribing, as limitations upon the powers of government, the freedom of mind and spirit secured by the explicit guaranties of speech and religion, [the framers] intended . . . any latitude for a legislative judgment that the compulsory expression of belief which violates religious convictions would better serve the public interest than their protection. . . . The Constitution expresses . . . a command that freedom of mind and spirit must be preserved, which government must obey, if it is to adhere to that justice and moderation without which no free government can exist."[67] In another dissenting opinion, Stone referred to the

[66] United States v. Carolene Products Co., 304 US 144, 152-53 n.4 (1938).
[67] Minersville School District v. Gobitis, 310 US 586 (1940).

freedoms specified by the First Amendment as having a "preferred position."[68]

Most surprisingly, Judge Hand, in a paper on Stone, published in 1946, shortly after Stone's death,[69] completely ignored the Holmes-Brandeis dichotomy between free-speech and "property cases," and also Stone's explicit restatement of Thayer. Judge Hand began this paper by relating how Holmes and Brandeis adopted Thayerism. "Their notion," he wrote, was that the Bill of Rights, in its vaguer provisions, "could not be treated like ordinary law; its directions were to be treated rather as admonitions of forbearance," as "merely a counsel of perfection and an ideal of temperance . . . whose infractions were . . . only . . . a matter of regret" not violations of the Constitution, that those provisions "forbade" only "statutes . . . which were so utterly outrageous that nobody could give" them "any rational support," and scarcely ever was such a statute enacted.

Judge Hand went on, correctly, to say that Stone, too, as a Justice, had adopted the Thayer thesis. For, in Stone's famous dissenting opinion in the *A.A.A.* case in 1936, he declared that the Court's majority, in knocking out the statute, were enforcing "their own predilections." "For the removal of unwise laws from the statute book," wrote Stone, "appeal should be not to the courts but to the ballot and to the processes of democratic government."[70] Stone was taking his Thayer straight.

So far so good. Now note Judge Hand's curious version of what happened in the free-speech and freedom-of-religion cases. Beginning, he said, in the later 1930's, with new Justices appointed by President Franklin Roosevelt, the Supreme Court's former minority view became that of a majority. The Thayer principle of judicial hands-off statutory validity was now dominant. Previously, said Judge Hand, the battle relative to this principle had been fought almost entirely over the constitutionality of statutes invading "property" rights. But, according to Judge Hand, there now arose a question theretofore little considered: did not the Thayer thesis apply also to statutes interfering with so-called "personal rights"

[68] Jones v. Opelika, 316 US 584, 600, 608 (1942). Consult Dunham, Mr. Chief Justice Stone, in Dunham and Kurland eds., Mr. Justice 47, 60-63 (1956).

[69] Chief Justice Stone's *Concept of the Judicial Function,* in The Spirit of Liberty 201 (Dilliard ed., 2d ed., 1953).

[70] United States v. Butler, 297 US 1 (1936).

—notably legislation interfering with free speech and freedom of worship? As Judge Hand told the story, Stone, always insisting on a "consistent application" of the Thayer hands-off principle, "could not understand how the principle which he had all along supported" could be differently applied when statutes dealt "with interests other than property," since to make such a differentiation would be to allow the judges, in respect of such statutes, to enforce "their own predilections." Judge Hand concluded that, because Stone "was throughout true to this view that . . . we should especially remember him with gratitude, and honor him as a judge."[71]

Here we have Judge Hand depicting Stone as ever loyal to Judge Hand's version of Thayerism, and therefore as opposed to those Justices—Black, Douglas, Rutledge, Murphy, and (at times) Jackson—who, according to Judge Hand, used it inconsistently when they faced legislation interfering with free speech and freedom of religion.

A biography often is an unconscious autobiography. So Learned Hand, purporting to describe Harlan Stone, instead described Learned Hand. For Stone was guilty of what Judge Hand regards as an inconsistency. Judge Hand, in his account of Stone's constitutional views, disclosed a surprising blind spot—at precisely the point where Stone's views strikingly differed from his own. The Justices whose position in free-speech cases Judge Hand criticized, have often, since 1938, acted on Stone's restatement of Thayer.

If Judge Hand's description did not fit Stone, it did indeed fit Justice Frankfurter.[72] In 1940, writing for the Court in the first "flag-salute" case, Frankfurter sustained the statute as not offending the First Amendment.[73] Three years later in the second flag-salute case[74] the Court over-ruled *Gobitis*. Now Frankfurter dissented. His reasoning was precisely that which Judge Hand applauds. The Court's power to nullify a statute, Frankfurter declared, "does not vary according to the provision of the Bill of Rights which is involved. . . . [E]ach specific Amendment, in so far as embraced within the Fourteenth Amendment, must be equally respected. . . . [E]ven though legislation relates to civil liberties, our duty of

[71] Hand, op. cit. *supra* note 69, at 206, 207.

[72] Justice Frankfurter's position on this issue is to be explored by Professor Herbert Wechsler in the November, 1957 issue of the Yale Law Journal, a symposium in honor of Justice Frankfurter's seventy-fifth birthday.

[73] Minersville School District v. Gobitis, 310 US 586 (1940).

[74] West Virginia State Board of Education v. Barnette, 319 US 624 (1943).

deference to those who have the responsibility for making our laws is no less relevant or less exacting." When, said Frankfurter, Holmes wrote for the Court that "legislatures are ultimate guardians of the liberties and welfare of the people in quite as great a degree as the courts," he did not mean "that, for only some phases of civil government, this Court was not to supplant legislatures and sit in judgment upon the right or wrong of a challenged measure. [Holmes] was stating . . . that responsibility for legislation lies with legislatures, answerable as they are directly to the people, and this Court's only and very narrow function is to determine whether . . . reasonable justification can be offered" for the legislation. The "narrow judicial authority to nullify legislation . . . is an undemocratic aspect of our scheme of government" since it "serves to prevent the full play of the democratic process." Accordingly, there must be "the greatest caution in" the use of that authority. Frankfurter then quoted at length a passage from one of Thayer's writings.[75]

Frankfurter's reference in that opinion to Holmes was surprising. For Frankfurter, in 1939, just before he became a Supreme Court Justice, had published an article demonstrating that "Holmes was far more ready to find [unconstitutional] legislative invasion" in the field of "civil liberties" than "in the area of debatable economic reforms."[76]

This brings me to the *Dennis* case.[77] As you know, it involved the conviction of some Communist Party leaders, under the Smith Act, for wilfully conspiring to "teach and advocate the overthrow and destruction" of the government "by force and violence" and "the duty" of so doing. In 1950, Judge Hand, on the appeal from this conviction, held for the Court of Appeals that the statute did not violate the First Amendment.[78] As an "inferior" judge, he had to deal with the "clear and present danger" test, a test contrived by Holmes and adopted by the Supreme Court in many decisions. Judge Hand interpreted this test to mean that, "In each case [courts] must ask whether the gravity of the 'evil,' discounted by

75 Id., at 648, 649, 650, 667.

76 Mr. Justice Cardozo and *Public Law, in Law and Politics* 92 n.2 (1939).

77 Dennis v. United States, 341 US 494 (1951). This article, of course, was prepared without the benefit of the numerous opinions on the Smith Act handed down by the Supreme Court during the October Term, 1956.

78 United States v. Dennis, 183 F (2d) 201 (CA 2, 1950).

its improbability, justifies such invasion of free speech as is necessary to avoid the danger."

I shall not discuss this interpretation of "clear and present danger." I do again emphasize the fact of Judge Hand's belief, previously and subsequently expressed with vigor, that the courts should never treat non-procedural provisions of the Bill of Rights as judicially enforcible commands. Possessed of that belief, it was pretty much a foregone conclusion that, if he possibly could, he would sustain the constitutionality of any federal statute interfering with free speech, no matter how undesirable he thought that interference.

In 1951, the Supreme Court affirmed Judge Hand's decision. Frankfurter wrote a concurring opinion. In effect, he rejected the "clear and present danger" test. Instead, he relied 100 per cent on his version of the Thayer doctrine. "The Smith Act and this conviction under it," he said, "no doubt restrict the exercise of free speech and assembly." He conceded that: "Suppressing advocacy of the overthrow [of the government by force] inevitably will also silence critics who do not advocate overthrow but fear that their criticism may be so construed." It "is self-delusion to think that we can punish [the defendants] for their advocacy without adding to the risks run by loyal citizens who honestly believe in some of the reforms these defendants advance. It is a sobering fact that in sustaining the conviction before us we can hardly escape restriction on the interchange of ideas. We must not overlook," he went on, "the value of that interchange." The "liberty of man to search for truth ought not to be fettered, no matter what orthodoxies he may challenge. Liberty of thought shrivels without freedom of expression. Nor can truth be pursued in an atmosphere hostile to the endeavor or under dangers which are hazarded only by heroes. . . . Without open minds there can be no open society. And if society be not open, the spirit of man is mutilated and becomes enslaved."[79]

Yet, in spite of these real dangers which he regarded as flowing from the statute, he concluded that the Court, acting democratically, could not declare it invalid. He described what, to him, was an inescapable paradox; the Court, "by recognizing the right of Congress to put some limitation upon expression," was seeking to

[79] 341 US 494 (1951).

"maintain and further" our democratic civilization, although "freedom of expression is the well-spring" of that civilization and although the Smith Act would undoubtedly, by creating fears, seriously impede free expression by non-communists not at all guilty of violating that statute. Nevertheless he asserted, "The democratic process . . . is not impaired or restricted" by the Smith Act. For he believed the Court was bound by his version of the Thayer principle. The Court, he said (quoting Brandeis and Holmes dissenting in a case unrelated to free speech or the like)[80] must not become a "super-legislature." The Court can properly set aside the legislative judgment "only if there is no reasonable basis for it." Most explicitly he rejected Stone's statements, theretofore accepted by a majority of the Court in decisions he cited, "that our function in reviewing statutes restricting freedom of expression differs sharply from our normal duty in sitting in judgment on legislation."

Let me now bring you back for a moment to Stone's dissent in the first flag-salute case. There he observed that, in several previous cases, the Court had vetoed statutes restricting freedom of speech or worship where there were "other ways," other "alternatives," to "secure the legitimate state and without infringing the asserted immunity."[81] Douglas, dissenting in the *Dennis* case, followed this lead. The government had argued, and the majority opinion made much of the argument, that the Communists had been guilty of "seditious conduct," of actions that were unlawful. Said Douglas, "There is a statute which makes seditious conspiracy unlawful," citing a statute which provides that it is a crime to "conspire to overthrow, put down, or destroy by force the Government of the United States." Had the defendants been convicted under that alternative statute, none of the fears inspired in other innocent citizens, as described by Frankfurter, would have ensued. The vice of the Smith Act, Douglas maintained, was that it criminalized advocacy—teaching, speech—not conduct. "Never until today," wrote Douglas, "has anyone seriously thought that the ancient law of conspiracy could constitutionally be used to turn speech into seditious conduct."[82]

Well, there you have markedly divergent judicial views about the meaning of the Thayer principle. Learned Hand and Frank-

---

80 Burns Baking Co. v. Bryan, 264 US 504 (1924).
81 Minersville School District v. Gobitis, 310 US 586 (1940).
82 Dennis v. United States, 341 US 494 (1951).

furter construe it one way; Stone, Black, Douglas and others construe it another way.

I shall not express my own view of the *Dennis* decision. But I do feel that it is absurd to say, as some have said, that only Communist sympathizers will disagree with that decision or with the rationale Frankfurter there employed. Surely Justices Black and Douglas cannot be so characterized.[83]

In holding the Smith Act valid, Judge Hand, of course, did not remotely intimate that he deemed it desirable legislation. The truth is that he loathes the popular mood which induced the enactment of that act. In so saying, I do not rely on private conversations with me. I can point to several articles he published since *Dennis*.

[83] I cite two eminent lawyers who have criticized the Dennis decision. Neither is, by any stretch of the imagination, a radical or subversive. Each detests, and is alive to the real internal threat of the purposes and conduct of the American Communist leaders; each believes that such conduct deserves severe punishment, but each regards the Smith Act as an unfortunate method of accomplishing that end. In 1953, about a year after the Supreme Court handed down the Dennis decision, Eugene Rostow took his stand with Stone. Rostow, *The Democratic Character of Judicial Review,* 66 Harv. L. Rev. 193 (1953). He deplored the notion that the judicial power to nullify legislation is undemocratic, that it has a "tainted" character. On the contrary, he asserted, the Supreme Court, in the exercise of this power, can have the "effect not of inhibiting but of releasing the dominantly democratic forces of American life." Had the Court reversed the conviction in Dennis, Dean Rostow maintained, it would have "forced the executive to prosecute the communists on the direct charge of a conspiracy to subvert the state" under another plainly valid statute. The Smith Act, which provided punishment not for so conspiring but for "teaching and advocating" subversion, embodied, Rostow observed, a principle which would have "jailed Calhoun" and "perhaps Thoreau." It would have jailed, too, "the participants in the Hartford convention" of the Federalists opposed to our 1812 war with England.

Professor Paul Freund, in 1953, also criticized Dennis, in the spirit of Stone's and Douglas' suggestions about alternative remedies. Freund, *Competing Freedoms in American Constitutional Law, in Conference on Freedom and the Law,* 13 U. of Chi. Conference Series 26 (1953). "The law," he wrote, "must be viewed in the light of the availability of less drastic means. . . . No one doubts that the leaders of a party which disciplines its members in espionage, sabotage and perjury, to say nothing of instruction in techniques of violence, can be punished for such activity. But the Smith Act was not so framed." Congress, he suggested, had inserted "the knife" too "far from the seat of the disturbance." The statute was "an excessively drastic curb on freedom of expression in order to reach an evil which could be attacked more directly. . . . What is disquieting is that the question of choice of means received such scant notice, and that the decision may support other restrictions on expression which would be unsupportable if subjected to a properly rigorous line of inquiry. . . . Indeed, for all that appears, it would seem that open advocacy of violent revolution, so far from producing the dangers apprehended, was rather a weakening factor in the life of the Party because of its repelling effect." Then Freund added a point which Morris Ernst has often urged, i.e., that "secrecy was the real threat." When speech is "covert," the "countercheck of the forum of ideas is by hypothesis lacking," wherefore "restrictions on such speech need not be subjected to a test . . . designed to foster open trading ideas."

In 1952, Judge Hand in effect admitted that the Constitution would not have been ratified, had it not then been promised that the Constitution would be amended promptly to include the Bill of Rights, and had it not then been believed that, as Judge Hand himself phrased it, all its provisions would be "mandates" against which "no statute should prevail."[84] There is every reason to think that statement historically accurate. Much popular opposition to the Constitution yielded only because of that promise and that belief. Moreover, such prominent men as Jefferson and Samuel Adams abandoned their grave doubts about ratification on the assurance that the courts would enforce the provisions of all the Amendments. When Madison, in the First Congress, advocated the first Ten Amendments, he said that "independent tribunals of justice will consider themselves in a peculiar manner the guardians of those rights; they will be an impenetrable bulwark against every assumption of power in the Legislative or Executive; they will be naturally led to resist every encroachment upon rights stipulated for in the Constitution by the declaration of rights."

Why, then, one may ask, should not the courts respect that history which discloses that the First Amendment was intended to be a legal "mandate" and not solely a "moral adjuration?"

Judge Hand thinks it folly to believe that the courts can save democracy. Of course, they cannot. But it seems to me that here, most uncharacteristically, Judge Hand indulges in a judgment far too sweeping, one which rests on a too-sharp either-or, all-or-nothing, dichotomy. In a posthumously published book, Justice Jackson similarly objected to the idea "that the Court can . . . supply . . . some clear bulwark against all dangers and evils that today beset us internally," that the "protection of civil liberties" should be left "wholly to the judiciary."[85] Obviously, the courts cannot do the whole job. But, just as obviously, they can sometimes help to arrest evil popular trends in their inception. Not only are the Supreme Court's opinions educational in a general way; they have also had discernible practical effects in stopping undemocratic tendencies.[86]

---

84 *A Plea for the Open Mind and Free Discussion,* in The Spirit of Liberty 274, 277 (Dilliard ed., 2d ed., 1953).

85 The Supreme Court in the American System of Government 58 (1955).

86 E.g., Hague v. C.I.O., 307 US 496 (1939). Consult also Freund, op. cit. *supra* note 83.

In a recent address,[87] Frankfurter, after quoting Judge Hand, noted, with marked pleasure, that no other English-speaking country has adopted anything like what Judge Hand calls the "imprecise" provisions of our Bill of Rights. Here Frankfurter virtually repeated something he had said in an article published in 1924,[88] i.e., that, without such provisions, "life and property [were] amply protected" in those countries, including South Africa. McWhinney pointedly comments: "There is perhaps today a special irony in the reference to South Africa."[89] Only recently at the Yale Law School, we heard from a brilliant South African lawyer how, absent a Bill of Rights in that unhappy land, each time its courts had interpreted a statute to protect legal equality, the legislature had at once enacted legislation to wipe out the democratic decision. When our Supreme Court, acting pursuant to our Bill of Rights, invalidates such a discriminatory statute, our legislatures cannot validly emasculate the decision. Whether, if supported by a Bill of Rights, like ours, the South African Court's decisions would have withstood the onslaughts of the regnant majority in the legislature, no one can say with certainty. But who can say that such decisions would not have done much to stem the terrifying growth of tyranny in that troubled land, a growth which, so many intelligent observers believe, may issue before long in a devastating civil war?

For a number of reasons, my own inclination is to disagree with Judge Hand's position that the First Amendment represents merely a "moral adjuration" addressed solely to the people and their elected representatives. However, so profound is my respect for his wisdom in general that my disagreement with him on this subject disturbs me. So I warn you not to make up your minds without much reflection.

Learned Hand and "The Common Will"

Judge Hand's reluctance to follow his own ideas of justice in opposition to the "common will," has led him to decide some naturalization and deportation cases which have provoked the

[87] John Marshall and the Judicial Function, in Of Law and Men 3 (Elman ed., 1956).

[88] The Red Terror of Judicial Reform, in Law and Politics 10, 16 (MacLeish & Prichard ed., 1939).

[89] *The Dilemma of Judicial Policy Making*, 39 Minn. L. Rev. 837, 847 n.22 (1955).

criticism of a wise lawyer-philosopher, Edmond Cahn, in general a warm admirer of Judge Hand. The statute requires that an alien, to become a naturalized citizen, must show that, for the five years immediately preceding his filing of a naturalization petition, he "has been and still is a person of good moral character." It also provides for the deportation of an alien who has been guilty of a conduct involving "moral turpitude." Judge Hand has treated the two standards as substantially identical. In deciding cases under either section of the statute, he has held that a jury, not a judge, is "especially the organ" to supply "the social sense of what is right,"[90] "the moral demands of the community."[91] The appropriate test is "the 'common conscience' prevalent at the time."[92]

Cahn criticizes Judge Hand on two grounds:

(1) A judge can seldom find out the prevalent " 'common conscience.' " Indeed, in some of his opinions, Judge Hand has so acknowledged, has admitted that no reliable opinion polls can inform the court of the "moral feelings prevalent in the community."

(2) Even if, says Cahn, the judge can ascertain those community feelings, he shirks his duty, if he shifts his responsibility to the community. "By subordinating his own moral principles to those of the marketplace," writes Cahn, "Judge Hand has seriously distorted the function of the court as pedagogue and moral mentor in a democratic society. I say he distorted the court's function, because instead of exercising such influence as he could to raise the morals of the community to a level approaching his own, he expressed rather an attitude of resignation. . . . By means of its legislation, the community says to the judge, 'Ascertain whether this man, has had a good moral character. . . .' Judge Hand's rationale would send that task back to the community."[93] Cahn thinks the judge should be ready to shoulder the responsibility which the statute "imposes on him."

William James once said that "a very real [moral] dilemma is . . . a unique situation. . . ." In 1951, Judge Hand, in one of the naturalization cases, repeated this sentiment, saying that "almost

90 United States v. Kennerley, 209 F 119, 121 (S.D. N.Y., 1913).

91 United States v. Levine, 83 F (2d) 156, 157 (CA 2, 1936).

92 Johnson v. United States, 186 F (2d) 588, 590 (CA 2, 1951).

93 Moral Decision: Right and Wrong in the Light of American Law 300, et seq. (1955).

every moral situation is unique."[94] Wherefore Cahn comments that, in determining whether a particular man has a "good moral character," there can be no community opinion, because the community, unlike a judge deciding that particular man's case, cannot have any attitude about that particular man's character. It is the judge's duty, says Cahn, to evaluate "the whole human personality that stands before him." The "community cannot conceivably know the myriad circumstances [of a unique individual biography]. The community may possibly pass an informed judgment on a single act; . . . [it] can never have the knowledge which the judge must glean and assemble in order to pass judgment on the totality known as 'character.'" The judge should take into account "[all] considerations having to do with upbringing, background, environment, and temptation; [all] considerations antecedent to the intention that accompanied the act; [all] considerations of reformation and personal rehabilitation; and [all] those most sacred considerations associated with repentance, mercy and forgiveness."[95]

Fair enough. But I would ask Cahn whether the judge can competently discharge that duty. Any discerning evaluation of a man's character would require a deep psychological probing of the man, a probing for which our present judicial techniques are hopelessly deficient. They might well be supplemented by calling in psychiatrists; but, as yet, the psychiatrists are at odds with one another concerning the methods of evaluating character. So, today the judge who judges á la Cahn engages in guesswork. Cahn escapes Judge Hand's dilemma but, as matters now stand, encounters another equally baffling dilemma.

Cahn himself notes a difference between (1) saying that good character means "as good in . . . character as the average citizen" and (2) saying that it means "good according to the judgment of the average . . . citizen." The distinction is a real one: The average citizen may demand a character, for purposes of naturalization, better than his own. So it may be, in the case of a judge whose moral standards—as revealed by his conduct or his proclivities—are lower than the community's average, that the administration of justice will improve if he accepts the admonition to consult the community's morality. Yet I admit that such an admoni-

[94] Johnson v. United States, 186 F (2d) 588, 590 (CA 2, 1951).
[95] Cahn, op. cit. *supra* note 93, at 309.

tion may encourage such a judge to become "pharisaical." Remember what Jesus said about the need to look at "the inside of the cup." Doesn't modern psychology disclose the danger that one may be excessively harsh in judging others whose conduct resembles that in which he has himself indulged or secretly longs to indulge? A troubled conscience can make a man a bigot as a judge. Shakespeare, centuries before "modern psychology," so perceived in *Measure For Measure.*

Cahn would say that, with such a judge as Learned Hand, the danger is just the opposite: highly sensitive and reflective, Judge Hand surrenders his exquisitely fine compassionate judgments to those that are crudely insensitive.

Whether or not you agree with Cahn's criticism of Judge Hand's decisions in the "good moral character" cases, I trust you'll recognize that Judge Hand's motive in those decisions springs from what Cahn terms his "democratic loyalty." Although Judge Hand usually finds the community standards undiscoverable in such cases, the reference to them does serve as a check on the assertion of his personal predilections. Important here is his distrust of his own infallibility. He likes to quote Cromwell: "I beseech you, man, in the bowels of Christ, have you never been wrong."

Tolerance in a judge, Judge Hand believes, breeds dispassionateness, detachment, essential to good judging. In a singularly insightful passage, stirred perhaps by the writings of the psychoanalysts, he wrote: "There are those who insist that detachment is an illusion; that our conclusions, when their bases are sifted, always reveal a passional foundation. Even so; though they be throughout the creatures of past emotional experience, it does not follow that that experience can never predispose us to impartiality. A bias against bias may be as likely a result of some buried crisis, as any other bias."[96]

He knows, however, that no man can always successfully control his deepest prejudices. So he is constantly watchful of, on guard against, his own. As nearly as any mortal can be, he is passionately dispassionate.

---

96 Thomas Walter Swan, in The Spirit of Liberty 209, 218 (Dilliard ed., 2d ed., 1953).

He opposes, vehemently, the idea that any eternal principles of justice exist. He does, also vehemently, insist that every society has fundamental attitudes. Those which our society has evolved, he treasures. Should they vanish, we will be in sad straits, he thinks. And today sometimes he apprehends that they may vanish, blown away in the current hurricanes of social intolerance. Nevertheless, it is one of his deepest convictions that judges cannot, and must not try—as judges—to save our people from their follies.

He has not, as a judge, always rejected his own judgments of what is right in favor of lower popular evaluations. I could point to many cases in which he has set his sights higher than the crowd's. In 1952, after expressing his scorn for the sort of judge who, disregarding the established legal rules, acts as a crusader for righteousness, Judge Hand confessed that sometimes he had "brought about desirable results at the expense of the rules, however flexibly one might interpret them."

Cahn could have found support for part of his criticism in Judge Hand's own writings. Thus you may recall that in his 1933 discussion,[97] Judge Learned Hand spoke of the belief of those who wrote the Constitution, in a "government by the people," through their legislatures, which would "express the common will." You might think that he glibly or naïvely slid over the concept of the "common will." But there he was talking popularly and in simple terms. Previously, he had twice searchingly considered that concept.

In 1932, he wrote that the "notion of a common will" had always "teased [the] political philosophers." He called it a "fiction," and said: "Just where that will resides, or how it is made manifest, is not too plain. . . ."[98] In 1929, he had explored the subject more intensively, asking *"Is There a Common Will?"* "If," he said, "by common will we mean the assent of a majority of men and women alive today," it "can be demonstrated that there is nothing of the kind." The "fact [is] that much of the law which governs the lives (citizens) is the *result* of compromises of conflicts long since dead. . . . To impute to [those now living] any actual assent is to create a fabulous entity. . . . Our common law is the stock instance of a combination of custom and its successive

[97] *How Far is a Judge Free in Rendering a Decision,* in The Spirit of Liberty 103 (Dilliard ed., 2d ed., 1953). See pp. 682-84 *supra.*

[98] *Democracy: Its Presumptions and Realities,* in The Spirit of Liberty 90, 95 (Dilliard ed., 2d ed., 1953).

adaptations. The judges receive it and profess to treat it as authoritative, while they gently mould it the better to fit changed ideas. . . . Sometimes for this reason we speak of the judges as representing a common will, and this was more nearly true before the advent of democracy, since they were of the class which alone had political power. It is a fiction to say so now." The judges "are not charged with power to decide the major conflicts." The legislature resolves them. But even if we were to say that in the legislature "we have an expression of the common will," we "should be wrong again." Some statutes do "carry something like the assent of a majority. But most legislation is not of that kind; it represents the insistence of a compact formidable minority. . . . The truth appears to be that what we mean by a common will is no more than that there shall be an available peaceful means by which law may be changed when it becomes irksome to enough powerful people who can make their will effective. We may say if we like that meanwhile everybody has consented to what exists, but this is fiction. They have not. . . ."

"Assuming it to exist at all, there is nothing more impalpable, nebulous and fugitive than the common will, as any political doctor will agree. . . . We can only ascertain it by counting noses, and when we have counted we do not agree on the meaning of the result."

What, then, is Judge Hand's answer to his own question concerning the existence of the common will? Here it is: "Of the contrivances which mankind has devised to lift itself from savagery, there are few to compare with the habit of assent, not to a factitious common will, but to the law as it is. We need not go so far as Hobbes, though we should do well to remember the bitter experience which made him so docile. Yet we can say with him that the state of nature is 'short, brutish and nasty,' and that it chiefly differs from civilized society in that the will of each is by habit and training tuned to accept some public, fixed and ascertainable standard of reference by which conduct can be judged and to which in the main it will conform." That standard, Judge Hand concluded, is to be found in what he called the "law."[99]

---

[99] Id., at 47, 51-52.

Learned Hand and Natural Law

A great man, such as Learned Hand, we should prize. Yet—as I'm sure he would tell you—you should beware lest you do him an ill-service by so venerating him that he will stand in the way of those who come after him, paralyzing them through awe of his achievements. Some men, wrote 17th century John Donne, "do not fill the place they are raised to"; but another man may "overfill his place. He may bring so much justice, so much integrity, to fill the place as shall . . . burthen the place . . ." and so become "a burthen upon his successor to proceed by example. . . ."

Learned Hand would be the last to claim perfection. Being human, he has his faults, of course. But no other judge has contributed as much of enduring value to his civilization. To borrow the words of Anatole France, "We owe him the gratitude due to minds that have fought against prejudices. . . . Men are rare who are free from the prejudices of their period, and look squarely at what the crowd dares not face." Judge Hand has a kind of courage seldom described and too seldom manifested—the courage to accept the fact that, as man is but a finite creature, there are some incurable defects in the solution of most human problems, and that life presents to us challenging uncertainties. This fact does not daunt him, soften him into a flabby defeatist, or harden him into a crusty cynic. A true liberal, he is no dogmatist. Himself dwelling in a temperate zone of attitudes, he has doubts about those who prefer the intemperate zones—excessively hot or excessively cold. He believes in government by discussion, agreeing with Pericles about the virtues of Athenian democracy when he said: "Instead of looking on discussion as a stumbling block in the way of action, we think it an indispensable preliminary to any wise action at all." Such a liberal has no list of fixed particularized ideas on which he insists as always wholly right or wholly wrong. He does not, phonograph-like, rattle off, with an air of infallibility, a long series of do's and dont's applicable in all circumstances. He is no slogan-addict. He looks upon liberalism as a mood, not as a system or a catalogue of precise commands. Nor will he forget that irrational extra-legal restraints may tyrannically do more than the edicts of government to narrow liberty; that among such extra-legal restraints are the irrational biased stereotypes of private groups, including the orthodox heresies and conformity-demanding taboos of rigid-minded pseudo-liberals.

Some persons denounce one who, like Learned Hand, accepts the fact of life's uncertainties, who fearlessly confronts man's limitations as a finite, mortal, human being. Themselves unable courageously to look at life as a drama full of contingencies, they resent it that any other can live without some assurance of cosmic guaranties.

This brings me, once more, to discuss Judge Hand's rejection of the idea of eternal principles of justice or morality. In this, he resembles Holmes. Since Holmes has been berated, on that account, as dangerously immoral, as an exponent of a cynical, sceptical, philosophy which leads to totalitarianism,[1] doubtless, ere long, Judge Hand will be similarly assaulted. I shall not here defend his repudiation of any form of Natural Law. I shall, however, question the suggestion that such a repudiation necessarily yields immoral, unjust, undemocratic conclusions.

I might begin with a counter-suggestion, by asking: Does adherence to a Natural-Law philosophy ensure morality, justice, devotion to democracy? Certainly not. Judge Manton adhered to that philosophy, and Judge Manton went to jail for taking bribes. The Italian philosopher, Del Vecchio, preached one version of Natural Law—and became a sponsor of Mussolini. Thomas Aquinas, the leading Natural-Law philospher, approved submission to despots. The lands which, in our times, succumbed to dictatorship were those where anti-relativism was far more popular than in those which resisted the dictators, e.g., America, in which flourished the pragmatism of William James, the arch-advocate of democracy and the dignity of the individual. I grant at once the unfairness of such an argument. I advance it merely to show the unfairness of those who assail men like Holmes or Hand because they do not espouse Natural Law.

It can be demonstrated that moral relativism neither implies nor induces cynicism or moral indifference. "Why," asks Oppenheim, "should an ethical relativist who has adopted the credo of democracy necessarily be a less enthusiastic defender of his convictions than a philosophic absolutist who claims these convictions

---

1 Consult, e.g., McKinnon, *The Secret of Mr. Justice Holmes: An Analysis*, 36 ABAJ 261 (1950); Palmer, Holmes, Hobbes, and Hitler, 31 ABAJ 569 (1945).

correspond to absolute truth? In Europe, the most ardent defenders of the democratic principle of individual dignity against the attacks by absolute monarchy, and subsequently by totalitarianism of the Right and Left, have come from the ranks of the liberal movements" whose "background has been traditionally one . . . of ethical relativism."[2] To "hold that value judgments cannot be *validated,* does not preclude anyone from *making* them," or mean that to utter them is meaningless.

Chesterton said that a man's philosophy is the most important fact about him. Once I endorsed that statement. I have come to doubt its wisdom, unless most carefully interpreted. For one should, I think, distinguish a man's formal philosophy from his actual working creed.[3] Influenced by their social heritage, or their teachers, men adopt, and express loyalty to, some particular system of ethics, or metaphysics, or ontology, or epistemology. Yet many a man, in the actual conduct of his life, negates the system to which he avows adherence. He takes over the language of some philosophic school, yet his verbal loyalty does not signify his acceptance of its spirit. He adjusts the system to his own unique inner needs, the product of his peculiar make-up and of his singular reactions to his experience. An ideal, become institutionalized, has many adherents who, while appearing, even to themselves, to accept it, inwardly dissent in varying degrees.[4] We all know men who talk like absolutists and act like relativists, or talk relativism but act on what they deem unalterable dogma. For example, as I've tried to show elsewhere,[5] Aristotle was a better legal pragmatist than John Dewey. It is notable that the "right wing" of a philosophic school is often closer to the "left wing" of an opposing school than to its own "left wing."

In short, when looking to a man's philosophy as a key to his character, one should search beneath his formal, spoken, avowals to discover, if one can, his living philosophy. I ask, then, whether any of Judge Hand's judicial decisions would have been one whit different had he talked in terms of Natural Law, had he declared

2 Oppenheim, *Relativism, Absolutism, and Democracy,* 44 Am. Pol. Sci. Rev. 951, 958 (1950).

3 Cf. Ramsdell, *Communication from a Christian Perspective,* 50 Relig. Education 335, 336 (1955).

4 Consult *Fate and Freedom* 103 (1945).

5 Modern and Ancient Legal Pragmatism—John Dewey & Co. v. Aristotle, 25 Notre Dame Lawyer 207, 460 (1950).

a belief in eternal principles of morality or justice? I can think of none. In this respect, at least, any sensible person should be a pragmatist. For pragmatism, wrote C. S. Peirce, "is only an application of the sole principle of logic which was recommended by Jesus: 'Ye may know them by their fruits.' "[6]

Horace Walpole said that "life is a comedy for those who think and a tragedy for those who feel." Learned Hand, who both thinks deeply and feels deeply, sees life as a marvelous comic-tragedy. He is not one who "despises men tenderly." He has a love for and an understanding of his fellow-creatures, like him, humanly fallible. I commend him to you as a great man and as our wisest judge.

[6] 5 Peirce, Collected Papers 402 n.2 (1934).

Adapted from Vol. 24, The University of Chicago Law Review (1957).

Arguments, Decisions and Opinions on Appeal

By Edson R. Sunderland

After the record on appeal has been prepared and filed in the appellate court, there are still three tasks to be performed in completing the proceedings for review: 1. Counsel must present to the court the facts and the law upon which they rely; 2. The court must consider the matters so presented and reach a decision thereon; 3. A record of the decision must be prepared and filed in the cause. Each presents difficulties.

The case may be presented by written brief or by oral argument or by both. In England the oral argument is the universal and exclusive method employed. In this country, on the contrary, the written brief is the universal and primary means for presenting a case on appeal, but it is not exclusive, and an oral argument may be, and usually is, added.

The Written Brief

The art of brief writing has not reached a high level of development in this country. Briefs are usually too long, devoid of style, and badly arranged. No other type of literary composition fails so generally to meet even the most elementary standards of literary form.

The problem of writing more effective briefs is primarily one for the individual brief writer, and yet something can be done by rules of court.

Prolixity, while it cannot be prevented, can be discouraged by a rule that no more than a designated number of pages in any brief shall be taxable as costs. This plan for limiting the length of briefs is recommended by the American Bar Association.[1]

So also, it has been found possible to eliminate some of the confusion which results from faulty analysis and bad arrangement

[1] 63 ABA Rep. (1938) 522, 608.

by a rule requiring concise and separate statements of the controlling points involved.

A technique for this purpose was devised by the Supreme Court of Pennsylvania. By rule of court it is required that the appellant shall, on the first page of his brief only, and without any other matter appearing thereon, set forth separately each question involved in the case, in general terms and without names, dates, amounts or other particulars, and whenever possible follow the question by a statement as to whether it was affirmed, negatived, qualified or not answered by the court below.

If such an analysis is made, and the controlling questions are stated, a brief supporting or opposing the answers to those questions as given by the court below can hardly fail to present an intelligible view of at least the main features of the case.

This plan has been followed in Connecticut, Michigan and Florida, with satisfactory results. It is simple and effective, and might well be used by brief writers as an aid in the preparation of briefs even though not required by the court.

The Oral Argument

Not all courts encourage the use of the oral argument. In some states it is not a matter of right but leave must in all cases be asked within a limited time. In many states the length of the oral argument is severely curtailed. A common deterrent is a real or supposed lack of interest in the oral argument shown by the appellate judges. Some of them frankly express doubt of its utility as currently employed.

On the other hand, members of the bar are almost unanimously in favor of preserving and encouraging the oral arguments as an aid to counsel in presenting his case. They are reluctant to rely upon written briefs alone, partly because they believe that the briefs can be effectively supplemented by oral explanation and partly because they are afraid that the briefs will not be read by all the members of the court.

The fear that only a single judge will read the briefs and record and will thereby exert a controlling influence over the decision of the case is widely prevalent among members of the bar. The feeling is fostered by the American practice of having one judge deliver the opinion of the court. The disquieting question constantly arises in the minds of defeated counsel,—How much knowledge of the case did the other judges possess as a basis for their concurrence?

When an oral argument is made, counsel at least knows that every judge who actually sat upon the bench heard what he said. The oral argument is therefore considered by the bar to be one of the most effective means for preventing "one-man" decisions.

Its intrinsic value in supplementing and clarifying the material in the brief depends, of course, on how the argument is presented. The average quality is poor, which may account for the low estimate of its usefulness held by many judges. But there can be no doubt that its possibilities are very great. To fully realize this one need only sit for a day in the English Court of Appeal, where the oral arguments constitute the sole means for bringing the views of counsel to the attention of the court.

If the oral argument is to perform the functions which in theory it ought to perform, its technique must be improved and the conditions necessary for its effective use must be determined and provided. This will require the close cooperation of bench and bar, for the presentation of the argument by counsel and its reception and use by the court are reciprocal processes.

Various methods for improving the effectiveness of the argument have been suggested and tried. Some of them are the following:

1. In order to eliminate the waste of time so commonly caused by discussion of trivial and uncontested matters, require each party to submit to the other, ten days before the hearing, a list of points to be urged, and allow no others to be discussed.

2. Organize the work of the court so that each judge will have an opportunity and will feel an obligation to become informed of the questions involved in advance of the argument.

3. Require the judges to designate in advance of the hearing the points upon which they would like to hear argument, and give counsel sufficient notice thereof.

4. Encourage more active participation in the argument on the part of the judges.

5. Allow more time for the oral argument, and if necessary for this purpose, provide that the court shall sit in divisions.

6. Require one of the judges to prepare a statement of the facts and the points involved to be read to court and counsel when the case is called, and to be thereupon settled in a form satisfactory to counsel on both sides before proceeding to the argument.

7. Employ the Pennsylvania rule already described, in order to provide the judges with a brief statement of the questions which can be quickly read before the argument.

8. Enable the judges to make effective use of the oral argument while it is still fresh in mind, by holding short and frequent sessions, and by finally disposing of the cases heard at one session before proceeding to the next; or by holding a conference immediately after the argument to arrive at a tentative decision.

Consideration and Decision by Court

This is a subject which is difficult to deal with because no one outside the membership of the court has any personal knowledge of how the judges prepare for the conference or what occurs when the conference takes place.

A conference is an inadequate safeguard against a "one-man" decision unless it is based on a prior study of the case by each judge. If one member of the court prepares the statement of facts or memorandum of opinion upon which the judges act in conference, he obviously holds a position of superior and perhaps controlling influence if the others are not able to fully check and verify his interpretation from their own investigation of the facts and the law.

A judge who has not read the record or briefs is naturally reluctant to oppose the views of a judge who has read them, with the result that the court is inclined to follow the lead of the judge who has specially studied and reported upon the case.

"One-man" influence over the conference at which the case is decided may be diminished by the oral argument, but this is not enough. There should be a sufficiently detailed study of the case by each one of the judges, prior to the conference, to give him the basis for an independent opinion in regard to it, and to enable him to participate fully and on equal terms in the discussion of the questions involved.

And not only should this preparation be made, but a procedure might well be adopted which would enable the minutes of the court to show that the provisions for securing such preparation had in fact been carried out. This would help to allay the doubts and suspicions which too frequently impair the confidence of the bar in the decisions of the court as the joint product of all the judges.

One Instance of Efficient Method

Such a procedure would not be difficult. The Circuit Court of Appeals of one circuit has employed the following plan. After the oral argument and on the same day, a preliminary conference is held. Each judge then prepares a separate written memorandum opinion covering the facts and the law, which invariably requires him to make an independent study of the record and briefs. A final conference then takes place at which each judge presents his view of the case and usually reads his memorandum opinion. The case is thereupon decided and one of the judges is assigned to write the opinion of the court.[2]

One of the associate and advisory members of the committee of the American Bar Asociation on Improvement of Appellate Procedure, who had enjoyed a broad experience as an appellate judge, expressed the view that no case should be called for oral argument or should be considered on briefs, until every judge had certified in writing that he had read the briefs and had examined the record in sufficient detail to fully understand the nature of the case.[3]

The Large Court Destroys Efficiency

Doubtless the tendency to "one-man" decisions is greatly increased by the heavy load of cases carried by many appellate courts. It is often impossible for each judge to find time to familiarize himself with the briefs and records in all the cases which he is required to vote upon at the conference.

This difficulty can be effectively met by organizing the court into a sufficient number of divisions.

Assume that a six-judge court will write 300 opinions a year. Working as a unit it will divide this load equally among its mem-

[2] 63 ABA Rep. (1938) 522, 611.
[3] 63 ABA Rep. (1938) 522, 611.

bers, each being assigned 50 opinions. This opinion load will not change if the court sits in two divisions, for each division will then write 150 opinions and each of the three judges in the division will still write 50 of them.

But every judge is also required to pass upon all the other cases coming before the court, in which he does not write opinions. These are the cases about which the bar is specially concerned. In the above-mentioned six-judge court sitting in banc, each judge would have to deal with 250 such cases. But if that court should sit in two divisions of three judges each, then each judge would have to deal with only 100 such cases, which would give him more than twice as much time for each one.

The advantage increases with the size of the court. If the court has nine members and each member writes 50 opinions, the docket will consist of 450 cases. This means that if the court sits in banc each judge will have to deal with 400 cases other than those in which he writes opinions, while if the court sits in three divisions of three judges each there will be only 100 such cases for each judge to deal with.

It is possible that the time gained by such an organization of the court would not be completely translated into a more extensive examination of briefs and records. But there can be no doubt that it would greatly reduce whatever tendency there is toward "one-man" decisions.

A practice which contemplates that every member of a large court individually shall read the briefs and record in every case coming before the court, calls for an enormous amount of duplication of effort which is difficult to justify. There should be *enough judges to provide adequate opportunities* for the development and discussion of different points of view. Beyond that additional judges contribute little except to an increased output. *It has never been seriously contended that the addition of more judges improves the quality of the decisions rendered.* Almost all the courts of last resort in the United States have been three-judge courts for considerable periods, and they were enlarged in size not because of dissatisfaction with the quality of the judicial service rendered, but because of the necessity of utilizing whatever advantage could be derived from a larger court in dealing with the increased load of business.

Three-judge Court Is the Best

A three-judge court is *ideal for the efficient handling of appellate business.* The English Court of Appeal has always sat in divisions of three judges, with complete satisfaction to the bar and the public. So do the federal Circuit Courts of Appeal, although the number of circuit judges varies from three to six and additional judges can always be called from the district bench to sit upon those courts. So far as the great mass of ordinary litigation is concerned, they are practically courts of last resort.

Coordination among different divisions of the same court, so as to eliminate inconsistent holdings and avoid decisions that do not in fact represent the views of all or a majority of the judges, is merely a problem of mechanical detail. Various plans have been successfully employed.

The objection often suggested that no appellate court ought to act, except through a majority of its members, is theoretical and traditional, and draws no support from the results of experience. The English Court of Appeal never sits with a majority of its members present, nor does the Judicial Committee of the Privy Council, and cases are constantly heard in the House of Lords by less than a majority of the judges.

The Opinion of the Court

The bulk of judicial opinions currently published is appallingly large. Many of them could be greatly reduced in length without impairing their value.

A mere order affirming, reversing or modifying a judgment is unsatisfactory to the parties, because it contains no showing as to what matters in controversy were actually considered and decided or what reasons influenced the court. Such a showing is generally considered a reasonable and proper protection against judicial oversight and error.

But an opinion containing such a showing may nevertheless be very short. Most cases involve no new principle or novel application of the law, but are controlled by simple and well established rules. In such cases it would seem sufficient to give a summary of the facts and a brief statement of the controlling propositions of law. If the case is one falling clearly within the rule stated in a prior case, a summary of the facts with a reference to the prior controlling decision would serve every purpose of a fuller discussion. Cases clearly controlled by statutes would fall in the same category. In most cases of the types here referred to, long and detailed recitals of facts tend to confuse rather than clarify. These proposals have been approved by the American Bar Association.[4]

Many cases involve merely questions of fact and the weight of evidence, and opinions in such cases hardly serve any useful purpose beyond demonstrating to the parties that the court understood the issues and gave them adequate attention. To do this will not necessarily require a long opinion.

A few cases involve difficult problems as to what the law is or ought to be, or whether and how it should be applied in novel situations. In such cases an exhaustive study need not be called for, with references to many cases. But even here it is easy to expand an opinion far beyond a proper length. The principle of stare decisis impliedly imposes upon the writer of the opinion the obligation to refrain from obiter dicta and to confine himself to the precise questions involved. Observance of this rule would go far to reduce the unnecessary length of opinions.

---

4 63 ABA Rep. (1938) 522, 613.

Adapted from Vol. 26, Journal of the American Judicature Society (1942).

The Ethics of Advocacy

The Art of Advocacy: Character and Skills for the Trial of Cases

By The Right Hon. Sir Norman Birkett, P.C.

It is now ten years since I first came to Toronto as a member of the English Bar, and upon that occasion I brought the cordial greetings of my colleagues working at the English Bar. Now, by an accident arising out of and in the course of my employment, I come as one of His Majesty's Judges; but I feel no essential difference. And whilst I bring the cordial greetings tonight of the Bench and Bar of England, I bring them with no less fervor than I brought them ten years ago.

And that, sir, illustrates the most important factor in any community of lawyers—the fact that whether you come from the Bar or whether you come from the Bench you share the same cordial feelings. It may serve as an illustration of the greatness of the work which was done, first of all in our own country in the Twelfth Century, when for the very first time the lawyers became a self-conscious community; when, for the first time men who were not in Holy Orders were permitted to practice at the English Bar. And from that early date in the Twelfth Century the promotion has always been from Bar to Bench. And by that simple thing, dependent upon the reforms of Henry II, the great community of lawyers within the community was formed; those traditions which we so much value were formulated; and through all the centuries they have been in operation.

It is quite true that if you have been at the Bar you know what the Bar thinks about the bench. We in England treasure very much the freedom of the Bar, in the various messes on circuit and elsewhere, to speak their minds about the Bench; and so the tradition grows from day to day. Mr. Justice Field, one of our old justices of days past, was so deaf that when he sat in the Court he once mistook a clap of thunder for an interruption by the witness.

And in Mr. Justice Field's day one barrister would say to another: "How are things in Field's Court?" And the answer invariably was: "Part heard."

The Ancient Story of the Deaf Plaintiff, Defendant and Judge

And speaking of the tradition that the Bar should have the license to speak freely among themselves about the judges, I was interested to observe, when looking into the Greek anthology the other night to find a particular quotation unconnected with the law, to find there the story which still circulates in England about the deaf judge, the deaf plaintiff and the deaf defendant. The judge took his seat upon the bench; the plaintiff and the defendant came before him; and the judge said: "You will begin."

The plaintiff had never heard a word, neither had the defendant, but he saw the judge's lips had stopped moving and said: "My Lord, my claim is a claim for rent."

Of course, the defendant never heard a word about this, and neither did the judge; but the plaintiff's lips had stopped moving, and the judge turned to the defendant and said: "What do you say to that?"

So the defendant, who had never heard a word, said: "My Lord, how can that be when I grind my corn at night?"

Of course, the plaintiff never heard a word about this and neither did the judge, but he saw his lips had stopped moving. The judge pulled himself together and said: "Well, I think this is a most difficult case but I see no useful purpose in reserving my judgment. As I have formed a clear opinion I propose to give expression to it. I have come to the conclusion that she is your mother and you will both maintain her." So the license to speak freely of judges is pretty ancient.

Then we had a perfectly delightful case of a very pleasant judge indeed who was trying a very complicated financial case. And he came finally to deliver his judgment and he said: "And so I come to the conclusion that I must find for the plaintiff, and I find for the plaintiff in the sum of 25,452 pounds, 16 shillings and 11 pence, but of course, if my figures aren't quite right, no doubt the counsel for the plaintiff and the counsel for the defendant will check me and correct me." Whereupon, the counsel for the plaintiff said to the counsel for the defendant in a loud whisper, "Why the damn old fool has added the date in," And the kindly judge, overhearing said: "So I have."

Our Profession Is Great Because It Is Devoted to Justice

Those are the kind of things which are only permissible and permitted when the community of interest between Bench and Bar is founded not upon the ephemeral things but founded upon something much more deep and much more lasting. And between the Bench and Bar in England, and I am sure between the Bench and Bar in Canada, there is that community of interest which is based upon one thing, namely, that our profession is devoted to the administration of the greatest thing in any civilized community—the administration of justice. And we in England pay great attention to tradition and to ceremonial. When the judge is going upon circuit, let us say to York to attend service in the Minster, he goes arrayed in full scarlet and ermine, and the stately procession through the ancient city of York brings all the populace to the street sides and they see the visible embodiment before them of the King's justice being brought to every part of the community. And though it is not for me to make suggestions with regard to procedure here or anywhere else, I can only say that the habiliments, the trappings, the ceremonial which is attendant upon the procession of the judges through the cities of our land, the pomp with which justice is administered, does certainly give not merely dignity to the Bench, but gives to the populace throughout our land a deep-seated admiration, which almost on occasion approaches reverence, for the value which the King's justice represents.

In these days of change, when the cherished institutions are in some danger from revolutionary hands, it is vital that that upon which everything else depends, the respect for law, for its administration, should be preserved; and the ceremonial and the tradition extending down through the ages, in my judgment, tends greatly to that end.

The links between Canada and Great Britain, and the links between the lawyers, are deep and lasting. We are members of a great profession, with a great history and a great responsibility. Every civilized community must—it is imperative—have within its borders a body of men trained in the law whose purpose is not merely to make money, not merely to seek and to win honor —though these things are not to be despised—but their purpose, the purpose of the community of lawyers within the community, is that the ordinary citizens shall always have at their disposal the man who can protect them, who can defend them, who can stand up before arbitrary power from whatever quarter it may come and assert the inalienable rights of the individual to the eternal freedoms. That is the center of all lawyer's work and the lawyer's ambition. And indeed, if you reflect upon it—I don't know how it is in Canada but in Great Britain where there is this deeply-rooted respect for the law, the lawyer himself is never likely to be a greatly beloved figure, and the real reason is because of one of the greatest virtues of our system.

The Advocate Cannot Be Judge of His Client's Cause

We in England have an unwritten law—the unwritten law is frequently much more powerful than the written—that every counsel, whoever he may be, has no right to decline any brief that may be offered to him except for good and sufficient reason. In my own practice at the English Bar, I have frequently had to undertake murder cases of the greatest complexity and difficulty, not because I wanted to but because of the unwritten law that I could not refuse them. It was Lord Erskine, perhaps the greatest advocate who ever trod Westminster Hall, the great Erskine, when he undertook the defense of Tom Paine—and you may read it in the State Trials—was the subject of the fiercest criticism by political parties in England because he undertook that defense. And on that memorable occasion in Westminster Hall, Erskine laid down the first rule with regard to the English advocate. "When the day comes", said Erskine in the course of that magnificent defence, "that the advocate in England is permitted to choose whom he will and whom he will not defend, and becomes not the advocate but the judge in the cause, at that moment the liberties of the citizens of England are at an end".

And that quality, the result of the unwritten law that the advocate trained in the law to defend the citizen shall be available to the citizen, is one reason why the lawyer in England is unpopular. Why, it is said, does the lawyer affect views in which he does not believe? He puts forward to the Court submissions which he may or may not think sound, but that is the rôle of the advocate. What the public will never understand is that the man who stands there to plead is not pleading his own view. He may be putting forward a view of which he profoundly disapproves; but he is putting forward, for the client, the view of the client.

We had a famous case in England of an advocate appearing for a prisoner, who in the midst of an impassioned speech to the Court stopped and said: "Now, Milord, I will lay aside the role of the advocate and I will assume the role of the man." And Milord upon the bench said: "You have no right to do any such thing. The only title by which you may be heard in this Court is that you speak as an advocate."

And the great Lord Brougham in his famous defense of Queen Caroline carried the doctrine to an extreme length when he asserted before the Court that the duty of a counsel to his client was so deep and so strong that it in fact over-rode his duty to his country. That is a proposition to which, I am quite sure, you of the Bar would not agree; but it is an illustration of the length to which the doctrine of the advocate speaking for the client may go.

And when you find great prose writers like Swift saying of advocates that they are men bred in the art of proving "that white is black and black is white, according as they are paid", it is because of the great virtue of the advocate that he is there to present the view of the client. And it leads me to say this further thing: Because of that duty, because of that responsibility, there are certain qualities of the advocate about which I hope you will allow me to say a word or two tonight.

Just let me say before I do it, that I don't pretend for one moment to give anybody advice about advocacy. I expect there are plenty of people who now hear me speak who are quite as competent to talk about the elements of advocacy as I am, but it is a subject on which we are all interested and therefore, perhaps, with humility and with deference, you will allow me to make a few observations about it.

There Is No One Pattern for Greatness as an Advocate

I have now been at the Bar and upon the bench for thirty-four years and I have seen almost every type of advocate in almost every type of Court. And I know at once there are no standards that you can lay down and say, if you want to be a great advocate, there is the pattern. It can't be done. There are diversities of gifts but the same spirit; and I have known in my time, men who could scarcely string a sentence together, who lacked all graces, and yet impressed the Court so that the Court strained to listen and to catch every word that was said. And I have known the impassioned orator who swept juries off their feet.

I was in the chambers of Marshall Hall and I shall never forget that very great man. There were times when Marshall Hall had very great failures, and there were times when he had the most resounding triumphs. To see Marshall Hall come into the Court surrounded by a retinue of people carrying pencils and air cushions and all sorts of things was an art in itself. Marshall Hall would sit there and he was not above certain, shall I call them, small tricks. This air cushion which he had—if the cross-examination of his client was getting pretty severe he would put the air cushion under his arm and go fsh! fsh! fsh! So that the cross-examining counsel was very greatly disconcerted. But I have heard Marshall Hall on some of the big cases, the defense of Fahmy at the Old Bailey, the defense of Greenwood, when Marshall Hall quoted to the jury that wonderful thing from Othello: "Put out the light, put out the light." To hear Marshall Hall on the full tide of his forensic oratory was a thing never to be forgotten.

These were great figures in my very early days. Edward Carson, the finest cross-examiner within my recollection at the English Bar, had a very attractive Irish brogue. You all know famous stories of Carson; you read them in the press: "Do you drink?" And the witness says: "That is my business." And Edward Carson says: "Have you any other?" But to hear it in the brogue, the effect was indescribable.

Rufus Isaacs was a great cross-examiner with an extraordinarily simple method of opening in his cross-examination. In the Seddon case, as you know, Seddon was charged with the murder of an old lady named Miss Barrow. On the opening of it in that crowded court—Seddon, the little, composed, ready, versatile prisoner; Rufus Isaacs at his very best, and he begins: "Seddon, did you like Miss Barrow?" And Seddon, surprised by the opening question, said: "Did I like her?" Said Rufus Isaacs: "That was the question". And in that simple, incisive, forcible, direct way one of the most wonderful cross-examinations in the world was begun.

Lord Hewart had an inimitable way with him. I remember a Greek witness called Pappinuckulous, a very undesirable man with a very bad character, and he was going to give evidence—at least, it was said that he was going to give evidence. And he used to come in at one door of the Court and probably leave by the other one. Upon one occasion he tried to push his way in to the front row of counsel which, as you know, in England is absolutely sacrosanct, and the usher put him out. All that went on under the observant eyes of Hewart. And at the supreme moment he came to the jury and said: "Members of the jury, then there was the witness, the Greek Pappinuckulous, sometimes coming through that door, sometimes going out through this other door; occasionally trying to push his way into the ranks of counsel, here, there and everywhere." And then, pointing to the witness box: *"but never there, never there."* The effect upon the jury was profound beyond all words.

Simple Speech Makes the Most Powerful Appeal in Court

And I once heard one of the most moving things I have ever heard in a murder trial by the advocate for the defense, words that I knew by heart, and yet the effect upon the jury was quite startling.

The moving finger writes; and, having writ,
Moves on: Nor all thy Piety nor Wit
Shall lure it back to cancel half a line,
Nor all thy Tears wash out a Word of it.

And that leads me to say that while there are no fixed standards for forensic oratory, and there are no patterns and no types to which the advocate must conform, yet I have found that it is simple speech that makes the most powerful appeal. Now when you think of it, you take the Gettysburg address. It is perhaps the greatest speech that ever fell from the lips of man. "Four-score and seven years ago our fathers brought forth upon this continent a new nation, conceived in liberty, and dedicated to the proposition that all men are created equal." Nothing could exceed it for simplicity. Take the Authorized Version of the Bible and pick where you will. Take the great stories of the Bible, such as the story of the Prodigal Son, and note this essential simplicity. It is the simple, direct, incisive speech that wins the great victories. And so it is in the Court. My experience has always been with regard to the great advocates that I have known that it was the element of direct, forceful, lucid, vivid speech, in all its simplicity that gave them their strength.

Most Cases Are Won by Preparatory Work

My own private view is that most cases are won before you go into Court. It is the preliminary, the preparatory work, the mastering of the brief so that every fact and every figure is in your head, that is all-important. I always found it most useful to have the essential things on a little sheet of my own, so that they could be referred to instantly at any critical moments in the case. The conference, as we call it in England, when you have your discussion with the experts, is of the utmost importance. For example, in the great murder trials it was often necessary to understand the effects of arsenic on the human body and to discover matters which were simply of vital importance as the case proceeded. One of the cases that I had to defend, a case which came from the West Country, was where a woman was charged with the administering of arsenic to various people. It was necessary that we should understand from the point of view of the defense, in every detail, the effect of the administration of arsenic upon the human body. And as you probably know, arsenic taken into the body has certain well-known pathological effects, but one thing is of the greatest importance, it comes down through the strands of the hair from the inside, from the inside. And your expert, by taking the strand of hair, can tell you when the arsenic was first administered and in what probable strength.

In this particular case it so happened that the body of one of the victims was exhumed in the Lewannick Churchyard and they decided to conduct the post-mortem in the churchyard. And by the strangest circumstances, the soil of that Cornish churchyard at Lewannick was charged and impregnated with arsenic, and it was the easiest thing therefore for the cross-examiner to say to the pathological expert from the Home Office, and to tell the jury, that in these organs of the body there were so many grains of arsenic, which might have come from the soil. How are you to know some of that arsenic was not deposited from the soil of the Lewannick Churchyard? That was easy, but the strands of hair, nothing would avail to say that the arsenic found there came from the outside. That came from administration from within. And so you perceive how in a case of that nature, and indeed in all cases, the preliminary work of conference, of understanding details that may perhaps never be used in the case, is of the utmost importance.

Importance of a Proper Opening Statement to the Jury

As I said before, all that side of the work of advocacy is an integral part of the mastering of the brief, the assimilation of the expert's knowledge in the conference room, then into the Court and the presentation of the case. We begin, as you know, by the leading counsel for the Crown, or leading counsel for the plaintiff, making a short opening statement to the jury in a jury case. And again, it would be almost a truism to say that more cases are won by a proper presentation of that opening statement than in any other way. The jury, fresh to the Court, fresh to the case, hear a presentation, and they are never, never likely to forget. Shaken they may be by cross-examination, by subsequent witnesses, but that first, clear, incisive impression made upon the jury is beyond all price.

Then there is the calling of witnesses, what we call the examination-in-chief—a most delicate and difficult task. And I have always found for my own part that, if you can so conduct your examination-in-chief that your opponent must sit still, that is a very great triumph; but if you so conduct yourself that you give your opponent the opportunity of protesting against leading questions or other irregularities your influence begins to go, your control over the jury begins to vanish. And I can not emphasize as much as I would wish the importance of paying attention to the proper examination-in-chief. Indeed, I would lay down for myself that a very sound working rule is so to conduct your case that the interruptions of your opponent are matters that will be frowned on by the Court.

Cross-Examination in the "Blazing Car Murder" Case

And then cross-examination — the thing which everybody thinks he can do so well and the thing that is rarely so very easy to do well. Sometimes you have a moment of inspiration. At one of our big murder cases, which is now fairly well known as the "Blazing Car Murder," a man called Rouse was accused of burning the body of his victim at a little village called Hardingstone in Northhamptonshire in the middle of the night. It was a most remarkable case. I wish I had time to tell you about it. The victim was never identified, although the case was discussed from one end of our land to the other. Nobody ever came forward anywhere to say they had ever known this unknown man, and there were all sorts of features of that kind. The question before the jury, raised by the defense, was whether the burning was accidental. There had been a joint—it was a Ford car—and there had been a joint where it was said that the petrol leaked and the heat of the car had made this joint much looser. That was the line upon which the defense was run. I was the counsel for the Crown and a man came in to the box for the defense who called himself an expert witness. As you probably have it in Canada and as we have it in England, any case of what I will call notoriety always brings people from all parts of the land volunteering to give evidence because of the kudos that their presence in the box gives.

This was a man exactly of that type. And there was I rising to cross-examine him, and whether it was inspiration or what it was I don't know, but my first question in the cross-examination of the man certainly wasn't in the brief. I said: "Tell me, sir, what is the coefficient of the expansion of brass?" And he didn't know. I am not sure that I did, but he couldn't ask me questions and I could ask him, and he didn't know. And from that moment, of course, it was easy.

Skillful Cross-Examination You Have to Get from Your Judgment

And the cross-examination to a very large extent must depend upon the kind of man you are. You can't get it from your brief; you must use your judgment. And above all don't ask the one question too many. They tell a grand story about a bastardy case in England where in the old days they used evidence of association as tending to show that the man accused was the father of the child. And in one of the country assizes towns there was an old farmer called to give evidence. He was cross-examined and the cross-examination proceeded upon these lines: "Well, sir, I suppose you were young once yourself?" "Yes sir," he says, "I was young once myself". "And I suppose you used to go walking through the lovely lanes and fields?"—"Oh yes," he says, "I walked the lanes and fields, all right". "And I suppose there were occasions when you went in those lanes and fields in the moonlight?"—"Oh yes," he said, "I went in the moonlight." "I suppose there were occasions when you had a girl with you?"—"Yes," he said, "there were occasions, I will admit, in these fields and lanes on moonlight nights when I had a nice girl with me." "Well," said the counsel, "I suppose there were occasions when you used to sit down on the hedge bottom on these moonlit nights with this nice girl?"—"Oh yes," he said, "we did that".

There he should have stopped. Instead of that, he asked one question too many; and he said to the old man: "Well now, tell me, there was nothing wrong about that, was there?" And the old man said to the judge: *"Am I bound to answer that question?"* No doubt, there are many classical illustrations of the man who in cross-examining gets all that he can ever wish to have, and who cannot restrain himself, and asks the one question too many.

The Advocate Must Be a Man of Complete Integrity

Then we have, of course, the final address to the jury when all the evidence is over, when everything is presented in its final form. All these things about which I do not presume to speak at any length are all essential parts of the work of the advocate, but the matters that I did just want to speak about in a general way, before I sit down, about advocacy are these—they are quite general. The first quality beyond all others in your advocate, whatever his type, the first quality is that he must be a man of character. Without that in the long run all else fails. The Court must be able to rely upon you. Your word must be your bond, and when you assert as a matter of fact, to the Court those matters which are within your personal knowledge the Court must be able to know that you in your integrity, on your responsibility as a member of a great profession, are being loyal to the Court.

You will forgive me saying it, but I am jealous of the very great reputation of the law. Its future is in our hands; and it is a solemn responsibility and duty cast upon every member of the practicing profession that in all he does, in his duty to the client, in his duty to the Court and in his duty to the State, he shall be above and beyond all other things a man of complete integrity. Whatever gifts or attributes he may possess, he shall have this supreme qualification that he is a man of integrity and a man of honor.

An Advocate Should Be a Man of Culture as Well as Character

The other general observation I would like to make with regard to the advocate is this: I think he must be not only a man of character but a man of culture. You may remember in Sir Walter Scott's *Guy Mannering* the figure of Counsellor Pleydell, who went into his room and there were all the great poets and writers on the shelf, and pointing to the books, he said: "These are my stock in trade."

There can be no doubt that whilst the knowledge of law and the training in law is essential, of itself it is insufficient. There must be the cultural background out of which springs the serene mind, the subtle understanding, the insight, that which differentiates man from man. "Two men look out through the same bars, one sees the mud, and one the stars." That cultural background is open to everybody. It may very well be that there are some here who have not had the opportunity of a classical education and been made familiar with all the great ancient writers; it may very well be so. We are not all so fortunate as to be born in circumstances which permit it. It may be, that many were unable, as indeed they were in England, to go to universities like Oxford and Cambridge and to spend the leisure years in reading, absorbing and imbibing. These are very great advantages but they are not possible for all.

But what is possible for all is that there should be a cultural background created by themselves. Take the whole field of literature and what a repository, what a treasure we have there. Take the Authorized Version itself of King James' Bible. Why, there are some men who have achieved very great fame who had little more cultural background than that very great book. Some of the greatest examples of oratory in our land and in our speech were given by John Bright, and if you will examine that oratory you will find it derives from the Authorized Version. His very great speech in the House of Commons on the Crimean War owed all its power to the narrative of Herod's slaying of the first born. Lincoln, President Lincoln, owed much to the same source. And to familiarize yourself with that great repository of English prose is in itself an education.

Familiarity with the Greatest Expressions in Speech Is Essential

Shakespeare! Even a nodding acquaintance with Shakespeare is of the greatest possible advantage to the advocate, for there speech has reached the highest form that we have ever known or are ever likely to know. And if we can get just a touch of historical background with it, it becomes most moving and most magical. A few months ago I was privileged to be in Shakespeare's birthplace, Stratford-on-Avon, and I reflected that it was at Stratford-on-Avon that Shakespeare came at the end of his short and crowded life, and it was at Stratford-on-Avon that he penned those memorable words in which he took farewell of all the imaginative beauty which he had created. For it was there that he wrote *The Tempest,* and into the mouth of Prospero he put perhaps the greatest form of speech we are ever likely to know:

You do look, my son, in a mov'd sort,
As if you were dismay'd: be cheerful, Sir.
Our revels now are ended. These our actors,
As I foretold you, were all spirits, and
Are melted into air, into thin air:
And, like the baseless fabric of this vision,
The cloud-capp'd towers, the gorgeous palaces,
The solemn temples, the great globe itself,
Yea, all which it inherit, shall dissolve,
And, like this insubstantial pageant faded,
Leave not a rack behind. We are such stuff
As dreams are made of, and our little life
Is rounded with a sleep.

To be familiar even for a moment with the greatest expression of that kind is, I think, not only a valuable addition to the advocate's art but an indispensable addition; and you no doubt have your own favorite passages in Shakespeare. The only other one I will quote is where I think the loveliness is still as perfect:

Sit Jessica: Look, how the floor of heaven
Is thick inlaid with patines of bright gold:
There's not the smallest orb which thou behold'st,
But in his motion like an angel sings.
Still quiring to the young-ey'd cherubins,—
Such harmony is in immortal souls;
But whilst this muddy vesture of decay
Doth grossly close it in, we cannot hear it.

I cite that merely to illustrate the admonition: Don't rely too much upon the law books. Our very dear friend George Pepper the other night made a beautiful speech at Osgoode Hall, and in the course of it he said: "If I were pressed I could tell you of every form of dower, dower at common law, and all the rest of it." And I said to George this morning: "My dear George, it was lovely to hear you, but let me tell you that in thirty-four years at the Bar I have never had one single case in which dower ever came into it."

And whilst these things are essential and training is invaluable, my advice is: Let your advocate be not merely a man of law—let him be a man of letters. Let him love the humanities, and from that springs the insight, the understanding and the judgment.

Cultivate and Love the Right Use of Words

The last thing that I would like to say to you, as a third matter for the advocate, is to cultivate the love of words. It is important to cultivate words, to select the right words, to put them in the right order, to know something of their meaning, of their association, of their sound. You know, it is a most fascinating world. Again take Shakespeare: "The *uncertain* glory of an April day." Nobody but a Shakespeare could have used the word "uncertain" to convey everything. Just think of it: "The uncertain glory of an April day." It is perfect.

And if you examine your Shakespeare you will find that is what Shakespeare was. He was a word lover. He invented, of course, a great many of the words which have gone into our common speech, simply made them up, but he also used the words of Romeo to Juliet on the balcony: "O, speak again, *bright* angel." Think of the use of "bright"—"O speak again, bright angel." Think how he used that word "bright" in so many places: "So quick bright things come to confusions," and so on.

That love of words, that discrimination in the use of words, is all essential to the advocate. The presentation of your case in the appropriate language, in the inimitable language, is part of the art of persuasion; and persuasion is the whole end of it, as I understand it. The Bar is the source and guardian of the virtue of the bench. It is the good Bar that makes the good bench.

And therefore it is the greatest possible pleasure to feel I have spent my life at the Bar; and now when I sit upon the bench, with occasionally a strong yearning to get back into the arena, nothing gives me greater joy than to see the young advocate presenting his case to the very best of his ability—immature it may be, but with all the signs of promise. And if I find, as I do find, an advocate with a nice sense of words who presents the argument in an attractive form, my heart warms to the advocate and I do my best to encourage and to help him on his way.

Adapted from Vol. 34, American Bar Association Journal (1948).

The Dialectic of Advocacy

BY ADLOW ELIJAH

TO MOST PEOPLE the courtroom epitomizes everything involved in the legal process. Actually very little litigation ever reaches the courtroom. From the statistics that are available it appears that no more than 10% of the writs entered in court ever reach the trial stage. Of these a fair proportion are settled before the tribunal has a chance to render a decision.

It would be wrong to assume from this that our method of administering justice is inefficient or unsuitable. Actually a multitude of factors are involved in the process of litigation and all of them play an important part in helping terminate a dispute. Those who are aware of these factors, be they professionals or laymen, exploit them in the manoeuvers that attend controversy. In some instances these practices are condemned as unethical and savoring of abuse of process. In others they are condoned as a proper exercise of one's legal rights. All of the practices, be they proper or improper, combine to make up that vast fund of expedients and devices which in the composite can be labelled the dialectic of advocacy.

Before exploring the substance of this dialectic it would be well to outline the variety of motives which help determine the tactics and strategy of a controversy. Some disputes arise from an honest difference of opinion as to the facts or the legal rights of the parties. No small amount of litigation presents the spectacle of parties approaching the discussion of their problem in a spirit of mutual respect and good will. Frequently the barrier to an amicable adjustment of the matter will be found in extraneous factors. An administrator of an estate will oppose a claim for services to the deceased even though he knows that the services were rendered. To protect himself from criticism by heirs he insists that a court find that the money is due and payable. Similarly, a corporation having many stockholders may be sued, and the officers, to avoid criticism for spending corporate funds in the payment of a claim, will prefer to let the matter be litigated, even though they recognize the merit of the claim.

Occasionally a situation arises that is without precedent, and the parties, being uncertain of the legal aspects, will litigate the matter, often by submitting the case on an agreed statement of facts. In this manner the adjustment is effected by transferring the burden from the parties immediately concerned to the court.

Most disputes, however, lack the congeniality described above. In fact, so far as the parties are concerned, a controversy is rarely the consequence of a misconception with respect to facts or law. At the bottom of most controversies will be found a determined insistence by one or both of the parties to have their own way regardless of the right or wrong of the situation. To achieve this, resort is had to those expedients which are the working tools of the advocate's art and which, for want of a better term, are here designated the dialectic of advocacy. Of what does this dialectic consist?

No description is possible unless we first summarize the implications of litigation. Certain of these implications are commonplace and readily recognized. For instance, a man says to another: "You owe me $25. If you don't pay me, I'll sue you." The man to whom this demand is directed immediately weighs the bother and expense of defending such a cause against the comparatively small amount which it would cost him to avoid all this trouble. Even if he is convinced that he is right and that he does not owe the claimant anything, he will in most cases pay rather than be annoyed. In this case the threat to resort to the courts has defeated the cause of justice.

In a like manner the "deadbeat" or slow payer has an advantage over his creditor who dreads the expense of litigation and the time lost in promoting it. When his debtor in response to his demand says, "Go ahead and sue me" he thinks twice before he calls upon his lawyer to start proceedings. The expense of litigation in time and money weighs heavily with thinking people in deciding whether to prosecute or defend a claim. Chronic litigants and unethical lawyers count heavily on these considerations in promoting groundless and in resisting just claims.

Aside from the expense involved in litigating a claim, there are other attendant embarrassments. A threat to trustee the wages of a debtor who may have a good defense against his creditor will often hasten the discharge of a debt for no other reason than the debtor dreads the thought of having his wages attached or the fact of his indebtedness being brought to the attention of his employer.

A threat to attach property at a time when the owner plans to transfer it has sufficed to force settlement of a groundless claim on many occasions. This expedient has served the interests of unconscionable brokers in pursuing groundless claims for real estate commissions. In my own experience as a lawyer, while representing the seller of property, I have made settlements with as many as three different claimants for a broker's commission on one transaction. If one would suggest that a courageous man would resist such baseless demands, the short answer is that to resist is to invite delay in effecting the transfer of property and to incur an expense out of all proportion to the satisfaction which eventual victory over the petty blackmailer affords. We must at all times keep in mind that, notwithstanding the justice of one's position, there is no assurance that justice will invariably prevail. There is little comfort in the occasional reminder that even judges and juries can be wrong.

If cold-blooded calculation will occasionally suggest that one forego a valid claim or submit to a groundless demand, then how much more persuasive will a suggestion of conduct be which has implications of social or financial embarrassment or ruin. Consider the many breach of promise cases settled before even a writ was served for the sole reason that the man dreaded the effect of a scandal on his social position or his business credit. Men have paid substantial sums, though innocent of blame, rather than become involved in matters so scandalous.

A great many people have an exaggerated idea of the amount of publicity which their appearance in court will receive, and hasten to settle a matter before it reaches the trial stage. Actually, this aspect of litigation is very much overestimated. Except in matters involving very prominent people, an amazing amount of sensational and scandalous matter passes through the courts without receiving the slightest attention from the press.

Many years ago, a very excited individual appeared in my office to consult me about a paternity case in which his son was involved. The man was on the verge of a breakdown. He walked back and forth expressing great apprehension with respect to the effect of the scandal on his family. One who listened to him would imagine that his name was a household word all over America. Finally I decided to set him aright on this aspect of his problem. My expedient to accomplish this was a simple one. After quieting him, I asked him, "What's the name of the Vice President of the United States?"

"Damned if I know," was his answer. "If you don't know the name of the Vice President, how many people do you imagine know who you are? Your're worried about an insignificant matter. The chances are no one will know about it except those whom you tell. Stop worrying about the scandal. It'll be forgotten sooner than you think." And it was. This man's viewpoint revealed a mental condition that has made it easy for many lawyers to quickly settle cases in which they were not invariably right.

When we use the word dialectic in connection with the legal profession we are concerned with the means of promoting the objectives of that profession. In a vulgar sense it refers to the "know how" of the lawyer's calling. Some people call them "the tricks of the profession", and no small portion of them are referred to in certain circles as "shyster tricks". But this by no means would preclude the employment of this dialectic in the furtherance of proper objectives. Just as a stubborn refusal to yield may discourage a worthy claimant from insisting on his due, a stubborn insistence on one's rights may suggest to a determined defaulter that it is futile to further resist an honest claim. The intangibles of advocacy are inextricably involved in uncertainty with respect to who is better served by this dialectic, the worthy or the unworthy.

Certain lawyers who have participated in unusually protracted proceedings enjoy a reputation which serves them well in their profession. Rather than become involved with them in burdensome litigation, parties will make great concessions in the interest of the settlement of disputes in which they represent parties. By the same token lawyers who are known to fight hard, to indulge in personalities, to badger witnesses, and to leave nothing undone to win will frequently obtain quick settlements from parties who shun these practices. The dramatics of the courtroom have implications which transcend the immediate cause in issue. It is a notorious fact that lawyers specializing in accident litigation will refuse to settle cases in which the liability is certain and the damages are great for the reason that a large damage award properly publicized will help them obtain good settlements in other cases in which neither the liability nor the injury are as clear-cut or well defined.

Perhaps nothing in the entire realm of advocacy serves the purposes of those determined to avoid a decision based on a clear-cut issue as does an insistence on the right to a trial by jury. Here is a method of reaching a decision that defies logical justification. Its shortcomings are notorious; the methods prescribed for its employment are cumbersome, slow, and costly. The mere request for a trial by jury suffices to postpone the trial for from two to four years. And yet plaintiffs as well as defendants, in important accident cases, prefer the jury trial. That both sides insist on this right poses one of the baffling paradoxes of the entire legal experience. We can well understand why the victim of an accident might confide in a jury, but the spectacle of an insurance company demanding a jury trial baffles explanation. Except for the delay which a jury trial entails, no other advantage accrues to the defendant. Possibly this delay suffices to make the claimant for damages more reasonable in his demands and thereby expedites an early settlement. Whatever the purpose may be, the demand for a jury trial serves some ulterior purpose of the lawyer who claims it and is another item in the inventory of the dialectic of advocacy.

Once a writ is served on a defendant and a controversy acquires a courthouse status, a vast variety of expedients become available to both claimant and respondent in their struggle for ascendancy. While pleadings are designed for the purpose of crystallizing the issue, this objective is rarely attained. Although a few causes will present a clear-cut issue, in most cases the parties appear more determined than ever to keep the matter as confused and complicated as conditions will permit. Some answers that have been filed to declarations are not without their humorous aspects. Consider the defendant in an action on a negotiable note who, in addition to a general denial of the plaintiff's allegations, further answered by

(1) Denying the signature;
(2) Denying that he received any consideration for the note;
(3) Alleging that the note was made on the Lord's Day and therefore, unenforceable;
(4) Claiming that the note was given for a gambling debt and therefore illegal and unenforceable;
(5) Alleging that he was a minor at the time of the alleged transaction and not liable on any contract made by him;
(6) And by further alleging that he has paid the note.

What little progress has been made in the development of legal procedure has been reflected in the simplification of our pleadings so as to keep these evasive practices down to a minimum. But plenty have survived to keep litigants in a chronic state of excitement. Consider the dilatory pleas, the interrogatories, the motions to strike out answers to interrogatories, and the many other devices which have a proper place in our procedural structure, but which, at the same time, can be used to wear down and exhaust an opponent. It would be error to assume that these practices are only resorted to by the "sharpers" of the profession. Actually the so-called better lawyers indulge in them as much, if not more, than do the more humble members of the profession. The amenities of the law have been enriched but little by the so-called big names at the Bar.

In perhaps no phase of litigation is more resourcefulness revealed than in the tactics employed to deny one a trial. It is then that doctor's certificates, engagements in other courts, the absence of witnesses, and a variety of other pretexts are invoked to postpone the actual hearing of the merits of the cause. Lawyers with an extensive practice are particularly well favored in this situation, and can always plead an actual engagement elsewhere as an excuse for securing a postponement. In some courts, certain lawyers have actually succeeded in preventing people from ever getting a trial by resort to this expedient. On the other hand, when the trial lists are handled by strong and competent judges the expedient loses its effectiveness. Judges have been known to order cases to trial with the suggestion that if the lawyer was busy elsewhere he engage other counsel to handle the matter.

To the average layman, the amount of work involved in the preliminaries of trial is overlooked as negligible. The pleadings, the hearings in the motion sessions, the markings for trial, and the postponements mean little to him: to the lawyers and their office attachés, they mean much. If parties wilt under the ordeal and settle on unfavorable terms, it is because, as the process unfolds, its drain on one's patience serves to cool the ardor to litigate. If the bulk of the causes entered in court are never tried, it is because the courthouse hardly serves to whet one's appetite for litigation. Hearings on motions are dull and uninteresting. Calls to a lawyer's office to answer interrogatories consume valuable time of the parties without affording any immediate prospect of satisfaction or relief. When finally one arrives in court with all his witnesses and learns that his opponent is engaged elsewhere, or is sick, or out of the city, he begins to think that his venture in litigation is a foolhardy enterprise. The corridors of courthouses everywhere echo with the complaints of those who doubt whether they will ever have their day in court. No small prejudice that exists against lawyers derives from the multitude of frustrated litigants whose hopes were shattered somewhere along the road leading to the courtroom. There may be exceptional instances in which this disappointment might be attributed to a default on the part of counsel, but the fact remains that in the majority of instances the condition is a normal consequence of what is commonly referred to as the "law's delays."

If the disappointments and vexations that one encounters along the road to the courtroom can prove so disheartening, what must the reaction of one be to the courtroom experience itself? How this unfolds depends on a variety of circumstances. In the first place, the judge who presides will determine to a considerable extent whether the cause will be disposed of with dispatch or whether it will drag along interminably. In the second place the competence of one's own counsel will have much bearing on how one's cause is presented. And, finally, the nature of opposing counsel becomes an important factor in determining how one's cause fares. If one has been fortunate in the choice of counsel, he will lose little by the absence of a worthy judge or by the presence of a vigorous opposing counsel. If he is fortunate enough to be served by an able attorney and, at the same time, to find an able judge on the Bench, he will be little discomfited by opposing counsel, no matter how vigorous he may appear. Such ideal conditions do not always appear. It is then that Mr. Litigant finds the courtroom a mighty uncomfortable place.

Many books have been written on the art of cross-examination. Strange to say few books, if any, have been written on the art of presenting one's own witnesses. Stranger still, is the fact that the gift of presenting a case clearly and effectively is almost as rare as the gift of cross-examination. As a consequence a great many litigants discover very quickly, after a trial has gotten underway, that it is not as easy to get over to the judge or to the jury their version of the cause in issue. Particularly vexing does it become when opposing counsel interposes objections in a manner to prevent any clear-cut account to be rendered to the court. It is here that the advocate exhausts his art to shape the evidence to serve his purposes.

With a strong judge presiding the danger from these practices is kept down to a minimum. Where weak men preside the danger of lawyers confounding witnesses and distorting the true picture is great. It is recorded of the great Chief Justice Shaw that when Rufus Choate argued certain evidence to the jury, the Chief Justice interrupted him to suggest that there was no such evidence. With such judges on the Bench the interests of justice were invariably protected.

A great many lawyers approach their courtroom responsibilities with dignity and respect, and with a desire to dispose of the matter at hand expeditiously. It is amazing how many cases are disposed of in less than an hour, once they have reached the trial stage, and the judge considers himself fortunate where lawyers with no other interest than to secure a decision present their witnesses, rebut opposing witnesses and then argue the merits of the cause. If all causes were handled in this manner, there would be no docket congestion and the court experience would have little of the threat which it now carries. Unfortunately, not all lawyers are content to dispose of matters expeditiously. Some lawyers are congenital exhibitionists and are determined to dramatize the most simple and commonplace situation into a cause célébre.

In my own experience as a judge, a lawyer whose opponent had not appeared in court with his parties on the day of trial and who had won his cause by default brought his parties forward and asked that they be sworn. When I advised him that no trial was necessary because of the defendant's default, he persisted in his demand for a trial. When I denied it to him, he took an exception to my ruling with a view to taking an appeal. This lawyer was unhappy because his client was denied an opportunity to watch him present a case. Disposing of the litigation was secondary to a desire to exhibit his talents as a lawyer.

On many occasions, counsel will confide to the judge that a certain decision is inevitable, but that they are continuing the trial with a view to impressing their clients with the amount of work involved. The motives for dragging out causes are not invariably associated with the client's interests. On many occasions in the past, lawyers who have prevailed in cases which they tried before me have nevertheless criticized me because they felt I was too insistent on their trying their cases expeditiously.

More than one lawyer has turned defeat into victory by the simple expedient of waiting out one of these time consuming types. It often happens that in dragging out a cause evidence crops up that was unexpected, and the tables are turned. It is this very contingency that encourages many lawyers, particularly lawyers whose cause appears hopeless, to drag out the process of examination or cross-examination in the hope of some fortuitous development. Resort to these tactics serves to wear out the parties, to exhaust their patience, and to hasten the settlement or abandonment of cases. Lawyers who are conscious of being in the right shun these practices and seek a speedy decision.

When a lawyer with a good case drags it needlessly, the condition can be attributed to incompetence and nothing more. The tricks of the profession are many; the expedients to which resort is had to attain a tactical advantage are well recognized; but the sad fact remains that many of the practices witnessed in the courtroom are attempted without design or motive. If they uncover anything favorable to the lawyer's case or embarrass the other side, the result is purely coincidental. It is amazing how much of the effort involved in the trial of a cause is without purpose or design.

When we speak of the dialectic of advocacy we speak of expedients consciously employed to attain a certain result. Quite frequently lawyers will claim credit for having planned an examination or cross-examination with certain objectives in mind, but the claim is inspired by hindsight. There are many lawyers, particularly among the older members of the Bar, whose patterns of behavior for handling causes are well known and whose methods of presentation can be predicted in advance. Some of these men are rough on an opponent. Their notoriety at the Bar often serves to hasten the abandonment or settlement of causes in which they represent parties. But the interests of justice suffer little under their efforts if the opponent is served by a competent counsel and if a capable judge presides over the trial of the cause. Lawyers have a legitimate right to aspire for the success of their clients, but a judge has a sworn duty to see that justice is done. A law suit is not a contest designed to reveal which side has the best, or the smartest, or the trickiest lawyer. Actually, the lawyer is a mere incident in a cause, and his interests as an advocate are secondary and incidental to the major public interests of seeing that justice is done between the parties. It is for this reason that the dialectic of advocacy, if it is to serve the interests of justice, must be employed in accordance with the rules and under the supervision of a competent judge.

Adapted from Vol. 36, Boston University Law Review (1956).

The Ethics of Advocacy

BY CHARLES P. CURTIS

I

I WANT FIRST OF ALL to put advocacy in its proper setting. It is a special case of vicarious conduct. A lawyer devotes his life and career to acting for other people. So too does the priest, and in another way the banker. The banker handles other people's money. The priest handles other people's spiritual aspirations. A lawyer handles other people's troubles.

But there is a difference. The loyalty of a priest or clergyman runs, not to the particular parishioner whose joys or troubles he is busy with, but to his church; and the banker looks to his bank. It is the church or the bank, not he, but he on its behalf, who serves the communicant or the borrower. Their loyalties run in a different direction than a lawyer's.

So too when a lawyer works for the government. His loyalties hang on a superior peg, like the priest's or the clergyman's. For it is fiction to say that he only has the government for his client. The government is too big. It absorbs him. He is a part of it.

Likewise with the general counsel for a corporation. His identification with his client is all but complete. Taft in some lectures at the Albany Law School,[1] referring to work in the legal department of a corporation, said, "Such employment leads to a lawyer's becoming nothing more than an officer of the corporation as closely identified with it as if he was the president, the secretary or the treasurer."[2] Indeed, he usually is a director or a vice-president.

Not so the lawyer in private practice. His loyalty runs to his client. He has no other master. Not the court? you ask. Does not the court take the same position as the church or the bank? Is not the lawyer an officer of the court? Why doesn't the court have

1 The Hubbard Lectures in May 1914.
2 Cheatham, *Cases and Materials on the Legal Profession* 60 (1938).

first claim on his loyalty? No, in a paradoxical way. The lawyer's official duty, required of him indeed by the court, is to devote himself to the client. The court comes second by the court's, that is the law's, own command.

Lord Brougham, in his defense of Queen Caroline, in her divorce case, told the House of Lords: "I once before took occasion to remind your Lordships, which was unnecessary, but there are many whom it may be needful to remind, that an advocate, by the sacred duty which he owes his client, knows in the discharge of that office but one person in the world—that client and no other. . . . Nay, separating even the duties of a patriot from those of an advocate, and casting them if need be to the wind, he must go on reckless of the consequences, if his fate it should unhappily be to involve his country in confusion for his client's protection."[3]

Lord Brougham was a great advocate, and when he made this statement he was arguing a great case, the divorce of Queen Caroline from George IV before the House of Lords. Plainly he was exerting more than his learning and more than his legal ability. Years later he explained to William Forsythe, the author of a book on lawyers called *Hortensius,* who had asked him what he meant. Before you read Brougham's reply, let me remind you that the king, George IV, was the one who was pressing the divorce, which Brougham was defending, and that George had contracted a secret marriage, while he was heir apparent, with Mrs. FitzHerbert, a Roman Catholic. Brougham knew this, and knew too that it was enough to deprive the king of his crown under the Act of Settlement. Brougham wrote:[4]

> The real truth is, that the statement was anything rather than a deliberate and well-considered opinion. It was a menace, and it was addressed chiefly to George IV, but also to wiser men, such as Castlereagh and Wellington. I was prepared, *in case of necessity,* that is in case the Bill passed the Lords, to do two things—first, to resist in the Commons *with the country at my back;* but next, if need be, to dispute the King's title, to show he had forfeited the crown by marrying a Catholic, in the words of the Act, "as if he were naturally dead." What I said was fully

3 Macmillan, *Law and Other Things* 195 (1937).

4 Lord Brougham to Wm. Forsythe in 1859, which he put into the third edition of his book, *Hortensius.* This is quoted in Cheatham, *Cases and Materials on the Legal Profession* 227 (1938).

understood by Geo. IV; perhaps by the Duke and Castlereagh, and I am confident it would have prevented them from pressing the Bill beyond a certain point.

Lord Brougham's menace has become the classic statement of the loyalty which a lawyer owes to his client, perhaps because being a menace it is so extreme. And yet the Canons of Ethics is scarcely more moderate, "... entire devotion to the interest of the client, warm zeal in the maintenance and defense of his rights and the exertion of his utmost learning and ability. . . ."[5]

You see how entire the devotion is, how single his duty is. How far must a lawyer accompany his client and turn his back on the court? Speaking of the New York Bar after the close of the Civil War, Mark Howe says, "Its morality and its principle descended to the level of the men by whom it was employed, and among the employers neither principle nor morality was evident. As a consequence, the lawyers lost the persuasion of their ancestors that the profession possesses other responsibilities than those owing to their clients. . . . . . . the leaders at the New York Bar had lost all sense that the law was for them what the church was for the clergy."[6]

I cannot forget what one of the very best Boston trustees once told me. He had, of course, in his many trusts large real estate holdings in Boston. He was a citizen of Boston. He told me once that he either refused to contribute to the campaigns of candidates for mayor or else he contributed to both of them, because, he said, "The assessments on the real estate I hold in trust, things being as they are in Boston, would be put in hazard if I were to come out definitely for a candidate and he lost." The better trustee, and he was a good trustee, the worse a citizen.

The person for whom you are acting very reasonably expects you to treat him better than you do other people, which is just another way of saying that you owe him a higher standard of conduct than you owe to others. This goes back a long way. It is the pre-platonic ethics which Socrates had disposed of at the very outset of the *Republic;* that is that justice consists of doing good to your friends and harm to your enemies. A lawyer, therefore, in-

[5] This is in the Fifteenth Canon, where what I have quoted is put in quotation marks; from what source I wish I knew.

[6] 60 Harv. L. Rev. 840 (1947).

sensibly finds himself treating his client better than others; and therefore others worse than his client. A lawyer, or a trustee, or anyone acting for another, has lower standards of conduct toward outsiders than he has toward his clients or his beneficiaries or his patrons against the outsiders. He is required to treat outsiders as if they were barbarians and enemies. The more good faith and devotion the lawyer owes to his client, the less he owes to others when he is acting for his client. It is as if a man had only so much virtue, and the more he gives to one, the less he has available for anyone else. The upshot is that a man whose business it is to act for others finds himself, in his dealings on his client's behalf with outsiders, acting on a lower standard than he would if he were acting for himself, and lower, too, than any standard his client himself would be willing to act on, lower, in fact, than anyone on his own.

You devote yourself to the interests of another at the peril of yourself. Vicarious action tempts a man too far from himself. Men will do for others what they are not willing to do for themselves—nobler as well as ignoble things. What I want to do now is to illustrate this in the practice of law by a number of perplexing situations. They raise ethical problems, but none of them, I think, has a simple right or wrong answer, and I know of no canons of ethics or morals which lead to any answer. How could there be when the cause of the perplexity is the difference between acting for another and acting for yourself?

II

I will start with the story of Sam the Lookout.

A distinguished New York lawyer was once called over to sit in a conference of admiralty lawyers with the crew of a ship which had been in a collision. The lawyers were going over the testimony which the members of the crew would give at the approaching trial. Finally they came to the lookout, and the Captain, who was asking the questions, turned to him and said, "You, of course, were up in the eyes on the forecastle keeping a sharp lookout." The seaman squirmed in his chair, twisted his cap, and said, "The truth is, Captain, I was in the head having a smoke." The lawyers leaned forward, but the Captain turned to reassure them. "That's all right, gentlemen, he'll testify that he was keeping a sharp lookout. Won't you Sam?" "No," said Sam, "I guess I can't do that."

And then, this lawyer said, such a storm of indignation burst over Sam as he had never seen. The Captain and the rest of the crew cursed him for betraying his ship. Let him go to the head if he had to. Let him even have his smoke if he must. But when he did let him also take the consequences. The collision was not his fault, they agreed. The fog was too thick for him to have seen the other vessel in time, but was he now going to let his own ship down? If he left his post on his own affairs, he had no right to make the ship pay the penalty. What if it was perjury? He'd taken that risk. Not the ship, but he had taken the risk of perjury.

The admiralty lawyers set back and listened. They seemed to recognize that there were peculiarities in the ethics of the sea which they could not but respect, though distinctly they were not a part of admiralty law. The meeting broke up with Sam still obstinately refusing to do what, the Captain insisted, any good seaman ought to know he was in honor bound to do.

Then I tried to find a situation in which a lawyer may be in duty bound to lie for his client. I asked an eminent and very practical judge. He told me he hoped I was joking. I went to two leaders of the bar, both ex-presidents of bar associations. One said, "No, I don't believe there is such a situation." The other said, "Why, of course, there are." But he has not yet given me one.

Finally I thought I had one. It was the case of a lawyer who, I felt very sure, had lied to me when he told me that he did not represent a certain man. I was secretary of the Grievance Committee of the Bar Association at the time, and I was trying to find out whether this man had been blackmailed by some other lawyers. I went to this lawyer and asked him. If he had even admitted to me that he had represented this man, I should have been pretty sure that the man had indeed been blackmailed, for I knew that he had not gone to his regular counsel, but to a different lawyer, in order to keep the whole affair secret. The lawyer told me he did not even know the man.

I recall thinking then that this lawyer was doing just right by lying to me, but I don't know who else agreed with me. My lawyer had gone on to make the same denial to the Grievance Committee, and later, when the Bar Association brought proceedings for his disbarment, in the course of those proceedings, persisted in his denial before the court itself. He was not disbarred, but he was subsequently reprimanded and suspended.[7]

I take it that it is inadmissible to lie to the court. A lawyer's duty to his client cannot rise higher than its source, which is the court. Perhaps my lawyer did wrong to lie to the Grievance Committee, but I am not so sure. I know he did right to lie to me, and I am inclined to hope that in his place I should have lied to the Grievance Committee as well.

It may be that it all depends on whether you are asked the question by someone who has a right to ask it. If he has no right to ask and if simple silence would, or even might, lead him to the truth, then, I believe your lawyer is in duty bound to lie. For the truth is not his, but yours. It belongs to you and he is bound to keep it for you, even more vigorously than if it were only his own. He must lie, then, beyond the point where he could permissibly lie for himself. But this only illuminates the problem from a different angle, the right to ask instead of the duty to answer. Let me give you a situation in which a lawyer must lie to someone who does have the right to ask him the question.

A lawyer is called on the telephone by a former client who is unfortunately at the time a fugitive from justice. The police want him and he wants advice. The lawyer goes to where his client is, hears the whole story, and advises him to surrender. Finally he succeeds in persuading him that this is the best thing to do and they make an appointment to go to police headquarters. Meanwhile the client is to have two days to wind up his affairs and make his farewells. When the lawyer gets back to his office, a police inspector is waiting for him, and asks him whether his client is in town and where he is. Here are questions which the police have every right to ask of anybody, and even a little hesitation in this unfortunate lawyer's denials will reveal enough to betray his client. Of course he lies.

And why not? The relation between a lawyer and his client is one of the intimate relations. You would lie for your wife. You would lie for your child. There are others with whom you are intimate enough, close enough, to lie for them when you would

[7] Some of these proceedings can be found in, In the Matter of Sleeper, 251 Mass 6, 146 NE 269 (1925).

not lie for yourself. At what point do you stop lying for them? I don't know and you are not sure.

To every one of us come occasions when we don't want to tell the truth, not all of it, certainly not all of it at once, when we want to be something less than candid, a little disingenuous. Indeed, to be candid with ourselves, there are times when we deliberately and more or less justifiably undertake to tell something less or something different. Complete candor to anyone but ourselves is a virtue that belongs to the saints, to the secure, and to the very courageous. Even when we do want to tell the truth, all of it, ultimately, we see no reason why we should not take our own time, tell it as skillfully and as gracefully as we can, and most of us doubt our own ability to do this as well by ourselves and for ourselves as another could do it for us. So we go to a lawyer. He will make a better fist of it than we can.

I don't see why we should not come out roundly and say that one of the functions of a lawyer is to lie for his client; and on rare occasions, as I think I have shown, I believe it is. Happily they are few and far between, only when his duty gets him into a corner or puts him on the spot. Day in, day out, a lawyer can be as truthful as anyone. But not ingenuous.

A lawyer is required to be disingenuous. He is required to make statements as well as arguments which he does not believe in. But the further his statements descend toward the particular, the more truthful he may be, indeed must be, because no one appreciates the significance of the particular better than a lawyer. In the higher brackets of generality, he has to be freed from his own beliefs and prejudices, for they are irrelevant, unless they are pressed into service for the client. But his insincerity does not extend to the particular, except, of course, particulars which do not belong to him, but are his client's secrets. Barring these, when he is talking for his client, a lawyer is absolved from veracity down to a certain point of particularity. And he must never lose the reputation of lacking veracity, because of his freedom from the strict bonds of veracity and of the law are the two chief assets of the profession.

I have said that a lawyer may not lie to the court. But it may be a lawyer's duty not to speak. Let me give you a case from the autobiography of one of the most distinguished and most conscientious lawyers I or any other man has ever known, Samuel Williston. In his autobiography, *Life and Law,* he tells of one of his early cases. His client was sued in some financial matter. The details of the claim are not important. Williston, of course, at once got his client's letter file and went through it painstakingly, sorting, arranging, and collating it. The letters, we may well believe, told the whole story, as they usually do in such a case. Trial approached, but the plaintiff's lawyers did not either demand to see the correspondence, nor ask for their production. "They did not demand their production and we did not feel bound to disclose them."[8] At the close of the trial, "In the course of his remarks the Chief Justice stated as one reason for his decision a supposed fact which I knew to be unfounded. I had in front of me a letter that showed his error. Though I have no doubt of the propriety of my behavior in keeping silent, I was somewhat uncomfortable at the time."[9]

This was a letter, a piece of evidence, a fact. Suppose it had been a rule of law. Suppose the Chief Justice had equally mistakenly given as a reason for his decision some statute or regulation which Williston knew had been repealed or amended, and it was not a letter but a copy of the new statute which he had in front of him. Williston would have interrupted the Chief Justice and drawn his attention to it. This is sometimes debated, but it is beyond dispute that this would have been Williston's duty, and there is no doubt at all that he would have performed it as scrupulously as he respected his duty to his client.

In the House of Lords, Lord Birkenhead observed in the course of a hearing, "Their Lordships were therefore very much in the hands of counsel and those who instructed counsel in these matters, and the House expected, and indeed insisted, that authorities which bear one way or the other upon matters under debate should be brought to the attention of their Lordships by those who are aware of those authorities. That observation was irrespective of whether or not the particular authority assisted the party who was aware of it. It was an obligation of confidence between their Lordships and all those who assisted in the debates in this House in the capacity of counsel."[10]

In that case Lord Birkenhead was referring to a statute. The Committee on Professional Ethics of the American Bar Associ-

[8] Williston, *Life and Law* 271 (1940).
[9] *Ibid.*
[10] Glebe Sugar Refining Co. v. Trustees of Greenock, 37 TLR 436 (1921).

ation has said that a lawyer has the same duty to advise the court of judicial "decisions adverse to his client's contentions." Mr. Robert B. Tunstall of the Virginia bar has pointed out that Lord Birkenhead was referring to a statute which was indeed so controlling that the House of Lords ordered the case reargued when it was finally brought to their attention. Mr. Tunstall thinks the opinion of the Committee of the American Bar Association went too far.[11] A lawyer surely has no duty to argue his opponent's case for him, nor should he be reproached for failure to suggest to the court an argument against him which his opponent has neglected.

But this distinction between statutes and precedents is not going to tell us how to reconcile a lawyer's obligations to the court with his obligations to his client. The Committee on Professional Ethics in its opinion said, "A lawyer is an officer of the court. His obligation to the public is no less significant than his obligation to his client. His oath binds him to the highest fidelity to the court as well as to his client. It is his duty to aid the court in the due administration of justice." And the Committee quoted one of the Canons of Ethics, "The conduct of the lawyer before the Court and with other lawyers should be characterized by candor and fairness."[12]

This is all very well, but you can't say that Williston was showing the highest fidelity to the court when he sat there with the letter in front of him. He was being faithful to his client, and uncomfortable that he could not be candid with the court. At first sight, the reasons which the Committee gave are not very helpful. If I ask you which of these two girls you love most, you are in effect declining to answer when you say, "Both." The Committee should have gone on to distinguish a lawyer's loyalties. The court has priority over the client in matters of law and the client has a priority over the court in matters of fact. The distinction is familiar enough to lawyers, and it is a useful distinction once we know what they mean by it, as I will try to make clear later. The point I want to make now is that the relations which a lawyer has with his client on one hand and his court on the other is somewhat

[11] See the remarks of Mr. Robert B. Tunstall of the Virginia Bar in 35 ABAJ 5 (1949).

[12] Opinion No. 146, Opinions of the Committee on Professional Ethics and Grievances 305 (1947).

bigamous, and it will continue to be until we can find a distinction between his loyalties as marked as their two objects.

Here is what Williston went on to say in his autobiography. "One of the troublesome ethical questions which a young trial lawyer is confronted with is the extent to which he is bound to disclose to the court facts which are injurious to his client's case. The answer is not doubtful. The lawyer must decide when he takes a case whether it is a suitable one for him to undertake and after this decision is made, he is not justified in turning against his client by exposing injurious evidence entrusted to him. If that evidence was unknown to him when he took the case, he may sometimes withdraw from it, but while he is engaged as counsel he is not only not obliged to disclose unfavorable evidence, but it is a violation of his duty to his client if he does so." And Williston concluded, ". . . doing something intrinsically regrettable, because the only alternative involves worse consequences, is a necessity in every profession."[13] It was a question, he said, of moral compromise, and he referred to a passage in Lecky's *The Map of Life.* This passage is worth quoting:[14]

> But at best there must be many things in the profession from which a very sensitive conscience would recoil, and things must be said and done which can hardly be justified except on the ground that the existence of this profession and the prescribed methods of its action are in the long run indispensable to the honest administration of justice.

"I must be cruel only to be kind," said Hamlet, on his way to his mother. And so likewise a lawyer has to tell himself strange things on his way to court. But they are strange only to those who do not distinguish between truth and justice. Justice is something larger and more intimate than truth. Truth is only one of the ingredients of justice. Its whole is the satisfaction of those concerned. It is to that end that each attorney must say the best, and only the best, of his own case.

This is not the method we have used in other endeavors, with not only more, but with conspicuous success. But the law has other things than success to think about. It must give the losing party, and his friends and his sympathizers, as much satisfaction as any

13 Williston, *Life and Law* 272 (1940).

14 Lecky, *The Map of Life Conduct and Character* 119 (1889).

loser can expect. At least the most has been said for him. The whole has been shaken out into the sun, and everyone concerned is given a feeling akin to the feeling of security which you get when you have told yourself the worst before you make a decision. The administration of justice is no more designed to elicit the truth than the scientific approach is designed to extract justice from the atom.

Advocacy requires a lawyer to start with something to be proved, and this is as true of facts as it is of propositions of law. When he goes to interview a witness as well as when he goes to the law library, he goes to get something. He will waste a lot of time if he goes with an open mind. He must, of course, first formulate the issue in his mind, but he does this only to make it the easier to find what lies on his side of the issue. He fixes on the conclusion which will best serve his client's interests, and then he sets out to persuade others to agree.

I do not believe there is any other way, even without an adversary, even without a judge to decide between you. Myself, I am quite incapable of entertaining a hypothesis and then testing it coolly and impartially to see whether it is true or whether it works. I have to take—I'd as soon be given—a preconceived notion and then do my best to prove it. I doubt very much whether there is such a thing as intellectual impartiality, an equilibrium of judgment. Not on this side of ignorance, or indifference, or imbecility. You have to be as eager in your thinking as in anything else. In other words, you have to be an advocate. Of course, I recognize that this demands a counterweight of candor to yourself. But neither eagerness nor advocacy makes candor impossible. And equilibrium is easier as well as more stable between two distant and opposed forces than when anything, big or little, is precariously balanced on the center of the seesaw.

III

The problem presented to a lawyer when he is asked to defend a man he knows is guilty or to take a case he knows is bad is perplexing only to laymen. Brandeis said, "As a practical matter, I think the lawyer is not often harassed by this problem, partly because he is apt to believe at the time in most of the cases that he actually tries, and partly because he either abandons or settles a large number of those he does not believe in."[15]

It is profoundly true that the first person a lawyer persuades is himself. A practicing lawyer will soon detect in himself a perfectly astonishing amount of sincerity. By the time he has even sketched out his brief, however skeptically he started, he finds himself believing more and more in what it says, until he has to hark back to his originial opinion in order to orient himself. And later, when he starts arguing the case before the court, his belief is total, and he is quite sincere about it. You cannot very well keep your tongue in your cheek while you are talking. He believes what he is saying in a way that will later astonish himself as much as now it does others.

Not that he cares how much we are astonished. What he does care is whether we are persuaded, and he is aware that an unsound argument can do much worse than fall flat. For it may carry the implication that he has no better one. He will not want to make it unless he really has no better.

This sort of self-sown sincerity, however, is seldom deep-rooted in lawyers, and it had better not be. If what Justice Darling said was cynical, it is also true. "I think," he said, "that most Counsel would be better advocates did they content themselves with simulating the belief instead of actually embracing it. The manifest appearance of a believer is all that is wanted; and this can well be acted after a little study, and will not interfere with that calmness of judgment which it is well to preserve in the midst of uncertainties, and which does not appear to be consistent with much faith."[16]

The classical solution to a lawyer taking a case he knows is bad is Dr. Johnson's. It is perfectly simple and quite specious. Boswell asked Johnson whether as a moralist Johnson did not think that the practice of the law, in some degree, hurt the nice feeling of honesty.

"What do you think," said Boswell, "of supporting a cause which you know to be bad?"

Johnson answered, "Sir, you do not know it to be good or bad till the Judge determines it. I have said that you are to state facts

[15] Brandeis, *The Opportunity in the Law,* 39 Am. L. Rev. 561 (1905).
[16] Darling, *Scintillae Juris* 90 (1914).

fairly; so that your thinking, or what you call knowing, a cause to be bad, must be from reasoning, must be from your supposing your arguments to be weak and inconclusive. But, Sir, that is not enough. An argument which does not convince yourself, may convince the Judge to whom you urge it: and if it does convince him, why, then, Sir, you are wrong, and he is right."[17]

Dr. Johnson ignored the fact that it is the lawyer's job to know how good or how bad his case is. It is his peculiar function to find out Dr. Johnson's answer is sound only in cases where the problem does not arise.

A lawyer knows very well whether his client is guilty. It is not the lawyer, but the law, that does not know whether his case is good or bad. The law does not know, because it is trying to find out, and so the law wants everyone defended and every debatable case tried. Therefore the law makes it easy for a lawyer to take a case, whether or not he thinks it bad and whether or not he thinks other people think it bad. It is particularly important that it be made as easy as possible for a lawyer to take a case that other people regard as bad. Otherwise, to take a current example, people who are now being charged with being Communists, who heaven knows need a lawyer, what with the capering of congressional committees, will find it hard to get counsel.

We want to make it as easy as we can for a lawyer to take a bad case, and one of the ways the bar helps go about it is the canon of ethics which says, "It is improper for a lawyer to assert in argument his personal belief in his client's innocence or in the justice of his cause."[18] It is called improper just so that the lawyer may feel that he does not have to. This, I think, must be its only purpose, for it is honored in no other way.

Listen to George Wharton Pepper's peroration to his argument on the AAA case.[19] Having argued that the AAA is unconstitutional, he proceeds most eloquently to express his own personal belief in the justice of his cause. "My time is fleeting and I must not pause to sum up the argument I have made. . . . But I do want to say just one final and somewhat personal word. I have tried very hard to argue this case calmly and dispassionately, and with-

---

[17] 2 Boswell, *The Life of Johnson* 47-48 (Hill ed. 1887).

[18] Canon 15, Canons of Professional Ethics of the American Bar Association.

[19] United States v. Butler, 297 US 1 (1936).

out vehement attack upon things which I cannot approve, and I have done it thus because it seems to me that this is the best way in which an advocate can discharge his duty to this Court. But I do not want your Honors to think that my feelings are not involved, and that my emotions are not deeply stirred. Indeed, may it please Your Honors, I believe I am standing here today to plead the cause of the America I have loved; and I pray Almighty God that not in my time may 'the land of the regimented' be accepted as a worthy substitute for 'the land of the free.' "[20]

To be sure, the Constitution was at stake, and constitutional law isn't law at all. But here is a canon which calls improper something which the most proper lawyers do. I suggest that its only purpose is to relieve lawyers of the necessity of expressing their opinion, so that they may never need express it unless they want to express it, and keep it to themselves whenever they choose. The canon gives a lawyer an excuse when his client wants him to espouse his cause, when all the lawyer wants to take is a case.

No, there is nothing unethical in taking a bad case or defending the guilty or advocating what you don't believe in. It is ethically neutral. It's a free choice. There is a Daumier drawing of a lawyer arguing, a very demure young woman sitting near him, and a small boy beside her sucking a lollypop. The caption says, "He defends the widow and the orphan, unless he is attacking the orphan and the widow." And for every lawyer whose conscience may be pricked, there is another whose virtue is tickled. Every case has two sides, and for every lawyer on the wrong side, there's another on the right side.

I am not being cynical. We are not dealing with the morals which govern a man acting for himself, but with the ethics of advocacy. We are talking about the special moral code which governs a man who is acting for another. Lawyers in their practice—how they behave elsewhere does not concern us—put off more and more of our common morals the farther they go in a profession which treats right and wrong, vice and virtue, on such equal terms. Some lawyers find nothing to take its place. There are others who put on new and shining raiment.

I will give you as good an example as I know that a lawyer can make a case as noble as a cause. I want to tell you how Arthur D.

---

[20] *Id.* at 44.

Hill came into the *Sacco-Vanzetti Case.* It was through Felix Frankfurter, and it is his story. Frankfurter wrote some of it in the newspapers shortly after Arthur's death, and he told it to me in more detail just after the funeral.

When the conviction of Sacco and Vanzetti had been sustained by the Supreme Judicial Court of Massachusetts, there was left an all but hopeless appeal to the federal courts, that is, to the Supreme Court. "It was at this stage," Felix Frankfurter said, "that I was asked if I would try to enlist Arthur Hill's legal services to undertake a final effort, hopeless as it seemed, by appeal to the Federal Law."

Frankfurter called Arthur Hill up and said that he had a very serious matter to discuss with him. "In that case," said Arthur Hill, "we had better have a good lunch first. I will meet you at the Somerset Club for lunch and afterwards you will tell me about it." They lunched together at the Somerset Club, and after lunch they crossed Beacon Street and they sat on the bench in Boston Common overlooking the Frog Pond. And Frankfurter asked Arthur Hill if he would undertake this final appeal of the *Sacco-Vanzetti Case* to the Supreme Court.

Arthur Hill said, "If the president of the biggest bank in Boston came to me and said that his wife had been convicted of murder, but he wanted me to see if there was any possible relief in the Supreme Court of the United States and offered me a fee of $50,000 to make such an effort, of course I would take the retainer, as would, I suppose, everybody else at the bar. It would be a perfectly honorable thing to see whether there was anything in the record which laid a basis for an appeal to the Federal Court.

"I do not see how I can decline a similar effort on behalf of Sacco and Vanzetti simply because they are poor devils against whom the feeling of the community is strong and they have no money with which to hire me. I don't particularly enjoy the proceedings that will follow, but I don't see how I can possibly refuse to make the effort."

If any of you have read Morgan and Joughin's book,[21] you will know that Arthur Hill was hired. He did get a fee. Arthur Hill took it as a law case. To him it was a case, not a cause. He was not the partisan, he was the advocate. I want to add just one other

[21] Morgan and Joughin, *The Legacy of Sacco and Vanzetti* (1948).

thing, that Arthur Hill said to me, years later. It sets a sort of seal upon his conduct in the case.

I used to meet him fairly often walking downtown, because we both often stopped at the Boston Athenaeum and we would go on downtown together. One morning I was stupid enough to ask him an indiscreet question. I had expressed my own opinion on the guilt or innocence of Sacco and Vanzetti. I said I thought that on the whole it seemed to me probable that they had been guilty, and I asked Arthur what he thought. Arthur looked at me, it was years later, twenty years later, and he smiled and said, "I have never said, and I cannot say, what I think on that subject because, you see, Charlie, I was their counsel."

I met Judge Thayer once. This too was some years after the trial. We were in his chambers in Boston settling an automobile accident case then on trial before him. We were all standing, and he was standing between me and the window, so that when I looked out the window behind him I saw the top of the Charlestown Jail where the death house was in the background of a sort of living portrait of Judge Thayer framed by the window. I wasn't thinking anything much about it until I realized that Judge Thayer was no longer talking about our case, but strutting up and down and boasting that he had been fortunate enough to be on the bench when those sons of bitches were convicted. I had a chill, and I comforted and warmed myself over thoughts of Arthur Hill.

I have talked perhaps too lovingly about the practice of the law. I have spoken unsparingly, as I would to another lawyer. In a way the practice of the law is like free speech. It defends what we hate as well as what we most love. I don't know any other career that offers ampler opportunity for both the enjoyment of virtue and the exercise of vice, or, if you please, the exercise of virtue and the enjoyment of vice, except possibly the ancient rituals which were performed in some temples by vestal virgins, in others by sacred prostitutes.

IV

Let us now go back and reconsider, and perhaps reconstruct, in the light of my examples and our discussion, this "entire devotion" which a lawyer owes to his client.

The fact is, the "entire devotion" is not entire. The full discharge of a lawyer's duty to his client requires him to withhold something. If a lawyer is entirely devoted to his client, his client receives something less than he has a right to expect. For, if a man devotes the whole of himself to another, he mutilates or diminishes himself, and the other receives the devotion of so much the less. This is no paradox, but a simple calculus of the spirit.

Good lawyers know this. It was true of Brandeis. His appointment to the Supreme Court was opposed for his sharp practices at the bar, for being a ruthless and unscrupulous advocate, for taking cases against former clients. So his opponents said. And yet Austen G. Fox, who led the fight against his confirmation by the Senate before the Senate subcommittee is quoted as saying, "The trouble with Mr. Brandeis is that he never loses his judicial attitude toward his clients. He always acts the part of a judge toward his clients instead of being his client's lawyer, which is against the practices of the Bar."[22] This remark loses nothing in Fox's obvious disapproval. Frederick P. Fish would never own any stock in a client's corporation. He said that he "never invested in a client." He would no more do that than a judge would hold stock in a corporation which was a party in a case before him.

Let me cite a third lawyer, for his name is synonymous with one of the big New York law firms to which Mark Howe was referring. The recent head of the firm, Robert T. Swaine, in his history of the Cravath firm, wrote that Paul D. Cravath "early came to believe that in most cases the client is best advised by a lawyer who maintains an objective point of view and that such objectivity may be impeded by any financial interest in the client's business or any participation in its management. Accordingly, he made it the policy of the firm that neither its partner nor its associates should hold equity securities of any client, or serve as a director of a corporate client, or have a financial interest, direct or indirect, in any transaction in which the firm was acting as counsel. Occasionally, more frequently in recent years, clients have insisted upon exceptions permitting partners to occupy directorships and own qualifying equity securities, but the exceptions have been few."[23]

---

22 Mason, Brandeis—A Free Man's Life 506 (1946).

23 2 Swaine, *The Cravath Firm* 9 (1948).

It takes nothing from the wisdom of Cravath's policy that it was based on experience. Swaine adds, "It was Cravath's experience in the Metropolitan matter that led to the rule that no member of the firm or staff may be a director of a corporate client, save in exceptional cases."[24] This was an unfortunate experience. Cravath was sued as a director in the Metropolitan Securities matter for an allegedly illegal redemption of some debentures. The suit was settled. Swaine gives a detailed account of the whole affair.[25]

Fish and Brandeis and Cravath knew that they could not give their clients the full measure of their services if they did not keep themselves detached. Thereby they were able to offer their clients what they had come to get—advice and counsel from someone above the turmoil of their troubles or at least far enough away from them to look at them. By not putting their emotions as well as their minds up for hire, they saved, for the client as well as for themselves, the waste of spirit which some lawyers confuse with devotion.

There is authority for such detachment. It is not Christian. Nor is the practice of law a characteristically Christian pursuit. The practice of law is vicarious, not altruistic, and the lawyer must go back of Christianity to Stoicism for the vicarious detachment which will permit him to serve his client.

E. R. Bevan, in his *Stoics and Sceptics,*[26] summarized the Stoic faith as follows: "The Wise Man was not to concern himself with his brethren . . . he was only to serve them. Benevolence he was to have, as much of it as you can conceive; but there was one thing he must not have, and that was love. . . . He must do everything which it is possible for him to do, shrink from no extreme of physical pain, in order to help, to comfort, to guide his fellow men, but whether he succeeds or not must be a matter of pure indifference to him. If he has done his best to help you and failed, he will be perfectly satisfied with having done his best. The fact that you are no better off for his exertions will not matter to him at all. Pity, in the sense of a painful emotion caused by the sight of the other men's suffering, is actually a vice. . . . In the service of his fellow men he must be prepared to

24 *Id.* at 68.
25 *Id.* at 45-69.
26 As quoted in 6 Toynbee, A Study of History 146-47 (1939).

sacrifice his life; but there is one thing he must never sacrifice: his own eternal calm."

But let the greatest modern Stoic of them all, because he outgrew it, tell us about himself. "I have been able," Montaigne said, "to concern myself with public affairs without moving the length of my nail from myself, and give myself to others without taking anything from myself. . . . We carry ill what possesses and carries us. Anyone who uses only his own judgment and address proceeds more gaily. He feints, he ducks, he counters at his ease, and according to the needs of the occasion. When he misses, it is without torment, without affliction, ready and whole for a new enterprise. The bridle is in his hand." And further on, "The mayor and Montaigne have always been two people, clearly separated. There's no reason why a lawyer or a banker should not recognize the knavery that is part of his vocation. An honest man is not responsible for the vices or the stupidity of his calling, and need not refuse to practise them. They are customs in his country and there is profit in them. A man must live in the world and avail himself of what he finds there."[27]

The Stoics gave us a counsel of perfection, but it is none the less valid. If a lawyer is to be the best lawyer he is capable of being, and discharge his "entire duty" to his clients, here in the Stoic sage is his exemplar. Here in Stoicism is his philosophy. Let him be a Christian if he choose outside the practice of the law, but in his relations with his clients, let him be a Stoic, for the better Stoic, the better lawyer.

A lawyer should treat his cases like a vivid novel, and identify himself with his client as he does with the hero or the heroine in the plot. Then he will work with "the zest that most people feel under their concern when they assist at existing emergencies, not actually their own; or join in facing crises that are grave, but for somebody else." I can't put it more neatly than Cozzens.[28] I can only add that this zest may deepen into a peculiar and almost spiritual satisfaction, as wide as it is deep. He will be taking T. S. Eliot's advice to readers of Dante. "You are not called upon to believe what Dante believed, for your belief will not give you a groat's worth more of understanding and appreci-

[27] IV Essais de Montaigne 152-53 et seq. (Charpentier, Variorum ed. 1876).
[28] Cozzens, *Guard of Honor* 479 (1948).

ation; but you are called upon more and more to understand it. If you read poetry as poetry, you will 'believe' in Dante's theology exactly as you believe in the physical reality of his journey; that is, you suspend both belief and disbelief. . . . What is necessary to appreciate the poetry of the Purgatorio is not belief, but suspension of belief."[29]

How is a lawyer to secure this detachment? There are two ways of doing it, two devices, and all lawyers, almost all, are familiar with one or the other of them.

One way is to treat the whole thing as a game. I am not talking about the sporting theory of justice. I am talking about a lawyer's personal relations with his client and the necessity of detaching himself from his client. Never blame a lawyer for treating litigation as a game, however much you may blame the judge. The lawyer is detaching himself. A man who has devoted his life to taking on other people's troubles, would be swamped by them if he were to adopt them as his own. He must stay on the upland of his own personality, not only to protect himself, but to give his client the very thing that his client came for, as Brandeis and Fish and Cravath and Montaigne so well understood.

I must refer again to the Stoics. In Gilbert Murray's small book, *The Stoic Philosophy,* he says, "Life becomes, as the Stoics more than once tell us, like a play which is acted or a game played with counters. Viewed from outside, the counters are valueless; but to those engaged in the game their importance is paramount. What really and ultimately matters is that the game shall be played as it should be played. God, the eternal dramatist, has cast you for some part in His drama, and hands you the role. It may turn out that you are cast for a triumphant king; it may be for a slave who dies of torture. What does that matter to the good actor? He can play either part; his only business is to accept the role given him, and to perform it well. Similarly, life is a game of counters. Your business is to play it in the right way. He who set the board may have given you many counters; he may have given you few. He may have arranged that, at a particular point in the game, most of your men shall be swept accidentally off the board. You will lose the game; but why should you mind that? It is your play that matters, not the score that

29 Eliot, Dante 42, 44 (1929).

you happen to make. He is not a fool to judge you by your mere success or failure. Success or failure is a thing he can determine without stirring a hand. It hardly interests Him. What interests Him is the one thing which He cannot determine—the action of your free and conscious will."[30]

But this is not a Stoic monopoly. "I want you to understand," Yeats wrote, "that once one makes a thing subject to reason, as distinguished from impulse, one plays with it, even if it is a very serious thing. I am more ashamed because of the things I have played with in life than of any other thing."[31] Yeats was no Stoic, as his shame shows.

The other way is a sense of craftsmanship. Perhaps it comes to the same thing, but I think not quite. There is a satisfaction in playing a game the best you can, as there is in doing anything else as well as you can, which is quite distinct from making a good score.

"Who can put life into . . . ?" Let us not brawl—
  But—No joy in crafts-goal well won?
No pleasure in pitching a neatly curved ball?
  No fun in the fact that good doing is fun,
That races, in part, are just there to be run?[32]

A lawyer may have to treat the practice of law as if it were a game, but if he can rely on craftsmanship, it may become an art, and "Art, being bartender, is never drunk; and Magic that believes itself, must die."[33] "Who sweeps a room as for Thy laws, Makes that and th' action fine."[34] I wonder if there is anything more exalted than the intense pleasure of doing a job as well as you can irrespective of its usefulness or even of its purpose. At least it's a comfort.

I have compared the lawyer to the banker who handles other people's money and to the priest who handles other people's spiritual aspirations. Let me go further. Compare the lawyer

30 Murray, *The Stoic Philosophy* 50 (1915).

31 Richard Ellmann quotes this from a letter which he says Yeats probably never sent. Ellmann, Yeats: The Man and the Masks 178 (1949).

32 A stanza from some verses by Diogenes J. S. Teufelsdrock, in the Harvard Law School Record for March 16, 1949.

33 Viereck, *Terror and Decorum* 53 (1948).

34 This is from "The Elixir" by George Herbert, Works of George Herbert 184 (Hutchinson ed. 1941).

with the poet whose speech goes to the heart of things. "Yet he is that one especially who speaks civilly to Nature as a second person and in some sense is the patron of the world. Though more than any he stands in the midst of Nature, yet more than any he can stand aloof from her."[35]

[35] VII Writings of Henry David Thoreau 289 (1906).

Adapted from Vol. 4, Stanford Law Review (1951).

The Art of Advocacy

BY LLOYD PAUL STRYKER

ON A LOVELY MAY MORNING in Long Island a week or two before the start of a much publicized trial, I was making my way toward the little church which has meant much to me. The Sunday bells were ringing as I walked up the steps and there encountered a charming lady whom I knew well.

Her face was a little flushed as she hurriedly exclaimed to me, "I don't like what you're doing." "What am I doing?" I asked. "You are going to defend that awful, guilty man," she answered. "But how do you know he is guilty?" I somewhat diffidently inquired. "How do I know he is guilty? How silly, of course I do! Haven't I been reading every word in all the papers?" "But haven't you discovered that newspapers are not always right? Don't you remember what the Paris press said about Dreyfus before his trial, and how they had to retract all they had said after his terrible ordeal at Devil's Island, and his ultimate though long-deferred, complete exoneration? God, whose church we are now entering, alone knows whether my client is guilty."

By this time, the choir, preceded by the Cross and the flag of our country, was about to march up to their appointed places. I found my pew and prayed that morning as I had never prayed before for strength, for courage, and for guidance, and as I prayed, I thought of the old hymn that my father loved and had taught me to love too: "In the hour of trial, Jesus, plead for me." I thought too of the many references in the Prayer Book to Christ as our mediator and advocate—an advocate who would help both the righteous and the sinner. I remembered the words of the Holy Communion: "If any man sin we have an advocate with the Father Jesus Christ the righteous."

With all my heart I believed that my client had not sinned, but if he had, I knew he had a far, far better advocate than I. If such an advocate would plead for him, who was I to decline?

And now the choir had finished the last note and we were exhorted: "Let us humbly confess our sins to Almighty God." Sins? Did these respectable people have sins? And as I reflected again upon this, we were on our knees, and as the Rector intoned, we followed in that most glorious of prayers: "Almighty and most merciful Father, we have erred and strayed from thy ways like lost sheep. We have followed too much the devices and desires of our own hearts. We have offended against thy holy laws. We have left undone those things which we ought to have done; and we have done those things which we ought not to have done; and there is no health in us. But thou, O God, have mercy upon us miserable offenders. Spare thou, O God, those who confess their faults. Restore thou those who are penitent."

Lost sheep! Offenders against God's holy laws! Miserable offenders! Even these, it seems, could look to God for restoration. Nice people—bankers and stockbrokers and lawyers and doctors—were these sinners? So it appeared, for there they were upon their knees, making confession of their sins. There was not, then, that sharp division between the righteous and the sinners, it seemed, for we had all strayed like lost sheep, and there was no health in any of us—even in attractive and beautiful women one meets at a dinner party, or in their healthy, tanned, and handsome husbands. God did not divide the world between the right and the wrong side of the tracks. We have all done those things which we ought not to have done, and left undone those things which we ought to have done, and there is no health in any of us. We are all criminals before God—offenders against His holy laws.

But my friend who criticized me at the church is not alone. From time immemorial, laymen have misunderstood the lawyer's role, have failed to grasp the true nature of his duty, and have never comprehended why a man accused, generally disliked and prejudged by the press, was nonetheless entitled to the defense of honest counsel. Few have read, and those who have care less about, the plain words of the United States Constitution, the Sixth Amendment to which commands that in every criminal prosecution the accused "shall enjoy . . . the assistance of counsel for his defense."

When a heinous crime has been committed, and the public, stirred to frenzy by the newspapers, has settled down on the belief that the accused is guilty, many otherwise fair-minded persons become enraged to see a respected lawyer undertaking the defense. They have never read, and if they had, would not agree with the Fifth Canon of Ethics which declares that "it is the *right* of the lawyer to undertake the defense of a person accused of crime, *regardless of his personal opinion* as to the guilt of the accused; otherwise, innocent persons, victims only of suspicious circumstances, might be denied proper defense. Having undertaken such defense, the lawyer is bound by all fair and honorable means to present every defense that the law of the land permits, to the end that no person may be deprived of life or liberty but by due process of law."

This rule of justice has obtained in England from the beginning; it still obtains there. "It is perhaps strange," writes Sir Patrick Hastings in his charming autobiography, "that the duties and obligations of a barrister are so little understood by the lay mind. So often the comment has been made, 'How can honest counsel defend or represent a cause in which he cannot possibly believe?' The answer is very simple. Counsel has no right to believe or disbelieve either his client or his case; he has a duty to perform; he must perform it. He alone has the right of audience in the superior courts of justice, and such right carries with it obligations that are well defined. He has been likened to a cabman on the rank. He is not entitled to refuse a fare, and he has no right to arrogate to himself the task of forming an opinion as to whether his client is innocent or guilty, truthful or a liar. His duty is quite simple. He is entitled to rely upon his solicitor's instructions, and within the conduct of those instructions to fight his cause to the best of his ability. There is only one rule of conduct that he ever need consider, that is to be just as honest and straightforward in his practice as he would be in his own private life. Then he cannot possibly go wrong."

More than a century and a half before Sir Patrick wrote these words in defense of his right and duty to represent an unpopular client, Erskine was saying to a London jury: "From the moment that any advocate can be permitted to say that he will or will not stand between the Crown and the subject arraigned in the court where he daily sits to practice, from that moment the liberties of England are at an end. If the advocate refuses to defend from what he may think of the charge or of the defense, he assumes the character of the judge; nay, he assumes it before the hour of judgment; and in proportion to his rank and reputation, puts the heavy influence of perhaps a mistaken opinion into the scale against the accused, in whose favor the benevolent principle of English law makes all presumptions, and which commands the very judge to be his counsel."

But perhaps the most classical statement on this subject was uttered by Dr. Samuel Johnson. You remember how Boswell one day asked him: "But what do you think of supporting a cause which you know to be bad?"—and how the author of the great dictionary answered him: "Sir, you do not know it to be good or bad, till the judge determines it. I have said that you are to state facts fairly; so that your thinking on what you call knowing a cause to be bad, must be from reasoning, must be from supposing your arguments to be weak and inconclusive. But, sir, that is not enough. An argument which does not convince yourself may convince the judge, to whom you urge it; and *if it does convince him,* sir, you are wrong, and he is right. It is his business to judge; and you are not to be confident in your own opinion that a cause is bad, but *to say all you can for your client,* and then hear the judge's opinion."

However, the most debated, and I think the most debatable, view of this subject was expressed by Brougham in his defense of Queen Caroline. Of all the cases about which I have ever read, including even those of Erskine, his defense of that much abused royal lady was the best conceived and the most brilliantly conducted; yet in his great final plea to the House of Lords there was an assertion, the correctness of which has ever since been debated.

In the midst of his summation, Brougham told the Peers that an advocate by the sacred duty which he owes his client knows, in the discharge of that office, but one person in the world, *that client and none other.* To save that client by all expedient means, to protect that client at all hazards and costs to all others, and among others to himself, is the highest and most unquestioned of his duties. And he must not regard the alarm, the suffering, the torment, the destruction which he may bring upon any other. Nay, separating the duties of a patriot from those of an advocate, and casting them if need be to the wind, he must go on reckless of the consequences, if his part it should unhappily be to involve his country in confusion for his client's protection."

What Brougham said there has been the subject of controversy ever since. I certainly do not agree that the duty of counsel is such as to override his duty to his country. "That is a proposition," said Sir Norman Birkett (later Lord Justice of Appeal) speaking before the Canadian Bar Association a few years ago, "to which the Bar of Canada would not agree." Neither would the Bar of the United States. It was, indeed, a proposition with which Brougham himself did not thoroughly agree, as he revealed many years after he enunciated it.

But to understand what Brougham wrote to Sir William Forsythe in 1859—nearly four decades after the Queen's trial—we must recall that King George IV was pressing for a divorce, although he himself had previously married Mrs. FitzHerbert, a Catholic, which marriage, if proved, under the Act of Settlement, would have deprived the King of his throne.

Referring to his celebrated speech, Brougham wrote Forsythe: "The real truth is, that the statement was anything rather than a deliberate and well-considered opinion. It was a menace, and it was addressed chiefly to George IV, but also to wiser men, such as Castlereagh and Wellington. I was prepared, *in case of necessity,* that is, in case the Bill passed the Lords, to do two things—first, to resist it in the Commons *with the country at my back,* but next, if need be, to dispute the King's title, to show he had forfeited the crown by marrying a Catholic, in the words of the Act, 'as if he were naturally dead.' What I said was fully understood by Geo. IV, perhaps by the Duke and Castlereagh, and I am confident it would have prevented them from pressing the Bill beyond a certain point."

No man or woman is so bad that something good could not honestly be said about him. Even the very bad may not be guilty of the crime of which they are charged. It is the duty of the advocate to say for his client all that could have been honestly spoken by the client himself in his own behalf had he been able. Judge Parry, an English judge, in his *Seven Lamps of Advocacy,* has written that "without a free and honorable race of advocates, there would have been little of the message of justice. Advocacy is the outward and visible appeal for the spiritual gift of justice. The advocate is the priest in the temple of justice trained in the mysteries of the creed, active in its exercises."

Yet reluctance to accept these views has ever been displayed by laymen. The hostility toward an unpopular defendant, more often than not, has been visited upon his counsel. Such was Erskine's fate when he defended Thomas Paine; such was John Adams' portion when he became counsel for the British soldiers charged with the Boston massacre. Such was thc reward of William Seward when, a hundred and eight years ago, in a little crowded courtroom, he stood up to defend a Negro by the name of Freeman on a charge of murder. His client was an emancipated slave. The man was deaf and obviously insane, but this, far from creating sympathy, seemed to accentuate the community's hostility for the poor Negro.

Seward's friends pointed out to him the unpopularity of the cause and how adverse an effect it might have on his political career. But Seward swept them all aside and gave the fullest measure of his strength and his entire devotion to this humble client. He told the jury that the most degraded human being in a civilized state is entitled to a hearing.

Finally, he closed, saying: "In due time, gentlemen of the jury, when I shall have paid the debt of nature, my remains will rest here in your midst with those of my kindred and neighbors. It is very possible they may be unhonored, neglected, spurned! But perhaps years hence, when the passions and excitement which now agitate this community shall have passed away, some lone exile, some Indian, some Negro, may erect over them an humble stone, and thereon this epitaph: 'He was faithful.'"

His prophecy was fulfilled. When he died, these words were engraved upon the marble over him. What better encomium could any lawyer have? What higher tribute than these words: "He was faithful."

Years, however, have not changed the public's willingness to visit its detestation of a client on the lawyer who defends him. How persistent is this point of view was recognized by the New York State Bar Association in July, 1952. Its *Bulletin* declared:

"Public misunderstanding of the lawyer's role in some recent cases indicates that the Bar should clarify and reaffirm its traditional obligation to represent and defend the unpopular. It has always been recognized in the profession that it is the duty of the Bar to see to it that even the most unpopular defendants and those charged with the most repellent of crimes can obtain a lawyer who will do what is possible and proper in their defense. From the earliest Colonial days, this has been a part of the tradition of the American Bar, even as it has in England. Indeed some of the most honored and memorable achievements of the Bar have been in connection with such causes. Adherence to this tradition is peculiarly necessary in times of great public impatience and concern, for in such times the pressure to dispense with ordinary safeguards of individual rights is most intense. . . . No lawyer doubts the duty; the problem is to make sure that it receives more than mere lip service."

And so, at their Saranac meeting, they adopted these resolutions:

Resolved,

1. That the New York State Bar Association recognizes that the right of counsel requires public acceptance of the correlative right of a lawyer to represent and defend, in accordance with the standards of the Bar, any client without having imputed to him his client's reputation, views, or character.
2. That the Association will support any lawyer against criticism or attack in connection with such representation, when, in its judgment, he has acted in accordance with the standards of the Bar.
3. That the Association will strive to educate the profession and the public on the rights and duties of a lawyer in representing any client, regardless of the unpopularity of either the client or his cause.

Echoing the same views, the Association of the Bar of the City of New York in January, 1953, adopted identical resolutions. Throughout the ages, popular distrust of lawyers has been fanned by novelists and dramatists, abetted in these latter days by columnists in many papers. We have learned to bear these strictures with composure, but when one of our own calling chooses to bring obloquy upon us, it is harder to endure. Such were my feelings when I came not long ago upon an article appearing in the December, 1951, issue of the Stanford *Law Review,* written by a Boston lawyer by the name of Charles P. Curtis.

In bald, plain terms he espouses the belief that a lawyer, in acting for others, has the right to lie for his client. "I want," he said in the beginning, "first of all to put Advocacy in its proper setting." If I thought he was right, I would even at this late day take up another calling. Surely all that I have said hitherto must indeed have been ill said if I have not made plain my belief that a good advocate must be an honest man. Ethics to an honorable man come naturally and without conscious effort —like good table manners or ordinarily decent behavior in polite society.

But listen to the views of Mr. Curtis. Having put advocacy in what he calls its "proper setting," he adds two platitudes with which no reasonable person could disagree: "It is a special case of vicarious conduct. A lawyer devotes his life and career acting for other people." True, but how should the lawyer act? Mr. Curtis tells us. "I don't see," he says, "why we should not come out roundly and say that one of the functions of a lawyer is to lie for his client." The occasions when he should do this, he says, are "rare." He should lie, we are told, only when "his duty gets him into a corner or puts him on the spot." A man whose business it is to act for others, the author of this article continues, "finds himself in his dealings on his client's behalf with outsiders, acting on a lower standard than he would if he were acting for himself, and lower, too, than any standard his client himself would be willing to act on, in fact, than anyone on his own." If this is the standard which Mr. Curtis has set for himself, it is one which should be repudiated with scorn and with contempt.

He gives a number of illustrations wherein a lawyer's lying for his client receives his hearty applause. He cites the case of a police inspector questioning a lawyer regarding the whereabouts of his client. "Of course he lies," says Mr. Curtis, adding, "and why not?" Still another sample of the ethics Mr. Curtis has espoused is the case of a lawyer who lied to him as a member of a grievance committee. "I remember thinking then," he writes, "that the lawyer was doing just right in lying to me, but I don't know who else agreed with me."

Well, I do not, for one, and there are others. Among these, none has spoken with more sincerity and authority than William Dean Embree, a member of a great New York law firm, a former president of the New York County Lawyers Association. "I thoroughly and vigorously disagree with Mr. Charles P. Curtis of the Boston Bar," writes Mr. Embree. "The lawyer owes entire devotion to the interest of his client," he continued. "He must use his utmost effort and all his ability for his client. This is the very heart of advocacy; this is the chief glory of the profession. But the lawyer is never required to resort to any step or procedure which impairs his own character or may weaken his standing in the profession or before the courts; no one can ever lie for his client without impairing his character and without weakening his standing in the profession and before the courts."

Mr. Curtis was graduated from Groton, from Harvard College, and from the Harvard Law School. Where, then, one wonders, did he acquire his views of legal ethics? Where was he taught that lying is a good thing? Surely not at Groton where Dr. Peabody impressed on every boy that one of the worst things he could become is a liar—not at Groton where not only lying was proscribed, but a peculiar opprobrium was reserved for the sneak who would lie to get out of a tight spot.

Surely Mr. Curtis did not learn at Harvard College that a liar should be countenanced, much less approved. And if, indeed, law was taught at the Harvard Law School in his day in what former Dean Pound has called the "grand manner," it would be a reflection on that much esteemed seat of learning to suggest that lying was applauded there.

I am light-years from suggesting that the writings of Mr. Justice Holmes, who was a kind of household god of the school where he once taught, could possibly be urged as a source to which approval of mendacity could be traced, but I have often wondered whether some of his assertions in the Holmes-Pollock letters might not be just a bit confusing to the youthful mind. "For my own part," wrote Justice Holmes, "I often doubt whether it would not be a gain if every word of moral significance could be banished from the law altogether, and other words adopted which should convey legal ideas uncolored by anything outside the law." As to ethics, he said, "I have called them a body of imperfect generalizations expressed in terms of emotion." Even in the domain of morals, he said that "it would be a gain, at least for the educated, to get rid of the word and notion of sin." He said he was "so skeptical as to our knowledge of goodness or badness of laws that I have no practical criticism except what the crowd wants."

That Holmes' suggested abolition "of every word of moral significance from the law" in any way prompted Mr. Curtis in his advocacy of lying, I do not believe. But, of this I am certain, that far better instruction can be found in the clear and unpretentious lectures of Lord MacMillan. His views of the connection between law and morals are poles apart from the Holmesian philosophy. "I maintain," he said, "that the ultimate justification of the law is to be found in moral considerations." The truth is, he declared, that "in the ultimate analysis the basis of the law is ethical, at first perhaps dimly perceived and concealed under much that is irrelevant, but increasingly realized as civilization advances and becomes self-conscious." Even in rules of law, he said, "which might appear to be morally indifferent . . . there is an ethical element. But when, as often happens from time to time," declared Lord MacMillan, "the law itself presents a choice whether one or the other principle is to be applied, then it seems to me that it is impossible, as it is undesirable, that the decision should not have regard to the ethical motive of promoting justice."

Ethics is the science of moral duty. It deals with the rules of conduct. Noah Webster, as a second definition of the word "ethical," gives this: "conforming to professional standards." The standards of conduct that lawyers must obey are as high, and are as generally followed, as the most exalted rules that govern any men on earth. All advocates are bound by these standards, and they must obey them. They may and should fight hard for their clients, but they must fight fairly. They may and should say all that honestly and honorably can be said for them. They may say it with fervor and all the persuasion in their power; but in saying it they may not deceive, they must not lie.

The advocate must never forget, said Judge Parry, that he is "not only the servant of the client, but the friend of the court, and honesty is as essential to true friendship as it is to sound advocacy." The arms which an advocate wields, said Lord Cochburn, "he ought to use as a warrior and not an assassin. . . . He ought to know how to reconcile them with eternal interests of religion."

Such an advocate was Thomas Erskine. It is just a hundred and sixty-three years ago that in defending Thomas Paine before Lord Kenyon and a jury, he declared: "I will ever and at all hazards assert the dignity, independence, and integrity of the English Bar, without which impartial justice, the most valuable part of the English constitution, can have no existence."

In America, where the stability of all departments of the Government rests upon the approval of the people, it is peculiarly essential that the system for establishing and dispensing justice be developed to a high point of efficiency and so maintained that the public shall have absolute confidence in the integrity and impartiality of its administration. The future of the Republic, to a great extent, depends upon our maintenance of justice pure and unsullied. It cannot be so maintained unless the conduct and motives of the members of our profession are such as to merit the approval of all just men. So runs the preamble of our Canons of Ethics.

I have been observing American lawyers for many years. I know that there is no other group of men in the United States whose record of devotion to their duty and whose obedience to their trusts is worthier of commendation. When one once thought to be an honest man turns out a rascal, he is driven from the Temple of Justice by the lawyers themselves. The conduct of the members of our profession, in general, has been such as to merit the approval of all just men.

And so, in the words of Erskine, I will ever assert the dignity, independence, and integrity of the American Bar.

Adapted from Ch. 14, "The Ethics of Advocacy," Simon & Shuster, N.Y. (1954).